# MOON HANDBOOKS®

# BRAZIL

## FIRST EDITION

## CHRISTOPHER VAN BUREN

COURTESY OF CHRISTIAN KNEPPER/EMBRATUR

AVALON TRAVEL

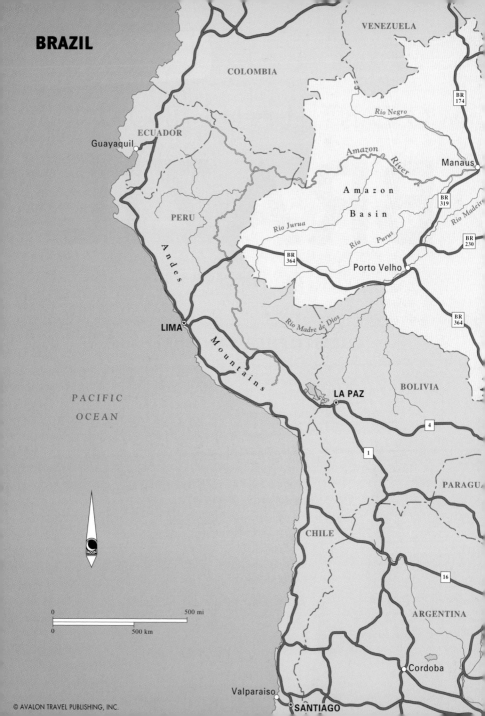

# CONTENTS

# Discover Brazil

# Explore Brazil

# Know Brazil

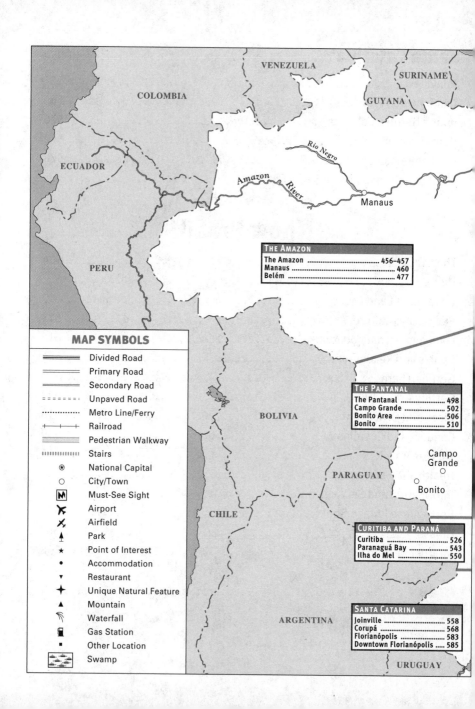

VENEZUELA

SURINAME

COLOMBIA

GUYANA

*Rio Negro*

ECUADOR

*Amazon* River

Manaus

PERU

## MAP SYMBOLS

| | |
|---|---|
| ≡ | Divided Road |
| = | Primary Road |
| = | Secondary Road |
| = = = = = | Unpaved Road |
| ·············· | Metro Line/Ferry |
| +—+—+ | Railroad |
| | Pedestrian Walkway |
| ⦙⦙⦙⦙⦙⦙⦙⦙⦙ | Stairs |
| ⊛ | National Capital |
| ○ | City/Town |
| Ⓜ | Must-See Sight |
| ✈ | Airport |
| ✕ | Airfield |
| ♣ | Park |
| ★ | Point of Interest |
| • | Accommodation |
| ▾ | Restaurant |
| ✦ | Unique Natural Feature |
| ▲ | Mountain |
| ⦆ | Waterfall |
| ▯ | Gas Station |
| ▪ | Other Location |
| 🪖 | Swamp |

BOLIVIA

Campo Grande ○

PARAGUAY

○ Bonito

CHILE

ARGENTINA

URUGUAY

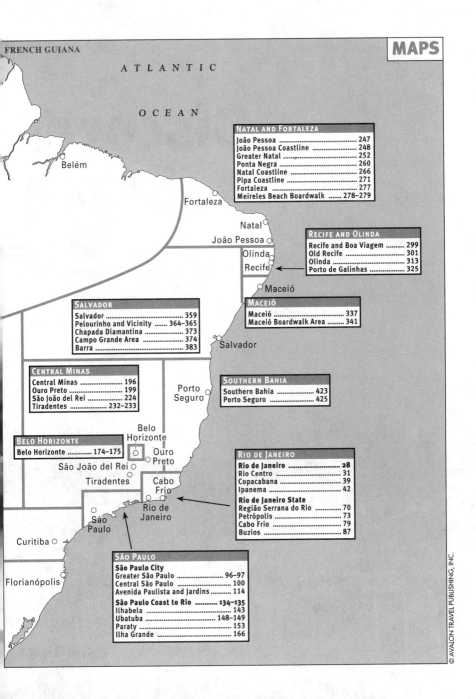

FRENCH GUIANA

**MAPS**

A T L A N T I C

O C E A N

Belém

Fortaleza

Natal

João Pessoa

Olinda

Recife

Maceió

Salvador

Porto Seguro

Belo Horizonte

Ouro Preto

São João del Rei

Tiradentes

Cabo Frio

Rio de Janeiro

São Paulo

Curitiba

Florianópolis

# Discover Brazil

Occupying almost half of the South American continent, Brazil is an enigma to its Spanish-speaking neighbors, and to the world beyond. It's a land where you can find modern computer assembly plants in the middle of the Amazon jungle, not far from aboriginal tribes that still dress in traditional jungle loincloths. It's a land where bustling concrete cities are barely able to keep tropical forests from encroaching and covering everything in green. It's the charming, rural hospitality you'll find in Minas Gerais, right alongside the most brutal driving conditions and aggressive drivers you'll find anywhere. And Brazil is a lot more.

Brazil is beautiful—with lush, tropical forests, thousands of bubbling waterfalls, silent caves and sparkling beaches, and vast fields of coffee and sugar that span like oceans. Brazil is also big—the fifth largest country in the world, offering travelers a plethora of options, destinations, and diversions. You may choose to stay on a working coffee plantation in the south of Minas Gerais and participate in the harvest. Or take a train ride through dramatic mountains, valleys, and rural farmlands reminiscent of northern Europe in the early 1900s. You might swim in a clear lagoon, then relax on an island's white beach with some Afro-Brazilian music and a cool caipirinha. Or walk barefoot into an ancient cavern and sit alone in pure darkness.

Brazil is diverse—and like its vast landscape, its people are diverse. Brazil is not just samba, Carnaval, and Copacabana. Its unique history has created an abundance of nationalities, cultural differences, language variations, regional customs, foods, and religions.

When the Portuguese began colonizing Brazil in 1504 with their official arrival in Porto Seguro, their intention was to extract as many riches as possible. The first attraction was the beautiful, red hardwood of the Pau Brasil tree. Later eyes turned to cocoa, sugar, and eventually the grand prize: gold and jewels. The northeast region is where the colonization first took hold; the cities of Salvador da Bahia and Recife/Olinda became major centers of the sugar and cocoa trade. To this day, sugar plantations blanket the hillsides of the northeast for as far as the eye can see. The region offers a three-dimensional view into the 16th and 17th centuries through its historical cities, colonial architecture, gold-laden churches, and age-old festivals.

The only place equal to Bahia in its association with all things Brazilian is, of course, Rio de Janeiro, the *cidade maravilhosa* (marvelous city). Thrust into the forefront by the great gold rush in Minas Gerais in the 18th century, Rio became the most important channel for extracting Brazil's great wealth. It wasn't until the Portuguese royal court spent its years of exile in the city, during Napoleon's scouring of Europe, that Brazil began its climb to independence. Rio gained a vast number of 19th-century buildings, parks, and grand public squares in the process. The museums and architectural complexes in downtown Rio de Janeiro take weeks to see completely. But competition from the city's 20th-century marvels is often a tempting distraction: the boardwalk of Copacabana, Carnaval, and the great monument of the Cristo Redentor, overlooking the city with arms open wide.

Brazil is quite literally inexhaustible—its vast tropical landscapes encompass the Amazon Jungle, the desert dunes of the Lençóis Maranhenses, and the largest wetlands in the world, the Pantanal, not to mention more than 7,000 kilometers of coastline. There are national parks where you can practice mountain climbing, rappelling, white-water rafting, and waterfall cascading. There are marine reserves where you can scuba dive with tropical fish, sea turtles, sharks, lobsters, and even visit wrecked ships on the sandy bottom of the ocean. Skin divers can snorkel in offshore reefs, natural pools, and underwater corridors, looking into the marine world as if into an aquarium. In Mato Grosso do Sul, there is a vertical cavern that is home to hundreds of red-breasted macaws; and it has a pool of crystal-clear water at the bottom. You can rappel down to get a closer look. In Chapada Diamantina you can hike up to the top of the *chapadas* (flat mountain mesas) and look out over the vast and rugged countryside. Then go for a swim in a lake of sparkling fresh water, surrounded by tiny fish nibbling at your arms and legs.

Brazil is alive; a country in constant movement, bubbling with excitement, activity and change. See for yourself.

Planning a trip to Brazil is usually an exercise in choosing priorities. Because Brazil is so large, just about any trip is going to be too short. It would take a couple of months just to see Brazil's principal attractions. Along with its size comes a huge diversity in its population. Its unique history has created an abundance of racial mixtures, cultural differences, language variations, customs, foods, and religions. Planning a trip to Brazil is usually an exercise in choosing your priorities and focusing in on the possibilities.

Brazil is officially divided into five regions, but these regions were not designed with tourism in mind, so most travelers end up dividing the country a bit more. First, there's Bahia, which boasts its Afro-Brazilian influences, historical cities, and monuments from Brazil's colonization period. Of course, there's also the unparalleled tropical coastline: a mix of quaint coastal villages, urban beaches, and untouched, virgin coast. The interior of Bahia is rich in eco-tourism and is home to many natural wonders. The center of Bahia is Salvador and you can visit the rest of Bahia from there.

Brazil's north coast requires a different travel strategy, as it consists of a string of coastal cities, each with kilometers of coastline around it. This area is known for its super-warm, super-clear water and is a haven for divers and beachcombers alike. Most travelers hop from one major hub to the next, all the way up or down the coast from Recife to Fortaleza.

The Amazon and Pantanal are Brazil's principal regions for those seeking nature and ecology. A trip to the Amazon region usually involves joining some kind of guided tour or boat excursion up the river. There are jungle lodges and different types of hotels in the cities of Manaus and Belém. The Pantanal, to the south, is a similar experience, with all visits hosted by guides through privately owned nature preserves. Most visitors enter and exit these areas in packaged (or at least self-contained) trips.

The southeast area is the most heavily populated region, containing three of Brazil's five largest cities: São Paulo, Rio, and Belo Horizonte. Because this region gives Brazil its reputation for being a dangerous country, most visitors end up breezing through here in just a few days or a week. But the area is loaded with history—from the historical gold-rush towns of Ouro Preto and Tiradentes in Minas Gerais to the lavish architecture of the coffee-boom era in São Paulo. The region also contains several national parks and some of the prettiest coastline in the country, including the historical port town of Paraty and the fabulous islands of Ilha Grande and Ilhabela. The best approach for this part of the country is to stick to the main areas and use trustworthy transportation. You can easily spend two or three weeks here, but it can be done in 10–14 days.

Finally, the south of Brazil is a region quite unlike the others. Here, you'll find high concentrations of German and Italian immigrants and, unlike in the other regions, these communities remain separate and distinct. You'll find German architecture in Joinville, Brusque, and Pomerode and Argentinean architecture along the Emerald Coast down to Florianópolis and even Rio Grande do Sul. The area is known for its rural villages, incredible national parks, and great waterfalls, such as the unequalled Foz de Iguaçu. Most visitors zig-zag their way down the coast to see most of the beaches and inland villages. The trip takes 10–20 days, depending on the angle of your zag.

## WHEN TO GO

The trick to visiting a tropical country is trying to avoid the rain as much as possible. In Brazil, that's fairly easy to do outside of the Amazon. The northeast coastline, from Fortaleza all the way to Bahia, is sunny until around March or April. The best months for the beach areas are September–December, when you'll get few crowds, low prices, and warm weather. Rio and São Paulo have heavy rains beginning in November and lasting through February, but the rains are not constant. It's always a crapshoot in the southeast region whether Carnaval (generally held in February) will be hot and wet or hot and dry. São Paulo and everything south of it gets quite cold in the winter (June–August), although many people still like to go south during those months. The best months for the south are March–May or during the peak-season months of January and February if you don't mind the crowds. Mangos are in season in December and January, along with cashews and most fruits. Coffee harvest takes place in June and July. There are wonderful cultural festivals during Holy Week (40 days after Carnaval) and in June (the Juninho festivals in the northern region).

The Pantanal and Amazon regions are best during dry season, which is June–September, unless you go for sportfishing, which is better in the wet season. Note that Brazilians have extensive holidays from just before Christmas through Carnaval. This is the peak season for most vacation spots throughout the country. Just after Carnaval is a good time to visit, as prices come back down and crowds disperse. Note that the big cities are probably best to visit during this peak season, since most Brazilians are leaving the cities and heading to the remote areas. You can get good deals in Rio and São Paulo during peak season. There is a special holiday in late October, which is when students take their spring break. It's called Semana do Saco Cheio (Fed Up Week). All beaches are crowded for 7–10 days, especially Buzios, Maresias, and Porto Seguro.

## WHAT TO TAKE

### Clothes
Outside of São Paulo and Rio, Brazilians generally dress casually. Typical social attire for men includes some type of jeans and a new, white tee shirt.

Short-sleeve button-down shirts are also popular and considered acceptable for business dress and dinner occasions. It's common to see bank officials wearing these types of clothes. Business suits are usually only worn by executives of large companies—and then only in the big cities. Women usually dress a bit snappier, with the latest jeans and pointed shoes with plenty of accessories. On the beach, Bermuda shorts are the most common for men, and women wear all sorts of sun dresses or netted bikini covers, draped sarongs, shorts, and skirts. Jeans are not a good choice for the beach because it's just too hot. Brazil is generally a warm country, but if you're planning to visit during the winter months (June–August), then you might bring one change of warm clothes—especially if you're traveling to any of the colder regions (São Paulo to the south and in the mountains). In São Paulo and the south of Brazil, you'll find that clothing is a bit more upscale and stylish, although nice jeans are always a good choice for men or women.

So what should you bring in terms of clothes? Simply put, as few items as necessary to get by. After the first few days, you'll want to wear the new clothes you bought in Brazil. After all, buying clothes is one of the greatest pleasures in traveling to Brazil. You can find well-made, inexpensive, and stylish clothes almost anywhere in the country. So come with your suitcase half empty, so you can return with it completely full.

Oh, about jewelry—don't bring any. You don't want to be calling attention to yourself by wearing some expensive watch or necklace. Do yourself a favor and leave the good stuff at home. If you don't have a cheap watch that you can use, you can buy one when you get to Brazil.

## Money

Don't bring traveler's checks. They are difficult to exchange in Brazil and they will cost you more than they should. The best way to get money while you're traveling is through the extensive ATM network. All major tourist areas and cities have international ATMs with the Plus and Cirrus systems. And they give you the best exchange rates, up to the minute. Just look for the Plus and Cirrus stickers on the ATM machines. Banco do Brasil is always a good choice (not all machines, but they usually have one or two) and the system called Banco 24 Horas, which is a network of ATMs that represent several different banks, including the Plus and Cirrus systems. You can also find Citibank offices in all large cities.

If you're heading to a small town or beach town, be sure to pull out some cash at the nearest large city when you arrive. Almost all small tourist destinations have a big-city hub nearby. Once you get to your destination, leave most of your cash in your hotel room or safe. You probably don't want to walk around with more than R$500 in your pocket at any time. Pay with your debit (or credit) card whenever you can, but don't let it leave your sight for too long. Even hotels and restaurants in small towns accept international credit cards (although not always, and exceptions are noted throughout the book). If you have credit cards that you don't intend to use in Brazil, leave them at home. All Banco do Brasil offices are Western Union agents, so you can receive money wires at any one of them.

Note: All prices in this guide are listed in Reals (R$). The currency exchange rate in Brazil fluctuates a lot (although it is supposedly stabilizing) so using Reals will help keep the majority of the prices listed accurate no matter what the rate. Keep in mind that Brazil experiences periods of inflation, so prices are liable to increase over time. Also, there are a few destinations, like the Amazon Region, that base their prices on the U.S. dollar. Prices in these sections are listed in dollars (and are noted as such) to keep them as accurate as possible.

## Papers and Documents

Bring your passport and driver's license for ID purposes. You should make at least two photocopies of your passport. Keep one copy at home. Keep another copy with you when you go out. Your original passport should stay in your hotel room or other safe location. You'll need the original only when entering and leaving the country, when presenting yourself to the federal police, or when doing any banking activities. For identification purposes, a copy is almost always acceptable. To make your copy even more acceptable, you can bring the original and a copy to any *cartório* office (like a notary public) and get the photocopy authenticated and stamped (Brazilians love to stamp things). The stamped copy can be used as the original in most cases. Every city has a *cartório* somewhere. Large cities have many. Bring a list of important phone numbers and addresses or email it to yourself. There are Internet cafés all over the country and a good Web-mail account comes in very handy when traveling.

Brazil is one of the few countries in the world that does not accept the standard international driving permit, which includes a Portuguese translation. Nevertheless, it can't hurt to get one and use it if you think you might drive in Brazil. Details on Brazilian driving permits and related issues appear in the *Know Brazil* section.

## Health Items

Naturally, you should bring anything you feel is necessary for your health and comfort. If you have drugs of a delicate nature, make sure you bring any doctor's prescription with you as there are some drugs available in the United States and Europe that Brazil has not authorized. This also works the other way around and Brazilian drugs are known for being low-cost and effective. If you think you might need a prescription filled in Brazil, then bring your doctor's prescription to the Brazilian Consulate when you make arrangements to go. They should be able to help you with a translation that will work in Brazil. Since brand names will not apply in Brazil, ask your doctor for the scientific name of your prescription.

## Special Items

More and more visitors to Brazil are bringing their international cell phones. Details on this and other business travel issues can be found in the *Know Brazil* section. Remember that Brazil uses both 110- and 220-volt electricity and some regions have both in the same hotel. Don't bother with plug converters as you can find them everywhere in the country.

## Gear

Heading to the beach? Even if you don't consider yourself a diver, you might consider investing in some basic diving equipment—like a mask and snorkel—or at least plan to purchase them here. Brazil has some of the best diving locations in the world—for casual snorkeling excursions and professional deep dives. Most of these diving locations will have equipment available, but you will be so much more comfortable with your own (not to mention that sense of personal pride as you break out your own gear). If you really want to get the most of the coast, invest in a scuba diving course before you leave home or plan to take one while you're here.

If you are thinking about doing some camping, then by all means, bring a tent and a lamp and maybe some pads. You can buy all this in Brazil if you prefer. Prices are generally hard to beat and if you happen to be landing in São Paulo, then you'll find some incredible deals on camping equipment. You probably won't need a sleeping bag, as a light blanket or cover will usually be enough (of course, you should check weather conditions, as the gear you choose should depend on your camping destination).

# The Regions

## THE SOUTHEAST

Most flights to Brazil land in either São Paulo or Rio de Janeiro, and it's here in the southeast region where most travelers begin their journeys in Brazil. Italian immigrants and rich coffee barons built the city of São Paulo into a rich mecca of commerce and culture. In the late 1800s, hoards of Italian immigrants flowed into the city to work in the coffee trade and the boom brought with it a wealth of architecture, monuments, parks, and city centers. Two spectacular examples include the Theatro Municipal and the Sala

São Paulo downtown. The city is also known for its incredible food, and its best restaurants are located in or near the Jardins area and in immigrant communities like Liberdade, the Japanese district. Many visitors drive from São Paulo to Rio de Janeiro along the coast, taking in some of the most beautiful beaches in the country along the way. Stops should include Ilhabela, the various beaches around Ubatuba, the historical town of Paraty, and the semi-deserted island of Ilha Grande. To the north of Rio, there's Cabo Frio, with its long stretch of blue water and white sand, and Buzios, with so many beaches and islands nearby.

A visit to the city of Rio de Janeiro should include a tour of the royal monuments and museums in the downtown area, such as the Theatro Municipal and Palá cio da Ilha Fiscal. Also obligatory is a visit to the Morro do Corcovado (Cristo) monument, a ride in the gondola to Pão de Açúcar, a stroll around the Jardim Botânico, and an afternoon walk along the Copacabana boardwalk. As you come inland from Rio to the state of Minas Gerais, stop at the Serra dos Orgãos National Park for some great hikes and adventure sports. Then, in Minas, you'll enter the gold-rush territory and the principal attractions are the mountain towns and villages where the gold rush took place. Don't miss Tiradentes, Ouro Preto, and Diamantina, three picturesque towns that processed literally tons of gold from 1700–1770. The sacred art and gold-leafed wooden sculpture in the churches of these towns is the most spectacular in the country.

## THE NORTHEAST

They say the wind caresses your skin in a special way in the northeast region. And when you sit in a beach cabana, with a cold coconut water, watching the palm trees blowing in the breeze, you'll begin to feel it. It's the feeling of paradise. But the northeast region is also the very heart and soul of Brazil's culture and reflects the country's turbulent history. In Salvador, the capital of Bahia and the heart of the northeast region, you'll see where slaves were publicly whipped at the *pelourinho,* or whipping post. You can also train with a Capoeira school or catch a Candomblé ritual in action. The beaches of Itapuã and Flamengo characterize the very essence of bossa nova and the islands and beaches to the south of Salvador are where you go to relax and enjoy the tropical breeze with a cold drink and shady umbrella. Highlights include the island of Morro de São Paulo and the quaint villages of Arraial d'Ajuda and Trancoso. Heading north from Salvador, you begin a journey along the northern coastal cities, each one with its own, unique personality. In Recife, you'll encounter some of the oldest monuments in Brazil, from the early days of the colonization and from the Dutch Invasion of 1629. The historical town of Olinda is a living museum with a couple dozen colonial churches and a rich tradition of arts and crafts. These cities are known to have the best cultural festivals in the country and Carnaval here is an unforgettable experience. Continuing north, you'll pass the pristine beaches and blue water around Maceió, one of the best-kept secrets of the Brazilian coastline. Natal to the north is famous for its mixture of huge, white sand dunes and blue ocean. The beaches here are some of the most spectacular in the country—the highlights being the reefs at Maracajaú and the island of Fernando de Noronha, famous for its daily visits by dolphins. By the time most visitors reach Fortaleza at the top of the country, they are surprised by the urbanization they find. The fifth-largest city in Brazil, Fortaleza is not always what travelers expect. But get out to the outskirts, especially way out to Jeriquaquara, and you'll be glad you came all this way.

## THE NORTH

If you take a boat along the Amazon River, you'll pass some of the densest jungle in the world along the largest and widest river in the world. You'll also see a number of towns and small cities along the banks of the river. Near Manaus, a city of almost three million inhabitants right in the heart of the jungle, you're likely to see pink river dolphins and *tucuxhi* dolphins (the world's only fresh-water dolphins) playing in the two distinct colors of water flowing side-by-side at the Meeting of the Waters, the beginning of the Amazon River. You'll paddle in a canoe past some of the largest water lilies in the world and see the eyes of the giant Caiman alligators staring at you in the night. The area is still home to numerous indigenous groups and some of them allow visitations by tourists. Downstream, in the Santarém area, you'll find the most beautiful fresh-water beaches of the region, where you can catch some sun for a day. You can also hike up to the oldest cave paintings in the Americas and see the incredible aboriginal pots and the ceramic art of the Tapajónica tradition, found in museums around the world. On the eastern edge of the Amazon Jungle is the Island of Marajó, where the bird species are as plentiful and varied as in the southern Pantanal. You can also get a close-up look at a working buffalo ranch. Nearby, the city of Belém marks the end of the Amazon Jungle, where the fresh-water rivers meet the ocean. Not to be missed is the great Ver-o-Peso market with foods, crafts, and herbal cures from the jungle on sale.

## THE CENTRAL WEST

Until recently, the central west region was known principally for Brazil's ultra-modern capital city, Brasilia. Today, visitors come from all over the world to visit the incredible flora and fauna of the world's largest wetlands, the **Pantanal**. Spanning 250,000 square kilometers (25 million hectares), the low plains of the Paraguay River Valley flood every summer, creating a huge series of waterways, lakes, and rivers. In the winter, the waters recede to create small lakes and pools and hundreds of species of birds come to feed on the fish that get trapped there. It's one of the world's most fascinating ecosystems. There are nature lodges there that will take you out for photographic safaris and river excursions and you're practically guaranteed to see giant storks, capybaras, giant anteaters, red-billed toucans, and the rare blue macaw. In the highlands, guarding the many rivers that feed into the Pantanal, is the town of **Bonito** with some of the country's most outrageous adventure sports, including fresh-water snorkeling, rappelling into silent caverns, scuba diving in underwater caves, horseback riding, and rafting. Not far to the north is the incredible **Chapada dos Guimarães,** with some of the tallest waterfalls in Brazil and some striking and dramatic landscapes.

## THE SOUTH

The southern region comes as a surprise to travelers who don't know the extent of Brazil's cultural diversity. The most noticeable difference is that the cities become cleaner, the poverty less dramatic, and the people more northern European in appearance. This is noticeable as soon as you enter **Curitiba,** the gateway to the south. The cities and small mountain towns from Curitiba to Porto Alegre are loaded with German immigrants and they tend to remain in separate colonies with all their cultural traditions intact. In the outskirts of Curitiba are Italian and German colonies with architecture, food, and traditions according to each. In most of these colonies, Portuguese was spoken as a second language until only a few years ago. On the way out of Curitiba, you can take a spectacular train ride through the mountains to the city of Paranaguá, one of the oldest coastal colonies in the south. Besides having some interesting colonial architecture, Paranaguá serves as a platform for visiting the Superagüi National Park, the Salto Morato Nature Preserve, and Ilha do Mel —the first two being pristine slices of the tropical countryside and excellent areas for hiking and camping. Ilha do Mel is a collection of charming island villages, beaches, and historical sights.

Heading south from Curitiba, into the state of Santa Catarina, German influences begin to get very definable in the mountain towns and villages. In the town of Pomerode, German is still the principal language of the inhabitants. Visitors can walk around the neighborhoods, sampling the food, culture, and crafts. In the village of Corupá near Joinville, you can also hike to dozens of waterfalls located deep in the mountains, beyond the many picturesque banana farms. On the coast from Joinville to Florianópolis is a string of beach towns that carry the mark of the original Portuguese settlers to the area. The area is called the Emerald Coast due to the sparkling green color of the water here. When you reach Florianópolis, a vast number of options are available—from urban beach towns to semi-deserted inlets surrounded by green mountains. A highlight here is the incredible seafood, prepared with locally harvested mussels, oysters, and fish.

Brazil being such a large country (slightly larger than the continental United States), this trip requires a lot of domestic flying. The best parts of Brazil are spread all over the country, from the great waterfalls in the south to the great Amazon Jungle in the north. In between, you'll see the world's largest wetlands (the Pantanal), the magical island of Fernando de Noronha, the sparkling city of Rio de Janeiro and the history and culture of Bahia. It's a lot to cover in 21 days, but this is a trip you'll never forget.

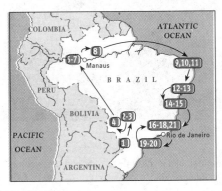

## DAY 1

Land in Rio or São Paulo and catch a flight to **Foz de Iguaçú,** where you'll take an afternoon look at the greatest waterfall in the world. Spend the night in Foz.

## DAY 2

Take a morning boat trip to the waterfall from either the Brazilian or Argentinean side, then hop an afternoon flight to Campo Grande, gateway to the **Pantanal,** where you'll catch a van directly to the Caiman Nature Reserve in time for the **night safari.**

## DAY 3

Enjoy a morning safari and excursions around Caiman. Take an afternoon swim back at the hotel before the large barbecue feast in the evening.

## DAY 4

Catch an early van to the city of **Bonito,** where you'll take nature excursions until the late afternoon.

## DAY 5

Choose a final nature excursion for the morning, then catch a van back to Campo Grande and a flight out to Manaus, in the heart of the **Amazon.** From Manaus, you take a boat straight to your jungle lodge for the next two days.

## DAYS 6 AND 7

A day and a night in the Amazon Jungle: river excursions, fishing for piranha, caiman focusing (scouting for alligators at night), jungle-canopy walks.

## DAY 8

Take a sunrise canoe excursion and jungle walks until lunchtime. Spend the afternoon visiting the sights in Manaus.

## DAY 9

Catch the morning flight to Natal and a direct connection to **Fernando de Noronha,** where you'll spend the afternoon and evening.

© CHRISTOPHER VAN BUREN

Caimans sit like stones in the waters of the Pantanal.

## DAY 10

Spend all day on the magical island of Fernando de Noronha, then catch a late-afternoon flight back to Natal. Check into your hotel in Ponta Negra and spend the evening out on the town.

## DAY 11

Rent a buggy for the day and visit the northern coastline, including Genipabu and Maracajaú. Go farther north to Galinhas if desired and time permits. Head back to Natal for the evening.

## DAY 12

Take the early flight to Salvador. Spend the day exploring Pelourinho and the afternoon at Solar de União to catch the Museum of Modern Art,

dinner, and a cultural show. Spend the evening in Pelourinho.

## DAY 13

Spend the morning in Bonfim and the Cidade Baixa, including the Mercado Modelo, then head to Flamengo Beach for lunch and down to Itapoã for the sunset. Don't miss the Acarajé de Cira in the Itapuã *praça*. The evening is your choice: Candomblé, Afro-Brazilian music and dance, or a cultural show.

## DAY 14

Take the scenic flight to Morro de São Paulo, check into your hotel, then spend the day exploring the village and beaches of the main island. Spend the evening in the village.

a mix of architecture in Pelourinho

## DAY 17

Take a sights and city tour of Rio de Janeiro. Spend the afternoon walking along the boardwalk from Copacabana to Ipanema.

## DAY 18

Catch more sights of Rio de Janeiro. For dinner, eat out in Copacabana or Ipanema.

## DAY 19

Catch the early bus to Paraty. Explore the Centro Histórico and have lunch on the island restaurant of Kontiki. Take an afternoon trip out to the waterfalls and *fazendas* inland or rent a car and visit the northern beaches. Spend the evening out in the Centro Histórico.

## DAY 20

Enjoy a full-day boat trip around the Bay of Paraty. Spend late afternoon and evening back at the Centro Histórico, shopping and eating.

## DAY 15

Take the Volta Ilha excursion around the island, and spend the evening in the village.

## DAY 16

Choose one of the morning excursions or just spend the entire day at Quarta Praia. Have lunch at the beach kiosk at Quarta Praia. Take a late-afternoon flight back to Salvador, then make a connection to Rio de Janeiro. Enjoy dinner in Ipanema.

## DAY 21

Spend the morning in Trindade exploring the village and beaches, then head back to Rio for your flight out.

© CHRISTOPHER VAN BUREN

These 14 days are designed to show you one of the richest strips of coastline in Brazil, including a day and a night in each of the two big cities to top things off. This is a very well-rounded trip that gives you a look at the big cities (including the famous sights of Rio de Janeiro), two large tropical islands, some of the best and most sparkling beaches on the coast, and an old, colonial Brazil via an 18th-century historical town. You'll need a rental car to complete this journey, and much of the driving takes place in the afternoons, when you can get some wonderful scenic views along the coastal highway.

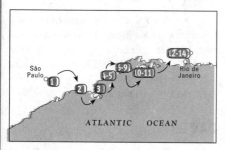

## DAY 1

Arrive in São Paulo, check into your hotel, then take a tour of the downtown area, including Sala São Paulo, the Pinacoteca, and the Mercado Municipal. Enjoy dinner out in Jardins, Pinheiros, or Vila Madalena.

## DAY 2

Treat yourself to early-morning shopping in Brás, then rent a car and make your way out of the city along the Rio–Santos coastal highway just after lunch. Drive up the coast to Cambury or Maresias for the afternoon and evening (about 3–4 hours driving).

## DAY 3

Lounge the morning away on the beaches of Cambury and Maresias, then drive to São Sebas-

tião and take the ferryboat to Ilhabela. Check into your hotel in the village, then explore the island for the rest of the day by car.

## DAY 4

Indulge in snorkeling, sunbathing, or hiking on the island until late afternoon. Then you're off to Ubatuba, three hours up the coast. Arrive in Ubatuba around nightfall. Stay in the Centro or Toninhas. Take an evening stroll along the boardwalk in the Centro.

## DAY 5

Explore Praia do Cedro, Praia Grande, Praia do Lázaro, and Praia Domingas Dias during the day. Enjoy dinner in town in Ubatuba or at the pier in Saco de Ribeira.

## DAY 6

Drive up the coast to explore Prumirim, Puruba, and the island of Couves (boat trip from Prumirim). Break out the snorkeling equipment for these spots.

## DAY 7

Spend the morning driving up the coast to Paraty (3 hours) and catch the inland tour of the waterfalls and *fazendas*. Then drive up to the northern beaches (Praia Grande or Iriguaçu) or south to Paraty-Mirim for the rest of the day (about thirty minutes drive). Head back to the Centro Histórico for the evening.

## DAY 8

Take a full-day boat excursion. Spend the afternoon and evening in the Centro Histórico. Go shopping.

## DAY 9

Hike to Praia do Sonho in the morning, then spend the afternoon exploring the village and beaches of Trindade. Eat dinner in Trindade or Paraty.

## DAY 10

Get up early (around 4:30 A.M.) for a drive to Mangaratíba to catch the 9 A.M. ferryboat across to Ilha Grande (leave your car at the port with the parking service). If you miss the boat, catch a private schooner in Mangaratíba or south in Angra dos Reis. When you arrive on the island, briefly explore the village of Abraão, then catch a boat tour out to Saco do Céu and surrounding beaches.

## DAY 11

Hike to Lopes Mendes, stopping at all of the fabulous beaches along the way. Take your time going out there, as you'll be taking the boat taxi back to the village for the evening.

## DAY 12

Hike to the Feiticeira waterfall then back to the village for a late lunch. Catch the 5:30 P.M. ferry back to Mangaratíba. Drive to Rio de Janeiro (4 hours) and return your car.

## DAY 13

Take a city tour of Rio. Spend the evening out in Ipanema or Leblon.

## DAY 14

Enjoy a morning stroll along the boardwalk from Copacabana to Leblon, then head to the airport for your flight home.

© CHRISTOPHER VAN BUREN

Stone streets lead through historic Paraty to the bay.

Most of the colonization of Brazil in the 1700s took place in the southeast region. The focal points were Rio de Janeiro, Paraty, and the gold towns of Minas Gerais. In this adventure, you explore these key locations with a focus on the natural beauty and cultural riches of the past and present. You'll see the famous monuments of Rio de Janeiro and the influence of the Portuguese royal court on the city, the beautiful beaches and historical port town of Paraty, and the rich culture and incredible food of the historical towns along the Royal Road in Minas Gerais.

boats docked in the Bay of Paraty

© CHRISTOPHER VAN BUREN

## DAY 1

Land in Rio and take the gondola at Pão de Açúcar, then a taxi up to Corcovado (Cristo monument). An afternoon walk along the boardwalk from Copacabana to Ipanema finishes the day. Choose between Ipanema and Leblon for an evening out.

## DAY 2

Tour the historical sights of Rio de Janeiro, including the two palaces, Theatro Municipal, National Library, and the churches of São Francisco and São Bento. If there's time, squeeze in the Museu Nacional de Belas Artes or the Museu Histórico da República. Spend the afternoon in the Jardim Botânical and an evening out in Ipanema.

## DAY 3

Catch an early bus to Paraty and take a walking tour of the Centro Histórico. Then catch an early-afternoon bus to Trindade to explore the beaches and do some snorkeling and sunbathing. Spend the evening back in the Centro Histórico.

The hillsides of Ouro Preto are a living museum.

## DAY 4

Enjoy a full-day boat excursion in the Bay of Paraty. Eat dinner and enjoy the evening in the Centro Histórico.

## DAY 5

Take a tour of the waterfalls and *fazendas* of Paraty, then take the afternoon bus to São João del Rei. Spend the evening strolling around the Centro Histórico of São João del Rei.

## DAY 6

Spend the day in Tiradentes with a walking tour of the sights, then return to catch the early evening bus from São João del Rei to Ouro Preto. Spend the evening out in Ouro Preto.

## DAY 7

Take a walking tour of Ouro Preto's churches and museums.

## DAY 8

Spend the morning in Lavras Novas and the afternoon in Cachoeira do Campo (both by taxi or guide) to see two different interior towns. Catch the bus after dinner to Belo Horizonte and go directly to Sabará. Spend the evening in Sabará.

## DAY 9

Take a walking tour of Sabará, then head back to Belo Horizonte in the afternoon to catch a flight to Rio and then back home.

© CHRISTOPHER VAN BUREN

# The Southern Tropics

For most travelers, the south of Brazil is one of the last places on the itinerary and it often never makes it on at all. But if you manage to squeeze in a visit to this vast and curious part of the country, this itinerary is designed to show you the best of the south in a fairly short period of time. In 10 days, you'll visit the incredible island of Florianópolis, work your way up the Emerald Coast, visit the German communities on the hillsides of Santa Catarina, and top everything off with a couple of days at Foz de Iguaçú, one of the natural wonders of the world.

## DAY 1

Land in Florianópolis and spend the afternoon in the old city center. Enjoy a sunset dinner at Mandalla Restaurante e Bar overlooking the lake. If you'd like, opt for a late night in the Lagoa neighborhood.

## DAY 2

Take the bus to Barra da Lagoa, where you catch a boat excursion to the Island of Campeche and enjoy some hiking and swimming on the island; then return for an afternoon on the Barra da Lagoa Beach or Praia Mole. Enjoy an evening downtown overlooking the bay.

## DAY 3

Catch the bus to Campeche Beach, then take the three-hour trail into Lagoinha do Leste Municipal Park. Picnic lunch at Lagoinha, then hike back to Pântano do Sul for a seafood dinner.

## DAY 4

Catch an early bus to Itapema and head directly to your hotel in Porto Belo. Spend the afternoon on the Island of Porto Belo and have dinner in Meia Praia. Alternative: Head directly to the Arvoredo Marine Preserve for scuba diving.

## DAY 5

Take the bus up to Balneário Camboriú. Check your bags at the bus station, then head over

the many beachgoers at Praia Laranjeiras

© CHRISTOPHER VAN BUREN

The best view of Foz de Iguaçu is from above, from a helicopter.

to the Parque Unipraias and take the gondola to Praia Laranjeiras (stopping at the park, of course). If you'd like, walk down to Taquarinhas and Pinha Beaches. Return in time to take an early-evening bus out to Joinville.

## DAY 6

Take an early bus to Corupá and spend the day at the Parque das Cachoeiras.

## DAY 7

Hike up to the Ano Bom waterfalls early, then catch the afternoon bus back to Joinville and then up to Curitiba. Enjoy dinner in the Santa Felicidade Italian colony.

## DAY 8

Take the Serra Verde Express train to Morretes with a return trip by van to Curitiba; then catch a late-afternoon flight to Foz de Iguaçu for the next two days.

## DAY 9

Enjoy a bit of sightseeing in Foz de Iguaçu.

## DAY 10

Spend the morning sightseeing in Foz de Iguaçu, then catch an afternoon flight to Curitiba or other final destination.

You could easily spend months exploring this part of the country, but this 14-day tour is a great distillation of the region. You get a look at the best of the *nordeste* in terms of history, culture, tropical beaches, and islands. You begin and end at the airport in Salvador, but if you can't find direct flights to Salvador, you can catch domestic flights from Rio or São Paulo.

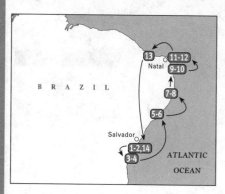

## DAY 1

Land in Salvador. Visit Pelourinho and the Mercado Modelo for the day. In late afternoon, catch a taxi to the Solar do União and Modern Art Museum. Enjoy dinner and a show (with a view of the bay) at Solar do União. Have a few drinks near your hotel (Barra, Costa Verde, or Campo Grande).

## DAY 2

Take a taxi tour of Bonfim and the museums in the Campo Grande area, then head straight to Flamengo for lunch on the beach and down to Itapuã for sunset and a taste of *Acarajé* in the Itapuã *praça*. Head back to your hotel to regroup for a night out in Pelourinho.

## DAY 3

Take a small plane to the island of Morro de São Paulo for the next two days. Explore the village

and sights. Take a late-afternoon walk along the three beaches, and eat dinner in the village.

## DAY 4

Take an island tour of Volta Ilha, enjoy the beaches, and spend the night in the village.

## DAY 5

After breakfast, walk around the beaches or village, then return by plane to Salvador and catch a flight to Maceió. Eat dinner in Maceió and then stroll the boardwalk.

## DAY 6

Day-trip to Maragogi to swim and snorkel along the reefs. Spend the evening in Maceió.

## DAY 7

Day-trip to Barra de São Miguel and Praia da Gunga, then catch the bus to Recife at around 5 P.M. (to arrive there around 10 P.M.). Spend the late evening near your hotel in Olinda.

## DAY 8

Take a city tour of Olinda and Old Recife. Spend the evening in Old Recife.

## DAY 9

Catch the bus or tour van to **Porto de Galinhas,** and take a long walk along the beach to Maracaípe (or take a dune buggy), where you can go snorkeling at the **Seahorse Reserve** and explore **Maracaípe village.** Spend the evening in the Porto de Galinhas Village.

in the shade at Praia do Flamengo

## DAY 10

Snorkel along the reefs at **Ipojuca.** In the afternoon, stroll around the village and take a walk along the beach to Cupe. Enjoy dinner in the village.

## DAY 11

Day-trip to **Carneiros Beach,** then catch the late afternoon bus back to Recife and an evening flight to **Natal.** Spend the final part of the evening on the **Ponta Negra boardwalk** in Natal near your hotel.

## DAY 12

Rent a buggy (with driver) for the day and visit the north coast, focusing on **Genipabu** and **Maracajaú** (for snorkeling). Spend the evening back in Ponta Negra, with dinner in the Rua Dr. Manoel A. B. de Araújo area.

## DAY 13

Day-trip to **Pipa,** with lunch and drinks at Praia da Pipa, then **swim with the dolphins** in the afternoon at Praia do Curral. Spend the evening in the Pipa village.

## DAY 14

Return to Natal for a flight to Salvador, then an afternoon or evening flight home.

the boat to Praia da Gunga

# Explore Brazil

# Rio de Janeiro

The images that come to mind when one thinks of Rio de Janeiro are many and varied, but one that always seems to appear is of the famous Copacabana boardwalk and the Copacabana Palace Hotel with its luxurious interior and high-rolling clientele. In its heyday, Copacabana (and the hotel in particular) was the setting of several Hollywood films, not to mention the playground of the actors themselves. Today, the Copacabana Palace remains the city's finest hotel, majestically overlooking the action on the boardwalk: beautiful women in the latest bikini fashions, athletes playing volleyball or demonstrating Capoeira on the sand, people jogging and cycling, and tourists from all nations congregating on the boardwalk to participate in the scene. And, like a director overlooking this stage, stands the Cristo Redentor high up on the Corcovado peak. To his left is the great historical center of town with a myriad of monuments and historical buildings from the glorious days of the 19th century, when Brazil was rich from the coffee boom and still bathing in the aftermath of the great gold rush of the 18th century. The 19th century brought many changes to Brazil, including its independence from Portugal and the end of its monarchy and formation of the republic. All this happened right here in Rio de Janeiro. To the Cristo's right is the famous Ipanema Beach,

# **M**ust-Sees

**Look for M to find the sights and activities you can't miss and N for the best dining and lodging.**

**M Palácio da Ilha Fiscal:** The palace is a pristine example of the neoclassic architecture favored by the Brazilian royal family in the late 1800s. The archways and hallways go on and on, while the outside is covered in ceramic tiles and perfectly-restored artistic details (page 30).

**M Museu Histórico da República:** This rich collection of historical furnishing and artifacts offers an intriguing insight into Brazil's history, from the early colonization to the present-day republic (page 36).

**M Morro de Corcovado and the Cristo Monument:** Rio's must-see panoramic lookout point is at the feet of the Cristo Redentor, Brazil's most famous monument. Standing on Corcovado Mountain, the Cristo looks down on Copacabana and the beautiful Rio coastline to either side (page 37).

© RIOTUR

**Copacabana Boardwalk**

**M Copacabana Boardwalk:** This four-kilometer stretch of beach is one of the most densely-populated areas in the world and is famous for its beautiful women in provocative bikinis, professional athletes playing volleyball in the sand, and celebrities walking or jogging up and down the boardwalk. The activity never stops at Copacabana (page 38).

**M Jardim Botânico:** This lush, tropical garden was create to suit the fancy of King João VI during his exile in Brazil in 1808. There are 8,200 different types of plants and flowers, many charming pathways, greenhouses, and thematic gardens (page 44).

**M Music and Dance:** There is something for everybody in Rio's hottest and most diverse night scene in **Lapa**. Listen to Brazilian roots music, dance the samba, or just watch the spectacle from a sidewalk café (page 47).

**RIO DE JANEIRO**

Rio de Janeiro

Palácio da Ilha Fiscal **M**

Music and **M** Dance

Museu Histórico da **M** República

Morro de Corcovado and the Cristo Monument **M**

Jardim Botânico **M**

Copacabana Boardwalk **M**

Lagoa Rodrigo de Freitas

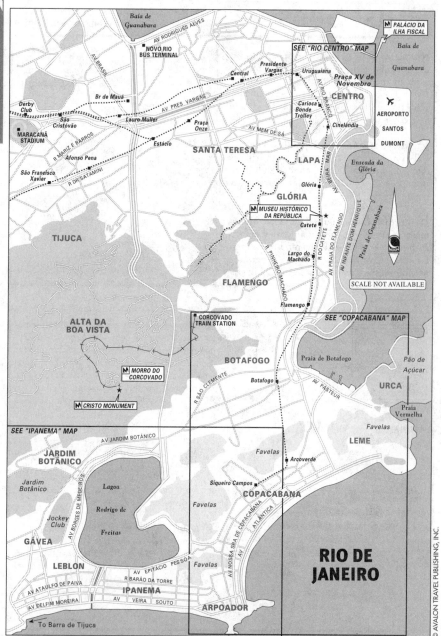

birthplace of bossa nova and home to many of the country's rich and famous. All this history is present here in Rio . . . in the buildings, in the landscape, and in the people themselves, who incorporate the traditional aspects of the city, while also encouraging its more modern, democratic traditions.

Not the least of these more democratic traditions is the popular festival of Carnaval, as much associated with Rio de Janeiro as Copacabana is. Carnaval is characterized by parades of highly costumed (or nearly naked) women dancing to samba rhythms, followed by elaborate floats that reach up to three or four stories tall, sparkling along the parade route. There are also many private galas and small, neighborhood festivities.

Over the years, Rio has not ceased to attract people from all over the world. Surfers come to join a great community of like souls who practice on the many great beaches in town and to the south; artists come to set up their ateliers in the bohemian neighborhoods, and wealthy playboys and debutantes continue to make Rio their home. Undoubtedly one of the world's greatest cities, Rio de Janeiro, like Paris, Rome, or London, is a place of dreams and fantasies.

## PLANNING YOUR TIME

With Rio's de Janeiro's recent bouts of violence and its overall reputation for crime, travelers are spending less and less time here than they used to. That's a shame, because Rio is loaded with natural beauty, history, culture, and attractions that continue to make this one of the world's great cities. Some travelers are so enthralled by Rio, they return here over and over to spend their vacations. But if you're set on breezing through Rio de Janeiro, it is possible to see most of the city's highlights in about three days. That may not sound like much for a city this abundant, but remember that Rio de Janeiro is relatively small and compact and there are only three principal areas that attract visitors: the historic downtown, Copacabana, and Ipanema (unless you're a surfer, in which case, you'd have to include Barra de Tijuca as a fourth). If you set yourself up in the Glória or Lapa neighborhoods

(where you can find reasonably-priced hotels) you'll be close to the metro line and will be able to access just about everything in the city with ease. On the other hand, some of the hotels in Copacabana may provide the kind of luxury experience you're looking for.

With that in mind, you'll want to spend part of your time checking out the historical sights in the old downtown area. Some of the 19th-century palaces, museums, and even coffee shops are spectacular. Take an afternoon walk along the Copacabana boardwalk and be sure to hit the high points (literally) of the city: the gondola to Pão de Açúcar and the view from the Cristo monument on Corcovado Mountain. These may require taxis to get to, since they lie just outside the main areas. Spend your evenings in Ipanema and Leblon with perhaps a happy hour in the Cinelândia area downtown. If you want to party, then a night in Lapa should probably be on the agenda. If you have a week to spend in Rio, then you'll be able to relax on the beach, take a walk in the park, or go on a guided tour of a *favela*. If you like to shop, then you should reserve a day for that activity, too.

You'll find Rio to be pleasant all year long, but the best time to visit is in the months leading up to and including summertime, September–March. The rainy season begins around the end of February, but it really hits in March and April.

## HISTORY

When gold starting pouring out of Minas Gerais in the early 1700s, the small and innocuous town of São Sebastião do Rio de Janeiro turned into the most important port town on the Brazilian coast, even surpassing Salvador in importance. It wasn't long before the Portuguese Crown took the capital of the colony away from Salvador and moved it to Rio de Janeiro. Roads connecting Minas Gerais (especially Ouro Preto) and Rio were constructed and traffic between the two regions grew exponentially over the next 70 years. Rio de Janeiro grew into the most important city in

Brazil. In 1808, the Portuguese court took an extended vacation in Rio, escaping the point of Napoleon's sword for a few years. Among the more important of these tourists was the Crown Prince himself, Dom João VI. The arrival of the royal family and court turned Rio into an imperial city, loaded with spectacular architecture, parks, and public facilities. It was Prince João himself who ordered the creation of the Jardim Botânico. While in Brazil, Prince João turned into King João VI. With his mother's death and the monarch and his court's returned to Portugal, Brazil was declared an independent nation—by the king's son, the prince of Portugal, who remained in Brazil to become the country's first emperor, Dom Pedro I. Naturally, the emperor and his new court set themselves up in Rio de Janeiro and his grand palace is open today for viewing. His son, Dom Pedro II saw the end of the monarchy in Brazil and the beginning of the republic, of which Rio de Janeiro was the capital from 1889 until 1960. By this time, the shift of power and economy was already leaning toward São Paulo and its booming coffee trade. The old presidential offices remain in Rio and are open to the public.

## Sights

### DOWNTOWN HISTORICAL DISTRICT

Many travelers come to Rio de Janeiro and never once set foot in the historical district. The beaches and attractions in the Zona Sul are so compelling that they overwhelm other agendas. That's a shame, because the historical architecture, museums, churches, age-old bars, and coffee shops in the downtown area make up the city's rich and fascinating history. Most of the main attractions are within a few city blocks of each other and you can easily create a nice walking tour of the area. I suggest starting at the pier with a trip out to the Palace on Fiscal Island. From there, you can make a J-shaped loop around the Centro Histórico. That puts you in a great area for sitting with a cup of coffee or cold drink at one of the city's legendary coffee shops or bars at the end of your tour. The sights in the following pages are arranged to facilitate such a walking tour. By all means, if you are compelled to walk down a particular street or other, go for it. The downtown area is safe during the day and full of historical architecture, colorful people, and interesting activities. That being said, a simple reminder can never hurt: Don't bring a lot of money, credit cards, or valuables with you on your walking journey downtown (or anywhere in Rio for that matter)—just enough for the day's activities.

### ⓜ Palácio da Ilha Fiscal

The marina area has a few different attractions to check out. First, inside the **Espaço Cultural da Marinha** (Av. Pres. Vargas, 9 A.M.–5 P.M. daily) is a small Maritime Museum with a few artifacts showing the history of sea navigation. Outside at the pier are two ships that are open for viewing: a battle ship and submarine. From the pier, you can take a boat across to the Fiscal Island, where you'll see the **Palácio da Ilha Fiscal,** one of the highlights in historic Rio de Janeiro. The palace was built by Emperor Dom Pedro II in 1889 and was used for about a week before Brazil was proclaimed a republic. After that, it was part of the marine base and later fell into disrepair. Restored in 2000, the palace is a beautiful gothic structure with many interesting stained-glass windows that show the life of Dom Pedro II and his family. Also restored were the ceiling panels and paintings on the walls and floors. The tiles on the outer walls shine with their original light green color. The architecture in general is fabulous. Inside the various rooms and hallways are permanent exhibitions related to the royal family, the palace itself, and the island. Visitation is guided and you should arrive early to get a seat on the boat, as it can get crowded (Sundays are less crowded). Boats leave at 1 P.M. and 4 P.M. Thursday and Friday,

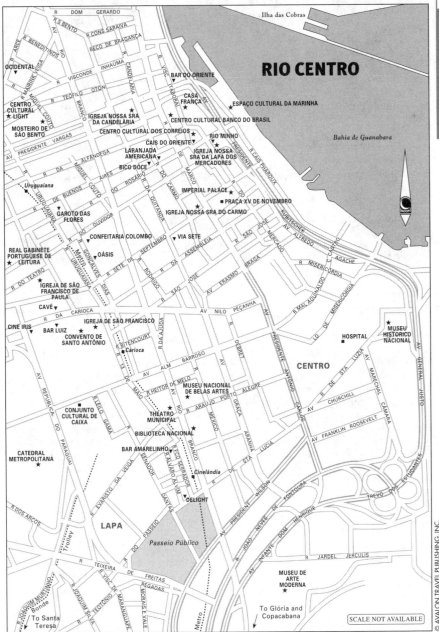

RIO CENTRO

sunset over the Guanabara Bay

COURTESY OF CHRISTIAN KNEPPER/EMBRATUR

1 P.M., 2:30 P.M., and 4 P.M. on weekends. The cost is R$8 for adults.

## Mosteiro de São Bento

On Sunday at 10 A.M. you can hear the Gregorian chants at the monastery of São Bento (Rua D. Gerardo 40, 7–11 A.M. and 2–6 P.M. Mon.–Sat. and from 8:15 A.M. Sun.), one of the most impressive baroque churches in the country. Built in 1663, the monastery contains detailing and sculptures with a mixture of dark jacaranda wood and gold leaf. Most impressive is the front altar and large paintings along the side altars. The pipe organ is a mixture of the original from 1773 and a new organ from 1945.

## Igreja Nossa Sra. da Candelâria

Built between 1775 and 1898 on the site of the first church in Rio, the Candelária church (Praça Pio X, Av. Rio Branco at Av. Pres. Vargas, 7:30 A.M.–4 P.M. weekdays and 7:30 A.M.– noon weekends) has a neoclassic design with numerous paintings and a marble interior. Highlights here are the huge, bronze sculpted doors and staircases.

## Galleries and Cultural Centers

Across Avenida Rio Branco (toward the ocean) is an area full of galleries and cultural spaces. First, there's the **Casa França** (Rua Visconde de Itaboraí 78, noon–6 P.M. Tues.–Sun.), which has temporary and permanent sculpture exhibitions in an 1820 neoclassic building. The building was designed as a fine arts school, but was used instead as a business center. Later, it served for a time as a customs house. Inside is a bookstore, coffee shop, and a lovely central atrium. Nearby is the **Espaço Cultural Banco do Brasil** (Rua Primeiro de Março 66, noon– 10 P.M. Tues.–Sun.), in a 1906 structure that was originally the headquarters of the Bank of Brazil but was reformed and turned into a cultural center. The building is fabulous; it has a theater, cinema, exhibition rooms, tearoom, and souvenir shop. It usually has some excellent national and international exhibits running. Inside is a restaurant/bar that is a popular spot for happy hour. Next door is the **Centro Cultural dos Correios** (Rua Visconde de Itaboraí 20, noon–7 P.M. Tues.–Sun.), an exhibition space with rotating exhibits that focuses on Brazilian sculptors and painters. They have

# THE ARCHITECTURE OF OSCAR NIEMEYER

The same elements that set the stage for bossa nova to emerge from Copacabana in the 1950s also paved the way for Brazil's most celebrated architect to rise to the top of his profession and scatter his works all over the bottom half of Brazil. Oscar Niemeyer was born in Rio and flourished in the cultural and economic boom there in the first half of the 20th century. It's difficult to find a capital city south of Rio de Janeiro that does not have some architecture of his design. Characterized by an ultra-modern, almost space-age treatment, huge open spaces, and geometric shapes, the works of Niemeyer stand out as some of the most daring and creative projects in the world of modern architecture. It seems that he went out of his way to break the rules and shock, creating buildings shaped like mushrooms, spaceships, cones, domes, and eyes. Whether or not you like his 1960s-style modernism, he certainly deserves a big C for "creative use of rebar, steal, and cement."

Some of Niemeyer's buildings are, indeed, monstrosities, such as his huge urban apartment complexes in Brasilia, São Paulo, and Belo Horizonte (known today as vertical *favelas*) and the out-of-place Grand Hotel Ouro Preto. In fact, one of the few structures that does not bear his grandiose and over-bearing thumbprint is also one of his greatest masterpieces: the small São Francisco church of Pampulha in Belo Horizonte. Other important Niemeyer structures include the governmental complex and Catedral Metropolitana in Brasilia, the waterfront complex in Niterói, and the Museu Niemeyer in Curitiba.

Oscar Niemeyer was born in Rio de Janeiro in 1907 and attended the Escola Nacional de Belas Artes. In 1939, he designed the Brazil pavilion for the New York World's Fair. His friendship with Joscelino Kubitschek—first as mayor of Belo Horizonte and later as president of Brazil—led to involvement in two of Kubitschek's visionary projects: the Pampulha Architectural Complex in Belo Horizonte and later the city of Brasilia. A member of Brazil's communist party, Niemeyer's projects were often disrupted and frustrated when Brazil's military dictatorship government took over in 1964, and the architect eventually left the country to set up office in Paris. Among his other professional accomplishments include work on the rebuilding of Berlin in 1954 and contributions to the Louvre in Paris.

10 exhibit halls and a concert hall for up to 200 people, where they often produce Brazilian musical performances. On the bottom floor, there is a nice coffee shop and a functioning office of the *correios* (postal service). Finally, there's the **Galeria Paulo Fenandes** (Rua do Rosário 38, noon–6 P.M. Tues.–Sun.) with contemporary works of art from local and national artists.

At this point, you might seek out the **Laranjada Americana** (Rua Buenos Aires 2C) for a fabulous orange juice. The shop, open since 1925, is in a great old building.

## Centro Cultural Light

Slightly out of the way at the top of old downtown is the Centro Cultural Light (Rua Marechal Floriano 168, tel. 21/2211-4822). The building was designed in American classic-style in 1911 and contains a number of spaces for exhibitions, concerts, and plays. There is an exhibition of antique photography showing Rio de Janeiro from the past. There are also artifacts and photos showing the Tramway Light and Power Company, the original inhabitants of the building, and there are paintings by Di Calvalcanti and others. There are often musical shows presented in the theater.

## Igreja Nossa Sra. da Lapa dos Mercadores

On the way down from the Centro Cultural do Correios in the direction of the Praça XV de Novembro is the small Lapa church (Rua do Ouvidor 35, 8 A.M.–2 P.M. daily). The small but charming church is full of marble and wood statuary and you'll enjoy walking along Rua do Ouvidor, one of the oldest in the downtown area, and checking out the old street lamps. The church played a minor part in the Chibata Rivolt of 1910, as it was hit by cannon fire from one of the ships at sea.

## Praça XV de Novembro

The *praça* that marks a major turning point in Brazil's history, moving from a monarchy to a republic, is right here in downtown Rio, in front of the old **Imperial Palace** (noon–6:30 P.M. Tues.–Sun.), home of the royal family from 1808–1889. Naturally, the *praça* was renamed in honor of the occasion, which took place in 1889, and the palace itself was promptly taken over by the state. Emperor Dom Pedro II and his immediate family went on an extended vacation. Inside the palace are a restaurant, food stands, and stores. Upstairs, they have stages for theater presentations and rooms for exhibitions. Nearby, you'll find other vestiges of the era, including the 18th-century **Arco do Teles** and an 18th-century *chafariz* (type of fountain that also served as a water supply). Exiting the *praça* toward Rua Primeiro de Março, you'll find the **Igreja Nossa Sra. do Carmo** (7 A.M.–5 P.M. Mon.–Fri.). Considered one of the finest baroque churches in the region, Carmo has a huge, vaulted interior that is rich in sculpture and ornamentation. It's worth crossing the busy boulevard for a look inside.

## Praça Floriano (Cinelândia)

During the golden days of Hollywood, Brazil was experiencing a cultural and economic growth period at the tail end of the coffee boom. Here in Rio, a number of things were occurring, including international recognition of the city— mostly due to the casinos in Copacabana. In the old downtown area, a number of movie houses were erected and the area that was Praça Floriano became known as Cinelândia. During the coffee boom just a few decades earlier, the *praça* had been chosen as the location of some important public buildings. Today, there is a convenient metro station right at Cinelândia and the area is buzzing during happy hour with various bars serving cold beer. There is often live music playing in the *praça* (usually samba).

The highlight of the *praça* is the grand **Theatro Municipal** (tel. tel. 21/2262-3935, 10 A.M.–5 P.M. Mon.–Fri.). The Theatro, built in 1909 at the height of the coffee boom, is a neoclassic building rich in wood, marble, and brass. There are stained-glass windows from Europe and *salas* rich in crystal and ornamentation. The best way to visit is to see an orchestral performance in the evening, but there are guided tours of the Theatro during the day (subject to cancellation for rehearsals). You can also catch a performance on Sundays at 10 A.M. and 5 P.M. Also in the Cinelândia area is the **Biblioteca Nacional** (Av. Rio Branco 219, 9 A.M.–10 P.M. Mon.–Fri. and 9 A.M.–3 P.M. Sat.), built in 1910 in a style to match the Theatro. It's said to be the second-largest library in South America and the eighth-largest in the world. Inside are numerous rare books (more than three million), all of which are available for viewing. Most impressive is the building itself with its grand marble staircase and columns. It's worth looking inside and they have guided tours for R$2.

Down the street a piece is the **Museu Nacional de Belas Artes** (Av. Rio Branco 199, 10 A.M.–5 P.M. Mon.–Sat., R$4 but Sundays are free), inside a 1908 building of renaissance style that was the city's fine arts academy until 1937, when it became a museum. It holds more than 14,000 pieces from national and international artists, with a special focus on the national artists (including works by Portinari, Segall, Calvalcanti, and Tarsila do Amaral, among others). There are also works by Picasso, Dali, Monet, and Rodin. Inside is a casual restaurant and souvenir shop.

When you're ready to take a break from all this history and art, have a seat at the **Bar Amarelinho,** a classic bar from the 1940s that sits in the Cinelândia Praça and usually attracts an international crowd. In the evenings, they have samba music and dancing, among other festivities.

## Praça da Carioca

If you see one church in the downtown area, make it the **Igreja de São Francisco** (Largo da Carioca, 11 A.M.–4 P.M. Wed.–Fri.). Recently restored, the church is a large and beautiful example of the baroque churches of the 17th and 18th centuries in Brazil, such as those found in Minas Gerais. In fact, some of the master artists and sculptors from Minas worked on this church, which was erected in 1657. The altars inside are replete with wood sculptures, covered in gold. There are numerous paintings along the walls and on the ceiling and a museum of sacred art inside. A metro station right at the Largo da Carioca makes it easy to get there and away. On the other side of the square from the São Francisco Church is the **Convento de Santo Antônio** (7 A.M.–6:30 P.M. Wed.–Sat. and 9:30–11 A.M. Sat.), which has its share of gold-covered sculpture lining the altars, along with Japanese sculpture from 1597 upstairs in the choir area. At the top of the square, you'll encounter the Rua da Carioca, which is full of food markets and various shops and is a great little stretch to explore. A highlight here is the age-old **Bar Luiz** (Rua da Carioca 39), which began in 1887 and has been the city's favorite German bar and eatery ever since.

## Rua Gonçalves Dias

If you walk up Rua Gonçalves Dias from the Largo da Carioca, you'll pass a number of cool shops. This is a great area for finding good deals on clothes. But the highlight of the street is the classic coffee shop and bakery, the **Confeitaria Colombo** (Gonçalves Dias 32). Used as the backdrop for numerous Brazilian films and soap operas, the café is a fantastic place to sit and have a refreshment. You can choose the upstairs balcony or downstairs in the main *sala*. A landmark in itself, the café is worth a visit for a cup of coffee and a look at the wonderful furnishings, including Belgian crystal mirrors and chandeliers. If you walk farther up Gonçalves Dias and turn right onto Rua do Rosário, you'll enter an area full of bookstores, restaurants, and coffee shops. You should find something here that interests you.

## Uruguaiana Metro Station Area

Finishing this sloppy loop around the downtown area, you come to a series of interesting sights around the Uruguaiana metro station. You can take the metro from Praça da Carioca to save both time and energy. The area around Uruguaiana is a bit nasty looking and filled with street vendors. First, there's the **Igreja de São Francisco de Paula** (Largo de São Francisco, 9 A.M.–1 P.M. Mon.–Fri.) from the 18th century. It has a rich baroque interior with some interesting detail work. More impressive is the **Real Gabinete Portuguese de Leitura,** Royal Portuguese Library, (Rua Luís de Camões 30, 9 A.M.–6 P.M. Mon.–Fri.), which has an impressive collection of books covering the high walls of the building's interior for many levels. The woodwork of the shelves and walkways is fantastic. Not far, you'll find a great place for a snack or refreshment, the **Penafiel** (Rua Senhor dos Passos 121), a Portuguese street café that serves some traditional recipes in an old building from the 19th century.

## Museu Histórico Nacional

Nowhere will you find a more complete collection of documents, art, artifacts, furnishings, and curiosities that shows the history of Brazil, from the colonization days to the beginning of the republic. Of special interest at the *museo* (Praça Mal. Ancora, 10 A.M.–5:30 P.M. Tues.–Fri. and 2–6 P.M. weekends, R$5 for adults, Sunday free) are the furnishings used by the royal family and the vast collection of old coins. The museum itself was once the arsenal complex for the country's soldiers, built in 1603, and an old prison.

## GLÓRIA, LAPA, AND SANTA TERESA

If you want to continue your walking tour of the historic downtown area, you can check out some of the attractions in the Lapa and Glória neighborhoods, starting with the **Museu de Arte Moderna** (Parque do Flamengo, noon–6 P.M. Tues.–Sat. and noon–7 P.M. Sun.). The modern building and grounds (landscaped by noted Brazilian artist Burle Marx) are the location of rotating exhibits from the collection of Gilberto Chateaubriand. His collection includes mostly Brazilian painters from the 1900s but also includes some international masters, such as Jackson Pollack and Picasso. There are also frequent guest exhibits of international status. Walking out the museum, you can stroll across the lovely grounds to the far side of the park and see the large WWII monument. Then cross the highway to the **Praça Paris,** where you'll see a garden inspired by gardens in Paris. There is an interesting view of the city buildings at one end of the *praça*. Continuing south, you can easily find your way to the Igreja Nossa Sra. Gloria do Outeiro, or simply the **Igreja da Gloria** (Ld. da Gloria 135, 8 A.M.–noon and 1–5 P.M. weekdays and 8 A.M.–noon weekends). Built in 1714 with an octagonal floor plan, the church is a delightful structure to observe from the outside. Inside, the highlights are the restored tiles that cover the walls.

## M Museu Histórico da República

From the Glória church, you can walk up to the metro station and take the train down to the next station, Catete, or take a taxi if you prefer. There, you'll find one of the most interesting museums in the city, the Museu Histórico da República (Rua do Catete 153, noon–5 P.M. weekdays and 2–6 P.M. weekends, R$5, Wed. free), which is inside the Palácio do Catete, built between 1858 and 1866. This is where Brazil's presidents worked and commanded while Rio was still the capital of Brazil (until about 1960). Inside, you'll see objects and documents from the history of the republic, including the bedroom and office of ex-president Getúlio Vargas, who shot himself on the eve of the military takeover in 1954, leaving a patriotic note behind. His bloodstained pajamas are on display. There is a bookstore and souvenir shop inside.

## The Trolley to Santa Teresa (Arcos da Lapa)

The neighborhood of Lapa sits between the downtown area and Santa Teresa and the best thing to do is pass over it in the **Bonde,** a trolley ride that goes from near the Catedral Metropolitana to the Santa Teresa neighborhood. The Bonde trolley begins at Rua Lélio Gama,

The best way to see the Arcos da Lapa is from below.

COURTESY OF EMBRATUR / DIVULGAÇÃO

near the Catedral Metropolitana, downtown and the Passeio Publico. It leaves every 15 minutes, 6 A.M.–11 P.M. Along the way, the trolley passes over the very photogenic Aqueduto da Carioca, more commonly known as the **Arcos da Lapa,** a Romanesque aqueduct built to distribute water from the Carioca River to the people living in Santa Teresa (then an upscale and noble neighborhood). The aqueduct was built in 1750 and today is used as a kind of bridge for the Bonde trolley. The best view of the aqueduct is from the bottom, of course, at the center of the Lapa activity—especially at night. The main area is along Rua Mem de Sá, but also includes the Passeio Publico.

The **Catedral Metropolitana** (Av. República do Chile 245, 7 A.M.–5 P.M. daily) is an enormous cone-shaped church erected in 1964 that holds up to 20,000 people. Inside are some interesting stained-glass panels and a small museum of sacred art.

In the neighborhood of Santa Teresa, you'll find the city's bohemian crowd. The area has attracted numerous artists and intellectuals and has a very alternative feel to it. There are numerous art galleries and ateliers, restaurants, and bars. It was once an upscale place to live but as it got boxed-in by the growing *favelas* on one side and the iffy Lapa neighborhood on the other, the upper class moved down the coast to Flamengo or Ipanema. They left behind some very cool 19th-century homes, which are still in use today. You probably don't want to just wander around this neighborhood, as it can be a bit unsafe. Instead, stick to the main street, Avenida Almirante Alexandrino, where you can walk around day or night without problem, and check out the bars and restaurants. To visit the bars and restaurants in other parts of Santa Teresa, you might consider taking a taxi.

## FLAMENGO AND BOTAFOGO

The area known as Flamengo was once a classy place. The president's office was nearby in Glória, and Flamengo housed a number of foreign consulates. Around the 1960s, everything moved out. The capital of Brazil moved to Brasilia and the upper crust moved down to Ipanema. Today, the area is home to the city's best economical hotels and restaurants. From here, the view of Urca and Pão de Açúcar from the coast remains unequalled. You can easily get here and away by metro if you want to come for drinks or food—or if you decide to stay in one of the hotels here and travel downtown or to Copacabana for the day.

Flamengo is home to one of the most spectacular palaces in Rio, the **Palácio das Laranjeiras** (1–4 P.M. Mon., Wed., and Fri., 9 A.M.–5 P.M. Tues. and Thur.). Still used as the governor's residence, the Palace also has rooms open to the public, with numerous works of art and furnishings from the 18th century. The building and interior are luxurious and interesting to see.

## ■ MORRO DE CORCOVADO AND THE CRISTO MONUMENT

Tirelessly watching over the craziness of Rio de Janeiro, the Cristo (9 A.M.–7 P.M. daily) has stood since 1931 redeeming the city and its inhabitants from the top of Corcovado Mountain. The famous monument, called Cristo Redentor (Christ the Redeemer), was designed to celebrate the 100 years of Brazil's independence from Portugal from 1822–1922. Better late than never; the 1,145-ton monument was lifted into place nine years later and has since become the very symbol of the city. Today, the Cristo Redentor is one of the world's most recognized monuments. It stands 38 meters tall on the top of the Morro de Corcovado, which is on the edge of the Tijuca National Park— the large mountainous area sitting right in the middle of the city. Many of the foothills of Tijuca are loaded with *favelas,* poor and lawless neighborhoods of Rio, practically at the very feet of the Cristo.

From the principal viewing deck at the feet of the Cristo, you get a magnificent view of the city, from the Zona Norte (at the left hand of Christ) to the Zona Sul (at the right hand of Christ). He stands, more or less, looking out in the direction of Copacabana (justifiably where

**The Cristo Redentor is one of the world's most recognized monuments.**

most of his attention is required). The monument was given some new features in 2000, including new lighting and new means of access to the top. You can now take one of the panoramic elevators up from the lower station, or take the high-tech escalator. If you prefer the original method, you can still climb the 222 steps, passing numerous souvenir shops and snack stands along the way. But first, you have to get up Corcovado Mountain to the lower platform and reception area. Access to the top of Corcovado Mountain is from the Flamengo neighborhood, where the streets begin their windy way up the hill. Many visitors take taxis up to the top (they are waiting at the bottom of the hill) or take one of the many vans that haul passengers in groups. The best way, however, is via the train that chugs up the hill (Rua Cosme Velho 513, tel. 21/2558-1329, www.corcovado.com.br). The station at the bottom was also recently revitalized and

contains shops, relaxation areas, and a photographic exhibition of the history of the monument. It costs R$20 and operates the same hours as the monument.

## PÃO DE AÇÚCAR

Despite the poverty, congestion, pollution, and other problems here, Rio is unarguably one of the most visually stunning cities in the world. Nowhere is this more apparent than from the top of Pão de Açúcar (Sugar Loaf), which jets out into the bay across from the Botafogo Beach. The gondola going up to Pão de Açúcar (8 A.M.–10 P.M. daily) goes in two stages, stopping first at the Morro da Urca, where you'll find a restaurant and souvenir shops. You'll also find an incredible view of the Guanabara Bay and a heliport. From there, you can jump the second stage of the journey, to the top of Pão de Açúcar, where the view is so awesome it makes you dizzy. From there, you can see all the way across the bay to the beaches of Niterói.

To get to the starting point at the base of Urca Mount, take a taxi or city bus (most say "Urca" on the front). You'll arrive at Avenida Pasteur 520. From there, you pay R$20 to make the trip, which leaves every half-hour with a group. The best time to go is at sunset, but any time on a clear day will make you happy. You might consider a second trip at night to see the city lights.

## ◼ COPACABANA BOARDWALK

The world's most famous beach boardwalk, Copacabana gained its greatest fame during Brazil's cultural boom in the first half of the 20th century. The Copacabana Palace Hotel, formerly a legendary casino, attracted playboys and debutantes from all over the world. Soon, this wide strip of white sand and blue waves became the summer playground for international travelers. The beach is the sight of international surfing competitions, beach volleyball and foot-volleyball competitions (a terrific sport to watch if you haven't seen it before), television shows, and Capoeira demonstrations

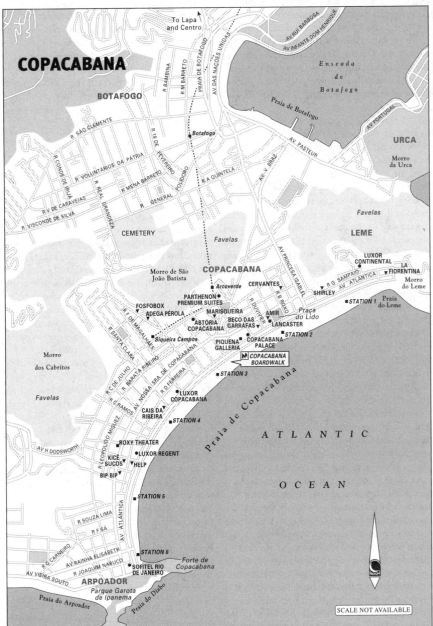

© AVALON TRAVEL PUBLISHING, INC.

every week during the summer. Residents of Rio come to the beach for morning and afternoon jogs and walks down the boardwalk and there are bike lanes for the many cyclists that come here. On Sundays during the summer, the city blocks one side of the street to traffic to facilitate all this movement and there are arts and crafts for sale and bikes for rent all day on Sunday.

The aforementioned activities notwithstanding, by far the most popular activity at Copacabana is people-watching and there are beach kiosks with tables and chairs overlooking the sand for just that purpose. It's common to see Brazilian celebrities and professional athletes walking here or playing foot-volley on the beach; many of them live right here in Copacabana. On the far side of the coastal highway are numerous condominium buildings (Paulo Coelho and Caetano Veloso are just two famed Brazilians with apartments overlooking the beach), top-end hotels, restaurants, bars, and stores.

At night, Copacabana becomes a cauldron of activities, most involving the tourist trade. If visitors are not being assaulted on one end of Copacabana (the north end), they are being hustled by prostitutes on the other (the middle and south end mostly). There are some popular dance clubs here, but most of them are packed with prostitutes and foreigners. The color of the night in Copacabana is definitely red and almost everybody on the street is looking to buy, sell, or steal something. The inland roads that parallel Copacabana (of which there are two main ones besides Avenida Atlântica on the coast) are generally less and less radical the more inland you go. The first street, Avenida Nossa Sra. de Copacabana, is the most active. You'll find restaurants, lunch buffets, markets, boutique shops, shopping malls, movie theaters, cheap hotels, expensive hotels. . . just about anything and everything is there. You can take this street all the way to the Praia do Diabo, where you can cross over into Ipanema. The next street is Rua Barata Ribeiro, which is a milder version of the other. The south end of Ribeiro goes into the tunnel that leads to Ipanema and you can pick up a bus going out that

way (better to go under than over, since the hill is home to two of Rio's grand *favelas*).

Note: The south end of Copacabana and the inland streets are relatively safe to walk around. The northern end is not. If you are staying in the northern end of Copacabana, be sure to take taxis to other parts of the city. Also, the ocean at Copacabana is generally considered to be polluted and not suitable for swimming, although sources differ on this point.

## Walking Tour of Copacabana

If you walk down the boardwalk in Copacabana, there are a few things you should be sure to include in your journey—occasionally coming in off the beach for a block or two to catch an interesting attraction on the inland streets. Before starting out, remember that this journey is farther than it appears on the maps and will take a few hours to complete. The same is true for a walking tour of Ipanema and Leblon afterward. If you're not up for a day on foot, look into renting a bicycle to make this journey.

At the very top of Copacabana sits the **Morro de Leme** and there's a trail that you can take out across the base of the mount to get a fabulous view of the beach. The trail is called the Caminho dos Pescadores (Fisherman's Way). Coming down toward the middle of the beach (between station 3 and station 2) is the famous **Copacabana Palace Hotel,** the first hotel built in Copacabana, in 1923. It was frequented by the likes of Marlene Dietrich, Clark Gable, Walt Disney, and Queen Elizabeth II. Fred Astaire and Ginger Rogers danced and filmed together inside. Today, it remains one of the city's most luxurious hotels, although the casino shut down in 1946. You can stop for an afternoon tea in their tearoom for only R$40. Reservations are recommended. Walk into town along Rua Paula Freitas up to Rua Barata Ribeiro, then turn left and continue until you see the **Baratos da Ribeiro Bookstore** (Rua Barata Ribeiro 354), where you'll find all kinds of treasures. Back toward the beach down at station 5, you'll find the **Roxy Theater** (Av. Nossa Sra. da Copacabana at Rua Bolivar), which was built in the

COURTESY OF RIOTUR

**Wavy patterns decorate the boardwalk at Copacabana.**

1930s and still shows art and feature films, including a 3 P.M. matinee. On the boardwalk, just south of the Othon Palace Hotel is the famous nightclub **Help,** which gets going every night around midnight with driving music and plenty of drinking and dancing. It is located in an old movie house. At the far end of the beach at station 6 is the Fisherman's Colony, where you can find the fresh catch of the day to take home with you.

Crossing from Copacabana to Ipanema on foot, you will walk past the southern end of Copacabana, where you'll see fishing boats and fishermen working their trade, as if from the first half of the 1900s. You'll see trees lining the point called Arpoador, where the **Copacabana Fort** (10 A.M.–6 P.M. Tues.–Sun.) is located. Built in 1914, the fort contains the **Museu Histórico do Exército** and some interesting German Krupp canons, along with maps and documents from Brazilian naval history. The fort offers an excellent view of Copacabana, which you can see from the patio of the Confeitaria Colombo coffee shop inside—an excellent place to sit for awhile. The walk out to the fort is also a pleasure.

## IPANEMA AND LEBLON

The point between Copacabana and Ipanema is a rocky area that attracts many couples at sunset, who sit overlooking the ocean, trying to avoid the beggars and street vendors who come around. There are many art galleries and shops around the point, particularly at Avenida Atlântica 4240, where several can be found in the same building. There is a park, called the **Parque Garota de Ipanema,** where you'll see arts and crafts vendors and a lovely, shady area with a blossoming tree.

You now begin your descent into Ipanema and Leblon, where the young and beautiful go to show off their bodies on the beach. There are sports and weight-lifting areas on the sand and more kiosks, bars, and restaurants on the boardwalk. The sections of Ipanema and Leblon beach are marked by the lifeguard stations, which are numbered. Different areas have different personalities and attract different crowds—from hippie surfer areas to gay and lesbian areas. The area at station 9, for example, is famous for its beautiful bodybuilders (mostly gay) and station 7 is where the surfers hang out. A walk down the boardwalk will reveal all. The water here is considered to be clean, but the waves are rough and the undertow can be dangerous, so take care if you go in.

Ipanema and Leblon are mostly residential areas for Rio's upper class and there are few hotels here. Most are high-end hotels and are located on the north end (closest to Copacabana). Restaurants and bars, however, are in abundance and the area is home to some of Rio's best eating and drinking establishments. The lower end of Leblon (as far down as Rua Dias Ferreira) is an excellent place to hang out; it has numerous restaurants, *lanchonetes* (snack stands), and bars with outdoor seating for watching the activities. There are numerous *praças* in Ipanema and Leblon and around

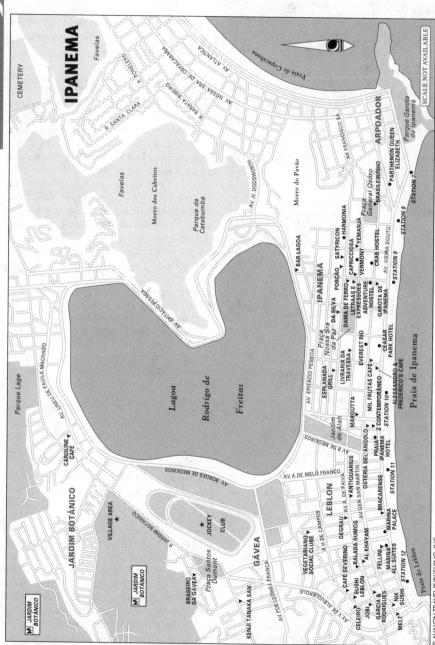

Rio de Janeiro

© AVALON TRAVEL PUBLISHING, INC.

COURTESY OF CHRISTIAN KNEPPER/EMBRATUR

**From the point at Arpoador you can look out at Leblon.**

these are great stores, flower stands, outdoor markets, and casual eateries. Check out the **Praça Nossa Sra. da Paz** and **Praça General Osóro,** where you'll find an outdoor flea market. A couple of kilometers from the beach sits Lake Rodrigo de Freitas, which is lined with upscale condominiums and restaurants and is a beautiful sight. On one side of the lake is the Gávea neighborhood, perhaps the city's most upscale district. The famous **Jockey Club** is there on the edge of the lake. It has several restaurants, shopping pavilions, and, of course, a racetrack and training grounds for the jockeys. Ironically, Gávea is at the foot of one of Brazil's largest and most dangerous *favelas,* Roçinha.

Separating Ipanema Beach from Leblon is a canal of water from the lake. Alongside the canal is the **Jardim de Alah,** a great place to stroll around or have a picnic. There are many great shops and restaurants near the Jardim.

## BARRA DE TIJUCA

Nearly everybody who has been there calls Barra de Tijuca the Miami of Brazil. It lies on the south end of Rio on a bar of land. On one side is the ocean and on the other is Lake Tijuca. It's full of high-rise buildings (mostly condos), shopping centers, clubs, and restaurants. Everything here is spread far apart and a car is absolutely necessary to get around. Unfortunately, driving to Barra de Tijuca is an exercise in frustration, since the few roads that go out there get seriously congested during peak hours. The restaurants and shopping centers in Barra are hardly worth the trouble of getting there. The area was designed as a residential district for the nouveau riche, and that's about all it is. The exception to this and the only attraction in Barra that pulls visitors down from Copacabana and Ipanema are the beaches. Here, the water is clear and beautiful and excellent for swimming and sunning.

### Beaches of Barra de Tijuca

**Praia Barra,** with its 14 kilometers of sand and heavy surf, has become a favorite among locals. The waves here make it great for surfing and there are bars and kiosks all along its extensive length. For this reason, it can get rather crowded on weekends. You can find surf shops all over the area. An extension of Barra is **Praia Recreio dos Bandeirantes,** also long and excellent for surfing. The huge expanse of the Barra and Recreio Beaches is frequented by cyclists and anyone interested in beach sports. **Praia do Pepê,** on the tip of Barra (closest to Ipanema), is perhaps the most popular and is frequented by Rio's famous sports and movie stars. There, you'll find water sports, like kite surfing and wind surfing. Beaches on the south end of Barra de Tijuca (Prainha, Grumari, and Abricó) are the most remote and can be almost deserted during the week, but they get plenty of surfers and sunbathers on weekends. **Praia Abricó** is the area's official nude beach, although topless women are not uncommon even in Copacabana.

## 🅼 JARDIM BOTÂNICO

Many cities in Brazil have botanical gardens, but none so special as the one here in Rio (Rua Jardim Botânico 920, tel. 21/2294-9349, www.jbrj.gov.br, 8 A.M.–5 P.M. daily). Covering 137 hectares on a hill behind Leblon, the garden was built by King João VI when the royal family came to live in Brazil in 1808. It features more than 8,200 species of flora, both Brazilian and international. There is a Japanese garden, an Amazon environment, an orchid garden, a rose garden, towering imperial palm trees, and greenhouses. One of the most intriguing greenhouses is full of carnivorous plants. There are water cascades and plenty of footpaths with excellent signage. The atmosphere is very tranquil and there are many peaceful areas to sit and observe nature. Other features include the **Botanical Museum** (11 A.M.–5 P.M. Wed.–Sun.), with documents and materials on display, and the **Museu dos Pilões** (8 A.M.–5 P.M. Wed.–Sun.), which was once a gunpowder factory and now has artifacts from archeological digs in the area. There are snack stands and souvenir shops.

Note that weekends in the summer can get crowded, so if you're looking for peace and quiet, you'd best go during the week. Access

COURTESY OF CHRISTIAN KNEPPER/EMBRATUR

the tree-lined streets of the Jardim Botânico

is via Leblon, next to the Jockey Club. On the road beside the garden (Avenida Pacheco Leão), there is a beautiful corridor of palm trees and you can walk around the neighborhood of Jardim Botânico to see the various art galleries and ateliers. The village is full of antique buildings and houses and is well worth a visit.

## PARQUE NACIONAL DE TIJUCA

To think that this vast forested area was once covered in coffee plantations gives one respect for the reforestation effort that occurred here at the end of the 19th century by order of Emperor Dom Pedro II. On the other hand, the 33 square kilometers of national park (the largest urban park in Brazil) was once only a small portion of the great Atlantic Rainforest that covered the entire area now known as the city of Rio de Janeiro. And the city was at risk of going completely dry due to the over-use of water by all these sugar and coffee plantations. Dom Pedro II decided to get rid of the farmers and put the monkeys and trees back up. It took 13 years and 100,000 saplings to get the monkey swinging, so to speak. Since then, it has received a number of updates and artistic touches, including the installation of bathrooms, reception facilities, and two restaurants.

Today, the Tijuca National Park (reception facilities: Praça Afonso Viseu, Alta da Boa Vista, tel. 21/2492-5407, www.sapnt.org.br, 8 A.M.–6 P.M. daily) is a great place to see some of the species from the original Atlantic Rainforest that was once here, including those cute miniature monkeys and plenty of plants and trees. There are trails going into the park, passing streams and waterfalls, and two of the three main sections of the park (the Floresta de Tijuca and the Serra da Carioca) are well patrolled by police. In the Serra da Carioca, you'll find several lookout points, including the Corcovado Mountain. You can hike to the **Dona Marta** lookout or the **Vista Chinesa** for a look over the city and coastline. You can also check out the very cool Mayrink Chapel, built in 1850 and sitting beautifully in the middle of the forest. In the Floresta de Tijuca area, you can hike up to the **Tounay Waterfall** and even go for a swim (don't forget your bathing suit). Another trail leads to the **Museu do Açude,** an interesting historical construction covered in antique Portuguese tiles. The administrative offices are at the entrance to the park, where you'll find two restaurants and plenty of shops and snack stands. One of the restaurants, called **Floresta,** is located in the slave quarters of an old coffee plantation. The best way to get there is by tour van, but there are buses that go to Alta da Boa Vista and can let you of at the park entrance. You can also take the metro to the Tijuca station (the last stop) and catch a cab from there.

# NITERÓI

An excellent way to spend a day in Rio is across the bay in Niterói, only 17 kilometers from Rio. Boats haul passengers between the two points throughout the day, every day. You can pick up a boat from the port near Praça XV de Novembro downtown. The trip takes about 40 minutes and costs around R$20 per person, depending on the type of boat you choose. There is also a bridge that goes all the way across the bay and you can find buses that cross it, leaving from the *rodoviaria* in Rio and heading to the *rodoviaria* in Niterói. Fortunately, many of Niterói's attractions are relatively close to the docks and the *rodoviaria* and you can walk or take a quick taxi ride to see them. The principal attraction near the docks is the complex of ultra-modern buildings of Oscar Niemeyer, Brazil's celebrated architect. The complex here is second only to the complex of government buildings he created in Brasilia— although the architect himself never got to see them completed. Finished only recently, and still undergoing some final touches, are some 10 constructions in the complex. Highlights include the **Catedral Metropolitana de Niterói,** which is a helmet-shaped building with interesting cathedral seating above the ground floor. Not one to practice favoritism, Oscar also created a Baptist church, called the **Catedral Batista,** which is located at the other end of the complex (known as the Caminho Niemeyer). There are two dome-shaped buildings, one of which is the **Fundação Niemeyer,** a museum dedicated to Niemeyer's work. Even the parking lot was designed as part of the complex.

By far the most interesting of the Niemeyer buildings in Niterói is a distance from the complex. The **Museu de Arte Contemporânea (MAC)** (Rua Visconde do Uruguai 288, 11 A.M.–6 P.M. Mon.–Fri. and 1–9 P.M. Sat.) houses a collection of contemporary art, mostly Brazilian, in a building that may be just as interesting as the art itself. The main hall is a round disk that sits on top of a cylinder, like a flying saucer on top of a pedestal. A large ring of windows circles the entire building, providing all sorts of interesting views of the bay and Niterói. The structure has earned a reputation as one of the world's most interesting examples of modern architecture and is now the *cartão postal,* or postcard (meaning the most widely recognized image), of Niterói.

## MARACANÃ

A thousand years from now, when archeologists look upon the ruins of Maracanã, they will figure it for a great temple built for the gods. In fact, Brazil's soccer players who frequent the huge stadium (Rua Professor Eurico Rabelo, tel. 21/2568-9962, 9 A.M.–5 P.M.) are often considered deities by the more fanatical fans. Holding some 114,000 people in a pulsating swarm, Maracanã, built for the 1950 World Cup, remains to this day the largest stadium in the world. But besides hosting soccer games, the stadium is used for major music concerts, including for the likes of Madonna and the Rolling Stones. Watching a game or concert there is a thrill. You can also visit the place during the day when there are no games to be played.

# Entertainment and Nightlife

Rio nightlife has its own personality and can be difficult to master. The city, while small and compact is very diverse and nightlife options are also small and diverse. Although there are a few big clubs and show bars (in Lapa, for example, as well as Melt in Leblon and Help in Copacabana), much of the action takes place in smaller venues all over town. Key locations are Lapa (with a rowdy and diverse crowd that includes a considerable gay scene), Ipanema (with small bars and music clubs, each with its own crowd), Gávea (with Irish pubs as well as large and small bars), and Copacabana (with its wild scene and an emphasis on sex clubs). There is also some activity in the downtown area at night, which mainly caters to professionals and a more mature crowd at traditional drinking establishments. The best calendar of happenings around town is in the *Veja Rio* magazine, which you can find at any newsstand for around R$6.

## SIDEWALK CAFÉS AND CAFÉ-BARS

### Downtown

There are plenty of classic bars and coffee shops downtown. Just walk around and you'll find them all over the place. One to look for is **Bar Amarelinho** (Praça Floriano 55), one of the oldest in town, which serves great draft beer, along with some great appetizers, in a casual but classical setting. Also, try **Bar Luiz** (Rua da Carioca 39), one of the city's oldest and a great place for German appetizers, beer, and conversation. It's also a happening spot for happy hour. Also in the downtown area is the **Ⓜ Bico Doce** (Beco das Cancelas), where you can get a variety of whiskies and great sausages. The **Garoto das Flores** bar (Praça Olavo Bilac 9) has been in town for 80 years and, along with beer and whiskey, serves some great home-style meals. It's in front of the flower market and has a great interior atmosphere. There are a bunch of café-style bars along Rua Miguel Couto, including the very popular **Ocidental** (Rua Miguel Couto 124), which serves a number of seafood appetizers. Finally, **Ⓜ Confeitaria Colombo** (Rua Conçalves Dias 32) is great for coffee and desserts and ispractically a tourist attraction with its 19th-century interior. It will take you back in time.

### Santa Teresa, Flamengo, and Botafogo

It's not easy to find all the great spots in this area, since they are spread all over. However, there are a couple of key areas, including the Largo do Machado, near the metro station, and the area at the bottom of the Urca and Pão de Açúcar mountains. The most popular areas are around the Arcos de Lapa and in Santa Teresa. Try the 100-year-old **Ⓜ Bar Brasil** (Av. Mem de Sá 90, Lapa) with its interesting interior and the **Carioca da Gema** (Rua Mem de Sá 79, Lapa), which is a very animated place where you can have a beer and check out the crowd. At night, they have live samba music and they also serve great food. In Santa Teresa, there's the **Bar do Arnaudo** (Rua Almirante Alexandrino 316, Santa Teresa) with Bahian food and a cool crowd. You can also look for **Adega do Pimenta** (Rua Almirante Alexandrino 296, Santa Teresa) for some German food and cold draft beers. There are more places in the Largo das Neves area of Santa Teresa.

**Bar Praia Vermelha** (Praça General Tibúrcio, Urca) at the base of Urca Mountain is an interesting place that's kind of hidden in the corner of the beach. Also, **Bar Garota da Urca** (Av. João Luis Alves 56, Urca), at the base of Pão de Açúcar, looks out over the bay. Finally, there's **Lamas** (Rua Mq. de Abrantes 18, Flamengo), which has been around since 1874 (in their downtown location) and has an interesting and eclectic crowd.

## Copacabana

There are more bars and cafés in Copacabana than you can probably count. Wherever you find yourself, there is probably some interesting establishment nearby. You can walk all along the boardwalk to check out the options on Avenida Atlántica, but it's probably not a good idea to traverse the entire length of the two inland streets. Instead, you can seek out **Bip Bip** (Rua Almirante Gonçalves 50), a tiny place a block from the beach near station 5, which has occasional live music. There's also **Beco das Garrafas** (Rua Duvivier), just off the beach, for a beer and look at the bossa nova days of the '50s. **La Fiorentina** (Av. Atlântica 458), on the boardwalk, is a good place to sip a beer and check out their collection of autographs from famous Brazilians. See how many you recognize. **N Adega Pérola** (Rua Siqueira Campos 138) is a popular place with a young, arty crowd. They have numerous types of appetizers, ready to serve.

## Ipanema and Leblon

Perhaps even more so than in Copacabana, Ipanema is loaded with coffee shops and simple bars. There are a lot of them around the *pra-*

*ças* and you can look for the very popular **Jobi** (Av. Ataulfo de Paiva 1166) for draft beer in a simple but cool atmosphere on the veranda or interior *sala*. **N Bracarense** (Rua José Linhares 85) also has a casual setting for sipping a draft beer. For an espresso and a good read, try the **Livraria da Travessa** (Rua Visconde de Pirajá 462), a bookstore/café with a great ambience and lots of books, including many in English. Also, the bookstore/café **Argumento** with Café Severino inside (Rua Dias Ferreira 714) is usually filled with young people until midnight. Staying with the coffee shop/bookstore theme, there's **Letras e Expressões** (Rua Visconde de Pirajá 276), which is popular all the time and especially on weekends. The bar **Garota de Ipanema** (Rua Vinícius de Morais 49) is where the lyrics to *Girl from Ipanema* were written. Formerly the Veloso bar, it's one of the oldest in the area. Finally, the **Botequim Informal** (Rua Humberto de Campos 646) is a simple place with great draft beer and sandwiches.

## BARS AND LOUNGES

In a perfect location on the beachfront is the **Bar D'Hotel** (Av. Delfim Moreira 696), inside the Hotel Marina All Suites. They have a retro ambience and serve all kinds of tropical drinks while you look out over the ocean. Another elegant place to look out over the activity on the boardwalk is the tearoom at the **Copacabana Palace.** You should call first or swing by earlier to let them know you'll be coming. Also check out the **Bar Lagoa** (Av. Epitácio Pessoa 1674) on the lake, a great bar—with delicious appetizers—that gets crowded at night and especially on weekends. It's one of the originals in the area. Don't get there too early; they start up around midnight.

## N MUSIC AND DANCE

Some of the best bars and pubs in Rio are in the Ipanema and Leblon areas. There you'll find all types of establishments, from elegant lounge-style bars to Irish pubs to Brazilian *choperias* to underground spin clubs. One of the clusters is on Rua Dias Ferreira at the far end of Leblon. Another is the vicinity of Praça Nossa Sra. da Paz. The city's most active area for music and dance is in Lapa, where the scene is a bit more eclectic and wild. The action spills out of the establishments and into the streets. Just go out to the Arcos da Lapa and start walking around. Get there around 11 P.M. and keep your eyes open and your wallet in a safe place (better yet, don't bring your wallet). The same is true if you visit the Santa Teresa area, which has plenty of bars and live music around the Largo de Guimarães and the Largo das Neves.

## Downtown

You can catch some jazz and bossa nova over the weekend at **Bar do Oriente** (Rua Visconde de Itaboraí 8, Centro). Check it out around 8 P.M. Also, the happy hour at Cinelândia usually continues well into the evening, so check

## A BRIEF HISTORY OF BOSSA NOVA

When you look back on it, it seems almost inevitable that something important was to come from Rio de Janeiro in the 1950s. Brazil was enjoying a time of prosperity and cultural growth under the presidency of Juscelino Kubitschek. Carmen Miranda had opened the doors to Hollywood and gotten the world to take notice of the big South American country and its music. Samba was sweeping the country as a popular music and dance form, and Copacabana was famous for its casinos and high-rolling jet set. Rio de Janeiro was full of nightclubs for all classes of people and musical tastes. American music scouts set up offices in town to help keep their ears to the music. Among the talent working these clubs were the likes of Antônio Carlos Jobim and João Gilberto—acquaintances at the time, although not exactly friends. Lena Horne, Sarah Vaughan, and Nat King Cole were among the musical presentations at the Copacabana Palace in those days.

João Gilberto was the son of a wealthy businessman from northern Bahia. His father played the sax and mandolin and was founder of his town's marching band. João got his first guitar at 14 and soon dropped out of school, formed a band, and began playing at parties and festivals in his hometown of Juazeiro. When his father learned that little João was not planning to continue his schooling but wanted instead to become a musician (synonymous with being a bum in those days), he cut off all financial support to his son. So began Gilberto's long history of leeching off others for support. Over the next 12 years, he would move from one handout to another, staying as long as anyone would support him, until eventually, practically nobody did. To make matters worse, João was rather fond of getting high on marijuana and sitting around playing his guitar and singing.

*Eu vim da Bahia cantar* (I came from Bahia to sing)/*Eu vim da Bahia contar* (I came from Bahia to tell my story)/*Eu vim da Bahia, mas um dia eu volto para lá* (I came from Bahia, but one day I'll return there)

Gilberto arrived in Rio with a government job set up for him by his family and a singing gig in a quartet called Garotos da Lua (Boys of the Moon), which played at various clubs in Rio and Petrópolis. He worked in the Cinelândia area, ironically, where all the popular music stores were located. Most of his time was spent in the stores and not at his desk. A year later, the Garotos da Lua got a record deal but on the day of the recording session, Gilberto was a no-show. He left the band the next day, after his band humiliated him for the no-show in front of the music store (where some of the band members worked). He was more interested in playing solo anyway and often promoted himself as a solo act on the band's time. Soon after leaving the band, Gilberto was fired from his job for not even pretending to show up to work.

out that area. An interesting club in the downtown area is inside the **Cine Iris** (Rua da Carioca 49, tel. 21/2266-1014), which is an adult theater, but they host a radical party once a month. Call for information.

## Lapa, Botafogo, and Flamengo

A favorite place for music and crowd-diving is the **Rio Scenarium** (Rua do Lavradio 20, tel. 21/3852-5516) in Lapa, where you'll find interesting interior decoration, live music, dancing, and plenty of sofas and places to relax and watch the crowd or the films that are constantly showing. They have three floors with all types of music, from Brazilian pop to samba and rock, and they are very GLBT-friendly. Call for the schedule of events. The bar **Mangue Seco** (Rua do Lavradio) is right in the heart of the action under the Arcos and has live music, seafood, and tables outside. During the week,

But Gilberto's great singing voice, guitar playing, and charming personality landed him plenty of contacts and gigs, and he spent the next few years scraping by on radio spots, ad jingles, and sit-ins for bands. As the story goes, one day he was kicked out of yet another friend's house and made his way to Antônio Carlos Jobim's place, then only an acquaintance from the club circuit. When he knocked on the door, Jobim's wife answered with the message, "Tom (Jobim) told me to tell you that he is not home." Gilberto later left Rio to play in Porto Alegre with some moderate success, but that success never quite translated to Rio de Janeiro and he left again to spend time with his sister in Diamantina, Minas Gerais. It's said that he hardly left her house, but spent every waking hour sitting and playing the guitar.

Meanwhile, Tom Jobim, the boy from Ipanema, had married young (at age 22) and was practically the opposite of Gilberto, concerned mostly with his domestic responsibilities and paying the rent. He worked as a pianist at night in any gig that would pay, from dive bars to the Copacabana Palace. He played frequently at the clubs on Beco das Garrafas (Bottle Alley), so called because residents threw bottles from the windows at the patrons as they made their way into the clubs. The alley was famous for its high-class prostitutes, jazz and swing music, and bohemian clientele. It was known by the musicians as Beco Joga Chave Meu Amor (Throw Your Keys My Love Alley). Jobim had acquired a decent amount of local recognition as a songwriter and piano player. He connected with poet and songwriter Vinicius de Morais, a government official who was to become his songwriting partner and later ambassador to France. By the time Gilberto returned to Rio, Jobim had already achieved quite a bit of success as a musician and songwriter.

Gilberto returned a bit more disciplined and determined, and his playing had changed and matured. His great singing and playing got him into professional gigs and recording sessions and his unique guitar style attracted some attention. People said it was like samba without the tambourines. One day, an important producer gave him an address on a piece of paper and told him to get in touch with this person to do some collaboration. The name on the paper was Tom Jobim. Their first recording together was Jobim's "Chega de Saudade" with Gilberto's "Bim Bom" on the B side. Slow to gather momentum in Brazil, the record got the attention of American scouts and within a year, Gilberto and Jobim were being produced in the United States. Gilberto's first royalty check from Verve/Polygram Records was around US$25,000 for his collaboration with Stan Getz.

*(Information cited from* Chega de Saudade: a história e as histórias da Bossa Nova, *by Ruy Castro, São Paulo, 1990.)*

they have live samba. Likewise, the **Emporium 100** and **Carioca da Gema,** both on Rua Mem de Sá in Lapa, offer a taste of samba. The **Asa Branca** bar has Brazilian pop music (MPB) and dancing right under the arches. For a helping of Brazilian roots music, try **Bar do Ernesto** in Lapa for some music known as *chorinho.* At the end of the night, there's **Nova Capela** (Mem de Sá 96), where artists go to pass the final hours of the night with more drinks and conversation.

The **Circo Voador** (Arcos da Lapa, tel. 21/2533-5873), or Flying Circus, has rock and funk concerts with some national names appearing from time to time. You should call ahead for tickets and to see who is playing.

With a few different environments, the **Cada da Matriz** (Rua Henrique de Novaes 107, tel. 21/2266-1014, Botafogo) keeps its music in the rock/pop flavors—both Brazilian and international. They have several DJs spinning their tunes and are generally open only on weekends.

### Copacabana

For a rock/underground scene, there's the **Fosfobox** (Rua Siqueira Campos 143); drum-n-bass and electronica night happens at **Sybno Music Club** (Av. Francisco Otaviano 20). There's also the famous **Help** dance club, which is as much a meat market as a dance club. Sex for sale is usually what's spinning there. It can be an interesting look into the modern Copacabana night scene, but if you venture in for a look, keep an eye on your pockets and don't accept a drink from anyone's cup or leave yours on the table unwatched. If someone tosses some *boa noite Cinderella* into your drink, you'll wake up the next day with no money and no good memories of the previous night.

### Ipanema and Leblon

**Melt** (Rua Rita Ludolf 47) has two levels and two different vibes. Music varies from electronic to samba-beat. You can also try the **Caroline Café** (Rua J.J. Seabra 10, Jardim Botânico, www.carolinecafe.com) for a similar experience

(run by the same group). The crowd at these two is generally the well-dressed Rio youth.

## AFTER HOURS

There are a lot of after-hours locations in Rio. It often seems like the entire city is engaged in activities of the flesh. Central meat markets include the bars and clubs along Copacabana beach, including Help on the south end near station 5. There are numerous strip clubs around Copacabana and plenty of them are also houses of prostitution. That's not to say that they aren't entertaining; most put on an incredible show.

The other popular center of everything goes is the Lapa area under the Arcos da Lapa. At night, this area lights up with transvestites, prostitutes, hippies, tourists, and all kinds of people who come to check it out. There are a number of bars in the area, where you can sit and watch the scene. The focal point is the area at Avenida Mem de Sá and Gomes Freire.

## GAY AND LESBIAN

During the day, station 9 on the beach of Ipanema is the central point for the beautiful boys. Afternoons and evening, the crowd simply moves a block or two inland around Ruas Farme de Amoedo and Vinicius de Morais. Check out **Bofetada** (Rua Farme de Amoedo) and **Dama de Ferro** (Rua Vinicius de Moraes 288) in Ipanema, which has DJs from Rio and São Paulo spinning techno and break beats. There's **Le Boy** (Rua Pompéia 102, Copacabana) and uptown, there's **Fundição Progresso** (Rua dos Arcos 24, Lapa). **Incontrus** (Praça Serzedelo Correia 15, Copacabana) has a very eclectic music menu and a predominantly gay crowd.

## POPULAR SHOWS AND SAMBA SCHOOLS

You don't think all those beautiful people dance down the Carnaval parade route in February without some practice, do you? In fact, the practice sessions begin around October and have become immensely popular shows for tourists and locals alike. The two largest and most popular practice arenas are those of the Mangueira and Salgueiro samba schools—two of the oldest and most traditional on the parade route. Their practice sessions take place on Saturday nights on the edges of town.

The **Mangueira** school practices in the Palácio do Samba (Sopé do Morro da Mangueira), which is in the Mangueira *favela* on the hillsides behind Copacabana near the São João Batista Cemetery. It's the most popular and crowded of the bunch. You'll see samba parades and dancing in full Carnaval costumes with music and drumming. It's always a spectacular event. You can reserve a table or box seats or just grab a seat in the stands with the crowd. The show starts around 10:30 P.M. and you should get there before 10 P.M. to make sure you get in. Mangueira has a downtown office at Av. Rodrigues Alves 733, tel. 21/2518-4088.

The **Salgueiro** school practices in the Tijuca neighborhood, which is on the far side of the Tijuca National Park beyond the last metro station. The **Portela** school practices in the Madureira neighborhood, slightly farther away from town. They also have a downtown office at Av. Rodrigues Alves 779, tel. 21/2233-1375. Both of these are very traditional schools and put on fabulous shows during practice season.

Remember that samba schools are based in *favelas* and you'll be entering the *favela* to watch these performances. The auditoriums are quite safe, but you should enter and exit by taxi. The best way to go is with a tour group, as they are known and recognized in the *favelas*. Try **Carioca Tropical Tour** (tel. tel. 21/2547-6327).

## CLASSICAL MUSIC

**Sala Cecília Meireles** (Largo da Lapa 37, tel. 21/2224-4291) in Lapa, has classical chamber music and popular music concerts. Call for programming. Popular and classical musical performances occur all over the city throughout the week. Check the *Veja Rio* publication for current listings, or pass by the various spaces while you're walking around town. Some of the concert spaces include the Espaço Cultural Banco do Brasil, Espaço Cultural do Correios, Centro Cultural Light, and the Imperial Palace downtown. You can listen to Gregorian chants at the Carmo church on Sundays. The **Theatro Municipal** downtown has opera and classical performances, as well as ballet and popular dance throughout the month. Most of their shows are excellent and worth a look.

## ART, THEATER, AND CINEMA

Besides the art museums and cultural centers listed earlier, there are numerous contemporary art galleries in Rio de Janeiro. Some represent internationally-known artists and others are more geared toward national talent. Many are worth a look inside to get a picture of the contemporary Brazilian art scene. A few of note include **Pequena Galeria** (Av. Atlântica 1782) in Copacabana and the gallery shopping at Avenida Atlântica 4240, where you'll find several galleries together in the same building near the Copacabana Fort. Also check out the galleries at Rua Visconde de Pirajá 82 in Ipanema and **Galeria de Arte Ipanema** (Rua Aníbal de Mendonça 27).

The **Conjunto Cultural da Caixa** (Av. República do Chile 230, downtown, 10 A.M.–6 P.M. Mon.–Fri. and 11 A.M.–3 P.M. weekends, free) is a type of cultural center with a focus on promoting contemporary (living) artists. They have a fabulous theater for plays and dance performances, a grand exhibition hall, and a small exhibition hall. Inside is also a coffee shop/bistro called Camarote Café.

If you want to know more about Brazil's Arte Naif painting, check out the **Museu Internacional de Arte Naif do Brasil–MIAN** (Rua Cosme Velho 561, Cosme Velho, www.museunaif.com.br, 10 A.M.–6 P.M. Tues.–Fri.). There you'll see a permanent exhibit of Naif art from all over Brazil and the world. There are more than 6,000 works.

The best place to get information about theater performances is in the *Veja Rio* magazine. Most performances will be in Portuguese, but some might be interesting to check out. Some of the more popular theaters include Teatro Ipanema, Teatro dos Grandes Atores, Teatro Leblon, and the cultural centers Banco do Brasil and Centro Cultural da Caixa. There are also plays going on at the Centro Cultural Light.

In Ipanema, there's the **Cineclube Laura Alvim** (Av. Viera Souto 176), right on the beachfront. In Leblon, there's **Espaço Leblon** (Rua Conde Bernadotte 26), with a couple of small theaters for artsy films, and **Cinema Leblon** (Rua Ataulfo de Paiva 391), with first-run and art films. You can catch a first-run film at the **Roxy Theater** (Av. Nossa Sra. da Copacabana at Rua Bolivar) in Copacabana.

# Festivals and Events

## CARNAVAL

If you asked people all over the world to name three things related to Brazil, about 98 percent would have Carnaval in their list. The biggest party in the world, Carnaval continues to draw international crowds to the many festivities across the country. Most people want to come to the mecca itself, to the party of parties, to Rio de Janeiro. Carnaval in Rio is officially four days in late February, but it starts well before that with warm-ups and practice shows. During the four days of Carnaval, everyone hits the streets to watch the street parades, enter private parties, or enter the holy of holies—the official parade route known as the Sambódromo. The Sambódromo is a large stadium built specifically for Carnaval (although it's used during the year for other events).

Carnaval always was and still is a festival for the masses. It occurs just before the 40 days of Lent and is, in effect, a final chance to sin before the spiritual trail ahead. The letting-it-all-out period in Brazil has been elevated to an art form (or lowered to a free-for-all, depending on your point of view) and Carnaval gets rowdy and often out of control for at least four days.

### Festival Galas and Carnaval Balls

Another popular way to pass Carnaval in Rio de Janeiro is in one of the private galas that occur all over the city. The galas range from raunchy to super-sophisticated and are located in restaurants, clubs, and hotels all along Ipanema, Copacabana, and Flamengo. These galas are generally expensive (the good ones) with price tags of R$150–500 per night. Highlights inside the parties often include costumed dancers, live samba music, drumming groups, strip shows, and specialty performers (magicians, clowns, etc.). There is always an edge of eroticism and sometimes more than an edge. Many parties are frequented by transvestites, as sexual expression is generally the theme of Carnaval.

### Marching in the Parade

You can participate in the parade by purchasing one of the costume kits from the school of your choice. Most of these should be purchased well in advance—not because they sell out but because prices go up the closer it gets to Carnaval. The best way to purchase your way into a samba school during the parade is through a local guide who can arrange the Brazil-side details. Check lists of guides at www.sindegtur.org.br/2004 and contact one or two to begin a conversation. If you want to get an idea about each of the schools and their previous getups, many of them have websites: Beija Flor (www.beija-flor.com.br), Caprichosos (www.caprichososdepilares.com.br), Imperatriz (www.imperatrizonline.com), Mangueira (www.mangueira.com.br), Portela (www.voodaaguia.com.br), and Salgueiro (www.salgueiro.com.br). The most popular schools will be the most expensive (Mangueiras, Salgueiro, Portela, and Beija Flor), ranging from R$250–600.

### Sambódromo and the Parade Route

Since around 1985, Carnaval in the Sambódromo has not changed much. Over the four official days of Carnaval, the 14 principal samba schools, along with a number of minor *blocos* (parade groups), dance down the parade route in outrageous costumes to the spine-tingling crack of Afro-Brazilian drumming. The costumes don't really change much from year to year. They always involve colorful hoop dresses for the *Bahianas* and a King and Queen of each school in lavish, birdlike garb, loaded with feathers and shiny things. These two dance out in front, twirling and spinning their way back and forth along the route. Then, doing the famous samba four-step on top of the floats and all around, are the dancers—semi-nude, voluptuous, and glamorous. It's similar each year, but stunning nonetheless. To see it live and up close is an emotional experience and you're sure to walk out half-deaf and in a kind of euphoric trance.

Unfortunately, the experience of the Sambódromo stadium has also gone unchanged for years. It's hot, crowded, and there are unbearable lines for bad food, worse beer, and filthy bathrooms. You're bound to sit next to loud and obnoxious people who throw food and chain-smoke the entire time. But it's the only place from which to see the parade in relative comfort and safety. The best idea is to try to get down on the floor as close to the parade as possible or on the lower edge of the stadium seats. The best days to go are on Sunday and Monday of Carnaval, when the grand samba schools go down the line with their head-spinning costumes and over-the-top floats.

Prices for seats in the Sambódromo vary depending on the day you go and where you sit. There are some 62,000 seats spread over 13 different stadium banks, called sectors. The banks at the end of the route are the largest and most crowded as this is the official judging area. However, the better seats are in the middle of the parade route in the smaller banks (3, 5, 7, and 9). These are also the locations of the box seats. On the ground level in front of each of these banks are more seats. Tickets usually get you in for eight hours, either during the day or at night. Scalpers sell tickets up to the last minute outside the stadium and around town, but you should be careful when purchasing these to make sure they are not counterfeit. Of course, you'll pay a premium for last-minute arrangements. Also, hanging around the outside of the Sambódromo during Carnaval is not the safest thing to do.

For information about the event and tickets, see the Riotur website (www.rio.rj.gov.br), which has a page dedicated to the current Carnaval event (Portuguese only). You can also get in touch with travel agents to arrange everything in advance, including tickets.

## Street Parades

There are a number of street parades that occur around town, outside of the Sambódromo madness. These are generally free or low-cost attractions that include costumes, drumming, music, and dancing. The street parades can be a bit dangerous if you are not participating in the parade with the *bloco* (group). Like all major Carnaval street scenes around the country, the Rio street parade consists of two groups: those inside the *blocos* and those bouncing up and down alongside the *blocos*. The bouncing bodies outside the rope are known as *pipoca* (popcorn) and are generally exposed to all sorts of assault and criminal activities. Since Carnaval always contains an erotic element, the tension among the masses can go off the meter. Single women and even couples are not advised to bounce around the street parades without participating in a *bloco*. Inside the rope, participants wear the tee shirts or costumes of the *bloco* and are somewhat protected by the group's security. You can purchase ingress into a *bloco* in advance or sometimes while they are marching along. There will generally be someone toward the back of the group making sales.

## NEW YEAR'S EVE

The largest outdoor bash in Rio next to Carnaval is Réveillon (New Year's eve). The event is marked by major fireworks shows that occur off the coastline near Copacabana and Ipanema. Besides the fireworks, there are stages on the beach with live music and dancing. Stands are lined up along the boardwalk to sell all types of alcohol and snacks and the crowd is unbearable. Like any free street party, Réveillon in Copacabana attracts a criminal element and you should be careful walking around. If you participate in the beach scene, don't put anything in your pockets and don't bring anything you wouldn't want to lose. The best way to enjoy the fireworks is from the comfort of a beachfront hotel, which you have to book about a year in advance. Of course, prices are three or four times the normal amounts. You can also check with hotels that have rooftop restaurants and pool areas, as they often throw parties in which you can participate for a fee. You'll probably pay about R$300–500 for the night (per person) with all drinks included.

## HALF MARATHON

More than 15,000 participants run along the coast of Rio de Janeiro from Leblon to the top of Flamengo in one of the world's most scenic half-marathon races. The international event attracts runners from more than 15 countries and you can reserve a position among them. The event takes place in September each year and is hosted by **yescom** (www.yescom.com.br). You can also get information from Easygoing Brasil (www.easygoing.com.br).

# Shopping

## OUTDOOR FAIRS AND MARKETS

You'll see people selling art, beach clothes, bikinis, jewelry, and just about every type of clothing and craft along the boardwalk in Copacabana on weekends. Officially, the market is located at the Praça do Lido at the far end of the boardwalk. During the week, you'll also find items for sale on the sand right by the boardwalk, particularly hammocks, towels, and sarongs. Don't forget the outdoor flea market on Sundays in Ipanema at the Praça General Osório, called the Feira Hippie. As its name suggests, it consists of many artsy-craftsy types of items and you should keep your eyes open when shopping here (as you should anywhere in Rio). There's another arts and crafts fair that takes place on Thursdays and Fridays from 8 A.M.–6 P.M. in Praça XV de Novembro downtown. The fair features works in leather, wood, ceramic, and silver, and there are numerous stands with regional foods for sale.

A true art fair takes place in the village of Jardim Botânico on the main walkway. The artists of the area display their paintings, drawings, and sculptures 6 P.M.–midnight on weekends. It's a great thing to do if you're after something different for an evening. Take a taxi there and back.

## BOUTIQUES

Ipanema is also the location of many boutique shops, including a festival of women's lingerie and beach fashions. The principal areas for these items are around the intersection of Ruas Garcia d'Avila and Barão de Torre. Also, try the **Galeria Ipanema 2000** (Rua Visconde de Pirajá 547). There are plenty of similar shops in Copacabana along Avenida Nossa Sra. da Copacabana without the brand names and high prices.

# Sports and Recreation

## TOURS AND EXCURSIONS

### Boat Trips

You can take an excursion on the 1910 tugboat *Rebocador Laurindo Pitta*. The boat leaves from the pier at the Espaçe Cultural da Mirinha and circles the bay. Trips leave at 1 P.M. and 3 P.M. Cost is R$6. There are also excursions out to Niterói and to the Island of Fiscal. Most leave from the pier in front of the Espaço Cultural da Marinha downtown.

The **Saveiros** (Rua Conde de Lages 44, Glória, tel. 21/2224-6990, www.saveiros.com.br, R$20 for adults) tour leaves from the marina at Glória and takes you all the way to Niterói to look at the coastline and beaches. It leaves at 9:30 A.M. every day and takes about two hours. **Marlin Yacht Charters** (Av. Infante Dom Henrique, Glória, tel. 21/2225-7434) has a morning and sunset cruise around the bay, passing Pão de Açúcar and other highlights. Boats leave at 9 A.M. and 5 P.M. The **Tocorimé Veleiro Oceânico** (Av. Infante Dom Henrique, tel. 21/2226-7921, www.tocorime.net) group has boats that go all the way to Ilha Grande off the southern coast of Rio de Janeiro state. They have smaller trips that go around the bay and to some of the small islands off Rio. Other companies offering extended boat trips from Rio include **Tropical Cruises Brasil** (tel. 21/2487-1687, www.tropicalcruises.com.br) and **Fantasia Turismo** (tel. 21/2549-0399, www.fantasiatur.com.br).

### City Tours

There are numerous guides in Rio that offer city walking and driving tours. Most of these need to be contacted in advance to make arrangements. Fortunately, the best guides—the ones registered with EMBRA-TUR—are all listed at the convenient tour-guide syndicate website: www.sindegtur.org.br/2004. There is an English page and you can enter criteria for choosing a guide in the Rio area. You can also find guides for hiking,

boating, and other tours, and get assistance with Carnaval, New Year's eve, and other special needs. Many guides are English-speaking and you can email them to begin a conversation.

### Favela Tours

The largest and most violent *favela* in Rio is Rocinha (see sidebar), sitting just above the Gávea neighborhood with a privileged view of the ocean—undoubtedly, some of the best real estate in the southern hemisphere. The *favela* is loaded with criminals, principally funded by drug traffic, who engage in regular wars with the Rio police (when they're not black-mailing Rio's government officials or rigging Carnaval). The neighborhood also has a commercial side and has become something of a tourist attraction, with regular visits by foreigners and Brazilians alike. They have their own cable TV station, which airs programs related to the *favela*. There are plenty of foreigners who live up there and they have become something of a legend with their studios and art ateliers and incredible views. They are generally married to someone from the *favela*. You can't exactly walk up into the *favela* on your own, but there are authorized guides who can take you in—generally without any risk or confrontation whatever. You have to be careful when and where you take pictures, but the guides will help with an orientation. Check with **Favela Tour** (tel. 21/3322-2727, www.favelatour.com.br).

### Helicopter Tours

You can pick up a helicopter tour of the city through **Helisight** (Rua Conde Bernadotte 26, tel. 21/2511-2141, 21/2259-6995, 21/2542-7895, www.helisight.com.br) at the heliport on Urca Mountain (the first stage of the gondola to Pão de Açúcar). A trip of about 10 minutes (R$100–150) takes a quick spin around Pão de Açúcar, the Cristo monument, and Copacabana. Longer trips take

# ROCINHA: NOW THE BIGGEST FAVELA IN TOWN

In Portuguese, the word *roça* literally means a tract of land that has been cleared for planting. It is also used colloquially to refer to any field or backwoods area and that is exactly what Rocinha (little *roça*) was in the late 1800s. It started as a settlement in a clearing near the sugar plantations where poor ranch hands and their families lived. At that time, Rio was a land of opportunity for Brazilians from all over the country and thousands of poor folks filed into the city to work in or around the sugar trade. When the financial crisis of 1929 occurred, Brazil's sugar business took a major hit. Thousands of workers were jobless practically overnight and many fled to the hillsides of Rio, where they were still close to the plantations, but didn't have to pay for rent or other services. The largest of these hillside communities was Rocinha in the far south end of the city.

And so began the poor neighborhoods of Rio de Janeiro, known as *favelas*. They are essentially squatter settlements; residents move in and find a corner of land on which to make a home—if you can call it that. Homes generally start out as large tents made of second-hand materials, like cardboard boxes, string and plastic bags. Over the years, the family will begin to swap these materials for sheets of wood, then ceramic blocks. A lucky few get water inside their homes by digging to the water table below, but most end up hauling it every day from streams nearby at the bottom of the hill. Eventually, a family might even get electricity through an illegal electric line tap, known as a *gato* (cat), or through an electricity reseller. Some residents or business owners on the edges of the *favelas* who get electricity from the city often resell it to families on the hillside, at a profit. Electric lines are over-tapped, streams are polluted, and public services are practically nil. The hillsides are communities with strong ties (many of them consisting of large extended families) and around 50–100 homes stacked on top of one another. As children grow and have their own kids, more houses get stacked

on. Combine a dozen of these hillsides and you have a *favela*.

In the 1990s, Rocinha went from around 12,000 domiciles to around 25,000, with an estimated population of 125,000 by the end of the decade. There are currently over 500 *favelas* in Rio, representing over 40% of the population of the city. The growth of the *favelas* in Rio is increasing at a rate of 30% per year, while the growth rate of the city is only around 11% annually. The *favelas* are literally taking over. Since the growth of drug trafficking in the 1970s, the *favelas* have been increasing in power and wealth and some say that the Rio government is badly corrupted by ties to the *favela* drug money. Besides the drug trade, *favelas* also dominate Carnaval and every samba school that heads down the parade route is based in one of the *favelas*. This is a legitimate source of income for the *favelas*, but also a source of political power struggles. In 2005, for example, the president of the Mangueira samba school was murdered for not choosing a drug trafficker's girlfriend to be the queen of the parade.

To protect their interests in what is essentially a feudal system, traffickers in the *favelas* operate sophisticated security forces, usually consisting of the neighborhood's youth, heavily armed and trained. They work long hours every day watching for intruders or other threats, including city police, residents of other *favelas*, or any unwelcome visitors. Street wars among the *favelas* and between *favelas* and the police are commonplace in Rio.

Although Rio's *favelas* are unique because of their privileged position on the hillsides overlooking the coastline and encroaching on the rich communities below, Rio is not the only place in Brazil with so many *favelas*. In fact, the highest concentration of *favelas* is located on the outskirts of São Paulo in the Jardim Angela *favela* (meaning circular brush area), the most dangerous *favela* in the world. Rio takes second place and the cities of Fortaleza, Curitiba, Belo Horizonte, Salvador, and Belém all have significant *favela* populations.

you all the way up or down the coastline, last up to two hours, and cost up to R$600 per person. There are several other trips in-between. Helisight has pads near Lake Freitas and in the Tijuca National Park near the Cristo monument.

## WALKING AND JOGGING

Most visitors end up doing most of their scenic walks right along the boardwalk from Copacabana to Ipanema. From the top of Copacabana all the way to the end of Ipanema is about nine kilometers. There are plenty of beach kiosks, bars, and juice stands for refreshing yourself along the way. Another favorite beachfront walk is along the Parque Brigadeiro Eduardo Gomes in the Flamengo neighborhood. If you walk along that part of the coast, I suggest that you start early and walk from north to south so you can keep the beautiful Pão de Açúcar in view as you go. Both of these paths are also great for jogging and you can even jog in your bathing suit, since you're right on the beach.

There's another walking and jogging path that goes from Praia Vermelha at the foot of the Urca Mountain all along its base. It's only open to joggers and it's very secure. A similar path goes from the top of Copacabana around the base of the Morro de Leme. This one is not as secure, but if you have nothing on you but your jogging suit, then you will probably not be an interesting target.

Finally, a favorite walking destination is around the Lagoa de Freitas, where you can take the nine-kilometer path around the lake. A final area for walking is along the coastline of Barra de Tijuca, where the beach stretches on for about 12 kilometers.

Every year, Rio hosts an international half-marathon run along the coastline of the city—from Flamengo all the way down to Praia de São Conrado. You can participate by getting in touch with the organizers at www.yescom.com.br or the English-speaking Easygoing Brazil agency (tel. 11/3801-9540, www.easygoing.com.br).

## SURFING AND BEACH ACTIVITIES

Most of the surfing in the city takes place around the *pontal* between Copacabana and Ipanema, known as Arpoador. There have even been competitions on the point, although the waves are not of international quality. Still, there are some great breaks and surfers hang out there waiting for the best conditions. On the other side of the Praça Garota de Ipanema are a number of surf shops where you can buy or rent boards. For better, longer waves, surfers head down to the Barra de Tijuca beaches or all the way down to Prainha, about 45 minutes to the south by car.

## CYCLING AND ROLLERBLADING

One of the most enjoyable ways to see the Rio coastline is by bike or blade. There is a bike lane all the way from the bottom of Leblon to the top of Copacabana. On Sundays, the traffic along this route is controlled and the area becomes a huge biking arena. You can rent bikes right on Avenida Atlântica by the hour. During the week, you can try **Pinarella** (Av. Atlântica 4240). There is also a terrific bike lane that goes around Lake Freitas and you can even rent bikes right on the lake at Mistura Fina "Café com Bicicleta" (Av. Borges de Medeiros 3207). Another great place to ride is along the shoreline of Flamengo and Botafogo, although you might want to take a taxi from Copacabana over to the Botafoto coast to avoid traffic. Taxi drivers might collect an extra fee for hauling your bike; ask ahead of time so you're not surprised. A great ride is the road going all the way along the beach at Barra de Tijuca. This is also a great place for in-line skating.

## HANG GLIDING, PARAGLIDING, CLIMBING

You can fly high above the southern beaches of Rio in a hang glider—even if you've never been in one before. Trained instructors can take you on a tandem flight from the ramp at

Pedra Bonita in the São Conrado hills. From there, you fly over Praia Pepino, where you can let go and take pictures (the instructor has the helm and you're strapped in). It's definitely a rush for anyone who has not flown before, and the view is hard to beat. You can just go out to the ramp where instructors are waiting on weekends, or call ahead to Bruno Menescal (tel. 21/3322-0266 or tel. 21/9962-7119).

If you're looking for a good climb, you can scale the face of Pão de Açúcar or the Corcovado Mountain. There are tall rocks in the Tijuca Park and other peaks to conquer on the north side of the city. The views are even better than those from the hang gliders. Excursions can be arranged with **Limite Vertical** (tel. 21/2527-4938, www.escaladarj.com.br).

## KAYAKING AND CANOEING

There are a few great kayak trips you can take around the bay and one of the best is only a half-hour row from Praia Vermelha, at the base of Urca, to the tiny island of Cotundaba. There, you'll encounter almost nothing but beautiful rocky inlets and clear water. You can get in touch with the **Federação de Canoagem do Estado do Rio de Janeiro** (Palácio dos Esportes Rua Visconde de Inhaúma 39, sala 606, Centro, tel. 21/2263-5276) in Praia Vermelha. You can find a listing of sportive organizations in Rio at www2.rio.rj.gov.br/smel/links.asp.

## SCUBA DIVING

If you're a diver, a great way to experience the coastline around Rio de Janeiro is on a dive excursion that leaves from the city. Excursions head out to local areas, such as the coast off Ipanema, the Cagarras Islands, and up to the beaches of Cabo Frio and Arraial do Cabo. Or you can go as far as Ilha Grande and Angra dos Reis on multi-day trips. Equipment and guides are part of the package. Try **Dive Point** (Av. Ataulfo de Paiva 1174, Leblon, tel. 21/2239-5105, www.divepoint.com.br) and **Diver's Quest** (Rua Maria Angélica 171, Jardim Botânico, tel. 21/2266-4041, www.diversquest.com.br).

## HIKING

Hiking in the Rio area is generally done in the Tijuca National Park, detailed earlier. There are numerous trails inside the park, including trails up to Corcovado and the Cristo monument. Some great trails are in the middle of the park and pass waterfalls and streams—or head out to some awesome lookout points. If you go to the park yourself, you can probably hike around without any problems and without a guide. However, you might consider consulting a guide or even hiring one to come with you. You'll probably feel much more comfortable accompanied by someone who knows the area well. Guides are most easily encountered at the two main mountaineering associations: **Centro Excursionista Brasileiro** (Rua Almirante Barroso 2, 8th floor, Centro, tel. 21/2252-9844, www.ceb.org.br) and **Centro Excursionista Carioca** (tel. 21/2255-1348). Call them to go to one of their meetings or just to ask about guides and hiking excursions. They are friendly and can communicate pretty well in English. You can also call the agency **Trilhas do Rio Ecoturismo** (Rua Francisca Sales 645, tel. 21/2424-5455, www.trilhasdorio.com.br).

Note: The Serra dos Orgãos National Park is only an hour away from Rio in the inland mountains and has numerous trails, white-water rafting, and other great outdoor activities. (See the *Rio de Janeiro State* chapter for details.)

# Accommodations

## FLAMENGO AND BOTAFOGO

Hotels in this area offer some of the best values in Rio. The problem is that you're not really close to anything. Still, you can catch the metro to the downtown area and the metro and taxi to Copacabana. If you stay out late in Ipanema, you'll have to catch a cab back to your hotel, which could cost as much as R$20.

### Under R$100

The **El Misti Hostel** (Praiade Botafogo 462, Casa 9, tel. 21/2226-0991, www.elmisti-hostel.com, R$40 pp) has six group rooms, kitchen facilities, a sitting room, three shared bathrooms, laundry service, bar, and restaurant. They are located near a metro station for easy access. Another hostel is the **Chave do Rio de Janeiro** (Rua Gal. Dionísio 63, tel. 21/2286-0303, www.riohostel.com.br, R$40 pp), with group rooms, laundry facilities, kitchen facilities, and TV room. The women's dorm has a private bathroom, but towels are extra. You can also check out the **Baron Garden Guest House** (Rua Barão de Guaratiba 195, Glória, tel. 21/2245-0040, www.baron-garden.com, R$45 for group rooms and R$120 for private rooms for two) for a spot between the Glória Church and the boardwalk. Check website for special rates for Carnaval and New Year's. Unfortunately, it's not super-close to any of the metro stations. Finally, the **Carioca Hostel** (Rua Marechal Cantuária 168, tel. 21/2295-7805, www.cariocahostel.com.br, R$35 for group rooms and R$110 for private rooms for two, breakfast included). gets you close to Pão de Açúcar, but take a taxi or bus to Copacabana.

### R$100–200

A good value is the **Imperial** (Rua do Catete 186, Flamengo, tel. 21/2556-0772, www.imperialhotel.com.br, R$125 s and R$135 d), in an old building with small but clean rooms, with air, TV, and phone, and decent facilities, including a pool and restaurant. **Hotel Flórida** (Rua Ferreira Viana 81, Flamengo, tel. 21/2556-5242, www.windsorhoteis.com.br, R$250–360) is a great place with good service and it's located near the metro station in Flamengo. They have a gym, pool, sauna, bar, and restaurant and rooms come with air, TV, and phone. **Hotel Novo Mundo** (Praia do Flamengo 20, Flamengo, tel. 21/2557-6226, www.hotelnovomundo-rio.com.br, R$165) has good facilities with 230 rooms, a restaurant, and bar. They are on a busy highway but very close to the beach and not far from the metro station.

### R$200–500

The **Hotel Glória** (Rua do Russel 632, Glória, tel. 21/2555-7272, www.hotelgloriario.com.br, R$225–425) is up near the old downtown area on a nice stretch of beach. They have a restaurant, bar, theater, pool, sauna, and gym.

## COPACABANA, IPANEMA, AND LEBLON

Hotels in the Copacabana area are tricky. Most of them are old and the buildings show it with run-down conditions and moldy rooms. A few have been remodeled and these are usually the better options. Of course, they are also the highest-priced options and compared to other locations in the city and in Brazil in general, they are not good values for the money. Still, if you want to be in a decent hotel in Copacabana, you're going to have to pay for it. The values in Ipanema are slightly better, since the hotels there are more modern and offer better facilities and conditions for the money. They are generally also expensive, but there are some low-priced hostels to check out.

### Under R$100

Budget hotels in this area are generally pretty ugly places, but at least the ones in Ipanema and Leblon are usually safe. Nothing budget in

Copacabana is in a safe area and some are right on the edge of the *favelas*. You should avoid hostels in Copacabana. In Ipanema, there's the **Harmonia** hostel (Rua Barão da Torre 175, tel. 21/2523-4905, tel. 21/2523-4904, www.hostelharmonia.com, R$40 pp). They have pretty unattractive facilities, but the location is great in Ipanema. There are several other hostels in Ipanema, including **Adventure Hostel** (Rua Vinícius de Moraes 174, tel. 21/3813-2726, www.adventurehostel.com.br, R$40 for group room or R$45 with air and R$120 for private double room, breakfast included), **Casa 6** (Rua Barão da Torre 6, tel. 21/2247-1384, www.casa6ipanema.com, R$45 for group room and R$120 for private double room, breakfast included), and **Crab Hostel** (Rua Prudente de Morais 903, tel. 21/2227-6130, www.crabhostel.com.br, R$40 for group room and R$120 for private double room, breakfast included). This last one is a long block to the beach on a busy street.

## R$100–200

Another good value for the location is **Vermont** (Rua Visconde da Pirajá 254, Ipanema, tel. 21/2522-0057, R$125). They are a couple blocks from the beach and have about 80 rooms with air, TV, and shared bath.

The hotel **Astória Copacabana** (Rua Rep. do Peru 345, Copacabana, tel. 21/2548-3838, www.astoria.com.br, R$165 s and R$205 d) is also a couple blocks from the beach and has a simple restaurant, bar, pool, sauna, and gym. Rooms come with air, TV, mini-bar, and safe.

## R$200–500

The **M Marina Palace** (Av. Delfim Moreira 630, Ipanema, tel. 21/2540-5212, www.hotelmarina.com.br, R$335) was the first hotel overlooking the beach at Ipanema and has recently been remodeled to include modern facilities, in-room Internet, pool, sauna, and gym. It's one of a few hotels on the beachfront at Ipanema. The **M Praia Ipanema Hotel** (Av. Vieira Souto 706, tel. 21/2540-4949, www.praiaipanema.com, R$385–455) is located near the Jardim de Alah and has a nice

view of Ipanema, including a terrific rooftop terrace. They have a pool, restaurant, and bar. Rooms come with air, TV, and phone. The **Lancaster** (Av. Atlântica 1470, Copacabana, tel. 21/2543-8300, R$245) is located in an old building with spacious but slightly dilapidated rooms. They have 70 rooms with air, TV, and phone. You can also take a look at the **Everest Rio** (Rua Prudente de Morais 1117, Ipanema, tel. 21/2525-2200, www.everest.com.br, R$357 for single room and R$385 for double room), which offers a pool, restaurant, and beach service. It's a city block from the beach.

The **Parthenon Arpoador** (Rua Francisco Otaviano 61, Copacabana, tel. 21/3222-9600, www.accorhotels.com) is a business-style hotel with 55 rooms, pool, sauna, gym, restaurant, bar, and cable TV. Rooms are clean and fairly modern. R$255 single and R$292 double for standard rooms. No breakfast included. Ask about weekend discounts. They also have a hotel in Ipanema called the **Parthenon Queen Elizabeth** (Av. Rainha Elizabeth 440, tel. 21/3222-9100, www.accorhotels.com) for R$335 single and R$375 double for standard rooms. Breakfast included. Ask about weekend discounts.

The Luxor Hotels group has three hotels in Copacabana, the **Luxor Regent** (Av. Atlântica 3716, tel. 21/2525-2070, regente@luxorhoteis.com.br), for R$310 single and R$338 double. Weekend packages for R$480. Ask about discounts for longer stays. There is also the **Luxor Copacabana** (Av. Atlântica 2554, tel. 21/2545-1070, copacabana@luxorhoteis.com.br), for R$242 single and R$270 double with a weekend package for R$436. Finally, they have the **Luxor Continental** (Rua Gustavo Sampaio 320, Leme, tel. 21/2546-1070, continental@luxorhoteis.com.br) for R$249 single and R$277 double with a three-day discount for R$182 per night. The first two are beachfront hotels, the second being the more modern of the two with better facilities. The third is on the far end of Copacabana, one block from the beach. It has the worst location but the best and newest facilities. They all have great views, pools, bars, restaurants, gyms, and all the facilities you'd expect from a luxury hotel. They have great breakfast buffets.

## Over R$500

**Sofitel Rio de Janeiro** (Av. Atlântica 4240, Copacabana, tel. 21/2525-1232, www.accorhotels.com, R$835–1200) has more than 300 rooms, with many overlooking the ocean at Copacabana. Rooms have air, TV, and phone, and the hotel offers a pool, sauna, gym, restaurant, and bar. The **M Marina All Suites** (Av. Delfim Moreira 696, Ipanema, tel. 21/2172-1100, www.marinaallsuites.com.br, R$550) has 40 rooms. Eight of them are "design suites," having been designed by Brazil's top interior artists. Many rooms have ocean views, as the hotel is right on the beach. This is where Arnold Schwar-

zenegger stayed when he was yucking it up in Rio (you saw the videos). Rooms have all the amenities and the hotel has a rooftop pool, sauna, gym, restaurant, and massage room. The **Ceasar Park Hotel** (Av. Vieira Souto 460, Ipanema, tel. 21/2525-2525, www.ceasar-park.com, R$495–795) has modern facilities with suites overlooking the ocean at station 9 in Ipanema (the most active area on the beach). Rooms have all the usual amenities and the hotel has a bar, restaurant, gym, and pool. Finally, you can stay at the **Copacabana Palace Hotel** (Av. Atlântica 1702, tel. 21/2235-7330, www.copacabanapalace.com.br, R$850–1800) for a brush against history. Rooms are spacious with period furnishings, air, TV, and phone. They have a gym, massage room, pool, and tennis court.

# Food

## COFFEE AND SWEETS

One of the city's best places for coffee and something sweet is the **Confeitaria Colombo** (Rua Gonçalves Dias 32, Centro, tel. 21/2232-2300, 8 A.M.–8 P.M. Mon.–Fri., 9:30 A.M.–5 P.M. on Sat.). The place is also a tourist attraction. They have a second location in the Copacabana Fort. You can also try the local favorite, **Alda Maria Doces Portugueses** (Rua Almirante Alexandrino 1116, Santa Teresa, tel. 21/2232-1320, 2–7 P.M. Sat. and Sun.). The specialty here is traditional Portuguese baked goods, including many pies and cakes.

In the Zona Sul (beaches), there's **Livraria da Travessa** (Rua Visconde de Pirajá 462, Ipanema, tel. 21/3205-9002, 9 A.M.–midnight Mon.–Sat., 11 A.M.–midnight on Sun.) for books, coffee, and sweets. Also, try **Café Severino** (Rua Dias Ferreira 714, tel. 21/2259-9398, 9 A.M.–midnight Mon.–Fri., 10 A.M.–midnight Sat. and Sun.).

## JUICE BARS

Rio de Janeiro is known for its plethora of juice bars—all along the beach areas of Copacabana and Ipanema with plenty of places downtown, too. Most of these are a block or two off the boardwalk. A couple worth noting are **Balada Sumos** (Av. Ataulfo de Paiva 620, Leblon, tel. 21/2239-2699, 7 A.M.–2 P.M. daily) and **Polis Sucos** (Rua Maria Quitéia 70, Ipanema). Also, **Kicê Sucos** (Rua Av. Nossa Sra. da Copacabana 1033, Copacabana, tel. 21/2522-1901, 8 A.M.–2 P.M. daily) has some good options, including *morango* (strawberry) juice. Downtown, there's the excellent **Laranjada Americana** (Rua Buenos Aires 2, Centro, 8 A.M.–5 P.M. Mon.–Fri.) for great juices.

## QUICK AND CASUAL

Remember that every one of the café-bars listed in *Entertainment and Nightlife* also serve great appetizers. They are often some of the best places for casual dining. There's also **Cavé** (Rua Sete de Setembro 137, Centro, tel. 21/2221-0533,

Rio de Janeiro

9 A.M.–7 P.M. Mon.–Fri., 9 A.M.–1 P.M. on Sat.) for great finger foods and **Cervantes** (Av. Prado Júnior 335, Copacabana, tel. 21/2275-6147, noon–3 P.M. Mon.–Thurs., noon–6 P.M. on Fri. and Sat., noon–2 P.M. on Sun.) for excellent sandwiches until the wee hours of the morning. In Ipanema, you can have a great sandwich with deli meats, sausages, and cheeses, at **M Alessandro & Frederico's Café** (Rua Garcia d'Avila 134, Ipanema, tel. 21/2521-0828, 9 A.M.–1 P.M. daily). Try a pizza at **La Mole** (Rua Dias Ferreira 147, Leblon, tel. 21/2235-3366, 11 A.M.–midnight daily) and you can eat at one of their sidewalk tables while looking out at the crowd.

You can get a falafel sandwich, made in Arabic fashion in pita or as a separate dish with hommus and salad, at **Amir** (Rua Ronald de Carvalho 55, Copacabana, tel. 21/2542-8575, noon–11 P.M. Mon.–Sat.). A meal costs around R$15. Remember wraps? You can get them at **Mil Frutas Café** (Rua Garcia d'Avila 134, Ipanema, tel. 21/2521-3841, 10:30 A.M.–midnight Mon.–Thurs., 9:30 A.M.–1 A.M. Fri.–Sun., about R$25 per person), along with ice cream, juices, and coffee.

## SELF-SERVICE

The lunch buffet at **Mala e Cuia** (Rua Visconde de Caravelas 180, Botafogo, tel. 21/2527-8800, noon–1 A.M. Mon.–Sat., noon–6 P.M. on Sun. R$20) features Comida Mineira, country cooking from Minas Gerais. You'll see plenty of meat and chicken dishes along with a buffet of side dishes, rice, and pasta. At night, they serve off the menu. It costs around R$15–25. The best buffet in town is at **M Fellini** (Rua General Urquiza 104, Leblon, tel. 21/2511-3600, 11:30 A.M.–4 P.M. and 9 P.M.–midnight Mon.–Fri., 11:30 A.M.–6 P.M. on weekends), where you'll find different themes each day of the week, from Spanish tapas to Italian dishes, to northern European recipes (like cured fish and meat pie). The buffet is always abundant and exotic with plenty of seafood and salad items. Open for lunch and dinner, it will set you back about R$25 per person. **Pergula** (Av.

Atlântica 1702, Copacabana Palace Hotel, tel. 21/2545-8744, 7 A.M.–midnight Mon.–Fri., noon–4:30 P.M. on weekends) has a lunch buffet with a view of the ocean for R$25, and **Da Silva** (Rua Barão da Torre 340, Ipanema, tel. 21/2521-1289, 11 A.M.–4 P.M. and 6 P.M.–2 A.M. Tue.–Sun., 11 A.M.–4 P.M. on Mon.) is a good choice if you're in the Ipanema area.

If you're downtown, you can try the self-service buffet at **Delight** (Rua Alvaro Alvim 37, Cinelândia, tel. 21/2518-7727, 11 A.M.–3 P.M. Mon.–Fri., R$20). They also have locations in Copacabana (Av. Nossa Sra. de Copacabana 391) and Ipanema (Rua Visconde de Pirajá 145).

## LOCAL FAVORITES

**Alfaia** (Rua Inhangá 30, Copacabana, tel. 21/2236-1222, 11 A.M.–midnight Mon.–Sat., 11 A.M.–11 P.M. Sun., R$35–50) is a small but charming place that specializes in fresh fish, squid, and other Portuguese favorites, including their specialty, *bacalhau* (a cod-like fish with a heavy taste). **Aurora** (Rua Cap. Salomão 43, Botafogo, tel. 21/2539-4756, 11 A.M.–midnight Mon.–Thurs., 11 A.M.–2 A.M. on Fri. and Sat.) is located inside an old warehouse with high ceilings and a great marble bar. They serve seafood and pasta dishes. An excellent place for a delicious fish stew is **Rio Minho** (Rua do Ouvidor 10, Centro, tel. 21/2509-2338, 11 A.M.–4 P.M. Mon.–Fri., R$20), which has been around since the 1800s. It's a great place to go between the downtown sights and cultural centers. One of the most sought-after places in town for fresh fish, oysters, mussels, and seafood in general (for around R$80–150) is **M Satyricon** (Rua Barão da Torre 192, Ipanema, tel. 21/2521-0627, noon–1 A.M. daily). Many a famous Brazilian and American has been there.

The Bahian restaurant **Yemanjá** (Rua Visconde de Pirajá 128, Ipanema, tel. 21/2247-7004, noon–midnight daily) serves traditional dishes like *vatapá* (a spicy fish and shrimp dish from Bahia) and seafood *moqueca* (a kind of fish stew). They also have several shrimp plates—just like in Bahia. Meals cost about R$55. You should also try **Aprazível** (Rua Aprazível 62, Santa Teresa, tel. 21/3852-4935, noon–midnight Mon.–Sat., 1–6 P.M. on Sun. Dinner only on Thurs., R$45) for a variety of Brazilian dishes and a terrific view from the hillsides of Santa Teresa. It's open for lunch and dinner.

You'll find Comida Mineira at the **Bar do Mineiro** (Rua Paschoal Carlos Magno 99, Santa Teresa, tel. 21/2221-9227, 11–2 A.M. Tue.–Thurs., 11–4 A.M. Fri. and Sat., about R$35 for dinner), a great place to have dinner before heading for the bars in the neighborhood. If you want Brazilian food and you're at the beach, try **Brasileirinho** (Rua Jangadeiros 10, Ipanema, tel. 21/2513-5184, noon–midnight Wed.–Mon., R$20) or **Degrau** (Av. Ataulfo de Paiva 517, Leblon, tel. 21/2250-3648, about R$20 for dinner). Both are popular for lunch but also serve dinner.

### Barbecue

For a huge Brazilian-style barbecue, you should check out **M Porcão** (Rua Barão de Torre 218, Ipanema, tel. 21/2522-0999, noon–1 A.M. daily), with numerous buffets offering salads, pasta dishes, fish, and deserts. These are to accompany the headline attraction: barbecued beef, pork, and chicken in a *rodísio*-style setup (items come off the barbecue regularly and are offered to you at your table). The quality and variety here are incredible. You pay one price—R$60 per person—and can stay and eat as long as you like. You can get grilled ostrich among more common meats at **Esplanada Grill** (Rua Barão da Torre 600, Ipanema, tel. 21/2512-2970). They're open from noon until the last client leaves. Meals cost around R$30. Another great barbecue grill for a reasonable price is **Braseiro da Gávea** (Praça Santos Dumont 116, Gávea, tel. 21/2239-7494, 11:30–1 A.M. Mon.–Thurs., 11:30–3 A.M. on Fri. and Sat.). They have plenty of barbecued beef, chicken, and pork and some special plates on the menu—for around R$22.

A great southern Brazil–style barbecue is at **Oásis** (Rua Gonçalves Dias 56, Centro, tel. 21/2252-5521, 11 A.M.–4 P.M. Mon.–Fri.), where you get a *rodísio*-style barbecue with various meat cuts and buffets. Open for lunch and dinner. The **Via Sete** barbecue (Rua Sete de Setembro 43, Centro, 8:30 A.M.–7:30 P.M. Mon.–Fri.) has a great selection of meats cooked over the flame. They have another location in Ipanema (Rua Garcia d'Avila 123).

## ITALIAN

Specializing in fish and seafood with an Italian emphasis is **Margutta** (Av. Henrique Dumont 62, Ipanema, tel. 21/2259-3718, 6 P.M.–1 A.M. Mon.–Fri., noon–1 A.M. on weekends, R$55). The place is small and charming with an excellent menu and great service. **Cipriani** at the Copacabana Palace Hotel (Av. Atlântica 1702, Copacabana, tel. 21/2548-7070, 12:30 P.M.–3 P.M. and 7 A.M.–midnight Mon.–Fri., noon–midnight on weekends) is one of the most elegant in the region, with a mixture of Italian and international cuisine. Reservations are required. It costs R$70–150 per person. Regarded as the best pizza in town, **Capricciosa** (Vinícius de Moraes 134, Ipanema, tel. 21/2523-3394, 6 P.M.–2 A.M. daily) cooks up about 30 combinations with fresh ingredients. Be ready for a crowd around dinnertime. A fine Italian restaurant with a great wine list is **M Garcia & Rodrigues** (Av. Ataulfo de Paiva 1251, Leblon, tel. 21/3206-4120, 6 P.M.–midnight daily). They have contemporary Italian dishes as well as rich and flavorful traditional Italian desserts. A meal is R$100–150. Finally, an excellent place for northern Italian food is the **Osteria Del'Angolo** (Rua Paul Hedfern 40, Ipanema, tel. 21/2259-3148, noon–4 P.M. and 7 A.M.–1 A.M. Mon.–Fri., noon on Sat. and Sun.). They charge around R$35 for a meal. Finally, there's **Quadrucci** (Rua Dias Ferreira 233, Leblon, tel. 21/2512-4551, noon–1 A.M. daily, R$45) with great food and a great location.

## ASIAN

The upscale sushi bar **Z Contemporâneo** (Rua Paul Redfern 37, Ipanema, tel. 21/2512-9494, 7–1 A.M. Mon.–Fri., noon–1 A.M. on Sat., noon–7 P.M. on Sun.) serves some interesting items, like shrimp termpura with curry and eel with foie gras. They also have some traditional sushi rolls. You won't get out of there for under R$100 per person. A popular sushi restaurant is **M Sushi Leblon** (Rua Dias Ferreira 256, tel. 21/2512-7830, noon–4 P.M. and 7–1:30 A.M. Mon.–Fri., noon–1 A.M. Sat., noon–7 P.M. on Sun.) on the south end of Leblon. They have good portions and get a good-looking crowd for dinner. It's about R$60 per person and is open until 1 A.M. If you're in the downtown area, check out **Cais do Oriente** (Rua Visconde de Itaboraí 8, Centro, tel. 21/2233-2531, noon–midnight Tues.–Sat., noon–4 P.M. Sun. and Mon., R$100 with music cover charge), with its international menu crossed with Asian. They specialize in seafood and shellfish and have live jazz upstairs on weekends.

A few more sushi restaurants around town include **Kenji Tanaka San** (Rua Professor Manuel Ferreira 89, Gávea, tel. 21/2274-2012, 7 P.M.–2 A.M. Tues.–Sat., 1 P.M.–2 A.M. Sun., R$70–150), **Nik Sushi** (Rua Garcia d'Avila 83, Ipanema, tel. 21/2512-6446, 11:30 P.M.–1 A.M. Tues.–Sat., 1:30–11 P.M. on Sun., R$35–80), and **Sansushi** (Rua Almirante Alexandrino 382, Santa Teresa, tel. 21/2252-0581, 7 P.M.–1 A.M. Tues.–Sat., 1 P.M.–midnight on Sun., R$50–100).

## PORTUGUESE

The beachfront **Cais da Ribeira** (Av. Atlântica 2964, Copacabana, tel. 21/2548-6332, 7:30 P.M.–midnight daily), inside the Hotel Pestana, is well-known for its Portuguese dishes, especially its seafood. A meal will run you R$60. Also in Copacabana is **M Marisqueira** (Rua Barata Ribeiro 232, Copacabana, tel. 21/2547-3920, 11 A.M.–midnight daily), a small place that has served some important people, including officials from the government of Portugal. It's reasonably priced at around R$25 per person. Another Portuguese kitchen is **Adega do Valentim** (Rua da Passagem 178, Botafogo, tel. 21/2541-1166, noon–1 A.M. daily). They have dozens of fish

recipes. An evening out will cost about R$40 for two. Everyone seems to think that **M Antiquarius** (Rua Aristides Espíndola 19, Leblon, tel. 21/2294-1049, noon–2 A.M. daily) is one of the best restaurants in the city. In fact, it's fabulous and the price—about R$35 per person—is reasonable. They specialize in dishes made with *bacalhau* (cod).

## OTHER INTERNATIONAL

For great food in the Spanish tradition, try the simple but excellent **Shirley** (Rua Gostavo Sampaio 610, tel. 21/2542-1797, noon–1 A.M. daily) in Copacabana. You'll find paella and plenty of different tapas, with a particular leaning toward fish. Expect to pay R$25 per person. You can find great German food at **Adega do Pimenta** (Rua Almirante Alexandrino 296, Santa Teresa, tel. 21/2224-7554, noon–10 P.M. Mon., Wed., Fri., noon–8 P.M. Sat., noon–6 P.M. on Sun.). Their menu is replete with German names, so you might have to ask what everything means. They work with plenty of pork, sauerkraut, meat, and potatoes and the place gets crowded at night. Meals cost around R$30. For Middle Eastern food, try **Al Khayam** (Av. General San Martin 889, Leblon, tel. 21/2249-9190, noon–1 A.M. Tues.–Sun., 6 P.M.–1 A.M. on Mon., R$25), and for Indian food, there's **Natraj Guilda's** (Av. General San Martin 1219, Leblon, tel. 21/2239-4745, 7 P.M.–midnight Tues.–Sat., noon–11 P.M. on Sun., about R$50 for two).

## VEGETARIAN

The restaurant **Vegan Vegan** (Rua Voluntários da Pátria 402, Botafogo, tel. 21/2286-7078, 8 A.M.–6 P.M. Mon.–Sat.) has absolutely no animal products or derivatives on the menu. You'll find soups, salads, and special dishes made with fresh, organic ingredients. They're reasonably priced at around R$22 per person. Another authentic veggie spot is **Vegetariano Social Clube** (Rua Conde de Bernadote 26, Leblon, tel. 21/2540-6499, noon–midnight

Mon.–Sat., noon–6 P.M. on Sun., R$25). Not exactly vegetarian, **Celeiro** (Rua Dias Ferreira 199, tel. 21/2274-7843, 10 A.M.–5 P.M. Mon.–Sat.) specializes in salads, with everything from curry chicken salad to marinated eggplant salad. They have around 50 different salads in their buffet at all times and there are always a few meat dishes, like lasagna or pasta. The place is small and gets crowded for both lunch and dinner. At around R$25 per person, meals are self-service style, *a-quilo* (by weight).

## Information and Transportation

## INFORMATION AND SERVICES

### Tourist Information

You'll find several tourist information booths at the Tom Jobim International Airport. In Terminal 1 and Terminal 2, you have booths at both the international flights (tel. 21/3398-4077, tel. 21/3398-2245) and national flights (tel. 21/3398-3034, tel. 21/3398-2246). They are all open 6 A.M.–midnight. The main bus terminal also has a booth (tel. 21/2263-4857, 8 A.M.–8 P.M.). There's also a booth in Copacabana at Station 6 (Av. Princesa Isabel 183, tel. 21/2542-8080, 9 A.M.–6 P.M. Mon.–Fri.).

### Communications

You can find Internet houses all over town, but especially in the Ipanema and Leblon areas. Also, most shopping centers have Internet houses and a lot of the coffee shop-bookstores have computers.

### Money

You'll find international ATMs all over Copacabana and Ipanema. Try the Banco do Brasil in Copacabana (Rua Nossa Sra. da Copacabana) and Leblon (by the lake). You'll also find ATMs at Shopping da Gávea. You can change money at most large hotels, although they will charge a large service fee if you're not registered at the hotel. There are money changers along Avenida Atlântica in Copacabana.

## GETTING THERE AND AROUND

Rio is host to more than one million foreigners per year and most of those come directly into the international airport, recently named Tom Jobim International (tel. 21/3398-5050). It's located on an island about 20 kilometers to the north of the city, on the northern tip of the downtown area. Local numbers for some major airlines include: Aerolineas Argentinas (tel. 21/3398-3520), Air France (tel. 21/2532-3642), American Airlines (tel. 21/2210-3126), Air Canada (tel. 21/2220-5343), Gol (tel. 21/3398-5131), JAL (tel. 21/2220-6414), Lufthansa (tel. 21/3687-5000), Swissair (tel. 21/3461-9343), TAM (tel. 21/3398-2133), United Airlines (0800-16-2323), and Varig (tel. 21/3398-2292).

### Metro

The metro (tel. 21/3982-3600 or 0800-595-1111) is a great way to get between the downtown area, Flamengo, Botafogo, and Copacabana. It's small and simple, but fast and safe. Unfortunately, the metro stops at the top of Copacabana. It runs from 5 A.M.–midnight Monday–Saturday and 7 A.M.–11 P.M. Sunday. There are buses that take passengers for free from the Estácio metro station downtown to the *rodoviaria* Novo Rio, called São Silvestre.

### Bus

The main bus terminal in Rio for buses to and from other cities is called Novorio (Rua Francisco Bicalho 1, www.novorio.com.br). Their website has information and times for all connections.

There are mini-buses with air-conditioning that circulate among the beaches, downtown, the airport, and the bus station for about R$3.50. You can find these on Avenida Atlântica in Copacabana. There are also municipal buses that do the circular route between downtown, Copacabana, Ipanema, and Leblon. They take a while to make an entire loop because of all the stops, but they cost under R$2 and are always coming. They generally say "Circular" on the front and you can ask at any bus stop along Avenida Atlântica in Copacabana, Avenida Visconde de Pirajá in Ipanema, and Avenida Adulfo de Paiva in Leblon. To get from downtown to Santa Teresa, take the Bonde trolley from the Passeio Publico area. To get downtown from Copacabana, Botafogo, Flamengo, or Lapa, take the metro.

To get to Pão de Açúcar, you can take the 107 bus from downtown (Rua Senador Dantas). This bus also passes Praia Flamengo (Avenida Augusto Severo) and Praia Botafogo on the way. The 511 and 512 go from Leblon (Avenida Visconde de Pirajá) past Ipanema (Avenida Ataulfo de Paiva) past Copacabana (Avenida Nossa Sra. de Copacabana), to Pão de Açúcar. To get to the Jardim Botânico, take the 170 bus from downtown (Avenida Rio Branco) or the 592 from Copacabana (Rua Barata Ri-beiro), Ipanema (Rua Prudente de Morais), or Leblon (Avenida Bartolomeu Mitre).

You can get to the train at Cosme Velho for a trip up Corcovado via the 180 bus, which leaves downtown (Avenida Rio Branco) and goes through Flamengo (Avenida Augusto Severo). The 584 gets you there from Leblon (Avenida Ataulfo de Paiva), Ipanema (Rua Visconde de Pirajá), Copacabana (Avenida Barata Ribeiro), and Botafogo (Praia de Botafogo).

To get south to Barra de Tijuca, take the 523 bus from Copacabana (Rua Barata Ribeiro), Ipanema (Avenida Vieira Souto), or Leblon (Avenida Delfim Moreira).

## Car

You should not attempt to drive around Rio. Instead, you can hire a taxi for an entire day for around R$200. There are also executive driving services available. If you want to rent a car to drive out of the city (to Paraty, for example), try Avis (tel. 21/3398-5012) or Localiza (tel. 21/3398-5445) at the airport.

# Rio de Janeiro State

Travelers visiting the city of Rio de Janeiro often overlook the incredible attractions just an hour or two away in Rio state. Along the coast north of Rio are beaches famous for their clear blue water and fine white sand. The long stretch of coast that is Cabo Frio remains one of the nation's most spectacular beaches, perfect for swimming, excellent for surfing, and a favored destination for getting some sun. The peninsula of Buzios has more than a dozen fab-ulous beaches, from the quaint and nearly deserted inlet of Ferradurazinha to the popular Tartaruga Beach with its excellent beachfront restaurants and offshore pools for snorkeling. In town, you'll find a shopping and night-life mecca. If you prefer quietude, choose a secluded hotel in the Ferradura area and get away from it all.

Just an hour or two inland of Rio are some of the most lush, tropical mountains in the

# **M**ust-Sees

**M Serra dos Orgãos National Park:** The Dedo de Deus (Finger of God) stretches high into the sky from the top of the mountain— a rock-climbers paradise—while the white waters of the Paquequer River hug the bottom of this dramatic mountain landscape, where you can go white-water rafting and rappelling down tall waterfall cascades (page 69).

**M Museu Imperial:** Emperor Dom Pedro II built this summerhouse in royal fashion, and the town of Petrópolis grew up around it. It contains many beautiful pieces from the imperial family and the building is a jewel in itself (page 74).

© CHRISTOPHER VAN BUREN

Dedo de Deus in Serra dos Orgãos National Park

**M Praias Brava, Conchas, and Peró:** Across the channel to the north of Praia do Forte are the most interesting beaches in the area. Take horseback rides, rent kayaks, or just lounge on the white sand and stare out at the calm, blue water (page 80).

**M Tartaruga Beach:** Whether you arrive by boat or via the long road that leads from town, your arrival at Tartaruga Beach will be filled with blue water, white sand, and excellent beach bars to serve you. Just offshore are some underwater reefs where you can practice the snorkeling arts or just go swimming with the fish. The following day, you can try Ferradura or João Fernandes beaches for another day in the sun (page 88).

**M Ponta da Lagoinha:** The pleasant walk out to Ponta da Lagoinha takes you to a landscape unlike any other on the coast of Brazil, beautifully dramatic and harsh. Stroll along the rim of the hills overlooking the ocean for one of the region's most beautiful views (page 90).

**RIO DE JANEIRO STATE**

Belo Horizonte

Serra dos Orgãos National Park

Museu Imperial

Cabo Frio

Tartaruga Beach

Ponta da Lagoinha

Rio de Janeiro

Praias Brava, Conchas, and Peró

ATLANTIC OCEAN

country. There, you can practice white-water rafting, mountain climbing, rappelling, and camping. The principal area is the Serra dos Orgãos National Park, where you'll encounter the Finger of God, among other spectacular sights. There are campgrounds right inside the park or you can stay in a hotel in the mountain town of Teresópolis. The area also has numerous hotel-*fazendas,* working ranches that provide great country meals and lodging for guests. Many travelers stay in Rio de Janeiro and take day or weekend excursions to the mountains or northern beaches, but for others, the mountains and northern beaches are the main attraction in the state.

## PLANNING YOUR TIME

A great way to see the attractions in the state of Rio de Janeiro is to create a 5–7-day trip that loops around the entire area, starting and ending in Rio city. You can go clockwise or counter-clockwise, and you can spend more or fewer days on the road, but the general idea is this: From Rio, head north to Buzios and get settled into your hotel. You'll be here for the next two or three days. Start by taking the boat tour that explores the islands and beaches on the north coast of the peninsula. You'll see the entire north coast and also get two opportunities to swim or snorkel in the transparent water. You can spend some extra time at Tartaruga and João Fernandes beaches and hike to the small inlets around them. The next day is yours to explore the peninsula as desired. Spend your third day in Cabo Frio at the various beaches there, including a night on the canal. From Buzios, you can head straight to Novo Friburgo in the mountains, where you can spend a day checking out the rural neighborhoods of the area. That night, head into Teresópolis and get ready for an early morning—you'll be hiking to the peaks and waterfalls in the Serra dos Orgãos the entire fifth day of your trip. Your sixth day can be spent at the bottom of the mountains, riding the white waters of the Paquequer River and swimming in the natural pools. The seventh and final day starts with a journey to Petrópolis, where you can visit the many 19th-century buildings and historical sights. From Petrópolis, you're only about 1.5 hours from your home base in Rio de Janeiro.

Tip: Be sure to plan ahead for the adventure sports part of this journey and make arrangement with guides at the park for rafting and overnight camping needs. The best guides are listed in this chapter.

# Região Serrana do Rio

About an hour and a half from Rio de Janeiro is a mountain range that offers some of the best action and adventure sports in the country. The mountains of the Serra dos Orgãos are filled with stone peaks for scaling and rappelling, rivers for rafting, waterfalls for swimming and cascading, and endless trails for hiking and camping in the Brazilian wilderness. Even if camping and hiking are not your main reason for coming, you'll likely find the landscape here dramatic and enchanting. The family of Emperor Dom Pedro II certainly did back in the mid-1800s. They made this area their summer playground, enjoying the mild summers while Rio de Janeiro was baking. There are numerous hotel-*fazendas* in the area, each with a different theme. Some are health spas, others working ranches, and still others are designed for recreation and leisure activities, like horseback riding, golf, and swimming. The area has everything from serious mountain adventures to relaxing and rejuvenating mountain getaways. You may want to return a few times to try it all.

## SERRA DOS ORGÃOS NATIONAL PARK

Only an hour from Rio de Janeiro in the high Orgãos Mountains is the Orgãos National

Rio de Janeiro State

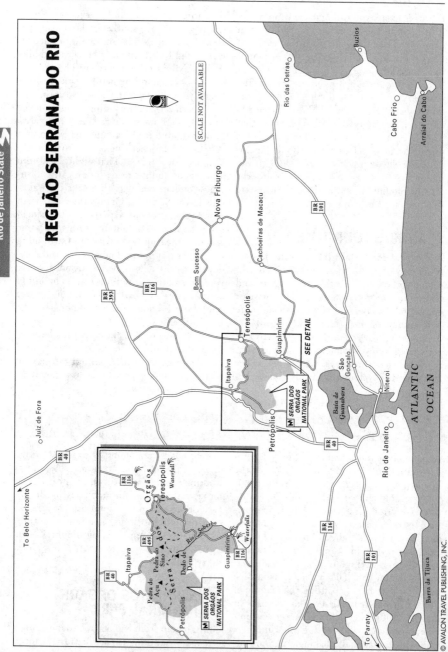

REGIÃO SERRANA DO RIO

SCALE NOT AVAILABLE

© AVALON TRAVEL PUBLISHING, INC.

the Orgãos Mountains

Park, one of the country's best options for adventure sports. Encompassing the majority of rock formations and peaks in the area, this national park is the main reason why visitors come to Petrópolis and Teresópolis, although many of the towns and communities outside the park have been working hard to attract tourists with their rural pleasures (country ranches, crafts, and restaurants mostly). The highlights of the national park are the incredible rocky peaks known to climbers all over the world. The most prominent of these is **Dedo de Deus** (Finger of God) in the form of a large finger pointing to the sky. The tip of the finger is 1,692 meters high and often scaled by expert climbers. You can hike to the base even if you don't plan to scale the big digit. Other peaks are known as **Pedra do Sino** (Bell Rock, 2,263 m), **Pedra do Açu** (Big Rock in the Tupi-Guarani language, 2,216 m), and **Dedo de Nossa Senhora** (Finger of Our Lady, 1,406 m).

You can also rappel down waterfalls and take a raft down the white waters of the Paquequer River. You can hike along the many trails in the park with cool waterfalls as your final destination or partake of a three-day hike across the park. There are a couple of campgrounds and lodges inside the park for overnight camping, plus guides that can take you through the adventures within.

Most of the trails, rivers, and waterfalls are accessible by starting at the visitor's center in Teresópolis, although there are also several hikes you can take from the visitor's center in Guapimirim. The visitor's center in Teresópolis has a pond, campground, lookout point, and several short trails.

The park is open Wednesday–Sunday, and visitors are allowed to enter and leave between the hours of 6 A.M. and 6 P.M. Staying the night in the park requires a camping permit (R$6 per person) that you should purchase the day before, after consulting with a guide. (Overnight stays require the presence of a guide and only 100 people are allowed to camp inside the park each night.) The office is open 8 A.M.–5 P.M. Wednesday–Sunday. If you arrive by car, you can park in the visitor's center for R$5. Basic entrance to the park is R$3 per person, on top of any camping permit you may purchase. If you plan to enter the park before the office opens, you should purchase your entrance the previous day. Some day hikes require that you start quite early, so this is a good thing to remember.

## Guides and Adventures

Many of the adventures in the park require the presence of a guide. Most guides are equipped to take you through the trails and campsites in the park, and most will provide cooking services along the way. If you are missing any equipment, they usually have rental equipment for anything you might need. Guides are also able to make arrangements for special adventures like white-water rafting (which takes place along the Paquequer River inside the park), rappelling, canyon scaling, and other radical endeavors. An activity known as cascading involves rappelling down a waterfall cascade. Here are some guides you can contact: **Mundo de Mato** (tel. 21/2742-0811, www.mundodemato.com.br), **Eco Trilhas** (tel. 21/2742-2478, www.ecotrilhas.com.br), and the **Centro de Excursionistas de Teresópolis** (tel. 21/2643-1777).

You can also look into visiting the **Campo de Aventuras Paraíso Açú** (Estrada do Bonfim 3511, tel. 24/2236-0003, www.campo-deaventurasparaisoacu.com.br), which is a park within the park where you'll find an infrastructure already in place for things like rappelling, cascading, and rafting. They also have a ropes course and paintball park. You can access the Campo de Aventuras off the Bonfim Trail near the Petrópolis side of the park (enter from Petrópolis).

## The Trails

There's a 30-minute hike on the Mozart Catão Trail that leads to a lookout point near the visitor's center. It's a great place to take pictures and see the city of Teresópolis from above. The trail to the **Véu da Noiva Waterfall** (35 meters high) takes about 1.5 hours and is a relatively light hike. Not far from there is the **Andorinhas Waterfall** at 15 meters. Swimming is permitted in both, so don't forget your

bathing suit. The Beija-Flor Trail (Hummingbird Trail) is a short but difficult path that is designed for bird-watching. It takes about 2.5 hours to complete. There are two swimming holes that are accessible from the Guapimirim visitor's center. One is only 15 minutes from the center and the other is 30 minutes. They are natural pools formed at points in the Soberbo River and are excellent for swimming.

From the Teresópolis visitor's center, you can take the Bonfim Trail to the highest peak in the park, the **Pedra do Sino,** which provides a spectacular view of the entire mountain range and its various peaks. You'll pass a couple of waterfalls and several viewpoints along the way. The trail is difficult and takes 5.5 hours to reach the Pedra. You should start this hike as soon as the gates open at 6 A.M. if you want to be sure to return before the gates close at 6 P.M. A similar hike goes up the Bonfim Trail from the Petrópolis side of the park as far as Pedra do Açu. That hike is about seven heavy-duty kilometers and takes eight hours to get there and back. If you want to walk the entire length of the Bonfim Trail, from Teresópolis to Petrópolis, you'll need a camping permit and a guide, as the 42-kilometer trail takes three days to complete. Along with the two major peaks mentioned earlier, you'll see the 500-meter drop of the Portal do Hércules Canyon.

# PETRÓPOLIS

Once the favored summer getaway of the imperial family, Petrópolis is known for its clean air, mountain vistas, and mild climate. Emperor Dom Pedro II built a summer palace here on a large piece of land passed to him by his father. That marked the beginning of the city of Petrópolis in 1843, as much of the court followed the emperor, building summer homes in the area and turning the place into a kind of royal village, known today as the Imperial City. The many elaborate 19th-century buildings in the old downtown area form the central attraction of Petrópolis, with the highlight being the old summer palace itself, now the Imperial Museum. In recent times, Petrópo-

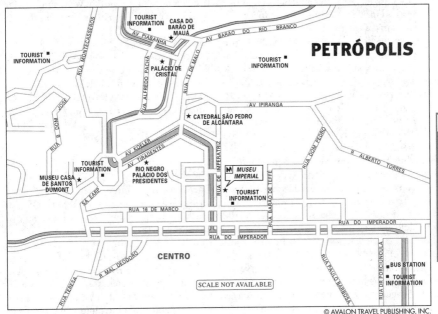

lis attracted the attention of Brazil's presidents and the old summer palace of the Barão de Rio Negro has been used as a presidential summerhouse since 1904.

Petropolis also attracted many foreign figures over the years and the German and Italian influences can be seen in some of the country homes in the area. With the construction of a railway and a couple of important highways connecting Petrópolis and Minas Gerais, the city grew into a major center of commerce and culture, which of course, attracted the likes of artists and intellectuals. Petrópolis was even the capital of Rio for a short time between 1894 and 1903.

Today, Petrópolis suffers from its great success. Being so close to Rio de Janeiro, it attracts bands of hoodlums who venture up from the big city in search of rich tourists. The clothing industry, for which Petrópolis is famous, results in the city's outskirts being filled with low-income workers. As these outskirts grow, so do the pollution, industrialization, and poverty. When you get off the bus in the Petrópolis

*rodoviaria,* you may wonder how such an ugly urban center could have possibly attracted presidents and emperors. The small stream going through town, once an abundant fresh-water source, is now a trickle of muck and sludge, an embarrassment to the noble mansions and palaces that stand on its borders.

No, Petrópolis is sadly not a place in which you will want to spend much of your time. It serves mostly as an interesting detour for those making their way to or from Teresópolis and the Orgãos National Park. A couple of hours visiting the main historical sights will probably be satisfactory.

## Historical Walking Tour

To see the historical buildings and museums of Petrópolis, a walking tour is usually suggested. If you are driving, try to park your car in one of the lots protected by security guards at one of the sights. The **Catedral São Pedro de Alcântara** (Rua Sao Pedro de Alcântara 60, tel. 24/2242-4300, 8 A.M.–noon and 2–6 P.M.

Tues.–Sun., free) features a French neo-gothic design and inside is the Imperial Chapel where the remains of the royal family are kept. Continue to the right down Rua 13 de Maio until you can make a U-turn over to Avenida Piabanha. Here you'll see the **Casa do Barão de Mauá** (Praça da Confluência 03, tel. 24/2246-9300, 9 A.M.–6:30 P.M. Sat. and 9 A.M.–5 P.M. on Sun., free), which is currently the headquarters of the Petrópolis Culture and Tourism Foundation. If you're not in town on a weekend, then just suffice it to look upon the building from the outside. The Baron built his summer home in a neoclassic style.

Continuing past the Baron's house, take your first left to cross over the waterway and down Rua Alfredo Pachá, where you'll find the **Palácio de Cristal** (Rua Alfredo Pacha, tel. 24/2247-3721, 9 A.M.–5:30 P.M. Tuesday–Sunday, free). The Palácio was built in 1884 to be an exhibition hall and to this day it serves as one. Today is houses art exhibitions and cultural events. The wrought-iron structure was prefabricated in France and the whole thing was the idea of the Conde D'Eu, brother-in-law to the emperor. Continuing down and to the left, you'll come to the Praça da Liberdade, where there is another tourist information center. Just off the *praça* is the **Museu Casa de Santos Dumont** (Rua do Encanto 22, tel. 24/2231-3011, 9:30 A.M.–5 P.M. Tues.–Sun., R$3), the former home of the father of aviation. Inside are personal artifacts from the life of Dumont. You can wrap up your tour with a visit to the **Rio Negro Palácio dos Presidentes** (Av. Koeler 255, tel. 24/2246-9380, 9 A.M.–5 P.M. Tues.–Sun. and noon–5 P.M. Mon., R$2) where Brazilian presidents have passed summer days until recent times.

## Ⓜ Museu Imperial

The Museu Imperial (Rua da Imperatriz 220, tel. 24/2237-8000, 11 A.M.–5:30 P.M. Tues.–Sun., R$8), once the summer palace of Emperor Dom Pedro II, is now a beautiful museum with pieces from the imperial era: jewels, furnishings, and works of art. The interior of the building itself is one of the main features.

Inside is a tea house and souvenir shop. There is also a tourist information center inside.

### Getting There

You can catch a bus to Petrópolis from Cabo Frio on the Transporte Única Petropolis line. Buses also leave from Rio de Janeiro every day. The bus to Teresópolis leaves from the bus terminal in Petrópolis at 5:45 A.M., 7 A.M., 9 A.M., noon, 3 P.M., 5 P.M., and 7 P.M. It takes about 40 minutes and costs R$8.50.

## TERESÓPOLIS

The mountains around Teresópolis are pretty serious business. They are steep, thick with brush, and topped by rocky peaks—but not *just* rocky peaks, these are huge rock formations that bring climbers from all over the world to scale them. At the base of these monsters are numerous rivers cascading through, presenting white-water rapids and lush waterfalls. In the midst of all this drama sits the city of Teresópolis, looking almost like the small mountain hamlet it once was. It was named in honor of Princess Teresa Cristina, wife of Emperor Dom Pedro II, and it was one of the royal family's favorite places to relax in the hills. The main attraction for travelers is the countryside. Tall stone peaks line up along the Orgão Mountains, each formation more interesting and impressive than the next. Mountain climbers have been coming here since the 1800s, when Austrian mountaineers came and fell in love with the area. Today, the Dedo de Deus and other formations challenge climbers of all levels. Most of the natural wonders here fall under the protection of the Serra dos Orgãos National Park, including the Paquequer River, where white-water rafting takes place. Teresópolis is the main entrance to the park and an agreeable place to stay while checking out its wonders. There are a number of hotels, *pousadas* (bed-and-breakfasts), and hotel-*fazendas* in the area, and you'll find some decent restaurants and bars in the main part of town. Teresópolis has one of the practice camps for the Brazilian national soccer team and many

**The Dedo de Deus is visible from Teresópolis.**

Brazilians and foreigners come to watch the team in action. The city hosts the Brazil Cup, an amateur soccer championship that gets national recognition.

## Shopping

There's a shopping center in the downtown area on Av. Lúcio Meira, but the best shopping is in the **Feirarte** outdoor arts and crafts fair on weekends and holidays from 10 A.M.– 6 P.M. (Praça Higino da Silveira, www.feirinhadoalto.com.br), where you'll find handmade clothing, food, and crafts at incredible prices. Check out the winter coats and bee products (honey, pollen, and Propolis).

## Sports and Recreation

There's a handy city tour that operates on weekends and takes you to the principal tourist sights around town. If you plan to do some serious hiking in the mountains, then the tour might pale slightly in comparison to the natural wonders you're going to encounter. Still, some of the tour's highlights include a stop at the best viewpoint of the Dedo de Deus peak (the Vista Soberba scenic viewpoint), a look at the Aranda Orchid Garden, and a quick tour of the visitor's center at the Orgãos National Park. You can catch the tour at the Fairarte *praça* on the south side of town (the park side). From the other end of town, you can catch the *Alto* bus (make sure you get the direct bus or you'll get a nice tour of the *bairros* in Teresópolis) to the Pracinha (or Fairarte *praça*). You have to walk through the art fair to the other side of the *praça* to catch the bus at Avenida Oliveira Botelho. The tour leaves every 45 minutes as long as there are enough people going. It costs R$3.

Would a round of golf in this crisp mountain air interest you? There's a golf course in the Vale do Paraíso neighborhood, which is on the north end of town.

## Accommodations

The youth hostel in town is called **N Recanto do Lord Hostel** (Rua Luiza Pereira Soares 109, tel. 21/2742-5586, ajteresopolis@bol.com.br, R$20 pp, R$15 with HI card) and is located at the top of the hill on the north end of town. They have a fantastic view of the city—one of the best in town—with the Dedo de Deus in the background. They have group and private

The Feirarte arts and crafts fair has some excellent buys on warm clothes and honey.

national park, then stay at the **Pousada Jardim Comary** (Rua Alfredo Timira de Carvalho 340, tel. 21/2642-7295, www.pousadajardim-comary.com.br, R$120). They don't have much in the way of character or charm, but the place is clean and well located. Better yet, stay right inside the park itself at the **Abrigo 4** (Parque Nacional, Av. Rotariana, tel. 21/3641-9095, parnaso1@terra.com.br, R$20). They have room for 30 guests and are 14 kilometers from the park entrance on the Bonfim Trail. They have support services for climbers.

If you like the idea of staying at a health spa in the country, then check out the **Hotel Fazenda Gaura Mandir** (Estrada Teresópolis-Friburgo Km 6.5, tel. 21/2644-6191, www.gaura.com.br, R$120–150). Along with lodging, they have a day spa that has 30 types of alternative therapies, including various types of massage, hot tubs, yoga, and herbal baths. They have an all-vegetarian kitchen, a pool, and a lake with waterfall cascade. Rooms are located in the main lodge and they have a couple of individual chalets.

## Food and Nightlife

The central area of Teresópolis is located toward the north end of town. It's an area of a few square blocks that is full of shops, restaurants, and bars. The main street is Avenida J.J.A. Regadas, which is where the Terminal Turístico is located (the main tourist information office). The next street, Rua E. Ducumunn is also a good place to find restaurants and bars, as is the Praça Higino da Silveira. There are also a couple of bars on the south end of town if you happen to be staying on that side. Try the **Taberna João Jurema** (Av. Oliveira Botelho 455, tel. 21/2642-4970, lunch and dinner daily) or the **Taberna Di Olicios** (Av. Oliveira Botelho 456, tel. 21/2642-4920, 11 A.M.–5 P.M. Wed–Fri., 11 A.M.–midnight Fri.–Mon.) around the Feirarte area.

For dining, you have several options spread all over town and into the suburbs. In the downtown area, there's the popular **Churrascaria Nino's** (Av. Delfim Moreira 722, tel. 21/2641-6150, 11 A.M.–midnight daily) bar-

rooms, mostly with shared bathrooms and a small breakfast included. Towels are R$1 extra and you might have to ask for extra bedding on cold nights, because they don't provide much. They have a comfortable TV room with a great view. Ask about group rooms. Also on the north end of town is the unique and interesting **Pousada das Mansardas** (R Wilhelm Christian Kleme 230 in the Ermitage neighborhood, tel. 21/3641-5102, www.mansardas.com.br, R$175). They have seven rooms in a large area with a pool and sauna. A decent downtown hotel is the **Hotel Rever** (Av. Delfim Moreira 634, tel. 21/2742-0176) which looks iffy on the outside but is actually somewhat charming on the inside. They have rooms with shared bath for R$41 and with private bath for R$57. Some rooms have fireplaces (remember, it gets cold here in the winter) and they give discounts on weekdays. Breakfast is included.

If you want to be as close as possible to the

the mountain hamlet of Teresópolis as seen from the Recanto do Lord Hostel

becue restaurant. They have a self-service-style setup for R$11 per kilo. There's another barbecue restaurant at the north end of the town, called **Night & Day** (Av. Lúcio Meira 1155, tel. 21/2643-4817, open 24 hours) that has a *rodísio*-style setup. One of the best options in town is **Pectopan Dona Irene** (Av. Ten. Luiz Meireles 1800, Bom Retiro neighborhood, tel. 21/2742-2901, noon–midnight Wed.–Sat., noon–4 P.M. Sun.) with authentic Russian food and vodka. Meals go for about R$50 per person. Another good bet is **Manjericão** (Rua Flavio Bortoluzzi de Souza 314, Alto neighborhood, tel. 21/2642-4242, 6–11 P.M. Thurs. and Fri., noon–midnight Sat. and Sun.), an Italian restaurant that uses all fresh ingredients and homemade pastas with herbs from their own garden. Pizzas are thin-crusted and delicious. Prices are around R$30 per person.

The road out to Nova Friburgo has a couple of interesting options that are not too far from town. Try **Fattoria di Teresa** (Estrada Teresópolis-Friburgo, Km 12, tel. 21/2644-6110, 11:30 A.M.–9:30 P.M. Sun.–Thurs., 11 A.M.–midnight Fri. and Sat.) for Italian food at around R$35 per person. The **Fazenda Genéve** (Estrada Teresópolis-Friburgo, Km 16, tel. 21/3643-6391, www.fazenda-geneve.com.br, call to make reservations) is great for anyone who loves meat.

### Getting There

The bus to Friburgo leaves Teresópolis at 7 A.M., 11 A.M., 3 P.M., and 7 P.M. and costs R$6. Buses go to Petrópolis at 6 A.M., 7 A.M., 9 A.M., 2 P.M., 3 P.M., 5 P.M., and 7 P.M. The cost is R$8.50.

## THE ROAD TO NOVA FRIBURGO

There are a number of things to do and see on the road from Teresópolis to Nova Friburgo (known as the Tere–Fri Circuit), but most of this territory requires that you have a car. If you're taking the bus to Nova Friburgo, it's not practical or advisable to stop along the way. About 12 kilometers from town on the RJ-130 highway heading out to Nova Friburgo, you'll come to the Mulher de Pedra turn-off. From there you can hike up to see the great stone figure of the reclining woman (Mulher de

Pedra means Stone Woman). You'll pass streams of clear, drinkable water along the way. There's also the Vale das Frades, which includes the Frades River at the bottom. This is a great place for swimming and enjoying the cascade of a waterfall. There are some water sports practiced here as well. Further up the road you'll come across all types of restaurants and viewpoints.

## NOVA FRIBURGO

In this mountain town, founded in the 1800s by a group of Swiss immigrants, you'll find an interesting mixture of elements. The town center is not unlike Teresópolis: urban, modern, and commercial. On the outskirts of town, especially in the neighborhoods of Lumiar and São Pedro da Serra, you'll find a kind of rural tourism not unlike that in the south of Brazil. The architecture of the area has traces of German and Swiss heritage and

the food is no different, with plenty of potatoes and fondue on the menu. The idea here is to get out of the center and off into one of the rural areas, where you can take walks through the natural wonders of the countryside. You'll also encounter plenty of art and artists here and the Sabor Mury district reveals the gastronomic arts in its many restaurants. There are numerous hotels and *pousadas* around town and along the Estrada Teresópolis–Friburgo. There, you'll also find a Swiss cheese farm, a Mink farm, and plenty of viewpoints and trails.

Nova Friburgo is best experienced with a car so you can drive in and out of the various districts and really enjoy the rural tourism. If you come in on the bus, then you might stick mostly to the Lumiar neighborhood and downtown, although you'll find buses going to any and all of the sights in town. Be sure to see the Parque São Clemente and the Praça Getúlio Vargas for a taste of the Nova Friburgo community.

## Cabo Frio

Visitors who come to Cabo Frio for the first time are surprised and usually repulsed by the city itself. Shortly afterward, upon stepping out onto Praia do Forte, visitors are stunned by the beauty of the coastline. The white sand and blue water continue on and on until they disappear out of sight. Most travelers, with the exception of scuba divers, prefer to visit Cabo Frio on day trips from Buzios, enjoying its fine beaches or partaking of a pleasant boat excursion around the islands and beaches. Lunch takes place on the boat or at a beach kiosk. At the end of the day, visitors can opt for a dinner along the canal or head back to Buzios for dinner.

A mass of tall concrete buildings and city streets, built without the slightest concern for aesthetic beauty, leave travelers shaking their heads in disbelief at the shameless lack of class found here. Cabo Frio is a favorite summer spot of Mineiros (people from the huge inland state of Minas Gerais). With no beaches

of their own, hundreds of thousands of Mineiros rush to this long strip of sand and blue water every summer in huge groups and pass their days on the beach. Mineiros are famous throughout Brazil for being somewhat frugal and this is evidenced in Cabo Frio by the fact that most of these visitors rent other people's homes during their stays here. As a result, there are not many good hotels or charming *pousadas* in Cabo Frio and about half of the residents of the city rent their houses or apartments out for the summer to make a few extra bucks. This means that thousands of inhabitants of Cabo Frio do not furnish or decorate their homes to any serious degree. And the city remains ugly inside and out.

The flux of summer vacationers gives Cabo Frio an all-or-nothing character. Either the beaches are packed and the crowds are throbbing in the streets at night, or they are abandoned and deserted with nary a kiosk open for business.

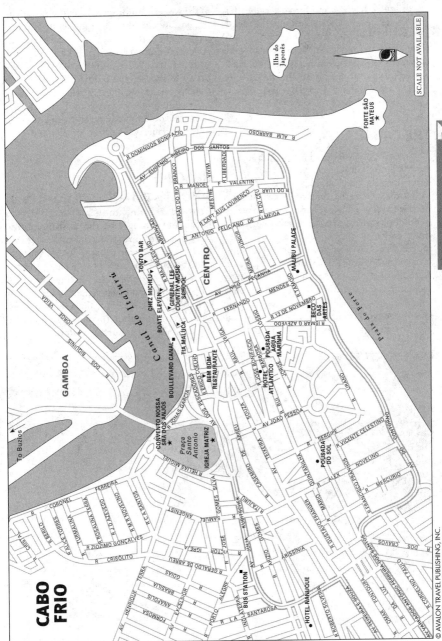

Rio de Janeiro State

CABO FRIO

SCALE NOT AVAILABLE

Ilha do Japonês

FORTE SÃO MATEUS

GAMBOA

Canal do Itajuru

To Búzios

R. JORGE VEIGA

R. DOS BIQUINIS

R. HELIAS MIGUEL

CONVENTO NOSSA SRA DOS ANJOS

Praça Santo Antonio

IGREJA MATRIZ

AV. TOMAS GARCIA

R. PESCADORES

R. LARGO COELHO

BOULEVARD CANAL

TIA MALUCA

BEM COM-RESTAURANTE

TONTO BAR

CHEZ MICHOU

BOATE ELEVEN

GENERAL LEE COUNTRY MUSIC SCHOOL

AV. ASSUNCAO

R. MAL. FLORIANO

CENTRO

AV. EUGENIO RIBEIRO

R. DOMINGOS BONIFACIO

DOS SANTOS

R. BARAO DO RIO BRANCO

R. MANOEL

F. VALENTIN

R. CAPT. MESTRE

R. AUG LOURENÇO

R. ANTONIO FELICIANO DE ALMEIDA

VIVIM

R. LIBERDADE

R. ALM BARROSO

R. DO LUAR

R. DO CEU

AV. NILO PECANHA

MENDES

FERNANDO

R. TAMOIO

R. TEIXEIRA JUNIOR

MALIBU PALACE

BECO DAS ARTES

R. 13 DE NOVEMBRO

R. ISMAR G AZEVEDO

Praia do Forte

R. VEIGA

R. COELHO

R. RUI BARBOSA

POUSADA AGUA MARINHA

HOTEL ATLANTICO

R. JOSE BONIFACIO

R. JORGE LOBO

R. URANO

AV. JOAO PESSOA

R. SOUZA

R. RAUL

R. CASSIANO DE ABREU

R. TEIXEIRA

R. JOSE GOMES SILVA

R. SAMUEL

R. ITALUNO

R. ANGENIST

R. VICTOR IGREJA

R. GERALDO DE ABREU

R. KUBITSCHEK

R. MARIO FRANEB

R. GUSTAVO FRANCO

R. FRANCISCO PRANHOS

R. QUINTANILHA

R. VICENTE CELESTINO

SERGIPE

NOVELINO

POUSADA DO SOL

ALEX

MERCURIO

R. CONTORNO

DOS CRAVOS

R. GOMES

ARDIO

ABISSINIA

R. FERREIRA

R. CORONEL

R. ALICE TORRES

R. BERILO

R. TURMALINA

R. ROSALINA TERRA

R. F.C.A. SANTOS

R. R.M.F. NOVELINO

R. ZIOZIMO GONÇALVES

R. CRISOLITO

R. CRISTAL

R. HENRIQUE TERRA

R. BRASILIA

R. ANAPOLIS

R. EXCELSIOR

R. PORTO ALEGRE

R. LA TERRA

R. GOIAS

R. FORMOSA

AV. INGLATERRA

SANTAROSA

BUS STATION

HOTEL NANUQUE

R. ROBERTO SILVEIRA

DA. LUZ

R. OMAR

R. CONSTANTINO PAULO

R. TENENTE ANTONIO FERREIRA DOS SANTOS

OBAR

DOS

For scuba divers, Cabo Frio offers a different experience, as the waters around the islands and Arraial do Cabo are replete with tropical plants, fish, and submersed ships from all kinds of wrecks that occurred here over the years. Special, dynamic conditions in the currents give the area a unique variety of marine life and a visibility of up to 25 meters.

## THE CANAL AREA

The most tourist-oriented area in Cabo Frio apart from the beaches is Avenida dos Pescadores along the canal, also known as the Boulevard Canal. There the inner edge of the street is lined with restaurants and bars, each with plenty of outdoor seating. On the canal itself, you'll find plenty of places with boats for hire, including the Terminal Marítimo, where you can find boat excursions of all kinds. Around Praça Santo Antônio sit the city's most historic buildings, including the Igreja Matriz and the Convento Nossa Sra. dos Anjos. The latter has a fantastic view of the canal from a high viewing deck, and a lower viewing area gives you a panoramic view of the western landscape. To get there, walk up the entrance road to the top (about 500 meters). At the bottom of this hill is the **Museu de Arte, Religiosa Tradicional** (Largo de Santo Antônio, tel. 22/2643-6898, 2–8 P.M. Wed.–Fri, 4–8 P.M. Sat. and Sun., R$32), which has some permanent exhibits of religious artifacts. The white bridge that crosses the canal from Cabo Frio heads over to the northern beaches or to Rio de Janeiro. The Rua dos Biquinis is just across the bridge to the right.

## BEACHES
### ⋈ Praias Brava, Conchas, and Peró

Across the channel to the north of Praia do Forte (and the city) are the most interesting beaches in the area, as much for the fact that they are less crowded than Praia do Forte as that they are surrounded by greenery and not by concrete. The first is Praia Brava, a small strip of white sand that attracts surfers to its strong waves. The next is Praia das Conchas, which is lined with permanent beach kiosks, more elaborate than those at Praia do Forte.

the canal at Cabo Frio

Here you'll find some tourist activities, like horseback rides and kayaks for rent. The Conchas beach is one of the prettiest, as it has calm, blue water in a quaint semi-circle formation. Although the water is somewhat cold, it's a great place to dive in and cool down. Finally, Praia do Peró is a long stretch of beach with plenty of bars and kiosks for getting out of the sun. It goes on for kilometers and there are some dunes nearby that you can explore. Access to these beaches is somewhat limited without a car and you may consider renting one for your stay here (also useful for tripping up to Buzios). There are buses that go out to the northern beaches from the *rodoviaria* or from Rua dos Biquinis. A taxi will cost around R$18 from the canal area and you can probably make a deal with a small boat in the canal to take you out to these beaches, then pick you up again at the end of the day.

## Praia do Foguete and Praia das Dunas

To the south of Praia do Forte, this stunning coastline continues another seven or eight kilometers under the names Praia do Foguete and Praia das Dunas, less frequented versions of Praia do Forte. Together these three beaches create a seemingly endless stretch of beach. Foguete has a slightly more aggressive surf than Praia do Forte, which makes it popular with surfers (especially wind and kite surfers as there are often strong winds here too). It's much less frequented than Praia do Forte, and continues to be popular with the local fishermen, who share the waters with the surfers. There are kiosks on Foguete in case you make your way down there and run out of food and water. The view from Foguete back to the city of Cabo Frio actually makes the city look pretty. Along the coastal road at Foguete are mostly small condos and summer homes in a smaller version of Cabo Frio itself. All along this area, you'll find large sand dunes, but especially at the Dama Branca dunes that mark the beginning of Foguete Beach. There, the dunes reach 20 meters and the sands are constantly blowing and shifting in the wind. Streets in this area are usually covered in sand.

The neighborhoods inland of these beaches are lower class and poor, which also keeps the crowds from encroaching. It's considered unsafe to walk around the dunes or even walk too far along the coastline down from Praia do Forte. To explore Praia do Foguete, it's best to get a bus or taxi. You'll take the main highway that goes out to Arraial do Cabo from Cabo Frio, called the Rodovia General Alfredo Bruno Gomes Martins. Given everything, you'll probably be happier heading up to the northern beaches instead.

## Praia do Forte

The main attraction in Cabo Frio, Praia do Forte is what keeps visitors coming back here year after year. It consists of 7.5 kilometers of fine white sand and bright blue ocean water, one of the most beautiful beach scenes in the Americas. At one end is the fort itself, called Fort São Mateus, sitting on a tiny island near the tip of the landmass. It was built in 1620 to protect the canal from the French, English, and Dutch pirates who made frequent attacks on the Portuguese colony during the 17th century. You can walk across a small bridge to the fort and check its various compartments, including the old prison chambers and main deck with canons. There is an exhibition hall inside with displays from local artists. The water around the fort is clear and shallow and is a popular place for swimming. Near the fort is one of the best beach bars in the area, called **Navegantes Bar.** The place is especially active during happy hour.

Dotted along the length of Praia do Forte are numerous small beach kiosks, almost more like temporary tents, that provide all types of food and drink for the crowd. In a singular act of genius, somebody decided that all of these tents should be white, to blend in with the sand. This is a small touch that has a large effect on the character of the beach. As extensive as it is, Praia do Forte gets so crowded during the peak season that it's difficult to find a spot on the sand. The kiosks stay busy all day long. Since the crowd consists mostly of Brazilians who come to rent other people's homes

© CHRISTOPHER VAN BUREN

**Praia do Forte in Cabo Frio**

for a week or so, there is a relatively small amount of support for international travelers. You'll need your own beach equipment, for example, as there are very few places with chairs and umbrellas available for rent. There are few public facilities and you may have to ask at one of the restaurants across the coastal road if you can use their facilities. In the off season, the beach is almost deserted and most of the kiosks close down.

Following the beach for about half of its length is the Avenida do Contorno, a fairly busy street that is lined on the inside with tall condominiums. The street sits above the beach on a small bluff and you have to walk down some steps to get to the sand. This serves to keep the beach insulated from the busy urban area. Add to that the many kiosks that block the view from the street. There is a new boardwalk and wooden deck that runs along the beach side of the coastal highway, looking over the sand and surf. About halfway down (from the fort) is a recently installed park and artificial lake with the only public restrooms within several kilometers. Slightly further down is the main tourist information center.

## ISLANDS

The most popular and visited of the islands around Cabo Frio is the Ilha dos Papagaios off the coast of Praia Brava. Many of the boat tours make a stop here for snorkeling or just swimming in the clear blue water around the island. Its neighbors, the Comprida and Dois Irmãos Islands, are popular locations for snorkeling and scuba diving excursions. Inside the canal is the Ilha do Japonês, which is a popular stop among the boat tours of Cabo Frio, but you can also go directly to the island and spend the entire day if you choose. The island has a sandy beach area with a couple of kiosks for snacks (seafood and crab) and drinks. The water is clear and calm.

## ARRAIAL DO CABO

With its turquoise waters, both shallow and deep, and various small islands and inlets, Arraial do Cabo is recognized as a scuba diver's haven. Although the water in these parts is colder than in other regions of Brazil (an average of 22°C), it offers remarkable clarity and a variety of sea life. The village and beaches of Arrial do Cabo are much less frequented than those of Cabo Frio and at times are almost deserted. The principal beach of Praia Grande, however, is decorated with beach bars and gets plenty of visitors during the summer months. Due to its position on the peninsula, it gets a great sunset over the ocean. There are several good boat excursions that leave from Praia dos Anjos near the village.

## ENTERTAINMENT AND NIGHTLIFE

Nightlife is active in the peak season and you hardly have to go looking for it. The best places are all along the Praia do Forte and at the canal restaurants. In low season, you might have a difficult time finding anything going on. You can try the **General Lee Country Music Saloon** (Av. dos Pescadores, Canal, tel. 22/2645-4380) on the canal road and **Boate Eleven** (Rua Major Belegard 590, Centro, tel. 22/2643-1985). Both open

their doors around 10 P.M. and go until sunrise daily in the peak season. On the low season, you should probably call to check hours of operation.

## FESTIVALS AND EVENTS

In keeping with its popularity with the Brazilian masses from Minas Gerais, Cabo Frio is a hugely popular place to spend Carnaval, Mineiro style. The hotels and *temporadas* (rented houses) book up months in advance and room capacities are maxed out. The four days of Carnaval, plus any extra days before and after to complete the weekend, find mobs of people on the beachfront and all over the streets of the city. The atmosphere is extremely festive and everyone is drunk and screaming or dancing. The city sponsors a few *trio elétrico* (semitrucks rigged with stages and sound systems for mobile music and dance performances) and most of the crowds hang around these. In terms of all-out parties in reasonably safe conditions, it's a decent event.

Rio de Janeiro State

## BIKINI HAVEN

Brazilian bikini fashions are famous the world over. Bikini manufacturers of all types and sizes are scattered throughout the southeast region—not just on the coastline. Key production areas include Belo Horizonte, Divinópolis, Petrópolis, Rio de Janeiro, and, topping them all, Cabo Frio. Known as the *capital da moda praia* (capital of beach fashion), Cabo Frio produces so much sexy swimwear that the city has an entire street dedicated to its manufacture and sale. Rua dos Biquinis is just across the bridge (Ponte Feliciano Sodré) from the canal area. On Bikini Street, you'll find dozens of shops and fashion centers with more bikinis than you can imagine at the best prices in the entire country. Most of the stores have their own, private labels and do their own manufacturing, so you won't find two stores with exactly the same thing. And prices are factory-direct.

Brazilian bikini styles are often too racy and

extravagant for foreign women, but many manufacturers have more conservative lines for international tastes. The famous *fio dental* model (literally, dental floss, but it translates to the g-string or thong style) would probably be censored in the United States but is quite common on Brazil's beaches. Ironically, as scandalous as Brazilian bikinis can be, Brazilian women are not as fond of nude beaches as foreigners are and most would never consider going topless on a public beach, much less frequent a nude beach. That explains the relative lack of nude beaches in Brazil. The most common bikini style, known as *amarradinho* (little string ties) can be encountered for as little as R$10. This style, too, is pretty revealing for foreign tastes. You'll find bikinis with hand stitching, beadwork, and even decorative painting, as well as belted bikinis, bikini shorts, mesh skirts, and all kinds of wonderful ways to adorn yourself while visiting Brazil's sensual beaches.

## SHOPPING

The street called Beco Das Artes is a small area filled with art studios, and it's one of the nicer places in town to walk around and window shop. It's not far from the Praia do Forte off Rua 13 de Novembro, just past the Malibu Palace Hotel. The studios are open mostly in the afternoon up to 9 or 10 P.M. On weekends, they open only in the evening. You'll find shops for bikinis and swimwear all over the Centro near the beach, but the best place is the Rua dos Biquinis (see sidebar).

## SPORTS AND RECREATION

### Boat Excursions

Excursions of all kinds leave from the Terminal Merítimo along the canal. The most common trips are in medium-sized boats that carry about 40 people at a time. A popular trip is a two-hour voyage that takes you out of the canal, around Praia do Forte, and over to Ilha dos Papagaios for a swim near the island. It costs around R$20 per person. A three-hour version includes a look at the various beaches to the north, with stops for swimming in Conchas and Ilha dos Papagaios. You also get a look at Ilha do Japonês on the way. This one costs around R$30. To hire a boat for your own agenda, you'll pay around R$40 per hour. You can also ask about taxi service to and from the beaches in the north. The Terminal is at Avenida dos Pescadores 1 (tel. 22/2645-2804, tel. 22/2644-4107). Miguel there speaks a bit of English. Some excursions take passengers up and down the canal at night to see the city lights from the water. Trips leave at 8:30 P.M., 10 P.M., and 11:30 P.M. The cost is R$25 per person, which includes a complimentary drink. You can get more information at the Restaurante Tia Maluca (tel. 22/9901-6952, www.tia-maluca.com.br) on the canal.

### Diving and Snorkeling

You can find some excellent diving conditions around Cabo Frio that you might even prefer over those in Buzios. Here, the water is around 22°C and has a visibility of up to 25 meters. The area is particularly rich in marine plants and corals. There are more than 80 different species of fish recorded in these waters, plus sea turtles, barracuda, eels, rays, and crustaceans. There are more than 80 locations that have pieces of wrecked ships and areas of shallow waters, from 5–15 meters. Deeper dives go down to 40 and 50 meters. Check details with **Cabo Frio Sub** (Rua Major Belegard 419, tel. 22/2643-1475, www.cabofriosub.com.br). You can also check with **Tridente Centro de Mergulho** (Rua Maestro Clodomiro Guimarães de Oliveira 362, tel. 22/2645-1705), located near the fort at the far end of town.

### Where to Dive

In Cabo Frio, the favorite spots are on the far side of the three islands off the north coast. In Arraial do Cabo, you can dive off Ponta da Jararaca, out to the remnants of a steam ship, wrecked here in 1923. The pieces are scattered around the point and there are many great species of fish in the area, too. On the inner coast of the Ilha dos Porcos, you can find sea turtles and other species with clarity of 15 meters and a depth of around 18 meters. A better place to swim with the turtles is at Ponta Leste and you can swim among sea horses at Cardeiros. Another shipwreck can be examined around 15 meters at Point Anequim and another from around 1839 is visible at 15 meters along the western coastline. There's an underwater cave, called the Gruda Azul that can be explored when conditions allow.

## ACCOMMODATIONS

Prices listed here are low-season rates; expect prices to double for peak season (December–February). A decent and economical hotel near the *rodoviaria* is **Hotel Nanuque** (Rua José Paes de Abreu 921, tel. 22/2645-2880, R$25 s, R$35 d with fan, and R$45 d with a/c). They have lots of rooms that are very simple, but clean. From here, it's a long walk to the canal area, but only a few blocks to the lower end of Praia do Forte. Also, the **Pousada do Sol**

(Rua Jorge Lóssio 1343, tel. 22/2645-3051, www.pousadadosolcabofrio.com.br, R$40 s and R$70 d) has decent rooms at a good price. They also have a pool and sauna. The service leaves quite a bit to be desired, however. Rooms have air and TV. It's located a couple blocks from the tourist information center. **M Hotel Atlântico** (Rua José Bonifácio 302, Centro, tel. 22/2643 0996, www.hotelatlantico.tur.br, R$35 s and R$50 d) has basic rooms with ceiling fans and TVs. Another relatively good bet is the **M Pousada Agua Marinha** (Rua Rui Barbosa 996, Centro, tel. 22/2643-8447, www.pousadaaguamarinhacabofrio.com.br, R$60). They have air, fan, TV, pool, and sauna. Finally, if you want the beachfront hotel experience, go for **Malibu Palace Hotel** (Praia do Forte, tel. 22/2645-5131, www.malibupalace.com.br, R$165). They have spacious rooms, pools, sauna, and game courts. It's kind of old and funky, but it's right on the beach at Praia do Forte.

## FOOD

The best place in town for a self-service lunch buffet is **Restaurante Kilo Junior** (Av. Barão do Rio Branco 8, tel. 22/2645-4167, open for lunch daily) behind McDonald's. You get a huge lunch for around R$10 per person. Two restaurant clusters in town are located on the canal road (mostly for dinner) and in the Praça Porto Rocha along the coast highway in the middle of Praia do Forte. Of course, there are also the many kiosks on the beach for a variety of lunch plates. Some places of note on the Boulevard Canal include **Chez Micheu Creperie** (Av. dos Pescadores, Canal, 6 P.M.–midnight daily in the peak season. In off season, you should call for hours) for crepes and pasta dishes and **Tia Maluca** for lobster, *moqueca* (fish stew) and cold beers. R$60 for two. You can also check out the **Tonto Bar** for pizza, beer, and festivities at night.

Around town, you'll find the **Bem Bom Restaurante** (Rua Bento José Ribeiro 129, tel. 22/2647-7206, 6 P.M.–midnight daily in the peak season, call for hours in the off season) for pasta and crepes in a nice environment.

## INFORMATION AND SERVICES

The main tourist information center is located off Avenida do Contorno about halfway down Praia do Forte and you should be able to find Internet cafés or LAN Houses along the coast highway along Praia do Forte. Try **Cyber Tel** for phone booths and Internet (Praça Porto Rocha 56, Centro, tel. 22/2649-7575, 9 A.M.–8 P.M. Mon.–Sat.). You can also check at the **Shopping da Praia** (Av. do Contorno 450) and **Cabo Frio Shopping** (Av. Teixeira e Souza 116, Centro) for Internet and international ATMs. Otherwise, there's a Banco do Brasil at Praça Porto Rocha 44, where you can change money and find ATMs. You can also change money at **Malizia Tour** (Av. Assunção 706, Centro, tel. 22/2623-2022) and the **Porto Búzios Viagens e Turismo** (Rua Silva Jardim 18, Centro, tel. 22/2643-6255).

## GETTING THERE AND AROUND

Buses leave from Rio de Janeiro for Cabo Frio on the Auto Viação 1001 line and from Belo Horizonte on the Útil line. You can get to and from Buzios on the *Buzios* bus that runs from the *rodoviaria* down Avenida Júlia Kubitschek every 20 minutes. The trip takes about 40 minutes.

If you want to rent a car here in Cabo Frio for trips up to the northern beaches, Arraial do Cabo, and Buzios, then look into **Casa do Buggy** (Av. Ver. Antônio Ferreira dos Santos 836, tel. 22/2645-3939, 8 A.M.–6 P.M. Mon.–Sat.) and **Localiza** (Av. Teixeira e Souza 1703, Braga, tel. 22/2643-9777, 8 A.M.–6 P.M. Mon.–Sat.).

# Buzios

Think of Buzios as the San Tropez of Brazil. Here Brazil's rich and famous come to shop, get *bronzeado* (bronzed) in the hot sun near a charming hotel, sample the gourmet lunches and dinners in the village, and shop some more. The village center is a theater of boutiques and restaurants (complete with lighting and stage sets) and a great place for an evening of music and dancing.

But that's probably not doing Buzios justice. There are also many simple destinations, semi-secluded beaches, and modest accommodations on the peninsula. It's easy to find something that suits your personal tastes. For many international travelers, the highlights are Tartaruga and Ferradura Beaches, two of the more accessible environments in Buzios. For others, the snorkeling and diving opportunities are the reason for visiting. Whatever your personal preference, you'll be pleased by the wide variety of options available. There are some excellent hikes along the dirt roads of the south shoreline that pass some awesome scenery.

## CENTRO

The Center of Buzios is what gives the entire peninsula its reputation as an upscale beach village for the rich and famous. The area is mostly a shopping and gawking district with fine boutiques, restaurants, and nightclubs that almost makes you feel like you're in an amusement park. Everything here is well produced, well designed, and well presented. This is also the principal nightlife zone and the options are numerous—from cozy, well-lit bars to nightclubs with live music and dance. During the day, you can shop for beachwear, tee shirts, furnishings, sunglasses, and so many other items in the many boutiques. There are ice cream parlors, Internet cafés, public bathrooms, and money exchange centers. Most of the area's top-end restaurants are here too, for lunch or dinner. The main street is called Rua das Pedras, but there are several side alleys and walkways

in the village center. Just walking around the village is great entertainment.

At one end of the center, near the Estrada da Usina, are some mid-range drinking and dining options, including a couple of pizza joints. There you'll also find outdoor temporary stands lined up on the street offering the usual selection of tropical drinks. This end is the last bastion of young, surfer activity in the Centro.

Along the coast from the Centro to the outer tip of the peninsula is a coastline called **Orla Bardot** (Bardot Coastline), in honor of Bridget Bardot, who is single-handedly responsible for turning Buzios from a small fishing area into a theater for the rich and famous. As you walk up the coast, you'll see a statue of the famous French actress and farther up, a series of three statues out in the surf, called the Three Fishermen. The beaches in the area near the Centro (Praia do Canto and Praia da Armação) are not recommended for swimming due to pollution and heavy boat traffic.

## JOÃO FERNANDES

Two of the most popular beaches for sunning and swimming are João Fernandes and João Fernandinho. Since there are quite a few charming *pousadas* in this area, these beaches tend to get a bit crowded in the summer months. This is also a popular place for rich Argentinean vacationers and there are several Argentinean-owned establishments here. The beach here is excellent for snorkeling as there are some small underwater reefs offshore. There are lots of beach kiosks and restaurants nearby. Some of the *pousadas* here are mid-range and some are top-end with ocean views.

## TARTARUGA

The most centralized location on the peninsula is the area called Tartaruga. It's basically a stretch of *pousadas,* restaurants, and other establishments along the Estrada da Usina as it

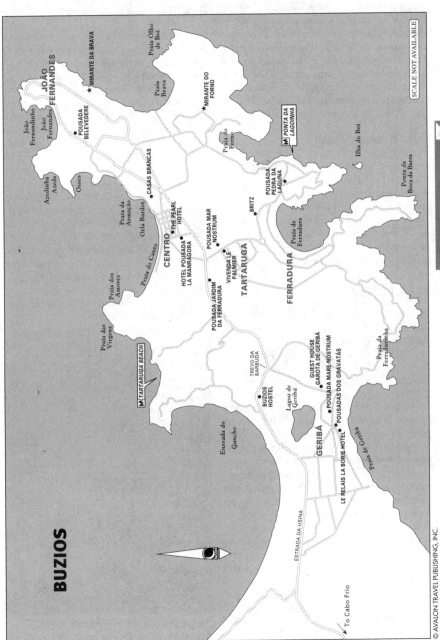

BUZIOS

JOÃO FERNANDES

João Fernandinho
João Fernandes
Azedinha
Azeda
Ossos

Praia Olho de Boi

MIRANTE DA BRAVA ★

POUSADA BELVEDERE

Praia Brava

MIRANTE DO FORNO ★

Praia do Forno

PONTA DA LAGOINHA M

Praia da Armação

Orla Bardot

CASAS BRANCAS

POUSADA PEDRA DA LAGUNA

Ilha do Boi

Ponta da Boca da Barra

Praia do Canto

THE PEARL HOTEL

CENTRO

POUSADA MAR NOSTRUM

BRITZ

HOTEL POUSADA LA MANRÁGORA

VIVENDA LE PALMIER

Praia de Ferradura

Praia dos Amores

Praia das Virgens

POUSADA JARDIM DA FERRADURA

TARTARUGA

FERRADURA

TARTARUGA BEACH M

TREVO DA BARBUDA

Enseada do Gaucho

BUZIOS HOSTEL

Lagoa de Geribá

GUEST HOUSE GAROTA DE GERIBÁ

POUSADA MARE NÓSTRUM

Praia da Ferradurinha

POUSADAS DOS GRAVATÁS

GERIBÁ

LE RELAIS LA BORIE HOTEL

Praia de Geribá

ESTRADA DA USINA

To Cabo Frio

N Rio de Janeiro State

SCALE NOT AVAILABLE

© AVALON TRAVEL PUBLISHING, INC.

makes its way down the middle of the peninsula out to the tip. Tartaruga is not the prettiest area in Buzios. There are no fabulous views and no beaches here. But the accommodations are the most reasonable in Buzios and you can easily walk to the Centro, Ferradura, and Tartaruga Beaches. It's even possible to walk to Geribá, although most people prefer to take a bus, since it's a long and uninteresting walk.

### Tartaruga Beach

Praia Tartaruga is an excellent beach for swimming, snorkeling, and laying out. There are several beach kiosks, clear water, and white sand. Although not the most crowded beach in Buzios, Tartaruga is popular and you may find crowds during peak season. You can access Tartaruga Beach by boat excursion or via the long road that leaves from the Estrada da Usina (about four kilometers).

## FERRADURA

Travelers who stay in the Ferradura Beach area often never visit other areas of Buzios. Ferradura is so beautiful and the *pousadas* here are so comfortable, there's really no reason to leave. The ocean is blue and clear, the waves are mild and the sand is white and wide and it goes on for about three kilometers. It's a perfect beach for swimming and catching some sun. On the left side, there is a row of beach bars that serve cold drinks and lunch plates and have shady seating on their patios. If you sit there, it won't take but a few minutes for the roving vendors to pass by, offering their beach dresses, sunglasses, cashews, and other items. There's a great hike that leads from the left side of Ferradura (behind the bars) up to Lagoinha.

Just inland, the area is rich in *pousadas.* They go all the way from the beach up to the Estrada da Usina. But this area is not very urbanized. Rather, this is a rural area. Some of the roads are dirt and there is plenty of open space. The main road into Ferradura is called Acesso a Ferradura. From there you'll reach a traffic circle from which you should go left and then right to enter the beach.

## GERIBÁ

One of the longest and widest beaches in Buzios, Geribá is a strange mixture of beachfront hotels (some mildly resort-like), residences, and simple beach flops on the inland streets. There are a few modest restaurants in the area, but most of the shops and activity are on the Estrada da Usina, at or near the **Trevo da Barbuda,** the main point of entry into Geribá Beach. In stark contrast to the Centro, there is really no town center here and it's difficult to find much in the way of shops or supplies. Everything here takes place on the expansive beach during the day, with the exception of the legendary **Pig Roast Luau** on Thursday nights at the Fishbone Café on the beach. The luau attracts folks from all over the peninsula and is a great nighttime adventure. The waves at Geribá are strong, but the water is clear and blue and you can certainly go in without worries as it's shallow for quite a ways. There is a lake in the Geribá area that is mostly surrounded by condominiums.

© CHRISTOPHER VAN BUREN

**the ruggedly beautiful coastline at Praia do Forno**

## OTHER BEACHES

Besides the aforementioned beaches, there are numerous beaches all along the edges of Buzios. The three beaches called **Ossos, Azeda,** and **Azedinha** are close together on the outer tip of the peninsula, past Armação and the Centro. All three are accessible via a small road that you can pick up behind the Igreja de Santa Anna. All three of these beaches have calm, crystal-clear waters that are great for scuba diving and snorkeling. In the low season, the Azeda and Azedinha beaches are nearly deserted. **Praia Brava** is one of the beaches most favored by surfers as it is long (two kilometers) and has strong waves. There are very few structures out there—just a couple of small kiosks. A 40-minute walk from the right side of Praia Brava leads to a tiny beach hidden in the most uninhabited part of the outer peninsula. The beach, called **Praia Olho de Boi** (Bull's Eye Beach), is the official nude beach in Buzios and a very enchanting place fenced-in by hills and a rocky shoreline. The **Praia do Forno** is on the inside of a picturesque bay that gets some very strong high tides. Near the beach at the innermost part of the bay, the water is calm and clear. There is a narrow strip of sand for lying out and no bars or kiosks of any kind. Finally, on a small but charming sandy inlet is the **Ferradurinha Beach,** accessible from the upper end of Geribá. The 300-meter beach is wide and sandy and the water is clear and calm. It's a great place for snorkeling.

On the northern coast of the peninsula, you might want to check out **Praia dos Amores,** a small strip of sand to the left of the Centro beach that you can access only by a short trail. Nevertheless, this is a popular beach as the water is clear and waves are minimal. **Praia das Virgens** (ironically located so close to Praia dos Amores) is a small, quaint beach with no structures and is very difficult to access. You can see if the trail from Amores is open or try the coastal access from Tartaruga Beach, which is only possible during low tide. Plan your trip to and from this beach with the low tide.

## ENTERTAINMENT AND NIGHTLIFE

Just about all the nightlife in town takes place in the Centro area. There, you'll find everything in the way of bars and clubs. Several sidewalk cafés make great people-watching perches and when you're ready for some music, you'll have several choices from which to choose. Just stroll around the village and look for the atmosphere you like. A note of caution: Prices here are as high as any you'll find in Brazil and make those great exchange rates seem almost non-existent.

A couple of recommendations: Try **Patio Havana** (Rua dasa Pedras 101, Centro, tel. 22/2623-2169, 5 P.M. until sunrise Mon.–Wed., 1 P.M.–sunrise, Thurs.–Sun.) for live jazz or blues music, including Brazilian pop and bossa nova. They have five different environments, among them an outdoor patio-bar, pool room, and restaurant. Also, **Chez Michou** (Rua das Pedras 90, Centro, tel. 22/2623-2169, 5:30 P.M. until sunrise Mon.–Wed., noon–sunrise from Thurs.–Sun., call for prices) has a stage with live music nightly, along with some great crepes. The Mexican Restaurant-Bar **Guapo Loco** (Rua das Pedras 253, tel. 22/2623-2657, 6 P.M. until the last client leaves daily) for has a wild night scene with tequila shooters, music, and Mexican food in a beautiful setting. For dancing, try the more electronic DJ club, **Privilege** (Av. José Bento Ribeiro Dantas 550, tel. 22/2623-0150, www.privilegenet.com.br, call for show times and prices).

Tip: You can pick up restaurant and bar ad cards in the finer hotels. These often have special offers for free drinks when you enter.

Remember that Thursday is the night of the Pig Roast Luau at the **Fishbone Café** right on the beach in Geribá. Not to be missed.

## TOURS AND EXCURSIONS

The **Buzios Trolly** (tel. 22/2623-2763, www.buziostrolly.com.br) tour of the peninsula leaves from the Centro and makes a circle around the peninsula, stopping at the main beaches along the way. The tour gives you a great overview of the peninsula in about two hours. the "Trolly" leaves at 9 A.M., noon, and 3 P.M. There are several other Buzios tours, including tours by buggy and van. Try **Buggycar Turismo** (Av. José Bento R. Dantas 1144, Armação, tel. 22/2523-2610, www.buggycar.com.br) and **Buzios Car Turismo** (Rua das Pedras 275, tel. 22/2623-2863, buzioscar@mar.com.br) for buggy tours and **Travel Bus** (Estrada da Usina 444, tel. 22/2623-2478, travelbus@alohanet.com.br) or **Travel Buzios** (Rua das Palmeiras 112 in Geribá, tel. 22/2623-2109, travelbuzios@uol.com.br) for tours by van.

You can take a boat trip out to a couple of the islands off the north tip of Buzios on the *Aloha* schooner. The boat leaves from the pier at Praia da Armação (Porto Valeiro) and visits all the beaches on the north edge of the peninsula (passing nearby from the ocean), as well as the Branca and Feia Islands. There are stops at the islands for snorkeling and at Praia Tartaruga (also for snorkeling). You can opt to stay at Tartaruga and pick up the next boat back. The trip includes masks, snorkels, an on-board bar, and a shower. Trips cost R$18–20 and take about 2.5 hours. Boats leave at 10 A.M., 1 P.M., and 3:30 P.M. The organization is called **Porto Veleiro Turismo** (Travessa de Santana 01, Praia da Armação, tel. 22/2623-5433, www.portoveleirobuzios.com.br). You'll find other organizations along Rua das Pedras downtown offering this same trip.

## SNORKELING AND SCUBA DIVING

You can bring your mask and snorkel with you to several of the beaches in Buzios and find great underwater aquariums. The principal beaches for this are Tartaruga, Azeda, João Fernandes, Forno, and Ferradurinha. Also, Ilha Feia (meaning Ugly Island, but it's actually the prettiest in the area) has excellent snorkeling. For snorkeling and diving excursions, check with **True Blue** (Rua J.B. Ribeiro Dantas 2, Centro, tel. 22/2623-2357, www.mar.com.br). They have courses, equipment, beginner dives, and excursions.

## HIKING

There are very few actual hiking trails in Buzios. Most of the peninsula is covered by roads, either paved or dirt. Still, you can get out to the far reaches of the peninsula by walking along some of these roads.

### Ponta da Lagoinha

One of the best walks goes from the left corner of Praia da Ferradura up to the **Ponta da Lagoinha.** During low tide, you can swim in the pool at this interesting rock formation. At the incoming tide, this area is a roar of white waves crashing onto the rocks. Either way, it's an amazing view. You can continue out to **Praia do Forno** along this beautiful coastline, then take a dirt road out to the point looking out over **Ilha do Boi.** From there, it's not far to the **Mirante do Forno,** one of the highest points on the peninsula. The hike is not difficult and takes about two hours each way. You can also turn in toward the Centro at any time along the way.

### Other Hikes

Another road leads from the other corner of Praia Ferradura out to the **Ponta da Boca da Barra,** which has an amazing viewpoint. This takes about 1.5 hours each way. A short walk from João Fernandes heads over to the **Mirante da Brava** viewpoint, where you get a view of Praia Brava and the outer edge of Buzios.

## ACCOMMODATIONS

There are *pousadas* and hotels spread all over the peninsula of Buzios, but they generally arrange themselves into five major clusters, corresponding to the five principal neighborhoods: Centro (top-end and mid-range hotels close to nightlife and shopping), João Fernandes (top-end *pousadas* with views of the ocean), Tartaruga (budget and mid-range *pousadas,* centrally located), Ferradura (quiet with charming mid-range *pousadas*), and Geribá (beachfront hotels and budget *pousadas* inland, no nightlife).

Note that prices given here are low-season

rates (unless otherwise noted). Prices go up 30–50 percent for peak season.

## Under R$100

The best economical place in Buzios is the **Pousada Jardim da Ferradura** (Av. Bento Ribeiro Dantas 1475, tel. 22/2623-2329, R$25 pp with discount for HI card holders). They have group and individual rooms, a community TV *sala*, a small pool, and a lovely tropical garden setting. Rooms are spacious and simple. Breakfast is included and they have discounts on boat excursions. The same owners have the **Buzios Hostel** (Rua Marisol 35 in Geribá, tel. 22/2623-6024), which is the same price. It's just off the Estrada da Usina near Shopping 5000.

In the Geribá Beach area, you have the **Guest House Garota de Geribá** (Rua Conceição 100, tel. 22/2629-8166, garotadegeriba@hotmail.com, R$60 s and R$70 d). The place is run by the Canadian immigrant David and his wife Núbia. It's simple and beachy, but clean and friendly and David speaks English. He also has a good bar. The **Pousada Mare Nostrum** (Rua Buritis 10, tel. 22/2623-7036, marenostrum@busiosonline.com.br, R$90) is a good value in the Geribá Beach area. It's a few blocks from the beach, but they have a comfortable atmosphere with clean, well-appointed rooms and a pool. An excellent breakfast is included and rooms have air, TV, fan, and mini-bar.

## R$100–200

There are two wonderful places to stay in the Ferradura Beach area. The first is **Ⓜ Vivenda Le Palmier** (Rua J VI no. 14, tel. 22/2623-2032, www.lepalmier.com.br, R$140 and R$225 in peak season) just off the Acesso a Ferradura road. They are a bit far from the beach, but they have a very cozy place with beautiful grounds, a library, and 16 rooms, each with a different aboriginal décor. Rooms come with air and loft. In the tropical yard, they have an indoor-outdoor bar, pool, pond, and massage room. Buffet breakfast is included. No service tax is included. Geraldina, the Argentinean owner, speaks English, French, and Spanish. The second place near Ferradura Beach

is **Ⓜ BRITZ** (formerly Sunshine Guesthouse, Rua da Paz 29, tel. 22/2623-5997, britz-buzios@hotmail.com, R$70 s and R$110 d). Britt, the Norwegian owner is very Zen and friendly. Her place is perched up on a hillside overlooking both Praia Ferradura and a lagoon in the area. She has eight unique rooms, a comfy area for sitting and reading, a pool, and a view deck. She is child- and gay-friendly, speaks English, and makes you feel very much at home. Peak season is double.

At the entrance to the Centro, you'll find the **Hotel Pousada La Mandrágora** (Av. Bento Ribeiro Dantas 1010, tel. 22/2623-1348, lamandragora@uol.com.br, R$160–175 standard and R$220 bungalow.). They have tennis and squash courts, yoga and samba classes, a gym, a pool, and a sauna. Rooms have air, TV, phone, and mini-bar.

## R$200–500

A beautiful hotel in an out-of-the-way location between Praia Ferradura and Ponta da Lagoinha is **Pousada Pedra da Laguna** (Rua 6 Quadra F, tel. 22/2623-1965, www.pedradalaguna.com.br, R$200 standard and R$350 suite with view). They have a huge pool area, impressive lobby, and a kind of Tex-Mex décor. Rooms are spacious, super-clean, and very comfortable with TV, phone, and ceiling fan. Suites have verandas with ocean views and large bathtubs.

In the João Fernandes area, there's the elegant **Pousada Belevedere** (Rua 1 Quadra C Lot 43, tel. 22/2623-2221, belvedere@mar.com.br, R$240). They have 12 rooms with air, TV, and phone, and boast ocean views, a pool, and bar. They offer transportation to the beach. Breakfast is included.

You can stay on the beach at Geribá in the **Pousadas Dos Gravatás** (Rua dos Gravatás 67, tel. 22/2623-1218, www.pousadagravatas.com.br, R$200 and R$250 with view). They have 56 rooms, many with ocean views. All have air, phone, cable TV, and mini-bar. Breakfast and lunch are included and they have two pools, a beach bar, sauna, gym, and two restaurants. Another beachfront hotel-resort in Geribá is **Le Relais La Borie Hotel** (Rua dos

Bravatás 1374, tel. 22/2623-1498, www.lab-one.com.br, R$330 or R$398 with ocean view). They have an excellent restaurant, pool, and beach access with beach service from their bar. Breakfast and dinner are included. They don't charge a service tax.

## Over R$500

**M Casas Brancas** (Morro do Humaita 10, tel. 22/2623-1458, www.casasbrancas.com.br, R$450–595) has a view of the Praia da Armação and is within a short walk to the Centro—perfectly located for anyone wanting to be in the heart of the action while still maintaining a luxury experience. Rooms have air, TV, and phone, and they offer a restaurant, bar, and lovely pool with a view of the ocean.

If you want to stay where the celebrities are, then look into **The Pearl Hotel** (Av. José Bento Ribeiro Dantas 222, tel. 22/2623-2856, www.thepearl.com.br, R$750–1025 s and R$825–1125 d) in the Centro area. This new, four-star luxury hotel was built out of a former shopping center and was designed and decorated to the nines. They have a restaurant-lounge (open to the public), a large, multi-level pool, poolside bar, spa, gym, and sauna. Rooms come in seven different categories.

# FOOD

## Asian

Japanese food is served at **Shiitake Cozinha Asiática** (Av. José Bento Ribeiro Dantas 412, tel. 22/2623-0125, 6 A.M.–midnight daily, R$70–140) in the Centro. They serve up sushi, tempura, and other traditional Japanese dishes, and they offer a lovely view of the ocean. You'll find Thai food in the Centro at **Sawasdee** (Av. José Bento Ribeiro Dantas 422, tel. 22/2623-4644, 6 A.M.–midnight, closed Wed., R$60), with typical semi-sweet dishes filled with mint, cilantro, and basil.

## Barbecue

The **Estância Don Joan** (Rua das Pedras 178, tel. 22/2623-2169, noon–midnight Wed.–Sun., 6 P.M.–midnight Mon. and Tue., R$60)

in the Centro specializes in Argentinean barbecued meat. They have a lovely ambience.

## International

A popular place for crepes is **Chez Michou Crêperie** (Rua das Pedras 90, tel. 22/2623-2169, 5:30 P.M. on Mon. and Tue., and noon Wed.–Sun.). They have a huge establishment with a stage and restaurant seating. For those with a hearty appetite, the **Restaurante Bavária** (Shopping no. 1, Centro, no phone, dinner daily) serves German cuisine and steak meals.

## Local Favorites

If you're in the Geribá area, be sure to pay a visit to **M Azulimão** (Av. Geribá 0, tel. 22/2623-8204, lunch and dinner daily). They have a casual, outdoor space with great seafood dishes, like salmon, shrimp, and oysters, plus many types of Brazilian fish. They have a super-special for R$15 per person and good grilled fish plates for only R$10. It's also a good place to sit and have drinks. The **M Bistro da Baiana** (Rua Manoel de Carvalho 11, tel. 22/2623-6285, 11 A.M.–midnight, no credit cards accepted) in the Centro serves traditional Bahian food, including *moqueca* (fish stew), *vatapá* (Bahia spicy fish and shrimp dish), and a variety of crab and shrimp dishes. It's very authentic. You get a view of the Armação beach along with your fresh fish or *moqueca*.

## Quick and Casual

There are some casual places to eat in the village area, including a couple of pizza restaurants at the entrance to the Centro, near the Estrada da Usina. The beach kiosks all over Buzios generally have seafood lunch plates, although don't count on these being cheap. The bars at Praia Ferradura have decent fish plates, as does the **Toca do Indio Quiosque** on the Geribá beach (open for lunch daily). The **Sol da Tartaruga** (open for lunch daily) has some great selections if you're on the Tartaruga beach. On the João Fernandes Beach, try **Cleopatra** (tel. 22/2623-2495, open for lunch daily). **Bananaland** (Rua Manoel Turibio de Farias 50, tel. 22/2623-0855, 11 A.M.–11 P.M.

daily) in the Centro has a self-service lunch buffet with plenty of salad items and meat dishes. The most economical options are in the Trevo da Barbuda area near Geribá. There you'll find some *lanchonetes* and simple self-service restaurants.

## INFORMATION AND SERVICES

The main tourist information office is in the Centro, at the far end in the small *praça* Santos Dumont. There's also an information booth at the entrance to town at the beginning of the Estrada José Bento Ribeiro Dantas (not to be confused with the Rua of the same name in the Centro). Internet cafés are all over the Centro, including **AlohaNet** (Av. José Bento Ribeiro Dantas 97, tel. 22/2623-4959) and **Posto Telefónico** (Av. José Bento Ribeiro Dantas 100, tel. 22/2623-4959). These places also have telephone booths and private phones for making international calls. Check their rates.

You'll find international ATMs in the Centro. Look for Banco do Brasil and Banco 24 Horas. There are several money changers in the Centro, including those who will take traveler's checks. Many of these are also tour agencies. Try **Malizia Tour** (Shopping Praia do Canto on Rua das Pedras, tel. 22/2623-2022, malizia@mar.com, 8 A.M.–10 P.M. daily).

www.buziosonline.com.br, www.buziosexplorer.com.br, and www.buziosturismo.com for information on hotels and Buzios in general.

## GETTING THERE AND AROUND

Many of the high-end hotels in Buzios offer transportation from the Buzios airport, Cabo Frio, or even as far as Rio de Janeiro—via third-party services. The services usually collect a fee of R$50–150. Check with your hotel about this when you make a reservation. Buses come from Rio de Janeiro into Cabo Frio on the Auto Viação 1001 line (tel. 21/2291-5151, www.autoviacao1001.com.br). From Cabo Frio, you can catch buses into Buzios every 20 minutes from the *rodoviaria*. From Rio, buses leave

at 6:30 A.M., 9:15 A.M., 11:15 A.M., 1:15 P.M., 3:15 P.M., 5:15 P.M., and 7:30 P.M. Buses return to Rio every two hours, 7 A.M.–7 P.M. You can reserve your tickets by phone using a credit card. The price is around R$25.

You can rent a car either in Cabo Frio or Buzios and drive back and forth. In Buzios, the organization called **Porto Veleiro Turismo** (Travessa de Santana 01, Praia da Armação, tel. 22/2623-5433, www.portoveleirobuzios.com.br) has cars and buggies for rent (a good way to get around in Buzios). Also **Buggycar Turismo** (Praia dos Ossos, tel. 22/2523-2610, www.buziosturismo.com) provides city tours by buggy, buggy rentals, trips to Rio and Cabo Frio, and other services. The same services are provided by **Buzios Car Turismo** (Rua das Pedras 275, tel. 22/2623-2863, buzioscar@mar.com.br). Compare prices at these three.

## RIO DAS OSTRAS

The village of Rio das Ostras grew up around the fishing trade and continues to this day with its fishing activities. There are a few interesting beaches in the region, including the principal beach, **Praia Rio das Ostras,** where you'll find numerous boats both on the sandy beach and out in the water. There are restaurants and beach bars along the two kilometers of sand and the left end is where you'll find the yacht club, where you can rent a boat or take an excursion. The water is emerald green and excellent for swimming. Beyond this beach is **Praia da Tartaruga,** a small inlet with shallow water. Around the perimeter are a few *pousadas* if you decide to stay the night here. Many of the beaches in Ostras are lined with private developments that make the beach less interesting for visitors. An exception is **Praia do Cemitério,** one of the more popular beaches in the area; it has kiosks and beach bars to make visitors feel more welcome. The water is clear and calm here.

Besides sitting on the beach or taking a boat excursion out to the nearby islands, you can also take buggy excursions along the coastline. Check with **Locatur** (tel. 22/2764-1359).

# São Paulo City

How do you put the third-largest city in the world in a nutshell? In the case of São Paulo, with two words: food and business. São Paulo is, first of all, a major business mecca. Just about everything that comes into or goes out of Brazil goes through São Paulo—and a huge portion of Brazil's own product-base is manufactured, in whole or in part, in São Paulo. Communications, automobiles, coffee, textiles . . . São Paulo stands in strong contrast to the Third-World images that most foreigners have of Brazil. Most foreigners (even Brazilians from other parts) are stunned by the efficiency and velocity of the São Paulo scene.

If you find yourself in this grand city, there's an 85 percent chance that you're here on some kind of business. Just keep in mind that the pleasure of doing business in São Paulo comes from all those incredible business lunches and dinners you'll be enjoying. The city's central area alone has more than 1,400 restaurants featuring more than 40 different types of foods. But if you're in São Paulo to take in some sights, you won't be disappointed. The city offers some charming neighborhoods (including several ethnic centers); museums focusing on Latin American art and culture; performance halls with internationally-renowned music groups; dance and theater groups; street fairs; shopping centers; and many parks and open spaces.

# **M**ust-Sees

**M Theatro Municipal:** As you walk through the doors of the Theatro, two huge sculptures of Atlantis glare down at you as if granting permission to enter. Inside is a visual feast, with marble floors, brass sculptures, and all the manifestations of a society riding a glorious cultural and economic wave (page 99).

**M Catedral da Sé:** The Catedral stands in the middle of downtown São Paulo and marks the center point of the city with its neo-Gothic presence. Inside, the church reflects Brazil's cultural diversity with stained-glass panels of French, Italian, and Brazilian design (page 99).

**M Banespa Building:** The magnitude of this vast megalopolis comes into view as you stand atop the Banespa building and look out on the 11 million inhabitants making their way up and down the city streets (page 102).

© CHRISTOPHER VAN BUREN

São Paulo City

view from Banespa building

**M Mercado Municipal:** One of the gastronomical centers of the city, the Mercado has more than 200 stands that sell all types of meats, cheeses, olives, nuts, wines, and, of course, coffee (page 102).

**M Museu de Arte São Paulo:** The MASP is the most important contemporary art museum in Latin America. It offers various collections of Brazilian and international art—an eye opener for anyone not familiar with the quality of the South American art scene (page 113).

São Paulo City

# GREATER SÃO PAULO

SEE "CENTRAL SÃO PAULO" MAP

SEE "AVENIDA PAULISTA AND JARDINS" MAP

BRÁS

To Guarulhos Airport

Armênia

Tiradentes

Luz

AV SEN QUEIROS

AV TIRADENTES

Praça da Luz

R BRIGADEIRO TOBIAS

São Bento

R RIBEIRO BADARÓ

Praça da Sé

Sé

Liberdade

CENTRO

AV IPIRANGA

Anhangabaú

Praça Ramos de Azevedo

AV RIO BRANCO

AL DINO BUENO

GLETE

AV RIO

AV DR CAXIAS

República

AV S LUIS

AV S JOÃO

AV NOVE DE JULHO

R BR DE CAMPINAS

AV CSO NEBIAS

AL NOTHMANN

AL RIBEIRO DA SILVA

Santa Cecília

AV MQ DE ITU

AV RADIAL LESTE-OESTE

To Zona Norte Bus Terminal

AV  RUDGE

R BARRA FUNDA

ELEVADO COSTA E SILVA

R DAS PALMEIRAS

AV MAJ SERTORIO

HIGIENÓPOLIS

R DONA VERIDIANA

R DA CONSOLAÇÃO

BELA VISTA

AV MQ DE S10 VICENTE

R DO BOSQUE

Mal Deodoro

AL BARROS

R IBIA DE ITU

R DR VEIGA FILHO

AV ANGELICA

R SABARÁ

R ITACOLOMI

R SERGIPE

R AUGUSTA

R CANECA

R BARATA RIBEIRO

VD PACAEMBU

R CNSO BOTELHO

AV HIGIENÓPOLIS

R BAHIA

R ALAGOAS

R MAYO GROSSO

R ITAJOBI

Barra Funda

AV PACAEMBU

R GUST AVO TEIXEIRA

AV DR ARNALDO

Clínicas

R TAGIPURU

AV FRANCISCO MATARAZZO

R TURIASSU

R ITAPICURU

R CARDOSO DE ALMEIDA

R DONA GERMAINE

R DR HOMEM DE MELO

R MINISTRO GODOI

AV ANTÁRCTICA

R TURIASSU

R JOÃO RAMALHO

AV SUMARÉ

R CAMPEVAS

R CAIUBI

R WANDERLEI

AV PAULO VI

R CAIOWAA

R ARIAÇAS

CERQUEIRA CESAR

Sumaré

R OSCAR

R CATÃO

FREIRE

R JOÃO MOURA

R ALVES GUIMARÃES

To Vila Madalena

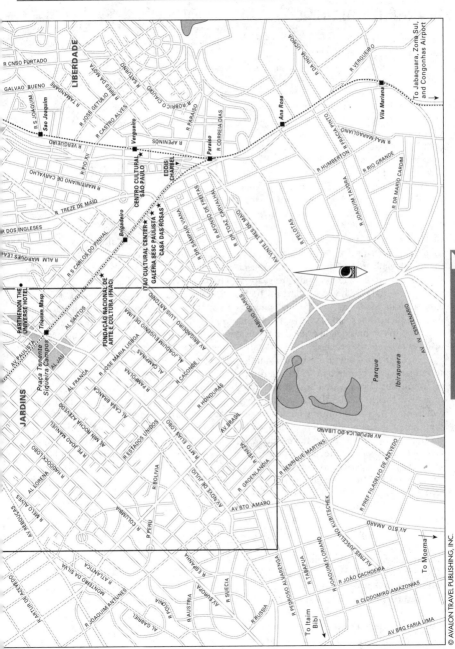

São Paulo City

© AVALON TRAVEL PUBLISHING, INC.

## PLANNING YOUR TIME

São Paulo is not really a tourist city, so it's relatively easy to see it's principal attractions in a couple of days. Such a visit would focus on the city center and Paulista areas, with a walking tour of each. Afterward, you'd have just enough time for a hop into Brás to do some shopping and head to Vila Madalena or Itaím Bibi for a night out.

If you're in town for a week or so, you might spend two days exploring the Centro Histórico, allowing you to really take your time in the museums and churches. You can take the little tours offered in the majority of these places. Then, you'll probably want to get to know the Jardins area and its many eating and shopping establishments. It's a great place to hang out, people-watch, and drink coffee. You'll have enough time to spend a day in the Zona Sul—starting or ending with a walk around the Parque Ibirapuera. Your nights can be spent sampling the various dining and nightlife hotspots: Jardins, Itaim, Moema, Vila Madalena, and Bexiga being the most frequented of them all. A final shopping excursion in the Brás neighborhood and you're ready to head for the beaches.

If you're in town on business, then your leisure time will probably be focused on dinner activities. Lucky you! You'll be spending most of your nights in the Jardins area, Pinheiros, and Itaim. These are the dining hubs, although there are great restaurants all over the city, including some great choices in the north region and, of course, Japanese food in Liberdade.

The city is temperate most of the year, with winter months (June–August) getting fairly cold, averaging around 19°C. The city can get pretty muggy during the summer (November–January) due to the smog and humidity. São Paulo has a reputation for being one of the world's ugliest cities. What with its polluted rivers, offensively poor air quality, and excess of high-rise buildings, it can seem like the ugly cousin of Los Angeles or Hong Kong. But the city's beauty does not reside in its natural endowments, nor in any special architectural charm. Rather, the beauty of São Paulo, for those who are open to seeing it, lies in its unique and special rhythms. Rhythms that can be heard in the people's conversations, in the daily business activities, in the nights out for dinner and drinks, and in the mornings riding the metro. São Paulo is not really a city to *see,* it's a city to *be in.* This is no more apparent than in the city's inhabitants themselves. Paulistas are extremely satisfied being in São Paulo. They are friendly, polite, generally sophisticated, and unparalleled at attending to the needs of others.

## HISTORY AND PEOPLE

As thousands of Italian immigrants were arriving in São Paulo to work in the coffee trade (mostly as a labor class), nobody imagined that they would change the face of the city to such a degree. But that's not all; they also changed the face of the typical Paulista. It's now a challenge to find a native Paulista who is not an Italian descendent.

Paulistas are very proud of their international roots, beginning with their Portuguese and indigenous ancestors at the beginning of the city's history. The Jesuit outpost of São Vicente, on the coast near São Paulo was one of the first European settlements in the southern region of Brazil (1532). Later, a group of these Jesuits established a monastery more inland, on a plateau between two rivers. This was the official foundation for the city of São Paulo in 1554. The Jesuits were expelled and re-instated to the monastery several times throughout the history of their work in São Paulo. In 1759, the Paulistas—colonists of Portuguese and native descent who considered themselves true Brazilians—attacked the Jesuits and managed to get them expelled for their anti-slavery politics. Those Paulistas formed the first groups of *bandeirantes* that made their way into Minas Gerais in search of gold.

The Italians came to town in the late 1800s. Later, during and just after WWII, a large number of Japanese entered Brazil, primarily in São Paulo. In the mid 1900s, an influx of Brazilians from the northeast of Brazil (Bahia mostly) added to the mix with their African, Dutch, and northern indigenous ancestries.

# Central São Paulo

At the height of the coffee boom in the 19th century, the old center was the financial and business nucleus of Brazil and a manifestation of the country's financial and cultural boom. Brazil was rich with architecture, theater, radio productions, films, and literature. Today, long after the coffee boom has settled down and been surpassed by other industries, the old center is still home to the country's stock market and most of the city's historical buildings and tourist attractions. The financial district has moved south to Avenida Paulista.

The old center is a bit run down these days, although efforts are being made to restore and renovate it. Hotels here are generally cheaper than in other areas, while some are still quite luxurious and make good alternatives to staying in the more expensive areas of the city, especially if your stay will be focused on the downtown sights. Some humble, economical hotels are also available in this area. During the day, the area is colorful but quite safe. At night, it's best to stick to main, well-lighted areas or take taxis. From Central São Paulo, you are close to just about everything in the city.

## THEATRO MUNICIPAL

When the Theatro Municipal (Praça Ramos de Azevedo, tel. 11/222-8698, tel. 11/223-3022, www.theatromunicipal.com.br) was constructed, São Paulo was in a glamorous phase. All that it lacked was a little European flair to give the city that special charm it needed. This fabulous opera house, inspired by the Paris Opera House, is a mixture of renaissance baroque and Roman styles. Built in 1903 and inaugurated in 1911, the Theatro functions to this day as the city's principal theater, presenting dance, opera, classical music, and pop music events all week long. The building itself and the various sculptures inside and out are well worth a look. Most impressive are the two breathtaking mosaics in the inner foyer at the top of the main staircase, depicting colorful

scenes from Wagner operas. Also impressive are the large sculptures of Atlantis, serving as pillars on the outside of the main entrance. Featured in the Theatro are operas at 6 P.M. every Monday, chamber music at noon on Thursdays, and pop music on the last Friday of each month at 1 P.M. There are presentations at 9 P.M. every night, sometimes featuring the São Paulo Symphony Orchestra or the São Paulo Dance Company, not to be missed. The Theatro is in easily accessed on foot from the Praça da República or Anhangabaú metro stations.

## CATEDRAL DA SÉ

The nucleus of old downtown is the Catedral da Sé (Praça da Sé, Centro, tel. 11/3107-6832), a neo-gothic church built from 1912–1954 (finished on Brazil's 200th birthday). It is 55 meters high and much of the marble and brass work inside was shipped in from Italy, including all of the yellow marble and the entire altar. The design of the church, however, is very Brazilian. This can be seen in the mixture of stained-glass styles and themes (featuring Italian, French, and Brazilian panels) as well as in the sculptures on the main pillars (in the form of Brazilian flora and fauna). The pipe organ (currently not functioning) is the largest in South America. In the *praça* just outside the Catedral, you'll see Marco Zero, the point from which distances in Brazil are measured. It is distinguished by a brass plate standing in the middle of a large compass inlayed in the *praça*'s floor. The church doors open at 8 A.M. (all three tons of them) with bells that ring out the Brazilian national anthem. Bells ring again at noon and briefly each hour. There are short tours offered for R$3, which will allow you to see the chapel room under the main altar with its various tombs. Vera, the principal guide does not speak much English, but she knows everything about the church and you'll get all the main points. Her tours are from 9:30 A.M.–4 P.M. The church is open from 8 A.M.–5 P.M. every day and has mass

São Paulo City

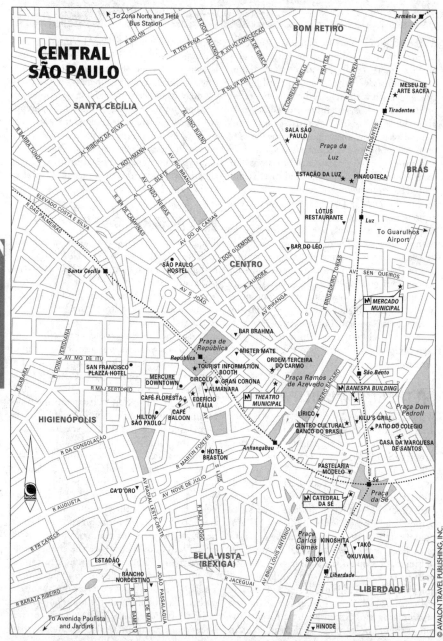

CENTRAL SÃO PAULO

© AVALON TRAVEL PUBLISHING, INC.

# SÃO PAULO'S COLORFUL NEIGHBORHOODS

If you want to fully capture the essence of São Paulo, you need to see and understand the various neighborhoods that interconnect to form this mammoth city. While enormous in geographic scale, São Paulo is easily accessible by metro. The system, recognized as one of the best in the world, is cheap, fast, clean, and safe and can take you as far as you'll want to go (or should go) in any direction. The basic divisions of the city are known simply as Centro, Zona Norte, Zona Sul, Zona Oeste, and Zona Leste and the metro forms a big cross, taking you in each of the four directions with the Centro at the epicenter.

**Centro:** Most probably where you'll spend the majority of your time, the center of São Paulo is a collection of neighborhoods, each with its own character. The **Centro Histórico** has most of the city's old buildings and churches, including the Theatro Municipal and Catedral da Sé. The area is in a constant state of upgrade, having suffered a heavy decline over the past fifty years or so, but you can walk around during the day without worry (nighttime is another story) and visit most of the area's offerings on foot. The **Liberdade** neighborhood is known as the Japanese district and is a haven for sushi lovers and anyone interested in Japanese culture. You can visit the shops and baths during the day and the sushi bars and restaurants at night. **Bela Vista** is the Italian district and, of course, a nucleus of great Italian food (although good Italian restaurants are spread throughout the city). At night, the area at Avenida 13 de Maio in Bela Vista becomes one of the city's night spots. Finally, the **Jardins** area along Avenida Paulista is the city's upscale, high-rise district with a rich concentration of shops, restaurants, and cafés. Here, you'll find the best selection of hotels. This area is also known simply as **Paulista.**

**Zona Norte:** The north part of the city is primarily a business district and often loaded with visitors from afar, due to its various convention centers and conference halls. It has several excellent hotels, designed for business travelers (comfort, technology, and access) and which are well worth considering as alternatives to the hotels in the Centro or Paulista (Jardins) areas. You can get great discounts here on weekends. The strip of restaurants and clubs on Avenida Luis Dumont Villares in the **Santana** neighborhood (at the Parada Inglesa metro stop) brings a crowd from all over the city. The Tietê metro stop is also the city's main bus station.

**Zona Sul:** Home to the Congonhas Airport (principal portal for domestic flights), the South Zone offers some of the largest and most impressive hotels in the region, golf courses, and great restaurants and night spots. Other highlights include the zoo and botanical gardens, the Boating Club, the Formula One track in the **Interlagos** area, and two concert halls: Credicard Hall and Tom Brazil, which feature a variety of shows all week long. This area begins at the Parque Ibirapuera and is home to three great neighborhoods for food and nightlife: **Moema, Itaím Bibi,** and **Brooklin.**

**Zona Oeste:** The farther west you go in São Paulo, the more you run into the city's bohemian side. This is probably due to the concentration of universities in the area. You'll also find a couple of interesting, alternative neighborhoods with great bars and restaurants, specifically **Pinheiros** and **Vila Madalena** (the latter being one of the best spots in the city for nightlife, with a slightly hippie style to it). Far out on the west side is the Butantã Institute for snake cures (open for viewing).

**Zona Leste:** The East Zone is the city's international portal, thanks to the Guarulhos International Airport. As a result of its presence, many new hotels have sprung up here offering competitive alternatives to the North and South Zone hotels. The **Brás** neighborhood, which is just one stop east of the Centro, is a major garment district with some of the best shopping in the city (although you have to look for the good shops).

São Paulo City

at 8:30 A.M.–noon weekdays; and at 9 A.M., 11 A.M., and 5 P.M. on Sunday.

## BANESPA BUILDING

The ride to the top of the Banespa building (Rua João Brícola 24, Centro, tel. 11/3249-7405, 9 A.M.–5 P.M. Mon.–Fri.) involves two elevators and a flight of stairs. At the top, you can look out over the entire city and watch its main arteries pulse with life. The tallest building in South America in its day (1939), the Banespa building is still home to the central offices of the Banespa bank, which allows visitors to ascend to the top of its headquarters (in small groups) and take in the view. They charge nothing for this and even provide a pair of binoculars at the top. It's one of the best (and cheapest) attractions in the downtown area. Next door is an excellent exhibition space with contemporary art showings and it's just around

an average day in São Paulo as seen from the top of the Banespa building

the corner from the stock exchange. To get to the Banespa building, walk out the doors of the Catedral de Sé, continue across the *praça* and down Avenida Boa Vista. You'll pass the Patio do Colégio museum on the right. Keep walking until you see the building on your left. You can also take the metro to the São Bento station, which is closest to Banespa.

## EDIFICIO ITÁLIA

If you want to have drinks while looking out over the city, the Terraço Itália Restaurante (Av. Ipiranga 344, tel. 11/3257-6566, lunch around 11 A.M. and dinner at 6 P.M.) is your best choice. The restaurant and bar at the top of this 41-story building (designed by Roberto Adler) offer the most spectacular, 360-degree view of the city (best seen at night). To enjoy this high perch, you must have dinner at the restaurant or drinks at the bar, resulting in at least R$25 per person. The management has gotten rather strict about this minimum, as they want to keep people from treating their establishment as a tourist attraction. The restaurant's lunch buffet runs R$35–45 per person and dinner goes for about R$80–110 per person. Live music plays Wednesday–Saturday. If you want to view the city at night or on weekends, the Banespa building will be closed and Edificio Itália, for R$25 in drinks, is your only option. It is very close to the Praça da República.

## MERCADO MUNICIPAL

Most major cities in Brazil have central markets, but none is so well housed as the Mercado Municipal (Av. Nova Cantareira 686, Parque Dom Pedro II, Centro, tel. 11/6203-8850, 6 A.M.–5 P.M. Mon.–Sat. and 7 A.M.–1 P.M. Sun.) in São Paulo. The building itself is a historical landmark, erected in the 1920s and 1930s in a mixture of neo-classic and gothic styles with some beautiful and well-preserved stained-glass windows in the front of the building. The windows depict scenes from the coffee trade and it's worth getting up on the mezzanine to get a better view of them. The huge warehouse has more than

12,000 square meters of space, more than 250 different vendors, and 14,000 visitors every day, with as many as 40,000 on busy days.

The Mercado is one of the central distribution points for fish, meats, cheeses, olives, oils, wines, and other food products in São Paulo. At night, restaurants come to make their wholesale purchases until the early-morning hours. During the day, the Mercado is open to the public and you can partake of some traditional lunch spots. The Bar do Mané (stand E14) is famous for its thick, deli-meat sandwiches (mortadella, a type of bologna, is their most famous, but they also have turkey and ham), which you can get hot or cold for around R$7. The Hocca Bar (G7) is famous for its *pastel de bacalhau* (fish pastry), as well as a variety of sandwiches, each for around R$6. The line gets long at lunchtime and on weekends, but it moves fast. While writing this book, the city was in the process of adding a mezzanine with several new restaurants and bakeries, which should be finished by the time you read this. To get there, take the metro to the Luz station and exit at Avenida Sen. Queirôz (up and to the right). Exit the station and turn right, then left down Avenida Sen. Queirôz until you see the Mercado towers on your right.

## PINACOTECA MUSEUM

The brick structure of the Pinacoteca (Praça da Luz 2, Centro, tel. 11/3229-9844, 10 A.M.– 6 P.M. Tues.–Sun.) was supposed to be finished with a smooth cement coating. Fortunately, it was never finished and recent reformations have turned the castle-like building into a great place to see art. The oldest art museum in São Paulo, the Pinacoteca building was begun in 1895 and designed by Ramos Azevedo, the same architect who designed the Theatro Municipal and the Mercado Municipal. The museum houses permanent and temporary art and sculpture exhibits with a specialty in 19th-century Brazilian paintings. There are also some wonderful European bronze pieces, including a few by Rodin and molds of the Atlantis statues from the Theatro Municipal that you can

see up close. The coffee shop inside is a comfortable, well-designed place for relaxing and the museum features a large outdoor sculpture garden with more than 40 sculptures and 1,200 more in rotation. The sculpture garden is free and the museum costs only R$4. For only R$1 more, you can visit the annex building, too. Saturdays are free. The Pinacoteca is closest to the Luz metro station. Exit the metro at Avenida Sen. Queirôz and turn left as you exit the station. You'll see a pedestrian overpass; the museum is just past it.

## SALA SÃO PAULO

With 1,501 seats, Sala São Paulo (Praça Júlio Prestes, Centro, tel. 11/3351-8282, tours: 12:30 P.M. and 4:30 P.M. Mon.–Fri., 2 P.M. Sat., and 1 P.M. Sun.) is the city's largest concert hall, created in the center atrium of the old train station's first-class passenger area. It was built during the coffee boom and sports many coffee themes in its interior. The architectural and acoustic achievements in covering the original garden (finished in 1999) are awe-inspiring. From the ceiling dangle numerous wood panels that can be raised or lowered depending on the musical dynamics desired. The seating and stage areas hold many interesting secrets in their design, from the choice of wood used to the shapes of the box seats. The floor of the entire hall floats on a cushion of rubber over cement, permitting trains to pass by without a hint of noise or movement inside. You can tour the Sala in Portuguese, English, or Spanish—best to call ahead. Better yet, go see a concert of the São Paulo Symphony Orchestra at 9 P.M. every Thursday or 4:30 P.M. on Saturdays. Cost is from R$22–70. At 11 A.M. on Sundays, you can catch a Pops performance for only R$2.

## OTHER SIGHTS

If you swing past the **Patio do Colégio** museum (Patio do Colégio 2, Centro, tel. 11/3105-6899, 9 A.M.–5 P.M. Tues.–Sun.,

São Paulo City

R$5) before actually taking the tour, the administration might be able to arrange an English-speaking guide for you. That would be a good thing, since a visit to the Patio is full of interesting details about the city's formation. Inside is a model of the city in the days of its founding, plus time lines and documents that bring you all the way to the present day. Upstairs are numerous artifacts from the city's history—mostly from the 19th century—including a beautiful silver and brass oratory of Middle Eastern design. The most interesting part of the tour is downstairs in the building's basement, which was once a crypt. Today it's an eerie exhibit hall for demonstrations of regional and indigenous arts and crafts. In the charming café garden area is an entombed stone and mud wall, which is said to be from the original Jesuit monastery that was the city's origin. Nearby is the **Casa da Marquesa de Santos** (Rua Roberto Simonsen 136 (behind and to the right of the Patio building), Centro, tel. 11/3241-4238, 9 A.M.–5 P.M. Tues.–Sun.), an example of São Paulo's urban architecture and social life from the 1800s. The Marquesa was one of Emperor Dom Pedro I's socialite lovers and she lived in this house from 1834–1867. During that time, the place was known fondly as the Palacete do Carmo, due to the many aristocratic parties thrown there—particularly when the emperor was in town. Besides showing construction methods of the day, the Casa houses exhibitions relating to São Paulo's history and a number of old photos.

The **Museu de Arte Sacra** (Av. Tiradentes 676, tel. 11/3326-1373, 11 A.M.–6 P.M. Tues.–Sun.) presents a collection of sacred art and furnishings from the various churches and religious monuments of Brazil's history. If you're planning a trip to Minas Gerais, then you can probably pass this up, since most of the country's important religious works are in the museums and churches of Minas. Sacred artifacts aside, you might want to take a look inside the **Ordem Terceira do Carmo** (Av. Rangel Pestana 230, Centro, 7–11 A.M. and 1–5 P.M. weekdays and 7–11 A.M. weekends) to see the great paintings

on the ceiling and the 800-pipe organ. Finally, the recently renovated **Estação da Luz** (Praça da Luz, tel. 11/225-0040, 11 A.M.–6 P.M. Tues.–Sun.) is one of the city's oldest train depots, created for carrying coffee from São Paulo to the port at Santos. The architecture is European-influenced and the building now links various methods of transportation, including trains, buses, and the metro. Inside are art exhibits, but the building itself is the most impressive work of art. It's located about ten minutes from the Sala São Paulo concert hall (by foot) and you can go directly there on the blue metro line to the Luz station.

# ENTERTAINMENT AND NIGHTLIFE

The city has several listings of current shows and events. The *São Paulo This Month* guide lists current music and cultural events and has a great map of the city. You should be able to find it at any magazine stand. A similar publication is the *Magazine Turismo & Hotelaria* (www.revistamagazine.com.br), available at hotels. The city's tourism office puts out *Cultura Dia-a-Dia,* which lists offerings at all the major spaces in town, including all the museums and exhibit halls. You can find this at the tourist information offices and museums. A more compact listing is the *Acontece em São Paulo* monthly folder, which lists all types of events and productions for the month. It's available at all tourist information booths. An informative website is http:\portal.prefeitura.sp.gov.brsecretariascultura.

## After Hours

The *Magazine Turismo & Hotelaria* (www.revistamagazine.com.br), available at hotels, has a huge section of ads from nightclubs and strip clubs. Try **TP—The Point** (Av. Alberto Ramos 130, www.thepointsp.com) for a night scene with everything under one roof.

## Art, Theater, and Music

Performances of the São Paulo Dance Com-

## SÃO PAULO SYMPHONY ORCHESTRA

Considered the most important symphonic group in Latin America, the São Paulo Symphony Orchestra presents almost 100 performances each concert season, most of them sold-out at the Sala São Paulo, which seats 1,500. Under the direction of Maestro John Neschling since 1997, the orchestra has grown to become a major world symphony and has toured Latin America, Europe, and the United States. They have recorded more than 20 CDs on the Swedish label BIS. The symphony incorporates a choral group for symphonic and chamber music, as well as chamber groups that interpret the music of Bach, Rossini, Mozart, and Brahms, among others. Their official website is www.osesp.art.br.

pany, Symphony Orchestra, Pops, and other classical music groups occur primarily in the Sala São Paulo and Theatro Municipal halls. The **Centro Cultural Banco do Brasil** (Rua Alvares Penteado 112, tel. 11/3113-3651, noon–8 P.M. Tues.–Sun.) has temporary art exhibits, music, theater, and cinema productions throughout the year. Most of these feature contemporary, living artists of national and international repute. You can pick up a copy of their monthly program guide at any of the tourist information booths or check www.bb.com.br/cultura. The building itself, built in the early 1900s in neoclassic style, is also impressive. Admission is free for art exhibits and R$4 for the cinema. Theater performances are R$15 and music is generally R$6.

### Bars and Clubs

The old downtown can be a little edgy at night and most travelers prefer to do their bar hopping in other parts of town. Nevertheless, there are a couple of options for downtown watering holes. Check out **M Bar Brahma** (Av. São João 677, tel. 11/3333-0855, 11:30 A.M.–2 A.M. Tues.–Sat., until midnight Sun. and 1 A.M. Mon.), a classic São Paulo bar

from the 1940s that still offers a taste of the old city. They have samba music on Wednesday nights and Sundays at 2 P.M. after their city tours, which run R$35 per person and start at 11 A.M. Another traditional bar is **Bar do Léo** (Rua Aurora 100, tel. 11/221-0247, 10:45 A.M.–8:30 P.M., until 4 P.M. Sat.) which has draft beer and a variety of appetizers and meals. You can also have drinks in the outdoor patio at **Café Baloon** (Av. Ipiranga 200, tel. 11/3258-7759, 7 A.M. until last client leaves daily), across from the Hilton Hotel. They have happy-hour specials on weekdays, starting at 5 P.M. On Mondays at 8:30 P.M., you can catch a more classical samba style at **Sapori di Rosi** (Av. Ipiranga 200, tel. 11/3120-4442, 7 A.M. until the last client daily) for R$10. Their specialty is happy hour. One of the most popular bars for the locals is the **Bar Barão** (Rua Barão de Duprat 561, tel. 11/3227-9687, 11 A.M.–9 P.M. Mon.–Fri., until 4 P.M. Sat.), which serves up draft beer and appetizers. The **Terraço Itália Restaurante** (Av. Ipiranga 344, tel. 11/3257-6566, lunch around 11 A.M. and dinner at 6 P.M.) has an elegant bar with an amazing view of the city. Minimum R$25 consumption.

The Bela Vista neighborhood around Avenida Treze de Maio is the city's Italian district (called Bexiga, beh-SHEE-gah) and home to many bars and clubs. Everything is located in a two-block area, so you can just walk along and choose the place you want. Bars with live music will require a cover charge or drink minimum, so ask the doorman at each place what the charges are. Most places will have people outside with flyers, trying to pull you in for a look. You can usually peek inside to see if it's something you like. You'll find a mixture of rock, blues, and oldies music in these places and they are usually packed on weekends. A taxi from República to Bexiga will cost around R$15. Most places get going around midnight and close when the sun comes up. The action is best Wednesday–Saturday, but some people feel that the Bexiga area is well past its prime and you'd be better off in Vila Madalena or Itaim Bibi for a night out.

São Paulo City

© CHRISTOPHER VAN BUREN

night falls on São Paulo

## Popular Shows

Large production Brazilian-style shows, featuring samba dancing, costumes, Capoeira demonstrations, and Maculelé knife dancing are presented in large concert halls in the Zona Norte and Zona Sul areas of the city. Smaller samba shows appear all over town, including one at the Bar Brahma. See www.sesc.sp.org.br for some additional information.

## Sidewalk Cafés

Near the Praça da República is the **Café Floresta** (Av. Ipiranga 200, tel. 11/3259-8416, 6:30 A.M.–1 P.M. Mon.–Sat., 8 A.M.–1 P.M. Sun.), which is at the base of the Edifício Itália and has a great view of the crowd passing by outside. It has its own brand of coffee and a variety of delicious sweets. One of the nicest downtown cafés for sipping coffee and reading something good is the **Café da Pinacoteca** at the Pinacoteca museum (Praça da Luz 2, tel. 11/3229-9844, Centro, 10 A.M.–5:30 P.M. Tues.–Sun.). The café in the **M Pátio do Colégio** museum (Av. Boa Vista, a few blocks from the Catedral da Sé, tel. 11/3106-4303, 9 A.M.–5 P.M. Tues.–Sun.) has a quaint

garden setting with excellent pastries and coffees (slightly expensive). It's one of the most relaxing settings for coffee and snacks in the downtown area. While you sip your Brazilian java, you can study the mud construction of the 16th-century wall that still stands at this site. There are good people-watching cafés in the shopping centers of the downtown area, including the small shopping center in front of the Theatro Municipal and in the mezzanine of the Mercado Municipal. Some of the bars listed in the *Bars and Clubs* section also make good daytime people-watching spots.

## FESTIVALS AND EVENTS

August is the month of the Festa da Nossa Sra. Achiropita (Av. Treze de Maio, www.achiropita.org.br), an Italian saint who is celebrated in two places in the world: Achiropita, Italy and São Paulo, Brazil. Every weekend in August from 8:30 P.M. to midnight, the Bexiga area fills up with visitors to partake of the many Italian food offerings. The lines are long, but the food is great and the festival is always a hit. They say it's the second-largest

## BRAZIL'S BLACK GOLD

While other South American countries produce that controversial white powder, Brazil has been busy producing its lucrative (and addictive) black powder since it was introduced into the country in 1727. Since then, coffee has become a national passion, not to mention an important export and once the driving force behind a great economic and cultural boom. Coffee is the principal reason why São Paulo grew into the most important financial center in Brazil and the third largest city in the world. At the end of the 19th century and part of the way into the 20th century, coffee overtook sugar as the country's leading agricultural product. Today, Brazil produces more than 25 percent of the world's coffee, making it the largest coffee producer on the planet. Almost every blended coffee in the world (mass-market, canned coffees, for example) and most espresso blends contain Brazilian coffee.

Originally oriented to mass production of Arabic beans, Brazil recently began competing in the world market with high-end and specialty coffees. Most are packaged for export to the United States and Europe, but some are destined for consumption right here in Brazil, particularly in the city of São Paulo. In fact, the hills of São Paulo state are known for producing the highest quality coffee in the country. Besides São Paulo, the hills of Paraná, Minas Gerais, Espírito Santo, and Bahia states are loaded with coffee plantations and some are becoming known for their special brews. Fortunately for Brazil's coffee trade, most of the coffee plantations are relatively small, with anywhere from 1–5 square kilometers of land. Only a small number of Brazil's plantations are large and industrialized and a rich future is brewing for specialty Brazilian coffees.

Brazilian coffee is generally rich and heavy, slightly sweet with very little acidity due to the natural drying methods used—for which Brazil's coffees are becoming famous. Despite the growth of specialty coffees and processing methods, Brazilian coffee is still used primarily as a foundation for blended coffee, often mixed with coffees grown in more traditional conditions, such as those from the higher altitudes of Central America. Such conditions are said to produce a cleaner and brighter flavor.

You might find it difficult to acclimate to the way in which Brazilians brew their coffee. Starting with the already rich and heavy beans, Brazilians brew their coffee using a fine espresso grind. This produces a strong, thick cup of crude-oil with a high octane kick. To this is added plenty of sugar, as Brazilians like their coffee very strong and very sweet.

The coffee harvest in Brazil takes place in June and July. You can stay at some coffee plantations during this season in the São Paulo and Minas Gerais regions.

popular festival in the city, next to Carnaval, of course. A large Carnaval festival takes place in the North Zone at the Anhambe convention center. It's not as large and well-known as the Rio de Janeiro Carnaval parade, but it's quite spectacular and has its own following. There are samba schools, floats, dancers, and everything you've come to expect from a Brazilian Carnaval. It's a great alternative to the over-the-top and often out-of-control Carnaval in Rio.

## SHOPPING

There's nothing more pleasant then strolling through an outdoor flea market on a Sunday morning. The old center in São Paulo has several. You can hit the Feira de Antiguidades on Saturday and Sunday in the Praça da República, Sunday being the more interesting day. Also on Sunday near the República area is a market of art and art supplies on Rua Marquesa de Itú, where you'll find paints, canvasses, frames, and every kind of material imaginable at incredible prices. Another antique fair takes place in the Bela Vista neighborhood at the Praça Dom Orione from 8 A.M.–5 P.M. on Sundays. Have a drink at the Café Mama D'Oro (Rua Fortaleza 288) which has outdoor seats that overlook the *praça* (get there early for a good seat). During the week, the area between República and the Praça da Sé down Rua Barão Itapitininga is a busy shopping district. Finally, the area around Avenida 25 de Maio (near the Mercado Municipal) is famous for cheap, imported goods from China and Paraguay—featuring many counterfeit goods. Keep your eyes open and your hands in your pockets when walking around this area and don't bring a camera or carry valuables. Rua Conselheiro Crispiniano is the place to find photographic equipment and supplies. You can find camping equipment in the Brás area on Rua Senador Queirôz and in Pinheiros at the Largo da Batata.

## ACCOMMODATIONS

### R$100

The **São Paulo Hostel** (Rua Barão de Campinas 94, tel. 11/3333-0844, R$25 pp for group rooms) is a new offering in the Hosteling International chain. They have seven floors with 125 rooms, open kitchen, phones, lockers, laundry facility, TV room, Internet room, and 24-hour front desk. They also make reservations at other hostels. Take the metro to the República station (which may require two or three trains, depending on your starting point) and exit at the Rua do Arouche side. Continue until you find the intersection of Avenida São João, Avenida General Osório, and Rua Barão de Campinas. Ask about prices for couples. A good choice for an economic, downtown hotel is the M **San Francisco Plazza Hotel** (Rua Marquês de Itú 271, tel. 11/3221-7001, tel. 11/3223-1220, R$45–60 s/d, breakfast included), just off the Praça da República. They have a nice atmosphere and rooms come with TV and phone.

### R$100–200

The **Hotel Braston** (Rua Martins Fontes 330, tel. 11/3156-2400, www.braston.com, R$100 s,

R$110 d and R$85 on weekends, R$250 suite) is a typical downtown offering—a touch of old world elegance with a hint of decay. They are well located and offer a piano bar in the large lobby, restaurant, sauna, and pool with bar area. Rooms are air-conditioned and most have bathtubs. Breakfast is an extra R$12 per person. Their breakfast and lunch buffets are great. The recently renovated **Hotel Gran Corona** (Rua Basilio da Gama 101, tel. 11/3214-0043, www.grancorona.com.br, R$90–135 s and R$100–155 d) is another classic establishment in the old style (overstuffed chairs, velvet drapes, and lots of glass and chrome). Their Gran Corona suite is only R$160 and the Presidential is R$180. Breakfast is included and they don't charge a service tax (so tipping is appropriate). Comes with cable TV, Internet access, and bathtubs in the rooms.

A classic-style hotel with modern facilities and expert management is the M **Mercure Downtown** (Rua Araújo 141, tel. 11/3120-8400, tel. 11/3747-7080, www.accorhotels.com, R$160 s and R$190 d on weekdays, R$92 s and R$112 d on weekends) just off the Praça da República. Rooms are ample, quiet, and have cable TV and 2-line phone. They have non-smoking rooms and wheelchair access, pool, and business center (extra cost). Breakfast is optional during the week and included on weekends. They also offer a city tour for R$35 Wednesday–Sunday.

### Over R$200

The **Hilton São Paulo** (Av. Ipiranga 165, tel. 11/3156-4300, fax tel. 11/3257-3033, R$450 s and R$500–600 d) is something of a downtown landmark. It's difficult to miss the tall round building just off the Praça da República. It has everything you'd expect from a Hilton, plus various restaurants and bars inside. Weekends are discounted.

## FOOD

### Middle Eastern

Near the Praça da República is a small, casual Lebanese restaurant called **Almanara**

(Rua Basilio da Gama, tel. 11/3257-7580, 11:30 A.M.–11 P.M. daily). They have typical Arabic dishes, like sesame chicken, hummus, and baba ghanoush for about R$20 per person, or you can sit at the counter and order some *esfihas* for around R$2.50 each. They also have locations in several shopping centers and in the Jardins area. **N Esfiharia Effendi** (Rua Dom Antônio de Mello 77, tel. 11/3228-0295, lunch only Mon.–Sat.) near the Luz metro station is actually Armenian in origin, serving the best *esfihas* in the city with imported spices. Meals are approximately R$15 per person.

## Brazilian

**Café Baloon** (Av. Ipiranga 200, tel. 11/3258-7759) across from the Hilton has a good self-service lunch from 11 A.M.–4 P.M., along with menu items. Lunch goes for about R$35 per person. Downtown near the Banespa building is **Kilu's Grill** (Rua 15 de Novembro 250, tel. 11/3041-1525), a typical Brazilian barbecue with good meats and a self-service lunch. Opens at 11:30 and runs around R$30 per person. In the Bela Vista neighborhood, **Rancho Nordestino** (Rua Manuel Dutra 498, tel. 11/3106-7257, 8 A.M.–2 A.M. Mon.–Thurs., 8 A.M. until last client leaves Fri. and Sat.,

4 P.M.–2 A.M. Sun.) serves traditional food from the northeast of Brazil, which is known for its use of hot spices, coconut milk, palm oil and dried meats. You also get types of *cachaça* to boot. R$25 per person.

## Chinese

**Lótus Restaurante** (Rua Brig. Tobias 420, tel. 11/3229-5696, 11:30 A.M.–3 P.M. Mon.–Sat. Coffee shop open 8 A.M.–6 P.M. Mon.–Fri. and 10 A.M.–4 P.M. Sat.) has a huge lunch buffet of Chinese and vegetarian dishes. You are sure to find a few that hit the spot. The restaurant is above a vegetarian market and close to the Luz metro station. Prices are approximately R$30 per person.

## Italian

There are probably more Italian restaurants than any other type of food in São Paulo. Ironically, the best places are not necessarily in the Italian district of Bela Vista. Some very traditional places are located downtown, such as **Ca' D'Oro** (Rua Augusta 129, tel. 11/3236-4300, noon–2:30 P.M. and 7–11 P.M. Mon.–Fri., 12:20–3 P.M. Sat. and Sun.), located between downtown and Avenida Paulista in an older part of town that becomes the city's red light district

**N São Paulo City**

# THROW ANOTHER PASTEL IN THE OIL FOR ME

No matter where you go in Brazil, you'll probably encounter the ubiquitous Brazilian *pastel*. Any small sidewalk food stand will have a deep fryer with these little square pastries puffing up in the hot oil. They're usually sold four or five at a time with a cup of juice or soda for a couple *reals*. In fancy neighborhoods, you might find *pastelarias* offering these hot finger foods with organic ingredients or creative combinations, like cinnamon and banana or chicken and cheese.

Undoubtedly Brazil's favorite hot snack, the *pastel* descends from the traditional Chinese spring roll. Having to adapt their traditional recipes to accommodate local ingredients, Chinese immigrants invented a number of some-

what different fried rolls, containing cheese, chicken, and *palmito* (heart of palm), among other local foods. However, the *pastel*'s popularity in Brazil is mostly due to Japanese immigrants who, attempting to pass for Chinese during WWII, opened diverse *pastelarias* featuring their modified "Chinese" spring rolls. As a result, they managed to escape much of the discrimination projected against them at the time. To this day, it is common to see Chinese and Japanese food served in the same establishment, something unheard of in other countries with significant Asian populations.

The pastel should be eaten hot, right as it comes out of the deep fryer. Look for establishments that have clean-looking oil.

at night. Nevertheless, the food and service are excellent and portions are traditionally abundant. Many plates are made for two, but you can order half portions if you're alone. You'll spend about R$40–70 per person. Right downtown near the Praça da República is **Circolo** (Av. Ipiranga 344, tel. 11/3257-1322), which has a great rotating menu and decent prices. Opens for lunch at around noon and serves dinner from 6–11. Approximately R$50 per person. **M Famiglia Mancini** (Rua Avanhandava 81, tel. 11/3256-4320, 11:30 A.M.–1 P.M. Mon.–Wed., Fri. and Sat., 11:30 A.M.–2 P.M. Thurs.) is in the Italian district of Bela Vista and is the foremost representative of Italian food in the area. Meals are abundant, prices good (approximately R$50 per person), and the atmosphere is cozy and traditional.

## Japanese

With all the Japanese immigrants in São Paulo, it's no surprise that Japanese food is abundant here. Sushi lovers will have a great time trying out the different sushi bars spread around town. Many of the best restaurants are in the Japanese neighborhood of Liberdade (but not all of them). A good choice is **Okuyama** (Rua da Glória 553, tel. 11/3341-0780, 11 A.M.–3 P.M. and 6 P.M.–midnight), which has great sushi at decent prices and is a favorite among locals. The owner is very welcoming. Try his Festival de Sushi dinner, which is a variety plate for around R$30. In the heart of the Liberdade area is **M Kinoshita** (Rua da Glória 168, tel. 11/3241-3586, 11 A.M.–2 P.M. and 6 P.M.–midnight), featuring Chef Tsuyoshi Murakami. He uses the best ingredients and offers an elegant experience. His sampler with various types of hot and cold dishes and a unique desert is R$140 per person. You can also sit at the sushi bar and order individual portions. Average price per person is around R$40. One of the oldest sushi restaurants in the area is **Hinodê** (Rua Tomás Gonzaga 62, tel. 11/3208-6633, 11 A.M.–2 P.M. and 6–11 P.M., hours slightly different on weekends), featuring sushi chef Sekai Skiguchi. He makes some American sushi favorites, such as cream

cheese rolls and has combination plates from around R$60–80.

## Lanchonetes and Casual

You should try the fresh juices at **Mister Mate** (Av. Ipiranga 913, Praça da República, tel. 11/3331-7610, 7 A.M.–10 P.M. daily) across from the Parque da República downtown. They have bad sandwiches, so save your appetite for somewhere else. But their juice combinations are out of this world. Try the Guaracaxi juice for starters or frozen *açaí*. Ice cream lovers may be disappointed with Brazilian *sorvete*, as it tends to be less creamy and less sweet than American or European ice cream. There is hope: a **Haagen Dazs** ice cream store in the Higienópolis shopping center (Av. Higienópolis 618, tel. 11/3815-9622, 10 A.M.–10 P.M. daily). A traditional bar and sandwich spot that is particularly great if you like pork is **Estadão** (Viaduto 9 de Julho 193, tel. 11/3257-7121, open 24 hours) in the Bela Vista area. Try the Pernil sandwich, which gives you a generous portion of pork on bread. The **M Pastelaria Modelo** (Praça da Sé 88, tel. 11/3241-2137, 7 A.M.–9 P.M. Mon.–Fri., until 6 P.M. Sat.) has been deep frying Brazilian finger foods for 90 years. Well located near the Catedral da Sé, the place is always crowded.

## Vegetarian

**Bio Alternativa** (Rua Maranhão 812, tel. 11/3825-4759, noon–3 P.M. Mon.–Fri., until 4 P.M. Sat. and Sun.) in Higienópolis near downtown is a true veggie restaurant with soy meats and all kinds of salads from organic greens, with no chemicals. They also have a selection of wonderful breads. Meals are approximately R$20 per person. In the Liberdade area, **Satori** (Praça Carlos Gomes 60, tel. 11/3242-9738, 11 A.M.–2 P.M.) is a macrobiotic establishment operating for more than 35 years. No chemicals are used in their greens and mineral water is used at all times. Dishes are approximately R$30 per person.

## Other

**Cecília** (Rua Tinhorão 122, tel. 11/3826-2973, noon–3 P.M. and 7–11 P.M. Tues.–Fri., lunch only noon–4 P.M. Sat. and Sun.) in the Higienópolis area has a Jewish (not kosher) menu and serves up large portions for around R$50 per person. For information on kosher restaurants and other topics, see the Hebráica Club (www.hebraica.org.br).

## INFORMATION

A tourist information booth is located on the corner of the Praça da República (tel. 11/231-2922) with maps, show listings, metro schedules, and other information. Another is located on Avenida Paulista (tel. 11/251-0970) near MASP. These are all open 9 A.M.–6 P.M. every day. There are also booths at the Guarulhos airport (tel. 11/6445-2945, 6 A.M.–10 P.M.), the Tietê bus terminal (tel. 11/3213-1800, 7 A.M.–10 P.M.) and the Pátio do Colégio museum (tel. 11/3105-6899, 9 A.M.–5 P.M. Tues.–Sun.).

Tourist bureaus include the **São Paulo Convention and Visitor's Bureau** (Av. Riberão Preto 130, tel. 11/5561-6650, www.spcvb.com.br), **Anhembi Tourist Information Center** (Rua Olavo Fontoura 1209, tel. 11/6971-5000, www.anhembi.terra.com.br), and the **American Chamber of Commerce in São Paulo** (tel. 11/5185-4688, www.amcham.com.br, saopaulo@cbre.com).

São Paulo is home to most international consulates. Some include:

- Argentina (Av. Paulista 2313, tel. 11/3082-7242)
- Canada (Av. Das Nações Unidas 12901, 16th Floor, tel. 11/5509-4321)
- France (Av. Paulista 1842, 14th Floor, tel. 11/3371-5400)
- Germany (Av. Brig. Daria Lima 2902, 12th Floor, tel. 11/3097-6444)
- Ireland (Av. Paulista 2006, 5th Floor, tel. 11/287-6362)
- Italy (Av. Higienópolis 436, tel. 11/3363-7800)
- Japan (Av. Paulista 854, 3rd Floor, tel. 11/3254-0100)
- South Africa (Av. Paulista 1754, 12th Floor, tel. 11/3285-0433)
- Spain (Av. Bernardino de Campos 98, tel. 11/3059-1800)
- United Kingdom (Rua Ferreira de Araújo 741, 2nd Floor, tel. 11/3094-2700)
- United States (Rua Henri Dunant 700, tel. 11/5186-7000)

## SERVICES

You'll find just about anything you need in São Paulo, the rest of Brazil certainly does. You just need to know where to look. For money issues, there are Citibank offices in the Paulista area (Av. Paulista 1111, tel. 11/5576-1000) and in the Higienópolis neighborhood, which is close to the Centro (Av. Angélica 1761, tel. 11/3256-2855). All banks in Brazil are open 10 A.M.–4 P.M. (except those that respect non-local time zones, as noted throughout this book). The Citibank site for Brazil is www.latam.citibank.com/brasil. Banco do Brasil offices downtown (Rua São Bento 483, tel. 11/3241-2048, 10 A.M.–4 P.M.) have at least one international ATM, equipped with Plus and Cirrus systems. Many of the Banco 24 Horas ATMs are equipped with Plus and Cirrus. They are in shopping centers and major commercial areas all over the downtown area. There are money exchanges along Avenida Ipiranga near the Edifício Itália building, but the best ones are in the Paulista area.

A good place for Internet connections downtown is **Baratofone** (Praça da República 76, tel. 11/3256-3578, 8 A.M.–10 P.M. Mon.–Fri., 10 A.M.–8 P.M. Sat., 10 A.M.–6 P.M. Sun.) across from the Praça da República. They also have private phones for international calls. You can rent a cell phone while you're in town from **Fast Cell** (Av. Doutor Guilherme Dumont Vilares 2450, tel. 11/3772-0777, 9 A.M.–6 P.M. Mon.–Fri., 9 A.M.–1 P.M. Sat.). This is an excellent way to keep in touch with family members in case you split up to explore different parts of the city. You can take the phone with you to other parts of the country, then drop it off again on your way out.

You can find a number of travel and car rental agencies on Rua da Consolação downtown.

The tourist police station is located in the Centro (Rua São Bento 380, tel. 11/3107-5642).

## GETTING THERE

### Buses

Buses to the city from the Guarulhos airport leave every half-hour from 5:30 A.M.–11 P.M. (tel. 11/5090-9225) and from the Tietê bus terminal every 45 minutes from 5:30 A.M.–10 P.M. (tel. 11/6693-1699). You can catch buses going to the airport from the Praça da República every 30 minutes and at most of the major hotels in the Paulista and downtown areas.

The Cometa (tel. 11/3868-5800) line leaves São Paulo for Belo Horizonte several times a day until midnight for around R$55. The Itapemirim (tel. 11/6465-8322) line goes to Brasilia. You can take Viação 1001 (tel. 11/6221-9596) to Florianópolis and Rio de Janeiro several time a day. The São Geraldo line (tel. 11/6955-1333) goes to Salvador along with the National line (tel. 11/6221-2928).

### Planes

Domestic flights leave from Congonhas airport (tel. 11/5090-9000) to Rio de Janeiro, Brasilia, Belo Horizonte, Porto Alegre, Curitiba, Salvador, and other major cities. You can get to Congonhas via taxi (around R$35 from Av. Paulista) or bus, which you can take from the Jabaquara metro station. Domestic carriers include VASP (tel. 11/5532-3838), Transbrasil (tel. 11/3228-2022), TAM (tel. 11/5585-1800), Rio Sul (tel. 11/5561-2161), and Gol (tel. 11/5033-4200). International flights leave from the Guarulhos airport (tel. 11/6445-2945). Some local numbers include:
- Aeromexico (tel. 11/3257-1022)
- Air Canada (tel. 11/3254-6630)
- Air France (tel. 11/289-2133)

- American Airlines (tel. 11/3214-4000)
- Argentina Airlines (tel. 11/3214-4233)
- British Airways (tel. 11/259-6144)
- Continental Airlines (tel. 11/2122-7500)
- Delta Airlines (tel. 08 00/221-121)
- Japan Airlines (tel. 11/251-5222)
- Lufthansa (tel. 11/3048-5800)
- United Airlines (tel. 08 00/162-323)
- Varig (tel. 11/5561-1161)

## GETTING AROUND

Most city travel is done with the metro and taxis. The metro operates 5 A.M.–midnight, and every metro stop is home to taxis and bus stops. With a few exceptions, such as Bexiga and the neighborhoods of the Zona Sul, you will usually be able to walk to your destination from the metro. A taxi from one of the four zones to the center will cost around R$25. Back and forth from downtown to the Paulista area by taxi will cost around R$10 each way. When taking taxis, try to avoid the 8 A.M. and 5 P.M. rush hours. If you're coming from a bus station or airport, look for the pre-paid taxis. They are the best during rush hours. There are three bus stations in the city. Most buses enter the city at the Tietê terminal, which is easily accessed by metro. Some lines dock at the Jabaquara or Barra Funda stations, which also have metro access.

You can hire a car and driver for less money than you might think. Some agencies offering this service include Brazilian (tel. 11/3772-7098), JS Turismo and Transportes (tel. 11/3082-4291), Vanvoar (tel. 11/5031-2222), and Gabriel Siderman (tel. 11/5543-3739). You can also pay a taxi about R$150–200 per day to be your personal driver. This is a common option among international business travelers staying in São Paulo.

# Avenida Paulista and Jardins

At the end of the coffee boom in the first half of the 20th century, São Paulo's old downtown went into a period of decline. But the city was not without resources. Replacing the coffee trade were a series of modern industries and agribusiness that dominate international trade to this day. Iron, steel, nickel, and aluminum lead the metallurgical sciences, while sugar, soy, and wheat became the important agricultural exports. Shoes came in from the south and manufacturing, including automobiles and airplanes, took place right in São Paulo itself. The nearby shipping village of Santos grew into one of the world's largest international ports. The city was in need of a new financial center. Avenida Paulista, the second of São Paulo's four business centers, literally sprouted up. With its many high-rise structures, the Paulista area is home to the headquarters of numerous financial, communications, and international import/export companies. Most of the city's banks have branches in this area and the majority of international consulates are either on Avenida Paulista or nearby. The area has a high concentration of art galleries, shops, hotels, and restaurants, which are mostly mid-range and high-end options.

The area begins just south of the Brigadeiro metro terminal at the Casa das Rosas, one of the original homes built along Avenida Paulista in 1935 and the only one still standing. Farther up Avenida Paulista is the Trianon/MASP metro station, where you'll find the MASP museum and the charming Trianon/MASP park in front of it. When you reach the Consolação metro station, you've hit the heart of the Paulista area. Just to the south side are numerous shops and restaurants, with a few on the north side as well. The Paulista area is busiest during business hours and on weekends can be quite calm. Most hotels have weekend discounts.

## ⋈ MUSEU DE ARTE SÃO PAULO

When you go to the Museu de Arte São Paulo (MASP) (Av. Paulista 1578, tel. 11/251-5644,

11 A.M.–6 P.M. Tues.–Sun., R$15 for adults, half price for students), you may wander around a bit, in search of the front door. The MASP is located in a modern structure, which is both above and below ground. The large cube-like building sits above ground on steel supports with a stairway and elevator as the main entrance. The elevator also takes you down to the basement, where there are more exhibits and lots of space. Touted as the finest museum of contemporary art in South America, MASP has an impressive collection of Latin American masterpieces as well as a few well-known European pieces by masters like Cézanne, Matisse, Monet, Picasso, Renoir, and Van Gogh. Exhibits appear in the large basement area, as well as on the main floors of the MASP building. The Trianon/MASP metro station is right in front of the museum.

## ENTERTAINMENT AND NIGHTLIFE

There are several monthly theater and show guides available with current listings. (See *Entertainment and Nightlife* in the *Central São Paulo* section for details.)

### Art, Theater, and Music

The **Centro Cultural São Paulo** (Rua Vergueiro 1000, tel. 11/3277-3611) in the Paraíso area (near the Paraíso metro station) is a cultural arts center with rotating art exhibitions, music, theater, and cinema productions. Their events appear in most of the monthly guides or you can stop by for a schedule and prices. The **Galeria SESC Paulista** (Av. Paulista 119, tel. 11/3179-3400, 10 A.M.–7 P.M. Mon.–Fri.) and the **Itaú Cultural Center** (Av. Paulista 149, tel. 11/238-1777, 10 A.M.–6 P.M. Mon.–Fri.). Naturally, hours vary depending on the event.) and the **Itaú Cultural Center** (Av. Paulista 149) have temporary art exhibitions on display. These are usually contemporary works by Brazilian artists, but exhibits can vary widely. Just

São Paulo City

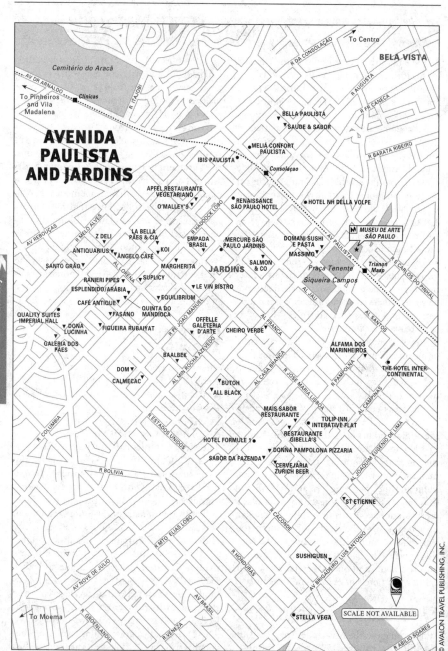

# AVENIDA PAULISTA AND JARDINS

BELA VISTA

To Centro

Cemitério do Aracá

AV DR ARNALDO

To Pinheiros and Vila Madalena

Clínicas

R DA CONSOLAÇÃO

R AUGUSTA

R FR CANECA

R BARATA RIBEIRO

BELLA PAULISTA

SAUDE & SABOR

MELIA CONFORT PAULISTA

IBIS PAULISTA

Consolação

AV REBOUÇAS

R MELO ALVES

AL LORENA

R HADDOCK LOBO

APFEL RESTAURANTE VEGETARIANO

O'MALLEY'S

RENAISSANCE SÃO PAULO HOTEL

HOTEL NH DELLA VOLPE

MUSEU DE ARTE SÃO PAULO

AV PAULISTA

Z DELI

LA BELLA PÃES & CIA

KOI

EMPADA BRASIL

MERCURE SÃO PAULO JARDINS

DOMANI SUSHI E PASTA

MASSIMO

Trianon Masp

R S CARLOS DO PINHAL

ANTIQUARIUS

ÂNGELO CAFÉ

SANTO GRÃO

MARGHERITA

JARDINS

SALMON & CO

Praça Tenente Siqueira Campos

SUPLICY

RANIERI PIPES

ESPLENDIDO/ARÁBIA

CAFÉ ANTIQUE

FASANO

LE VIN BÍSTRO

EQUILIBRIUM

AL JAU

AL SANTOS

QUINTA DO MANDIOCA

QUALITY SUITES IMPERIAL HALL

DOÑA LUCINHA

FIGUEIRA RUBAIYAT

OFFELLE GALETERIA D'ARTE

CHEIRO VERDE

AL FRANCA

ALFAMA DOS MARINHEIROS

R PAMPLONA

THE HOTEL INTER-CONTINENTAL

GALERIA DOS PÃES

R PE JOÃO MANUEL

AL MIN ROCHA AZEVEDO

BAALBEK

AL CASA BRANCA

R JOSÉ MARIA LISBOA

AL CAMPINAS

R COLUMBIA

DOM

CALMECAC

BUTOH

ALL BLACK

R ESTADOS UNIDOS

MAIS SABOR RESTAURANTE

TULIP INN INTERATIVE FLAT

RESTAURANTE GIBELLA'S

HOTEL FORMULE 1

DONNA PAMPOLONA PIZZARIA

SABOR DA FAZENDA

CERVEJARIA ZURICH BEER

R BOLIVIA

AV JOAQUIM EUGENIO DE LIMA

ST ETIENNE

R CACONDE

R MTO ELIAS LOBO

SUSHIGUEN

To Moema

AV NOVE DE JULHO

R GROENLANDIA

AV BRASIL

R VENEZA

R HONDURAS

AV BRIGADEIRO LUIS ANTONIO

STELLA VEGA

R ABILIO SOARES

SCALE NOT AVAILABLE

© AVALON TRAVEL PUBLISHING, INC.

walk in for a look. Admission is free and they are practically next door to each other. A few doors down is the **Casa das Rosas** (Av. Paulista 37, tel. 11/288-9447, 1–8 P.M. Tues.–Sun.), one of the early mansions built along Avenida Paulista in the 1930s still standing. It was designed by Ramos de Azevedo, who also designed the Pinacoteca, Mercado Municipal, and the Theatro Municipal. Today it's an art gallery with temporary exhibitions on display. The **Museu Brasilleiro da Escultura** (Rua Alemanha 221, tel. 11/3081-8611, 10 A.M.–7 P.M. Tues.–Sun.) has frequent sculpture and ceramics exhibits. Call first to see what's happening there. The **Fundação Nacional de Arte e Cultura (Fnac)** is a book and CD mega-store with a concert and exhibit hall. They have two locations in São Paulo at Av. Paulista 901 (tel. 11/2123-2000) and at Av. Pedroso de Morais 858 in Pinheiros (tel. 11/4501-3000). These locations host various music, theater and film events, as well as art and photography exhibits. Look for their *Encontros* monthly catalog at tourist information booths for listings.

Besides all these museums and exhibition spaces, the Paulista area is home to most of the city's best contemporary art galleries. Many are close enough to one another that you can create a nice walking tour to see them. You might start at the **Monica Filgueiras** gallery (Rua Bela Cintra 1533, tel. 11/3081-9492, 11 A.M.–7 P.M. Mon.–Fri., until 1:30 P.M. Sat.), where you can pick up a copy of the *Mapa Das Artes São Paulo*, a map of the area showing the locations of all museums and art galleries. Some good galleries to include in your tour are **Galeria Luisa Strina** (Rua Oscar Freire 502, tel. 11/3088-2471, 10 A.M.–7 P.M. Mon.–Fri.), **Arvani Galeria de Arte** (Rua Oscar Freire 540, tel. 11/3082-1927, 10 A.M.–10 P.M. Mon.–Fri.), **Arte Aplicada** (Rua Haddock Lobo 1406, tel. 11/3064-4725, 10 A.M.–7 P.M. Mon.–Fri.), and **Nova André Galeria** (Rua Estados Unidos 2280, tel. 11/3081-6664, 10 A.M.–8 P.M. Mon.–Fri.).

## Bars

One of the best smoky blues bars in the Paulista area is the **Ranieri Pipes** bar (Al. Lorena 1221, tel. 11/3062-5504, 8 A.M.–midnight Mon.–Sat.), which has live jazz music on weekends and a great jazz-blues atmosphere. They offer a full bar with wines and mixed drinks. It's a great place for a late-night drink. **Cervejaria Zurich Beer** (Rua Pamplona 1551, tel. 11/3885-0510, noon–1 A.M. daily) has outdoor seating and a friendly atmosphere. You can get draft beer and various appetizers from R$15–30 each. The best happy-hour hangout is a cluster of bars on Alameda Juaquim Eugénio de Lima at Avenida Paulista. They all have outdoor seating, sandwiches, appetizers, and various kinds of beer, both draft and bottled. The prices are good, so the area fills up pretty quickly after work until around 8 P.M. **Bar Balcão** (Rua Dr. Melo Alves 150, tel. 11/3063-6091, 6 P.M.–2 A.M. daily) is a great spot for meeting people while having a drink or two; it's best for happy hour during the week.

Finally, one of the hottest discos in the area, playing a variety of dance music from the '70s through contemporary times, is **Cambridge** (Av. Nove de Julho 210, tel. 11/3259-6585, www.bardohotel.com.br, 6 P.M. daily) in the old Hotel Cambridge.

**O'Malley's** (Al. Itú 1529, tel. 11/3086-0780, 11:30 A.M. until the last client leaves) is a good Irish pub with a decent selection of beer and cigars along with blues music. They will pick you up at your hotel if you're staying in the Paulista area. Another Irish pub in the area is **Finnegan's** (Rua Cristiano Viana 358, tel. 11/3062-3232, hours of operation vary slightly every day but are roughly 6 P.M.–2 A.M.), which has become something of a landmark. Naturally, there are plenty of different beers from which to choose. Finally, **All Black** (Rua Oscar Freire 163, tel. 11/3088-7990, 6 P.M.–4 A.M.) is an internationally frequented Irish pub with plenty of international beers from which to choose.

## Clubs and Discos

In the Paulista area, the **Atari Club** (Al. Lorena 2155, tel. 11/3085-0424) plays '80s underground music with lots of dancing and drinking. The **DJ Bar Club** (Al. Franca 241,

São Paulo City

## OPEN 24 HOURS

If you're looking for a late-night snack, there are plenty of establishments in São Paulo to serve you:

- **Black Dog** (Al. Joaquim Eugénio de Lima 565) for late-night hot dogs and people-watching.
- **Galeria dos Pães** (Rua Estados Unidos 1645) for sandwiches and pastries near Avenida Paulista.
- **Brasserie Bela Vista** (Al. Campinas 150) for Italian food any time, especially after a night out in the Bexiga neighborhood.
- **Pasta e Pizza** (Rua Barão de Capanema 206) for lasagna, ravioli, and pasta at sunrise.
- **Bella Paulista** (Rua Haddock Lobo 354) for sandwiches and pastries in the Jardins area.

tel. 11/3106-2846) has several environments, from disco to punk, live music, and a wide variety of customers, including some gay, lesbian, bisexual, and transgender (GLBT). These are late-night clubs that generally don't get rolling until around midnight and go until the sun comes up. Call for specific times.

If you're into electronic music, you can find plenty around town, especially in the Vila Olimpia area (Zona Sul), and at the **SoGo Mix Club** (Al. Franca 1368, tel. 11/3061-1759), the **House Lounge Bar** (Av. Brigadeiro Faria Lima 4467, tel. 11/3044-0112), serving up some lounge music on weekends, and **Ultralounge** (Rua da Consolação 3031, tel. 11/3083-6088). Keep in mind that these kinds of clubs appear and disappear with the change of the wind, so call first if you can.

The area's best underground bar is M **Bar da Dida** (Rua Dr. Melo Alves 98, tel. 11/3088-7177, 6 P.M.–1 A.M. Tues.–Sun.), which serves great caipirinhas and snacks until the very late hours. It's a small and interesting space.

## Gay and Lesbian

The circuit of GLBT bars and clubs is around the Cerqueira Cesar area and Ruas Frei Caneca and Consolação. Check out **Director's Gourmet** (Al. Franca 1552, tel. 11/3064-7958),

**Hertz** (Al. Itú 1530, tel. 11/3064-2088), and **Pride** (Al. Itú 1576, tel. 11/3085-1213), all open 9 P.M.–3 A.M. Tuesday–Sunday. A couple more are **RITZ** and **Mestiço** both in the Jardins area.

## Sidewalk Cafés

As the nucleus of the Brazilian coffee trade, São Paulo has a reasonable amount of cafés from which to choose, particularly in and around Avenida Paulista. Walk down any street and you won't have to go far before passing a café. A small shopping gallery at Avenida Paulista 1499 is almost half filled with cafés (including some Internet cafés). Here are a few worth mentioning.

**Suplicy** (Al. Lorena 1430, tel. 11/3061-0195, 8 A.M.–midnight, 9 A.M.–1 A.M. Sat. and Sun.) is a great place for American and European-style coffee. It has a clean, modern interior and great sweet snacks, too. Though slightly expensive, it has the very best coffee. **Equilibrium** (Rua Augusta 2420, tel. 11/3081-2742, 10 A.M.–11 P.M. Mon.–Sat., until 9 P.M. Sun. and 6 P.M. Mon.) at the corner of Al. Tietê has gourmet sweets and a selection of healthy appetizers, like soy-meat pastels and light sandwiches. It also has lunch plates and is a good spot for people-watching. **St. Etienne** (Al. Joaquim Eug. De Lima 1417, tel. 11/3819-2578, 6 A.M.–11:30 P.M. Mon.–Fri., opens 7 A.M. Sat. and Sun.) has some excellent French-style baked breads and sweets, plus an ample outdoor seating area for hanging out and drinking coffee or beer. You can order off the menu or choose something from the inside bakery. They have real croissants, too. **Ângelo Café** (Al. Lorena 1271, tel. 11/3081-5464, 9 A.M.–11 P.M. Mon.–Thurs., until midnight Fri. and Sat.) is an Argentinean café with great surroundings and a great selection of coffee drinks. It's always crowded on weekdays. Finally, M **Santo Grão** (Rua Oscar Freire 413, tel. 11/3082-9969, 9 A.M.–1 A.M. Tues.–Sun. and noon–1 A.M. Mon.) has a great space with a terrace and lounge area and a large communal table upstairs. It makes a great hangout for coffee. If you're into authentic Italian *sorvete,* try

**Offelle Galeteria D'Arte** (Al. Lorena 1784, tel. 11/3088-8127, 1 P.M.–midnight Mon.–Thurs., 1 P.M.–1 A.M. Fri. and Sat., and noon–11 P.M. Sun.) with numerous flavors, including many using tropical fruits.

## SHOPPING

You can shop the high-end boutiques in the Jardins area starting at Rua Peixoto Gomide and going to Rua Bela Cintra, the shops getting more expensive as you go. The prime real estate is around the intersection of Haddock Lobo and Oscar Freire, where you'll find the choicest restaurants, art galleries, shops, and cafés. There are some less expensive shops along Rua Augusta where you can actually find some good deals on no-name items.

## ACCOMMODATIONS

Since the Paulista area (and São Paulo in general) is oriented to business travel, you should always check into weekend discounts if your trip happens to fall on a weekend. When possible, weekend rates are included in the following list.

### R$50–100

Some of my favorite hotels are the Ibis hotels by Accor. They have a no-frills, streamlined system with one type of room for a single price. Rooms do not include breakfast, but it's available for an extra fee, as are refreshments from their bar/lounge and Internet access. Rooms are clean and modern with phones, comfortable beds, and gas-heated showers. The ⓜ **Ibis Paulista** (Av. Paulista 2345, tel. 11/3523-3000, www.accorhotels.com, R$79 s or d) is near the Consolação metro station and perfectly located in the Paulista area. Make reservations way ahead because this place is always booked up. If you can't get into the Ibis, then try the **Hotel Formule 1** (Rua Vergueiro 1571, tel. 11/5085-5699, tel. 11/5575-8122, www.accorhotels.com, R$69 for up to three people), which is run by the same company with the same streamlined idea, except that

these hotels are even more streamlined. There are public telephones on each floor (no phones in the rooms) and the price is good for up to three people per room. Rooms come with a TV, a double bed and a single bunk above it. Internet, breakfast, and refreshments are all extra. It's well located next to the Paraíso metro station. There is another Formule 1 going up on Avenida Nove de Julho on the far end of the Jardins area. It will probably be finished by the time you read this. Check the Accor site for details.

Another great value is the **Aclimação Hotel/Flat** (Av. Armando Ferrentini 668, tel. 11/3346-7799, www.ezhoteis.com.br, R$60 s and R$79 d with no breakfast included) in the Paraíso area, just around the corner from the metro station. Rooms are equipped with kitchen facilities (pots and pans are available for a fee for 24-hours), phone, and TV. They also have an excellent pasta bar for dinner, a pool, sauna, and Internet room (extra fee for Internet). They also have a van that takes guests to and from the metro station every half-hour.

### R$100–200

Personally, I think this is the best price range for cost/benefit in São Paulo hotels. You can pay less and get a lot less or you can pay more for a luxury experience. The **Parthenon The Universe Hotel** (Rua Pamplona 83, tel. 11/3178-2828, www.accorhotels.com, R$125 s and R$135 d weekdays, R$80 and R$90 weekends) is perfectly located a few blocks north of Avenida Paulista near the Consolação metro station and surrounded by quaint bars, restaurants, and snack stands. The hotel features a gym, pool, and sauna, plus an excellent restaurant for breakfast (included), and a lunch and dinner buffet (a great deal at R$15 per person). They also offer daily and nightly sightseeing trips for guests. Rooms have air, cable TV, in-room Internet connections, some kitchen facilities and voice mail. Non-smoking rooms are available. Another excellent and brand-new Parthenon hotel is the ⓜ **Stella Vega** (Rua Salto 70, tel. 11/3055-2500, R$98 on weekdays and R$78 on weekends), well located on the northern tip of the Parque Ibirapuera and within walking distance to the Jardins area, too (up Avenida Brigadeiro Luis Antônio). Rooms are small but well designed, quaint, and squeaky clean. Amenities are similar to the previous listing, including an excellent restaurant for breakfast and lunch.

The **Meliá Confort Paulista** (Rua Haddock Lobo 294, tel. 11/3123-6200, paulista@meliaconfort.com.br, R$100 s and R$145 d) is only a block from Avenida Paulista on the downtown side. It's a few years older than the Parthenon hotels and a bit more worn down but still offers excellent service and accommodations, with cable TV, 2-line phones, non-smoking rooms, indoor pool, and gym. Don't forget to ask about weekend discounts. The **Tulip Inn Interative Flat** (Rua Jose Maria Lisboa 555, tel. 11/3059-6500, www.interativeflat.com.br, R$175 s and R$195 d on weekdays) is a modern facility in the heart of the Jardins area. They have three types of rooms, including a luxury suite with outdoor Jacuzzi. All have cable TV, air, and in-room Internet access. The restaurant serves breakfast (included). A final entry in this category is the **M Hotel NH Della Volpe** (Rua Frei Caneca 1199, tel. 11/3549-6464, www.nh-hotels.com, R$185 weekdays and R$130 weekends for standard rooms; R$255 and R$155 for suites). This newly renovated hotel is a couple blocks from Avenida Paulista near MASP. It has a sophisticated interior with well-appointed rooms, cable TV, in-room Internet, air, pool, and sauna. The restaurant serves an abundant breakfast buffet (included) and crepes for dinner (R$25). The service is stellar.

## R$200–300

**Quality Suites Imperial Hall** (Rua da Consolação 3555, tel. 11/3061-1320, www.atlantica-hotels.com, R$210–265 d) offers a luxury, business-oriented experience for a reasonable price. It's near Rua Oscar Freire, where you find the largest concentration of restaurants and shops in the Jardins area. They have cable TV, air, voice mail, some mini-kitchen facilities, bathtub, in-room Internet connection, non-smoking rooms, pool, sauna, and fitness

center. They offer excellent service with an entire floor for women's beauty and health, and a free 15-minute massage for all guests. They have three types of double-occupancy rooms. The hotel's fabulous French restaurant, **Marcel,** serves lunch and dinner for around R$55 per person with excellent salmon and lamb plates. Open from noon–3 P.M. for lunch and 7 P.M.–midnight for dinner. The **M Mercure São Paulo Jardins** (Al. Itú 1151, tel. 11/3089-7555, www.accorhoteis.com.br, R$200–280 d) is an excellent choice in this price category and will almost make you feel like you're in the Marriott. It's located right in the middle of the action in the Jardins area. They have excellent facilities and service and a top-notch restaurant on the ground floor.

## Over R$300

The Marriott **Renaissance São Paulo Hotel** (Al. Santos 2233, tel. 11/3069-2233, www.mariottbrasil.com, R$850–1500 d) is the city's luxury choice. Located in the prime real estate section, a block from Avenida Paulista on the corner of Avenida Haddock Lobo and Alameda Santos, it's walking distance to everything interesting in the Paulista area. Just a few of their offerings include specialized executive check-in with English-speaking employees, in-room Internet, bathtubs, spa, café bar, racquetball courts, jogging track, sauna, pool, and massage room. Their restaurant and café are top notch. The lunch buffet has daily themes and costs R$48 per person. **The Hotel Inter-Continental** (Al. Santos 1123, tel. 11/3179-2600, www.interconti.com, R$850 d) is another top-end entry.

# FOOD

## Middle Eastern

**Arábia** (Rua Haddock Lobo 1397, tel. 11/3064-4776, noon–3:30 P.M. and 7 P.M.–midnight) is a high-end Lebanese restaurant with well-known favorites, such as hummus and baba ghanoush, plus some interesting new items, like their salad with pomegranate. Try their sampler plate for R$45. **Baalbek** (Al. Lorena 1330, tel. 11/3088-8127, 8 A.M.–9 P.M. Mon.–Fri., until 6 P.M. Sat.) is a small place with tables arranged in a small corridor and patio area. But the food is wonderful and authentic, including dishes with lamb and sesame sauce. Meals are approximately R$25 per person.

The Arabic (mostly Lebanese) district of São Paulo is in the Paraíso area. There, near the Formule 1 hotel, you'll find a number of restaurants and cafés serving all kinds of Eastern dishes and desserts. A super-authentic and low-priced example is **Eddis Charbel** (Rua Domingos de Moraes 144, tel. 11/5573-7543, 6 P.M.–midnight Mon.–Fri., 6 P.M.–1 A.M. Sat.), which has incredible sweet sesame cakes and Habibi sandwiches. Prices are around R$6 per person. There's no formal seating.

### Churrasco (Barbecue)

**Figueira Rubaiyat** (Haddock Lobo 1738, tel. 11/3063-3888, noon–3 P.M. and 7 P.M.–midnight) is a well-known Brazilian-style barbecue in the heart of the Jardins area. You get all types of meats, chicken, and fish, and then more meat. You can sit inside, or under the large shade tree on the outdoor patio. It offers excellent service and a good wine list. Prices are around R$60–150 per person. For an excellent atmosphere and great meats and other dishes, try the **La Caballeriza** (Alameda Campinas 530, tel. 11/3285-6189). The Argentine owners Leandro and Manoel invested in the decoration and location, which are both top-notch. It's a great spot for business dinners. Lunch buffet is from noon–4 P.M. for R$20 per person. Dinner runs around R$60.

### Comida Mineira (Brazilian)

**⅗ Dona Lucinha** (Rua Bela Cintra 2325, tel. 11/5051-2050, noon–3 P.M. and 8–11 P.M. Tues.–Fri., lunch only until 4:30 P.M. Sat. and Sun.) has earned a reputation for some of the best Comida Mineira (country cooking from Minas Gerais) in both São Paulo and Minas Gerais. The original restaurant in Belo Horizonte is always packed, so Dona Lucinha (herself) moved to São Paulo to open another. You'll find typically hearty portions and savory, saucy dishes for approximately R$45 per person. A

self-service restaurant with country cooking is **Sabor da Fazenda** (Av. Pamplona 1834, tel. 11/3884-9190, self-service lunch only 11 A.M.–4 P.M. daily), with recipes from all over Brazil, cooked in copper pans over a wood-burning oven. Meals run about R$40 per person.

### Italian

**Cantina do Piero** (Rua Haddock Lobo 728, tel. 11/3062-9635, noon–midnight), located across from the Renaissance hotel, serves authentic Italian cuisine with huge dishes. It's become a tradition in the area. One of the most award-winning restaurants in São Paulo (not just in the Italian category) is **Fasano** (Rua Vitório Fasano 88, tel. 11/3062-4000, 7:30 P.M.–1 A.M. Mon.–Sat.). Located in the Fasano Hotel, it is a dining experience of the finest quality. Although principally Italian, many dishes cross boundaries, such as the tuna steak encrusted with Sicilian lemon and served with potato and asparagus. Reservations are recommended. Meals are R$70–150 per person. In the style of Fasano, but smaller and slightly less expensive, is **Palazzo Grimaldi** (Al. Santos 1826, tel. 11/3284-0311, noon–3 P.M. and 7:30 P.M.–1 A.M. Mon.–Fri., 7:30 P.M.–1 A.M. Sat., noon–5 P.M. Sun.) from a former Fasano chef, who makes many exceptional dishes in the Italian-fusion fashion, specializing in seafood. Prices run R$45–80 per person. Yet another of the city's finest Italian restaurants is **⅗ Massimo** (Al. Santos 1826, tel. 11/3284-0311, noon–3 P.M. and 7:30 P.M.–midnight Mon.–Fri., lunch only until 4:30 P.M. Sat. and Sun.) near MASP, specializing in Northern Italian food and Italian wines. Meals are R$55–95 per person.

### Japanese

Visit **Koi** (Al. Tietê 360, tel. 11/3081-1414, noon–midnight Mon.–Sat. and 1–11 P.M. Sun.) for excellent and creative sushi dishes in a modern atmosphere. It's a very artistic place both in decoration and food. Try the Acelgamaki special. For an all-you-can-eat sushi lunch at R$27, try **Domani Sushi e Pasta** (Rua Peixoto Gomide 1002, tel. 11/3171-3727, 11:30 A.M.–3 P.M.

and 6 P.M.–midnight Mon.–Sat.). They have a decent variety of items at an excellent price, including several good pasta plates. **Butoh** (Rua Peixoto Gomide 1797, tel. 11/3082-1750, noon–3 P.M. and 7 P.M.–1 A.M. Mon.–Sat.) is a popular sushi bar with live music and charming atmosphere. The chef has some interesting inventions worth trying. It's approximately R$60 per person. **M Sushiguen** (Av. Brigadeiro Luís Antônio 2367, tel. 11/289-5566, 11:30 A.M.–2 P.M. and 6–11 P.M.) near Avenida Paulista is for true sushi lovers. Sushi chef Mitsuaki Shimizu is the sensei of many of the city's chefs and he whips up some interesting recipes, including his famous Tirashi Sushi mixtures. The tuna and salmon melt in your mouth.

### Lanchonetes and Casual

In the Jardins area is **M La Bella Pães & Cia.** (Rua Bela Cintra 1491, open 24 hours) where you can belly up to the counter and order one of their delicious sandwiches with a fresh fruit juice. A great, quick lunch spot, it also has a good bakery for breads and sweets. **Bella Paulista** (Rua Haddock Lobo 354, tel. 11/3214-3347, open 24 hours) is just a couple blocks from Avenida Paulista on the downtown side. They have a bakery and market with a café area that serves sandwiches, deli items, and even dinner plates. A similar place is the **Galeria dos Pães** (Rua Estados Unidos 1645, tel. 11/3064-5900, open 24 hours) at the bottom of the Jardins area. They have some great sandwiches. The **St. Etienne** bakery (Al. Joaquim Eug. De Lima 1417, tel. 11/3819-2578, 6 A.M.–11:30 P.M. Mon.–Fri., opens at 7 A.M. Sat. and Sun.) has seating for dinner and beer. You can order from the menu or from the bakery, which has French breads and croissants, among other things. They have a great outdoor seating area for hanging out. **Empada Brasil** (Rua Augusta 2212 near Al. Franca, tel. 11/3061-9591, 9 A.M.–8:30 P.M. Mon.–Fri., until 7:30 P.M. Sat.) has some of the best *empadas* (small meat pies) in the state, filled with shrimp, salmon, chicken, cheese, and other goodies. In the heart of the Jardins area is **M Z Deli** (Al. Lorena 1689, tel. 11/3088-5644, 11:30 A.M.–6:30 P.M. Mon.–Fri., 11:30 A.M.–4:30 P.M. Sat.), a traditional Jewish deli with some of the finest salads and small hot dishes you've ever tasted—using quality ingredients and creative cooking. They offer an executive plate for $25 or all-you-can-eat buffet for R$30 per person.

### Pizza

**Donna Pampolona Pizzaria** (Rua Pamplona 1115, tel. 11/3285-2001, 6 P.M.–1 A.M.) near Alameda Franca has a luxurious interior and offers a fine-dining pizza experience for around R$25–40 per pizza. A more accessible option is **M Margherita** (Al. Tietê 255, tel. 11/3086-2556, 6:30 P.M.–1 A.M. Mon.–Sat.) with a variety of crunchy pizzas and cold beers. It gets crowded for dinner with as much as an hour wait, but it makes one of the best pizzas in the area, with all fresh ingredients. Pizzas range from R$20–40.

### Portuguese

**Alfama dos Marinheiros** (Rua Pamplona 1285, tel. 11/3884-9203, noon–3 P.M. and 6 P.M.–midnight Mon.–Fri., noon–midnight Sat. and Sun.) is a Portuguese-style seafood eatery with plenty of fried fish plates, a wonderful fish soup, and plenty of shellfish options. They have live Portuguese music Thursday–Saturday. Slightly expensive, but worthwhile at around R$50 per person. One of the most celebrated Portuguese restaurants in São Paulo is **Antiquarius** (Al. Lorena 1884, tel. 11/3082-3015, noon–3 P.M. and 7 P.M.–1 A.M. Tue.–Sat., noon–6 P.M. Sun., 7 P.M.–1 A.M. Mon.) with a rather formal, luxurious atmosphere and impeccable service. They have such interesting dishes as duck risotto and grilled octopus, with plenty of other fish and meat dishes. Meals cost R$80–120 per person. Reservations are recommended.

### Seafood

**M Salmon & Co.** (Al. Jaú 1199, tel. 11/3085-1419, noon–3 P.M. and 6–11 P.M. Mon.–Fri., noon–11 P.M. on Sat., noon–5 P.M. on Sun.) is a small, cozy place that serves up great seafood—specializing in, you guessed it, salmon. For the price, it's one of the best, most elegant restaurants you'll find in the area. **Le Vin Bistro** (Al Tietê 184, tel. 11/3082-3951, noon–midnight Mon.–Thurs., Fri. and Sat. until 1 A.M. and Sun. until 11 P.M.) has fresh oysters for about R$25 a dozen. For lunch, they serve up authentic French dishes from the menu and a self-service buffet open noon–3:30 P.M. They specialize in seafood. Some outdoor seating is available on the front sidewalk patio.

## Self-Service

At **Mais Sabor Restaurante** (Rua Pamplona 1466, tel. 11/3052-3003, 11 A.M.–3 P.M. Mon.–Fri.) you'll find dozens of different salads along with light chicken dishes in a self-service style. They claim to be a vegetarian restaurant, but hard-core vegetarians may differ. Still, they offer a healthy lunch buffet for around R$10 per person. The country-style **Quinta do Mandioca** (Rua Oscar Freire 726, tel. 11/3064-4999, lunch only Mon.–Sat.) serves Brazilian dishes in a self-service lunch buffet for around R$20 per kilo. They offer a great location and comfortable surroundings.

## Sunday Brunch

The **Terraço Jardins,** located in the opulent Renaissance Hotel (Al. Santos 2233 at Rua Hoddock Lobo, tel. 11/3069-2233) has a jazz brunch on Sundays from noon–4 P.M. For R$65 per person, you have access to several huge buffet tables and food preparation stations (omelets, crepes, etc.). They have an incredible selection of fruits and sweets, too.

## Vegetarian

The **Apfel Restaurante Vegetariano** (Rua Bela Cintra 1343, tel. 11/3062-3727, lunch only 11 A.M.–3:30 P.M. Mon.–Fri., noon–4 P.M. Sat.) offers daily vegetarian-style specialties, including some veggie Brazilian dishes. **Saude & Sabor** (Rua Luis Coelho 214, tel. 11/3237-4306, 11 A.M.–3 P.M. Mon.–Fri.) is a very reasonably priced veggie option near the Conceição metro station. Lunch is only R$10 per person for a complete buffet of salads, hot dishes, and soups. **Cheiro Verde** (Rua Peixoto Gomide 1413, tel. 11/289-6853, noon–3 P.M. Mon.–Fri., noon–5 P.M. Sat. and Sun.) is an all-natural restaurant with no meats and no chemicals. They use mineral water in all dishes and have been around for more than 20 years. Meals cost approximately R$35 per person.

## Other International

**Calmecac** (Rua Padre João Manoel 861, tel. 11/3082-2720, noon–2 A.M. daily) offers some pretty authentic Mexican food by Brazilian standards (amazingly, there are very few good Mexican restaurants in Brazil). They have all the Mexican standards, tequila shooters, and Mexican beer. It's a great night spot on weekends, when they also have a mariachi group for a R$4 cover charge. **Café Antique** (Rua Haddock Lobo 1416, tel. 11/3062-0882, noon–3 P.M. and 7 P.M.–midnight Mon.–Fri., noon–4:30 P.M. and 7 P.M.–1 A.M. Sat.) is a classic French restaurant with a refined atmosphere and a great wine list to accompany the French cooking. Mealso run R$70–125 per person. For a more modern French experience, try the oft-awarded **Laurent** (Al. Lorena 1899, tel. 11/3062-1452, noon–3 P.M. and 7 P.M.–midnight). French chef Lauret Suadeau uses a variety of local ingredients in his French cuisine. Available on the menu are foie gras, duck, and fish dishes, along with decadent desserts. It costs approximately R$90 per person. There are few Indian restaurants in São Paulo, but one of the best is located in the Paraíso area, called **Tandoor** (Rua Dr. Rafael de Barros 408, Paraíso, noon–3 P.M. and 7–11 P.M. Tues.–Sat., noon–4 P.M. and 7–10 P.M. Sun., dinner only 7–10 P.M. Mon.). They have typical, spicy dishes, including tandoori chicken, lentils, and naan bread with yogurt sauce, to name a few. Prices are R$50 per person.

One of the city's most contemporary restaurants is **N D.O.M.** (Rua Barão de Capanema 549, tel. 11/3088-0761, noon–3 P.M. and 7 P.M.–midnight Mon.–Fri., 7 P.M.–1 A.M. Sat.), which is something of a showcase for chef Alex Atala, whose culinary inventions are frequently out of this world. Coming out of nouveau cuisine, the dining experience is also an exhibit and can sometimes leave you a little hungry, though creatively satisfied. Still, for world-class fusion food and great desserts, it's not to be missed. The experience starts at around R$100 per person.

## INFORMATION

The tourist information booth in the Paulista area is located in front of MASP. You can also walk into most of the better hotels in the area and ask for information, pamphlets, or directions. Most are very happy to help.

## SERVICES

You can change money at a number of private agencies, including **Gama** (Rua Augusta 2690 loja 101, tel. 11/3083-5633), **Astor** (Av. Paulista 1499 loja 10, tel. 11/288-3588), and **Action** (Rua Augusta 2766, tel. 11/3086-1966). All of these are open during regular Brazilian business hours: 9 A.M.–6 P.M. Mon.–Fri., 9 A.M.–4 P.M. Sat. Most of these offer good rates and no commissions. For larger exchanges, go to **Banco do Brasil** (Av. Paulista 2163, tel. 11/3066-9203, 10 A.M.–4 P.M. Mon.–Fri.) near the Consolação metro station, which charges a commission, but offers the best rates. They also have international ATMs. There is a **Banco 24 Horas** ATM in the Jardins area (Rua Oscar Freire 450) which has the Plus and Cirrus systems and a **Citibank** (Av. Paulista 1111, tel. 11/5576-1000, 10 A.M.–4 P.M. Mon.–Fri.).

**Cybor Games and Internet** (Rua Augusta 2346, tel. 11/2123-0702,cyberian.com.br) is open 24 hours with lots of computers and private telephones. It costs approximately R$3 per hour. Another is the **Cyber Café** (Avenida Paulista 1499, loja 19, tel. 11/3253-0645, 9:30 A.M.–11 P.M. Mon.–Fri. and 9:30 A.M.–10 P.M. Sat.) with computers for R$4 per hour, including scanner, web cam, and fax. They are inside a small shopping center that is full of small cafés.

## GETTING THERE AND AROUND

You get to the Paulista and Jardins areas via the metro. The three stations, Brigadeiro, Trianon/MASP, and Consolação, stop along Avenida Paulista. The area is fairly compact and most territory can be covered on foot. However, getting to and from the extreme ends can involve quite a trek. The green metro line runs all the way down Avenida Paulista. This is a good way to lop off a chunk of time and energy from your walking tour of the area. Going the other way (north–south), such as from Avenida Paulista to Avenida Estados Unidos, is farther than it looks on the maps (about 2.5 kilometers), and the only shortcut is by taxi—well worth catching on your way back, which is uphill. A taxi to and from the old downtown area will cost around R$10–15. It's perfectly safe to walk around the Paulista area at night. Just keep an eye out if you turn down Rua Augusta toward the downtown area, as this is the city's red light district.

# Zona Sul

The South Zone of the city is large and spread out. This section starts at the Parque Ibirapuera, which is at the base of the Paulista/Jardins area, and focuses on the three principal neighborhoods of Moema, Vila Olimpia, and Itaim Bibi, all of which offer an assortment of restaurants, bars, clubs, and shops, featuring some of the best restaurants in the city. The Morumbi neighborhood is home to the city's largest football stadium and the oft-mentioned Brooklin is mainly a business center with plenty of eating options for lunch. Farther south lies the Congonhas Airport area, which is a decent place to find hotels. Even farther south are the zoological and botanical parks.

Mostly, visitors and residents of São Paulo come to Zona Sul for nightlife activities in the three aforementioned neighborhoods. However, there are a few daytime excursions and sights worth checking here, such as the Parque Ibirapuera and its museum spaces. If you're actually staying in the southern region, then you're probably doing business in the area, perhaps in Brooklin. Not to worry, the surrounding areas provide plenty of diversion and sightseeing, even if you never make it into the downtown area.

## PARQUE IBIRAPUERA

São Paulo's Central Park, Ibirapuera (Av. Pedro Álvares Cabral, tel. 11/5574-5177, 6 A.M.–8 P.M. daily) is a great place to stroll in the morning or afternoon. It is home to the Bandeiras Monument, built to pay homage to the groups of Paulistas who entered the country's interior regions in search of gold and jewels. The monument shows a group of indigenous, black, and Paulista adventurers on route to Minas. The Bandeiras Monument sits just outside the park's northern entrance. Another monument in the park is the Obelisk, which commemorates the 1932 revolution for a new Brazilian constitution. Nearby is a wonderful fountain that lights up in colors at night. There are walking and jogging trails, a lagoon, food kiosks, reading areas, a Japanese pavilion, and a planetarium. The Modern Art Museum (MAM) and Museum of Contemporary Art (MAC), which are also inside the park, are covered separately.

## MUSEU DE ARTE MODERNA

The Museu de Arte Moderna (MAM) (tel. 11/5549-9688, noon–6 P.M. Tues., Wed., and Fri., noon–10 P.M. Thurs., and 10 A.M.–6 P.M. Sat. and Sun.) is located in the Ibirapuera park in the Oca building, a dome-shaped structure of modern architectural design. The dome houses a large collection of Brazilian modern art pieces from the late 1800s to the present. The MAM has more than 2,000 pieces, spread around the city in affiliate branches, such as the **MAM Higienópolis** (Av. Higienópolis 698, 10 A.M.–6 P.M. Tue.–Sun.).

## MUSEU DE ARTE CONTEMPORÂNEA

The companion structure to the Oca dome in the Parque Ibirapuera is the Pavilhão da Bienal. This building houses a large part of the vast collection of modern art pieces in the permanent collection of the MAC (tel. 11/3091-3039, 10 A.M.–7 P.M. Tues., Wed., and Fri., 11 A.M.–8 P.M. Thurs., and 10 A.M.–4 P.M. Sat. and Sun.). Adjoining the Pavilhão is a sculpture garden with modern pieces on permanent exhibit. More works in the collection can be seen at the MAC facility in the Cidade Univeritária (Rua da Reitoria 160, 10 A.M.–7 P.M. Tue.–Fri., 10 A.M.–4 P.M. Sat. and Sun.).

## ESTADIO DO MORUMBI

The largest stadium in São Paulo, Morumbi Stadium is home to the state championship soccer matches between the Palmeiras, Corinthians, São Paulo, and Santos teams. Many famous players came from these teams. To see a game here, check the schedules in ticket offices or call BR-Arts (tel. 11/9196-7766), a service that will pick you up at your hotel, take you to the game, and bring you back again, safely and soundly. The stadium is located in the Praça Roberto Gomes Barbosa in Morumbi (tel. 11/3749-8000). Avoid taking public transit to and from the stadium, as the fans get very rowdy and destructive on route.

## FUNDAÇÃO MARIA LUÍSA E OSCAR AMERICANO

Fundação Maria Luísa E Oscar Americano (Av. Morumbi 4077, tel. 11/3742-0077, 11 A.M.–5 P.M. Tue.–Fri., 10 A.M.–5 P.M. Sat. and Sun.) in the Morumbi area is this huge mansion and grounds that make up this Foundation. Inside is a collection of Brazilian art from the period between 1822, with Emperor Dom Pedro I, through 1889, when Brazil became a republic after Emperor Dom Pedro II. There are also many furnishings and documents from the same period.

## ZOO, ZOO SAFARI, AND JARDIM BOTÂNICO

In the far south of the city, a vast green area holds the city's zoos and botanical garden. It's probably worth trying to see two of these in the same trip, perhaps having lunch in the garden with its many green areas, trails, and lagoons. The Jardim Zoológico (Av. Miguel Stefano 4241, Agua Funda, tel. 11/246-0811, 9 A.M.–5 P.M. Tues.–Sun., R$7 for adults) is home to more than 2,000 species of birds, mammals, and reptiles. The Zoo Safari (Av. do Cursino 6338, Agua Funda, tel. 11/6336-2131, 9:30 A.M.–4:30 P.M. Wed.–Sun., R$40 per car with up to five people) has large cats and bears in semi-confined spaces with other species roaming free. Tours take you through open spaces near the animals. The Jardim Botânico (Av. Miguel Stefano 3031, Agua Funda, tel. 11/5073-6300, 9 A.M.–5 P.M. Wed.–Sun., R$2) is rich in green spaces, gardens, greenhouses, and ponds. Numerous species of Brazilian fauna are present with a special highlight on the orchid garden.

## ENTERTAINMENT AND NIGHTLIFE

### Bars and Clubs

Itaim Bibi and Vila Olimpia are two areas very near each other that have the city's most "see and be seen" establishments. This is where young people go to show off their new clothes and cell phones, while sipping an expensive draft beer. The music and dance clubs are large and impersonal and have large consumption minimums, pretty much killing any bar hopping you might want to do. Still, this may be just the club action you're seeking. A few examples include **Boogie** (Rua Alvorada 515 tel. 11/3044-9669, opens at 10 P.M., R$40 in consumption), which plays retro '80s and '90s music. **Disco** (Rua Pro. Atilio Innocenti 160, tel. 11/3078-0404, 11 P.M. until sunrise Thurs.–Sat.) has a mix of music and a consumption minimum of R$60. Other locations include **Club** (Rua Gomes de Carvalho 560,

tel. 11/3842-2820) and **Vinyl** (Rua Gomes de Carvalho 799, tel. 11/3845-8555). All of these are open 11 P.M. until sunrise Thursday–Saturday. You get a good idea of the place via its name. Here are a few more: **E-Muzik** (Rua Lourenço Marques 265, tel. 11/3045-7128), **Ibiza** (Rua Casa do Ator 1169, tel. 11/3045-0388), and **Liquid Lounge** (Av. Helio Pellegrino 801, tel. 11/3849-5014). All are open 11 P.M. until sunrise Thursday–Saturday.

If you just want to have drinks, try **Azucar** (Rua Dr. Mário Ferraz 423, tel. 11/3078-3130, 7 P.M. Mon.–Sat.) is a 1950's Cuban-style bar that's good for meeting people and **All of Jazz** (Rua João Cachoeira 1366, tel. 11/3849-1345) is the area's only jazz bar. Couples of all ages go dance cheek-to-cheek at the **Passatempo** (Rua Jerônimo da Veiga 446, tel. 11/3079-5054, 9 P.M.–5 A.M. Tues.–Sat.) in Itaim Bibi.

The Moema area attracts a slightly more relaxed (read: mature) crowd with its various pubs and restaurants. There is a small *praça* with several food and drink offerings, called the Largo de Moema (also known as the Praça Nossa Sra. Aparecida). There, you'll find some of the town's best restaurant and bar choices, like **Companhia Cervejaria Imperial** (Largo de Moema 76, tel. 11/5056-0207), one of my personal favorites. It's a spacious place with draft beer and a small Museu da Cerveja upstairs showing photos and equipment from the beer industry in Brazil. They also have whiskies, smokes, and a few German food items on the menu. Opens at 11 A.M. until the last person leaves. On the other side of the *praça* is **A Estalagem** (Av. Moema 2, tel. 11/5051-8415, 11–1 A.M. weekdays and until 2:30 A.M. weekends), which is more of a dinner-and-drinks place, but you can just go in for drinks, especially at happy hour. They have a full bar and lots of seating. Also in this *praça* are Chinese, Japanese, and Brazilian restaurants. One of the most popular drinking holes in Moema is **Dona Flor** (Rua Canário 480, tel. 11/5052-5729, from 5 P.M. weekdays and from noon weekends), which is located in a huge, classic building that fills up with crowds all week long.

For music in the Moema area, try the **Bourbon Street Music Club** (Rua das Chanés 127, tel. 11/5095-6100, www.bourbonstreet.com.br, 9 P.M. daily). They have shows every night. On weekends, you should purchase tickets early, either online or by phone. Also **Rock Brasil** (Rua Canário 1274, tel. 11/5042-3838, 10 P.M. until sunrise Thurs.–Sat.) and **Blackmore Rock Bar** (Al. Dos Maracatins 1317, tel. 11/5041-9340) serve up, you guessed it, rock and roll.

Tip: Those attracted to the Moema scene generally go dancing in the Vila Madalena area (Zona Oeste), where there are more bars and many dancing establishments.

## Popular Shows

**Tom Brasil** (Av. Bragança Paulista 1281, tel. 11/5644-9800, tel. 11/2163-2221) in Vila Olimpia is a favorite event among international visitors. Every Wednesday night you can watch a traditional samba show by the samba school Mangueira, complete with drumming ensembles and costumes. It's just like Carnaval in Rio de Janeiro, only safer and in a more controlled environment. **Credicard Hall in Morumbi** (Av. Das Nações Unidas 17955, tel. 11/6846-6010) is another concert hall with live music performances and popular shows. Check monthly guides for current programs.

## ACCOMMODATIONS

**Hilton São Paulo Morumbi** (Av. Das Nações Unidas 12901, tel. 11/6845-0000, www.hilton.com) has luxurious rooms and services available for around R$450–800. In the same area is the **Grand Hyatt São Paulo** (Av. Das Nações Unidas 13301, tel. 11/6838-1234, www.saopaulo.hyatt.com) has rooms for R$520–600. The **Estanplaza Berrini** (Av Eng. Luiz Carlos Berrini 853, tel. 11/5509-8900, www.estanplaza.com.br) has rooms for R$260 single and R$395 double. **Best Western Brooklin** (Rua Princesa Isabel 340, tel. 08 00/153-733, www.fresp.com) goes for R$230 single and R$265 double.

In Moema, you can try the **M Quality Moema** (Av. Rouxinol 57, tel. 11/3054-6100, www.atlantica-hotels.com) for around R$120 on weekends and R$160 during the week, or the **Blue Tree Towers Ibirapuera** (Av. Ibirapuera 2577, tel. 11/5091-1700, ww.bluetree.com.br) with rooms for R$120–250. The **M Sofitel São Paulo** (Rua Sena Madureira 1355, tel. 11/5574-1100, www.accorhotels.com, R$700) is on the southeast corner of the Parque Ibirapuera with a luxurious interior and many amenities. More economic options include the **Novotel São Paulo Ibirapuera** (Rua Sena Madureira 1355, tel. 11/5574-9099, www.accorhotels.com, R$180–225) connected to the Sofitel and one of the many Parthenon hotels in Moema, Itaim Bibi, and Vila Olimpia. These are always reliable and a good value. Check www.accorhtels.com for details. The **Campobelo Plaza** (Rua Demóstenes 748, tel. 11/5536-9922, www.campobeloplaza.com.br) has rooms for R$160 single and R$190 double.

## FOOD

### Brazilian

**M Dona Lucinha** (Avenida dos Xibarás 399, tel. 11/5051-2050, noon–3 P.M. and 8–11 P.M. Tues.–Sat., noon–4:30 P.M. Sun.) opened her third country-cooking restaurant in Moema after the first two (in Belo Horizonte and the São Paulo Jardins area) were smashing successes. Comida Mineira is hearty and savory with plenty of variety. Most dishes are cooked in clay or brass pots and you serve yourself *a vontage* (as much as you like). Meals are R$35 for dinner, R$25 for lunch. **Varanda Grill** (Rua General Mena Barreto 793, tel. 11/3887-8870, noon–3 P.M. and 7–11:30 P.M. Tues.–Fri., noon–midnight Sat., noon–6 P.M. Sun.) in Itaim Bibi serves beef in three styles: American, Brazilian, and Argentinean. You can get a New York porterhouse steak cooked exactly as you like or try other cuts. Many dishes are enough for two. Closed for dinner on Sundays. Prices run R$30–60. For a Brazilian seafood experience, try **Badejo** (Al. Dos Jurupis 813, tel. 11/5055-0238, noon–3 P.M. and 6 P.M.–midnight Tues.–Fri., noon–midnight Sat., noon–6 P.M. Sun.) in Moema, which serves its specialty, *moqueca,* a sort of fish stew, along with a variety of fish plates—meals go for around R$70.

## Italian

A most interesting modern Italian spot is **Supra** (Rua Araçari 260, tel. 11/3071-1818, noon–3 P.M. and 7:30 P.M.–midnight Tues.–Fri., 7:30 P.M.–1 A.M. Sat., noon–5 P.M. Sun.) in Itaim Bibi. Chef Mauro combines traditional cooking with creative touches. Meals end with a cheese plate—now that's civilized! Prices are around R$50 per person. Another artsy Italian restaurant is **Bellalluna** (Rua Inhambu 1318, tel. 11/5041-3939, 6 P.M.–1 A.M.) in Moema, which has a similar combination of modern and traditional cooking, like their salmon risotto with mango flambé and a host of thin-crust pizzas. Meals are about R$45. For a late-night or early-morning meal in Moema, try **Vila Conte 24 Horas** (Avenida Macuco 579, tel. 11/5054-0166). They serve salads, pastas, meat, and fish dishes along with some interesting inventions—for around R$30. The breakfast buffet is 6–10 A.M. for R$12.

## Japanese

There are almost as many Japanese restaurants in the Zona Sul as in the Japanese district of Liberdade, and some of the best are south of center, like **Ν Nakombi** (Rua Peketita 170, tel. 11/3845-9911, noon–3 P.M. and 7 P.M.–2 A.M. Mon.–Fri., noon–2 A.M. Sat., noon–midnight Sun.), a hip sushi spot, created by sushi chef Ignacio Ito, who serves numerous combinations of tuna and salmon, along with other varieties. Prices range from $50–100. **Shimo** (Rua Jerônimo da Veiga 74, tel. 11/3167-2222, noon–3 P.M. and 7 P.M.–midnight Mon.–Fri., 7 P.M.–1 A.M. Sat. and Sun.) in Itaim Bibi is a place for advanced sushi eaters, as the sushi chef offers numerous imported treats, along with such things as giant squid and red snapper. Expect meals from R$60–150. For sushi with art and music in a unique décor, try **JAM Warehouse** (Rua Lopes Neto 308, tel. 11/3079-4259, noon–3 P.M. and 7 P.M.–1 A.M. Mon.–Fri., 7 P.M.–1:30 A.M. Sat. and Sun.). They have live music almost all the

time and serve sushi individually or in combinations—from R$25–150.

## Lanchonetes and Casual

At **Deli Diet** (Rua Jerônimo da Veiga 457, tel. 11/3168-4422, noon–3:30 P.M. Mon.–Fri., noon–5 P.M. Sat. and Sun.) in Itaim Bibi, you'll find healthy, low-cal salads of all types, combining chicken and tropical fruits in amazing ways—R$20 per person. **Trio** (Rua Gomes de Carvalho 1759, tel. 11/3845-0979, noon–3:30 P.M. Mon.–Fri., noon–5 P.M. Sun.) is another lunch buffet in a spacious setting with a variety of salads and hot dishes. Meals cost about R$30 per person.

## Pizza

The only thing that Paulistas consume more than beer is pizza and some of the best pizza joints are in the South Zone. **Ν Bráz** (Rua Graúna 125, tel. 11/5561-1736, 6:30 P.M.–midnight Mon.–Thu., 6:30 P.M.–1:30 A.M. Fri. and Sat.) in Moema creates its combinations with the freshest of ingredients. Try the Margherita (mozzarella with tomato and fresh basil). Pizzas range from R$20–40. Another Moema pizza house is **Estação Vila Moema** (Rua Jacutinga 187, tel. 11/5055-7077, 5 P.M.–midnight Mon.–Thu., 5 P.M.–1:30 A.M. Fri. and Sat.), which is located in a fabulous building with great seating possibilities. Pizzas are thin crusted with a variety of toppings and go for around R$35. Finally, **Grappa Pizza Burger** (Rua Leopoldo Couto de Magalhães Júnior 710, tel. 11/3071-0391, 6 P.M.–midnight Tue.–Sun.) in Itaim Bibi serves several types of grappa along with its pizza combinations. They also serve hamburgers and sandwiches made with pizza dough (and why not?). Meals are around R$38.

## Other International

An excellent Arabic experience is **Ammoul** (Al. Dos Arapanés 539, tel. 11/5051-1662, noon–3 P.M. and 7–11 P.M. Mon.–Fri., noon–11 P.M. Sat., noon–5 P.M. Sun.) in Moema. They serve inventive Lebanese dishes, like their Esfiha sandwich filled with meat, sesame paste, and pomegranate juice. A meal will set you back

## ESCAPES FROM SÃO PAULO

To get away from the city scene for a weekend, São Paulo residents have several options just a few hours from the city. Here are some of their favorite escapes.

**Brotas:** Lying in the São Paulo countryside about 250 kilometers northwest of the city, Brotas is the most popular nature escape for Paulistas of all ages, especially young singles who flock to the area every sunny weekend and holiday. Highlights include numerous rivers and waterfalls and the many adventure sports available in the area, including white-water rafting, hang gliding, paragliding, rappelling, cascading, and ropes courses (which Brazilians call *arvorismo*). The center of town offers great food and nightlife options, and there are numerous hotels and *pousadas*, but they fill up fast on holidays, so plan ahead. Buses leave from the Barra Funda bus station in São Paulo (11/3612-1717) and cost around R$25. The trip takes four hours. For a place to stay, check out the **Pousada Villa da Serra** (Rua Nabor Marques 497, 14/3656-1092, www.pousadavilladaserra.com.br) and the **Estalagem Quinta das Cachoeiras** (Rua João Rebecca 225, 14/3653-2497, www.quintadascachoeiras.com.br). The best way to go is with a packaged tour by an agency in the city.

**Campos do Jordão:** More than a million visitors from São Paulo and Rio cram into this quaint Swiss village during the peak month of July, when the **Festival de Inverno** (Winter Festival) is in full swing. The town's many fine restaurants and beer gardens are packed and the festival brings music, dance, and folkloric presentations to the streets and stages of town. One of the most active spots is the **Choperia Baden** (Rua Djalma Forjaz 93) in the center of town, with several types of fresh-brewed beers. Besides eating, drinking, and enjoying the Swiss architecture and culture (don't miss the **Palácio Boa Vista**), you can play golf, go on horseback rides, hike up canyons, and participate in ropes courses. You can also hike up to the **Pedra do Baú** for a wonderful view or ride a bike around town to visit the many shops. You can rent a bike at the **Pedal Shop** (Av. Brasil 108, Capivari, 12/3663-6388). The best time to go is just after the peak season, in August, when crowds disperse and prices go back to normal (which is still high for Brazil). For a place to stay, check out the **Krishna Shakti Ashram** (Estrada da Minalba, 12/263-3168), which is part ashram and part inn. You can also try **Matsubara** (Rua Prof. José Paulo 80, 12/3263-3177). R$380 standard double, includes breakfast and dinner. Prices vary depending on the season, so call first to confirm. Note: Bring warm clothes when visiting in the winter.

**Monte Verde:** A smaller and more rustic version of Campos do Jordão, Monte Verde lies only 65 kilometers from Campos do Jordão and 165 from São Paulo. Most of the streets in town are dirt roads and the activities are much more rural: horseback rides, hikes, and adventure sports. You can also take a plane ride over the hills. Hotels and restaurants are made in the Swiss and German styles and you'll find the crowds and prices here a lot more bearable. Try the **Pousada Cantinho da Raposa** (Rua Represa Nova 488, 35/3438-1540) or **Nico on the Hill** (Av. das Montanhas 2440, 35/3438-1730). For more info, check the website www.monteverde.art.br.

São Paulo City

---

about R$30 per person. **Tantra** (Rua Chilon 364, tel. 11/3846-7112, noon–3 P.M. and 6 P.M.–midnight) in Vila Olimpia offers a true Mongolian barbecue in an Indonesian bungalow décor. You choose your own meats and veggie items and present it to the chef, who whips it up on the Mongolian grill, all for only R$35 per person. Menu items are also available, like salmon cooked in banana leaves and other tasties. At **Brooklyn** (Rua Baltazar Fernandes 54, tel. 11/5533-4999, 8 P.M.–1 A.M. Mon.–Sat.) in the Brooklin neighborhood, you get dinner and a show, with the waiters singing Broadway tunes between service. The food is contemporary fusion with such dishes as shrimp risotto with a clove cashew sauce and roasted onion stuffed with meat and squash with sweet and sour beets. Prices are in the R$40–75 range. If you can't make it all the way to Brooklin, try **Ruella** (Rua João Cochoeira

São Paulo City

1507, tel. 11/3842-7177, noon–3:30 P.M. and 8 P.M.–1 A.M. Mon.–Fri., 1 P.M.–2 A.M. Sat., 1–5 P.M. Sun.) in Vila Olimpia. They have a contemporary French menu with creative conjurings, along with classics like medallion de foie gras. Meals run around R$40–75.

**Azur** (Rua Cr. Mário Ferraz 490, tel. 11/3167-0100, 6 P.M.–2 A.M. Mon.–Sat. and noon–5 P.M. Sun.) is a bar and Spanish restaurant in the Itaim Bibi area. They have various tapas, including spiced potatoes or goat cheese, served generally as appetizers. Entrees focus on paella (chicken, seafood, or mixed), which serve two. Meals are R$60–85 with an appetizer.

## INFORMATION AND SERVICES

There are no formal information posts in the Zona Sul for foreign visitors. The area is mostly geared toward Brazilian visitors or business travelers. Check at major hotels for maps and guides.

## GETTING THERE AND AROUND

You'll find it a bit more difficult to get to the Zona Sul than other areas of São Paulo because of its lack of metro access. The best thing to do is take a taxi from the Paulista area, which will cost around R$15 to Moema and R$25 to Itaim Bibi. It's farther than it looks on the map, so don't try walking, and you probably won't like the city buses that cut through Moema, either—they take forever and are always fighting traffic. The light blue metro line, which stops in Vila Olimpia, is accessible only from the distant Barra Funda station (red line).

# Other Neighborhoods

## PINHEIROS

Pinheiros is a sort of extension of the Paulista area, but perhaps a bit less glamorous. It's more like a real neighborhood where people actually live. For visitors, Pinheiros is a destination for good restaurants at prices that beat the Paulista area hands down. One of my favorites is **Rosmarino** (Rua Henrique Monteiro 44, tel. 11/3819-3897, www.rosmarino.com.br, 6:30 P.M.–midnight), in a wonderful backyard garden setting, with well-appointed tables reminiscent of restaurants in San Francisco and Paris. The owner/chef has an excellent menu with pastas, fish, and chicken dishes, as well as a small but good wine list and excellent desserts. A meal costs around R$45 per person. Another Italian offering is **Palliano Ristorante** (Rua Lisboa 284, tel. 11/3088-4376, noon–3:30 P.M. Mon.–Fri., noon–5 P.M. Sat.), with daily specials featuring modern Italian dishes and desserts at very reasonable prices (R$20–40).

In Pinheiros, you'll find one of São Paulo's most celebrated Japanese restaurants, **Jun Sakamoto** (Rua Lisboa 55, tel. 11/3088-6019, 6 P.M.–1 A.M. Mon.–Sat.). At Jun, you have to reserve a seat at the sushi bar as there are only eight and they are always in demand. At the bar, you will be obligated to have the chef's choices (a sort of sampler that runs around R$150), which will span the spectrum of tastes and textures. At the tables, you can order normally from the menu. Dinner should cost you around R$120 minimum. If you're tired of the same ol' pizza combinations, try **I Vitelloni** (Rua Conde Silvio Alvares, tel. 11/3813-1588, 7 P.M.–midnight Tue.–Sun.), which conjures such pizzas as asparagus with *presunto* (prosciutto) and shiitake mushrooms with mascarpone and garlic. Meals go for R$35. For a taste of Bahia in São Paulo, try **Espírito Capixaba** (Rua Francisco Leitão 57, tel. 11/3062-6566, noon–3 P.M. and 6:30–11 P.M. Tue.–Sat., noon–6 P.M. Sun.), which serves fish soups and *moqueca* (fish stew) Bahian style. Expect to pay R$70 for two people.

Pinheiros is more endowed with restaurants than with bars and clubs, but there are a few good options to check out after dinner. **Ampgalaxy** (Rua Fradique Coutinho 352, tel.

11/3062-5850, noon–sunrise) is one of the city's most happening dance clubs, sporting electronic music, house, disco, and techno in a special mixture of dance club, bar, and fashion boutique. The clientele is a fashion-savvy, retro-techno punk set, if one were to put a label on it. International DJs are known to frequent the place. There's a R$10 entry fee with a R$20 consumption minimum. **Finnegan's** (Rua Cristiano Viana 358, tel. 11/3062-3232, 6 P.M.–2 A.M. Mon.–Sat., 7 P.M.–1 A.M. Sun.) is the best place for a Guinness beer and Irish Whiskey and **Teta** (Rua Cardeal Arcoverde 1265, tel. 11/3031-1641, 4 P.M. Mon.–Sat.) is the place for bossa nova and jazz and German draft beer.

Although Pinheiros is well located between Vila Madalena and the Paulista areas, it has, unfortunately, almost no decent hotels. You're best bet is to seek a hotel in the Paulista area or downtown. Pinheiros is conveniently located below the Clínicas metro station, where you can get off the metro and catch a taxi to your favorite restaurant.

## VILA MADALENA

In the 1970s, Vila Madalena became crowded with students and artists, mostly due to the nearby campus of the University of São Paulo. To this day, the neighborhood is known for attracting the city's hippie/bohemian crowd and the local art ateliers, bars, and restaurants reflect this. Vila Madalena is one of the city's most popular nightlife centers, with numerous bars and restaurants attracting a somewhat artistic, alternative crowd.

At night you can walk up and down the streets to find the place that suits you. Some suggestions: **Astor** (Rua Delfina 163, tel. 11/3815-1364, 6 P.M.–3 A.M. Mon.–Thu., noon–4 P.M. Fri. and Sat., noon–7 P.M. Sun.) for a '50s-style décor with food and drinks. **Bar do Sacha** (Rua Original 89, tel. 11/3815-7665, noon–1 A.M. daily) is a simple bar with a good, upbeat vibe. **Empanadas** (Rua Wisard 489, tel. 11/3032-2116, noon–1 A.M. Mon.–Thu., noon–3 A.M. Fri. and Sat.) is another informal bar that is always crowded, with most customers ordering the tasty empanadas. **Samba** (Rua Fidalga 308, tel. 11/3819-4619, noon–2 A.M. Tue.–Sat., 5 P.M.–2 A.M. Sun., noon–3 P.M. Mon.) has live samba music at night and during the day on Saturdays in a quaint and informal setup. Finally, tucked away in a side alley is **Tocador de Bolacha** (Rua Patrizal 72, tel. 11/3815-7639, 5 P.M.–midnight Tue.–Sat.) off Rua Harmonia. The owner spins oldies and jazz tunes on an antique juke box for the few tables full of customers eating and drinking inside. A great find.

There are just as many options for food. **M Matterello** (Rua Fidalga 120, tel. 11/3813-0452, noon–3 P.M. and 7 P.M.–midnight) is a restaurant with a lot of character. It's decorated with recycled materials in a semi-Gothic style. They serve fresh pasta dishes and you can view every recipe. Their wine list has more than 500 labels from R$20–200. Meals cost R$25 per person. For pizza, try the popular **D'Antigona** (Rua Aspicuelta 713, tel. 11/3812-6402, 5 P.M.–midnight Mon.–Sat., 5 P.M.–2 A.M. Fri. and Sat.), which heats up your pie in an iron pan in a wood-burning oven to achieve a fresh and crunchy pizza. Barbecued meats are a specialty of the southern regions of Brazil (influenced by Argentina) and **Leôncio** (Rua Girassol 284, tel. 11/3812-7309, 11:30 A.M.–11:30 P.M. Tue.–Fri., 11:30 A.M.–6 P.M. Sat. and Sun.) is in that southern tradition, with skewers of meat leaning against an open fire. It's an excellent choice for carnivorous types. Prices are around R$40. A natural foods restaurant in the area is **Alternativa** (Rua Fradique Coutinho 910, tel. 11/3816-0706, noon–4 P.M. daily), which has three lunch choices, all with brown rice and lentils. They use soy milk in dishes and desserts, including their homemade ice cream. Expect to pay around R$18.

You can get to Vila Madalena by metro, stopping at the Vila Madalena station, the last stop on the green line. From there, you can walk to the nucleus of the action, which mostly takes place at night. A taxi back to the Paulista area will cost about R$8 and to downtown about R$15.

## ZONA NORTE

At the farthest tip of the blue line metro (at the Tucuruvi station) is the distant Zona Norte of São Paulo. From the station, you can walk down Avenida Luiz Dumont Villares, past numerous restaurants and bars to the principal hotel in the area, the Parthenon Nortel. Within walking distance from the Nortel (farther away from the metro) is the area's principal daytime diversion, the Shopping Center Norte, with hundreds of shops, restaurants, cafés, and playgrounds to keep you occupied. The Zona Norte is also home to the largest city park in South America, the Ortoflorestal Parque, which has many species of flora and fauna, including wild monkeys.

Although a few kilometers from downtown São Paulo, the **Parthenon Nortel** (Av. Luiz Dumont Villares 400, tel. 11/6972-8111, www.accorhotels.com) is an excellent place to stay, especially on weekends when heavy discounts apply and local pubs are hopping with crowds. Even Paulistas from other parts of the city spend the night here after partying at nearby pubs (the breakfast buffet is fabulous after a night on the town). During the week, the hotel serves its business customers, who are in the Zona Norte participating in a convention at one of the convention centers nearby. The hotel has two pools, two saunas, two gyms, a jogging track, in-room Internet connections, a restaurant, bar, and meeting facilities. They also provide a van to and from the shopping and convention centers. Standard rooms are R$129 single, R$142 double and R$87 on weekends. Suite with kitchen is R$117 single, R$128 double and R$97 on weekends. Breakfast is included.

Along Avenida Luiz Dumont Villares, you'll find numerous dining and drinking options, from sidewalk snack stands to classy restaurants. You can walk down the street at around 9 P.M. and check out the options. Some places to note include **Adega Original** and **Taberna,** which have inviting atmospheres and good-looking crowds. A few kilometers from this area is the famous beer bar **Ⓜ Frangó** (Largo da Matriz 168, tel. 11/3932-4818, 11 A.M.–midnight Tue.–Sun.), which offers a sampling of numerous international beers that are difficult to find in Brazil. It's always crowded and fun.

## BRÁS

Brás has long been São Paulo's principal shopping area, both for wholesale and retail clothing and textile items. Today, the face of Brás is changing slightly with the arrival of new restaurants, principally Japanese. If you're up for a shopping adventure, then Brás holds a lot of promise and great deals—just be sure to shop around for the best stores with quality goods, as there are numerous low-end stores with questionable quality. A few to check out include **Lemier Jeans** (Rua Maria Marcolina 513, tel. 11/6291-9677, 9 A.M.–7 P.M. Mon.–Fri., 9 A.M.–2 P.M. Sat. and Sun.), which is wholesale-only with a minimum of 12 items paid in cash (ask for the cash, *a vista,* discount). **Store-tex Jeans** (Rua Maria Marcolina 418, tel. 11/6694-1127, 9 A.M.–7 P.M. Mon.–Fri., 9 A.M.–2 P.M. Sat. and Sun.) and **Litani** (Rua Maria Marcolina 525, tel. 11/6694-1925, 9 A.M.–7 P.M. Mon.–Fri., 9 A.M.–2 P.M. Sat. and Sun.) offer wholesale and retail prices and cash discounts. Pull plenty of cash from the ATM before leaving for Brás, take one credit card (about half of the stores accept cards), and leave everything else at the hotel.

To get to Brás, take the red line metro to the Brás station. Follow the crowds out of the station, past the trains, and out the building to the right. Make your way through the tents and food stands to Rua Maria Marcolina (second left), where you turn left and keep walking. Don't let yourself get too flustered or distracted by the intensity of this area. Just walk calmly and keep your eyes open. Getting back to the metro is a bit of a trick, because you have to walk all the way around the station to the entrance on the other side, traversing some pretty funky territory. I suggest that you catch a cab back to the station. From the shopping area, a cab should cost about R$8.

For a lunch break in the Brás area, try Rua Oriente 500 in the upstairs food court. There is a good self-service option there.

## INSTITUTO BUTANTÃ

Not far from Pinheiros (a bit farther west and across the river) is the **Instituto Butantã** (Av. Vital Brasil 1500, tel. 11/3726-7222, 9 A.M.– 5 P.M. Tue.–Sun.), which attracts a large number of visitors from all over the world. The Butantã Institute is principally a center for venom and anti-venom research and is recognized internationally as a principal laboratory in the field. The Institute allows visits and hosts tours of its facilities, which focus on snakes and serpents.

## EMBU DAS ARTES

If you don't have a chance to see Minas Gerais on your visit to Brazil, then Embu das Artes, about 30 minutes from São Paulo makes a great alternative. This artist enclave began growing in popularity in the mid-1990s and is now a popular tourist attraction outside of São Paulo. Many of the galleries in Embu have locations in Minas Gerais (generally in Tiradentes or São João del Rei), so you know you're getting authentic Mineiro arts and crafts. Some specialties include wood paintings and sculptures, terra cotta figurines, and the famous *namoradeiras* (busts of love-struck women made to sit in a window sill, facing outward toward the street). You can walk around the quaint streets, lined with buildings from the 18th and 19th centuries, including the Church of Rosário, one of the Jesuit structures in the São Paulo area. On

© CHRISTOPHER VAN BUREN

*namoradeiras* **waiting in the window in Embu das Artes**

weekends, there is an outdoor arts and crafts fair in addition to the many permanent shops in the central area. There are plenty of restaurants; one good option is **O Garimpo** (Rua da Matriz 136, tel. 11/4704-6344, call for hours), with a varied menu. You can take an excursion to the Cidade das Abelhas to see a bee farm and its honey production facilities. Just check in at the tourist information office in the center of town for details on vans leaving for this site.

# São Paulo Coast to Rio

It may seem ironic that between Brazil's two largest and most industrial cities is a coastline of unparalleled beauty and variety with some of Brazil's finest beaches. Spanning the 429 kilometers of coastline are beaches and tropical islands, both urbanized and semi-deserted. Some areas are practically unknown and untouched—such as the far side of Ilha Grande or the beaches north of Ubatuba—and stand in sharp contrast to the major metropolitan areas nearby. This is where the bustle of the city comes to a screeching halt. Most will find that the beaches get prettier the closer you get to Rio, with a coastline that is clear and blue-green. If you're into water sports or diving, there are many areas for both along the way.

Highlights along this stretch of coastline include the islands and beaches of Ubatuba, the Paraty Bay, and Ilha Grande. In the morning at Ubatuba, visitors distribute themselves among the many different beaches to the north and south of town, depending on their particular mood that day. There's everything from quiet sandy inlets to party beaches to remote and semi-deserted areas that are excellent for scuba diving and long walks on the sand.

# **M**ust-Sees

**M Ilhabela's Outer Beaches:** The second largest island off the coast of southeastern Brazil, Ilhabela offers more than 45 kilometers of beaches with a charming village center. Spend the day on **Jabaquara** or **Praia da Fome**, and be sure to check out the waterfalls nearby (page 144).

**M Ilha Anchieta:** Travelers who see the Paraty Bay for the first time stand in awe of the incredible tropical beauty here. The bay is spotted with dozens of islands and pristine beaches, and Ilha Anchieta is one of the nicest (page 147).

**M Ubatuba's Northern Coastline:** Unknown to most foreign travelers, the coastline around Ubatuba has some of the finest beaches and diving spots in the nation and Praia Lázaro is one of its best examples, with charming beach kiosks under the shade of tropical trees—an excellent beach for swimming and sunbathing (page 148).

© CHRISTOPHER VAN BUREN

Paraty Bay

**M Paraty's Centro Histórico:** In the 1700s, Paraty was the most important port in the southern hemisphere. Loads of slaves and supplies from Europe came in, while tons of gold and precious stones went out. Today, the town is an open-air museum of colonial architecture (page 155).

**M Trindade:** The village of Trindade, 30 kilometers south of Paraty, is famous among surfers. Besides having some of the most beautiful beaches in the region, with clear, blue-green water, it also has a small beach where the waves get up to five meters high (page 158).

**M Lopes Mendes:** Are you into semi-deserted beaches with crystal-blue waters on the edges of a tropical island? Lopes Mendes beach is a hike, but the tropical surroundings along the trail make for an exciting journey (page 166).

**SÃO PAULO COAST TO RIO**

Belo Horizonte

Paraty's Centro Histórico

Trindade

Ubatuba's Northern Coastline

São Paulo

Lopes Mendes

Ilha Anchieta

Ilhabela's Outer Beaches

ATLANTIC OCEAN

São Paulo Coast to Rio

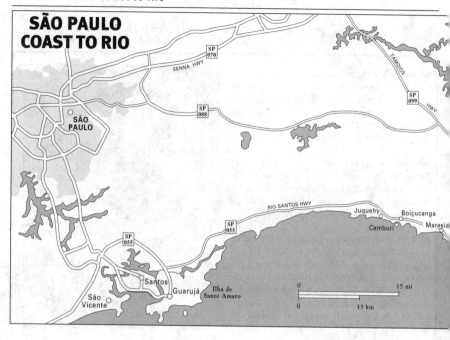

Similarly, Paraty offers a variety of beaches north and south of the main village. In this case, the village is a historical town from the Brazilian gold cycle of the 1700s. Its churches and monuments line the stoney streets of the Centro Histórico and light up and night with restaurants and bars. The water here is especially warm and bright green and the beaches are calm and shady. Ilha Grande, the largest island off the coast of Brazil, offers some of the most beautiful beaches in the country and many that require long hikes or boat trips to reach. The scuba diving options around the island are among the best on the São Paulo coast.

## PLANNING YOUR TIME

The trip between Rio and São Paulo has many potential stops along the way. You can try to hit a lot of these spots or focus on just a few. A good amount of time to plan for this journey is 10–14 days, although you can do it in 6 or 7 if you just hit the hottest spots. If you rent

a car, you can make some short stops to get to know the more remote beaches along the way. Driving is generally simple and straightforward (once you get out of the city) and if you take it easy on the windy coastal roads, you won't have a single problem. It's definitely the recommended way to see this part of the coast. There are also buses that will take you from one major point to the next or you can join a packaged tour departing from one of the big cities, which offer their own transportation options. Traveling by bus, you should probably stick to a few major points to enjoy them to the fullest. Going north from São Paulo, the most interesting points include **Ilhabela, Ubatuba, Paraty,** and **Ilha Grande,** with the last two being the best of all. Each of these is worth 3–4 days of exploration. If you have only 7–10 days, then don't even bother with the rest.

The entire coastline of Brazil has a peak period in the summer (December–February) when prices nearly double and crowds quadruple. Reservations are recommended dur-

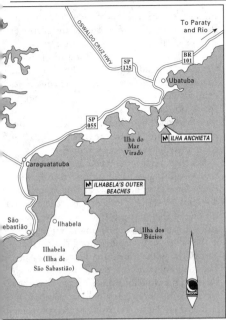

© AVALON TRAVEL PUBLISHING, INC.

a peak month with peak-season prices due to Brazilian and international holidays. Temperatures range from 15°C in the winter months (June–August) to 40°C during the summer. At around 25°C, the water temperature is not as warm as that of the northeast beaches (Salvador, Natal, or Fortaleza for example), but can hardly be considered cold. The area between Rio and São Paulo is especially affected by Brazilian holidays, since these beaches are frequented by residents of the two big cities. Any sunny weekend could bring crowds to the more popular beaches and the peak season of December–February brings higher prices and packed hotels, in spite of the fact that this is the beginning of the rainy season, which lasts until around April.

Note: A great travel itinerary for this region is detailed in *Southeast Coast* in the *Discover Brazil* chapter. Also, the agency **EasyGoing** (Rua Cristiano Viana 1182, tel. 11/3801-9540, www.easygoing.com.br) in São Paulo offers packages to Guarajá, São Sebastião, Ilhabela, and all over this part of the coast, with English-speaking guides, generally leaving from São Paulo. They have a trip called the Brazilian Ride that goes from São Paulo to Rio de Janeiro in eight days, covering the two cities plus Ilhabela and Paraty. Call or email them to discuss their options.

ing this period, or, better yet, move your trip up a month to hit the beginning of the season, when the beaches are not crowded and the weather is warm and clear. September–November are great months to visit. Winter months can be cold and rainy. Nevertheless, July is still

# Guarujá

One hour from São Paulo by car, Guarujá is a small island that parallels the coast for about 20 kilometers. The far side of the island was once a Paulista beach haven, where the middle and upper-classes from the city would go for the weekend, giving them a kind of Rio de Janeiro experience right in São Paulo. After the secret of Guarujá got out, the place became over-crowded, over-built, and generally lost its edge. As is all too common on the Brazilian coastline, when one location starts going downhill, the crowd moves up or down the coast to develop another location. In this case, the mid-

dle class went north to Maresias and Buzios. What's left behind in Guarujá is a mixture of urbanized and private beaches, boardwalks, and boat harbors, not completely without redeeming qualities. If you know where to go, you can find great beaches, boat trips, and shops in which to pass your time—all within a day's trip from São Paulo.

Like all beaches along the coast from São Paulo to Rio, Guarujá gets crowded in the summer (December–January), on weekends, and during holidays. Because of its proximity to both Santos and São Paulo, Guarujá is pretty much crowded all the time and unbearable on summer weekends. Most of the beaches attract a young, surfer-type crowd and some are places just to see and be seen, or for, as Brazilians say, *paqueta* (flirting). Remember that prices go up during peak season, although most people don't spend the night in Guarujá anyway, so hotel prices are usually unimportant.

## THE TOWN

Originaly the home of indigenous people, the Island of Santo Amaro as it was originally known was chosen by the Jesuits as a great site to set up shop and start converting the native peoples. It was a small base of operation in the New World. They set up a couple of chapels and went to work on the natives. But the plight of the Jesuits in São Paulo was rather troublesome and the island remained relatively unoccupied until the 1800s, when it was used as a site for military bases. It also became a center for whaling activities that were flourishing on the Brazilian coastline in the mid-1800s. At the end of the 19th century, a commercial interest thought the island would make a great Rio de Janeiro for Paulistas and they got together with American companies to build a hotel, casino, and a few dozen upscale homes to get the dice rolling, as it were. The project was fairly successful and the village of Guarujá turned into a sort of Riviera of the Paulista coast. Most passengers came from the port at Santos, a port city that was then experiencing an enormous boom due to the coffee trade (to this day, Santos is the busiest commercial port in the world). Today, the town of Guarujá is the central meeting place for those visiting the island. Young Brazilians frequent the bars and restaurants of the *vila* to see and be seen by their counterparts, particularly on the appropriately-named Rua Rio de Janeiro.

## THE BEACHES

All of the beaches around the city of Guarujá (the *vila*) are urbanized and crowded during the summer. There are boat excursions from there to some of the other beaches around the island (although most boats depart from Praia Perequé), as well as water sports and plenty of surfing. This goes for Praia da Enseada, Pitangueiras, Astúrias, and Praia do Tombo. **Praia da Enseada** is the largest beach on the island and is not as good for surfers due to its calm waters. Instead, the beach is used for all types of other water sports. You can swim in these waters without worry and there are many restaurants and bars on the shore to keep you company when you come up for air.

Beaches north of the *vila* are more popular for sunning and swimming, starting with **Praia Sorocotuba,** which is a tiny beach that does not get quite as crowded as some others. It's one of the prettiest beaches on the island and you have to descend a small trail to get to it. The remaining beaches along the northern part of the island are mostly fenced-in by private condominiums that restrict access through their property. That simply means that they are accessible most easily by boat because entering by land means crossing private property to get to the beach (Brazilian beaches cannot be owned, but the land up to the beach can be, thus blocking access except by boat). The beaches of **São Pedro, Iporanga,** and **Praia Branca** are a few highlights on the north coast. They offer semi-private, semi-deserted settings, but are popular for surfing in the peak season. If you have a car, you can usually enter by land via one of the condominiums (private communities), which allow a number of visitors to cross through every day. It's their way of demonstrating that they are not restricting access to the beach, which they technically don't own. Just drive out the Estrada do Pernambuco toward the tip of the island and watch for beach signs. You may have to chat with a gate guard to let you through to the beaches. It's unlikely that you'll have any problems getting through. At the end of the Estrada, near the ferryboat to Bertioga, there is a trail that leads back to Praia Branca, avoiding all entry restrictions. It takes about 15 minutes, it's easy to find, and is very nice.

The other way to the private beaches is to hire a boat and enter by sea. Boats leave from

Praia Perequé, where there is also a tourist information center. Try Marcus (tel. 13/9712-1904), who can take you all around the island or just to one of the beaches for an extended stay. He speaks some English and charges about R$20 per hour or R$80 for a day.

## ACQUA MUNDO

You can see more than 700 types of marine animals, fish, and alligators at Acqua Mundo (Av. Miguel Stéfano 2001, Praia da Enseada, tel. 13/3351-8793, 10 A.M.–8 P.M. Mon. and Thurs., 10 A.M.–midnight Sat., and 10 A.M.– 11 P.M. Sun.), the largest marine aquarium in South America. They have shark tanks, penguin habitats, sea turtles, and hundreds of species of fish. Their largest tank, which hold 900,000 liters of salt water, has an entire underwater world of sharks, rays, and many plant species.

## SHOPPING

There is a *feira de artesanato* (arts and crafts fair) at Pitangueiras Beach. It's a warehouse full of clothing and crafts that operates 4– 10 P.M. Thursday–Tuesday. It also contains snack stands and places to sit and rest your feet. Not to be outdone, the arts and crafts fair at Praia de Astúrias, just a few kilometers away, has its own selection of goodies and is open 2– 11 P.M. Thursday–Tuesday.

## ACCOMMODATIONS

Most people don't stay in Guarujá (unless they have a private beach condo), but return to São Paulo at the end of the day, fighting the traffic the entire way. Nevertheless, if you're set on spending the night on the island, you can try

**Delphin** (Av. Miguel Stéfano 1295, Praia da Enseada, tel. 13/3386-2112, www.delphinhotel.com.br, R$185). They have a pool, bar, restaurant, and beach service. Rooms are old, but clean and have air, TV, and phone. Also, **Canto da Enseada** (Rua São Paulo 132, Praia da Enseada, tel. 13/3392-2984) costs around R$120.

## FOOD AND ENTERTAINMENT

The most active area for bars and nightlife activities is Rua Rio de Janeiro in the *vila*, but you'll also find plenty going on around the urban beaches near the *vila*, including outdoor café/bars and even a few discotheques. Look for **The Phoenix** (Av. Miguel Stéfano 1087, Praia da Enseada, tel. 13/3355-4192, after midnight until sunrise). You can find great seafood at **Rufino's** (Av. Miguel Stéfano 4795, Praia da Enseada, tel. 13/3351-5771, lunch and dinner daily) and **Dalmo o Bárbaro** (Estr. De Pernambuco Km 14.5, Praia do Pereque, tel. 13/3351-9298, lunch and dinner daily) two well-known establishments on the island.

## GETTING THERE

You can catch a bus out to Guarujá from the Tietê bus station in São Paulo. Check the Ultra line, which leaves daily 5:30 A.M.–9:30 P.M. You can also take a ferryboat from Ponta da Praia in Santos.

## GETTING AROUND

The Perequé bus goes north from the *vila* or any of the urban beaches to Praia Perequé every 20 minutes. From there, you can take a boat up to the northern beaches, or catch the Bertioga bus going north.

# São Sebastião

The area called São Sebastião is a large municipality that stretches over 45 kilometers of beach with the city of the same name at the top. Getting from one end of this county to the other takes about an hour by car, as the road is windy and hilly. The city of São Sebastião is an industrial and commercial center with a small historical center near the ocean. As you come up the coast from São Paulo, you'll pass numerous fishing or surfing villages nestled in the inlets along the coast. If you're blowing through this area on your way up the coast, then be sure to hit **Barra do Sahy,** with its beaches and islands; **Camburi,** a small and romantic beach village; and **Maresias,** a popular beach town for young Brazilians. Many visitors arriving in São Sebastião are actually heading to the more popular resort island of **Ilhabela,** which is accessible by ferryboat. Neither the island nor the mainland is easily traversed without a car, but the mainland beaches are perhaps a bit easier to visit by bus. If you were going to rent a car at any time during your stay in Brazil, this would be a good time.

If, like many Brazilians who visit this part of the coast, you're merely taking a weekend away from work in São Paulo, then I suggest a stay at one of the nicer hotels in either Barra do Sahy or Camburi. Stay there a couple of days, enjoying the local beaches and restaurants. Another night or two in Ilhabela and you've seen the best of the region.

## JUQUEHY

Coming up the coast from São Paulo, the first beach town to consider visiting is Juquehy, a long stretch of sandy beach with a small town area near the surf. This beach is best for sunning, swimming, and taking long walks. There are no kiosks on the sand. In town, you'll find restaurants and shops with local handicrafts.

## BARRA DO SAHY

Just up from Juquehy is **Barra do Sahy.** With its calm, blue waters and white sand, this is one of the prettiest beaches in the area. Beach kiosks offer snacks, drinks, and areas to sit. The south side of Barra has a rocky area with tide pools that offer excellent diving, and the village around the Sahy River has some good restaurants. There are decent options for staying the night here.

## CAMBURI

Camburi is a cute beach town that has a rustic feel to it. It consists of a single dirt road that parallels the beach. On either side of the road are the various *pousadas* (bed-and-breakfasts) and restaurants the village has to offer. Some are quite nice, but you can also find campgrounds and low-cost lodging. The far end of the road, when you cross a small bridge, the village officially becomes Camburizinho (Little Camburi). The beaches have small waves and are great for sunbathing and lounging. There are no kiosks, or *barracas,* on the beaches here, but the better hotels offer beach service, which means they provide chairs, umbrellas, and food and drinks for their guests. During the low season, you'll want to ask your hotel if they are offering beach service, because the town can be somewhat dead during this time (not necessarily a bad thing). Camburi is a place for couples wanting a little romantic getaway. You should stay at a cozy *pousada* and spend your time laying on the beach or swimming in the hotel pool. If you want surfing, snorkeling, or nightlife, there are other places more interesting to visit on the São Paulo coast (like Maresias, Ubatuba, or Ilhabela).

About three kilometers from Camburi is the town of Boiçucanga. Here you'll find more restaurants and low-cost dining options. You'll also find more stores and urban activities. There are some economical accommodations here and the beaches are good for swimming and surfing. Beware: Although it's only three kilometers between Camburi and Boiçucanga, taxis will charge you as much as R$25 for the trip back and forth. This is simply because they are. The highway between the two areas is not safe for pedestrians. Unfortunately, it's this type of opportunism that dampens Brazilian tourism. Buses run along the main highway all day long and into the night.

Note: You'll see Camburi spelled Cambury on many materials and maps. Both are acceptable.

## MARESIAS

When São Paulo's middle-class youth stopped going to Guarujá Island (near São Paulo), they started coming to Maresias beach. During the peak season and on sunny weekends, this is the playground of the "see and be seen" set. The beaches fill with parties, surfers, and martial artists showing off for the crowds. It's the most active beach scene in the area and has been the site of international surf competitions. If you're not into this type of scene, you probably want to visit this beach in the off season and during the week, when the beachfront hotels are quiet and cheap. The town of Maresias has a variety of restaurants and shops and there are hotels, restaurants, and bars all along the beach. On the opposite side of the coastal highway are more shops, ice-cream stores, and restaurants, including some fast-food options—Shopping Maresias, across from the main *praça*, is a good example. The surf at Maresias is a good place for beginning surfers. You can find shops in town that will rent equipment for the day.

## ENTERTAINMENT AND NIGHTLIFE

Each of the small hamlets along the coast has its own particular nightlife. Most activity occurs on weekends and during peak season, though the Maresias area has some action all year-round. Beach parties are common in Maresias, and the bars along the coastal highway fill with visi-

tors. One excellent point is **Os Alemão** (Rua Francisco Leitão 57, tel. 11/3062-6566, noon–3 P.M. and 6:30–11 P.M. Tue.–Sat., noon–6 P.M. on Sun.) a beach bar with breakfast and lunch offerings and crowds at night. They are on the south side of the beach (where most of the action is) next to the Maresias Beach Hotel. In Camburi, the **Saquaritá Bar** (Rua José Inácio, pass the bridge on the Estrada to Camburi and turn right at the Bradesco ATM) has good crowds at night with music, pool tables, and reasonable prices. It's not a fancy place.

## RECREATION AND OUTDOOR ACTIVITIES

During peak season and on sunny weekends, you'll find kite surfing and other water-sport options on the beaches of Maresias. There are hiking opportunities in the wilderness area near Camburi (the best place for information on this is at the Camburi Hostel, which is listed in the *Accommodations* section) and you can find boats to take you snorkeling off the islands of Barra do Sahy.

## ACCOMMODATIONS

The best accommodations on the São Sebastião coast are in the towns of Camburi and Maresias. Using these locations as a base, you can drive (or take the bus) to the other beaches for day trips and dining options.

### Camburi

In Camburi, a great place to stay (keeping the couples theory in mind) is ▶ **Vila Bebek Hotel Pousada** (Rua do Zezito 251, tel. 12/3865-3320, www.villabebek.com.br, R$200–270 weekdays and R$230–320 weekends), which offers a great getaway for two. Although not a beachfront hotel, they make up for that in charm and great facilities, including a tropical pool, bar, restaurant, and lounge area. The service is excellent and not overbearing. No children under 12 allowed. For a beachfront experience, try the **Novo Cambury Praia Hotel** (Estrada do Camburi 247, past the bridge, tel. 12/465-1452, www.novocambury.com.br). It is the only hotel in town with a beach view and private beach entrance. They have basic rooms without views for R$140–160 or two suites with beach views for R$180 (low season). The **Pousada Camburizinho** (Estrada do Camburi 200, tel. 12/3865-1276, www.pousadacamburizinho.com.br, R$110) is a cozy option on the main road with a pool area. A good mid-range option is the **Pousada do Rosa** (Rua das Rosas 139, tel. 12/3865-1412, www.pousadadorosa.com.br, R$75–90 weekdays, R$110–135 weekends), a cute and cozy inn with pool, sauna, computer room, and areas for hanging out. Beach service is available on weekends.

Lower-cost options in Camburi include the **Camburi Hostel** (Rua Tijucas 2300, tel. 12/3865-1561, www.ajcamburi.com.br), which is in the Sertão do Cacau area, about ten minutes inland from the Camburi beach area (by car) in a wilderness setting. They have great facilities, breakfast, and laundry service, and they host wilderness hikes. Some transportation service to the beach is available. Rooms for groups, couples, and families are available from R$25 per person in low season. Also available is **Camping Camburi** (Estrada do Camburi 932, tel. 12/3865-1312, www.campingcamburi.cjb.net), which is generally full of surfers or completely empty. It is walking distance to the beach and has an area for pitching tents for R$14 per person and a few rooms for 2–3 people for about R$45.

## Maresias

If you stay in Maresias, check out the **Maresias Beach Hotel** (Av. Francisco Loup 1109, tel. 12/3891-7500, www.maresiashote.com.br); which is one of the most frequented on the beach. They have 100 rooms, most with beach views, a great pool with outdoor bar, and a large grassy area for hanging out, or you can just walk out to the beach for a dip. Rooms are R$150–300 weekdays and R$520–800 for weekend packages (Friday and Saturday nights). A more reasonably priced beachfront hotel is the M **Coconuts Hotel** (Av. Francisco

Loup, tel. 12/3865-7875, www.coconutshotel.com.br, R$105–135 weekdays and R$150–195 weekends). They have a huge pool area, restaurant, and beach access. Rooms come with either ceiling fans or air-conditioners.

# FOOD
## Camburi

There are several top-end restaurants in Camburi that are known for their good food and service. A couple to note are **Restaurant Manacá** (Rua do Manacá 102, tel. 12/3865-1566, lunch and dinner starting at 1 P.M. Fri.–Wed., dinner only on Thursday. Call to confirm as hours vary depending on the season), which is reputed to be one of the best in Brazil. The hosts, Edinho (little Ed) and Wanda, serve a contemporary fish cuisine in a tropical garden setting with a flair for the creative (like shrimp flambé with *cachaça* and mint risotto). Dinner will cost around R$120–180 for two. **Aqua** (Estrada do Camburi 2000, tel. 12/3865-1866, lunch and dinner starting around 1 P.M. daily) at the end of the beach with a wonderful ocean view, has an Italian flair with fine pasta and fish dishes for around R$60 for two. They also offer a Sunday brunch (peak season) from 11 A.M.–2 P.M. for R$35 per person.

A good mid-range option is the **Restaurante Antigas** (Rua Reginaldo Flavio Corrêa 190, tel. 12/3865-1355, lunch and dinner starting at 1 P.M., closed Mon. and Thurs.) with fish, beef, and risotto options for around R$25–35 per person. There are several other options all along the Estrada do Camburi that you can check out as you walk. A great spot for an economical lunch is **Saquaritá** (Rua José Inácio 29, Camburi, tel. 12/3865-4414, lunch and dinner daily). They have set plates with fish or chicken from R$5–22. It's also a great place to sit and have a beer and it's open during low season. During peak season, it has a happening night scene.

## Maresias

A stroll up the coastal highway will give you a good idea of the restaurants, cafés, and *lan-*

*chonetes* in town. On the beach side, you'll find mostly top-end restaurants with ocean views and more sophisticated menus. On the other side is a mixture of mid-range and low-end eateries, including pizza, fast food, and ice cream. Some places to check out include **Barra Maresias** (Av. Dr. Francisco Loup 333, tel. 12/3465-6721, lunch and dinner daily starting at noon) for fish and **Mescalina** (Av. Dr. Francisco Loup 722) for an international menu. The restaurant district in Maresias is one street inland from the coast highway toward the south end of town.

### São Sebastião City

The city has some decent places for lunch, including great low-cost plates in the old center area, which is within walking distance from the bus station. Go out and to the left, then left at the main avenue for a few blocks. Turn right and walk a couple blocks until you find the old center. **Restaurante São Sebastião** (Praça da Matriz, lunch only from noon–3 P.M.) has an executive lunch for R$8 that is enough for two people. There are other offerings in the same *praça*—all are simple, but delicious. Dinner options are not good in the city.

## INFORMATION AND SERVICES

You might find some tourist information at the bus station in São Sebastião, which has a small office staffed during the day. The best tourist information centers are in Ilhabela and Maresias. In Maresias, the tourist information center is easily located in the main *praça* on the beach side of the highway (tel. 12/4656-6767, www.maresias.tour.br). Check out www.praiasonline.com.br for information about the São Sebastião area. Internet can usually be found at the hotels and *pousadas*. There are some Internet cafés in São Sebastião city on the way to the Centro Histórico from the bus station. Most offer connections for about R$3 per hour.

## GETTING THERE

Buses from São Paulo stop in the bus terminal, where you can catch a bus to one of the beaches down the coast. If you're going to Ilhabela, most buses from São Paulo will let you off at the ferry stop, where you can walk to the harbor and catch the boat. Otherwise, you can take a taxi from the bus terminal to the ferry. You can catch a bus from the terminal going north to Caraguatatubas, where you can transfer south to São Paulo (buses take the inland route) or north to Rio.

## GETTING AROUND

You can rent a bicycle at **Maresias Bike** (Rua dos Navegantes 562 at the corner of the main highway, tel. 12/3865-5289, 9 A.M.–7 P.M. Mon.–Sat., 10 A.M.–5 P.M. on Sun.). Rentals are R$3 per hour or daily for R$10. Call **Translado e Taxi** (tel. 12/9767-8407) for transportation within Maresias and between Maresias and all nearby towns. They also have packaged tours.

There is a "circular" bus that makes the 1.5-hour trip up and down the coast all day long and into the evening, but it's not a trip you want to take often. Besides being crowded with locals, the buses have drivers who seem to go out of their way to make the trip as uncomfortable as possible, driving their buses like race cars down the treacherous mountain road. You can catch this bus at the *rodoviaria* (the main bus station) and all along the coast highway.

# Ilhabela

The original inhabitants of Ilhabela were simple people who lived off fishing and wild harvesting and made their homes around the edges of the island. To this day, the outer rim of the island is mostly inhabited by families of the island's original inhabitants, still fishing the waters for sustenance. During the 19th century, the island was known for its sugar harvest and especially for its fabulous *cachaça*. There was also some large-scale sardine fishing here, as well as coffee plantations. When tourists from São Paulo began to pay attention to the place, they generally built their establishments along the inner rim of the island, facing the mainland. Since the 1950s, the inner rim has been growing in popularity and is now the location of the island's principal village, the village of Ilhabela. (The actual name of the island is Ilha de São Sebastião, but everyone knows it as Ilhabela.) The village is where most of the hotels are located and almost all of the shops and restaurants. Today, the island's principal economy is tourism.

There are some 40 kilometers of coastline divided almost in half by the area called Barra, which is where the ferryboat comes into port. From Barra, you can drive along the coastal road to the north (toward the village) or to the south (toward the village of Borrifos, which is a small settlement of local inhabitants). The beaches along this inner coastline (especially near the village) are the most popular, the easiest to reach, and the most frequented by visitors and inhabitants alike. There are plenty of places to go fishing, sailing, and scuba diving. The beaches to the south are slightly less crowded than those in the north. There are hotels and *pousadas* all along the coast with the highest concentration in the north around the village. On summer weekends, the place is packed, the single coastal road gets gridlock, and there are no rooms available in town. Lines of cars wait to take the ferryboat from São Sebastião to add to the crowd. Many are just staying for the day. During the week, the village

is about half full and the beaches in the south are semi-deserted.

There is a dirt road that heads straight across the island from Barra to the outer rim and the Baía de Castelhanos. The road requires a 4-wheel-drive vehicle and even so, gets treacherous during the rainy season. These conditions help to maintain the pristine conditions of the outer coastline. There are no hotels there and the scenery is fantastic. You can hike along a trail to the Gato Waterfall or take boat excursions to the beaches that face the open ocean. There are great places for snorkeling and scuba diving all over the island, including several shipwrecks around the southern end.

## INNER BEACHES

The beaches along the inner rim of the island are the most frequented, since there is a coastal road that connects them and the water here is calm and tranquil. Most people arrive on the island by car and the coastal road can get pretty crowded on weekends and during the peak season. On off-season weekdays, you can drive up and down the island with no problems and there are buses that make the trip every half-hour. If you take the bus, be prepared to do some walking once you get to your chosen beach as everything is spread apart and designed for people with cars. As a general rule, the beaches on the south coast are more desirable for laying out and enjoying a swim in the ocean. Highlights include **Praia Feiticeira,** which has several beach kiosks to serve visitors and a trail that heads up to the Três Tombos Waterfall and pools. Also, check out **Praia do Julião,** which requires a short hike along a trail from the road or a walk along the rocks from Praia Grande. There are rustic beach kiosks here that may not be open during the low season. This is one of the more secluded beaches on the inner coast. **Praia Grande** is the longest beach on the island at two-thirds of a kilometer (small compared to other beaches on the Bra-

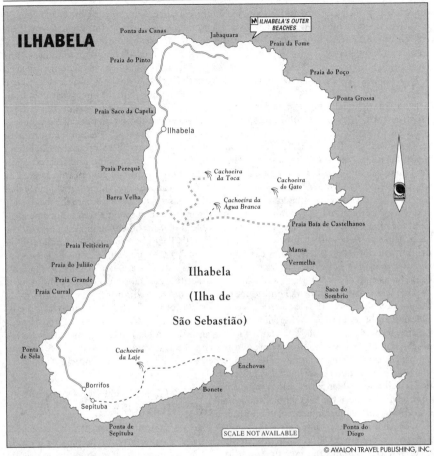

ILHABELA'S OUTER BEACHES

**ILHABELA**

Ponta das Canas
Jabaquara
Praia da Fome
Praia do Pinto
Praia do Poço
Ponta Grossa
Praia Saco da Capela
Ilhabela
Praia Perequê
Cachoeira da Toca
Cachoeira do Gato
Barra Velha
Cachoeira da Água Branca
Praia Baía de Castelhanos
Praia Feiticeira
Mansa
Vermelha
Praia do Julião
Praia Grande
Saco do Sombrio
Praia Curral
Ilhabela
(Ilha de
São Sebastião)
Ponta de Sela
Cachoeira da Laje
Enchovas
Borrifos
Bonete
Sepituba
Ponta de Sepituba
SCALE NOT AVAILABLE
Ponta do Diogo

São Paulo Coast to Rio

zilian coast). The beach has a small boardwalk, several bars, and even areas for volleyball and other sand sports. The beach is one of the exit locations for diving excursions, although **Praia Curral** is closest to the shipwreck offshore and is one of the main departure points for divers. Curral is loaded with bars and restaurants along its 400 meters of pink sand. There are beach chairs, tables, and outdoor showers here. During the peak season, Curral is one of the busiest beaches on the island. **Praia Veloso** is the last beach that the coastal road reaches and is a calm and quiet place to hang out. There are no structures or crowds here.

Beaches along the northern half of the island include **Praia Perequê,** which is a popular place for kite surfing on windy days. The beach is right on the coastal road and there are bars and kiosks spanning its length. The many palm trees right on the sandy beach provide shade and turn what would otherwise be a mundane beach into a pleasant landscape. **Praia Saco da Capela** is a popular beach that is visible from the coastal road. There are a couple of hotels here that have beach restaurants open to the public. This is a good beach for relaxing and hanging out, although the presence of traffic on the coastal road makes it less attractive than other beaches, such as **Praia do Pinto,** which is not visible from the road. Pinto has a wide stretch of sand and some kiosks to keep the visitors cool and happy.

# Ⓜ OUTER BEACHES

The outer beaches are the most dramatic and pristine, since they are difficult to reach. The main way to get to these beaches is to circumnavigate the island by boat. Starting at the top of the island, the most interesting beaches are **Jabaquara,** which is a favorite location for diving and underwater fishing (with harpoon). The beach itself is long and beautiful and there is a river that empties into the ocean here, forming a small fresh-water lake. There are a couple of beach bars that serve lunch and drinks. You can access this beach by car along the dirt road that continues after the main coastal road ends or take a boat with or without the snorkeling option. **Praia da Fome** is one of the prettiest beaches on the island and is accessible only by boat. There is a waterfall here and the river feeds into the ocean. The nearby **Praia do Poço** is also accessible only by boat and is a great place for diving activities. The inhabited beach on the outer coastline is **Praia Baía de Castelhanos,** which is where the road from Barra ends. It's one of the largest beaches on the island with about one kilometer of white sand. This beach is popular with surfers as the waves here are strong. From here you can hike to the Gato Waterfall. Finally, the **Saco do Sombrio** is a great place to sit and watch the boats come in and out of the harbor. The clear water here also makes it popular among divers.

# WATERFALLS

Mountain peaks and waterfalls are the highlights of the forested area of the island's interior. There are four principal waterfalls that are open to visitation. The **Cachoeira da Água Branca** is located off the dirt road that heads across the island, called the Estrada Para Castelhanos. Along this road you'll come to the main entrance to the Ilhabela State Park. From the entrance, you can park and hike about 30 minutes up to the waterfalls, where you'll encounter several cascades and pools for swimming. You can drive out to the entrance in any type of car (beyond that, you'll need a 4-wheel-drive vehicle). If you don't have a car, you can take a bus out there or check with the tour agencies in the village for excursions by jeep and other transportation options. On the way to the Agua Branca Waterfall, you can turn off the *estrada* and head up to the **Cachoeira da Toca,** one of the more popular waterfalls for swimming and playing in the water. The water cascades down a slippery rocky slope that is used as a slide. Watch where the locals slide down first, then give it a try at the same location. It's located about eight kilometers off the Estrada Para Castelhanos. The **Cachoeira do Gato** is a 40-minute hike from the left end of the Baía de Castelhanos. It's one of the most beautiful waterfalls on the island and it has a nice pool for swimming. The **Cachoeira da Laje** is located in the southern part of the island and requires a 1.5-hour hike from the village of Sepituba. You can swim at the waterfall and continue your hike another 1.5 hours to either Enchovas or Bonete Beach.

# ENTERTAINMENT AND NIGHTLIFE

The only nightlife on the island occurs in the village, particularly in the bars on Rua do Meio, where you'll find some live music on weekends and during the peak season.

# SPORTS AND RECREATION
## Excursions

The most popular excursions are by boat, taking you around to the outer beaches. The longest trip takes you all the way around the northern tip of the island and down to the Saco do Sombrio, stopping at several beaches along the way, including Jabaquara, Fome, Poço, and Castelhanos. There are stops for swimming and snorkeling. The trip takes all day (10 hours) and leaves around 9 A.M. Another trip takes you around the southern tip of the island, passing the inner beaches to the south of the village, rounding the tip of the island, and stopping at both Bonete and Enchovas for a swim. This trip also takes 10 hours and leaves at around 9 A.M. A smaller trip is the schooner excursion from the Engenho d'Agua over the tip to Jabaquara, where you can swim in the ocean and have lunch. This trip takes only four hours and leaves twice a day at 10 A.M. and 2 P.M. It requires a minimum of 10 passengers and costs around R$35. Besides these packaged trips, you can hire a boat to take you out to any beach on the island and create your own agenda. With 4–6 passengers, the price is reasonable.

You can take a jeep across the island to the Baía de Castalhanos. The trip includes about an hour of off-roading and a hike up to the Gato Waterfall. It takes all day and costs around R$35. There are many tour agents and services in town. A couple of services to check out are **Bestboats** (tel. 12/9146-5555, www.bestboats.com.br) and **Fenix** (tel. 12/3896-3549, fenix@fenixbarcos.com.br). Contact these via telephone or Internet. For jeep excursions, try **Lokal Adventure** (Av. Princesa Isabel 171, Pereque, tel. 12/3896-5777, www.lokaladventure.com.br).

## Sailing

By far the most popular activity on Ilhabela is sailing. Every year in July, the island hosts International Sailing Week, one of the largest sailing competitions in the world. You can reserve a room during this week and rent a boat to sail out and watch the competition up close. Besides this, you can rent a boat or take a sailing class at any time on the island. The most common areas for sailing are **Praia Pequeá**, which has the Projeto Navegar, a sailing and kayaking school. Also, the **Engenho d'Agua** is the busiest sailing port and home to the **Ilhabela Yacht Club** (tel. 11/5502-6720).

## Diving and Snorkeling

Although clarity in this region varies, depending on the tide and season, the island is a favor-ite spot for snorkeling and scuba diving. The most popular places for both are the beaches along the northern tip of the island, including Jabaquara, Fome, and Poço. Here, it's possible to see sea turtles and even dolphins. Diving and snorkeling excursions frequent these places, as well as the beaches on the south end of the island, which are home to the most accessible shipwrecks (of which there are 20 in these waters). Dive schools are all located in the village and you can discuss the options with them in their offices. There is also **Colonial Diver** (Av. Brasil 1751, tel. 12/3894-9459, www.colonialdiver.com.br) in the Pedras Miúdas Beach area.

## Trails

There are numerous trails around the island and some of them are easy enough to take without a guide. Most, however, require a guide to keep you from getting lost in the forest. One popular hike is from the Estrada Para Castelhanos to the Agua Branca Waterfall. It's about six kilometers along a dirt road with the waterfall as your reward. Another trail takes you out to the Laje Waterfall from the village of Sepituba on the southern tip of the island. It takes about one hour to get to the waterfall and another 1.5 hours to reach the Bonete or Enchovas Beach. The 45-minute hike from Castalhanos to the Gato Waterfall is a favorite on the island, although it's not an easy trail. The short hike includes some steep climbs.

If you like panoramic views, then you can take the four-hour hike up to the Pico do Baepi, which overlooks the village and the entire channel. The hike should be taken with a local guide. You can also take the 22-kilometer trail that goes from Castelhanos to Praia Serraria. It takes about six hours to complete, so you should arrange a boat pickup at Serraria to bring you back. You can also take this trail on a mountain bike, which you may be able to rent from one of the tour agencies in the *vila*. Try **Lokal Aventure** (Av. Princesa Isabel 171, Pereque, tel. 12/3896-5777, www.lokaladventure.com.br).

If you want to spend the day walking along the outer beaches of the island, you can start at

Castelhanos, then walk down to Praia Mansa, Praia Vermelha, and Praia da Figueira. The entire hike takes about 3.5 hours (one way), but you'll probably want to stop at each of the beaches for a swim and look around. Plan on spending an entire day doing this.

Note: If you plan to hike on Ilhabela or go out to the more remote areas, be sure to bring insect repellant with you, as the bugs here are abundant.

## ACCOMMODATIONS

One of the quaintest *pousadas* on the island is **Porto Pacuíba** (Av. Leonardo Reale 1578, Praia do Viana, tel. 12/3896-2466, www.portopacuiba.com.br, R$225), which is on the beach about three kilometers from the village. They have an incredible view of the channel, beach access, and very charming installations with Northern European touches brought in by the German owners. They have a restaurant (with European and Brazilian cuisine), bar, pool, and sauna. Rooms have air, TV, and phone. They only accept multi-day packages in the peak season, but remain open-ended in the off season. Another excellent choice is the **Pousada do Capitão** (Rua Almirante Tamandaré 272, Praia da Itaquanduba, tel. 12/3896-1037, www.pousadadocapitao.com.br, R$165 low season, R$245 peak season). They have comfortable beds, air, TV, phone, pool, and sauna. They don't accept children, so this is a great choice for couples wanting a little romance.

More economical options include **Pousada Saco do Sombrio** (Rua Arapongas 326, Praia Itaguaçu, tel. 12/3896-1951, www.sacodosombrio.com.br, R$165). They have a bar, pool, air-conditioning, TV, and phone. Most of the rooms have a terrific view of the canal. Also, try **Vilamar** (Av. Dos Bandeirantes 55, Praia da Itaquanduba, tel. 12/3896-2622, www.hotel-vilamar.com.br, R$125–198), which is a great place for families as their rooms hold up to six people. They have a pool, restaurant, bar, air, TV, and phone. Some rooms have hot tubs.

## FOOD

In the village, you'll find all kinds of food establishments at all kinds of prices. For a quick snack, try **Borrachudo** (Rua Dr. Carvalho 20, tel. 12/3896-1499, breakfast and lunch daily), which has burgers and sandwiches. You can get a good, cheap lunch at **Cheiro Verde** (Rua da Padroeira 109, tel. 12/3896-3245, lunch and dinner daily) in the village. There is also a pizza joint called **Pier Pizza** (Praça da Bandeira, tel. 12/3896-6079, lunch and dinner daily) that gets crowded at night. **Free Port Café** (Rua Dr. Carvalho 112, Village, tel. 12/3896-2237, 11 A.M.–11 P.M. Sun.–Thurs., 11–1 A.M. on Fri. and Sat.) is a great place to sit and have a cup of java. The interior is charming and interesting, made to resemble the interior of a ship.

There are restaurants spread around the beaches of the northern part of the island. One of note include **Viana** (Av. Leonardo Reale 1560, Praia Viana, tel. 12/3896-2598, lunch–midnight), which serves a variety of seafood with interesting recipes, including shrimp in orange sauce and fresh fish in white wine sauce. The place gets crowded, so get there early. Another popular place is **Bacalhau** (Av. José Pacheco do Nascimento 7942, Praia do Curral, tel. 12/3894-1754, 10 A.M.–midnight), which is a beach restaurant that stays open until midnight in the peak season. Their specialty is, you guessed it, fish. You can also try **Pitanga** (Av. Pedro de Paula Morais 435, tel. 12/3896-2156, 10 A.M.–midnight) in the Saco da Capela for a variety of fresh fish. They're open until midnight during the peak season.

## GETTING THERE AND AROUND

You get to Ilhabela via the ferryboat from São Sebastião, whether you're arriving by car or on foot. Buses coming from São Paulo leave from the Tietê terminal on the Litorânea Transportes Coletivos line.

Buses go to Agua Branca in the geographic middle of the island from either Barra (the ferryboat port) or the *vila,* every half hour from 6 A.M. until about 1 A.M. and return at the same times. Buses go up to Armação at the northern tip from the *vila* almost every hour from 5:40 A.M.–10:40 P.M. You can catch a bus going along the south coast every half hour from 6 A.M.–12:30 A.M. leaving from Barra. Buses cost just under R$2.

# Ubatuba

A bit less famous than some of its neighboring beach regions, Ubatuba is every bit as interesting, if not more so. Traversed by the tropic of Capricorn, Ubatuba is the recipient of many tropical downpours and is known to locals as Uba-CHUVA, *chuva* meaning rain. Nevertheless, this region is a delight and offers something for everyone: urban beaches, secluded beaches, beaches for hanging out in the shade of a kiosk with a cold drink, and small fishing and boating villages. The wilderness in this area is said to be part of the original *Mata Atlântica,* or Atlantic Rainforest (although I wish I had a dollar for every time I heard that claim in Brazil), and offers some beautiful vistas and wildlife hikes. In addition, you'll find great places for biking, swimming, surfing (waves up to four meters), and diving. You can also find boats to will take you out to the nearby islands or to some of the many diving spots where the water is clear and blue. Ubatuba's town center is medium-sized and offers a variety of hotels, shops, restaurants, and markets. The beaches downtown are urbanized, but pretty. Unfortunately, they are only for viewing, due to polluted conditions. The boardwalk area is usually crowded on weekends and presents a variety of activities, food stands, and shops. There is a skate park and children's amusement park on the boardwalk.

The most accessible hotels and *pousadas* are in the downtown area. If you're based there, you can catch buses or take taxis or boats to the neighboring beaches to the north and south. There are also accommodations (often more interesting than those downtown) in the beach outskirts, principally in Praia Grande and Saco da Ribeira.

## PROJECT TAMAR AND THE AQUARIUM

In the town center are two interesting marinelife exhibits. The Projeto TAMAR (Rua Antonio Atanázio 273, tel. 12/3832-6202, 10 A.M.–6 P.M. daily) is a protection organization for sea turtles, based in Praia do Forte, Bahia. Their Ubatuba location has several tanks with turtles on display and information about the turtles, which spawn on the beaches of Ilha Anchieta. (For more information on TAMAR, see the *Salvador* chapter.) The Aquarium (10 A.M.–8 P.M. every day but Thurs.) is an exhibit of sea life with more than 70 different species, including penguins in a temperature-controlled environment. Both the Aquarium and TAMAR are located in the town center at Praia Itaguá.

## SACO DA RIBEIRA

This fishing port is where you can charter a boat to the Island of Anchieta, Praia das Sete Fontes, or for a fishing or diving excursion. The village here has its own special charm and offers a few good accommodations and a couple of good restaurants (for fish, of course). You can walk to the south end of town along the inner pathways, then turn right to make your way to Praia Lázaro, passing numerous *pousadas* and homes for rent along the way.

## ◪ ILHA ANCHIETA

Like many coastal islands, Anchieta was once home to a prison. Today, the prison is an old ruin and attracts visitors from the mainland—that, and the pristine beaches of white sand and clear water around the island. Take a boat from the Saco da Ribeira for about R$20 (see

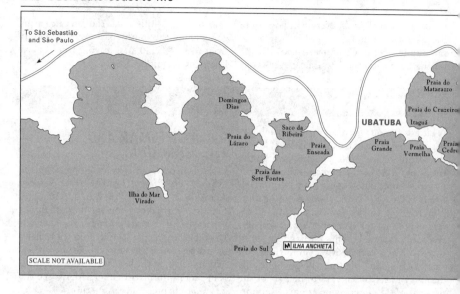

To São Sebastião
and São Paulo

Domingos
Dias

Praia do
Lázaro

Saco da
Ribeira

Praia
Enseada

Praia das
Sete Fontes

Ilha do Mar
Virado

Praia do Sul

**M** ILHA ANCHIETA

UBATUBA

Praia do
Matarazzo

Praia do Cruzeiro

Itaguá

Praia
Grande

Praia
Vermelha

Praia
Cedro

SCALE NOT AVAILABLE

*Boat Excursions* below for details) and don't forget the snorkeling equipment (usually included on the boat) as the island has some great diving areas and frequent visitations by marine turtles. There are kiosks and places to eat on the beaches and near the pier, or you can bring you own lunch from the mainland. Don't miss **Praia do Sul** on the south side of the island. The island is closed on Wednesdays.

## WATERFALLS

The Ubatuba region has several waterfalls. Worth visiting are the **Cachoeira da Escada** at the northern end of the region, just past the village of Picinguaba. The **Cachoeira do Ipiranguinha,** just inland from Ubatuba and on the way to the Horto Florestal wildlife park, is seven meters high with a pool of water suitable for swimming. It can get crowded with families during summer weekends. The **Cachoeira do Promirim,** to the north near the Promirim Beach, is nearly 20 meters high, with water falling to a cool pond in the middle of the tropical forest. It's also good for swimming and close to some worthwhile beaches. Start out early to take in all three of these in one day.

## NORTHERN COASTLINE

The first interesting beach to the north of Ubatuba is **Praia Itamambuca,** famous for its surfing conditions and competitions. At the mouth of a river that flows into the ocean here, you'll find a beautiful scene of clear water and shade under some large trees. Beach kiosks serve cold beer and snacks and there are plenty of beautiful people here. Just a bit farther up the road is **Praia do Felix,** which is also frequented by surfers and is a great place to hang out. Next are the beaches of **Promirim** and **Purubá.** To get to these beaches, you have to cross a channel of water by boat from the north. These are beautiful and nearly deserted in low season. A great way to see this area is take a boat excursion from the Itaguá beach in Ubatuba to the Promirim beach and island, with options for snorkeling and swimming around the island (see *Boat Excursions* below for details).

The town called **Vila Picinguaba** is a charming piece of Brazilian Ilha Anchieta beach culture and home to the beautiful **Praia da Fazenda** and the Bicas River. Just passing the area by car or bus, you can already get an

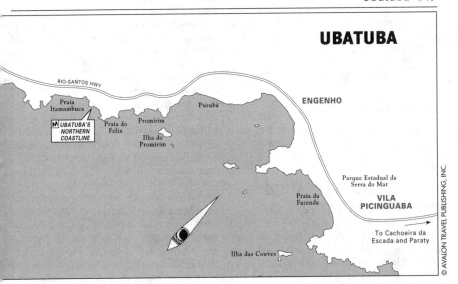

# UBATUBA

© AVALON TRAVEL PUBLISHING, INC.

São Paulo Coast to Rio

incredible view of this inlet. Home to traditional Brazilian families, Picinguaba is a bit less frequented by tourists than the beaches on the southern coastline. From here you can hire boats to take you out to the nearby islands, with **Ilha das Couves** being the highlight for snorkeling and clear-water swimming conditions (bring your own food and water). Not far to the north is the **Cachoeira da Escada.**

Making up more than 80 percent of the Ubatuba region, the **Parque Estadual da Serra do Mar** offers trails and a rich collection of flora and fauna from the original Atlantic Rainforest. It includes the Praia da Fazenda Beach and the Village of Picinguaba. Guides are available in the village or check with your hotel in Ubatuba.

## SOUTHERN COASTLINE

The southern beaches begin with **Praia Vermelha** and **Praia Cefro,** which are on the peninsula separating the town of Ubatuba from the southern coast. These are beautiful and almost always uninhabited. To get to these two beaches, you have to hike from the south side of Ubatuba or hire a small boat from Itaguá. **Praia Grande**

is a stretch of six kilometers of white sand and blue water with plenty of tourists, beach kiosks, and water sports. It's probably the most popular beach in the Ubatuba area and its southern end is situated right off the highway.

You can take the one-hour hike from the Saco da Ribeira to **Praia das Sete Fontes** on the tip of a peninsula. The beach is excellent for sunbathing and is one of the stops on the boat excursion that visits the Island of Anchieta. One of the prettiest beaches in Ubatuba, **Praia do Lázaro** is a lovely walk from the Saco do Ribeira. Near the middle of the long stretch of white sand is a charming kiosk where you can sit and have lunch or drinks into the night. The calm, blue waters make for excellent swimming. Just to the south is the small and charming beach of **Domingos Dias.** A bit more private than Lázaro, Domingos Dias is one of the best beaches in the area. It's about a 20-minute walk from Lázaro along the coast.

## ENTERTAINMENT AND NIGHTLIFE

Nightlife activities occur mostly in the town center, where you'll find a few bars, cafés, and clubs, many of them facing the water on the coastal highway. The **Beethoven Music Bar** (at Shopping de Madeira center, tel. 12/3835-1275, 8:30 P.M. daily, Wed.–Sat.) has live jazz, blues, and rock nightly.

## SHOPPING

Most shops are in the downtown area near Praia Itaguá. There you'll find boutique shops with clothes, bikinis, and souvenirs.

## SPORTS AND RECREATION

### Boat Excursions

Boats to Ilha Anchieta and other islands around Ubatuba generally leave from either the Centro beaches or the Saco da Ribeira. Most boats have a minimum of 10–15 people and it can be difficult to find a full boat during the week in low season (some companies only operate on weekends). Cost is from R$12–20 to Anchieta. Try **Mykonos Turismo** (tel. 12/3842-0329, www.mykonos.com.br), which has large boats leaving at 8:30 A.M., 10:30 A.M., 12:30 P.M., and 2:30 P.M. during peak season and 11 A.M. only during low season. Remember that the island is closed on Wednesdays. Also, **Fountains Turismo** (tel. 12/3842-0608) has fishing and island tours on weekends leaving from the Saco da Ribeira.

### Trails

The Corcovado Trail, which begins in the Parque Estadual da Serra do Mar is an advanced hiking experience with five hours of uphill climb to the highest peak in the region. Thankfully, there is a swimming hole near the top, which is an excellent place to refresh after taking in the incredible view (at an altitude of more than 1,000 meters). A smaller and less radical trail is the 45-minute hike from the Saco da Ribeira to the Praia do Flamengo or the one-hour hike along the Praia Sete Fontes Trail. There are also numerous trails in the Horto Florestal area.

### Surfing and Diving

Surfing is best at Praia Itamambuca, which has hosted international competitions, although there are good surfing and very cool beaches along the northern coast. Check out Praia Itamambuca and Praia Félix.

The best diving locations include Ilha Anchieta and the islands off Prumirim Beach and Praia da Fazenda in the northern waters. Most of these are best accessed with guides, which include transportation by boat, along with equipment if needed. Check with **Omnimare** (Rua Guaicurús 30, Centro, tel. 12/3832-2005, www.omnimare.com.br). They offer beginner dives as well as full courses and dive excursions for experienced divers. Also, try **Scubatuba** (Av. Beira Mar 126, Praia Lazaro, tel. 12/3842-2655, www.scubatuba.com.br) for beginner dives, lessons, and excursions. Finally, there is **Bixodagua** (Av. Andrelino Miguel 151, Praia do Lázaro, tel. 12/3842-2636, www.bixodagua.com.br), which specializes in night dives. Also check the site www.divebrazil.com for information.

## ACCOMMODATIONS

Most hotels are either downtown or on the south end of Praia Grande, in Toninhas and Enseada Beaches. Hotels in the beach areas are generally better values, giving you more for the price. In the downtown area, the most charming *pousadas* are toward the south side of town in the older area near the Aquarium. Some good options include the **M Pousada Don Diego** (Rua Guarani 782, tel. 12/3832-2338, www.pousadadondiego.com.br, R$60 s/d low season), which is charming, well located and affordable. They have laundry service and offer their own boat trips. A similar option is the **Pousada Cavalo Marinho** (Rua Guarani 757, tel. 12/3832-2041, www.pousadacavalomarinho.com.br, R$60 weekdays and R$140 weekends during low season), which is a beachfront hotel with a pool and very clean rooms. You can also try **Pousada Serramar** (Av. Leovigildo Dias Vieira 218, tel. 12/3832-3949, R$55 s and R$70 d) a small, new *pousada* with TV and air-conditioning. Singles can try the **Hotel Charbel** (*praça* Nóbrega 280, tel. 12/3832-1090, www.saocharbel.com.br, R$40 s and R$70 d), which is a slightly less-attractive but affordable offering.

A couple of options in the Toninhas area include the **Wembley Inn** (Praia das Toninhas Km 8, tel. 12/3442-0198, www.wembley-inn.com.br, R$135 in low season). They have a great location with views of the beach, restaurant, bar, beach service, and pool. Rooms have air, TV, and phone. One of the most charming places in town is at Toninhas Beach, called **Recanto das Toninhas** (SP-055 Km 6.5, tel. 12/3442-1425, www.toninhas.com.br, R$155 low season and R$325 peak season). They have restaurants, bars, pool, and beach service. Rooms have air, TV, and phone. Finally, the **Pousada Ancoradouro** (Praia das Toninhos Km 7, tel. 12/3442-0657, R$85) has beach service, restaurant, bar, and pool.

The area between Saco da Ribeira and Praia Lázaro has a few *pousadas*. One of the most interesting is **Albatroz Pousada** (Rua Tapiá 156, tel. 12/3842-2853, www.pousadaalbatroz.com.br, R$80 s/d). They have a tropical jungle motif, outdoor barbecue areas, pool area, and rooms with ceiling fans and kitchen facilities. Rooms hold up to 5 people. Negotiate group rates.

## FOOD

A great place for pizza, lunch or dinner, is the **Pizzaria e Restaurante Orégano** (Av. Leovigildo Dias Vieira 1116, Itaguá, tel. 12/3832-1614, open lunch and dinner daily). **Marlin Azul** (Rua Guaraní 525, tel. 12/3832-6920) offers a great self-service lunch starting at 11 A.M. for only R$7 per kilo and pizza in the evenings starting at around 6 P.M. Since you'll most likely be on one of the beaches during the day, you'll be having lunch at the beach kiosks. Most have fish lunches with rice and beans for two people or other specialties. More popular beaches, such as Praia Grande, also have restaurants near the beach and inside most of the *pousadas* nearby. They are all happy to have you come in and check out their restaurants.

For dinner, try **Rei do Peixe I and II** (Rua

Guaraní 480, tel. 12/3832-3272, 11:30–12:30 A.M. daily). They whip up a variety of fish plates from R$25–60 for two people. Also, **Peixe com Banana** (Praia do Cruzeiro, on the beach, tel. 12/3832-1712, noon–11 P.M., closed Wed.) serves some typical, local dishes, including fish with banana.

## INFORMATION AND SERVICES

There is a tourist information office on the beach in the downtown area, open from 8 A.M.–6 P.M. with a long lunch break. The city website is www.ubatuba.sp.gov.br. Internet services are available at **Surf Net** (Rua Guarani 620, 11:30 A.M.–11:30 P.M.) and **Microage Informática** (Av. Prof. Thomaz Galhardo 64, 9 A.M.–10 P.M. daily and 4 P.M.–10 P.M. Sun.).

International ATMs are located in the town center. Look for Banco do Brasil and Banco 24 Horas near the *praça* and on the boardwalk. Most hotels and some restaurants take credit cards. Money changing is usually available at travel agencies if you get stuck.

## GETTING THERE

Buses going south from Paraty leave from the main bus terminal every day. From São Sebastião, you need to catch the bus to Caraguatatuba, then transfer to Ubatuba. Direct from São Paulo, you can catch the Litorânia Transportes line to Caraguatatuba and then transfer up to Ubatuba. There are also some direct buses from São Paulo and Rio to Ubatuba.

Buses to Paraty leave from the Rodoviaria São José (Av. Prof. Thomaz Galhardo 513) at 9:40 A.M., 4:45 P.M., and 8:40 P.M. for about R$7.

## GETTING AROUND

Like many small, tourist towns in Brazil, Ubatuba does not have a huge infrastructure for travel within the region. Moreover, taxis often over-charge or outright rip you off (like showing up with time already on the meter). Just remember to ask for prices before getting in. Remember not to ask a taxi driver for recommendations on anything. Buses going up and down the coast leave from the rodoviaria or you can walk out to the highway and catch a bus in either direction. Buses south go to Lázaro or Maranduba and you can get off anywhere along the line. These buses go from about 4:30 A.M.– 11:30 P.M. and cost about R$2.

To rent a car in Ubatuba (a great way to get back and forth to the distant beaches), get in touch with rental agency **Localiza** (Av. Guaraní 194, Airport, tel. 12/3833-7200 8 A.M.– 5:30 P.M. daily).

# Paraty

The first and foremost attraction in Paraty is the Centro Histórico, a colonial village that, during Brazil's gold rush period (called the Gold Cycle), was the most important shipping center in Brazil (not necessarily the largest, which was in Salvador). Paraty was important for getting the country's natural riches out to Europe. There are a few historical sights to visit in town, including some colonial churches, but today Paraty is mostly a tourist center, full of shops, genuinely great restaurants, dance clubs, bars, and ice cream stores. Shops offer a variety of local arts and crafts, including a few decent art galleries. There is also a tradition of street activity in the center, and you'll find native Guaranis selling baskets and other hand-made goods on the stone streets, along with local hippies selling jewelry and art. On busy nights, you'll probably see more than one outdoor performance by local students.

Paraty is one of Brazil's most sparkling coastal jewels. Its waters are blue-green and warm and splash onto a number of remote beaches and islands, great for exploring, swimming, and diving. The tourist infrastructure is fairly well organized and you'll find fine restaurants, economic eateries, and plenty of watering holes both day and night. When you're not checking out the town, the main activity is to visit the islands and beaches in the bay. Most of these are accessible only by boat and most have spectacular tropical settings, as beautiful as any you'll see in Brazil. There are also beaches accessible by foot, including Praia do Pontal, closest to town, and Jabaquara, a short distance to the north. By bus or car, you can visit numerous beaches to the south, including Sonho, which requires a one-hour hike after exiting the bus, and Trindade, which offers its own restaurants and accommodations, along with three or four different beaches (including one for advanced surfers). Farther up the coast, north of Paraty, you can find some of the region's best beaches, specifically Prainha and São Gonçalo, both accessible by bus. Finally, Paraty offers some inland pleasures, including a couple great waterfalls, hiking trails, and hotel *fazendas* (hotel ranches).

After arriving and getting settled in your *pousada,* the best thing to do is explore the old town center. Shop, have dinner, and visit the nearby beaches if you have time. Spend your first full day on one of the boat trips out in the bay. Be ready for plenty of swimming and snorkeling. In the evening, walk around the Centro Histórico to select a restaurant and see the happenings at night. Your next day can be spent at one of the more distant beaches, such as Trindade or São Gonçalo. Repeat this step for as many days as you like or until you see all the beaches you want. If you are traveling with a group, you can charter your own small boat to any destination(s) in the bay, spending your time as you see fit. Night trips on the bay are excellent options for *festas* (parties). For an inland break, check out one of the jeep trips to the nearby waterfall and inland *fazendas.*

## HISTORY

Once there were seven strategic outposts, or forts, protecting the bay at Paraty. One was

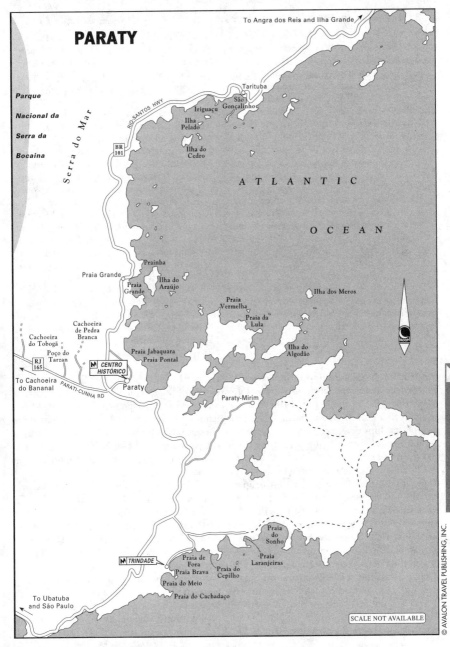

# PARATY

To Angra dos Reis and Ilha Grande

Parque

Nacional da

Serra da

Bocaina

Serra do Mar

RIO-SANTOS HWY

BR 101

Tarituba

São Gonçalinho

Iriguaçu

Ilha Pelado

Ilha do Cedro

ATLANTIC

OCEAN

Prainha

Praia Grande

Praia Grande

Ilha do Araújo

Ilha dos Meros

Praia Vermelha

Praia da Lula

Cachoeira de Pedra Branca

Cachoeira do Tobogã

Poço do Tarzan

RJ 165

Praia Jabaquara

Praia Pontal

Ilha do Algodão

CENTRO HISTÓRICO

To Cachoeira do Bananal

PARATI-CUNHA RD

Paraty

Paraty-Mirim

São Paulo Coast to Rio

Praia do Sonho

TRINDADE

Praia de Fora

Praia Brava

Praia do Meio

Praia do Cepilho

Praia Laranjeiras

To Ubatuba and São Paulo

Praia do Cachadaço

SCALE NOT AVAILABLE

## PETROBRÁS AND THE COAST OF RIO

Besides being one of the most beautiful stretches of coastline in the country, the coast of Rio de Janeiro is also where most of the country's offshore oil production—almost 80 percent—is located. That number is likely to grow, as more offshore oil and gas fields have been located and are likely to be explored over the next five years. Most of the new fields are located in the Campos Basin, along the coast north of the city of Rio de Janeiro. This region was mostly responsible for Brazil's dramatic increase in domestic oil production in the 1990s.

But along with the increase in production came an increase in consumption. Brazil is the largest energy consumer in South America and the third largest in all the Americas, next to the United States and Canada. But in the latter half of the 1990s, Brazil's energy self-sufficiency increased to approximately 80 percent, with a goal of 100-percent self-sufficiency by 2006. Both an increase in production and a leveling of consumption are responsible for this change. Besides oil and combustible fuels, which represent just over half of all energy consumption in the country, Brazil also relies heavily on hydroelectric power and has the world's largest and most productive hydroelectric plant, located in the state of Paraná, not far from Foz de Iguaçu.

Currently, Brazil imports oil, principally from Africa and the Middle East, and has the second-largest oil reserves in South America, next to Venezuela. Until recently, Brazil's oil production and exploration was the jurisdiction of the government-created monopoly Petrobrás. But in 1997, new laws were established to break the Petrobrás monopoly and attract foreign investment in the oil exploration and production sectors. This foreign investment has been minimal. State and federal taxes and regulations have stifled interest in offshore drilling, while Petrobrás remains the dominant force in the country, with most of the best prospective fields. Nevertheless, both Shell and Texaco have made investments in new fields in the Campos Basin, including an underwater gas field containing around 60 billion cubic feet of natural gas. In all, the Campos Basin in Rio de Janeiro holds an estimated 15 trillion cubic feet of natural gas.

---

constructed on high ground in Paraty itself. The others were spread around the bay—in Angra dos Reis, on the Island of Ilha Grande and on other islands—strategically placed to spot pirate ships entering the bay. Paraty was the most important shipping port at the time and the primary cargo was gold. Lots of gold.

The area of Paraty and Angra dos Reis was originally occupied by the Goianás people. Paraty is an indigenous word for a fish that was plentiful in the waters of the region. In Tupi-Guarani, it means bay or gulf. In the late 1500s, the Goianás around the Paraty bay sought out the help of nearby Portuguese settlers in their defense against the Tamóios. The settlers noted the convenient location of the area and its main trail, which led toward São Paulo (later dubbed *Facão*, or Big Knife Trail). Around 1636, the now-mixed population was mostly clustered on the far side of the river to the north. They erected a chapel in the name of São Roque, which gave the area its first identity. Later, the population separated from Angra dos Reis and moved its nucleus to its current position. Another church was built, to the patron saint of Nossa Sra. dos Remédios, which is currently the site of the Matriz Church in the Paraty square.

Around 1660, Paraty was recognized and given autonomy under the name Nossa Sra. Remédios de Paraty, or simply Vila Paraty. The city consistently benefited from its fortunate location between Rio de Janeiro and São Paulo. In the early days of the Gold Cycle, as Brazil's interests were moving from Bahia to the southeast, Paraty became the principal port of entry between Minas Gerais and Europe and a weigh station for the nation's gold trade. During this period, Paraty was famous for its production of *cachaça* (sugarcane rum). When São Paulo took over in the late 1700s as the dominant force in the coffee trade, Paraty became an important station for coffee on its way to Rio de Janeiro. This and its *cachaça* trade became the city's principal activities, since the Novo Caminho (New Road), which connected Rio and Minas Gerais directly, had eliminated Paraty as an important port. At the end of the 19th century, railroads made Paraty unimportant as a stop between São Paulo and Rio, removing Paraty from the coffee trade. The city fell into a period of disrepair and its population declined to a mere 600 inhabitants. Since the 1950s, Paraty has begun a new life as a tourist village and national monument.

## HISTORICAL SIGHTS
### Centro Histórico
The town center is a historical monument, sporting architecture from Brazil's colonial period. Today, the center is a well-preserved tourist area, full of good restaurants, bars, and shops with local handicrafts, souvenirs, clothes, and other items. You can walk around the streets of the town in an hour or two, but be sure to wear tennis shoes or other walking shoes as the stone streets are difficult to navigate. In the rainy season, the streets fill with water and people are forced to walk along the sides. The center is usually full of street vendors, artists, and performing groups. The main *praça* features the town's principal church and many sidewalk cafés. Past the *praça* is the bridge that leads to the closest beach (Pontal) and, slightly farther up the road, to the Jabaquara beach. There are many *pousadas* near these beaches.

### Matriz de Nossa Sra. dos Remédios
The main church in Paraty, the Matriz, occupies the main *praça,* where once stood two other, smaller chapels, in 1646 and 1712. Considered too small, the 1712 chapel was replaced by the Matriz church in 1787. It underwent many reforms over the years until it was finally finished in 1873. A typical baroque church of the region, the Matriz is not as spectacular or well preserved as similar churches in

São Paulo Coast to Rio

© CHRISTOPHER VAN BUREN

**narrow cobblestone streets of historic Paraty**

Minas Gerais. Still, it's well worth a look inside, where you'll see marble and wood sculpture on the altar.

### Igreja de Nossa Sra. do Rosário

Part of the family of Rosário churches, built by the brotherhood of black slaves originating from Ouro Preto, the Paraty Rosário church is small and humble, but no less interesting than its larger counterparts.

### Igreja de Nossa Sra. das Dores

Filled with 19th-century furniture and adornments, the Igreja das Dores was originally constructed in 1800 as a church for the white elite of Paraty. Restored in 1004, the church stands on the bank of the bay near the town's principal pier and is a clear landmark as you approach Paraty by boat.

### Igreja de Santa Rita

Built in 1722, the Santa Rita church is the oldest church in Paraty and once served as the main church, until the Matriz was built. It was built by free men of mixed race and contains catacombs in its external grounds. It is of typical Jesuit style, with its three windows and one door in front. Today, it serves as the Museu de Arte Sacra and holds some antique furniture and silver pieces.

### Forte do Defensor Perpétuo

One of the more interesting structures of Paraty, the Forte was built in 1702 and reformed in 1822. Most interesting is its positioning in the town on the hill between Pontal and Jabaquara beaches, where it gains an incredible view of the bay. It was once part of a network of seven outposts that defended the city and its gold trade from invasion by sea. Only this fort remains. Today it serves as the Center for Art and Popular Culture.

## WATERFALLS

The most frequented waterfall of the area is the **Cachoeira do Tobogã.** There you'll find a large, clear pool surrounded by stones and lush vegetation. The falls themselves hit a large cluster of rocks that form a slippery slide into the pool. Locals commonly practice the art of rock sliding. You can, too, but be prepared for a few bruises afterward. Nearby is the **Poço do Tarzan** (Tarzan's Well) waterfall, which presents a rope from which you can swing and drop into a clear pool—shouting like Tarzan as you swing. These are both along the road from Paraty to Cunha and can be visited by car, van, or tour group. The **Cachoeira de Pedra Branca** presents a spectacular series of falls and pools of varying sizes, surrounded with large stones and tropical forest. Many of the pools are excellent for swimming and diving from the rocks. Access to this waterfall is on foot, from the Fazenda Murycana, which is about seven kilometers from Paraty along the Paraty–Cunya road and accessible by car or van from the city. From the *fazenda,* you walk about one hour on the Pedra Branca trail, which follows a river most of the way. The **Cachoeira do Bananal,** which is also along the Paraty–Cunha road, is accessed via the Fazenda do Bananal. It has a 15-meter drop, which presents an amazing show of nature. It's best accessed with a tour group. Finally, there are a few waterfalls in the Trindade area, including Codós, Cachadaço, and Pedra que Engole (meaning, the stone that swallows, and best accessed with a guide). These are inland from the village of Trindade, following Rua da Cachoeira to the right.

If you're a waterfall lover, don't stop with these. There are at least six other waterfalls in the Paraty and surrounding areas. Some others to note include Usina, Iriri, and Lage de Pedra.

## BEACHES
### Islands and Beaches in the Bay

There are numerous islands and secluded beaches in the Paraty area. Most are accessible only by boat. Most packaged trips include four or five principal stops in the bay, so you'll get a good idea of what's available. Be sure not to miss Praia da Lula and Praia Vermelha, two beaches great for swimming. There are also several islands with restaurants that may not be part of your boat trip, but you can go back another day with a more customized tour. Be sure to ask your captain the details as you pass by.

## Pontal and Jabaquara

The Pontal beach is closest to the Paraty center, easily accessed on foot by crossing the bridge on the north side of town and following the road to the right. Pontal is not the prettiest beach in the area, but it does offer a few kiosks for sitting and gazing out to the islands. Three kilometers to the north of town is Jabaquara beach and neighborhood. The beach is more frequented than Pontal and offers some kiosks and campgrounds. At the far end of its two-kilometer extension are therapeutic mud pools, where you can dip yourself any time of the day or night. The mud baths are principally used during Carnaval festivities when locals go running through the town as cave people, covered in mud. The mud serves to make the local waters a bit less clear than other beaches, but the water is warm and friendly.

## Praia Grande and Prainha

Ten kilometers north of Paraty, Praia Grande is a small stretch of beach that serves a local fishing community. The water is blue-green and shallow. On the left side of the beach is a trail that leads to Prainha, a more popular beach outpost. Prainha has beach bars and campgrounds to offset its clear, shallow waters and white sand. It's excellent for swimming and sun bathing. Buses leave for Prainha approximately every hour from the Paraty bus station.

## Iriguaçu

Less frequented than Prainha, Iriguaçu (about 31 kilometers north of Paraty) offers warm waters and dark sand, stretching for about one kilometer. On the far end, the Iriguaçu River meats the ocean in a cool mix. Small boats can take you out to the nearby island of Cedro, which is great for sunbathing and swimming. You can access this beach via the bus to São Gonçalinho.

## São Gonçalinho

Not far from Iriguaçu on the northern coast of Paraty is the popular beach of São Gonçalo, covered in fruit and palm trees with a few beach kiosks and campgrounds. From here,

© CHRISTOPHER VAN BUREN

São Paulo Coast to Rio

Praia do Sonho

you can take a small boat to the Ilha dos Pelados (Island of the Naked). There, you can take it all off while ordering a cold drink from one of the kiosks. You can also catch a van with one of the tour agencies, which makes trips out to this beach.

## Paraty-Mirim

The small settlement of Paraty-Mirim is about 17 kilometers south of Paraty and is home to a small beach of clear, warm water. On the far end is the mouth of the Paraty-Mirim River, where you can splash in fresh or salt waters. There is a small church worth visiting at the near end of the beach. Buses leave from Paraty every 45 minutes and pass through a Guarani reservation.

## Praia do Sonho

The bus going south to Praia do Sonho from Paraty will drop you off at its final stop, a small settlement that is essentially home to Dona Joana, her 13 children, 30 grandchildren, and 23 great-grandchildren. Passing through the middle of the settlement and uphill, you must walk about 1.5 hours through the Cairuçu wildlife reserve to reach the Praia do Sonho on the other side. Well worth the trouble, Sonho is a beautiful stretch of white sand and calm, blue water. On weekends, there should be a few rustic kiosks open that can make lunch or sell you a beer or soda. On weekdays, you might find one kiosk open. If you have a tent, you can camp on this beach in the campgrounds for about R$14. Bus 1040 leaves the Paraty station every 40 minutes, starting at 5:15 A.M. The last bus back is at 11:20 P.M.

## ☒ Trindade

Approximately 30 kilometers south of Paraty, Trindade is a village and coastal region offering some of the prettiest beaches in the area. Footpaths connect most of the beaches and the small village has a few accommodations and restaurants. The first beach is Praia Brava, which is a small, sandy strip surrounded by lush vegetation and a small stream that empties into the ocean. Praia do Cepilho is famous with surfers, as it often produces waves of up to four

meters (not for beginners). The village itself is on the banks of Praia de Fora and if you walk down Rua das Cachoeiras to the left, you'll hit Praia do Meio, one of the prettiest in the area with white sand and warm, blue waters. This is the most popular beach for sunbathing and swimming. Farther down the trail is Praia do Cachadaço, which has excellent pools for snorkeling with a wide variety of colorful fish and sea life. Finally, the Praia da Figueira is a small, hidden strip of sand and clear water that is often used for nude sunbathing. Nearby are more pools for snorkeling.

The bus from Paraty, called Paraty–Trindade, leaves every 40 minutes starting at 5:20 A.M. The last one back is at 11:20 P.M. You can get off at Praia Brava, which is before the end of the line. Be sure to ask the driver to stop for you. After the Praia Brava stop, the bus will drive through a stream of water before stopping in the village. You can walk to Praia do Meio from there. Boats are also available to give tours of the coastline and guides can take you out to the waterfalls. If you fall in love with the area, you can stay at one of the *pousadas* there (see *Accommodations* later for details).

# ENTERTAINMENT AND NIGHTLIFE

## Sidewalk Cafés, Bars, and Clubs

Nightlife in Paraty centers on the Centro Histórico and the many bars, clubs, and restaurants there. It's small enough that you can just walk around and find the atmosphere and crowd that suits you. You'll find crowds of people seated outside at the bars next to the Igreja Matriz. On weekends, these bars can get very crowded, so it's good to arrive early if you want a good seat outside. Other bars can be found all around the center, with a variety of styles. There are music and dance clubs scattered around the center. Just walk around and listen for the music you like. Most have cover charges or consumption minimums and get started around midnight.

The Jabaquara area is known to have beach parties on weekend nights. These usually include music and take place near the beach kiosks. To get there, walk through the Centro Histórico and across the bridge to the far side of town. Keep walking for about 15 minutes until you reach the Jabaquara area. To return, you can try one of the motorcycle taxis, which bring you back to the center for about R$6. A more sophisticated night can be spent on a boat in the bay. Check out night trips at the pier or through agencies.

## Theater and Shows

The most interesting show in town is the **Teatro de Bonecos,** or puppet theater (Rua Dona Geralda 327, tel. 24/3371-1575), which presents shows at 9 P.M. every Wednesday and Saturday. Tickets are available at the theater, tour agencies, and in many hotels.

# SPORTS AND RECREATION

## Boat Excursions

Catching a boat out to the islands is easy. Just visit the many agencies along Avenida Roberto Silveira to get an idea of the various trips offered and the prices of each. Each agency has its own boat (small or large) and packages its own particular set of island and beach attractions. You can reserve a place at one of the agencies, or just go out to the pier at 10 A.M. or 11 A.M. (the main departing times) and find a boat and package that looks good to you. Most trips cost around R$25 and include four or five stops with about 45 minutes at each. You'll get back to town around 4 P.M. Small boats can adjust their trips to the particular tastes of the passengers, staying longer or shorter at certain stops. If you have four or more people, you can even charter your own boat and assemble your own trip (key spots are listed throughout this chapter). Large boats offer the advantage of a more stable ride and perhaps better galley facilities. Diving into the ocean from atop a large boat is also a special thrill. Lunch is sold on board and will cost R$10–25, depending on the agency and number of people. You are usually allowed to bring your own lunch and small cooler, which is a good idea, since most boats will charge around R$6 for a can of beer. You can also have lunch at one of the island restaurants or beach kiosks, which will cost at least as much, but they offer a one-of-a-kind lunch experience. Be sure to negotiate the price, including lunch, before you get on board. Ask if snorkeling equipment is included (if not, there are shops near the pier where you can rent equipment).

One of the largest agencies is **Albatroz** (Av. Roberto Silveira 55, tel. 24/3371-2370), which has several large boats for bay tours and vans for trips to Trindade and the *fazendas* and waterfalls. **Aguia Tour** (Rua Jango Padua, tel. 24/3371-2733) near the bus station has a boat for bay tours, scuba diving tours, and vans for visiting the more distant beaches. They also rent bikes, dune buggies, and motorcycles. **Alcance Turismo** (Av. Roberto Silveira 86, tel. 24/3371-6442) has a safari jeep for trips to the *fazendas* and waterfalls, plus several hiking trips.

## Diving and Snorkeling

The best spot for surfing is Praia do Cepilho in Trindade. There's not much surfing around Paraty itself or in the northern beaches. Snorkeling and diving spots are numerous and if you're serious about diving, get in touch with one of the dive schools in town. Some great spots are Ilha Comprida and Ilha dos Ratos in the bay and Praia da Cachadaço in Trindade. Try **Adrenalina Mergulho** (tel. 24/9215-5802, www.adrenalinamergulho.com.br, call to set up a meeting at your hotel). You can get diving equipment and paraphernalia at **Seven Seas** (Rua da Lapa, Centro, www.sevenseasparaty.com.br).

## Fazendas

There are a number of working *fazendas* (ranches) in the hills just inland of Paraty. Many of these have working *cachaça* stills and provide samples along with excellent meals. You can find packaged excursions that go out to these *fazendas* and maybe out to one of the waterfalls before or after. Check with the guides listed in this chapter. Check out the **Fazenda Murycana** (tel. 24/3371-1153, www.murycana.com.br, 10 A.M.–6 P.M.

snorkeling in Paraty Bay

© CHRISTOPHER VAN BUREN

daily), which has an excellent *cachaça* that you can sample. They also have a small museum, homemade sweets, and country food at their restaurant. There's also **Coqueiro Fazenda Cabral** (Trevo de Paraty im 6.5, tel. 24/3371-1579, 8 A.M.–6:30 P.M. daily), which provides a tour of their still and production facilities. They have several different types of *cachaça* that you can try.

## Hiking

There are hiking trails all over the Paraty area, including the 1.5-hour hike to Praia do Sonho, the hike to the Cachoeira de Pedra Branca, and the trails in Trindade. You can also check with some of the adventure-tourism agencies for information about trails into the wildlife reserve area and to more hard-to-reach waterfalls.

## ACCOMMODATIONS

*Pousadas* in Paraty vary widely in style and quality. Most increase their rates 50–150 percent for peak season and major holidays. Here is a good selection from which you can choose.

### Under R$50

**Pousada Ace Hostels** (Rua João Luiz do Rosário at Rua Jango Pádua, tel. 24/3371-2684, www.acehstels.com, R$18 s and R$22 d) is a low-cost option with dorms and private rooms. They offer kitchen facilities and lockers. There are a couple of campgrounds in Paraty, including **Big Camping** (corner of Rua Onze and Av. Roberto Silveira, for more camping information, see www.paraty.com.br/trindade/f_camping.htm), which provides spaces for R$12 per person and some rooms for R$45 double occupancy. Rooms do not have bedding or towels.

### R$50–100

The **M Pousada Solar do Algarve** (Rua Derly Helena 28, tel. 24/3371-1173, www.solardoalgarve.com.br, R$30 s, R$50 d in low season) is well located just outside the historical center. It's small and quaint with lots of plants. On the same street is the **M Pousada Marendaz** (Rua Derly Helena 09, tel. 24/3371-1369, www.paraty.com.br/marendaz.htm, R$50 d), which is run by two sisters in a very homespun style. They have a dozen or so rooms in two stories situated around a charming quad.

Rooms have ceiling fans and include a decent breakfast. **Pousada Sonho Meu** (Rua João Luiz do Rosário, tel. 24/3371-2069, www.paraty.com.br/sonhomeu.htm, R$40–60 d) is on the main road just outside the historical center and has basic rooms.

## R$100–200

You can stay in the *pousada* of the Brazilian royal family (descendants of Dom Pedro II), which owns the **Pousada do Príncipe** (Av. Roberto Silveira 289, tel. 24/3371-2266, www.pousadadoprincipe.com.br, R$90 s and R$110 d). Ironically, it's not the most "royal" of the Paraty accommodations. They have a pool and modern facilities with TV and air conditioning in the rooms. In the Pontal beach area is the new and charming **Pousada Aldeia Paratii** (Alameda Princesa Isabel, tel. 24/3371-2689, www.paraty.com.br/aldeiaparatii.htm, R$80 s, R$130 d), which has seven suites with TV and air-conditioning, king-sized beds, a pool, a good breakfast, and very clean facilities.

One of the nicest *pousadas* in the Paraty Centro Histórico is the **Pousada Porto Imperial** (Rua Ten. Francisco Antônio, tel. 24/3371-2323, www.pousadaportoimperial.com.br, R$140 d and R$210 suite), which is in a historical building with several colonial-style rooms that will make you feel like you are back in colonial Brazil. In the area just past the bridge heading to Praia Pontal, along the banks of the River Pereque-Açú are a couple of resort-style *pousadas*. **Pousada La Cigale** (Av. Otávio Gama, tel. 24/3371-1884, R$70 double occupancy) has rooms with TV and air-conditioning, pool, wet sauna and a great breakfast buffet. The **Pousada Paisagem** (Rua das Acácias 03, tel. 24/3371-1602, www.paraty.com.br/paisagem.htm, R$85–125) is a similar offering without the pool and sauna facilities.

One of the coziest places to stay is at the **M Pousada do Ouro** (Rua Dr. Pereira 145, Centro, tel. 24/3371-2033, www.pousadadoouro.com.br, R$135–165). They are located in an 18th-century building with a lovely courtyard garden. Make sure you get a room in the main house. They have a pool, gym, restaurant, sauna,

bar, and rooms have air, TV, and phone. You'll like the energy at the **M Pousada Arte Urquijo** (Rua Da. Geralda 79, Centro, tel. 24/3371-1362, www.paraty.com.br/urquijo.htm, R$195). They have six rooms in an 18th-century building with beautiful wooden floors. They don't accept children under 12.

### Over R$200

A great place to stay in Paraty is at the **M Pousada Padieiro** (Rua do Comércio 74, Centro, tel. 24/3371-1370, www.pousadapadieiro.com.br, R$225). They are in the Centro Histórico in a colonial-style building with very cozy rooms that offer great comfort in an old-fashioned setting. They have a pool, sauna, and bar. Rooms have air and TV and they don't allow children under 15.

## FOOD

The best way to approach the selection of restaurants in the Centro Histórico is to walk around town, look into the restaurants that catch your eye and check out their menus. Shopping for restaurants is actually a great goal to have as you stroll around town, checking out the nightlife. Remember that there are also numerous restaurants outside of the Centro Histórico, including some that are situated on islands and others at the local *fazendas*. Following is a selection to get you started.

### International

The often-recognized **Porto Restaurante** (Rua do Comércio 36, tel. 24/3371-1058, noon–midnight daily), has been listed in various magazines as one of the best in Brazil. They offer a mixture of Brazilian and international cuisine with a flair for the artistic and creative. They have an extensive wine list and English is spoken. Meals are approximately R$60 per person. **Sushi Paraty** (Praça da Bandeira 01, tel. 24/3371-3161, noon–3 P.M. and 7 P.M.–midnight daily) near the pier offers traditional sushi and some Chinese dishes for around R$45 per person. **Thai Brasil** (Rua Dona Geralda 345, tel. 24/3371-0127, 6 P.M.

Mon.–Sat.) has a romantic, artistic atmosphere and an open kitchen where they prepare various dishes from the East. It's open 6 P.M. until the last person leaves and costs around R$40 per person. Out along the road to Cunha is a well-known *fazenda*-style restaurant, called **M Vila Verde** (tel. 24/3371-7808, 11 A.M.–5:30 P.M. Tue.–Sun.). Look for the sign on the road after you pass the Murycana turn off. If you're driving, park on the side of the road (at the sign) and walk down to the brook where you'll find the entrance to the restaurant. They have an international menu, and meals run about R$60 per person. It's also easy to reach by taxi.

### Island Restaurants

On the little Ilha do Catupão, across from the Praia da Lula, is a restaurant with a deck that looks out onto the water. You have to arrive by boat for lunch, which is served from 11 A.M. until around 4 P.M. Check with one of the tour agencies for information on getting there. The **Kontiki** restaurant (tel. 24/9999-9599, tel. 24/3371-1666) is on the Ilha Duas Irmãs, which is a small island in the bay. They offer all kinds of fish dishes and Mediterranean cuisine in a fabulous tropical/Mediterranean atmosphere. You can catch their private ferry from the pier to the island. Reservations are recommended. The best idea is to have lunch there, as you'll be able to appreciate the view.

### Regional Food

You can have dinner at the **Fazenda Murycana** (Estrada Paraty–Cunha, Km 06, tel. 24/3371-1153, 10 A.M.–6 P.M. daily) which is on the way to some of the waterfalls in the region. The *fazenda* serves typical regional dishes, along with their special brand of *cachaça*. You can have dinner after playing in the waterfalls, or head out there just for dinner. Call them for transportation options. **A Teresa Resto-Bar** (Rua da Lapa 256, tel. 24/3371-6273, 11 A.M. daily) offers all kinds of meat, chicken, and fish dishes cooked in traditional Brazilian styles. They also have many vegetarian dishes and a

decent wine list. If you like the idea of dining at a beach kiosk, you can try the **Quiosque do Beto** (tel. 24/3371-1661) on the Jabaquara beach. They make good seafood dishes for a reasonable price (around R$18 per person). It's very casual. Open for lunch and dinner starting around noon.

## INFORMATION AND SERVICES

Tourist information is available at the main entrance to the Centro Histórico on the corner of Avenida Roberto Silveira and Rua Domingos Gonçalves de Alporo There you can get maps, pamphlets, and questions answered. Walk up Avenida Roberto Silveira (away from the Centro Histórico) to find various tour agencies, offering everything from boat tours to hikes and safaris. There are a couple more in the Centro Histórico near the Dores church.

Internet services are available all around town, including a couple near the Matriz church *praça* (in the Gina Pizza Restaurant) and one across from the Pousada Marendaz on Rua Derly Helena 09 for about R$4 per hour. There is another across from the bus station for R$4 per hour. These services are all run by ParatyWeb (tel. 24/3371-2499, www.ecoparaty.com/cyber). Their three locations are: in front of the main plaza in the Quero restaurant (10–2 A.M. daily), in the brand new Restaurante da Gina (Rua Dr. Samuel Costa 245, noon–midnight daily) and in Placa Informática next to the bus station (9 A.M.–6 P.M. daily).

There are banks all along Avenida Roberto Silveira, including a Banco do Brasil office with international ATMs. Most establishments accept credit cards and the large tour agencies will exchange money.

## GETTING AROUND

You can walk all around the Centro Histórico as far as the Jabaquara beach. To see remote beaches, you'll need to rent a car, catch a bus, join an excursion with one of the tour agencies in town or take a boat from the Paraty pier or river. Buses go up and down the coast from the *rodoviaria* to Trindade, Paraty-Mirim, and Laranjeiras to the south and São Goncalinho and Prainha to the north. Most buses begin around 6 A.M. and cost around R$3. Boat trips to these beaches will vary in price. Northern trips are easier than southern trips due to the configuration of the coastline. You can prob-ably find a trip going north from the pier or charter your own boat with four or more people. By car, it's possible to get anywhere around the bay within 20–30 minutes.

Heading to the waterfalls is possible by car or tour van. Most are in the same region, off the highway that goes from Paraty to Cunha.

## Angra dos Reis

The once-noble city of Angra dos Reis is now a run-down, foul-smelling industrial port town. Its beaches are polluted and swarming with *urubú* (a type of vulture prevalent in Brazil) and the town center has almost nothing of its origi-nal charm left (just enough to reveal that it once had some charm). For tourists, Angra dos Reis is simply a launch pad to the various islands in the bay—some of the more secluded being fre-quented by Brazil's rich and famous. Not the least of these islands is **Ilha Grande,** accessible from Angra dos Reis by ferryboat or one of the regular schooners that make the trip.

If you miss the 3 P.M. ferryboat to Ilha Grande for some reason (easy to do when catch-ing buses from other towns, like Paraty), then you can either take one of the private boats across, which leave throughout the day for around R$25 per person (if they have enough passengers), or stay the night in Angra dos Reis. Should you end up passing some time in Angra, here are a few suggestions.

### SPORTS AND RECREATION

The thing to do in Angra dos Reis is get out of there, preferably by boat. The principal destina-tion is Ilha Grande, but there are many islands in the bay. Some of the most interesting are small islands just south of Angra and the Ilha da Gipóia. You can find tourist agencies with boat trips all around the town center, which is very near the docks. You can also find infor-mation at the bus station and the main tourist information office, which is located between the bus station and the town center.

Some of the island tours that do not in-clude Ilha Grande are pretty spectacular and may even be worth spending a night in Angra. Check with **Passeios Marítimos** (Av. Julio Maria 54, tel. 24/3365-7003) for some op-tions or **Mar de Angra** (Av. Julio Maria 16, tel. 24/3365-1097). For experienced scuba div-ers, the islands and coastline around Angra are a paradise. Some of the country's best diving spots are here and, once you get away from the Angra shoreline, the water gets clear and clean. Check with Diver's Trip (Rua José Pereira Carneiro 152, Monsuaba, tel. 24/3361-7560, www.diverstrip.com.br) for more information on diving excursions in the area, or get in touch with any of the schools in Ilha Grande (listed later in this chapter).

The countryside around Angra dos Reis is pure tropical beauty and there are numerous old trails that can be used to explore the area, including visiting some of the nearby water-falls. A good resource for organizing a trek around Angra is **Andarilhos de Mambucaba** (Rua Roraima 12, Mambucaba, tel. 24/3362-9469, tel. 24/9991-8024, call first to arrange a meeting in town).

### ACCOMMODATIONS

The **Angra Hostel** (Praça da Matriz 152, tel. 24/3364-4759, R$18–22 pp for group rooms) is a good, economical option that is not far from the town center or the boat to Ilha Grande. They can help you with connec-tions out of town or to Ilha Grande. The **Lon-dres Angra Hotel** (Av. Raul Pompéia 75, tel. 24/3365-0044, R$50–70 s and R$70–85 d) is located in the center of town and has decent

São Paulo Coast to Rio

rooms with cable TV, phone, and air-conditioning. Finally, the **Palace Hotel** (Rua Coronel Carvalho 275, tel. 24/3365-0032, R$70 s and R$80 d) has rooms with cable TV, phone, and air-conditioning.

## FOOD

There are restaurants and casual eating options all around the town center. One of the best, with its self-service lunch deals, is at the **Londres Angra Hotel** (Av. Raul Pompéia 75, tel. 24/3365-0044), which is around R$12 per kilo.

## INFORMATION AND SERVICES

The tourist information office (Rua Caravelas, tel. 24/3364-4759) is at the entrance to town, coming from the main bus terminal. It's in one of the few restored colonial buildings in town. They have good information on boat excursions, resorts, and Ilha Grande. It's open from 8 A.M.–5 P.M. There is also information at a small counter in the bus terminal. There is an Internet gaming station (LAN House) just behind the tourist information office, which also serves for Internet connections (if you can take the kids shouting constantly). It's about R$3 per hour. A couple of good sites for information on Angra are www.angraonline.com and www.angra_dos_reis.com.

You can find quiet phones at the Telemar post on Av. Raul Pompéia 97 on the left side past the Londres Angra Hotel. There are several banks in the town center. Banco do Brasil (corner of Rua do Comércio and Rua Raul Pompeia) has Plus and Cirrus systems on some of its ATMs and you can find travel agents who will exchange money for you.

## GETTING THERE

Most buses coming into Angra are coming from either Rio de Janeiro or Paraty. The Viação Costa Verde line makes the trip from Rio to Paraty and back, stopping in Angra. There is also the Colitur line that goes from Paraty to Angra and back. If you come from Belo Horizonte on the Util line (the "Angra dos Reis" bus), you will arrive very early in the morning. This gives you plenty of time to check out the various options for getting to Ilha Grande or some other island. You may have to kill a few hours in Angra. A leisurely walk around town can help with an hour or so. Also note that the nearby town of Mangaratiba (about 20 minutes drive to the north) has a 9 A.M. ferry to Ilha Grande.

## GETTING AROUND

The bus from Paraty will take you all the way to the town center, where you can walk a short distance to the docks and catch the ferry boat to Ilha Grande. Other buses will probably let you off at the main bus terminal. It's possible to walk from the bus station to town if you're not carrying a lot of luggage. Otherwise, you can take a taxi for about R$8 or one of the many buses heading in that direction from the street in front of the station (catch the bus on the opposite side of the street). You will pass the tourist information office on the way into town. Once you are in town, it's a short walk to the docks.

# Ilha Grande

A lot of people come to Ilha Grande not knowing what to expect. Since it's such a large island (the third largest in Brazil, next to Florianópolis and Ilhabela) and so close to the large, industrial areas of Brazil, many visitors expect to see some type of urbanization here. Roads, at least. In fact, Ilha Grande is like an oasis in the busy ocean between Rio and São Paulo. It marks the northern end of the Paraty Bay, one of the most beautiful places in the country. And it has remained relatively untouched by modernization, aside from a few minor conveniences, like air-conditioning, Internet, and credit card access. Banks, however, have not quite arrived on the scene, so remember to bring cash with you when you visit.

The nucleus of Ilha Grande is the small village of Abraão, which was once a defense outpost for the bay, protecting the precious cargo going in and out of the area (gold, sugar, and coffee for starters), mostly from pirates, but also from organized invasions. Now it is home to dozens of quaint *pousadas* and restaurants. Thankfully, the town cannot grow much, since it is surrounded by tall hills. That and the difficulty of getting supplies to the island help keep things moving slowly. Abraão is one of the most charming island towns you'll ever see, but if you prefer seclusion, there are a number of *pousadas* around the perimeter of the island and even some campgrounds. It does not take a lot of effort to get away from the crowd. Although Abraão is irresistible, you'll want to make your way to some of the beaches around the island, of which there are many.

You can visit the beaches by boat or on foot, although some of the more remote beaches can take up to eight hours hiking—the really remote beaches take a couple of days. Even the shorter hikes can be rather arduous at times due to the hot, tropical conditions and steep inclines. One day, you can walk to Lopes Mendes, which takes you past Palmas and Mangue-Pouso. Another day, you can head in the opposite direction (south) and visit Praia Preta and the Feiticeira Beach and Waterfall. You can also hang out at the beaches in Abraão. To really relax and enjoy some time at these beaches, you'll need more than a couple of days on the island. In fact, you could spend months exploring the island's many remote beaches, but to do it justice will take you around 5–7 days. There are many great diving locations off shore (including two sunken ships) and plenty of local dive masters to take you out. The water is generally warm, at around 25°C average temperature.

## ABRAÃO

The village of Abraão is easily traversed on foot. There is a main road that runs from the pier up into the village. First, you'll see the church and main *praça*. Around the *praça* are a few good restaurants for lunch and late-night beers. There are also some boutique shops and souvenir shops here. Continue up the road to pass the main restaurant row. There are several options here, including some Internet cafés. When you reach the intersection, you can turn left to head down the back road through the village. You'll pass numerous *pousadas* (practically every structure in town that is not a restaurant is a *pousada*). The next intersection takes you back to the beach (to the left), past more restaurants and *pousadas*. If you keep walking straight, you'll pass the youth hostel on your left and eventually hit the trail that goes to Lopes Mendes Beach.

Walking along the beach, you'll see several beachfront *pousadas* and more restaurants. You'll also pass the Jardim Buganville, which is a path that leads to, you guessed it, more boutique shops, restaurants, and *pousadas*. Despite this proliferation of *pousadas* in the last couple of years, the town is still as charming as can be. This is partially due to the lack of cars on the island and the presence of so much sand. During low season, the competition among *pousadas* keeps prices quite reasonable.

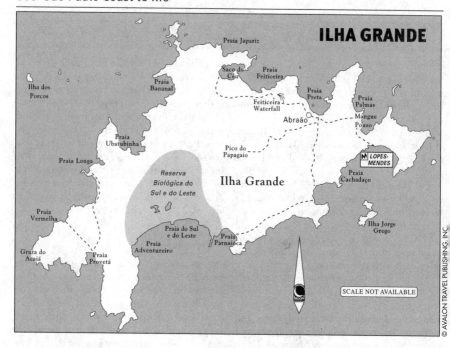

ILHA GRANDE

Praia Japariz

Saco do Céu

Praia Feiticeira

Ilha dos Porcos

Praia Bananal

Praia Preta

Praia Palmas

Feiticeira Waterfall

Abraão

Mangue Pouso

Praia Ubatubinha

Pico do Papagaio

LOPES-MENDES

Praia Longa

Reserva Biológica do Sul e do Leste

Ilha Grande

Praia Cachadaço

Praia Vermelha

Praia do Sul e do Leste

Ilha Jorge Grego

Gruta do Acaiá

Praia Provetá

Praia Adventureiro

Praia Parnaióca

SCALE NOT AVAILABLE

© AVALON TRAVEL PUBLISHING, INC.

## THE EASTERN TRAIL AND BEACHES

The most popular trail on the island is the hike to Praia Lopes Mendes, said to be one of the prettiest beaches in Brazil. The trail takes you past a few other beaches that might tempt you for a couple hours of swimming and relaxing. My suggestion is to take this trail without the main goal being the arrival at Praia Lopes Mendes. Instead, consider all the beaches along the way to be part of the goal and spend as much time as you like at each one. The pleasure is spending the day on the trail, not at Lopes Mendes per se.

### Lopes Mendes

Often noted as one of Brazil's prettiest beaches, Lopes Mendes is a 1.5-hour hike from Abraão up and back down one of the island's smaller peaks. Lopes Mendes is one of the most popular destinations on the island and can get crowded in peak season. Along the way, you'll pass the Pal-mas and Mangue-Pouso beaches and get a good look at Abraãozinho from above. The tropical surroundings along the trail are home to numerous bird species and you might even spy some small monkeys along the way. When you finally make it to Lopes Mendes, you will set eyes on a stretch of blue water and white sand that is a rare commodity. There are no kiosks on this beach, so you'll need your own towel or blanket for sitting. Some locals sell drinks and sandwiches from coolers, in case you didn't eat at one of the beaches along the way. The trail and beach stops to Lopes Mendes are worth an entire day, if you take it slow and enjoy all the beaches.

### Mangue and Pouso

Mangue and Pouso are two beaches, separated by some rocks and a pier. Both have calm, warm waters and shady kiosks for getting out of the sun for awhile. Since they are on the way to the famous Lopes Mendes beach, they can get somewhat crowded during peak season, but most people mistakenly spend most of

the coastline along Ilha Grande

their time at Lopes Mendes and pass through Mangue and Pouso rather quickly. Although Lopes Mendes is a visual marvel, I personally prefer these two beaches, which have more relaxed atmospheres. The kiosk/bar at the entrance to the trail up to Lopes Mendes is a great place to hang out and have lunch.

## Palmas

Palmas is a pretty little beach that is perfect for a morning swim. The kiosk in the middle of the beach is run by friendly folks and offers a cold drink or even lunch if you stay around that long. This is the first major beach stop on the trail to Lopes Mendes and most people pass through quickly. However, it's well worth a couple hours visit. When you come down the trail to the beaches, there is a fork to the left that leads to a cute little beach that is worth checking out.

## THE WESTERN TRAIL AND BEACHES

The trail that runs to the west from Abraão first passes along the beaches just outside of the village, particularly Praia Preto, one of the most popular beaches for sunning and kicking back, just about one kilometer from the end of the village. The trail also passes the Feiticeira Waterfall (after an uphill climb), which is a great place to cool off in a fresh-water pool. You then descend to the Feiticeira Beach where you can relax for awhile at one of the rustic kiosks. This part of the trek takes about an hour and involves a bit of a climb and descent. Along the way, you're likely to see monkeys and tropical birds if you're not too noisy as you hike. The next leg of the journey lasts about two hours and takes you to the Saco do Céu, one of the prettiest areas on the island, with calm waters that are begging for you to come in and cool off. There are kiosks on the beach and even *pousadas* in the area, in case you decide to spend the night. If you keep going on the trail, you'll arrive at Praia Japariz, where you can take another rest and grab a snack before heading back. A great alternative to hiking out there and back is to take a boat out and hike back, or vice-versa. There are boats in Saco do Céu and Japariz waiting to bring folks back from the hike, but check with guides in

a most pleasant day at Palmas Beach

© CHRISTOPHER VAN BUREN

São Paulo Coast to Rio

Abraão before leaving to make sure. The trail, by the way, continues all the way to the far tip of the island, passing some of the more remote beaches along the way.

## REMOTE BEACHES

You shouldn't miss some of the remote beaches if you can help it. One of the most beautiful is called Cachadaço on the far side of the island. It has the bluest water you'll ever see and a charming beach with rocks along the edges. There is a difficult trail that heads over the peaks and down to this beach. Another must-see beach is Parnaióca, farther along the same trail. This beach was once home to the largest community on the island and there are ruins of an old church left behind. Today there are only a few people living there, but the beach is still beautiful, tranquil, and practically deserted. It's a long hike out to Parnaióca and you should consider going by boat.

## ENTERTAINMENT AND NIGHTLIFE

Any nightlife that exists on the island occurs in Abraão and generally revolves around food and

drinks. There are no shows or discos, but some of the principal bars stay open late. Just walk down the main road to see what's happening.

## SPORTS AND RECREATION
### Boat Excursions

Boat excursions are popular on the island, since they are the easiest way to get to the various beaches (and the only way to get to some). Popular excursions take you along the same basic routes as the trails detailed earlier. By boat, you'll stop at the principal beaches along the trajectory, with a stopping point at Saco do Céu or Pouso Beach for you to get out and hike or hang out on the beach. Depending on the arrangement, you can take the same boat back, catch a different boat, or hike back. All of these arrangements are possible. You can also take a boat out to the more remote beaches. Highlights include Praia Bananal, Ubatubinha, Praia Longa (also called Lagoa Verde), and Praia Vermelha. These take hours to reach by boat and sometimes include an overnight stay at one of the *pousadas* in the area.

### Hikes

The two hikes mentioned earlier are the most

boats waiting for passengers in Paraty

a dive with **Ilha Grande Dive** (tel. 24/3361-5512, igdive@bol.com.br, 8 A.M.–noon and 4–10 P.M. daily). The dive master there is Alexandre Faria, who is one of the most experienced on the island. They have night dives, beginner dives, courses, and excursions for experienced divers. Finally, there is **Ocean** (Enseada do Bananal in the Pousada Sankay, tel. 24/3365-8496, www.ocean.com.br, call to make an appointment) with similar services.

## ACCOMMODATIONS

Starting with the low-cost accommodations, the first *pousada* to note is also one of the most interesting options in town. The ℕ **Pousada L'Albergue** (Av. Getúlio Vargas, tel. 24/3361-5217, R$20 s, R$30 d with breakfast buffet) is on the far end of town (to the left of the pier) and set way back on a large piece of property. It offers a very quiet and tranquil atmosphere for an excellent price. The **Pousada Over Nativa** (Rua Getúlio Vargas 517, tel. 24/3361-5108, www.overnativa.com.br, R$15–30 pp) is run by the always-happy Marcio, who can get by speaking English, Spanish, and French. His rooms have TV and air-conditioning or ceiling fans. His is a good place for solo travelers. The **Pousada dos Meros** (Av. Getúlio Vargas, tel. 24/3361-5214, www.pousadadosmeros.com.br, R$45 d weekdays and R$60 weekends) has basic rooms with ceiling fans, a tree-filled garden area, and laundry facilities. In their front yard is an excellent crepe kiosk. The **Pousada Mara e Claude** (Rua da Praia 333, tel. 24/3361-5922, tel. 24/3361-5899) is an excellent choice for a beachfront hotel. The very friendly Mara will take care of everything you need and her husband Claude is French and speaks English. They have three rooms with ocean views and three without. Rooms have fan, TV, and most have gas-heated showers. R$60 double without view and R$90 with view. In peak season, prices go up to R$150. They don't accept credit cards yet.

The **Pousada Casablanca** (Rua da Praia 34, Jardim Buganville, tel. 24/3367-2363,

common day hikes in the area. You can take longer hikes around the island that include overnight stays at campgrounds and *pousadas* along the way. It's a great way to see the island but requires a little planning ahead of time. Check with **Ilhagrande Adventure** (Rua Getúlio Vargas 35, Abraão, tel. 24/3361-5590, www.ilhagrandeadventure.com, 9 A.M.–9 P.M. Mon.–Sat.) for information on putting a long hike together. They also rent equipment if you decide to camp along the way.

### Snorkeling and Diving

There are some amazing dives around Ilha Grande, including clear pools, shipwrecks, a helicopter wreck, underwater caves, and remote islands. Principal areas for diving include the perimeter of the Jorge Grego Island, the Palmas Island, and the area off the Adventureiro Beach, called the Adventureiro Marine Park. Besides numerous species of tropical fish, you're likely to see rays, eels, and even dolphins. Check with **Ilha Grande Diving and Fishing** (Trav. Buganville 5, tel. 24/3361-5877, www.divingfishing.com.br, 8 A.M.–8 P.M. daily). You can also schedule tel. 24/3361-5040, www.casablancapousada .com.br, R$70 s, R$80 d) is a pretty *pousada* close to the beach (down the Buganville Shopping Alley). It has clean, white walls, a great sitting area in their patio café, and TV and air-conditioning in their rooms. They accept most credit cards. The **ℕ Pousada Paraíso** (Rua Getúlio Vargas 249, tel. 24/3361-5606, R$70 s, R$100 d) is a clean and well-maintained establishment with 19 rooms containing TV, air-conditioning, and gas heating. They also have comfortable beds and a nice breakfast. Finally, the luxurious and healthy **Sítio do Lobo** (Enseada das Estrelas, tel. 24/3361-4438, www.sitiodolobo.com.br, R$480 standard and R$750 for a suite) is a remote resort with an alternative feel. They offer all meals (healthy style), kayaking, hiking, yoga, Tai-Chi, massage, and their own boats to take you around the island. All this in an island setting with air-conditioned rooms, phone, Internet, and pool.

## FOOD

A good option for pizza is **Fogão de Lenha Pizzaria** in the main *praça* (tel. 24/3361-5097, 11 A.M.–midnight daily). They serve pizzas of all kinds, including some sweet pizzas. Dinner will run about R$18–40 for two. One of the best places for fish along the main street is **Resta 1** (Rua Prof. Alice da Silva, tel. 24/3361-5873, 11 A.M.–midnight daily). They have a great *refeição* (lunch plate) for only R$7.50 and dinner plates go for around R$30 for two. Try the *filet de peixe resta 1* with shrimp sauce. A great place for drinks and crepes is the crepe kiosk at the **ℕ Pousada dos Meros** (Rua Getúlio Vargas, tel. 24/3361-5214, open 24 hours). They have outdoor seating in a tropical setting and the fattest crepes you've ever seen, filled with all kinds of ingredients. Crepes run R$7–10 and the place is open late. It's a great place for meeting others on the island.

One of the best restaurants in town, offering a cozy atmosphere and great lighting, is **ℕ Canoa Restaurante** (Rua da Praia, tel. 24/3361-9907, 6 P.M.–midnight daily). They serve seafood, chicken, salads, and pasta for around R$30–50 per person.

## GETTING THERE

The ferry from Angra to Ilha Grande leaves at 3:30 P.M. Monday–Friday and 1:30 P.M. weekends and holidays. The weekday boat leaves Ilha Grande for Mangaratiba at around 5:30 P.M. to return again at 10:30 A.M. the next day (leaving from Mangaratiba at 9 A.M.). It then sets sail for Angra dos Reis at 10 A.M. to start the cycle over again. The ferry costs only R$4 per person. If you miss this boat for some reason (easy to do when catching buses from other towns, like Paraty), then you can either take one of the private boats across, which leave throughout the day for around R$25 per person, or stay the night in Angra dos Reis.

## GETTING AROUND

There are only two ways to get around on Ilha Grande, by land or by sea. You can hike around the island, using the numerous trails that circumnavigate the place and take you past most of its beaches and alcoves, or you can take a boat to the various island hot spots, heading directly to the beach of your choice or touring the jagged circumference of the island in search of the perfect beach. For a notion of the size of the island, it will take you at least three days to hike around it and the trails are not flat and smooth. With the tropical sun and often humid conditions, some of the longer hikes are for serious trailblazers. A boat tour of the perimeter takes two days and you can either sleep on the boat or stop at one of the more remote *pousadas* along the way. These options can be worked out with your guide. Of course, you can choose specific locations to visit by boat, making the trip faster and more targeted. There are also small, packaged tours that visit the coastline to the north or south of Abraão. Thankfully, if you can hike to one of the beaches near Abraão, you can catch a boat taxi back to town. So relax and enjoy the beach; if you're too tired to hike back, just catch the boat taxi.

# Belo Horizonte

The third-largest city in Brazil by population, Belo Horizonte, or B.H. (bee-ah-GAH) to the locals, is nestled in the hills of the Serra do Curral, a small mountain range for which the city was originally named Curral D'El Rei (King's Corral). The city is situated in a triangular position with Rio de Janeiro to the east and São Paulo to the south. Belo Horizonte, while not as evolved as São Paulo or as picturesque as Rio, offers some interesting attractions that will take you off the tourist track for awhile. First and foremost, Belo Horizonte is a shopper's dream. The garment district, called **Barro Preto,** offers some of the best deals on clothes in the entire country. The city offers several active street fairs with wonderful hand-crafted items at excellent prices, even for Brazil. And the basics of dining, groceries, and accommodations are 10–30 percent less expensive than in the other cities. If you get carried away, you can look around for some good deals on extra luggage.

Belo Horizonte is also home to all kinds of great food products, including sweets, bottled waters, beef, and the famous Brazilian *pão de quejo* (cheese bread), which was invented here. And while the city may not offer the breadth of international cuisine that São Paulo offers, Comida Mineira is well known and loved throughout Brazil as the best country cookin' available.

Belo Horizonte, with 3.2 million people is

# Must-Sees

**M Barro Preto Garment District:** The city's bustling garment district, Barro Preto has nearly 1,000 stores and outlets for all types of clothing, from casual beachwear to jeans to formal evening gowns. You'll find factory and discount outlets, fabric and supply stores, indoor malls, and collectives (page 176).

**M Feira de Artes e Artesanatos:** On Sunday mornings, a huge section of the city's main boulevard becomes one of the largest outdoor flea markets in Latin America. As its name suggests, most items are handmade by local artisans, but you'll also find great deals on clothes, shoes, and accessories (page 177).

**M Mercado Central:** A labyrinth of isles full of meats, cheeses, fruits, and vegetables, this public market is one of the most interesting in the country. Besides the food, there are also wines, *cachaças,* health foods, pots, pans, wicker furniture, and, of course, live animals. It's a wonderful slice of the local culture (page 177).

**M Savassi Clubs and Discos:** The Savassi area is the city's upscale center, sporting numerous sidewalk cafés, boutique stores, art galleries, design centers, restaurants, and bars. In addition, a number of classy nightclubs have recently sprung up, making the area a great nightlife destination (page 184).

**M Sabará:** Long before Belo Horizonte existed, Sabará stood as one of the five most important gold towns in Minas Gerais. At its peak, its gold production surpassed that of Ouro Preto, and the vestiges of this era remain intact. Colonial architecture, gold-lined churches, and lavish public buildings . . . it's all within an hour of Belo Horizonte and can be seen in a single day (page 190).

**BELO HORIZONTE**

Sabará
Barro Preto Garment District
Belo Horizonte
Mercado Central
Feira de Artes e Artesanatos
Savassi Clubs and Discos

Rio de Janeiro

ATLANTIC   OCEAN

still considered by residents of São Paulo and Rio to be something of a farming town, full of *caipiras* (country folk) transporting their cattle and chickens to and from the city by mule. Indeed, you can still find, on the outskirts of town, country farmers with mule carts moving their cargo precariously down city streets (taking the right-of-way over the cars). But Belo Horizonte is, in truth, a bustling metropolis with a crowded city center, an international airport, several upscale neighborhoods, and ev-

erything you would expect from a major city. Life in B.H. has actually become somewhat stressed and agitated in the past 10 years or so, making these simple, country folk something of a terror behind the wheel. Driving in Belo Horizonte is, to be sure, an exercise in insanity and self-restraint. Combine this pent-up, urbanized stress with the sincere but insufficient attempt at urban planning and you have one of the most challenging and awe-inspiring street scenes in Latin America.

Belo Horizonte

## PLANNING YOUR TIME

Most travelers spend no more than two or three days in Belo Horizonte and usually not all at once. The largest city in the region, B.H. serves as the hub for travelers going to and from the historical towns, farming villages, and industrial centers that surround it. That makes it common for travelers to come back to B.H. two or three times during their exploration of the region, spending just enough time to re-stock any necessities, get to know one or two neighborhoods or sights, and perhaps partake of a new restaurant. Then it's off to the historical towns or mountains. There's no reason to hang around in Belo Horizonte longer than is absolutely necessary.

If you find yourself in Belo Horizonte for a more extended period, you could plan a couple of day trips to some of the small towns within a day's reach from the city. **Sabará,** a mere 20 minutes by bus from the B.H. *rodoviaria* (bus terminal), offers a taste of the region's historical architecture, and the nearby **Gruta da Lapinha** will give you a feel for the region's hillsides and natural caves.

Generally temperate, Belo Horizonte is most pleasant March–September, the dry season. Temperatures during this time can get well into the hot zone, reaching as high as 42°C, but usually hover around 30–36°C. The rainy season, October–February, brings a consistent and moderate rain with patches of sun every week or so. During the peak of the rainy season, it's not uncommon to experience heavy, tropical downpours that bring floods and landslides. On a clear day, the city appears a sparkling metropolis with many tall buildings climbing up and down its hills. On such a day, you'd do well to find a majestic viewpoint in the south hills of the city and take in the bird's eye view.

## HISTORY

In the late 19th century, Belo Horizonte, then known as Arraial de Belo Horizonte (Belo Hor-izonte Settlement), was selected as the site for the new state capital, largely due to it's central-ized location in the state. A train line was ex-tended into the village and the Praça da Estação was built. Thus the city began, and continues to this day, as an almost schizophrenic mix-ture of technology and modernity placed on top of simple, traditional origins. At the time of the city's creation, Minas Gerais was suffer-ing from a fragmentation brought about by the excessive mining activities in the region. Ouro Preto was then the state capital and had once been the central mining town in the state, with a population greater than that of Rio de Ja-neiro (although as much as 60 percent of those were slaves). Then the small town of Sabará took the lead in gold production and was be-ginning to urbanize the region. Belo Horizonte was conceived as the unifying, governing city that would bring a new order and prosperity to the region.

The Praça da Estação quickly became the central point for the people of Belo Horizonte and the train line brought progress to the new center. Soon parks, churches, and *avenidas* sprouted up all over the city—starting with the Parque Municipal and the Praça da Liber-dade, which soon became the civil center with its governor's palace and state buildings. In the 1930s came an industrial boom and, to keep it lit up and running, the creation of Brazil's first state energy company, CEMIG. By 1942, this growth had reached its culmination in the cre-ation of the Lagoa da Pampulha and it's artistic and architectural annexes. The 1940s mark the city's peak years and B.H. saw a time of great cultural and industrial growth under the gov-ernment of Juscelino Kubitscheck, who went on to become president of Brazil. In the '60s and '70s, the city's population more than dou-bled and the short road to over-urbanization began. Today, the city suffers from a grave lack of public services, infrastructure, and just plain good housekeeping, although there are some independent efforts being made to restore the city's once-beautiful profile.

# BELO HORIZONTE

AV DO CONTORNO

AV FRANCISCO SALES

EZEQUIEL DIAS

Parque Municipal

FEIRA DE ARTES E ARTESANATOS

AV DOS ANDRADAS

Hotel Othon Palace

TOURIST INFORMATION BOOTH

POST OFFICE

HOTEL WIMBLEDON

R DA BAHIA

PENA

ALL-FACE

SERRANA PLACE HOTEL

AFONSO PENA

DE LIMA

PIZZA PEZZI

PRAÇA DA ESTAÇÃO

MUSEU DE ARTES E OFÍCIOS

R ESPÍRITO SANTO

AV AMAZONAS

Praça Sete

@COM INTERNET

TELEMAR

SHOPPING CIDADE

AV SÃO PAULO

NATURALMENTE

AV AUGUSTO DE LIMA

SPETACULO GRILL

POUSADINHA MINEIRA

R ARAXÁ

R GUAICURUS

R GUAJAJARÁS

CENTRO

R CAETÉS

AMBASSY HOTEL

R DOS DUMONT

COMODORO TOURIST HOTEL

BANG BANG BURGER

R CURITIBA

R 21 DE ABRIL

TOURIST INFORMATION BOOTH

BUS STATION

HOTEL MADRID

R DO ACRE

R DOS SANTOS DUMONT

R DOS CARIJÓS

AV OLEGÁRIO MACIEL

R DOS TAMOIOS

R DOS TUPIS

R DOS GOITACAZES

MERCADO CENTRAL

AV DOM PEDRO II

BARRO PRETO

GARMENT DISTRICT

AV BIAS FORTES

Praça Raul Soares

RIO GRANDE DO SUL

R MATO GROSSO

R DOS GUAJAJARÁS

AV DO CONTORNO

ARAGUARI

FOGÃO DE LENHA

HOTEL BH PALACE

To Confins Airport

# Downtown Belo Horizonte

The downtown area is primarily commercial, but also has a number of residents in its dark and ominous high-rise buildings. With a few long-standing exceptions, such as the classic Othon Palace Hotel, accommodations in this area are in the lower price ranges. Like many city centers, central Belo Horizonte is mostly a run-down, low-rent district that offers its principal attraction during the day—great shopping. Likewise, most of the good restaurants in this area are lunchtime offerings.

## PRAÇA SETE AND NEARBY SHOPPING

The main center of activity in the downtown area (aside from the bus station) is Praça Sete de Setembro, or simply Praça Sete. Marked by an obelisk commemorating Brazil's independence on September 7, 1822, the *praça* is basically the intersection of several main boulevards (the biggest being Avenida Afonso Pena and Avenida Amazonas) where one can walk in any direction and find an endless array of stores. If you're walking around ths area, you should either continue uphill on Afonso Pena toward the Parque Municipal (away from the bus station), where you'll pass the **Igreja São Jose** (worth a quick look inside), or turn west along **Rua Rio de Janeiro**, where you'll pass the Shopping Cidade indoor mall and plenty of small shops and eateries. Although not a dangerous area during the day, keep your eyes open for the possible "grab-and-run" or "traffic-jam" tricks played on crowded streets.

If you turn down **Rua dos Carijós** from Praça Sete, you'll pass a busy shopping district. A right turn on **Rua Paraná** will take you past some of the discount clothing outlets that line both sides of the street, all the way back to the *rodoviaria*.

### Ⓜ Barro Preto Garment District

With nearly 1,000 stores and outlets, Barro Preto offers everything from casual beach wear to jeans to formal evening gowns and business suits. You'll find numerous factory outlets that offer quantity discounts for resellers, plus fabric and supply stores, indoor malls, and collectives. Many stores do not accept credit cards and there aren't many banks in the immediate vicinity, so if you bring cash for a little shopping spree, be sure to catch a taxi to avoid walking through the surrounding neighborhoods. Keep in mind that stores in this area sell to resellers from all over the state and are not particularly oriented to tourists. And remember to always ask for a discount when paying cash. Some stores of note include **Flair** (Rua Goitacazes 1128, tel. 31/3272-6728) for inexpensive Lycra and cotton blends, **Climary** (Rua Araguari 363 near Rua Goitacazes, tel. 31/3271-6604) for a variety of beach and gym wear, **Carbono Ligítimo** (Avenida Augusto de Lima 1131, tel. 31/3275-8910) for great kids clothing (wholesale only, R$250 minimum), and **America Latina** (Augusto de Lima 1134, tel. 31/3275-1514) for jeans and a little of everything. All of these stores are open 9 A.M.–7 P.M. Mon.–Fri. and 9 A.M.–2 P.M. on Sat.

## PARQUE MUNICIPAL AND THE PALÁCIO DAS ARTES

Not far up Avenida Afonso Pena from the *rodoviaria* is the Parque Municipal, which offers a momentary respite from the frantic city scene. You might even bring a snack into the park to have a makeshift picnic under one of the huge rubber trees. The central park of Belo Horizonte, this quaint garden is located downtown along the main street of Avenida Afonso Pena, about a 15-minute walk from the bus station. Especially beautiful in the early morning when the city is waking up, its exotic trees and windy paths make a pleasant opening of the day. The Parque Municipal is open from 8 A.M.–6 P.M. Tuesday–Sunday.

Bordering the park on Avenida Afonso Pena is the city's principal tourist information center and the Palácio das Artes, which frequently hosts music and theater performances in its large and small theaters, art exhibits of national stature in its various *salas,* and other special events in it's ample facilities. Its cinema plays artistic films and has a coffee shop in the waiting area downstairs. You can check its calendar online at www.palaciodasartes.com.br and purchase tickets on-site, 9 A.M. –6 P.M. daily.

## Feira de Artes e Artesanatos

On Sundays, Avenida Afonso Pena around the Parque Municipal turns into one of the largest and most frantic outdoor flea markets in South America, locally known as the Hippie Fair. The fair has more than 1,000 stalls full of handcrafted jewelry, furniture, clothing, accessories, household items, crafts, and paintings. You'll find some really different stuff too, like handmade flags, original toys, plastic, and ceramic items. There are lots of food stands, but if you prefer a complete lunch, then you should hit the self-service restaurants in the Shopping Cidade mall (Rua Rio de Janeiro 910) when you're finished with the fair. Better yet, the view of the fair from the Othon Palace Hotel restaurant is unbeatable (Av. Afonso Pena 1050). The shoulder-to-shoulder crowds at the market can be overwhelming to some, so be careful not to get too flustered, as it makes you more vulnerable to theft. Take plenty of breaks in the *lanchonetes* alongside the stands to regroup. The fair goes from 7 A.M.–2 P.M. but most of the stands are already breaking down by 1 P.M.

## Mercado Central

Located at the end of Avenida Curitiba near Praça Raul Soares is the Mercado Central (7 A.M.–6 P.M. Mon.–Sat. and 7 A.M.–noon Sun.), a large indoor market that carries everything from fruits and vegetables to local cheese, *cachaça,* sweets, meat, and spices. You'll also find handcrafted furnishings, health food stores, healing-herb vendors, chickens, roosters, and dogs. The many dive bars offer a taste of local *boteco* cuisine (a long-standing B.H. tradition) along with cold beer. It's a bit of a madhouse, and you're sure to get lost inside, but it's

a terrific slice of B.H. life. Note that prices on pots, pans, and handcrafted items are usually better in the small towns around Minas from which they come.

## PRAÇA DA ESTAÇÃO (TRAIN STATION)

One of the city's original *praças* and points of business and commerce, the Praça da Estação (Rua Varhinha 235, tel. 31/3213-0003, 1–6 P.M. Tue.–Fri., 1–6 P.M. on Sat., R$3), went into a gradual state of decay, along with the neighborhood in which it is located. Happily, Angela Gutierrez, daughter of the rich and powerful train baron, Flavio Gutierrez, through her cultural institute has recently completed a total renovation of the station, the annexed buildings, and the grounds. Today the site is home to the **Museu de Artes e Ofícios,** two exhibition halls, a café-restaurant, a garden and meeting area, a restoration lab, and various training rooms. The next step is to clean up the surrounding neighborhood. It's located at the base of Avenida Amazonas, near the *rodoviaria.* To get there, walk directly down Avenida Amazonas (do not take the side streets) and take a taxi after dark. Better yet, take a taxi any time, especially if you're carrying bags or anything valuable. The renovated station is beautiful and worth a look.

### Mangabeiras Park

At the foot of the Curral Mountains lies the vast Mangabeiras Park. It's main entrance area was designed by noted landscape architect Burle Marx and is home to dozens of sculptures from Brazilian artist Ricardo Carvão. You'll find several picnic areas, fountains, a restaurant, and many food and drink kiosks. The rest of the park grounds, which you can see from the park's bus tour, offer more picnic areas, streams, and sports facilities. The park's many playgrounds are an attraction for travelers with youngsters (the best playground being the last on the tour).

Catch the 4108 or 4103 (blue) "P. Mangabeiras" bus anywhere along Avenida Afonso

Pena. It will take you all the way up to the park, passing the **Praça do Papa,** which offers an excellent view of the city and some of its most spectacular homes. When you reach the park, head for the information kiosk and purchase a park bus ticket for R$1. You don't want to wander far from the main grounds on foot as the park can be somewhat dangerous in the remote areas. There are guards at all main facilities and bus stops and you can exit and reenter the bus at will with your pass. No time to plan a picnic? Just pick up a roasted chicken and some sodas on Rua Curitiba near the *rodoviaria* before catching the bus up Afonso Pena.

## MUSEUMS

Belo Horizonte is not known for its fabulous museums, so if you're passing through the city to one or more of the historical towns in the region, you might save up your museum stamina for the small towns. The exception may be the newly renovated **Museu de Artes e Ofícios** in the train station (Rua Varhinha 235). It holds more than 2,000 pieces relating to fabrication and industrialization from the 19th and 20th centuries, such as a *cachaça* still, early textile mills, and jewelry-making and metallurgical objects. If you have time to kill, try the **Museu Mineiro** (Av. João Pinheiro 342, tel. 31/3269-1168, 10 A.M.–5 P.M. Tues.–Fri. and 10 A.M.–4 P.M. weekends). Sunday is free and all other days are only R$2.

## ENTERTAINMENT AND NIGHTLIFE

Most shows and activities around town are listed in one of two monthly guides: the *BH Guia Turístico* or the *Programe-bh*. Both can be found at the tourist centers.

### Cafés and Bars

The best bars and cafés in the city are in the Centro Sul area, but if you want to stick to the downtown area, there are a few good choices, including **Café Kahlúa** (corner of Rua da Bahia and Rua dos Timbiras, tel. 31/3222-5887, 8 A.M.–9 P.M. Mon.–Fri.), one of the city's best spots for coffee, a good read, and, if you're so inclined, a good smoke. They offer coffee from around the world and from some of the best plantations in Minas Gerais, as well as real cappuccino and mocha coffees, cigars, and gourmet sandwiches. A more bohemian-style café-bar is **Café Cultura** (Rua da Bahia at Rua dos Aimorés, happy hour at 6 P.M. and stay until midnight Mon.–Fri.) with jazz performances on weekends. The restaurant-bar at the **Othon Palace Hotel** (Av. Afonso Pena 1050, tel. 31/3247-0011, 24 hours) is a great place for drinks and a view of the city at night.

On the way up Afonso Pena toward Mangabeiras Park is **Bonomi Café and Bakery** (Av. Afonso Pena 2600, tel. 31/3261-3460, 8 A.M.–11:30 P.M. Tue.–Sun., noon–11:30 P.M. on Mon.) at Praça Benjamin Guimarães. Bonomi is reminiscent of the bakery-cafés in northern California, with its spacious, country-style interior, red wines by the glass, and some of the best breads and baked goods in the city. It's one of the few places in town where you'll find authentic croissants and cheesecake. In the same area is the **K-bob Restaurant** (Av. Afonso Pena 2483, tel. 31/3224-2100, lunch staring at noon daily), a large outdoor seating area, full bar, and menu items in the Arabic tradition.

**La Greppia** (Rua da Bahia 1196 near Augusto de Lima, tel. 31/3222-1461) is open 24 hours for draft beers and late snacks. Late-night burgers and beer are served up at **Bang Bang Burger** (Rua São Paulo 679 near Praça Sete, tel. 31/3212-1468, 9–1 A.M. daily). You'll find one or two 24-hour restaurants on Avenida Amazonas where it meets Praça Raul Suares, but take a taxi to avoid walking around there at night.

### Music and Shows

There are often great dance pieces and music concerts going on in town. Some of the more common locations for these events include the café at the **Centro de Cultura Belo Horizonte** (corner of Rua da Bahia and Av. Augusto de Lima, tel. 31/3277-4014, 9 A.M.–9 P.M. Mon.–Fri., 9 A.M.–6 P.M. on Sat., 2–6 P.M. on Sun.), the **Casa do Baile** (Av. Otacílio Negrão de Lima 751, Pampulha, tel. 31/3277-7443,

9 A.M.–7 P.M. Tue.–Sun.) in the Pampulha area, the **Museu Histórico Abílio Barreto** (Av. Prudente de Morais 202, Lourdes, tel. 31/3277-8573, 10 A.M.–5 P.M. Tue.–Sun. and until 9 P.M. on Thu.), and the concert hall **Marista Hall** (Av. Nossa Sra do Carmo 230, Savassi, tel. 31/3228-7500, www.maristahall.com.br, call or see site for show times and prices). Each of these places has its own calendar of events.

## Theater and Cinema

There are many theaters in town as B.H. is known for its great theater and dance companies. Pieces will be in Portuguese, but if you're interested, some of the better locations include the **Teatro do Palácio das Artes** (Av. Afonso Pena 1537, tel. 31/3237-7399), **Teatro da Cidade** (Rua da Bahia 1341, tel. 31/3273-1050), and the **Teatro Minascentro** (Av. Augusto de Lima 785, tel. 31/3498-1807). There are often short theater pieces in the outdoor theater in the **Teatro Francisco Nunes** inside the Parque Municipal on weekends (tel. 31/3224-4546). Every 15 days, there's an evening serenade in the Parque de Mangabeiras that's worth catching if you're in town (see www.parquemangabeiras.com.br). You can catch a mainstream movie, usually in English with Portuguese subtitles, at the **Shopping Cidade Cinema.**

# ACCOMMODATIONS

If you stay in the downtown area, you'll be within walking distance of most of the city's best shopping, including the Barro Preto district and the area around Praça Sete toward Rua Paraná (and all along Rua Paraná). If you stay in the south-central neighborhoods, such as Savassi or Lourdes, you can take a nice walking tour to see the various cafés, clubs, and boutiques in the area. The *praça* Savassi is the area's central hub and is host to several great cafés with patios for hanging out and watching the locals.

## Under R$25

The hostel **Pousadinha Mineira** (Rua Araxá 514, tel. 31/3423-4105, tel. 31/3423-1406, pousadinhamineira@terra.com.br, R$13) has group rooms with shared bath for four, six, and eight people. There are separate dorms for men and women. Bedding is available for R$3 if needed. The facilities include Internet, TV, and a sitting room. Another hostel is the **Chale Mineiro** (Rua Santa Luzia 288, tel. 31/3467-1576, R$13 with HI card or R$17 without) in the Santa Efigênia neighborhood, not far from both the Center and the Savassi areas. They have 54 spaces, a game room, and a pool with barbecue.

Note that most rooms in the downtown area for less than R$25 are in relatively unsafe or unclean neighborhoods. Hence, if you are set on saving money, it's recommended that you check out low-cost lodging in the outskirts of town, where you can find clean rooms for low prices.

## R$25–100

**Hotel Madrid** (Rua Guarani 12, in front of the *rodoviaria,* tel. 31/3201-1088, R$25 s or R$35 d with shared bath, R$30 and R$40 with private bath) is in a sleazy area, but it's close to the bus station, and it's clean and cheap. It also includes *café da manhã* (breakfast). They accept cash only. The **Ambassy Hotel** (Rua Caetés 633, tel. 31/2122-0001, reservas@ambassy.com.br, R$50 s and R$65 d) includes bathtubs in some of its rooms. The building has old '50s-style architecture and decoration, which can look somewhat worn (definitely not the Jetsons). This place takes cash only, too. It's clean, quiet (relatively, for the area), and safe. The **M Comororo Tourist Hotel** (Rua Carijós 508, tel. 31/3201-5522, R$60 s, R$60–90 d) is a nice alternative with its wooden floors and clean facilities. They have air, cable TV, and a restaurant on the top floor where breakfast is served (included). The **Serrana Place Hotel** (Rua Goitacazes 450, tel. 31/3274-6020, www.hotelserrana.com.br, R$75 s, R$88 d) has a sauna, pool, and restaurant.

**Hotel BH Palace** (Avenida Augusto de Lima 1147, tel. 31/3335-3717, www.hotelbhpalace.com.br, R$100 s and R$115–140 d weekdays, R$60 s and R$70–95 d weekends) is in the Barro Preto area and generally services professionals doing their wholesale buying in

## COMIDA MINEIRA: MENU SURVIVAL GUIDE

### Appetizers and Snacks

**Pão de Queijo:** a special mixture of bread dough with cheese and *polvilho* (*casava* or manioc meal). The typical translation, simply cheese bread, does not do justice to this unique creation. A Brazilian favorite, *pão de queijo* is a cheesy, chewy bread ball with a slightly crunchy outer crust. Great *pão de queijo* can be found all over Minas Gerais. Try to find a batch that just came out of the oven.

**Pão de Queijo Reicheiado:** *pão de queijo,* but larger and filled with grated chicken.

**Torresmo:** deep-fried pigskin. You either love it or you don't.

**Biscoito de Polvilho:** deep-fried manioc meal with last night's beef or pork fat mixed in for flavor. They are light and crunchy, melt in your mouth, and leave a heavy taste of beef or pork fat behind.

**Empada:** a small pie or tort, usually filled with chicken, cheese, or heart of palm.

**Pastel:** a type of fried spring roll filled with ground beef, chicken, cheese, and other creative combinations.

**Pastel Assado:** an oven-baked meat pie with plenty of breading.

**Cigarrete:** ham and cheese, rolled, breaded, and deep fried.

**Misto Quente:** a hot ham and cheese sandwich.

**Coxinha:** grated and spiced chicken in a breading and shaped like a giant teardrop (actually, it's supposed to be a chicken drumstick) and deep-fried.

### Side Dishes

**Couve:** finely-chopped kale, sautéed with plenty of garlic and salt. This is generally a very salty accompaniment to meats or carbohydrates.

**Angú:** blocks of cornmeal with a pudding-like texture, usually to accompany saucy dishes as an extra carbohydrate to soak up the flavorful sauce. A version called *angú á Baiana* comes with ground, spiced beef on top.

**Feijão Tropeiro:** dry meat, hard-boiled egg, *torresmo,* kale, onion, bacon, sausage, and herbs mixed together with beans and cornmeal. A more homespun version is known as *mixidão* (big mixture) and can include any leftovers thrown into the pan with rice and beans and the other ingredients.

---

the area. Therefore, weekends are highly discounted. They offer rooms with three single beds, a business center, and a restaurant.

### Over R$100

The long-standing **N Hotel Othon Palace** (Avenida Afonso Pena 1050, near the park, tel. 31/3247-0000, www.hoteis-horthon.com.br, R$90–110 s, R$120–150 d, and R$650 presidential suite) is one of the city's landmark hotels and has hosted many important Brazilian and international guests. The hotel offers all amenities, including massage service and a business center. All cards accepted.

    **Hotel Wimbledon** (Avenida Afonso Pena 772, tel. 31/3222-6160, www.wimbledon.com.br, R$135–196 s, R$163–230 d) has small rooms, but is clean, noise-free, and modern. There is a pool on the terrace,

and all rooms come with sauna and jet bath as well as cable. Finally, the **Quality Hotel Afonso Pena** (Av. Afonso Pena 228, tel. 31/3263-1300, www.atlanticahotels.com.br) specializes in business travelers. They have in-room Internet, king-size beds, ironing equipment, a fitness room, sauna, pool, and business center. Double rooms are R$150 or R$130 for businesses.

## FOOD

### Barbecue

**Spetaculo Grill** (corner of Rua Guajajaras and Rua Curitiba, tel. 31/3272-7595, 11–1 A.M. Mon.–Sat.) is hopping every night with the locals. It's not fancy, and the neighborhood is a little sketchy at night, but the barbecued meats are great and the beer is cheap.

## Main Courses

**Frango com Quiabo:** spiced chicken simmered and mixed with sautéed ochre.

**Frango a Molho Pardo:** chicken with a rich, dark brown sauce, usually made with tomato but traditionally with chicken blood.

**Vaca Atolada:** cooked beef with manioc in a thick beef sauce.

**Abobrinha:** squash with pork ribs and a light sauce, usually served inside the gourd itself.

**Traíra:** fried, salted fish, generally served whole on a platter for two to share.

## Soups

**Canja de Galinha:** thick chicken soup, usually with rice and topped with chopped green onions.

**Sopa de Batata com Carne:** potato soup with beef, chicken, or pork, usually made with a corn-flour base.

**Caldo de Manjoca:** manioc soup, usually made with a corn-flour base, beef broth, and spices.

**Caldo de Feijão:** bean soup, usually spiced with pork. Some versions are so good they are the highlight of the meal. Others are just every-day bean soup. The best can be found in small, humble establishments.

**Rabada:** a Brazilian version of ox-tail soup with manioc.

**Feijoada:** a thick stew made with the unwanted parts of a pig, beans, and spices.

## Sweets

**Broa de Fubá:** pound cake made from corn-meal, not unlike cornbread.

**Goiabada:** guava preserves served with cheese. You can find this in blocks or jars in small markets throughout Minas Gerais.

**Pudim de Leite Condensado:** creamy white pudding served with cinnamon on top.

**Pudim de Pão:** thick, hard pudding made with condensed milk and bread.

**Doce de Leite:** A regional favorite, *doce de leite* is used in many ways and for many types of desserts. It's simply milk and sugar heated until it becomes thick and frosting-like. It's usually eaten with cheese for desert but can also be found in markets in blocks and jars.

**Bolo:** cake.

## Natural Foods

**Naturalmente** (Rua Rio de Janeiro 1197, near the Shopping Cidade, tel. 31/3213-7029, 11:30 A.M.–3 P.M. Mon.–Sat.) offers organic veggie and macrobiotic lunches from about R$8.

## Quick and Casual

The *lanchonetes* along Avenida Afonso Pena are usually fresh and cheap. If you like *salgados* (Brazilian finger foods), these are the places to go in the downtown area. It's perfectly OK to ask the clerk which items are the freshest (*"Qual está mais fresquinha?"*) before making your selection. Remember that you pay first in these places, so practice saying the names of the items you want so you know what to say when you get to the window. A simple but nourishing lunch is available for less than R$5 at **33 Paraná** (Rua Paraná 33, open for lunch only from 11 A.M.–3 P.M.) near the *rodoviaria*. Similar lunch values are commonplace in and around the Mercado Central with a *prato feito* or PF (ready-made plate) featuring pork, beef, or chicken. Finally, you can't beat the oven-roasted pizza by-the-slice at **Pizza Pezzi** (Augusto de Lima at Espirito Santo, tel. 31/3222-7272), but you may have to stand up and eat it. Open day and night.

Fresh juices can be ordered on the spot at many *suco* stands along Afonso Pena, particularly in and around Praça Sete and in the Mercado Central. You can usually get your choice of fruits mixed with milk or water. They'll add loads of sugar unless you tell them, *"Sem açucar, por favor!"* You haven't lived until you've tried avocado juice with milk and sugar (Brazilians will look at you strangely if they see you eating avocado with salt).

**Belo Horizonte**

## Self-Service

The best self-service value in town is at **Ⓜ Fogão de Lenha** (Rua Araguari 246, tel. 31/3271-3087) in the Barro Preto district. They have a huge variety of dishes for under R$6 per kilo. They serve lunch only from 11 A.M.–3 P.M. every day including Sunday. Cash only. An excellent self-service-style lunch can be found at the **All-Face** (Avenida Augusto de Lima 120 near Rua da Bahia, no phone, lunch only Mon.–Sat.). The name is a play on the word *alface,* meaning lettuce. As the name implies, they have a healthy selection of veggie items. If you like pasta, **La Greppia** (Rua da Bahia 1196 near Augusto de Lima, tel. 31/3222-1461, 24 hours) has 15 different kinds to sample in their pasta *rodísio,* (a rotisserie-style, all-you-can-eat barbecue) starting at 7 P.M. every night. Only R$7 per person. Dinner off the menu runs about R$15.

At the far end of Avenida Afonso Pena where it intersects Avenida do Contorno is **Ⓜ Aromi** (Av. Afonso Pena 3126, no phone, lunch only from 11:30 A.M.–4 P.M. Mon.–Fri., and noon–4 P.M. on Sun.), one of the best self-service restaurants in town with a creative selection of dishes for a reasonable *a-quilo* (per-kilo) price. You'll probably get out of there for less than R$15 per person and the food is worth twice that.

On weekends, your only good option downtown is the food park on the bottom floor of the Shopping Cidade mall on Rua Rio de Janeiro. There you'll get a decent self-service lunch at any hour of the day.

## INFORMATION

Tourist information booths, sponsored by Belotur, can be spotted all around the downtown area, including at the Confins airport (open 8 A.M.–10 P.M.), the *rodoviaria* (8 A.M.–8 P.M.), the Parque Municipal (8 A.M.–8 P.M.), and the Mercado Central (8 A.M.–6 P.M.). You'll find copies of their excellent B.H. monthly guide, theater schedules, brochures, maps, and maybe even English-speaking clerks. The Secretary of Tourism (SETUR) is located in the Praça da Liberdade (tel. 31/3272-8674, www.turismo.mg.gov.br, 9 A.M.–6 P.M. Mon.–Fri.) They also have offices in the Savassi area. The **Belo Horizonte Convention and Visitor's Bureau** (BHCVB; Rua Aimorés 981, 8th floor, at Rua Pernambuco in Funcionarios, tel. 31/3213-5150, www.bhcvb.com, 9 A.M.–6 P.M. Mon.–Fri.) can help with group events, accommodations, and all sorts of trip assistance.

## SERVICES

### Documents and Officialdom

The federal police station is at Rua Nascimento Gurgel 30 in the Gutierrez neighborhood. There you can extend your tourist visa for an additional 90 days. Consulates in B.H. include the following:

• Argentina (Rua Ceará 1566, 6th floor, tel. 31/3281-5288)

• Canada (Rua Rio Grande do Norte 1164, Conj. 502, tel. 31/3261-1017)

• France (Rua Tomé de Souza 1418, tel. 31/3291-5187)

• United Kingdom (Rua dos Inconfidentes 1075, Conj. 1302, tel. 31/3261-0226)

• Japan (Rua Prof. José Vieira de Mendonça 3011, tel. 31/3499-9620)

---

## CELEBRATING THE GREASY SPOON

If you have a sense of adventure along with an iron stomach, you might be interested in the annual **Festival da Cumida di Buteco** (roughly translated, Festival of the Greasy Spoon). Here, you'll find some special and secret family recipes, traditional foods, and mysterious concoctions of the common people of Minas. The festival itself takes place in May, when the 31 greasy spoons gather to offer their special dishes. The exact date and location can be found at the official website: www.comidadibuteco.com.br. There, you'll also find a list of the previous year's participants and winners, so you can catch a cab and go visit them any time of the year to sample their winning recipes.

- Switzerland (Rua Paraiba 476, sl. 1002, tel. 31/3261-87732)

## Internet and Communications

Internet services can be had at @.com Internet (870 Rua Rio de Janeiro, upstairs, tel. 31/3274-0668, 9 A.M.–11 P.M. Mon.–Fri., 9 A.M.–8 P.M. on Sat.). They charge around R$3 per hour. Notebooks are welcome. Inside Shopping Cidade at the **Leitura** bookstore on the top level is another, slightly more expensive one. You'll find private phone booths at the **Telemar** (dial 103 for information, 8 A.M.–4 P.M. Mon.–Fri ) office on the corner of Rua Rio de Janeiro and Rua dos Tupis. There, you can also buy all denominations of phone cards for the public phones. Ignore the vendors outside the building and go directly inside to the desk to purchase.

## Money

The city's main branch of **Banco do Brasil** is located at Rua Rio de Janeiro 750. They offer all financial services, including money exchange, cashing traveler's checks, money wires, and ATMs with Cirrus and Plus systems. Note that all Banco do Brasil offices are Western Union agencies, although not all change dollars. **Citibank** is located at Rua Espirito Santo 871 and has similar services and English-language ATMs.

## Post Office

You'll find post offices all over the downtown area. Some convenient locations include the *rodoviaria* (2nd floor), the main branch at Avenida Afonso Pena 127 in front of the park, and in the Shopping Cidade mall at Rua Rio de Janeiro 910, which is open 9 A.M.–10 P.M. Monday–Saturday.

## Miscellaneous

The hospital district is along Avenida do Contorno and Avenida Francisco Sales in the São Lucas neighborhood. Public bathrooms are practically non-existent in Belo Horizonte (and Brazil in general). You'll find them at the *rodoviarias* (usually for a small fee), shopping malls, and parks. One of the few self-service

laundry facilities in the city is **LaundroMat** (Rua Rio de Janeiro 1348, tel. 31/3274-1768). They charge R$6 per "basket" for washing and another R$6 for drying. A basket holds up to eight kilos. They also pick up and deliver for a small extra fee. Most other laundry facilities are not self-service and the best ones (including dry-cleaning) are in the Savassi and Lourdes area.

# GETTING THERE

## Buses

Most all buses land at the *rodoviaria* downtown. If you're coming from Rio, you can get off early in the Savassi area. From the *rodoviaria,* you can catch a bus (usually the next one leaving if so desired) to just about anywhere in Brazil.

## Planes

Flights will arrive in Belo Horizonte at either Confins International Airport. From Confins, there are two buses to the city. The Expresso Unir leaves throughout the day until 10:30 P.M. for R$4.75 to the *rodoviaria*. Be careful not to catch the *Executivo* that goes to the *terminal Turistico JK*. You can also catch the municipal (red) bus 2261 "Belo Horizonte" for R$2.75 (pay inside the bus) at 8:30 A.M. and 3:30 P.M. at the front end of the loading/unloading zone at the airport. The same buses leave the *rodoviaria* to return to the airport. Buy tickets to Confins at Expresso Unir, booth 11, at the *rodoviaria*. You can book flights at any travel agency in town.

## Trains

Once a day, the passenger train Vitória/Minas leaves Belo Horizonte from the train station near the Praça da Estação at 7:30 A.M. going northwest to João Monlevade, Itabira, Ipatinga, Governador Valadares, and Vitória with many stops in-between. It's slow going, but the price is right at only R$24 economy class to Vitória. Buy your tickets at the station. The same train returns from Vitória at 7 A.M. and arrives in B.H. around 8 P.M.

Belo Horizonte

## GETTING AROUND

Most everything in the downtown area is within walking distance. Avoid walking in the areas immediately surrounding the *rodoviaria*, except to walk straight up Avenidas Afonso Pena or Paraná, and don't even think about the northeast quadrant between Avenidas Amazonas and Afonso Pena (to the left of Afonso Pena as you leave the *rodoviaria*). At night, take taxis, unless you're very close to your hotel or sticking to the main streets. Several buses go from the *rodoviaria* up Avenida Afonso Pena, including the 4108 and 4103 "P. Mangabeiras" buses, or you can share a taxi at the base of Afonso Pena for the price of a bus fare.

# Savassi and Centro Sul

The most active neighborhood in Belo Horizonte and the most visited by tourists, Savassi is technically not a neighborhood at all, which is why you don't see it on most city maps. The name comes from the neighborhood's first bakery, owned and operated by the Savassi family and still heating their ovens to this day. The so-called *praça* is the intersection of two major boulevards (Getulio Vargas and Cristóvão Colombo) and two smaller streets. At these eight intersection points, and lining the streets in all eight directions, are numerous cafés, shops, and restaurants—eight directions in which to shop, eat, and hang out.

The Travessa Bookstore & Café, for example, is right in the heart of the Savassi quad and is often frequented by some of Belo Horizonte's artist set. The locals are known to café-hop, making the rounds and partaking of the various morsels available at each. At night, Savassi lights up with options, including many of the city's best restaurants and nightclubs. During the week, you might catch an art opening at one of the many galleries in the area. A pleasant walk down Rua Antônio de Albuquerque from Savassi to Lourdes will place you in a neighborhood that offers a little of everything: restaurants, galleries, a small park, boutique stores, beauty salons, and a couple of good nightclubs. The Lourdes area is home to several excellent hotel-flats within walking distance to the shops and restaurants.

## SIGHTS

The only true historical sights in the Savassi area are conveniently bunched together at the Praça da Liberdade. The Palácio da Liberdade, the governor's office (tel. 31/3250-6011), is open once a month to visitors, or you can just look from the outside. There, you'll find the Geology Museum (tel. 31/3271-3415, 9 A.M.–5 P.M. Thu.–Sun., free) at the Escola de Minas Gerais. Other government buildings from the 1920s are nearby and you can't miss the '60s-style apartment building of famed architect Oscar Niemeyer. These are all pretty much best observed from the outside—so a quick walk around the park will reveal all. The park itself is at its best when all lit up for Christmas.

The Museu Abilio Barreto (Av. Prudente de Morais 202, tel. 31/3277-8573, 10 A.M.–5 P.M. Wed.–Sun. and until 9 P.M. Thur.) offers a bit of the history of Belo Horizonte via photographs, sketches, texts, and artifacts from the region. The building and grounds are charming and the upstairs café is one of the nicest in the area. They also have a hall for contemporary art exhibitions. However, if it's contemporary art you like, check out the many fine galleries around Centro Sul. A few of note include Galeria Regard (Marilia de Dirceu 226, tel. 31/3292-2530), Quadrum Galeria (just up the street at Avenida Prudente de Morais 78, tel. 31/3296-4866), and the Palácio de Leilões (Gonçalves Dias 1866 near Rua Rio de Janeiro, tel. 31/3291-2343). All of these are open regular business hours (9 A.M.–6 P.M. Mon.–Fri., and 9 A.M.–2 P.M. on Sat.).

## ENTERTAINMENT AND NIGHTLIFE
### Clubs and Discos

The nightclub scene in Belo Horizonte is plen-

© CHRISTOPHER VAN BUREN

**The architecture of Oscar Niemeyer stands at Praça da Liberdade.**

tiful and mixed. If you know where to look, there is something for everyone. The upscale clubs usually have a consumption minimum, which, if you stay the entire night, will not be difficult to exceed. However, these minimum fees make it expensive to barhop, an international tradition that has not taken hold in Brazil. (Brazilians not only like to stick to one place for the entire evening, they also tend to return to the same place every weekend.) Most clubs give you a ticket that they stamp each time you order and it can be extremely expensive if lost (as much as R$300). Clubs usually get started around midnight and go until the sun comes up.

The Savassi nightclub cluster is on Ruas Tomé de Souza and Sergipe, west of the *praça*. There you'll find several options, including **Café Cancun** (Rua Sergipe 1208, tel. 31/3287-3223), which opens for music around 9 P.M. They have a R$15 consumption minimum for women and R$25 for men, with an additional

R$5 entry charge. Reports are that the crowd at Cancun can be a bit snooty. The **Pop Rock** (Rua Sergipe 1211, tel. 31/3284-8006) across the street has live cover bands and large crowds, so on weekends it's best to swing by during the day to get tickets or call tel. 31/3284-8006 (R$5 entry with R$20 consumption on weekends and a flat R$10 on weekdays). **Bwana** (Rua Tomé de Souza 1145, tel. 31/3281-2339) is a club with a slightly harder edge, sporting pop and Brazilian *axé* music (a type of country) for a R$25 consumption on weekends. Drinks range from R$3–10. Not far from these spots is **Lunico** (Av. do Contorno 5727, tel. 31/3264-5867, www.lunico.com.br, shows start around 11 P.M.), a jazz and rock venue. Jazz is usually played on Wednesdays with rock on Thursdays. Weekends are a crapshoot. Music starts at 11 P.M. but they also have a Japanese/Thai restaurant attached if you want to fuel up before all that jazz.

### Late Night and After Hours
The **Republica do Café** (Av. do Contorno 5757, tel. 31/3225-5151) is usually hopping late at night until the wee hours. They offer food, beer, and wines 24 hours a day. The scotch bar/strip club **Aphrodite** (Rua Martins de Carvalho 30 at the top of Afonso Pena, tel. 31/3072-4031, www.aphrodite.com.br, starts around 11 P.M. every night) caters to a sophisticated audience and closes its doors at 11:30 P.M. Another adult club is the **Crystal Night Club** (Rua Rio Grande do Norte 1470, tel. 31/3221-9856, www.crystalnightclub.com.br, starts around 11 P.M. every night). The **Cantina de Cida** (Rua Antonio de Albuquerque 156 in Savassi, tel. 31/3292-8153, 24 hours) is an all-night self-service restaurant and crowded late-night hangout on the weekends. Finally, you can order take-out pizza or Chinese food at any hour of the day or night at **Pizza Sim!** (tel. 31/3386-8699), probably the city's lowest-priced and most-requested pizza.

### Sidewalk Cafés and Bars
What Belo Horizonte lacks in tourist attractions, it makes up for in variety of bars and

Belo Horizonte

*cervejarias* (there are said to be more than 8,000 bars in the downtown area). **Café com Letras** (Rua Antônio de Albuquerque 781, tel. 31/3225-9973, 9 A.M.–11 P.M. Mon.–Fri., 9 A.M.–11 P.M. on Sat.) is one of Savassi's original tourist coffee shops. You can often find tables full of backpackers on any given day or night. They offer a full lunch menu, great sweets, and a selection of wines. They also offer books in English, art exhibitions, and Internet connections (expensive at R$2 per 10 minutes). It's open every day until midnight with live jazz on Sundays. The **Café da Travessa** (Rua Pernambuco, tel. 31/3223-8090, 9 A.M.–11 P.M. Mon.–Fri., 9 A.M.–11 P.M. on Sat.) in the Savassi quad is a local hangout for coffee or beer and books and is the most strategically located of the Savassi cafés. You can sit outside on their patio and watch the Savassi scene passing by. Upstairs is a contemporary art gallery and scotch bar. **Status Café** (Rua Cristóvão Colombo 280, tel. 31/3261-6045, 9 A.M.–midnight daily ) is a great bookstore-café with live music nightly (usually jazz) and great coffee and treats. It's open 7 A.M.–midnight. Around the corner is the **República do Café** (Avenida do Contorno 5757, tel. 31/3225-5151) a pleasantly appointed café-bar with excellent wines, pasta dishes, and sweets—not to mention an attractive crowd. It's open 24 hours. In Lourdes, **Bendita Gula Bar-Café** (Marilia de Dirceu 94, tel. 31/3491-7800) offers wonderful sweets along with a calm atmosphere and Internet connections.

### Theater and Cinema

The fine-arts cinema **Cine Belas Artes** (Rua Gonçalves Dias 1581, a block from the Praça da Liberdade, tel. 31/3213-5594) plays a variety of foreign and Brazilian films and has a great coffee shop waiting area. American films are in English with Portuguese subtitles. Another cinema for alternative flicks is the **Savassi Cineclube** (Levindo Lopes 358, tel. 31/3227-6648) with films starting from 2:30–8:30 P.M. There are current movies at the **Diamond Mall** (Avenida Olegário Maciel at Rua Gonçalves Dias, tel. 31/3292-9026).

## SHOPPING

The best boutiques in Savassi are generally in the network of streets between Savassi and Lourdes. You can just stroll along the avenues and do some quality window-shopping or venture in for some great deals. The **5th Avenue Shopping Center** (Rua Alagoas 1314) is host to the All-Face self-service restaurant (third floor), many good shops, and a tourist information booth. They also have quiet public phones.

A nice walking/shopping tour is to stroll from Savassi into Lourdes. Start by walking down Antônio de Albuquerque and turn right at Rua Rio de Janeiro, then left again on Rua Felipe dos Santos or Rua Professor Antônio Aleixo. The shops get more glamorous the closer you get to Lourdes. When you reach Rua Marilia de Dirceu, you have arrived. Now you can pause for an espresso and a pastry or a few of the city's best *pasteis* at **Pastelaria Marilia de Dirceu.** Lourdes also has some of the city's finer restaurants and art galleries. Cross Avenida do Contorno to continue your walk up Avenida Prudente de Morais, where you'll pass more shops, cafés, Quadrum Galeria de Arte, and the Museu Abilio Barreto with its lovely upstairs café. End of tour.

The **Diamond Mall** (Avenida Olegário Maciel and Rua Gonçalves Dias) is a full-scale indoor mall experience. It features a wonderful fruit and vegetable market, movie theaters, and a well-stocked food court.

## ACCOMMODATIONS

There are no budget hotels in the south-central area. Most accommodations run around R$80–150 with a few higher-priced exceptions. Most offer weekend discounts of about 10 percent and you can add a third person for about 25 percent extra. Of course, any discount or special deal has to be demanded when you check in or make reservations. All hotels charge at least 5-percent service tax, usually 10-percent. Those charging more or none at all are noted herein.

One of the best choices for clean, modern, and

well-priced facilities is the **M Ibis Accor Hotel** (Avenida João Pinheiro 602, tel. 31/3224-9494, www.accorhotels.com, R$89 s/d), perfectly located near the Praça da Liberdade. It's one of a growing number of streamlined hotels and offers one style of room. Breakfast is not included but there is a bar and 24-hour food service. The **Hotel Savassi** (Claudio Manoel 1144, tel. 31/3261-3266, R$95 s and R$115 d) is reasonably close to *praça* Savassi. They have a pool, sauna, and Internet (extra). The **Boulevard Hotel** (Avenida Getúlio Vargas 1640, tel. 31/3269-7000, www.boulevardhoteis.com.br, R$135 d) is well positioned in the Savassi area. It has large, clean rooms, a nice café with business center, restaurant, pool, and gym. There are weekend discounts. The **Royal Savassi** (Alagoas 701, tel. 31/3247-6999, www.royaltowers.com.br, from R$130 s and R$150 d) has a cool Mediterranean-style restaurant and bar, a gym, and a business center. There are plenty of cafés and restaurants nearby. Check out Surubim na Brasa for fish or Xanadu for food and beer.

In the Lourdes area, the **M Promenade Platinum** (Av. Olegário Maciel 1748, tel. 31/3348-3400, www.promenade.com.br, R$140 s, R$165 d) is a brand-new, super-clean hotel with complete pool, sauna, and gym facilities and a business center. The **São Francisco Flat** (Avenida Alvares Cabral 967, tel. 31/3330-5600, www.sanfranciscoflat.com.br) is one of the better flat deals on the block. They offer large, clean rooms (some with kitchen facilities) for about R$110 and a spacious two-story duplex with kitchen for R$155. Amenities include pool, sauna, gym, and a decent restaurant. The same organization has two other flats in the area, including the **St. Paul** (Rua São Paulo 1636, tel. 31/3291-5559, www.saintpaulresidence .com.br) and the **Aspen Sport Flat** (Rua Cristina 1163, tel. 31/3296-8855, www.aspensportflat.com.br). Both are slightly smaller and less expensive than the São Francisco.

## FOOD

### Barbecue

In the Savassi area, you'll find some excellent grilled meats and fish. At **M Surubim na Braza** (Av. Alagoas 601, tel. 31/3261-9707, open for dinner daily), they serve up only one type of fish (*surubim* is a mild, meaty, white fish) either off the barbecue grill or in a kind of stew called a *moqueca*. Most meals are good for two people, but they also have dishes for individuals. The cost is around R$15 per person and well worth it. The Lourdes area offers **Cia do Boi** (Avenida Curitiba 2069, tel. 31/3292-4372), with fresh-grilled meats by the kilo, draft beer, and (limited) outdoor seating. Dinner will run around R$12–20 per person. It's open every night from 6 P.M.

By far the most memorable dining experience in Belo Horizonte is to be had at **M Porcão** (Rua Raja Gabaglia 2985, tel. 31/3293-8787), meaning big pig, up in the city's south hills. It is primarily a *rodísio*-style barbecue but also offers fresh fish catches of the day, a buffet table fit for a king, scotch bar, sushi bar, and dessert bar. It has several huge dining areas and some of the finest views of the city (day or night). There is a wine cellar, playground for the kids, and valet parking. You pay R$40, stay as long as you like, and eat as much as you want (drinks and desserts not included). It opens at 11:30 A.M. for lunch and continues non-stop until the last person leaves, although doors close at midnight. No reservations required. If you want to hear some music after dinner, the **Alambique** is a short walk up the road.

### International

**M Vecchio Sogno Ristorante** (Rua Martim de Carvalho 75, tel. 31/3292-5251) is one of the city's finest gourmet venues, offering a selection of Italian dishes, chef specials, fine wines, and desserts. The owner-chef is known in Brazil as one of the best and it shows in his artistic creations and fresh ingredients (he does wonders with mushrooms). Dinner prices are R$40–R$60 per person. It's up the street from Lourdes in the Praça da Assembléia (where the city's movers and shakers hang out). The restaurant opens at 10 A.M. for lunch and continues until the last person leaves. Reservations are recommended, but you can also just pop in for

## FOODS FROM THE MINAS COUNTRYSIDE

### Ora Pro Nóbis

It's said that any family with an *ora pro nóbis* plant in the yard will never go hungry or be under-nourished. The leaves of this plant are super-rich in proteins and amino acids and can be used for human and animal consumption. Studies show that the leaves contain 25-percent highly digestible proteins, along with one of the highest quantities of Lysine available in any known plant. Part of the cactus family, *ora pro nóbis* is not known to have any toxic qualities and is used in recipes containing chicken, beef, and pork and in various types of salads. It's not commonly found in supermarkets and is not commercially grown, but some fancy restaurants in Minas Gerais and São Paulo use it in special dishes.

### Jaboticaba

*Jaboticaba* is a grape-like fruit with a flavor unlike anything you've ever tasted. Because of its tough skin and large seed inside, you must squeeze the fruit into your mouth, suck the juice and spit out the seed. It quickly becomes a kind of obsession and a kilo of the succulent little fruit can easily disappear in no time. *Jaboticaba* trees, which are really large bushes, take up to 15 years to produce the fruit, which sprout out like knobs along its many trunks and branches. The peak season for *jaboticaba* is October–December. At this time of the year, it's common to find street vendors selling bags of the little jewels for around R$3.

### Taioba

The leaf of the *taioba* plant is similar to kale but much larger. It is used like kale in recipes and is often just chopped and sautéed with garlic and oil. It has a wonderful buttery flavor, along with that green, leafy taste of the countryside. Families in Minas Gerais often plant *taioba* in their yards, as it's difficult to find in supermarkets. You might find it in some self-service restaurants specializing in authentic Comida Mineira.

drinks and appetizers in their piano-bar area. Another Italian offering, **Saatore** (Av. Alvares Cabral 1181, tel. 31/3339-3180, lunch and dinner Mon.–Fri., dinner only on Sat., and lunch only on Sun.) attracts connoisseurs from all over the city—not just guests of the Hotel-Flat in which the restaurant is located. Dishes range from R$20–50 per person. It opens for lunch and dinner. No reservations required.

## Local Favorites

One of the city's largest and most active spots for beer and food is **Sushi Beer** (Rua Tomé de Souza 1121, tel. 31/3282-7755, happy hour and dinner Mon.–Fri., lunch on Sat. and Sun.). At night, the place comes alive with three different environments—an outdoor pizza pub looking onto the street, an indoor restaurant with set dinner plates, and a hopping, self-service sushi restaurant in its spacious back patio. The size of this place is impressive, yet on Fridays and Saturdays, it's still a good idea to make reservations, because it packs 'em in. Sushi sells for about R$25 per kilo. Voted the best happy hour in B.H., **M Maria de Lourdes** (Rua Barbara Heliodora 141, tel. 31/3292-6905, dinner Mon.–Fri., lunch and dinner on Sat. and Sun.) is crowded in the late afternoon and evening. Owned by the city's only microbrewery (Krug Bier), the restaurant offers four types of fresh beers (the premium amber is excellent) and a variety of dishes in the Comida Mineira tradition, including several flavors of Feijoada (a kind of chili or spicy stew made with pork parts). Dinner runs around R$10–25 per plate.

Up in the São Bento neighborhood is the

city's only microbrewery, **Krug Bier** (Av. Paulo Camilo Pena 736, tel. 31/3286-0061, www.krug.com.br, opens at 6 P.M. Mon.–Fri., 1 P.M. on Sat. and Sun.). A partnership among two Brazilians and two Austrians, Krug offers four quality microbrews. The malt is shipped in from Austria to make their amber bock and their wheat beer has a terrific, slightly tart flavor. You can sit and taste the beers or order dinner or appetizers. While you're there, you can tour the brewery if you like.

### Pizza

The thin-crust pizza is always crunchy at the upscale (and slightly pricey) **Pizzeria Marilia** (Rua Marilia de Dirceu 189, Lourdes, tel. 31/3275-2027, lunch and dinner Mon.–Sat.). Offering a variety of fine wines and wonderful outdoor seating in the heart of Lourdes, they serve plates off the menu for around R$15–25. A pizza will cost about the same.

### Quick and Casual

**TiaClara** (Antônio de Albuquerque 617, tel. 31/3221-7966, near *praça* Savassi) is a glorified *lanchonete* with the best *salgados* and *doçes* (savory and sweet finger foods) in town—for only about three times more than other places (but worth it). The **Pastelaria Marilia de Dirceu** (Marilia de Dirceu 70, tel. 31/3335-2700, 8 A.M.–8 P.M. Mon.–Sat., 10 A.M.–7 P.M. on Sun., approximately R$6 for snacks) is consistently voted the best *pastelaria* in the city, no doubt due to its fresh ingredients and clean conditions. Try the *pastel com frango e catupiri* (fried spring roll with chicken and cheese) and the sweet banana pastel. The **Atelier do Pão** (Rua Barbara Heliodora 34, in Lourdes, 8 A.M.–8 P.M. daily) has a few patio tables where you can munch some of their great breads or sandwiches. Try their *pão napolitana* (bread stuffed with savory ingredients) for a savory snack.

### Self-Service

In the heart of Savassi is a terrific self-service restaurant, called **M Chico Savassi** (Rua Fernandes Tourinho 219, 11:30 A.M.–4 P.M.

daily). They offer numerous dishes, spacious facilities, and live music on weekends. **Café Cancun** (Rua Sergipe 1208, in Savassi) has lunch starting at noon Tuesday–Sunday with a Brazilian/Mexican buffet from R$14–20 per person. A true vegetarian lunch is available at **Mandala** (Rua Claudio Manuel 895, near Rua Rio Grande do Norte in Savassi, tel. 31/3282-2173, 11 A.M.–5:30 P.M. daily). Menu items are R$6–18, with daily specials. Chicken and fish are available, too.

# INFORMATION AND SERVICES

## Internet

A great Internet café is the **Internet Club** (Rua Fernandes Tourinho 385, near Sergipe in Savassi, tel. 31/3297-9002, www.internetclubcafe.com.br, 9 A.M.–8 P.M. Mon.–Fri., 9 A.M.–6 P.M. on Sat.). They have several computers (about R$5 per hour), coffee, treats, and, of course, a nice selection of shoes. The bookstore **Leitura** (Avenida Cristóvão Columbo 167, tel. 31/3287-2002, 9 A.M.–8 P.M. Mon.–Fri., 9 A.M.–6 P.M. on Sat.), just off *praça* Savassi, has computers for rent upstairs for about R$3 per hour.

## Money

**Citybank** (Rua Cristóvão Colombo 323) has 24-hour ATM access with both Plus and Cirrus machines (in English). **Banco do Brasil** (Rua Sergipe 1052 at Cristóvão Columbo) has at least one Cirrus and Plus machine. Another branch is at the corner of Rua Antônio de Albuquerque and Avenida da Bahia. In Lourdes, there are a few banks with international ATMs on Rua Raja Gabaglia, just up the hill from the Praça da Assembléia. You can cash American Express traveler's checks at 626 Rua Paraíba, *loja* 4, in Savassi.

## Post Office

The most convenient post office in the Savassi area is just up Rua Pernambuco from the Travessa Bookstore & Café at Rua Pernambuco 1322.

## GETTING THERE

At the entrance to the *rodoviaria,* you can catch the SC04 circular bus to the *praça* Savassi (the bus passes from left to right as you leave the *rodoviaria* and goes up Rua Curitiba). The circular SC02 will drop you off in Lourdes at Rua Santa Catarina. You can catch these same buses back to the center on the SC01 circular around Avenida do Contorno. A taxi from the *rodoviaria* to Savassi costs approximately R$10. You can find taxi points all along Avenida Afonso Pena and at many intersections in town. Buses coming from Rio pass directly through the Savassi area, so you can disembark before getting to the *rodoviaria* and take a quick cab ride to your hotel.

# Near Belo Horizonte

## PAMPULHA

Pampulha is an upscale district on the outskirts north of Belo Horizonte. Built around an artificial lake, the area is mostly suburban and not well configured for travelers. You need a car to get around and even getting to and from the main tourist attractions (the museum and church) is not as easy as it should be. There are buses that service the area, but nothing specifically for going between the attractions, except for organized tours or taxis (more on this later). On top of all this, the lake suffers from a raw sewage pollution problem so you may just end up leaving Pampulha off your list of Belo Horizonte sights. If you are flying in or out of B.H. and want to stay near the airport, then you might take a look at the Pampulha restaurant offerings to pass the time until your plane leaves. Pampulha is about 45 minutes by bus from downtown and about R$18–28 for a taxi—depending on which side of the lake you come from. From the Confins International Airport, Pampulha is slightly more than halfway to downtown.

Principal attractions in Pampulha are the buildings of the architectural complex spread around the lake, built by architect Oscar Niemeyer in partnership with landscape artist Roberto Burle Marx and other artists. The most interesting is the **Igreja São Francisco de Assis** (Av. Otacílio Negrão de Limão, no number, Pampulha, tel. 31/3441-9325, R$3, 8:30 A.M.–5 P.M. Mon.–Fri., closed at noon for lunch), which, after years of neglect, has recently reopened as a museum.

There are some great places for dining in the Pampulha area. The **Atelier G21** (Rua Marcos de Oliveira 50, tel. 31/3475-3870, after 6 P.M. Wed.–Sun.) offers a complete artistic experience in its food, atmosphere, and backyard sculpture garden. Go for dinner or just have drinks at the bar or in the garden. The **Restaurante Xapuri** (Rua Mandacaru 260, tel. 31/3196-6198) is near the zoo at the Pampulha lake. They offer traditional Comida Mineira and are open from noon Tuesday–Sunday.

## ⓜ SABARÁ

Sabará is a mere 25 kilometers from Belo Horizonte and is home to many historical structures, including eight baroque churches, two of which are among the most celebrated in the region. The churches were built during various stages of the region's mining activity. Shortly after the initial explorations for gold and minerals in the late 1600s, three key settlements grew to become the first official villages of the gold trade in 1711. These three villages were Mariana, Ouro Preto, and Sabará. Toward the latter phase of the mining era, Sabará had become the most productive and most populated of the three (this wave moving away from Ouro Preto, which dominated the early phases). By the end of the 1700s and in the early 1800s, Sabará housed almost 20 percent of Brazil's 2.85 million inhabitants and its activity greatly increased the urbanization of the region, including networks of roads to other states and through the new state capital, Belo

## THE SOUTHERN CROSS

As famous as it is, the Southern Cross is not as easily identified as you might think. There are many stars in a triangular, cross-like formation down here in the southern hemisphere. The identifying characteristics of the Southern Cross include a pink-colored star at its top point, a bluish star at its bottom point, and the somewhat faint star on one arm. In the summer, it's usually lying on its side and is more upright in the winter. It can often be seen even when other stars are faint.

Horizonte. Today, Sabará is a miniature version of Ouro Preto, sitting on the banks of the brown waters of the polluted and diminishing Rio das Valhas, once a majestic waterway of the gold trade.

Besides its historic architecture (more than just the churches), Sabará offers a taste of the culture of Minas Gerais, with its various festivals, arts and crafts, and, of course, regional foods. Your trip to Sabará will show you a poorer side of Minas Gerais through the bus windows.

Among the most impressive baroque structures to visit in Sabará is the **Igreja Nossa Senhora do Ó** (9 A.M.–5 P.M. Mon.–Sat., closed for lunch), built in the growth phase of the region's mining activities, in 1717. Crested with gold leaf, adorned with rich and colorful paintings, and strong in European and oriental influences, the church of Ó is a small jewel among Minas's historical churches and has a place among Brazil's most important historical structures. The **Igreja Nossa Senhora do Carmo** (Largo Nossa Sra. do Ó, no phone, 9 A.M.–6 P.M. Tues.–Sat. and 1–6 P.M. Sun.), in contrast, is from the final stages of the mining era, built in 1773 and containing important sculpture works of Aleijadinho. If you have the time and stamina to see more baroque buildings, you'll find many other attractions noted in the city's brochure available weekdays at the Secretary of Tourism (Rua Dom Pedro-II 223 near Praça Santa Rita, tel. 31/3672-7690, www.sabara.mg.gov.br). The city is planning to put up a tourist information booth one of these days. When it does, information will be available on weekends, too. But everything in town is easy to find if you ask around.

After touring the churches, you might take a little walk around the town, viewing the shops, restaurants, and activities offered. Some places of note include the **Restaurante 314 Sabarabuçu** (Rua Dom Pedro II 279, tel. 31/3671-2313, 11 A.M.–midnight Wed.–Mon., 11 A.M.–6 P.M. on Tue.), offering Comida Mineira with barbecue, pizza, and a full bar. The self-service price is R$12.90 or R$18.50 on weekends. Also, **Cê Qui Sabe** (Rua Mestre Caetano 56, tel. 31/3671-2906, 11 A.M.–11 P.M. Tue.–Sun., 11 A.M.–4 P.M. on Mon.) is another self-service offering just off the Praça Santa Rita. The price is R$12.90 per kilo. Finally, if you have some extra time, try **Jotapê** (Rua José Vaz Pedrosa 367, in the Pompéu district, tel. 31/3671-2445, 8 P.M. until sunrise on Fri., 11 A.M.–8 P.M. on Sat. and Sun.) on the outskirts of town (you'll need to take a taxi). They offer Comida Mineira, self-service (of course), and homemade *cachaça*, along with live music on weekends.

If you miss the last bus or otherwise decide to stay the night in town, you can stay at the **Pousada Solar dos Sepúlveda** (Rua da Intendência 371, tel. 31/3671-2708, R$85 double), which is in the center of town.

Sabará has several festivals during the year. The most notable include the Festival of Ora Pro Nobis, a super-high-protein leafy food from which many dishes are made. The city celebrates this traditional food in May. The Festival of Jabuticaba, in November, is something to catch if possible. This unique and tasty fruit becomes the basis of liqueurs, cakes, pies, jellies, jams, ice cream, and much more. Every year on July 17 is the city's birthday festival, which includes live music in the *praça* and lots of activity in town. Finally, the Festival de Artesanato in August is replete with handcrafts, paintings, and other artworks. The city gets crowded and exciting. For exact dates and other details, see the city's tourism site at www.sabara.mg.gov.br.

To get to Sabará from Belo Horizonte, take

the Viação Cisne from the *rodoviaria* for around R$5. The municipal bus 1059 is R$2 and leaves from Avenida do Contorno at the corner of Rua Caetes every 15 minutes, starting at 5:45 A.M. You can also get to Sabará from Caeté for R$2.10 and enter town near the Church of Ó; just tell the driver you want to get off at the church. Otherwise, ask for the stop near the center of town. See details in the Caeté section. The last 1059 leaves Sabará at 10:30 P.M.

## CAETÉ

Another village built in the beginning of the mining era, Caeté (meaning virgin forest in a native language) was built around 1706 in a dense forest area near the Piedade mountain range about 56 kilometers from Belo Horizonte. The town's principal attractions are its expansive views at the nearby Serra do Piedade peak. During the day, you can take in a panoramic view from the summit of the mountain, and at night, the observatory of UFMG (Federal University of Minas Gerais) provides a view of the southern stars. For most visitors, Caeté is just a half-day trip.

Take the Saritur bus from downtown Belo Horizonte at the *rodoviaria*. The 5504 municipal bus from Belo Horizonte will drop you at the foot of the mountain for R$3.15 before turning to enter the town. Be sure to ask the driver to let you off at the *pé da serra* (foot of the mountain). Then you walk about 45 minutes up the hill to the top, which has a historical church and a restaurant and grounds. You can catch the same bus back to B.H. or take it to the Caeté bus station (for another R$3.15 or take a taxi for about R$15—call tel. 31/3651-2887). In front of the station, catch the Sabara-Caete bus (a white-knuckler ride) to Sabará for R$2.10. The bus to Sabará leaves weekdays at 5 A.M., 7 A.M., 11 A.M., 1:30 P.M., 3:40 P.M., 6 P.M., and 9:10 P.M. On weekends: 7:20 A.M., 10 A.M., 1 P.M., 3:40 P.M., and 6 P.M.

A memorable tour could be arranged, beginning with sunrise on the Serra da Piedade peak, then a hop over to the Museu de Cachaça before heading to Sabará for lunch and sightsee-ing. In the late afternoon, you're back in Belo Horizonte. You can make a deal with a taxi driver or call one of the guides at **Andarilho da Luz** tours (tel. 31/3494-2727) to set it up.

## GRUTA DA LAPINHA

A calm, middle-class town about one hour from downtown Belo Horizonte by bus, Lagoa Santa is built around a natural lake. Originally, the city grew up around the aeronautic industries brought on by the airport and nearby military installations. In the past twenty years of Brazil's democracy and capitalism, though, the city has experienced a boom in *lotimentos* and *condominios* (planned subdivisions), making the town a favorite choice for middle- and upper-class Brazilians to build their country houses and make their weekend getaways.

The **Gruta da Lapinha,** a natural mineral cavern more than 500 meters long and 40 meters deep, is considered an important scientific archive, since it was here that Dr. Peter Lund discovered a 10,000-year-old human skull in 1934. The only real tourist attraction in Lagoa Santa, the *gruta* has 6 openings and 11 galleries and is one of the few caves that visitors can enter and exit at different openings. Guides take small groups into the caves every day, 9:30 A.M.–4:30 P.M., for about R$5. The *gruta* facilities include a museum, restaurant, and picnic grounds. Get there by catching the Lapinha bus at the Lagoa Santa bus station or the Praça Dr. Lund for R$1.40 (pay inside the bus). It leaves about every 40 minutes.

If you want a quick snack, try the *pão de queijo reicheiado* (cheese bread stuffed with grated chicken) at the **Panificador Tutti Pane** in the Praça Dr. Lund. More formal lunch and dinner offerings can be found lakeside, just down from the *praça,* including pizza, pasta, and Comida Mineira.

There's a 1001 bus every two hours from the *rodoviaria.* Buy your ticket at the counter a few minutes before departure for about R$4. You can also catch the 2220 inter-municipal bus (the red one) a block north of the *rodoviaria* at 920 Rua Caetés for about R$3.

There's usually a line forming but plenty of room. The buses run every 20 minutes. (Note that it's best to avoid this municipal bus during rush hours: 9 A.M. and 5 P.M.) If you want to continue traveling north, away from Belo Horizonte, you can either return to the city and select one of the Passaro Verde destinations up the main highway or pick up the Viação Serro milk run north from the Lagoa Santa *rodoviaria* toward Serro. The last bus back to Belo Horizonte is at 11 P.M.

## GRUTA DO REI DO MATO

Stalagmites and stalactites meet in two large columns in one of the galleries inside this cave. Spanning 220 meters, the *gruta* is near the city of Sete Lagoas (Seven Lakes), which has a laid-back feel and some wonderful lakeside bars and eateries and, if you stay late, a few decent hotels. The town is uphill to the left of the *rodoviaria* within walking distance. You'll know when you reach the lake (one of the seven). You don't have to enter the city if you want to see the cave, just take the Sete Lagoano from the Belo Horizonte *rodoviaria* for R$8 and ask the driver to let you off at the *trevo da gruta*

(roadside stop at the cave). You'll have to cross the highway to get to the cave. An alternative is to go all the way to the Sete Lagoas *rodoviaria* and take the Fazenda Velha *lotação* (VW Bus) for R$1, which will drop you off at the front door of the Gruta. The same van will bring you back to Sete Lagoas, where you can catch the bus back to Belo Horizonte. Tourist information is available at tel. 31/3772-2197.

## GRUTA DA MAQUINÉ

Dicovered in 1825 by a local farmer, and mapped by Dr. Lund in 1834, the Gruta da Maquiné is one of the more spectacular in the region. It is 650 meters long and has seven galleries with colorful stalactites and stalagmites. It's located near the town of Cordisburgo, but you don't have to enter the town to get to the caves. Just take the Sete Lagoano for R$17.50 from the *rodoviaria* at 6:30 A.M. or 12:30 P.M. Monday–Saturday and noon only on Sunday. The same bus leaves Maquiné at 4:20 P.M. There is a restaurant and *pousada* at the cave site. The cave is open every day 8 A.M.–5 P.M. Entry is R$8. Tourist information is available at tel. 31/3779-7483.

# Central Minas

Although the entire state of Minas Gerais offers attractions, it's the central area that really holds the most for travelers—with its numerous historical sites, beautiful landscapes, legends, and mysteries from a time when what happened in Brazil changed the entire world forever. The amount of gold and jewels extracted from Minas Gerais from 1700–1770 was nothing short of staggering and the gold rush (which is called the Gold Cycle in Brazil) left behind dozens of churches and architectural monuments. Nonetheless, the most significant attractions of this region are not the churches and museums, but the old colonial towns in which they reside. While Ouro Preto, for example, has many important historical monuments, it's really the town itself that captures the imagination and holds a kind of mystery and poetry in its streets and hillsides. The sleepy town of Tiradentes is home to the most spectacular church in the entire region, the Igreja do Matriz do Santo Antônio (the second most gold-laden church in Brazil), but the magic of your voyage to Tiradentes begins when you settle into the town itself, feel its quiet repose, and experience the hospitality of the locals and their passion for the place.

Of course, there is history at every turn,

# Must-Sees

**Look for M to find the sights and activities you can't miss and M for the best dining and lodging.**

**M Igreja Nossa Sra. do Rosário:** Many visitors remember this as their favorite church in all of Central Minas, probably because of its charming round design and the way it sits humbly in the Largo do Rosário *praça*. It is one of the principal churches of the brotherhood of black slaves (page 202).

**M Igreja São Francisco de Paula:** The hills of Ouro Preto are a museum in themselves and no better seen than from the grounds of the Igreja São Francisco de Paula in the afternoon sun. From this perch, you have more than a 180-degree view of the city (page 202).

The Igreja São Francisco de Paula has an incredible view of the Ouro Preto hillsides.

© CHRISTOPHER VAN BUREN

**M Igreja do Antônio Dias:** This is one of the few churches in Central Minas that is not dripping in gold. There is a different feel to the statuary here (of which there is an enormous amount, each highly detailed) because of their simple, wood finish. Manoel Francisco, the father of Aleijadinho, was responsible for its reconstruction. Inside is the Museu de Aleijadinho (page 203).

**M Santuário do Senhor Bom Jesus de Matosinhos:** The most important works attributed to Aleijadinho, the *12 Profetas*, in the Santuário, are masterpieces of sculpture. Legend has it that the artist placed many hidden symbols and messages within their design (page 220).

**M Maria Fumaça:** The train ride from São João del Rei to Tiradentes is a short but magical journey through the Tiradentes valley and over the Rio das Mortes (River of the Dead) (page 226).

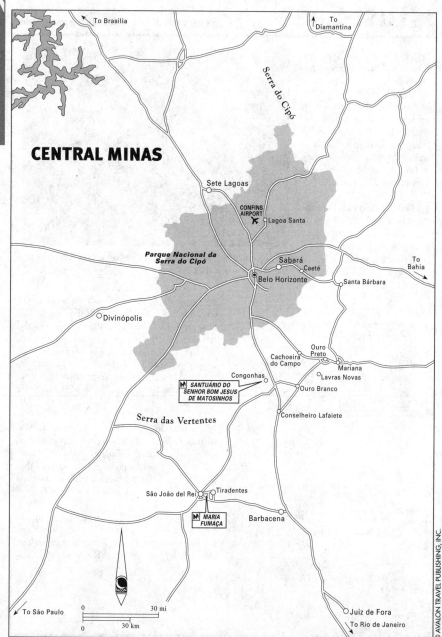

# CENTRAL MINAS

To Brasilia

To Diamantina

Serra do Cipó

Sete Lagoas

CONFINS AIRPORT

Lagoa Santa

Parque Nacional da Serra do Cipó

Sabará

Caeté

To Bahia

Belo Horizonte

Santa Bárbara

Divinópolis

Ouro Preto

Cachoeira do Campo

Mariana

Congonhas

Lavras Novas

SANTUÁRIO DO SENHOR BOM JESUS DE MATOSINHOS

Ouro Branco

Conselheiro Lafaiete

Serra das Vertentes

São João del Rei

Tiradentes

MARIA FUMAÇA

Barbacena

To São Paulo

0        30 mi

0        30 km

Juiz de Fora

To Rio de Janeiro

mostly from the years leading up to and during the gold boom. When you realize that this area produced in the 18th century as much as the rest of the world produced from the 16th to the end of the 19th centuries combined, you begin to imagine what frenzy must have taken place here. Now add the political (and spiritual) influences of the Catholic church, European colonization, and the realities of the slave trade and you have a most fascinating trip ahead of you.

Naturally, you should check out some of the churches, museums, and historical sites of the area. But be warned: There are dozens of them and after awhile they all begin to look the same, interesting as they may be. So this chapter will steer you to the most important and interesting of the bunch, while mentioning some of the side options that you might find worth exploring. Aside from these historical sites, you may want to see some of the natural wonders, including some of the exhilarating waterfalls and mountain vistas. Also, take some time to visit the local artisans, whose crafts can be found in shops throughout the region and in street fairs and festivals—from the stone pots and pans in Cachoeira do Campo just outside of Ouro Preto to the pewter factories in São João del Rei.

## PLANNING YOUR TIME

If you have the time and stamina, it's well worth seeing all the major towns described in this chapter and a couple of the minor ones. But if time is limited, then your choice is really between visiting one of two major groups: One group includes Ouro Preto, Mariana, and Congonhas (with some small villages in-between). The other includes São João del Rei, Tiradentes, and Congonhas. Either of these groups can be seen in 3–4 days. Add an extra day or two if you plan to do some hiking or horseback riding.

Since these two groups offer very similar experiences in terms of historical sites and monuments, you should try not to squeeze too many of these towns into one trip. With a mass of baroque images in your head, you may end up unable to remember which was in what church. And you certainly want time to enjoy the special cafés and stroll through the towns, looking into the various shops. If you have an extra day, use it getting to know the surrounding areas of your chosen group, visiting a waterfall, or hiking to a mountain peak.

To those who enjoy packing as much as possible into a short trip, it is certainly possible to see Ouro Preto, Congonhas, São João del Rei, and Tiradentes in one five-day trip. Just limit your museum choices to the few that really attract you and remember that most of the churches are best seen from the outside anyway. The exceptions are noted throughout this chapter.

Central Minas is a mountainous area with various ranges bumping into one another. Spotted along these hills and valleys are the many cities and towns that you will be visiting. The good news is that this topography makes for some picturesque vistas and horizon lines. The not-so-good news is that you can never be completely sure what the temperature will be from one town to the next. Towns in the higher altitudes, such as Ouro Preto, can have their own micro-climates, with cold fronts in the winter—reaching as low as 5°C—and extreme hot spells in the summer, as high as 35°C. Often, when it's raining in Belo Horizonte, it can be clear and crisp in Ouro Preto and vice-versa. The average temperature for the region is around 17°C in the winter and 28°C in the summer. The months of June–September are usually quite hot, so be sure to pack sunscreen and appropriate attire. You'll want a decent jacket in the winter months of July and August.

## Ouro Preto

Walking slowly up and down these steep, stony streets went Brazil's religious, political, intellectual, and artistic elite. As the center of Brazil's mining activities, Ouro Preto provided the only official mint in the region (Casa dos Contos) and the largest government chambers (and jailhouse) in Brazil at the time. Upon its stony hills sit 13 baroque churches spanning all phases of the Brazilian mining era, several museums, a fine arts college, and one of the world's most recognized schools of geology and mining. Ouro Preto offers an ample selection of hotels, dozens of small *pousadas* (inns), campgrounds, and two youth hostels. Its restaurant selection ranges from cheap-and-delicious to five-star elegant, most being somewhere in-between. Its hilly topography gives the city a charming mountain village appearance. Many of the city streets, lined with square stones placed in the 1700s, can be quite challenging to ascend. It's possible to walk from the highest point in town to the lowest in a couple hundred meters of cobblestone. Just be sure you have good walking shoes. The hillsides around Ouro Preto are part of a protected wildlife reserve and offer numerous waterfalls (some decent for swimming) and trails for hiking and horseback riding.

Ouro Preto began as a mining town and continues with its mining activities to this day. It is the home of several major metallurgical interests, including ALCAN, AçoMinas, and SAMARCO, employing a large percentage of the city's 68,000 inhabitants. The soap stone and talc mining in and around Ouro Preto has given rise to an indigenous form of sculpture, including wonderful stone and clay pots and pans for cooking. Art and theater have always been part of the city's history. Besides being the birthplace of Antônio Francisco Lisboa, Brazil's Michelangelo, it has been home to several of Brazil's most famous painters, including Alberto Guignard. The school of theater is the impetus behind the many theater pieces produced during festivals yearround. In fact, with all the educational institutions in Ouro Preto, the city has become something of a college town and most nighttime activities (outside the major festivals) are held in the many *repúblicas* (frat houses) around town and are dominated by young people. The city is said to have one of the highest beer-consumption-per-capita ratios in the country. You get the idea.

Wonderful any time of the year, the city does have a rainy season, September–December, which is perhaps the least desirable time to visit. In the winter (June–August), it can get quite cold, being at an altitude of about 1,100 meters. Temperatures range from 16–28°C normally, with winter nights hitting a low of 2°C at times. The famous Festival de Inverno (Winter Festival), which originated in Ouro Preto (although has now spread to many other towns) is still one of the city's principal events. It happens all during the month of July. Summers are clear and hot with temperatures hovering around 25°C. The summer season offers the grand festival of Carnaval, for which Ouro Preto earns a reputation as one of the rowdiest cities outside of Rio de Janeiro.

Ouro Preto is probably the most spectacular and beloved of Brazil's historical towns, having gained official status as a world historical monument by UNESCO—recognizing it as one of the world's most prized and well-preserved historical sites. Sadly, recent political tides have put tourism and the city's preservation behind other interests and Ouro Preto may lose its official UNESCO title. Its tourism infrastructure tends to be a bit lower-end than that of its rival towns, Tiradentes and São João del Rei. Still, Ouro Preto's historical and cultural heritage along with its special mountain charm continue to make it one of Brazil's favorite travel destinations.

Despite its revered place in Brazilian history, Ouro Preto offers only about two days and one night of normal sightseeing for most visitors, especially if they have other historical towns on their agendas. One can see only so many

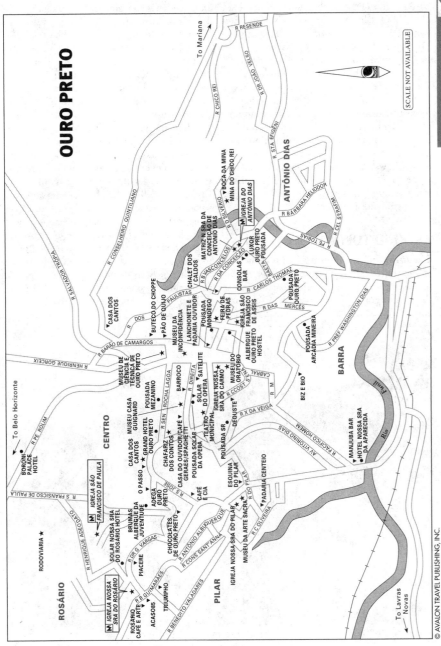

OURO PRETO

SCALE NOT AVAILABLE

© AVALON TRAVEL PUBLISHING, INC.

baroque churches and abandoned gold mines, after all. Outside of major festivals, Ouro Preto's night scene centers on a single street (Rua Direita) and a somewhat rowdy *boteco* (dive bar). If you're young, single, or like to party (all of the above?), then you'll probably find Ouro Preto an excellent harbor for several days—your fondest remembrance being, perhaps, a lovely romance. During festivals, your options are vastly different and your nights could be filled with music, dancing, theater, and art. The *prefeitura* (mayor's office) frequently produces shows in the main square (Praça Tiradentes) and the city is generally full of tourists, street vendors, art exhibitions, and of course, lots of students and beer.

## AROUND TOWN

The main square in Ouro Preto is dedicated to the confederate Tiradentes, who is known for leading an anti-taxation movement against the king of Portugal and, in effect, a Brazilian independence movement. He was hanged in Rio de Janeiro and his head was returned to Ouro Preto for public display. The *praça* features a statue of Tiradentes and is the main access point to the rest of Ouro Preto. You are likely to see a stage set up in the *praça*, as musical and political events are often held there. In the *praça* itself, you'll find doors to the **Museu da Inconfidência** (the old senate building and jailhouse), the **Museu de Ciência,** the **Escola de Minas** (Federal University of Minas Gerais), a tourist information office, money changers, and some uninteresting restaurants and bars. In the *praça,* you can usually find hippies selling their handmade wares and sometimes demonstrations of Capoeira, juggling, or music. When popular bands play in Ouro Preto during festivals, the *praça* can get so crowded that it takes more than 30 minutes to walk across it. If you happen to be in the *praça* at one of these moments, keep an eye on your valuables as you traverse.

To the right of the *praça* is the street known

The streets of Ouro Preto are lined with 19th-century architecture.

as **Rua Direita** (Right Street), officially known as Rua Conde de Bobadela, although many Ouro Preto residents don't even know its official name. It is full of shops, bars, and restaurants. At night, Rua Direita is the only major action in town, centered on a few bars about halfway down the street. Although this nightlife generally involves a young crowd, there are plenty of options for a more mature audience, too. Also in this direction, you can access the **Teatro Municipal** (Latin America's oldest theater); **Rua São José,** which offers up most of the city's banks and a number of shops and restaurants; and eventually the **Igreja do Rosário,** the **Igreja do Pilar,** and their accompanying *praças.*

To the left of Praça Tiradentes is Rua Claudio Manoel, which leads to the **Feira das Pedras** (Largo do Coimbra, 9 A.M–6 A.M. daily), a flea market of handmade stone works in the Ouro Preto tradition. The outdoor market faces one of the town's principal *chafariz* (a type of fountain that usually taps a natural spring), called the **Chafariz do Largo do Coimbra** and which is still used by residents and travelers as a source of drinking water. Also in this direction, you'll find the **Igreja São Francisco de Assis,** the **Matriz de Antônio Dias,** the **Mina de Chico Rei,** and many *pousadas.*

Tip: For the best photographs, note that the sun hits the Rua Direita–side of the city in the morning and the Rua Claudio Manoel–side in the afternoon. There is something special about Ouro Preto's hillsides in the afternoon sun. Aleijadinho planned all three of his São Francisco de Assis churches (in Ouro Preto, São João del Rei, and Tiradentes) to face west so the afternoon sun would illuminate their facades.

## CHURCHES AND MUSEUMS

Ouro Preto's churches are all privately owned and operated. Each has its own particular hours and price of admission, but most ask for just R$1–3 to enter. Most of these churches were built by sects, or brotherhoods, contributing their gold to create what were in effect power centers (and profit centers) for their particular group. The churches also displayed the brotherhood's social, economic, and racial status. Most of the churches also cap entrances to a network of tunnels that runs under the hills of Ouro Preto and even directly under Praça Tiradentes. Although said to have been mines, these tunnels were probably used to contraband gold, hiding it from the Portuguese government, in the guise of church activity. It is said that the Mina do Chico Rei stretches under the *praça* until it intersects this network of tunnels. At the hotel Solar do Rosário, you can see where the construction of the hotel's modern annex broke into one of these tunnels running between the Rosário and São José churches, both of which were built by brotherhoods of black slaves. Notwithstanding these efforts, most of the gold from Brazil found its way to Rome and England and sits there to this day.

### Casa dos Contos

It's difficult to imagine how much gold went through the doors of this old stone building. The Casa dos Contos (Rua São José 12, tel. 31/3551-1444, 12:30–5 P.M. Tues.–Sat. and 9 A.M.–3 P.M. Sun. and holidays, R$1) was originally the city's administrative offices, the gold exchange office, and, of course, the location for collecting taxes. It also served a time as slave quarters and a jailhouse. Today, it is home to the Museu da Moeda (money museum), which you can see exactly what the gold nuggets, coins, and government notes looked like during the gold rush period. It also houses an art gallery, usually featuring contemporary Brazilian artists, and the Ouro Preto branch of the Receita Federal (the Brazilian IRS), still collecting taxes from this building.

### Igreja Nossa Sra. do Carmo

From a distance, Igreja Nossa Sra. do Carmo (Largo de Coimbra, tel. 31/3551-3282, R$3, 1–4:45 P.M. Wed.–Sun.) appears to be one of the largest churches in Ouro Preto, sitting to the right side of the Museu da Inconfidência (as you face the museum). Actually, this is an optical illusion, as the church is built on a slightly higher plateau than the surrounding buildings. Begun in 1766, it is considered to be one of Aleijadinho's principal architectural works, although it does not offer many sculptural works. Inside, the church is one of the few in Ouro Preto with a brightly painted interior. Within the church grounds, you can also find the **Museu do Oratorio.**

## Igreja Nossa Sra. do Pilar

The Pilar Church (Rua Henrique Adeodato, no number, Pilar, no phone, 9–10:45 A.M. and noon–4 P.M. Wed.–Sun., R$3)is the third-most opulent church in Brazil, the first two being in Salvador and Tiradentes, respectively. Its many sculptures, images, and icons hold more than 430 kilos of gold leafing. It is indeed one of the most impressive churches in Minas Gerais from the inside. Built between 1711 and 1733, Pilar is a perfect example of Brazil's baroque architecture and the incredible wealth of the era. Be sure to go upstairs for the view from above (not all churches allow this). Below the church is a basement full of sacred art pieces called the **Museu da Arte Sacra,** featuring mostly silver religious pieces and linens used by the priests.

##  Igreja Nossa Sra. do Rosário

Considered by many to be the most enchanting of all the churches in Ouro Preto, Rosário (Largo do Rosário, no phone, noon–4:45 P.M. Tue.–Sat., noon–3:30 P.M. on Sun., mass starts at 4 P.M. on Sun., free) is the only church built in a round format. It was influenced by Italian architectural designs of the same period, which were sent to Ouro Preto by the Catholic Church. Built in 1709 by the brotherhood of slaves of the Rosário, the church holds a special place in Ouro Preto history.

## Igreja São Francisco de Assis

One of the most mysterious churches of the era, Ouro Preto's Igreja São Francisco de Assis (Largo de Coimbra, tel. 31/3551-3282, R$3, 8:30–11:45 A.M. and 1:30–4:45 P.M. Wed.–Sun.) is one of three churches dubbed São Francisco de Assis that are said to feature the architectural and sculptural works of Aleijadinho. The others are in São João del Rei

© CHRISTOPHER VAN BUREN

Igreja do Rosário is one of the most charming churches in Ouro Preto.

(the most spectacular of the three) and Tiradentes. All have a similar structural designs, use of soapstone sculpture on the face of the building (in rococo style), and feature wooden sculptures inside without gold leafing. This one is the smallest of the three. Its outside sculpture work is said to be full of secret symbolism designed by the artist and which can be seen in the light of different times of the day, as the sun casts its shadows on the face of the church. (Blur your eyes on the sculpture work above the doorway and you may see the face of Jesus looking back at you.) It's best seen at 5 P.M., when the light of the afternoon sun hits the face of the building.

## Igreja São Francisco de Paula

Positioned on a hilltop near the main bus station, the Igreja São Francisco de Paula (Rua Henrique Adeodato, no phone, R$3, 8:30–11:45 A.M. and 1:30–4:45 P.M. Wed.–Sat. and

# THE MYSTERY OF ANTÔNIO FRANCISCO LISBOA

Recognized as Brazil's greatest sculptor, Antônio Francisco Lisboa, commonly known by the derogatory nickname Aleijadinho (the little cripple), was the son of a Portuguese architect who moved to Ouro Preto in 1724 on the wave of the gold rush. Like so many Portuguese settlers, Manuel Francisco added his contribution to the rich mixture of races that exists in Brazil with his child, Antônio, born to one of his slaves, Isabel, in the city of Ouro Preto around 1730. (Antônio took on the name of Lisboa—his father's birthplace—after his father's death in a confusing and somewhat mysterious alteration of documents.)

Growing up around the tools, artists, and architectural circles of the day, Antônio also studied religion, music, and Latin, all of which would find their way into his works. His racial mix excluded him not only from certain social circles but also from official recognition as a master architect and sculptor. His name does not appear on a single architectural or artistic contract involving a church construction or reform. In fact, the few written references to Aleijadinho indicate that he was most likely an assistant or auxiliary to the master architects.

Around the age of 40, Aleijadinho began suffering pain throughout his body, which was originally thought to be syphilis and arthritis. Most recent analyses (of his exhumed body) attribute his illness to porphyria, a debilitating disease that often affects the hands. Shortly thereafter, the sculptor could not walk without the help of his two slaves. His hammer and chisel were said to have been strapped to his hands so he could continue working. Work was, by this point, his obsession and his primary means of interfacing with the community. Nevertheless, Aleijadinho managed to travel among the historical towns of Minas Gerais, adding his masterpieces to the many baroque churches.

Although it is not always known which works can be attributed to which artists, there has been a great study of the works of Aleijadinho, and modern masters have attributed certain works to the legendary sculptor—a difficult task, since much of the sculpture of the time was done by groups working together. Aleijadinho is said to have been the designer behind many churches and sculptural works and his signature characteristics are well cataloged. His greatest works were his last, created around 1800 in the town of Congonhas, shortly before the end of his life in 1814. He died in Ouro Preto, close to where he was born, his sickness leaving him bedridden. He and his father are entombed inside the church at the Matriz de Antônio Dias in Ouro Preto.

Because of the mysterious lack of documentation showing his participation in the works of the day and strange alterations in his birth and death records, some believe he never existed or was nothing more than an assistant his entire life. These disbelievers also find it incredible that a man inflicted with such a crippling disease could have been responsible for so many works attributed to him.

1:30–4:45 P.M. Sun.) is one of the most majestic churches in Ouro Preto, owing to its fortunate position overlooking most of Ouro Preto from one of the town's high points. Indeed, a visit to this church consists mostly of walking around it to take in the near 180-degree view. It's one of the city's newest churches, begun in 1804, and also one of the best photo ops and most romantic perches in town.

## M Igreja do Antônio Dias

One of the few churches in Minas Gerais that is not dripping in gold, the Igreja do Antônio Dias (Praça Antônio Dias, tel. 31/3551-3282, 8:30–11:45 A.M. and 1:30–4:45 P.M. Wed.–Sun., R$4 or R$1.50 for students) began in 1699 as a small chapel, commissioned by Antônio Dias himself, the man responsible for discovering all this gold. At the time, the town was just a small settlement. Later, after the settlement of Antônio Dias had grown to become Vila Rica, the chapel was reconstructed to include a new temple and a matrix of offices and functions. The reconstruction was initiated in 1727 by Manoel Francisco, father of Antônio Francisco, who is assumed to be the

Central Minas

© CHRISTOPHER VAN BUREN

looking out over Igreja do Antônio Dias

famous Aleijadinho. Today, the church houses the **Museu do Aleijadinho** as well as his and his father's tombs, which are set into the church floorboards, as was the custom to honor rich patrons. Aleijadinho and his father rest inside the church sanctuary in the floor of the right-hand causeway, near the first archway if you were to enter the church from the front door (which you don't). The sculpture work inside the church, although probably not that of the master Aleijadinho but of his teachers, is impressive in its quantity and detail. The museum has a few works of Aleijadinho and many works that are thought to be his. The sculptures with porcelain eyes are particularly eerie and intriguing.

### Other Churches

There are many other churches and chapels spread around Ouro Preto, some requiring taxis or guides to find. Most are small and not as spectacular as those mentioned previously, but some have interesting historical significance and if you're particularly interested in such things, you may find some of them worth scouting out. Check with the folks at the in-

formation center in Praça Tiradentes for details and guides.

### Museu Casa Guignard

For art lovers, the Museu Guignard (Rua Direita 110, tel. 31/3551-5155, 12:30–6:30 P.M. Tues.–Fri. and 9 A.M.–3 P.M. weekends and holidays, free) is a most interesting stop on their walk through Ouro Preto. It provides a special view into the history of art in Brazil. The museum houses the paintings, sketches, personal letters, and documents of one of Brazil's most respected artists, Alberto da Veiga Guignard. The museum and grounds were once the artist's residence and, in 1987, were inaugurated as the Guignard Museum. Guignard was the professor of many of Brazil's well-known artists and his works influence Brazilian art to this day. He painted in a kind of Chagall-like, loose expressionism.

### Museu de Ciência e Têcnica de Ouro Preto

One of the most interesting things about the Museu de Ciência e Têcnica is its location in the old governor's palace, built by Manoel

Francisco at the top of the *praça*. A stroll up the ramp to the doorway will give you a bird's-eye view of the *praça* and surrounding hillsides. Stroll up in the morning and then compare the view again later in the afternoon. You'll see two different images of Ouro Preto. Today, the building is primarily used by the Federal University in Ouro Preto and it offers a museum with two main sections: The Mineralogy and Natural History section (noon–5 P.M. Wed.–Sun.) has thousands of stones on display, along with pieces from the mining and metallurgy industries. The Design, Topography, and Astronomy section (8:30 A.M.–11 P.M. Saturday) offers, among other things, a look at the Ouro Preto observatory, whose dome can be seen from outside the building.

### Museu da Inconfidência

The most recognized museum in Ouro Preto, the Inconfidência (Praça Tiradentes 139, tel. 31/3559-1121, noon–5:30 P.M. Tues.–Sun., R$5 or R$2.50 for students) displays a collection of religious and cultural artifacts from the 18th century, including furniture, sculptures, large religious works, silver works, and paintings. The collection resides in the original government chambers, begun in 1784 and which boasts the country's largest jailhouse of the time. The construction was interrupted so many times, however, that it took until 1846 to finish and was often accused of having somewhat barbaric conditions inside. In 1944, it became a museum.

### Museu do Oratório

This unique museum (Casa do Noviciado in the Nossa Sra. do Carmo Church listed earlier, www.oratorio.com.br, 9:30–5:30 daily, closed for lunch, R$2) was inaugurated in 1998. It is the world's only museum of *oratórios*, displaying more than 160 of them, all from the personal collection of Angela Gutierrez. Said to have once been the temporary home of Aleijadinho, the building sits beside the Igreja Nossa Sra. do Carmo and can be accessed by entering the church grounds. It brings together various types of oratories from vari-

ous moments of (primarily) Brazilian history, made from all kinds of materials. All of them are interesting, but the miniature ones made from matchbooks and bullet shells are perhaps most memorable.

## ARCHITECTURE AND MONUMENTS

### Bridges

There are six stone bridges in Ouro Preto, built between the years of 1744 and 1806. The oldest and most picturesque is the bridge at the Casa dos Contos, which offers a special view from either side (up or downstream) and a beautiful photo op in the morning light. Another interesting bridge can be found in the Rosário neighborhood. When you reach the Igreja do Rosário, you turn left at the bottom of the *praça,* then take the first right going steeply downhill. Your next right takes you onto a narrow path that leads to a very polluted stream and the lovely Rosário bridge that crosses above it, built in 1753.

### Buildings

The **Teatro Municipal** (Rua Brigadeiro Musqueira, in front of the Igreja Nossa Sra. do Carmo, tel. 31/3559-3224, noon–6 P.M. daily) is the oldest functioning theater in South America. This former opera house was built in 1770 and is almost identical to the one in Sabará. It's small and very charming and there's not a bad seat in the house. Pass by during the day for information about plays and events showing or check www.ouropreto.com.br for listings.

### Chafarizes

A *chafariz* is a small structure that caps a natural spring and turns it into a kind of fountain. Ouro Preto has so many of these structures (some wet, some dry) that it makes other historical towns look silly for making such a fuss over the one or two they have. As you walk around town, you will see these structures. The most impressive is the **Chafariz dos Contos** in the Praça Reinaldo do Alves de Brito, at the bottom of Rua Sen. Rocha Lagoa. While you may or may not want to drink from the ones still active, you can use them to cool yourself down on a hot day. Ouro Preto boasts some of the best and cleanest water in the region and residents of the city pay nothing for it. Some neighborhoods still get their water from 18th-century sources, such as wells or springs coming out of abandoned mines.

## Mines

The **Mina do Chico Rei** is a small, abandoned gold mine (and accompanying restaurant) with an interesting history. The mine itself was hidden by brush and stone in the back of the old house. In 1948 when the house was sold, the children of the new owner discovered the mine while playing in the back yard. After some study of city documents, it was determined to be the mine of the famous Chico Rei, the African king/slave who purchased his own freedom and began his own mining efforts. The house was later turned into one of the city's hot night spots with a bar and live music. Today, the owners have closed the bar (too rowdy) and opened a lunch venue, **Boca da Mina** (Rua Dom Silverio 108, tel. 31/3552-2866, 8 A.M.–5 P.M. daily).

There is a little town between Ouro Preto and Mariana called Passagem de Mariana (Mariana Passage). There's really nothing much in the town, but it's home to one of the most interesting (and newest) old gold mines in the area and, they say, one of the largest. Called the **Mina de Passagem de Mariana** (Rua Eugênio Eduardo Rapallo 192, Passagem, tel. 31/3557-5000, 9 A.M.–5 P.M. daily, R$15—a bit steep but probably worth it), the mine produced more than 35 tons of gold ore during its time in the early 1800s. You enter the mine via a trolley once used to remove the ore and descend a short distance into the dark, cold cave. Inside is a natural pool of water so clear and calm it's practically invisible. If you go when there are not many

## LEGENDS OF THE SLAVE TRADE

Only a few of the slaves in Brazil were used for domestic servitude. The great majority were males brought in to work in the mines, road construction, and other laborious activities of the great expansion. Conditions were harsh, to be sure. But in the early days of the gold boom, Portuguese laws concerning slaves were somewhat liberal and slaves were even allowed to purchase their own freedom. These laws were soon toughened after **Chico Rei,** a former tribal leader in Africa, purchased his freedom and later that of many others. Together, they formed the roots of a free black brotherhood in Minas Gerais, called the Brotherhood of Nossa Sra. do Rosário. Legend has it that Chico Rei hid gold dust in his fingernails and hair until he had collected enough to liberate himself and others.

The legend of **Zumbi,** who lived prior to Chico Rei, tells of an African leader who escaped and lived in the hills of Minas Gerais, coming down at night to free others from his tribe. This group of escaped slaves lived in the hillsides on what could be found or stolen and represented the first *quilombo,* or community of exiled slaves.

There are also many stories of European settlers mixing with their black slaves, creating one of the three principal racial mixtures in Brazil, the mulatto (traditionally a mixture of Spanish or Portuguese with African). The legend of **Chica da Silva** tells of a Portuguese governor in the diamond trade in the town of Diamantina who fell in love with a beautiful African slave and made her his wife. Chica da Silva became one of the most powerful black women of the time and used her power and money to build a large plantation, erect a church, and acquire many slaves of her own. She was known for her eccentric power plays and the governor finally left her to return to Portugal. She ended up poor, homeless, and crazy.

visitors, you might be able to bribe the guide into letting you enter the water—an unforgettable experience. Bring a towel and be ready for a cold exit.

## ENTERTAINMENT AND NIGHTLIFE

### Bars

Being something of a drinking town, Ouro Preto is full of all kinds of bars and watering holes, the most frequented being on Rua Direita. The **Barroco** (Rua Direita 106, 11–2 A.M. or until the last one leaves) is the town's most famous *boteco* (simple bar) and offers a very mixed crowd, including a lot of international travelers and locals. Sometimes it can get pretty rowdy and sometimes it's just full of students from the local universities. It has some of the finest finger foods in the region, like their famous *coxinha* (grated chicken in breading). Across the street is the **Satelite,** which is a *boteco* that also serves pizza and sandwiches. It's usually less rowdy than the Barroco and has better bathrooms. There are other dive bars in the *praça* and, for that matter, all around town. You can find a decent party crowd at the **Esquina do Pilar** (diagonally behind the Pilar church, noon–midnight Mon.–Sat., noon–6 P.M. Sun.), which serves drinks and offers some simple menu items. If you're in town on Sunday, most places are going to be closed. Your best bet is to hop over to Mariana in the afternoon and partake of the festivities in the *praça*.

Mid-range options include the **Buteco do Choppe** (Rua Barão de Carmargos 126, tel. 31/3551-4733, from 4 P.M. daily), which has live music most nights and draft beer flowing. It's a good option if you're not into the Rua Direita scene. **Consolas Bar** (Rua da Conceição 18, tel. 31/3551-4175, from 6 P.M. until the last client), offers food and drinks all night long for a slightly older, but generally very cool crowd. Get there early on weekends.

More sophisticated offerings include the many scotch bars in town, such as the one in the **Hotel Solar do Rosário** (Rua Getúlio Var-

gas 270, tel. 31/3551-5200) or the **Grande Hotel Ouro Preto** (Rua Sen. Rocha Lagoa 164, tel. 31/3551-1488), which offers a wonderful view of the town, or the outdoor patio at **O Passo** (Rua São José 58, tel. 31/3552-5089). You can also have drinks at the **Acaso 85** restaurant (Largo do Rosário 85, tel. 31/3551-2397), which has a wonderful patio bar area, or at the **Solar do Opera** café on Rua Direita 75.

### Clubs and Discos

Ouro Preto has very few dance locations. Every few years one pops up and soon closes its doors. Special dance events are held at random intervals at the **Caim,** which is a large space above the university cafeteria in Praça Tiradentes. It usually features hordes of people and unbearably loud rock cover music. Check the posters at the Barroco bar on Rua Direita for this and other possibilities while you're in town. You can also check the flyers at Cyberhouse on Rua Direita or with the Universidade Federal de Ouro Preto website: www.ouropreto.com.br.

There is a dance club for the locals. It's a popular club, which means it's for the masses. But if you're young, adventurous, and would like to try dancing *forró* (a type of Brazilian swing dance) then you might go out on a limb and pay them a visit. Called **Segunda Sem Lei** (Lawless Monday), it happens every Monday night starting at around 11 P.M. near the entrance to town (just ask the taxi driver, because you don't want to go by any other means, and be careful not to offend any of the locals). There is a small cover charge and inside, you can get drinks and appetizers.

### Music and Theater

There are shows of all kinds happening at festival times, but off-season, you'll have to look around for them. For local listings, the best place to check is the ouropreto.com.br site or directly at the tourist information center in the *praça*. You can also swing by the convention center's **Parque Metalúrgico** (Rua Diogo de Vasconcelos 328, near the train station), which has the city's largest theater facility, and ask for current listings. Don't forget to stop by the

**Teatro Municipal** in front of the Igreja Nossa Sra. do Carmo for their current listings.

## Sidewalk Cafés

Just looking for a cup of java and a snack? Ouro Preto has a few cool café hangouts, starting with **Café Geraes** (Rua Direita 122, tel. 31/3551-5097, 11 A.M.–11 P.M. daily). They have good sweets, good sandwiches, and decent coffee. A seat by the window lets you gaze out at the Rua Direita movement. Also on Rua Direita is the **Solar do Opera** café (Rua Direita 79, from noon), which has a slightly more elegant ambience in which to taste its coffees and snacks. At around 8 P.M. it becomes a full restaurant. A relative newcomer in town is the café **Chocolates de Ouro Preto** (Rua Getúlio Vargas 66, on the way to Rosário, tel. 31/3551-7330, 9 A.M.–8 P.M. Mon.–Fri., 9 A.M.–10 P.M. on weekends), which features quality chocolate marvels made on-site along with hot chocolate, coffee, and appetizers. Continuing along the road to Rosário, you reach the Rosário church and the little *praça* in front. There you find the **Rosário Cafée Arte** (Largo do Rosário 99, no phone, 9 A.M.–6 P.M. Mon.–Sat.) with its great vantage point looking back up the hill. They have coffee, sweets, and a gallery of art representing regional artists.

## FESTIVALS AND EVENTS

The **Festival de Inverno** is probably the most interesting of the festivals in Ouro Preto, being focused on art, music, and cultural events and lasting most of the month of July. There are scheduled events every day, some in established locations (such as plays and concerts) and others on the streets of the Centro Histórico (such as parades and performances). Just about every weekend during the festival there are free shows taking place on the outdoor stage set up on Praça Tiradentes. It's easy to find schedules of events around town. What's difficult is getting a room, so plan early for this festival. Festival information is at www.ouropreto.mg.gov.br.

**Festival de 12 Outubro** is a national holiday celebrated in Ouro Preto because of its coincidence with the birthday of the Escola de Minas. It's marked by theater and music demonstration inside the school (and open to the public) and parties around town. **Carnaval** in Ouro Preto is a bawdy, rowdy affair, crowding the streets of the Centro Histórico with hordes of young people in costumes or bathing suits generally drunk from all-day drinking fests. The streets are nearly impossible to navigate, as the crowds can be shoulder to shoulder and pulsating to some music or other (usually not anything so agreeable as samba, rather some horrible Brazilian rock or metal). Some events take place in other neighborhoods, including parades with floats and drumming. There are a great number of assaults during Carnaval and an excess of testosterone. Still, it can be a great time if you are young, single, and looking to unleash your wild side for a few days. The official dates of Carnaval change from year to year, so consult online sources for exact dates.

**Semana Santa** is the Brazilian Easter festival, which occurs exactly 40 days after Carnaval. In Ouro Preto, it is marked by the making of "carpets," which are artistically drawn on various streets in the city center (the streets leading up to the churches) using colored sawdust. Each family is responsible for a portion of the carpet. It's a wonderful experience to stay up all night and watch the various carpets being made. The next morning, a parade of parishioners marches up to the churches on the carpets with people hanging out their windows throwing confetti. The carpets are gone by mid-day.

**New Year's Eve,** called *reveillon,* is a single evening that is not unlike an evening of Carnaval. The events occur mostly around Praça Tiradentes, including concerts and fireworks. The *praça* gets so crowded that walking from one side to the other can be a major part of the evening. There are also some private parties that you can enter for a fee, usually R$100–500 for the night (all food and drinks covered). These usually occur in restaurants and hotels around town. Ask at local establishments a week or so ahead of time if they host one of these or know where such parties will be held.

## SHOPPING

Ouro Preto has numerous shops and art ateliers. The crafts most commonly associated with Ouro Preto include soapstone and talc sculptures, stone and clay pots and pans, furniture, tapestries made of natural fibers, and, of course, jewelry. You can find great handmade stone pieces all over town and especially in the Feira de Pedras in front of the São Francisco de Assis church. But if you want the truth, the best place to buy stone sculpture and stone or copper pots and pans is in the nearby town of Cachoeira do Campo, about 20 minutes by bus from Ouro Preto. Naturally, the trip is only worth making if you're planning to make a somewhat large purchase or if you just want to go see what they have and visit the little town. If you choose to purchase stones in Ouro Preto, be sure to purchase from a reputable source, such as one of the main stores or a reputable merchant. It helps to know a thing or two about gems. Shop the various stores in town and call João the guide as another source (tel. 31/9961-2939) for comparison. He speaks English and has contacts at the mines. Always negotiate prices.

Ouro Preto is proud of its imperial topaz, which is a tri-colored stone found only in this region. It's a semi-precious stone and difficult to find outside of Ouro Preto.

## RECREATION AND OUTDOOR ACTIVITIES
### Alternative

After walking up and down all those Ouro Preto hills, you might want to visit the **Shivam Yoga Center** (Praça Reinaldo Alves de Brito 47A, tel. 31/3551-3337) for massage, yoga sessions, tarot, Ayurvedic analysis, or acupuncture. Stop by to schedule a session. The **Zen Buddhist Monastery** (Rua Chuí 390, Morro São Sebastião, tel. 31/3551-6102, templozenpicoderaios.com.br) is a great place for meditation and contemplation. You can even stay the night. It's a bit far from the center, but that's probably a good thing for a Zen center. It has a nice view of the city. Do not attempt to go there on foot. A taxi is recommended.

### Hikes and Horseback Excursions

Some of Ouro Preto's best hikes and waterfall sights are around the town of Lavras Novas, which is normally a day-trip option for anyone staying in Ouro Preto. However, more and more, visitors are turning Lavras Novas into the principal attraction and Ouro Preto into the day trip. Check out the Lavras Novas section later in this chapter and decide for yourself.

Note that the neighborhoods around Ouro Preto, including to some degree the entire city of Mariana, are rather poor. Passing through these areas on hiking excursions—even with a guide—can lead to unpleasant criminal encounters. Reports of assaults around Ouro Preto (even inside the city limits) are on the rise. Anybody walking away from the main areas with backpacks are easily spotted and followed. The town's principal hike (to the Pico do Itacolomi) is unsafe, even with a guide. If you attempt any excursions around Ouro Preto, you should never hike to or from any of these locations. They should be accessed only by car (your guide's car). Once you arrive at a national or state park, you can usually relax and enjoy yourself, as there are guards at the entrances and exits.

The **Cachoeira das Andorinhas** is easily accessed by taxi (in case you don't have a guide) and protected by guards during normal daylight hours (6 A.M.–6 P.M.). The area along the river presents many small waterfalls and pools. As you follow the river, you'll find a medium-sized waterfall of about 10 meters and later, one that reaches 40 meters, said to be one of the tallest in the area. There are also some interesting rock formations, plants, and wildlife—including great numbers of swallow-like, black and white birds, called *andorinhas,* in the summer months. The **Parque Estadual do Itacolomi** is, unfortunately, only accessible on foot and getting there means traversing some pretty unsafe territory. Even groups with Brazilian guides are assaulted on the trails going to the peak and the state park beyond. It may be

**Central Minas**

awhile before the infrastructure is sufficient for travelers to feel safe going to and coming from this location. Save your excursion time for less risky experiences.

## ACCOMMODATIONS

Ouro Preto's many hotels and *pousadas* are clustered in and around the city center with a couple of exceptions on the far outskirts of town. All accommodations have peak-season and off-season rates and prices go up anywhere from a smidge to a lot. Peak season is any festival or holiday. A list of festivals follows, but be sure to ask when you make your reservations. Prices in this section are off-season rates.

### Under R$50

Ouro Preto has two official hostels. The **Albergue Ouro Preto Hostel** (Rua Costa Sena 30, in the Praça das Pedras, tel. 31/3551-6705, www.albergue@feop.com.br) has group rooms of 4–12 people with shared bathrooms for R$25 per person (R$20 with HI card). Its only private room goes for R$55. It includes breakfast and a beautiful view of the São Francisco de Assis church. The *pousada* **Brumas Albergue da Juventude** (Ladeira de São Francisco de Paula 68, tel. 31/3551-2944, brumasonline@hotmail.com) is centrally located just below the Igreja São Francisco (the one next to the *rodoviaria*). Just walk from the *rodoviaria* past the church to the left and downhill. The *pousada* is on the left.

One of the lowest-priced hotels in the city is the **Hotel Nossa Sra. da Aparecida** (Praça Cesário Alvim 21, tel. 31/3551-1091, R$10 pp with shared bath and R$15 with private bath). It's across from the Praça da Estação.

If you're into roughing it a little, you can pitch a tent at **Camping Clube do Brasil** (Rodovia dos Inconfidentes, Km 93, tel. 31/3551-1799, R$14 pp), on the road before you enter the city. They have a large space with plenty of room and electricity for the camping spaces. They offer a basic breakfast during peak seasons and you can use the kitchen for your other meals. There are bathrooms and showers

and a guard who will keep your valuables safe for you. Reservations are not required.

The **M Pousada Mezanino** (Rua Sen. Rocha Lagoa 131, tel. 31/3551-1289, R$40 pp s/d) is very well located on the street parallel to Rua Direita. It's a colonial-style inn with simple but cute rooms.

### R$50–100

The **Pousada SR** (Rua Xavier da Vega 506, tel. 31/3552-6512 or tel. 31/3552-6086, srpousada.com.br, R$40 s, R$60 d) has small but very cozy and well-decorated rooms. The **Pousada Ouro Preto** (Largo Musicista José dos Anjos Costa 72, tel. 31/3551-3081, pousadaouropreto@barroco.com.br, R$40 s and R$70 d) is one of the city's most advertised inns. It has a nice view if you get one of the rooms looking out over the town below and 14 other clean but not particularly impressive rooms. To get there, just follow Rua Claudio Manoel off Praça Tiradentes until it goes downhill and passes at the foot of the *pousada*. One of the quaintest *pousadas* in Ouro Preto is the **M Pousada Arcadia Mineira** (Rua Xavier da Veiga 125, tel. 31/3551-2227, R$50 s, R$80 d). They have excellent service and style. They are about a five-minute walk to Rua Direita, but there is a small stretch that has no lighting and gets kind of eerie at night.

### R$100–150

The **Boroni Palace Hotel** (Rua Padre Rolim 580, tel. 31/3551-5001, www.boroni@feop.com.br, R$95 s and R$130 d) is located next to the *rodoviaria*. It is a relatively new hotel and as such offers some fairly modern facilities, including in-room Internet connection. They also have an excellent map of Ouro Preto in their hotel brochure. Pick one up even if you're not staying there. The **Hotel Colonial** (Rua Trav. Pe. Camilo Veloso 26, tel. 31/3551-3133, www.hotelcolonial.com.br, R$70 s and R$90 d), the first right going down Rua Direita, is in the center of the action. During festivals that means it can be a bit noisy but it also means you don't have to walk far to get home after dinner and drinks. Rooms are simple and clean.

Also in the heart of the action is the **Pousada Solar da Opera** (Rua Direita 75, tel. 31/3551-6844, www.hotelsolardaopera.com.br, R$96 s, R$108 d, R$144 garden suite). On the top end of this price category is the **M** **Hotel Arcanjo** (Rua São Miguel Arcanjo 270, tel. 31/3551-4121, arcanjohotel.com, from R$145 standard and R$165 suite), just before the *rodoviaria* as you enter the town. The building and ambience are wonderfully colonial gold rush, cozy, and elegant, and they have a working fireplace in their main sitting room.

### Over R$150
Perhaps the best value in this price range is the four-star **M** **Solar Nossa Sra. do Rosário Hotel** (Rua Getúlio Vargas 270, tel. 31/3551-5200, www.hotelsolardorosario.com.br, R$150 standard, R$250 master suite). Their original *casarão* (big house) was built in the 1800s and was recently augmented to offer 46 rooms, a pool, sauna, a restaurant, and solarium (the only hotel in this price range with these amenities). The rooms vary in size and style, being more modern in the new wing. There's a 10-percent service tax (they have excellent service, including help with money exchange and guides). Weekends are about 25-percent more. The **Luxor Ouro Preto Pousada** (Rua Dr. Alfredo Baeta 16, tel. 31/3551-2244, www.luxorhoteis.com.br, R$170 standard, R$200 small suite, and R$270 master suite) is adjacent to the Antonio Dias church. Rooms are spacious and simple. The house has many rare works of art, including some painted directly on the walls in the rooms. Finally, the **Pousada Mondego** (Largo de Coimbra 38, tel. 31/3551-2040, www.mondego.com.br, R$205–275 and R$410 presidential suite) is one of the town's prettiest options and has hosted presidents, famous musicians, and other VIPs in its colonial-style rooms. They have a wonderful collection of art and a great view of the São Francisco de Assis church. Each room is different. They have a 10-percent service charge.

### Just Outside of Town
The **Hotel Fazenda Campo Grande** (Estrada Antônio Pereira, Km 4, tel. 31/3551-5828, www.fazendacampogrande.com.br) is a colonial country house about 4 kilometers from Ouro Preto that offers a bit of peace and quiet for their guests. They have no TV or mini-bars in the rooms to keep the atmosphere very rural. Nevertheless, they offer a pool, sauna, massage kiosk, and outdoor facilities along with all-cotton bedding in their rooms. They supply guides for visits to Ouro Preto and the surrounding mountains.

Finally, the *cachaça*-maker **Gota de Minas** (an excellent brand of *cachaça*, available only in the Central Minas area) offers a rural-style *pousada* at their facilities (Sítio do Sapê, tel. 31/3468-5852, www.gotademinas.com.br). Along with their active *cachaça* stills, they offer pool, sauna, small fishing ponds and a restaurant that serves great Comida Mineira. Their rates include breakfast, lunch and dinner (and probably plenty of *cachaça*) for about R$180 double occupancy. Children stay either for free or very cheap, depending on their age.

## FOOD
### Comida Mineira
One of the most Ouro Pretan lunch experiences is at the **M** **Boca da Mina** (Rua Don Silveiro 108, tel. 31/3552-2866, 8 A.M.–5 P.M. daily). It's at the mouth of the Mina do Chico Rei and offers excellent lunch plates of lamb, chicken, and sausages for around R$22 per person. You'll feel like you're eating inside the cave. If you want to experience Ouro Preto the way the old nobility did, then try **Acaso 85** (Rua Largo do Rosário 85, near the Igreja do Rosário, tel. 31/3551-2397, from 8 P.M. to the last client) for an elegant dinner that will take you back in time. The space is so compelling that you will find yourself more interested in the surroundings than in the food, which, while not Ouro Preto's finest, is quite adequate for the occasion. Reservations are not required except during festivals. In a more modern atmosphere, the restaurant at the **Grand Hotel Ouro Preto** (Rua Sen. Rocha Lagoa 164, tel. 31/3551-1488, noon–11 P.M. daily) offers an elegant lunch or

dinner experience with a view of the town for around R$13 per person. Boasting its very Mineiro specialty dishes, such as *frango a molho pardo* (chicken in brown sauce) and *feijoada* (pork stew). The **Casa do Ouvidor** (Rua Direita 42, tel. 31/3551-2141, 11 A.M.–3 P.M. and 7 P.M.–10 P.M.) is a large space with lots of tables, specializing in Comida Mineira, including grilled meats and chicken, for an average price of R$25 per plate.

## International

A few mid-range restaurants for dinner include **Spaghetti** (Rua Direita 138, tel. 31/3552-2373, from 6 P.M.), with Italian dishes in large portions (many are made for two), good service by Paulinho, and, in the evenings, live guitar music. The owner, Peter, is an Italian immigrant. He offers a full bar and a selection of pizzas. It can get crowded on weekends. One of the most interesting dinner experiences can be had at **Consolas Bar** (Rua da Conceição 18, tel. 31/3551-4175, from 6 P.M.), alongside the Antonio Dias church. They specialize in brick-oven baked pizza, but have a variety of *porções* (appetizers), too. It's small and cozy with a friendly local crowd. Another Italian offering (mostly pizza) is the new **O Passo** (Rua São José 58, no phone, 6 P.M. until the last client daily). They have an authentically antique atmosphere and offer dinner for R$12–15. On a warm night, you can sit on their veranda and watch the movement below. The **M Chalet dos Caldos** (Rua Carlos Tomaz 33, tel. 31/3551-1614, dinner only, Tue.–Sun., approximately R$20 per person) offers mostly soup dishes, from *canja de galinha* (chicken soup) to *caldo de feijão* (bean soup with bacon). It's in a wonderful stone building just below the Feira das Pedras.

In the Rosário neighborhood near the Igreja do Rosário is **M Piacere** (Rua Getúlio Vargas 241, tel. 31/3551-4297, 7 P.M.–midnight Tues.–Sat. and noon–3:30 P.M. Sun., R$35 per person), with an excellent selection of Italian dishes and wines. Run by a German immigrant and her Italian husband, Piacere offers the best Italian food in town. In the same neighbor-

hood is the new **Triumpho** restaurant (Largo do Rosário 02, tel. 31/3552-6774, from 7 P.M. daily), featuring a variety of international cuisine for around R$18 per person. This is another wonderfully Ouro Pretan atmosphere with its stone columns and dungeon-like interior. It has live music most nights.

Ouro Preto's best wine list can be found at **Deguste** (Rua Cel. Alves 15, tel. 31/3551-6363, 11:30 A.M.–midnight daily) in front of the Igreja Nossa Sra. do Carmo. The building is a classic; they have a lunch buffet for R$20 per kilo; and there's live music in the evenings with plates averaging R$30. **O Profeta** (Rua Direita 65, tel. 31/3551-4556, 11 A.M.–10 P.M. Mon.–Thu., 11 A.M.–midnight Fri.–Sun.) has a slightly more upscale menu at around R$20–55 per person. Reservations are recommended during festivals.

## Lanchonetes and Casual

There are *lanchonetes* all over town, serving up the usual assortment of *salgados* (savory finger foods), tasty juices, and sweets. Worthy of special note include the **Barroco** bar (Rua Direita 106, no phone, 11 A.M. Mon.–Sat., 8 P.M. on Sun., about R$10 for snacks) for the best *coxinha* in the entire region (a secret family recipe) and the **Satelite** (Rua Direita 95, tel. 31/3551-4625, 11–2 A.M. or until the last one leaves) across the street for custom sandwiches and pizza at all hours of the day and night. Also, **Pão de Queijo** (just off Praça, 8 A.M.–8 P.M. daily) has fresh juices and various mixtures for different effects (relaxing, energetic, etc.). The **Lanchonete e Padaria Ouvidor** (corner of Praça Tiradentes and Rua Claudio Manoel, 24 hours) is open until the wee hours with finger foods and an excellent *torta de frango* (chicken pie) when it's fresh out of the oven. The best breakfast counter is at the **Padaria Centeio** (Praça da Prefeitura behind the Igreja do Pilar, Rua do Pilar 138, tel. 31/3552-2908, 6 A.M.–10 P.M. daily). Try their *Cigarrete* (pronounced see-gah-HECH) with a cup of coffee.

You can get a cheap-and-delicious *prato feito* at the **Manjuba Bar** (Praça Cesário Alvim 43, no phone, 8 A.M.–midnight daily, and lunch is served around 11 A.M. for about R$6), across from the Praça da Estação. Be sure to get there early for a seat, as it's popular with the locals.

## Self-Service

There are many mid-range options in town. Starting more or less in the center of town, a few of the most popular that are open for lunch and dinner include **Quinto de Ouro** (Rua Direita 76, tel. 31/3552-2633, 11 A.M.–3 P.M. weekdays and 11 A.M.–4 P.M. weekends), with a full self-service buffet of Comida Mineira for around R$18 per kilo or all you can eat for R$15 per person. **Adega Ouro Preto** (Rua Teixeira Amaral 24, tel. 31/3551-4171, noon–4 P.M. daily and 6 P.M.–11 P.M. Wed.–Sat.) has a great lunch spread for R$12 all you can eat, and the place itself is an interesting stone and wood building—very Ouro Preto. Dinner is off the menu and goes for around R$24 for two people. Another entry is **Maximus Colonial** (Rua Direita 151, tel. 31/3551-3143, lunch daily starting at 11 A.M.), offering about the same types of dishes as the others (Comida Mineira, mostly) at about the same price. There is also **Café e Cia** (Rua São José 187, tel. 31/3551-0711), which offers a great spread of cheeses, olives, and cold cuts along with their hot dishes. They open at 11:30 A.M. for lunch and keep the dishes fresh all day long. Dinner starts around 6 P.M. and is served until midnight. They even have a computer for Internet connections in the front.

For a lunch or dinner self-service buffet, check out **Casa dos Contos** (Rua Camilo de Brito 21, tel. 31/3551-5359, 11:30 A.M.–5 P.M. Mon.–Wed. and 11:30 A.M.–10 P.M. Thur.–Sun.), off the *praça* toward Mariana. Rebuilt from old slave quarters, the building itself is practically a tourist attraction. They offer an all-you-can-eat Comida Mineira lunch for R$20 per person. Dinners are R$15–20 per person.

## INFORMATION

Tourist information, including brochures, maps, and festival agendas, is available at the information office at the entrance of the city (Rua Padre Rolim, tel. 31/3551-2655, 8 A.M.–8 P.M.). There is another office in Praça Tiradentes 41 (tel. 31/3559-3269, 8 A.M.–8 P.M.), which is easier to access on foot. Finally, there's the main office of tourism (Rua Claudio Manuel 61, tel. 31/3559-3213, 9 A.M.–6 P.M. Mon.–Fri.).

You can ask about guides at the information office, at any hotel, or at the *rodoviaria*. For a well-rounded view of the city and entry into some working mines, get in touch with João Pereira (tel. 31/9961-2939 or tel. 31/3552-2877, ctopjb@feop.com.br). He's fun-loving and knows all about the city. He'll take you around in his Rural (Brazilian off-road vehicle), show you the best deals on precious stones, and share a *cachaça* with you. The guide Fernando can fix you up with the best eco-tours on foot. He works with the Ouro Preto Hostel but works independently, too.

The Federal University in Ouro Preto hosts a website, listing just about every hotel, *pousada,* and restaurant in the city. It will also give you current information about festivals and shows in town: www.ouropreto.com.br. Other sites that have information on Ouro Preto include the www.terra.com.br city guide, www.estrada-real.org.br, and the www.cyberhouse.com.br site, which is hosted by the Cyberhouse LAN house in town.

## SERVICES

**Banco do Brasil** has ATMs with Cirrus and Plus systems, but remember to get money out before the tellers close at 10 P.M. During business hours (10 A.M.–4 P.M. Mon.–Fri.) they will also exchange dollars. For small exchanges, you're better off trying the man called Bigode (bee-GODJEE, meaning mustache) at Minas Gemas in Praça Tiradentes 62, or your hotel (if you're staying at a good one). Cash traveler's checks in Belo Horizonte before leaving for Ouro Preto.

There are Internet cafés scattered around town. The prices in Ouro Preto are much higher than in Belo Horizonte, up to R$10 per hour. The most ample connection is at **Cyberhouse** (Rua Direita 109, tel. 31/3552-2404, www.cyberhousebr.com, 10 A.M.–8 P.M. daily), across from the Barroco bar. Down the street is **Raitai Lan House** (Rua Paraná 100, tel. 31/3551-5151, raitai.com, 9 A.M.–10:30 P.M.) for R$6 per hour.

You can get your laundry done at the *lavanderia* in the Praça da Estação. They charge by the kilo. The only quiet public phone in the city is in the mini-mall on Rua São José just past Banco do Brasil.

## GETTING THERE

Passaro Verde has buses running between Ouro Preto and Belo Horizonte throughout the day. Most go directly to Ouro Preto, but a few are destined for Mariana and stop in Ouro Preto. The trip takes one hour and 45 minutes. Conventional buses run about R$12 one way and an executive bus will cost around R$15. Remember to ask if you want or don't want an executive bus. During festivals and holidays, the buses can get very crowded and only have space *de pé* (on foot), which you probably don't want, unless you're in a hurry to leave town. You can probably negotiate a taxi to Belo Horizonte for around R$80.

From Belo Horizonte to Ouro Preto, buses run about every hour from 6 A.M.–11 P.M. Leaving Ouro Preto for Belo Horizonte, buses run from 6:30 A.M.–10:30 P.M. Going south, you can catch the Vale do Ouro bus from Mariana (via Ouro Preto) to São Paulo and get off in Congonhas, Lafayete, or São João del Rei. It leaves Mariana 7 A.M., 5:30 P.M., 6:25 P.M., and 8 P.M. These buses pass through Ouro Preto about 20 minutes later. There are bus lines running from Ouro Preto to other cities, including Rio de Janeiro. Check times at the *rodoviaria* (tel. 31/3559-3252).

If you're coming from São João del Rei, catch the Viação Vale do Ouro coming from São Paulo and going to Mariana, stopping in Ouro Preto. It passes through São João del Rei several times during the day. Check at the *rodoviaria* for details (tel. 32/3371-5119).

## GETTING AROUND

Except for its steep inclines, Ouro Preto is a town that's easy to access on foot. Everything is nearby, if at a different altitude. That being said, there are many occasions when you will want to take a taxi, such as when you're carrying luggage or late at night. Taxis are easy to find in the Praça Tiradentes and any hotel or restaurant will be happy to call one to pick you up. The taxi station in Praça Tiradentes is tel. 31/3551-1977 and at the *rodoviaria*, tel. 31/3551-2675. Taxis in Ouro Preto do not use meters. They charge about R$8 to take you short distances and R$12 for long distances. Ask the driver for a price before you get in and don't hesitate to check with a different taxi driver for a competitive rate. Always negotiate prices for special trips. Ouro Preto is rife with little *mafias*, a word commonly used in Brazil for cartels and closed, private interest groups (especially in the area of tourism), so it's best not to ask taxi drivers for suggestions on anything because you'll just get the suggestion that pays the best kickback. Besides taxis, Ouro Preto offers micro-buses, called *turins*, for the locals. At only R$.60, they are an excellent way to get around. Although Ouro Preto is a quaint little mountain town, it can be dangerous at night or in remote areas. Don't walk around with valuables showing, unless you stick to the main traffic areas and don't bring a lot of money or valuables with you at night.

Mariana and Lavras Novas are day trips from Ouro Preto. Municipal buses leave for Mariana every 20 minutes from the *rodoviaria* or at the bus stop on Rua Cons. Quintiliano (the street on the right side of the old governor's palace, just off the *praça*). The trip takes about 30 minutes and costs about R$2.50. The first bus leaves Ouro Preto at 6 A.M. and the last bus from Mariana to Ouro Preto leaves at midnight. A taxi to or from Mariana will cost around R$20. The two cities are in the process of building a train line between them called Linha Azul da Vale. It will leave for Mariana from the Ouro Preto Praça do Estação.

Lavras Novas is more difficult as the schedule is more limited. Mondays, the bus leaves at 6 A.M., 8 A.M., 2 P.M., and 5 P.M. Tuesday–Friday, buses leave at 6:50 A.M., 2 P.M., and 5 P.M. Saturdays, buses leave only from the train station at 4 P.M., and Sundays at 9 A.M. from the station.

Coming back to Ouro Preto, buses leave Mondays at 5 A.M., 7 A.M., 10 A.M., and 3 P.M. Tuesday–Friday, buses leave at 5:45 A.M., 10 A.M., and 4 P.M. Saturdays, they leave at 5:45 P.M. and Sundays at 5:30 P.M.

# Mariana

Mariana is officially among the oldest historical towns in the central region of Minas Gerais. Gold was first discovered here at the Pico do Itocolomi, which is part of the Mariana municipality. It wasn't long, however, until Ouro Preto superceded Mariana in mining activities. Mariana became something of a satellite to Ouro Preto, as it is to this day. The birthplace of baroque artist Manoel da Costa Athayde—the most celebrated baroque painter of the gold era and whose works appear on canvases and sculptures throughout the state—Mariana offers many works of art and is known for its artists and wood sculptors to this day. It makes a terrific half-day trip when you're staying in Ouro Preto. That's about all the time you need to see the local culture, the few attractions, and perhaps partake of a meal at one of the restaurants (there are several good ones). For young, singles action, Mariana is the place to go on Sunday afternoons, as the Praça Gomes Freire (also known as the Praça do Jardim, or Garden Square) fills up with young beauties (male and female) from the region.

## SIGHTS

In the main *praça*, called the Praça Claudio Manoel, is the **Catedral Basílica da Sé** (7 A.M.– 6 P.M. Tues.–Sun., R$1). The church's 12 altars are covered in gold leafing, and crystal chandeliers hang from the ceiling. It's a great example of gold rush wealth and, having been reconstructed many times, shows the evolution of baroque art in Minas. On the first Saturday of each month, this church hosts organ concerts by keyboardists Elisa Freixo and Josinéia Godinho, two of the country's most recognized organists. The organ itself, with more than 1,000 pipes, was made in Germany in 1701 and brought to Bra-

zil as a present from the king of Portugal to the bishop in Mariana at the time. Concerts begin at 11 A.M. on Fridays and noon on Sundays and last about one hour, R$8 entry; call tel. 31/3558-2785 or check orgaodase.com.br for more information. The **Museu Arquidiocesano de Arte Sacra** (Rua Frei Durão 49, tel. 31/3557-2516, 8:30 A.M.–5 P.M. Tues.–Sun., closed for lunch, R$3) is perhaps the second most interesting attraction in the city. It contains sacred objects, antique clothing, and sculptures of the gold era. Also on display are paintings of master Athayde. At the entrance is a sculpted fountain, attributed to Aleijadinho.

Other churches in Mariana include the **Igreja São Francisco de Assis** (Praça Minas Gerais, 9 A.M.–5 P.M. Tues.–Sun., R$2), the final resting place of Athayde (in the floorboards of the church). The **Igreja Nossa Sra. do Rosário** (Praça do Rosário, no phone, 10 A.M.–4 P.M. Mon.–Fri., free) was built by the Rosário brotherhood of black slaves in Mariana. It's not as architecturally gratifying as the Rosário church in Ouro Preto, but is interesting due to its exclusive use of statuary showing Afro-Brazilian imagery.

## OUTDOOR ACTIVITIES

As with most outdoor activities around Ouro Preto, hiking around Mariana is best done with a guide and, even then, only in the most secure locations. (See the *Ouro Preto* section for a list of these locations.)

## ACCOMMODATIONS

One of the cheapest hotels in Mariana is the **Hotel Muller** (Av. Getúlio Vargas 34, tel.

31/3557-1188, R$20 pp with shared bath and R$25 with private bath). It's on the other side of the stream, not far from the center. The **Hotel Central** (Rua Frei Durão 8, tel. 31/3557-1630, R$30 pp) is also on the far side of the stream close to the center. It's a funky but interesting place and easy to access.

One of the more interesting colonial-style offerings is the **Hotel Providência** (Rua Dom Silvéro 233, tel. 31/3557-1444, R$25 s and R$45 d), which used to be a Catholic boarding house for women. It has 22 rooms, a pool, and a volleyball court. The **Pouso da Typographia** (Praça Dr. Gomes Freire 220, tel. 31/3557-1311, R$60 s and R$80 d) is one of the nicer places in town in a restored colonial house in the center.

## FOOD

Mariana has a surprisingly ample selection of restaurants and *lanchonetes,* some rivaling the offerings in Ouro Preto. If you spend a half-day in Mariana, you might consider staying for dinner to enjoy one of these eateries.

There is a simple, diner-style restaurant near the main bus stop coming from Ouro Preto (not the *rodoviaria*), called **Dois Irmaos** (9 A.M.–1 A.M. daily). They serve great appetizers, including a wonderful *porção de frango,* a roasted half-chicken with onions and spices, for about R$6. There are several *padarias* (bakeries) near that same bus stop, in front of the tourist information center, where you can compare *salgados* and sweets for a quick snack.

Arriving in the Praça Gomes Freire, you can taste great Comida Mineira at the lunch buffet **M Rancho da Praça** (Praça Gomes Freire 108, tel. 31/3558-1060, 11:30 A.M.–3:30 P.M. and 5:30 A.M.–1 A.M.) for around R$7 per person. At night, they serve a selection of soups for R$2 and selected regional dishes off the menu for around R$18 for two people. Another self-service buffet is **Lua Cheia** (Rua Dom Viçoso 23, tel. 31/3557-3232, lunch from Sun.–Thu., dinner on Fri. and Sat.), which offers many regional favorites for around R$9 per kilo. One of the best deals in town.

The restaurant **M Uai Zé** (Av. Getúlio Vargas 32, tel. 31/3557-2899, 11 A.M.–3 P.M. and 6–10 P.M.) near the Hotel Muller offers self-service lunch and dinner for R$13 per kilo. They also have pizzas. **Tambaú** (Travessa São Francisco 26, tel. 31/3558-2370, 6 P.M.–2 A.M. Mon.–Sat.) is a dinner spot just off the Praça Gomes Freire going uphill toward the São Francisco church. They have some Cuban dishes and a self-service buffet for R$8 per person. There's some outdoor seating.

The only semi-international offering in town is **O Bistrô** (Rua Salomão 61-A, tel. 31/3557-4138, 6 P.M.–midnight Tue.–Fri, noon–midnight on weekends), at the end of the street, just off the Praça Gomes Freire on the left side (downhill). They have sushi and various pasta dishes along with Comida Mineira. The atmosphere is comfortable and cozy. The average price per person is around R$15.

## INFORMATION

The tourist information office (Praça Tancredo Neves, tel. 31/3557-1158, 8 A.M.–5 P.M. Mon.–Fri.) is across the street from the main bus stop coming from Ouro Preto. They have maps and information on hotels and guides. You can check the city's website for information at www.mariana.mg.gov.br. Most of the guides in Ouro Preto can cover Mariana with no problem.

## GETTING THERE

Buses leave Ouro Preto for Mariana every 20 minutes from the *rodoviaria* or the bus stop next to the Federal University. The price is about R$2.50 and it takes about 30 minutes. The bus stops at the Mariana *rodoviaria,* which is actually quite far from the center of town. Don't get off there. Keep going until the bus enters the town, crosses the overpass, turns right, and stops. This is where most people will exit the bus. To your left is the tourist information office. The center of town is straight ahead and to the right.

Coming from Belo Horizonte, you can get a direct Passaro Verde bus a few times during the day, or just go to Ouro Preto and take a local bus between the two towns. From São João del Rei, catch the Viação Vale do Ouro coming from São Paulo to Mariana. It passes in São João del Rei a few times per day. Check the *rodoviaria* for details (tel. 32/3371-5119).

## GETTING AROUND

Everything in Mariana is within walking distance. If it's not, then you don't want to go there unless you are with a guide.

# Lavras Novas

The simple mountain town of Lavras Novas offers a most beautiful landscape both in and around the town. On a foggy day (of which there are many, especially from January–April), you can warm up with savory soup in one of the country-style restaurants. When the sun is shining and the clear blue sky is above, you can take a mountain hike to one of the waterfalls or go on an excursion by horseback. The town has only one main street and one small, historical church. You can walk from one side of the town to the other in about 15 minutes. In spite of its size, Lavras Novas has some surprisingly good restaurant options and stores selling locally made arts and crafts.

As noted in the Ouro Preto section, Lavras Novas has recently become the preferred location for folks coming from Belo Horizonte and wanting a quiet getaway or an exhilarating hike to one of the nearby waterfalls. Being such a popular little town, it can get rather crowded on weekends, and you might want to make reservations ahead of time at the *pousada* of your choice (if your stay includes a weekend, which it probably should since the town can be pretty dead during the week and some establishments don't even open their doors). Some of Brazil's rich and famous have purchased property in the town, making it something of a bedroom community mixed with the original country folks who have lived there for generations, many being descendents of the original slaves who made their way there in the early 1700s to create the village (such villages are known as *quilombos*).

## SIGHTS

Lavras Novas, while offering only one small chapel (the **Igreja do Cristo Redentor** in the middle of town) and no official museums or historical sights, is itself a wonderful historical artifact. As you walk around town, remember that this was once a village of runaway slaves with little or no access to Ouro Preto. It wasn't long ago that phone lines were brought into the town and there is only one public telephone to this day.

## ENTERTAINMENT AND NIGHTLIFE

There's not much to do nights in Lavras Novas during the week, but on weekends it's another story. Saturday night, for example, the **Peixaria's Bar** (Rua Nossa Sra. dos Prazeres 701, stop by for information about current shows) offers all-night *forró* dancing with live country music. The music starts at 10 P.M. and goes until sun up. The **Bar Ieieca** (Rua Nossa Senhora dos Prazeres 497, 11 A.M.–midnight on weekends. Weekday hours vary), pronounced yeh-YEH-kah, near the entrance of town (before the church) is a great night spot for drinks and appetizers with a great rustic interior. You can also have dinner and drinks (or just drinks) at one of the many restaurant-bars in town.

## RECREATION AND OUTDOOR ACTIVITIES
### Horseback Rides

Excursions by horse are a common way to see the countryside around Lavras Novas. The main rides take you out along the Serra do Trovão mountains, where you can see the hillsides and waterfalls. The trip takes about 1.5 hours and at the end, you reach the peak with a 360-degree view. For details, check with your hotel or call tel. 31/3554-2114 or tel. 31/3295-2344, or check www.lavrasnovas.com.br/cavalgadas.htm.

## Trails and Waterfalls

The **Cachoeira do Falcão** is a principal watering hole for swimming and lounging around in a bathing suit. It's in a nearby town called Chapada, which is between Ouro Preto and Lavras Novas. On foot, you follow the road back to Ouro Preto until the Chapada turnoff to the left. When you arrive in the small town of Chapada, you'll need to follow a trail off to the right (beside the town's principal bar) for about five minutes until you hit the waterfall.

The **Cachoeira do Pocinho** is a beautiful walk to a small waterfall, not far from town. Begin at the Pousada Palavras Novas, following the trail that begins beside the *pousada*. Turn left at the third wooden post and continue for about 15 minutes. Finally, the **Cachoeira dos Três Pingos** is easily accessed. Just continue past the end of town (past the bar Kokopelli). At the first crossroads, turn left and continue for about 100 meters. The entire walk takes about one hour.

You can get information on guides at any of the major *pousadas* in town or by calling tel. 31/9105-9140. Any guide from Ouro Preto will also be able to show you the waterfalls and attractions of Lavras Novas.

## FESTIVALS AND EVENTS

The biggest festival in Lavras Novas is the **Festival da Nossa Sra. dos Prazeres,** which takes place on the second weekend of August and turns this sleepy town into a major party zone. Other festivals include New Year's Eve, Carnaval, and Easter festival in April, 40 days after Carnaval. The town also participates (in its own way) in the Festival de Inverno and the Festival de 12 de Outubro along with Ouro Preto. See www.lavrasnovas.com.br for details on these and other events. Remember that all hotels will cost more during festivals and require advanced reservations.

## ACCOMMODATIONS

With the boom of tourism in Lavras Novas, many of the locals have converted their homes into *pousadas,* or else erected small chalets on their land to offer the upscale visitors. Many brand-new *pousadas* have popped up in and around town as well. There are so many, it's difficult to make a choice. The following descriptions should give you a good head start.

The **Pousada Carumbé** (Rua Projetada 220, tel. 31/3554-2105, www.carumbe.com.br, R$95–110 d weekdays and R$135–155 weekends) is a reasonably priced place with 20 suites overlooking the mountains. They have a pool and sauna and their restaurant serves breakfast until noon (included). The rooms are simple, but clean and comfortable. On weekends, the restaurant turns into a popular tavern with live music. They usually require weekend packages with reservations and partial payment up front. **Pousada Palavras Novas** (Rua Nossa Senhora dos Prazeres 1110, tel. 31/3554-2025, tel. 31/9987-0033, www.ouropreto.com.br/palavrasnovas, R$90–120 double) is a well-known reference point in town. It has a panoramic view of the surrounding hills and a cozy, country-style environment. They offer a heated pool, sauna, and sitting room with fireplace. The **Villa Kokopelli Pousada e Restaurante** (Rua Nossa Senhora dos Prazeres 114, tel. 31/9961-1331, tel. 31/3554-2165, R$100 standard double, R$150 for a chalet) is another key location—at the end of town where the street ends. They have a wonderful view of the surrounding mountains and various types of rooms, including private suites, a deluxe chalet, and their more economical *casa* with shared facilities and optional breakfast.

The **Pousada Serra do Luar** (Rua Nossa Sra. dos Prazeres 119, tel. 31/3554-2021, tel. 31/9961-2474) is an economical option with seven suites for around R$60 with TV and mini-bar and R$40 without. They also have cabanas for R$70–90 for up to six people. They provide excellent hospitality in a simple country setting. The **Pousada Menestrel** (Rua Alto do Campo 287, tel. 31/9667-2075, tel. 31/9621-2150, R$100 weekdays or R$120 weekends) has several chalets with TV, mini-bar, and kitchen facilities. Many have a great view of the mountains. Weekend packages run about R$220.

## FOOD

The **Restaurante Serra do Luar** (Rua Nossa Senhora dos Prazeres 488, tel. 31/3554-2021, call for hours) offers lunch at an incredible price. You get a typical country-style self-service lunch for R$5 per person. Even if you're not staying at their *pousada,* you might enjoy lunch or dinner at the **Carumbé** (Rua Projetada 220, tel. 31/3554-2105, www.carumbe.com.br, call for hours), which offers great Comida Mineira for around R$12 per plate. Likewise, the **Villa Kokopelli Pousada e Restaurante** (Rua Nossa Senhora dos Prazeres 114, tel. 31/9944-5278, call for hours) is a great food and entertainment option at night, even if you're staying at a different *pousada.* They have a great rustic atmosphere and authentic Comida Mineira. They're also open for self-service lunch. The **Taberna Casa Antiga** (Rua Alto do Campo 215, tel. 31/3554-2040, lunch only on Fri.–Sun.) has an elegant dinner with a cozy, candlelit atmosphere. They

offer music and theater shows on weekends and holidays.

## INFORMATION

Lavras Novas does not have a tourist information center, being so small with everything so easy to find. Just ask around and you'll get information on just about anything. Don't be afraid to ask at a hotel where you are not staying; everyone is happy to help and show off their lovely town, and you're more likely to find English speakers at the hotels. You can also check at the city's website: www.lavrasnovas.com.br.

## GETTING THERE

You can get to Lavras Novas from Ouro Preto several times each day, with additional options on Mondays. (See the *Ouro Preto* section under *Getting Around* for full details.)

## GETTING AROUND

There are no taxis in Lavras Novas because there is nowhere to drive, except back to Ouro Preto. Everything is accessible on foot or on horseback. Be sure to take a guide with you.

# Congonhas

In the early 1700s, Portuguese settlers lined the banks of the Maranhão River searching for gold, like they lined hundreds of rivers throughout Minas Gerais in those early gold-rush days. Congonhas soon became one of the region's most opulent cities. Local legends recount how, after strong rains, gold could be seen blanketing the city streets. Today, the settlement around the Maranhão River is one of the oldest and most treasured historical towns in Brazil. About 1.5 hours by bus from Belo Horizonte and only about 45 minutes from Ouro Preto, Congonhas offers just one primary historical-architectural complex atop its highest peak. But the treasures inside this complex

include some of the most important sculpture works in the Americas.

Most travelers don't spend more than a single day in Congonhas and leave before nightfall—off to one of the other, perhaps more robust, historical towns in Minas. Nevertheless, there are a couple of good hotels and a couple of good restaurants in town in case the 12 Prophets talk you into staying the night.

## SIGHTS
### Igreja Nossa Sra. da Conceição
A typical baroque church built on the top of a hill, the Igreja da Conceição (Praça Sete de

Central Minas

# THE ESTRADA REAL

Once gold was discovered in the hills of Minas Gerais, masses of miners, architects, artists, governors, and, of course, slaves, flowed into principal towns by the tens of thousands. Ouro Preto was the central and most productive of the gold towns, with Sabará and Diamantina to the north and Congonhas, Tiradentes, and São João del Rei to the south. The main ports for export of all this gold were in the cities of Rio de Janeiro and Paraty, both in Rio de Janeiro state directly south of Ouro Preto.

With so much commerce between Minas Gerais and Rio, two new roads opened up to aid exchange and, more importantly, collect taxes and tolls on that exchange. The roads led from Ouro Preto to Paraty and the city of Rio de Janeiro. The Estrada Real (Royal Road), made Rio the most important port in Brazil, taking the title away from Salvador. In 1763, Rio de Janeiro officially became the capital of Brazil although Ouro Preto had a larger population (about 130,000 to Rio's 50,000). To get around the road taxes, bands of *tropeiros* (literally, troupers), moving supplies and animals between the two regions, would forge new pathways to circumvent the toll stations. The region was soon rife with small towns dotted along the Estrada Real, which are recognized to this day as part of the *tropeiro* culture. Also part of the culture is a tradition of country cooking that arose from the necessities of eating on the trail.

Most of the gold rush was concentrated on the sandy banks of the region's many rivers. A few random gold veins were discovered in the hills and many large and deep mines were carved out of the rock. Gold was found in the form of nuggets, flakes, or dust and brought to one of the gold exchange offices where one-fifth would be taken for the king. Although gold bars were commonly forged, there was, up until the early 19th century, a liberal use of sheets of solid gold.

The massive extraction of gold from Minas Gerais occurred in the span of a single generation and is said to have indirectly financed the British industrial revolution. King João V was fortunate enough to have been the ruler of Portugal during most of this 70-year period and he used his riches to buy his great fidelity to France and the Catholic Church. But it was the king's imprudent commercial treaties with England that ended with most of Brazil's gold making its way to Great Britain.

---

Setembro, no phone, 8 A.M.–6 P.M. Mon.–Fri., 8 A.M.–9 P.M. on Sat. and Sun., closed for lunch) was built in 1734 and shows heavy signs of age and deterioration. From the inside, it's not one of the most impressive churches in the area, but the view from the grounds is wonderful and you can see all the way across to the Basílica and *Capelas* on the opposite hillside. From the main bus stop, dropping you off in the center of town, you turn right up the cobblestone street (left takes you to the Basílica) and walk up, up, up to the church.

## Romaria

Romaria was built in 1932 to provide lodging for the pilgrims who made their way to Congonhas for the Jubileu festival that occurred there (and still does to this day). The entire structure was demolished and later rebuilt as a cultural space and governmental offices. Here you can find the Museu Sacro and Museu da Mineralogia (no phone, 9 A.M.–6 P.M. Mon.–Fri.), two small collections from the mining era. Romaria is easily spotted on the right side of the Basílica as you walk up to the *praça*.

## Santuário do Senhor Bom Jesus de Matosinhos

The principal attraction of Congonhas and the primary reason for visiting the town is the Santuário (Praça da Basílica, tel. 31/3731-1591, no hours available), situated at the top of the city's highest peak. Begun in the mid 1700s and completed with its final artistic touches at the end of that century, it consists of three primary elements: the Basílica, the

## MYSTERY AND SYMBOLISM OF THE 12 PROPHETS

The last and most astonishing works of Aleijadinho are undoubtedly the 12 Prophets and the 66 wooden figures in the chapels at the Sanctuary of Congonhas. Although there are few documents that prove Aleijadinho's participation in artistic works around Minas Gerais, experts have identified the artist's signature elements, which are embedded in the works at Congonhas. Also embedded in these works is a political and social commentary by the artist through his use of artistic symbolism. For example, since the church forbade artists to sign their works, it is said that Aleijadinho chose the 12 Prophets (from 16 biblical possibilities) to spell out his name with their initials. Furthermore, the face of Amos is said to be a self-portrait of Aleijadinho and is the only prophet made from a single stone. Aleijadinho shows this figure wearing pants and dressed differently (more humbly) than the others, perhaps alluding to the artist's humble status. Most of the figures have physical deformities in their hands or feet, which are visible only at close inspection.

The statue of Daniel is considered by some to be the greatest of the 12. He has a mysterious portal in his back, said to be the hiding place for treasure (a technique commonly used in the contraband of gold) or perhaps merely the artist's tools. The prophet Jonus offers a secret homage to the Minas Confederacy, which attempted Brazilian independence under the leadership of Tiradentes. His face is said to be a portrait of Tiradentes, and his head is turned upward almost as though he were being hanged (which was, indeed, the fate of the famous confederate).

Finally, the four prophets standing farthest away (closest to the church doors) are larger than those in front, giving the impression when approaching the church that all the prophets are the same size. In fact, the four rear prophets are larger than the others and considered the major prophets in biblical terms. The prophets on the left side offer optimistic messages and those on the right are the bad-news prophets.

The Prophets look mysteriously over the *praça*.

© CHRISTOPHER VAN BUREN

*12 Profetas*, and the *Capelas dos Passos*. The Basílica is the unifying structure of the *santuário* and the principal church of Congonhas. It rests at the far end of a *praça*. Its architectural design was inspired by two churches in Portugal. Inside, the church is a perfect example of baroque-turned-rococo style of design but it's not the interior that will call your attention.

What makes the Basílica church (and the town itself, for that matter) special are the sculptures of Antônio Francisco Lisboa, better known as Aleijadinho, including his grandest of works, the 12 Prophets. Well worth the hike up to the *praça*, the prophets find themselves arranged at the entrance of the church,

casting their ominous glances in all directions. Aleijadinho carved the four major prophets and eight of the 12 minor prophets in soapstone toward the end of his life in the years 1800–1805. Already crippled and unable to walk or hold his sculpting tools, he created the prophets while suffering from a sickness that would take his life only nine years later. Naturally, many of his designs were at this point carried out by his disciples, but experts believe that the four major prophets were rendered by Aleijadinho himself. The 12 Prophets confirm Aleijadinho's status as a sculptor of international, historical stature.

Slowly, the statues are being restored and debate continues about whether or not to replace the originals with replicas. The deterioration you see in the images is said to be weathering of weak elements in the stone, which will not continue to deteriorate. The largest threat to these works is, unfortunately, vandalism.

The third key element of the Santuário consists of the *Capelas dos Passos* and accompanying sculptures. In 1796, Aleijadinho and his crew began these 66 separate life-sized works in wood for the six individual chapels positioned in the sanctuary grounds. The six chapels follow the Catholic tradition of the stations of the cross, from the passion of Christ. Together with the 12 Prophets, these works represent the largest collection of baroque statuary in the Americas.

## FESTIVALS AND EVENTS

Perhaps it goes without saying that the principal event in Congonhas is **Semana Santa** (Holy Week), which occurs 40 days after Carnaval, around March or April, when a reenactment of the passion of Christ is played in the *praça* at the *Capelas dos Passos*. September 7–14, the town celebrates the festival of **Jubileu**, which brings thousands of religious pilgrims to the Basílica to pray and atone. It's one of the largest pilgrimages in Minas Gerais.

## ACCOMMODATIONS

A decent mid-range hotel is the **Hotel dos Profetas** (Avenida Júlia Kubtischeck 54, less than R$40 s and R$60–90 d), or **Hotel dos Profetas** (Av. Júlia Kubitschek 54, Centro, tel. 31/3731-1352, www.hoteldosprofetas.com.br, R$60–120 d). At the top of the hill looking over the Basílica square is the historical **Hotel Colonial** (Praça da Basílica 76, tel. 31/3731-1834, www.hotelcolonialcongonhas.com.br, R$50 s with shared bath and R$85–105 d with private bath), freshly restored and managed by the friendly Senhor Eduardo.

## FOOD

There are a couple of restaurants at the Basílica square, including one inside the Hotel Colonial, which is quite well appointed. A more casual, self-service offering is across the street at **Restaurante Cova do Daniel** (Praça da Basílica 76, tel. 31/3731-1834, 11 A.M.–8 P.M. daily) and *lanchonetes* are sprinkled throughout the town.

## INFORMATION AND SERVICES

The Secretaria Municipal de Turismo is located in the Romaria buildings near the Basílica square and can be reached at tel. 31/3731-3100. An Internet service is located on Rua Dr. Vitor de Freitas. A good site for information is www .congonhas.mg.gov.br.

## GETTING THERE

From Belo Horizonte, you can catch one of the Sandra buses directly into Congonhas. They cost around R$12 and leave at 6:15 A.M., 10:15 A.M., and 2:15 P.M. At the *rodoviaria* in Congonhas, catch the yellow "Congonhas" bus to the center. If you miss one of the Sandra buses, you can catch any bus going to Juiz de Fora, Barbacena, or São João del Rei and ask to get off at the Congonhas roadside stop (*trevo de Congonhas*). Buses going south to these cities include Atual, Sandra, and Util. From the roadside stop, walk down toward the town and keep an eye out for the yellow "Congonhas" bus, which will pick you up and take you past the *rodoviaria* to the center.

Sandra buses leave Congonhas for Belo Horizonte at 6 A.M., 11 A.M., and 5 P.M. Sunday and holiday schedules are different, so check times when you arrive. If you miss the last direct bus, there are several *em transito* (coming through town from another town), with the last one leaving at 8:45 P.M. If all else fails, you can go to Lafeyete every hour until around 11:30 P.M. and catch all kinds of buses from there.

## GETTING AROUND

Everything in Congonhas is accessible on foot—except perhaps getting to and from the bus station at the entrance of town. For this, there are many buses running up and down the road in and out of town. A taxi will run you about R$10–15 from the Basílica to the bus station.

# São João del Rei

Nestled in the hills of Central Minas about 900 meters above sea level is the historical town of São João del Rei. Not as famous for tourism as its neighbor Tiradentes or its rival Ouro Preto (240 kilometers away), São João experienced an era of modernization and the historic city center became a mixture of modern and historic architectures, a fact that is used against the town in terms of tourism, perhaps because this mixture makes the town less picturesque than other towns. In truth, São João del Rei is one of the finest historical towns in Central Minas. It's home to two of the most beautiful churches in the region from the outside and one of the most spectacular on the inside. Everything in the Centro Histórico, where you will most likely be staying and walking around, is easily accessible by foot. Besides its many churches and museums, the Centro Histórico has many old, colonial buildings to admire from the outside as you stroll around town. You'll find wonderful places to sit and have coffee or drinks and more than a few decent restaurant choices, all moderately priced.

The people of São João del Rei are largely descendents of the original Paulistas (mixed Portuguese and native indigenous settlers from São Paulo) who came to the town during and after the Gerra das Emboabas, the Brazilian civil war. This explains why São João and Tiradentes have a slightly more upscale image than the more Mineiro historical towns of Ouro Preto and Congonhas.

São João del Rei is a fairly small town, with about 65,000 inhabitants. It has mild weather most of the year, with very pleasant summers. Temperatures range from 5°C in the winter to as high as 38°C in the summer, but the average is a pleasant 29°C.

## CHURCHES AND MUSEUMS

São João del Rei is almost equal to Ouro Preto in its historical significance and has some of the most beautiful churches in the entire region. They are all within walking distance from one another in the old city center. Five principal churches were positioned in the city center to form a cross with Mercês at the top, São Francisco de Assis at the bottom, Carmo and Rosário forming the two arms, and the Pilar Matrix at the heart.

Note: All churches and museums in this city are open noon–5 P.M. Tuesday–Sunday (unless otherwise noted). All but one or two are priced R$2–5 to enter—the remainder are free and noted herein.

### Capela Nossa Sra. do Bonfim

Way up on the hill above the Igreja São Francisco de Assis (Praça Frei Orlando, Centro, 8–11 A.M. and 2–4 P.M. daily) sits this small chapel with its simple interior, built in 1769. Although not officially recognized as such, it makes a better base to the "cross" formed by the city's five principal churches. The grounds in front of the church provide the best view of the city center. Just walk past the Igreja São Francisco de Assis (on either side) until you get to the top of the hill.

### Igreja Nossa Sra. do Carmo

Carmo (Largo do Carmo, Centro, 7–11 A.M. and 5–8 P.M. daily) faces the Rosário church on the other end of the avenue. It is one of the more striking churches on the outside, with its mostly white facade shining in the light of the sun. Even on the inside, the church uses bright blue and white coloring, which are striking as you enter, since one becomes accustomed to seeing so many dark, rococo images in Minas Gerais.

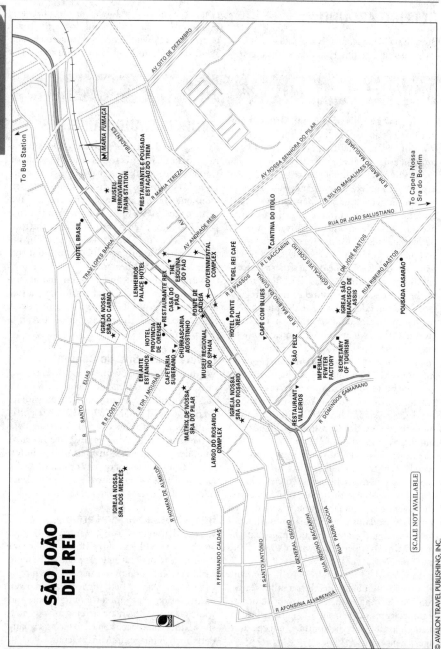

**SÃO JOÃO DEL REI**

To Bus Station

Central Minas

To Capela Nossa Sra do Bonfim

SCALE NOT AVAILABLE

© AVALON TRAVEL PUBLISHING, INC.

## Igreja Nossa Sra. dos Mercês

Mercês (Praça D. Pedro II, Largo das Mercês, Centro, 7–11 A.M. and 5–8 P.M. daily) was first a small chapel and grew to become the church that exists today. Not one of the more striking churches in the city, still, Mercês has its charms, principally its location on a hill behind the Matrix do Pilar. The Mercês sect has a celebration on September 8 every year and the festival at this church in São João del Rei lasts the entire month with music, dancing, fireworks, and religious ceremonies.

## Igreja Nossa Sra. do Rosário

Sitting on the opposite end of Av. Getúlio Vargas from the church of Carmo, Rosário (Praça Embaixador Gastão da Cunha, Largo do Rosário, Centro, 8–11 A.M. Tue.–Sun.) is not one of the most beautiful churches in the region and offers no particularly special features. It is, however, historically significant as

© CHRISTOPHER VAN BUREN

**Imperial palm trees line the *praça* at the Igreja São Francisco de Assis.**

one of the brotherhood of Rosário churches, built in 1719.

## Igreja São Francisco de Assis

The São Francisco church is, as Brazilians say, the *cartão postal* (postcard) of the city. It is also the largest and most impressive of the three principal São Francisco de Assis churches in Minas Gerais and probably one of the most beautiful baroque churches in the entire country. It also happens to be the tallest baroque church in Brazil and possibly in all the Americas. It was built in 1749–1774 by the grandest names in Brazilian baroque architecture, principally Francisco de Lima Cerqueira. It is one of the few sights where Aleijadinho is documented to have been seen working (in this case, as one of the assistants to the main architect, supporting the fact that he was probably not officially recognized as a master architect).

In the front garden area is a group of Imperial Palm trees, which reach as high as (or higher than) the church itself, giving the entire image a magnificence unlike any other church in the country. These palms are not indigenous to Brazil but were, in fact, a gift from the Brazilian Emperor Dom Pedro II on the city's incorporation in 1838. The only others in Brazil that reach this height are in the Jardim Botanico in Rio de Janeiro (also gifts from around the same time). The facade of the church (which is best viewed in the afternoon when the sun hits it) contains a beautifully sculpted portal topped by the crowning jewel, literally a crown sculpted from a single block of stone.

The Igreja São Francisco de Assis is also one of the most impressive churches on the inside, containing massive and intricate works of wood sculpture, treated and painted to look like stone. The effect is so well done that it's difficult to determine if the works are stone or wood even to the touch.

## Matrix de Nossa Sra. do Pilar

Pilar (Rua Getúlio Vargas, Centro, 6–11 A.M. and 5:30–8 P.M. daily) began as a simple wooden chapel built by the São Paulo *bandeirantes* at the beginning of the 18th century. In 1721, it was reconstructed as part of the larger plan of the city with an architectural design by Francisco de Lima Cerqueira. Inside are large, impressive works of art and a typical baroque design to the altars and pulpit.

## Maria Fumaça

Maria Fumaça (Smokey Mary) is the name of the train that has hauled travelers and cargo along the windy tracks between São João del Rei and Tiradentes for more than 100 years. The train itself is a functioning, antique steam locomotive, now running on oil. In the train station complex is a museum featuring old train cars and wagons, documents, and photographs from the train's history. (For details on taking Maria Fumaça to and from Tiradentes, see the *Getting There* section.) The museum is open from 8 A.M.–5 P.M. Monday–Sunday and is closed for lunch.

### Museu Regional do SPHAN

Inside one of the most impressive mansions in the city, which was built in 1859 for a rich coffee baron, the Museu Regional (Rua Marechal Deodoro 12, Largo Tamandaré, tel. 32/3371-7663) is a collection of furniture and sacred art pieces from the gold era through the 1800s. The house and pieces are pristine and well presented.

## ARCHITECTURE AND MONUMENTS

The two bridges that cross the *corrego* (waterway), splitting the Centro Histórico into two parts, are rich with history and give the city its special trademark. They were both built in stone with three arches and the more impressive of the two, the **Ponte da Cadeia** (the Jailhouse Bridge) was built in 1849 after the original wooden bridge collapsed, dropping a group of worshipers into the *corrego*. The **Governmental Complex** is a series of colonial buildings near the Ponte da Cadeia that are currently used as government buildings, including the present-day mayor's office. These are easily spotted on the south side of the *corrego*. The most striking of these buildings is

probably the **Teatro Municipal,** which was renovated in 2003 and hosts some of the city's most important musical and theatrical events. The **Largo do Rosário Complex** is a set of buildings in front of the Igreja Nossa Sra. do Rosário, which includes the Museu da Arte Sacra and the Capela Passo, among other buildings that are now shops.

## ENTERTAINMENT AND NIGHTLIFE

### Bars and Clubs

**Café com Blues** (Rua Tiradentes 792, evenings from 8 P.M.) is a small, cool jazz club that has live jazz shows from time to time. It's a nice place to have drinks. The **Cantina do Italo** (Rua Gabriel Passos 317, tel. 32/3371-8239, 11 A.M.–midnight, closed Tue.) is one of the city's older establishments and a great place for drinks in a dusty, dark atmosphere.

### Sidewalk Cafés

**Del Rei Café** (Av. Tiradentes 553, tel. 32/3371-1368, 9 P.M. until the last client nightly) is one of the best locations to sit and people-watch while sipping something. They have a little of everything. Throughout the day, you can order coffee, drinks, and snacks. At lunchtime, they have a simple lunch offering with an executive *prato feito* for R$5. At night, you can sit and have draft beer or more coffee. The **Esquina do Pão** (Av. Hermilio Alves 136, tel. 32/3371-2359, 6 A.M.–11 P.M. daily) near the Teatro Municipal is an excellent choice for coffee and bread items, including sweets. They have a cozy interior and are well located on the south bank of the *corrego*. Across the *corrego* is the **Casa do Pão** (Rua Pres. Tancredo Neves 37, tel. 32/3372-1576, 7 A.M.–8:30 P.M. daily), another very good coffee and snacks offering with excellent stuffed breads. **Cafetaria Soberano** (Rua Artur Bernardes 49, at Rua Arthur Bernardes, Centro, tel. 32/3371-4487, lunch and dinner daily) is another good option.

### Theater, Music, and Cinema

The old **Teatro Municipal** (Av. Hermilio Alves

170, tel. 32/3371-3704), near the train station, is a fully restored colonial building that offers music and theater performances on a regular basis. There are usually pamphlets for current shows at the major hotels, or swing by for details. On Sunday mornings at 9 A.M., the Igreja São Francisco de Assis hosts a choir performance as part of their mass. There is also live music throughout the city on weekends. Check the dinner spots along Rua Tiradentes and Rua Getúlio Vargas. The movie theater at Rua Tiradentes 380 plays current films three times per day at 3 P.M., 7 P.M., and 9 P.M.

## RECREATION AND OUTDOOR ACTIVITIES

Most of the hiking and other outdoor activities in São João take place in the stretch of land between this town and Tiradentes and are best accessed from the Tiradentes side. (See the *Tiradentes* section for more details.)

## FESTIVALS AND EVENTS

São João has various festivals throughout the year. The most significant include the city's birthday on December 8th, which includes a variety of activities and fireworks. **Carnaval** in S.J. is hearty, with plenty of partying and street parades. It's a less rowdy version of the Ouro Preto or Diamantina Carnaval festivals, though. Like most of the historical towns in Minas, S.J. celebrates **Semana Santa** (holy week) with a lot of musical and religious activities. Finally, the **Festival de Inverno** in July brings theater, music, and other cultural events to the city. More current events and festivals are listed at the city's website: www.saojoaodelreisite.com.br.

## SHOPPING

The city of São João del Rei is known for its many pewter factories. In the early 1900s, a British pewter smith came to town and began his factory of high-quality pewter, which today still operates as the **Museu do Estanho** (Av. Leite de Castro 1150, tel. 32/3371-8000, 9 A.M.–6 P.M. Mon.–Sat., 9 A.M.–4 P.M. on Sun.) and associated shops. The museum offers an interesting view of pewter manufacturing and makes a great side trip out of the old center. Other factories with shops attached appear throughout the town, including the **Imperial Pewter factory** and store (Rua Padre Jose Maria Xavier 132, tel. 32/3372-1465) and **Em Arte Estanhos** (Av. Getúlio Vargas 73) near the Igreja Pilar. The arts and crafts of the area are also represented in São João, and you'll find interesting wood sculptures and *namoradeiras* (carved busts made to sit on a windowsill, looking onto the street with a wistful, love-struck look) throughout town. The busy commercial center in town, where you'll find all sorts of modern products, is off Avenida Presidente Tancredo Neves past the Hotel Brasil.

## ACCOMMODATIONS
### Under R$50

One of the best low-cost offerings in town is the antique **Hotel Brasil** (Av. Presidente Tancredo Neves 395, tel. 31/3371-2804, hotelbrasil@ig.com.br, R$13 pp with shared bath, R$20 pp with private bath) right across the *corrego* from the train station. You can't miss the old building. No breakfast is included. The **Hotel Provincia De Orense** (Rua Mal. Deodoro 131, tel. 31/3371-7960) is not fancy. It has basic rooms for R$17 single or R$35 double and slightly more luxurious rooms (with TV and mini-bar) for R$30 single and R$50 double.

### R$50–100

Near the train station is the **Restaurante e Pousada Estação do Trem** (Rua Maria Tereza 45, tel. 32/3372-1985, www.pousadaestacaodotrem.com.br, R$40 pp). They have cute, clean rooms. The restaurant offers a self-service lunch and turns into a crepe and pizza spot at night. The **Lenheiros Palace Hotel** (Av. Pres. Tancredo Neves 257, tel. 32/3371-8155, www.mgconecta.com.br/lenheiros, R$60 s, R$95 d, and R$150 suites) offers small but clean rooms and a couple of suites with great views of the *corrego* and train station.

## R$100–150

One of the best colonial-style hotels in town is the **⋈ Pousada Casarão** (Rua Ribeiro Bastos 94, tel. 32/3371-7447, R$66 s, R$110 d standard, and R$121 d suite). They have 19 rooms with mini-bar, telephone, and TV. The hotel has a nice breakfast, a pool, and a game area with pool table. It's very comfortable and spacious and practically next door to the Igreja São Francisco de Assis. The **Hotel Ponte Real** (Av. Eduardo de Magalhães 254, tel. 32/3371-7000, R$90 s, R$130 d, and R$160 suite) is in the middle of the governmental complex, near the Ponte da Cadeia and faces the *corrego*. You couldn't get more centrally located. It's a relatively modern facility with cozy, well-insulated rooms, central heating and air-conditioning, and a pool. It also offers a cool scotch bar for late-night drinks. Finally, the **⋈ Pousada Beco do Bispo** (Beco do Bispo 93, tel. 32/3371-8844, R$80 s, R$125 d) is one of the most charming facilities in town. They have one style of room with air-conditioning, mini-bar, phone, and TV. They also have a pool and a sitting room with a working fireplace. You can ask for a discount if there's nothing special happening in town.

### Just Outside of Town

The **Cabana do Rei** (Av. Pres. Castelo Branco 2002, tel. 32/3371-8888, R$60 s and R$120 d) is about seven kilometers from São João del Rei in the direction of Tiradentes. (Take the road to Agues Saints to the 10 Km point). They offer 12 *apartamentos*, 9 chalets, a restaurant, and pool. The chalets are spread around a large area with a view of the mountains and plenty of privacy. The room comes with breakfast in the morning and soup, fries, and snacks at night. Rooms are a bargain if you don't mind being so far from town.

The **Pousada Recanto das Andorinhas** (Rua Luís Giarola 336, Colônia do Marçal Km 4, tel. 32/3371-7201, R$50 s, R$90 d, R$125 chalet) has two-story chalets for up to six people each. They also have a pool and restaurant. They are about 20 minutes from either São João del Rei or Tiradentes (in a triangular position).

## FOOD

### Quick and Casual

The best cheap lunches can be found at the café-bakeries listed earlier in this section under *Entertainment and Nightlife*. Besides these, a cheap eatery worth mentioning is the *boteco* on Rua Getúlio Vargas 96, which offers a R$2 *prato feito*. Not a bad choice if you're bent on economizing.

### Self-Service

The city's best self-service buffet is at the **⋈ Restaurante Rex** (Rua Marechal Deodoro 124, tel. 32/3371-1449, lunch and dinner Tue.–Sun.), which offers great Comida Mineira, including a terrific *frango com quiabo* (chicken with Ochre) for about R$14 per kilo. Another good self-service with barbecue is the **Churrascaria Agostinho** (Rua Arthur Bernardes 45, tel. 32/3373-5200, lunch and dinner daily), which has a decent variety of Comida Mineira along with grilled meats for about R$13 per kilo. They also have menu items for R$12–28 for two people. Finally, the **Restaurant Villeiros** (Rua Padre Jose Maria Xavier 132) has a great self-service lunch for around R$14 per kilo and many menu items for an average of R$12 per person.

## INFORMATION

There is a very simple office of the **Secretary of Tourism** (Praça Frei Orlando 90, tel. 32/3372-7338, 8 A.M.–5 P.M. Mon.–Fri.) right next to the Igreja São Francisco de Assis. They have maps of the city and can answer questions. The building is also home to the small **Museu Municipal Tomé Portes** (tel. 32/3372-7338, 8 A.M.–5 P.M. Mon.–Fri.), which only takes a few minutes to see. When you arrive in town at the *rodoviaria* (Praça Dr. Antônio Viegas), there is a tourist office in the corner that has maps and basic information about the town. If you can't find a good map at any of these tourist points, just try any of the larger hotels in the area. The Lenheiros Palace Hotel has a city map in its hotel brochure and also offers copies of the little city guide, which has a simple but effective map inside. The city website is www.saojoaodelreisite.com.br.

## SERVICES

Internet services are all over town. **NetCyber** (Rua Tiradentes 798, 9 A.M.–8 P.M. daily, no phone) has several computers for about R$5 per hour. There is also **City10 Internet** (Av. Andrade Reis 120, tel. 32/3371-8810, 9 A.M.–8 P.M. daily). The *rodoviaria* also has several computers available for R$3 per hour.

**Banco do Brasil** on Av. Hermilio Alves near the train station has international ATMs with the Plus and Cirus systems (the 4th and 6th machines on the left side). During the week, you can change money there too or at **Tiradentes Viagens e Turismo** (Av. Tiradentes 600-A, tel. 32/3371-9586, 9 A.M.–6 P.M. Mon.–Sat.). The post office is also on Av. Tiradentes on the far end, toward the train station.

## GETTING THERE

Viação Vale do Ouro buses leave from Mariana to São Paulo (Santos), stopping in Ouro Preto about 20 minutes later, and then hitting São João del Rei. They leave Mariana every day 7 A.M., 5:25 P.M., 6:25 P.M., and 8 P.M. Viação Sandra leaves Belo Horizonte for São João del Rei every two hours, starting at 6 A.M. with the last bus leaving at 8 P.M. Monday–Friday. Check at the *rodoviaria* for more times and weekend schedules. From Congonhas, the Viação Sandra leaves at 5 P.M. Saturday–Thursday and at 6 P.M. and 10 P.M. on Fridays.

From São Paulo, take Gardenia to São João at 8 A.M., 10 A.M., 8 P.M., 9:45 P.M., and 10 P.M. Sunday–Friday. Saturday hours are throughout the day, starting at 9 A.M. and ending at 10:30 P.M. From Rio, take the Paraibuna line starting at 8:30 A.M. with the last bus leaving at 11 P.M.

Leaving São João for Congonhas, you take the Viação Sandra at 12:30 P.M. direct or one of the buses to Belo Horizonte that leaves every two hours beginning at 6 A.M., with the last bus leaving at 7 P.M. You can get off in Congonhas or go all the way to Belo Horizonte. To Rio, the Paraibuna line leaves at 7 A.M., noon, 4 P.M., and midnight. To São Paulo, take the Gardenia at 8 A.M., 10 A.M., 8 P.M., 9:45 P.M., and 10 P.M.

Between São João and Tiradentes, there are two lines: Presidente and Vale do Ouro. They both leave the São João *rodoviaria* about once an hour from 5:50 A.M.–7 P.M. They both cost about R$2. It's 14 kilometers between the two towns, so you can take a taxi if you like. It will cost you around R$35.

The Maria Fumaça train operates Friday–Sunday. It leaves São João for Tiradentes at 10 A.M. and 3 P.M. and leaves from Tiradentes at 1 P.M. and 5 P.M.

## GETTING AROUND

Getting from the *rodoviaria* to the center, you can catch one of the yellow buses for about R$1.50 in front of the *rodoviaria*. Ask for the Centro Histórico. You can return to the *rodoviaria* from the bus stop in front of the Igreja São Francisco or in front of the Maria Fumaça train station. The trip takes only a few minutes. A taxi between the *rodoviaria* and the center should cost around R$7. When in the center of town, everything is within easy walking distance. It's safe to walk around town at night.

# Tiradentes

Easily the most quaint and well-preserved of the Minas Gerais historical towns, Tiradentes was first a town rich in gold, known as the Vila de São João del Rei. Its riches brought about a growth in culture and architecture that remains to this day. Tiradentes is perhaps best known as the birthplace of the *inconfidente* (confederate rebel) and martyr Joaquim José da Silva Xavier, who was known as Tiradentes. Tiradentes is a small colonial town nestled in the Serra São José mountains, a sleepy mountain range that divides the town from its neighbor São João del Rei. Today, Tiradentes is famous for its many festivals and events, which bring national and international visitors to the town several times per year, mostly to partake of the excellent restaurants and visit the many historical churches and monuments. The town also offers a great selection of country-style inns and many cafés and bars for hanging out. If your trip includes festival months, be sure to reserve your hotel accommodations well in advance and be prepared for prices doubling and tripling. The Festival of Gastronomia may well be worth it.

The climate in Tiradentes is generally mild–warm (25–35°C) getting into the hot temperatures November–February. Rainy season, like most of Minas Gerais, hits December–March.

## SIGHTS

### Casa da Câmara Municipal

On the hillside going up to the Matriz church, you'll pass the old city hall and town chambers (Rua da Cámara, no phone, 9 A.M.–4 P.M. Mon.–Fri.), which were used to receive governors and emperors visiting the city beginning in 1718. It's a wonderful example of colonial civil architecture and a quick stop on your way to the Matriz church.

### Igreja Matriz do Santo Antônio

The Matriz church (Rua da Cámara, no number, no phone, 9 A.M.–5 P.M. daily) is the second most gold-draped church in Brazil. Sitting atop one of the high points in Tiradentes, it looks protectively out over the town. The walk up to the church is full of interesting sights and shops and there are other sights up at the top once you get there. Inside the Matriz is a rich display of gold-leaf statuary, paintings, and a Portuguese pipe organ installed in 1788. Standing at the steps in front of the church, you get a wonderful view of the town from the outdoor sundial sculpture (1785). Built from 1710–1752, the Matriz is full of details and perhaps worth having a guide show you around. Every Saturday at 7 P.M., the church has its mass, open to the public.

### Igreja Santíssima Trindade

Behind the Matriz church, a bit farther up the road is this church (Rua Santíssima Trindade, no phone, 8 A.M.–5 P.M. daily),

the grassy grounds of the Santíssima Trindade church

## THE INCONFIDENTES

Led by children of the rich and elite from Minas Gerais, the *Inconfidencia Mineira* was an attempt at turning Brazil into a great independent nation. These intellectuals were inspired by the French Revolution and American independence and met to discuss their plans first in the town of Tiradentes and later in Ouro Preto. Three of the most important names associated with this movement were Joaquim José da Silva Xavier, known as Tiradentes (literally, pull-tooth, as he was a trained dentist), Claudio Manoel de Costa, and Tomás Gonzaga—three wealthy landowners fed up with paying taxes (a whopping 15 percent, we should all be so oppressed) to the Portuguese government. They were also upset by the gold quotas required by the Crown and the threats associated with their collection. Tiradentes was imprisoned in 1789 and hanged in Rio de Janeiro as the leader of the movement. His head was put on public display in Praça Tiradentes in Ouro Preto. He is recognized principally in Minas Gerais, although his death also falls on the same day as that of President Tancredo Neves (ironically, from the same region as Tiradentes in Minas Gerais). The two are remembered together on April 21.

built in 1810 from the scribbled plans of designer Manuel Victor de Jesus. The interior of the church is simple. More memorable are the lovely grounds around the chapel, including the fresh-water wells, which are still used to this day.

### Igreja São Francisco

This is the third of the São Francisco churches said to be designed (although not necessarily built) by Aleijadinho. They all have similar structures and front portals and all face west to capture the afternoon sun. This one, on Alto de São Francisco, is the smallest of the three, but not the least interesting—beautiful from the outside and not disappointing on the inside. Worth a look, especially if you've seen (or will see) the other two. Hours of operation are not well indicated and its likely you will view it only from the outside.

### Largo das Forras

The main town square, Largo das Forras, is surrounded by colonial buildings which now serve as restaurants, hotels, and government buildings. Among the most interesting include the current mayor's offices, built in 1720, and the chapel Senhor Bom Jesus da Pobreza (9 A.M.–5 P.M. Wed.–Mon.), built in 1771. They're on opposite ends of the *praça*. In the center is a charming garden area in which you can sit and rest your eyes on the various buildings around you.

### Museu Padre Toledo

The first meeting place of the *inconfidentes* was this colonial mansion (Rua Padre Toledo 190, tel. 32/3355-1549, 9 A.M.–4 P.M. Wed.–Mon.), home of *inconfident* Padre Toledo from 1777–1789. Today, the house is a museum filled with colonial art and furnishings. Especially interesting are the ceiling panels, which are a rich display of artworks. You can easily find the museum on Rua Padre Toledo next door to the Igreja Evangelista.

### Rua Direita

One of the principal streets in Tiradentes, Rua Direita offers a rich collection of architectural buildings, including the **Igreja do Rosário** (Praça Padre Lourival, no number, no phone, noon–4 P.M. Wed.–Sun) built 1708–1719 for and by black slaves with its statuary depicting mostly black culture and images. Also along Rua Direita is the **Cadeia Pública** (old jail house) (Rua Direita, no number, no phone), and the **Centro Cultural Ives Alves** (Rua Direita 168, tel. 32/3355-1604, 10 A.M.–6 P.M. Tues.–Sun.), which functions as a theater and music hall (pass by during the day for current listings or check www.centroculturalyvesalves.org.br).

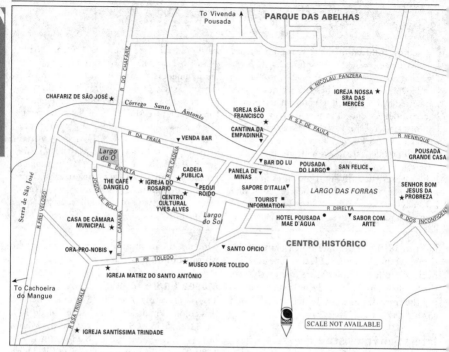

Map labels:
To Vivenda Pousada
PARQUE DAS ABELHAS
R. DO CHAFARIZ
CHAFARIZ DE SÃO JOSÉ ★
Córrego Santo Antonio
R. NICOLAU PANZERA
IGREJA NOSSA ★ SRA DAS MERCÊS
IGREJA SÃO FRANCISCO ★
CANTINA DA EMPADINHA ▼
R. DA PRAIA
VENDA BAR ▼
R. S. E DE PAULA
R. HENRIQUE
POUSADA GRANDE CASA
R. DA CADEIA
Largo do O
BAR DO LU ▼
POUSADA DO LARGO ●
SAN FELICE ▼
R. DIRELTA
CADEIA PUBLICA
PANELA DE ▼ MINAS
THE CAFÉ ▼ DÁNGELO
★ IGREJA DO ROSARIO
▼ PEQUI ROIDO
SAPORE D'ITALIA ▼
LARGO DAS FORRAS
SENHOR BOM JESUS DA ★ PROBREZA
R. JOGO DE BOLA
Serra de São José
R. FREI VELOSO
CENTRO CULTURAL YVES ALVES ■
TOURIST ■ INFORMATION
R. DIRELTA
R. DOS INCONFIDE...
CASA DE CÂMARA MUNICIPAL ■
Largo do Sol
HOTEL POUSADA ● MAE D'AGUA
▼ SABOR COM ARTE
R. DA CAMARA
ORA-PRO-NOBIS ★
▼ SANTO OFICIO
CENTRO HISTÓRICO
R. PE TOLEDO
★ MUSEO PADRE TOLEDO
To Cachoeira do Mangue
IGREJA MATRIZ DO SANTO ANTÔNIO ★
R. SSA TRINDADE
★ IGREJA SANTÍSSIMA TRINDADE
SCALE NOT AVAILABLE
MOON

# ENTERTAINMENT AND NIGHTLIFE

## Cafés and Bars

The town's principal café hangout is **Sapore D'Italia** (Praça Largo das Forras, tel. 32/3355-1846, 10 A.M.–11 P.M. weekdays and until midnight on weekends), which is perfectly positioned overlooking the main square for great people-watching. It has a great outdoor seating area and they offer coffee, drinks, smokes, sandwiches, and appetizers. They also have a selection of ice cream. **The Café Dángelo** (Rua Direita 176, tel. 32/3355-1611, 10 A.M.–11 P.M. weekdays and until midnight on weekends) is a small but elegant tea and coffee room with a garden view. They also serve various alcoholic beverages.

An excellent drinking establishment is the **Venda Bar** (Rua Ministro Gabriel Passos near the *praça*, tel. 32/3355-2142), just off the square. They have live solo music acts most nights, a selection of appetizers, and a collection of old radios on the wall for interesting viewing. The bar and restaurant **Sabor com Arte** (Praça Largo das Forras 66-B, tel. 32/3355-1886, 6 P.M.–midnight Mon.–Fri., 11 A.M. until the last client leaves on weekends) is a popular night spot. You can have dinner and drinks, or just drinks. Dinner is around R$19 per person and features pizza, pasta, and soups. They have live music on weekends. A great place for having drinks and listening to music is the **Bar e Restaurante Pequi Roido** (Rua Direita 224, tel. 32/3355-2774, noon–11 P.M. Mon.–Fri., noon–2 A.M. on weekends). They have a great patio area and host live jazz and bossa nova groups just about every night. They also serve lunch and dinner for about R$13 per person.

The **Centro Cultural Yves Alves** (Rua Direita 168, tel. 32/3355-1604, centroculturalyvesalves.org.br) hosts music and theater pieces on weekends and sometimes during the week.

To Cruz do Carteiro and
Calçadão dos Escravos

**TIRADENTES**

R. FRANCISCO P. DE MORAIS

DON
JIXOTE
USADA

R. ANTONIO TEIXEIRA CARVALHO

• POUSADA MARIA BONITA

POUSADA VILA REAL •  • POUSADA DA SIRLEI

Rio das Mortes

AV. GOV. ISRAEL PINHEIRO

■ TRAIN STATION

**ALTO DA TORRE**

HOTEL SERRA VISTA •

POUSO DI
BARTOLOMEU

To São João del Rei,
Casa da Pedra Caves

© AVALON TRAVEL PUBLISHING, INC.

Take a look at their current schedule as you pass by on your way to the sites.

## FESTIVALS AND EVENTS

The Tiradentes film festival, **Mostra de Cinema,** is recognized as one of the country's best film events. It takes place in January. Late February sees the passing of **Carnaval,** which is a lively event in Tiradentes, marked by parades and parties. Forty days after Carnaval is **Semana Santa** (Holy Week) which brings many street parades to town, along with festivals centered around the churches. The **Jubileu** festival in May/June brings religious pilgrims to town to celebrate at the Santíssima church with many bonfires. In July is the **Julho em Tiradentes** festival, which is a version of the Ouro Preto Festival de Inverno, a cultural and artistic festival that lasts the entire month. The principal festival in August is the **Festival de Gastronomia,** which

has given Tiradentes its reputation as one of the gastronomic centers of Brazil. In May/June is the **National Motorcycle and Antique Car Encounter.** December brings **Christmas** with lights throughout the town.

## SHOPPING

Tiradentes is home to numerous artisans. The special crafts of the region include wood sculpture, furniture, terra cotta figurines, and paintings on wood and canvas. There are many arts and crafts shops spread around town and most offer the same types of items (but possibly from different artists). So as you stroll around town, peek into the craft stores to get a look at the many offerings, then make your selections. One wood sculpture shop worth noting is the **Galeria de Artes e Móveis** (Praça Cberó da Liberdade 100, tel. 32/3355-1725, 10 A.M.–8 P.M. Mon.–Sat.), which displays the work of the late sculptor Fernando Araújo Gomes. His altars are magnificent and the atelier is something like a museum.

## RECREATION AND OUTDOOR ACTIVITIES

The countryside around Tiradentes offers many opportunities for hiking and exploring. One of the most rewarding is the hike to the **Cachoeira do Mangue.** This three-hour hike starts at the far west end of town and takes you through one of the early gold trails, along the slave trail (paved in stone by slaves working the gold trade) to the Mangue waterfall. Farther up are more natural pools, known as the **Balneario das Aguas Santas.** Here, you'll find some tourism infrastructure, including a playground, game areas, and water bikes. This area is also accessible directly from São João del Rei off the main highway. It's possible to take this hike without a guide if you are the adventurous sort. Otherwise, a guide is recommended. Take insect repellent, good shoes, and a swimsuit. The trail through the **Calçadão dos Escravos** (also known as the Trilha do Carteiro) is easily found entering the mountains on the east side of town. The hike, which takes about four hours, takes you through an area paved in stones by slaves working the gold trade. Farther along the trail are natural pools and the **Cruz do Carteiro,** marking the grave of a historical messenger of Tiradentes.

An interesting half-day trip is a visit to the **Casa da Pedra** caves, which can be a bit tricky to find without a guide. Here are the directions if you want to give it a try on your own: Catch the Presidente bus toward São João del Rei on the road going out of town past the train tracks (on the way to the heliport and the Alto da Torre neighborhood). Ask the driver to let you off at the *trevo da pedra* (roadside stop at the stone), from which you walk about one kilometer perpendicular to the highway and then turn to the right to follow the road. The caves will appear on your left just after the turn of the road. The caves are not extensive, but very interesting and are lit from openings above. There are guides at the main entrance to the caves, which offer to take you through the area for R$5. They also offer low or high repelling activities at the cave site. You can schedule with them in advance at tel. 32/8813-9894.

If you are very adventurous and happen to visit the caves on a weekend, you can follow the Maria Fumaça train tracks back into town. To find the tracks, you have to walk out of the cave entrance under the barbed-wire fence and past the mining station (which is closed on the weekends, making this possible). Just past the station, you hit the tracks and follow them to the right. Remember that the trains will pass through around 10:20 A.M., 1 P.M., 2:20 P.M., and 5 P.M., which is extremely important when you are crossing the short but narrow wooden bridges on foot (you don't want to have to jump into the Rio das Mortes, or River of the Dead, to avoid the train, do you?).

A good tour agency for hikes and ecotourism is **Caminhos e Trilhas** (Rua Antonio Teixeira de Carvalho 120, tel. 32/3355-2477).

Colonial buildings overlook Rio das Mortes in old Tiradentes.

## ACCOMMODATIONS

Hotels and *pousadas* in Tiradentes fall mostly into the mid-range category, with a few offerings on the low and high ends of the spectrum (although there is nothing extremely cheap or incredibly expensive). Keep in mind that everything in Tiradentes is more expensive during the festivals, and hotels go up 50–200 percent, depending on the festival. Almost all hotels require that you purchase a block, or package, during festivals and make you pay as much as half up front. On weekends, you'll pay about 50 percent more than on weekdays. Prices listed herein are non-festival prices with weekend rates noted separately.

### Under R$100

The **Pousada da Sirlei** (Rua Antônio Teixeira Carvalho 113, tel. 32/3355-1440, www.pousadadasirlei.com.br, R$66 d) is one of the lowest-priced options in town. It's not fancy, but has everything one needs to sleep and bathe. They also have a pool, breakfast area, and TVs in the rooms. You can have up to five people in a room. It's near the train station, past the main *praça*. The **Hotel Serra Vista** (Av. Governador Israel Pinheiro 196, tel. 32/3355-1404, www.serravista.com.br, R$35 s weekdays and R$55 s weekends, R$77 d weekdays and R$110 d weekends) is a slightly kitsch, low-cost offering with a pool and sauna (and even a water slide). The **Vivenda Pousada** (Rua José Batista de Carvalho 39, tel. 32/3355-1982, www.pousadavivenda.com.br, R$60–110 weekdays and R$80–130 weekends) is one of several newer hotels in an area called Parque das Abelhas (Park of the Bees), on the foothills of the Serra de São Jose. They have small rooms, but all are clean and freshly painted. They offer a pool with sauna, as well as breakfast and a bar at night. They also have a massage room and charge R$35 for an hour massage. The **Pousada Maria Bonita** (Rua Antônio Teixeira de Cavalho 134, tel. 32/3355-1227, R$100 d) is also on the way to the train station and is at the top end of the low-priced hotels. They have a villa-style setup with a pool and

café in the middle. Rooms are small but cute. The lowest priced hotel that's in the center of town is the **Pousada Grande Casa** (Rua dos Inconfidentes 447, tel. 32/3355-1251, R$100 d) near the main *praça*. It's in the back of an antique store and has a pool and sauna.

### R$100–200

One of the most charming hotels in Tiradentes is the 🅜 **Pouso di Bartolomeu** (Rua Herculano dos Santos 377, tel. 32/3355-2142, pousodibartolomeu@portaltiradentes.com.br, R$120–180 s and R$140–210 d) in an area called *Alto da Torre* (High Tower) past the train station on the far side of town. It's a bit farther from the center of town than other offerings, but what you get is a cozy, quiet country inn with a fantastic view of the town and the mountains behind it. Rooms are perfectly appointed with four-poster beds, mosquito netting, and all-new facilities. There is a pool and sitting room and the owner, Carlos, has an interesting selection of art on the walls, all from local artists. The high-end master suite has a bathtub whirlpool.

The **Pousada Vila Real** (Rua Antônio Teixeira Carvalho 126, tel. 32/3355-1292, www.pousadacasarao.com, R$99 s and R$135–180 d) is well located, just past the main *praça* and is the *pousada* of the chefs during the city's Festival de Gastronomia in August. They offer a large backyard with pool, game area, kitchen facilities, and sitting areas. They also have an indoor pool, a restaurant, and a tearoom with fireplace. A large and somewhat newer hotel is the **Don Quixote Pousada** (Rua Francisco Pereira de Morais 69, tel. 32/3355-1929, www.pousadadonquixote.com.br, R$130–150 weekdays and R$180–200 weekends). They have beautiful facilities, a scotch bar, sitting area, and restaurant.

**Hotel Pousada Mãe D'Água** (Largo das Forras 50, tel. 32/3355-1206, www.pousadamaedagua.com.br, R$66–100 s, R$154–165 d) is strategically located in the main *praça*, with all the restaurants and bars. It's an older building, but refurbished to be comfortable and spacious (including gas-heated showers). They have several rooms and are open to negotiating rates. They have an indoor pool, sauna, and garden area. On the other side of the *praça* is the **Pousada do Largo** (Largo das Forras 48, tel. 32/2255-1166, R$60 s and R$120 d) with a few small rooms. You can negotiate for up to four people per room.

### R$200 and Up

The **Pousada Pequena Tiradentes** (Av. Gov. Israel Pinheiro 670, tel. 32/3355-1262, www.pequenatiradentes.com.br, R$250–500) is built like a small village with numerous chalets and small buildings. They have a pool with swim-up bar, jacuzzi, sauna, outdoor bar and barbecue area, and several boutique shops. They also have a café and a restaurant for lunch buffet and dinner. It's like a little Disneyland village. Rooms have satelite TV and gas-heated water. The deluxe rooms have fireplaces and bathtubs. They also have rooms with lofts for up to five guests. It's about 10 kilometers from town, but they have a private van to bring you back and forth.

## FOOD

Eating in Tiradentes generally means opening the wallet a little. There are very few low-cost restaurants in town. The good news is that Tiradentes is home to some of the best restaurants in the country, gastronomy being one of the town's proud traditions.

### Comida Mineira

The self-service restaurant **Panela de Minas** (Rua Ministro Gabriel Passos 23, tel. 32/3355-1217, 11 A.M.–11 P.M. Tue.–Fri., 11:30 A.M.–4 P.M. on weekends) is a typical buffet with excellent Comida Mineira. Well-positioned, just off the main *praça*, it offers the self-service price of R$20. They serve lunch only. The **Ⓜ Restaurante Ora-pro-nobis** (Rua da Câmara 88, 10 A.M.–5 P.M. Tue. and Wed., 10 A.M.–midnight Thu.,–Sun.) is a small and charming restaurant on the street going up to the Igreja Matriz do Santo Antônio. They serve

meals off the menu for around R$20–55 per person, including meals with *ora pro nobis*, a high-protein leafy green, when in season.

### International

For Italian food, **San Felice** (Largo das Forras 86, tel. 32/3355-2340, 6 P.M.–midnight Tue.–Fri., noon–1 A.M. on weekends) offers a decent menu at about R$20 per person. They also serve trout and great salads. Well-located in the main *praça,* they are open for lunch and dinner. **Ⓜ Santo Oficio** (Rua Padre Toledo 366, tel. 32/3355-2031, dinner starting at 7 P.M. Tue.–Fri., lunch and dinner on weekends) is an elegant, gourmet dining experience with an international menu. Their menu changes regularly, but they specialize in fish and fowl. Meals range from R$25–65 per person.

### Quick and Casual

A simple *boteco* with snacks and appetizers is the **Bar do Lu** (Rua Ministro Gabriel Passos 80, no phone, 10 A.M.–10 P.M. daily). Around the corner is the **Cantina da Empadinha** (10 A.M.–10 P.M. daily ) also with small meals and low prices. Both are best for lunch. Next door to the Cantina is **Sucos e Cia** with great juices on a hot day.

## INFORMATION

Tourist information is available in the mayor's office building in the main town square (Largo das Forras). There are no international money machines in Tiradentes at this time, so its best if you get money in São João del Rei before coming. Most good restaurants and hotels take credit cards. If you have foreign money, you can exchange it at **Tiradentes Viagens** (Rua Inconfidentes 211, tel. 32/3372-3153).

## GETTING THERE

The main entry to Tiradentes is from São João del Rei, either via the Maria Fumaça train (on weekends) or via van or municipal bus. The train leaves from the far side of São João del Rei at 10 A.M. and 2 P.M. Friday–Sunday and holidays. The Presidente bus line leaves from the bus station about every hour, starting at 5:50 A.M. and ending at 7 P.M. Monday–Friday for R$2. The Vale do Ouro line also has buses every hour for just over R$2 and leaves from the same bus station. These are slightly more comfortable. A taxi from São João to Tiradentes will cost around R$35.

## GETTING AROUND

You can access everything in Tiradentes on foot. However, you may want to ride around town in a horse buggy, which will take you on a general overview of the city, starting from the **Maria Fumaça** train station.

Maria Fumaça

© CHRISTOPHER VAN BUREN

Central Minas

# Natal and Fortaleza

Clear, warm water, white sandy beaches, and giant sand dunes are a few of the things commonly associated with Natal and Fortaleza on Brazil's Northeast tip. More than one million visitors come to the region each year to take advantage of the perpetually warm weather, crystalline waters, cozy hotels just a few steps from the beach, and local arts and crafts. The beaches are pristine and the water is warm and clear and the presence of underwater reefs just offshore makes snorkeling and diving two of the most popular activities among tourists. Others include kicking back in the sun, drinking cold beverages, and eating the local fish and shrimp. Driving along the coast over the great sandy dunes is also a favorite sport in the region.

Natal has two urban centers, the cities of Natal and Ponta Negra, the latter being the main area for food, entertainment, and accommodations. The Ponta Negra beach is well worth a day of body surfing, sunbathing, and shopping. The beaches north and south can be visited by van or dune buggy in daylong or

# ust-Sees

**Look for M to find the sights and activities you can't miss and Ⓝ for the best dining and lodging.**

**M Genipabu:** Whether by dune buggy, camel, or on your own two feet, a trek across the dunes of Genipabu is unforgettable. There are charming beach kiosks, warm waters for swimming, and sandy dunes to roll around on (page 266).

**M Maracajaú:** An aerial photo of the *parrachos* (reefs) in Maracajaú will give you an idea of how large this area is. Spanning some 13 square kilometers, it's the largest cluster of offshore reefs in Brazil and perfect for snorkeling and scuba diving (page 267).

**M Praia da Pipa:** Charming during the day, the village of Pipa takes on a most special atmosphere at night. Lights glow from the restaurants and shops and people stroll along the main road without a care in the world (page 270).

© CHRISTOPHER VAN BUREN

**Trek the dunes of Genipabu by camel.**

**M Iracema:** *The New York Times* called it one of the most intense night spots in the world. That's just the west end at Iracema. Farther east, the boardwalk is just a tad calmer, with arts and crafts fairs, restaurants, and lots of people jogging and sitting at the beach bars (page 276).

**M Praia do Futuro:** The challenge here is deciding on which part of the beach you want to sit and relax for a few hours. There are more than 50 beach bars stretched across almost eight kilometers of sand and surf. Choices range from rowdy and crowded to calm and tranquil—but you're sure to find tasty boiled crab wherever you end up (page 279).

**M Jeriquaquara:** Something happens when you get this close to the equator. You lose track of time and leave pressures way, way behind. Now imagine a tropical beach village with no streetlights, a few charming inns, and lots of sun and sand (page 291).

**NATAL AND FORTALEZA**

ATLANTIC OCEAN

Jeriquaquara Ⓜ

Fortaleza

Iracema — Ⓜ
Praia do Futuro Ⓜ

Maracajaú
Genipabu

Praia da Pipa Ⓜ Ⓜ

Natal

João Pessoa

Recife

**Natal and Fortaleza**

half-day trips. There you'll be snorkeling, riding buggies across sandy dunes, skiing down sandy hills into warm water, and of course, eating and sunbathing at the beach kiosks. Known as the City of the Sun, Natal is located on the elbow of Brazil—the northeastern tip—the point closest to Africa and Europe. It's about 15 degrees south of the equator, where the days are long and the sun shines more than 3,000 hours each year. It has a rainy season from April–June. The rest of the year, tropical rains come and go quickly. The average temperature is 27°C, although on summer days, it normally hits the 38°C mark. The water is a soothing 26°C.

As for Fortaleza, it's difficult to decide whether the highlight here is the incredible nightlife in Iracema and Praia do Futuro; the seafood at the beach kiosks in Praia do Futuro; or the incredible arts, crafts, and clothing available for such great prices all over this region. For sure, the area's beaches also rank among the top attractions. What these beaches may lack in clarity of the ocean water (compared to Natal's beaches) is offset by their pristine conditions and the abundance of variety they offer. Indeed, in the 500 kilometers of coastline from Jeriquaquara to Canoa Quebrada, there are some 50 or so beaches worth visiting. The lack of a coastal highway linking these beaches keeps them pure and relatively unpopulated, if a bit more difficult to visit.

Most every coastal city in Brazil has an alternative beach village on the far outskirts of town with its own restaurants and hotels. In the case of Natal, this would be Pipa, about 85 kilometers to the south and well worth a couple nights' stay. There, you can go diving, surfing, and partake of the excellent nightlife activities. It's one of Brazil's most charming beach villages; even dolphins and sea turtles come to visit. Fortaleza has two villages on the outskirts, one in each direction. Canoa Quebrada lies to the east and Jeriquaquara is way out on the western shores. Both are worth overnight visits.

If you want for adventure, then a trip from Natal to Fortaleza might be in order. You can also travel south to see the highlights of the city

of João Pessoa on an overnight excursion. But the greatest highlight of this area is the famous island paradise of Fernando de Noronha, where the beaches are perfect, the water is as clear as any in the southern hemisphere, and 1,000 dolphins come to visit every morning at sunrise.

## PLANNING YOUR TIME

The best of the region is centered in Natal and you should probably start there. Natal has enough variety along the north and south coastline to hold you captive for quite awhile. To really explore the city, Ponta Negra, and the north and south coasts, you'll need 5–7 days. That includes a couple of days to check out Natal and Ponta Negra both at night and during the day, another 2–3 days to explore the north and south coasts, and time left over for a day and a night in Pipa. If you have a couple more days in your agenda, spend them in and around Pipa. The right amount of time in Natal depends on your personal preferences. If you are into snorkeling and diving activities, for example, then Natal may keep you busy longer. If you have 10 days or more, Fortaleza is not all that far away and has its own set of beaches to discover. The nightlife there is over the top, but you can also head out to the remote beach villages for a more secluded experience. The best is Jeriquaquara. You'll need an extra 3–5 days for the Fortaleza area. About three hours to the south is the city of João Pessoa, which is worth a day and night if you want a change of pace.

### Beach Excursions

One thing to decide is exactly how you want to see the north and south coasts around Natal. The best thing to do is rent a buggy each day or as a package for your entire time here. That gives you the freedom to come and go as you please and visit the areas that suit your fancy. You can also take the packaged buggy trips that explore the entire *litoral norte* (north coast) or *litoral sul* (south coast) in one day each. You leave in the morning by dune buggy or van (or boat in some cases), drive to several beaches, stopping for an hour or less in each key location, and return in the late afternoon. These trips give you a good overview of the coastline. For some, that's enough. Others like to return to their favorite spots to spend more time. Some trips go directly to one or two hot spots and stay there an entire day. An example is a full-day snorkeling trip to Maracajaú in the north or a half-day trip to Pirangi in the south. Details and suggestions on the various boat and buggy trips that you can take appear throughout the Natal section of this chapter.

Unlike the beaches around Natal, the Fortaleza beaches are spread very far apart, making it difficult to see more than two or three of them in the same day. In fact, you'll find that most excursions from Fortaleza focus on 1–3 locations in a day-long excursion from morning to late afternoon. Another effect of this distance is that dune buggies are not the principal means of travel to the beaches. Instead, you take a van or bus to your chosen destination and hire a dune buggy from there, if you choose. Travel between beaches is made more difficult due to the lack of a coastal highway, present in most other coastal regions of Brazil. Thankfully, Fortaleza is just too full of sand dunes to make a coastal highway feasible—so the beaches remain separate, difficult to get to, and pristine. Just remember that unless you have your own car, it's not easy to move from beach to beach. Packaged trips by van are pretty economical, but you're usually stuck with their schedule, so choose your excursions carefully. Although tour vans are comfortable and excellent, many travelers rent cars or buggies to explore the beaches. If you take this options, be sure to rent a car and not a buggy, as the high winds and whipping sands can be extremely uncomfortable in a dune buggy. Don't bother driving to Jeriquaquara as the road is tricky and you won't be able to do anything with your car once you get there. Better to take the bus.

## HISTORY

Contrary to popular belief, Brazil was actually discovered here in Fortaleza and not in South-ern Bahia, as has always been assumed. In fact, when Pedro Alvares Cabral cheerfully marked the discovery of these lands, Vincent Pinzon, captain of the *Niña* (one of Christopher Columbus' fleet) had already set foot on Brazilian ground several months before, on April 22, 1500. Although the entry appears in Spanish navigational records, the discovery was never announced due to treaties with the Portuguese, which gave Portugal preference to territories below the equator. In 1534, the Portuguese Crown divided up the new colony into 15 territories and gave what is currently Ceará to Antônio Cardoso de Barros, who never once set foot on Brazilian soil.

The French were not so happy with this division of the world between the Spanish and Portuguese and began infiltrating the colony. Portuguese colonists and French pirates continued fighting over this territory for the next 100 years. They were clamoring over the natural riches in the area, particularly Pau Brasil, the beautiful, hard, red wood coveted in Europe. Neither the French nor the Portuguese made much progress in colonizing and populating this vast region. Not the least of their problems was the native Potinguares people, a somewhat aggressive tribe influenced by the warnings of the French to beware of Portuguese domination. By the end of the century, however, the Portuguese, under the leadership of Captain Jerónimo de Albuquerque, indigenous on his mother's side, successfully negotiated with the Potinguares and the Forte dos Reis Magos was built to stand off further colonization efforts by other nations. The city was officially founded on Christmas day, 1599, hence the name Natal, meaning Christmas. The French were soon expelled and the Portuguese began colonizing the area. But the far northern reaches in the area known today as Ceará, remained brutal and untamed and Cardoso and his followers were never very successful in making a stronghold there. In 1603, a band of indigenous people and 65 Portuguese made their way up to the northern region to set up a government once and for all. Along the way, they were attacked by French pirates and suffered heavy losses, but

## FORRÓ: THE PEOPLE'S DANCE

The popular Brazilian dance style, *forró*, is something between swing and salsa dancing. Pairs make fast turns with tricky handwork. It's sexier than swing, but not quite as sexy as salsa. The dance was invented during the war, when American soldiers and local Brazilians got together to let off steam. The Americans created these large dance parties and invited everyone in the area, saying that the dance was "for all," which over time turned into *forró* (pronounced fo-HO). It's a popular dance style to this day in Brazil, practiced mostly by the common folks. The typical *forró* music arrangement includes an accordion, a triangle, and a bass drum. More modern versions include other instruments, like a guitar, but the rhythm is the same simple quarter-beat. One of the most traditional *forró* bands is called **Trio Forrózão** and a more modern *forró* is played by **Falamansa**. The dance itself is a modified two-step with fancy turns. An adept couple can be a joy to watch.

in the end they were victorious and the territory was named Nova Lisboa. It was not long before these pioneers were devastated by drought in the region and only six were able to crawl back to Natal alive.

The population of Natal remained small and the city itself innocuous until the time of WWII, when Franklin Roosevelt realized the strategic importance of the point in his attack on the Nazis in Europe. He and Brazil's Getúlio Vargas traded favors: Brazil gained a metalworks industry and the United States gained a couple strategic airbases during the war. Thus, American cultural influence in Brazil began with 10,000 American soldiers. Today, Brazil is one of the world's leaders in iron and steel production and Coca-Cola is only one of many large American companies in Brazil.

## Fernando de Noronha

Most visitors who come to the island for the first time are left truly speechless by the incredible beauty of this place. Fernando de Noronha is one of those special places in the world where the magic of nature is so close and so brilliant that it feels unreal. It's known to be a paradise for divers, but it's really a paradise for anyone who visits (of course, almost anyone who visits can participate in a scuba dive). First, the island is home to large families of sea turtles that reproduce on the sands of the island's outer beaches. What makes people goofy with joy are the dolphins that come to relax every day in one of the large bays on the island's inner edge—more than 1,000 of them. They head out again in the afternoon for a night in the ocean. The island's many beaches and swimming inlets are some of the most beautiful you'll ever see anywhere in the world. The water is blue and the sand is white and fine. Ev-

erything is surrounded by green vegetation and rock formations. There are two small villages where most of the *pousadas* are located and you can walk along trails to the various beaches and peaks. The island is only 17 square kilometers (roughly seven kilometers long by 2.5 wide) and has a population of 3,000. There are a few dirt roads and one paved highway, seven kilometers long. Fernando de Noronha sits 360 kilometers from Natal, a distance that kept the island remote and undeveloped during the ugly years of tourism and industrialization in the area. Today, it is a protected marine sanctuary and the few privileged folks who live on the island protect it with voracity as wild as the island itself. Visitations are limited and even certain beaches have limited access or are completely restricted.

The island was officially discovered in 1503 and was occupied intermittently by French and

Dutch pirates until about 1737 when it was occupied by the Portuguese and used as an island prison (a common use for remote islands). The island's natural forest was removed to keep the prisoners from creating boats and escaping, hence the vegetation on Fernando is oddly bereft of trees. It was used for a short time by the Americans in 1942 as a military base (along with the city of Natal) and finally stopped operating as a prison in 1972. In 1988, it became a national aquatic park.

The best time to visit is October–January, when the ocean is calm and the water is clearest. Unfortunately, this is also the peak season and the island is often a destination point for cruise ships coming from São Paulo or other southern locations. Other good months to visit are during the dry season of September–March, when the island is beautiful, the weather is fine, and the crowds are minimal. Note that the island restricts the number of visitors per day, so it's important to plan your trip ahead of time—especially if you are traveling during the peak months.

## VILLAGES

The population of the island is kept under control (although I'm not exactly sure how) and almost all of the inhabitants live in the three villages of Remédios, Floresta Nova, and Trinta on the northwest end of the island. Technically, the villages, the airport, and the sandy inner coastline are all outside of the national park area and constitute the most urbanized parts of the island. All of the *pousadas* and restaurants are located in this section too—mostly in Vila do Trinta, but also along the roads and paths all around. In the Vila dos Remédios, you can visit the **Igreja dos Remédios**, built in 1772, the ruins of the **Forte dos Remédios**, and the **Museu Histórico**, which has a few artifacts from the island's history.

## BEACHES

There are 16 beaches on Fernando de Noronha and most of the sandy ones are on the inner coastline, called the *Mar de Dentro*. The most popular is **Praia do Cachorro**, which has reefs for snorkeling and very calm and clear water. Walking south from Cachorro along the inner coastline, you come to **Praia do Meio** and **Praia da Conceição**, two beaches with waves big enough for surfing. At this point, you can see one of the island's landmarks, the Morro do Pico, a large rocky peak that looks back to the mainland. Next is **Praia do Boldró**, which is an excellent place to scuba and skin dive and is the site of the ruins of an old fort. From there, you can see one of the island's natural landmarks, the two small rocky islands called Dois Irmãos. Two highlights include the **Baía dos Porcos** and **Baía do Sancho,** both with excellent rocky reefs and calm water. These are two of the most visually stunning beaches on the island. There is a trail from the Vila dos Remédios that runs all along the inner beaches past Baía do Sancho. A walk along this trail is a perfect way to spend the day, although it can take several hours. After Sancho comes the Baía dos Golfinhos, which is completely off-limits to tourists.

On the outer rim of the island, you'll find a limited number of accessible beaches as most of this part of the island belongs to the national park. At the northern tip of the island, the beaches are very rocky and swimming is not permitted due to dangerous conditions. However, the **Praia da Atalaia** is open to groups of 20 at a time. The highlight here is the incredible snorkeling along underwater trails and rocky reefs. The picturesque **Baía do Sueste** is open for swimming and even sea turtles partake of the pleasure there. Swimming among the turtles is a great possibility. Finally, the beaches of Caracas and Leão are only open for viewing as these are principal locations for the spawning of sea turtles.

## OBSERVING THE DOLPHINS

There are few places in the world where you can see so many dolphins at one time—and so close. It's not a chance occurrence on Fernando de Noronha, but an everyday event. Every morning at sunrise, about 1,000 dolphins come into the Baía dos Golfinhos after a night out in the open ocean. The bay is their favorite location to play and reproduce. There is a great viewpoint in the hills on which you can sit and watch the grand entrance at sunrise. In the early afternoon, they make their way back out to the open sea and it's at this time you can take a small boat out to wait for them. They pass right alongside the boat in great numbers, jumping and spinning out of the water, almost as if they enjoy the company. The boat trip goes from the Santo Antônio pier on the northern tip of the island all the way down the inner coast to the dolphin swimming hole. It costs R$35 per person and takes about four hours. Organizations that offer this excursion include The **Projeto Golfinho Rotador** (tel. 81/3619-1295) and **Abatur** (tel. 81/3619-1307).

## DIVING AND SNORKELING

There are three dive schools on the island, all equipped and ready to take visitors—whether experienced divers or novices—out under the water. For novices, the event is known as a scuba baptism, a first-time dive. Usually, such baptisms are performed in swimming pools, but here in Noronha, you can take your first dive in the greatest underwater preserve in Brazil. The baptism dives include several hours of instruction on land and participants are always under the watchful eyes of the instructors. Scuba diving is so associated with Fernando de Noronha that it would be a crime not to offer this underwater experience to all—and a bigger crime not to try it out while you're here. The dive masters will also film your dive for a souvenir. You get a baptism dive of about 30 minutes with an instructor and all equipment and transportation for about R$165 (including an island tax of R$10). You're guaranteed to see sharks (up to two meters long), colorful fish, coral reefs, and perhaps turtles.

For experienced divers, the most popular location is around the islands north of Fernando de Noronha, where the water clarity is up to 50 meters and the temperature is a toasty 25°C. You have a good chance of diving among dolphins here, plus many other species. There are two shipwrecks around the island. One is about 60 meters deep and with a visibility of 50 meters, you can almost see it from the surface

of the water. But not quite. The other is near the pier at only seven meters. You cannot dive around the Baía dos Golfinhos and there are folks watching to make sure nobody does.

The dive instructors are easy to find on the island, but in case you want to make prior arrangements, the dive schools are **Águas Claras** (tel. 81/3619-1225), **Atlantis** (tel. 81/3619-1371), and **Noronha Divers** (tel. 81/3619-1112).

## TRAILS

There are trails all over the island and you can walk to the tops of most of the peaks to get panoramic views. The main trail goes from Vila dos Remédios all the way down the sandy beaches of the inner coastline for about six kilometers. There is another trail that goes up into the hills on the south side of the island, called the Capim Açu Trail. This one requires the presence of one of the island's certified guides. There are also a lot of dirt roads that lead to interesting places and great vistas. These are easily found, branching off the main highway.

## NIGHTLIFE

Difficult to believe, but yes, the remote and pristine island of Fernando de Noronha has a nightlife. It takes place every night at the **Bar do Cachorro** (Mirante do Cachorro, tel. 81/3619-1232, 10 P.M. until sunrise), which overlooks Praia do Cachorro. The program? Open-air *forró* dancing. You'll learn some of the steps in just a few minutes of practice. At 9 P.M. every night, there are talks by the local ecology groups, such as IBAMA (Instituto Brasileiro da Meia Ambiente), TAMAR (Projeto Tartaruga Marinho), and PGR (Projecto Golfinho Rotador).

## ACCOMMODATIONS

*Pousadas* on the island are generally very rustic and most don't even offer air-conditioning. Still, you'll be so tired by all that interaction with nature that you'll probably not notice any discomfort. One of the best is **M Pousada Solar dos Ventos** (Est. do Sueste, tel. 81/3619-

1247, tel. 81/3619-1347, R$385), with individual chalets and a few more rooms that overlook the Baía do Sueste. They offer rustic but comfortable and charming facilities with breakfast and dinner included. You'll also be comfortable at the **Pousada da Morena** (Rua Nice Cordeiro 2600, Floresta Nova, tel. 81/3619-1142, R$200). They have six rooms with air, TV, and phone. Finally, ☑ **Pousada Zé Maria** (Rua Nice Cordeiro 1, Floresta Nova, tel. 81/3619-1258, www.pousadazemaria.com.br, R$398) was one of the first on the island and has undergone a great transformation. It has 14 cozy chalets with air and TV.

**Hotel Esmeralda do Atlântico** (Al. do Boldró, tel. 81/3619-1255, R$185) has 41 rooms with air, phone, and transportation services. Finally, the **Pousada das Flores** (Rua D. Juquinha, Vale do Trinta, tel. 81/3619-1224, R$175) has five rooms with air, TV, and phone. They also have a small pool.

## FOOD

Most hotels and *pousadas* on the island offer their guests a *meia pensão,* meaning that breakfast and dinner are included in the fee. When you find yourself wanting lunch or dinner out, try the **Creperie das Artes Creperie das Artes** (Floresta Nova, tel. 81/3619 1120) for sweet and savory crepes or **Soparia Aconchego** (Vila do Trinta, tel. 81/3619-1306) for a varied menu of fish and fowl. You can also head over to the airport to enjoy the seafood at ☑ **Restaurante Ekologicus** (Estrada Velha do Sueste, Sueste, tel. 81/3619-1290, lunch and dinner daily) which has lobster for R$50 for two. Also, the great self-service buffets at the **Pousada Zé Maria** (Rua Nice Condeiro 1, tel. 81/3619-1258, 24 hours) and the **Hotel Esmeralda do Atlântico** (Boldró, tel. 81/3619-1255) are open to the public, although it's best to let them know you're coming.

## INFORMATION AND SERVICES

You can visit the tourist information center, **Centro de Visitantes** (Al. do Boldró, tel.

84/3619-1171, 8 A.M.–10:30 P.M.), but any of the hotels or establishments can give you information about the tours and options there. There are no international banks, so draw cash out in Natal (or Recife) before you come.

Besides the hefty airfare, there is a tax to stay on the island, charged per day. The tax is a disincentive to stay a long time. One day is R$23; one week is R$87; 10 days is R$110. If you stay longer than 10 days, the price begins to go up: 15 days is R$295 and a month is R$1,465. A good website for information about the island is www.noronha.com.br.

The island has a list of rules and regulations that visitors must follow. Most are pretty obvious, such as not removing plants or animals (including shells) from the island. Others are interesting to note. For example, it's forbidden to visit the small islands around Fernando, and the various, aforementioned off-limits beaches. It's also forbidden to climb the rock formations or swim with the dolphins in the Baía dos Golfinhos.

## GETTING THERE

Packages from Natal are available at most of the agencies listed in the Natal section. Let them know if you plan to scuba dive or take a boat trip while you're visiting the island (of course, you are) so they can plan ahead. Try **Mauricio Travels** (Av. Erivan França 35, Strandboulevard, Ponta Negra, tel. 84/3219-5486, www.vacationsbrazil.com) or the agency inside the **Lua Cheia Hostel** (Rua Dr. Manoel A. B. de Araújo 500, tel. 84/3236-4747, www.luacheia.com.br).

TRIP Linhas Aéreas (Av. Prudente de Morais 4283, Lagoa Nova, tel. 84/3234-1717) goes between Natal, Fortaleza, and Fernando de Noronha. Also the Nordeste line goes from Recife to the island (tel. 11/5561-2161).

## GETTING AROUND

The island is small enough that you can walk to its major points, and this is one of the most interesting ways to see the island. However, if your feet tire, you can rent a dune buggy to traverse the greater distances. They cost about R$100 per day and there is even a paved highway on the island that runs seven kilometers, constituting the smallest federal highway in Brazil. There are also buggy taxis and a couple of *kombis* (VW vans) that take people to the extreme ends of the island.

# João Pessoa

For travelers coming south from Natal, the next coastal city on the route is João Pessoa. Likewise, for those choosing to travel north along the coastline, João Pessoa falls just after a trip to Recife. It does not enter the journals as one of the most popular or most visited places on the coastline and many travelers pass through quickly on their way between Natal and Recife. João Pessoa makes a good overnight excursion from either of these cities for travelers who are not necessarily making their way up or down the coastline. Although the city has many sandy beaches to the north and south, the truth is, an overnight trip (two days and one night) is probably enough to take it all in. Public transit in João Pessoa is not very good, so the best way to get around is by car or tour van. In fact, this is one of the few cities that might actually be best when visited in a packaged tour, since you'll get to see all the highlights in a quick sweep. Take a day trip to the southern beaches and another out to the two major highlights of the area: Picãozinho, a rocky island that is great for snorkeling, and Ilha de Areia Vermelha, a sandbar out in the ocean that, during low tide, becomes a great beach for hanging out, swimming, and snorkeling. A guided tour can also take you through the handful of sights in the downtown area, which is about seven kilometers from the beach.

Unfortunately, João Pessoa is not geared toward international travelers and most of its attractions, boardwalks, and beaches are designed to be used by the 600,000 residents of the city. There are few hotels in the area, and on weekends, the entire coastline is packed with locals, from the northern point all the way to the beaches in the south. Afterward and well into the week, the beaches remain filthy with trash and empty coconut shells. The lack of beach kiosks on the northern coastline means that there's nobody to clean up the mess. The southern coastline is much better, as there are beach bars that keep the beaches in better shape. On weekdays in the off season, the beaches are practically deserted. Remember that weekends and major holidays get radically crowded with the sweaty, steamy masses.

## ILHA DE AREIA VERMELHA

One of the two most popular attractions in João Pessoa is a sandbar that sits a few kilometers off the northern coastline and pokes its head up out of the water at low tide. During the summer, scores of boats wait for the tide to drop and take passengers out to the sandbar to walk around, swim in the shallow water, partake of the temporary beach kiosks that sell beer and coconut water, and snorkel in the reefs nearby. It's a mass of people huddled around a single sandy island in the middle of the ocean. Interesting, but a bit over-populated with boats and bathing suits. The water along the north coast, however, is as blue as anything you'll ever see and that might be worth a trip out to the red, sandy isle. Boats leave from Praia do Camboinha and Praia do Poço for about R$15 per person and stay around two or three hours on the island. Times differ depending on the tide.

## PICÃOZINHO (CORAIS)

The second of the city's favored attractions is another island that sits about one kilometer off the main beach of Tambaú. This one is made of rocks and forms various natural pools that can be explored with a mask and snorkel. The water is clear and warm and there are plenty of fish that come around, as the locals provide

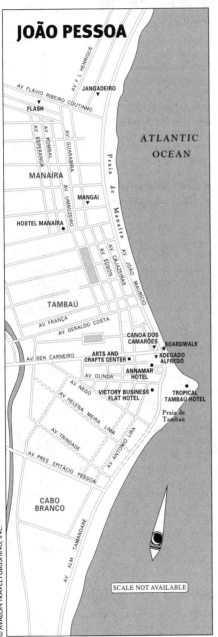

# JOÃO PESSOA

ATLANTIC OCEAN

AV FLÁVIO RIBEIRO COUTINHO

AV F L HENRIQUE

JANGADEIRO

FLASH

AV ESPERANÇA

AV POMBAL

AV GUARABIRA

AV UMBUZEIRO

MANAÍRA

MANGAI

Praia de Manaíra

HOSTEL MANAÍRA

AV EDSON

AV CAJAZEIRAS

AV JOÃO MAURÍCIO

TAMBAÚ

AV FRANÇA

AV GERALDO COSTA

CANOA DOS CAMARÕES

BOARDWALK

ARTS AND CRAFTS CENTER

ADEGADO ALFREDO

AV SEN CARNEIRO

ANNAMAR HOTEL

AV OLINDA

AV NEGO

VICTORY BUSINESS FLAT HOTEL

TROPICAL TAMBAÚ HOTEL

AV HELENA MEIRA LIMA

Praia de Tambaú

AV TRINDADE

AV ANTONIO LIRA

AV PRES EPITÁCIO PESSOA

CABO BRANCO

AV ALM TAMANDARÉ

SCALE NOT AVAILABLE

snacks for them. The trip is generally made by catamaran from the pier at Tambaú, but you should reserve a place with **Brunettur** (Av. Nossa Sra. dos Navegantes 104, tel. 83/3227-0709, www.brunettur.com.br), because of high volume in the peak season and extreme low volume in the low season (the boats might not be leaving for lack of passengers). The trip takes about three hours and costs R$20 per person.

## TAMBAÚ BEACH AND BOARDWALK

The main beach area and boardwalk is called Tambaú. There you'll find a long pier that extends ominously into the water. On the boardwalk, there are restaurants, bars, and cafés offering all kinds of seafood and drinks. The principal crossroads is at Avenida João Maurício (the coastal highway) and Avenida Sen. Rui Carneiro. The boardwalk is most active in this area and there are kiosks that extend onto the beach on the south side of the pier. The boardwalk also runs north all the way to Avenida Flavio R Coutinho, where you'll find the Mag Shopping Center. Along the way, there are numerous kiosks overlooking the beach from the boardwalk.

Around the main intersection at the boardwalk (Av. Sen. Rui Carneiro), you'll find a shopping center with a tourist information booth. There are souvenir shops and Internet cafés there. If you walk through the center, you'll reach the Mercado de Artesanato Paraibano in a small, circular building. Inside are handcrafted clothes and some arts and crafts.

## PRAIA DO JACARÉ

There is a tradition in João Pessoa that takes place every afternoon at the fresh-water beach of Jacaré. Years ago, a local sax player began playing Ravel's Bolero every day at sunset at the Jacaré Bar and it began to attract crowds. Soon the sax player had a live band accompaniment for the spectacle. Not wanting to be left out of the classical fever, neighboring bars began putting bolero music on at sunset and

JOÃO PESSOA COASTLINE

Costinha
PB 25
Cabadelo
Ilha da Restinga
FERRYBOAT
Ilha de Areia Vermelha
Praia Tamboinha
Praia do Jacaré
BR 230
Praia de Bessa
SEE "JOÃO PESSOA MAP"
Praia de Manaira
João Pessoa
Praia de Tambaú
Picãozinho (Corais)
Praia do Cabo Branco
← To Natal
Praia do Seixas
PB 8
Praia Jacumã
BR 101
Praia Tabatinga
SCALE NOT AVAILABLE
Praia Tambaba
↓ To Recife

MOON

© AVALON TRAVEL PUBLISHING, INC.

## BEACHES OF THE SOUTH COAST

The most beautiful beaches in João Pessoa are on the south coast. There, you'll find a long stretch of sand that is divided by rocks, rivers, and inlets into several different beaches, each with its own special personality. The first, called **Jacumã,** is situated under a cliff that looks out over the blue water. It has fine sand and plenty of room for the many people who frequent the place. There is a large bungalow-style kiosk there and coconut trees on the plateau above. Farther south is **Tabatinga,** which is more easily accessible from the street and also has a large beach bar. From Tabatinga, you can walk down to the locally famous **Tambaba Beach,** said to be the first nude beach in the northeast of Brazil. It still functions as a nude beach, with plenty of people partaking of the pleasure. There is a security guard at the entrance to keep single men from entering and to guarantee that everyone enters nude and without cameras. Unfortunately, they cannot maintain total control over the peepers who hang out on the cliffs above the beach. You enter via a cement staircase that goes over the rocky barrier between Tabatinga and Tambaba. The beach itself is small and full of rocks and small inlets where people lay out in the sun. There is a large beach bar to serve you (the waiters are clothed in case you were wondering). The water along this part of the coastline is fairly rough and not the best for swimming, but many people go in a few meters to cool off.

It's difficult to get to the south coast if you don't have a car or tour group. Buses leave from the *rodoviaria* downtown and circle around the outer edge of the city to come up on these beaches from the south. It's a heck of a long way to go. The beaches are a bit too far for a taxi ride (about 50 kilometers). The best way to visit is with a tour group or buggy trip.

now the entire area is known for its sunset observations with the classical music of Ravel. Get there early to get a seat because it's a favorite spectacle among locals and visitors alike. The sunset over the river is indeed lovely. Jacaré is located about 17 kilometers north of the city on the river-side of the peninsula. To get there by car, take BR-230 up the coast to the Jacaré exit. You can also catch the Cabedelo/Pr. do Jacaré bus from the *rodoviaria* or the Parque Salon de Lucena downtown. A taxi from Tambaú Beach will cost around R$20.

## SIGHTS DOWNTOWN

The city of João Pessoa is the third-oldest capital city in Brazil, founded in 1585. There are

Natal and Fortaleza

plenty of colonial buildings in the downtown area, including a couple of interesting baroque churches from Brazil's discovery period. Highlights include the **Theatro Santa Rosa** (Praça Pedro Américo, tel. 83/3218-4384, 2–6 P.M. weekdays and 4–8 P.M. on weekends), a baroque theater with impressive architecture and interior. There is also the **Parque Solon de Lucena,** the main downtown park, which has a man-made lake and lots of green area around it. Finally, you can check out the **Igreja São Francisco** (Praça São Francisco, tel. 83/3218-4505, 9 A.M.–noon and 2–5 P.M. daily), one of the oldest churches in the area, dated from 1589–1779. Inside are beautifully carved altars, covered in details and gold leaf. There are Portuguese tiles lining the walls and adjacent rooms with sacred art and contemporary exhibits.

## EXCURSIONS

In a valiant attempt to create some kind of tourist infrastructure in the city, several tourist agencies offer excursions in the area. In fact, joining one of these packaged excursions is just about the only decent way to enjoy this city (the other way is to visit the city on a packaged tour from Natal or Recife, which offers you a similar experience). The most common tours include trips to the Ilha de Areia Vermelha, including transportation to Camboinha Beach and a speedboat out to the sandbar. The trip takes about three hours and costs around R$35 per person. You can also get to Camboinha Beach on your own and catch a boat going out to the island for about R$15 per person.

Another trip is a ride up the north coast in a dune buggy. The north coast beaches are marked by some of the bluest water and most spectacular surf in the area. Unfortunately, the infrastructure there is almost nil (actually, it might be better if it were nil, as the bars and kiosks along this part of the coast are pretty ugly). A ride up in a buggy is a good way to see the best of the northern peninsula. It takes about four hours and costs R$100 for up to four people. There is also a mini-bus that goes up the north coast. You can catch this on Avenida Argemiro de Figueiredo for R$1. It's called the Cabedelo bus. Get off at Jacaré to see the sunset, the *balsa* to catch the ferryboat across the channel, Praia Formosa for an interesting and beautiful beach (except on weekends), or the *ponto* to go all the way to the fort on the tip of the peninsula.

Buggies and vans also go out to the south coast, which is more popular. You can spend the day walking among the various beaches of the south coast, or just spend the day nude at Tambaba.

Another popular package is the city tour, where you stop at several of the major points around the area, including the lighthouse of Cabo Branco (the most eastern point of Brazil, which is closer to Africa than to the capital city of Brasilia) and several downtown monuments. It takes most of the day and costs R$35 per person.

There are several tour agents near the boardwalk area of Tambaú and around the landmark Hotel Tambaú. Try **Trailer Tour** (Praia Tambaú, tel. 83/9982-2583), which has buggies for R$120 for up to four people or **Brunettur** (Av. Nossa Sra. dos Navegantes 104, Tambaú, tel. 83/3227-0709, www.brunettur.com.br), which has buggies and vans for packages and also rents buggies for the day.

## ACCOMMODATIONS

Most visitors stay around the Tambaú area or within walking distance to it. This keeps you close to the nightlife and tour agencies, in case you want to catch an excursion out to the south coast or downtown. There are some good deals farther north, but they are a bit remote. They can be good if you spend a lot of time on the Vermelha sandbar, which is off the northern coast.

### Under R$100

One of the best deals in the area is the **Ⓜ Annamar Hotel** (Rua Santo Antônio 36, Tambaú, tel. 83/3247-3011, www.annamar.com.br,

Natal and Fortaleza

R$80 s and R$100 d). They are a block off the boardwalk of Tambaú near the Arts and Crafts Center. They have simple but clean and modern facilities, air, TV, pool, and a breakfast buffet (included). If you want to be close to the Cabedelo area, to be closer to the sandy Ilha de Areia Vermelha, then check into the **Formosa Apart Hotel** (Av. Cassiano da Cunha Nóbrega 555, Praia Formosa, tel. 83/3228-2555, formosa@netwaybbs.com.br, R$80–100). Their location makes them a bit more competitive. They have 27 rooms with balcony, air, TV, phone, and some have small kitchen facilities. Their (rooftop) pool has a wonderful view of the ocean and they are practically on the beach itself. They also have a bar and restaurant.

One of the most economical places to stay is the **Hostel Manaíra** (Rua Major Ciraulo 380, tel. 83/3247-1962, www.manairahostel.br2.net, R$20 pp or R$45 for a private room). It's a few blocks off the beach in the Manaíra area, about 20 minutes' walk from the Tambaú boardwalk area. The building is nice and clean and they have group and private rooms, a nice pool area, breakfast buffet (simple but fresh), and a cozy TV room. They offer Internet (extra) and use a hospital service to sterilize their sheets and pillow cases (the owners are doctors), perfect for hypochondriacs.

### R$100–200

A very nice hotel that is well located near the Tambaú boardwalk is the **M Victory Business Flat Hotel** (Av. Almirante Tamandaré 310, Tambaú, tel. 83/3247-3100, www.victoryflat.com.br, R$120 s and R$140 d). They have 60 rooms with a small kitchen area (coffee maker, mini-bar, and microwave), air, TV, and phone. Facilities include a restaurant, rooftop pool and sauna, beauty salon, Internet (extra), and a tour agency. There's a 25 percent service charge. Breakfast is included. In the Cabo Branco Beach area, just south of Tambaú, is the simple, but very clean, beachfront **Netuanah Praia Hotel** (Av. Cabo Branco 2698, tel. 83/3247-3373, www.hotelnetuanah.com.br, R$165–

215). They have rooms with ocean views, an excellent breakfast buffet (included), air, TV, stereo, in-room Internet (extra), pool, and poolside bar.

### Over R$200

If you want to stay in the landmark resort hotel, the one that looks like a bottle cap on the beach, check out **M Tropical Tambaú Hotel** (Av. Almirante Tamandaré 229, tel. 83/3247-3660, www.tropicalhotel.com.br, R$190–435). There, you will enjoy the type of atmosphere that Brazilians love. Everything is provided inside the hotel, including areas to relax by the pools, restaurants, bars, boutique shops, gym, game areas, and more. Some rooms have ocean views, and sizes and styles vary (as do prices).

## FOOD

There are a lot of restaurants around the pier at Tambaú, but also some decent offerings up and down the coast. In the Manaíra area, there's **Flash** (Rua Juvenal Mario da Silva, tel. 83/3246-3625, 8 P.M.–midnight daily, R$10) with good seafood. A bit farther up is the beachfront restaurant **O Jangadeiro** (Rua Argemiro de Figueiredo, tel. 83/3246-2526, around R$20 per person) with a casual, beachy atmosphere. Back at Tambaú, you can try **Canoa dos Camarões** (Av. João Maurício 121, tel. 83/3247-2055, 11 A.M.–midnight daily, R$45 for two), specializing in shrimp, shrimp, and shrimp. The **Mangai** restaurant (Av. Gen. Edson Ramalho 696, Manaíra, tel. 83/3226-1615, 11 A.M.–10 P.M. Tue.–Sun.) has regional foods in a buffet-style lunch and dinner. The price is excellent at around R$20 per person. Also, you can try **Tábua de Carne** (Av. Sen. Rui Carneiro 648, Tambaú, tel. 83/3247-5970, 11 A.M.–11 P.M. daily, R$15 per person) for meats and regional dishes. Finally, there's **M Adega do Alfredo** (Rua Coração de Jesus, Tambaú, tel. 83/3226-4346, lunch and dinner Tue.–Sun.) for a varied menu, including regional and international foods.

## INFORMATION

There are tourist information booths at the main bus station and airport. There is also a tourist office in Tambaú at the **Centro Turístico**

**Tambaú** (Av. Almirante Tamandaré 100, tel. 83/3247-0505, 8 A.M.–7 P.M. Mon.–Sat.). To rent a car, you can contact the tour agencies listed earlier, or **Avis** (tel. 83/3247-3050) and **Localiza** (tel. 83/3232-1130).

# Natal City

The city of Natal is not the principal destination for visitors to this region—at least not anymore. Up until 2000, it was a tourist hot spot. You can still see many of the hotels and restaurants along the main boardwalk area (from Praia do Forte to Praia dos Artistas), but they are now inexpensive alternatives to the Ponta Negra establishments. Like many coastal cities in Brazil that experienced extreme growth in the 1990s, Natal did not properly care for its sewage and waste problems and its beaches suffered the consequences. Now unswimmable due to pollution, Natal's urban beaches are visited primarily by low-income Brazilians from the region. That means the area is also more dangerous for tourists. Tourism moved south to Ponta Negra, where the water is still clean.

On the positive side, Natal's urban beaches are still beautiful to look at and there are some interesting and inexpensive dining and hotel options in the area. On the other side of the river, just north of Natal is Praia Redinha, the first beach on the northern coastline and an excellent swimming and sun-bathing option, especially if you're staying in the city of Natal.

Coming in off the beaches of Natal, there are a few interesting historical sights worth a look and some additional hotel and restaurant options that might lure you away from Ponta Negra with their excellent values. If you have a rental car, then staying in the city of Natal is a perfectly good option, since you'll be able to get around to the various restaurants downtown and in Ponta Negra without a hassle. You may consider staying in the city if you are traveling in a group of four or more, as you will be able to split taxi fares. A final motive for staying in the city is if you're simply not into the

wild night scene of Ponta Negra and prefer a more tranquil visit. But if that's the case, then I suggest you stay in Pipa or one of your other favorite beaches, away from the city.

## FEIRA DE ARTESANATO

The Feira de Artesanato is located on the coastal road (Av. Pres. Café Filho) at the beginning of Praia dos Artistas. Along the many corridors of booths, you'll find tee shirts, terra cotta and wood sculpture, clothes, leather goods, trinkets, and food items. In the front of the market is a booth that sells several types of roasted cashews, cashew wine, *manteiga de garrafa* (butter with clear butter oil), *dendê* (palm oil), fruit syrups, and *cachaça* (sugarcane alcohol).

## NATAL AQUARIUM

This small but interesting exhibit (Av. Litorânea 1091, Redinha Nova, tel. 84/3224-2177, www.aquarionatal.hpg.ig.com.br, 8 A.M.–6 P.M. daily) features more than 30 different aquariums with tropical fish species and special shark and seahorse tanks. They also have reptile and monkey habitats. It's not far from the city at Praia Redinha. To get there, you should take the ferry across the Rio Potengi. The best plan is to combine this visit with a trip to the Redinha beach. There are also buggy trips that stop at Redinha and the aquarium on their way up the northern coast.

## CENTRO DE TURISMO

The **Centro de Turismo** (Rua Aderbal de Figueiredo 980, tel. 84/3211-6218, 9 A.M.–6 P.M. Mon.–Sat.) is housed in the old jailhouse

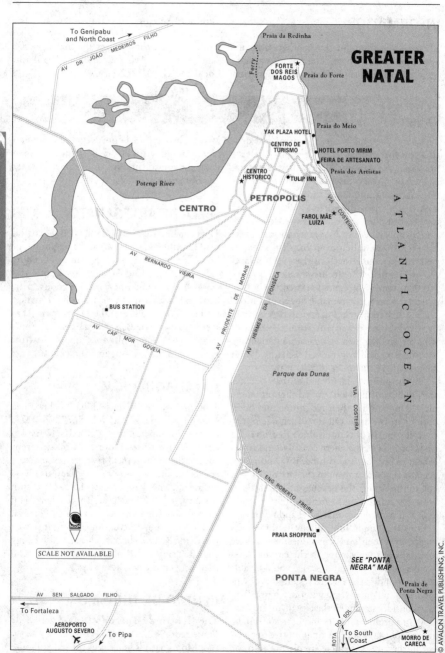

Natal and Fortaleza

**GREATER NATAL**

To Genipabu and North Coast

AV DR JOÃO MEDEIROS FILHO

Praia da Redinha

Ferry

FORTE DOS REIS MAGOS ★

Praia do Forte

Praia do Meio

YAK PLAZA HOTEL

CENTRO DE TURISMO ■

HOTEL PORTO MIRIM ■

FEIRA DE ARTESANATO ■

Praia dos Artistas

CENTRO HISTORICO ★

● TULIP INN

Potengi River

**CENTRO**

**PETROPOLIS**

FAROL MÃE LUÍZA ★

VIA COSTEIRA

A T L A N T I C   O C E A N

AV BERNARDO VIEIRA

AV PRUDENTE DE MORAIS

AV HERMES DA FONSECA

■ BUS STATION

AV CAP MOR GOVEIA

*Parque das Dunas*

VIA COSTEIRA

MOON

SCALE NOT AVAILABLE

AV ENG ROBERTO FREIRE

PRAIA SHOPPING ■

*SEE "PONTA NEGRA" MAP*

**PONTA NEGRA**

Praia de Ponta Negra

AV SEN SALGADO FILHO

← To Fortaleza

ROTA DO SOL

To South Coast

AEROPORTO AUGUSTO SEVERO ✈

To Pipa →

MORRO DE CARECA ★

© AVALON TRAVEL PUBLISHING, INC.

with a great view of Natal's urban beaches. It was reopened in 1976 as a center for tourism, with local artisans showing their works, restaurants, and a dance hall. It's the best place to get local arts and crafts. The hall functions on Thursday nights at 10 P.M. for *forró* dancing. It's popular with the locals and tourists alike (mostly Brazilians). They offer some limited transportation options from local hotels. Call for details or ask at your hotel.

## FAROL MÃE LUÍZA

Sitting high above the Via Costeira highway that connects Natal and Ponta Negra is Natal's old lighthouse (tel. 84/3201-0477, 2–5 P.M. Sundays). It offers an incredible view of the coastline and marks the edge of the Parque das Dunas (Av. Alexandrino Alencar, no number, Morro Branco, tel. 84/3201-3985, 8 A.M.–6 P.M. Sundays), an urban park with sand dunes, lunch establishments, and hiking trails. The Parque is not really a major draw, but if you're into scenic views, then a visit to the Farol might be in order.

## FORTE DOS REIS MAGOS

Natal's most recognized monument, the fort (Av. Presidente Café Filho, no number, tel. 84/3202-9013, 8 A.M.–4:30 P.M. daily) was built in 1598 and later rebuilt in 1958 with stones from the nearby reefs, whale oil, and lime. It was constructed in one of South America's most strategic locations, on the point of the continent closest to Europe. Following Portuguese tradition, it was designed in a lopsided star shape with its 14-meter-high walls facing the ocean, the Potengi River, and the sandy tide pools. Inside is a small museum. You can walk to the fort along the beach at low tide if you don't mind walking past some mean-looking groups of people to get there. Better to take a taxi to the riverside entrance and walk along the causeway to the fort. Since the fort is still used by the military, it is prohibited to go near it at night. Don't even think about it!

## CENTRO HISTÓRICO

The Natal Centro Histórico, now part of the Cidade Alta neighborhood, has a number of

The Forte dos Reis Magos sits on a rocky reef jutting out into the ocean.

historic buildings, mostly from the 1700s. One of these monuments is the **Igreja Santo Antônio** (Rua Santo Antônio 698, Cidade Alta, tel. 84/3211-4236, 6 A.M.–7:30 P.M. daily) a simple, baroque-style church from 1776. The adjoining **Museu de Arte Sacra** houses a few religious pieces of art from churches of the same era. If you're in the downtown area for shopping, take a look at the old *praça,* the current location of the *profeitura,* or office of the mayor (Rua Santo Antônio 698, 6 A.M.–5:30 P.M. daily), and the many old buildings around it.

## URBAN BEACHES

The urban beaches of Natal extend from Praia do Forte on the northern tip near the fort about four kilometers south to Praia dos Artistas. Between these two points is Praia do Meio (Middle Beach). It's not exactly clear where one beach ends and the other begins, as it's really just one long stretch of coastline. What makes this area interesting is the formation of *recifes* (rocky reefs) just off the shore that have the effect of blocking the ocean at low tide, cre-

## POLLUTION ON BRAZIL'S BEACHES

How can something so beautiful be so polluted? That's sometimes the reaction from foreigners looking out on the urban beaches throughout Brazil. The water is blue and often clear—how can it be so dirty? Often, it takes nothing more than a walk along the beach to realize what goes into the ocean. Soon, you have to walk across a little stream of water entering the ocean from a concrete pipe in the nearby retaining wall. Usually, you can smell the little stream long before you see it. It's not always sewage—at least, not from the homes and businesses nearby. What's running untreated into the ocean is the runoff from the streets. Not so bad? If you've seen a city street in Brazil after a weekend of festivities, then you know that it might as well be raw sewage. It's customary in Brazil, even somewhat celebrated, for men to relieve themselves in public places. With all the beer drinking that goes on and the incomprehensible lack of public facilities, you can imagine what just one weekend must add to the runoff water. Culturally, Brazilians learn to throw anything and everything into the street, from food wrappers to, well, who wants to think about those details? There is not a city in Brazil that cleans its streets using public services. Everyone is responsible for their little piece of the sidewalk. And people do, in fact, wash down their 3–5 meters of sidewalk every day. A myriad of soaps and cleansers carry the filth down into the urban waterways through the covered holes

in the streets, called *bocas de lobo,* or mouths of the wolves.

Besides the runoff water, many coastal cities have little or no sewage-treatment facilities and the massive urbanization of Brazil only exacerbates the problem. Most of Brazil's population resides near the coast. Since there are no federal programs to provide sewage treatment, it's up to the cities to make these investments. Needless to say, only the most modern cities and successful tourist towns have sewage treatment. Some that do include Rio de Janeiro, Salvador, Morro de São Paulo, Cabo Frio, Buzios, Balneário Camboriu, and Florianópolis. Other large cities are lagging way behind.

But that's not the worst of the problem. These are things that might, someday, be controlled through education and public services. The real seven-headed beast is the lack of infrastructure in the poor areas of the country. Imagine this: *Favelas* (poor areas) are usually found on high ground. Rivers and streams run from the high ground to the ocean. You get the idea. There is absolutely no incentive for a poor family to stop throwing its garbage into the stream and no penalty that would deter them from doing it. Enforcement of any such measure would be a joke. What to look out for are beaches with rivers opening into them. Often, those rivers are not clean and not treated.

For a look at how Brazil's beaches get cleaned up, see the sidebar *The Water's Fine: Salvador's Coastal Clean-Up* in the *Salvador* chapter.

ating a series of shallow, very warm tide pools along the sandy beach. At high tide, the ocean crashes in and fills the pools again. These reefs are present off the shoreline of a great many beaches in Brazil, from Natal down to Southern Bahia. But nowhere do they form the kinds of shallow pools that you find in Natal. Here the reefs are higher and there are no other inlets for the water but over the reefs at high tide. Consequently, a relatively small amount of water makes its way onto the beach, forming these pools. If they weren't polluted, they would be terrific for swimming. Nevertheless, you'll see plenty of locals enjoying the warm waters of the pools with their families.

Praia dos Artistas is the principal area for hotels, restaurants, and other services in the city of Natal. Here, you'll find the Feira de Artesanato and some informal restaurants in front of the *feira* with great views of the ocean. There are a few beach kiosks that enter the sandy beach from the sidewalk, but these are not as picturesque as the kiosks in Ponta Negra and most visitors don't spend all that much time here.

## ENTERTAINMENT AND NIGHTLIFE

There are several nightlife options in the city of Natal. First, you have the bars and clubs in the Praia dos Artistas area, namely **Chaplin** and **Hooters** (A. Pres. Café Filho 27, Chaplin tel. 84/3202-1199, Hooters tel. 84/3202-1199, from 10 P.M. Thurs.–Sat.), at the tip of Praia dos Artistas. These have rowdy Thursday-night dance parties with women entering free of charge. They are part of the same establishment.

Redinha beach, just on the other side of the river to the north, has an active late-afternoon scene. There, you'll find a long stretch of simple bars that look out on the beach. There is always music playing, sometimes live. From the ferry port, walk to the right along the beach until you see the first few bars. You can keep walking around the point, where there are even more beach bars with music and festivities. The ferry operates 6 A.M.–9:30 P.M. After that, you'll have to find a boat to take you back

to shore or catch a taxi, buggy, or bus back the long way via the Estrada da Redinha, also known as Avenida João Medeiros Filho.

You can catch a number of presentations at the **Zás-Trás Shopping Show** (Rua Apodi 500) from around 8 P.M.–midnight. At 10:30 P.M., the dance shows begin, including northeast Brazilian dancing with native tribal costumes and influences, Maculelê knife dancing, and Capoeira. It's in the Tirol neighborhood downtown, about a R$10 taxi ride from Praia dos Artistas.

## FESTIVALS AND EVENTS

During the entire month of June, the **Festas Juninhas** occupy the streets and *praças* of the city. Bands, parades, and arts and crafts exhibits occur every weekend and some throughout the week. In the middle of November, the neighborhoods of Tirol and Petrópolis in Natal have **pre-Carnaval** festivities. Look for these around the second weekend in November. Weekends in December, you can go out to Pirangi for the **Festa do Cajueiro** at the world's largest *cajueiro* (cashew tree), which is lit up like a Christmas tree, with music and festivities all around. Natal's largest festival is **Carnatal,** which is their off-season Carnaval, during the first half of December. Parades, parties, music, and dancing take place in the streets of Natal, principally Avenida Prudente de Morais and Amintas Barros. Ponta Negra is the place to experience **New Year's Eve.** There, you have 24 hours of festivities, water games, and music, culminating in fireworks at night. In late February or early March, **Carnaval** takes place all over the city, but it's Ponta Negra that serves up the most activity with parades, live music, and street parties. There are also activities at Redinha.

## SHOPPING

There are several shopping centers in Natal if you like visiting modern malls. The best is the **Alamanda Shopping Center** (corner of Av. Alfonso Pena and Rua Serido) in the Petrópolis neighborhood, which is an upscale district for shopping, café sitting, and dining. The commercial center of Natal is the area called Cidade Alta, which is between Avenida Rio Branco and Avenida Prudente de Morais. There you can find the best prices on clothing, swimwear, shoes, cameras, and accessories. There are also countless *lanchonetes* for a quick meal and several Internet cafés. It's about a half-hour walk from Praia dos Artistas (walk up Avenida Getulio Vargas and into town and not around the Forte) and usually packed with locals doing their shopping. You'll find the best souvenirs at the **Feira de Artesanato** at Praia dos Artistas and the **Centro de Turismo.** The best deal on tee shirts is at the main bus station on your way out of town. They sell good-quality shirts with artistic designs for R$7–10 each.

## BUGGY EXCURSIONS

In Natal, visiting the outlying beaches usually means hopping aboard one of the guided trips created for tourists. Trips are made by air-conditioned vans, dune buggies, and boats. There are numerous agencies offering dozens of packaged trips to the beaches. Most of the agencies offer about the same thing for the same price with small differences for optional services, such as using *lanchas* (speedboats) instead of smaller boats and whether or not equipment is included. Many agencies work together, passing clients back and forth to make sure vans and buggies are full. You can also hire out a buggy for the day, with a driver, and choose your own agenda.

If you're selecting an agency on your own (as opposed to going through your hotel or travel agent), try to find an agency with credentials from SETUR (Secretário de Turismo) or EMBRATUR (Empresa Brasileira de Turismo). These have better guides and are able to access areas that are off-limits to pirate *bugeiros* (buggy drivers). When choosing an agency, be sure to ask whether the lunch stop includes several options or just one restaurant and whether snorkeling equipment is included in the price. If you don't have four people in your party for one of the buggy trips, your choices are to wait

for others to fill your trip or pay for the entire buggy anyway. As a single, I once split a trip with a very nice Brazilian couple, which put three people in the vehicle (a comfortable number). Problem is, the single rides in the front the whole time. If you are trying to split a buggy, you should leave your name and hotel phone number with several agents the night before. Following are some agencies to check out:

**Natal Vans Turismo** (Av. Ayrton Sena 880, N. Parnamirim, tel. 84/3091-1180, tel. 84/9983-4076, www.natalvans.com.br) offers various trips by van and a good Maracajaú trip with optional scuba baptism. **Marazul Turismo** (Rua Manoel Sátiro 75, Ponta Negra, tel. 84/3091-2450, tel. 84/3988-4787, www.passeiodebuggy.com.br) has vans and buggies with a great *litoral norte* trip and full-day trips to Pipa and Galinhos. **PorpinoTur** (Rua Pedro Fonseca Filho 8864, Ponta Negra, tel. 84/3082-0341, tel. 84/9981-8553) has good full-day trips to Pipa and Maracajaú, including full scuba diving trips. **Marina Badaué** (Rua Principal, no number, Praia de Pirangi do Norte, tel. 84/3238-2066, www.marinabadaue.com.br) offers boat trips to Pirangi in the south, with diving and snorkeling off the boat. Finally, **Mauricio Travels** (Av. Erivan França 35, Strandboulevard, Ponta Negra, tel. 84/3219-5486, www.vacationsbrazil.com) has a wide variety of full-day and half-day trips, but they tend to be much more expensive than other agencies and set their prices in euros. You can find most of these agencies in the Ponta Negra boardwalk area.

**Star Buggy** (Praia dos Artistas, tel. 84/3202-4313, tel. 84/3982-1343) offers a good rate on a *litoral norte* full-day trip (you start closer at Praia dos Artistas instead of Ponta Negra), which goes through nine beaches to Muriú, including snorkeling and dunes. Also, The **Association of Buggy Owners and Drivers (APCBA)** (Rua Projetada 405, Genipabu, tel. 84/3225-2077) is located in Genipabu, in case you want to rent a buggy from Genipabu for a trip farther north.

Now it's just a matter of deciding which trips to choose. Descriptions of the beaches and suggestions for trips are in the *Beaches Near Natal* section. If you prefer unguided trips (and who doesn't like to come and go as they please?), then your choices are somewhat limited. There are a few van services that drive up and down the coast and can drop you off at any of your chosen beaches for around R$10. The problem is that you still have to operate on a schedule, as the van returns at specific times later in the day. Still, what you do in-between is your own choice. Almost everything you can do on a guided trip, you can arrange on your own at the destination. One such operator is **Ismael** (tel. 84/9973-3320). You can also try **Claudio** (tel. 84/9997-6602). Best to call the night before. Municipal buses can get you to Genipabu, Galinhos, São Miguel do Gostoso, and Touros, which are all distant beaches to the north (except Genipabu). To the south, only Pipa has municipal bus service. Details and schedules appear with each beach description later in this chapter.

Your best option for making your own schedule is to rent a car or buggy and drive yourself. This gives you total freedom. You can hire a buggy for the day, with a driver, paying the full daily price of R$160–180. You can do this with any number of passengers up to four (five including the driver) and it lets you dictate where you go and how long you stay in each place.

## OTHER EXCURSIONS

**Vitoria Regia Turismo** (Av. Roberto Freire 2250, Shopping Tour, Ponta Negra, tel. 84/3081-4216, tel. 84/9994-8748, www.vitoriaregiaturismo.com.br) offers a rappelling excursion with equipment and instructors. They also have buggy trips, horseback riding, and service to Fernando de Noronha. You can take a night trip by boat around the Natal harbor and Rio Potengi, with plenty of partying on board. Check **Iate Santa Catarina** (Av. Hermes da Fonseca 509, Petrópolis, tel. 84/3202-2741, tel. 84/9921-3221) for boat tours. The **Ma-Noa Water Park** (Praia de Maracujaú, no number

tel. 84/3234-9321, 10 A.M.–4 P.M. daily) has water slides and lots of pools for playing in the water. Great for kids. It's located inland at the Maracajaú beach.

## ACCOMMODATIONS

The best hotel with a view of Praia dos Artistas is the **Ⓜ Yak Plaza Hotel** (Av. Pres. Café Filho 25, tel. 84/3202-4224, www.yakplaza.com.br, R$80 s/d). They have the nicest facilities with air-conditioned reception area, two pools, and a deck area overlooking the ocean. Rooms are spacious with air, TV, phone, and safe. Another decent hotel on this beach is **Hotel Porto Mirim** (Av. Pres. Café Filho 682, tel. 84/3615-1730, R$60), which has a small pool and small rooms with no views, but the hotel is clean and comfortable.

In town, you have the very presentable **Tulip Inn Potengi Flat** (Rua Potengi 521, tel. 84/3211-3088, www.potengiflat.com.br, R$180) located at the Praça Civica (the main downtown square) within walking distance to Praia dos Artistas. They have large, modern rooms with TV, air, veranda, and dining table. They offer a pool, sauna, and restaurant for guests.

## FOOD

Some of the best restaurants in the city area are located along Avenida Gov. Silvio Pedrosa, which is in the direction of the Via Costeira, within walking distance from Praia dos Artistas. One example is **Stravaganzza Pizzaria & Restaurante** (Av. Governador Silvio Pedroza 15, Areia Preta, tel. 84/3202-3736, noon–midnight, Tue.–Sun.) which serves huge portions (enough for two) of fish and shrimp, as well as numerous pizza combinations. Some of their specials include fish in shrimp sauce and shrimp with Greek rice. It should cost around R$20 for two. The most spectacular restaurant in Natal (and Ponta Negra) is **Ⓜ Mangai** (Av. Amintas Barros 3300, tel. 84/3206-3344, 6 A.M.–10 P.M., Tue.–Sun.), which serves regional dishes in a self-service buffet spread like

fresh fish for lunch on the beach in Natal

you've never seen. The variety of meat, pasta, rice, and vegetable dishes goes on and on. They also have a *tapioca* (a type of crepe) station that whips up combinations as you wait. The décor is somewhere between Disneyland cheesy and Brazilian country. The restaurant (which has an affiliate in João Pessoa) raises its own beef and chicken. Meals are about R$25 per person. It's in the Lagoa Nova neighborhood not far from the Zás-Trás Shopping Show, in case you want to catch a show after dinner.

In the upscale shopping district is **Buongustaio Ristorante** (Alfonso Pena 444, tel. 84/3202-2667, 6 A.M.–midnight Mon.–Sat., noon–4:30 P.M. on Sun.) with an outdoor patio, bar, and full Italian menu. It costs around R$35. For sushi, try **Ira Chai Sushi** (Rua Trairi 714, tel. 84/3222-4660, noon–3 P.M. and 6 P.M.–1 A.M.), which has two floors and sushi for R$38 per kilo. Mondays, they have a sushi *rodísio* (sampling) for R$29.

## INFORMATION AND SERVICES

The tourist information booth at Praia dos Artistas is generally useless, but you can take a look just in case. The best information is at the **Centro de Turismo** (Rua Aderbal de Figueiredo 980, tel. 84/3211-6218, 9 A.M.–6 P.M. Mon.–Sat.).

The **Cyber Container Café** (Av. Pres. Café Filho 680, tel. 84/3202-7932, 9 A.M.–10 P.M. daily) is usually bustling with computer users. It's located on the coastal road near Praia do Meio. There are others in Cidade Alta.

## GETTING THERE

From the airport, which is in the extreme south of the city, you can catch buses directly to Ponta Negra or downtown. A taxi to Ponta Negra from the airport will cost around R$35 and slightly more to downtown. Domestic airlines that service Natal include TAM (tel. 84/3643-1624), Varig (tel. 84/3644-1252), and Vasp (tel. 84/3643-1137).

From the *rodoviaria* (bus station), which is in the west end of town, you can catch buses to downtown Natal or Ponta Negra. A taxi from the *rodoviaria* to either of these points will cost around R$20.

## GETTING AROUND

Natal is a small city and it's possible to walk around most of it. From the Praia dos Artistas, you can walk up to the center of town, all the way to the historical part if desired. You can also walk to the fort along the beach at low tide (although this is not recommended due to the possibility of assault). You should take a taxi to the ferry that crosses Rio Potengi to Praia Redinha, mostly because the area around there is a bit sketchy. There were some attempts at restoring the old buildings along Rua Chile, but it appears that the effort did not catch on and eventually lost its steam. Taxis from one end of town to the other should cost around R$10–15. A couple of phone numbers for taxi service are Cidade Taxi (tel. 84/3223-6488), Disque Taxi Natal (tel. 84/3613-0811), and Rádio Taxi (tel. 84/3221-5666). If you're somewhere on the north coastline and need a taxi, call Radio Taxi Litoral Norte (tel. 84/3214-2317).

You can catch buses down the Via Costeira to Ponta Negra for less than R$2. The best bus is number 56. A taxi from Praia dos Artistas to the beginning of Ponta Negra will cost around R$12.

Buggy rentals are available at private agencies all along Ponta Negra. Details are in the Ponta Negra section. Local numbers for national car rental agencies include Avis (tel. 84/3644-2500), Hertz (tel. 84/3207-3399), Localiza (tel. 84/3206-5296), and Yes (tel. 84/3219-4001).

# Ponta Negra

The Venice Beach of South America, Ponta Negra is an artsy, edgy, beach scene with an incredible mixture of elements. You'll find every class and style of person walking along the boardwalk, from groups of international and Brazilian tourists to the local hippies trying to sell them art, bikinis, hats, jewelry, or tee shirts. Hotels range from beachy budget flops to five-star resorts. The surf is blue and mild and good for swimming (unpolluted, they say), except that there are usually so many surfers in the water, you can't find a place to enter safely. In compensation, there are plenty of beach bungalows for sitting in the shade with a cool coconut water. The center of Ponta Negra can get somewhat congested and rowdy, while the more remote north end is upscale and calm. Since the entire area is easily traversed on foot, nobody on the beach escapes the many *ambulantes,* hawkers that make their living interrupting people on the beaches every five minutes for a possible sale.

At night, the Ponta Negra area is Natal's most active and agitated scene. At its best, it's a small, urban party town full of bars and restaurants with crowds of international travelers enjoying themselves in low or high gear. Barhopping is a favorite activity until the dance clubs open at around midnight. There's a little something for everyone and a lot of character at every turn. At its worst, Ponta Negra is a slightly sleazy beach scene with plenty of prostitution, drugs, and opportunism. These activities extend themselves into the area's dance clubs. Thankfully, you can avoid most of this pretty easily, simply by not making yourself available to it (prostitutes and drug dealers don't force themselves on anyone).

Ponta Negra's principal natural attraction, Morro de Careca (Bald Hill) is on the south side of the beach with a strip of sand running vertically down the middle to the water, like a reverse Mohawk. It was once a popular activity to slide down the sandy hill into the warm water below, but due to heavy erosion of its surface from excessive use, it now sits a unique landmark and a reminder to preserve our environment. (For sliding down sandy hills into warm ocean water, you need go no further than the Genipabu beach to the north of Natal. Praia de Jacumã to the north also has this thrill.)

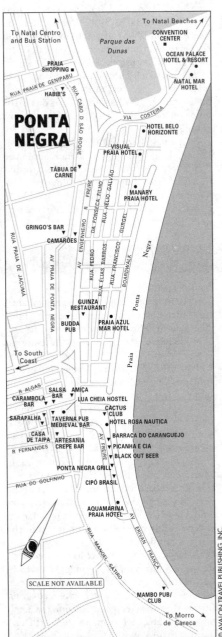

## PONTA NEGRA

To Natal Centro
and Bus Station

To Natal Beaches

Parque das
Dunas

CONVENTION
CENTER

OCEAN PALACE
HOTEL & RESORT

NATAL MAR
HOTEL

PRAIA
SHOPPING

RUA PRAIA DE GENIPABU

HABIB'S

RUA CABO DE SÃO ROQUE

VIA COSTEIRA

HOTEL BELO
HORIZONTE

VISUAL
PRAIA HOTEL

TÁBUA DE
CARNE

R FREIRE

DA FONSECA FILHO

RUA HELIO GALVÃO

MANARY
PRAIA HOTEL

GRINGO'S BAR

CAMARÕES

AV ENGENHEIRO

RUA PEDRO

RUA ELIAS BARROS

RUA FRANCISCO

GURGEL

BOARDWALK

Negra

RUA PRAIA DE JACUMA

RUA PRAIA DE PONTA NEGRA

GUINZA
RESTAURANT

BUDDA
PUB

PRAIA AZUL
MAR HOTEL

Ponta

Praia

To South
Coast

R ALGAS

CARAMBOLA
BAR

SALSA  AMIÇA
BAR

LUA CHEIA HOSTEL

SARAPALHA

TAVERNA PUB
MEDIEVAL BAR

CACTUS
CLUB

HOTEL ROSA NAUTICA

CASA
DE TAIPA

R FERNANDES

ARTESANIA
CREPE BAR

AV FREIRE

BARRACA DO CARANGUEJO

PICANHA E CIA

BLACK OUT BEER

PONTA NEGRA GRILL

RUA DO GOLFINHO

CIPÓ BRASIL

AQUAMARINA
PRAIA HOTEL

RUA MANOEL SÁTIRO

AV ERIVAN FRANÇA

SCALE NOT AVAILABLE

MAMBO PUB/
CLUB

To Morro
de Careca

© AVALON TRAVEL PUBLISHING, INC.

# ENTERTAINMENT AND NIGHTLIFE

The area along the boardwalk in the center of town is full of bars and restaurants. Most are a mixture of both. This main street is called Avenida Erivan França. There are also a number of spots along the main highway (Av. Engenheiro Roberto Freire) just inland from the beach. Another, more charming area for restaurants and bars with a great ambience is on a street called Rua Dr. Manoel A. B. de Araujo, which intersects Avenida Engenheiro Roberto Freire. This area is well worth a visit at night. Dance clubs appear mostly along Avenida Engenheiro Roberto Freire. For the most part, you can walk around and between these areas and get a good idea of what they offer. Here are some recommendations:

Most of the bars on the boardwalk are also restaurants and are listed in the *Food* section. The **Cactus Pub** (Av. Erivan França 5, tel. 84/3219-6399) is the first bar on the boardwalk and sits facing the lifeguard station. They have a Mexican-style menu, which is nothing to put in your postcards to home, but at night, they get a number of visitors coming to drink their beer (Canadian beer, not Mexican). A great sidewalk bar that has the best people-watching vantage is **Black Out Beer,** which serves beer on tap and in small bottles. They are about halfway down the boardwalk area. These places are open all day and all night. The **Mambo Pub/Club** is at the far end of the boardwalk and is a disco that opens around 11 P.M. and goes until the sun comes up, just about every day of the week.

On the inland highway, Avenida Engenheiro Roberto Freire, is **Ilha da Fantasia** (Avenida Engenheiro Roberto Freire 174, tel. 84/3219-3230, 8 P.M. until sunrise) an American-style bar, that serves cocktails and plays rock music. Also along the highway is **Amiça** (Avenida Engenheiro Roberto Freire 3004, tel. 84/3215-0395, 11 P.M. until sunrise), the most dance-oriented singles club in

**Beach umbrellas decorate Praia Ponta Negra.**

the area. It gets going around midnight and costs R$10–35 to enter, which makes it one of the better places in town. The **Budda Pub** (Avenida Engenheiro Roberto Freire 9102, tel. 84/3219-0033, 11 P.M. until sunrise, R$7 cover charge) presents live rock and R&B music every night during peak season and on weekends in low season.

In the area along Rua Dr. Manoel A. B. de Araujo, you'll find the **Taverna Pub Medieval Bar** (Rua Dr. Manoel A. B. de Araujo 500, tel. 84/3236-3696, 11:30 P.M. until sunrise) under the Lua Cheia Hostel, which is built like a castle. The pub presents local musical groups in a great setting without the edgy pick-up scene that occurs in the other clubs. You can swing by the hostel during the day to pick up discount tickets. Also in this area is the **Salsa Bar** (Rua Dr. Manoel A. B. de Araujo 176, tel. 84/3236-2573, from 7 P.M. until sunrise Tues.–Sun.), which has great outdoor seating and Latin music to go with their tropical drinks. The **Carambola Bar** (Rua Dr. Manoel A. B. de Araujo, 6 P.M.–4 A.M.) serves fruit juices and sandwiches.

**Guinza Restaurant** (Via Costeira 4, tel. 84/3219-2002, dinner daily) is a mixture of sushi bar, beer-and-cigar bar, and dance club. Presentations of belly dancing appear on the dance floor and live bands play mostly blues oldies. It's located on the northern end of Ponta Negra on the Via Costeira highway, just off Av. Engenheiro Roberto Freire on the way to Natal. A long but pleasant walk from the boardwalk area.

## SHOPPING

In Ponta Negra, shopping takes place on the boardwalk itself with the street vendors and in the little shops dotted along Avenida Erivan França. There is a shopping mall, **Praia Shopping** (Avenida Engenheiro Roberto Freire 8790), just past Habib's going out of Ponta Negra toward downtown Natal.

## ACCOMMODATIONS

The accommodations in Ponta Negra are more expensive than hotels in downtown Natal, but you usually have to pay more to be close to the action. Besides hotels, the majority of agencies that offer day trips to the outlying areas are set up in Ponta Negra. Hotels here, like most on the Brazilian coast, nearly double their prices for peak months, which are generally mid-December through the end of February and the month of July. Unfortunately, some hotels have a take-advantage-of-gringos attitude and raise their prices at will for foreigners. Some establishments publish their prices in dollars or euros to avoid low periods in the exchange rate—a practice which is borderline dishonest in this writer's opinion, since their expenses fluctuate relative to the Brazilian *real,* not the dollar. Following are some hotels that are fairly trustworthy. Prices here are for low season and breakfast is always included unless noted otherwise.

## Under R$100

The **M Lua Cheia Hostel** (Rua Dr. Manoel A. B. de Araújo 500, tel. 84/3236-4747, www.luacheia.com.br, R$30 pp group rooms and R$65 d) is becoming legendary, perhaps because it looks like something out of legend. It's built like a large castle inside and out, including a small mote. Guests stay in group or double rooms along corridors of brick and stone. In the middle is an open atrium and the dungeon area is the popular Taverna Pub, a meeting place for travelers of all sorts. In the vicinity of the castle are several charming restaurants and bars that maintain the low-lit atmosphere of the street. Despite all this medieval monkey business, the management at Lua Cheia is efficient and professional. An excellent value and location is the **M Hotel Belo Horizonte** (Rua Francisco Gurgel 8852, tel. 84/3219-4188, www.hotelbelohorizonte.com.br, R$82 d), which is American-owned and -operated and sits about one kilometer from the Ponta Negra center at the beginning of the Via Costeira highway. The pool and outdoor bar area look out over the ocean. They do not charge a service tax.

## R$100–200

In the center of the action is the **M Hotel Rosa Nautica** (Rua Erivan França 150, tel. 84/3219-2515, www.rosanautica.com.br, R$95 s and R$120 d), with rooms overlooking the ocean and nightlife in the village. They have Internet service and offer day trips and buggy rentals. The **Aquamarina Praia Hotel** (Av. Engenheiro Roberto Freire 22A, tel. 84/3219-5546, www.hotelaquamarina.com.br, R$60 and R$120 d) is on the highway just inland from the beach and offers rooms with TV and kitchen facilities for up to four people. There's a view of the ocean from the veranda. The **M Visual Praia Hotel** (Rua Francisco Gurgel 9184, tel. 84/3646-4646, www.visualpraiahotel.com.br, R$193 d) is another beachfront hotel just outside the boardwalk area in Ponta Negra with a lovely pool and front deck where breakfast is served. They also have beach service (in front of the hotel) and ample rooms with beach views.

## R$200–500

Walking away from the center of Ponta Negra toward Natal, the **Praia Azul Mar Hotel** (Rua Francisco Gurgel 92, tel. 84/4005-3555, www.praia-azul.com, R$195 with no view and R$270 for an ocean view) is the last hotel with a sidewalk passing in front. The location is excellent, being far from the noise of the nightlife center, but close enough to walk to it (about one kilometer). They have a pool, restaurant, and beach access. Rooms come with air, cable TV, microwave, and mini-kitchen.

## Over R$500

One of the most charming (and expensive) hotels in Ponta Negra is the **M Manary Praia Hotel** (Rua Francisco Gurgel 9067, tel. 84/3219-2900, www.manary.com.br, R$490 s and R$550 d for standard rooms, R$595 s and R$685 d for a suite), which leaves nothing to be desired. Their rooms are spacious and cozy with excellent beds and amenities. Their restaurant is excellent and serves a dynamite breakfast buffet (included) and the pool area is so beautiful that you might not even want to leave for the beach. They have an ocean-view sunning deck and their own agency for day trips to other beaches.

© CHRISTOPHER VAN BUREN

The restaurants and bars along Rua Dr. Manoel A. B. de Araujo are the most charming in Natal.

## Resort-Style Hotels

There are several resort-style hotels along the stretch of beach between Ponta Negra and Natal, which is accessed by the Via Costeira highway. The beaches in this area are not the best for swimming, but are pretty and as good as any for getting some sun. These hotels generally have a huge number of rooms and a somewhat over-the-top infrastructure (several pools, sauna, game areas, etc.). One of the closest to Ponta Negra is the **Natal Mar Hotel** (Av. Sen. Dinarte Mariz 8101, Via Costeira, tel. 84/3219-2121, www.natalmarhotel.com.br, R$300 d), about an hour walk to Ponta Negra on the beach. One of the best in this category is the **Ocean Palace Hotel & Resort** (Via Costeira, Km 11, tel. 84/3219-4144, www.oceanpalace.com.br, R$350 d), which has a stellar deck and pool area overlooking the ocean, outdoor bar, 24-hour service, sushi bar, and large rooms with verandas overlooking the ocean.

## FOOD

Restaurants in Ponta Negra are numerous, if mostly limited to seafood. You can have lunch at one of the boardwalk establishments overlooking the beach, or you can eat at one of the beach kiosks, which usually serve up a few fish and shrimp plates. Of course, the beach kiosks close at sundown, but the boardwalk options are open all day and night. Some great options are clustered along the highway just inland from the boardwalk. These are generally open noon–3 P.M. and 6 P.M.–midnight. Exceptions are noted herein.

### Crepes and Tapiocas

**Cipó Brasil** (Av. Erivan França 5, tel. 84/3219-6368) has an interesting, if cheesy, décor with banana trees and a sand floor. They serve up pizza in their wood-burning oven and a series of crepes for around R$9 each. The best place in all of Brazil for a traditional *tapioca* (northeastern Brazilian-style crepe) is the **◪ Casa de Taipa** (Rua Dr. Manoel A. B. de Araujo 130, tel. 84/3219-5798) near the castle. They have a cozy, beachy atmosphere and serve more than 30 kinds of sweet or salty *tapiocas* for around R$11 each. The **Artesania Crepe Bar** (Rua Senador Teotonio Vilela 146, Ponta Negra, tel.

## OCEAN FARMING IN BRAZIL

Natal and its northern reaches are great places for eating shrimp and lobster. The waters in this area are warm and rich in crustaceans. There are many farms in the open ocean north of Natal, including a large offshore shrimp farm in Praia Muriú. The lobsters in this area are small and it's not uncommon for a person to eat three or four in one meal. Keep in mind that during January–April, lobster hunting is prohibited as this is their reproduction period. You will most likely get frozen lobster during these months. Crabs are generally hunted in the marshes and mangroves around lakes and rivers that empty into the ocean. These northeastern Brazilian crabs are called *guaiamum* and are small and bluish. They don't really offer much meat, but what they have is quite tasty. Crabs reproduce in February and since there is no organized prohibition of crab hunting during this season, you might want to voluntarily refrain from ordering the little critters if you're in town that month.

Cultivation of shellfish dates back to the 13th century in France, where oysters and shellfish were cultured and harvested along the banks of Brittany. In the 19th century, it had become an important practice throughout Europe. Following suit, the fishing communities in South America, particularly Argentina and Chile, began cultivating shrimp and shellfish. In Brazil, oysters and mussels are grown off the coast of Santa Catarina—specifically around the Santa Catarina Island near Florianópolis. By the late 20th century, the world was producing more than 10 million tons of cultured shellfish, and by 2000, the volume surpassed 32 million tons. Besides the Santa Catarina coast, there are *fazendas marinha* (ocean farms) in Cabo Frio, Rio state, and along the northeast coastline, particularly around Natal.

84/3219-5343) in the castle area serves more traditional crepes along with music and drinks.

## Lanchonetes and Casual

There are plenty of simple sandwich and burger joints along the boardwalk. Most have seating on the sidewalk and plenty of hippies hanging out there. The cost for eating cheaply is that you'll be bombarded with people trying to sell you things. Other casual burger and sandwich places are located on Avenida Engenheiro Roberto Freire. There is a **Habib's** (Av. Engenheiro Roberto Freire 8790, Praia Shopping, tel. 84/3215-0580, lunch and dinner daily) fast food restaurant on the far end of Avenida Engenheiro Roberto Freire going toward downtown Natal. **O Sandwich** (Avenida Engenheiro Roberto Freire 2920, tel. 84/3236-2667, lunch and dinner daily) is another good option.

## Meats and Barbecue

**Ponta Negra Grill** (Av. Erivan França 20, tel. 84/3219-3714) is a three-story, wooden structure that looks out on the beach and serves up grilled meats. Open for lunch, but mostly a dinner place. Meals cost about R$25 per person. **Tábua de Carne** (Av. Engenheiro Roberto Freire 3241, tel. 84/3642-1138) serves a number of meat dishes (including the famous local dish, *carne de sol,* or sun-dried meat) with manioc, rice, beans, and other accompaniments. It should set you back about R$25.

## Seafood

**Barraca do Caranguejo** (Av. Erivan França 1180, tel. 84/3219-5069) on the boardwalk has an all-you-can-eat shrimp lunch for only R$15 per person. **Picanha e Cia** (Av. Erivan França 8876, no phone) cooks up various meats or fish in small slices to present as an appetizer or with accompaniments for a full meal. It's about R$20–30 for two people. One of the most famous shrimp restaurants in the area is **Camarões** (Av. Engenheiro Roberto Freire 2610, tel. 84/3219-2424), which serves a multitude of shrimp dishes with various sauces for about R$55 for two. **Samô** (Av. Engenheiro Roberto Freire 9036, tel. 84/3219-3669) is another shrimp and fish establishment with great dishes that serve two. Meals cost about R$45 for two.

## INFORMATION AND SERVICES

There is information available all along Avenida Erivan França, particularly in the travel agencies. Note that these are all private and will give you information with a commercial interest in mind. The nearest public information booth is in the Praia Shopping Natal (Av. Engenheiro Roberto Freire) on the way to downtown Natal from Ponta Negra.

The post office (8 A.M.–5 P.M. Tues.–Fri.) is also located in the Praia Shopping mall. You'll find international ATMs at the Praia Shopping and Natal Shopping Centers. The Banco do Brasil ATM in Ponta Negra also has international access.

The tourist police are located in the Praia Shopping mall (tel. 84/3219-5559).

## GETTING THERE AND AROUND

You can catch a bus or taxi to Ponta Negra from the airport or *rodoviaria*. A taxi will cost around R$35 from the airport and R$25 from the *rodoviaria*. (For information on domestic carriers, see the *Natal* section.)

Within the Ponta Negra area, everything is accessible on foot. It's perfectly safe to walk around at night. To get to downtown Natal (such as the bus station), you can catch a number of buses on Avenida Engenheiro Roberto Freire. Surprisingly, getting to the Praia dos Artistas is not as easy. Buses run infrequently down the Via Costeira. To catch one of these buses, your best bet is to wait at the first stop along the Via Costeira as it turns away from Avenida Engenheiro Roberto Freire. A taxi into Natal will run about R$12–15.

# Beaches Near Natal

The beaches north of Natal are some of the most interesting and popular in the area. There are many ways to visit them, either in packaged tours of the entire north coast, day trips to specific beaches, or on your own by bus, car, or private van. There is so much to see in this direction that a sampler tour is a good idea to give you an overview of the territory. You can then go back and visit your favorite destinations on full- or half-day excursions.

## NORTH OF NATAL

On a sampler of the *litoral norte,* you visit nine beaches (sometimes twelve), including Genipabu, Pitangui, Jacumã, and Muriú. Along the way, you ride through several sand-dune areas and inland lakes. You'll stop for a half-hour to 45-minutes at each major point along the way with a longer lunch stop at one of the beaches (not included). I personally prefer the trip that does not go as far as Maracajaú, leaving it for its own, special trip, which it deserves.

### Redinha

Redinha is the closest beach to the north of Natal, and the entryway to the north coast, just across the River Potengi. To get there, you must cross the river by *balsa* (ferryboat), which takes about ten minutes and costs R$5 for cars and R$1 for foot passengers. The Redinha beach is popular for swimming and sunbathing, with a series of kiosks on the tip that looks back at Natal and the Forte dos Reis Magos. The water is not clear, but very warm. Medium-sized waves make it popular with beginning surfers. Plenty of small boats are docked here and are used by the local fishing community. Within walking distance from the beach is the old church and the Natal Aquario. In the late afternoon, Redinha is an active party spot, especially on weekends. Live music and activities in the beach bars are common. A popular food

NATAL COASTLINE

São Miguel des Touros

Zumbi

Pititinga

MARACAJAÚ

BR 101

Muriú

Jacumã

To Fortaleza

Pitangui

GENIPABU

Redinha
Praia do Forte
Praia dos Artistas

Natal

Parnamirim

Ponta Negra

Cotovelo

Pirangi do Norte
Pirangi do Sol

Tabatinga

Buzios

Barreta

BR 101

Tibau do Sol

Goianinha

Pipa

Barra do Cunhaú

Bahia Formosa

To João Pessoa

SCALE NOT AVAILABLE

item that you can order in the bars along the river is a *tapioca* with *agolinha* (fried needle-fish). The *balsa* operates 9 A.M.–9:30 P.M. every day and boats run every 20 minutes. From the docking point, walk to the right along the beach to get to the main area.

##  Genipabu

Camels in Brazil? Actually, they look right at home on the huge sand dunes of Genipabu. About 30 kilometers north of Natal, Genipabu is probably the area's most popular destination. It offers a little of everything. Start with the enormous sand dunes (more than 50 meters tall and often extremely steep). These lie between the calm, warm ocean and an inland, fresh-water lake, resting among the white dunes. Along the beach are several beach bars with tables and umbrellas for food and drinks. You can walk from your table to the top of a tall dune, where you find the camel rides. A slow walk across the dunes is around R$20 for 10 minutes or R$40 for 30 minutes (prices go up in peak season). Slide back down the dune at the ski-bunda station, where locals will arrange a board for you to use to ski down the sand on your butt.

Buggy rides, whether you hire one from Ponta Negra or arrange one at Genipabu, will take you over a series of dunes with names like Devil's Cauldron and Hollywood Success. You will be asked if you want the ride *com ou sem emoção* (with or without emotion). You can pretty much imagine what the difference is. Just be sure that your sunglasses are on tight and don't wear a hat unless it straps onto your head. Drivers are trustworthy and very familiar with the territory. Only drivers with credentials are allowed into the Genipabu dunes. If you arrive in Genipabu on your own, you can arrange a buggy to take you farther up the coast from here. Ask at your beach kiosk for *vovô* (tel. 84/3225-2015). There is a great little shopping area near the beach bars with more buggy agencies. One half-day buggy package to try goes to Genipabu from Ponta Negra, letting you get to know the many options here, have lunch at one of the kiosks, and ride the dunes there and back again, with a visit to the inland lake.

Natal and Fortaleza

the postcard-perfect point of Genipabu

To get to Genipabu by bus, you can catch the Extremoz line from the Natal bus station every 45 minutes from 5 A.M.–8:30 P.M. Get off at the last beach stop, near the restaurant Terra Nossa.

## Pitangui

Forty-five kilometers from Natal, Pitangui beach is calm and less crowded than other beaches. Here, the water is great for swimming and the inland lake offers an overhead cable for swinging and diving into the water. Lakeside bars have tables in the water, where you can relax with a cold one while dipping your fee in the water.

## Jacumã

The principal attraction at Jacumã (49 kilometers from Natal) is the large fresh-water lake that sits among the area's many tall dunes. Here you'll find everything well organized for the tourist. You can slide down a tall dune into the fresh water or ride a cable over the lake and drop in. Everything is organized for safety and ease. You can hike to a local waterfall over dunes and through tropi-cal forest—just ask for a guided hike to the Cachoeirinha do Rio Pratagi. Most packaged tours of the *litoral norte* make a stop here at Jacumã. All costs at Jacumã are extra.

## Muriú

One of the best locations on the north coast for diving and snorkeling, Muriú is about 50 kilometers from Natal and far less popular than its rival Maracajaú. In low season, Muriú is practically deserted. After stopping on the beach, you board one of the small boats to visit the natural pools and reefs about one kilometer from shore. Afterward, be sure to partake of the fish and shrimp from the local fish farms. The restaurants are simple, but the shrimp is abundant. A good diving excursion from Ponta Negra includes a stop at Muriú before moving on to Maracajaú for a second dive.

## Maracajaú

The north coast's most popular snorkeling spot, Maracajaú sits about 63 kilometers from Natal and offers the most extensive span of rock and coral reefs in the country, some 13 square kilometers of them. Here the water is transparent,

© CHRISTOPHER VAN BUREN

**Camels are a common means of transportation at Genipabu.**

warm (around 28°C), and shallow (1–3 meters deep), making it perfect for viewing tropical fish and lobsters. The main diving area, called *Parrachos,* is about six kilometers from the shore and you can take a fast or slow boat out there for a swim. Afterward, try a fresh fish meal at one of the beach kiosks. On the full-day excursion by van (R$60), you drive to Maracajaú, then take a small boat out to the reefs for several hours of snorkeling. Some agencies offer optional scuba baptism (beginner) dives here and this is a privileged way to try scuba (normally baptisms are done in swimming pools). Try to get a boat that has a covered area on board and consider wearing a tee shirt in the water to keep from burning your back while you're busy snorkeling.

For experienced divers, there are two shipwrecks worth exploring. One is the São Luiz, which went down in 1911 and rests on the sandy bottom, about 30 meters deep, among lobsters and numerous species of fish. The other is called *O Comandante Pessoa,* which sank in 1942 and is a bit more advanced.

## São Miguel de Touros
Marking the tip of Brazil, where the coast changes directly from north/south, to east/west,

Touros is a calm and tranquil place that looks out over the Atlantic Ocean toward Africa. If you want to see as far as possible, then you can climb to the top of the enormous lighthouse, the largest in Brazil and one of the largest in the world. Some 62 meters high, the lighthouse offers an incredible view of the planet's curving surface. You can climb its 300 or so steps from 10 A.M.–2 P.M. Saturday and Sunday. It sits on the Praia do Calcanhar, the most popular of the area. If you want swimming and diving action, the nearby Praia de Perobas has rocky reefs that you can visit by boat (check with the restaurant Polo das Aguas). Praia São José is a nearly deserted beach with calm water, great for swimming. If you decide to spend the night here instead of rushing back to Ponta Negra, try the **Sinos de Vento Pousada** (Praia de Garças, tel. 84/3263-2353, www.sinosdevento.com.br, R$80 d). They have a quaint setup and all rooms have a view of the ocean.

## Galinhos
The 3,000 inhabitants of Galinhos are slowly becoming more accustomed to visitors. Their remote fishing village has been growing in popularity over the years. There are perhaps a dozen *pousadas* there now, offering humble

lodgings with ocean views. Still, because of the difficulty in arriving in Galinhos, it remains a secluded place among the dunes, some 170 kilometers from Natal. You need a good off-road vehicle or a boat to get there. There is only one road in town and you can catch one of the mule taxis to get to your *pousada*. The Galinhos Praia is the principal beach and has calm, warm water and fine, white sand. Among the many things to do in town, a mule ride along the beach to visit the lighthouse and a buggy trip over the dunes to visit the salt fields are two of the highlights. A half-day boat trip up the local river is also an interesting excursion. At night, some of the town folk gather in the small *praça* to have a beer and watch TV.

You might want to spend a night here and enjoy an entire day of activities in the area. You can stay at the simple but charming **Chalé Oasis** (Beira Rio, tel. 84/3552-0024).

There are day trips to Galinhos from Ponta Negra. By van, you drive directly to Galinhos. There you take a boat out on the ocean, visiting the coastline. Some trips include an overnight stay at a local *pousada*. You can take a bus to Galinhos from the Natal *rodoviaria*. The Cabral line leaves Natal at 3:15 P.M., 6 P.M., and 8 P.M. It takes three hours and costs R$18. Buses return at 5:30 A.M., 6 A.M., 8 A.M., 9 A.M., noon, 3 P.M., and 5:30 P.M. The direct bus leaves at noon weekdays and at 6:30 A.M. Sundays. This strange schedule is not made for tourism. It was created to help folks from Galinhos and surrounding areas arrive in Natal in time for work.

### The Road to Fortaleza

Past Galinhos, there are no interesting spots for tourists. Macau is mainly home to a salt company and the ocean is beautiful but unswimmable due to the presence of sharks. Plus, the winds here are very unaccommodating—you can pour yourself a beer and actually miss the cup. The inland city of Mossoró holds no attractions for the traveler except as a lunch stop on the way to Fortaleza. Avoid the packaged trips from Natal to Fortaleza. It's much better to go to Fortaleza on your own and visit the nearby beaches from there. After Galinhos to the north, there's nothing worthwhile until Canoa Quebrada, which is best visited from Fortaleza.

## SOUTH OF NATAL

Many agencies offer guided tours of the entire south coast either by boat or buggy. The buggy trips visit about 12 beaches south of Natal—all the way to Pipa—from around 8 A.M.–4 P.M. You drive much of the way on the highway, visiting Pirangi, Tabatinga, a dune area, and an inland lake. Personally, I prefer the boat tour of the south coast, which goes as far as Pirangi, leaving Pipa for its own, special trip.

### Cotovelo

One of the least-frequented beaches on the south coast, Cotovelo has small waves, shallow water, and white sand and makes a good swimming beach. There are beach kiosks and restaurants and in the little town inland are more food options. To the north, you can see the colorful cliffs of the Barreira do Inferno. It's easy to reach by taxi from Ponta Negra if you want a day at the beach with no agenda. Tip: Bring the phone number of your taxi driver, so you can call him to come pick you up later.

### Pirangi

About 28 kilometers from Natal, Pirangi do Norte and Pirangi do Sul are mostly destinations for diving and snorkeling. Boats park about one kilometer offshore where there are reefs and pools excellent for diving, and they generally never touch land—partially because the beach itself is not suitable for swimming or sunbathing due to both rocky conditions and pollution from the incoming river. The little town of Pirangi, just inland, is where you encounter the world's largest *cajueiro* (cashew tree), which produces more than 100,000 cashews each season. Near the tree is a charming cashew and crafts fair (R$24 per kilo for cashews). It's a great gathering place for night *festas* during the summer season (December–February), which is also cashew-harvest time.

If you arrive from the highway, you can hire one of the boats on the beach to take you out to the pools. Otherwise, there are great half-day boat trips that stop at the pools offshore.

## Buzios

About 35 kilometers from Natal, Buzios is a favorite destination for surfing and water sports, such as wind surfing and kite surfing. There is a stretch of beach with strong waves for surfers and other stretches with calm water for the other sports. Although not the best beach for swimming, due to strong currents and an uneven floor, there are beach kiosks that will help you cool down after heavy sunbathing activity.

## Tabatinga

Tabatinga, some 40 kilometers from Natal, is a beach made for viewing from above. Its rocky coast makes it unsuitable for swimming, but the frequent appearance of dolphins feeding and playing in the waters offshore make it a popular lookout point. On the cliffs above the beach are restaurants and bars that offer excellent views, like Pico de Mirante Restaurante, which serves fish plates and cold beer for around R$25 for two.

## Barreta

Approximately 48 kilometers from Natal, this beach is calm and uncrowded, with dunes and fresh water lakes nearby. There are tide pools and the water is clear and warm. At the Carcará lake, you can swim in transparent water and eat fresh fish, cooked to order at the simple bars on the lake's edge. These bars keep live fish and shrimp in the lake for clients to choose for lunch.

## Tibau do Sul

Clear, warm water, beautiful beaches, and cliffs overlooking dolphins swimming offshore are some of the pleasures of this area, just 75 kilometers from Natal, near Pipa. Tibau do Sul sits on the edge of Lake Guaraíra, which empties into the ocean and offers a picturesque scene, along with excellent diving and snorkeling activities. You can stay at one of the *pousadas* in Tibau or in Pipa nearby.

# Pipa

Pipa's small, innocuous village is calm and quaint during the week. On weekends, it lights up with surfers, young people, and travelers from all over the world, there to catch a glimpse of the charm. Originally a hippie/surfer outpost south of Natal, Pipa has recently been discovered. It's now full of small *pousadas,* excellent restaurants, and classy boutiques. But the surfers and youth have not run away. On weekends, they occupy the town from morning to night. The village in Pipa is only the beginning. What really draws attention to this part of the world are the many different beaches, many of which are frequented by dolphins that have no fear of the humans swimming with them. Sea turtles come to spawn on the beaches north and south. When you're not kicking back on the sand or swimming with the dolphins, you can take a ride across the dunes, snorkel in the rocky reefs offshore, or take a kayak up the river on a nature safari.

Most people get to know Pipa in a couple of days at the end of their trip to Natal. But to really do justice to the place, you'll need 2–3 days.

## SIGHTS AND BEACHES
### M Praia da Pipa

Also known as the Praia do Centro, this is the main spot for beach-sitting activities. Here, a small swath of sandy beach is packed with beach bars (the only beach in the area with kiosks on the sand) that extend into the water itself during high tide. There are plenty of seats, but they still fill up on weekends and during peak season, as this is the gathering place for tourists, surfers, and locals. Beer, fried fish, live

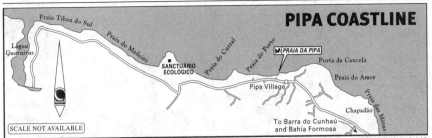

PIPA COASTLINE

Praia Tibau do Sul

Lagoa
Guaraíras

Praia do Madeiro

SANTUÁRIO
ECOLÓGICO

Praia do Curral

Praia do Porto

PRAIA DA PIPA

Porta da Cancela

Praia do Amor

Pipa Village

Chapadão

Praia das Minas

SCALE NOT AVAILABLE

To Barra do Cunhaú
and Bahia Formosa

© AVALON TRAVEL PUBLISHING, INC.

music, and fashion swimwear are the diversions at Praia da Pipa. The water is warm and shallow, but you'll want to avoid the boats that park offshore. There are plenty of inlets for swimming and exploring at low tide. If you can't find a seat on the main beach, walk out to the left to find one of the bars positioned higher up on the cliffs, overlooking the ocean. The cobblestone street that descends to the beach from the far end of the village passes numerous shops and private stands with clothes and local arts and crafts.

## Praia do Porto

Praia do Porto is an extension of Praia da Pipa and a good alternative to the masses that form there. At Porto, you'll find rocky waters not great for swimming (unless you swim out farther from the shore where the boats are), and several *pousadas* and beach bars set up on the cliffs. Most of the area's boats are anchored here.

## Praia do Curral

This beautiful stretch of beach, about one kilometer long, has warm, shallow waters with almost no waves. It is frequently visited by dolphins in the afternoon, but the water is slightly murky green, so it's not possible to see clearly if you swim out to say hello to them. They may come up around you without your knowing—you may hear them breathing nearby and just catch a glimpse as you turn to look. On active days, they are leaping out of the water, playing with tiny fish before eating them. It's easy to swim out to the dolphins as they come in very close to shore, even to the areas where a human

can stand up. The beach itself is quiet and deserted in low season. There are no kiosks here, so bring your own water and refreshments. During low tide, you can walk between the Curral and Pipa beaches in about 30 minutes.

## Santuário Ecológico de Pipa

About three kilometers out of town toward Tibau do Sul is the Santuário Ecológico de Pipa, which is a large wildlife area with numerous trails in which to get lost. If you find your way to the cliffs, you'll get some excellent scenic views. On the northern end of the sanctuary is an access path going down to Praia do Madeiro. It's open from sunrise until 5 P.M. You can enter the sanctuary from the beach if desired. It costs R$4.

## Praia do Madeiro

This stretch of beach is not unlike Curral: shallow, warm, and milky green. But these waters are not frequented by dolphins as much as they are by sea turtles, who make their pilgrimage from the sandy shore to the ocean during the summer months, December–February. The beach itself is calm and practically deserted, since most travelers don't come out this far. Access to the beach is possible at low tide via Praia da Pipa (about a 45 minute walk) or via the access trail at the Santuário Ecológico de Pipa.

## Praia Tibau do Sul

Also known as Cacimbinha, this beach is tranquil and great for swimming, with dolphins often playing offshore. You have to descend down some steep cliffs to get there, but there are rope handrails to help you. Once you get

The charming village of Pipa is full of shops and restaurants.

to the beach, you are privy to one of the most beautiful spots in the Pipa/Tibau area. A few simple kiosks sell fish lunches and beer. This beach is six kilometers from Pipa and you can get there via the local *kombis* (VW buses) that run up and down the coastal highway all day long and well into the evening.

## Lagoa Guarairas

Along the shores of this beautiful lake that opens into the ocean is the town of Tibau do Sul. Here you'll find some charming dining establishments looking out over a breathtaking scene. It's a perfect place to catch the sunset after a long day at the beach. You can swim in the lake or take a boat out snorkeling in the middle of the lake near shallow sandbars. Nearby are the Malembar dunes, where you can catch a buggy ride. Try **Ponta do Pirambu** (Rua Sem Pescoço 252, tel. 84/3246-4333) for a fabulous infrastructure. In the town of Pipa, you can find *passeios* (excursions) that include a lakeside visit and a romp around the dunes. You can also catch a *kombi* to the shores of Lake Guarairas.

## Ponta da Cancela

Also known as the Ponta do Cabo Verde, this area is a hot spot for snorkeling, with numerous underwater reefs and rocky pools. It's only a short walk from the Pipa beach at low tide. You can also take the coastal road and descend at the point.

## Praia do Amor

Just on the other side of the Ponta do Cabo Verde is the Praia do Amor, the most popular beach for surfing in Pipa. Waves are strong here and the water is clear and blue. It's also a great beach for sunbathing and relaxing. There are no kiosks, but locals sell sodas and coconut water from coolers. You can walk here on the coastal highway. Just follow the surfers.

## Chapadao

Looking out over Praia do Amor, the Chapadão is a series of cliffs that are easily accessible on foot, about two kilometers south of Pipa. This is an excellent viewpoint and very romantic at sunset.

## Praia das Minas

This five-kilometer stretch of beach lies at

© CHRISTOPHER VAN BUKEN

**Boats sit offshore from Pipa Beach after the day's fishing activities.**

the bottom of rocky cliffs and can be difficult to access. For that reason, it's a favorite for nudists. The water is warm and clear and the beach is wide and sandy. Here, the sea turtles are frequently found making their nests, which hatch little turtles in the summer months. On the far end is the Praia de Sibaúma, perhaps the best piece of this stretch of beach.

## Barra do Cunhaú

Just a bit south of Praia das Minas, the coastal highway ends at the River Curimataú. There you can take a ferryboat across to Barra do Cunhaú, where you'll find marshes filled with crabs, tide pools, and beautiful beaches. You can hire a boat to take you to the pools for a snorkeling experience or up the river for a water safari. The village of Cunhaú has several establishments for lunch, including **Punto Massimo** (Av. Beira Mar), which serves a variety of seafood and pasta dishes. Only about 12 kilometers from Pipa, Cunhaú makes a great half-day trip. No need for a guided tour, you can catch a *lotação* (local van) to the ferry and go from there.

## Bahia Formosa

About 25 kilometers from Pipa, Bahia Formosa is a stunning series of uninhabited beaches, frequented by dolphins and sea turtles. Boats wait off shore to take you out to the dolphins, where you can stay until sunset. Here, the beaches are also frequented by surfers and there are a few simple restaurants and *pousadas* in case you want to spend the night. If you don't, then be sure to come early for a full day of enjoyment until sunset. You'll be back in Pipa for the night scene.

## ENTERTAINMENT AND NIGHTLIFE

Speaking of the night scene, Pipa is an entirely different place at night. The village lights up with charming boutiques, restaurants, and street vendors, and it seems like everyone in the village is walking up and down the main street. It's easy to find a place you like—just walk around and choose. There are a few side streets that you should explore, so don't just stay on the main drag. A couple of interesting places include the

© CHRISTOPHER VAN BUREN

Praia do Curral is a great place for a walk along the shoreline.

**Blue Bar** (Galeria dos Cores, Av. Baía dos Golfinhos), which plays loud rock music to swarms of visitors until the wee hours. It's got very cool interior décor. **Garagem** (Ladeira do Cruzeiro) is a great place for drinks overlooking the ocean during the day. But it's also popular at night—especially during the full moon, when they have special parties under the natural moonlight. From the main road, turn toward the beach at the "Book Shop" and continue walking down the steps. The rowdiest night spot in Pipa is **Calangos** (Av. Baía dos Golfinhos), on the far end of town. The place gets going at around 2 A.M. when the other bars close their doors. Sundays, they play *forró* dance music and every other day it's a mixture of rock, blues, reggae, and funk.

## OUTDOOR ACTIVITIES

In Pipa, it's possible to do more than surf. Buggy excursions can take you to all the beaches in Pipa and over the dunes of Malembar in Tibau do Sul. It's also possible to take a kayak up the Guarairas Lake and the Rio Curimataú. Boat trips are available to take you all over the coastline, stopping for diving and swimming in the offshore pools. All of this and more is offered by Pipa's foremost tour agency, **Aniyami** (Av. Baía dos Golfinhos 985, tel. 84/3246-2606). They have English- and Spanish-speaking guides. Other agencies can be found along the main village road.

## ACCOMMODATIONS

A decent hotel and a good value is the simple but cozy **Pousada Aconchego** (Rua do Céu 100, tel. 84/3246-2439, conchego@bluemail.ch, R$40 s, R$60 d). They offer individual chalets with ceiling fan, veranda, and hammock. Breakfast is included. **The Oasis Hotel Pousada** (Baía dos Golfinhos 672, tel. 84/3246-2203, oasis@digi.com.br, R$130 d) is located right in the middle of town in the back of a mini shopping gallery. It has a pleasant, tropical décor with a nice pool, garden area, and individual chalets. Rooms have air, king-size bed, and hammocks. Breakfast is included. ⓜ **Pousada Tartaruga** (Av. Baía dos Golfinhos 508, tel.

84/3246-2385, tartarugapipa@uol.com.br, R$185 d) is a charming place just outside the noise of the village center. They have 10 chalet-style rooms with comfortable beds, air, TV, and patio with hammock. The rooms surround a small and inviting swimming pool. To the side is the breakfast deck overlooking the pool where Anna and Tatiani serve an excellent breakfast buffet.

If it's the very best you're after, then you should stay at the ℕ **Toca da Coruja Pousada** (Av. Baía dos Golfinhos 464, tel. 84/3246-2226, www.tocadacoruja.com.br, R$360–850), one of the best *pousadas* on the entire Brazilian coastline. Their huge area is half wildlife preserve and half super-charming *pousada,* with individual chalets, from simple and tropical to super-romantic bungalows. They have a lovely pool and deck area (open 24 hours) with a tropical bar nearby (also 24 hours). One of the finest restaurants in Pipa, it offers three different breakfast buffets for guests (included) with sweet crepes and fried bananas in cinnamon made to order. The rooms have gas-heated water, air, cable TV, and mosquito netting on the comfortable beds. Some rooms include indoor/outdoor shower and a large deck with bathtub and hammocks. You take a long, raised, wooden walkway past wild miniature monkeys to get there. You won't ever want to leave.

## FOOD

A popular café-style eatery is **Casa de Farinha** (Av. Baía dos Golfinhos) on the far end of town. They have Brazilian finger foods, sandwiches, and soft drinks. **Espaço Verde** (Av. Baía dos Golfinhos, from 11:30 A.M. for lunch), located where the avenue forks to the right on the far end of town, has a self-service lunch buffet with a variety of dishes for R$16 per kilo. The fish meals at the beach kiosks on Praia da Pipa are not bad and cost around R$20 for two people.

For dinner, there are numerous restaurants in town. Walk around and look at the menus to help you decide. Here are some suggestions: **São Sebastião** (Rua do Céu) has a cozy interior with a variety of fish and meat dishes for around R$25 per person. ℕ **Vivenda** (Av. Baía dos Golfinhos) specializes in pasta dishes and grilled meats. Their interior decoration is charming and comfortable. Meals are about R$35. **Vila Rocky Point** (Largo São Sebastião) overlooks Praia da Pipa on the path down to the beach. It has a great view and plates for around R$25. Recently reformed. **Panela de Barro** (Rua do Cruzeiro 52) makes up a darned good *moqueca* (fish stew) in a traditional manner with modern touches. This and other dishes from the region are about R$40 for two. **Caligula** (Av. Baía dos Golfinhos) makes a decent pizza and has a great atmosphere. Pizzas are around R$20. Finally, the ℕ **Toca da Coruja Restaurant** (Av. Baía dos Golfinhos 464) at the beginning of town is open to the public and has an excellent menu in a romantic, tropical setting. You have to walk pretty far down their entrance road to get to the restaurant. Meals cost around R$55.

## INFORMATION AND SERVICES

There is no official tourist information at Pipa, but you can get some basic help at the **Pousada Tartaruga** (Av. Baía dos Golfinhos 508, tel. 84/3246-2385). There is a Banco do Brasil across from the bus station at the entrance to town. At the time of this writing, their ATM was not equipped with international systems, but it's worth checking when you get to town. Otherwise, Pipa has no banks. Most establishments accept credit cards, but cash is difficult to come by. Be sure to bring it with you. Sometimes the credit card system is down and cash is the only payment method possible.

A couple websites for information on Pipa are www.pipa.com.br and the Toca da Coruja site: www.tocadacoruja.com.br.

## GETTING THERE

You can take day trips to Pipa by van or buggy. Some trips go almost directly to Pipa, while others are *litoral sul* packages, which include

Pipa with a half-dozen other destinations. The Pipa-only trip is usually made by van. Most of your time is spent exploring the beaches and village of Pipa. This trip (for around R$40) is worthwhile if you don't plan an overnight visit to Pipa, which it deserves. Boat trips at Pipa are optional once you get there. Otherwise, you're usually on your own for the day. Buses leave for Pipa from the main bus station in Natal on the Oceano line (tel. 84/3205-3833, tel. 84/3203-2440, www.expresso-oceano.com.br) for about R$12. Buses leave about every hour from 7:15 A.M.–6:45 P.M. Monday–Saturday

and 8 A.M.–6:30 P.M. Sunday. Return buses leave Pipa from 5 A.M.–6 P.M. Monday–Saturday and 7:30 A.M.–6 P.M. Sunday.

## GETTING AROUND

You can walk anywhere within the village in no time. For distant beaches, you can either schedule an excursion with one of the agencies or get a ride with the *lotação* (privately run vans) that go back and forth along the highway for R$1. Keep in mind that they cram people into these vans to maximize profits. Not exactly comfortable.

# The City of Fortaleza

The French pirates who navigated the waters around Fortaleza in the 1500s, were so enchanted by the place that they made it a main base of operation for years. Legend has it that they buried treasure in the coastal dunes, although you don't see locals digging around in search of it. There are more obvious treasures available for the taking, like the emerald waters and shiny white sandy beaches. Much of Fortaleza's history is linked to the construction and disposition of the city's principal monument, the Nossa Sra. da Assunção fort, which was built in 1649 by the Dutch during their 20-year dominance over the Portuguese in Brazil. After taking over the Portuguese-constructed forts in Natal, Porto Seguro, and Salvador, the Dutch built the Fortaleza fort (called Fort Schoonenborch) as a symbol of their dominance over the Portuguese. By 1654, the Portuguese had won back their dominance in Brazil and expelled the Dutch. The city grew up around the fort and continued until its present-day population of more than 2 million inhabitants. The existing fort was built in 1816 on the site of Fort Schoonenborch.

What you are likely to see of the city of Fortaleza are the beaches and coastal roads that span the nearly 40 kilometers of urban coastline. This coastline is divided into two parts: east and west of the lighthouse. The east side is where you find most of the hotels, the ac-

tive boardwalk of Meireles, and the restaurant-filled area of Iracema. This side is also home to the city's museums, culture centers, and craft markets. The water here is blue and beautiful. Unfortunately, it's also polluted and not appropriate for swimming.

You'll see large industrial ships docking around the lighthouse area, which is not a good area to explore on your own due to risk of assault. Instead, jump over to the west side of the lighthouse to Praia do Futuro, where so many people spend their daylight hours among the numerous beach bars and kiosks. Although the water here is a bit rough, it is clear and clean and good for cooling off. Other highlights in the city of Fortaleza include the outrageous nightlife in Iracema and the active boardwalk scene in Meireles Beach, especially in the afternoon.

## ◪ IRACEMA

Iracema Beach is not so much for daytime use, but for its over-the-top night scene. During the day, you can walk along the sandy beach and admire the ocean (blue and vast). A few beach bars at the entrance to the main area (as you enter Iracema from Meireles Beach) serve cold beer and lunch with a view of the ocean, both day and night. There are some interesting stores and surf shops in this area,

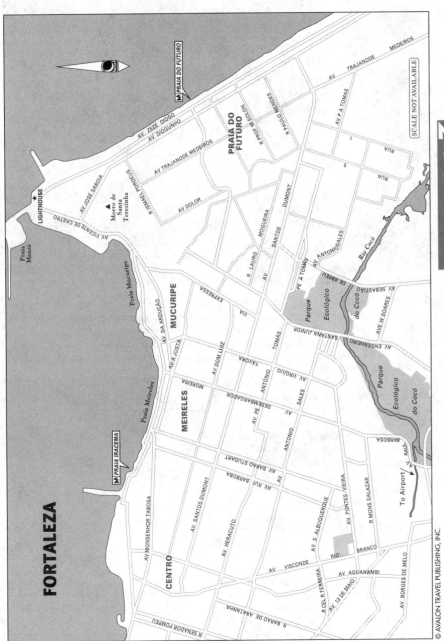

FORTALEZA

SCALE NOT AVAILABLE

LIGHTHOUSE

Praia Mansa

Praia Mucuripe

Praia Meireles

M PRAIA IRACEMA

M PRAIA DO FUTURO

CENTRO

MEIRELES

MUCURIPE

PRAIA DO FUTURO

Morro de Santa Terezinha

Parque Ecológico do Cocó

Parque Ecológico do Cocó

Rio Cocó

To Airport/

AV. ZEZE DIOGO
AV. DIOGUNHO
AV. TRAJANODE MEDEIROS
AV. TRAJANODE MEDEIROS
AV DOLOR
AV. JOSÉ SABOIA
AV. VICENTE DE CASTRO
AV. DA ARDUÇÃO
AV. A JUSTA
AV. MOREIRA
AV. DOM LUIZ
R. ISMAEL PÓRQUS
VIA EXPRESSA
R. LAURO
AV. SANTOS
AV. MOGUEIRA
DUMONT
TÁVORA
AV. ANTONIO
AV. DESEMBARGADOR
AV. SALES
AV. VIRGILIO
TOMAS
AV. PE A TOMAS
AV ANTONIOSALES
DE ABREU
AV SEBASTIAO
AVE W SOARES
AV ENGENHEIRO
SANTANA JUNIOR
AV. TRAJANODE MEDEIROS
AV. A TOMAS
RUA 1
RUA 5
R. PAULO MENDES
R. PROF W MOSSON
AV BARBOSA
AV RAUL
R. MONS SALAZAR
AV. PONTES VIEIRA
AV. S. ALBUQUERQUE
AV. RUI BARBOSA
AV. BARÃO STUDART
AV. ANTONIO
AV. SANTOS DUMONT
AV. HERACUTO
AV MONSENHOR TABOSA
R. SENADOR POMPEU
R. BARÃO DE ARATANHA
R. CEL R. FERREIRA
AV. 13 DE MAIO
AV. VISCONDE
RIO BRANCO
AV. AGUANAMBI
AV. BORGES DE MELO

© AVALON TRAVEL PUBLISHING, INC.

Natal and Fortaleza

© CHRISTOPHER VAN BUREN

**The beaches of Fortaleza stretch along the urban coastline.**

and you can walk out to the pier for a great view of Fortaleza, so it's not all bad during the day. Don't get wet, however, because here the ocean is polluted and not appropriate for swimming (the same is true of all the beaches to the west of the lighthouse).

Around sunset is when Iracema opens its arms (at the least) to visitors. Many people watch the sunset from the pier before choosing a restaurant for dinner. Around the pier area is a feast of restaurants and bars with a number of dance clubs thrown in to boot. There are crowds every night, sampling the diverse cuisine, which runs the spectrum from pizza and beer (mostly around the pier) to sushi and Brazilian *churrasco* (barbecue). Just walking around the area to choose a restaurant is an experience to remember. On the streets you'll find artists, performers, and a lot of people trying to lure you into their restaurant.

For singles, the Iracema scene presents a wide variety of options—from bars to dance clubs. But be warned; prostitution is the norm in clubs here. Ladies of the evening enter clubs early to avoid cover charges, then spend hours hanging around the windows, to tempt single

tourists inside. You'll see bars and clubs with nothing but single women inside until around 11 P.M., when men start entering.

Finally, Iracema is where most of the economical hotel options are located, including

the city's youth hostels. Some of these options are not half bad.

## MEIRELES BEACH BOARDWALK

The main boardwalk area in Fortaleza is essentially the 3.5-kilometer span of Meireles Beach. One side of the avenue, called Avenida Beira Mar, is lined with mid-range hotels and the other side (the beach side) is lined with beach bars, restaurants, small kiosks, shady areas for sitting, and artists selling their wares. Here, you'll see lots of people swimming in the ocean, but at close examination, you'll find that they are mostly low-income Brazilians. Rest assured the water here is quite polluted. If you partake of a cold drink at one of the beach kiosks, you'll also have to fend off the endless flow of people hawking everything from sunglasses to lobsters. Every night, the **Feira de Artesanato,** which is in the main *praça* on the Meireles Boardwalk, presents dozens of local craftspeople selling their handmade clothes and jewelry. Prices are good and you won't be bombarded with salespeople as you walk around (not as much as on the beach anyway). Starting around 5 P.M., the city's tour guides line up on the street by the Feira de Artesanato to present their excursion options. Locals from the area make a practice of jogging and walking up and down the boardwalk in the afternoon, making the area even more active.

## MUCURIPE

Mucuripe Beach is separated from Meireles by rocky tide pools that are interesting to explore (with shoes). The boardwalk activity from Meireles extends into this area, which, otherwise, has fewer beach bars and kiosks and is, therefore, slightly calmer. Most of Fortaleza's luxury hotels are along this stretch of Avenida Beira Mar. The ocean here is not appropriate for swimming.

##  PRAIA DO FUTURO

The principal attractions on these eight kilometers of wide, sandy beach are the numerous *barracas* (beach kiosks), lined up one after the other—more than 50 of them—and spread over most of the eight kilometers. Amazingly, each *barraca* manages to create its own style, from the kind of beach furniture it uses to the

surrounding trees (or lack thereof). Most of these establishments are permanent structures with kitchen facilities in which they cook their seafood marvels, featuring those small Brazilian crabs (only about R$3 each). The most popular of these *barracas* are **Chico do Caranguejo** and **Tropicália,** which pack in the beachgoers and provide food and cold beer, live music, fashion shows, and massages. These also provide table safes for storing your valuables while you dip in the water (the only unpolluted beach in the city). Shady umbrellas, tables, and chairs are a given all along this beach. Vendors are less aggressive here and you can actually have a casual conversation without being interrupted every few minutes. Still, you have to practice saying *não* and wagging your finger to fend them off.

The ocean here is blue and beautiful, but, unfortunately, a bit too rough for any real swimming or water sports. But the water is warm, so don't be afraid to go in up to your waist or thereabouts. The festivities go until around 3:30 P.M. when, tanned and stuffed with crab, the crowd makes its way back to Meireles and Iracema.

Thursdays, the main kiosks go on until late evening with live music productions. Grab a cool, outdoor shower at one of the beach bars and get ready for round two.

One warning: Do not walk all the way to the east end of the beach (toward the lighthouse) past the last of the kiosks, as this part can be dangerous due to risk of assault. Just inland from this area is a fairly large slum. You can walk as far as your legs will take you in the other direction.

You can get to Praia do Futuro by taxi (about R$12 from Iracema) or bus (catch one along Avenida Abolição). Look for the Top Bus line Centro/Praia do Futuro. It seems like there should be more options for getting between Praia do Futuro and Meireles, but transportation options are somewhat limited in Fortaleza.

## SIGHTS

### Centro Cultural Dragão do Mar

Fortaleza gained this modern cultural center (9 A.M.–5 P.M. Tues.–Thurs. and 2–9 P.M. weekends) in the 1990s and it remains one of

one of the many beach bars at Praia do Futuro

the finest in Brazil. The space includes theaters, an amphitheater, a cinema, a library, art galleries, bars, museums, and a planetarium. Around the complex are numerous historical buildings from the town's humble beginnings. You can walk between the center and the Iracema restaurant area. On weekends, there are free music events in the afternoons and evenings. They publish their own monthly *Agenda Cultural* with show listings, which you can find in hotels and tourist information booths.

### Fortaleza de Nossa Sra. de Assunção

The 10th Regiment of the Brazilian military still uses the Fortaleza de Nossa Sra. de Assunção (9 A.M.–5 P.M. weekdays), built in 1816, as a base of operation, but they share it with visitors during the day. It's located near the Centro Cultural Dragão do Mar, just past the Iracema restaurant area.

### Museu de Ceará

Located in a historical building that was once the city hall, the museum (Rua São Paulo 51, 8:30 A.M.–5 P.M. Wed.–Fri. and 8:30 A.M.–noon, R$2) has a collection of anthropological and historical pieces, including fossils, antique clothing, and furniture.

### Theatro José de Alencar

A mixture of neoclassic and art nouveau, the Theatro building (Praça José de Alencar, tel. 85/3252-2324, guided tours every hour 8 A.M.–5 P.M. Mon.–Fri.), located past Iracema, is an architectural monument of the early 20th century. Built in 1908 with a metal structure imported from Scotland, the Theatro hosts music and cultural events and art exhibitions throughout the year.

## ENTERTAINMENT AND NIGHTLIFE

Nightlife activities occur at Iracema and Meireles beaches, with a Thursday-night option at the kiosks of Praia do Futuro. Iracema is the

## WHO OWNS THE BEACHES IN BRAZIL?

In spite of the fact that many of Brazil's beaches look like they are privately owned, Brazilian law establishes all beaches as public property. More specifically, beaches are the property of the municipality in which they are located, controlled by the *prefeitura* (city hall, or mayor's office). The land up to beach (up to but not including the sandy part, although the interpretation varies) can be owned and fenced off. However, it is illegal to block public access to the beach. Of course, this is sometimes a very fuzzy issue, since some natural conditions make it nearly impossible to access certain beaches anyway. But technically speaking, you can enter any beach in Brazil from the ocean and nobody can stop you. In the bay near Paraty, most of the islands are privately owned, but boats take you out to the beaches on those islands, where you can kick back without asking anybody's permission.

Furthermore, most of the *barracas* (beach kiosks), shade umbrellas, and beach chairs are the property of the *prefeitura* and are only rented out to families or individuals to manage. That's why you can sit in just about any beach chair (if it's on the sandy part of the beach) without obligation to order anything from the adjacent bar or kiosk. In fact, you can order from the shrimp or lobster vendors who pass by on foot if you like or even break out your own food. Those running the *barracas* cannot obligate you to use their services because you happen to be sitting in their area.

There are some exceptions. At Pajuçara Beach in Maceió, locals bring tables and chairs to the beach on weekends and sell beers from coolers stashed in their cars. This is, of course, not legal. Some *barracas* are privately owned—along with a piece of property leading up to the beach. Some of these *barracas* get to be rather large and sophisticated, such as those at Praia do Futuro in Fortaleza and in the cities of Maceió, Porto Seguro, and Arraial d'Ajuda. These beaches are famous for their *super-barracas,* some of which have become tourist attractions themselves.

more racy of the two areas, with its clustering of dance clubs and bars. After dinner, Iracema is mostly for young singles action. Remember that there is a lot of prostitution and plenty of theft in these clubs. Keep your eyes open as more than a few gringos have been slipped a Mickey (a drug known in Brazil as *boa noite cinderella*) during a quick trip to the bathroom. They wake up the next morning with no money, no watch, and no pride. If you want to play these radical singles sports, remember not to leave your drink on the table unwatched, don't accept a drink from anyone else's cup, and bring only as much money as you can afford to lose.

The most radical of the Iracema dance clubs is **Pirata,** which is right on the water and operates only on Monday nights, presenting *forró* dancing. You pay approximately R$30 to enter and you should swing by early to get your pass, as scalpers sell *entradas* for as much as R$60 at the last minute. If you want to go to Pirata, my suggestion is to get there early, have some drinks and dances, take a photo, and leave before 1 A.M. when things start getting sleazy. A couple more places in Iracema: **Kaipiras** is a good bar with a bungalow theme, pool table, and barbecue. **Lupus** is a microbrewery restaurant and discotheque, catering to upscale Brazilian tastes: It's fashionable, has everything under one roof, and it's expensive.

The nightlife in Meireles is centered on food. Restaurants stay open late, serving up drinks and dishes for the crowds. Everything along the boardwalk stays open late, and there are restaurants and bars on the other side of the street, too. Try **Beira Mar Grill e Sorvetaria** on the boardwalk for an ice cream. Also, the intersection of Avenida Beira Mar and Avenida Des. Moreira has a number of restaurants that are good for drinks and appetizers (dinner here is not the best).

On Tuesday nights, the **Oasis Club** at the Praia do Futuro features live bands playing oldies music. It's on the beach with the kiosks. Thursday nights, the kiosks stay open with late-night music and activities.

## FESTIVALS AND EVENTS

There are small festivals going on throughout the year in Fortaleza, but with all the crowds and usual activities going on, you might not realize anything special is happening. One festival you can't mistake is **Fortal,** Fortaleza's off-season Carnaval, which the city celebrates the last week of July. Thousands of people fill Avenida Beira Mar to watch the bands and parades. **Carnaval** itself occurs in late February or early March and is spread throughout the city.

## SHOPPING

The secrets of the needlework and lacework in Ceará have been passed down for generations. Originally, it was an Arabic craft, descended from the Portuguese and is, to this day, one of the area's great treasures. Called *labirinto,* it is generally made with white cotton or synthetic fibers and comes in various forms: pillow covers, cup holders, doilies, and table runners. You can find handmade crochet and lacework throughout the city, especially in the arts and crafts fairs. You'll also find leather work, clothing, wood sculpture, and pottery at excellent prices. Some locations include the **Central de Artesanato do Ceará** (Av. Santos Dumont 1589 and in the Centro Cultural Dragão do Mar), the **Feira de Artesanato** on the boardwalk in Meireles (daily at sundown), the **Centro de Turismo** and adjoining shops (Rua Senador Pompeu 350), past Iracema, and at the **Mercado Central** (Av. Alberto Nepomuceno 199). You'll find handmade sand paintings (the kind inside glass jars) at Praia Morro Branco. There is a center of lacework in the Prainha Beach area.

## SPORTS AND RECREATION
### Beach and City Excursions
Visiting the beaches is the principal activity in Fortaleza. This is done by van, bus, or rental car. Van excursions can be made through an agency (there are many, all along Avenida Beira Mar and on the inland highways, Ave-

nida Abolição and Avenida Monsenhor Tabosa) or directly with a representative, when parked along Avenida Beira Mar in the afternoon. The main agency offering van trips is **OceanView** (tel. 85/3219-1300), which has a booth right on the boardwalk at Meireles. Many other agents resell the OceanView excursions or pass their clients to OceanView when they don't have enough to warrant a trip of their own. There is not much variation in the trips or prices and if you go directly through a representative, you can't even be sure if you're getting the exact vehicle that you sign up for—since passing clients back and forth is a common practice. Trips cost R$15–30, depending on the beach, type of van, and guide. The best guides are registered with EMBRATUR and work for OceanView and **SunnyTour** (Av. Prof. Aderbal Nunes Freire 4097, tel. 85/3272-5754). Another good agency is **Limatur** (Av. Almirante Barroso 977, tel. 85/3219-0087). All of these can be spotted in the afternoon at Meireles boardwalk. Some beaches can be visited by municipal bus, including the Vitoria line, which goes to Cambucu.

You can take a boat trip around the city beaches. Schooners leave in the morning from 10 A.M.–noon or at sunset from 4–6 P.M. The sunset trip is the best. Try **LocaMar** (Rua Oswaldo Cruz 01, tel. 85/3242-9326) in Meireles. They embark at the beach in Meireles, around Avenida Beira Mar 4444. Also, **Ceará Saveiros** (Av. Beira Mar 4293, tel. 85/3263-1085). They both will pick you up at your hotel.

Many agencies offer a city tour for R$25. It lasts about 3.5 hours and you get to see many points of interest that you would probably not otherwise see, like the Farol do Mucuripe, which requires passing through a dangerous part of town, not appropriate to try on your own, and the Museu da Arte e Cultura, which is on the opposite side of town.

### Scuba and Snorkeling

A good source for surf, scuba, and snorkeling information and excursions is the **Bio Board** store and agency (Av. Beira Mar 914, tel. 85/3219-8585) in Iracema. They can hook you up with everything you need for these water sports. They have a great juice bar upstairs looking out over the beach. For more serious scuba excursions and lessons, including a dive to a sunken WWII ship, get in touch with **Projeto Netuno** (tel. 85/3264-4114). Cambucu is the best beach for water sports, with an infrastructure for kayaking, windsurfing, and kite surfing.

### Water Slides

Fortaleza is proud of its water park, **Beach Park,** on the far west side of the city. It is said to be the largest coastal water park in the country (there are bigger water parks inland). The park has slides as high as 40 meters (that's more than 10 stories high). You can take a van excursion out to the park for around R$15 (not including the park entrance fee of R$50, which does not include lunch at another R$15–25). If you have a group of four or more, take a taxi out to the park for about R$60 roundtrip. That way, you come and go when you want.

## ACCOMMODATIONS

With a few exceptions, hotels in Fortaleza are divided into three groups. The economical hotels are mostly located in the Iracema area; mid-range hotels can be found in Meireles Beach area; and the top-end hotels are clustered around Mucuripe Beach. Hotels in Fortaleza are generally medium or high-rise buildings with no particular personality—a very urban scene. They double their prices for peak season and most charge a 10-percent service tax on top of the room fee. They all include breakfast with the room. Economical hotels generally have Brazilian-style showers, while mid-range and top-end hotels offer gas-heated water. All exceptions to these rules are listed herein. Prices listed are low-season rates.

### Under R$100

The **Pousada Atalaia** (Av. Beira Mar 814, tel. 85/3219-0755, www.alburguedajuventudeatalaia.com.br, R$45 s and R$60 d) is part of the Hosteling International chain and has a small but cozy setup at the near end of Iracema Beach. Rooms are clean and the *pousada* is well frequented. My only gripe is that you have to pay to store your bags there, even for a few hours until your room is ready. That's low. The **Turismo Praia Hotel** (Av. Beira Mar 894, tel. 85/3219-6133, www.turismopraiahotel.com.br, turismopraia@bol.com.br, R$40 s and R$55 d) is also located on the beachfront of Iracema with simple rooms and no service tax during low season. Beds are not all that comfortable, but the price and location are great. Avoid the other HI hostel, **Albergue Praia de Iracema** (Av. Almirante Barroso 998, tel. 85/3219-3267, www.alberguepraiadeiracema.com.br, R$25 pp) unless you can't find another cheap place to stay. This place is run-down and rooms are large but uncomfortable.

The **Colonial Praia Hotel** (Rua Barão de Aracati 145, tel. 85/4005-4644, www.colonial-praiahotel.com.br, R$80 s and R$90 d) was once a Best Western, which is apparent by its two-story horseshoe layout with a pool in the center (why do they do that?). Nowadays, it's a clean, well-run, and economical hotel just off the beach of Iracema. They have an excellent breakfast buffet. Rooms have air, cable TV, phone, and access to two pools, a patio bar, and restaurant. The "Best Value for the Money" award goes to the **M Ibis Accor Hotel** (Rua Dr. Atualpa Barbosa Lima 660, tel. 85/3219-2121, www.accorhotels.com, R$60 s and R$70 d). They have a streamlined management style with excellent service, very knowledgeable employees, and money-changing service. The entire hotel is new and clean with modern conveniences, including a pool, café, and gas-heated water. Some rooms have an ocean view. Breakfast is not included but available for an additional R$8 (better to walk around the corner to the bakery, where you can get a variety of goodies for breakfast—turn left out the hotel, then another left until you reach the intersection).

A good, economical hotel is the **Vila Azul Praia Hotel** (Rua Paula Barros 251, tel. 85/3242-8855, www.hotelvilaazul.com.br, R$89). They have a small, somewhat older building but offer good service, a decent break-fast, 24-hour room service, Internet (extra), and an excellent location on the edge of Mei-reles and Iracema.

## R$100–200

The **M Sol Jangada Fortaleza Hotel** (Av. Da Abolição 3035, tel. 85/3466-4400, jangada.for@solhotels.com.br, R$100 d) is a clean and relatively modern facility with gym, pool, sauna, and restaurant. Rooms have cable TV, air, phone, gas-heated water, and in-room Internet. The **MareDomus Hotel** (Av. Almirante Barroso 1030, tel. 85/4005-4500, www.maredomushotel.com.br, R$150–180) is in the Iracema area, just off the coastal road. They have decent facilities, with gas-heated water, air, and TV, and are well located. The **Plaza Praia Suites** (Rua Br. de Aracati 94, tel. 85/3455-1616, www.plazasuites.com.br, R$105–140 d) offers a flat-style room with kitchen facilities, ocean views, air, cable TV, and gas-heated water. They have a pool on the top floor with an incredible view and 24-hour room service. There's a great breakfast buffet (included).

The **Praiano Hotel** (Av. Beira Mar 2800, tel. 85/3242-9333, www.hotelseara.com.br, R$135 d) is located in front of the Feira de Artesanato in Meireles and has rooms with ocean views, air, TV, and a pool area.

**Hotel Luzeiros** (Av. Beira Mar 2600, tel. 85/3486-8585, www.hotelluzeiros.com.br, R$150 d, R$350 master with view) is an elegant hotel in Meireles with a nice pool area and artistic interior design. They offer excellent service and a breakfast buffet. Their beachfront location offers many rooms with ocean views, all with gas-heated water, air, and TV. Another beachfront number is the **Hotel Beira Mar** (Av. Beira Mar 3130, tel. 85/3242-5659, www.hotelbeiramar.com.br, R$100 s, R$115 d, R$150 suites with ocean views). They have an impressive reception area with a café in front, pool, and restaurant. Rooms have cable TV, air, and gas-heated water. Some rooms have in-room Internet access. An abundant breakfast buffet is included. Prices go up 30–40 percent in peak season.

**Seara Praia Hotel** (Av. Beira Mar 3080, tel.

85/3242-9555, www.hotelseara.com.br, R$125) is well located in Mucuripe with spacious but drab rooms. They have a nice rooftop pool and hot tub, plus a gym and recreation area.

### R$200–500

The hotels along the beachfront at Praia Mucuripe are luxurious and modern with great service. If you can treat yourself to one of these hotels, you certainly won't be disappointed. Besides great rooms and service, they all offer excursion services, assistance with car rentals, and excellent restaurants.

The **N Ceasar Park Hotel** (Av. Beira Mar 3980, tel. 85/3466-5000, www.ceasarpark-for.com.br, R$350) is one of the most luxurious on the boardwalk. It has all the amenities you can imagine and an excellent location, plus three good restaurants serving Japanese and regional food. The **Othon Palace Hotel** (Av. Beira Mar 2500, tel. 85/3242-7777, www.hoteis-othon.com.br, R$350) is part of the luxury Othon chain, which has hotels in all major cities in Brazil. They have a great restaurant, bar, pool, and game room. Rooms have air, TV, phone, and they have non-smoking floors. One of the best on the beach is the **Meliá Confort** (Av. Beira Mar 3470, tel. 85/3466-5500, www.melia.com.br, R$350–550). They have everything, including a pool, two restaurants, and all kinds of beautiful guests. Finally, try the **Marina Park** (Av. Presidente Castelo Branco 400, tel. 85/3455-9595, www.marinapark.com.br, R$350) if you want a resort-style experience. They have an ocean view, a restaurant, bar, recreation area, pool, gym, and fishing pond. Their 315 rooms have air, TV, and phone.

## FOOD

No matter where you go to eat, you're likely to see *moqueca* on the menu. A regional favorite, *moqueca* is a rich fish stew made with coconut milk and thick palm oil. The fish is usually a meaty, white fish and you get huge chunks of it, together with vegetables, potatoes, and other ingredients. It is a dish for two. Some restaurants make a *lite moqueca,* with soy milk

as an alternative to coconut milk and olive oil instead of palm oil. These are generally made to suit the foreign palette (traditional *moqueca* has been known to weigh heavy on the foreign stomach). Another regional favorite is crab— those tiny, blue crustaceans that flourish in the northeast of Brazil, due to all the marsh lands in this region.

The most interesting restaurants are in the Iracema area and are mostly frequented for dinner, although many are open for lunch. There are some worthwhile places in Meireles and a few spread around town. Most people have lunch at whichever beach they happen to be at. Of course, crab at Praia do Futuro is a well-known favorite. Hours of operation for restaurants are generally noon–3 P.M. and 6 P.M.–midnight. Exceptions are noted herein.

### Casual Dining

There are some great deals on pizza and soda along the pier at Iracema. Pizzerias there usually offer some kind of special, such as a pizza and 2-liter soda for R$10. There are some casual eateries, including a couple bakeries along Avenida Monsenhor Tabosa. There you can find pre-made sandwiches or have them heat up a *misto quente* (hot ham and cheese) on the spot. You'll find *lanchonetes* with typical lunch plates in the Mercado Central. A great place for frozen *açaí* and other juices is above the **Bio Board** store (Av. Beira Mar 914, 9 A.M.–9 P.M.).

### International

The best Italian restaurant in town is **Pulcinella** (Rua Osvaldo Cruz 640) in Meireles. They offer pasta dishes, seafood, and grilled meats, along with some imported wines. Meals are around R$40. There are sushi restaurants and Portuguese food options in the Iracema area; however, they are not known to be the best options in town. Instead, try **La Paella** (Rua Idelfonso Albano 603, Meireles) for Spanish food or **La Marine** (Av. Pres. Castelo Branco 400) for French food. This one is located inside the Marina Park Hotel and has an excellent ocean view. There is also **La Nuit** (Rua dos Tabajaras 440, Iracema) for French food.

Japanese cuisine is available in the Hotel Cesar Park at **Mariko** (Av. Beira Mar 3980), which has good sushi, but comes off a bit pricey. A better value is **Mikado** (Av. Br. de Studart 600) for around R$40 per person.

### Seafood and Regional Food
**Sobre o Mar** (Rua dos Tremembés 2) in Iracema has a beautiful location with two floors overlooking the ocean. The all-wood structure is elegant and perfect for lunch or afternoon drinks, when you can still see the ocean. Lobster and crab meals are around R$35 per person. They have a great executive lunch plate for only around R$10. Next door is **M A Taska,** which serves char-broiled lobster and seafood in a more casual atmosphere. Plates are about R$25 per person. **Marquinhos** (Av. Beira Mar 4566) in Mucuripe has some good fish and shrimp plates. They are on the boardwalk near the Othon Palace Hotel. Meals go for around R$35. One of the city's most well-known seafood restaurants is **Osmar** (Morro de Santa Terezinha), which is on the hill near the lighthouse. In their simple environment, they serve excellent lobster with butter sauce, shrimp with garlic sauce, and fried fish—all for around R$20 per person. Take a taxi to and from the Morro de Santa Terezinha.

There are two great restaurants with regional dishes in Iracema. **Colher de Pau** (Rua dos Tabajaras 412) serves the famous *carne de sol* (dried meat) in various ways for around R$20 and **La Bhéme** (Rua dos Tabajaras 380) has a few different *moqueca* dishes for around R$30 for two.

## INFORMATION AND SERVICES

The **Centro de Turismo** (Rua Senador Pompeu 350, 8 A.M.–6 P.M. Mon.–Sat. and 8 A.M.–noon Sun.) has information and maps for visitors. It's located in a historical building that was once the city jail and includes adjoining shops and museums, such as the Museum of Popular Art and Culture. It's worth a visit while you're out on that end of town, checking out the Theatro José de Alencar and the Fortaleza.

There is an information trailer at the Feira de Artesanato in Meireles. However, it's often unmanned and lacks information. Instead, try the OceanView Turismo office in the same *praça*. It is not a tourist information office, but there they have most any information you need.

**Aldeia Zen** (Rua Julio Ibiapina 89, tel. 85/3242-6334) is a massage and bodywork space. They offer a 5-hour package for only R$100 and you can use your hours for just about any of their services, including shiatsu, lymphatic massage, and Swedish, among others.

The tourist police are at tel. 85/3261-3769. A good website for information on Fortaleza is www.ceara.com.br/fortaleza.

### Consulates
There are numerous foreign consulates in Fortaleza. Some of them include:
- Austria (Rua Kasel 391A, Parque Manibura, tel. 85/3278-6251)
- Germany (Rua Dr. José Lourenço 2244, tel. 85/3246-2833)
- Belgium (Rua Eduardo Garcia 909, tel. 85/3261-2451)
- Spain (Av. Santos Dumont 2727, sala 211, tel. 85/3264-0055)
- United States (Rua Nogueira Acioly 891, tel. 85/3252-1539)
- France (Rua Boris 90, tel. 85/3254-2822)
- Great Britain (Sede Grupo Edson Queiroz, Praça da Imprensa, tel. 85/3466-8888)
- Netherlands (Av. Pe. Antônio Tomás 386, tel. 85/3461-2331)
- Italy (Rua E 80, Pq. Washington Soares, tel. 85/3273-2606)

## GETTING THERE

All the domestic airlines in Brazil fly into Fortaleza, including Vasp, Varig, and TAM. If you come from Rio or São Paulo, you can check out the discount airlines, Fly (tel. 11/3256-0370) and ViaBrasil (tel. 0800/124-848). Buses come from all over the country, as well. From Natal, the Viação Nordeste line has five or six buses leaving every day for around R$55. Times are 5:15 A.M., 9 A.M., 3 P.M., 9:15 P.M., and midnight (the last two are not available on Saturdays). Every day at noon, there is an executive bus for R$70. The Fortaleza *rodoviaria* is at tel. 85/3256-2100.

## GETTING AROUND

Avenida Beira Mar is about five kilometers long, from Iracema to Mucuripe. For most, that's well within walking limits, especially in the cool of the evening. However, to get to Praia do Futuro, you should get a taxi, which will cost around R$12. There are also buses running to Praia do Futuro along Avenida Abolição and Avenida Santos Dumont every 15 minutes for less than R$3. Whether or not you choose to walk from one end of Praia do Futuro to the other (eight kilometers), is another thing altogether. Most of the action in Praia do Futuro is slightly east of the middle.

Although it's popular to rent a dune buggy for cruising around the beaches of Fortaleza, you're probably better off with a normal car. High winds and sand make an open-air buggy impractical on the highways. Rental-car agencies at the airport include **Avis** (tel. 85/3477-1303), **Hertz** (tel. 85/3477-5055, tel. 85/3477-5051, tel. 85/3242-5425), and **Localiza** (tel. 85/3477-5050). **Loca Buggy** (Av. Abolição 2950, tel. 85/3242-6945) rents cars, jeeps, and buggies. Buggies go for about R$100 per day and R$.50 for each kilometer over 50. Jeeps are R$350 per day for 200 kilometers and R$1 each additional. Use this to compare with other rental services. There are several along Avenida Abolição and in the Meireles boardwalk area. A few of note are **Fortaleza Rent-a-Car** (Av. Abolição 3524, tel. 85/3263-2981), **Aldeota Locação e Turismo** (Av. Abolição, 3802, tel. 85/3263-4200), and **Sol Rent-a-Car** (Av. Monsenhor Tabosa 1181, tel. 85/3219-4433).

# Beaches Near Fortaleza

## EAST OF FORTALEZA

The São Benedito bus line (tel. 85/3272-1999) runs buses to the eastern coastline of Fortaleza. You can get off at just about any of the beaches you like, but with so many stops, be prepared for a long trip if you're planning to hit distant shores. The cost is R$3–15.

### Caponga

Locals go out to Caponga on weekends because it has plenty of kiosks and restaurant options; many are quite economical. During the week, it's relatively peaceful and the water is great for swimming. Trips often combine this beach with a stop in Prainha and its Centro das Rendeiros, an arts and crafts center where lacework is created every day. Of course, the results are all for sale.

### Morro Branco and Fontes

These two beaches go together, since they are near one another and excursions are designed to take you through them both. You start at the little town of Marina de Morro Branco, looking out over the ocean from the cliffs above. There you can watch local artisans making sand paintings in jars using the colored sand of the region. The small jars cost only R$5. From there, you descend to the beach through a series of sandy cliffs that overlook the ocean. You will hear the words *"No Limite"* (pronounced noo leeMEECH) a lot at this point. This was the name of a popular reality TV show that was filmed among these cliffs. If you hired a buggy for the day (worthwhile at about R$25 per person), you will then be driven along the coast to see a cave that is visible only at low tide and drips fresh water from the ceiling. Then it's off to a fresh-water lake in the middle of the dunes and a sandy, ski-bunda slope. Finally, it's back to a beach resort for lunch. If possible, combine the Morro Branco/Fontes excursion with another beach, as there is plenty of time after lunch to see another one. But you're also

© CHRISTOPHER VAN BUREN

**the sandy cliffs of Morro Branco, east of Fortaleza**

welcome to hang out at the resort and enjoy their lovely pool.

## Canoa Quebrada

In the '70s, Canoa Quebrada was another hippie, surfer town on the far outskirts of a large coastal city, in this case, Fortaleza. But like many hippie towns along the coast of Brazil, this one grew into a popular tourist village. Now the town is full of bars, restaurants, and *pousadas* with tourists visiting in busloads from Fortaleza for the day. Water sports are popular here, including paragliding and the banana-boat experience (being pulled behind a speedboat on a cylindrical tube). You can rent an all-terrain vehicle to explore the dunes and beaches or take a buggy trip to Ponta Grossa (the best excursion offered), where you can have lobsters for lunch at a beachfront kiosk. At night, most of the tourists go back to Fortaleza and leave the place more quiet and peaceful. If you have decided to sleep over, you can spend the late afternoon watching the tide roll in, then catch the beautiful sunset over the water from atop a tall dune. The next morning, you'll have time to

walk down to the semi-deserted beach and enjoy a nice swim before the day's tourists arrive from the city.

The most popular beach is **Canoa Quebrada Praia,** which gets crowded on weekends and summer days. It's right in front of the village. To the right is **Majorlândia,** about eight kilometers away. There you'll find a simple fishing village and some local sand paintings. Next is **Praia Lagoa do Mato,** which has sand dunes and beautiful coconut trees all around. About 50 kilometers to the east is **Ponta Grossa Beach,** with dunes, red-rock cliffs, and a small fishing village nearby. There are also some reefs offshore for snorkeling and guides can take you out from the village. The next beach to the east is **Redondas,** also excellent for snorkeling.

Most accommodations are clustered around the Canoa Quebrada Praia, the most popular of the beaches. Here, you find white sand and calm waters, perfect for swimming. On full moons and during peak season, this beach is the spot for night beach parties with live music and dancing. These parties are called luaus but have little resemblance to a Hawai-

Natal and Fortaleza

© CHRISTOPHER VAN BUREN

**Kite surfing is the water sport of choice at Cambucu Beach.**

ian luau. The rest of the time, you'll find night activities on Broadway, where there are several different bars for the choosing.

The best hotel in the area is the **Best Western Canoa Quebrada** (Av. Porto Canoa 500, tel. 88/3421-9000, www.portocanoa.com.br, R$185), which is right on the beach and has a large patio area that is open to the public. Their facilities include beach service, pool, tennis, and transportation in their little golf carts. Some *pousadas* in Canoa Quebrada include **Pousada Lua Morena** (in the village, tel. 88/3421-7030, www.luamorena.com, R$65 s, R$85 d) with individual chalets and swimming pool. Some rooms have an ocean view. **Pousada Latitude** (Praia Canoa Quebrada, tel. 88/3421-7041, R$60 s, R$75 d) is in the active beach area. They have TV, air, and a bar. Finally, **Pousada California** (Praia Canoa Quebrada, tel. 88/3421-7039, R$65 s, R$80 d) has more than 20 small rooms with air and TV. They also have a swimming pool and bar.

Have lunch at a *barraca* on whichever beach you happen to be on at lunchtime. For dinner, however, try **Artesanal** (Praia Canoa Quebrada) for fish, pasta, and various other dishes. Also, **Bistrô Natural** (Rua Dragão do Mar) in the village has a decent menu at a good price.

Day trips to Canoa Quebrada go for around R$30. You can catch a bus from the Fortaleza bus terminal on the Nordeste line (about R$10) or the São Benedito and Guanabara lines (about R$12). These buses take you as far as Aracati, where you can catch a bus every hour into Canoa Quebrada for less than R$3 or take a taxi for R$20.

## WEST OF FORTALEZA
### Cambucu

About 30 kilometers from Fortaleza, Cambucu is probably the most popular beach destination outside of the city. Here you'll find a cluster of large beach kiosks that serve lunch and cold beer—either out on the sand or up in the comfort of their structure. Walk along this part of the beach and a representative from every restaurant/kiosk will greet you and invite you into his place, which he will swear is the cheapest on the beach. Other options include kite surfing and wind surfing (with lessons if desired), buggy rides, horseback rides (somewhat lame, by appearances), para-jeep rides, and plenty of secluded coast in both directions for getting away from the crowds. The water is warm and shallow, with mild waves, in most parts. One of the best places to make camp is at the last establishment on the beach, **Velas do Cambucu.** Here, they have great outdoor seats with plenty of shade, a pool, and lockers for keeping your stuff safe. All available for their customers (i.e., anyone sitting and ordering from their bar, although you are not obligated to have lunch there, but can walk to one of the other kiosks nearby). They also offer buggy trips for R$20 per person.

You can get to Cambucu by city bus. Take the Vitoria (tel. 85/3342-1148) line on Avenida Abolição at 8 A.M., 10:40 A.M., or 1:10 P.M. for less than R$4 (more buses during peak season). Take it to the last stop, which is right in front of the Velas do Cambucu restaurant. Return buses leave at 1 P.M.,
2:30 P.M., and 5 P.M. Packaged excursions go to Cambucu for around R$15.

## Taiba

Tall windmills capturing thermoelectric energy along the dunes near the ocean stand in strong contrast to the humble fishing village that is Taiba. Some 67 kilometers from Fortaleza, Taiba is a good beach to visit, due to its white, sandy beaches and calm waters. You can take the Brasileiro bus line (tel. 85/3256-4483) to Taiba from Fortaleza for less than R$5.

## Lagoinha

Fenced-in by large dunes, Lagoinha has only one road accessing it from the main highway. As such, it remains an almost virgin beach in parts and definitely one of the prettiest beaches on the Fortaleza coast. *Jangadas* (small fishing boats) are a common sight here, as fishermen come in and out with their daily catches. On the right side of the beach sit a few restaurants and *pousadas*. Trips to Lago-

ATVs are just one of the diversions at Cambucu Beach.

© CHRISTOPHER VAN BUREN

inha leave from Fortaleza for about R$25 and stay the entire day.

# JERIQUAQUARA

When Jeriquaquara (or Jeri to the locals) obtained electricity only a few short years ago, everyone thought it was on its way out. Modern civilization had arrived to destroy the unspoiled feeling of the place. Surprisingly, Jeriquaquara remains a tropical paradise on the upper coast of Brazil—maybe just the paradise you've been looking for. But paradise is not easily attained. Some 320 kilometers (six hours by bus) from Fortaleza, Jeri is too far for a simple day trip. In fact, most visitors to Fortaleza never make it to Jeriquaquara, as it requires an overnight stay (although the more savvy visitors go directly to Jeri and stay there the entire time). To really do it right, you should hang out for at least two days. Besides some of the most beautiful beaches surrounded by fluffy sand dunes and palm trees, you'll find some of the friendliest, most laid-back people in the world. Although Jeri has several charming *pousadas* and a few sandy streets lined with bars and restaurants, it still has a very undiscovered feel to it. Perhaps because signs of progress have not spoiled the place. Electric lines, for example, were installed underground, making it possible to see the stars at night—an obligatory part of any tropical paradise.

Accommodations in Jeriquaquara are not outrageously expensive, nor is the food. What you'll find a bit excessive are the prices for transportation to the major beaches and lakes. Buggies, which are about the only way to get around, cost R$120–180 for standard trips that last about a half-day. It's best if you can put together a group of four people to split the cost and also dictate what you want to see and for how long. Otherwise, the buggy drivers will take you on their programmed trips.

## Buggy Excursions

After hiking up one of the tall dunes to get a view of the coastline, the best way to get to know Jeri is by dune buggy. Not to be missed is the ride out to **Lagoa Paraíso** and **Lagoa Azul,** two fresh-water lakes in the middle of the dunes, formed by rainwater. Paraíso is clear and blue and fantastic for swimming, with white sand and charming beach bungalows selling refreshments—it's even better than the ocean. The lake is surrounded by coconut trees and small boats pass along the surface. Motorized water vehicles are prohibited, so it remains peaceful. Lagoa Azul is equally clear and beautiful and you can go out to a sandbar in the middle, where there is a restaurant with tables and chairs partially in the water. You can rent a mask and snorkel and check out the underwater world. Buggy rides to Lagoa Paraíso and Lagoa Azul cost around R$120 for four people. Again, if you are in a group, you can dictate where you'd like to go and how long you'd like to stay.

Several of the Jeri beaches are worth exploring and you can walk to one of the most popular, called **Pedra Furada.** A canoe trip costs around R$15 and renting a ski for surfing the dunes is about R$5 per hour. Windsurfing equipment is also rather expensive at about R$150 per day, but Jeri is an excellent place for practicing the sport—given the constant winds. In the late afternoon, go up the tall dune called *Duna do Por do Sol* to look out over the beach and the boats coming in from their day of fishing. The sunset from there is spectacular. And it's still free.

## Accommodations

In spite of its distance from Fortaleza, Jeri still manages to draw plenty of tourists during peak season. Reservations at *pousadas* are recommended. Remember that prices go up significantly during peak season (December–February). Try the **Pousada do Cajú** (on the main road, tel. 88/9962-9099, R$55 d in low season). They have ceiling fans in the rooms. The **Pousada Calanda** (in the village, tel. 88/3669-2285, R$40 or R$55) has simple rooms with ceiling fan or air-conditioning. The **Jerimar** (tel. 88/3961-0102, R$55 d)

© CHRISTOPHER VAN BURFN

Boats rest on the beach, awaiting their captains at Canoa Quebrada.

hotel is in the village and has air-conditioning. The nicest hotel in Jeri is **Vila Kalango** (on the beach, tel. 88/3669-2290, R$100 d), with charming chalets, ocean views, and ceiling fans. They have an excellent view of the sunset from their restaurant.

## Food and Nightlife

The **Seu Antonio** bakery opens at 2 A.M. with hot bread and sweets—a great stop after a late night in the bars. The **Restaurante Savannah** (Rua do Forró) has Arabic sandwiches in pita bread for around R$6, among other treats. An economical lunch plate is available at **Nativa's** in the village. They have a *prato feito,* or PF, for around R$6. For more sophisticated digs, try the **Restaurante Sabor da Terra** on the main street (Rua do Forró) with fish and fowl plates for around R$20. One of the best restaurants in town is **Chocolate** (Rua do Forró 213) for their great seafood paella, shellfish, and pasta dishes. The main bar in town is **Planeta Jeri,** where they play music until late at night. Rua do Forró has the most animated night scene in Jeri. You can

check in the various establishments for flyers announcing beach parties (luaus), which occur regularly. It's a good idea to bring a flashlight with you when you go out at night in Jeri as there are few streetlights.

## Information and Services

There are no banks in Jeriquaquara, so it's a good idea to bring cash, particularly in small bills (nobody likes to change large bills). Plenty of places accept credit cards, but not all. Since most of the residents in Jeriquaquara are foreigners, you'll have no problem finding someone who can speak to you (in your own language) about everything the town has to offer.

## Getting There and Around

There are several ways to arrive at Jeriquaquara. The most common is to catch one of the buses leaving Fortaleza, which offer one-way passage for around R$35. One company offering this is Redenção (tel. 85/3256-2018, in Jeri: tel. 88/3669-2000). Buses leave at 9:30 A.M. and 5:30 P.M. You can also rent

© CHRISTOPHER VAN BUREN

**horseback rides on the beach at Fortaleza**

a dune buggy to make the trip. Just remember that the final few kilometers are sandy, off-road conditions. Most of the tour agencies in Meireles offer Jeriquaquara packages for around R$160 per person, which includes transportation, accommodations, and some light, guided tours. A final option is to fly. A small plane takes about one hour to make the trip (it's another hour from the airport to Jeriquaquara) and charges around R$500. Try Corretas Linhas Aéreas (tel. 85/3272-3288).

# Recife and Olinda

Recife and Olinda have changed a lot over the years. During the first half of the 20th century, when Brazil was enjoying a sort of cultural renaissance (centered mostly in Rio de Janeiro and São Paulo), Recife became known as the Copacabana of the northeast, mostly due to the Praia Boa Viagem. In fact, Boa Viagem was the only real attraction in town; Olinda and the old city center were in a bad state of disrepair. But in the 1980s, the local government began a series of restorations and today Old Recife is a colorful and pristine flash of colonial Brazil. There you can see architecture from the early

days of the colonization, such as the complex of buildings along Rua Bom Jesus. The great government buildings around Praça da República almost take you back in time, and the waterfront complex from the 1700s along Rua da Aurora is a work of art.

Olinda's restoration lagged behind somewhat, even after being named a World Heritage Site by UNESCO in 1982. But one by one, the historical churches and monuments of the town are being restored and you can even see the restoration laboratory in action in the Amparo church. The restored main

# Must-Sees

**M Old Recife:** Mixed in among the modern high-rise buildings and traffic lights of downtown Recife are dozens of 17th-, 18th-, and 19th-century buildings, faithfully restored, looking every bit as majestic as they did hundreds of years ago—except at night, when they light up the city with a flash of old, colonial Brazil (page 300).

**M Convento de São Francisco:** As the church comes into view perched on an Olinda hillside with its back to the ocean, you realize that this was indeed a perfect spot to build the first village in the territory. More than 450 years later, visitors walk up the same steep streets to this convent that sits overlooking the same blue ocean (page 314).

Convento de São Francisco

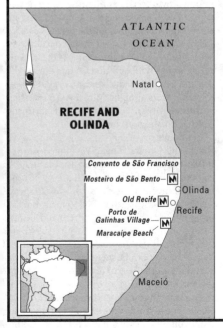

**M Mosteiro de São Bento:** The winner of the "Most Stunning Baroque Altar" award goes wholeheartedly to the main altar in the Igreja São Bento. Standing some 14 meters high, the intricate carving and gold leaf may bring you to your knees, if not to pray (page 315).

**M Porto de Galinhas Village:** After a long day swimming and snorkeling along the reefs offshore, there's nothing better than to choose your favorite perch, and watch the village light up for the evening (page 324).

**M Maracaípe Beach:** At high tide, the Maracaípe River basin fills with ocean water, the crabs come out to feed, and you can go snorkeling in search of the seahorses that flourish in these waters (page 328).

COURTESY OF CHRISTIAN KNEPPER/EMBRATUR

Recife and Olinda

Recife and Olinda

altar in the Mosteiro São Bento is one of the finest specimens of baroque sacred art in the world.

Recife borrows its name from the large *arrecifes* (rocky reefs) that sit some 200 meters from shore and block the incoming tide, making the surf calm and tranquil. The natural formation of these reefs creates something of a bay where the city's two principal rivers empty into the ocean. There, the reefs almost totally block access between the mouths of the rivers and the ocean, making the area a perfect shipping port. Inside the reefs are two islands where Old Recife and the new downtown shake hands. To the north is the Island of Itamaraca, home to one of the offices of the Peixe Boi Eco-Center, a habitat and preservation center for the sea cows of Brazil's northern coastline (a salt-water cousin to the manatee). This is also a great area for scuba diving. The southern coast is full of picture-perfect beaches, some deserted and some semi-urbanized. The water is extremely warm and clear and snorkeling excursions are a highlight at many of the beaches. One of the must-sees of the area is Porto de Galinhas, a quaint coastal village along the southern shores of Recife that has one of the best reef areas for diving and snorkeling in the country, plus seahorse preservation areas and plenty of radical water sports and inviting beach kiosks.

One of Brazil's largest and most turbulent cities, Recife suffers from a few modern problems. Pollution of the area's rivers and canals makes it difficult to get away from the stench. These conditions make Praia de Boa Viagem a great place for a half-day walk along the boardwalk and nothing more. Keep in mind that weekends can get crowded with locals. Within the city you have traffic, noise, and crime.

This mix of attractions and repulsions makes Recife a challenging destination for foreigners. But with a little planning and some good background information, it's possible to have a smooth trip through the area with a minimum of inconveniences and a maximum of pleasures.

## PLANNING YOUR TIME

Many travelers are baffled by Recife and Olinda and spend their first few days just getting a handle on the place. The three main areas—Olinda, Old Recife, and Boa Viagem—are spread about 10 kilometers apart. Transportation between them is not as obvious or as easy as it should be and where you choose to sleep ends up having a big influence on how you approach your entire visit.

Here's a piece of advice to help you get the most out of this area: Forget about Boa Viagem, except for a possible dinner out. Focus instead on Old Recife and Olinda. Most guides will tell you the opposite, suggesting that you set up camp in Boa Viagem and take day trips into the downtown area and Olinda. This is probably because Boa Viagem is full of hotels and restaurants. But the truth is, you'll be much happier staying in Olinda or in a hotel in downtown Recife and taking one half-day trip to Boa Viagem to see the beach. Despite everything you hear about the place, Boa Viagem is not where you want to spend your time. Most likely, you'll be checking out the historical sights of Old Recife and Olinda during the day and heading to the bars and restaurants in the same areas at night. When you're satisfied with those areas, you'll want to head to the beaches north and south of the city.

Four days is a decent amount of time to see Recife and Olinda. That gives you one day to walk around Old Recife and another day to walk the town of Olinda (with plenty of time for coffee breaks along the way). You can spend a half-day on the beach in Boa Viagem and the other half checking out the Brennand installations on the outskirts of town (or substitute this for a full day at the beach if you prefer). Your final day can be spent at the Praia Maria Farinha and the Island of Coroa do Avião to the north—if you get up early enough to catch the catamaran tour. Spend your nights in Old Recife and Olinda. By the end of these four days, you'll be ready for some fresh air. . . literally! Thankfully, the beach villages of Porto de Galinhas and Tamandaré are nearby to offer just what you're looking for. Plan another 2–4 days for those.

## HISTORY

Captain Duarte Coelho was not thrilled when he finally came to settle onto his Brazilian lands, given to him by King João III to govern and populate for the Portuguese Crown. Fourteen other Portuguese captains were given lands in Brazil. Coelho's particular slice—the part that would become the state of Pernambuco—was riddled with marshlands and occupied by numerous indigenous tribes. After several lackluster attempts at establishing a stronghold on his land, he finally made his way to a summit overlooking the ocean. Leading up to the summit were numerous hills, each with an excellent view of the coast—perfect for keeping an eye out for intruders offshore. That was 1535. In 1537,

the village of Olinda was founded on Coelho's chosen site.

The Olinda colonists got into the sugarcane business and were soon supplying Portugal with the stuff. The satellite port of Recife was established to support sugar plantations around Olinda, which had become the capital of the Pernambuco territory. Olinda's success and popularity grew. By the early 1600s, Olinda had come to be known as Little Lisbon. Churches and seminaries were built upon the many hilltops and as a result, art, sculpture, music, and architecture flourished in their connection to the churches. Only Salvador, to the south, rivaled Olinda in its successful colonization efforts and lucrative exports.

It wasn't long before the Dutch decided they wanted a piece of the action and, starting in Salvador in 1624, began a series of attacks on the coastal cities of Brazil. They arrived in Olinda in the year 1630 and burned it to the

### THE HISTORY OF PERNAMBUCO ACCORDING TO SAMBA

Samba lyrics often recount the stories of Brazil's history. This one, called "Onde O Brasil Aprendeu a Liberdade" (Where Brazil Learned Freedom), is a perfect summary of the history of Pernambuco. It was written in 1971 by Martinho da Vila, one of Brazil's most beloved *sambistas.*

*Aprendeu-se liberdade* (They learned freedom)/*Combatendo em Guararapes* (At war in Guararapes)/*Entre fleshas e tacapes* (Among arrows and clubs)/ *Facas, fuzis e canhões* (Knives, rifles and cannons)/*Brasileiros irmanados* (Brazilians in brotherhood)/*Sem senhores, sem senzala* (Without lords, without slave quarters)/*E a senhora dos prazeres* (And the lady of pleasures)/ *Transformando pedra em bala* (Turning stones into bullets)

*Bom Nassau já foi embora* (Good, Nassau has now gone away)/*Fez-se a evolução* (Made himself an evolution)/*E a Festa da Pitomba* (And the Festa da Pitomba)/*É reconstituição* (Is the reconstruction)

*Jangadas ao mar!* (Boats to the ocean!)/*Para buscar lagosta* (To pick up lobsters)/ *Para levar para festa* (To bring to the party)/*Em Jaboatão* (In Jaboatão)

*Vamos preparar* (Let's prepare)/*Lindos Mamulengos* (Beautiful Mamulengos, or celebration dolls of Olinda)/*Para comemorar* (To celebrate)/*A libertação* (The liberation)

Martinho da Vila, "Onde O Brasil Aprendeu a Liberdade," 1971 ground in 1631. Setting up their headquarters in the port town of Recife, they ruled for the next 20 years in Brazil, until Portuguese colonists, together with native tribes, succeeded in dislodging them from power and regaining control of the industries of Pernambuco. The nine-year insurgence was known as the Pernambuco Restoration, beginning in the nearby city of Jaboatão dos Guararapes. The same scenario was played out in other territories from Salvador to Fortaleza.

During the 20-year reign of the Dutch, Recife received a heightened degree of economic and cultural attention. The Dutch constructed new roads, *praças,* and buildings, as well as a series of bridges connecting the islands of Recife with the mainland. The ruling Count Mauricio de Nassau even imported a beer factory to

support the many festivities that occurred in the city. Olinda and the sugar plantations were all but forgotten, replaced by a new social class of merchants. When the Dutch were expelled in 1654, they had already changed the landscape of Olinda and Recife. Naturally, the sugar barons of Olinda began the reconstruction of their industries, but they were now competing with the new ruling class in Recife. The standoff between Recife and Olinda culminated in a series of battles called the Gerra dos Mascates, leaving the entire region suffering economically. Emerging from the wreckage (with the help of the Portuguese Crown) was the port city of Recife, with Olinda all but abandoned. Olinda remained in decay until 1982, when it was named a Cultural Heritage Site by UNESCO and gained new life as a tourist destination.

# Recife and Boa Viagem

Recife is one of Brazil's five largest cities, with about two million people in the city itself and almost four million inhabitants in the greater Recife area. It has a major international airport with flights coming from all over Europe, and an economy based primarily on commerce and service industries, including tourism. Its historical monuments and *praças* are largely from the period of the Dutch Invasion and the years following their expulsion from the region. Most of these monuments are clustered in Old Recife. During Brazil's cultural renaissance in the early 1900s, the Boa Viagem area emerged as a upscale neighborhood for the area's new rich, a sort of Copacabana in the northeast. Recife has a vast infrastructure of culture, education, leisure, and commerce, but a lot of this is difficult to access and we visitors end up focusing on the coastal region.

## PRAIA DE BOA VIAGEM

Ever since surfers were attacked by sharks inside the reefs of Praia Boa Viagem, the beach does not get as many tourists. The worst period was in the 1980s. Now there are signs posted all

along the beach warning of shark sightings and prohibiting anyone from surfing or swimming. Nobody ever thought sharks would come inside the reefs. It's a shame, because Boa Viagem was

COURTESY OF CHRISTIAN KNEPPER/EMBRATUR

Praia Boa Viagem is known as the Copacabana of the northeast region.

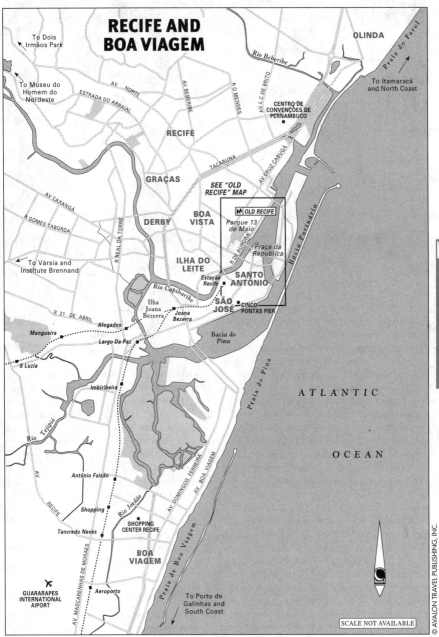

RECIFE AND BOA VIAGEM

To Dois Irmãos Park
To Museu do Homem do Nordeste
OLINDA
Rio Beberibe
Praia do Farol
AV NORTE
ESTRADA DO ARRAIAL
AV BEBERIBE
R.O. MENDES
AV L C DE BRITO
To Itamaracá and North Coast
CENTRO DE CONVENÇÕES DE PERNAMBUCO
RECIFE
TACARUNA
AV CRUZ CABUGÁ
GRAÇAS
SEE "OLD RECIFE" MAP
OLD RECIFE
Bacia Portuária
AV CAXANGÁ
DERBY
BOA VISTA
Parque 13 de Maio
R. DE AURORA
R GOMES TABORDA
R REAL DA TORRE
R DA TORRE
Praça da República
To Vársia and Institute Brennand
ILHA DO LEITE
Rio Capibaribe
Estação Recife
SANTO ANTÔNIO
R 21 DE ABRIL
Ilha Joana Bezerra
Joana Bezerra
SÃO JOSÉ
CINCO PONTAS PIER
Afogados
Largo Da Paz
Bacia do Pina
Mangueira
S Luzia
Imbiribeira
Rio Tejipió
Praia do Pina
ATLANTIC
OCEAN
Antônio Falcão
AV RECIFE
AV DOMINGOS FERREIRA
AV BOA VIAGEM
Rio Jordão
Shopping
SHOPPING CENTER RECIFE
Tancredo Neves
AV MASCARENHAS DE MORAES
BOA VIAGEM
Praia de Boa Viagem
GUARARAPES INTERNATIONAL AIPORT
Aeroporto
To Porto de Galinhas and South Coast
SCALE NOT AVAILABLE
MOON

Recife and Olinda

© AVALON TRAVEL PUBLISHING, INC.

the beach at Boa Viagem

once a popular urban beach and an excellent place to get away from the bustle of Recife's agitated downtown area.

Often compared to Copacabana in Rio de Janeiro, the eight-kilometer span of sand and boardwalk that is the Praia de Boa Viagem is, indeed, very reminiscent of its Rio de Janeiro counterpart. Tall buildings line the opposite side of the coastal highway (mostly upscale condominiums), while the beach itself is a wide stretch of sand going on and on for several kilometers. Small, permanent *barracas* (beach kiosks) are spaced evenly along the boardwalk—each one exactly like the next—and offer coconut water, juices, and other refreshments. Like in Copacabana, the kiosks do not extend onto the beach itself and they do not have kitchens for preparing meals. Despite the fear of sharks and polluted conditions, Boa Viagem fills up with locals on weekends and holidays, bringing thousands of people to play volleyball and soccer on the sand or just lie out in the sun. And lots of people venture into the water with no fear of sharks. On weekdays, the area is strangely quiet and motionless—with the exception of some jogging and bike riding along the boardwalk in the late afternoon.

The streets of Boa Viagem—from the coastal highway (Avenida Boa Viagem) to Avenida Domingos Ferreira—are dotted with hotels, restaurants, and shops. There is no central *praça* or principal avenue that houses most of these establishments. Instead, they are spread across the eight kilometers of Boa Viagem, along three main highways that run parallel to the coast and the many side streets that connect them. It's way too spread out and not very interesting to attempt a walking tour of the area. You probably won't even want to walk very far down the beach boardwalk, as there is very little difference between one end of the beach and the other. When you get as far as the Praça de Boa Viagem, about halfway down the beach, you've pretty much seen how it goes.

## OLD RECIFE

Recife's Portuguese merchants and landowners (known as the *mascotes*) set up their businesses

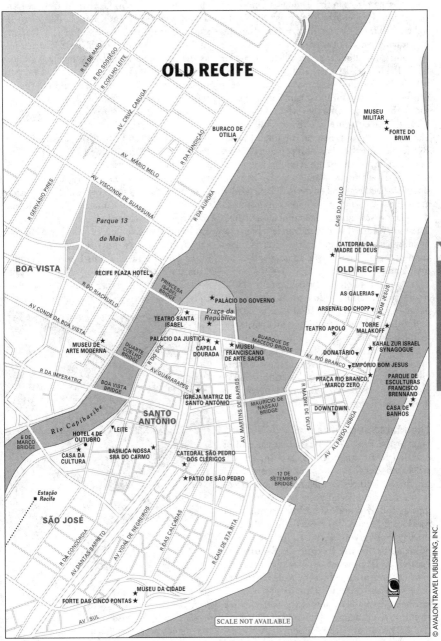

OLD RECIFE

R 13 DE MAIO
R. DO SOSSÊGO
R. COELHO LEITE
AV. CRUZ CABUGÁ
R. DA FUNDIÇÃO
BURACO DE OTILIA
MUSEU MILITAR
FORTE DO BRUM
AV. MÁRIO MELO
AV. VISCONDE DE SUASSUNA
R. GERVÁSIO PIRES
R. DA AURORA
CAIS DO APOLO
Parque 13 de Maio
CATEDRAL DA MADRE DE DEUS
BOA VISTA
RECIFE PLAZA HOTEL
OLD RECIFE
R. DO RIACHUELO
PRINCESA ISABEL BRIDGE
PALÁCIO DO GOVERNO
AS GALERIAS
R. BOM JESUS
AV. CONDE DA BOA VISTA
TEATRO SANTA ISABEL
Praça da República
ARSENAL DO CHOPP
TEATRO APOLO
TORRE MALAKOFF
MUSEU DE ARTE MODERNA
DUARTE COELHO BRIDGE
PALÁCIO DA JUSTIÇA
CAPELA DOURADA
MUSEU FRANCISCANO DE ARTE SACRA
BUARQUE DE MACEDO BRIDGE
DONATÁRIO
KAHAL ZUR ISRAEL SYNAGOGUE
AV. RIO BRANCO
EMPÓRIO BOM JESUS
R. DA IMPERATRIZ
R. DO SOL
AV. GUARARAPES
BOA VISTA BRIDGE
PRAÇA RIO BRANCO, MARCO ZERO
PARQUE DE ESCULTURAS FRANCISCO BRENNAND
IGREJA MATRIZ DE SANTO ANTÔNIO
AV. MARTINS DE BARROS
MAURÍCIO DE NASSAU BRIDGE
R. MADRE DE DEUS
CASA DE BANHOS
Rio Capibaribe
SANTO ANTÔNIO
DOWNTOWN
6 DE MARÇO BRIDGE
HOTEL 4 DE OUTUBRO
LEITE
CASA DA CULTURA
BASÍLICA NOSSA SRA DO CARMO
CATEDRAL SÃO PEDRO DOS CLÉRIGOS
AV. ALFREDO LISBOA
Estação Recife
PATIO DE SÃO PEDRO
12 DE SETEMBRO BRIDGE
SÃO JOSÉ
R. DA CONCÓRDIA
AV. DANTAS BARRETO
AV. VIDAL DE NEGREIROS
R. DAS CALÇADAS
R. CAIS DE STA RITA
MUSEU DA CIDADE
FORTE DAS CINCO PONTAS
AV. SUL
SCALE NOT AVAILABLE

Recife and Olinda

and meeting places in the shadow of Olinda on the Ilha do Recife, now known as Old Recife. When the Dutch planted their own seeds in Recife, leaving Olinda in ashes, Old Recife became the strategic port of the area and left Olinda far behind. The activity grew and the island soon became the location of important government offices for the region. Inhabitants erected their shops, theaters, and churches (and a synagogue) along the streets and *praças*. By the 1800s, Old Recife extended well beyond the small Ilha do Recife and onto the adjacent Ilha Joana Bezerra, known today as the Santo Antônio neighborhood. Today, these two islands, together with the Boa Vista neighborhood on the mainland nearby, are home to the city's most important historical buildings, *praças,* and architectural monuments. These are scattered among the modern high-rise buildings, city streets, and traffic. Several bridges connect these islands to one another and to the mainland on either side.

It's possible to create a walking tour of Old Recife and even include a great deal of the Santo Antônio and Boa Vista areas. If you prefer the packaged city tour, which visits the major sights in about 3–4 hours, you can arrange it at practically any hotel, even if you're not staying there. It leaves in the morning and again at around 2 P.M. for about R$35 per person. (See also *Outdoor Activities* for details on city tours.)

### The Marco Zero Area

Start at the **Praça Rio Branco** at the end of Avenida Rio Branco; this is a point known as **Marco Zero,** the point on the map from which all distances in the area are measured. It was also the official point where Old Recife was founded and where the original pier was located, controlling traffic in and out of the bay. Today, you can take a boat from this point across to the **Parque de Esculturas Francisco Brennand,** a permanent exhibit of sculptures installed on the reefs in front of the Island of Recife. It's actually pretty interesting to take a boat across the water to see a sculpture garden on a narrow reef. Where else will you get that experience? A bit far-

ther north on Avenida Alfredo Lisboa is the **Torre Malakoff** and observatory (Rua do Observatório, 10 A.M.–8 P.M. Tues.–Fri. and 2–7 P.M. weekends). Built in 1855, it stands as the first stargazing tower in the Americas with a small dome that once opened for gazing activities. Today, you can climb to the top terrace to view the city with the telescopes provided. Entrance is free.

### Rua Bom Jesus (Rua dos Judeus)

Parallel to Avenida Alfredo Lisboa is Rua Bom Jesus, where you'll see numerous old buildings that have survived since the 17th century. Beginning with the Dutch occupation, this street was the commercial center of Old Recife and was known as Rua dos Judeus due to the numerous Jewish-owned establishments here. This was also the location of the first Jewish synagogue in the Americas, **Kahal Zur Israel Synagogue** (Rua do Bom Jesus 197, tel. 81/3224-2128, 9 A.M.–5 P.M. Mon.–Fri., 3 P.M.–7 P.M. on weekends, R$2). Destroyed in the early 1900s, the

the Sunday art fair at Rua Bom Jesus

COURTESY OF CHRISTIAN KNEPPER/EMBRATUR

site is now a cultural center with information about the Jewish participation in the city's history and some interesting ruins. It's said that from this nucleus, some 23 Jews left to create the first synagogue in New York City.

Today, Rua Bom Jesus is loaded with bars and restaurants that come alive at night with outdoor parties that extend into the side streets with dancing and live music. On Sundays, the street hosts an arts and crafts fair, along with more live music and outdoor festivities.

## Forte do Brum

On the northern end of the island is the **Forte do Brum,** built in 1629 out of stones from the local reefs. Its purpose was to fend off attacks from the Dutch who overtook the fort only two years later. Inside is the **Museu Militar** (9 A.M.–4 P.M. Tues.–Fri. and 2 P.M.–4 P.M. weekends) with artifacts from the Brazilian participation in WWII, interesting perhaps to WWII history buffs.

## The Apolo Area

Coming back south along Avenida Cais do Apolo, you'll pass the **Catedral da Madre de Deus** on the right (Av. Cais de Apolo, 8 A.M.–noon and 2–4 P.M. Tues.–Fri., 8–10 A.M. Sat., and 9–11 A.M. Sun.). Turn down to Rua do Apolo to check out the **Teatro Apolo** (Av. Cais de Apolo, tel. 81/3224-1119, 8 A.M.–6 P.M. Mon.–Fri.) before making your way back to Avenida Rio Branco and the **Buarque de Macedo Bridge.** Here you can cross over to the Santo Antônio area to continue your tour.

# SANTO ANTÔNIO AND BOA VISTA

Santo Antônio is an extension of Old Recife and your tour of the area should include some of the major attractions here. You can extend your walking tour from Old Recife until your feet get tired and you decide to see the last few sights by taxi.

## Praça da República

Leaving Old Recife across the Buarque de Macedo Bridge, you enter directly into the **Praça da República.** The *praça* features several gardens; an amazing, giant baobab tree; and fountains and sculptures surrounded by a beautiful architectural complex from the early 1800s. One of the buildings in the *praça* is the **Teatro Santa Isabel,** which was reconstructed in 1876 after the first *teatro* burned in 1869. This second *teatro* contains numerous sculptures, crystal chandeliers, and rich interior decorations. It functions to this day as one of the city's classical theaters, hosting events and shows throughout the year. The **Palácio do Governo,** also known as the **Palácio do Campo das Princesas,** is another monument in the Praça. Built in 1841, the Palácio functions as government offices. You can take a peek inside at the inner foyer and grand staircase. A few steps away is the **Palácio da Justiça** (1930), built to commemorate the presidency of Getulio Vargas. It houses the city's courthouse and is best viewed from the outside, where you'll see two important sculptures on the face of the building. At night, the building and dome-shaped cupola are lit up, along with fountains nearby in the *praça* gardens.

## Capela Dourada

One of the most interesting churches in Recife, the **Capela Dourada** (Golden Chapel, Rua do Imperador, tel. 81/3224-0530) was built between 1696 and 1724. Inside, you'll find one of the finest baroque altars in Brazil, sculpted in cedar with gold leaf. Adjoining the chapel is the **Museu Franciscano de Arte Sacra** (8–11:30 A.M. and 2–5 P.M. Mon.–Fri. and 8–11:30 A.M. Sat., R$2), with various religious artifacts from the 18th and 19th centuries and a host of other structures making up the Conjunto Franciscano do Recife.

## Rua da Aurora

Making your way to the western end of the Praça da República, you'll find **Rua do Sol** and the **Princesa Isabel Bridge,** one of the two oldest bridges in the area. Built in 1643 by the Dutch, it has sculpted figures at each end

**government buildings at the Praça da República**

and lanterns that light up at night. From the middle of the bridge, you have a view of both sides of the River Capibaribe. On the side facing the rising sun is Rua da Aurora with its many colorful, 18th-century buildings. On the side facing the setting sun is Rua do Sol and the modern side of the city. For the best photos, get there early in the morning to catch the sun gleaming on the fronts of the historical buildings. Your next stop is the **Museu de Arte Moderna** (Rua da Aurora 256, tel. 85/3423-2095, noon–6 P.M. Tues.–Sun., R$1) at the far end of Rua da Aurora. Here you can either walk down Rua da Aurora or down Rua do Sol. The latter has a better vantage point from which to see the historical buildings reflecting in the water. Either way, the museum is located near the next bridge, Ponte Duarte Coelho. Inside are works from various contemporary Brazilian artists, including Pernambuco artist Francisco Brennand, whose ceramic sculptures appear all

over the city. Occasionally, the museum has international exhibits.

## Casa da Cultura

From the Museu de Arte Moderna you can walk or take a cab to the **Casa da Cultura** (Rua Floriano Peixoto, tel. 81/3223-2850, 9 A.M.–7 P.M. Mon.–Sat. and 10 A.M.–3 P.M. Sun.). There, you'll find the grand, cross-shaped structure that was built in 1855 as the city prison. Its cross-shaped design helped guards keep an eye on the four cell-lined corridors from the middle point. In 1973, the prisoners were relocated and the prison became a shopping and cultural center. Now the cells have been converted into arts and crafts shops, art galleries, money exchanges, and a tourist information booth. A second story was added with panoramic elevators to access them. In the large patio area appear music and dance performances daily. One of the old cells re-

historical buildings line Rua da Aurora

## THE STORY OF FREI CANECA

When Prince João VI returned to Portugal in 1821 from his 13-year exile in Brazil, he had already become King some three years earlier. His son, Dom Pedro I, stuck around in Brazil for awhile and shortly thereafter, in 1822, declared Brazil's independence from Portugal. Pernambuco, along with a few other territories in the northeastern region, rejected Dom Pedro's new constitution and formed a separatist movement, called the *Confederação do Equador*. A key figure in this movement was a missionary named Frei Caneca. His ideas and writings on the subject of a new republic were literally revolutionary and when the short-lived revolt ended in 1825, Frei Caneca was on death row in the Forte das Cinco Pontas in Old Recife. Figuring a public hanging would be inappropriate for a man of the cloth, the government resolved that he would be executed by firing squad. This took place on the eastern wall of the fort, where there now stands a bust of the famous rebel.

mains intact and you can keep an eye out for it as you walk around the center.

### Forte das Cinco Pontas

In many ways, the Dutch were more forward-thinking than the Portuguese were. This can be seen in the additions they made to the city, including an observatory, several bridges, a commercial center, and the **Forte das Cinco Pontas** (Praça das Cinco Pontas, tel. 81/3224-8492, 9 A.M.–6 P.M. Mon.–Fri. and 1–5 P.M. weekends). At the time, the only potable-water supply for the growing city of Recife was in the far south side of the island. To protect this source of water—and the southern waterways of the city at the same time—the Dutch built the Fort of Five Points out of mud and organic matter during their period of domination (specifically in 1630). The wells were well maintained and always kept full. In 1677, the Portuguese rebuilt the fort out of stone in a four-pointed design, hence resolving the question of how this four-sided structure could have gotten its name. The current structure was once a prison and location of the famous execution of Frei Caneca. Inside the fort is the **Museu da Cidade** with documents and artifacts from the city's formation and turbulent history. Since the fort is on the far side of the city, far from other attractions, you should probably take a taxi there and back.

### Churches

Not far from one another in the middle of the Santo Antônio district are three historical churches. The **Basílica Nossa Sra. do Carmo** in the lovely Praça do Carmo towers above the adjacent buildings on the site where the Palácio Boa Vista (palace of Count Mauricio de Nassau) once stood. The church and convent was erected from 1687–1767 in a determined effort to replace the palace with a catholic monument. There, the famous Frei Caneca took his monastic vows. The **Patio de São Pedro** is a historical *praça* that is lined with colonial houses from the 18th century. There, the **Catedral São Pedro dos Clérigos** stands with its beautifully restored baroque architecture.

Inside is a pulpit and altars with numerous gold-covered carvings and large paintings from the 1700s. Most impressive is the massive carved front door. At night, the church and *praça* light up with restaurants and bars serving until late evening and providing an interesting alternative to the movement on Rua Bom Jesus in Old Recife. Finally, the **Igreja Matriz de Santo Antônio** stands tall in the Praça da Independência where once stood the Dutch armory. The Portuguese built this church in 1790 in their typical baroque style as part of their frenzy to replace all the important Dutch constructions in town. Inside are altars lined with carvings and covered in gold.

## OUTSKIRTS

In an area called Várzia, on the far outskirts of town are the installations of Francisco and Ricardo Brennand. The **Oficina de Cerâmica Francisco Brennand** (access via Av. Caxangá, Várzea, tel. 81/3271-2466, 8 A.M.–5 P.M. Mon.–Fri., R$3) is a huge sculpture garden built around the grounds of the family's *olaria* (ceramic factory and kiln). More than 2,000 ceramic works are on display in the area's warehouses and gardens, as well as numerous paintings that form the basis of Brennand's sculptures, which are both bizarre and erotic. Francisco is often seen walking around the gardens in his hat and long, white beard. The **Instituto Ricardo Brennand** (Alameda Antônio Brannand, Várzea, tel. 81/2121-0370, 8 A.M.–5 P.M. Mon.–Fri.) is a type of museum and private collection of medieval armor and battle gear. Comprising one of the largest private collections of its type in the world, it displays some 2,000 pieces, including a gothic altar, English stained glass, tapestries, and animal armor. There is also a collection of paintings by Dutch artist Franz Post. The building in which Brennand houses his collection is in the form of a medieval castle, complete with a lake, gardens, and plenty of tropical forest nearby.

Examples of the Afro-Brazilian and indigenous cultures from the northeast of Brazil are on display at the **Museu do Homem do Nor-**deste (Av. 17 de Agosto 2187, Casa Forte, tel. 81/3441-5500, 11 A.M.–5 P.M. Tues., Wed., and Fri., 8 A.M.–5 P.M. on Thurs., 1–5 P.M. on Sun., R$3). You'll find colorful ceremonial clothing, crafts, toys, and musical instruments from the 17th and 18th centuries. There is also a well-preserved carriage from the 1800s and personal effects of Dom Pedro I.

## ENTERTAINMENT AND NIGHTLIFE

### Bars and Cafés

The two main nightlife centers in town are Rua Bom Jesus in Old Recife and the Patio de São Pedro in Santo Antônio, the latter being the calmer of the two. They both offer numerous bars and restaurants for sitting, talking, and watching the movement on the street. Both areas also have live music on weekends (and some days during the week). Try the **Arsenal do Chopp** (Praça do Arsenal da Marinha 59 on Rua Bom Jesus, tel. 81/3224-6259, 5 P.M. until the last client), which fills up at happy hour with folks drinking draft beer both indoors and along the sidewalk. Here you have an excellent view of the old buildings along Rua Bom Jesus. The **Empório Bom Jesus** (Rua Bom Jesus 187, tel. 81/3424-7474, 9 A.M.–6 P.M. Mon.–Thurs., 9 A.M. until the last client on Fri., 4 P.M. until the last client on weekends) serves coffee, drinks, and appetizers in a charming, colonial house with a small souvenir shop in the back. It's a good place to get a cocktail and watch people pass by. You can try a sweet and potent *maltado* at **As Galerias** (Rua Bom Jesus 35, lunch and dinner daily). This is a famous regional drink made with malt, banana, and peanut, although the true recipe is a secret of the owners. A British-style pub called **Downtown** (Rua Vigário Tenório 105, Old Recife, tel. 81/3424-6317, 10 P.M. until the last client Wed.–Sun.) has live music, snooker tables, and an upstairs area with tables looking out on the passersby. Live rock and jazz plays on weekends. And if you just want to hang out with the crowds at a local dive bar, then look for **Burburinho** on Rua Bom Jesus (Rua Tomazina 106, tel. 81/9944-8446, 5 P.M. until the last client on weekdays and noon until the last client on weekends).

If you're looking for a good drinking establishment in Boa Viagem, try **Boteco** (Av. Boa Viagem 1660, tel. 81/3325-1428, 5 P.M. until the last client on weekdays and noon until the last client on weekends), which has a popular happy hour with draft beer and excellent Brazilian *salgados* (finger foods). Another popular spot for drinks from happy hour until late night is **Biruta Bar** (Rua Bem-te-vi 15, tel. 81/3326-5151, 5 P.M. until the last client on weekdays and noon until the last client on weekends, closed Mon.). They have a rustic wooden interior and a terrace area on the second floor. Try their Caipifruta Pernambucana for a great local cocktail. Across from the Hotel Tivoli (Rua Tenente João Cicero 47, 5 P.M. until the last client on weekdays, noon until the last client on weekends) is the **Choperia,** a pleasant patio for beers and grilled meat. They have a great happy-hour special of two beers for the price of one.

## Night Excursions

A great way to see the Recife night scene is from the various waterways around the islands. You can take a nighttime catamaran ride around the islands, visiting several important points and looking out onto the city from the water. The boat leaves from the pier at Cinco Pontas near the Forte das Cinco Pontas and costs R$20 for the 1.5-hour tour. Afternoon tours at 4 P.M. are also available, but night tours, leaving at 8 P.M., are more interesting. For reservations, call tel. 81/3424-2845.

## Theater, Music, and Events

Look for a copy of the *Agenda Cultural* for current listings of music, theater, and dance shows all around town. Informal shows take place in the *praças* around town, including the Marco Zero *praça* in Old Recife, the Casa de

# REGIONAL DANCES AND FOLKLORE

If you're in town during any of the major festivals, you're certain to see one or more of the regional dances and the lavish costumes used in them. Here's a little primer to enhance your understanding of these folkloric dances: **Maracatu** is a dance that originates in Recife. It was originally created to honor Nossa Sra. do Rosário dos Negros but soon digressed into a more rowdy celebration. A parade of participants, dressed in colorful costumes from Brazil's Afro-Brazilian roots, makes its way down the street. Some of the characters portrayed by the costumes include the Tupi people, country farmers, and a queen who carries a *boneca* (large papier mâché doll) on a pole, representing Nossa Sra. do Rosário. The music and drumming are intense. This dance is commonly performed by *blocos* (parades of participants) during Carnaval.

The **Bumba Meu Boi** dance celebrates our connection to the earth and our ability to cultivate it. It opens with a story from the farming culture: A black man steals a steer from a white man's farm because his wife is pregnant and wants to eat its tongue. After the steer is dead, the farmer demands that the thief bring it back to life, which he does. The scenario is played out with music and dance and numerous costumed figures, including the steer. When the steer rises to life again, the crowd goes wild with festivities. *Bumba* is a type of large kettledrum and *boi* is the word for steer.

One of the most popular dances in Pernambucano folklore is the **Coco de Roda.** Here, a large group dances into the shape of a wheel, clapping and stomping to imitate the sound of a coconut cracking, hence the name of the dance. In the center, a solo figure dances and sings verses that are repeated by the crowd until the wheel is fully formed. At that point, the person in the middle is replaced by another. A slightly different version is the **Ciranda** dance, in which a circle of participants sings a particular verse. Each new round, a person from the ring is pulled into the center until everyone is in the center and the dance starts again.

Cultura, and others. You can also check listings at www.recife.pe.gov.br/agendacultural.

## FESTIVALS AND EVENTS

People from Recife will tell you that Brazil's best and most authentic **Carnaval** celebration is right here in town. Without a doubt, the Recife Carnaval is one of the three most intense in the country (the other two being in Salvador and Rio de Janeiro). It opens with a sunrise gathering at the Forte das Cinco Pontas, where the streets begin to clog with people at around 7 A.M. From there, the Gala de Madrugada begins to move down the streets of Recife—a *bloco* (parade of participants) that grows to include as many as one million people. By the time the *bloco* begins throbbing down the street, the rest of Old Recife is already full of people and festivities. But Carnaval takes place all over the city on numerous preset stages, city streets, and along the Praia de Boa Viagem. It's a mix of costumes, music, and dance from Pernambuco's cultural roots—sometimes organized and often just loose on the streets.

Another popular festival in Recife is **Semana Santa** (Holy Week), when hundreds of actors and participants join together to reenact the passion of Christ. The main procession takes place at the Marco Zero *praça* in Old Recife. The **Festa de Nossa Sra. do Carmo** takes place in the Praça do Carmo on July 8–16. The *praça* fills with food stands, cultural and folkloric presentations, and, of course, ceremonies in the Basilica do Carmo church. During the **Encontro Pernambucano de Cirandas** (every Saturday in October on the Island of Itamaracá) the special dance and music tradition of the Cirandeiros is practiced and celebrated—a dance that involves the building of a wheel, costumes, and special songs. **New Year's Eve** fireworks can be seen all along the coast of Recife, from Olinda to Praia de Boa Viagem. An excellent place to view them would be from a boat out in the ocean. If that's not possible, then the Praça Marco Zero is a good bet.

## SHOPPING

Just in case visitors were about to think that **Rua Bom Jesus** in Old Recife was only for nightlife activities, the neighborhood put together an arts and crafts fair from noon–8 P.M. on Sundays. Along with the various stands are music, dance, and theater performances. More arts and crafts can be found in the many shops at the **Casa da Cultura.** The **Shopping Center Recife** in Boa Viagem (Rua Padre Carapuceiro 777, tel. 81/3464-6123, 10 A.M.–11 P.M. Mon.–Sat., noon–8 P.M. on Sun.) is one of the best modern shopping malls, with many film-developing labs, movie theaters, two food courts, and even a sculpture garden outside. You can look for *carqueja* and *boldo*—two great herbal remedies found only in Brazil—at the **Mercado de São José** (Praça Dom Vital, tel. 81/3445-599, 6 A.M.–5:30 P.M. Mon.–Fri. and 6–11 A.M. Sun.) in the Santo Antônio neighborhood. The Mercado is a great place for off-the-wall products, healing herbs, consultations of the tarot and runes, and crafts and food products. The iron building was finished in 1875 and designed by two French architects. Inside are more than 500 stands.

Saturdays along the **Boa Viagem boardwalk,** you'll find arts and crafts stands, art exhibitions, and food. Every afternoon at 4 P.M., the **Praça da Boa Viagem** (boardwalk where it crosses Avenida Barão de Souza Leão) has an arts and crafts fair with items from the region's folk festivals, clothing, and leather works.

## OUTDOOR ACTIVITIES

Besides walking on the beach of Boa Viagem and in the old city center, outdoor activities in Recife are somewhat limited. City tours of Old Recife leave in the mornings and afternoons and you should book your reservation the day before. During low season, your tour may be cancelled if there are not enough sign-ups. A full-day tour of Old Recife and Olinda is offered by **Martur** (Rua Nilo Dornelas Câmara 90, tel. 81/3463-3636, 8 A.M.–6 P.M. Mon.–Sat.). They also offer boat tours to Porto de

Galinhas (worth more than a day), the Ilha de Itamaracá on the north coast, and Tamandaré on the south coast.

Boat tours to the Ilha de Itamaracá and Coroa do Avião leave from the pier at Cinco Pontas near the fort. The full-day tour includes an on-board bar and swimming net that dips into the water below the catamaran, a good value at R$30 per person. For reservations, call tel. 81/3424-2845.

The **Parque Dois Irmãos** (8 A.M.–4 P.M. daily), about 40 kilometers northwest of the city, has hiking trails, lakes, a zoo, and botanical garden in its 360 hectares of plants and trees. You can catch a bus to the park from the Parque 13 de Maio and from the airport.

You can take scuba diving lessons and excursions with **Pernambuco Scuba** (Rua Ricardo Hardman 105, Aflitos, tel. 81/3267-0088, www.pernambucoscuba.com.br, call to make an appointment). There are some great diving spots around the Island of Itamaracá on the north coast, including several sunken ships.

## ACCOMMODATIONS

Most accommodations in Recife are in the Boa Viagem area. There you'll find hotels in just about all price ranges. Many hotels in the downtown area are business hotels, generally among the mid-range offerings, and often have weekend discounts. Remember that accommodations in Olinda are often preferred over those in Recife and Boa Viagem, so be sure to check the *Olinda* section for details. Prices go up slightly during the peak season, which is December–February. All hotels charge a 10-percent service tax. Exceptions are noted herein.

### Under R$100

In Boa Viagem: First, avoid the **Albergue de Juventude Maracatus do Recife** (Rua Dona Maria Carolina 185), part of the Hostelling International chain, as it has filthy conditions. You won't want to sleep on the beds they have there. A better bet for a low-cost room is the **Pousada Casuarinas** (Rua Antonio Pedro Figueiredo 151, tel. 81/3325-4708,

www.pousada-casuarinas.com.br, R$50 s, R$65 d). This place has a few small rooms with verandas overlooking a small garden, air, and TV. Another HI hostel in the area is the **Boa Viagem Hostel** (Rua Aviador Severino Lins 455, tel. 81/3326-9572, www.hostelboaviagem.com.br, R$25 pp). They have a pool, Internet, kitchen facilities, and group rooms. The **Navegantes Praia Hotel** (Rua dos Navegantes 1997, tel. 81/3325-2689, tel. 81/3326-9609, R$60 s, R$75 d) offers basic rooms with air and TV, a tiny pool out back, and a reasonable breakfast. They can arrange city tours and other trips if desired (most hotels can). Ask for a discount if making reservations in advance. The **Hotel Tivoli** (Rua Tenente João Cicero 47, tel. 81/3465-7400, www.hoteltivolirecife.com.br, R$79 s, R$89 d) has clean rooms, a small pool on the top floor, and good service. A modern hotel with clean rooms and good facilities is the 🄼 **Onda Mar Hotel** (Rua Ernesto de Paula Santos 284, tel. 81/3465-2833, www.ondamar.com.br, R$80 d). They have an excellent breakfast buffet in their café, a rooftop pool with ocean view, and an Italian restaurant with live music on weekends.

In Downtown Recife: The **Pousada Villa Boa Vista** (Rua Miguel Couto 81, tel. 81/3223-0666, www.pousadavillaboavista.com.br, R$75 s, R$85 d) is located between Old Recife and Olinda in the Boa Vista neighborhood. It has a charming courtyard area in an old colonial house. They serve an excellent breakfast buffet. The 🄼 **Recife Plaza Hotel** (Rua da Aurora 225, tel. 81/3231-1200, R$95 s and R$115 d) is in the Boa Vista area near the Duarte Coelho Bridge. They have air, TV, a pool, and sauna. **Hotel 4 de Outubro** (Rua Floriano Peixoto 141, tel. 81/3424-4477, R$60 s, R$75 d) was built in 1964 near the Casa de Cultura. They have 35 rooms with air, TV, and phone. Nothing fancy.

### R$100–200

In Boa Viagem: The **Holiday Inn Recife** (Av. Eng. Domingos Ferreira 3067, tel. 81/2122-3939, www.modesto.com.br, R$110 standard, R$126 luxury suite, and R$155 deluxe suite with view) has large, clean rooms with air and gas-heated water. Some rooms have ocean views. The facilities include a pool, café, three bars, and a gym. They don't charge a 10-percent service tax. The **Mar Hotel Recife** (Rua Barão de Souza Leão 451, tel. 81/3302-4444, www.marhotel.com.br, R$135 d) has three pools with waterfalls and fountains. Rooms have small verandas and many have ocean views. The restaurant on the top floor has a panoramic view of Boa Viagem. The **Parthenon Navegantes** (Rua dos Navegantes 1706, tel. 81/3466-1185, navflat@cyb.com.br) is a clean and modern facility with well-appointed rooms and a good breakfast buffet. R$160.

In Downtown Recife: The **M Parthenon Metropolis** (Rua Estado de Israel 203, tel. 81/3413-1900, flatmetropolis@cyb.com.br) is a business hotel that serves for tourism, since it's relatively close to Old Recife. Located in the Ilha do Leite neighborhood on the northern mainland west of Boa Vista, the hotel offers a pool, gym, sauna, Internet room (extra), bar, café, and excellent breakfast (included). A taxi from the hotel to Old Recife is about R$10. R$150. The **Comfort Hotel Ilha do Leite** (Rua Sport Club do Recife 75, tel. 81/3416-7700, chilhadoleite@atlantichotels.com.br) has rooms with air, cable TV, and in-room Internet. The hotel features a sauna, non-smoking rooms, and a restaurant with 24-hour room service. R$265.

## R$200–500

The five-star **M Hotel Atlante Plaza** (Av. Boa Viagem 5426, tel. 81/3302-3333, www.atlanteplaza.com.br, R$200 d) is on the beachfront in Boa Viagem. They have more than 200 rooms, two pools, a non-smoking level, gym, 24-hour room service, and well-appointed rooms with gas-heated water. Glass elevators take you up to your floor with a view of the ocean.

## FOOD

### Barbecue

The traditional Brazilian barbecue is a foodfest that should not be missed. There are several good locations to participate in this dining experience. In Boa Viagem, the best is **M Porção** (Av. Eng. Domingos Ferreira 4215, tel. 81/3465-3999, 11 A.M.–midnight daily). They have a *rodísio*-style setup (you are served various cuts of meat at your table throughout the evening) with several self-service buffets, including pasta, green salads, fish, cheese, and desserts. Meals cost around R$65. In the Derby neighborhood, just west of Boa Vista you'll find **Spettus** (Av. Agamenon Magalhães 2132, tel. 81/3423-4122, 11 A.M.–1 A.M. daily), which is also a *rodísio*-style barbecue that specializes in fine cuts and cured meats. It costs about R$35.

### Casual

There are casual restaurants and quick *lanchónetes* all over the downtown area. You will have no trouble finding a self-service lunch or *prato feito* (ready-made plate) in Old Recife at the Marco Zero *praça* or all over the Santo Antônio area, especially near the Praça da República and the Mercado São José. Try taking the boat from Marco Zero to the reefs across the water, where you'll find the restaurant **Casa de Banhos** (Molhes do Porto do Recife, Brasilia Teimosa, tel. 81/3075-8776, noon–11 P.M. Wed.–Fri., noon–7 P.M. on Sun.) with *moqueca* dishes that serve two hungry people for R$25.

In Boa Viagem, an excellent choice for self-service lunch or dinner is **M Chica Pitanga** (Rua Petrolina 19, tel. 81/3465-2224, 6 A.M.–10 P.M. Mon.–Sat., 11:30 A.M.–4 P.M. on Sun.). Their buffet is filled with salads, grilled meats, seafood, and pasta dishes. Get there early to avoid crowds. A meals costs R$25. A good lunch-only buffet in Boa Viagem is **Papaya Verde** (Av. Pe. Bernardino Pessoa 287, tel. 81/3325-6198, 11:30 A.M.–3 P.M. daily). They have an enormous buffet table with plenty of variety. It costs around R$25.

### International

**Hakata** (Rua Viscondessa do Livramento 182, tel. 81/3421-7299, lunch and dinner daily, open late on weekends) in the Derby area west of Boa Vista offers an all-you-can-eat sushi experience along with their Asian buffet. They have a daily self-service lunch. Closed Sundays. Meals cost R$35. A local favorite for Portuguese food is **Tasca Restaurante Portuguesa** (Rua D. José Lopes 165, tel. 81/3326-6309, 6 P.M.–midnight Tues.–Sun.) in the Boa Viagem area. The small converted home is an elegant place for dinner and wine. It should set you back around R$50. An excellent Italian restaurant is **Buongustaio** (Av. Eng. Domingos Ferreira 467, tel. 81/3327-5001, 7 P.M.–midnight Mon.–Sat.) in Boa Viagem, with a variety of well-prepared pastas, seafood, and grilled meats. Meals run about R$45.

### Regional

**Donatário** (Rua Bom Jesus 237, tel. 81/3424-9591, lunch and dinner daily) specializes in seafood, particularly shrimp and lobster. They are located near all the action in Old Recife. Meals are R$60. Another regional favorite (this one located in an old colonial house along Rua da Aurora) is **O Buraco de Otilia** (Rua da Aurora 1231, tel. 81/3231-1528, lunch Sun.–Fri.). They have regional fish and meat dishes for about R$60 in an elegant setting. One of the most famous restaurants in the downtown area is **Leite** (Praça Joaquim Nabuco 147, tel. 81/3224-7977, lunch Sun.–Fri.), which has been around since 1882 and served many famous Brazilians. The building and interior are all rich and antique, and the food is classically Pernambucano. You'll spend around R$50 per person. In Boa Viagem, the regional favorite is **◪ Bargaço** (Av. Boa Viagem 670, tel. 81/3465-1847, noon–midnight daily) on the north end near Pina. This beachfront restaurant serves all the obligatory favorites, such as *moqueca de camarão* (shrimp and fish stew). They also have oysters and mussels from the south of Brazil. Get there early for a seat outside. Meals are R$50.

## INFORMATION AND SERVICES

There are tourist information offices at the Guararapes airport (tel. 81/3341-6090), the main Terminal Rodoviaria (bus station, tel. 81/3452-1892), and in the Praça de Boa Viagem (Av. Boa Viagem at Rua Barão de Souza Leão, tel. 81/3463-3621). You can also find information at the Casa de Cultura (tel. 81/3224-2850). The tourist police are at tel. 81/3464-4088 or tel. 81/3326-9603. Hospitals are all located in the Ilha do Leite area, west of Boa Vista.

Money is available at ATMs all over downtown Recife (look in Banco do Brasil offices for the Plus and Cirrus signs). You can change money at the *cambio* offices in the Casa de Cultura. The best Internet connections are in the shopping malls around town, such as Shopping Center Recife. They cost around R$8 per hour. There is also a connection at the Torre Malakoff and in Olinda.

A good website for information about Recife is www.recife.pe.gov.br (in Portuguese).

## GETTING THERE

Most flights will come into the Guararapes International Airport, which is very close to the Boa Viagem area. From the airport, you can catch vans and buses into Boa Viagem, Old Recife, or Porto de Galinhas. Local numbers for some domestic carriers include Gol (tel. 81/3464-4793), TAM (tel. 81/3464-4257, tel. 81/3327-8320), Varig (tel. 81/3464-4809, tel. 81/3464-4450), and Vasp (tel. 81/3464-4931, tel. 81/3216-2051).

If you arrive by bus, you will disembark at the main bus station, which is way, way out of town to the west. There is a storage area for luggage, which charges around R$3 per bag per day. You'll want to go directly to the metro (less than R$2), which connects to the bus station, and catch the train to downtown Recife. You want to get off at the last stop, which is the Estação Recife. From there, you can catch a taxi to Old Recife (R$8), your hotel in the Ilha do Leite area (R$8), Boa Viagem (R$15), or Olinda (R$18). There are buses in front of the downtown metro station that go to Boa Viagem, Olinda, and Porto de Galinhas. You can walk from the metro station to the Casa da Cultura, but you might prefer to take a taxi, since the area is a bit rough.

To get back to the Terminal Rodoviaria from the downtown metro station, be sure you take the red line, which leaves from the right side of the station. Get off at the *rodoviaria*. It's quite easy.

## GETTING AROUND

Buses between Olinda and Boa Viagem are called Rio Doce/Piedade and run all day for around R$2.50. The trip takes about 20 minutes. To arrive in Olinda, make sure you get off at the Praça do Carmo. It's easy to pass it up. Driving around the Recife/Olinda area is not recommended even if you're going to Porto de Galinhas or other distant beaches. You're better off taking a bus or tour van (from the airport, preferably) and renting a vehicle when you get to your destination. If you need a vehicle in Recife, try **Avis** (tel. 81/3462-5069), **Hertz** (tel. 81/3338-2103), **Localiza** (tel. 81/3341-2082), **Yes** (tel. 81/3341-4565, tel. 81/3341-3400), or **Master** (tel. 81/3341-1944).

# Olinda

After less than 100 years of glory, the entire village of Olinda was burned almost entirely to the ground. It's many churches and government buildings lay in ruin and the town's hold on the sugar trade was broken forever. Even after the resilient Pernambucanos rebuilt their village some 23 years later, after the Dutch Invasion had ended, it never regained its political or economic hold over Recife. Thus began its long, slow decline into obscurity. Today, it is rising once again from the ashes as a major tourist attraction and cultural nerve center. Undergoing a series of reforms, Olinda is slowly being restored to its old glory atop the many hillsides north of Recife overlooking the blue Atlantic. The restored churches are often so picture-perfect that they make the unrestored monuments all the more painful to see.

Old Olinda functions almost completely on tourism and the people in town are eager to show their wares or provide their services for any visitor entering the town. This includes children who attach themselves to you as self-appointed tour guides, reciting memorized phrases about the various sights and attractions. If you're not interested in their services, you could pretend you don't understand a word they are saying (and maybe you don't). Most have not yet memorized their lines in English. But in case they have, pretend you speak Polish.

As you walk the streets of Olinda, passing or entering the various churches and monuments, you'll also see an uncanny number of art galleries and craft markets. Arts and crafts, it seems, have gone well with tourism and now everyone in town has an atelier in his home or place of business.

You'll probably find it difficult to see everything you want to see in one day. That's not because there is too much to fit into a single day, but because hours of operation are not synchronized to allow for a single-day visit to everything. Some churches can be seen only on Sundays and others only during the week. One suggestion is to plan your walking tour of Olinda based on the hours of operation of the monuments you'd like to see. Olinda is small enough that you can walk back and forth many times to catch the different operating hours. Most likely, you will still run into a few locked doors. In the following pages, you'll get a good idea of which monuments are worth seeing on the inside and which are adequate from the outside. If you are staying at one of the hotels in Olinda, then you can easily return to complete your tour another day. The hotels in Olinda generally offer more for the money than those in Boa Viagem and there are some excellent economical options in town. Nights are often full of performances in the *praças* around town and there are many bars and casual hangouts along the coastal highway (Avenida Beira Mar) at the foot of Old Olinda.

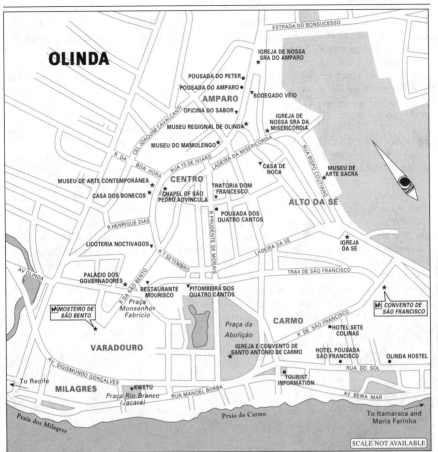

OLINDA

IGREJA DE NOSSA
SRA DO AMPARO

POUSADA DO PETER
POUSADA DO AMPARO
BODEGADO VÉIO
AMPARO
OFICINA DO SABOR
MUSEU REGIONAL DE OLINDA
IGREJA DE
NOSSA SRA DA
MISERICÓRDIA

MUSEU DO MAMULENGO

CASA DE
NOCA
MUSEU DE
ARTE SACRA

MUSEU DE ARTE CONTEMPORÂNEA
CENTRO
MUSEU DE ARTE CONTEMPORÂNEA
CASA DOS BONECOS
CHAPEL OF SÃO
PEDRO ADVÍNCULA
TRATORIA DOM
FRANCESCO
ALTO DA SÉ

POUSADA DOS
QUATRO CANTOS

LICOTERIA NOCTIVAGOS
IGREJA
DA SÉ
LADEIRA DA SÉ

TRAV DE SÃO FRANCISCO
PALÁCIO DOS
GOVERNADORES
RESTAURANTE
MOURISCO
PITOMBEIRA DOS
QUATRO CANTOS
CONVENTO DE
SÃO FRANCISCO
Praça
Monsenhor
Fabrício
Mosteiro de
São Bento
Praça da
Abolição
CARMO
HOTEL SETE
COLINAS

VARADOURO
IGREJA E CONVENTO DE
SANTO ANTÔNIO DE CARMO
HOTEL POUSADA
SÃO FRANCISCO
OLINDA HOSTEL
RUA DO SOL

To Recife
KWETÚ
TOURIST
INFORMATION
MILAGRES
Praça Rio Branco
(Jacaré)
RUA MANOEL BORBA
AV BEIRA MAR

Praia dos Milagres
Praia do Carmo
To Itamaraca and
Maria Farinha

SCALE NOT AVAILABLE

© AVALON TRAVEL PUBLISHING, INC.

Recife and Olinda

# CHURCHES

If you wonder what such a small town was doing with so many churches and chapels, you need only remember that this colonial society was divided into many different groups and social classes. The order of Carmelita Brasileira had a church; the brotherhood of black slaves had a church; even single men and musicians had their own church. Each skin color and social caste (often one and the same) had a church to protect the interests of the group. Churches served as political power centers within the overall guidelines of the Catholic religion and

influences of the Portuguese Crown. Various convents and monasteries were erected to keep the population on the straight and narrow, given the many windy roads in Olinda. All in all, some 35 churches and chapels decorate the streets—including some of the oldest churches in the country, dating back as far as 1534.

Many churches in Olinda carry two dates of construction: that of the original construction and another indicating its reconstruction after the Dutch Invasion. History buffs and church buffs will enjoy seeing all of these buildings and their interiors (those open to viewing), but most people will find them somewhat repetitious and prefer to concentrate on the most significant among them. Not all of the churches have been restored and some are painfully dilapidated, as are some of the colonial homes around town. If you have time, check out all of the following. If time is short, be sure to see the Convento de São Francisco, the Igreja da Sé, and the Mosteiro de São Bento.

## Convento de São Francisco

To get the full effect of this architectural masterpiece (Rua São Francisco 280, tel. 81/3429-0517, 8 A.M.–noon and 2–5 P.M. Mon.–Fri. and 8 A.M.–noon Sat.), one should approach it from above, from the Travessa de São Francisco, and not from below via Rua de São Francisco. This way, you see the convent set perfectly against the blue ocean and framed with palm trees. The first Franciscan convent in Brazil, São Francisco was constructed in 1585 and almost completely destroyed by the Dutch in 1631. It was rebuilt in the last half of the 1600s. It consists of two small chapels and the **Igreja**

**Nossa Sra. das Neves.** Although most impressive from the outside, the inside is covered in blue Portuguese tiles and has a richly painted ceiling, depicting the holy family. Paints were made of bull's blood, egg yolk, and whale oil. Mass is at 8 A.M. and 7 P.M. on Sundays, 5 P.M. on Saturdays.

## Igreja e Convento de Santo Antônio de Carmo

The first church you'll see as you make your way into town, Carmo (Praça do Carmo) is one of the largest and most picturesque in Olinda. Fully restored in the last few years, the church was originally built in 1588, though it was practically destroyed in the early 1900s and left to deteriorate. Today, it houses the Olinda office of IPHAN, a government agency responsible for the protection and preservation of Brazil's cultural patrimony. The Igreja do Carmo is best viewed from the outside. Find a great vantage point at the top of the *praça* looking out upon the church with the ocean in the

view from above the Convento de São Francisco

background and palm trees all around. It's one of the most photographed monuments in the area. You can see Carmo on the inside during Sunday mass at 11 A.M.

## Igreja de Nossa Sra. do Amparo

All of the literature on this church (Largo do Amparo, tel. 81/3429-7339, 7:30 A.M.–1 P.M.) says that it was founded by single men and musicians around 1613. For its many-colored altars, carved pulpit, and gold leaf, Amparo is worth a visit. The date on the face of the current structure (rebuilt after the first was burned down) is 1644, a date disputed by historians who don't believe that the Dutch would have allowed for its reconstruction while they were still in possession of the territory (they were expelled in 1654). It sits at the top of Olinda on the far end of Rua do Amparo, where you will certainly find yourself after checking out the shops and art galleries. Inside is the restoration laboratory of the city of Olinda. Mass is at 5 P.M. on Sundays.

## Igreja de Nossa Sra. da Misericórdia

This rather simple-looking church (Rua Bispo Coutinho, Alto da Sé, tel. 81/3429-2922, 11:30 A.M.–12:30 P.M. and 5:30–8:30 P.M. daily) is full of surprises on the inside. Its main altar is amazingly detailed with painted and gold-leafed wood and ceramic tiles. Panels of blue Portuguese tiles line the walls, and in the back is a large baptismal made of carved stone. Originally serving as the town hospital, Misericórdia was built around 1540 and again in 1654. There are no visiting hours, but the church is open for mass on Sunday at 7:30 A.M. on Sunday and at 6:20 A.M. on Saturday. Daily prayer sessions take place at 11:45 A.M.

## Igreja da Sé

Built originally out of mud and organic matter, the Igreja da Sé (Rua Dom Helder Camara, tel. 81/3271-4270, 8 A.M.–noon and 2–5 P.M. daily) has undergone numerous renovations and two complete reconstructions. The original mud parish was erected in 1540, only to be leveled and reconstructed 40 years later in stone. It was given three side altars covered in wood carvings and draped in gold. In 1631, it was completely destroyed by the Dutch and underwent its second reconstruction in 1656. Since then, it has received numerous renovations, including a complete retooling of its facade. Since 1918, it has been the official cathedral of the Archbishop of Olinda and Recife and was home to the Archbishop Dom Hélder Câmara, who spoke out against the torture of political prisoners by the Brazilian military government in the 1970s. He was also accused by the archdiocese of promoting communism in Brazil. He is entombed in the church near the main pulpit. A great arts and crafts fair occurs every afternoon near the church.

## Mosteiro de São Bento

On your walking tour of the Olinda churches, don't miss the inside of the Mosteiro de São Bento (Rua de São Bento, tel. 81/3429-3288, 8–11:30 A.M. and 2–4 P.M. daily), for it's on the inside that your jaw will surely drop to the floor. The main altar, covered in wood carvings and dripping with gold, is considered one of the most beautiful baroque altars in the world. Fully restored in 2001 by an American team, it was sent to New York in 2002 for an exhibit of Brazilian sacred art at the Guggenheim. Given that it stands some 14 meters tall and is more than 12 tons of wood and gold, the altar was dismantled into 52 separate pieces for shipping. It has since been restored to its original home in the São Bento church. São Bento was built in 1761 in the location of an earlier church that was first built in 1599 and again in 1654 after the Dutch Invasion. At 10 A.M. on Sundays, the Benedictine monks perform Gregorian chants during mass—worth catching, no matter what your religious bent may be.

## MUSEUMS AND GALLERIES

The only things that outnumber the churches in Olinda are the artists. Nobody knows for sure how many there are, since a great many of them work inside their homes. Ateliers are spread all over town, but the main cluster is located on **Rua do Amparo,** along with restaurants and *pousadas.* In fact, most of the restaurants and *pousadas* on Rua do Amparo are also galleries or ateliers. Of note are the **Goya Restaurant** (Rua do Amparo 157, tel. 81/3439-4875), with paintings by the owner/chef; the **Pousada dos Quatro Cantos** (Rua Prudente de Moraes 4211, Carmo, tel. 81/3429-0220), exhibiting excellent paintings by the owner's daughter; the **Pousada do Peter** (Rua do Amparo 215, tel. 81/3439-2171), decorated with works by the owner, Peter Bauer; and the **Atelier Iza do Amparo** (Rua do Amparo 150, tel. 81/3429-2357) with works on canvas and clothing by the entire resident family. As you walk the streets of Olinda, merely peek inside the windows and doorways of the open houses and you're sure to find many more artists and their ateliers. They will all be more than happy to show you inside.

The **Museu de Arte Contemporânea** (Rua 13 de Maio, tel. 81/3429-2587, 9 A.M.–5 P.M. Tues.–Fri., 2–5 P.M. on weekends), in front of the stairs, hosts exhibitions by local contemporary artists. The building was once the ecclesiastical jailhouse, built in 1764. Across the street is the charming **Chapel of São Pedro Advíncula,** where the prisoners were allowed to pray (or perhaps forced to pray). The museum and the chapel are both open from 9 A.M.–1 P.M. Tuesday–Friday and 2–5 P.M. on weekends. While you're there, climb to the top of the stairs in front of the museum for a thrill. At the top is a small terrace and chapel used during Holy Week. Turn to the left to find an arts and crafts market just up the road.

Besides painters, there are numerous artisans in town. Popular crafts include carved wood panels (sometimes painted), carved wood miniatures, ceramics, and the famous Mamulengo puppets. The **Museu do Mamulengo** (Rua do Amparo 59) has more than 900 puppets on display, some dating from the 1800s. The puppets are used in folk festivals to act out comedies and folk legends. One of Olinda's artisans, **Silvio Botelho,** is rather famous for his huge

*bonecos* (dolls or puppets) that are worn on the streets of Olinda during Carnaval. You can see these at his **Casa dos Bonecos** (Big Dollhouse, Rua do Amparo 45, tel. 81/3439-2443, 8 A.M.–1 P.M. and 2–5 P.M. daily, R$2).

## OTHER SIGHTS

If you're into lighthouses, you might enjoy seeing the **Farol de Olinda** (Rua Ruth Costa Rodrigues), which is located on the far north side of town just past the Seminário de Olinda. Like many of the monuments in Olinda, the lighthouse is best viewed from above. Its black and white stripes are something of a trademark and you'll see the tower portrayed in miniature all over the arts and crafts fairs in town. It's not open for public visitation. The **Museu Regional de Olinda** (Rua do Amparo 128, 9 A.M.–5 P.M. Mon.–Fri. and 2–5 P.M. weekends, R$2) is located in a colonial building used by the church in 1745. Today, it houses furniture, religious art, and artifacts from the city's history. The **Museu de Arte Sacra** (Rua Bispo Coutinho 726, 9 A.M.–1 P.M. Tues.–Fri., R$1) is located on the north end of town and contains some religious sculpture and pieces from churches that no longer exist. There is nothing here any more impressive than what you can see in the principal churches around town, but if you happen to be descending Rua Bispo Coutinha on your way to the Igreja da Sé, then pop in for a look. Built in the 1700s as the governor's mansion, the **Palácio dos Governadores** (Rua de São Bento 123) is used to this day as government offices. You cannot go inside for viewing, but it's enough to walk past on your way to the São Bento church and sit for a moment in the *praça* in front and check out the complex from the outside. During festivals, this *praça* is spinning with activity, being one of the few level areas in town.

## ENTERTAINMENT AND NIGHTLIFE

If you happen to be in town during festival time, or on a weekend in the summer, then

**17th-century buildings line the streets of Olinda**

your nightlife options are pretty wide open. Just about everywhere you walk in town has something going on. All the bars and restaurants are loaded with people and the *praças* around town are alive with music and dance. During normal months, you can find activities around the main *praças* at night (especially the outdoor market at the Igreja da Sé) and along Avenida Beira Mar, the coastal highway at the north end of town. A few other key locations are spread throughout the town, but you may have to walk around a bit to find the action on any given night. There are no particular theaters, cinemas, or concert halls in Olinda, so shows are generally presented in the town squares. On Friday nights in the summer, starting around 10:30 P.M., the streets fill with musicians romancing the town with their serenades. Two main groups roam the streets (trying to avoid each other) and sing for anyone who wants to listen. They go well past midnight.

The central dive bar in town, where local artists mix with the tourists, is the **Bodega do Véio** (Rua do Amparo 212, tel. 81/3429-0185, 8:30 A.M.–11 P.M. Mon.–Sat., 8:30 A.M.–2 P.M. on Sun.). There is no place to stand at the bar itself, so people spill out onto the street with their cups of beer. If you get there early enough (or late enough), you might find a spot in their adjacent hillside veranda, which offers a great view of the street below. They have a few appetizers, like cheese and salami. Another casual place, though not quite as bohemian, is the **Licoteria Noctivagos** (Rua 13 de Maio 3, tel. 81/3429-6248, around 5–11 P.M. daily). The specialty here is homemade liqueur using such ingredients as ginger, coffee, and tropical fruit. The secret recipes were handed down from the slaves of Old Olinda. The ambience is nothing special, but it's an interesting place to sit and taste some special juices. Another dive bar experience is **Pitombeira dos Quatro Cantos** (Rua 27 de Janeiro 128, tel. 81/3439-4939, 4 P.M. until the last client Mon.–Fri.) near the Igreja de São Pedro Apóstolo. There is always activity here, including live music on Thursday nights. Again, this is nothing special in the atmosphere department. A final entry in the "simple bars" category is the *lanchonete*/bar in the Praça do Carmo at the entrance to town. In the afternoons and evenings, this *praça* has a casual but nice feeling to it and you can sit and have a drink and snack while watching the main road into Olinda.

Some places with more atmosphere are located along Avenida Beira Mar at the bottom of the hill just north of town. Practically in front of the lighthouse, there is a *praça* that fills with food and drink stands at night. You'll find several places to sit and have a drink in this area, both in the *praça* and farther up the coastal highway. One of the best is the **Marola Bar e Restaurante** (Trav. Dantas Barreto 66, tel. 81/3429-7079, 4 P.M.–midnight on Mon., 10 A.M.–midnight Tues.–Sun.), which is on the beach side of the highway, overlooking the ocean. They have great seating for drinks and serve a killer *peixada* (fish stew) for around R$22 for two people. Live music plays Thursday–Sunday. It can get pretty windy in the afternoon, but it calms down around 8 P.M.

## FESTIVALS AND EVENTS

There is something about historical towns in Brazil that call attention to themselves during **Carnaval.** Indeed, Olinda has become one of the most sought-after places to pass the festival. The streets throb with parades and parties and people generally letting loose. There are numerous *blocos* that parade up and down the streets with costumes and regional dances. Visitors can join any of these parades just by showing up. One of Olinda's signature events is the parade of giant dolls. Carnaval is opened with the call of the Homem da Meia Noite (Midnight Man), one of the special giants whose job is to wake up the town for the opening of the festival. At other times during Carnaval, the streets are filled with these giants. **Holy Week** in Olinda is celebrated with a procession that marches from the São Pedro church to the Igreja da Sé. There is also a reenactment of the passion of Christ that stops at various points in town. On August 6, there is a large festival at the Igreja da Sé, the **Festa do Senhor Salvador do Mundo.** Processions, presentations, and live music join the many stands in the arts and crafts fair at the church. Of course, Olinda has to have at least one festival of art

and that's **Arte em Toda Parte,** which takes place in November, usually from the 25th to the end of the month or beyond. Each weekend, there are public displays of art, both inside the galleries and establishments as well as on the streets. Olinda participates in the **New Year's Eve** festivities with a fireworks show. It's best viewed from the hills of Olinda.

## SHOPPING

For only a few dollars in most cases, you can take home with you a handcrafted souvenir from Olinda. Not only will you be patronizing the arts, but you will also be helping support the families involved in creating and marketing these regional treasures. Besides the aforementioned ateliers on **Rua do Amparo,** you should pay a visit to the **Centro de Artesanato** (Largo do Varadouro, 9 A.M.–5 P.M. Mon.–Fri.), in front of the São Bento church, also known as the **Mercado Eufrásio Barbosa.** Besides local arts and crafts, you'll see performances of regional dances, including *maracatu, ciranda,* and *coco de roda.* These occur mostly during peak season and festivals. The building itself was once the Royal Customs House. The **Mercado da Ribeira** (Rua Bernardo Vieira de Melo, 9 A.M.–6 P.M. daily), at the top of the stairs, was a 16th-century slave market and is now a center of arts and crafts from the region. Maybe the most interesting market is the **open market** at the Igreja da Sé. Every day at 4 P.M., the *praça* fills with stands exhibiting regional arts and crafts, food, and homemade liqueurs. On Sundays, there are Capoeira demonstrations and *maracatu* dances there.

## ACCOMMODATIONS

Rooms in Olinda go up 25–100 percent in peak season, except during Carnaval, when they triple and quadruple. If you want to experience Carnaval in Olinda, it's a good idea to call way ahead of time for reservations. There are a few hotels in the modern part of Olinda, which is not too far from the Centro Histórico. These do not increase in peak season and could be great

© CHRISTOPHER VAN BUREN

traditional wood carvings of Olinda

options for Carnaval, too. Several well-priced hotels appear at the entrance to Olinda on Rua do Sol, which runs parallel to the coastal highway, Avenida Beira Mar. The economical hotels usually have Brazilian-style water heaters and all hotels charge a 10-percent service tax. Exceptions are noted herein.

## Under R$100

The **N Hotel Pousada São Francisco** (Rua do Sol 127, tel. 81/3429-2109, www.pousadasaofrancisco.com.br, reservas@pousadasaofrancisco.com.br, R$60 s and R$85 d) has an excellent structure with 45 rooms, restaurant with regional cuisine, pool, sauna, and laundry service. Rooms are simple, but clean and modern. They come with air, TV, and phone. The **Olinda Hostel** (Rua do Sol 233, tel. 81/3429-1592, www.alberguedeolinda.com.br, alberguedeolinda@alberguedeolinda.com.br, R$25 group room, R$65 private room for two) is one of the better hostels in Brazil. It has a nice pool area with hammocks and reading tables as well as group and private rooms for couples or families. They can connect you with various excursions and transportation options to the

outlying beaches. In the heart of Old Olinda is the **Pousada do Peter** (Rua do Amparo 215, tel. 81/3439-2171, www.pousadadopeter.com.br, R$50 s and R$70 d during high or low season), which is installed in an old colonial manor. Not as well appointed or as sophisticated as its neighbor, Pousada do Amparo, Peter nevertheless offers a good value for its location. Out back, you get a panoramic view of Olinda and Recife beyond the pool area.

## R$100–200

Installed in a large historical manor, the **N Pousada dos Quatro Cantos** (Rua Prudente de Moraes 441, tel. 81/3429-0220, www.pousada4cantos.com.br, hotel@pousada4cantos.com.br, R$90 s and R$105 d, R$125 suites, and R$180 luxury rooms) offers a touch of Old Olinda at a very reasonable price. Almost all their rooms are different and range from simple and charming to a spacious loft in the attic overlooking the town. They have a courtyard with a huge shade tree, a breakfast den and a patio area overlooking the courtyard. The pool area is also quite charming, although not particularly private. Another charming installation

poolside cabana at the Pousada do Amparo

© CHRISTOPHER VAN BUREN

at the foot of Old Olinda is the **Hotel Sete Colinas** (Rua de São Francisco 307, tel. 81/3429-6055, www.hotel7colinasolinda.com.br, R$155 d in high or low season), with a huge pool and garden area looking out on the São Francisco church. Rooms have modern facilities with air, TV, and phone.

The **Parthenon Quatro Rodas Olinda** (Av. José Augusto Moreira 2200, tel. 81/3431-2955, 4rodas@cyb.com.br, www.accorhotels.com, R$65 s and R$85 d) is located in the Casa Caiada neighborhood about five kilometers north of Old Olinda and overlooks the beach. They have a modern facility with a pool, sauna, gym, restaurant, and Internet (extra).

### R$200–500

If you want to treat yourself to a first-class experience in the midst of old, colonial charm, check into the ⋈ **Pousada do Amparo** (Rua do Amparo 191, tel. 81/3439-1749, R$170 s, R$210 d, and R$315 suite). The *pousada* is located in a colonial manor in the center of town. It has a view of Olinda and Recife in the distance out back. Each of the 11 rooms is unique and they all have modern conveniences like hot

tubs, air, phone, and cable TV. The beds are super-comfortable with fine bedding materials. Outside, there is a quaint garden patio, a pool, and a kiosk bar. They serve an abundant breakfast buffet with many regional treats and a wine cellar with a cozy tasting room. Children under 6 are free and they don't charge a service tax. At the time of this writing, they were opening a second location nearby with another eight rooms.

## FOOD

### International

Two of the more popular restaurants in town, possibly due to their privileged locations along Rua do Amparo, serve contemporary international food. ⋈ **Goya** (Rua do Amparo 157, tel. 81/3439-4875, noon–midnight Wed.–Mon.) has contemporary cuisine made by two Dutch chefs (and artists, of course). Both the food and the art are well prepared and abstract. Meals cost around R$45. The second restaurant on this street is the **Oficina do Sabor** (Rua do Amparo 335, tel. 81/3429-3331, noon–4 P.M. Mon.–Fri., noon–1 A.M. on Sat., noon–5 P.M.

on Sun.), an elegant place with a lovely interior and patio seating out back. The house special is *jerimum* (pumpkin), cooked in various ways, including with shrimp and lobster. They have a good wine list (for Brazil). A meal will set you back R$80. The **Tratoria Dom Francesco** (Rua Prudente de Morais 358, tel. 81/3429-3852, noon–3 P.M. and 7 P.M.–midnight Mon.–Fri., 7 P.M.–midnight on Sat.) is set in a small, very quaint Italian kitchen. They have only a few tables, so you may have to wait for an opening, or make a reservation. For a real tossed salad of cultures, try **Ꮇ Kwetú** (Av. Manoel Borba 338, tel. 81/3439-8867, noon–4 P.M. and 6:30 P.M.–midnight Thurs.–Mon., 6 P.M.–midnight on Wed., closed Sun.) near the front entrance of town at the Praça Rio Branco (also known as Praça do Jacaré). Here you have a Belgian chef, creating French, Indian, Moroccan, and Thai dishes in an African ambience. The *kuetú* means "our house" in an ancient language of Zaire. Meals cost about R$60.

### Quick and Casual

Informal and inexpensive eateries are clustered along Rua Beira Mar, the coastal highway, at the entrance to town. You can stroll along the coastal highway going north until you see the many offerings. Hamburgers and caipirinhas are the mainstay.

### Regional

A local favorite that is becoming legendary in Olinda is **Casa de Noca** (Rua Bertioga 243, tel. 81/3439-1040, 11 A.M.–midnight daily). It's slightly difficult to find because it looks like any other house on the street. But in the far back is a patio area where they serve up a single dish: *carne de sol* with cooked cheese and boiled *macaxeira* (manioc root), smothered in liquid butter. One plate offers enough sustenance for three people. It's not high-brow by any stretch but it certainly fills the stomach, maybe even a little too much—you may need a stretcher to carry you out of there if you have a sensitive digestive system. One plate is a mere R$12. The **Restaurante Mourisco** (Rua 27 de Janeiro 7, tel. 81/3429-

1390, noon–3 P.M. and 7–11 P.M. daily) is located near the Praça dos Governadores in an 18th-century building of Moorish design. The inside is filled with trees and cozy places to sit. They offer fish, meat, and chicken dishes with a regional flair. Open for lunch and dinner. It costs around R$35 per person.

## INFORMATION AND SERVICES

The tourist information office is located at the entrance to town in the Praça do Carmo. From there, you can begin your walk up into the hills of town. There are no banks in Old Olinda; you should do your banking in Recife before coming here. If you need a bank, your best bet is to catch a bus from Olinda to either the Centro de Convenções toward Recife or to the Tacaruna Shopping Center. You can catch a bus from the top of Rua do Amparo that goes there. There are Internet cafés at the Praça do Carmo and one or two along Rua do Amparo.

## GETTING THERE AND AROUND

The Rio Doce/Piedade bus line goes from Praia de Piedade in Recife, past downtown Recife, and past Olinda to the Rio Doce bus terminal about 20 minutes north of Olinda. It costs around R$2.50. To get off in Olinda, tell the cashier that you want the Praça do Carmo. A taxi from downtown Recife to Olinda will cost around R$15–18. Within the Centro Histórico of Olinda, everything is accessible on foot.

To go north to Maria Farinha or the Island of Itamaracá, you have two options, both involving two buses: First, you can catch the bus from the top of Rua do Amparo to the Tacaruna Shopping Center. From there, you cross the highway and catch the Pau Amarelo to Maria Farinha. Your second option is to catch any bus on the coastal highway in front of Old Olinda that is going north through the Casa Caiada neighborhood. Get off at any stop in Casa Caiada and switch to the Casa Caiada/Maria Farinha line. A taxi from Olinda to Maria Farinha will cost around R$40, a reasonable option for small groups.

# Beaches Near Recife

## NORTH OF RECIFE

### Maria Farinha and Coroa do Avião

The first worthwhile destination north of Recife/Olinda is Maria Farinha, which is at the mouth of the Igarassu River. Because the river flows slightly northward as it hits the ocean, the land forms a sort of point, which is Maria Farinha. On one side of the point is the calm river with many small wooden piers stretching out into the water. Boats wait around the piers to take tourists out on excursions. On the other side of the point is the vast, blue ocean with small waves breaking on the shore, leaving masses of seaweed on the sand. You can walk around the point from the ocean to the river and back. The very tip is filled with seaweed and the water is shallow and breaks sideways across the landscape.

If you like looking out on the ocean from a secluded and shady beach bungalow—with sand under your feet, a warm breeze in the air, and only the sound of birds and the ocean to keep you company—then stop for awhile at the **Club 3** beach bar (tel. 81/3436-7481) on the ocean side. It's not a fancy place, but they have a very special location. Weekends get crowded around lunchtime until dusk. They make some decent fried fish, although you should be prepared to wait awhile as the kitchen is rather slow. But who's in a hurry? They have rooms available with noisy ceiling fans, fleas, and lots of mosquitoes for around R$45 double.

The key attraction in Maria Farinha is the **catamaran tour** that takes you to the **Coroa da Avião** island. Actually, it's more like a large sandbar in the middle of the ocean. At low tide it's a great place to kick up some white sand and dip into the water. A green strip in the middle of the island (the part that remains above sea level), has some permanent island bars that serve drinks and lunch. Your tour continues with a visit to the **Island of Itamaracá** to see **Fort Orange** on the south-most tip. Catamaran tours leave from the pier at Cinco Pontas near the Forte das Cinco Pontas in Recife. You can also take a bus to Maria Farinha and catch the catamaran tour that leaves from the **Amoaras Resort** (Rua Garoupa 525, Maria Farinha, tel. 81/3436-1221, hotel@hotelamoaras.com.br, R$130–160 d with a nice breakfast), which is on the river side of Maria Farinha. The buses are a bit tricky: From Olinda, catch the Rio Doce/Casa Caiada bus to any bus stop in the Casa Caiada area. Transfer to the Casa Caiada/Maria Farinha bus from there. Ask to be let off at the *entrada para Maria Farinha* (entrance to Maria Farinha). At this bus stop (or in front of the small market up ahead), you can catch a VW bus for R$1 to the final stop in front of the *padaria* (bakery), where you then walk a short way to the Amoaras Resort. The entire trip will take about two hours. Call in advance to reserve a location and ask if they have enough people to make the trip, as they don't leave with fewer than 8 or 10 people. The trip is R$25 per person and leaves between 9 A.M. and 10:30 A.M., so you have to get up early to make all these connections. You can also stay a night at the Amoaras Resort, which has a great pool and bar area and two restaurants.

If you miss the boat and have a group of four or more, then you can probably find a private boat to take you to the island for about the same price. Just ask around. On the far shore of the river, across from Maria Farinha, there are two nice beaches for swimming and sipping something cold under an umbrella. Your catamaran trip might include a visit to these beaches on the way to Coroa da Avião. If not, you can hire a small boat to take you across. Negotiate the price.

Note: There are no banks at Maria Farinha, so be sure to hit the ATM for cash before you leave.

### Ilha de Itamaracá

The most interesting destination on the north coast of Recife is the Island of Itamaracá. About 50 kilometers from Recife, the island was once

the point at Maria Farinha

a major outpost during the early colonization period. Around the island were many sea battles between the Portuguese and the Dutch. In fact, there are several sunken ships in these waters and farther south toward Recife, excellent places for scuba diving. There are 11 main beaches on the island—all along the side facing the open ocean. On the north-most tip is **Praia Fortinho,** which has calm waters and semi-deserted beaches and a few beach bars. Several Recife residents keep summerhouses here. Further south is the **Praia do Sossego,** one of the nicest beaches on the island with calm, shallow water and no crowds. In the middle of the island are the **Quatro Cantos** and **Pilar** beaches, the most urbanized beaches of the island. They have reefs not far offshore that make the area popular for diving and snorkeling. Equipment and guides are available in the area. The most popular spot for swimming and sunbathing is **Praia Baixa Verde,** just south of Pilar. Here the water is calm and there are plenty of beach kiosks to make life comfortable. Most of the hotels on the island are in this vicinity or just a bit farther south.

Note that the beaches on the north end of the island are not safe after sunset. It's best to visit the island during the day and return to Recife or Olinda at night. Unless you have a car, you should stick to the middle and southern beaches.

At the south-most tip of the island are two important attractions. The first is the **Peixe Boi Eco-Center** (Estrada do Forte, Praia do Forte Orange, tel. 81/3544-1056, 10 A.M.–4 P.M. Tues.–Sun.), a habitat and research center for the preservation of sea cows. Inside the center are nurseries, habitats, and presentations about these awesome animals. The second attraction at the south tip is **Forte Orange** (Estrada do Forte, tel. 81/9935-1925, 9 A.M.–4:30 P.M. daily), originally built by the Dutch out of mud and grass, then destroyed and rebuilt out of stone by the Portuguese in 1654. Inside are arts and crafts shops and a small museum with artifacts from the time of the Dutch Invasion. The beach around Forte Orange is beautiful and excellent for swimming. From here, you can catch excursions out to the Coroa de Avião island.

(See *Outdoor Activities* in the *Recife* section for information on excursions to the Ilha de Itamaracá.)

## SOUTH OF RECIFE

The first beaches worth visiting south of Recife are Gaibu, Calhetas, and Cabo de Santo Agostino. This entire stretch of coastline is often referred to as **Cabo de Santo Agostino,** probably because the highway goes to there, passing up the other beaches above it. For this reason, it's not easy to get to Gaibu and Calhetas from Recife—you have to backtrack a bit. But the journey is well worth it, as these are two of the nicest beaches on Recife's south coast. **Gaibu** has an alternative, hippie feel to it from the surfer crowd that frequented the place in the '70s. On one side is the open ocean, where surfers practice their sport. The other side has calm, clear waters for swimming and boats that will take you out to pools for snorkeling. There are plenty of beach bars to keep you company and even some *pousadas* in case you decide to stay the night. **Calhetas** is a small and charming beach with clear waters that stay warm all the time. The beach bars are also small and charming. Day trips to Calhetas leave from Recife for around R\$30. Check with your hotel for details. If all else fails, call the **Navegantes Praia Hotel** (Rua dos Navegantes 1997, Boa Viagem, tel. 81/3325-2689, tel. 81/3326-9609) and sign up with one of their tours. Note that you can visit the beaches of Cabo de Santo Agostino by dune buggy from Porto de Galinhas on full-day trips that cost around R\$80–120 for up to four people.

# Porto de Galinhas

Easily the most sought-after destination on the coast of Pernambuco, Porto de Galinhas has grown into a high-volume tourist village with dozens of hotels, resorts, restaurants, and, of course, beaches to explore. During the summer months, weekends in the village can get pretty crowded. In fact, it's best to avoid weekends altogether, as Galinhas is also popular year-round with the locals, who come to spend a day at the beach with a minimum of expenditure. The town limits the number of buses that enter the village, which helps keep the masses to a minimum. If you happen to be in town on a sunny weekend or in peak season, there are numerous remote beaches for avoiding crowds. Just catch a buggy and head on out. The farther you go away from the village, the more tranquil and deserted the beach will be. Some local favorites are Muro Alto to the north and Maracaípe to the south, both offering water sports, clear and warm water for swimming, and beach kiosks for relaxing with a cold one. These beaches are still fairly close to the village and can get crowded during peak season and weekends. Farther out are the beaches of Calhetas to the north and Carneiros to the south, which will be much less crowded. They make excellent day trips. At night, most of the locals have gone home and the village belongs to the tourists once again. Of course, on weekdays, everything is more calm and easygoing.

You can easily spend 3–4 days getting to know Porto de Galinhas and the surrounding areas. You might even think about spending a night in Tamandaré, so you can really check out the beaches and islands on the south coast.

## PORTO DE GALINHAS VILLAGE

While it has grown significantly over the past five years, the village of Porto de Galinhas retains its charm and character. One of the most popular activities is to walk up and down the streets of the village, looking in the various shops and perhaps stopping for coffee or juice along the way. There are numerous shopping *galerias* around town and about 20 *praças* where you can sit and rest in the shade (the *praças* are numbered 1–20). There are many boutique shops in town that offer specialty items, arts, and crafts from the local area. You can even find shops with simple offerings and modest prices if you look around. Another shopping village is at the far end of Maracaípe Beach with more rustic, handmade crafts from local artisans.

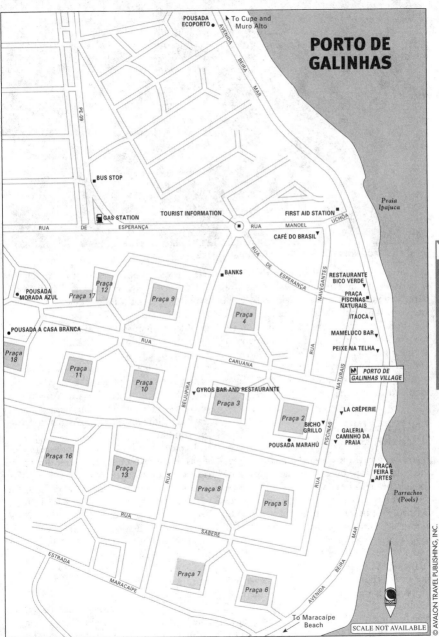

local arts and crafts in the Porto de Galinhas village

At night, another walk around the village is in order, as the atmosphere changes after dark. Restaurants begin to fill with people, the streets are illuminated with colored lights from the shops, and the energy of a night on the town is in the air. Choosing a restaurant or bar is a great goal to have as you walk around town and get to know the establishments. There is something for every taste, both in the way of food and atmosphere.

## SNORKELING AT IPOJUCA BEACH

If you walk on the main road directly through the village to the ocean, you will drop onto Ipojuca Beach. The center of activity in Porto de Galinhas (in the daytime), Ipojuca Beach is filled with things to do. Beach bars line up along the shore above the sand and offer all kinds of drinks and seafood lunch plates. Some have live music playing. Others have tables and chairs on the sand, so you can stay as close to the water as possible. The water on the left side of Ipojuca is warm and shallow and there is a sandbar that extends into the water some 50 feet, making it look like you're standing up in the middle of the ocean. As you walk to the

left side of Ipojuca, waiters at the beach bars will try to lure you into their chairs with a cold drink and a menu of lunch choices. Remember that while seated at a beach table, you are free to order from anyone passing by with a cold coconut water or other delight. But be careful of salespeople who come close to your table to make a sale. Some have been known to slip on your sandals (sitting under the table, perhaps?) while demonstrating their wares. Anything on top of the table is in a perilous position. Don't leave anything on the table unattended, even for a minute.

To the right side of Ipojuca sit the main tide-pools. Boats wait out in the water during low tide to take passengers out to see them. They are about 30 meters offshore and make up one of Brazil's most popular *parrachos* (rocky reefs). Second only to the reefs at Maracajaú in Natal, the Ipojuca formation is so extensive that it's more like an underwater rock garden, spanning some three square kilometers of shoreline.

The pools are like natural, saltwater aquariums the size of football fields, and snorkeling among them is an experience you should take with you when you go. For those uncomfortable in the water, there are pools so shallow during low tide that a person can stand up on

## SNORKELING IN THE PARRACHOS

**P**arrachos are clusters of rocks in the ocean, usually found in shallow, sandy areas. They are rich in sea life and perfect for fishing and snorkeling. Brazilians also call these formations *piscinas naturais* (natural pools) because the rock formations leave large pools between them. The pools usually have soft, sandy bottoms. During an extreme low tide, parts of the reefs are exposed above the water and it becomes tricky to navigate through the pools, even in the small *jangadas* (flat boats) that the fishermen and local guides use. However, this is the best time for snorkeling. The reefs are covered in algae, seaweed, and pointed sea anemones that make it difficult to walk safely and comfortably over them. That's usually not a problem, since most visitors are interested in swimming in the large pools, particularly around the edges of the rocks, where most of the colorful fish and sea life can be found. Here are some tips for getting the most out of the *parrachos*:

• Invest in your own snorkeling equipment. The best prices are in the United States, since much of the equipment is made there. However, you can purchase everything in Brazil (in the city if possible) at fairly decent prices. With your own equipment, you'll be much more prepared for and comfortable on diving excursions,

and you can take advantage of beaches that do not have snorkeling equipment available.

• A set of small swimming fins can be a lot of fun and enhance your control and speed under water. Large fins can be cumbersome in the *parrachos*. If you don't use fins (or even if you do), be sure to purchase a pair of surf booties to protect your feet from the reefs. Invariably, there will be times when you have to stabilize yourself with your feet and the rocky reefs can be sharp and dangerous. Buy booties and fins together for a proper fit. Many people prefer diving with simple swimming goggles and no snorkel. This provides more freedom while swimming around the pools.

• Remember that your back is exposed to the sun while you snorkel. Wear a tee shirt or use waterproof sunscreen on your neck, back, and legs. Men with facial hair (particularly mustaches) often have trouble with water entering the mask. After many uncomfortable dives, I now shave all my facial hair when heading to the *parrachos*. You can also apply Vasoline to your mustache to help seal the mask to your lip.

• For some of the deeper pools, a set of diving weights can help you dive down under the water for a look at the sandy bottom and the bottom-dwelling animals. You can rent these from scuba shops in the area before heading out to the pools.

---

the sandy bottom, stick his snorkel-clad face in the water, and watch the show standing up. Another popular approach is to swim normally around the pools with only the aid of small, underwater goggles. This leaves you very free and unfettered.

The pools are not far from shore and good swimmers can actually swim out to them in about 10 minutes. However, taking a *jangada* out to the pools has many advantages, including having somewhere to put your mask when you want to take it off for a few minutes. The *jangada* drivers charge about R$8 to take you out and back—a total of two hours.

The thrill of the pools at Ipojuca (and else-

where in the area) comes at low tide. When you arrive in town, ask at your hotel or at the beach for a basic timetable. And remember that the tide comes in an hour earlier or later every day, depending on whether the moon is waxing or waning. The best time to go out is early in the morning (the first low tide of the day) when the fish are hungry and the waters are undisturbed.

## CUPE

A stroll along the shore from Ipojuca to Cupe takes about 1.5 hours. If you make it all the way to the Pontal do Cupe (the point at the far end), then you'll be able to cool off with a dip in the water and pools. Unfortunately, the surf between Ipojuca and the Pontal is way too rough for swimming and a handful of international tourists have even drowned there over the years. Still, the main reason for heading to Cupe is to enjoy the walk itself. The beach is extensive and beautiful, if unswimmable. You'll pass a number of beachfront hotels on the way; the area from Cupe to the village is loaded with accommodations. You'll also pass an extensive coconut plantation that makes a picturesque addition to the shoreline.

## MURO ALTO

The award for "Warmest Water on the Brazilian Coastline" goes to Praia Muro Alto in Porto de Galinhas. The reefs at Muro Alto (High Wall) form a thick wall that completely blocks the incoming surf. The result is a pool of water—about 100 meters wide and two kilometers long—that is so calm and warm, you'll forget that it's part of the ocean. The average water temperature is 29°C. Most people huddle

around the southern tip, where the pool comes to an end at the reefs. This is the warmest and calmest part, and temporary beach kiosks are set up here with tables and shade umbrellas. The north end of the beach is used for noisy water sports involving motorized vehicles, but if you like getting away from the crowds, then the northern stretch is where you want to go. It's noisier but has fewer people, and you can walk past the motor activities to a quiet part near the point.

Most people spend about half a day in Muro Alto before heading to another beach, but if you are particularly fond of the clear, warm water here, then a full day in Muro Alto is perfectly within reason.

## ⚑ MARACAÍPE BEACH

At high tide, ocean water spills into the Maracaípe River basin and causes a sort of high river tide as well. Called the Pontal de Maracaípe, the area is a kind of saltwater marshland. Clusters of trees and shrubs that grow in these waters form islands where crabs and sea

Muro Alto beach

horses flourish among the tall root systems. Where the river passes so close to the ocean that only a sandbar separates the two, *jangadas* (flat boats) take small groups up the river to search for sea horses and relax at the floating bars that anchor themselves around the islands. They charge R$6 per person for about two hours. The water is warm, clear, and *salobra* (semi-salty); the bottom is pure sand; and there are no large fish in the waters. Still, snorkeling up in the dark, swampy root systems can be creepy for some. To maintain the sanctity of this sea horse habitat, the *jangadas* have no motors. Instead, they are propelled by pushing off the bottom of the river with long sticks. The only other vehicles allowed up the river are kayaks, which are available for three-hour river excursions—four people at a time for R$12 per person. For information, call tel. 81/3552-1111. A final option at the sandbar of Maracaípe Point is to sip a cold beverage while sitting at a table, waist-deep in the river. It's extremely refreshing and if you stick around until sunset, you're in for an amazing show.

The Maracaípe River basin is actually at the far end of Maracaípe Beach. Along the beach itself are numerous kiosks, beach bars, and shops. You'll find convenient outdoor showers and restaurants for lunch. The last bar before the river has excellent spicy fish soup. There is a small village toward the south end—the Vila de Todos os Santos—which has arts and crafts stands during the summer months and on weekends. The surf along this beach is pretty rough and not recommended for swimming. Water sports, on the other hand, are very popular here, particularly surfing and kite surfing. In fact, Maracaípe Beach has been the location of several international surfing events.

If you like to walk along the beach, you can walk all the way from Ipojuca Beach at the village of Galinhas to Maracaípe. It's about six kilometers and takes around two hours. Maracaípe and the Pontal can easily occupy an entire day in Porto de Galinhas. For that reason, the half-day buggy trips that include Maracaípe will probably leave you wanting more.

**cooling off with a cold one at Maracaípe**

## SARRAMBI

If you want to get to the deserted Island of Santo Aleixo, the best launching pad is Sarrambi Beach. Here you'll find boats to take you on a variety of excursions, passing different islands of the coast and stopping at clear pools for snorkeling. The beach is fairly popular with surfers (not as popular as Maracaípe) as it has medium-sized waves and a wide stretch of sand. The road from Porto de Galinhas passes through the town of Sarrambi and then makes its way through a private condominium to gain access to the beach. This path is necessary because buggies are not allowed onto the beaches in this area, a distinct difference from most of the beaches in the northeast region.

## ILHA DE SANTO ALEIXO

Ever thought about being stranded on a deserted island? Well, this may be your chance, although it's unlikely you'll get stranded here. About eight kilometers of the coast near the town of Barra de Sinharim, the Ilha de Santo Aleixo is privately owned and 100-percent deserted. There are no structures of any kind, so you have to think about what you're gong to bring with you (what book would you take to a deserted island and so on). Water, for one, is a good idea. You can hike all around the island, including a trek up to the tallest peak, where you get an incredible view of the island and the blue ocean all around. You may actually wish you were stranded here. Since beaches in Brazil cannot be owned (the sandy part), the owners cannot prevent you from docking on the island, even in your own boat. You can take an organized excursion from Sarrambi, which is a five-hour tour (I know what you're thinking) for R$25 per person. There are tours that leave from Porto de Galinhas for R$30 per person. You can also call tel. 81/3552-1111 or tel. 81/2455-2765 for more options. Tours also leave from Tamandaré for about R$35 per person.

## TAMANDARÉ

Many well-to-do families from Recife and all over Pernambuco have summer homes in Tamandaré. It seems to be in style. The town itself has very little to offer travelers, but there are two very popular beaches along the northern coast. The first is **Praia Tamandaré,** where you'll find calm water, beach bars, and natural pools just offshore at low tide. In the summer and on weekends, this beach gathers crowds and you'll find various water sports practiced here (available for participation). A number of *pousadas* line themselves up along the beach in case you want to spend the night. About seven kilometers to the north is **Praia dos Carneiros.** To get there by land, you have to pass through a private resort. This is not all bad. The resort makes a few great services available for those on the beach, such as bathrooms, a bar, and a restaurant. Because they charge a service fee for this, the beach is wonderfully free of riff-raff and in pristine condition, looking like it must have in the early 1500s, when it was discovered. Situated at the mouth of Rio Formoso, Carneiros has transparent, warm water and at low tide, natural pools reveal themselves just off shore. Paradise is always just a bit more expensive.

Buggy trips in Tamandaré take you to Praia dos Carneiros (and a few local sights) for R$25 for up to four people. Trips take around 2–3 hours. You might prefer to just pay a buggy like a taxi to drop you off at Carneiros for the day. You can arrange return trip at the resort on the beach. Another buggy trip takes you to two different beaches and a waterfall. A four-hour trip costs R$60 for up to four people. You can also take a boat excursion; there are three offered, mixing up the different beaches and islands of the area, including one excursion that passes through Carneiros and another that goes out to Ilha de Santo Aleixo. Prices vary, but the average is R$30 per person.

## BUGGY EXCURSIONS

Porto de Galinhas has a relatively strict system of registration for *bugeiros* (buggy drivers). The town's 200 or so registered drivers are all authorized to enter into the beach areas (not on the beaches themselves) and they have a few standards to keep up, like the quality of their buggy and some mild tourism training. All registered *bugeiros* have a *credenciado* sign on their vehicles. Buggies have set excursions, but also double as taxis, so you can set up your own excursion if you like. Almost all prices are pre-established. The main trip is a two-hour sampler of Cupe, Muro Alto, and Maracaípe for R$60 for up to four people. If you have fewer than four, try to negotiate a discount. Most likely, you'll want something more than this sampler, like a full day in Maracaípe or a trip to Tamandaré. All of this can be arranged and negotiated with the *bugeiros*. You can count on a full-day trip to Tamandaré costing around R$120–160 for up to four people. Full-day trips to Calhetas or Carneiros are R$100–120 and a full day in Muro Alto or Maracaípe goes for R$40–50. A quick ride to your hotel in Cupe from the village will cost R$7–10 by buggy or taxi. A ride to Muro Alto is R$15. Buggies are on duty 24 hours and are easily spotted on the streets of the village, especially near the gas station at the entrance to town. Their organization is at tel. 81/3552-1930.

## SCUBA DIVING

Diving activities are abundant in these parts. You can take a scuba baptism (beginner) dive in the clear pools offshore or, for those already licensed, join an excursion to any number of spots from 4–40 meters deep. There are a few shipwrecks offshore that are available for exploring and some night dives offered. Get in touch with **Atlantic** (Av. Beira Mar, tel. 81/3552-2327, www.atlanticdiving.pro.br),

## WHAT'S WITH THOSE BIG CHICKENS, ANYWAY?

When Kiki Zonari was the Minister of Tourism in Galinhas, she had the idea to turn the unpopular *galinhas* image (*galinha* meaning chicken) into a favorable town mascot. Today, besides cute little chicken images in every souvenir shop in town, there are huge chickens sculpted out of palm-tree stumps lining the village streets. You can't miss them. Kiki is responsible for that, too. As head of tourism for the town, she gave great incentives to any artist who created chicken art. To start the ball rolling, she lured a sculptor from Olinda who was working with palm-tree fiber to the area. Since Kiki was the granddaughter of a palm tree baron and had a huge coconut plantation in Porto de Galinhas, her promise of an endless supply of palm trees was enough to get the artist to move down the coast. His outdoor atelier is just north of town in the beginning of the Cupe Beach area.

Kiki took charge of tourism when the town was not as popular as it is today. One of her first missions was to clean it up and make it presentable to an international crowd. That meant getting some kind of limits on the number of *farofeiras* who frequented the town on weekends. These are folks from the surrounding neighborhoods and towns who visit the beaches on the weekends, and have a rowdy, destructive bent.

Kiki's first move was to demand that each bus line entering the city present all documents required by law for operating. That eliminated most of the busses right off the bat. She then prohibited dune buggies from driving on the beaches, another provision of Brazilian law that most beach towns simply ignore. Buggy drivers were up in arms at the change in policy. But to protect their interests, Kiki started an association of certified buggy drivers and restricted access to some beaches—only certified drivers could enter. That helped placate them a bit. Finally, she went after the city's image and spruced up the streets and public spaces. That's where the chickens come in.

located in front of the Peixe na Telha restaurant. They have English-speaking guides available.

## ENTERTAINMENT AND NIGHTLIFE

The village has something going on almost every night. First and foremost, the various bars around town are always alive with people after dark. Some bars turn into dance clubs by arranging a little space on the floor and hiring some live music. Some places to check out are **Bicho do Mato** (Rua das Piscinas Naturais, tel. 81/3552-1290, 8 P.M. until the last client daily) inside a small shopping galeria. There, the tables fill with people of all ages around 10–11 P.M. and their patio becomes a dance floor with live music. There's a R$10–15 consumption minimum. Get there early to get a good table. Also, **Mameluco Bar** (on the beach at Ipojuca, tel. 81/9113-3636) has beach-bash parties starting at happy hour. For a more dance-club scene, try the **Hotel Village** (PE-09, Km 5.5, tel. 81/3552-1038, starts around 11 P.M. and goes until sunrise) on Tuesday and Thursday for *forró* dancing or **PontX Club** (Travessa dos Navegantes, tel. 81/3552-3032, starts after 11 P.M. and goes until sunrise) for disco and lounge music Monday–Saturday.

Nightlife spots in Porto de Galinhas are known to come and go, so walk around town and visit the various *praças* to find current spots. You can also ask at your *pousada*.

## FESTIVALS AND EVENTS

In the last week of June, the village celebrates something called **Porto Forró**. There are music shows, boat races, and street festivities.

## ACCOMMODATIONS

Hotels are situated along the beaches from the Porto de Galinhas village to Muro Alto. The village has mostly economical and mid-range options, while the northern beaches have mid-range to luxury hotels.

### Under R$100

Down a sandy road several blocks from the beach is the **Pousada A Casa Branca** (Praça 18, tel. 81/3552-1808, www.pousadaacasa-branca.com.br, R$25 pp), part of the Hostelling International chain. They have good facilities with group and private rooms. A private room with air-conditioning is slightly more.

About two kilometers north of the village at the beginning of Cupe Beach is the **Ⓜ Tabajuba Pousada** (PE-09, Km 6.5, tel. 81/3552-1049, www.tabajuba.com.br, info@tabajuba.com.br, R$175 d, R$250 in peak season). It is in an area loaded with economical and mid-range options, but Tabajuba stands out as one of the best. They have a friendly atmosphere, 24-hour ice-cream access, pool, beach access, and an excellent café/restaurant for breakfast (included). They do not allow children under 12 (it's designed for couples). **Pousada Marahú** (Praça 2, tel. 81/3552-1700, www.pousadamarahu.com.br) is well located just outside the village center and within walking distance to everything. They have clean rooms a good breakfast and pool. What more could you want? R$95. At the edge of the village is the **Pousada Morada Azul** (Praça 20, tel. 81/3552-1143, www.moradaazul.com.br, R$85 d, R$150 peak season) with pool, TV, air, and a quaint breakfast.

### R$100–250

The **Ⓜ Tabapitanga Pousada** (PE-09, Km 4, tel. 81/3552-1321, www.tabapitinga.com.br, info@tabapitinga.com.br, R$300–400) is the special passion of Kiki Zonari and her American husband Scott. Kiki's place is among the most charming in Galinhas. Rooms are individual cottages with comfortable beds, TV, air, and gas-heated water. She also has an excellent breakfast buffet, pool with tropical bar, and beach service in front of the hotel. It's located at the far end of Cupe Beach. A taxi into the village from the hotel is R$10. The **Hotel Solar Porto de Galinhas** (PE-09, Km 7, tel. 81/3552-0001, www.solarportode-galinhas.com.br, R$200 d, R$300 peak season) is at the beginning of the Cupe Beach just north of the village (walking distance along the beach to the village). It offers a beachfront location with a great pool area and options for daytime excursions (buggy, jet ski, etc.). Rooms have air and TV. Every room in the **Pousada Ecoporto** (PE–09, Km 6.5, tel. 81/3552-1781, www.ecoporto.com.br, R$135 d, R$235 in peak season) has a view of the ocean. So does the lovely pool area. And if you want to get even closer, they have a beach kiosk and beach service in front of the hotel.

## R$250–500

At the far end of Praia Cupe, in the middle of a large coconut grove is the  **Hotel Pontal de Ocaporã** (PE–09, Km 4, tel. 81/3552-1400, tel. 81/3552-0088, www.ocapora.com.br, info@ocapora.com.br, R$250 d and R$450 beachfront suite, R$390 and R$550 during peak season), a large hotel that does not sacrifice anything in the way of charm. The rooms are built in pairs, each pair in its own separate chalet; some chalets have ocean views. There

the grounds at the Hotel Pontal de Ocaporã

© CHRISTOPHER VAN BUREN

is a beautiful pool area with three pools and a tropical bar and patio. They have a fourth pool that looks onto the ocean, and there's beach service in front of the hotel. The restaurant is top-notch and serves one of the finest breakfast buffets (included) you'll find on the coast of Brazil. Their service in general is excellent. The only thing that does not quite match the rest of the package is their handling of transportation into town. You end up having to take a taxi (at a slight discount) there and back every time you want to go into town. There is a van that makes the trip twice a day for R$2, but it doesn't always leave when you want to go. Otherwise, this hotel is a jewel.

Drop into the **Nannai Beach Resort** at Muro Alto beach (Praia de Muro Alto, Ipojuca, tel. 81/3552-0100, www.nanai.com.br, R$585 standard, R$1325 luxury bungalow during low season, prices go up about 40 percent during peak season) even if you don't have the money to stay there. It's worth a look. It is inspired by the Bora Bora hotels in Thailand, with hundreds of square meters of swimming pool circling the property and passing the many bungalow apartments, which are constructed on stilts. Your stay there includes breakfast and dinner for around R$600 per day. Right next to the main beach in Muro Alto is another resort hotel that is quite famous in the area, the **Summerville Beach Resort** (Praia de Muro Alto, tel. 81/3302-5555, www.summervilleresort.com.br, R$550–900 double). It's a fully-equipped resort that does not expect you to ever want to set foot outside of the property. There are numerous bars, restaurants, and activities during the day (archery, gymnastics, games, etc.). At night, they have live music and dancing. Rooms are bungalow-style with air and TV. And, of course, the pool is enormous. Breakfast and dinner included.

## FOOD

### International

**La Crêperie** (Rua Beijupirá, tel. 81/3552-1831, 6 P.M.–midnight on weekdays and 2 P.M.–midnight on weekends, from R$12 per person) has been in the village for more than 10 years serving crepes and salads. On Tuesdays, they have an all-you-can-eat menu for a set price, along with live music. They have a cozy patio with a great atmosphere at night. The beachfront restaurant ⋈ **Itaoca** (Rua da Esperança, tel. 81/3552-1309, 10 P.M. until the last client daily), on the right side at the water, has a perfect location with a deck overlooking the beach. They serve a variety of international dishes, including fish and paella. You can sit on the deck or inside.

### Quick and Casual

All along **Rua da Esperança** are restaurants, pizzerias, *lanchonetes,* and every type of café and burger joint you can hope for. You're sure to find something in your price range with the atmosphere you want. Look for the roasted chickens during lunch and dinner at the **Bar do Marcelo** (*saida para Mariana,* exit to Mariana, tel. 81/3552-1830, 10 A.M. until the last customer daily). They're only R$14 and its enough for two. There's an excellent kiosk at the end of Rua da Esperança (near the beach), called **Café do Brasil,** that serves coffee, coconut water, and drinks. They have a cool, tropical kiosk setting. Other great cafés are spread around the shopping *galerias* in town. Take a look down Rua das Piscinas Naturais for the **Galeria Caminho da Praia** for a number of quaint places.

### Regional Favorites

One of the most popular places for seafood is ⋈ **Peixe na Telha** (Av. Beira Mar, tel. 81/3552-1323, 9 P.M. until the last client daily, R$20), which serves, among other things, fish stew on a *telha* (shingle). It's overlooking the beach and prices are higher than other options in town, but probably worth it. The **Restaurante Bico Verde** (Rua da Esperança, tel. 81/3552-1309,

10 P.M. until the last client daily, R$25), the last restaurant on the left, serves fish for lunch, right on their beachfront patio. They also have services for beachgoers, such as showers and lockers. It's open Monday nights for dinner and shows. For grilled meats in the Brazilian tradition, try **Tio Dadá** (Rua da Esperança 167, tel. 81/3552-1319, noon until the last client daily, R$20). They have a pleasant atmosphere and live music on weekends.

## INFORMATION AND SERVICES

The tourist information office is in the middle of Rua da Esperança where it forks on its way to the beach. You can't miss it. There is another tourism office along Rua da Esperança on the right side, just before the fork in the road, where you'll find better maps and materials. You'll find Internet services all along Rua da Esperança. Most offer connections for around R$12 per hour. Just look for the signs.

There are ATMs on Rua Bejupirá that have international systems. You can also exchange money inside Banco do Brasil. The small post office is on Rua da Esperança just past the tourist information office. A first-aid station (how civilized!) is on the Ipojuca Beach, along the northern end (to the left).

## GETTING THERE AND AROUND

Buses leave Recife for Porto de Galinhas about every 45 minutes, starting at around 6 A.M. and ending at 8:20 P.M. The best place to catch the bus is at the airport, but you can also get on at the beginning of the line in front of the downtown metro station. The cost is R$4. Buses returning to Recife leave every 45 minutes from 4 A.M.–6:15 P.M. from the highway PE–09 (in front of the gas station). (See *Buggy Excursions* earlier for information on getting around.)

# Maceió

If you add up all the factors that make a great coastal region in the northeast of Brazil—things like clarity of the water, variety of beaches, nightlife options, charm, safety, quality, and variety of food, and so on—Maceió may very well come out in the top position. Surprised? Most travelers are when they see what the Maceió region has to offer. The city itself sits in the middle of the Alagoas coastline with almost 200 kilometers of coast to the north and south. The water in Maceió is surprisingly blue and clear and it gets even better as you go farther north or south. The coastline is loaded with reefs that break the incoming tide (making the surf on the beaches both calm and warm) and provide great snorkeling and scuba diving areas—among the best in the country.

Some of the remote beaches are nearly deserted while others have options for tourists, like beach bars, restaurants, boat excursions, and hotels. What's best about this region is that it's not as "discovered" as some other places in the northeast—so you'll find fewer crowds, lower prices, and better overall conditions. Highlights include the Pajuçara Beach and its offshore reefs in the city of Maceió itself. There you can do some snorkeling in the sparkling green waters of the area. Praia da Gunga and Barra de São Miguel to the south are also important to put on the agenda as they are two of the

# Must-Sees

ᴹ **Pajuçara Beach:** People come to this part of the Brazilian coast to see the clear, blue surf and perhaps go snorkeling along the fantastic underwater reefs just off the coast. The reefs, a mere 20 minutes from shore by *jangada,* offer some of the finest snorkeling and swimming in the country (page 340).

ᴹ **Ponta Verde:** Most of the nighttime action in Maceió is centered along the boardwalk from Ponta Verde to Jatiúca. Here, the beach bars are also some of the city's best full-scale

© CHRISTOPHER VAN BUREN

**the water so blue at Pajuçara**

restaurants, and the sweet *tapiocas* (Brazilian crepes) are not to be missed (page 342).

ᴹ **Lake Mundaú Boat Trip:** They say you can't see the sunset from the eastern Atlantic coast, but the sunset tour on Lake Mundaú proves them wrong. After tripping around the islands and beaches of the Mundaú waterways, you can catch the sun slowly slipping behind the palm tress and into the calm ocean (page 346).

ᴹ **Maragogi:** If you thought the Pajuçara reefs were a thrill, wait until you explore the reefs of Maragogi. If you start with the morning low tide, you'll miss the crowds and get the best conditions (page 350).

ᴹ **Praia da Gunga:** The best way to get to Gunga is by boat from Barra de São Miguel. When you get there, you'll see one of the most picturesque tropical beaches in northern Brazil. You can take a kayak across the mouth of the river, hire a small boat to take you across, or hop aboard a large schooner that also takes you up the river (page 355).

Maceió ᴹ

**Natal**

**Recife**

**MACEIÓ**

Lake Mundaú Boat Trip

Ponta Verde — ᴹ○ Maceió
  Pajuçara Beach
  *Praia da Gunga*

ᴹ *Maragogi*

ATLANTIC
OCEAN

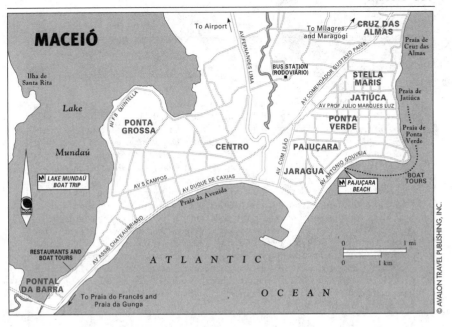

most pristine beaches on the Brazilian coastline. Maragogi to the north is an alternative beach village with a little of everything: semi-urban beaches with plenty of bars and shops, remote beaches for getting away from the crowd, and offshore reefs for some of the best snorkeling in the area. These are actually only a few of the many great beaches in the area.

Like the entire northeast coast of Brazil, Maceió is best visited just before peak season, September–December. Peak season in Maceió is not as packed as in other locations, so you might even find the summer months (December–February) agreeable, although prices do go up, and reservations are a must.

## PLANNING YOUR TIME

There's no better way to see Maceió and the surrounding beaches than to pack an overnight bag and make your way up and down the coast, spending a night (or two) in key locations along the way. After visiting the north coast, come back for a day in Maceió to regroup and then

set out for the south coast, or vice-versa. How much time you spend doing this depends on how many stops you decide to make, but a reasonable amount of time would be 7–8 days. First, spend a day and night in Maceió to see the main beaches and boardwalk. The next day, head out to the south coast: a day and a night in Praia do Francês, Barra de São Miguel, and Jequiá (maybe spending the night in Penedo instead of Jequiá). Back in Maceió, you can spend a half-day at Praia da Sereia, which is only 13 kilometers from the city, before packing your bag again for the north coast. Spend a day and a night in Milagres (one of the best places to stay) or Maragogi before coming back to Maceió to catch the sunset at Prainha. Of course, you can choose other beaches as key points and mix and match them as desired. The descriptions in this chapter will help guide you.

A lot of travelers approach Maceió a different way: They set themselves up in a hotel in the city and take a series of day trips to the principal beaches north and south, spending nights back in the city. The farthest beach to

## COMPARING BRAZIL'S NORTHEASTERN COASTAL CITIES

**Salvador**

The largest of the northeastern coastal cities, Salvador is difficult to compare to the rest, as it is home to so much variety and diversity. The beaches in the city itself—especially Itapuan and Flamengo on the north end—offer some lovely options for swimming and hanging out. The main attraction of Salvador is the culture and history encountered at every turn, but especially in the old centers of Pelorinho and Bonfim. There is a wide variety of hotels, from luxury to economical. Remote beaches up the coast offer some OK swimming, but the water is not as clear as in Natal or Maceió. The remote village of choice is Praia do Forte, which is very charming, if a bit overproduced. Swimming is not great there either, but there are several excursions and the TAMAR sea turtle reserve to keep you occupied. To the south of Salvador is the island of Morro de São Paulo, which has a charming village, great beaches, boat excursions, clear water in places, reefs for diving, and a variety of inns, although nothing extremely economical. **Summary:** Salvador offers some of the best cultural attractions in Brazil, along with some very decent beaches at the north end of town. Prices are a bit higher here for hotels and restaurants, but the options are endless. To the south are the best beaches and islands. There are several remote villages: Praia do Forte, Morro de São Paulo, and Itacaré.

**Maceió**

Maceió is about half the size of Fortaleza and slightly bigger than Natal. The difference is that the city itself is home to some of the most beautiful beaches in the area, especially Pajuçara, which is not polluted and has excellent reefs offshore for diving and swimming. The boardwalk is active day and night, but does not get quite as rowdy as the Fortaleza or Ponta Negra (Natal) boardwalks. Still, nightlife is active and varied. The water here and in the outlying beaches is clear and warm and offers some of the best diving and swimming on the coast. The nearby beach village is Praia do Francês, which is somewhat rundown. Excursions by van go out to the various beaches from the city and return for the evening, but there are some quaint places to stay in the remote beach areas, particularly Milagres and Barra de São Miguel. Hotels in Maceió are about like those in Fortaleza. **Summary:** This is a perfect combination of city and remote beaches, with enough variety to suit all tastes, and the water here is perfectly warm and clear. The only drawback is the lack of a good remote village.

**Recife**

Recife is one of Brazil's largest cities and it offers very little in terms of urban beaches, as its main beach, Boa Viagem, is polluted and frequented by sharks. The center of activity is on the island of Old Recife, where the old, historic buildings are mixed in with modern high-rises. There are numerous monuments, museums, and historical buildings here, and that's not even counting the nearby historical town of Olinda, which is a UNESCO Cultural Heritage Site. Carnaval in Recife is possibly the best in Brazil. Activities include boat excursions along the city's waterways and boat trips up the coast to beaches and the Tamandaré Island, which has some good swimming and diving options. The village of Porto de Galinhas to the south is the best remote area, with excellent diving and swimming options and several great beaches with warm, clear water. With the exceptions of Tamandaré and Porto de Galinhas, Recife's outlying beaches are not as attractive as those in other cities. **Summary:** The city of Recife (and neighboring Olinda) is more about culture and history than about the beach. For beach activities, you should leave Recife and head to Porto de Galinhas or the island of Tamandaré.

## Natal
Natal is a medium-sized city with very little of interest in the city itself. Its urban beaches are pretty but polluted. Most activity and the wild nightlife scene are in Ponta Negra, which has a slight hippie feel to it. Beaches to the north and south have warm, clear water and excellent pools for diving and swimming—some of the best in the country. Common excursions include dune buggy rides and boat trips to diving spots. Several lakes offer swimming and sand-skiing activities. Hotels in Ponta Negra are slightly expensive, but cheaper options can be found in the city of Natal. Some quaint *pousadas* can be found in remote beaches, especially to the north. The best satellite village is Pipa. **Summary:** Natal offers a great variety of remote beaches, clean water, diving, swimming, and dune buggy excursions. The nightlife in Ponta Negra is ample enough to suit all tastes.

## Fortaleza
Fortaleza has an over-the-top nightlife in Iracema, with some (slightly) more tranquil options along the Meireles boardwalk. Praia do Futuro is the only unpolluted urban beach. It has a rough surf and 8 kilometers of beach bars. The ocean in Fortaleza and in the surrounding beaches is not as clear as Natal, or even Salvador, and afternoons can get windy with very rough surf all along the coastline. There are no particularly good diving options or ocean excursions. Most activities take place on the beaches (dune buggies and water sports) or in the city. Fortaleza is three times the size of Natal and almost as big as Recife. Hotels are large and not particularly charming, but modern and affordable. The best satellite village is Jeriquaquara. **Summary:** Fortaleza has the frenzy of a large city, with a night scene that can be too much for many people. Outlying beaches are beautiful but don't wow visitors as much as those in Natal, primarily due to the lack of clarity of the water.

the north (Maragogi) is only 2.5 hours by car, and Penedo is only 3.5 hours to the south. The proximity of these beaches makes day-tripping a reasonable technique, especially if you like festive nights—something the small beach towns cannot always offer.

If you have more time to spend, there are certainly more beaches along the north and south coasts to keep you occupied. And a couple extra days in the city of Maceió would also be well spent.

## HISTORY

Maceió grew up in the 19th century from its massive sugar exportation via the Port of Jara-guá, which still functions today as a major shipping port. The city's sugar port grew to the point that the city overtook the economy of its neighbor Marechal Deodoro, which was capital of the state of Alagoas at the time. Marechal Deodoro never really recovered and today is a somewhat poor fishing town with a number of old buildings from its glory days. The old city center in Maceió and the port area of Jaraguá retain some of the old buildings from the sugar trade—the oldest in the city. Over the years, Maceió lost two of its three major beaches to pollution, including Jatiúca, once the favorite of them all. Urban planning arrived just in time to save the last beach, Pajuçara, from the same fate.

## The City of Maceió

Residents of Maceió and people from the state of Alagoas in general, are some of the nicest and most helpful people you're going to meet in Brazil. They are not traumatized by the big-city madness that characterizes the large coastal cities of Rio, Recife, and Fortaleza. They generally love to talk, especially if the subject is their lovely city. With about 650,000 inhabitants, Maceió is one of the smaller capital cities of the northern coastline. It has more than 20 kilometers of urban beaches and is surrounded by beautiful blue water, islands, and offshore reefs. The two principal urban beaches are Pajuçara and Ponta Verde, which have restaurants and bars open 24 hours a day. The old city center is still an active commercial area and is home to several historical monuments, including the architectural complexes at the **Praça Deodoro** and the **Praça Dom Pedro II.** The architectural complex in the neighborhood of Jaraguá also comes alive at night as one of the city's best nightlife centers. The south part of the city is characterized by waters of a different kind—with two lakes that empty into the ocean and several islands clustered around the inlets.

##  PAJUÇARA BEACH

They say that Pajuçara is the only beach in the city that is OK for swimming. Both Praia da Avenida (all 10 kilometers of it) to the south and Praia Ponta Verde to the north are polluted. It's true that the water in Pajuçara is a stunningly beautiful shade of blue that just beckons you to dive in. Don't ask about its close proximity to the other, polluted beaches; and ignore the signs that advise against swimming after heavy rains. That might make you somewhat dubious of its chemical properties. Still, hoards of people swim out in the Pajuçara waters every day. During the week, it's calm and beautiful. The restaurant/kiosks along the boardwalk provide excellent seating—both on and off the sand—along with a variety of seafood dishes for lunch (you can't escape the *moqueca,* or fish stew; it's on practically every menu in the city). The other side of the coastal road is lined with mid-range hotels that overlook the ocean and in the middle of the highway is a grassy meridian where you'll find some convenient ATMs. Strolling along Pajuçara is a favorite activity for visitors and locals. The city's principal tourist information booth is located in the

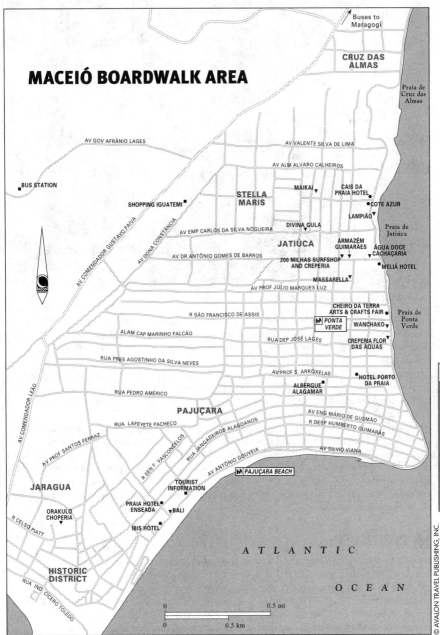

MACEIÓ BOARDWALK AREA

Buses to Maragogi

CRUZ DAS ALMAS

Praia de Cruz das Almas

AV GOV AFRÂNIO LAGES

AV VALENTE SILVA DE LIMA

AV ALM ALVARO CALHEIROS

BUS STATION

MAIKAI

CAIS DA PRAIA HOTEL

STELLA MARIS

COTE AZUR

SHOPPING IGUATEMI

LAMPIÃO

AV COMENDADOR GUSTAVO PAIVA

AV DONA CONSTÂNCIA

Praia de Jatiúca

DIVINA GULA

AV EMP CARLOS DA SILVA NOGUEIRA

JATIÚCA

ARMAZÉM GUIMARÃES

ÁGUA DOCE CACHAÇARIA

AV DR ANTÔNIO GOMES DE BARROS

200 MILHAS SURFSHOP AND CREPERIA

MELIÁ HOTEL

MASSARELLA

AV PROF JÚLIO MARQUES LUZ

CHEIRO DA TERRA ARTS & CRAFTS FAIR

Praia de Ponta Verde

R SÃO FRANCISCO DE ASSIS

PONTA VERDE

WANCHAKO

ALAM CAP MARINHO FALCÃO

RUA DEP JOSÉ LAGES

CREPERIA FLOR DAS ÁGUAS

RUA PRES AGOSTINHO DA SILVA NEVES

AV PROF S ARROXELAS

HOTEL PORTO DA PRAIA

RUA PEDRO AMÉRICO

ALBERGUE ALAGAMAR

AV COMENDADOR LEÃO

PAJUÇARA

AV ENG MÁRIO DE GUSMÃO

RUA LAFEYETE PACHECO

R DESP HUMBERTO GUIMARÃES

RUA JANGADEIROS ALAGOANOS

R SEN F VASCONCELOS

AV SILVIO VIANA

AV PROF SANTOS FERRAZ

AV ANTÔNIO GOUVEIA

JARAGUA

TOURIST INFORMATION

PAJUÇARA BEACH

PRAIA HOTEL ENSEADA

BALI

ORAKULO CHOPERIA

IBIS HOTEL

R CELSO PIATT

ATLANTIC

HISTORIC DISTRICT

OCEAN

RUA IND CICERO TOLEDO

0        0.5 mi
0        0.5 km

Maceió

© AVALON TRAVEL PUBLISHING, INC.

© CHRISTOPHER VAN BUREN

**fresh coconut water at Pajuçara Beach**

middle of the three kilometers of the Pajuçara boardwalk. On the beach near the tourist information office are numerous *jangadas,* (small boats) that sit waiting to take tourists out along the shoreline or to the rock and coral reefs two kilometers out to sea. The reefs are excellent for snorkeling and diving.

On Sundays, the city blocks off the street from traffic and the area here turns into a kind of street fair. The entire weekend brings thousands of local residents to the beaches and there is hardly a seat available at the beach bars or a section of sand that is not filled with screaming kids. The weekend is a good time to head out to the remote beaches.

## ⓂPONTA VERDE

Despite how lovely the Pajuçara Beach is, the happy masses hang out here at Praia Ponta Verde. The beach bars here are more integrated with the beach and provide a very festive atmosphere—some have large, shady areas with palm trees and grassy knolls. The

beach itself is extensive and the kiosks and restaurants are spread out at intervals along its boardwalk. Here, you'll find some of the best restaurants in the city—both on the beach and on the inland roads, and they all stay open late at night. It's interesting just to walk along the boardwalk at Ponta Verde, by day or by night.

Ponta Verde has a huge variety of hotels in all price categories. Some are on the coastal highway overlooking the ocean, but most are just a few streets inland. Along with all the other beaches in the city, Praia Ponta Verde gets crowded with locals on weekends—most setting up camp on the sand, where there is no obligation to buy anything from the beach bars. If you decide to stay in the city on a weekend, you can avoid the masses by sitting at one of the bars during the day.

The ocean at Ponta Verde is not recommended for swimming due to pollution and excessive algae that builds up along the shore. Nevertheless, you'll find hundreds of people playing in the water here, usually on weekends.

**Families hunt for mollusks at Barra Nova.**

## JATIÚCA

Continuing the beachfront restaurants and bars from Ponta Verde, Jatiúca is slightly less congested than Ponta Verde, but still offers an active night scene for anyone willing to stroll that far along the boardwalk (it's only about two kilometers long). Probably the most polluted beach in the city, Jatiúca suffers from an excess of untreated run-off from the streets of Maceió. Walking up the beach from Ponta Verde, you can begin to smell the evidence. For this reason, it's best to stick to the boardwalk in Jatiúca. Ironically, hotels in this area are generally mid-range and top-end entries, such as the Meliá Beach Resort, which marks the beginning of Jatiúca Beach, and the Jatiúca Resort Hotel, which marks the end. Toward the end of the boardwalk, there is the popular Lampião beach bar (Av. Alvaro Otacílio, Jatiúca, tel. 82/3325-4376, 9 P.M. until the last customer daily), which has music and dancing every night, beginning at 9 P.M. Next to Lampião are several *tapioca* kiosks that, collectively, are a favorite spot among locals for great, inexpensive, Brazilian crepes. The sweet ones are the best.

## PONTAL DA BARRA, BARRA NOVA, AND PRAINHA

Way down on the southern tip of the city, the land forms a narrow point that separates the ocean from Lake Mundaú, called Pontal da Barra. There are numerous islands just off the point and in the lake, the largest of which is the Ilha de Santa Rita, which serves as a kind of stepping stone for crossing the waterways formed by the two lakes (Mundaú and Manguaba). In this area you'll find some interesting excursions and options for hanging out and observing the surroundings. First, on the lake side of the *pontal* itself are several bars that host boating excursions to the various islands. You can choose the 9 A.M. or 2 P.M. trip, depending on whether you want to watch the sunset from the boat or from the bar. You may also be able to arrange other excursions from this area, such

Maceió

as a trip out to Prainha, which is a sandbar that extends out into the ocean and is a great place for watching the waves and the sunset. Two restaurants in this area are the Restaurante Peixarão and the Restaurante Maré.

As you cross the island of Santa Rita by car, you'll see numerous fruit stands just off the highway, where you can get mangos, papayas, and all kinds of locally-grown fruits. You can also get a bundle of live crabs, recently caught in the local marshes. On the south end of the island is the Barra Nova area, where you can turn off the highway and have lunch or drinks while watching local families search for mollusks and crabs in the marshy waters. The restaurant here is called **Restaurante Ilha do Fantasia** and they make a decent fish lunch. (It's possible to have a bus or van drop you off at the Barra Nova stop. From there, you can walk toward the south end of the island, past the fruit stands, and turn into the restaurant on foot.)

Leaving the island to cross over to the south side of the continent, you can pull off to the right to access the Massagueira area, which has a number of lakeside bars, or to the left to head out to Prainha, which is an idyllic location for sitting in the water and watching the palm trees bend in the breeze. The options in this area are difficult to access without a car, but there are some buses that pass directly in front of the Pontal da Barra restaurants. You can catch the Santuário/Pontal bus in Pajuçara on Rua Quintino Bocaiuva (three streets inland from the boardwalk). Buses and vans going south to Praia do Francês or Marechal Deodoro can drop you off at Barra Nova or Prainha.

## ENTERTAINMENT AND NIGHTLIFE

The boardwalk in Ponta Verde is the most accessible scene for bars and hangouts, both during the day and at night. All along the boardwalk are places for sipping something and watching the crowd pass by. Across the highway are numerous other bars and cafés. Just walk up one side and down the other to find a place you like. At the far end of Jatiúca

Beach boardwalk is the famous **Lampião** beach bar, which has music and dancing every night starting at 9 P.M. Another popular area for clubs and bars is the Jaraguá historic district, which is near the shipping port of Jaraguá at the south end of Pajuçara. Here, the historical buildings have been restored and turned into great bars and restaurants with a varied crowd. Some dance clubs are also in the area. Try **Orakulo Choperia** (Rua Barão de Jaraguá 717, tel. 82/3326-7616, 6 P.M. until the last customer leaves, closed Tues. and Sun.) for draft beer and live music in one of four different environments. Finally, the Stella Maris neighborhood near Shopping Iguatemi has some night spots, including the popular **Maikai** (Rua Alfredo G. de Mendonça, tel. 82/3325-7565, 6 P.M.–midnight daily), which has several environments for dancing, drinking, and listening to music.

## FESTIVALS AND EVENTS

In June, the region celebrates the **Festival de Juninha** in the city and in numerous small towns all over the coastline. The main event is regional food. In Maceió, there are stands set up all along the boardwalk, and around the downtown area. Many outdoor stages have *forró* music and dancing. The festival takes place in the last half of June. On the second to the last weekend in November, the city celebrates its off-season Carnaval, called **Maceió Fest**. Stages are set up in Pajuçara and in the Jaraguá area, along Rua Ind. Cícero Toledo. National-level bands and performers come to celebrate and the very famous pop star Djavan is usually present, as he was born in the city and keeps a house in Barra de São Miguel. Traffic gets nasty and crowds are thick in the *praças* and festival areas during this weekend, but the party is terrific—usually including fireworks displays and parades. The parades usually begin in the Pajuçara area and march up the coast. You can participate (join a *bloco*) for about R$100, which gives you the right to march with the group, using the group's tee shirt. As with most Carnaval events in the

# LAMPIÃO, THE OUTLAW HERO

It takes at least a generation for cruel bandits to become mythological heroes, but that's what happened to Lampião and his gang, who scoured the countryside of Brazil's northeast region around Maceió and Recife, killing police and the rich and powerful in his wake. Today, he is remembered as the Rei do Cangaço (King of the Outlaws). Lampião's most heroic gesture was his Robin Hood–like distribution of wealth, from the large landowners and cattle ranchers to the poor folks of the Pernambuco countryside. Lampião frequently sacked small towns and raided the rich and powerful, killing cattle and torturing his rivals and enemies in some very cruel ways—a dagger in the throat, cutting ears off, gouging eyes out, raping, torturing, and hanging were some of his favorite tactics. He made frequent attacks on the police, using his knowledge of the countryside to escape. From 1920 to around 1938, Lampião, the small and gangly boy from the country, was the most feared bandit in Brazil.

Lampião, a nickname that means lantern, was born Virgulino Ferreira da Silva, the third in a family of eight siblings. He started his gang with a couple of brothers and cousins in order to attack his neighbor and rival, whom he claimed had stolen some animals from his family. He had been working as a kind of local distributor, using his family's horses and burros to transport goods from the train station to individual farms in Pernambuco and neighboring states. In this fashion, he came to know the countryside and each ranch that sat upon it. Lampião was vengeful and full of hate. He swore to avenge his father, who was shot by police in their search for young Virgulino and his brothers after their run-in with the neighbors. He, his wife, and most of his gang died in a police raid at dawn in 1938.

country, joining a *bloco* is the safest way to enjoy the festival, since there is security inside the group. If you just want to walk alongside the parade, you should be careful not to bring any valuables with you. To join a *bloco,* just ask anyone in the *bloco* for details. They usually sell their uniforms right on the spot.

## SHOPPING

There is a great arts and crafts market on the coastal highway in Ponta Verde. Called **Cheiro da Terra** (Smell of the Earth; Av. Álvoro Otacílio 2500, tel. 82/3034-0339), the permanent market has more than 200 stands with tee shirts, trinkets, jewelry, and local crafts. They also have the **Museu do Cangaço** (Outlaw Museum), which has a photographic history of the famous outlaw Lampião. Starting at 8 P.M., they present music and dance events. If you call them, they will come pick you up at your hotel. The downtown area (or Centro), is the main commercial center, with all kinds of shops for clothing, swimwear, film and camera supplies, shoes, and household supplies. Here you'll find the best prices, but be prepared for a congested street scene. People downtown have nothing to do with the beach scene or tourism, so don't wear your bathing suit if you come into this area. While you're there, check out the **Mercado do Artesanato de Maceió** (Av. Alvaro Otacílio 2500, Jatiúca, tel. 82/3325-5931, 10 A.M.–11 P.M. daily). The best indoor shopping mall in the city is **Shopping Iguatemi** (Av. Gustavo Paiva 2990, tel. 82/3357-1010, 10 A.M.–11 P.M. Mon.–Sat., 3–10 P.M. on Sun.) in the Stella Maris neighborhood, but you won't find much there that you can't find in Ponta Verde and along the beaches.

## EXCURSIONS

Right off the coast of Pajuçara and Ponta Verde are massive rock formations under the water, called *parrachos*. These rocky reefs form beautiful *piscinas naturais* (natural pools) with sandy bottoms, that are fabulous for snorkeling and swimming. The water is shallow at low tide and the reefs are full of tropical fish and sea life. Boats leave from the main *praça* at Praia

Maceió

fresh fruit for sale near Lake Mundaú

Pajuçara (roughly in the middle of the beach) to take groups out to the pools in small *jangadas*. The excursion includes snorkeling equipment, but it's always a joy to have your own. The two-hour excursion costs about R$15 per person.

Vans, boats, and off-road vehicles are all waiting to take passengers out of the city to the outskirts on various excursions. The most common, of course, are trips to the various beaches north and south of the city. For examples, you can visit Praia do Francês, Barra de São Miguel, and Gunga in a single trip for only R$15 per person. Individual trips to these beaches are about R$15 as well. An excursion to Maragogi goes for R$25 per person (snorkeling not included). You'll also find packaged excursions to historical towns, such as Penedo.

## Lake Mundaú Boat Trip

A popular boat trip is the 9 Island excursion in Lake Mundaú, which leaves from the Pontal da Barra area (the southern tip of the city) and takes passengers up the waterways past nine different islands and a couple of beaches (with stops for swimming). It's R$25 per person. Different tour agencies provide slight vari-

ations on the same trip. Check out **Pôr do Sol Turismo** (Rua Alipio Barbosa 421, Pontal da Barra, tel. 82/3336-3038), and **Marcão Turismo** (Rua Residencial Repouso da Gávea 24, Pajuçara, tel. 82/3231-0843, www.turismomaceio.com.br).

**Eco Aventura** (tel. 82/9341-9896, henrique@master-mcz.com.br) takes small groups on a 4-wheel-drive through the countryside and sugarcane fields to the Carro Quebrado Beach. **Gato do Mato** (Rua Nova Brasilia 242, Cruz das Almas, tel. 82/9972-0902, www.gatodomato.com, reservas@gatodomato.com) offers a series of high-adventure trips, including rappelling, mountain biking, kayaking, and hiking.

## ACCOMMODATIONS
### Under R$100

The youth hostel **Albergue Alagamar** (Rua Pref. Abdon Arroxelas 327, tel. 82/3231-2246, R$35 s and R$45 d with a small breakfast included) is well located a few streets inland in Ponta Verde. It has spacious rooms for two, three, and four people, ceiling fans (some rooms have air), kitchen facilities, laundry, and a TV room. The **Hotel Porto da Praia** (Rua Abdon Arroxelas 128, tel. 82/3327-2823, www.hotelportodapraia.com.br, reservas@hotelportodapraia.com.br, R$85 s and R$95 d) in Ponta Verde is a slightly older hotel, but it's fairly well kept and clean, and well located. They have a great breakfast buffet (included) and rooms with air, TV, phone, and 24-hour room service. The **Ibis Hotel** (Av. Dr. Antônio Gouveia 277, tel. 82/3327-6699, www.accorhotels.com, R$69) is in the Pajuçara Beach area overlooking the ocean. They are well managed and have rooms with air, cable TV, and phone. They also have a pool, bar, money-exchange service, and non-smoking rooms. Breakfast is optional.

An excellent beachfront hotel in Jatiúca is the **Cais da Praia Hotel** (Av. Alvaro Otacílio 4353, tel. 82/3235-3013, www.caisdapraia.com.br, reservas@caisdapraia.com.br, R$65 d in low season and R$120 in high season). It's a small building with about 32 rooms, a quaint pool, and comfortable reception/lounge. The rooms have air, cable TV, phone, and many have ocean views. Breakfast is included. Finally, you can rent a room in the **Côte Azur** building (Av. Alvaro Otacílio 3567, tel. 82/3231-6577, www.fontesimobiliaria.com.br, R$560 per week peak season and R$650 per month low season), which is a residence apartment with full kitchen facilities on the Ponta Verde Beach.

## R$100–200

The **Praia Hotel Enseada** (Av. Dr. Antônio Gouveia 171, tel. 82/3231-4726, www.hotelenseada.com.br, reservas@hotelenseada.com.br, R$100 in low season and R$190 in high season) is overlooks the Pajuçara Beach and is a relatively modern facility. They have decent rooms and service. They are connected with the hotel at Praia Gunga and offer special trips for their guests to the Gunga Beach. Their luxury rooms are on the top floors with ocean views and go for about 10 percent more.

## R$200–500

The **N Meliá Hotel** (Av. Alvaro Otacílio 4065, tel. 82/3355-2020, www.meliamcz.com.br, R$195–255 d) marks the beginning of Jatiúca Beach and is one of the more luxurious hotels in the area, with three restaurants (including sushi), a large pool area with outdoor bar, a game room, and tennis court. Rooms have cable TV, air, phone, and some have ocean views. Luxury suites are also available.

# FOOD
## Casual
Just inland from the Jatiúca Beach is **200 Milhas Surfshop and Creperia** (Av. Dr. Antônio Gomes de Barros 234, tel. 82/3325-7071, 9 A.M.–11 P.M. Mon.–Sat., 5–11 P.M. on Sun.), which has a cool atmosphere for sitting and ordering one or more crepes with a cold beer. A popular place for late-night *tapiocas* (Brazilian crepes) is at the far end of Jatiúca, where several *tapioca* stands appear at night. They will whip up several combinations of sweet or salty *tapiocas* for about R$2.50–4.50 each. A more formal place for crepes (meaning it's in a permanent building) is the **Creperia Flor das Aguas** (Av. Alvaro Otacílio 3309, tel. 82/3231-2335, noon–11 P.M. Mon.–Fri., 4–11 P.M. on weekends) in Ponta Verde. They make the more traditional, French-style crepes along with Belgian waffles and other sweets. Speaking of sweets, you can get a number of ice cream dishes at **Bali** (Av. Dr. Antônio Gouveia 451, tel. 82/3231-8833, 3–11 P.M. daily) in the Pajuçara Beach, near the Ibis Hotel.

## International
One of the most well-known places in town is a Peruvian restaurant, called **N Wanchako** (Rua São Francisco de Assis 93, tel. 82/3327-8701, noon–3 P.M. and 7 P.M.–midnight Sun.–Fri. and 7 p.m.–midnight Sat.) in Jatiúca. They serve all types of traditional Peruvian dishes, including a fantastic seviche for about R$50 per person. For great Italian food in a cozy environment, try **Massarella** (Rua José P. Magalhães 271, tel. 82/3235-6000, noon–midnight Tues.–Sun., closed Mon.) behind the Meliá Hotel in Jatiúca. They serve a variety of pizzas and pasta dishes for around R$35 per person.

## Local Favorites
A Brazilian bar and restaurant that specializes in Comida Mineira (country food from Minas Gerais) is **Agua Doce Cachaçaria** (Av. Alvaro Otacílio 3977, tel. 82/3235-5580, 11:30 A.M. until the last client daily, R$30) in Jatiúca. Besides their buffet dinner and lunch, they have more than 200 different types of *cachaça* (sugarcane liquor) and live music on Wednesday and Friday nights. Another restaurant and *cachaçaria* in Jatiúca is **N Divina Gula** (Rua Eng. Paulo B. Nogueira 85, tel. 82/3235-1016, 11:30–1 A.M. Tues.–Sun., R$15), which has a rustic but elegant atmosphere and menu. They are the recipients of several national food awards. **Armazém Guimarães** (Av. Dr. Antônio Gomes de Barros 188, tel. 82/3325-4545, 6 P.M.–midnight daily) in Jatiúca is a large and festive pizza joint with a large variety of pizza combinations and cold beer for R$15–20 per person.

## INFORMATION AND SERVICES

The main tourist information booth is located about mid-way along the Pajuçara Beach boardwalk. They have excellent maps and materials. You can call the bus station at tel. 82/3221-4615. The **Cybercafé** (Rua Emp. Carlos da Silva Nogueira 192, tel. 81/3235-5334, 8:30 A.M.–10 P.M. Mon.–Fri., 2–8 P.M. on Sat.) in Jatiúca is a great place for sipping coffee while getting some computer work done. In Ponta Verde, try **Net Paper** (Av. Alvaro Otacílio 3587, tel. 82/3231-4927, 9 A.M.–7 P.M. Mon.–Sat., closed for lunch) inside the Côte Azur building. There is a call center on the Jatiúca boardwalk just past the Meliá Hotel, where you can make quiet, international calls.

## GETTING THERE AND AROUND

A lot of international visitors from northern Europe fly directly into Maceió's international airport. American travelers, however, usually have to catch a domestic flight from another city or take a bus from Recife. The Real Alagoas line goes to Maceió from Recife approximately every two hours, from 7 A.M.–4 P.M., and again at midnight. This is the standard bus for R$26. An executive bus leaves Recife at 8 A.M., 1:30 P.M., and 7 P.M. daily.

Although Maceió is a large city, most of the areas that you'll be visiting are accessible on foot, including the entire boardwalk from Pajuçara to Jatiúca. That's a good thing, too, because there is no convenient public transit that goes up and down the coast between the beaches. As strange as that seems, it's not unlike many other coastal cities in northern Brazil. You can cut through Ponta Verde to get between the Pajuçara and Ponta Verde Beaches, lopping off a great deal of time and distance. Long distances, such as back and forth to the bus terminal or to the Pontal da Barra boat trips, should be covered in a taxi or rental car. From the main bus terminal, you can get to all beaches up and down the coast and to the airport.

Driving around the city of Maceió is nasty. Closed roads, detours, and traffic jams make it a convenience not worth recommending. But if you want to drive to the beaches up or down the coast, then you can look into **Avis** (tel. 82/3214-4110), **Localiza** (tel. 82/3325-5523), **Rentacar** (tel. 82/3327-3388), and **Unidas** (tel. 82/3325-5642). Most of the car-rental agencies have lots and offices in the Jatiúca Beach area. You can walk up the boardwalk and find several.

# Beaches North of Maceió

The best way to see the north coast of Maceió is by car. This leaves you free to stop at any time to check out the beaches, then start up again to continue on your journey. Some of the beach hotels have extensive properties and walking from the front gate to the reception area can be a hike in some cases. Still, there are several transportation options if you want to remain unencumbered by a vehicle. First, you can take the Atlántica (tel. 82/3325-2018) bus from the main bus station in Maceió to Porto de Pedras, stopping at most of the beach villages in-between. It takes about two hours to make the trip and costs R$8.50. Buses leave at 9 A.M., 11:20 A.M., and 4:20 P.M. daily. If you plan it right, you can catch the early bus to your first destination, then pick up a later bus to keep going north that same day.

Another option is to get to the **Posto Mar Azul** (the gas station on the north end of Maceió near the Via Box supermarket), where you can catch a *lotação* (group taxi) for about R$10 per person. For R$30, they'll leave on the spot with whomever is inside.

To get past Porto de Pedras (to Japaratinga and Maragogi), take the bus or *lotação* to the *balsa* (ferryboat) in Porto de Pedras, which is probably the end of the line. You then take the ferry for free across the river or hire a private boat for R$1 to take you. On the other side, you have to wait for another *lotação* or taxi that can take you to Japaratinga or to the bus stop in

Japaratinga, where you catch the bus to Maragogi. Just explain that you're going to Maragogi and they'll set you on your way. There are also direct buses to and from Maragogi and Maceió. In a car, you just cross on the ferryboat and keep driving, turning right at the highway that leads to Maragogi. More details appear in the following descriptions.

## PRAIA DA SEREIA AND IPIOCA

These two beaches actually belong to the city of Maceió and are easily accessed by car, bus, or taxi from the city. Praia da Sereia (Mermaid Beach) is famous for its large rocky reef just a stone's throw offshore. On the reef is a sculpture of a mermaid and you can swim out to see her up close. The pool formed by the reef is shallow, warm (a steamy 30°C year-round) and clear. On the beach, the white sand crunches under your feet as you walk. There are a number of bars that serve drinks, appetizers, and seafood lunch plates at tables on the sand. Being so close to Maceió, this beach can get rather crowded on weekends and dur-

ing the summer. Ipioca Beach is not as popular, but offers a beautiful strip of sand and water and a picturesque colonial church that you can visit.

## BARRA DE SANTO ANTÔNIO AND ILHA DA CROA

The Santo Antônio River empties into the ocean here and divides the area into two parts: On the south side is Barra de Santo Antônio and on the north is Ilha da Croa. Both have some tourist attractions, including boat trips up the river to see the flora and fauna of the area, buggy rides, and even ultralight rides. There are also reefs that form offshore during low tide and which are great for snorkeling. A ferryboat can take you from one side to the other.

## SÃO MIGUEL DOS MILAGRES

If you're not staying at a *pousada* along the beach at Milagres, then you probably should come into the little town called Porto da Rua

a shady cabana at Pousada da Toque

and make your way directly to the beach. There are a few places to sit, order lunch or a drink, and make camp while you play in the water. (If you are in the mood for something nicer, don't hesitate to walk into either of the *pousadas* listed later to have lunch or dinner at their respective restaurants, which are open to the public.) To the right of this little village is a long stretch of virgin beach. At low tide, a wonderful series of pools form just inside the barrier reef and you can catch a small boat out to them for some snorkeling activities. Even if you don't want to snorkel, just going out to the pools for a swim is a great thing. If you wear tennis shoes, you can actually swim and walk out to the pools. They are warm, shallow, crystal-clear, and there are several areas with a variety of fish to observe. The left side the beach comes to a point at the edge of a river. At low tide, this area becomes an extensive, shallow pool and great fun for swimming and splashing. There are also excursions that take you to the south waters and beaches around the mouth of the Camaragibe River. These excursions are not well organized, so you have to ask around for a guide.

There is no infrastructure in Milagres and no beach kiosks for sitting on the sand, so the real pleasure here is staying at one of the beachfront *pousadas*. That way, you can take advantage of the facilities while enjoying the pristine beaches and natural pools. The coziest and most charming of the Milagres *pousadas* is **Ⓜ Pousada da Toque** (Rua Felisberto de Ataide, Praia do Toque, tel. 82/3295-1127, tel. 82/9991-2168, www.pousadadatoque.com.br, R$175–300), perhaps one of the most enchanting places to stay on the entire Brazilian coast. Individual chalets are set among tropical plants and animals and they have super-comfortable beds, gas-heated showers, CD players, and in-room DVD (with an extensive library of disks). The DVD players are a good idea since there is no nightlife in this area. Some of the larger suites have their own pools. The *pousada* also has a large deck and pool area, outdoor bar, and an excellent restaurant that receives the owners gourmet touch (everything on the menu is

top-notch—R$40–80 for two people). Their breakfast is served in a covered bungalow and is prepared with special homemade bread (outrageously good), cheeses, fruits, and regional dishes. Besides offering impeccable facilities, the owner, Nilo, and his staff make you a part of the family with a special friendliness and hospitality from the northeast.

Just up the beach from Nilo's place is the **Pousada Côte Sud** (Praia de Porto da Rua, tel. 82/3295-1283, pousadacotesud@uol.com.br, R$110 d), which is run by Corinne, a charming French immigrant who has set up her place here in Milagres. Corrine offers simple but comfortable chalets, a fabulous French restaurant, and plenty of charm.

## JAPARATINGA

If you've made it this far, then you might as well take a look at the beaches of Japaratinga, some of the most beautiful and rustic coastline in Brazil. There are plenty of hotels and *pousadas* here, but there is no real tourist infrastructure, so the area remains somewhat inaccessible for foreigners. The beaches are practically virgin with clear water and pools for snorkeling. There is a small town with simple restaurants, bars, and shops, but most of the *pousadas* are on the road coming into town. You can check out the **Hotel Bitingui** and the **Estalagem Caiuia** if you want to spend a night here. Both have clean and cozy facilities. Take a look at the site www.ahmaja.com.br for information on these and other hotels in the Maragogi and Jabaratinga areas.

## Ⓜ MARAGOGI

What brings people all the way to Maragogi is not the town itself. Despite the low-priced cafés and Internet connections in the village or the beach bars and boutique shops along the boardwalk, Maragogi is not a town that calls attention to itself. The highlight here is the popular **Galés**, a sandbar surrounded by rock formations that present themselves at low tide about six kilometers off the coast and which make an excellent playground for swimming and snorkeling. In the morning, at the first low tide of the day, boats will take you out to the pools to visit the fish for around R$15 for two hours, including equipment. You can get information about tides at any of the hotels or just ask one of the guides. If you have time after a trip out to Galés, visit one of the beaches in Maragogi, such as São Bento, with a small village and sandbar about two kilometers offshore.

There are several hotels along the boardwalk. If you decide to stay the night here, check out **Solar da Praia** (Av. Senador Rui Palmeira, tel. 82/3296-2025, solardapraia.com.br, R$35 s and R$50 d), which has clean facilities and rooms.

You can catch the Atlântica bus from the Maceió bus terminal to Maragogi at 7 A.M., 9 A.M., and 2:45 P.M. daily. The return bus leaves at 5 A.M., 10 A.M., and 4 P.M. daily. The trip takes three hours and costs R$12.

# Beaches South of Maceió

To reach the southern coast of Maceió is best done by car. This lets you stop and go at will and also look into the various nooks and crannies of the coastline, such as the small stopping points in the Barra Nova area. Since the south coast is not all that extensive in terms of distance, you can hire a taxi for the day and explore all the beaches you like. Buses go from the main bus station in Maceió to Barra de São Miguel, which stops in Praia do Francês. You can also find private vans (white VW buses) that pick up passengers all along the south road for R$3 per person. These are frequent and cheap, but often very crowded.

## PRAIA DO FRANCÊS

In the 1980s, Praia do Francês was a major attraction on the coast of Alagoas. Despite its name (which simply pays homage to the French pirates who traded in these parts in the 16th century), the destination was particularly frequented by Portuguese and Italian tourists, as well as vacationers from inside Brazil. It consists of a single beach, divided into two parts. One part has calm waters and an energetic beach scene; the other part has strong waves and nothing major happening on the beach. The village area, which starts at the beach and continues inland for a few blocks, has numerous *pousadas,* shops, and restaurants.

Praia do Francês originated like many beach villages in Brazil. First, surfers and hippies discover the little fishing village and start coming to commune and practice their sport. Soon, small shops and food kiosks sprout up along the small streets of the village to cater to the many surfers visiting the place. Arts and crafts vendors hang out among the crowd to sell their wares. Some of the old, local establishments go in for a renovation and suddenly there are some interesting restaurants and permanent beach bars in town. At this point, it becomes an interesting destination for professionals from the nearby urban areas to spend their weekends and vacations. Everybody with property in the main village turns their home into a *pousada* or boutique shop and international investors start buying up lots to build larger hotels. That was Praia do Francês in the '80s.

At this point, if the local government does not get involved in protecting and caring for their little coastal jewel, it will invariably turn sour. Hoards of youth from the surrounding area flock to the beach on weekends to see whose car has the loudest music system. They don't patronize the shops or eat in the restaurants. Many don't even buy their beer from the local bars, but bring their own in coolers. The idea is to see and be seen by everybody you already know back home. The area fills with noise, trash, and urine, and soon these weekends of out-of-control youth represent the only income the village has. Hotels and restaurants go up for sale. This is Praia do Francês today.

Until the powers that be decide to take better care of the place, Praia do Francês is probably only interesting for a half-day visit. The

kayaks for hire at Praia do Francês

village shops are worth a look and prices here tend to be better than in the beaches farther south. If you don't like the idea of staying in the big city of Maceió, then you could consider making Praia do Francês your home base for visiting the southern coast. You'll find lots of economical hotels here and during the week, the place is calm and uneventful. Driving south from here is a breeze.

## The Beach

If you come to town on a sunny weekend or during the summer season, you're bound to find the place bustling with action. Surfers ride waves on the south side of the beach, where there are no bars on the beach and no reefs in the ocean to calm the waves. The north side is packed with folks sitting at the many large beach bars that overlook the ocean. The surf on this side is calm and the water is warm and great for swimming. A belt of reefs blocks the incoming tide on this part of the beach. The beach bars are stacked one after the next for about a quarter mile, or about 800 meters. You can walk along the beach and see them all from below. You'll want to arrive early to get a seat at

your favorite establishment because the crowd descends on the beach with a fury. You'll find water sports available in this area, including windsurfing and kite surfing. Buggies park on the beachfront path for anyone interested in a joy ride. If you walk north past the bars for about another three kilometers, you'll reach the mouth of the Manguaba River, where there are some simple restaurants that serve lobster, crab, and shrimp (all from local waters).

**Cristal Mar** (tel. 82/9908-9446) offers boat excursions out past the reefs to an area that is great for snorkeling, with clear water and natural pools.

If you happen to be in town during the week in the off-season, then you may wonder what happened to the place. It has a strange emptiness to it. Most everything is open and operating, but there is a notable lack of customers. Maybe you'll like it better this way.

## The Village

During busy season, the village is active day and night. There are restaurants of all types and price points, hotels, and bars. Boutique shops, predominantly near the beach, sell colorful swimwear, crafts, and other souvenirs. If you stroll up Rua Carapeba (where Bruce's Burguer is located), you'll find a couple of art galleries mixed in with the hotels. Pay a visit to the very friendly Rosa Maria at the **Mulher Endar** café (Rua Carapeba 27, tel. 82/3260-1795), *pousada,* and art studio. Her café opens at around 2 P.M. and is a charming place to have coffee, especially in the evening. Her art studio is open all day and features sculpture from a local master of wood carving (Mestre Deodato). Her *pousada* is listed under *Accommodations.* You can also drop in on Marisa at the **Bêmeos Mosaico** studio (Rua Carapeba 133, tel. 82/3260-1727, no specific hours available, just pass by as you stroll around the village), where she and her husband make great art from small pieces of tile. Their work can be seen all over town. They also have a rustic, dial-up Internet connection, but it's the only game in town.

## Accommodations

Rosa Maria has four rooms for rent in the back of her café/gallery, called **Mulher Endar** (Rua Carapeba 27, tel. 82/3260-1795, R$80 d). Rooms include breakfast at the café. One of the coziest places in town is the **Pousada Graciosa** (Rua Cavalo Marinho 21, tel. 82/3260-1197, R$70 d, R$140 peak season), on one of the side streets crossing Rua Carapeba. The all-brick structure has about a dozen rooms situated around a courtyard garden, adding a sense of privacy. The rooms are simple but clean and comfortable, just like the rest of the place. They can arrange boat and buggy excursions. The **Pousada Le Soleil** (Rua Carapeba 11, tel. 82/3260-1240, www.pousadalesoleil.kit.net, R$45 s and R$50 d, R$90 and R$100 during peak season) is perhaps the cleanest and most modern in town. Their rooms are simple, but the facilities and service are trustworthy.

## Food and Entertainment

There are economical places to eat all along the main street coming into town, called Avenida Caravelas. You'll find pizza, burgers, and a Brazilian barbecue. You'll also find a bakery and deli where you can buy makings for sandwiches. Farther up the same road is **Taipas** (Av. Car-

avelas, tel. 82/3620-1609, noon–10 P.M. daily) with Comida Mineira. The two most popular restaurants in town for a sit-down meal are **Chez Patrick** (Rua Maresia), which serves French cuisine in a cozy ambience and **Padrino** (Rua dos Corais), across from Pousada Le Soleil, which serves Italian food. The latter is a good place for late-night drinks, as is **Bruce's Burguer** (Rua dos Corais, open lunch and dinner daily, R$8). Nothing happens on the beach at night, as the city government removed the lights that once lit up the beach. Nobody seems to know exactly why.

## Information

Another great endowment from the local government is that there are no banks in Praia do Francês and almost nobody takes credit cards. Apparently, the whole phone system required to support the credit card system is in process, and that's what everybody tells you when you ask if they take credit cards (*"Está no proceso"*). Unfortunately, the nearest bank with international ATMs is in Maceió. For information on excursions and car rentals, check with Ricardo at **Cancun-Tur** (tel. 82/9307-6657, kellerrico@ig.com.br, call to schedule a meeting).

### Getting There and Around

Buses leave from the Maceió bus station going south down the coast. Look for buses marked "Marechal" and "B. São Miguel." They cost about R$3 each and leave about every 20 minutes. Be sure to ask for the Praia do Francês exit. There are private vans and cars that will take you to Maceió for about R$3. Just wait at a bus stop on Avenida Caravelas and one will drive by. Note that the vans can get pretty crowded, as the drivers like to cram as many passengers in as possible. A taxi between Maceió and Praia do Francês will cost R$15–25 depending on your destination in Maceió.

## BARRA DE SÃO MIGUEL

On your journey down the southern coast of Maceió, Barra de São Miguel is the first

© CHRISTOPHER VAN BUREN

low tide at Barra de São Miguel

destination that offers uncrowded, pristine beaches, the kind everyone is looking for. In fact, the beauty and variety of this area is one of the best-kept secrets of the Brazilian coast. You will not find water more transparent and warm or beaches more picture-perfect than here in Barra de São Miguel and its neighbor Praia da Gunga. Like much of the coastline in the Brazil's northeast region, here, offshore reefs block the incoming tide and form a long, narrow pool of calm, clear water. The pool receives both ocean water and river water, making it exceptionally clear and clean. Called Lagoa do Roteiro, the pool is quite shallow, perfect for swimming along with the tiny fish that come up around you. At low tide, you can walk out onto the reefs for kilometers and check out the small crabs and tropical fish in the pools left behind by the tide. Out farther, near the barrier reef, you can partake in some excellent snorkeling activity (you should bring your own gear). If you like strolling along the shoreline, there is plenty of that to go around, and simple beach kiosks are clustered around the *vilarejo* (village) area, where you can order lunch and drinks on the sand or on a shady patio overlooking the water.

You'll probably find Barra de São Miguel an excellent place to hang out for a night or two—there is certainly plenty to keep you captive, and you won't find a more agreeable place on the southern coast of Maceió.

## Excursions

On the beach in front of the *vilarejo*, you can rent a kayak to paddle out to the reefs for snorkeling or, if you're in good shape, out to **Praia da Gunga** some 30 paddling minutes away. You can go with or without a guide for around R$10 per hour (negotiate a discount for more than three hours). Boats of various sizes are also available to take you around these waters and to Gunga for the day. These cost around R$20 per person. Another trip will take you to the **Isle of Tres Corações,** where you can walk around the shallow waters and sandy beaches at low tide.

If you want something drier and less strenuous than paddling a kayak some three kilometers up the mouth of the river separating São Miguel and Gunga (with the Ilha Tres Corações in the middle), then you might enjoy a trip in a large schooner. This excursion leaves from the *cais* (pier) downtown and not from the village area.

You can visit Praia da Gunga and other parts of Barra de São Miguel by buggy. Just ask around at the *vilarejo* for Aluisio (tel. 82/9313-4958).

## The Village and Town Center

Barra de São Miguel is not a sophisticated place. Both the village and town center are small and rustic. The village is just a couple of streets near the main beach. There, you'll find some shops and simple restaurants that operate mostly during the day. There are also a couple of hotels near the village. About three kilometers south is the town center, where you'll find a couple of banks, a post office, more simple restaurants, several small markets, and the *cais*, where you can catch a boat excursion.

## Accommodations

The first hotel in town (about three kilometers before the village) is the **BrisaMar Pousada** (Rua Margarida Oticica 38, Barra de São

Miguel, tel. 82/3272-2030, R$50 s and R$70 d, approximately R$80 and R$125 in peak season), one block away from the beach at a more turbulent (and deserted) section of the coastline. You can walk along the beach from the hotel to the village in about 45 minutes. The owner of the BrisaMar is an extremely friendly and helpful guy named Edival, who will set you up with anything you need while you're in town. His *pousada* is small and charming with clean rooms, hammocks, a swimming pool, and a darned good breakfast (included). The most modern hotel in Barra de São Miguel is in the village area on the beach and is called the **Village Barra Hotel** (Rua Senador Armon de Mello 65, tel. 82/3272-1000, www.villagebarrahotel.com.br, hotel@villabarrahotel.com.br, R$107 d and R$160 suite). The place was recently renovated to include three floors of modern rooms overlooking the beach, a large reception area and *sala*, and a beautiful pool and patio overlooking the ocean. The hotel has its own boat for excursions (extra) and beach service.

## Food and Entertainment

When it's open, the **Canoa Restaurante** in the town center is probably the best in town. They serve the regional favorite *sopa de maçune* (pronounced ma-SOO-nee), a rich soup made from small mollusks found in the local waters. (In the summer, Barra de São Miguel celebrates the Festival of Maçune.) Lunch options in the village include the beach kiosks, which serve fish and fries, and the **Lanchonete do Aluisio** (Rua Medina Cavalcante Silva, tel. 82/3272-3019, 11 A.M.–5 P.M. and 7–11 P.M. Tues.–Sun.), a simple place with excellent food at an excellent price. Try the *peixada* fish soup. Aluisio stays open for dinner, too, and is the town's principal buggy driver. He does not speak English, but is a very accommodating guy. There are restaurants at Praia da Gunga in case you head there for the day.

In the month of December, a place called **Nilquin** produces folklore festivals, dances, and events in their large *fazenda* (country farm), which is not far from the village. During the year, they produce *forró* dancing

on Saturday nights. Besides this, there is no nightlife in town.

## Information

Ask at your hotel for information on anything you need while in Barra de São Miguel. There is a Banco do Brasil in the town center with an international ATM.

## Getting There and Around

Buses from Maceió, marked "B. de São Miguel," leave from the main bus station for about R$3. If you're staying at the BrisaMar hotel, make sure you ask to get off before the *vilarejo*. You can get around town by buggy or by walking. You can take a private *lotação* (group taxi service) back up the coast to Praia do Francês or Maceió. Your hotel can call one for you.

## ◪ PRAIA DA GUNGA

The reef at Barra de São Miguel runs parallel to the coast for about six kilometers until it bumps into a sandy point on the other side of the river's mouth, called the Praia da Gunga. The reef divides Gunga Beach into two parts: the part inside the reef, which has calm ocean and river water, and the part outside the reef, which has large waves and rough surf. Both sides are beautiful and you can walk between them in a few seconds. The wavy side has several small beach bars near the point and then stretches on for about two kilometers to the next point. The entire stretch of beach is fenced-off by a palm tree grove. The calm side has small kiosks that serve beer, coconut water, and various lunch plates. You can find a nice, shady table, then take a Jet Ski out for a 10-minute ride. If you do not want to drive, then take a ride on a banana boat. Buggy excursions also leave from Gunga to various spots nearby.

During the week in the off-season, Gunga is not crowded and the kiosks have limited selections. But the sandy point is as picturesque as any tropical beach you're ever likely to see. If you decide to stay for a second day, set yourself up in a hotel in Barra de São Miguel.

a perfect day on the perfect beach, Gunga

## BARRA DE JEQUIÁ (DUAS BARRAS)

Jequiá is situated where the river Jequiá flows into the ocean. Before it does, it makes a couple of flashy serpentine turns that form two sandy bars on which you can hang out and relax in the sun. There are beach kiosks and restaurants for lunch and the water is excellent for swimming and the whole area is wonderfully picturesque with palm groves lining the beach and plenty of sand and blue sea. From here, you can take a boat excursion up the river, an unforgettable experience. Barra de Jequiá is about 50 kilometers from Maceió off the main highway (101). Excursions come here from Maceió, Praia do Francês, and Barra de São Miguel.

## PONTAL DO CURURÍPE

Like most of the hot spots on the south coast of Maceió, Cururípe is situated at the mouth of a river. The point at which the river and ocean meet is a sandy area with shallow waters and warm tide pools created by offshore reefs. The area is perfect for swimming and there is a small village with arts and crafts and a small lighthouse. The water is transparent and shallow, but there are no kiosks or beach chairs in which to catch a moment of shade. That will certainly change as more people find there way here from Maceió.

Also in Cururípe is the Praia da Lagoa do Pau. This beach has mild waves and warm, shallow water that is good for swimming. On the beach are large bars that double as complete restaurants and serve the popular *moqueca* fish stew, Bahian style, with coconut milk and palm oil. You can take buggy trips and other excursions from here.

# Salvador

It's difficult to think of a place in South America more rich in history, more steeped in art and culture, more tied to the conquest of liberation than Salvador da Bahia. Many consider Salvador to be the very pulse of Brazilian culture, the grand palace overlooking Brazil's ethnic landscape. Salvador's heart remains in Africa and the African influences here are strong and colorful, having been filtered through almost three centuries of slavery and hardship. Today, Salvador celebrates its liberation with music, dance, art, festivals, and traditional religious ceremonies. The streets of Pelourinho, the Centro Histórico, vibrate with history, music, art, and food—both during the day and at night.

The night scene in Pelourinho is a non-stop festival of the senses. Besides the historical buildings throughout the Centro Histórico, there are numerous museums, architectural monuments, and baroque churches to explore.

Now let's talk about the beaches: Salvador is guardian of the All Saints Bay, which is home to several tropical islands. On some islands, you can sit on a sandy beach and look across the bay at the Salvador skyline. Others offer more secluded experiences. Up the northern coast of Salvador are the famous beaches of Itapoã and Flamengo, both with excellent beach bars for relaxing in the shade. There are also restaurants and a variety of hotels.

# Must-Sees

Look for **M** to find the sights and activities you can't miss and **N** for the best dining and lodging.

**M** **Igreja e Convento de São Francisco:** If you've never seen hundreds of kilos of pure gold splashed over the walls and altars of a 17th century church like it was paint, then you should not miss the São Francisco Church and Convent. Don't let the humble exterior fool you; going inside is like walking into the king's jewelry box (page 366).

**M** **Mercado Modelo:** It's an obstinate person, indeed, who can resist purchasing a little something at the Mercado Modelo. The place is bursting with Bahian arts, crafts, clothing, jewelry, leather goods, and trinkets—two floors and more than 250 stands full of goodies. There's a restaurant out back and an international ATM in the front in case you need to refuel (page 369).

© CHRISTOPHER VAN BUREN

Igreja e Convento de São Francisco

**M** **Morro de São Paulo Beaches:** Walk the beaches or take a speedboat around the island, and you may see dolphins heading out for the night while flocks of snowy egrets come in (page 399).

**M** **Maraú Peninsula Lakes and Beaches:** The lakes and beaches on this peninsula are vast and varied, and beaches like **Taipu de Fora,** have amazing underwater reefs and tide pools for snorkeling. (page 410).

**M** **Praia da Concha:** You'll probably wonder how you can go about staying in one of these beach cabanas for the entire summer. This is a perfect slice of tropical Bahia. When the sun begins to set, you'll see the Capoeira artists practicing their craft, silhouetted against the palm trees, the surf, and the horizon (page 412).

ATLANTIC OCEAN

Fortaleza

**SALVADOR**

Maceió

Igreja e Convento de São Francisco
Mercado Modelo
Praia da Concha
Morro de São Paulo Beaches
Salvador

Maraú Peninsula Lakes and Beaches

Porto Seguro

Belo Horizonte

Salvador

# SALVADOR

To Mangue Seco
and North Coast

Jacuípe

Interlagos

Jauá

Camaçari

Dias
d'Ávila

Ipitanga

Flamengo

Stella Maris

Simões Filho

Itapoã

Pituaçu

SALVADOR

Armação

Jardim de Alá

Campo
Grande

Pelourinho

Pituba

Barra

Ondina

Bonfim

Candeias

Ilha de
Maré

Madre
de Deus

Ilha do
Frade

Baía de Todos
os Santos

Bom Despacho

Mar Grande

Vera Cruz

Penha

Barra do Pote

Conceição

Barra Grande

São Francisco
do Conde

Itaparica

Ilha do
Medo

Ilha de
Itaparica

To Morro de São Paulo Beaches,
Praia da Concha, and Maraú

Conceição
de Salinas

Pirajuía

Tribatuba

Catu

Cacha-Pregos

Canal de
Itaparica

Maragogipe

Jaguaripe

To Itacaré and Ileus

A T L A N T I C    O C E A N

2 mi

2 km

Salvador

© AVALON TRAVEL PUBLISHING, INC.

Geographically, Salvador lies on the tip of land that separates the Atlantic Ocean from the Bay of All Saints. The most interesting elements of the city are concentrated on the coastline and the city can be divided into three parts: the coastline along the ocean (Flamengo Beach, Itapoã Beach, and the Blue Coast areas); the coastline along the bay (Pelourinho, Cidade Baixa, Bonfim, and Campo Grande vicinity); and the point in-between (Barra). This chapter uses these three basic divisions.

## PLANNING YOUR TIME

There is so much to do and see in Salvador that planning takes on a new dimension. Most visitors not only want to see Salvador, but also some of the islands in the bay (especially Morro de São Paulo) and some of the northern coastline (especially Praia do Forte). Here's my advice for setting yourself up in Salvador: Get a decent hotel along the bay in the Campo Grande area and take taxis back and forth to Pelourinho and Bonfim to see the sights and nightlife. You can walk around these areas once you get there (Bonfim only during the day, please), and it's easy to catch a taxi back from Pelourinho at any time of the day or night. You can walk to many of the sights in the Campo Grande area, since you'll be staying right there. Hire a taxi to take you on a tour of the few distant sights between your hotel and Pelourinho—or to the sights in Barra.

Next, move your base to Itapoã for the next day or two. Besides enjoying the Itapoã and Flamengo areas, you can make day trips to the north coast. This is a good time to rent a car, so you can come and go as you please. When you're ready, catch a small plane from the airport (not far from Itapoã) to Morro de São Paulo for the final few days of your trip. I personally can't imagine a better Brazilian vacation.

For a more economical version of this trip, just substitute a hotel in the Barra neighborhood and catch the frequent buses back and forth from Pelourinho and Bonfim. You can splurge for a taxi if you end up staying out too late. For the sights between Barra and Pelourinho, take a bus to the Carlos Costa Pinto Museum and walk from there up to the São Pedro Fort, passing various sights along the way. Take a taxi to the final few sights on the way to Pelourinho. You can take day trips to Itapoã and the northern beaches and catch a boat across the bay to Morro de São Paulo. Voila! A perfect trip on a budget.

A couple more tips: Try to avoid the city beaches on weekends, unless you like rubbing elbows with the masses. This is especially true in the summer months. Weekdays in the summer are best for visiting the Salvador coast. On weekends, you can head up to the northern coast or to Morro de São Paulo or even take a trip to Itacaré to the south. Itapirica Island has wonderful beaches but will also be very crowded on the weekend, although less so than the coast of Salvador. A weekend exploring Pelourinho and the museums in Campo Grande is a decent option. Many churches and museums are closed on Monday or Tuesday, so these are perfect days to hit the beaches. If it's raining when you wake up, don't despair. Most likely it will pass in a couple of hours, so keep you plans intact. Remember that any place you have to pay to get into will be safer than those you don't. That means that it's safer to sit in the actual area belonging to the beach bar, rather than on the sandy beach. The same is true for any sidewalk establishments in town.

The best time to visit Salvador is October–December, part of the dry season. The months of December–March are also good in terms of weather, but things can get a bit crowded at this time, as these are holiday months for Brazilians (at least until Carnaval in February). During these months, prices go up in most hotels. The rainy season begins full-on in March and goes until June. Of course, you'll get rainy periods during any of these times and some years have seen endless storms throughout October and November, but this is not the norm. Salvador is always warm and tropical with plenty of humidity.

## SALVADOR SURVIVAL TIPS

Around Pelourinho and the Cidade Baixa, you'll encounter a lot of poverty. Most likely, you'll be approached by children with their hands out and sad looks on their faces. Still, the beggars generally don't present a threat. Whether or not you decide to give money is your own personal choice. Most experts feel that giving money is a bad idea, as it encourages more begging. Some travelers give food items, articles of clothing, and useful objects instead of money.

Street vendors can be an annoyance, especially those handing out the *fitinhas* (strips of colored ribbon in reverence to *O Senhor do Bonfim*) and wanting to shine your shoes. These can be rather insistent and will often start placing a ribbon around your wrist or sitting down and shining your shoes even after you've said *"não obrigado(a)"* several times. They may guarantee that you don't have to pay, that it's a gift, or that they just want to show you a sample. If you let them, you will end up in their debt. It's best to be firm and persistent with your nos. If you are sitting at a table outside, then you can enlist the help of the waitstaff with a hand gesture and a beseeching *"por favor. . ."*

On the beach, be careful of cheese vendors and anyone coming to your area to sell something (sunglasses, peanuts, etc.). With great sleight of hand and misdirection, they are known to snatch stuff from your table or towel area as they demonstrate their wares. If you put your shoes on the sand near your table, they might even walk off in them without you knowing it until later.

In Salvador, most foreigners stand out no matter what they do to blend in. The best protection is to not walk around dangerous areas. Of course, that means cutting out a lot of adventure, so if you are the adventurous type, here's some different advice: Don't walk around with anything of great value on you. That includes a watch, credit cards (keep them in your hotel if you can), passport (use a copy), and camera (OK, you have to have a camera, but keep it tucked away in your pack). You can keep money in your shoe, in a money belt, or an inside pocket. Keep a few bills in your front pocket (with your hand in it) or any other pocket that zips or buttons. If it looks like you have a wad of bills folded up in your pocket, then redistribute the bills.

Sounds dangerous? It's really not. Just be smart about where you go and when. If you feel that you are entering a bad part of town, then hail a taxi and ride comfortably to your destination.

## HISTORY

One of the first cities to be developed in Brazil, Salvador's official founding is 1549, when Captain Tomé de Souza came to govern the land given to him by King João III of Portugal. It was a dubious honor, but certainly better than suffering the Inquisition back home. Others had failed at keeping the colony free of French pirates and other invaders—not to mention populating the territory and converting indigenous tribes. The first captain to be given the territory of Bahia, Francisco Pereira Coutinho, shipwrecked in the Bay of All Saints

a year after he came to govern the territory. He was captured and later eaten by the Tupinambá people. They knew who he was. The good captain Tomé de Souza was now to be governor of the territory and governor-general of the entire Brazilian colony. He established Salvador as the capital city, made his home in the area that is now Pelourinho, and built a palace for himself out of mud and sticks. That palace was eventually to become the Palácio Rio Branco on the edge of present-day Pelourinho.

Tomé de Souza arrived with his small fleet of ships carrying a troupe of workers (smiths, masons, etc.), numerous Jesuits for converting the native inhabitants, and a small flock of prostitutes. So it was that Salvador's inception was marked by a mixture of Catholicism, indigenous enslavement (those who did not convert), and bawdiness. When the slaves proved insufficient at working in the new sugar mills, cocoa harvesting, and Pau Brasil cutting (a tree used for its hard wood and for the die made of its red bark and seeds), African slaves were imported to take over. Between 1600 and 1888 (when slavery was finally abolished in Brazil) almost 1.5 million African slaves were brought to Brazil.

Salvador was the nucleus of the colony and its sugar production, and it was here that African slaves were most severely treated. A kind of resistance movement grew among the slaves that found its way into their religion (mixing African Candomblé with Catholicism), music, and dance (Capoeira evolving out of an African fighting technique and practiced through "dances" in the slave communities).

Salvador soon became the most important trading port between Brazil and Europe in the 16th and 17th centuries—until Rio de Janeiro usurped its position in the early 1700s as a result of the gold rush in Minas Gerais. But Salvador remains a kind of cultural capital of Brazil, with its mix of African, Portuguese, French, and Dutch influences—along with the native tribal races that were already flourishing on the continent.

## Pelourinho and Bonfim

Over 800 colonial mansions and Baroque churches lean against the hillside of the old city center of Pelourinho. It was here at the Largo do Pelourinho where slaves and outlaws were publicly whipped (the word *pelourinho* means whipping post). During its heyday, Pelourinho was the center of Salvador, the capital city of the colony and home to the richest sugar and cocoa barons of the time. It was also home to the country's most active international port, located strategically inside the Bay of All Saints. Now a UNESCO World Heritage Site, Pelourinho is a living museum, with numerous buildings from the 16th and 17th centuries fully restored to their original beauty and charm (there are always buildings undergoing restoration in Pelourinho, as the job is practically endless). During the day, you can walk the streets, looking into the many clothing and art shops, restaurants, museums and churches. At night, Pelourinho offers up music and dance events in its many public squares, as well as a non-stop street scene that passes in front of the many sidewalk café/bars that decorate the streets. The Laranjeiras areas is loaded with charming restaurants that seat their guests outside on the sidewalk or inside their colonial manors. A number of programmed events take place during the week, like cultural performances at the SENAC theater or concerts by Olodúm and other groups. Just outside the Centro Histórico, you can watch a native Candomblé ritual.

Originally, this principal area of Salvador consisted of a high and low city, called Cidade Alta and Cidade Baixa. Today the famous Lacerda Elevator carries over 50,000 people every day between the two. At the bottom, where all of the shipping activity took place, are more churches, the Mercado Modelo for regional arts and crafts, and the Maritime Terminal, where you can catch a boat to one of the islands in the bay. The Cidade Baixa extends westward to the area known as Bonfim, a neighborhood famous for its Afro-Brazilian festivals and home to the famous Bonfim Church.

On the other side of Pelourinho (toward the ocean) the monuments, churches and museums continue all the way down the coast to the Campo Grande neighborhood (mainly along Av. Sete de Setembro). Some highlights here include the Museum of Modern Art and the nearby Solar do União performing arts center. Two of the city's best museums are here (Carlos Costa Pinto and Bahian Art Museum) as well as the Praça Castro Alves and the modern Castro Alves Theater.

# CHURCHES

## Catedral Basilica de São Salvador

As you walk into the main *praça* of Pelourinho, called the Terreiro de Jesus, the Catedral Basilica (Centro Histórico, tel. 71/3321-4573, 9–11 A.M. and 2–5 P.M. daily, R$1) will be on your left. You can't miss it; it's the largest and most impressive church in the *praça*, built in the early 1600s, not long after the founding of Salvador. Much of the original construction was lost to fire in the early 1900s, but the church was rebuilt and stands as an example of baroque architecture and sacred art in South America. The church was originally built as a Jesuit school (until the Jesuits were ousted in the mid-1600s) and above the entrance doors are carvings of three Jesuit saints. Inside, you can look down to see the marble floors, or up to see the beautifully painted and carved ceiling. Side altars are loaded with gold-covered wooden sculpture and hand-painted ornamentation, and represent a mixture of styles, from baroque to neoclassic.

The highlight is the front altar with a hand-carved arch and many wood carvings. In the back of the church is a collection of religious paintings and Portuguese tiles. With its two towers, marble floors, tropical wood, gold leafing, and paintings, the Catedral Basilica is considered one of the country's most beautiful churches. It is often used by Brazil's rich and famous for wedding ceremonies. You can attend mass on Sundays at 10:30 A.M. with baroque music presentations.

## Igreja da Ordem Terceira de São Francisco

This church (Rua Inacio Acccioli, tel. 71/3321-6968, 8 A.M.–5 P.M. Mon.–Fri. and 7 A.M.–noon Sun., R$3), located next to the São Francisco Convent, has the date 1703 carved into the facade. It's the only church in Pelourinho with hand-carved stone in the front. The ceilings are beautifully painted with several interlocked panels and the altars are filled with typical baroque carvings covered in gold. Upstairs is a museum with numerous paintings (check out the gold-leaf frames) and an enormous banquet table for 30.

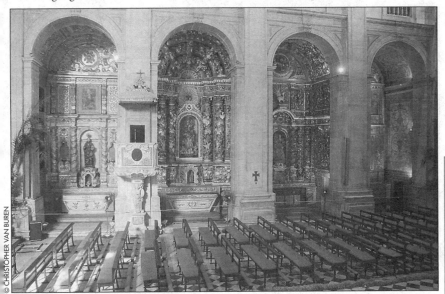

gold-leaf altars in the Catedral Basilica

Salvador

Salvador

# PELOURINHO AND VICINITY

Baía de Todos os Santos

To Bonfim and Ferryboat →

SANTO ANTÔNIO

CARMO

POUSADA HILMAR ●

R. DE QUEIROZ

★ IGREJA E ORDEM TERCEIRA DO CARMO

BAIXA DOS SAPATEIROS)

R. DO CARMO

LAD. DO PILAR

IGREJA DO SANTÍSSIMO SACRAMENTO DO PASSO ★

R. DO PASSO

R. DO JULIÃO

R. DO ALVO

PELOURINHO

PRAÇA DO REGGAE ★

★ TEATRO DE ARENA DO SENAC

★ LARGO DO PELOURINHO ARCHITECTURAL COMPLEX

UAUÁ ▼

Praça do Pelourinho

★ CASA DE JORGE AMADO

★ MUSEU DA CIDADE

★ COOKING SCHOOL AT SENAC

LARGO BERRO D'ÁGUA ▼

R. DO TABOÃO

IGREJA NOSSA SRA DO ROSÁRIO ★

R. LAFAYETE

CORS.

■ GONÇALVES MONORAIL

CABRAL

R. DOS PADRES

R. MIGUEL CALMON

R. CONS DANTAS

R. PEDRO

AV. ESTADOS UNIDOS

MARTINS

PINTO

R. PORTUGAL

R. JOÃO

CIDADE BAIXA

AV. DA FRANÇA

■ TERMINAL MARÍTIMO

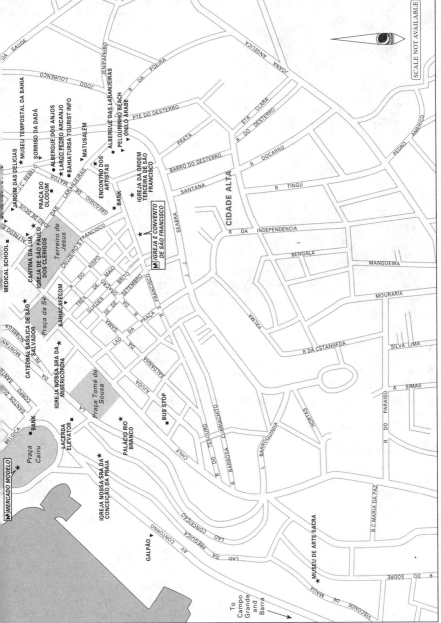

SCALE NOT AVAILABLE

Salvador

© AVALON TRAVEL PUBLISHING, INC.

The Igreja da Ordem Terceira de São Francisco with its carved façade.

### Igreja de São Pedro dos Clérigos

Not necessarily one of the most exciting churches in the Centro Histórico, São Pedro (Terreiro de Jesus, tel. 71/3321-0966, 1–5 P.M. Mon.–Fri.) is worth peeking into as you walk across the Praça Terreiro de Jesus. It's one of the few churches in the rococo style.

### Igreja e Convento de São Francisco

Also known as the Gold Church, the Igreja São Francisco (Cruzeiro de São Francisco, tel. 71/3322-6430, 8:30 A.M.–5 P.M. Mon.–Sat.) is drenched in gold leaf, hundreds of kilos of it. The many wood sculptures on the altars—representing cherubs, angels, saints, flora, and fauna—are all draped in gold and surrounded with detailed ornamentation in gold and white. The simple gold-and-white motif is offset by the dark jacaranda wood used in the hand railings and altar pews and a few simple blue Portuguese tiles above the altars. The ceiling

and entrance are covered in baroque paintings. Considered the richest church in Brazil, São Francisco was finished in 1723, its rather humble outer facade hiding the incredible riches within. The adjoining convent has an entrance hallway covered in blue Portuguese tiles from the 1500s, and the theme continues to the outer patio area.

### Igreja Nossa Sra. da Misericordia (Santa Casa)

Flanking the Monument to the Fallen Cross is the Santa Casa de Misericordia (Rua Chile, Praça da Sé, tel. 71/3322-7666, 8 A.M.–5 P.M. Mon.–Fri.), a 17th-century construction with 18th-century reforms. The house contains a collection of sacred art, sculpture, colonial furniture, and artifacts from the colonial period. Even if you're not up for checking out more religious art and sculpture (you might want to save your stamina for the Sacred Art Museum and principal churches), it's worth at least stepping into the entry hall to check out the interior of the building.

### Igreja Nossa Sra. do Rosário

At the bottom of the hill, on the far end of Pelourinho sits the Igreja do Rosário (Largo do Pelourinho, tel. 71/3326-9701, 7:30 A.M.–6 P.M. Mon.–Fri. and 7:30 A.M.–noon weekends), built in the 1700s by free slaves. Like most churches of the brotherhood of Rosário (brotherhood of black slaves), this church is on the outskirts of town and uses a mixture of themes, both African and Catholic. The facade is a mixture of baroque and rococo architecture with East Indian influences in the spires. At the time of this writing, this church was closed for restorations, which have been known to take years to complete in Pelourinho.

### Igreja Nossa Sra. da Conceição da Praia

Although it is sitting here in Salvador, overlooking the Bay of All Saints, this church (Praça Ramos de Queirós, 6:30–11:30 A.M. and 3–5:30 P.M. Tues.–Fri. and 6:30–11:30 A.M. Sat.–Mon.) was actually built in Portugal. It was

**Igreja e Convento de São Francisco in Pelourinho**

prefabricated there and brought to Brazil by boat to be reconstructed in its present location in 1736. The ceiling features a painting by José Joaquim da Rocha (1772). On January 1 each year, boats take off from the pier in front of this church, carrying sacred icons to the Igreja da Boa Viagem in Bonfim.

# MUSEUMS

### Casa de Jorge Amado

Located at the top of Largo do Pelourinho, the Casa de Jorge Amado (Largo do Pelourinho 51, tel. 71/3321-0122, 9 A.M.–6 P.M. Mon.–Sat.) was once the very spot where slaves were whipped in public at the *pelourinhos* (whipping posts). If you look around on the stone street in front of the place, you'll find part of the original stone platform where the *pelourinhos* actually stood. In 1987, the house opened as a foundation dedicated to the preservation and study of the novels of Jorge Amado (the background of each story is on display at the museum), who lived in Salvador all his life and finally acquired and lived in this house until his death. Many of the author's books are set

in old Pelourinho and characters are often based on personalities from Salvador. The second most interesting thing about the Casa is the air-conditioned café inside the building, which is a great place to cool off and grab something to drink. Inside is also a souvenir shop and gallery.

### Museu Abelardo Rodrigues

Not unlike the Museu de Arte Sacra, the Abelardo Rodrigues Museum (Rua Gregório de Matos 45, tel. 71/3321-6155, 1–7 P.M. Tues.–Sat., R$1) houses a collection of statuary, paintings, and religious artifacts from Salvador's colonial period, said to be the largest private collection in Brazil. As impressive as the artifacts themselves is the building, with its massive stairway entrance and old, wood floors. It maintains elements from the 17th and 18th centuries and was used as a seminary and home for rich families visiting Salvador. The museum is mercifully small and easy to see in about 20 minutes. Step out to the patio area upstairs to get a view of the north side of Pelourinho, where most buildings have not been restored.

Salvador

## Museu de Arte Sacra

This old convent (Rua do Sodre 276, Cidade Alta, tel. 71/3243-6310, 11:30 A.M.–5:30 P.M. Mon.–Fri., R$5) houses one of the country's largest collections of sacred art and sculpture, specializing in baroque sculpture (of course). After seeing so many baroque churches in Pelourinho and the Cidade Baixa, you might be reluctant to see a museum full of baroque religious images. But this one is worth a visit—if not just to sit in the garden and look out over the bay. The beautiful building and garden (finished in 1685) sit just outside Pelourinho on Rua do Sondré toward Campo Grande, but is easy to reach on foot or by taxi. Next door is the Santa Tereza Church.

## Museu da Cidade

Next to the Casa de Jorge Amado in a beautiful colonial manor is the Museu da Cidade (Largo do Pelourinho 3, tel. 71/3321-1967, 9:30 A.M.–6:30 P.M. Mon., Wed., Thur., and Fri., 1–5 P.M. Sat., and 9 A.M.–1 P.M. Sun., R$1). The museum houses a collection of Bahian artifacts, such as paintings, tapestries, antique furnishings, and traditional Bahian clothing. There are collections of dolls and art relating to Candomblé dieties, or Orixás.

## Museu Tempostal da Bahia

Inside this old building (Rua Gregório de Matos 33, 1–7 P.M. Tues.–Sun., free) is a private collection of antique postcards from Bahia, most in pristine condition, that is more interesting than you might imagine. You can see the entire collection in about 15–20 minutes.

# ARCHITECTURE AND MONUMENTS

## Gonçalves Monorail

If you get bored riding the Lacerda Elevator, you can take your next trip between Cidade Alta and Cidade Baixa in the Gonçalves Monorail (7 A.M.–5 P.M. Mon.–Fri. and 7 A.M.–1 P.M. Sat.), known as the Plano Inclinado do Gonçalves or the Gonçalves Teleférico. The upper station is directly behind

Colonial architecture lines the streets of Pelourinho.

Salvador

the Basilica Church in the Praça da Sé and the lower station is on Rua Francisco Gonçalves, just north of the Mercado Modelo. All this for a mere five centavos. It is often closed during lunch hours.

## Lacerda Elevator

In the 15 seconds it takes to descend from Praça Tomé de Souza in Cidade Alta (High City) to the Praça Cairu in Cidade Baixa (Low City), you will have traveled more than 70 meters in one of the tallest public elevators in the world. Some 50,000 passengers make the trip every day (about 120 at a time) using the four elevator cars. Cars one and two are from the 1929 reconstruction of the original 1872 elevator. It was not made with tourism in mind, so there are no scenic views from the elevator cars. There are lookout points inside the tower before you get into the elevator, but the best angle is actually from the Praça Tomé de Souza outside, where you can see the elevator tower with the great Bay of All Saints just beyond and Forte São Marcelo in the middle of the water, right in front of you. It's especially lovely at dusk. The elevator was renovated—although not rebuilt—in 1993 to update its mechanics and add two more cars. Originally, the site was used to raise and lower cargo with ropes and pulleys, and before that, slaves would ride mules up and down the hill, carrying heavy loads.

## Largo do Pelourinho Architectural Complex

The most famous and photographed of the Pelourinho colonial buildings, the complex along the side of the Largo do Pelourinho is, indeed, a picture-perfect example of architecture from the 17th and 18th century in Brazil. Most of the buildings are privately owned, but you can enter the SENAC Cooking School and Restaurant for a look inside (and a terrific lunch buffet). It is here in the Largo do Pelourinho where Carnaval and other festivals occur with huge congregations of people filling the praça and live music coming from a tall stage in front of the Casa de Jorge Amado.

## Mercado Modelo

At the bottom of the Lacerda Elevator and across the highway sits the Mercado Modelo (Praça Visconde de Cayru, tel. 71/3241-0242, 9 A.M.–7 P.M. Mon.–Sat., 9 A.M.–2 P.M. on Sun.), built in 1861 and originally used as the customs house for shipments coming into port. In 1971, the building was converted into the present-day Mercado only to be destroyed by fire in 1984. Quickly rebuilt, the Mercado functions again as a center of Bahian arts and crafts with more than 250 stands. Here you'll find Capoeira pants, lacework, jewelry, wood carvings, Bahian traditional clothing, trinkets, musical instruments, souvenirs, and much more. Prices here are about the same as in Pelourinho, but don't be afraid to bargain, especially for jewelry and handcrafts. In the back is a covered patio area, where you can relax and have lunch or a cold drink. In the *praça* in front of the market, you'll find more arts and crafts stands with a host of hippie-style items and occasional Capoeira demonstrations and live music. There is a Banco do Brasil ATM machine here that has the Plus and Cirrus systems. You'll see armed police hanging around the *praça* during the day, but don't be caught here at night—or anywhere around the Cidade Baixa for that matter.

## Palácio Rio Branco

Marking the eastern edge of Pelourinho (or the entrance to the city, depending on your point of view), the Palácio Rio Branco (Praça Tomé de Souza, Cidade Alta, tel. 71/3321-0204, 10 A.M.–noon and 2–6 P.M. Tues.–Fri.) stands as a fabulous example of Brazilian architecture from the early 1900s. Before the current building was constructed in 1919, the site had a number of previous incarnations. In 1549, at the founding of the city of Salvador, the building, then made of mud and clay, was the headquarters of the governor-general of Brazil, Tomé de Souza, and administrative offices for the Portuguese Crown in Brazil. Later, the building was renovated and served as the town prison, then as temporary living quarters for Emperor Dom Pedro II. After this, the building fell into disrepair and eventually burned down in 1912. The current building, known as the Palácio Rio Branco, was used as government offices and tourism offices. In the middle of the 20th century, the building again fell into disrepair (along with the rest of Pelourinho) until it was restored in 1983 as a museum and government memorial. It houses government documents and artifacts, but the primary attraction is the building itself, which has a fabulous iron and brass staircase leading to the upper floors and a patio from which you can view the Bay of All Saints.

## Terminal Merítimo (Maritime Terminal)

The terminal is not a tourist attraction so much as a point of reference for almost any boat excursion you might take in Salvador. Here, you'll find all types of boats offering trips to the islands in the Bay of All Saints. The terminal (Avenida da França, no number, Cidade Baixa, tel. 71/3216-7045) is directly behind the Mercado Modelo.

## Terreiro de Jesus Medical School

The first school of medicine in Brazil, this early 19th-century building (Terreiro de Jesus, 9 A.M.–5 P.M. Mon.–Fri.) is currently undergoing renovations by the state of Bahia and private parties (and has been for quite a few years). Part of the building houses three small museums. The **Afro-Brazilian Museum** (tel. 71/3322-8070, R$2) contains religious and spiritual art and artifacts from African and Afro-Brazilian origins, including sculptures, pottery, paintings, and crafts. There is also a collection of photographs. The **Archeology and Ethnology Museum** (tel. 71/3321-3971, R$1) reveals more works of art, photos, and some artifacts. The **Medicine Memorial** ( tel. 71/3321-0383, R$2) houses mostly books and texts about the beginnings of medicine in Brazil.

## BONFIM

Every year in January (two Thursdays after January 6, to be exact), thousands of devotees and spectators take part in a religious and

Historical buildings line the hillsides of Pelourinho.

Salvador

festive procession from the Igreja Nossa Sra. da Conceição da Praia to the **Igreja Nossa Senhor do Bonfim** (Largo do Bonfim, tel. 71/3316-2196, 8 A.M.–noon and 2–5 P.M. Tues.–Sun.), a distance of some six kilometers. Upon reaching the Bonfim church, the Bahianas empty large water pots onto the steps of the church to commence the *lavagem do Bonfim* (washing ceremony). The tradition was begun in 1804 by a devotee who vowed to wash the entire church in gratitude for returning uninjured form the war with Paraguay. Others began to repeat his devotion in gratitude for the blessings bestowed upon them during the year. The tradition turned into a sort of Bahian, Candomblé festival, with its mixture of Catholic saints and Orixás (African deities). As such, the Archbishop in 1889 prohibited the Bahianas from entering the church and, to this day, the washing takes place on the front steps, along with a massive festival that includes food, samba, Capoeira, and plenty of *cachaça*. You can visit the Bonfim church and its miraculous back room where pilgrims come for healings of all kinds.

Near the Ponta de Humanita in Bonfim is the **Forte Monte Serrat** (Rua Santa Rita Durão, no number, tel. 71/3313-7339, 9 A.M.–5 P.M. Tues.–Sun., R$1), which has an amazing view of the Bay of All Saints and the coastline of Salvador. The fort was built in the 1600s and currently houses a display of cannons and other weapons of war. Not far from the fort is the **Igreja Nossa Sra. da Boa Viagem** (Largo da Boa Viagem, tel. 71/3314-1800, 7:30 A.M.–1 P.M. Mon.–Fri. and 7:30 A.M.–5 P.M. weekends), which is the ending point (and party point) for the Mariner's Festival on January 1 every year. It's also interesting in that the front of the church faces the bay, which makes it most attractive from the water. Built in 1741, the church features panels of blue Portuguese tiles from the 18th century.

## CARMO AND SANTO ANTÔNIO

The Santo Antônio district, along with its neighbor Carmo, are on the far side of Pelourinho.

After walking through town and down the hillside of the Largo do Pelourinho, you come to what appears to be the end of town. This is the beginning of the Carmo district. Continue up the hill, known as the Ladeira do Carmo, and you'll come to a number of interesting sights. Further up is the Santo Antônio district, which is known for being a more economical place to stay and eat. Highlights of the area include the **Igreja do Santíssimo Sacramento do Passo** (Largo do Passo), which has been closed for restoration for several years and might open any day now. It has three floors of beautifully carved statuary and gold leaf. A grand staircase takes you up to the church from the left side of the Ladeira do Carmo. It was built in 1737 on one of the most picturesque points of the city, overlooking both Pelourinho to one side and the Cidade Baixa to the other. Next is the **Igreja e Ordem Terceira do Carmo** (Largo do Carmo 9, 9 A.M.–1 P.M. and 2–6 P.M. Monday–Saturday), one of the more opulent churches in Pelourinho. Inside this drab facade is a lavishly carved and gold-covered interior. It's at the very top of the Ladeira do Carmo. Continue along Rua do Carmo and you'll pass the Boqueirão Church, built in the 1700s, plus many old, original buildings. Farther up, you'll finally land in the Praça Santo Antônio, where you can enjoy a wonderful panoramic view of the area, including the Fort Barbalho to the north.

## CAMPO GRANDE

The sights in this region extend from the end of Pelourinho to the Campo Grande neighborhood, which is east, toward the tip of Salvador. As such, they are a bit too spread out to visit on foot and it's best to take taxis between them. Try to time it so that you can spend the afternoon at the **Solar do União,** a cluster of colonial buildings that includes an antique manor, slave quarters, and chapel. Also housed here is the **Museu de Arte Moderna** (Av. do Contorno, tel. 71/3329-0660, 1–6 P.M. Tues.–Fri., 1–7 P.M. on weekends, free) with works from famous Brazilian masters, including Portinari, Di Calvalcanti, and Tarsília de Amaral, among others.

Salvador

# CHAPADA DIAMANTINA

One of the most sought after places for hiking, camping, and adventure sports lies in the interior of Bahia, known as Chapada Diamantina. There, the dramatic countryside is filled with great stone mesas and sprawling valleys. Rivers and waterfalls carve their way through the stones, forming pools and caverns along the way. You can hike along these waterways, swim with the fish in the ultra-clear pools, and climb to the top of the mountain mesas, or *Chapadas*. The Chapada known as **Morro do Pai Inácio** is a favorite spot for hang gliding and rappelling. It also affords a panoramic view of the entire region from 1170 meters high.

Other highlights include the **Cachoeira da Fumaça** (Waterfall of Smoke), where from 340 meters high, the water cascades down and turns to smoke before hitting the ground. There are over 100 caves in the area, many with clear, silent lakes inside and even cave paintings. The **Lapa Doce** cave is one of the most impressive, with its towering ceilings and huge tunnels. The Torrinha cave is one of Brazil's longest. You can access most of the area's caves from the town of Iraquara, 80 kilometers north of Lençóis.

## Guides and Excursions

The best way to see the Chapada area is on guided excursions. You can find guides with transportation in the main points of entry, particularly in Lençóis. Guides offer all sorts of excursion packages, grouping together adventures relatively close to one another with a variety of hiking, swimming, and cave dwelling. You can move to one of the other points of entry to continue your adventures with new guides, or make a package deal with your guide to include more distant sites. Packages usually start in the morning and return at sundown. The average price is R$60–120. Some guides offer overnight camping excursions through the park. Most offer equipment for rent, transportation and all food. The cost is from R$80–250. Be sure to use guides that are registered with the state or associated with a reputable *pousada*. Most *pousadas* will recommend guides with whom they work on a regular basis. With a group of four people, you can usually tailor your package to suit the group. For example, you can spend an entire day exploring caves. If you are traveling alone or with one other person, ask your *pousada* if they can put you together with another group. Do this as soon as you get into town.

## Points of Entry

The primary point of entry into the Chapada Diamantina is through the town of **Lençóis** approximately 350 kilometers west of Salvador. Lençóis sits on the northern tip of the Chapada Diamantina National Park and you can access most of the attractions of the area from this base of operation. The town also offers some bars and nightlife options, in case you have energy after a day of hiking and adventure. There are also historical sites in town, mostly from the diamond exploration era of the 18th century. The town of **Caeté Açu** is close to many of the area's natural treasures, including the Cachoeira da Fumaça and the Vale do Capão. From the town or **Andaraí**, you can see the Marimbus wetlands, where you can observe a variety of flora and fauna on a canoe safari. You can also head out to the Poço Encantado (Enchanted Well) and the Poço Azul. The historical town of **Mucugê** is worth a look and perhaps even an overnight stay. Nearby you'll find plenty of rivers and waterfalls.

## Where to Stay

In Lençóis, check out the **Canto das Águas** (Av. Senador dos Passos, Centro, tel. 75/3334-1154). In Caeté Açu, try **Pousada Candombá** (Rua das Mangas, Vale do Capão, 75/3344-1102). If you prefer, you can probably find a hotel or *pousada* upon arriving in town, depending on the hour of your arrival and excluding peak season (mid-December through mid-February).

Don't miss the outdoor sculpture garden and be sure to have dinner at the Solar do União's restaurant with its beautiful view of the bay and folkloric show at sundown (9 P.M. Mon.–Sat., reservations tel. 71/3329-5551, R$36). Farther down the coast toward the ocean is the **Praça Castro Alves,** with its many trees and impressive monument by the Italian sculptor Pasquale Di Chirico. On the far end is the **Teatro Castro Alves** (for schedule and ticket information: tel. 71/3339-8014, www.tca.ba.gov.br) where large-scale performances are presented, including classical and international music and dance concerts. Not far from the *praça* is the **Forte São Pedro** (Rua Visconde de São Lourenço, tel. 71/3336-9588, 8 A.M.–6 P.M. daily), which was built in the early 1700s as part of the city's defense system.

Farther down Avenida Sete de Setembro (the street in front of the Praça Castro Alves) are two museums. First is the **Bahian Art Museum** (Av. Sete de Setembro 2340, tel. 71/3336-9450, 2–7 P.M. Tues.–Fri., 2:30–6:30 P.M. Sat.–Sun., R$3, free Thurs.), which has works from Bahian artists dating from the 1700s. There are also sculpture works, stamp collections, and historical documents. The museum is housed in a beautiful manor from the 1920s. Down the street is the **Carlos Costa Pinto Museum** (Av. Sete de Setembro 2490, tel. 71/3336-6081, 2–7 P.M. Wed.–Mon., 2:30–6:30 P.M. Sat.–Sun., R$5, free Thurs.), which houses collections of decorative pieces and jewelry in gold, silver, ivory, and bronze. There are also furnishings and paintings from the 1600s through the 1900s.

## ENTERTAINMENT AND NIGHTLIFE

Pelourinho is all about nightlife. When the sun goes down, the streets of the Centro Histórico light up with music, sidewalk cafés, and a high-energy night scene in general. Some stores stay open until late at night, but in compensation for the ones that close, a troupe of street hawkers descends on the town to sell wares to tourists. It's common to see drumming groups marching up and down the streets, pounding out traditional Afro-Brazilian rhythms from Bahia. The famous Bahianas in traditional white hoop dresses sit in front of food stands with interesting items for sale (typically sweets or *Acarajé*). There is so much stimulus going on all around that just sitting with a cold beer and watching the scene take place in front of you is a fabulous way to pass the night. If you're in the mood for dancing, there is always something going on in town. Dance, music, and cultural performances take place daily and it's a good idea to check out the various theaters around town to see what's going on that night. A good and easy-to-understand music and theater guide is the *Bahia Cultural,* which has a section called *Pelourinho Dia & Noite* in the back with a cultural calendar for the month. See if you can pick up a copy of this at the tourist information office. A more complete guide is the *Guide do Ócio,* which you can find at magazine stands for R$3.50, but it's not easy to understand, since it covers arts and entertainment for the entire city. It has a small section in English in the back.

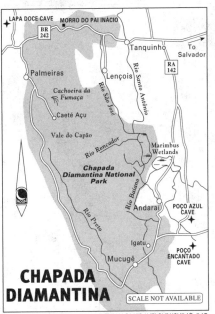

LAPA DOCE CAVE    MORRO DO PAI INÁCIO

BR 242

Tanquinho

To Salvador

RA 142

Palmeiras    Lençóis

Rio Santo Antônio

Cachoeira da Fumaça

Rio São José

Caeté Açu

Vale do Capão

Rio Roncador

Marimbus Wetlands

**Chapada Diamantina National Park**

Rio Baiano

Andaraí    POÇO AZUL CAVE

Rio Preto

Igatu

Mucugê    POÇO ENCANTADO CAVE

MOON

# CHAPADA DIAMANTINA

SCALE NOT AVAILABLE

© AVALON TRAVEL PUBLISHING, INC.

Salvador

## Music and Dance

Want to shake it to some Afro-Brazilian rhythms? There are several key spots for music and dance in Pelourinho—and they all have something going on every night. Most live music starts around 11 P.M. and goes until at least 3 or 4 A.M. The first one to check out is the **Largo Berro D'Agua,** which is a small *praça* closed-in by colonial buildings on all sides. There are tables for sitting and dining, while watching and listening. Or you can just stand around the perimeter along with the crowd. You can enter the Largo through the restaurants on Rua Alfredo Brito (the second block from the main *praça*) or from the street entrance off Rua J.C. Rabelo. Entrance is free. Another place for music and dance is the **Largo Tereza Batista,** which is accessible from Rua João de Deus or through the shops on Rua das Laranjeiras. Entrance is usually free, but sometimes there is a minimal charge. Inside are plenty of tables and space for dancing. If you don't find what you like at either of these locations, look into the

**Largo Pedro Arcanjo,** which is located on Rua Gregório de Mato 24.

Two more spaces for music concerts include the **Praça do Olodúm** (at the top of Rua João de Deus, also known as Largo Teresa Batista), which hosts the Olodúm drumming group on Tuesday nights for around R\$30 per person. It's a loud and wild show with everyone standing up or dancing to the rhythms (and drinking). The energy is high and it goes all night long. The second space is the **Praça do Reggae** (Largo do Pelourinho near the Rosário Church), which specializes in Brazilian and Jamaican reggae music. Swing by during the day to see if there is something happening that night or ask at the tourist information office. The entrance fee varies, depending on the group performing.

## Sidewalk Cafés and Bars

One of the most popular ways to pass the night in Pelourinho is to hop from one *praça* to the next, sampling the food and drinks (and watch-

ing the street scene) at each location. There are numerous locations for hanging out on the street with a drink or appetizer. One of the most frequented locations is **Rua J. C. Rabelo** (from the main *praça,* go down Rua Alfredo Brito and turn right at the first corner). There, you'll find a sidewalk full of tables and chairs, mostly filled with international tourists. Traditionally dressed Bahian women lower baskets of food from second-story windows to the waiters below. Sit there long enough and you'll hear a drum group pass in front of you. Nearby is the Largo Berro D'Agua.

Another strategic point is the confluence of Rua João de Deus and Rua Gregório de Matos. There, at the small, triangular *praça* that forms from the joining of the two streets, you'll find another cluster of sidewalk cafés. Overlooking the main *praça* is the **Cantina da Lua** (Terreiro de Jesus, tel. 71/3241-7383, open 11 A.M. daily), which has a slightly more controlled environment with live music on their outdoor patio.

For a more mellow experience, try the **Bahiacafe.com** Internet café (Praça da Sé 20, across from the Palácio Arquiepiscopal). They have good coffee drinks, sweets, and computers for Internet connections.

## Theater and Shows

Traditional dance and cultural shows, including Capoeira and Maculelé demonstrations take place at the **Teatro de Arena do Senac** (Largo do Pelourinho 19, tel. 71/3324-4520), at the base of Rua Gregorio de Mato. There are also shows from time to time on the outdoor stage at the Praça da Sé. All formal productions are listed in the *Bahia Cultural* monthly guide. Large-scale productions take place at the **Teatro Castro Alves** (Praça 2 de Julho, Campo Grande, tel. 71/3339-8000), which is about halfway to Barra in the Campo Grande neighborhood. Most of their productions are well worth a look.

# FESTIVALS AND EVENTS

First, there are the festivals of the individual Orixás in the **Candomblé rituals.** You should call ahead for the specific dates or check with the Federação Baiana do Culto Afro-Brasileiro

© CHRISTOPHER VAN BUREN

Salvador

Afro-Brazilian dance performances in Pelourinho

(see the *Catching a Candomblé Ritual* sidebar for details). If you don't speak Portuguese, then have your hotel look into this for you. Another famous religious festival is the **Lavagem do Bonfim,** which takes place in the second week of January in the Cidade Baixa. It's a pseudo-religious procession and major *festa* with plenty of dancing and drinking. The largest single festival in Brazil is **Carnaval** in Salvador—even larger than that in Rio de Janeiro. Carnaval takes place sometime in February (the date moves each year) and consists of music, dancing, parades, and swarms of sweaty people hopping up and down on the streets of Salvador. There are always fireworks on the bay during **New Year's Eve** and the Praça Tomé de Souza is an excellent place to watch them. Another great viewpoing is the Solar do União restaurant patio. The following day is the day of the *Procissão do Senhor do Bom Jesus dos Navigantes,* or **Mariner's Procession,** with boats that travel from the pier in Cidade Baixa to the Boa Viagem Church in the Bonfim area—with a great party at the destination.

## SHOPPING

Arts and crafts are some of Pelourinho's most plentiful offerings. Just walking around the streets of the Centro Histórico, you'll see numerous art galleries, crafts shops, and outdoor craft fairs. Some focal points include the shops along the Terreiro de Jesus (in front of the Catedral Basilica), where you'll find clothing, leather goods, and jewelry. The shops along Rua Alfredo Brito are also good for art, leather goods, and musical instruments. A great shop for quality fabrics with Afro-Brazilian designs is **Didara** (Rua Gregório de Matos 20, tel. 71/3321-9428, 9:30 A.M.–10 P.M. Mon.–Fri., 10 A.M.–6 P.M. Sat., 9:30 A.M.–4 P.M. Sun.). You should not miss a visit to the **Mercado Modelo** (Praça Visconde de Cayru, tel. 71/3241-0242, 9 A.M.–7 P.M. Mon.–Sat., 9 A.M.–2 P.M. Sun.), at the bottom of the elevator and across the highway, where you'll find basically the same stuff you see all around town, but in a marketplace setting and in great quantities. There, you'll also find more traditional souvenirs, such as tee shirts, coffee mugs, and such. There's a great patio for

handmade jewelry for sale on the streets of Pelourinho

Salvador

having lunch, when you need a break from shopping. The **Arts and Crafts Institute of Mauá** (Rua Gregório de Matos 27, tel. 71/3321-0168, 9 A.M.–6 P.M. daily) has fine works of terra cotta, porcelain and wood, among other things. There is an **arts and crafts fair** on Rua Gregório de Matos between the Cruzeiro de São Francisco and Rua Laranjeiras. You can get Cuban and other international cigars at the **Dom Inácio Tabacaria** (Rua das Laranjeiras 25, tel. 71/3321-0168, 9 A.M.–10 P.M.).

Coming out of Pelourinho on Rua Chile, then onto Avenida Sete de Setembro, you'll pass a busy commercial center with shops for the masses. Here you'll find household items, shoes, clothes, consumer electronics, and just about everything else for the day-to-day. When you get to the Praça da Piedade, turn left onto Rua Junqueira Ayres and pass the Igreja da Piedade, which is wonderful to look at from the outside. You'll see Shopping Lapa on your left and then Shopping Piedade further down on the left. Besides these, the best shopping mall is in the Barra area.

## ACCOMMODATIONS

Hotels in the Pelourinho area are known for being somewhat low-end. The area is full of hostels and cheap flops—not necessarily all bad. But staying in Pelourinho means not getting much sleep due to the noise and constant movement in and out of the hotel. The best hotels are in the Campo Grande area, also known as the Vitória neighborhood. By far, the greatest number of hotels are on the Atlantic coast, starting in Barra and going all the way to Itapoã. These areas are covered in separate sections later in this chapter. Remember that economical hotels always have Brazilian-style electric showers, while mid-range and high-end hotels have gas-heated water. All charge a 10-percent service tax, so tipping is not required. Prices listed are for low season and generally go up about 25 percent for peak season. You should inquire about prices for the Carnaval week, which are often more than triple the normal rate and require reservations a year in advance.

## CATCHING A CANDOMBLÉ RITUAL

African rituals and spirituality have found avenues for expression in even the most prohibitive environments. New Orleans and the southern United States have their voodoo rituals and here in Salvador da Bahia, Candomblé is the principal spiritual practice from Africa. Originating from Western Africa, Candomblé centers around the worship of several powerful guides, or saints, called Orixás. Since slaves were not permitted to practice Candomblé freely, they invented a way to worship their deities while appearing to worship Catholic saints. Each Orixá was linked to a particular saint and, while worshipping the saint, the devotees were actually worshiping their Orixá.

Each devotee has a principal Orixá as her personal protector and guide (the principal roles in Candomblé are all occupied by women). They are known as the children of that particular deity (a child of Oxalá or Xangô, for example). The elders of the religion, known as mothers and fathers, incorporate, or channel the Orixás during ritual dances designed to induce trance. The Orixás will have messages and teachings for particular devotees, often asking for offerings or giving special advice.

The best way to see a Candomblé ritual is during one of the Orixá festivals (each deity has a festival on a particular date). Tourists are permitted to watch, provided they do not bring cameras or wear shorts or other beach clothes. You can also catch a smaller incorporation dance just about any time of the year in the outskirts of town, at centers called *terreiros*. Rituals usually start around 8 P.M. For details, get in touch with the **Federação Baiana do Culto Afro-Brasileiro** (Rua Alfredo do Brito 39, Pelourinho, tel. 71/3321-0145, 8 A.M.–noon Mon.–Fri.) or ask at the tourist information office in Pelourinho. They can provide you with schedules and locations of the *terreiros*. There will be a fee involved and you should not bring a camera.

## Under R$100

Right in the heart of Pelourinho is the **Albergue dos Anjos** (Rua Gregório de Matos 15, tel. 71/3322-7486, www.alberguedosanjos.com.br, alberguedosanjos@terra.com.br, R$20 pp with breakfast and R$15 without), which was recently remodeled. They only have group rooms. They charge you R$5 for a towel. Their coffee shop downstairs is a pretty good place to hang out, even if you don't stay there. The best hostel in town is the N **Albergue das Laranjeiras**, or Laranjeiras Hostel (Rua da Ordem Terceira 13, tel. 71/3321-1366, R$20 pp for group rooms, R$38 s, R$50 d with shared bathroom, and R$65 d with private bathroom), at the corner of Rua Laranjeiras. They have a 24-hour reception area with English-speaking attendants, group rooms, double rooms, and triple rooms, Internet connections (extra), and a great café downstairs for hanging out with fellow international travelers. Prices go up about 25 percent during peak season. Private rooms are almost always booked up, so call in advance if you want one of those. The place can get a bit noisy due to a nearby Olodúm practice room, but you don't exactly stay in Pelourinho to get sleep, now do you?

In the Santo Antônio area, there are a few more economical options. The best is **Pousada Hilmar** (Rua Direita de Santo Antônio 136, tel. 71/3243-3959, www.pousadahilmar.hpg.com.br, R$25 s, R$45 d), which has small rooms, but they are clean and quaint.

## R$100–200

A decent place in a slightly older building is the **Hotel Bahia do Sol** (Av. Sete de Setembro 2009, tel. 71/3338-8800, www.bahiadosol.com, R$85 s and R$95 d), which is well located in the Campo Grande/Vitória area. They have air, TV, phones, 24-hour room service from their coffee shop, and breakfast (included). They do not add a service tax. The most professional hotel on the block in Campo Grande is the N **Sol Victória Marina Hotel** (Av. Sete de Setembro 2068, tel. 71/3336-7736, www.solbahia.com.br, solmarina@solbahia.com.br, R$179 d, R$230 in peak season). They have a beautiful pool with a view of the bay and the Island of Itapirica, spacious rooms, two restaurants, a coffee shop, and 24-hour room service. There is also a pier below the hotel with a bar on it and the hotel has a cable car that lowers you to the pier. Rooms have air, TV, safe, and phone. About half have ocean views.

## R$200–500

If you want to be closer to Pelourinho, try N **Redfish** (Rua Ladeira do Boqueirão 1, tel. 71/3241-0639, www.hotelredfish.com, R$200–285), inaugurated in 2004 by an Englishman and his Bahian wife. They have eight rooms with air-conditioning. The place is small, clean, and quaint. It's on a small street going up to the Santo Antônio district. Right across from the Praça Castro Alves is the well-known **Tropical da Bahia Hotel** (Av. Sete de Setembro 1537, tel. 71/3255-2000, www.tropicalhotel.com.br, R$225–295). Although in need of a bit of renovation, the hotel is still one of the better luxury options in the area, with a perfect location. They have air, TV, phone, non-smoking rooms, three restaurants, several bars, and a swimming pool.

# FOOD

## Bahian Favorites

A number of good restaurants are clustered together at the end of Rua Laranjeiras. They open around 11 A.M. for lunch. Most people sit outside on the sidewalk tables, but they all have room indoors as well. Some worth looking into include **Encontro dos Artistas** (Rua das Laranjeiras 13, tel. 71/3321-1721), which specializes in *moqueca* (Bahian fish stew made with coconut milk and palm oil) and fresh fish for around R$25–50 for two. **Pelourinho Beach** (Rua Santa Isabel 2, tel. 71/3321-8668) has a slighly more sophisticated menu with *moquecas, ensopadas* (a light version of the *moqueca*), Italian brochettes, and pasta dishes for around R$20–45 for two. **Matusalém** (Rua das Laranjeiras 28, tel. 71/3321-5598) also serves *moqueca* along with Comida Mineira (country cooking from Minas Gerais); fish and pasta dishes go for around R$30–65 for two.

One of the coziest and most sophisticated dining experiences is the garden restaurant **N Jardim das Delicias** (Rua João de Deus 12, tel. 71/3322-7068, noon–midnight daily). The restaurant is set inside an antique store with a backyard garden patio where you can enjoy regional foods for about R$35–60 per person. The restaurant **Uauá** (Rua Gregório de Matos 36, tel. 71/3321-3089, lunch and dinner Tues.–Sun.) specializes in meat dishes, including dried lamb, for around R$45 for two.

Perhaps the most famous place in town with locals and tourists alike is **N Sorriso da Dadá** (Rua Frei Vicente 5, Pelourinho, tel. 71/3321-9642, 11 A.M.–midnight daily), meaning the smile of Dadá, the lovely Bahian owner. (Currently her smile is amplified by the braces on her teeth, but that does not stop her from gracing her guests with her famous *sorriso*.) Dadá's specialty is seafood and her lobster plates are very popular and only R$30 per person. There's also a favorite eatery in the Cidade Baixa, which attracts many local personalities, called **Galpão** (Av. do Contorno 660, tel. 71/3321-9642, 11 A.M.–midnight daily). They serve regional foods in a contemporary fashion and have excellent desserts. Take a taxi there and back. A meal will set you back about R$65 per person.

## International

In the Laranjeiras restaurant cluster, there is an Arabic restaurant called **Onilo Arabe** (Rua Francisco Muniz Barreto 44, tel. 71/3495-3578) with Moroccan couscous, *kibes* (mixed meat), and *esfihas* (Arabic pizzas). They have belly dancing on Saturdays at noon and 4 P.M. It costs R$20–45 for two. One of Pelourinho's more popular Italian restaurants is **Mamabahia** (corner of Rua Alfredo Brito and Rua J. C. Rabelo, tel. 71/3322-4397, lunch and dinner daily). They have international cuisine with an Italian slant for around R$20–35 per person. There is a Jamaican restaurant in the Jacuzzi Suite Hotel, called **Quilombo do Pelo** (Rua Alfredo de Brito 13, tel. 71/3322-4638, lunch and dinner daily). The name refers to a Pelourinho slave outpost.

## Quick and Casual

If you're just interested in a quick snack, try the bakery on the northwest corner of the Praça Terreiro de Jesus (next to the São Pedro dos Clerigos Church). There you can get hot and cold sandwiches, as well as Brazilian finger foods. They are open until 9:30 P.M. or later if crowds warrant. At night, the sidewalk bars all serve appetizers. You should probably avoid the sidewalk *Acarajé* stands, unless you can see that the oil they are using is fresh and clear. Casual lunch plates can be found all over town at the bars and self-service diners. There are a couple near the Cruzeiro do São Francisco (upstairs). There is a great self-service lunch restaurant on Rua da Ajuda, across from the Praça da Sé for about R$16 per kilo. You'll see lots of locals inside.

One of the best self-service lunch places in Pelourinho is the **Cantina da Lua** (Rua Alfredo Brito at the Praça Terreiro de Jesus, tel. 71/3241-7383, open 11 A.M. daily). Their buffet is located upstairs and they have a number of great dishes for about R$16 per kilo. Another excellent self-service buffet is the **N cooking school at SENAC** (Praça José de Alencar 13, tel. 71/3321-5502, lunch and dinner daily), at the bottom of the Largo do Pelourinho. They serve more than 40 different dishes with desserts.

## Sweets

You can cool off with a natural, tropical-fruit-flavored ice cream at **Le Glacier Laporte** (Largo do Cruzeiro do São Francisco 21, tel. 71/3266-3649, 9 A.M.–9 P.M. daily) located in front of the São Francisco Church. French-owned and -operated, the shop has various ice creams made with local fruits, such as coconut, *jaca, cajú,* and *graviola*. Try them all if you can. There is nothing artificial added. The oldest ice cream parlor in Pelourinho is **A Cubana** (Rua Alfredo Brito 12, tel. 71/3322-7000, 8 A.M.–9 P.M. daily), which also serves local flavors as well as the old standards. For coffee and sweets, try **Bahiacafe.com** (Praça da Sé 20, tel. 71/3322-1266, open 8 A.M. daily), across from the Palácio Arquiepiscopal.

## INFORMATION

The official tourist information office in Pelourinho is **Bahiatursa** (Rua Laranjeiras 12, tel. 74/3321-2133, 8:30 A.M.–10 P.M. daily), at the corner of Rua Gregório de Matos. There is another information office inside the Lacerda Elevator tower (at the top). There are Bahiatursa offices in the main bus terminal and at the airport, so you can pick up materials wherever you enter the city. You can try calling Disque Turismo by dailing 131. You might even get an English-speaking attendant who can give you information about current shows and concerts. They can also recommend good restaurants and hotels. Some good websites about Bahia and Salvador include www.bahia.com.br, www.pelourinho-virtual.com.br, www.salvador2003.com, and www.emtursa.ba.gov.br.

Salvador is home to several international consulates. Here are some addresses:
• France (Travessa Francisco Gonçalves 1, Comércio, tel. 71/3241-0168)
• Germany (Rua Lucaia 281, salas 204–206, Rio Vermelho, tel. 31/3247-7106)
• United Kingdom (Avenida Estados Unidos 4, suites 1109–1113, Comércio, tel. 31/3243-9222)
• United States (Avenida Antônio Carlos Magalhães, Edifício Cidadela Center 1, suite 410, Pituba, tel. 71/3358-9166)

You can extend your passport at the Federal Police station (tel. 71/3242-9996), which is in the Cidade Baixa on the way to Bonfim. You can catch a bus or taxi from the bottom of the Lacerda Elevator. The tourist police (tel. 71/3322-1188) are located at the Largo do Cruzeiro de São Francisco, across from the São Francisco Church. There is a police post behind the Catedral Basilica in the Praça da Sé.

## SERVICES

There are several Internet cafés in Pelourinho. The most complete is **Internet Café.com** (Rua João de Deus 2, tel. 71/3321-2147, 9 A.M.–9 P.M. daily). They have several computers and good snacks. **Bahiacafe.com** (Praça da Sé 20) has several computers and a great environment for sipping coffee. There is also a computer at the Laranjeiras Hostel.

You'll find a **Banco do Brasil** with international connections in front of the São Francisco Church and Convent. Another is located in front of the Mercado Modelo. There is also a **Banco 24 Horas** in the main *praça,* Terreiro de Jesus, that has the Plus and Cirrus systems. The post office is across from the São Francisco Church.

**Bahia Ticket Travel Turismo** (Largo do Pelourinho 7, tel. 71/3322-0809) is a car rental and tour agency with many packaged tours. Most of their tour packages are abusively expensive (better to hire a taxi or arrange your own transportation), but they can help with car rentals, domestic flights, and **daily lockers** to store your stuff while you walk around town. They also sell tickets to selected shows and have telephone booths for international calls (compare their prices first). An interesting urban tour is offered by **Tours Bahia** (Largo do Cruzeiro de São Francisco 4, tel. 71/3322-4383). They take a small group in a jeep to various suburbs and historical sights around Salvador—outside of Pelourinho.

There are a number of shipwrecks in the Bay of All Saints popular with serious scuba divers. Check with **Bahia Scuba** (tel. 71/3321-0156) or **Dive Bahia** (tel. 71/3264-2820). There is also great diving and snorkeling on the island of Morro de São Paulo.

Want to get cornrows in your hair? It's a process that takes 4–8 hours, depending on your hair and the size of the braids you want. You can make an appointment with one of Brazil's most celebrated stylists at the **Instituto Kymundo de Cultura Afro-Brasileira** (Rua Frei Vicente 4, Pelourinho, tel. 71/3321-8332).

## GETTING THERE

The main number for the airport is tel. 71/3204-1010. Domestic flights come from all over Brazil via Vasp (tel. 71/3204-1304), Varig (tel. 71/3340-4371), and TAM (tel. 71/3342-

0123). Discount carriers include Gol (tel. 71/3204-1603) and Nordeste (tel. 71/3204-1050). From the airport, you can catch a taxi to the city center for around R$60 or to the upper coast (Itapoã, for example) for R$40. Buses run from the airport to Barra and Cidade Baixa (Praça Cairu, at the location of the Lacerda Elevator) all day long. These take about an hour to reach their destinations but they only cost around R$3 for the executive bus.

## GETTING AROUND

You can easily walk around Pelourinho and even check out parts of the Cidade Baixa (such as the Mercado Modelo) on foot. If you head to Bonfim, I suggest you take a cab or bus and don't stay after dark. The Bonfim area is not as safe as Pelourinho, so don't bring your credit cards or a lot of money with you. It's possible to walk from Pelourinho as far down as the Praça da Piedade (and nearby shopping centers) or the Solar de União, but most people prefer to take a cab. You might consider taking taxis to tour the city as well, since packaged tours are usually not competitively priced. A taxi from Barra to Pelourinho will cost R$12–15 and from the Cidade Baixa to Bonfim it's another R$12–15. Feel free to negotiate packages with taxi drivers for a single price *sem taxímetro* (sayn tax-EE-mee-troo; meaning with the meter off).

Buses go to all corners of the city from the Pelourinho bus stop, which is down Rua Chile and to the left (just ask as you walk out of town along Rua Chile; it's easy to find). You can also catch a number of buses from the gas station at the lighthouse in Barra. To head to the northern beaches, make your way to Barra (the bus stop after the Morro do Cristo) or the *rodoviaria* to catch buses from there. From the *rodoviaria,* you can catch buses up the coast to Praia do Forte and other northern beaches.

I don't recommend renting a car to get around in Salvador, except maybe if you are staying in the Costa Azul or Itapoã. Even then, I don't suggest driving in the city very often—the rental car is better for going north to the remote beaches and for getting around in the Itapoã area. For the price and frustration factors involved, you're better off taking taxis around the city. You can rent a taxi for an entire day for a package price of around R$200, which is not a bad idea if you're going to and from the *rodoviaria,* airport, or other distant locations. Packaged tours can get you more comfortably to Praia do Forte (see *Services* or ask at your hotel). If you insist on renting a car, some local numbers include **Avis** (tel. 71/3377-2276), **Hertz** (tel. 71/3377-3633), **Localiza** (tel. 71/3332-1999), and **Unidas** (tel. 71/3377-1244).

Salvador

# Barra

The very tip of the Salvador peninsula (if you can call it that) is the area called Barra. It's marked by the largest and most significant fort in northern Brazil. The Barra neighborhood is where the beaches begin—and they continue north up the Atlantic coastline to Itapoã and Flamengo. As you turn from the bay side of Salvador to the ocean side, you'll notice a great difference in atmosphere. First, you come down off the hills to sea level. The sun seems to beat down hotter and the temperature goes up. The vibe in Barra is definitely more beachy and most of the action takes place on the coastal highway.

## THE BEACH

Barra is a busy beach just about every day of the year. It is situated in front of one of the most active areas on the coastline for hotels, bars, and restaurants. During the day, the Barra beach is a place to kick back and get some sun on the sand. You won't be there but two minutes before you'll be interrupted by someone selling something: roasted peanuts, sunglasses, sunscreen, and roasted cheese. The water in Barra and all of the beaches of Salvador is mercifully pollution free, due to a major clean-up program initiated by the mayor. The city installed sewage treatment facilities in every beach from Bonfim to Itapoã and you can swim anywhere on the Salvador coast, with the exception of Boca do Rio (the river does not get treated before it empties into the ocean). Of course, there are many beaches that you should not visit due to risk of assault, such as anything within 20 kilometers of Rio Vermelho Beach.

If you go into the water in Barra, just be sure that you have someone to watch your stuff. If you are alone on the beach (perhaps watching somebody's stuff), be aware of people who may try to distract you from what you are watching over. Some of these misdirection schemes are performed in pairs, so if one person approaches you, open the eyes in back of your head. There is almost no risk of outright assault on the Barra beach during the day.

## SIGHTS

Barra is more about beaches and less about sights than Pelourinho. You may also find yourself in Barra because of the abundance of hotel options there. Still, there are a couple of sights worth checking out. First and foremost is the **Santo Antônio da Barra Forte,** also known as the Farol da Barra (or Barra Lighthouse). It is perhaps the most important fort in Brazil's history. It was here that the Dutch first invaded Brazil (unsuccessfully) in 1624 and then again (successfully) in 1629. It has played an important role in the protection of the Bay of All Saints since its construction in the mid-1500s. Inside the fort is the **Nautical Museum** (9 A.M.–7 P.M. low season, 9 A.M.–9 P.M. summer, closed Wed., R$4), which has a bunch of artifacts from a 16th-century Portuguese ship that sank offshore, as well as nautical maps and historical documents. Most impressive is the view from the lighthouse platform, which lets you see both the bay side and ocean side of the coastline. There is a small coffee shop inside the fort. The second most interesting fort in Salvador is also in the Barra region, called the **San Diogo Forte** (9:30 A.M.–noon and 1:30–5:30 P.M., closed Mon.). It overlooks the Barra Port at the end of Avenida Princesa Isabel. Next to this fort is the Instituto Mauá. Finally, on the hill above Barra is the **Igreja Abadia da Graça** (Largo da Graça, Graça neighborhood, 8–11:30 A.M. and 2–5 P.M. Mon.–Sat.). This church was built in 1557, making it one of the city's oldest original structures. It's small and not as flashy as the churches in Pelourinho, but if you want to check it out, you can get a taxi from the Barra neighborhood.

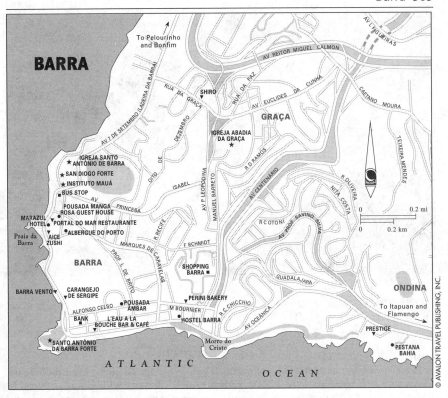

## BARRA

To Pelourinho and Bonfim

AV L FIGUEIRAS

AV REITOR MIGUEL CALMON

RUA DA GRAÇA

SHIRO

RUA DA PAZ

AV. EUCLIDES DA CUNHA

CAETANO MOURA

GRAÇA

IGREJA ABADIA DA GRAÇA ★

R D RAMOS

AV 7 DE SETEMBRO LADEIRA DA BARRA

R. OLIVEIRA

TEIXEIRA MENDES

OITO DE DEZEMBRO

AV P LEOPOLDINA

AV CENTENÁRIO

NITA COSTA

★ IGREJA SANTO ANTÔNIO DE BARRA
★ SAN DIOGO FORTE
★ INSTITUTO MAUÁ
■ BUS STOP

ISABEL

MANUEL BARRETO

R C OTONI

0        0.2 mi
0        0.2 km

● POUSADA MANGA ROSA GUEST HOUSE
AV. PRINCESA

MARAZUL HOTEL ●
● PORTAL DO MAR RESTAURANTE
● ALBERGUE DO PORTO

R. RECIFE

F SCHMIDT

AV. PROF SAVINO SILVA

Praia da Barra
AICE ZUSHI

MARQUES DE CARAVELAS

BARRA

PROF L. DE BRITO

SHOPPING BARRA ■

GUADALAJARA

ONDINA

BARRA VENTO ▼
▼ CARANGEJO DE SERGIPE

● POUSADA AMBAR

● PERINI BAKERY

R C CHICCHIO

To Itapuan and Flamengo

ALFONSO CELSO
BANK ■
L'EAU A LA BOUCHE BAR & CAFÉ ●

M BOURNIER

● HOSTEL BARRA

AV. OCEÂNICA

PRESTIGE ●

★ SANTO ANTÔNIO DA BARRA FORTE

Morro do Cristo

● PESTANA BAHIA

A T L A N T I C      O C E A N

© AVALON TRAVEL PUBLISHING, INC.

# ENTERTAINMENT AND NIGHTLIFE

## Music and Dance

There is a dance club called **Pedra da Sereia** (Rua Pedra da Sereia 66, tel. 71/3336-0553, open 11:30 P.M. daily) in the Ondina neighborhood. It's all Bahian music and dance and it gets rowdy on weekends. For something a bit more mellow, try the **French Quarter Café** (Av. Otávio Mangabeira 2323, Rio Vermelho, tel. 71/3240-1491, open 5 P.M. daily).

Outside of town in the Candeal neighborhood (near the Parque da Cidade) is the Candyall Guetho Square, which is home to the other drumming group in Salvador, **Timbalada** (tel. 71/3276-7298, www.timbalada.com.br). Every Sunday, the group performs at the square. Get there early to avoid lines.

## Sidewalk Cafés and Bars

Barra is filled with sidewalk cafés and bars. Just take a walk along the coastal highway from the beginning of Barra (let's say, from the gas station at Avenida Princesa Isabel) all the way to the Monte Cristo. There are bars all along the inland side of the highway. One of the most frequented of these bars (especially at night) is **Carangejo de Sergipe** (Av. Oceanica, tel. 71/3245-9826, open 10 A.M. daily), which is near the Monte Cristo. Folks sit on the sidewalk patio, eat crab (the house specialty), and sip beers until the wee hours. You'll spend about R$36–60 for two to have dinner here. Across from this place is **Barra Vento**

**Salvador**

**Praia Barra**

(tel. 71/3247-2577), the only restaurant/bar on the beach side of the highway. This is a slightly more upscale location and it's a privileged place to be on New Year's Eve. They book their tables for the night a year in advance.

There are also a number of sidewalk bars on Avenida Almirante Marques de Leão, including some interesting options on the small streets that connect Almirante Marques to the coast highway—in particular, **L'eau a la Bouche Bar & Café** and its neighbors. They serve crepes and bottled beer and their neighbor has live music starting at 11 P.M. every night (the beer is actually cheaper at the neighboring bars, if you don't care about the crepes).

A great place for juices and late-night hanging out is the **Restaurante Sol Potente** (Av. Sete de Setembro 3835, 24 hours). They cater to a healthy/hippie crowd and have a great view of the ocean from their deck.

## FESTIVALS AND EVENTS

Barra is one of the key locations for **Carnaval** in Salvador. The crowds congregate all along the coastal highway up to the Monte Criso. The official parade goes from Ondina to Rio Vermelho.

## SHOPPING

There are shops all along **Avenida Sete de Setembro,** the coastal highway at Barra. If you want a more formal shopping experience, then **Shopping Barra** (Av. Centenário 2992, tel. 71/3264-4566) is within walking distance. It's one of the best shopping malls in Salvador and has a tourist information booth inside, as well as movie theaters and Internet cafés. There are also some excellent lunch buffet restaurants in the food court and a bank of relatively quiet public phones. The best way to enter is from Rua Miguel Bournier. You'll enter at the arts and crafts fair, which is in the east wing. This fair has some of the same items that you'll find in the Mercado Modelo and probably at about the same prices. Another arts and crafts fair is at the Instituto Mauá (Praça Azevedo Fernandes 2), across from the gas station. Again, the merchandise here is similar to that of the Mercado Modelo at about the same prices, but it's worth a look.

# ACCOMMODATIONS

## Under R$100

There are a lot of economical accommodations in the Barra area. The best hostel in the area is ◪ **Albergue do Porto** (Rua Br. de Sergy 197, tel. 71/3264-3131, www.alberguedoporto.com.br, R$18–23 group room and R$70 private room). They have cute rooms, decorated by the owner herself, a communal kitchen, and a cable TV room. Most rooms are collective, but they have a couple of rooms for couples. Breakfast is included. Another hostel in the area is the **Hostel Barra** (Rua Dr. Artur Neiva 4, tel. 71/3245-2600, reservas@alberguebarra.com.br, R$25 pp group room, R$55 private room with fan, and R$65 private room with air), which is located near the Morro do Cristo. They have group and private rooms with a small breakfast and free Internet included. **Pousada Ambar** (Rua Afonso Celso 485, tel. 71/3264-3791, www.ambarpousada.com.br, R$25 group room low season and R$32 peak season, R$60–70 s and R$70–90 d) is a simple place, but it's clean and quaint. It's run like a hostel, but it's really a hotel, full of international travelers (the owner, Christine, is French). They have 12 private rooms and one group room. In the lobby is a communal TV room.

## R$100–200

The ◪ **Pousada Manga Rosa Guest House** (Rua Cesar Zama 60, tel. 71/3267-4266, www.mangarosa.com, reserve@mangarosa.com, R$100–120 standard, R$180 suite) is located in a restored colonial building a block from the beach in Barra. Their rooms are charming and well appointed, with air, ceiling fan, and TV. They also have a restaurant on the premises and the owners operate a beachfront café down the street. On the top floor is a special room with a terrific veranda and laundry facilities. Internet and breakfast are included.

The **Vila Galé Hotel** (Rua Morro do Escravo Miguel 320, tel. 71/3236-8888, www.vilagale.pt, R$185) has a great view of the ocean and new installations with 225 rooms. They offer a bar, restaurant, pool, sauna, gym, and game room. Rooms have air, TV, and phone.

## R$200–500

The **Marazul Hotel** (Av. Sete de Setembro 3937, tel. 71/3264-8200, reservas@marazul-hotel.com.br, R$190 s and R$210–280 d) is right on the beachfront in Barra. It's a large, semi-modern building with 116 rooms, a pool, restaurant, 24-hour room service (no service tax), a large café/bar, central air, cable TV, in-room stereo, and a business center with Internet access. You can watch the sunset over the ocean from their upstairs pool area. Rooms are not particularly charming, but are clean and professionally appointed.

One of the finer hotels in the area is the **Bahia Othon Palace** (Av. Oceânica 2456, Ondina, tel. 71/3203-2000, www.hoteisothon.com.br, R$425–850), with almost 300 rooms, many overlooking the ocean. They have a great restaurant and bar, pool, sauna, and all the first-class services you would expect from a luxury hotel.

# FOOD

There are numerous casual places right in the Barra area and a few upper-end restaurants, too. But most of the finer restaurants are just up the road in the Costa Azul area—near the many fine hotels, of course. It's worth taking a taxi to that area to get a good meal, if you're not already stationed there at one of the hotels. There are also some worthwhile restaurants in Rio Vermelho, but bed aware that this can be one of the most dangerous areas in Salvador; getting to and from the Rio Vermelho area should be done only by taxi (both ways).

## Bahian Food

Bahian food is rich in spices and loaded with shellfish. One place to get a lot of both is **Abrolhos Café** (Rua Fonte do Boi 24, Rio Vermelho, tel. 71/3334-8829). It costs about R$40 for two people. A great place for *moqueca* (fish stew) is **Ki-Mukeka** (Av. Otávio Mangabeira 136, Armação Beach, tel. 71/3461-7333,

11 A.M.–midnight daily, R$30). They make an authentic fish or seafood stew or a lighter version, called *ensopada*.

## International

If you like the idea of eating sushi while looking out over the sunset in Barra, then head over to the **Aice Zushi** (Av. Sete de Setembro 3959, tel. 71/3359-5628, lunch and dinner daily) where you can get combo plates for two for around R$60. Be sure to get there well before sunset. Their adjoining restaurant upstairs is called **Pereira** and they have some wonderful fish, such as their salmon with mushrooms in teriyaki sauce. Meals cost R$40 per person. But if it's sushi you're after (forget the view), then try **Shiro** (Rua da Craça 181, Graça neighborhood, tel. 71/3337-3732). They have the sushi experience you need for about R$75 for two people. An excellent Italian restaurant in the Costa Azul area is **Cantina Cortile** (Rua Adelaide Fernandes da Costa at the Parque Costa Azul, tel. 71/3341-3572, noon–1 A.M. daily). Try their pasta with prawns and cognac. It should cost around R$60 for two people.

If you're up for some artistic contemporary cuisine, then try **Prestige** (Av. Oceânica 3001, Ondina, tel. 71/3331-9708, 7 P.M.–midnight Tues.–Sat.). There, you can get filet of ostrich in shitake sauce and wild rice. A meal will set you back R$55.

Note: There are pizza and Chinese restaurants near the Morro de Cristo area but none are worth a visit. You'd do better to go to **Companhia da Pizza** (Rua Oswaldo Cruz 266, tel. 71/3334-6807, lunch and dinner Tues.–Sun.) at the Praça Brigadeiro Farias Rocha in Rio Vermelho. They make a crunchy, thin-crust pizza with toppings like salmon, buffalo ricotta, and sun-dried tomatoes. A pizza for two costs R$15–25. It's worth the taxi ride to get there.

## Quick and Casual

If you want to make a picnic with some fabulous cheeses, olives, breads, salads, and baked goods, then head over to the **Perini Bakery** (Av. Centenario 200, 6 A.M.–10 P.M. Mon.–Fri., 6 A.M.–2 P.M. Sat.–Sun.), near Shopping Barra. They also have imported wine, peanut butter (difficult to find in Brazil), and other imported goods. There are numerous sandwich shops and cheap lunch eateries on the streets of Barra. Check out the options along Rua Almirante Marques de Leão (the Sheik Restaurant has an all-you-can-eat lunch buffet for R$6) and Rua Miguel Bournier near Shopping Barra. There are plenty of places with economical lunch plates near the gas station at Avenida Princesa Isabel. Tip: You might prefer to get your sandwich to go and have your lunch at the lighthouse or Monte Cristo to take in a view of the ocean. The inexpensive sandwich shops do not always have the most desirable environments for eating.

For good food in a simple atmosphere, try the **Portal do Mar Restaurante** (Av. Sete de Setembro 510, tel. 71/3267-6250), which serves great seafood for about R$15 per person. Also check out the food at **Carangejo de Sergipe**, listed under *Sidewalk Cafés and Bars*. Don't forget that the food court in Shopping Barra has some excellent lunch buffets on the first floor.

## INFORMATION AND SERVICES

There's a tourist information booth in Shopping Barra on the fist floor, but a better office is in the Instituto de Mauá arts and crafts market across from the gas station at Avenida Princesa Isabel. Any of the good hotels in this area can give you information and advice on tours, transportation, and restaurants in the Barra area.

There is a Citibank with international ATM systems near the lighthouse at Avenida Almirante Marques de Leão 59. There are other ATMs with Plus and Cirrus in Shopping Barra. Shopping Barra also has a post office.

## GETTING THERE AND AROUND

You can get a bus into Barra from the *rodoviaria* or the airport. They take a long time to arrive, but they only cost around R$3 for the executive bus. A taxi from the *rodoviaria* will cost about R$15–25 and from the airport, about

R$35–45. There are many bus stops in Barra and there are some subtle differences between them. For example, to go up Avenida Sete de Setembro (say, to the Carlos Costa Pinto Museum), you should catch the bus at the gas station on the corner of Avenida Sete de Setembro and Avenida Princesa Isabel. To go directly to Pelourinho, you can catch a bus at the above stop, or at the lighthouse, which will turn inland and take a bit longer. You can catch a bus to either Praça da Sé, which is in the Cidade Alta, or to Praça Cairu, which is at the elevator in Cidade Baixa. To go north to Itapoã or Flamengo, catch the bus at the stop just after the Monte Cristo, as they turn onto the coastal highway from Avenida Centenário. I recommend taxis for going back and forth between Barra, the Costa Azul, and Pelourinho at night. Going between Barra and either of these locations is about R$12.

# Itapoã and the Costa Azul

*Passar uma tarde em Itapoã* (To spend the afternoon in Itapoã)/*Ao sol que arde em Itapoã* (In the sun that shines in Itapoã)/*Ouvindo o mar em Itapoã* (Listening to the ocean in Itapoã)/*Falar de amor em Itapoã* (To talk of love in Itapoã)

*Vinicius de Moraes,* Tarde em Itapoã

When Vinicius de Moraes wrote these lines, Itapoã was relatively unknown except to the locals. Today, it stands as a paragon of the coast of Bahia—cool, jazzy, shady, and middle-class. Vinicius was not the only famous bossa nova artist from Bahia. João Gilberto was also a child of the state, as was Caetano Veloso, Gilberto Gil (currently serving as Minister of Culture for the government), and many artists who are famous nationally. Besides a classy, shady set of beaches, Itapoã offers a great *praça* where you can get the country's best (make that the world's best) *Acarajé* and a cold beer to go with it. There are also clubs for dancing the night away to regional music.

Many of the city's most luxurious hotels are located along the Costa Azul area. Perhaps because the ocean view is something to marvel over. Or perhaps because the location is desirable, with access to the northern beaches, Barra, the airport, and across town to the *rodoviária* and Centro Histórico (that's if you have a car, of course). The Costa Azul begins around Praia Pituba, which is a decent beach for swimming and kicking back. The farther north you go, the better it gets. South of Pituba should be avoided, especially the area around Rio Vermelho. You should take taxis through this section (between Pituba and Ondina).

## ITAPOÃ BEACH

In these times of hip-hop and funk, the Itapoã Beach still has a relaxed, bossa-nova feel to it. Perhaps that's because of the numerous shade trees that separate the sandy beach from the houses just inland. A sandy footpath winds through the trees and takes you all the way up and down the Itapoã shoreline. Along the way, you'll pass among the *barracas* (beach bars) that are permanently set up in the shade. There are places to sit, open-air showers for cooling off (or washing off after a swim in the ocean), and even public bathrooms (a rarity in Brazil). Except on weekends, when the masses invade just about every beach on the Salvador coastline, Itapoã is a very civilized place to sit and watch the tide with a cold tropical drink of some kind. The best beach *barraca* in which to do this is the **Barraca Morena de Itapoã,** which is the most elaborate wooden structure on the beach, run by Patrick, the Dutchman. In the summer season (during the week), this and the other beach bars get rather crowded with international tourists, lovely young Bahian women, and surfers. Patrick hosts live music 1–4 P.M. on Saturdays and Sundays.

You can walk along the sand to the small lighthouse and check out the *barracas* on the far side, which is actually the beginning of the

Stella Maris beach. The tide here is said to have too much undertow to be good for swimming. The beach bars at Stella Maris do not present the same shady areas as in Itapoã, but they have their own particular charms all the same.

## FLAMENGO BEACH

About 20 minutes north of Itapoã by bus is Praia do Flamengo, presenting a different type of sun-and-sand experience. Here, you'll find a wide strip of sand that goes on for several kilometers. On the small hill or incline that overlooks the sand are numerous *barracas,* elaborate structures that serve not only as places to sit under a shade umbrella, but also as full-scale restaurants. There are plenty of plants and trees in and between the *barracas* that give Flamengo a peaceful, comfortable ambience with a different feel to it than in Itapoã. As in Itapoã, weekends get crowded with locals, but weekdays are quite calm in low season and the beach seems almost deserted. Weekdays in the summer months are active and full of excitement here. A great *barraca* here is **Barraca Quissamã,** which is operated by a couple from Rio de Janeiro. They have an excellent structure with comfortable seating at the *barraca* or in beach chairs on the sand out front. They also have a shower, clean bathrooms, and a great bar and restaurant. Lunch is slightly expensive at R$40–70 for two. The most popular *barraca* is the **Barraca do Lôro**.

## ACARAJÉ DA CIRA

Far from being just a food stand, the Ararajé da Cira *barraca* has become something of a legend in Salvador—known for having the best *Acarajé* in Bahia (and therefore in the world). Dona Cira uses all fresh ingredients in her mixture, including fresh roasted shrimp—headless but with skin intact—and fresh palm oil. Her recipe for the breading is a secret. You can watch them frying up by the hundreds as the line continues to move past Cira at the cash box. Across from her stand (the one with the red canopy and long line) is the inland center of activity in Itapoã—a traffic circle that is home to two bars that fill the circle with tables and chairs every afternoon. On weekend nights, it's difficult to find a spot anywhere in the circle. But don't fear, there are alternatives in every direction, especially to the south along the boardwalk. But Cira remains the best. If you try *Acarajé* once in your life, try Cira's in Itapoã.

## LAGOA DO ABAETÉ

If you walk up the hill from the Itapoã traffic circle (away from the ocean), you will soon come to the Lagoa do Abaeté. This small lake has become a recreation center for locals and tourists wanting a little fresh water as a change of pace. All around the lake are bars and cafés with live music at night. There is a stage area for larger productions and there is always something going on here on summer nights. It's a lot cheaper here than on the Itapoã boardwalk, so the *lagoa* tends to have a more *popular* (meaning for the masses) crowd. There are buses that turn up the hill and pass the lake in just a few minutes in case you don't want to walk.

## COSTA AZUL

The area between Pituba and Piatá Beaches is known as the Blue Coast. The beaches here are lovely to look at from a beachfront hotel window and are some decent urban beaches for swimming and sunning—especially if your hotel is right nearby. The highlights in this area, besides the hotels, are the restaurants and bars that are dotted along the coastal highway. There are also a few interesting parks for taking morning or afternoon walks. For example, the **Parque Aeroclube**, which is part of the Aeroclube Plaza Show complex, is a large grassy area along the coast. The **Parque Costa Azul** and **Parque Jardim dos Namorados** also afford nice walks in the afternoon (although you'll probably prefer walking along the Itapoã Beach).

## ENTERTAINMENT AND NIGHTLIFE

When the beach bars close for the evening, the crowd moves to the traffic circle and the boardwalk area south of the circle to continue the festivities. If you can't find a place at the traffic circle (first choice), then walk south until you find a place that suits you. There is always something going on at the lake, too. When you're ready for some dancing, there are two places within a stone's throw from the circle: **Jangada** and **Lingua de Prata** (Silver Tongue). These are both on the boardwalk area south of the *praça* and offer similar music and dance atmospheres. Generally, the music is Bahian *axé* or *forró*; you may not recognize much of it, but you can dance to it all the same. If being in Itapoã puts you in the mood for bossa nova and jazz, then a trip down the coast to Rio Vermelho and the **French Quarter Café** is what you need (details in the *Barra* section).

One of the best places in town to hear rock music is the **Rock in Rio Café,** located inside the **Aeroclube Plaza Show** complex (Av. Otávio Mangabeira 6000, Costa Azul area). The complex is a kind of entertainment center with bars and clubs and it gets rowdy on weekend nights.

You can catch a Bahian folk presentation with dinner at the **Casquinha de Siri** restaurant (Av. Actávio Mangabeira at Praia dos Coqueiros, tel. 71/3367-1234), which specializes in crab and other seafood. It's just a few kilometers down the coast in the Piatá Beach area. Dinner and a show will cost around R$60 per person.

## SHOPPING

Most shopping is done along the boardwalk area starting at the traffic circle/*praça* and working south. There are a couple of mini-malls along the way with boutique shops, particularly the **San Felipe Center,** directly across from the circle. To the north of the *praça* is another small shopping mall, called **Shopping do Farol.** From Itapoã, you can get to Shopping Iguatemi near the main bus terminal for about R$15 by taxi, and the **Aeroclube Plaza Show** complex to the south has a number of shops mixed in with the restaurants and bars. Other than that, there is not really much to buy in Itapoã, except another beer at the beach *barraca*.

## ACCOMMODATIONS

### Under R$100

There are very few low-end hotels in the Itapoã area, but one that stands out is the **Pousada Betel** (Rua Betel 6, tel. 71/3249-2700, pousadabetel@terra.com.br, R$40 s and R$50 d), on the Ladeira do Abaeté going west toward the lake from the *praça*/traffic circle. The hotel is located on an ugly street, but it has a tall wall around it and inside there is a pool and several simple but clean rooms.

### R$100–200

The coziest little inn in Itapoã is the ◪ **Encanto de Itapoan** (Rua Nova Canaã at the Farol de Itapoã, tel. 71/3285-2505, www.encantodeitapoan.com.br, info@encantodeitapoan.com.br, R$180 s and R$210 d), run by the delightfully British Janet and her Brazilian husband Otacílio. It is perfectly located near the lighthouse, where you can walk to just about everything in Itapoã—either on the beach or via the inland streets. The *pousada* is clean and air-conditioned, and the rooms have cable TV, gas-heated showers, and comfortable beds. There is a nice pool area where they serve an ample breakfast (included). Janet can help you with anything concerning Itapoã, including car rental, restaurant selection, and bus schedules. The **Mar Brasil Hotel** (Rua Flamengo 44 at the Farol de Itapoã, tel. 71/3285-7339, www.marbrasilhotel.com.br, marbrasilhotel@terra.com.br, R$120–140 standard and R$140–170 suites with kitchen, depending on the season) is a decent choice if the Encanto de Itapoan is full. They have a medium-sized facility with two pools, a restaurant, and a distant view of the ocean. Rooms have air, cable TV, and Internet connection. Some rooms have full kitchen facilities and a view of the ocean. A nice breakfast buffet is included.

In Flamengo Beach, you can stay at the

**Pousada do Sarafina** (Rua Antonio Augusto Machado, tel. 71/3374-3010, www.sarafina.com.br, sarafina@sarafina.com.br, R$150). They have a main house and a couple of large apartment hotels in the back by the pool. Be sure to get a room in the main house. Rooms have TV and air, and breakfast is included.

At the bottom of the Costa Azul in the Pituba Beach area is the **Golden Park Hotel** (Av. Manuel Dias de Silva 979, tel. 71/3240-5622, www.goldenparkhotel.com.br, R$145–225). They have 90 rooms (some with ocean views) with air, cable TV, and phone. The facilities include two restaurants, a pool, and a bar.

## R$200–500

At the top of Itapoã, just past the *farol* (lighthouse) is the well-known **Ⓝ Hotel Sofitel** (Rua Passárgada, tel. 71/3347-8500, www.accorhotels.com, reservas@svn.com.br, R$365–450) offering one of the best resort-type experiences in Salvador. They provide a luxury experience with comfortable rooms, nonsmoking floors, three restaurants, bars, a pool, a sauna, golf, a jogging track, a gym, and a tennis court. Rooms have air, cable TV, and ocean views (not all rooms). Their location is calm and quiet.

## FOOD

Besides the famous *Acarajé* in the *praça* at Itapoã, there are several places to get a casual lunch plate or snack—first and foremost, at the beach kiosks. There are also economical lunch plates available in and around the *praça*. The farther south you walk, the more you'll find inexpensive options. In Flamengo, the beach *barracas* are the main offering and they do not offer the best bargains for a simple lunch—although they make some great fish plates and side dishes, like french fries. If you're on a budget, try the *lanchonete* **Lá em Casa** (Rua Prof. Antônio Augosto Machado), just off the main road going into the Flamengo Beach area—you may have to ask around. They have an executive lunch plate for R$7, which is enough for two people. There is an Internet café next door.

There are several options in the Itapoã area for dinner. For a decent pizza dinner, **Fratello** (about 15 minutes north of the *praça* on foot, near the gas station) is a good choice and has a nice atmosphere. It makes a nice walk from the *praça* when you're ready for dinner. In the same basic area is one of Salvador's finest restaurants, called **Mistura Fina** (across from the gas station). This place has an elegant atmosphere and a gourmet menu with seafood dishes and contemporary cuisine. You'll spend about R$30–60 per person here, but it's worth it.

For a great Brazilian barbecue, the place to go is **Boi Preto** (Av. Otávio Mangabeira, Armação Beach area, tel. 71/3362-8844), meaning black bull. This is a classic *rodísio*-style restaurant, which means that waiters bring meats from the grill to your table and you decide if you want some of it or not. In addition, there are buffets for salads, sushi, pasta, and desserts. Chicken and fish also available at the buffets. Finally, a local favorite for Bahian food is **Yemanjá** (Av. Otávio Mangabeira 4655, Armação Beach area, tel. 71/3461-9008). They have numerous fish and seafood dishes in rich, Bahian sauces and spices, such as shrimp flambé in white onion and butter sauce. Dinner will cost around R$50 for two people.

## INFORMATION AND SERVICES

The nearest tourist information center is in the convention center near the Aeroclube Plaza Show. There is also an information booth at the airport, but your best bet is to ask at your hotel if you're staying in the Itapoã area. There are Internet houses on the second floors of Shopping San Felipe and Shopping do Farol. The latter also has a phone center where you can make international calls in private booths.

You can find an international ATM at the gas station near the Itapoã lighthouse and at the airport and *rodoviaria*. All car-rental agencies are at the airport. Telephone numbers are listed under *Services* in the Pelourinho section.

## GETTING THERE AND AROUND

From the Barra neighborhood, take the airport or Itapoã bus at the first bus stop past the Morro do Cristo. The airport bus will turn just before Itapoã, so ask to get off at the Itapoã exit. You then cross the street to catch a micro-bus that says "Flamengo/Farol" or "Itinga/P. do Flamengo." These buses will take you past Itapoã (where you can get off) or all the way to Flamengo. They cost about R$1.50. To get off at Itapoã, look for the main *praça*, which is a small traffic circle filled with tables and chairs and people drinking beer. That's your stop. From the airport, there are buses to Itapoã that pass Flamengo first. A taxi from the *rodoviaria* will cost about R$15–20 to Itapoã and about the same from the airport. Take the micro-bus between Itapoã and Flamengo. The trip takes longer than you might think.

# North of Salvador

## JACUIPE BEACH

There is a marina here with lots of motors winding—from the many water sports going on offshore. Of course this makes the tide a little oily, especially when low. High tide is better for swimming.

## GUARAJUBA BEACH

The Guarajuba area is marked by real estate developments. That's because of the new Ford plant that went in nearby, making this a middle-class beach. As such, it's actually pretty nice and quiet with fewer people than other beaches on the north coast. Good for a day of sunning and swimming.

## ITACIMIRIM BEACH

There are a few interesting beaches in this area, including some decent places for snorkeling in some offshore reefs and a couple of beaches for surfing. The center here is a small fishing village, which is still active and you can find a great selection of seafood at the local establishments.

## PRAIA DO FORTE

In the last 20 years, Praia do Forte has grown into one of Salvador's most beloved remote beaches. It consists of the EcoResort, a huge resort that comprises about half of the land in the area and which is responsible for the commercial growth of the area; a charming village with numerous shops, restaurants, and *pousadas*; and the TAMAR sea turtle preserve, famous for its work with numerous species of sea turtles. It's gotten to the point where mass tourism has made Praia do Forte almost too well-produced. It all begins to look like a facade in Disneyland or something—with too many souvenir shops and restaurants that don't really merit the prices they charge. But the payoff from all this well-developed tourism is a clean and crime-free village that is good for the local economy. Plus, any gripes are quickly and easily forgotten when you stroll around village or get lost on the incredible kayak expeditions around the lake. Praia do Forte remains one of Salvador's best remote beach villages. Most visitors from Salvador just spend the day here and return to the city for the evening. One day is enough time to do some snorkeling in the pools (trade this for a whale-watching excursion in the winter), visit the TAMAR project, and have dinner at one of the restaurants in the village. That certainly gives you a quick overview of the place, but an overnight stay with a second day to wander up the lakes and rivers by kayak would be even better.

### The Village

The village itself consists of a single street that is lined with coffee shops, *pousadas,* restaurants, and boutiques. The street is known as both Avenida ACM and Alameda do Sol. It's an extremely charming and well-kept place. On one end of the village (the entrance) is the Eco-Resort and on the other end is the TAMAR Project headquarters. The village is where many of the local residents work and make their crafts or sell their homemade foods. You'll see artists and craftspeople all over the village, as well as natives selling food and trinkets in the streets. Once dependent on a humble fishing industry, the village's fishermen have traded in their nets and taken up more lucrative work in the tourism business. As such, the people of the village are generally happy and friendly. It doesn't take long to walk up and down the village street and choose a comfortable spot for lunch or snacks. There are plenty of bars for cooling off with a cold beer and coffee shops for an afternoon pit stop.

## TAMAR Project

Biologists are still baffled at how adult sea turtles make their way back to the same beach upon which they were born and struggled to make their way into the ocean, some 25 years before. Victims of poaching and hunting (for

the eggs and adult shells and meat), the sea turtles of Brazil were nearly extinct by the middle of the 20th century. Today, thanks to IBAMA and its TAMAR Project, nearly five million turtles have been released into the ocean off Brazilian shores.

The TAMAR (TArtaruga MARinha) Project has a few important installations scattered around the Brazilian coastline, including in Ubatuba near São Paulo, Pipa near Natal, and their main office here in Praia do Forte, Bahia, one of the turtles' favorite nesting areas. Their reason for being is to protect and assist the lives of the sea turtles that live off the coast of Brazil. Here in Praia do Forte, the turtles make their nests along the sandy beaches to the north, right in front of the TAMAR headquarters, now only possible after years of intervention and community awareness. Every year between September and March, people come to watch the little turtles break out of their eggs and make the perilous journey into the ocean. Less and less, they require the assistance of the TAMAR researchers.

When the turtles are not in hatching season, you can still see them in various stages of life in

a resident of the TAMAR Project

# THE SEA TURTLES OF BRAZIL

Of the seven known species of sea turtles in the world, five can be found off the coast of Brazil. Hunted almost to extinction in the 20th century, these charming and docile creatures have inhabited the planet for around 150 million years, having survived and adapted to all sorts of harsh conditions. Today, with the help of Brazil's TAMAR project, there are millions of turtles roaming the shallow waters along much of the Brazilian coastline. They frequent the many islands off the coast and the females choose certain beaches on which to hide their eggs. Males, however, never leave the water. They are known to migrate for thousands of kilometers to their favorite eating and mating areas. They often spend several hours copulating, and the females will always return to the beach from which they were spawned to lay their eggs. This occurs at around 25 years of age. Females lay 300–500 eggs over a two-week period. About a month later, the little turtles emerge from the sand and make their way to the water. Approximately two in every thousand eggs will survive to adulthood.

An amphibious reptile, the sea turtle is believed to have adapted from its land-going cousins. Most of them have long front feet that act almost like paddles or fins for propelling them through the water. Their back feet are usually smaller than the front and overall, they are larger than land-going turtles. The largest sea turtle is the **leatherback,** which has a soft, pointed shell that reaches up to two meters in length. This turtle can weigh as much as 750 kilos. It is not found in Brazil as much as other species but can be spotted in the open ocean and sometimes spawns on the beaches in the southeast region. More common to Brazil is the **green turtle,** the second-largest of the bunch, which can be found around the islands along the north coast of Brazil. The green turtle can reach up to 350 kilos and 1.5 meters in length. The most endangered of the Brazilian sea turtles is the **hawksbill turtle,** known in Brazil as the *tartaruga de pente* (comb turtle), owing to its beautiful and highly-valued shell.

Sea turtles are calm and non-aggressive and it's possible to dive in and swim with them in some areas of the country, such as Fernando de Noronha, the Abrolhos Islands, and Campeche Island in Florianópolis.

the TAMAR habitats. Besides being a research center, the TAMAR Project opens its facilities to visitors. Inside are aquariums and habitats for turtles of all sizes. There are also incubators right in the sand. Besides the turtles, there are numerous fish tanks and even shellfish pools. It takes about 45 minutes to walk around and another 45 to make your way through the incredible souvenir shop, which has all kinds of items featuring their turtle art. At the entrance to the park is an area with tables and chairs facing the ocean. A kiosk, called the **Bar do Souza,** serves food and drinks. It's one of the most popular places to sit and watch the tide come in or out. You can enter this bar area from the TAMAR park or from the beach.

## Nature Excursions

The beaches at Praia do Forte are not the best part of the place. They are narrow and the water is not particularly clear (some days more so than others). There is, however, a section of the beach that has a series of tide pools offshore. These are excellent for snorkeling and exploration. You can walk to this area—just go out of the village to the beach and turn left. Walk for about one kilometer and you'll see the pools offshore. There are guides on the beach who can set you up with equipment for snorkeling, or you can prearrange a trip to the pools from a tour agency in the village or your hotel. If you have your own equipment, then just dive in and enjoy the warm water. The **Tourist Center** (in the village, tel. 71/3676-1091, www.prdoforte.com.br) offers a number of excursions from Praia do Forte, including a trip to Mangue Seco for five hours and a schooner trip to two nearby islands (snorkel and lunch included). These trips are offered just about every day. In the winter months of July and August, they also offer whale-watching tours that go from 9 A.M.– 2 P.M. for R$130 per person. The group **Portomar Passeios Turisticos** (tel. 71/3676-0101, www.portomar.com.br) offers kayak excursions up the Timeantube River (a great water safari for photography and bird-watching), a snorkeling excursion to the offshore pools, and off-road biking excursions in the surrounding hills. If you stay at the local youth hostel, they give you a discount on their excursions.

For a real thrill, you can take a small plane around the coastline—either to Salvador to the south or Mangue Seco to the north. Check with **Fly and Fun** at the Aeródromo Praia do Forte (tel. 71/3676-1540, www.flyandfun.com.br, flyandfun@bol.com.br).

Finally, there are about a dozen special excursions offered to guests of the Eco-Resort, such as walks around the Juara Lake, a quadricycle ride to the Aruá Lake, horseback riding along the beach and dunes, and beach excursions in search of sea turtles.

### Garcia D'Avila Castle Ruins

Sitting quietly on top of the plateau that overlooks Praia do Forte, with a view of the entire coastline, is one of the oldest stone structures in Brazil, the Garcia D'Avila Castle. Built in 1549 by Governor-General Tomé de Souza's official storekeeper, the castle was passed down through 10 generations of Garcia D'Avilas until it was finally abandoned in the early 1800s. The castle was the nucleus of one of the largest estates in Brazilian history, spanning some 800,000 square kilometers and more than 100 farms (mostly sugar). In addition to the castle, there are items from the Garcia D'Avila family that were found at the site, turning the place into a kind of museum. On Monday, Wednesday, and Saturday mornings at 9 A.M., you can catch Capoeira exhibitions in the amphitheater in front of the castle. The best time to visit the castle is just before sunset, so you can see the colored rays of the sun beaming onto the castle walls and into the courtyard. The view of the coastline is also a winner. You can visit the castle on

foot from town or take one of the local taxi carts from the entrance of the village.

### Whale-Watching

During the winter months in the southern hemisphere, humpback whales make their way north from the cold southern waters in search of warmer waters in which to spawn. Some of their favorite digs include the warm waters off the coast of Brazil. Whales can be spotted from Santa Catarina in the south all the way to northern Bahia. By September, the young calves can be seen swimming in mother's milk and playing with their parents. The large whales often dive out of the water, spinning in the air and landing with a great splash. They spray jets of water some three or four meters. They are friendly and often swim alongside the boats, even with their calves. Thankfully, the humpbacks are fairly well protected today, but in the past this was not so true. Brazil was one of the world's cruelest and most productive harvesters of whale products, especially in the southern states.

Going on a whale-watching excursion from Praia do Forte is almost a guaranteed way to see some of these creatures, as they hang out in the waters offshore until their calves are strong enough to resist the colder waters in the south. With the engine off, boats get quite close to the whales, creating a sensation you will never forget.

### The Praia do Forte EcoResort

When Klaus Peters, a Brazilian of German descent and industrialist from São Paulo, visited the small fishing village of Praia do Forte in the 1970s, he decided he had to buy as much of it as he could. At that time, there was only one *pousada* in town and just a few small businesses. His half-million-dollar investment got him 30,000 hectares, what today comprises almost half of the Praia do Forte area. He built himself an ecoresort, in part to preserve the wildlife and environment he purchased and in part to develop it. His *pedacinho* (little piece) incorporates about 12 kilometers of beach, part of the Timeantube Lake, the Timeantube and Pojuca Rivers, a large area covered in sand dunes, and the marshlands around the mouths of the rivers. The rest is history. His resort has grown to develop 90,000 of the 250,000 square meters of land and has 250 guest rooms (with cable TV, air, phone, and hair dryer), a modern convention center with 200 seats, a shopping village, travel agency, fitness center and spa, playgrounds, some five swimming pools with poolside bars, and two serious restaurants. It's impressive how the main restaurant/buffet maintains its extremely high quality of food and service while attending such enormous quantities of people. Indeed, breakfast and dinner at the EcoResort win first prize in the "Best Hotel Breakfast Buffet" and "Best Hotel Dinner Buffet" in Brazil awards, in this author's opinion.

The resort hosts numerous nature excursions for only a few *reals* each and, since Klaus owns most of the nature around there, the majority of these excursions are available only through the resort for their guests.

## Accommodations

The **Albergue Praia do Forte** (Rua da Aurora 3, tel. 71/3676-1094, www.albergue.com.br) is about 300 meters from the beach and has 24-hour reception, laundry service, Internet access (extra), group and private rooms with bathrooms in the rooms, and an open kitchen for guests. Another economical option that is slightly off the main road is **Ⲯ Pousada Solar das Estrelas** (Alameda das Estrelas 31, tel. 71/3676-0274, solardasestrelas@hotmail.com.br, R$60–80, depending on length of stay). It has a decent infrastructure with moderately charming rooms, fan, and TV, but no breakfast. There are two places right in the middle of the action on the main drag. First, **Pousada Ogum Marinho** (Av. ACM, tel. 71/3676-1165, www.ogummarinho.com.br, pousada@ogummarinho.com.br, R$120 with air and R$105 with ceiling fan) is located on the TAMAR side of the village and has a cool restaurant in the front of the building. They also have rooms with air, TV, and varanda with hammock. Second, the **Sobrado da Vila Guesthouse** (Av. ACM, tel. 71/3676-1088, www.sobradodavila.com.br, R$132 d or R$185 suite for

up to four people) is on the entrance side of the village and includes a large barbecue-style restaurant that is busy all day long and rockin' at night. All rooms have air, TV, and phone.

The **Pousada Casa de Praia** (Praça dos Artistas, tel. 71/3676-1362, www.casadepraia.tur.br, R$110 s and R$120 d) is close to the TAMAR Project and has 20 rooms with air and TV. It's comfortable and cozy with breakfast included. The **Ⲯ Pousada Praia do Forte** (Av. Do Farol, tel. 71/3676-1116, www.pousadapraiadoforte.com.br, R$240) was the first hotel in the area. It's located next to the TAMAR Project and has 20 chalets that can hold up to four people each. Most rooms have air, TV, and phone. They have a pool and restaurant with ocean view. A more modern facility is the **Pousada Farol das Tartarugas** (Rua Martim Pescador, tel. 71/3676-1512, www.faroldastartarugas.com.br, R$200 s and R$240 d). They have a two-story building with rooms facing the large pool (upper rooms have ocean views). Rooms have air, TV, and phone. They have their own, private access to the beach, where the turtles spawn. Breakfast is included.

Finally, if you want the first-class experience in Praia do Forte, then spend a day or two at the **Praia do Forte EcoResort** (Av. do Farol, tel. 71/3676-4000, www.ecoresort.com.br, reservas@ecoresort.com.br, R$800–1500). A full description appears previously. Your stay includes breakfast and dinner (all-you-can-eat with beer and sodas included), yoga and exercise activities, nightly music around the pool area, and kayaks for daily excursions. Other excursions and services are extra (R$8–20).

## Food and Entertainment

There are numerous restaurants, bars, and coffee shops along Avenida ACM and it's fun to walk up and down the street to make your selection. Here are just a few ideas: For coffee and desserts, try **Tango Café.** For simple sandwiches at a prices, try **Pudim** (located in the art avenue that crosses Av. ACM). Burgers and sandwiches are R$3–5 each. A comfortable place for drinks and a healthy salad is **Ⲯ O Europeu Bar and Restaurante.** They have a great location on the main street where you can watch the crowd pass by. A decent Italian restaurant with a great view of the street from above is **Skipper** (Av. ACM about halfway down). They have some vegetarian dishes and pastas for about R$40 for two people. The owner is friendly and gracious. One of the most popular places in the village is **N Sabor do Forte** on its nice corner lot with ample outdoor patio seating. They have a number of excellent meat, chicken, and fish dishes for around R$25–50 for two.

During the day, the restaurant/bar inside the TAMAR Project is the most popular spot for sitting and watching the ocean with a cold beer. You can use these facilities without having to pay to enter the park. In the evening, you can check out the scene at **Sobrado da Vila Guesthouse** at the entrance to the village. They have a large open area for eating and drinking and offer live music on weekends. The first place in town is the **Restaurante do Souza** with live music on weekends and plenty of outdoor seating.

### Information and Services

The information booth is right at the entrance to Avenida ACM. There, you can also find taxis and quadricycles for daily excursions. These modes of travel can be a bit expensive, but think of them as excursions and not just transportation. There is a Banco do Brasil with international ATM along the village road.

### Getting There

Buses leave from the entrance to town to Salvador all day long for around R$5. There is one that originates at Praia do Forte (you can buy tickets right at the bus stop or on the bus) and another that comes from the north (purchase passage inside the bus). You can never be sure which bus will come first, so if it's not crowded, just catch the first one that comes. Note that the last bus leaves at 6 P.M., which is a great way to get people to spend the night, but probably also ends up pushing people out of the village before they want to go. For this reason, it's not a bad idea to find a packaged excursion to Praia do Forte that leaves after dinner, or rent a car for the day.

## SÍTIO DO CONDE

The most popular attraction in Sítio do Conde actually comes about five kilometers before the town itself, in an area called Barra do Itariri. Barra is located at the mouth of the Itariri River, where you can partake of beaches on the ocean or along the river. You can take a swim in either salty or semi-salty water and visit the many bars and restaurants that have sprung up in the area to serve visitors. If you want a more secluded beach experience, make your way to Sítio do Conde, and walk along the beaches past Poças and all the way to Barra de Siribinha, which is at the mouth of the Siribinha River and surrounded by huge dunes, cashew trees, and mangroves. On the way back, stop at one of the beach kiosks at Poças Beach for lunch. Try the *moqueca* made with fish brought in by the local fisherman. If you prefer, you can take a dune buggy out to the beaches near town and they'll take you on a coastal excursion for about R$20 per person. You can also take a boat trip up the Siribinha River with one of the locals at Poças Beach.

Sítio do Conde is about 212 kilometers from Salvador along the BA-099 highway. You can get there by bus on the Expresso/Linha Verde and the São Luis lines, which leave from the Salvador *rodoviaria* several times during the day up to about 6 P.M. The tourist information office in Sítio do Conde is DENIT (tel. 71/3115-2159). There are *pousadas* at the entrance to town, between the Barra do Itariri and Sítio do Conde.

## MANGUE SECO

Travelers heading to the beaches north of Salvador come to an end of the road at Mangue Seco. Located on the tip of a long peninsula, Mangue Seco represents the northern-most beach in Bahia and is known for its huge dunes that are always blowing and changing position, all the way down to the ocean. Also in this area are the Rivers Fundo and Real, offering calm water and marshlands for the town's fishermen, while the ocean provides strong waves that attract surfers. In the Rio Fundo, you might catch a rare appearance by a manatee, as this is one of the few rivers outside of the Amazon region in which the mammal makes its home. The village of Mangue Seco is small and rustic, and the town remains somewhat isolated due to its unique position on the tip of the peninsula and its abundance of sand dunes, which make it difficult to build roads. All along the beaches, you'll find humble dining establishments that serve up the local fish, crab, and shellfish.

Nights in Mangue Seco are calm and relatively uneventful, except for a single beach bar in Alcobaça Beach (the principal beach for surfing) that has live music starting at midnight on summer weekends.

## Morro de São Paulo

Locals loosely refer to the Archipelago of Tinharé as Morro de São Paulo. Actually, the archipelago consists of three principal islands, separated by small channels of ocean water so narrow that they appear to be rivers. There are also 23 smaller islands (mostly uninhabited) dotting the waters around these three landmasses. The **Island of Cairu** was the first to be inhabited and is home to the area's government offices. As such, Cairu Island and the city of Cairu are more urbanized than the rest of the archipelago and you'll see cars and buses there (although not many). Cairu is also home to some of the oldest architecture in Brazil. The **Island of Tinharé** is the largest of the three and is home to the Village of Morro de São Paulo, where just about all of the tourism in the area is located. There are five principal beaches on this island, including three popular beaches near the village and two semi-deserted beaches a bit farther away. The first three beaches are dotted with bars, restaurants, and *pousadas* and are active both day and night—each one with its own, special personality. The **Island of Boipeba** is farthest south. Its principal feature is a small and super-charming village on the northern tip, which is used as a stopping point for many boat tours that circumnavigate the islands.

All totaled, the Archipelago of Tinharé, or Morro de São Paulo, presents a collection of attractions that is difficult to match anywhere along the coast of Brazil: beautiful beaches, two quaint villages, a small historical town, and several interesting monuments. All this on a tropical-island setting in Bahia. Sound like paradise? Morro de São Paulo is probably about as close as it gets.

### THE VILLAGE

If you arrive by boat, you'll exit the pier and walk up and to the left. Then, you turn right and go up, up, up until you're at the top of the village, marked by the **Igreja Nossa Sra. da Luz** and a small *praça* across from it. The *praça* has shops and a couple *pousadas*. If you follow the footpath leading through the *praça,* you'll arrive at the lighthouse. More on that later. To continue into the village, you now start walking downhill. Just as you pass the **tourist information office** on your left, you'll arrive at the main square, called Praça Aurellano Lima, marked by the **Pousada and Restaurante Casarão,** a key point in town for music and shows. Here, in front of the Via Brasil Restaurante (the best pizza in town), you'll find an arts and crafts fair every afternoon and evening that doesn't rain. Continue walking downhill to see the main stretch of the village, where most of the restaurants and many of the *pousadas* line themselves up. You'll also find tour agencies and scuba diving schools as you walk. When you reach the steep, rocky, downhill slope, you are on your way to the first beach, called Primeira Praia.

The village is full of life every day and night. You'll find some decent lunch venues here

Salvador

(although you'll probably have lunch right on the beach at one of the kiosks), and at night, the place lights up with activity from about dinnertime to 10 or 11 P.M., when the party moves either to the local dance clubs or back down to the beach. There are a number of *pousadas* in the village and they are pretty good options, since the village quiets down around midnight. The exceptions are the *pousadas* along the path to the lighthouse (across from the church), since they are on the way to and from the main dance club.

## THE LIGHTHOUSE AND THE FORT

The path to the lighthouse is directly across from the church (Igreja Nossa Sra. da Luz, built in 1845 and recently restored) at the top of the village. The entire hike takes about 20 minutes. Just follow the path faithfully until you reach the *farol*. As you begin the journey, you'll pass an excellent lookout point to the right just past the *praça,* where there is a break in the vegetation. On the left, you'll pass an interesting wall that supports the roots of a rubber tree (or is it the tree that supports the wall?). Further up on the left is the city's main disco. Keep walking until you reach the lighthouse. Unfortunately, it is not open for visitation, but there are footpaths going to the left and right that both lead to amazing lookout points. Go to the left and down to get an idea of how big the ocean is. You'll come out above the fort (which you'll be able to see below you) and with a view of the ocean that goes on for kilometers. You can also see the north side of the island and the Canal de Taperoá to the left. There is no formal structure here, so be careful of vertigo as you enjoy the view. To the right of the lighthouse, the path leads to the lookout point called **Belvedere do Farol.** Here you can see the postcard image of Morro de São Paulo and get the picture yourself. You will also get a glimpse of the local miniature monkeys that frequent the lookout point, begging or stealing food from the tourists. On a clear day, the three principal beaches are all lined up and sparkling below you. On busy, sunny days, you'll have the opportunity to ride the cable from Belve-

the fort at Morro de São Paulo

dere point over Primeira Praia (one of the highest cable rides in the world, they say) and drop into the ocean of Primeira Praia from a relatively low point at the end of the line. The ride costs R$20 per person and includes a boat rescue from the water. It's fairly radical.

A different path leads to the fort. After walking off the main pier and walking through the archway entrance to the village, you take a sharp left turn. The path there follows some 600 meters of short, stone wall built as part of the fortress, originally to secure the island from French pirates. Later, the fort was adapted to protect Salvador from invasions by the Dutch. This, of course, failed as the Dutch invaded successfully in 1629. The fort itself is in ruins, but many of the walls and archways still stand overlooking the ocean. The scene is classic and beautiful—almost more so than if the fort were 100-percent intact. It was the custom in those days to add whale oil to the mixture of stone and lime when building these structures, in the belief that the oil strengthened the walls. In fact, it did not, but it did make the walls more waterproof and therefore last longer. The fort is a great place to view the sunset and if you forgot to bring a picnic, there are usually young island boys selling sodas and snacks at the entrance to the fort.

## ℕ MORRO DE SÃO PAULO BEACHES

The three main beaches of Morro de São Paulo are called Primeira, Segunda, and Terceira Praias. Just about everything on the island is located by the name of the beach (or village) in which it's found ("My hotel is on Terceira Praia," or "I'll meet you at Primeira Praia and we'll head into the village for dinner"). You can walk from the beginning of Primeira Praia to the end of Terceira Praia in about 45 minutes. Each of the three beaches has a unique personality. **Primeira Praia** is the smallest and, in many ways, the most quaint. It is especially interesting during low tide, when you can walk back and forth between Primeira and Segunda Praias (at high tide, the area between these two

beaches is used for beginning scuba diving lessons) and even from Primeira Praia all the way around the point to the bottom of the fort. Just be sure not to get caught there after the tide comes in. There are a number of boats docked in the waters of Primeira Praia and many of these belong to the tour agencies in the village. There is a very quaint beach kiosk at Primeira Praia with a tranquil view of the ocean. Above the beach, a trail leads past some *pousadas* and casual eateries. Here, you'll also find scuba diving clubs and tour agencies.

**Segunda Praia** is the most active of the three. Here, you'll find the best swimming conditions (calm waters blocked by offshore reefs and no boats) and people playing sports on the sand (which can actually be somewhat invasive and a hassle to avoid). All along the inside of the beach are shops, bars, restaurants, and *pousadas.* These bars provide the late, late night party action for the island, which is why the *pousadas* here are not necessarily the best options on the island. They are, ironically, some of the more expensive places. At night, a slew of temporary *barracas* appears in front of the bars, offering all sorts of tropical fruit drinks (with or without alcohol). The far tip of the beach is a tree-covered area called the Ilha de Saudade, which is not really an island at all. There is an excellent place for snorkeling just off the point in the direction of Segunda Praia.

On the way to **Terceira Praia,** you'll pass some small beach kiosks that sell drinks and appetizers. Then, as you enter the third beach, you'll notice that it has a completely different feel. First of all, the beach is lined with *pousadas.* Some are excellent economical options for being right on the beach. There are also a number of places to sit and have a drink while looking out on the water, which is full of boats here. The swimming here is not bad if you don't go out to where the boats are.

## FOURTH AND FIFTH BEACHES

Whereas the first three beaches total about three kilometers of coastline, the fourth and fifth beaches consist of a long stretch of sand that goes on for about six kilometers. But you need not walk all the way down the beach to enjoy yourself here. That's because the best beach on the island for sunning and swimming is Quarta Praia. If you walk to the far end of Terceira Praia and cross over onto Quarta Praia, you'll come to the **Barraca da Piscina,** which is a great structure that serves folks going out to swim in the natural pools just off the coast of Quarta Praia. They have plenty of shade umbrellas and beach chairs for sitting out. Plenty of people spend a few hours walking past Terceira Praia and all the way across Quarta and Quinta Praias (Quinta Praia is also known as Praia do Encanto). These are spectacular at low tide, offering up shallow waters, sandbars, and natural pools that are excellent for snorkeling. There are not many kiosks or *barracas* to serve you once you get past Quarta Praia, so bring your own water if you decide to head out there. Your reward, if you get as far as Praia do Encanto, is that you'll encounter the **Hotel Praia do Encanto,** where you can have lunch or drinks and get a ride back into town on one of their regular trips. While you're there, check out their *cachaça* still (with free samples of their different *cachaças*) and their resident artist, with an atelier and shop on the grounds (see *Accommodations* for more details).

## FONTE GRANDE AND THE GAMBOA VILLAGE

Back up at the top of the village, at the Restaurant and Pousada Casarão, you'll notice a road the exits the *praça* to the left side of the Casarão. This is called **Rua da Fonte Grande** and it leads to the back side of the village and eventually to the village of Gamboa. The back side of the village is where you'll find the historic **Fonte Grande,** built in 1747 as a water source for the people of the island. It taps a natural spring that still works to this day—and the dome-shaped roof was designed to capture rainwater to augment the spring. The water runs into a well, or pit, into which residents dunk their pots. Unfortunately, the water here is no longer drinkable, but the system is still intact. From Fonte Grande, you can turn up Rua do Porto de Cima (marked with a sign indicating the direction of Gamboa). The highlight here is to take the trail down to the beaches, which are accessible only at low tide, so plan your excursion with this in mind. The trail will lead you to **Praia do Porto** and you can walk to the left to get to **Praia de Gamboa,** two beaches that will have few tourists and sparkling, greenish water. If you want to walk all the way to the village of Gamboa, you'll find a few humble *lanchonetes* for snacks and that's about it. If you get stuck here after the tide comes up, you can try to arrange a boat back to the main pier by one of the locals. The ferryboat that goes between Morro de São Paulo and Valença stops in Gamboa both coming and going, so this is also a possible return trip.

## THE CITY OF CAIRU

About the same size as the Village of Morro de São Paulo (7,000 inhabitants), Cairu is an interesting mixture of modern and colonial architecture. It is home to the city government and has a bridge that allows cars to enter from the continent—although it is far from being an active urban center. The principal economic activities of Cairu consist of fishing and harvesting palm oil. Cairu has the special distinction of being the second oldest city in Brazil with a founding date of 1507 (second to Porto Seguro, where Brazil was said to have been discovered, although it's now known that the Spaniards set foot in the Fortaleza area in the year 1500, one year before the Portuguese). Cairu is generally a stop on the *Volta Ilha* boat tour, where passengers walk up the small hill to the oldest convent in Brazil, still standing and in excellent condition. The highlights in the convent are the many walls covered in blue Portuguese tile and the restored side altar in the small chapel. Although this is about all most visitors ever see of Cairu, it's said to have some interesting sights for anyone wanting to spend more time there.

## ENTERTAINMENT AND NIGHTLIFE

There is a certain rhythm to the nightlife on the island and it goes in stages. After a day at the beach, the town gathers at the Praça Aureliano Lima to check out the arts and crafts fair and later, choose a restaurant for dinner. If you're there at sundown, walk over to the **Pousada Passargada** across from the Igreja Nossa Sra. da Luz to enjoy the sunset and a coffee from their outdoor patio. They also have excellent *pão de quejo* (cheese bread). The **Pousada Casarão** has folk shows right outside on their patio, every day that doesn't rain. Dinner should go until about 10 –11 P.M. Afterward, anyone interested in dancing heads over to **Morcego** (bat), which is along the path toward the lighthouse, just past the cemetery (a creepy place that is open if you want to check out the abandoned crypt—assuming you're into that kind of thing). Morcego bar and discotheque is not creepy at all, but is well located toward the top of the hill away from the *pousadas* to minimize the noise factor. Live music and dancing goes on until about 1–2 A.M., at which point the festivities move to the Segunda Praia bars. That goes until sunrise, which is stunning as it comes up over the ocean. You can head over to Segunda Praia after dinner if you want to avoid the crowd. It's a pretty cool place to have a drink at any time of the day or night. The best of the Segunda Praia bars is **Clube do Balanço,** which has good food and clean toilets.

There are stands selling fruit cocktails, caipirinhas, and other delights all along the main road through the village—from around dusk to midnight. These are usually cheaper than the stands at Segunda Praia.

An alternative to the Segunda Praia scene is the **Pousada Canto da Sereia,** which is on Rua da Fonte Grande. They have live music every night and a good crowd forms there.

## FESTIVALS AND EVENTS

The week after Carnaval is a peak time on the island. People flock to the island to recuperate after the heavy partying during Carnaval in Salvador.

## EXCURSIONS

The most popular island excursion is a full-day boat trip around the Island of Tinharé. Called **Volta Ilha,** this trip begins at Terceira Praia (although they will pick you up at Quinta Praia if you happen to be staying there) and takes a complete trip around the island. You'll have several interesting stops along the way. First is a stop about one kilometer off the beach of Garapuá for some excellent snorkeling and swimming among the fish in the underwater reefs and pools. The quantity and variety of fish here is excellent and if crowds warrant, there is also a floating bar that awaits you there.

Without actually docking at Garapuá, the boat excursion continues to the northern tip of the Boipeba Island. You get off at a secluded beach called **Praia Tassimirim** where locals are ready for you with beers, fried lobster, and shrimp. The beach here is narrow and when the tide comes in, they hang their plastic tables and chairs in the trees for safe keeping. Tip: If you like lobster, have lunch here. It's about R$20 per person for a plate full of lobster meat. Well worth it. The next leg of the journey is a 20-minute hike along the beach to the village of Boipeba, also known as the *Boca da Barra* (Mouth of the Sandbar), where there are several beach bars lined up to serve you fish, lobster, and all kinds of lunch plates for around R$10–15 per person (most plates are made for two, so if you're alone, ask for a *meia porção*). If you're on a budget, then just keep walking along the beach until you come to some smaller and cheaper places. You can swim in the waters here or just sit in the shade and enjoy the view. The village here is small and charming with a number of great *pousadas* in case you want to spend the night. In fact, it's a common practice to cut the *Volta Ilha* excursion in half at this point and spend the night on Boipeba, then pick up the second half of the excursion the next afternoon. I highly recommend this, but you should set it up ahead of time with the

putting tables and chairs away for high tide

boat captain and be sure to reserve your hotel on Boipeba the morning of your excursion.

After lunch in Boipeba, the journey continues with a trip up the Rio do Inferno all the way to the village of Cairu, where you stop to see the old convent. On the way back down the hill to the boat, you might stop for an ice cream at one of the local shops. Then you continue your journey up the Canal de Taperoá and back to the pier at Morro de São Paulo. All this for R$50 per person, snorkeling equipment and lunch not included. An excellent group offering this excursion is **Quarta Praia Sul** (Rua da Prainha 75, Primeira Praia, tel. 75/3652-1284, www.quartapraiasul.com.br), which has a modern *flexiboat* that is perfect for making this journey.

The fishing village of **Garapuá** is an excellent place to stay while you're on the island. Some of Brazil's rich and famous stay there, as it's one of the island's most remote locations. You can get to the village via horseback or 4-wheel-drive vehicle with the tour group **Quarta Praia Sul** for approximately R$25 per person. Another tour offered by the same group is the **Trilha do Mar Sea Trak**. On this

6.5-kilometer hike along the canal at Praia do Encanto, you'll see three of the island's ecosystems: the marshlands, the forest, and the channel. An English-speaking guide (or Spanish or German) will explain the various flora and fauna along the way. It costs approximately R$15 per person. A final excursion, exclusive to the Quarta Praia Sul group is the **Galeão** trip. On this excursion, you take a fast boat from the main pier to the São Francisco Church that sits high on the hill overlooking the Canal de Taperoá on the western tip of the island. From here, you can see as far as Cairu and past the Morro de São Paulo village. On the way back, you stop at Manguinho Island to watch the snowy egrets come home for the evening, decorating the trees in a splash of white feathers. You may also catch some dolphins swimming in the channel, as they come in from the ocean in the afternoon and are often spotted near Manguinho. This trip costs approximately R$25 per person.

Another group offering excursions around the Island of Tinharé, hikes to the island's waterfall, and trips to Cairu and Boipeba is **Madalena Tur** (Rua Segunda Praia, tel. 75/9148-3234, www.madalenaturismo.com.br). You can also check at the tourist information center at the entrance to the village.

The best group for scuba diving adventures (and lessons) is the **Cia de Mergulho** (Rua da Primeira Praia at the Pousada do Farol, tel. 75/3652-1200, www.ciadomergulho.com.br, ciadomergulho@ciadomergulho.com.br). They have a series of trips and courses, including a 40-minute beginner dive in the ocean for R$90. For experienced divers, they combine two dives for R$145 with equipment. A full course is R$650 and takes five days, but what a great way to spend a week on the island. Note that the months November–March are the best for diving, as the water is clearest. Try to plan your trip around the full or new moon.

If you like having one person take care of all your needs—hotels, transportation, tours, and whatever else comes up—then get in touch with Jody at **Batuke Turismo** (tel. 75/3652-1611, batuke@neth.com.br, www.morrodesaupaulobahia.com.br). He can set up your entire island trip from beginning to end and even find long-term accommodations if you're interested in staying for awhile. He's a nice, honest guy and accepts credit cards.

## ACCOMMODATIONS

If you stay in the village, you'll be able to choose from some of the quaintest options on the island. You'll also be close to everything and halfway between the pier and the beaches. The down side is that it can be a bit noisy in the village, but most of the noise heads to the beaches after midnight. There are only a few hotels in Primeira Praia, but they have excellent locations at the base of the village and overlooking the beach at the same time. Primeira Praia is also a very quiet beach at night. I don't recommend the hotels on Segunda Praia, since they are expensive and should be economical due to the inconvenience of the noise on the beach from around midnight to sunrise. Terceira Praia has a huge variety of hotels and is a favorite place to stay for many people. It is far from the noise of Segunda Praia and the village

and offers many beachfront accommodations for reasonable prices.

### The Village

A good deal for a *pousada* around the back side of the village is **Canto da Sereia Bar and Pousada** (Rua da Fonte Grande, tel. 75/3652-1018, www.cantodasereia.com.br, sereia@cantodasereia.com.br, R$40 s and R$55 d). Run by a Chilean couple, the *pousada* is a three-story structure built around a large mango tree. The rooms are all pretty much the same: simple and clean with no particular charm. Their bar and restaurant (serving Chilean food) gets quite crowded at night. Breakfast is included.

At the top of the hill near the church is the **Pousada Passargada** (Rua Caminho do Farol 1, tel. 75/3652-1069, www.pousada-passargada.com.br, ppassargada@uol.com.br, R$90 d low season and R$150 peak season). Besides having an excellent deck for watching the sunset with a cup of coffee, their *pousada* has some decent rooms, some with views. The **Ⓜ Pousada Solar do Morro** (Praça Aureliano de Lima 155, tel. 75/3652-1057, www.pousada-solardomorro.com.br, reservas@pousadasolardomorro.com.br, low-season/peak-season prices: R$120/R$180 standard, R$175/R$250 luxury, and R$200/R$300 suite with veranda) has a perfect location at the *praça* that marks the beginning of the village (right behind the arts and crafts fair). They have 14 quaint rooms built at various levels on the hillside. Their rooms have comfortable, kind-sized beds, satellite TV, and bathtub with jets. They have a pool with poolside bar and are joined at the hip with the Via Brasil restaurant next door (the owners are sisters), where you can get food sent up to your room if you like.

Finally, you might like the idea of staying in the most famous of the island's *pousadas,* the **Pousada O Casarão** (Praça Aureliano Lima 190, tel. 75/3652-1049, www.ocasarao.net, info@ocasarao.net, R$200). They have a large facility with two pools, a restaurant, six rooms in the main house and 10 chalets with balcony, air, TV, and hammocks. They are perfectly located at the top of the *praça* in the village.

## First, Second, and Third Beaches

Laura and her husband José Carlos will treat you like family at their *pousada* **Via Brasil** (Primeira Praia, 76, tel. 75/3652-1218, www.pousadaviabrasil.com.br, reservas@pousadaviabrasil.com.br, R$80–120 low season and R$130–180 peak season). They have turned their small place into a very comfortable and charming hotel in an excellent location at First Beach. They have six rooms (the top two have views of the ocean) with air, TV, very comfortable beds, and gas-heated water. Breakfast is served on their deck with a view of the ocean and movement on the street below. Ask about single rates.

A great place for single travelers and backpackers is the **Recanto das Estrelas** (Terceira Praia, tel. 75/3652-1328, R$30 pp with breakfast). It's down a small and charming sandy alley off the beach along with a few other economical hotels. The **Pousada Minha Louca Paixão** (Terceira Praia, tel. 75/3652-1318, pousada@minhaloucapaixao.com.br, R$135 with view and R$105–120 without) is one of the more charming places on Third Beach.

They have beachfront rooms with views of the ocean. They also have a cozy restaurant that is not just for guests of the *pousada*. A very cool place to stay at the Third Beach is the **Vila Guaiamú** (Terceira Praia, tel. 75/3652-1035, www.vilaguaiamu.com.br, edoardo@vilaguaiamu.com.br, R$160), which, besides being a *pousada,* is an area of preservation for the local *guaiamú* crabs that are pretty much just considered food in these parts. You'll see more crabs—and big ones—in the hotel's extensive preserve area and you may get to know some of them by name. The place has several chalets that contain two or three rooms each and a charming indoor/outdoor restaurant with lovely Bahian women serving the food—and no crabs on the menu.

## Praia do Encanto

If you want a more quiet and private experience on the island, then you might consider getting set up at the Praia do Encanto. The most likely choice for a hotel there is the **Hotel Praia do Encanto** (tel. 75/3652-2000, tel. 75/3652-1288, www.praiadoencanto.com.br,

Primeira Praia from above

Salvador

otel@praiadoencanto.com.br, R$126). The otel is made up of a series of quaint, individual halets (great for couples) spread across a large eachfront property. They have two pools, a eachfront kiosk/bar, and a restaurant for break-ast (included and quite ample) and dinner. The wner, Luciano, purchased the land in the '80s when residents of the island thought he was nuts or purchasing so far away from the village. He has filled the place out with a great infrastruc-ture, a resident artist and gallery, and a truck that makes regular trips into town throughout he day and night (both for guests and for lo-cals). Luciano also makes a wicked homemade cachaça, which you are free to sample as much as you like (the high-octane is the best). Luciano knows everything about the island and is re-sponsible for the **Quarta Praia Sul** tour group. The hotel is close to the island's airport in case you fly into town and the beach in front of the hotel goes out for kilometers at low tide.

### Boipeba

A great place to stay in the Boipeba Village is **Horizonte Azul Pousada** (tel. 75/3653-6080, pousadahorizonteazul@uol.com.br, R$80). They have a hillside property comprising a few chalets and apartments with a very relaxed, spiritual feeling. There is also a campground on the Boipeba beach with some great locations for pitching tents, including atop a wooden tower (R$10 pp or R$20 with breakfast). It's located past the beach bars/restaurants on the left.

## FOOD

All the restaurants along the village road are open for lunch and dinner. You'll find a vari-ety of places with both regional and interna-tional food. The quality of these places is all about the same with the exception of the sushi restaurant upstairs on the main road, which is over-priced and serves microscopic portions of fish. You can find a variety of lunch options on First, Second, and Third Beaches (First and Third Beaches having the most economical op-tions). Also, the restaurants down Rua da Fonte Grande are interesting and have better prices for

lunch than those on the main village road. If you hang out at the **Barraca da Piscina** on Fourth Beach during the day, then you can partake of one of their seafood lunch plates.

Dinner in the village presents several good places to check out. For the best pizza in town and plenty of other good dishes, try the ⚠ **Restaurante Via Brasil** (Praça Aureliano de Lima 155). They have a great location over-looking the *praça* and the service is excellent and friendly. The owners also run the Pousada Via Brasil on the First Beach. Try the inter-esting and delicious chocolate pizza for desert, called *doce de Laura*. Meals cost R$15–25 per person. The **Restaurante Bemmequer** (Rua Caminho da Praia) has great grilled meats and seafood dishes for around R$50 for two.

## INFORMATION AND SERVICES

There is an international ATM at the Mercado Estevan on the main street in the village. It ac-cepts Visa, MasterCard, Plus, and Cirrus. The problem is that it does not always work and the market closes at 9 P.M. Most decent hotels on the island will accept credit cards, but you are well advised to bring plenty of cash with you.

As you get off the boat and drag your bags down the pier, you will probably be approached by young island boys with wheelbarrows offer-ing to haul your bags to your hotel. Unfortu-nately, there is no alternative to this service, so if you are bag-laden (and that's not a personal insult), you should probably take one of them up on a lift. Be careful to ask the price before giving them your bags. The going rate is R$5 per bag and you should probably carry any small bags yourself or you'll get charged for them, too.

Note that very few of the pay phones on the island work properly, so if you need to make phone calls, you'll need to use your hotel's phone or one of the expensive call centers along the main village road.

A good website for information about the island is www.morrodesaopaulo.com.br. Also, the site of the Hotel Praia do Encanto, www.praiadoencanto.com.br, has lots of in-formation (in Portuguese), and you can try

**Salvador**

www.morro.com.br for a good general overview of the island.

## GETTING THERE

There are basically three ways to get to Morro de São Paulo: the fast-and-expensive way, the medium way, and the slow-and-cheap way. That is, by plane, by direct speedboat, or by a combination of land and sea via the town of Valença. Even if you're not the type to splurge on unnecessarily luxurious travel, you might consider getting to the island by plane. Besides getting to the island, you also get a short aerial tour of the coastline between Salvador and the archipelago. On a clear day, this 30-minute trip is worth the price, even if it were just a sightseeing tour; getting you to the island is an extra benefit. On a rainy day, speedboats don't make the trip to the island, so going by plane or the long way (land and sea combination) will be your only options. Check with **Aero Star** in Salvador (Praça G. Coutinho, tel. 71/3377-4406, aerostar@e-net.com.br, www.aerostar.com.br) or on the island (Rua Caminho da Praia, in the village, tel. 75/3652-1112). Another company is **Adey** (tel. 71/3377-2451 in Salvador). The flight costs around R$250.

Speedboats leave for the island from the Terminal Merítima several times per day, 9 A.M.–2 P.M. The trip takes about two hours and costs R$45 per person. The last speedboat back from the island leaves the pier at around 5 P.M. During peak season, you should get your tickets 24 hours in advance.

The slow way to the island involves catching a speedboat, catamaran, or ferryboat to the Island of Itaparica. From there, you catch a bus to the town of Valença, where you pick up a catamaran to Morro de São Paulo. The trip takes around six hours and costs a total of R$25 per person. Boats getting to Itaparica leave from the Terminal Marítima starting at about 6 A.M. There are also ferryboats that leave from a different dock (closer to the Bonfim area) for only R$4. You should leave by 1 P.M. at the latest if you want to take this route. In Valença, you'll transfer to another bus that takes you to the pier, where you wait for the boat taxi from the island, which runs every 30 minutes, 6 A.M.–5 P.M. The last ferry boat from Itaparica to Salvador (the last leg of your return trip) is at 11 P.M. so you can take the last boat off the island to Valença and still get all the way to Salvador. The bus terminal on the Island of Itaparica has buses that go south to Itacaré and Ileús, if you're interested in continuing south instead of returning to Salvador. You can also catch these buses in Valença.

## GETTING AROUND

The few remote locations on the island that are not reachable on foot are reachable by *jardineira* (tractor taxi). You can catch the tractor just behind Segunda Praia at the Terminal de Mangeira.

# Itaparica and the Bay of All Saints

For the residents of Salvador, the Bay of All Saints provides a number of options for rest and relaxation away from the city. Most visitors head to the island of Itaparica, where there are numerous beaches with beach bars and restaurants to serve guests. The beaches of Itaparica are probably even more popular than those on the mainland and the island was chosen by Club Med as their first resort location in Brazil. The phenomenon of Club Med became so popular in Brazil that within a short time, there were three major resorts on the Brazilian coastline. Today, the coast is rife with resort-style hotels and Club Med has two in Bahia alone (the other is in Arraial d'Ajuda). Besides the beach island of Itaparica, the bay is home to many small, tropical islands, including the islands of Frade and Maré. These are particularly interesting for scuba divers, but also present some interesting historical villages, small fishing towns, and tropical flora. In the south corner of the bay is the city of Jaguaripe, where you can find various waterfalls along the Jaguaripe River and a simple tourism infrastructure to take you out on nature excursions.

The Bay of All Saints was the most active marine port in the southern hemisphere during the 17th and 18th centuries. It saw boats filled with sugar and cocoa leaving for Europe and boats filled with African slaves coming in. It's one of the largest bays in the world, with more than 1,100 square kilometers of water, 56 islands, and numerous rivers and marshlands feeding into it.

# ITAPARICA

Every weekend in the summer, boatloads of people from Salvador descend on the beaches of Itaparica to partake of the great view of Salvador across the bay. There are rocky reefs blocking the ocean waves from many of the beaches and the water is calm and warm. This also makes great offshore pools for snorkeling and scuba diving. The beaches are the most popular part of the island, but there are other attractions as well. Namely, the island has one of the most important bus terminals in the area, where you can catch buses traveling south down the coastline. Buses coming from the city of Salvador travel along the highway and not along the coastline and take a long detour to get around the inside of the bay. Despite its busy bus and ferryboat terminal, Itaparica is a simple place, and its inhabitants are principally involved in the fishing trade and tourism. The main population centers are spread along the outer coastline, where most of the beaches are also located. The largest centers are Porto Santo and Bom Despacho, where the ferryboat and bus station are located. The best beaches are farther down the island.

## Beaches

Many of the popular beaches on the island are huddled around the populated end of the island, near Bom Despacho and the town of Itaparica. One of these is called **Praia do Forte,** a very small inlet surrounded by trees and brush near the São Lorenço Fort on the innermost tip of the island. **Praia do Boulevard** is a pretty beach that is super shallow during low tide and you can walk way out into the bay. There are numerous summer-

houses in this area and the beach is popular in summer. You can see the city of Salvador across the bay while sitting on the beach. The **Praia da Ponta do Mocambo,** also known as Praia dos Namorados, is semi-deserted due to the difficulty in accessing it. In the summer, it is often used as a nude beach. One of the most popular beaches for tourists is **Ponta de Areia,** which has no waves and warm, shallow water, perfect for swimming. Boat excursions from Salvador often stop here to let passengers off for awhile. There are beach kiosks to serve you. Just a bit farther south is **Amoreiras Beach,** which also has a number of beach bars to serve visitors. You can have lunch here with a variety of seafood and crab options along with cold beer and tropical drinks. There are shady almond trees to keep you cool when you're not laying out in the sun.

## Sights

You can take a bus out to the **Centro Histórico** from the Bom Despacho station to see the old fort and antique village that remain there. The streets of the old village are strangely peaceful and tranquil and they sit only nine kilometers from the port. Not far from there, you can check out the **Fonte da Bica,** a mineral water spring that is said to have rejuvenating powers. The structure around the spring was built in 1842, and you can still drink the water. From the Centro Histórico, you can walk to the fountain, which is on Avenida 25 de Outubro. Nearby, in the city of Itaparica, you can find boat tours to take you out to **Ilha do Medo,** a two-hour excursion that shows you the flora and fauna of the beautiful little island. It sits just 3.5 kilometers from Itaparica. It's best to go during high tide.

## Information

You can get to Itaparica by catamaran from the Centro Nautico, which is located behind the Mercado Modelo. The boats leave throughout the day for only around R$8 per person. The trip takes about 30 minutes. You can hire a speedboat to take you across in about 15 minutes if you prefer. You can also take the ferryboat from the ferry terminal (west of the Centro Nautico). The trip takes about

Salvador

45 minutes. Once you're in Bom Despacho, you can find buses and vans to take you around the island.

## ILHA DE MARÉ

This little island in the middle of one of the most active bays in the hemisphere is amazingly rustic and untouched by civilization. The inhabitants have resisted modernism for centuries and continue in their traditional ways, mostly surviving off the land and sea. Only 20 minutes by boat from Salvador, the island has semi-deserted beaches and small beach villages that appear to be suspended in time. The best beaches are Santana, Itamoabo, and Praia Grande. Around the island are areas that are excellent for scuba diving. You can get to the island by taking a bus to São Tomé de Paripe. Boats leave for the island just about every hour, 8 A.M.–6 P.M.

## ILHA DOS FRADES

Covered in thick forest and protected as an ecological preserve area, the Island of Frades is one of the most beautiful in the bay. On all sides, there are sandy beaches and some have simple bars and restaurants that serve lobster, crab, and seafood from local waters. Some of the more popular beaches include Paramana, Loreta, Viração, and Praia da Costa. During the slave trade, the island was used to quarantine the slaves before taking them to market in Pelourinho. You can also visit the old ruins of the quarantine area. In addition, there's an old flour mill and two small chapels.

You get to Frades via the Island of Madre de Deus, which is connected to the mainland by a bridge. At the port on Madre de Deus, you can negotiate a boat trip across to Frades. The average price is about R$10 per person, depending on the size of the group.

## NAIF PAINTING AND TRIBAL ART

How do you critique an art style that has no connection to classical art forms and whose artists have no formal training whatever? Such is the aptly named Art Naif (from the French *naïve*), which grew up in the countryside throughout the Western world. Today, it is prevalent throughout South America and is particularly common in Brazil, where a familiarity with European classical styles is a luxury that much of the population cannot afford. Although Art Naif can be found in many countries around the world, Brazilian Art Naif is considered by some experts to be a distinctly national art form, since it evolved in Brazil with no reference whatever to the outside.

Brazilian Art Naif is characterized by simple forms and an almost childlike approach to design and color. There is usually little or no color mixture and no attention paid to perspective, composition, or balance. Most works are landscapes or cityscapes, rife with people and animals in everyday situations. Often, the scenes depict popular festivals, Capoeira dances, or farming activities. Colors are bright, primary, and vibrant with very little variation in the mix.

Art Naif is said to have its roots as far back as cave painting, where perspective and color were also not the principal preoccupation of the artist. For this reason, Naif art is often associated with primitive art forms and even tribal art. Such associations may be more appropriate than connecting it to the European Primitivists, Rousseau, Gauguin, or Monet, since Art Naif is not a movement or counter-academic in any way. It is, in fact, a pure art form that stands on its own merits and should be critiqued by its own standards. What standards are those? Experts generally look for spontaneity, simplicity, and freedom of expression when evaluating the works of Naif artists. If this sounds like something your child might create, you're not far from the mark. Art Naif is, in fact, considered a bridge between the child and the adult. Some say that it begins where childhood leaves off.

For more information about Art Naif, see the **Museu Internacional de Arte Naif do Brasil–MIAN** in Rio de Janeiro (Rua Cosme Velho 561, Cosme Velho, www.museunaif.com.br, 21/2205-8612, 10 A.M.–6 P.M. Tue.–Fri., noon–6 P.M. on weekends).

# JAGUARIPE

Some of the earliest colonists made their home here on the southern end of the Bay of All Saints, where the local indigenous groups were fierce and quarrelsome. More than a few of those early colonizers were served up for lunch. It's said that the original village here had a series of tunnels underneath, in which the Portuguese inhabitants would hide during attacks by the indigenous people. You can walk around the town, which is divided into a high and low village (like Salvador and many other cities on the Bahian coast). There are small chapels and structures used in the shipping trade, for which the city is most famous.

## Excursions

The best way to visit the town is by guided tour, either from Salvador (which includes boat transportation) or in the city of Jaguaripe itself. One popular excursion that leaves from Jaguaripe is a boat trip out to the Ponta and around the inner coast of Itaparica. At low tide, the area called the Ponta (Point), is a popular place to visit and swim. A bar of sand stretches some 20 kilometers into the bay. There are also excursions out to the nearby waterfalls. The Tiriri Waterfall, for instance, is on a working flour mill that is open to the public. From the mill, you hike 40 minutes up to the falls on the bank of the Jaguaripe River, surrounded by green, tropical vegetation. Another option is to take a boat trip up the Jaguaripe River to the city of Nazaré, passing mangroves, and many vistas along the way. The trip may also include a visit to the small islands off the point of Jaguaripe and even pass through the archipelago between Itaparica and the mainland.

# Barra Grande and the Peninsula de Maraú

Although Barra Grande is actually close to Salvador and, in particular, Morro de São Paulo, it is most often and most easily accessed from Itacaré in the south. The area includes three main towns, the Camamu Bay with its many islands and inlets, two fresh-water lakes, and kilometers of sandy beaches lined with palm trees and tropical forest. The area is not as built-up for tourism as its neighbors, the Bay of All Saints and Itacaré, which makes it more of a tropical paradise in many ways. The beaches are mostly virgin and deserted and the villages are untainted by commercialism. Although most people see the peninsula on a one-day tour from Itacaré, the area deserves another day or two of exploration—at the very least, to catch a boat tour up the channels and waterways of the Camamu Bay, but a day or two on the virgin beaches of the peninsula are also unforgettable. Without a doubt, a few days in this region will take you far away from the rest of the world.

Keep in mind that Barra Grande is almost deserted during the low season and many of the establishments do not operate. Bars and restaurants may require reservations in low season, just to alert them of your presence. During peak season (December–February), everything is in full working condition. Don't let that stop you from coming during low season, however, as this is a wonderfully peaceful time to visit. Just call ahead to let everyone know you'll be in town.

## CAMAMU, BARRA GRANDE, AND MARAÚ

The main town on Camamu Bay is Camamu itself. From here, you can catch boat excursions or simple transportation to various points in the bay, such as Barra Grande. The town of **Camamu** was founded by Jesuits around the same time as Salvador and suffered much of the same fate as Salvador in terms of attacks by pirates and the Dutch. Like Salvador, it also grew rich from its exports (mostly manioc root) and had an active port. Since Camamu has no beaches or tourist attractions as such, most people simply use it as a launching pad to the peninsula and excursions around the bay. The town of

Salvador

**Barra Grande** is the most popular place for tourists. It has a number of restaurants and *pousadas* and there are several beaches nearby with pristine conditions. The main village beach is **Mangueiras Beach** and it has a calm surf and a few beach kiosks to serve refreshments while you pass the afternoon and watch the incredible sunset. The town is a mixture of a humble fishing village and tropical paradise for tourists and international immigrants. As such, it retains a very traditional look and feel, while also offering some amazing food and accommodations. The village of **Maraú** is closest to Itacaré on the south part of the bay (actually it's on the edge of the Maraú River, which feeds into the bay). You need an off-road vehicle to get there and that keeps the village small and undeveloped.

## THE CAMAMU BAY AND ISLANDS

You can take boat trips around the bay, visiting the various islands and even going all the way up the bay to where river water empties into the bay in a beautiful waterfall, called the Cachoeira do Tremembé. Boats pass under the small waterfall and cool off the passengers at the end of the trip upriver. Trips leave from Camamu and Barra Grande and are generally only available during the summer months, when demand is high enough to fill a boat. If you have a group of people (4–6), you can probably hire out a boat almost any time of the year. The cost will vary from R$200–300 for a day (for the entire boat), depending on the agenda. Small boat trips can take you out to the islands closest to Barra Grande, such as the Ilha do Goió, for around R$80. If you only have two people in your party, the prices will be the same. Highlights in the bay include the **Ilha da Pedra Furada,** a small island with a natural spring and beautiful beaches. One small kiosk serves drinks and appetizers during peak season. At low tide, you can walk along a sandbar to the stone arch that gives the island its name. The **Village of Sapinho** (meaning little toad) has restaurants that specialize in seafood harvested from the local waters. Nearby

is the **Island of Goió,** which has several interesting beaches and lots of marshes full of lobsters and crabs. You may decide to stay at one of the *pousadas* on **Ilha Grande,** the largest island in the bay and the most populated, with about 2,000 inhabitants, mostly families in the fishing trade. You can walk around the island on the various trails and you won't see a single car—only beautiful beaches and views of the ocean and bay.

A couple of agencies that provide boat and 4-wheel-drive excursions in Barra Grande include Camamu Adventure (tel. 73/3255-2138), Natur E Mar Turismo (tel. 73/3255-2343), and Maris Turismo (tel. 71/3255-2348).

## Ⓜ MARAÚ PENINSULA LAKES AND BEACHES

The lakes and beaches of the Maraú Peninsula are vast and varied. Starting at the top is the **Barra Grande Beach,** with beach kiosks for tourists hanging out for the afternoon. On the ocean side of the peninsula is the famous **Tres Coqueiros Beach,** with its picturesque white sand and palm trees. Here, you'll find some *pousadas* and restaurants in case you want to stay a bit longer. Continuing down the coast is **Taipu de Fora,** a long expanse of sand and surf that has some amazing underwater reefs and tide pools for snorkeling. The **Cassange Beach** is on the coast of a narrow strip of land between the Cassange Lake and the ocean. You can walk between them, switching from salt water to fresh water for your swimming pleasure. Finally, the beaches closest to Maraú include **Arandi** and **Algodões,** which have long, extensive stretches of sand and a light surf that is perfect for swimming. Offshore are some reefs and pools for snorkeling.

## ACCOMMODATIONS

The most elaborate accommodation on the peninsula is at **Kiaroa Beach Resort** (Praia dos Tres Coqueiros, tel. 71/3272-1320, www.kiaroa.com.br). They have an incredible view of the ocean at the secluded Tres Coqueiros Beach.

The grounds also include a coconut plantation and some tropical forest. They offer a pool, sauna, restaurant, bar, diving equipment, and excursions, and they have a small landing strip for small planes coming from Salvador or Ileus. The place is oriented to couples and does not allow children under 14. Their rooms are rustic-style chalets made out of wood and are equipped with air-conditioning, TV, and phone. Prices are established through multi-day packages and should be negotiated with their reservation center. In the village of Barra Grande is the ℕ **Pousada dos Tamarinhos** (Rua José Melo Pirajá 21, tel. 71/3258-6064, www.pousadadostamarindos.com.br, R$165–255), which offers about 20 rooms of Japanese architecture and design. They have a large outdoor space that's very close to the beach and full of tropical trees and plants. Rooms have air, TV, and phone. They have a restaurant featuring Japanese cuisine and a bar. Prices vary depending on the season and length of stay. Finally, you can stay near the *lagoa* at **Pousada Logoa da Cassange** (Praia do Cassange, Km 19, tel. 71/3258-2166, www.maris.com.br, R$185). They have about 15 lovely chalets with air, ceiling fans, and verandas overlooking the lake and beach. They offer transportation into town and have a bar and restaurant.

## FOOD

There are bars and restaurants in all of the hotels and *pousadas* in Barra Grande and along the peninsula. There are also a few special places to note in the village of Barra Grande itself. You can get a great cup of coffee at **Café Latino** (Rua Dr. Chiquinho 9) with various blends and flavors. They also have a menu with excellent pasta dishes. For lunch or dinner, try **Tubarão** (Praia Barra Grande). They cook up lobster, crab, and seafood risotto. It's on the beach near the pier at Barra Grande. Another great place to eat is the Japanese restaurant in the **Pousada dos Tamarinhos.** They serve authentic Japanese food in a lovely environment and are open to the public.

## INFORMATION

The easiest way to get to Barra Grande is to drive or take a bus to Camamu. From Salvador, you should take the ferry to Itaparica and then catch a bus (from Bom Despacho) down to Camamu. The trip takes about two hours, not including the ferry. From Camamu, you take a boat across to Barra Grande. There are slow boats (1.5 hours) and speedboats (30 minutes) that make the trip from the main pier in Camamu. You can also come up from Itacaré by 4-wheel-drive vehicle on a one-day or multi-day excursion.

There are no international banks in Barra Grande and many of the establishments there do not accept credit cards, so make sure you get money before you leave Salvador or Itacaré. A great website for information on the Barra Grande area is www.barragrande.net.

# Itacaré

Positioned between Salvador and Southern Bahia, Itacaré is not unlike many other surfing villages in Brazil (especially Pipa, Arraia d'Ajuda, and Trindade), radiating a kind of hippie, alternative vibe. But Itacaré is not just for surfers. In fact, only two of the seven principal beaches are used for the practice of the sport. The rest offer a variety of lounging, swimming, and sunbathing activities—not to mention eating and drinking in the shade of a beach kiosk. But the alternative feel to the town extends into almost every corner, regardless of the price range. Besides an ample selection of economical eating, drinking, and sleeping holes favored by surfers and hippies, there are also a number of charming restaurants, bars, and *pousadas*. Besides performances of Capoeira and Maculelé knife dancing, you'll find yoga classes, massage therapists, and nature excursions in the tropical surroundings.

The best time to go is between October and February, with the latter half of this period being the peak season (higher prices and more crowds, but great weather and everything functioning at high velocity). The months of August and September are best for whale-watching. There are also whales in July, but the months of June and July see heavy rains and half the town closes down for the low season.

## THE VILLAGE

The main road through the village (Rua Pedro Longo) is lined on both sides with establishments catering to both the local surfers and visiting tourists. You'll see simple bakeries and *lanchonetes,* restaurants, pizza stands, coffee shops, bars, arts and crafts shops, clothing stores, tour guides, and *pousadas.* They appear one after the next from the **Praça Santos Dumont** (the main *praça* in town, also known as Praça do Cachorro) all the way down **Rua Pedro Longo** until it changes into the Caminho das Praias. You can spend quite awhile walking up and down this street, checking out the various shops. At night, this is where the action begins, and the restaurants and bars start filling up after dark. There are other interesting roads in the village, such as Rua Lodônio Almeida, which is home to the town's best and fanciest restaurants. There are also more shops and tour guides up this road and along Rua Ruy Barbosa, which crosses it and leads to the village church. This is the location of the old village center, Praia Coroinha, where many of the locals live and work.

## N PRAIA DA CONCHA

There are only a few beaches in Brazil that have the kind of large yet charming beach kiosks that you find here on Praia da Concha. Although they line the inside of the beach with almost no breaks between them, the kiosks (which they call *cabanas*) have a special, inviting atmosphere about them. This may be because each one is designed and constructed in a unique way, either out of wood or with some

tropical motif or other. Although most are two-stories tall, they generally have an open-air construction with no cement floor (just sand), which means that they don't block access to (or view of) the beach from the sandy road behind them but allow people to walk right through them onto the sand in front. These are small touches that have made a huge difference in retaining the charm of Itacaré (something more beaches in Brazil ought to do). The two best cabanas for good lunch menus are the **Cabana do Amigão** and **Ximbica.** Because of these cabanas, Praia da Concha is easily the most popular and crowded beach in Itacaré. In peak season, this one-kilometer stretch of beach can get rather packed with visitors. The ocean here is a gray-brown color and not particularly transparent or beautiful. Still, the water is warm and the sand is soft and pink. In the afternoon, you can watch the sunset over the water and catch groups performing Capoeira on the sand.

Besides the sandy road that runs behind the cabanas all along Praia da Concha, there is another road inland that parallels the beach and is full of *pousadas.* At about the middle of the beach, there is a road that goes straight back and off to the other beaches in the south. This passes the **Mar e Mel Restaurante** (one of the town's key night spots), an area with numerous new *pousadas,* and then meets up with **Caminho das Praias** (the main village road), which continues all the way to the beaches.

## RESENDE, TIRIRICA, COSTA, AND RIBEIRA BEACHES

The only way to access the many small beaches along the south coast of Itacaré is by walking south along the **Caminho das Praias.** The beaches are all separated by rocks or marshes that jet out into the ocean, forming sandy inlets between them. As such, the beaches are all quite small and separated from one another. However, these separations are not insurmountable and you can walk between the first three beaches (Resende, Tiririca, and Costa) across the rocky divisors. The first beach you'll come to is called **Resende.** Here, you'll find a wide sandy inlet with a mild surf (some beginning surfers here, but not too many) and shallow waters that are excellent for swimming. Inside the sandy beach is a grassy area that is great for setting up camp and having a picnic. On weekends and during the peak season, this beach gets pretty crowded, as it's the closest and largest beach on the south shore.

Most of the surfing gets done at **Tiririca Beach,** just south of Resende. Here, you'll find some of Itacaré's most charming beachfront *pousadas,* built up all along the steep hillside that leans over the small, sandy beach. The many wooden dwellings huddled together over the small beach make for a very cozy environment. The waves here are the best in the area and many of the *pousadas* make surfboards available to their guests. If you don't surf, you can take lessons at the surf school. There are also outdoor showers, bars, and restaurants with decks to look out at the surfers and sunbathers.

Crossing over the rocky divisor or south along the Caminho das Praias, you'll next come to **Costa,** the smallest beach on the south coast. Here, the waves are small and the water is shallow, but the lack of any kiosks or structures makes this one of the less-frequented beaches. Continue walking along the road until you reach the bank of a small stream, emptying into the ocean. On the other side is **Praia Ribeira.** You can cross the stream by walking right through it, or walk upstream to the small bridge. Here in Ribeira, you'll find a rustic beach with excellent swimming conditions, medium-sized waves, and humble kiosks to serve you cold coconut water, beer, and lunch. Note that the prices at these simple-looking beach cabanas are every bit as high (or higher) than those at Praia da Concha. Because the food here is not really worth the price, a good option at this beach is to snack on the fresh *pasteis* that are made to order. They cost about R$1.50 each.

The Caminho das Praias comes to an end at Ribeira, but there is a trail that continues through a private property that leads to the Prainha and São José Beaches.

# PRAINHA AND SÃO JOSÉ BEACHES

The magic of the southern beaches of Itacaré is the mixture of tropical forest and sandy beach. In one easy hike, you can go from a waterfall in the thick tropical brush to the salty ocean lined with palm trees blowing in the wind. You can access the southern beaches on foot as far as Praia São José. After that, the beaches are accessible only from the main highway, BA-011, that goes from Itacaré to Ileús. For that, you need to rent a car or join a packaged excursion (see *Remote Beaches* and *Excursions and Day Trips* for more details).

To reach the beaches south of Ribeira, you have to hike through private property. As a result, you have to pay an entrance fee—not to enter the beach, but to cross the property. This is probably illegal in Brazil, since one cannot restrict access to the beach. But nobody has bothered to contest it, and it serves to keep the beaches more private and cleaner. Besides, the fee is only about R$3 per person. What's annoying is that if you don't have a guide to take you through the brush, you will be hounded at the start of the trail (at Ribeira) to pay R$20 (per couple, they say) for a child to lead you through. These prices fluctuate depending on the size of your group, the age of the child, and the time of day. In other words, it's probably just an organized scam aimed at tourists and gringos. You are not obligated to take a guide across to **Prainha,** but you might want one the first time you go. After making the trip once, you can easily make your own way through the brush the second time. The hike to Prainha takes about one hour and a fair price for a guide to take you across is R$20 for an entire group. Prainha Beach has kiosks and plenty of shade umbrellas for hanging out. The surf here is strong, so this beach is frequented by surfers.

From Prainha, you can walk about 20 minutes to **Praia São José** to the south. The beach here is dominated by folks using the **Itacaré EcoResort,** an excellent place to stay if you want the very best of Itacaré. Even if you're not staying at the resort, you can pay R$40 for a day-use of their facilities, which are extensive.

## REMOTE BEACHES

Some of the best beaches in the area are far south and accessible from the main highway going toward Iléus. The best way to visit these beaches is via a guide and tour van. You can also hire a taxi to take you out there and arrange a pick-up later in the day. This way, you don't have to think about anything but enjoying the sun and surf. You can also spend a night at the Txai Resort to fully enjoy the beaches and waterfalls of the area. **Praia Jeribucaçu** is a nearly deserted beach surrounded by palm trees and situated at the mouth of the Jeribucaçu River, which has a waterfall upstream. You can walk to this beach from the highway along a trail that takes about one hour or via the waterfall trail that takes a bit longer. **Praia Havaizinho** is also accessible from the highway, where you hike about 20 minutes down to the beach. Access is restricted by private property and they charge R$5 to enter the beach, but it's worth every penny. The beach is beautiful and surrounded by trees and dense tropical forest. From this beach, you can walk about 20 minutes (to the left side of the beach and into the forest) to **Praia Engenhoca,** which is also a paradise and semi-deserted. These are both well worth visiting by car, tour group, or even taxi.

The **Itacarézinho Beach** is a long strip of sand with the **Txai Resort** nearby. You can use the resort services for a price and even take a trip out to the excellent **Tijuípe Waterfall,** which is a good place for swimming and sunning. Packaged excursions take you to the waterfall and beach here on a day trip from Itacaré.

## ENTERTAINMENT AND NIGHTLIFE

### Cafés and Café-Bars

The beach bars at Praia da Concha and Praia Tiririca serve drinks until sundown and are great places to hang out in the afternoon. There are some great bars and sidewalk cafés along Rua Pedro Longo that are open from about noon until the last person leaves in the evening. This is the place to hang out for the evening. **Casa Mineira** at the end of Rua Pedro Longo serves draft beer, sandwiches, and other snacks. There are coffee shops and bars with patios overlooking the street on Rua Lodônio Almeida, like the **Armazém de Minas Café,** which has coffee drinks, including an iced cappuccino. Looking out at the Coroinha Beach, just past the church *praça* is **Botecaré Bar** (Av. Castro Alves), which is frequented by the locals.

Note that most of the restaurants listed under *Food* are also great places to have drinks and hang out for the evening.

### Capoeira and Other Shows

You can catch an informal Capoeira demonstration in the afternoon at Praia da Concha. For a more formal demonstration, head to **Mar e Mel** (behind Praia da Concha, tel. 73/3251-2380) on Tuesday, Thursday, and Saturday nights at around 5 P.M. The Capoeira is top-notch and they also demonstrate Maculelé knife dancing. The restaurant charges a R$5 cover for the show. During peak season, the bar opens at noon, but the show starts in the evening. They also have music and dance after the Capoeira. Saturday night *forró* dancing at Mar e Mel is among the best in town.

### Music and Dance

Nights are hopping at the boardwalk of Praia Croinha. Crowds form around 10 P.M. to the live music performances lining the street. You'll find dancing all along the way. Also, on weekend nights at around 10 P.M., you'll find music and dancing at the **Cabana dos Corais** on the beach at Praia da Concha.

## SHOPPING

Most of the shops in town are dotted along the two main roads in town: Rua Pedro Longo and Rua Lodônio Almeida. You'll find great arts and crafts, swimwear, and clothing. The best tee-shirt shops are on Rua Lodônio Al-

## CAPOEIRA, SALVADOR'S DEADLY DANCE

You'll be walking along the streets of Pelourinho and there, in one of the *praças*, a group of Brazilians crowd around two people fighting—or is it dancing—in the street. It's almost hypnotic to watch. First, there's the music, clapping, and chanting—all led by the sound of the *berimbau* and a couple of simple drums—that draw you closer. Then you see the movements of the players, fast and enthralling, flourished with high kicks, gymnastic handstands, and cartwheels. At times, the two contenders are dancing together, spinning, and kicking over each other's head. At other times, each one appears to be doing his own thing, standing on his head or hands.

At its foundation, Capoeira is a martial art of attack and defense, but it contains many aspects of dance and demonstration, mostly created to hide the fact that it is indeed fight training. The practice of Capoeira was prohibited in Brazil until 1937 and anyone caught practicing the sport faced a prison sentence. So Capoeira was practiced in secret and camouflaged with music and dance movements. Behind these flourishes are movements of attack, takedowns, and dodges that form the basis of the martial art.

Capoeira is based on fighting techniques from Angola and other parts of Africa, brought into Brazil with the slaves. In the early 1900s, the sport underwent a major metamorphosis at the hands of master Manoel dos Reis Machado, known as Mestre Bimba. Bimba took the train-

ing he received from original Angola masters and transformed it into the Capoeira seen today, known as Brazilian or Regional Capoeira. He ran a physical education and cultural center in Bahia where he created techniques for teaching Capoeira and its ethical foundations. His students included doctors and lawyers from the middle class and soon Capoeira was on its way to becoming an art practiced internationally.

Like most martial arts, or arts in general, practitioners of Capoeira are very plugged into the lineage of teachers, following each school back to its original master and his relationship to Bimba or another great master. Likewise, there are dissenting opinions about techniques, and Regional Capoeira is not the only game in town. The practitioners of Capoeira Angola (also known as Traditional Capoeira) believe that their version is the purest. It's known to be more aggressive. The grandfather of Traditional Capoeira was Mestre Pastinha, who lived at the same time as Bimba.

There are numerous schools in Salvador and you can take lessons for a day, a week, or years if you like. The price is reasonable at around R$30 per lesson, but you can discuss monthly fees if you're staying around long enough. For information about schools and teachers, see www.capoeirista.com. You can also swing by the **Bimba Academy** (Rua das Laranjeiras 1, Pelourinho, tel. 71/3492-3197) to watch a demonstration every night at 6 P.M. or discuss classes.

---

meida. All along the beaches and streets of town, you won't be able to avoid the many hippies selling their handmade jewelry (it all looks the same, but some of it's interesting). One of the best shops is **Aquarela do Brasil** (Rua Lodônio Almeida 121).

## EXCURSIONS AND DAY TRIPS

Itacaré has everything you can imagine in terms of excursions and adventures. There is white-water rafting, rappelling down a rocky waterfall, hikes of all levels, off-road vehicles, canoeing, cycling, snorkeling, and scuba div-

ing. The diversity of the coastline here is amazing and you can find just about any type of beach you are looking for—from completely deserted to swinging! There are numerous tour agents in town, and you can spend a few hours comparing their excursions and prices. Here are a few top choices to get you started:

### Alternative
The **Pousada Ilha Verde** (Rua Ataide Setuba) offers various classes and groups in which you can participate while you're in Itacaré, even if you're not staying at the *pousada*. Classes include yoga, bio-gymnastics, Capoeira, samba,

## THE WATER'S FINE: SALVADOR'S COASTAL CLEAN-UP

In 1990, Salvador had the dubious distinction of being the largest city in South American without sewage treatment facilities. Rivers that were once transparent and loaded with fish had become flows of raw sewage. The Tororó Dyke that runs through the middle of the city was a central passageway for sewage emptying into the bay. In fact, there were some 100 key points for sewage to enter into the bay. Public health was seriously compromised and conditions began to take a toll on tourism. Nothing clears a coastline of tourists like polluted beaches. Over the course of 10 years and 600 million dollars, the government of Bahia managed to turn Salvador into one of the best examples of sewage treatment in the entire country. Today, there are only two points where sewage enters into the bay and most of the beaches from Bonfim to Flamengo are clean and safe for swimming once again.

The project, called Bahia Azul, engaged in a massive clean-up of the city, principally through the installation of a sewer system to which most of the coastal region could connect. Installation of the system was slow and disruptive, but the inconvenience to traffic and residents has paid off. Today, the system is almost 80-percent complete and expectations are that more than 85 percent of the homes in Salvador will be connected. Already the Tororó Dyke no longer receives sewage and is on its way to becoming clean again.

The biggest problem with the new system is convincing families in poor neighborhoods to connect. Many families can't even pay their water bills, much less incur costs to connect to a sewage system. Investing in sewage treatment is far from the concerns of these needy families. Incentive programs are helping, but connections to the system remain low in poor areas, as low as 8 percent. The incentives themselves require a great deal of explanation. In areas where the incentives were highly promoted, connections to the system rose significantly.

and drumming. They also have great areas for meditation and massage. Talk to Simon.

### Beach Trips

One great trip is a day in the southern destination of Itacarézinho. The excursion includes a stop at the **Tijuípe Waterfall** and several hours of sunbathing at the **Itacarézinho Beach.** If you don't like the idea of hiking for an hour to get to Prainha and then São José Beach, a great self-made excursion is to take a taxi out to the **Itacaré EcoResort** at São José Beach. For R$40 and the price of the taxi (about another R$30 roundtrip from the bus terminal), you can spend the entire day in great luxury and leisure. One idea is to catch a taxi out and walk back along the beach and Prainha Trail. Another trip you can take by taxi is out to **Havaizinho.** Have the taxi drop you off at the beginning of the trail and then pick you up

again at a set hour later in the day. This should cost around R$10–15 each way.

### Snorkeling and Scuba Diving

One of the best day trips from Itacaré is the 4-wheel-drive, off-road excursion to the northern peninsula of Barra Grande. The trip takes you to several bodies of water, each offering delicious snorkeling and swimming conditions in underwater reefs and pools. The tropical surroundings along the way are sometimes rugged and always breathtaking. There are a couple variations on the trip, but the basic agenda includes a visit to the **tide pools at Maraú,** a stop at the **Lagoa do Cassange** and the **tide pools at Taipus de Fora,** and **Lagoa Azul.** Some trips also include a stop at the historical village of **Barra Grande** at the top of the peninsula. You leave in the morning and return at the end of the day, happy and tired. There is a version

Salvador

of this trip that just goes out to Maraú for half a day of snorkeling and other versions that don't go all the way to the village of Barra Grande. This trip costs R$65–95 per person.

If you like the idea of exploring Barra Grande, then you can catch a small plane out there for R$50 per person, one way. Spend the night out there or return later that day.

A good guide for snorkeling and scuba diving excursions (including the Barra Grande trips) is Beto at **Beto's Cyber Site** (Rua Pedro Longo 71, tel. 73/3251-3094, www.betoicacare.com). He is a dive master and also runs a cyber café in town. He knows all about the waters in and around Itacaré, including where you can swim with the dolphins and catch the best views of the whales. Another guide for trips up to Maraú, rafting, and air transportation is Paulo at **Raiz Ecoturismo** (Rua João Pessoa, tel. 73/3251-2474, www.raizecoturismo.kit.net).

## Waterfalls, White Water, and Canoes

You can opt for a few different **canoe adventures.** The most accessible is a trip up the **Rio das Contas** to the **Cleandro Waterfall** (R$8 entry to the waterfall). Along the way, you see the marshland ecosystem of the area. This goes for around R$35 per person. There are white-water rafting trips along the Rio das Contas up around the Taboquinhas village area (about 27 kilometers from Itacaré). You go out to the village by van or jeep and raft down a short but exciting piece of the river. This goes for about R$60 per person. A great agency for the more radical excursions is **São Miguel Aventuras** (Av. Castro Alves 535, tel. 73/3251-3109, www.saomiguelaventuras.tur.br). You can also check at **EcoTrip** (tel. 73/3251-2191, www.ecotrip.tur.br).

You can rent a bike and ride around the entire village of Itacaré for about R$15 for the day. You can find bike shops on Rua Pedro Longo.

## Whale-Watching

In the winter season, you can take excursions out to the whales that hang out in the warm waters of Southern Bahia. A full-day excursion on a special speedboat costs around R$100 per person. The agency **Aquamar Itacaré** (Rua João de Souza, tel. 73/8801-0819), near Banco do Brasil, has special discounts for kids and seniors.

# ACCOMMODATIONS

There are many streets, beaches, and hilltops on which you can find hotels throughout Itacaré and each area has its own personality. If you stay on the main streets of the village, you will find some charming and low-cost *pousadas* and you will be close to everything. The downside it that you will also hear everything that goes on in the village from sunrise to sunset. This is the main reason for the cost differential. The exception is the Pousada Ilha Verde, which is on the edge of the village and rather quiet. There are numerous *pousadas* on the left (west) end of Praia da Concha and along the *condominium* (subdivision) behind the beach (inland). These are some good options for staying close to the action of the village and the beach, however, they are not beachfront accommodations and can suffer from some noise on rowdy nights. *Pousadas* in Praia Tiririca are some of the best beachfront options you'll find in Itacaré and are usually pretty quiet at night. They are often booked way in advance. Finally, there is an area that has been seeing new hotel constructions over the past couple of years and is loaded with options. This is the area between Praia da Concha and Rua Pedro Longo. This area is one of the quietest in town, but most of the *pousadas* there lack character.

## Under R$100

Down at the far end of Praia da Concha off one of the inland roads is the vary nature-oriented **Pousada da Lua** (Praia da Concha, tel. 73/3251-2209, www.pousadadalua.com.br, R$70 d low season and R$150 peak season). The place is run by the half-Scottish Sandy and his wife Claudia. Sandy speaks perfect English and has built a *pousada* in the middle of the trees near the beach. His rooms are large and the suites have a loft, kitchen facilities, TV, mosquito netting, and ceiling fan. Although it's close to Praia da Concha, you are away from the noise here.

A cute place on the main village road is the **Pousada Maresia** (Rua Pedro Longo 388, tel. 73/3251-2338, maresiapousada@bol.com.br, R$50 with ceiling fan and R$60 with air and TV). Although they get some noise at night, the rooms are spacious, clean, and economical—good if you like being right in the center of the action. Breakfast is included. Another economical option in the center of the action is the **Pousada Pituba** (Rua Pedro Longo 371, tel. 73/3251-2050, www.pousadas.itacare .com.br/pousadapituba, R$20 pp). They have simple rooms with breakfast included. Rooms have ceiling fans.

If you don't want to spring for the Pousada Sage Point, but like the idea of a charming, rustic atmosphere on Tiririca Beach, then go for the **Pousada Hanalei** (Praia da Tiririca 35, tel. 73/3251-2311, juniorsampaio@hotmail.com, R$50 studio, R$130 suite). Built on a rocky incline above the beach, the *pousada* makes use of various nooks and crannies with rooms, bathrooms, and offices. Everything is made out of wood and most rooms have ocean views. It's really quite a special place. Each room is different and they range from a single, cozy studio to a suite with loft and air-conditioning. They also have a chalet that holds up to six people. Breakfast is included and they have surfboards for rent for their guests.

The **M Pousada Sítio Ilha Verde** (Rua Atayde Setubal, tel. 73/3251-2056, ilhaverde@ uol.com.br, R$60, R$70, and R$120 s and R$80, R$90, and R$150 d low season) is a large tropical estate with an alternative feel to it. The owners, Nicole and Christof, are both French and they have put together a wonderful *pousada* with plenty of space for meditation, relaxation, swimming, and exercising. They offer several different activities, including yoga, meditation, Capoeira, and dance classes. Their swimming pool and deck are beautiful and spacious and the entire place gives off a wonderful, inviting vibe. They are located on the edge of the village about 5 minutes' walk to Rua Pedro Longo and the restaurants in a quiet part of town. Rooms are comfortable and cozy and come with ceiling fan, air, or luxury suite. Peak season rates are about 30 percent higher. This is an excellent place for a small group.

## R$100–200

The **Papa Terra Pousada** (Praia da Concha, R$100 low season and R$187 peak season) has a large area with a swimming pool, grassy outdoor seating areas, sauna, game room, and restaurant. They have 28 rooms with air, TV, phone, and veranda. They also have two *casas* that are equipped for large groups. This place is very popular with Brazilians and is always crowded.

## R$200–500

The **M Pousada Sage Point** (Praia da Tiririca 65, tel. 73/3251-2030, falacom@pousadasage-point.com.br, R$219–550 d low season) is a beachfront inn that has a wonderfully rustic feel, with heavy wooden stairways and hand railings. Each room is different and some make you feel like you're in a treehouse. Everything is first-class and luxurious in a charming, rustic way. An abundant breakfast buffet is included on their indoor-outdoor restaurant area that overlooks Praia Tiririca. This is easily the best on the beach.

The **Itacaré EcoResort** (Praia São José, tel. 73/3251-3133, www.ier.com.br, reservas@ ier.com.br, R$350 d) is one of the most luxurious places to stay in Itacaré. It is right on the São José Beach with its own lake, restaurants, bars, and swimming pools. Rooms are spacious and modern with air, TV, and phone. Accommodations include huge breakfast and dinner buffets. There are discounts for long stays.

# FOOD

## Pizza and Other International

The **Pizzaria Boca de Forno** (Rua Lodônio Almeida) is one of the most popular places in town. They have a tropical motif inside and plenty of tropical drinks that they whip up for their guests. They also have a cozy coffee shop on the side. They get fairly rowdy and crowded at night and it's a good place to meet other travelers. **Pizza a Metro** (Rua Pedro Longo) has square pizza sold by the meter. They have a great corner lot in a perfect area for people-watching. Get a seat in their outdoor patio area. The pizza is thick-crust and they have lots of different toppings. For a sophisticated dining experience, try **Casa Sapuchia** (Rua Lodônio Almeida 84). They serve French and Brazilian dishes.

## Quick and Casual

For a quick snack, you can try the *Acarajé* in the Praça do Cachorro. It's actually very fresh and well pepared and rivals the *Acarajé* in Salvador. The Bahian owner is easy to spot on the side of the *praça,* sitting at her food stand. You can also get snacks and sandwiches at the **Padaria Casa Mineira** (Rua Pedro Longo). They have pizza slices, Brazilian finger foods, and pre-made meat pies and sandwiches. You can sit outside on their deck and eat. You can find self-service lunches in the Praia Coroinha area, including **SenZala** (Av. Castro Alves), which has a huge variety of dishes.

## Regional Favorites

On the beach at Praia da Concha is **Cabana do Amigão,** one of the beach *barracas,* where you'll find the best *caldo de sururu* (fish soup) in the area and a great view of the ocean. They are open until sundown. Also, try the **Ximbica** *barraca* (Praia da Concha) for *caldo e peixe vermelha* (red fish soup), which is one of the tastier fish from the region. This is also more of a lunch and early-dinner place.

In the old village along Coroinha Praia, you'll find some more humble restaurants that serve excellent food at good prices. Look for **Dedo de Moça** (Rua Plinio Suares 26), which has regional dishes with fish, banana, and coconut. Also, try **Casarão Amarelo** (Av. Castro Alves), one of the town's landmark restaurants in the old village. They have international and regional foods, good prices, and a great view of the ocean from their deck. **Tia Dete** (Av. Castro Alves), near gas station, has Bahian food,

fried fish, and *moqueca.* This place is known to charge a special price for gringos using a different menu with higher prices on it, a relatively common practice in Brazil's tourist towns. Still, the value is pretty good here and the food is great.

One of the more popular places in town is **La In Restaurante** (Rua Lodônio Almeida 166) for Bahian food, including *moqueca de peixe* (fish stew). They have one of the most elegant and well-decorated interiors in town. Finally, **O Restaurante** (Rua Pedro Longo) is great for grilled fish with banana, one of the local dishes.

# INFORMATION AND SERVICES

There is no official tourist information office in Itacaré, but you can find information and maps at all the tour agencies along Rua Pedro Longo. You'll have no trouble finding Internet cafés all along Rua Pedro Longo. The Banco do Brazil office is on Rua João de Souza (to the left as you go up Rua Lodônio Almeida). A couple of websites for Itacaré include www.itacare.com and pousadas.itacare.com.br. You can also check out www.barragrande.net, which has a page for Itacaré in English.

# GETTING THERE

The main point of access to Itacaré is through the city of Ileús. You can rent a car in Ileús and drive up the BA-011 highway, stopping from time to time to take in the incredible view of the ocean below. There are also buses that make the trip from the Ileús bus terminal. Buses leave every hour, 6:40 A.M.–12:40 P.M. then 2:10 P.M., 3:10 P.M., 4 P.M., 4:40 P.M., 5:40 P.M., and 8:30 P.M. A taxi from Ileús to Itacaré costs around R$100.

You can get to Ileús from Salvador on a direct bus from the Salvador *rodoviaria.* This is the fastest and most comfortable way to go. The cost is around R$50. A cheaper, but more tedious route is down the coast. For this, you need to catch a bus on the Island of Itapirica. The cost is R$25.

Leaving Ileús to go south to Porto Seguro requires a long journey on a pothole-ridden highway. Buses leave from Ileús at 7:15 A.M., 2:15 P.M., 4:15 P.M., and 5:15 P.M. The price is R$24. You can take a small plane to Porto Seguro directly from Ileús. Check with local tour agencies for pricing and scheduling information.

## GETTING AROUND

Everything within the village of Itacaré, as far as the Ribeira Beach, is accessible on foot. You can rent a bicycle to get around town or to the more remote locations by the river. You can take taxis to some of the remote beaches or go with a group tour.

# Southern Bahia

The southern part of Bahia is an interesting mixture of modern and traditional influences. You'll find many of the things that the Bahian coast is famous for: Bahianas in traditional white hoop dresses serving regional foods in the *praças* of the small villages, 17th-century religious architecture from Brazil's colonial period, beautiful sandy beaches lined with palm trees, and various islands and offshore reefs in which to swim and snorkel (or scuba dive). The people here in Southern Bahia are laid-back and relaxed. The rest of Brazil pokes fun at the slow-moving Bahianos, swinging in their hammocks and waiting for the sun to pass overhead. But everybody wants a little part of it. Who wouldn't?

But Southern Bahia has a more modern side, too—particularly in the city of Porto Seguro. There, you'll find a very urban atmosphere with a festive beach experience unlike any other in the world. The main attractions are the three huge structures on the beaches of the northern coastline. The structures, called *super barracas,* are enormous two- or three-story beach bars, each with three or four outdoor stages presenting non-stop music and dance. For sure, the sand and surf in Porto Seguro is secondary to the festivities at the *super barracas.*

South of Porto Seguro, the climate changes at the villages of Arraial d'Ajuda and Trancoso.

# Must-Sees

Look for **M** to find the sights and activities you can't miss and **N** for the best dining and lodging.

**M** **Passarela de Alcool:** Every night just after sundown, the Alcohol Pass lines up with stands on one side and the permanent shops on the other. Besides incredible local arts and crafts, you can try a seafood *moqueca* and a *capeta* cocktail (page 424).

**M** *Super-Barracas:* The *super-barracas* (beach bars) host all kinds of activities, and most notably they have continuous stage shows featuring different types of music and dancing (page 427).

**M** **Praia do Espelho and Excursions to the South:** The best tide pools and underwater reefs in the area are at Praia do Espelho. Wade among the sandy tide pools, and you'll find enough sea life to keep you busy for hours (page 432).

The Barraca do Sting is a favorite spot on Arraial's Praia do Delegado.

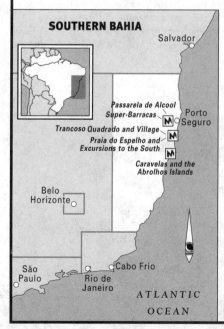

**SOUTHERN BAHIA**

Salvador

Passarela de Alcool
Super-Barracas

Trancoso Quadrado and Village

Praia do Espelho and
Excursions to the South

Porto
Seguro

Caravelas and the
Abrolhos Islands

Belo
Horizonte

São
Paulo

Cabo Frio

Rio de
Janeiro

ATLANTIC
OCEAN

**M** **Trancoso Quadrado and Village:** Most visitors drop their jaw when they reach the far end of the Quadrado, which overlooks the ocean. The view here is world-class. Below you, the Rio Trancoso glides toward the ocean with a couple of serpentine turns between sandbars and past tall palm trees (page 444).

**M** **Caravelas and the Abrolhos Islands:** Swim with sea turtles and dolphins in clear, shallow waters. Considered one of the 10 best spots in the world for scuba diving, the Abrolhos Islands are part of a protected marine park that sits about 70 kilometers off the coast of Brazil (page 451).

© CHRISTOPHER VAN BUREN

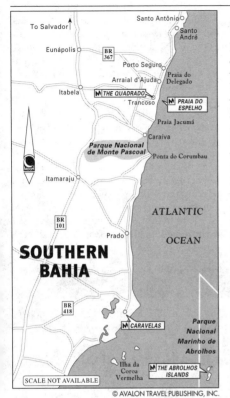

To Salvador
Santo Antônio
Santo André
Eunápolis
BR 367
Porto Seguro
Praia do Delegado
Arraial d'Ajuda
THE QUADRADO
Itabela
Trancoso
PRAIA DO ESPELHO
Praia Jacumá
Caraíva
Parque Nacional de Monte Pascoal
Ponta do Corumbau
Itamaraju
ATLANTIC
OCEAN
BR 101
Prado
SOUTHERN BAHIA
BR 418
CARAVELAS
Parque Nacional Marinho de Abrolhos
Ilha da Coroa Vermelha
THE ABROLHOS ISLANDS
SCALE NOT AVAILABLE

© AVALON TRAVEL PUBLISHING, INC.

## PLANNING YOUR TIME

First of all, try not to visit this area on the weekend. Everything here is designed for weekday visits—especially the nightlife options. The beaches along the entire southern coast fill with thousands of locals on the weekends and some become almost unbearable in terms of crowds and noisy masses of people who have no business wearing those little bathing suits anyway. Weekdays in the months just before and after the peak season (as always, mid-December through mid-February) are the best times to visit. If you happen to be in town over the weekend, use these days to take the more extended (and more expensive) excursions to the remote areas of Southern Bahia. You won't be missing anything in town. During the week is another story altogether and you'll find semi-deserted conditions just a kilometer or two away from the principal areas.

For reasons detailed in the Porto Seguro section, I suggest you spend no more than a day and a night in Porto Seguro. That's enough time to get a glimpse of the amazing *super-barracas* and hit the Passarela de Alcool in the evening. Next, move your base of operation down to Arraial d'Ajuda for the next few days. You can spend your days on the beaches of Arraial d'Ajuda or take day trips to the beaches north or south. Spend your nights in the charming village of Arraial d'Ajuda. I guarantee, you'll prefer the quaint atmosphere of Arraial d'Ajuda over that of Porto Seguro.

Here's a better idea: Don't even stay in Porto Seguro, but go directly to Arraial d'Ajuda. You can take the ferryboat over to Porto Seguro for a day, if you're curious about the *super-barracas* and night scene there. Now, instead of taking planned excursions to the outlying beaches, why not rent a car or buggy and drive down the coast to Trancoso, Jacumá, Caraíva, and even as far as Caravelas? If you have more time (and are here between July and November) arrange a diving and whale-watching excursion from Caravelas to the Abrolhos Islands—the kind that lets you stay overnight on the boat. It's something you'll never forget.

There, you find a smaller, more charming atmosphere with small roads leading past the many quaint *pousadas,* shops, and restaurants. The beaches, too, are quainter, due to their smaller and more personalized beach kiosks. Naturally, you pay a bit more for the charm and quality of options that these towns have to offer, but most international visitors prefer the village atmosphere.

Finally, in the more distant south are small fishing villages and experiences that bring you closer to the marine world. The more elaborate excursions in these areas will give you something to remember for a lifetime—tropical islands, deserted beaches, whales splashing in the ocean, and kilometers of palm trees lining the coast.

# HISTORY

Alveres Cabral was probably off course when he "discovered" the land that is now known as Brazil. But his discovery was recorded and christened The Land of Vera Cruz and claimed for the Portuguese Crown. Cabral had arrived with a fleet of 13 ships and set his foot upon Brazilian soil in the place that is known today as Porto Seguro (the Safe Port). Today, the entire south coast of Bahia is called the Discovery Coast due to the many early voyages made here. Ironically, it was Amerigo Vespucci's discovery of the Bay of All Saints up near present-day Salvador that would mark the continent with its current name, America. The Discovery Coast would play a secondary role in the drama that was to come: the colonization and exploitation of Brazil.

Villages and ports sprouted up along the coastline and sugar soon overtook wood and cocoa as the principal export to Europe. The village of Porto Seguro is home to some of the country's oldest houses, churches, and monuments. They remain standing on the plateau overlooking the ocean, a great vantage point from which to spot the English, French, and Dutch ships that might sail in to threaten Portugal's hold on the colony. Indeed, the Discovery Coast and the entire northeastern coast of Brazil was the stage of many skirmishes and all-out battles for control of the new land. Add to this the precarious relationships with the indigenous tribes (often attacking from the other side) and you have an idea of the free-for-all that was the discovery and occupation of South America. And it all happened right here in Southern Bahia.

## Porto Seguro

Visitors arriving in Porto Seguro for the first time are often surprised by what they see. It's a common misconception that Porto Seguro is a quaint, Bahian-style beach village. Porto Seguro has a very particular appeal. Specifically, it appeals to young, working-class Brazilians. It offers everything that this group desires: sun and sand, mobs of people dancing and pulsating together, and lots of food and cold beer. As famous as it is, and as appealing as the beach-blanket party atmosphere can be, most foreign visitors end up spending their time in the villages of Arraial d'Ajuda and Trancoso to the south.

Of course, that doesn't mean you should avoid the place, as there are some redeeming factors—like the excellent prices for food and accommodations, including many resort-style hotels. Another great thing about Porto Seguro is the quantity and variety of shopping you'll find there. Shops line the coastal road and in the evening when the Passarela de Alcool revs up, you'll find even more stands with local artisans selling their wares. Finally, you should not miss the historical city of Porto Seguro, which rests on the high plateau, watching over

the city and beaches below. The view alone is worth the hike up there.

## PASSARELA DE ALCOOL

It's ironic that the Passarela de Alcool, or Alcohol Pass, did not get its name because of all the alcohol that gets sold there every night. Rather, the name was given to this particular road back in the 1800s because it was the principal passage by which alcohol was carried down to the port for shipping out of the city. Today, the area is Porto Seguro's main spot for eating, drinking, shopping, and drinking some more. The Passarela is lined with shops, restaurants, and temporary stands that sell jewelry, clothing, crafts, and traditional Bahian cocktails. It has become difficult to define exactly where the official pass begins and ends; the area has spilled over onto the streets leading up to the original road and even along one or two of the side streets. After dark, the first signs of festivities are noticeable at the Praça da Paz (with the large clock sculpture in the middle) as you walk through town along Avenida 22 de Abril (with the ocean to your left). The *praça* is not

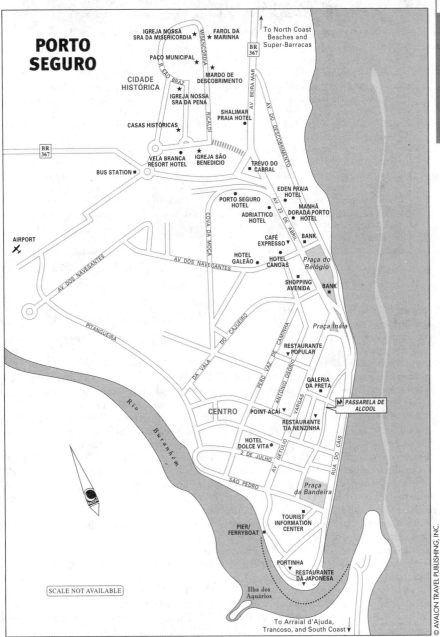

PORTO SEGURO

To North Coast Beaches and Super-Barracas

BR 367

IGREJA NOSSA SRA DA MISERICORDIA

FAROL DA MARINHA

PAÇO MUNICIPAL

MARDO DE DESCOBRIMENTO

CIDADE HISTÓRICA

IGREJA NOSSA SRA DA PENA

SHALIMAR PRAIA HOTEL

CASAS HISTÓRICAS

BR 367

VELA BRANCA RESORT HOTEL

IGREJA SÃO BENEDICIO

BUS STATION

TREVO DO CABRAL

EDEN PRAIA HOTEL

PORTO SEGURO HOTEL

MANHÃ DORADA PORTO HOTEL

ADRIATTICO HOTEL

CAFÉ EXPRESSO

BANK

AIRPORT

HOTEL GALEÃO

HOTEL CANOAS

Praça do Relógio

AV DOS NAVEGANTES

SHOPPING AVENIDA

BANK

PITANGUEIRA

Praça Inaia

RESTAURANTE POPULAR

GALERIA DA PRETA

PASSARELA DE ALCOOL

CENTRO

POINT AÇAI

RESTAURANTE TIA NENZINHA

HOTEL DOLCE VITA

2 DE JULHO

SÃO PEDRO

Praça da Bandeira

Rio Buranhém

TOURIST INFORMATION CENTER

PIER/ FERRYBOAT

PORTINHA

RESTAURANTE DA JAPONESA

Ilha dos Aquários

SCALE NOT AVAILABLE

To Arraial d'Ajuda, Trancoso, and South Coast

© AVALON TRAVEL PUBLISHING, INC.

# PORTO SEGURO, LAND OF THE VACATION PACKAGE

Brazilians love doing things in large groups; so when it comes time to plan a vacation, more than a few seek out agencies that offer pre-packaged trips that include transportation, accommodations, food, parties, and everything else that might be needed. Among the most frequented group-vacation spots throughout the 1980s and 1990s was Porto Seguro. In fact, so many Brazilians chose Porto Seguro for their group vacations that the large travel agencies from São Paulo, Rio, and Belo Horizonte began investing in the place, purchasing or building hotels by the dozens to offer to their clients. Today, a majority of the hotels along the principal beaches of Porto Seguro are owned and operated by travel agencies and are occupied principally by Brazilian *pacoteiros* (package users). The hotels cater so much to their package clients that you might even feel a bit slighted if you stay there as an autonomous guest. Everybody at the hotel seems to know one another and they head out to the beaches and nightclubs together. So much of Porto Seguro is made for these clients, who frequent the place only during peak vacation months, that there is almost a disincentive to arrive alone and out of season. Thankfully, we visitors have Arraial d'Ajuda and Trancoso to the south to offset the situation in Porto Seguro.

the official start of the Passarela, but there are several restaurant/bars there with outdoor seating and live music to deter you for awhile. Keep walking, passing the intersection of Avenida 22 de Abril and Avenida Getúlio Vargas, where you'll see a large sculpture of a mermaid in the small Praça Ináia. (The sculpture may also represent the Candomblé deity, Iemanjá, a sort of goddess of the sea.) Keep walking straight and you'll come to Avenida Portugal, which is, officially, the Passarela de Alcool.

The Passarela warms up every night at around 5 P.M. and goes until about 11 P.M. It's not a late-night party zone. Rather, it's where the crowd *begins* the evening's activities. There is a small amusement park with a Ferris wheel around halfway down the Passarela, and just prior to the park, there is a strip of restaurants with outdoor seating where you can eat and watch the mob. Here you'll find the famous *barraca* (tent) **Help,** which was one of the first on the Passarela and still the best place to get drinks, especially the traditional **Capeta.** At the far end (the calm end, relatively speaking), you walk into an area lined with 17th-century cottages that are now restaurants, artist ateliers, and boutique shops. This is called the **Praça da Bandeira.** There are places to sit and relax for

awhile in this area—before you make your way back up the Passarela for the second round.

## BEACHES AND BARRACAS

Up the northern coast of Porto Seguro, the beaches stretch on for kilometers. There is little difference among the beaches along this 10-kilometer stretch. They all have fairly wide strips of fine sand with medium-sized waves and semi-blue, semi-clear water (depending on the season). If you're looking for charming tropical beaches with white sand and coconut trees blowing in the gentle breeze, this is not the place to come. Rather, what makes these beaches popular are the many *barracas* (beach bars) dotted along the coastline. Three of these *barracas* have grown up to become *super-barracas,* multi-level centers of activity at three principal beaches along the northern coastline. Between these *super-barracas* are several mere mortal beach bars with lunch menus, cold drinks, tables, chairs, and beach service.

### Praia do Curuípe and Itacimirim

A day at these beaches might not seem all that different from a day on any other beach on the Brazilian coastline. Here, the scene moves along a bit slower than at the *super-barracas* and the beach kiosks are of a normal size, offering shade under the palm trees, cold drinks, and decent lunch plates. The beaches here are great for swimming, with small waves and warm water. Some of the beach bars available here include Mayumi, Ponto das Tartarugas, and João de Sunga (the largest is across from the Hotel Solar do Imperador). These are good beaches to retreat to, if you need a break from the *super-barracas* to the north.

## Super-Barracas

The *super-barracas* host all kinds of activities: Most notably, they have continuous stage shows (from morning to sundown), featuring different types of music and dancing. The have several environments for drinking and eating, including service on the sandy beach where there are plenty of lounge chairs and shade umbrellas. The activities spill out onto the beach and even to the ocean where you can usually partake of water sports, like kite surfing and banana-boat rides. It's non-stop high energy and it's all sponsored by the *super-barraca*. There are three *super-barracas* on the north coast: **Tóa Tóa** is the first one, located at Praia Mundaí about six kilometers from town. **Axé Moi** is next, located at Praia Taperapuã about seven kilometers from town. The farthest is **Barramares** at Praia Barramares, about 10 kilometers away. It's difficult to say which is better or worse since they all have about the same kind of activities and attract the same type of large crowds during the day—mostly young, adolescent Brazilians and a few scattered international tourists. The question is not which *barraca* is best, but whether or not you like the *super-barraca* scene at all. To best answer this question, its worth visiting one of these mega–beach bars during the day. If you don't like the energy there, you can probably find a smaller, cozier beach bar nearby, or (if you have a car or don't mind paying for a taxi) continue north to the more charming beaches near Santa Cruz de Cabrália and Santo Antônio.

On weeknights, the *barracas* have a rotating schedule to produce super-luau beach parties.

Each of the three *super-barracas* has a different night and they never overlap. They even coordinate nights with other clubs in town. The night scene is a mega-version of the day scene. They generally break out the main stage for the *axé* dancing groups and get ready for crowds that number into the thousands during peak season. To keep the ugly masses out, there is a cover charge to enter the luau (around R$25, but women usually get a heavy discount). The *barracas* encourage you to purchase your tickets through a tour guide or at your hotel. This is partially to respect the vacation-packaging system of Porto Seguro.

## CIDADE HISTÓRICA

Amidst all the wild beach parties, rowdy nightclubs, and the Passarela de Alcool, there is a calm and quiet historic town center sitting peacefully at the top of the plateau overlooking all of Porto Seguro. This is the original location of the village of Porto Seguro, the oldest city in Brazil. The view from the Cidade Histórica (also called the Cidade Alta) leaves no doubt in your mind why the spot was chosen. And the area is perfectly preserved, looking pretty much like it did in the early 1500s. Many of the small, historic dwellings are still inhabited by traditional families of Porto Seguro; others have been turned into shops, selling tee shirts and crafts, all made locally.

Like many port towns, including Salvador, Porto Seguro consisted of both a Cidade Alta (High City) and a Cidade Baixa (Low City). Here, the Cidade Baixa was where the port and the shipping activities took place. At that time, the primary goods were Pau Brazil (a coveted dark red hardwood used in Europe for furniture and die), sugar, and cocoa. At first, the Aimores people were friendly and helpful to the Portuguese colonists and even helped them secure the coast around Porto Seguro. Later, they learned that the colonists did not necessarily have their best interests at heart and the Aimores turned somewhat hostile toward the Portuguese and other visitors. Today, you can see some Aimores hanging around the historic

© CHRISTOPHER VAN BUREN

the picturesque houses of the Cidade Histórica

city, selling traditional indigenous clothing, jewelry, and trinkets.

You can walk around the Cidade Alta in an hour or so. It's small and simple. A highlight in the old city is the large rubber tree that sits in a large grassy area at one end of the town. All along this grassy area sit old, historic buildings in pristine condition. Another highlight is on the opposite end of town, where you can sit and look out over the ocean from the high plateau near the lighthouse. At the end of town, near the lighthouse, are some simple shops and stands where locals sell pure cocoa powder (ask for it without sugar if you want the pure stuff), cocoa beans, and other natural herbs. There is a small square in the middle of town that is lined by old buildings now converted into shops. Inside the square, you can sit in the shade. There is also a main church and a museum inside the old jailhouse.

Walking to the Cidade Histórica from the lower city is not difficult. The best way is to climb the long stairway across from the Trevo do Cabral (the *praça* with the statue of the pointing man). The stairway is pretty run-down, but it's perfectly safe during the day. You can also take a taxi around to the back side. The old city is near the *rodoviaria* and there are buses that go there all day and night. You can pick them up on Avenida 22 de Abril.

## ILHA DOS AQUÁRIOS

The tiny island of Pacuio (also known as Ilha do Pirata, but most commonly called Ilha dos Aquários) sits on the far side of Rio Buranhém, almost directly across from the ferryboat that heads over to Arraial d'Ajuda. The island is most famous for its parties on Friday nights that spin up several types of music, from techno to Brazilian *axé*. The party takes place around the island's principal attractions, the 220,000-liter salt-water aquarium and two other, smaller aquariums that are home to various types of fish, sharks, lobsters, and other marine animals. You can head over to the island on the Cia do Mar schooners that are docked near the ferryboat. For more details, check with **Cia do Mar** (Praça dos Pataxós 15, tel. 73/3288-2107).

# CACAO: BRAZIL'S ORIGINAL GOLD DUST

Chocolate, or more specifically the cacao fruit, first appears on our radar in Egypt in the 16th century B.C. Little is known of its use in Egyptian culture, but the first known cultivation of the fruit was by the Aztec culture of around 600 A.D. The Aztecs and Mayans believed that their ancestors brought the cacao seeds from paradise, where the god Quetzcoalt presented the fruit as a gift. This fruit bestowed wisdom and power upon all who ate it or, in most cases, drank it.

In Southern Bahia, cacao (or *cacau*, as it's spelled in Portuguese) created something of a revolution in the area. Although sugar was the region's principal cash crop, cacao played an important part in exports to Europe. In the years before Spain managed to steal a number of seedlings in an act of bio-piracy, the fine powder came mostly from South America, with Southern Bahia being among the main producers. Cacao is not easy to cultivate. Trees are sensitive to weather and temperature and prefer to be surrounded by other trees. The cacao industry in Southern Bahia was consistently riddled with problems and hardships. Nevertheless, the European market for cacao powder increased throughout the 18th and 19th centuries, although it was still used principally by the rich. It wasn't until the 20th century that chocolate was mass-produced and industrialized. By then, Spain had created and lost its vast monopoly of cacao production, which it had established in Africa and Malaysia. Today, most of the cacao produced in the world comes from these same African nations, although it is believed that the plant originated in the Amazon region.

## SANTO ANTÔNIO AND THE EXTREME NORTH

Way past the popular beaches of Porto Seguro to the north are two areas known as Santo Antônio and Santo André. Together, these two areas provide a completely different experience of the southern coast of Bahia. First, there are wonderful beaches with excellent conditions for swimming and simple but inviting kiosks. In particular, the **Praia do Santo André, Praia das Tartarugas,** and **Praia Santo Antônio** are excellent choices. The atmosphere here is more relaxed and laid-back than the party-till-you-puke energy of Porto Seguro. The food is excellent and the beers are ice-cold. The area surrounding the beaches is green and full of coconut trees. A major highlight of the area is the sandy island of **Coroa Alta,** which brings boatloads of people from Porto Seguro every day. You can swim and snorkel in the shallow waters of the island. In the Cabrália area just a short distance to the south, you'll find a long coastline of sandy beaches, some of them nearly deserted and others with just a small kiosk or two. Check out the **Praia dos Lençóis** for a good example. Here, you'll also find the **Fazenda Mãe Tereza,** a private sanctuary that opens its gates to the public. Inside you can hike around the *fazenda* with or without a guide pointing out the flora and fauna of the area. You can also take a canoe trip up the river to a fresh-water swimming hole, check out the various crab habitats, or learn about the harvesting and processing of palm oil, a principal ingredient in Bahian cuisine. Your entrance fee of R$30 includes lunch at the *fazenda*.

A final option in the extreme north of Porto Seguro is a trip out to the **Jaqueira Reservation.** Here, the indigenous groups have created their own attraction for visitors, offering a look into their culture and native lands. The first 30 minutes of your visit will be a presentation by the indigenous guides (Portuguese only). Afterward, you will hike along trails into the reservation, where you'll see one of their rituals and get the opportunity to taste some of their cuisine. Be aware that this experience is very produced and does not exactly look like a visit to an authentic indigenous village. Still, it does provide a look at the culture from one point of view.

Southern Bahia

## RECIFE DE FORA MARINE PARK

One of Brazil's official marine parks, Recife de Fora is a great place to check out marine life with a mask and snorkel. The park encompasses 17.5-square kilometers of reefs and underwater rock formations that are home to various species of marine life. The water is 1–6 meters deep and very clear. You'll see various types of fish, crustaceans, coral (18 different types), squid, octopus, and sea turtles. The diversity and visibility are both excellent and the area can be appreciated by both skin divers and scuba divers—although the most common activity in the area is snorkeling. Most trips out to the park leave at low tide to take advantage of the better visibility and you're advised to bring tennis shoes or diving booties in case you have to step on the rocky reefs (which you should avoid doing anyway, but it happens).

## ENTERTAINMENT AND NIGHTLIFE

There is almost nothing but nightlife in Porto Seguro and it's wild and well organized. Each night of the week belongs to a different club or *super-barraca*. The party just moves from one to the next during the week. The Passarela do Alcool goes all week long (including weekends), but it ends at around 11 P.M. so as not to interfere with the club schedule. It's almost too well organized. And the offerings are all pretty much the same: *axé* music and dance, some techno, and some *forró*. It's made to appeal to young Brazilians visiting Porto Seguro on a packaged trip, and not to visiting foreigners. If you're young and single, you might be able to wedge yourself into the scene with some broken Portuguese. Otherwise, the scheduled Porto Seguro night scene will probably not serve your cup of tea.

Happily, there are a few clubs in town that are not part of the main Porto Seguro itinerary and are open at different times during the week—providing some alternatives to the main schedule of events. One is called **Porto Night** (Av. dos Navegantes 613, tel. 73/3268-2828,

## NIGHTLIFE IN PORTO SEGURO

Nightlife is serious business in Porto Seguro. Each night a well-produced *festa* appears in one of the main party spots in town. There are six principal locations for music and dance; they all have about the same mixture of elements. Here is a quick reference to the Porto Seguro night scene. See also: www.portonight.com.br.

**Monday:** The Alcatraz club hosts Monday nights with the usual collection of Bahian music and stage dancing, *forró*, and techno.
**Tuesday:** The Transilvania club has several environments for dancing, including techno, *forró*, and *axé* group dancing. Characters dressed in vampire suits roam the party and other diversions await.
**Wednesday:** The *super-barraca* Barramares has their luau at night. You'll find the usual stage and group dancing, plus smaller stages with guitar music, *forró* dancing, folkloric demonstrations, and fireworks.
**Thursday:** This is the night of the Tóa Tóa luau at Praia Mundaí. There, you'll find group dancing with Bahian *axé* music, Capoeira demonstrations, and lots of eating and drinking.
**Friday:** Head over to Ilha dos Aquários for a mixture of *axé* music, techno, and traditional guitar music. You can check out the aquariums when you're not dancing.
**Saturday:** The American Bar at the edge of town has a typical bar and live music scene (for a change). They have a large-screen TV and a variety of dance music.
**Sunday:** Nothing happens on Sunday. This is a good time to head south to Arraial d'Ajuda.

www.portonight.com.br, 9 A.M.–6 P.M. Mon.–Sat.) and another is **Cia do Mar** (Praça dos Pataxós 15, tel. 73/3288-2107, 9 A.M.–8 P.M. Mon.–Fri.). There are also bars that stay open late in the Praça da Bandeira area.

## SHOPPING

Shopping takes place all over town and especially in the shops that line Avenida 22 de Abril and the Passarela do Alcool, all the way to the tip of the city where the ferryboat docks. The Passarela do Alcool is especially active after dark, when locals set up stands to sell clothing and arts and crafts on the street. There is an arts and crafts market inside the tourist information office at the far end of the Passarela do Alcool (and past the Praça da Bandeira). You'll find the atelier of Bahian artist Menelaw Sete directly across the street from the Praça da Bandeira. Sete is recognized nationally for his cubist works—in the tradition of Picasso. There is an interesting art gallery, featuring many Bahian artists, called **Galeria da Preta** (Av. Portugal 148, tel. 73/3268-2375, 10 A.M.–midnight daily). They are open daily until around midnight and are located at the beginning of the Passarela. The best deals on tee shirts can be found in the Cidade Histórica (although there are some very cool tee-shirt designs in the shops around the Praça da Bandeira) and the best shopping mall in town is **Shopping Avenida** (Av. 22 de Abril), which has coffee shops, boutique stores, ice cream shops, and a good Italian restaurant upstairs. You can find Cuban and other international cigars and smokes at the **Officina Café e Tabacaria** inside the Shopping Avenida mall.

# ACTIVITIES AND EXCURSIONS

Trips up and down the coast leave from the various piers at the southern tip of Porto Seguro. Here you'll find excursions that visit all of the popular outlying areas, from Santo Antônio in the north to Caraíva and even the distant Caravelas in the south. There are tour agencies all over town, including several right around the pier area, that can arrange tickets and passage for you. A few possibilities are **Cia do Mar** (Praça dos Pataxós 15, tel. 73/3288-2107) which has schooners or small speedboats. **Passeios** (Av. 22 de Abril 286, tel. 73/3288-5898) has a variety of trips both by van and boat (not their own boats). Prices given in this section are mostly based on this company's price list. You can try **Yes Tours** (Rua Rui Barbosa 15, tel. 73/3288-3363,

www.yestours.tur.br), located at the southern tip of the city near the boats. They offer every tour you can imagine, but their prices are a bit higher than the others. Finally, the group **Luanda** (Av. 22 de Abril 172, tel. 73/3268-3723) has boat excursions to all the major locations, plus an extended trip to Abrolhos.

## Excursions to the North

A day trip to **Santo Antônio** drops you off at the extensive beach, where you can spend the day kicking back at the beach kiosks and swimming in the ocean. For only R$20 per person (lunch not included), it's a great way to see this northern beach and the town of Santo Antônio. An alternative version of this trip is made by boat, 45 minutes up the coast to **Coroa Alta** for a swim. Here the water is shallow due to a huge sandbar in the ocean. You also get a chance to sit at the beach cabanas on Praia de Santo André and have lunch, plus stop at the small island Ilha Paraíso to look at the local culture, crafts, and foods. This trip is around R$25 not including lunch. It lasts pretty much all day. For one of the best snorkeling excursions in the region, you'll want to take the trip to **Recife de Fora,** a large area of tide pools and underwater reefs that presents a huge diversity of fish and sea life. Trips from Porto Seguro by schooner cost about R$25 per person, not including equipment. The trip lasts about five hours. There are also trips that drive up the coast and then embark on a boat out to the reefs. This version costs about R$20 per person and lasts only four hours. Time of day varies on these trips depending on the tide (low tide is required).

You can also take excursions up to the **Parque Ecológico do Santuário** and the **Fazenda Mãe Tereza,** where you can hike along trails and enjoy great boat trips along the river. The *fazenda* charges around R$30 per person to spend the day and a packaged tour with transportation will cost around R$60.

Finally, you can visit the indigenous groups in the **Jaqueira Reservation** in a van with a tour guide for about R$25. The trip lasts about three hours. Snacks at the reservation are extra.

### ⊠ Praia do Espelho and Excursions to the South

Day trips from Porto Seguro go by van to **Arraial d'Ajuda** and/or **Trancoso** just 20 minutes to the south. These trips are designed for folks staying in Porto Seguro on vacation packages, since, by far, the preferred method for visiting these two locations is to stay a couple of nights in Arraial and rent a car or buggy and drive to Trancoso for a day. On this packaged excursion, you visit the old, historic centers of both Trancoso and Arraial, with enough time to walk the beaches of Trancoso. It costs about R$20 per person. Lunch in Trancoso is extra. A more interesting excursion is the visit to **Praia do Espelho** and **Curuípe**. Some versions of this trip pay a visit to the town of **Caraíva** as well. The beach at Praia do Espelho is one of the prettiest in the area and some say in all of Brazil. It is lined by shady trees and the water is clear and blue with offshore reefs that make for great snorkeling and diving. During low tide, you can walk right from the beach to the reefs. There are palm trees and sandy cliffs all around. This is a beach you might want to visit more than once. The price of this excursion is about R$35 per person and there are versions that go by van or by boat. Snorkeling equipment is not included but available for an extra R$5–10.

You can take a long trip out to the **Abrolhos Islands** from Porto Seguro. You should plan well ahead for this as it takes a couple of days and requires some equipment. The trip usually has a tour and overnight stay in Caraíva, then heads out to the islands early the following morning. There are tourist versions and scuba diver versions of this trip. Of course, the diver versions are a bit more intense and should be booked through one of the dive schools in Porto Seguro or Arraial d'Ajuda.

### Local Trips

Several agencies offer city tours that take you up to the historical village for a look at the monuments and indigenous arts and crafts. The trip usually continues up the coast to give you a quick look at the principal beaches of the area, all the way to **Coroa Vermelha,** where Cabral and his crew had their first mass on the newly discovered continent. The trip takes half a day and costs around R$30. Another local tour is a trip out to the **Ilha dos Aquários,** also known as Ilha do Pirata. Most of these are not guided, since you can usually just show up at the pier and head on over to the island to look at the fish.

## ACCOMMODATIONS

Most of the hotels in the city of Porto Seguro are in the northern end of town, starting at Avenida dos Navegantes and following Avenida 22 de Abril. Some of these are economical and others are mid-range. Most of the upper-end hotels are up around the beaches, including some large, resort-style offerings, except for the Vela Branca Resort, which is in the old village area. Porto Seguro works primarily via vacation packages and many hotels are owned by travel agencies. The agencies create packages that include special hotel rates. The agency you use determines the hotel you get. Still, a stray foreigner or two can show up and get a room for a decent rate in low season. Rates listed here are all for low season. Count on them doubling during the peak months of December–February.

### Under R$75

The **Porto Seguro Hostel** (Rua Cova da Moça 720, tel. 73/3288-1742, www.portosegurohostel.com.br, R$20 pp) offers group rooms with air, 24-hour reception, food station, pool, and laundry room. They accept credit cards, and breakfast is included. **Eden Praia Hotel** (Av. 22 de Abril 45, tel. 73/28-1367, www.edenhotel.com.br, R$60) is a beachfront hotel on the north end of town near the Trevo do Cabral (next to the American Bar). They have a great location and a relatively cozy atmosphere. Despite being on the ocean, they don't offer much in the way of ocean views. Still, they have super-clean rooms and a pool. Breakfast is included. Next door is the **Manhã Dorada Porto Hotel** (Av. 22 de Abril 133, tel. 73/3288-2171, www.manhadourada@bol.com.br, R$30 s and R$50 d), which offers similar conditions with perhaps a slightly more cozy look and feel, but slightly less efficient management.

One of the best values in this price range is the  **Hotel Canoas** (Av. dos Navegantes, tel. 73/3288-2122, www.portohoteis.cjb.com, hotelgaleao@bol.com.br, R$40 s and R$50 d). They have a quaint lobby as well as a breakfast area, pool, and simple rooms. The same group has a second hotel on the same street called Hotel Galeão, which is also fairly quaint and costs the same. Finally, toward the Passarela de Alcool is the very charming and economical **Hotel Dolce Vita** (Rua Itagibá 67, tel. 73/3268-4443, www.hoteldolcevita.com.br, R$30 s and R$40 d, R$60 d in peak season). They have a garden-manor style with 24-hour reception area, pool, outdoor barbecue area (in case you're inclined), and small but cozy rooms with air, TV, and safe. Breakfast is included. Go to the Ferris Wheel, turn right, and walk two blocks.

## R$75–150

The **Adriattico Hotel** (Av. 22 de Abril 1075, tel. 73/3288-1188, contato@adriaticohotel.com.br, R$80 d) is right on the main road in town with a charming breakfast loft that overlooks the street.

The hotel facilities include a pool, game and TV room, sauna, and transportation to Taperapuan Beach. Rooms are clean and relatively modern (gas-heated shower), with air and TV. There's also the **Taperapuan Praia Hotel** (Av. Beira Mar 5299, tel. 73/3679-2449, www.tme.com.br/taperapuan, tph@tme.com.br, R$100 d), at the Taperapuan Beach.

## Over R$150

The **Shalimar Praia Hotel** (Av. Beira Mar 1, tel. 73/3288-7000, tel. 73/3288-2001, www.shalimar.com.br, R$165) has an excellent location at the beginning of the Av. Beira Mar as it goes up the coast. They have 120 rooms with air, TV, and phone. Some rooms have ocean views. Plus, they have a bar, restaurant, pool, and game room. The deluxe, over-the-top resort hotel of Porto Seguro is **Sued's Plaza** (Av. Beira Mar 6931, tel. 73/3288-7900, reservas@suedsplaza.com.br, R$185–225), which is located at Taperapuan Beach. It's huge, with a recreation area, pools, restaurant, bar, beach service, and gym. Rooms are simple but clean and fairly modern, with air, TV, and phone. The best

view from the Vela Branca Resort Hotel

of the luxury hotels is **Vela Branca Resort Hotel** (Rua Doutor Antônio Ricaldi 177, Cidade Histórica, tel. 73/3288-2318, www.velabranca.com.br, R$195 s and R$235 d), which has a five-star pool and patio area, gym, restaurant and buffet, tennis courts, and playground for children. Rooms are comfortable and fairly modern, with air, cable TV, and phone. Their double rooms have lofts for holding up to two more people. They offer a *meia pensão,* which includes breakfast and dinner for about R$18 per person extra—an incredible deal if you plan to be around for dinner. Their breakfast buffet (included) is outrageously good.

## FOOD
### Coffee and Sweets
A good place to sit at the bar and have an espresso with something sweet is **Café Espresso** (Av. 22 de Abril 1077, 8 A.M.–6 P.M. Mon.–Sat.). They also serve cold drinks and sandwiches. The best ice cream store in town is on the second level of Shopping Avenida, at the front of the building. It has a view of the street below. You'll find all kinds of regional desserts for sale at night along the Passarela do Alcool. There are puddings, pies, and cakes

that might suit the foreign palette, along with coconut and peanuts mixed with **rapadura** (pure cane sugar). You might even be able to find some pure cane sugar for sale in blocks. Also keep an eye out for *caldo de cana,* which is pure sugarcane juice, squeezed right in front of you. Most of the simple *lanchonetes* make it.

### International
At the point of the city, practically in the very farthest end, is the **Restaurante da Japonesa** (Rua Saldanha Marinho 38, tel. 73/3288-2592, 6 P.M.–midnight daily). They have traditional Japanese dishes and sushi for around R$35 per person.

### Quick and Casual
For a healthy self-service lunch and fresh juices, try **Point Açaí** (Rua General Freitas 42, tel. 73/3288-0202, 8 A.M.–11 P.M. Mon.–Sat., R$7). Their specialty is frozen *açaí* juice, which is a nutritious and fruity drink containing protein, fiber, calcium, magnesium, iron, and vitamins C and E. They also serve the delicious *cupuaçú* juice, which is a regional fruit that is often used for juice and ice cream. They mix these drinks with pure *guaraná* syrup, which is what gives them that special energy kick! Noon–4 P.M. they have a self-service lunch buffet with many healthy dishes. The best

## THE CAPETA: A JOLT OF ENERGY AND SOMETHING MORE

If you go out at night in Southern Bahia, you're likely to encounter the region's most popular and traditional cocktail, the Capeta. The two key ingredients in the Capeta, pure cocoa powder and *guaraná,* are powerful stimulants. Considering that Porto Seguro's nightlife just gets started at around 1 A.M., it's no wonder that the Capeta is a favorite among the local cocktails. Besides being stimulants, the Capeta's ingredients are considered to be aphrodisiacs and have been used for centuries by the native groups of the Amazon region as such. The most authentic Capetas can be found along the **Passarela do Alcool** in Porto Seguro, but the **Cactus Club**

in Arraial d'Ajuda makes a wicked version, too. The secret recipe goes something like this:

1 teaspoon of unsweetened cocoa powder
¼ teaspoon of powdered *guaraná* or 2 tablespoons of *guaraná* syrup
1 cup of vodka
¼ cup of condensed milk
3 cups of crushed ice

Mix all ingredients together in a blender for 30 seconds. Drink immediately. Serves two. Note: You can find *guaraná* syrup at **Point Açaí** (Rua General Freitas 42, Porto Seguro).

place in town for a cheap and delicious self-service lunch is the **Restaurante Popular** (Rua Manoel Cancela 22, Praça da Forum, tel. 73/3268-0236, lunch daily). They have traditional fish, beef, and chicken dishes with rice, beans, salad, and other accompaniments for R$5 per person, all-you-can-eat.

### Regional Food

**Portinha** (Rua Saldanha Marinho 32, tel. 73/3288-2743, noon–10:30 P.M. daily) is at the far tip of the city near the ferryboat. They have one of the best self-service buffets in the city with fish, beef, and chicken dishes, salads, and pasta plates. They also have an ample dessert table. All for about R$20 per person. The best place along the Passarela do Alcool is the well-known **Ñ Restaurante Tia Nenzinha** (Av. Portugal 170, tel. 73/3288-1846, noon–midnight daily). They have traditional meat and seafood dishes, including fish or seafood *moqueca* (fish stew), *vatapá,* and shrimp pie. They also serve lobster and fresh fish plates. Meals are approximately R$40 per person.

## INFORMATION AND SERVICES

The main tourist information center is in the southern tip of town just past the Praça da Bandeira. They have all sorts of pamphlets and information. There are several Internet cafés in town. The **Internet Point** (Av. dos Navegantes 90, tel. 73/3268-4191, call for hours) has high-speed connections and phone booths for private calls. There are a couple more along the north end of Avenida 22 de Abril. The

Banco do Brasil is located at Avenida 22 de Abril and Avenida dos Navegantes on the ocean side. They have international ATMs. There are other ATMs near the Praça da Paz.

## GETTING THERE

Porto Seguro is 705 kilometers from Salvador. It has a fairly well-equipped airport that receives flights from all over the country. Most flights into town are with Nordeste (tel. 73/3288-3131), but you can also get here on TAM (tel. 73/3288-4926) and Vasp (tel. 73/3288-1205). Arriving by bus from Salvador, you can take the Aguia Branca line (tel. 71/4004-1010), which leaves from the main bus terminal several times a day.

## GETTING AROUND

You can easily walk around the lower city of Porto Seguro on foot—from the Trevo do Cabral to the ferryboat that goes across to Arraial d'Ajuda. You'll need a taxi, bus, or tour van to take you to the beaches along the north coast. There are buses that go up and down the coast all day until early evening. You can catch these across from the Shalimar Hotel. You might want to take a bus or taxi to and from the *rodoviaria.* Although it is within walking distance, the heat and uphill climb make it a bit uncomfortable during the day and it's probably not a good idea to walk there at night. Likewise, the stairway that goes up to the Cidade Histórica is OK during the day, but should be avoided at night.

# Arraial d'Ajuda

Most travelers who come to the south of Bahia remember Arraial d'Ajuda as their favorite place on the coast. It has a kind of rustic charm to it that seduces just about everyone who comes here. It's difficult to say whether the highlight is the village itself or the beaches. Thankfully, you don't have to choose between them. You can spend your days on the many different beaches of the area and your nights enjoying the pleasures of the village. Highlights on the beach include the fabulous beach kiosks at Mucugé Beach and the stroll you can take from Mucugé to Pitinga to the south. Likewise, a stroll along the northern beaches takes you past some great kiosks, beach bars, and swimming areas that will probably delay you for awhile. In town, you'll see one of the oldest villages in the country, in pristine condition. You'll find local handcrafts and taste the regional cuisine at restaurants of all kinds. The new part of the village has some of the most quaint and cozy restaurants and hotels in Bahia. Nights are magical here.

If you make Arraial d'Ajuda your base of operation while in Southern Bahia, you'll be able to schedule excursions from here or take the 30-minute trip up to Porto Seguro to work with an agent there. One of the best scuba diving schools is right here in Arraial and you can rent dune buggies here for trips down to Trancoso and the distant south. Hotels in the village come in a variety of sizes, styles, and prices and you'll certainly find something in your budget.

Arraial became a popular beach village over the last 10–15 years. Before that, it was frequented mostly by hippies, surfers, and Argentineans. There is still a very hippie feel to the place, mixed with a lot of international influences, too. One of the interesting influences is the world music that you'll hear all over the village and on the beaches. Another is the incredible variety of restaurants.

## OLD VILLAGE/NEW VILLAGE

Arraial d'Ajuda means Settlement of Help, and the original village center is, indeed, a kind of small settlement on top of the bluff overlooking the beautiful ocean. (As a side note, the village was not named because of its helpful nature, but was in honor of one of the principal ships, *Ajuda,* that landed here in the discovery). There really wasn't much to it, just a few small houses and a village square. But as time and tourism moved on, the village extended in the direction of the beach. Now the old part and the new part form a kind of L-shape where the old village leads up to and along the top of the plateau and the new village goes back down toward the beaches on the other side. Both parts are full of restaurants and shops, but the old village houses these shops in small, historical buildings while the new village has modern, well-decorated structures made to be charming and attract customers. The restaurants and shops in the old village are, naturally, cheaper than those in the new village. For sure, you'll want to spend some time walking around both.

As you enter the town of Arraial d'Ajuda, you'll most likely enter through the old village. The main road up onto the bluff passes under the old **Igreja Nossa Sra. d'Ajuda** (Our Lady of Help Church) past the **Banho da Santa.** The Banho is really just an outdoor shower/bath that is used by hippies and poor villagers. However, legend has it that anyone who bathes there will return to Arraial d'Ajuda.

When you finally make it up into the village, you'll arrive in the old town square, **Praça Brigadeiro E. Gomes,** which is a grassy area with shade trees and a relaxed atmosphere. One side of the *praça* is the main bus stop in town, so if you arrive by bus, you'll likely get off right there. Bordering the *praça* are numerous colonial buildings, the 16th-century type—small, boxy houses with a window and door in front, colorfully painted, and facing the *praça.* Although most of these have been converted into simple boutique shops, you can still see residents of the town sitting at their windowsills, staring onto the *praça*. On the far end of the *praça* is the Nossa Sra. d'Ajuda Church, which is open for visitation from 8 A.M.–5 P.M. daily, closed for lunch. More impressive than the church is the view from behind the church. From there, you can see the entire northern coastline of Arraial. If you turn right on the road behind the church (rightly named, **Rua Bela Vista**) you will come to a couple of very nice and simple *pousadas* and a couple of bars with incredible views.

Another highlight of the old village is the road that extends from the *praça* to the new village, called **Rua Broduei** (that's phonetic Brazilian for Broadway). This part of the old village is quite popular for restaurants and shops and some economical eateries, such as a bakery and *lanchonete* on the end near the *praça*. When you reach the end of Rua Broduei, you'll come into the **Praça São Braz,** which is the final part of the old village. Here, you'll find more quaint colonial buildings, currently in use by the city government, post office, and such. This is also called the Praça Hippie, since it's usually filled with hippies selling their handmade jewelry. Since they are not allowed to sell on the streets in town or on the beaches, they took over the *praça* as a place to set up shop. An unfortunate side effect is that they work aggressively to pull potential customers (can you say gringos?) into the *praça* from the streets nearby. If you walk near the Praça Hippie, you'll undoubtedly make one or two new friends there. The hippies and surfers actually "discovered" Arraial d'Ajuda back in the 1970s and are now being pushed out by all the upscale progress and evolution in the village.

As you walk from Praça Hippie toward the ocean, you'll be walking through the new village. Here you'll find more *pousadas,* boutique shops, and restaurants, but the offerings are mostly upscale and charming. Thankfully, the atmosphere here maintains its village look and feel and, although the construction is more modern, everything is quite charming and inviting. It's worth spending an afternoon walking along the main village road, the **Estrada do Mucugé,** to check out the many shops there. Evenings in this part of the village are buzzing with people choosing restaurants and places to sit for the evening to watch the movement on the street. The far end of the Estrada do Mucugé bumps into Mucugé Beach.

## SOUTHERN BEACHES

The main beach in Arraial is **Praia do Mucugé,** at the bottom of the Estrada do Mucugé just below the village. Due to its proximity to the village, it is by far the most popular and crowded of the beaches here. There are plenty of beach bars with plenty of beach chairs and umbrellas to keep the sun off. Some trees line the area around the *estrada* and give the whole place a nice, relaxing feel. This is a great place to spend the afternoon after walking along the northern or southern coastline for several kilometers. A cold beer and a shady tree are just what you'll be looking for. To the south (right) of Mucugé is the **Praia Parracho,** which is a bit more extensive than Mucugé, with its beach bars more spread apart. However, there are some large beach bars here, in the tradition of Porto Seguro, and they can get rowdy during peak season. You can easily walk between these two beaches. The water here is not as warm or as clear as in other parts of the country, but on a sunny day in the summer months, it can turn a beautiful blue-green.

It's easy to walk from Mucugé all the way to **Praia Pitinga,** about 1.5 kilometers (30 minutes) away. You'll cross a small stream that empties into the ocean and several beach bars. Pitinga is the location of the town's most charming and luxurious beachfront *pousadas,* and the beach bars along the way are also slightly higher-end. Check out the Paraíso Restaurant with its wooden chairs and large sitting area. Also the São Tropez Praia Hotel has a large area with restaurants and bars. You can enter from the beach or from behind on land. The Cabana Grande is the largest beach bar in the area, a younger cousin to those in Porto Seguro. This one also gets rip-roaring during

the deck at Pousada Pitinga

peak season but is mercifully silent during the off season. The best place to stop for a drink is on the deck at the **Pousada Pitinga,** marking the far end of Pitinga.

A much farther trek (about seven kilometers) is the stroll to **Praia Taipe** and the **Lagoa Azul.** The *lagoa* itself is dry, but the sandy cliffs, called *falesias,* make for a striking scene. The beach here is one of the most deserted in the area and is well worth a visit, as it's also one of the prettiest. This is about the final point to which most people care to walk along the southern coast of Arraial. However, a few daring folks make the 14-kilometer haul all the way down to Trancoso. You'll have to cross a few small rivers that empty into the ocean, but otherwise, it's quite possible to accomplish in about five hours with a canteen of water, a hat, and plenty of sunscreen. There are kiosks along the way for filling up and resting your feet and you'll pass the large Club Med establishment about halfway down. You can catch a bus or taxi back from Trancoso.

Note: If you like the idea of walking along the beach at night, be sure to bring a flashlight; there are no lights to guide you (but for the beckoning moon), as the beach bars are all shut down for the evening. It's perfectly safe to walk along these beaches at night, although you should be aware that some stretches will have plenty of water splashing in at high tide. At night, the walk along the northern coast is probably a bit more straightforward than on the southern coast.

## NORTHERN BEACHES

Walking up along the northern beaches is a must while you're in Arraial. First, the beaches themselves are long and excellent for swimming—with clear, warm water that is generally shallow and calm. Plus, there are kiosks spread at intervals all along this part of the coast, many associated with some *pousada* or other (but the kiosks are always open to the public, so make yourself at home or, as the Brazilians say, *fique a vontade*). Some women even go topless on these beaches. The walk all the way to the top, which is marked by the Pousada Aquarela, is about six kilometers (two hours walking). Along the way, you'll pass the **Arraial Ecoparque,** which has very little "eco"

beaches at the northern tip of Arraial d'Ajuda

about it. It's really just a huge water park with slides and attractions marketed to Brazilians visiting Porto Seguro on vacation packages. If you like the idea of exhilarating water slides, then check it out (you have to enter from the road on the other side). You'll also pass the **Praia do Delegado**, which is full of beach *barracas,* chiefly, the legendary **Barraca do Sting,** which is an excellent choice for sitting and sipping a cold coconut water or something stronger. The beach in front of his *barraca* is an excellent choice for swimming, as the water is shallow and calm there. If Sting himself is around, you'll see why he got his nickname; as he does, indeed, resemble the famous pop star. He serves great fish lunches and organizes boating excursions up the Santa Cruz River.

You can cut in from the beach to the inland road at the Barraca do Sting or any number of other trails along the northern beaches. If you go all the way to the end, you'll cut in at the Pousada Aquarela, right at the location of the ferryboat to Porto Seguro.

There is a northern road that parallels the beach from Arraial d'Ajuda to the ferryboat. Along this road are numerous *pousadas* and a

few interesting shops, restaurants, and bars. The best place to come in from the beach and have a look around is at the Barraca do Sting. Just inland from Sting's place is the cozy Santa Fe Hotel, with an excellent restaurant/bar (open to the public, of course). There are also shops and art galleries in the vicinity. A late-afternoon walk along the northern beaches is one of the best excursions you can take in Arraial. The wind comes up a little and blows the sand around your feet, as the tide goes way out, revealing the shiny, sandy ocean floor.

## ENTERTAINMENT AND NIGHTLIFE

When the beach bars close for the evening at around sundown, the village road begins to light up. People hit the village shopping for a restaurant or bar or just walking around to take in the charm of the place. Things really get moving at around 10 P.M. and it's a good idea to already have chosen your spot by then, as the best seats in the best restaurants go fast.

You might notice an unusual amount of world-beat and drum-and-bass music in Arraial d'Ajuda. It seems that all the bars and beach kiosks are playing some kind of electronic groove music. It has become something of a tradition in town—brought in by the Spanish and Argentinean immigrants. It serves as another reminder that you're in a more hip part of Southern Bahia.

### Cafés and Bars

There are bars all along the village roads and *praças.* Many are also restaurants and are listed in the *Food* section. Be sure to walk into the **Beco das Cores** area, which is basically a small, dead-end road that crosses the main village road (Estrada do Mucugé). Cars are not allowed on this road and entrance is marked by an archway. Inside are several great bars and restaurants, including a sushi bar and some live music.

Every afternoon starting at around 2 P.M. the **Cactus Club** (Estrada do Mucugé 590, no phone, 2 P.M.–midnight daily) has live rock and blues music in on their patio that overlooks the ocean. The atmosphere here is young, casual, and very cool. It's a great place to end the afternoon or begin the evening. They make a great Capeta cocktail. A personal favorite is the **Girassol** (Estrada do Mucugé, no number, tel. 73/3575-1768, 11 A.M.–midnight daily) bar located down a small *galeria* of shops on the corner of Rua Amendoeiras and the Estrada do Mucugé. There is a large, new restaurant in front and shops lining the other side of the pathway. At the end of the pathway is the Girasol bar. Don't confuse this with the Gerasol restaurant, which is farther down the Estrada do Mucugé and not at the end of a pathway.

Also, on the road behind the church in the old town square (Rua Bela Vista), there is a small jazz bar called the **Blue Bar.** It opens only during peak season—nights only—but it offers a different kind of atmosphere. Down the road, at the end of Rua Bela Vista is a *cachaça bar* called **Nos de Bahia** (no phone, 5 P.M.–midnight Thurs.–Sat.) Get there in the late afternoon when they are just opening for the evening to get a shot of their incredible view along with their *cachaça.*

### Music and Dance

During peak season, the two large beach bars offer late-night music and dancing in the Porto Seguro style. These are located on Praia Parracho and at the beginning of Pitinga. The offerings are generally Bahian *axé* music and dance or electronic music. If you're really interested in Brazilian music and dance, then a trip up to Porto Seguro would be in order for the evening. Remember that the ferryboat back and forth operates 24 hours a day, so *fique a vontade!* However, Arraial has some pretty rockin' options of its own—a bit more sophisticated than those of its neighbor and probably appealing more to foreign tastes. There's nothing that goes on in town that is not known to anyone interested. People will pass you fliers and billets as you stroll the streets—especially if you look like the profile of their place. The principal location for late-night groovin' is the **Plato Espaço Bahia** (Estrada do Mucugé 500, no phone, 11 P.M. until sunrise) located on the descent to Praia Mucugé. They often have techno or other music that starts at about midnight and goes until sunup. There is often regional music going in the outdoor stage at the Shopping d'Ajuda in front of the Gandaya burger joint. You can catch some authentic samba music and Capoeira demonstrations in front of the Sky Lanches diner at the end of the Estrada do Mucugé near the Praça Hippie. Everything else will be revealed as you walk around town.

## SHOPPING

In my opinion, the best shopping is in the old village, but by all means check out the more upscale offerings all along the Estrada do Mucugé, too. An interesting shop in the Praça Brigadeiro E. Gomes is the **Casa de Renda** (no phone, 10 A.M.–6 P.M. Tues.–Sun., closed for lunch) with handmade and hand-painted fabrics. There is also a well-stocked souvenir store on the far corner of the *praça,* opposite the church. While you're hanging around the old town *praça,* take a look inside the **Claudio Macedo, Atelier de Madeira** (no phone, hours are unpredictable, but it's generally open from 10 A.M.–4 P.M. Tues.–Sun.) to see some interesting wood sculptures.

## EXCURSIONS

Excursions available in Arraial d'Ajuda are pretty much the same ones available in Porto Seguro. Whether you book your excursion in Porto Seguro or Arraial is just a matter of comparing prices and options. Some agencies in Arraial are just reselling an excursion that leaves from Porto Seguro anyway, so be sure to ask about the details. There are tour agencies all along the main village road.

The one thing that is probably better to book in Arraial d'Ajuda is a rental car or dune buggy. Most likely, you'll be taking the buggy south to Trancoso and beyond, so renting it in Porto Seguro to the north is pointless. One excursion that is specific to Arraial is a horseback ride down the southern coast. Check with local agencies for details.

If you are a diver, you might consider working with **Arraial Dive** (Estrada do Mucugé 471, tel. 73/3575-2666, arraialdive@bol.com.br), since they are one of the three official groups in the area that have certified dive masters (the other agencies resell their excursions). The other two are in Porto Seguro, but the folks at Arraial Dive are excellent, professional, and speak English and German. They offer a full course in English for R$800 (4–5 days), and a beginner dive for R$100 in the ocean or a swimming pool. Dive excursions generally go from 9 A.M.–3 P.M. and take in two spots (including one of the two shipwrecks in the area) for about R$120, including a simple lunch. Talk to Osmar or any of the dive masters there.

## ACCOMMODATIONS

The most economical accommodations in town are generally in or around the old village. A couple of excellent choices are found on Rua Bela Vista behind the old church. Mid-range and high-end options are spread throughout the new village with some good deals to be found along Alameda dos Flamboyantes, which runs parallel (sort of) to the main street in town, Estrada do Mucugé. Some of the most comfortable and charming accommodations can be found at Praia Pitinga, which you can access from a dirt road that runs parallel to the beach, called Estrada para Praia Pitinga. Finally, there is a vast array of hotels and *pousadas* on the road that runs from the ferryboat into town. This road parallels the northern beaches of Arraial and is an excellent alternative to staying in the village. Prices here are generally economical and the area is excellent for hanging out.

### Under R$100

One of my favorite economical *pousadas* in town is the very artsy Ñ **Tubarão Pousada** (Rua Bela Vista 210, tel. 73/3575-1086, www.tubarao.arraialdajuda.com, tubarao@arraialdajuda.com, R$40 s and R$60 d, R$100), owned by an Argentinean couple. They have a pool and simple but cozy rooms on a very quiet street behind the old church. Farther down on the same

street is the **Pousada Alto Mar** (Rua Bela Vista 114, tel. 73/3575-1935, R$15 pp group room, R$25 private room without breakfast, R$30 with breakfast), which is run like a hostel (it's better than the horrible hostel in town), with group rooms, community spaces, kitchen facilities, and so forth. They have barbecues during the week, a large breakfast with lots of regional treats, and free Internet service for guests. Laundry services are also available. You get a very local flavor in the **Pousada da Aninha** (Rua dos Flamboyantes, tel. 73/3575-1079, R$40 d). The owner, Aninha, is a traditional Bahiana and offers small but clean rooms with TV, ceiling fan, and breakfast included. She also has a small pool.

If you want to be close to the northern beaches (not a bad idea), then you have an alternative selection of *pousadas* from which to choose. The best economical option that does not feel economical is the Ñ **Pousada Agua Marinha** (Estrada da Balsa 2340, tel. 73/3575-1228, www.pousadaaguamarinha.com, peter@tinet.org, R$50 s and R$70 d low season, R$85 s and R$100 d peak season). This is a simple, down-to-earth place with a pool, breakfast area, TV room, and several chalet-style buildings, each with two or three rooms. Rooms have air, ceiling fans, and verandas with hammocks. The owners, Peter and Vera, are as sweet as can be. They are located about 50 meters from the beach. Larger suites are just slightly more expensive.

### R$100–200

A terrific mid-range option with an interesting style and decoration is the **Pousada Bemvira** (Al. dos Flamboyants 54, tel. 73/3575-1714, www.bemvira.com.br, reservas@bemvira.com.br, R$60 s and R$70 d low season, R$120 s and R$140 d peak season). They are well located near the village road and offer air or ceiling fan, TV, and terrace with hammock. They have a pool and poolside bar. The **Coqueiros Hotel Pousada** (Al. dos Flamboyants 55, tel. 73/3575-1229, www.pousadacoqueiros.com.br, coqueiros@pousadacoqueiros.com.br, R$100 d low season and R$170 peak season) has an excellent location near the village and a mixture of Southwestern and tropical design (it works, actually, and they're not the only ones who are doing it either). Rooms are colorful, well-appointed, and clean and come with air, TV, phone, and safe. The *pousada* has a pool, restaurant, sauna, bar, and TV room.

The award for the "Best Pool with an Ocean View" goes to the **N Hotel Paraíso do Morro** (Estrada do Mucugé 471, tel. 73/3575-2423, www.paraisodomorro.com, paraiso@paraisodomorro.com, R$130 standard and R$200 suite). They have a perfect location—on the beach side, with a view of the ocean—on the main village road as it goes down to the beach. Their grounds are well kept and their rooms are cozy and clean. They have a corner luxury suite that has a most excellent view of both the pool and the ocean. Rooms have TV, hydro-massage tub, king-size bed, and air. Try to get the one on the corner.

### R$200–500

If you're into a romantic tropical setting, cozy chalets with decks that overlook the ocean, air conditioning, TV, music, and sitting area, then check into one of Arraial's best hotels, the **N Pousada Pitinga** (Praia Pitinga 1633, tel. 73/3575-1067, www.pousadapitinga.com.br, pitinga@pousadapitinga.com.br, R$235–350). This place is a dream. They have a beautiful pool that's available 24 hours, an excellent restaurant for lunch or dinner (open to the public and one of the best in Arraial, but most people don't go there unless they are staying at the *pousada*), a sun deck, breakfast loft, and super-comfortable TV room. If you get the second story of one of the chalets, you'll have a wonderful view of the ocean from your front deck. The service is excellent and personal and somewhat hands-off. Although it's only about 1.5 kilometers from the village, taxis gouge you for R$15 to make the trip. During the day, it's an easy walk along the beach.

Along the road that goes past the northern beaches to the ferryboat, you'll find several *pousadas*. The best among them is the **Estação Santa Fé Hotel Pousada** (Estrada do Arraial 2020, tel. 73/3575-2237, www.santafehotel.com.br, reservas@santafehotel.com.br, R$195 low season and R$280 peak season). This place has a Southwestern design with a lovely lobby and a large pool area and restaurant. They have a Jacuzzi, poolside bar, and plenty of room for relaxing.

## FOOD

With all the lovely restaurants in Arraial, it's amazing that so many of them offer mediocre food and mediocre service. Truly great restaurants are difficult to find, like oysters among the many clams on the beach. The true test of service is, of course, when you have a problem or complaint. Just watch how fast that I'm-your-best-friend service turns sour. Apparently, there are still not enough restaurants in town to create the kind of competition that produces excellence. Nevertheless, here are some winners among the contestants.

Note: Be careful when selecting a table that is right on the Estrada do Mucugé. If you are too close to the street, you may be hit by a wave of exhaust when a lovely off-road vehicle stops right in front of your table. Since Arraial has not yet prohibited traffic along the main street, it's better to be slightly in from the street itself. Hours in this section are for the peak-season (Dec.–Feb. and July), and many establishments reduce their hours during the low season or close completely. Since the village is relatively small, you can easily walk around to see which restaurants are operating if you're visiting during the the low season. Just be aware that your options will be much fewer.

### International

A favorite top-end restaurant in town is **Aipim Restaurant** (Beco do Jegue 181, tel. 73/3575-2655, 6 P.M.–1 A.M. daily), located on a street crossing the Estrada do Mucugé. They have a decent international-style menu in a somewhat elegant setting. Meals cost around R$50 per person. If you're into meat, try the Argentinean barbecue restaurant **Boi Nos Aires** (Estrada do Mucugé 200, tel. 73/3575-2554, 5 P.M.–midnight Mon.–Thurs., 2 P.M.–1 A.M. Fri.–Sun., closed Mondays during low season). They have a key location with a large indoor-outdoor dining area and plenty of great candlelight for ambience. They serve Argentinean and Chilean wines. A meal is about R$40 per person. For an elegant setting with a very accessible menu, try the **Estrela Restaurante** (Beco das Cores 201, tel. 73/3575-2655, 6 P.M.–midnight daily). They specialize in fish, but have pasta and other dishes. It will set you back about R$30–50 per person.

### Local Favorites

One of the most popular places in town among the locals is the **Portinha Self-Service Restaurante** (Rua do Campo 01, tel. 73/3575-1289, noon–midnight) just outside of the Centro. They have excellent self-service dishes with a huge variety of meats, salads, and pastas. Each night, they have a different theme, such as Chinese, Arabic, or Italian. The price is R$20 per person. Another local favorite is the small **Ñ São João Restaurante** (Praça Brigadeiro Eduardo Gomes 41, tel. 73/3575-1191, noon–11 P.M. daily during peak season. Closed on Sundays in the low season) in the old town square near the church. This place was around before Arraial became popular. It was once the owner's house. They serve regional dishes and make their own liqueurs. It should cost around R$20 per person.

### Quick and Casual

For a quick snack, try the *lanchonetes* at the Praça Hippie just as you enter the Estrada do Mucugé. There, you can find fast, cheap, and delicious pizza slices, *pasteis* (Brazilian deep-fried spring rolls), and traditional Brazilian finger foods. Around lunchtime, they have self-service buffet lunches with barbecued meats. There are also casual places along Rua Broduei.

### Regional Food

A good selection for seafood and a variety of Brazilian dishes is **Manguti** (Estrada do Mucugé 99, tel. 73/3575-2270, 2 P.M.–midnight, closed Tues.), which has good food at an excellent price. It also has a cozy, village atmosphere. They are open for lunch and have great executive lunch plates for around R$10.

The most celebrated restaurant in town and a sure bet to win you over with magnificent seafood is **Ñ Rosa dos Ventos** (Al. dos Flamboyantes 24, tel. 73/3575-1271, 5 P.M.–midnight Mon.–Sat., 2 P.M.–11 P.M. on Sun. Closed Thurs.). The Austrian-owned establishment is open only during peak season (escaping the cold winter in Austria, no doubt) and has wonderful fresh fish plates, like grilled catch-of-the-day in banana leaves with pineapple. You'll spend about R$60 per person.

## INFORMATION AND SERVICES

There is no official tourist information office in Arraial d'Ajuda, but you can get information at any of the tour agencies. There are Internet services all around town. On the Estrada do Mucugé, you'll find CyberPoint, which always has people inside. There are ATMs in the Shopping d'Ajuda and if you run into any trouble, just head back to Porto Seguro to withdraw cash. The post office is on the far side of the Praça Hippie. For dune buggy rentals, try **Buggy Mania** (Estrada do Mucugé 250, tel. 73/3575-3000).

## GETTING THERE AND AROUND

You get to Arraial d'Ajuda from Porto Seguro via the ferryboat that operates 24 hours per day. It costs R$2 to get to Arraial and it's free to get back to Porto Seguro. Once you get to the Arraial side, you can take a taxi to the village for R$10. If your hotel is on the northern coast, then you can probably walk to it. If you have a lot of luggage, the taxi driver will charge you the same R$10 to go one kilometer to your hotel (we don't need no stinkin' taxi meter). There are buses from the ferry that leave every 20 minutes to the village and others that go to Trancoso. Finally, you can wait for 10 people (not difficult in peak season) and fill up a *kombi* (VW bus) that will take the group into the village (or drop you off earlier) for R$1 each.

# Trancoso

The pace of life in Trancoso is always calm and laid-back. Even in peak season, the little village does not get too stirred up. Here, the *pousadas* are spread around the old village and along the beaches. And those are the two most important parts of Trancoso. The village is where you'll find shops, *pousadas,* and restaurants in quaint, 16th-century constructions, not unlike the Cidade Histórica in Porto Seguro. But unlike the old village in Porto Seguro, the Trancoso Quadrado (as the main village square is called) is a place to pass the late afternoon and evening. During the day, most folks are enjoying the many beautiful beaches below (like its neighbors, Trancoso is built upon a high bluff overlooking the sea). Trancoso is quite a bit smaller than Arraial d'Ajuda, with fewer establishments. Some prefer the quietude and minimalism of Trancoso—and find the establishments more quaint and inviting. Others find Trancoso a bit too high-brow, since it is frequented by Brazil's rich and famous, caus-ing the finer restaurants and *pousadas* to demand higher prices.

## THE QUADRADO AND VILLAGE

The small square that is historical Trancoso, called the **Quadrado,** was once the only civilization for kilometers and kilometers. On horseback, the trip to Porto Seguro to sell sugar and cocoa products took an entire day. But life in the Quadrado was slow and simple. As you walk into the square, you can imagine how life here must have been. The place is intact, with its small structures perfectly restored and functioning as restaurants or *pousadas.* At the far end of the square, toward the cliffs that overlook the ocean, is the town church, looking exactly as it did in the 1500s. As you walk toward the cliffs, you'll pass locals (including indigenous people) selling rustic jewelry and other items in the square. The quality of these

the Trancoso Quadrado

handmade goods is generally much higher than that of neighboring towns, so if you're going to do some purchasing, Trancoso is the place to do it. Most visitors drop their jaw when they reach the far end of the Quadrado, which overlooks the ocean. The view here is world-class. Below you, the Rio Trancoso glides toward the ocean with a couple of serpentine turns between sandbars and past tall palm trees. You might want to hang out at this viewpoint for awhile to drink it in. Later, you can walk down to become a participant in the scene.

The Quadrado used to be the only part of the village and was home to 12 traditional families that lived quite isolated from the rest of the world. Families would arrange marriages between young men and women only if they lived on opposite sides of the square. The principal economy of the village was, of course, fishing. The village was discovered in the '70s, along with much of the Southern Bahia coastline. In the '80s, it underwent a major transformation, with the addition of electricity, telephones, and, little by little, investors from other parts of Brazil, who built their *pousadas* and restaurants in town. Today, the Quadrado remains much as it did before civilization hit. No outdoor lights are allowed in the square and, if you want to walk around the area at night, you might want to bring a flashlight.

On the other side of the Quadrado, away from the ocean, is the new part of the village, known as the **Bosque** area. An extension of the Quadrado, this is where you'll find some of the town's more well-decorated restaurants and boutique shops. The entire Bosque area consists of just a few streets: the main road entering the town and a few others forming a single square block.

## BEACHES TO THE NORTH

The beaches in Trancoso are slighly less populated than those in Arraial, but the layout is similar. In Trancoso, however, the northern and southern beaches are separated by the Trancoso River, which you can cross either by swimming or by taking a small boat for R$1.

Of course, you can also hike up to the village, go across, and head back down the other side.

The main beach, **Praia dos Nativos,** is below the village on the north side and has most of the establishments, beach bars, and activities. The north coast has long stretches of sand and surf and is great for swimming—especially at low tide. These are also terrific beaches for unforgettable sunrise and sunset walks. The farthest you probably want to walk to the north is to **Praia Rio da Barra,** which is one of the prettiest beaches in the area, at the mouth of the Barra River. The river bends a few times before it reaches the ocean, where it opens into a large lake. The entire scene is lined with palm trees and there are few visitors here during low season. Still, there is a beach kiosk to help you refuel for the walk back. It's about four kilometers from the village (1.5-hour walk) and you'll pass some lovely coconut groves along the way (but few or no beach kiosks).

To get down to the northern beaches, just

Praia dos Nativos from the Quadrado lookout point

take the road on the left side of the village (as you enter the town) and cut through to the ocean at Praia dos Nativos. You'll see the signs. Unfortunately, this little walk downhill can be annoying, due to the many badly mannered drivers going back and forth along this dirt road. If you're sensitive to dust and easily angered by rudeness, then take a taxi to the beach.

## BEACHES TO THE SOUTH

On the south side of the village are beaches with slightly more turbulent waters, although they are nevertheless excellent for swimming. The water here is clearer and bluer than on the north coast, largely due to the many rivers that flow into the ocean along this part of the coast. The first beach you come to on the south coast is **Praia dos Coqueiros.** Here, you'll find plenty of beach bars and shady umbrellas and chairs. The farther you walk south from here, the more sparse the beach kiosks become and the more deserted the beaches. You'll pass **Praia do Rio Verde** as you continue south, which is just past a small river opening (which you can cross on foot). After the river, you walk onto an excellent stretch of beach—with warm, blue water and medium-sized waves. This was once a nudist beach, known as Praia do Nudismo. Today, you might come across a few people looking to revitalize the practice (*fique a vontade,* OK?) but mostly it's just a great place to swim and get some sun. At the far end of this beach is the best beach kiosk on the coast, the **Pé Na Praia** *barraca*. It has an excellent position on the beach with plenty of wooden chairs, hammocks, and places to lay out on a straw mat or sit and sip a cold one. They usually have some kind of electronic groove music going, which puts you in a great, relaxed mood (or maybe that's the beer).

If you walk further south, you won't come across anything but lovely sand and surf for about five kilometers. This is a good place to get away from the crowd. There are reefs just offshore in this area, and the beach is slightly murky with seaweed and kelp (evidence of the reefs). You can go snorkeling out in these waters, and in peak season, you will find groups of people doing just that—on some excursion or other. It doesn't look so inviting from the beach around the point (called **Ponta de Itapororoca**), but once you get out beyond the barrier reefs, you'll understand the attraction. Again, there are no kiosks around this area until you get all the way to **Praia Jacumã,** where you'll find some great beach bars at the Jacumã coconut plantation. There are also more natural tide pools for snorkeling at Jacumã and boats to take you out. If you don't like the idea of walking on your own all the way to Jacumã to go snorkeling, then join an excursion from Trancoso or Arraial d'Ajuda that visits these pools. Alternatively, you can take a taxi or bus from Trancoso directly to Jacumã to spend the day there. South of Jacumã are the very sought-after **Praia Curuípe** and **Praia do Espelho,** which receive visitors from Porto Seguro excursions. If you get to Jacumã, you can walk to these two beaches in about 30 minutes.

To get to the southern beaches from the village, take the trail that leads from the right side of the Quadrado down until you reach the sand and surf. You can't miss it.

## ENTERTAINMENT AND NIGHTLIFE

There's not a lot going on at night in Trancoso. Most of the night activity winds down around 11 P.M. after everyone has eaten and had some after-dinner drinks. Individual hotel bars often stay open all night. There is one late-night club in town called **Para Raio** (across from the Padaria Pandoro, tel. 73/3668-1025, call for current schedule, 7 P.M.–sunrise). They have drinks, Italian food, house music, Brazilian beats, and live shows in peak season.

## SHOPPING

Shopping takes place primarily in the Quadrado during the day and just outside it on the way to the Bosque village area at night. Most of

## EXCURSIONS

If you're staying in Trancoso, then you can connect with one of the local tour agencies to select from just about any of the tours offered in Porto Seguro and Arraial d'Ajuda. The largest in town is **Trancoso Receptivo** (Quadrado, tel. 73/3668-1333, www.trancosoreceptivo.com). Besides booking excursions, they also provide reservation services at hotels, car rentals, and transportation to and from the airport in Porto Seguro. You can rent a car or buggy from Trancoso for a personalized trip farther down the coast.

## ACCOMMODATIONS
### The Quadrado and Village

Start with the  **Pousada Puerto Bananas** (Quadrado 234, tel. 73/3668-1017, www.portobananas.com.br, reservas@porto-bananas.com.br, R$96 s and R$120 d for standard rooms, R$230 *casa* chalet), on the south side of the Quadrado. It's a rustic space with simple, but quaint chalets designed for couples or groups. There are no phones or TVs in the rooms. Their *casa* chalet has kitchen facilities and an upstairs loft and houses up to six people. It's run by a young couple, Christof (from France) and his Brazilian wife. Christof speaks English. The **Pousada do Quadrado** (Quadrado, tel. 73/3668-1808, pousadado-quadrado.com.br, R$149 low season and R$249 peak season) has a large piece of land on the south side of the Quadrado with semi-Indonesian landscaping. They have a dozen or so chalets with air, TV, and comfortable beds. You might avoid the **Pousada El Gordo,** because, although one of the most beautiful installations on the Quadrado, it has a rather snooty Portuguese owner and staff, leaving something to be desired in the service department, especially for the price.

One of the nicest places to stay in Trancoso if you have a group, is in one of the **Casas de Lia** (near the Quadrado on the road to Praia dos Coqueiros, tel. 73/3668-1143). Lia has built two cottages on her lot, which she rents out to groups

Handmade crafts are for sale on the beach.

the regional arts and crafts you'll come across are sold on blankets on the ground or simple stands, but many of these items are very well made. In particular, check out the jewelry made with the red seeds from the Pau Brasil tree. Although using the wood of the tree is prohibited in Brazil, the seeds are free to be harvested and commercialized. Local artisans turn them into all kinds of beautiful tribal jewelry.

There are some boutique stores in the Quadrado, including **Etnia** (Quadrado, tel. 73/3668-1137, 9 A.M.–6 P.M. daily), a home furnishings store created by an Italian designer, who also owns the Pousada Etnia at the entrance to town. A great place for colorful fabrics and pillows is **Cobras & Lagartos** (no phone, 9 A.M.–6 P.M. daily) and don't miss the arts and crafts store **Santo do Pau Oco** (Quadrado, tel. 73/3668-1121, 9 A.M.–6 P.M. daily), with irresistible wood carvings and other crafts from all over Bahia.

© CHRISTOPHER VAN BUREN

**the grounds at Pousada Estrela d'Agua**

and families. They are fairly large and can hold up to six people each. Her property is in a perfect location just off the Quadrado along the pathway that leads to the southern beaches. It looks, rightly so, like someone's house, but you'll see a small sign to help you figure out that you've arrived. One of her cottages has a view of the ocean and goes for R$260 per night, including full cleaning and cooking services. The other is spacious, but has no ocean view and goes for R$170 per night.

A top choice for anyone seeking style and décor is **N Etnia** (Rua Principal, tel. 73/3668-1137, www.etniabrasil.com.br, R$240–350 low season and R$350–450 peak season). Here, you'll find a thematic-style inn, each chalet (called a bungalow) with its own decoration—from Mediterranean to tribal to Moroccan. They have a pool area with a great poolside bar, a garden for lounging, and a therapy center upstairs (massage, yoga, etc.). All rooms have air, mosquito netting, comfortable beds with Italian linens, and Swedish down pillows. Some rooms have lofts. A path behind the *pousada* heads down to the southern beaches. The owner, André, speaks English.

One of the more economical options in the village is the **Pousada Hibisco** (Rua Bom Jesus, tel. 73/3668-1117, www.pousadahibisco.com.br, R$70–95), which is on the road just as it starts its descent to the northern beaches. The *pousada* has several chalets and a simple breakfast with regional delights.

## On the North Coast

The north coast is known to have the most elaborate (and expensive) *pousadas* in the area. There's no particular reason why they are all in this area, since the beaches here are not necessarily the best. Perhaps it's because this area is quieter and more deserted than the south coast. At any rate, the best entry in this area is the **N Pousada Estrela d'Agua** (Estrada do Arraial, tel. 73/3668-1030, www.estreladagua.com.br, reservas@estreladagua.com.br, R$350–550). This is a semi-resort-style place, meaning that it offers everything you need to never have to leave the grounds. But it's not really a resort; it's more of a large, beachfront garden village. It was once the home of the famous Brazilian pop singer Gal Costa, but it traded hands and now the original house serves as the restaurant. They have two beautiful pools with views of the ocean, a poolside deck, two outdoor bars, and beach service. The beach just to the left of the hotel is a great place to go swimming. Right in front of the hotel, the water is a bit choppy and the floor quite uneven. But you'll probably like the pools better anyway. Rooms are arranged in clusters, each cluster is a separate building. Rooms include air, mosquito netting, comfortable king-size beds, and TV. The breakfast buffet is amazing and the service is top-notch. The only thing missing is a complimentary van to take you to the village and back—especially at night, but that's a minor complaint.

## On the South Coast

A great place along the south coast is **Bahia Bonita** (Praia Rio Verde, tel. 73/9993-0771, www.bahiabonito.com.br, R$65 low season and R$135 peak season). Here, you'll find chalets just a stone's throw from the ocean. Each one is spacious and comfortable, if rustic. The grounds are all sand and grass. The **Aldeia do Sol** (Praia Rio Verde, tel. 73/3668-1984, www.aldeiadosol.com.br, R$90 s and R$110–180 d) is another beachfront option that has two lodges with several rooms in each. Top-level rooms have ocean views. They also have a pool and barbecue area. Their beach kiosk serves drinks and is open to the public.

## FOOD

For a simple snack or sandwich, try **Padaria Pandoro** (Rua Principal, no phone, 6 A.M.–10 P.M. Mon.–Sat., 6 A.M.–2 P.M. on Sun.) just outside the Quadrado in the village. They have good pizza slices, breads, deli items, and sand-wiches. You can also buy the fixings for a picnic here. They have a great outdoor area for eat-ing and drinking into the evening and you'll have the opportunity to make friends with all of the dogs in town. For regional food, try **Capim Santo** (Quadrado, tel. 73/3668-1122, 5 P.M.–midnight Mon.–Sat., R$30). They have a nice atmosphere and decent fish and seafood. One of the more celebrated places in town is **O Cacau** (Quadrado, tel. 73/3668-1268, 6–11:30 P.M. Mon.–Sat., R$25), which makes Bahian dishes with a flair of creativity. They're a bit more expensive, but excellent. The pizza restaurant called **Maritaka** (Rua Carlos Alberto Parracho, Bosque, tel. 73/3668-1258, 5 P.M.–midnight Wed.–Mon., R$25) has a wonderful atmosphere and serves only pizza. It's a great place to have a beer and snack in the early af-ternoon. **Sabor do Mundo** (Parque Municipal, Bosque, tel. 73/3668-1191, opens for dinner daily with several vegetarian dishes, R$35) is run by a Dutch immigrant. He serves interna-tional cuisine in a very nice atmosphere. Finally, for excellent Japanese food, try **Aki Sushi Bar** (Rua Principal, tel. 73/3668-2340, dinner daily, starting at around R$50 per person) at the en-trance to the village. The sushi is good and you get a decent amount for the price.

## INFORMATION AND SERVICES

There is no tourist information office in Tran-coso, but you can get information at the agen-cies in town. There is an Internet connection in the village near the Padaria Pandoro and they can help you with information, too.

There are no international ATMs in Tran-coso, so come prepared with plenty of cash. Many establishments accept credit cards, but not all. And often the system is down. If you are desperate, ask at the Padaria Pandoro if they can use their system to get you some cash.

## GETTING THERE AND AROUND

As with Arraial d'Ajuda, most visitors come to Trancoso via Porto Seguro. If you want a pick-up service, call **Trancoso Receptivo** (tel. 73/3668-1333, www.trancosoreceptivo.com). Otherwise, you can catch a bus directly from Porto Seguro to Trancoso. A taxi will cost around R$60, including the ferryboat ride. For a taxi in Trancoso, call tel. 73/3668-1260.

Most beaches are within walking distance from the Trancoso village, but if you want to head as far south as Praia Jacumã (or beyond), then you should take a van or rent a buggy.

# The Extreme South of Bahia

## CARAÍVA

There are no paved streets in Caraíva and gas generators produce the electricity for the village (hotels and *pousadas* have their own generators). Most visitors pass through town during the day on an excursion from Trancoso or Arraial d'Ajuda, hitting Praia do Espelho on the way. An overnight stay in Caraíva is only for those who are serious about getting away from it all. The beaches around Caraíva are isolated and the village is peaceful and quiet. During the day, you can check out the arts and crafts from the local Pataxó people, who sell their wares in town, or take a walk along the incredible beaches to the north or south. You can also find some excellent snorkeling in the area—some of the best in Southern Bahia. And don't think there's no nightlife. The locals dance *forró* most every night with local musicians. If you're staying at one of the *pousadas* on the beach, then you can enjoy an evening overlooking the ocean at your *pousada*'s beach bar.

### Beaches

You can get to the beaches around Caraíva on foot, by boat from the village (down to the mouth of the river and out to the ocean), or on horseback. The River Caraíva empties into the ocean here and locals spend their days fishing and collecting crabs and shellfish in the semi-salty waters. At the mouth of the river is **Praia Satu,** one of the visual highlights of the area. Here, the river serpentines into the ocean and forms two flat sandbars. All around are coconut-tree groves. One of the most popular beaches is **Praia do Curuípe,** to the north, which has two rustic beach bars that offer fried fish and cold beer for lunch. You can walk for kilometers along the beach beside the groves of coconut trees. The **Praia do Espelho** is one of the principal destinations in Southern Bahia for snorkeling, and excursions come here from Porto Seguro and Arraial d'Ajuda. At low tide, the reefs are accessible and make for ex-

cellent diving conditions. At high tide, you'll see why this is called Mirror Beach. You can get to both Curuipe and Espelho by boat from Caraíva, which lets you get out there early, before the excursions from the north arrive. You can find some more excellent reefs for diving and snorkeling off the **Ponta do Corumbau,** about 35 kilometers to the south of town. The reefs here are similar to those in the Abrolhos Islands. You'll also find indigenous groups selling their crafts in the small fishing village. The best way to see this beach is by taking a boat from Caraíva that includes a snorkeling excursion. The trip takes about four hours.

### Food and Accommodations

You can stay at the **Pousada Vila do Mar** (Praia de Caraíva, tel. 73/3223-0662, www.pousada-viladomar.com.br, viladomar@hotmail.com, R$110), which has 14 rooms on the beachfront with king-size beds, air, cable TV, and minibar. They have a pool, Jacuzzi, and beach bar. Breakfast buffet is included. You can stay at the very quaint and rustic **Pousada Lagoa,** (Foz da Lagoa, tel. 73/9985-6862, www.caraiva.com.br, R$75), which has four rooms and four bungalows with very rustic conditions (no hot water in the shower, but you won't want hot showers in the summer). The place is right on the beach, with seven square kilometers of space. They offer their own excursions all over the Caraíva area.

If you want to stay near Praia do Espelho, you can have one of the nicest rooms in the area at **M Pousada do Baiano** (Praia de Curuipe, get there through the Outeiro das Brisas complex, tel. 73/3668-5020, www.pousadadobaiano.com, R$185). The place is very cozy and quaint and has 20 rooms that face the ocean. They have a charming restaurant/bar area on the beach that offers comfortable chairs and hammocks for kicking back with a cold drink. Rooms are clean and comfortable and have king-size beds, hot tubs, ceiling fans, TVs, and phones.

All of the hotels on the beachfront have beach bars and restaurants that are open to the public. Each of the hotels listed previously has such an offering and you can walk along the beach and find more.

## Information

You can arrange excursions from the village of Caraíva. The best ones are by boat and take you to the beaches north or south of the village. You can also find windsurfing and catamaran trips around Caraíva Beach.

The best way to get to Caraíva is by buggy from Arraial d'Ajuda or Trancoso. You take the BR-101 highway from Itabela to the Caraíva turn-off. It takes about two hours to get there. Note that the Caraíva turn-off is a dirt road and it can be difficult to access the town during or after heavy rains. You can take a bus to Caraíva from Itabela. Check the Viação Aguia Branca line.

## MONTE PASCOAL

This rocky mountain sits about 200 kilometers south of Porto Seguro and was the first land that Alveres Cabral saw when he approached the shores of South America. As such, this place holds a special place in the heart of Brazilians. The area is protected as a wildlife sanctuary and national heritage site and includes the Pataxó Indian Reservation along with 144 square kilometers of Southern Bahian flora and fauna. Inside the park are various species of animals, including sloths, jaguars, hawks, armadillos, and porcupines.

You can get to the park from the highway BR-101. At kilometer 796, turn off and continue about 15 kilometers to the entrance of the park. You can also take an excursion from Caraiva that includes a guide. At the entrance, you can arrange for guided tours or assistance with scaling the face of Pascoal. You can also arrange an excursion from Caravelas.

## CARAVELAS AND THE ABROLHOS ISLANDS

Imagine swimming with sea turtles and dolphins in clear, shallow waters some 70 kilometers from shore with only a mask and snorkel. Most visitors who come out here are serious about wanting to see marine life in action. And that's what they get. Considered one of the 10 best spots in the world for scuba diving, the Abrolhos Islands are part of a protected marine park that sits about 70 kilometers off the coast of Brazil, specifically, off the coast near Caraíva. The five islands form a kind of semicircle in the ocean, having once been the upper rim of a volcano. The floor of the volcano, or the area that was once the inside, is a kind of shallow crater in the middle of the ocean, as shallow as one kilometer in some parts. You can enjoy snorkeling here as much as experienced divers enjoy their deep scuba journeys. Among some of the species you might see are barracudas, sharks, dolphins, turtles, and eels. The islands and marine area around it comprise almost 266 square nautical miles of underwater paradise. Included in this area is the Timbebas coral reef, the largest reef in the south Atlantic, taking up a mere 32 square miles of the park. If that's not enough, there are several shipwrecks in the area for advanced divers to check out. The islands were perilous to sea captains as the reefs and shallow waters around the islands are deceiving and unexpected. In fact, the name Abrolhos, comes from the contraction of *abra olhos* (open eyes), given to the island by Portuguese sailors.

As a marine preserve, the area is protected from any type of fishing activities, and visitors are required to adhere to a few basic rules to limit their impact on the place. In the middle of the preserve area is the Island of Santa Barbara, the only inhabited island out there, currently being used by the Brazilian navy and, in spite of its location in the middle of the Archipelago, the island is strictly off-limits.

### There Be Whales Here

The only place where the *Megaptera novaeangliae* whales hang out when the waters of the southern Antarctic region begin to freeze is in the area around the Abrolhos Islands. They arrive around July to give birth in the warm waters of the region, then stick around until

December to give their calves a chance to build up the layers of fat that insulate them from the cold waters of the south. The temperature and depth of the Abrolhos waters are perfect for the nursing period.

When the calves are born, they weigh around 1.5 tons and reach as much as five meters in length, whereas a full-grown whale can reach up to 40 tons and 15 meters. In the months July–November, you're almost guaranteed to encounter these whales, which often leap out of the water to spin in the air. Around 2,000 whales are known to frequent these waters during the mating and nursing season.

## Information

You can arrange a trip out to the park from Caravelas via speedboat that leaves early in the morn-ing and returns in the late afternoon. The trip takes 2.5 hours each way. You can also take a slow boat (four hours), or schooner (six hours). The schooner trips often stay overnight in the area and give you a chance to see more of the archipelago. The cost varies depending on the package you arrange, whether or not you'll be using diving equipment, and how much time you plan to spend. Meals are generally included in the package. Contact **Abrolhos Turismo** (Praça Dr. Embassay 8, tel. 73/3297-1149, www.abrol-hosturismo.com.br) for excursions out to the islands and **Paradise Abrolhos** (tel. 73/3297-1433, www.abrolhos.com.br) for diving excursions. You can also try **Princesa de Abrolhos** (tel. 73/3297-1777) for information on scuba diving. Dive schools and guides from Arraial d'Ajuda can also take you out to Abrolhos.

# The Amazon

One of the most memorable things about a visit to the Amazon is what you hear in the jungle. There are the mysterious sounds inside the forest at night, when the many nocturnal creatures are roaming about, and at sunrise, when a myriad of birds take off over the jungle canopy. Some of the jungle birds are remarkably vocal, such as the flocks of bright green parrots or red macaws that scream out their wild complaints as they fly overhead. Everything in the Amazon seems larger than life, amplified and exaggerated. The colors are brighter, the temperature hotter, the plants bigger, and the fish tastier than you could have imagined. After you get settled in, you'll be ready for some adventure. You'll float in a canoe across a large, still lake to see lily pads the size of coffee tables and then, as night falls, you'll hear the sounds of the jungle change from day to night. You'll see the glowing red eyes of the caiman (kin to the alligator) sitting motionless in the water at night and feel the tug of a piranha at the end of your fishing line. High up in the jungle canopy, you'll walk across suspended footpaths to observations towers, where you'll spot monkeys, birds, and even giant sloth. In the morning, the pink river dolphins perform acrobatics around the lakes and at the Meeting of the

# Must-Sees

The Amazon

**M** **Teatro Amazonas:** If you see one attraction in the city of Manaus, make it the Teatro. This luxurious theater exudes the great rubber boom in its rich design and imported furnishings. It's still used for presentations of opera and Brazilian music (page 462).

**M** **The Meeting of the Waters:** The dramatic difference between the cold, muddy water of the Solimões and the warm, smoky water of the Negro continues even after they join to become the Amazon River. Pink river dolphins like to come here to play in the two different sides (page 463).

**M** **Jungle Hikes and Canopy Walks:** Hikes along the jungle floor should probably be guided, and some reach up into the high canopy, either using observation towers or suspended walkways (page 468).

**M** **Swimming with the Piranha and Dolphins:** Swim with the pink river dolphins at the Meeting of the Waters and other popular swimming holes all over the area (page 469).

**M** **Mercado Ver-o-Peso:** The central market in Belém, one of the largest in Brazil, just keeps going on and on . . . fresh fish, strange varieties of jungle fruit, indigenous ceramics, and plant medicines from the ancient wisdom of the Amazon. It's all held in an architectural complex that has elements from the 17th, 18th, and 19th centuries (page 478).

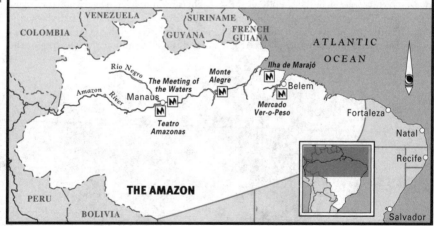

Waters, where the Amazon River is born out of two completely different streams—one creamy white with mud and sediment, the other dark and warm, like tea.

Almost 60 percent of the Amazon Jungle lies within Brazil's borders and about 50 percent of Brazil is part of the Amazon Jungle. In other words, the amount of Brazil that is not part of the Amazon is about equal to the amount of Amazon Jungle that is not inside

Brazil. Without a doubt, the Amazon is Brazil's most important national treasure, and national responsibility. It comprises almost two million species of plants and animals, one-fifth of the fresh water on the planet, and about as many secrets and mysteries as there are stars in the sky.

With an average temperature of 27°C, the Amazon can easily hover around 40°C during the day. Humidity chimes in at around 80

**N Ilha de Marajó:** There are only two places in the world where you can find the beautiful and endangered blue macaw: in the Pantanal and on the Island of Marajó near Belém. Flocks of pink flamingos gather around the lakes, and the morning flight of bright green parrots from the Papagaios Island is a rush of pure delight (page 490).

**N Monte Alegre:** Down the Amazon River by boat, Monte Alegre sits in the shadow of some tall, tropical mountains. Up in those looming mountains are some of the oldest cave paintings in the Americas, around 12,000 years old.

COURTESY OF EMBRATUR/DIVULGAÇÃO

a typical Amazon jungle lodge

Besides the cave paintings, you can hike to numerous waterfalls and beautiful vistas (page 494).

## Best Jungle Lodges

**N Acajatuba Jungle Lodge:** Made entirely of wood and jungle plants, the Acajatuba sits on the side of a wide area in the river, with incredible views. Rooms are joined in small groups and offer comfort in a rustic setting. Their restaurant has a panoramic view of the area (page 472).

**N Amazon Ecopark Lodge:** One of the most elite lodges in the jungle, the Ecopark has long stretches of suspended trails that lead to its Primate Rehab Center, where you can watch the monkeys all day long. They also have a beautiful restaurant and plenty of excursion options. Manaus is only 20 minutes away by boat (page 472).

**N Ariaú Jungle Towers:** The largest lodge in the Central Amazon, Ariaú is a series of jungle cabanas that combine to offer the most complete set of options in the jungle. They have extensive suspended trails up in the jungle canopy and seven separate observation towers (page 472).

**N Juma Jungle Hotel:** The most rustic of the bunch, this hotel offers simplicity and great contact with the jungle canopy. The entire hotel is built on stilts and they offer an excellent set of excursions for their guests (page 473).

The Amazon

percent. There are only two seasons in the jungle: the rainy season and the very rainy season. The wet season is at the end of Brazil's summer, December–May, when temperatures are cooler and heavy rains occur daily, a constant series of downpours. The "dry" season is June–November, when rains come on quickly and heavily and pass just as quickly. This is when it gets hot. Corresponding to these two seasons goes the level of the river—changing as much as 10 meters in depth between the two periods. During the wet season, the Amazon River and its tributaries bulge with water and cover the sandy beaches that appear in the Central Amazon during the dry season. Temperatures average 28°C in the wet season and 36°C in the dry season with humidity ranging from 80–90 percent.

The **Central Amazon** region is where two big rivers cut through the jungle, then meet

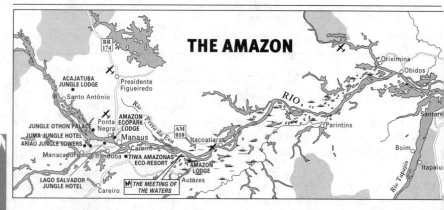

up to form the Amazon River. There are vast areas that are off-limits to visitors, due to their native inhabitants or sensitive ecosystems (or both). But within the region are also numerous ecological preserves and national parks encompassing hundreds of square kilometers of virgin forest. Along the waterways are numerous jungle lodges, where visitors can stay in relative comfort (or total comfort in some cases) and organize their various safaris and excursions into the jungle and along the rivers. The capital of the state of Amazonas, the largest state in Brazil, and home to most of the Brazilian Amazon, is Manaus, a large city of almost three million inhabitants. Manaus is a shocking contrast to the surrounding environment. Many visitors want to get as far from it as possible, to experience the untouched aspects of the jungle. But there are many other cities and towns in the Central Amazon region, including São Geraldo da Cachoeira to the east, with a population of almost 80 percent indigenous or *caboclo* (indigenous and Portuguese mix), and the city of Parintins to the west, with its great Festival of the Ox. In between are numerous small towns and villages.

Venturing out to the eastern edge of the Amazon is a mixed bag of nuts, as the attractions come in three different categories: urban, rural, and jungle. There are dense jungle areas, vast wetlands, and huge rivers that rush past archipelagos and island straits on their way to the Atlantic Ocean, where they are received in a great wave of resistance, known as the Pororoca. On the other hand, there are also urbanized areas and popular beaches (with kiosks, restaurants, and beach activities on weekends). Between these two extremes, you'll also find working buffalo ranches and rural areas, where you'll see the great mixture of cultures from the region—from aboriginal groups to descendents of the European colonizers. Nowhere is this culture more visible than in the arts and crafts you'll find in the small towns and public markets.

The **Eastern Amazon**'s major city is Belém, with four centuries of historical architecture, a story spanning the city's development up to the present day. Around Belém, much of the focus is on the beaches—both fresh- and salt-water—that rest along the banks of the many islands and waterways of the area. Some of these (mainly those on Mosqueiro Island) are urbanized and extremely popular with the city's residents, especially on weekends in the dry season. The best beaches are the ones most difficult to reach: along the coast of Marajó Island and on the Island of Cotijuba. Of course, even better beaches are farther out still, in the vicinity of Santarém, 50 hours by boat upriver. In Santarém, you'll also find some of the region's best pottery and some interesting jungle excursions, including animal-observation safaris, fishing trips, and hikes out to some ancient cave paintings.

Perhaps the most sought-after destination in

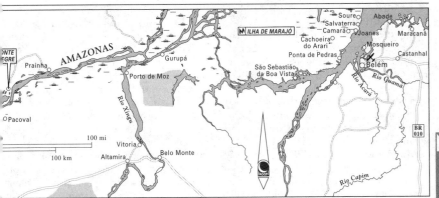

© AVALON TRAVEL PUBLISHING, INC.

the Eastern Amazon is the Island of Marajó, where you'll find a bit of everything that's great in the region: semi-secluded fresh-water beaches, great ceramic pottery employing techniques passed down from the ancient aboriginal tribes, and jungle safaris featuring egrets, storks, blue macaws, caimans, monkeys, sloths, and many more animals of the forest.

## PLANNING YOUR TIME

### The Central Amazon

There are several ways to pay a visit to the Central Amazon region around Manaus and they differ according to your accommodations. Staying in a hotel in Manaus allows you to create your own agenda of excursions and tours, even on the spot while you're in town. This is what many visitors do when their trip to Manaus is short, requiring that their journeys lie within a few hours of the city. This is the best way to visit the jungle without a packaged agenda—although all hotels will try to sell you on their packages. Most create packages together with third-party guides and tour agencies, taking you around to the principal sights of the area: the Meeting of the Waters, city tour, Praia Ponta Negra, and Parque de Janeiro. You can also shop for your tours when you arrive in Manaus if you want to keep things open-ended.

Staying in a jungle lodge is the preferred option, as it gets you the deepest into the jungle. Most lodges have their own restaurants and excursions (both river trips and jungle hikes) and you generally spend your time at the lodge or on their excursions, since most are well out of town and some are downright hidden out in the jungle. Obviously, your trip is determined almost completely by the quality and style of the lodge. Lodges work with packages, and you can purchase packages as small as a single day. Some lodges allow day visits by people who are not staying at the lodge but want to see and sample its facilities for the day. Most of these day visits have day-use fees and include lunch.

The third method is to stay on a floating hotel, which is a combination of excursion and accommodation. This means you'll be spending all of your time with the hotel's guided tours, whether onboard or off in the jungle. Some of these floating excursions are long (like a trip between Belém and Manaus) and others are short (just around the major Manaus attractions, for example).

How much time you spend in your chosen accommodation and which one you choose depends mostly on your budget. If you have time, a good idea is to combine these trips; spend two days and two nights in Manaus, taking the city tour and seeing the popular attractions in the area, then move to a jungle lodge for a more in-depth look at the jungle, or take a boat up Rio Negro on a multi-day excursion to São Gabriel da Cachoeira. Mixing and matching is a great way to go.

## The Eastern Amazon

To get the most out of the Eastern Amazon region, you'll want to concentrate on the highlights of the area and avoid the rest. Boat trips that take you out to the various islands and beaches can take hours to get back and forth, so any casual journey or excursion can easily end up eating an entire day. Excursions to popular beaches and along well-trodden trails are often underwhelming.

My advice is to use Belém as it has always been used: as a launching pad to other parts of the jungle. While you're in the city between connections, go ahead and check out the sights around town. A few hours of sightseeing upon your arrival and a few more when you return from Marajó, for instance, will be enough to check out the Ver-o-Peso market, waterfront architectural complex, and Emílio Goeldi Museum—the main attractions in town.

From the city of Belém, you can find more wonders of the Amazon, including the magical island of Marajó. The island is home to numerous working buffalo ranches and private lodges, from where you can take safaris into the environment, spotting monkeys, alligators, sea turtles, and hundreds of species of tropical birds (including the rare and beautiful blue macaw). You can also take boat excursions from Belém that pass Marajó as they make their way upstream into the jungle. The best time to visit this area is between August and December, the dry season.

Another favorite excursion from Belém is to the beaches on the Island of Cotijuba and the early-morning bird-watching trip to Papagaios Island. After that, a multi-day boat trip (or better, a quick flight) to Santarém is usually the next step in the journey toward Manaus.

Plan for two half days in Belém, two days and two nights on Marajó, and two days in Santarém for a total of five days. If you take a boat from Belém to Santarém, you can add another two days to the trip.

## The Latest in Jungle Fashion and Gear

The key to packing for the jungle is to concentrate on your gear and not on your cloth-ing. Besides, you can find great outfits in cotton and blended fabrics right in Manaus, including light safari pants and hats. You'll want to wear long pants when you're out in the jungle and shorts around town or on the boat. The great thing about Manaus is that it is not infested with mosquitoes. In fact, due to the acidity of Rio Negro, there are very few mosquitoes to bother tourists. Nevertheless, you should bring insect repellant for the other interesting insects in the region. Also, don't forget sunscreen, waterproof hiking boots, and maybe a pair of water galoshes. You may also want to bring a head lamp, good binoculars, rain suit or hooded rain cape, large ziplock bags in which to keep your dry socks and underwear, and a water bottle. You should have a pair of light tennis shoes for walking around the city and dry areas and a bathing suit for swimming with the dolphins and piranha (they don't bite hard). Bring a hammock if you plan to spend the night in the jungle, in which case you should also bring mosquito netting for your head so you can sleep at night (not many mosquitoes is not the same as no mosquitoes). Many lodges that offer overnight campouts in the jungle also have their own equipment and hammocks. You can buy hammocks right in Manaus and you can get other gear at any fishing and hunting store in Brazil. If you fly into Rio, São Paulo, or Salvador, there are many from which to choose.

If you have a camera or computer equipment with you, you might consider bringing along dry packs to keep the moisture away. Absorbent cloth carrying bags also help.

## Vaccinations

The most common concern of those visiting the Amazon region is the contraction of malaria, and many travelers bring malaria pills or take shots before coming. Until recently, malaria was rarely seen in Brazil and hardly an issue in the Amazon. But a recent outbreak in Minas Gerais (interior state) has brought about a renewed awareness of the sickness and it might not be a bad idea to bring along some pills. What the Brazilian Minister of Health recommends most strongly when visiting the Amazon is a yellow fever vaccination. A recent outbreak of the disease caused a bit of a scare throughout the country and vaccinations were administered nationally in 2001. Anyone entering the northern states of Brazil was required to be vaccinated as well. Likely, you will be stopped upon entry into Brazil or at the very least into the northern region and asked for your yellow fever vaccination card. You can receive the vaccination here in Brazil if you prefer, but you'll need to get your shots 10 days before entering the jungle.

# Manaus

How far can you walk into the jungle? The answer must certainly be *as far as Manaus,* because if you go any farther, you'll be walking *out* of the jungle. Manaus is about as deep inside the Amazon as you can get—in its very bosom, surrounded on all sides by thick tropical forest. The city is positioned close to the confluence of the two rivers that combine to form the Amazon River: the dark and ominous Rio Negro and the muddy Rio Solimões. In essence, Manaus is located at the beginning of the Amazon River. Interestingly, many of the most popular river excursions go up Rio Negro rather than down the Amazon (at least those leaving from Manaus).

In the city of Manaus, there are a few interesting sights, including some historical buildings, vestiges of the rubber trade of the early 20th century. You'll get an idea of how much money British and American interests brought into this area (and yet only a small portion of the value that was extracted). There are also interesting open-air markets and craft fairs, plus an assortment of museums and ecological research centers. The Duty Free Zone is a major shopping area that extends the tourism of the area into the industrial zone, where all kinds of electronics and household products are made. Many visitors are surprised at the size of this jungle city. With almost three million inhabitants, Manaus is one of Brazil's 10 largest cities and was the second city in Brazil to get electricity. In spite of its jungle surroundings and strong aboriginal influences, Manaus is a large, modern city.

Another thing that surprises first-time visitors is the number of beaches on the outskirts of town. Formed along the sandy banks of the Rio Negro during the dry season (July–November), these beaches resemble any typical beach on the ocean. There are even beach kiosks, shade umbrellas, and beachfront hotels to complete the picture. The river is so wide here that it resembles the ocean and while the river is low, the sand along its banks is exposed, creating long stretches of beach. Some of these sandy strips near Manaus have been developed into popular leisure zones and many are frequented by the residents of the city on weekends (with all that that implies: crowds, noise, trash, etc.).

But by far the most compelling attractions of Manaus are the excursion that go up (or down) the river and out into the jungle, by day and by night. Most of the official areas—nature preserves and national parks—are accessible only by boat and the types and styles of river excursions are practically endless. There are multi-day riverboat journeys, day trips to protected wildlife areas, and even deep jungle adventures. You can opt to spend your nights on one of these riverboats or stay in a comfortable hotel in the city and take day trips up and down the river. Many visitors end up opting for one of the lodges located well inside the jungle, 20–400 kilometers from the city. These lodges generally provide their own excursions, treks, native village visits, and animal encounters for their guests.

## HISTORY

It may seem out of place, a city of three million inhabitants in the middle of the dense jungle.

The area along Rio Negro was inhabited by the Manaus people, who made their homes along the sandbars and riverbanks around the Meeting of the Waters. A few adventurous colonizers made their way to the location to set up a small village as a field station for the wild harvesting of fruits and nuts. The village grew slowly over the years and a small fort was built there to protect the region from the English, French, and Dutch pirates that often attacked the coast. Then, around 1850, when steam ships were beginning to travel the rivers of the world, bringing the English, Americans, and Europeans to all corners of the globe, a new interest was placed on Manaus. At that time, it was a small town with only 250 homes and 3,000 inhabitants. Still, it was the principal city of the region, then known as the Lugar da Barra (Place on the Bar). With the increased traffic into the region, the jungle's natural riches became a principal export and source of wealth for the city. Principal exports at the time were nuts, cocoa, *guaraná*, and rubber. By 1888, rubber would take over as the new gold because of the increasing demand of the modern world. The region supplied the raw material for the American tire companies Dunlop and Michelin. And so began an era of great wealth and growth for the city of Manaus in the middle of the Amazon Jungle.

The demand for the latex was seemingly unquenchable and the city's economy was based almost entirely on it. To get a piece of the great boom, poor farmers from the northeast of Brazil made their way into the jungle. Few were able to make the transition successfully and most ended up on the outskirts of town, poorer than they were back home. And so the poor neighborhoods of Manaus began. Around 1912, the clock struck 12 and the great gala came to an end, much faster than it began. American companies switched suppliers and began to import their latex from Asia, where labor was even cheaper than in Brazil. The entire region went into an economic meltdown that lasted until 1967, when the Zona Franca (Duty Free Zone) was created. The Zona Franca gave Manaus a new economic base, supplying tax-free imports to the Brazilian market. As demand increased within the country, the zone soon became home to numerous assembly plants for international companies to make their goods right on the spot.

The last chapter is familiar to most Westerners: During the 1980s and 1990s, a growing awareness of our global interconnectedness and fragility brought a new focus to the region and the world began to pay a lot of attention to just what Brazil was doing with the Amazon Jungle, the world's second-largest wildlife area and home to unfathomed natural riches.

## SIGHTS IN CENTRAL MANAUS
### Alfôndega and Floating Pier
Prefabricated in England, the Alfôndega Customs House (Rua Marquês de Santa Cruz, no phone, 8 A.M.–1 P.M. daily), was reconstructed in 1912 near the Port of Manaus to receive and process shipments to and from all over the world. It stands as one of the principal buildings from the Rubber Cycle in Manaus and is located right on the waterfront. Nearby, the floating pier was created to receive large ships during all phases of the river's flow—which can vary up to 10 meters in depth. The pier and port area is a bustling side of Manaus, with workers loading and unloading goods and tourists boarding for their river excursions. It's worth stopping for awhile to observe the activities and take some pictures.

### Mercado Municipal
Do you want to find some Cat's Claw or Devil's Scratch to take home with you? You'll find these and many more jungle remedies right here in the Mercado Municipal (Rua dos Barés 46, 8 A.M.–6 P.M. daily), standing in the same location in front of the Rio Negro since 1882. Besides herbal cures and the native medicine men and women selling them, there are arts and crafts from the region, spices, all kinds of fruits you've never seen before, and fresh fish from the rivers. There is a restaurant inside that cooks up some of these fish during lunch.

The Amazon

## Palácio Rio Negro

Built from 1900–1910, the Palácio (Av. 7 de Setembro 1540, tel. 92/3232-4450, 10 A.M.– 5 P.M. weekdays and 4–9 P.M. on weekends) is one of the city's primary cultural centers. It contains exhibition halls and presentation rooms for its many permanent and temporary exhibitions. Inside is the Museu de Numismática and the Radio and Film Museum. It's located just outside the old Centro area.

## M Teatro Amazonas

Easily the most striking building in Manaus and one of the most important neoclassic monuments in Brazil, the Teatro Amazonas (Opera House) (Praça São Sebastião, tel. 92/3232-1768) is a reminder of the great wealth extracted here from the rubber boom of the late-19th and early-20th centuries (known in Brazil as the Rubber Cycle, or *Ciclo de Burracha*). Overshadowed by the great coffee boom in the southeast region, the Rubber Cycle was a relatively quiet extraction of natural latex from the *serigueira* tree mostly by the American companies Dunlop and Michelin. The growth that followed is well captured in the great Opera House. Almost everything used to build the great theater was imported from Europe, such as the Portuguese and Italian marble in the entry hall and stairway. In the theater area is a gold Venetian chandelier and a painted mural backdrop depicting the Meeting of the Waters. There are three levels of box seats in the theater. The floor in the noble hall is made of 12,000 interlaced wooden panels (no glue or nails used). The only thing in the Opera House not imported are the rich wooden hand runners and railings, made from local jacandara wood, which was used throughout Brazil and heavily exported to Europe. From the outside you can't miss the theater's central dome, which is covered with 20,000 glazed tiles in the colors of Brazil.

You can visit the house from 9 A.M.–4 P.M. Monday–Saturday on a 20-minute guided tour or visit during one of the traditional presentations (known as Livro Vivo), which occur at 2 P.M. on Fridays and 10 A.M. and 11 A.M. on Saturdays. The cost is R$6. There are also performances in the evenings and a Festival of

Teatro Amazonas

Opera during April and May, when there are numerous performances from national and international groups.

## MUSEUMS

There are two fairly interesting museums in Manaus and they are both rather far from the downtown area, so you might look for a city tour that includes them if you're interested in visiting. The city buses that go out to these museums are comfortable but slow and you could spend that time on more interesting excursions. The **Museum of Natural Sciences** (Estrada de Belém, no number, tel. 92/3644-2799, R$3) is located in the Cachoeira Grande colony (one of the city's Japanese districts) and features aquariums of regional fish, including a piraruca (the world's largest fresh-water fish) tank. There is also an arts and crafts store in the museum, which is open from 9 A.M.–5 P.M. Monday–Saturday. The **Museu do Indio** (Rua Duque de Caxias 356, Praça 14, tel. 92/3635-1922, 8:30–11:30 A.M. and 2–4:30 P.M. Mon.–Fri. and 8:30–11:30 A.M. on Sat., R$4) has several exhibit rooms with artifacts from the local tribes. You'll find fishing and hunting equipment, ceramics, crafts, and ceremonial artifacts. There is information about the psychotropic rituals using the ayahuasca vine and other native plants.

## PONTA NEGRA BEACH

Brazilians love their beaches and when it became possible for residents of Manaus to frequent a long strip of sand along the riverbank some 13 kilometers from the city, they were hit with a sort of beach fever and turned the area, once inhabited by the Manaus people, into one of the city's hottest tourist attractions and nightlife centers. Ponta Negra beach, a wide strip of sand right in the middle of the Amazon Jungle, is complete with beach bars, restaurants, shade umbrellas, and volleyball courts. There is a first-aid station and the city's largest hotel and convention center, the Tropical Manaus Eco Resort. Nearby is a public theater

where music and popular shows are presented all year long and especially during festivals.

Afternoons at the beach are relaxing and beautiful and the sunset over the river is something to put on your agenda. At night, Ponta Negra lights up with activity in the restaurants and bars and is the only place in town that stays up late. You can get to Ponta Negra by taxi or look for a tour van leaving from Manaus for the day or half-day. You can also opt to stay at a Ponta Negra hotel. A great idea is to combine an afternoon at Ponta Negra with a morning of sightseeing and shopping in the city.

## OTHER BEACHES ON RIO NEGRO

Ponta Negra is not the only sandy bank along Rio Negro. Other beaches, or *banhos* (baths), are being developed for the city's tourism trade. Some of these include **Praias Tupé** and **Arrombado,** an hour from the city by boat. At Tupé, there is a nature preserve with plenty of jungle plants nearby. During the week, it's nearly deserted, but on weekends it fills with locals. Along the Estrada do Tarumã, leading out of town, are a number of beaches, including **Tarumã** and **Tarumāzinho Beaches** and the **Almas Waterfall.** Finally, there's the **Amarelinho Beach** in the Educandos neighborhood with a couple of good restaurants and an excellent view of the sunset. If you don't have a rental car to make the trips out to these beaches, then the best way to visit is by tour van or bus. You can also hire a boat to take you out.

## ◪ THE MEETING OF THE WATERS

For eight kilometers, the waters of Rio Negro and Rio Solimões flow side-by-side without mixing, as if getting used to each other. This interesting phenomenon, known locally as the *Encontro das Aguas,* is one of the area's principal attractions, only 10 kilometers downstream from Manaus. Full-day excursions take visitors down to the meeting to observe the two distinct colors, speeds, and temperatures

## THE MAGICAL PINK RIVER DOLPHIN

Among the strangest and most enchanting creatures of the Amazon is the beautiful and intelligent pink river dolphin (*Inia geoffrensis*), or *peixe boto* as they are known in Brazil. You can't miss them as they play and perform acrobatics in the waters of the Central Amazon Region. They are often spotted along the Rio Negro from the Meeting of the Waters to the Anavilhanas Archipelago upriver, but they are also found in Venezuala, Peru, and throughout the Amazon region. At times, they can be seen swimming alongside river boats or hunting for fish around the *igarapés* (still waters along the banks of the rivers). They are extremely intelligent (their brain is about 40 percent larger than the human brain), very playful, and very communicative.

The *boto*'s shocking color comes with age. A full-grown adult is bright pink, reaches almost three meters in length, and weighs up to 200 kilos. This makes it among the largest of its species, including ocean-going dolphins. Aside from its shocking color, the *boto* looks very much like its ocean-going cousins, but with a few particularities no doubt evolved to suit its fresh-water environment. In particular, its body is more flexible and "bent" than other dolphins, giving it extra maneuverability in the intricate waterways of the Amazon. Instead of a dorsal fin, it has a pronounced ridge along its back. Another difference is that the *boto* usually swims alone or in pairs, a behavior attributed to its relative lack of natural predators.

The *boto*'s biggest enemy is the local fisherman. Excessive fishing of the Amazon River Basin diminishes the *boto*'s food supply and makes hunting difficult. Dolphins also get caught in fishing nets and drown. In a note of karmic justice, the *boto*'s hunting practices frustrate the fishing methods of the locals. The *boto* herds fish into shallow waters where it captures them, whereas fishermen depend on calm conditions and fish that are not being pursued by a *boto*.

Apart from its rivalry with fishermen, the *boto* has enjoyed a special relationship with indigenous groups of the Amazon, who consider it taboo to hunt or eat the animal. The *boto* plays a large role in native lore and is considered a magical and powerful being, not all that different from humans. Legend has it that the *boto* occasionally takes on the guise of a human and hangs around the river banks looking for young women to seduce. A bastard child is usually the result. Its reputation as a lover has given it the name *boto amorador* (lover *boto*) among local tribes and has made it the primary scapegoat for all unwed mothers. Women are warned against swimming near the riverbanks and riding alone in canoes. But the *boto* can also take the form of a beautiful woman who seduces the men of the region. Any man fortunate enough to encounter such a creature will forever be protected by her when in the waters of the Amazon.

---

of the rivers flowing together. The tea-colored waters of the Rio Negro (a comfortable 28°C) and the milky, muddy waters of the Solimões (fast and cold at 22°C) finally get together downstream. Such is the formation of the Amazon River. At the meeting, it's common to see numerous pink river dolphins playing in the waters. They enjoy both of the rivers, navigating primarily by sonar. Excursions to the Meeting usually include views of huge water lilies and even short hikes into the jungle near the confluence at the January National

Park. Boats leave from the floating docks in Manaus at 9 A.M. and return around 4 P.M. with lunch included. There are all types and sizes of boats that make the trip. The cost is around R$65.

## INPA SCIENCE WOODS

Located within the city limits, the Bosque de Ciência (Rua Otávio Cabral, no number, Petrópolis, tel. 92/3643-3293, www.inpa.com.br, 9–11 A.M. and 2–4 P.M.

Tues.–Fri. and 9 A.M.–4 P.M. weekends, R$2) is a small research center of the National Amazon Research Institute (INPA). The area consists of 13 hectares of natural forest and habitats for giant otters, manatees, alligators, and other species. There is a bee exhibit and trails that lead past monkeys, sloths, and countless tropical bird species (including parrots and toucans). There is also the Casa de Ciência, which displays research projects involving the Amazon's flora and its use in medicine and industry, and the Jardim Botânico, with numerous species of plants and flowers from the jungle. INPA is located in the Petrópolis neighborhood on the east side of the city. To get there, you can catch a bus on Av. 7 de Setembro (many have INPA written on them) or take an organized city tour that visits INPA.

# MINDÚ PARK

The suspended walkways of the Mindú Park (Av. Perimetral, Parque 10, tel. 92/3236-7702, 8 A.M.–5 P.M. Tues.–Sun., R$2) are a great way to see the forest without actually interfering with it. They also put you high into the canopy, where most of the action takes place in the Amazon. The Park, created in 1996 in an area of 330,000 square meters, provides a simple and elegant way to view the Amazon's great flora and fauna. Besides the suspended walkways, there are paved trails that lead through various ecosystems, including planted forest, dry land forest, and flooded forest. There is also an area that suffered an illegal deforestation in 1989. The park is a refuge for the endangered miniature monkey, the bare faced tamarin, which only exists in the forest around Manaus. The park also contains a bookstore, tourist information center, and outdoor theater for lectures and presentations. The architecture is designed to integrate with the environment. You'll also find gardens of medicinal and aromatic herbs from the jungle. The best way to see the park is on a city tour package. However, there are buses that go out from the Centro.

# ADOLFO DUCKE BOTANICAL GARDEN

To help keep Manaus's urban sprawl in check—at least in the direction of the Meeting of the Waters—the Adolfo Ducke Forest Preserve (Rua Uirapuru 1, Cidade de Deus, tel. 92/3681-2282, R$5) was created with almost 100 square kilometers of protected forest near the eastern edge of Manaus. Inside the preserve is a botanical garden, occupying about 500,000 square meters (500 square kilometers), where visitors can hike along eight different jungle trails and observe the many species of plants and animals that live in the region. Entry into the garden requires a guide.

# ANAVILHANAS ARCHIPELAGO

Around 100 kilometers from Manaus up Rio Negro is the world's largest group of fresh-water islands, the Archipelago of Anavilhanas. The islands are long strips of land covered in virgin forest and they form a giant maze of waterways for almost another 100 kilometers up the river. Navigating among these islands requires a great deal of skill and familiarity with the area. Among the islands live hundreds of animal species, such as huge snakes, iguanas, and alligators. There are also several varieties of monkeys and water mammals, such as the pink river dolphin, the *tucuxi* dolphin, and the manatee. The giant river fish, the pirarucu, is also abundant here. During the dry season, the water level drops by nearly 10 meters and great sandy beaches appear around many of the islands. Thankfully, the entire area is a protected ecological research preserve and tourists can only pass through by boat. The area is restricted to research professionals that are approved by IBAMA (Brazilian Institute for the Environment).

# PARQUE ECOLÓGICO DE JANEIRO

The most frequented of the natural parks near Manaus is the Parque Ecológico de Janeiro, about 25 kilometers downstream from the city

# THE MANATEE:
# LARGEST RESIDENT OF THE AMAZON RIVER

The life of a Peixe Boi (sea cow, or *Trichechus manatus* in scientific language) is rather laid-back. This docile and inoffensive creature spends about a third of each day feeding on various water plants growing in the deep Amazon waterways. It usually swims alone but sometimes meets with others at warm swimming holes or rich feeding grounds. Another third of the manatee's time is spent playing and socializing and the rest is spent sleeping or relaxing near the top of the water or motionless on the bottom. Scientists believe that manatees are intelligent animals, capable of passing information between them, such as the locations of feeding grounds or directions through complicated waterways. They also communicate in times of danger, warning others to stay away or setting up meeting locations for when the danger has passed. Because they are creatures of habit, returning frequently to the same swimming and feeding grounds, local guides are proficient at finding the creatures and bringing groups in for a look. They are especially plentiful in the Archipelago of Anavilhanas about 100 km from Manaus and are among the most charming and delightful animals in the Amazon Region.

The Brazilian Peixe Boi looks quite different than its North American cousin. It's much thinner for one thing, and almost completely black. Its face looks like that of a walrus with no tusks. Although slightly chubby and slow in appearance, the Peixe Boi is actually a powerful swimmer and can reach up to 25 km per hour in the water. It uses its powerful tail for both propulsion and direction. Besides the small population of Peixe Boi in the Central and Eastern Amazon Regions, the creature can also be found in the ocean along the shores of Northern and Northeastern Brazil.

Hunted practically to extinction, the Peixe Boi is now on the Endangered Species List. Females give birth to only one cub per year and their gestation period is longer than that of a human: about 13 months. They do not have a particular mating season, so cubs are born throughout the year. They remain with their mothers for two years, when they begin to feed on the surrounding plant life. Brazil's Projeto Peixe Boi (www.projetopeixe-boi.com.br), part of the government environmental group IBAMA, is responsible for maintaining and protecting the species and even rehabilitating young, orphaned cubs. The headquarters are located on the Island of Itamaracá, north of Recife in the state of Pernambuco (see the *Recife* chapter for details on visitations) and has offices and rehabilitation centers in Manaus and Belém.

(past the Meeting of the Waters). Excursions through the park are often combined with the Meeting of the Waters. You can take a small canoe along the shallow, swampy waterways, passing numerous species of birds and jungle plants. Make your way to the huge Queen Victoria water lily in a lake inside the park to see lily pads that reach up to two meters in diameter. The area consists of more than 90 square kilometers and contains several types of Amazonian ecosystems: the *igarapé* (swamplands), *vársia* (lowland growth area), and dry land forest. You can easily find an excursion leaving from the port at Manaus. Most leave at 9 A.M.

## ZOO

If you come to the end of your stay in the Amazon and you don't feel that you got to see enough animals, then swing by the Manaus Zoo (Estrada da Ponta Negra, Km 13, tel. 92/3625-2044, 9 A.M.–4:30 P.M. Tues.–Sun.) for a look at more than 300 species, including monkeys, jaguars, giant otters, snakes, alligators (caimans), and tortoises. You'll get a good, close look at all kinds of jungle species. It's located near the Ponta Negra Beach along the Estrada da Ponta Negra, 13 kilometers from downtown.

# SHOPPING

You can find indigenous arts and crafts at the **Museu do Indio** and in the **Mercado Central**. You will likely be approached by native people selling rustic jewelry all over town and at the Ponta Negra Beach area. For Brazilians, Manaus represents an area of great shopping possibilities. The **Zona Franca de Manaus** (Duty Free Zone) was created in 1967 to inspire the movement of imported goods into Brazil. The success of the project resulted in the creation of an entire industrial center in the city, where products are manufactured for the Brazilian market. Everything from computers to refrigerators is made in Manaus and the economy of the area has been greatly stimulated as a result. The zone is scheduled to be discontinued in 2013, when tax incentives will return to normal on products sold here. Most likely, the movement of imported goods will decline, but the manufacturing sector should continue as usual. For the foreigner, the Duty Free Zone does not affect purchases, which are subject to the import regulations of their own countries. However, certain products manufactured in Manaus may carry competitive prices for visitors and a walk around the city's commercial zone may be of some interest.

# MANAUS JUNGLE EXCURSIONS

As already noted, most jungle lodges and floating hotels will offer packages that include everything, including your jungle excursions. However, if you stay in town and end up planning your own excursions, you should be careful when shopping for a tour agency. Remember that the best ones are certified by EMBRATUR or the city's own Manaustur or some other governmental agency. The EMBRATUR website is www.turismo.gov.br in case you want to check anybody's credentials. There may be times when you want a simple boat taxi to some beach or jungle lodge and you may end up using an unofficial, local guide. The best advice is to ask other travelers for their recommendations or ask at any tourist agency for a reputable *barceiro.* Do not try to economize by going with an unknown or unauthorized guide as you can end up putting yourself at great risk. You can call or email Manaustur (tel. 92/3622-4886, info@manaustur.com.br) with questions about guides and excursions.

## Bird-Watching

The best way to see tropical birds is in one of the national parks. You can see plenty of species in the Mindú Park and the small INPA grove, as they are sanctuaries for birds and other animals. Catching rare birds out in the jungle can be difficult and you will probably be more successful on a bird-watching excursion, with a guide that is experienced in finding the flocks. Often, just waiting around your jungle lodge is a great way to catch birds coming and going. When successful, you'll be able to spot egrets, toucans, various species of hummingbirds, red macaws, blue and yellow macaws, parrots, and more.

COURTESY OF EMBRATUR/DIVULGAÇÃO

**Flocks of green and yellow macaws are commonplace in the Amazon.**

The Amazon

## Caiman Night Focusing

At night, the canoes take off from the lodge or floating hotel to pass along the river near the *igarapés,* the shallow, swampy margins of the rivers, where the caimans hang out. These large crocodilians can reach up to six meters in length here in the Amazon and are capable of eating any large animal. Thankfully, they are rather timid and dislike humans, who make a lot of noise and splash around a lot in the water. The caiman prefers to sit motionless, like a stone in the water, waiting for its prey to pass close enough to grab with a quick turn of the head. Most common meals are fish and birds. They're easy to spot as you pass along in a small canoe (just about the size of a big caiman), as their eyes glow in the dark when you shine a light on them. Caiman focusing is an old hunting technique for capturing the animals, where a light is shone into the *igarapé* to see the many pairs of red orbs just above the surface of the water. The caiman is abundant in the Amazon and is found in Peru, Columbia, and Ecuador. Smaller caimans are found in great quantities all the way down in the southern Pantanal in Brazil and Paraguay.

## Canoe Trips

The best time to head out onto the river is at sunrise, when birds are active and the jungle is buzzing with life at the dawn of a new day. Typical day journeys go out into the tributaries and smaller waterways off Rio Negro and even into the *igarapés* to see the many plants and animals. There are great canoe trips around the Parque de Janeiro that pass the Lagoa da Vitória Regia (Queen Victoria Lake) and most jungle lodges and floating hotels have specific canoe trips and interesting areas to explore for their guests. Besides the sunrise excursion, the most interesting is at sunset and into the evening—combined with a caiman focusing ritual—giving you the intriguing sensation of night falling upon the jungle.

## Fishing for Piranha

One of the more popular jungle excursions involves throwing a piece of meat into the water on a hook and waiting for that unmistakable tug of the red or black piranha. The black piranha is the largest, but the red piranha is the most aggressive. Most jungle lodges offer some type of piranha fishing excursion; the floating hotels always have such activities; and you can find individual excursions at the agencies in town. For serious fishing pleasure, there are multi-day fishing trips that take you way up the river to designated fishing areas (the areas rotate during the year to allow species to replenish themselves). You can even fish for the great pirarucu at certain times of the year. Check with the tour agencies for specific trips being offered.

## Indigenous Village Encounters

Most of the jungle lodges have connections with indigenous villages and bring small groups of visitors around to visit and observe their ways of life. There are numerous villages around Manaus and they range from well-produced demonstrations for the tourists to authentic aboriginal villages. Generally, the farther out into the jungle you go, the more authentic your experience will be. Of course, there are tribes that are protected and visitations are heavily restricted. Until around 2000, there were even some tribes untouched and unseen by foreigners.

Some towns outside of Manaus are surrounded by native villages, such as São Gabriel das Cachoeiras and Silves (in opposite directions). Jungle lodges in the large jungle preservation areas, such as Mamirauá and Jaú, are also more likely to bring you in touch with the jungle's human inhabitants. Lodges that specialize in indigenous encounters include Juma Jungle Hotel and Guanavenas Lodge.

## Jungle Hikes and Canopy Walks

Most jungle lodges have their own jungle hikes—some even take guests out for overnight stays. The most interesting of the jungle walks are the ones that reach up into the high canopy, either using observation towers or suspended walkways. These are almost always associated with jungle lodges, who build their own structures in their piece of the jungle. Some of the best walkways are at the Ariaú Jungle Towers, the Juma Jungle Hotel, and the Guanavenas Jungle Lodge. The Amazon EcoResort also has suspended trails along with their extensive facilities for leisure activities. They accept day-use visitations. Finally, the Mindú Park also has suspended walkways that are open to visitors.

Hikes along the jungle floor should probably be guided, unless they are on the grounds of a jungle lodge or in one of the smaller city parks. These hikes are excellent for photo safaris and bird-watching. An interesting excursion is a hike out to one of the old *seringais* (rubber tree groves) still producing rubber for a specialized market. Night walks are usually not recommended; the best nocturnal excursions are by canoe or floating hotel. That being said, there are tours that take you out to sleep in the jungle. Generally, you bring a hammock and sleep between two trees. This special excursion can be an eerie experience for most city folk and you'll need to bring some special items for the occasion.

## Jungle Lodge Visits

Some of the larger and more structured jungle lodges are attractions in themselves. You can arrange day trips to visit the lodges, partake of their suspended trails and observation decks, and experience their slant on the local cuisine. Trips usually leave in small groups from the docks and cost around R$65 per person. The most sought-after lodges for day trips include the Amazon Eco-Resort and the Ariaú Jungle Towers. Contact the hotel directly for more information or check with a tour agency in Manaus.

## N Swimming with the Piranha and Dolphins

Generally, visitors are reluctant to jump into the Rio Negro or Amazon River and splash around, although it's perfectly safe to do so away from the *igarapés* (shallow, swampy areas). Locals are known to swim with the pink river dolphins at the Meeting of the Waters and there are popular swimming holes all over the area—in the lakes and tributaries along Rio Negro mostly. In spite of this abundance of opportunity, most foreigners are timid about swimming, except when at the beaches on the margins of Rio Negro. Still, if your guide dives in, you can probably dive in too. There are numerous swimming holes around Manaus and along the excursion routes that are regularly used for cooling off.

Despite their fierce reputation, the piranha do not generally nibble on human flesh. The black piranha is mostly a fruit eater and the smaller red piranha prefers insects and pieces of other fish. Attacks on humans swimming in the river are almost unheard of and you'll see locals jumping into the river without a single thought of peril.

# ENTERTAINMENT AND NIGHTLIFE

Bars and restaurants do not stay open late in the Centro area of Manaus. After dinner, your best bet for a night scene is in the Ponta Negra Beach area, where bars and clubs continue all night long.

## Bars

One popular bar in the Ponta Negra area is **Porão do Alemão,** or The German's Cellar (Estrada da Ponta Negra 1896, tel. 92/3238-4504, 6 P.M. daily). They have German food and plenty of beer flowing. Another place to check out is **Spa Musical** (Estrada da Ponta Negra 5049, tel. 92/3625-8056, call for hours).

## Music and Dance

In the downtown area, there's **BoiArts** (Rua José Clemente 500, tel. 92/3637-6807, 6 P.M. daily) and **Boite dos Ingleses** (Boulevard Vivaldo Lima 33, tel. 92/3232-6793, 6 P.M. daily). Also, check into the stage show at **Zolt** (Rua Monsenhor Coutinho 275, tel. 92/9119-1069, call for show times) downtown.

In the beach area of Tarumã is the **Tukannu's Club** (Avenida do Turismo 3156, tel. 92/2659-5000, 6 P.M. daily). In Ponta Negra, you can look for **Coração Blue** (Estrada da Ponta Negra 3701) and the **Studio Tropical** (Tropical Hotel, Estrada da Ponta Negra 9015), which has a very mixed crowd, mostly tourists from the hotel.

## FESTIVALS AND EVENTS

Together with the rest of Brazil, the Amazon region, and Manaus in particular, celebrates **Carnaval** at the end of February each year. In the city, there are parades and parties with their own version of the Samba Schools of Rio de Janeiro. Most of the activity takes place around the Ponta Negra area, but the entire city is abuzz with festivities. In May, the Ponta Negra area is the location of the **Festival de Toadas** (Festival of Sounds), and musical performances occur nightly throughout the month. June is the month of the **Amazon Folkloric Festival,** which is a colorful display of traditional costumes and dances. This is also known as the Festival de Juninho. There is a **river parade** on June 29 and the **city's birthday celebration** on October 24. **Christmas** brings lights and public performances in the Ponta Negra area.

The most popular and spectacular festival in the Amazon Region is the **Ox Festival in Parintins,** about 350 kilometers east of Manaus downstream along the Amazon River (about 45 minutes by plane or 24 hours by boat). The festival is akin to Carnaval in Rio de Janeiro, with groups, or *blocos,* parading down the *bombódromo* (grand parade arena) in dazzling costumes with huge floats, depicting all kinds of superb fantasies. At its foundation, the festival celebrates the traditional return of the ox to the festival grounds to perform a northern version of the *Bumba Meu Boi* dance. Festivals like this take place in the northeastern and southern regions of the country, but nowhere is it so elaborate as here in Parintins. The city is divided into two parts, red for the Caprichoso ox and blue for the Garantido ox. The parade is a competition between the two sides. More than 60,000 people come to observe the parade every night during the last three nights of June. Prior to the official festival, however, visitors can come and observe practice sessions starting around the end of April. These sessions take place in practice areas, but are almost as rich as the festival itself, with costumes and floats and lots of parties.

## ACCOMMODATIONS IN MANAUS

Most of the hotels in Manaus and all of the jungle lodges set their prices in dollars to avoid having to change their prices constantly as the exchange rate changes. That's because most of their customers are Europeans and Americans and they can charge accordingly. Manaus is known for having one of the most dollar-based economies in Brazil. Like it or not, prices in Manaus don't fluctuate with the Brazilian currency. Many of the jungle lodges even have offices (or at least contact information) in the United States. Consequently, prices given in this section are in U.S. dollars.

### Under US$50

The **Ibis Accor Hotel** (Av. Mandii 4, Bola da Suframa, tel. 92/3612-6234, www.accorhotels.com, US$29) is a great value with 120 rooms offering air, TV, and mini-bar. They have a restaurant and bar, and breakfast is not included. It's located a bit far from the tourist area near the docks, as it serves business travelers coming into Manaus to work with the Zona Franca. If you don't mind being in the industrial center, it's a good value. **Líder Hotel** (Av. Sete de Setembro 827, downtown, tel. 92/3633-1326, US$35–49) is conveniently located on one of the city's main avenues. They offer nothing special, but rooms have air, TV, and phone.

### US$50–100

The **Hotel Novotel** (Av. Mandil 4, tel. 92/3237-1211, www.accorhotels.com, US$65–95) has decent facilities and is located near the downtown area. The **Best Western Manaus** (Rua Marcilio Dias 217, Centro, tel. 92/3622-2844, www.bestwestern.com.br, US$79) will make you feel at home with their standard Best Western layout and service. They're located right on the waterfront. The **Plaza** (Av. Getúlio Vargas 215, tel. 92/3232-7766, US$65) has a pool and restaurant, and air, TV, and phone in their rooms.

## US$100–250

The most elaborate hotel in the city is the **Tropical Hotel Manaus** (Estrada da Ponta Negra 9015, tel. 92/3658-5000, tropicalhotel.com.br, US$135–310), with more than 600 rooms, many overlooking the river. It's about 20 minutes from downtown Manaus in the Ponta Negra Beach. They have modern facilities with pool, restaurant, bar, gym, and sauna, and their rooms have air, TV, phone, and Internet access. The **N Holiday Inn Taj Mahal** (Av. Getúlio Vargas 741, downtown, tel. 92/3633-1010, US$110–165) has a revolving restaurant on the top floor that gives you a 360-degree view of Manaus and the rivers around it every 45 minutes. They also have a pool, and rooms have air and TV.

## FLOATING HOTELS

There are several riverboats that offer from one day to a week onboard, floating around the Amazon. Trips that stay around the Manaus area (the majority) are usually around 2–5 days, while some trips take four or five days and travel from Manaus to other cities. Two good destinations for floating trips include Parintins and Santarém. Anything farther than that can get tiresome. If you want a taste of the jungle-boat experience, many of them offer a single night's stay. The floating hotels offer complete services: breakfast, lunch, dinner, and excursions. The trips that hang around Manaus will likely visit the Meeting of the Waters, the Parque Ecológico de Janeiro, and the Archipelago de Anavilhanas (longer trips). In addition, they almost all offer sunrise and sunset canoe trips and fishing for piranha.

The **N Tucano** (Ecotour Expeditions, Jamestown, RI, tel. 401/423-3377, www.naturetours.com) is a medium-sized boat (80 feet) with nine cabins that hold two people each. Cabins have private facilities and are air-conditioned. They have an observation deck on top, as well as a balcony on the mid-deck and a reasonably spacious dining room with plenty of windows to see out onto the jungle. They work with well-trained guides who generally speak English, and they offer a variety of packages, 2–10 days. The **Agencia Serpe** (Rua Marquês de Sta Cruz, Centro., tel. 92/3231-1236, tel. 92/3622-1555, serpe@argo.com.br, contact for prices) has river trips that go from Manaus to Belém, passing several smaller towns along the way, including Parintins, Santarém, Monte Alegre and others. The trip takes 84 hours to complete and there are many adventures along the way.

The **Amazon** group (you can get more information on this group at their site www.amazonclipper.com.br) has three different ships, typical of the Amazon River safaris. All of them offer air-conditioning (at night) and private bathrooms in their cabins. They have viewing decks around the perimeter of the boat. The top deck has a panoramic view and includes a bar and dining area. They use mineral water in their kitchen and cook regional foods. Packages vary according to the number of days you purchase. Their Amazon River package is two nights and costs around US$375, while their Rio Negro package is three nights and costs US$500. Their **N Clipper Premium** is a modern vessel that is small enough to go up into the small tributaries of the area. Nevertheless, the rooms and group areas are more spacious than the older ship. Packages on the Premium ship are about US$100 more than the others.

The **Amazonia Expedition** is a ship for groups of 10–16 people that will create a trip according to your specifications. The boat is small and the rooms are tight, but they have a sun deck on top and all the necessary facilities for an extended excursion. The cost for 10 people is US$1,250 per day. The **Victôrica Amazônica** has a similar setup, but the boat is much more modern and spacious. All cabins have air and private bathrooms. For 14 people, the cost is US$1,750 per day. The **Cassiquiari** is a smaller boat for groups of 7–12 people in eight cabins with private bath and air-conditioning. The cost is US$1,000 per day for seven passengers. Finally, the *Santana* is a modern yacht with luxury facilities for up to 12 people. It has six double cabins with private baths and air-conditioning. Most rooms are large enough to add a third person. They have small inflatable boats for special river excursions. They charge US$2,400 per day for up to 12 people.

A good place for information and bookings of the above ships is www.viverde.com.br. They have a page in English.

## JUNGLE LODGES

Staying at a jungle lodge puts you directly in touch with nature—even if your lodge is one of the more luxurious in the region. Generally, the lodges are located out in the jungle along the banks of the rivers. Most lodges will provide you with everything you need during your stay. That always includes breakfast and usually lunch and dinner, too. They also offer transportation to and from Manaus (usually by boat) for your arrival and departure, but most have limits on the amount of baggage you can carry on the boat, so pack light when visiting the Amazon. Excursions may be included in the price or treated separately, depending on the package. Almost all lodges offer jungle hikes, nighttime caiman focusing, canoeing along the shallow marshes, bird-watching, fishing for piranha, and visiting to indigenous villages. The only thing that changes is the location of these activities and the quality and style of the lodge. Note that most jungle lodges, including the most luxurious, offer cold-water showers. That's all you're going to want.

### Ⓜ Acajatuba Jungle Lodge

About four hours from Manaus by boat, the Acajatuba Jungle Lodge (Lago Acajatuba, tel. 92/3233-7642, www.acajatuba.com.br) is situated on the bank of a large river formed by Rio Acajatuba, a tributary of Rio Negro. The views here are incredible and their 20 cabanas (40 rooms)—made entirely out of wood and jungle

fibers—offer a rustic experience, with the comfort of air and private baths. All of their structures are built above the jungle floor and are connected by suspended walkways. The restaurant has a fantastic view of the lake and jungle. A one-night package goes for around US$180 double occupancy, with some excursions included.

### Ⓜ Amazon Ecopark Lodge

The Amazon Ecopark Lodge (Igarapé do Tarumã, tel. 92/3234-0939, tel. 21/2275-6544, www.amazonecopark.com) has 20 rustic chalets with 60 rooms that offer air, phone, and hot-water showers. The chalets are spread over a large area, offering a sensation of semi-seclusion. Their restaurant is up in the canopy with a beautiful jungle view. They are only six kilometers from Manaus (30 minutes by boat). Suspended trails enter their piece of the jungle, where they have a Primate Rehabilitation Center to reintroduce illegally-captured monkeys into the jungle. They also offer plenty of jungle-excursion packages, focusing on their monkey park and canoe trips. A one-night package goes for around US$240 for two.

### Amazon Lodge

One of the original jungle lodges in the Amazon region, the Amazon Lodge (Lago Juma, Km 80, tel. 92/3656-6033, US$465 for three days and two nights. For price and booking information, contact the Natural Safaris Agency at marketing@naturalsafaris.com.br) continues to offer one of the best experiences in the jungle. They are about four hours from Manaus down the Amazon River, situated along one of the smaller tributaries on the edge of a private preserve of 10 square kilometers. They have 18 double rooms, built on stilts above the river with shared bath facilities. Rooms are very rustic, both aesthetically and functionally. They have a restaurant area and veranda for relaxation, as well as suspended trails and a 45-meter-tall observation tower.

### Ⓜ Ariaú Jungle Towers

The Ariaú Jungle Towers (Lago Ariaú in Iranduba, tel. 92/3622-5000, tel. 92/3232-4160,

www.ariau.tur.br, treetop@ariautowers.com.br)
is the largest of the jungle lodges in the Brazilian Amazon. It has more than 200 rooms,
two restaurants, four bars, a pool, a spa, and
group areas. It's built along the banks of the
Ariaú Lake, situated 2.5 hours from Manaus
by boat near the Archipélago das Anavilhanas.
(You can also get there by speedboat in an hour
or helicopter in 15 minutes.) It's practically a
tourist attraction in itself, with more than eight
kilometers of suspended walkways at the top of
the jungle canopy, 40 meters above the jungle
floor. They also have seven separate observation towers, connected by the walkways. Everything is made out of wood and stone and some
of the structures are on stilts above the water.
Their rooms range from standard with cold
showers to large suites and luxury suites with
Internet access. They also have their version
of a presidential suite, called Tarzan's House,
which is a large, multi-level suite with two
rooms and a bathtub.

They supply all types of excursions for their
guests and day visitors and have English-speaking guides. Their office in Manaus is located
at Rua Silva Ramos 42. A one-night package
is US$300. Day visits are US$115.

## Guanavenas Jungle Lodge

If your idea is to get way out of sight, then you
might consider the Guanavenas Jungle Lodge
(Silves, tel. 92/3528-2110, tel. 92/3656-1500,
www.guanavenas.com.br), about 365 kilometers downstream from Manaus near Silves.
The lodge is located on a small island and has
a kind of resort atmosphere to it. They have
a 30-meter wooden observation tower and
many jungle excursions in the local area. The
main lodge is made of wood and stone and
has a group sitting area and 70 rooms spread
over 25 cabanas, offering air, TV, video, and
verandas. They also have two pools, tennis
courts, and a restaurant. The best way to
get there is by boat, which takes five hours
from Manaus. Their office in Manaus is at
Rua Constantino Nery 5256 in the Flores
neighborhood. A two-night package goes for
about US$315.

## Juma Jungle Hotel

On the bank of the Juma River, about 80 kilometers from Manaus (three hours by boat) is
the simple and rustic Juma Jungle Hotel (Lago
do Juma, Zona Rural, tel. 11/3872-0362,
tel. 11/3088-1937, www.venturas.com.br,
sofia@jumahotel.com.br). Built entirely on
stilts, the hotel puts you right inside the jungle canopy. They offer all the usual excursions
and excellent contact with native tribes. They
have only eight chalets, each with private bath.
A two-night package is around US$350.

## Jungle Othon Palace

With only 22 rooms, the Jungle Othon Palace (Igarapé do Tatu, tel. 92/3633-6200, tel.
92/3234-0173, www.junglepalace.com.br,
junglepalace@internext.com.br) is one of the
most luxurious and interesting in the area, although not one of the most beautiful visually.
It literally floats on top of the river in a sta-
tionary position, built on top of an old ferryboat. All rooms have verandas, air, TV, and
phone and the hotel offers a pool, massage
room, game room, meeting rooms, and an excellent restaurant. They offer the usual jungle
excursions, plus horseback rides. Their office
in Manaus is at Rua Saldanha Marinho 700. A
one-night package is around US$175.

## Lago Salvador Jungle Hotel

On the banks of the Salvador Lake, about
45 minutes out of Manaus past Ponta Negra
Beach, is the Lago Salvador Jungle Hotel
(Lago Salvador, www.salvadorlake.com.br,
lagosalvador@internext.com.br; for booking information, contact the Fontur Agency
at fontur@fontur.com.br, tel. 92/3658-3052,
tel. 92/3659-5119, R$495–1000). They have
suspended canopy trails and ropes courses in
the trees, and they offer rafting excursions,
jungle walks, canoe trips, and piranha fishing.
Their cabanas are spread out, each containing about 12 rooms (there are 50 total) with
air, TV, and phone. They also have a restaurant (a short hike to get to it), massage room,
and game room.

### Tiwa Amazonas Eco-Resort

On the other side of Rio Negro (across from Manaus) is the new Tiwa Amazonas Eco-Resort (Margem direita do Rio Negro, tel. 92/3088-4676, www.tiwaamazone.nl), one of the newest and most modern in the region. It looks across at the city with the jungle behind it and you get there in 20 minutes, crossing Rio Negro by boat. They have 62 room built in stilts above the water, with many individual chalets for up to four people. They offer long stretches of suspended canopy trails, 25 meters high, with rope-course activities at the end. They have a restaurant, lovely pool, and massage room. They accept day visits and often produce dance or live music shows at night. A one-night package runs US$200.

## FOOD

Naturally, the most interesting and savory meals in town are the ones prepared with local ingredients—particularly the local fish (the best is grilled *tambaqui* or *tucunaré*). If you're staying at a jungle lodge, you'll likely have all your meals prepared for you, so if you don't like fish, you'd be well advised to check the menu with the lodge before signing on. The best restaurants are spread all over the city, so you should be prepared to take a taxi there and back.

### International

It wouldn't be Brazil if there weren't at least one Portuguese kitchen in town. The best in Manaus is **M Bernardino's** (Rua Pará 555, Vieiralves, tel. 92/3233-7300, 7 P.M.–2 A.M. Mon.–Fri., noon–2 A.M. on Sat., noon–4 P.M. on Sun.). Meals are R$45 per person. Also, try **Agua na Boca** (Rua Pará 415, Vieiralves, tel. 92/3232-6383, 11:30 A.M.–3 P.M. and 6:30–11:30 P.M. daily) for a varied menu of local and international cuisine.

### Japanese

There are two major Japanese neighborhoods in Manaus and they are both located in the industrial part of town. Japanese food is authentic and the fish is fresh. Try **Nippon** (Avenida Darcy Vargas 734, Casa 2, Chapada, tel. 92/3084-7735, 11 A.M.–3 P.M. and 6:30–11 P.M. Mon.–Fri.) and **Suzuran** (Rua Teresina 155, Adrianópolis, tel. 92/3234-1693, 11 A.M.–3 P.M. and 6:30–11 P.M. daily except Tuesdays).

### Quick and Casual

If you're not having lunch as part of your day's excursion package, then you can check out some of the offerings in town. Some are also open for dinner: **Açaí & Cia** (Rua Acre 98, Vieiralves, tel. 92/3635-3637, 9 A.M.–midnight Mon.–Sat., 3 P.M.–midnight on Sun. and Mon., R$20) is great for fresh juices and snacks. They are open late. Try **Kilo Center** (Rua Dez de Julho 203, downtown, tel. 92/3622-6948, lunch only from Mon.–Sat., R$15) for self-service lunch and dinner and **Coqueiro Verde** (Rua Ramos Ferreira 1920, downtown, tel. 92/3633-2151, 11 A.M.–11 P.M. Mon.–Sat., 11 A.M.–4 P.M. on Sun.) for typical Brazilian self-service. Best for lunch, but is also open for dinner. Meals are around R$15.

### Regional Favorites

To get a taste of the local fish, cooked up Amazon-style, try **M Restaurante Canto da Peixada** (Rua Emílio Moreira 1677a, Praça 14 de Janeiro, tel. 92/3234-3021, 11 A.M.–3 P.M. and 6:30–11:30 P.M. Mon.–Sat.). It runs about R$20 per person. Also, there's **Restaurante Panela Cheia** (Rua Washington Luís 292, Planalto, tel. 92/3238-4234, 11 A.M.–4 P.M. and 6–11:30 P.M. Mon.–Sat., 11 A.M.–4 P.M. on Sun., R$20) and **La Barca** (Rua Recife 684, tel. 92/3642-3040, 11 A.M.–3 P.M. and 7–midnight Mon.–Sat., 11 A.M.–4 P.M. on Sun., R$20), both with great fish. One of the best is **M Bons Amigos** (Rua D-8 1923, Conj. 31 de Março, tel. 92/3237-7476, 11 A.M.–midnight Mon.–Sat., 11 A.M.–5:30 P.M. on Sun., R$25).

## INFORMATION AND SERVICES

The main tourist information office is **Manaustur** (Av. 7 de Setembro 157, downtown, tel. 92/3622-4925, tel. 92/3622-4886, 8 A.M.–noon and 2–5 P.M. daily). You can also call tel. 92/3652-1120 any time during the day or night. Travel agencies that service Manaus include **Selvatur** (Praça Adalberto Vale 17, Centro, tel. 92/3622-2577, selvatur@henig.com.br) and **Amazon Explorer's** (Rua Nhamundá 21, tel. 92/3633-3319, amazonexplorers@internext .com.br). You can also try **Nature Safaris** (tel. 92/3656-6033, www.naturesafaris.com.br). Note that tour agencies often work exclusively with certain hotels, so you may not get unbiased information when contacting these groups.

Manaus has several of the world's consulates. Following are some of them:

• Austria (Rua 5 no. 4, Quadra E, Parque 10, tel. 92/3236-6089)

• Belgium (Residencial Murici 13, Quadra D, Parque 10, tel. 92/3236-1452)

• Spain (Alameda Cosme Ferreira 1225, Aleixo, tel. 92/3644-3800)

• France (Avenida Joaquim Nabuco 1846, Bloco A 2, tel. 92/3233-6583)

• Great Britain and Northern Ireland (Avenida Eduardo Ribeiro 520, No. 1501, downtown, tel. 92/3622-3879)

• Netherlands (Rua Miranda Leão 41, downtown, tel. 92/3622-1366)

• Italy (Rua Belo Horizonte 240, tel. 92/3611-4877)

• Japan (Rua Fortaleza 460, tel. 92/3234-8825)

• United States (Rua Recife 1010, Adrianópolis, tel. 92/3633-4907)

There are Internet connections in the Ponta Negra area and some LAN Houses spread around town. You can also try **Amazon Cyber Café** (Av. Getúlio Vargas 626, Centro, tel. 92/3232-9068, 9:30 A.M.–11 P.M. Mon.–Sat.).

## DEEPER INTO THE CENTRAL AMAZON

Some 66 miles north of Manaus, **Presidente Figueredo,** is known for the numerous waterfalls around town, many offering areas to sit and have a snack between dips in the great pools, although many are completely natural with no tourist facilities whatsoever. The falls in this area are not tall, but many offer excellent swimming pools and cold-water showers in the cascades, which are best during the rainy season (December–May). Two of the more popular falls include Iracema and Cachoweira do Santuário, both located on private lands that are open to public visits for a small fee. You should also pay a visit to the Maruaga Cavern while in town. Another popular activity in town is fishing, and you can head out to the lake to catch *tucunaré,* which is one of the best fish for grilling and soups. You can also find some excellent bird-watching excursions in the area.

**São Gabriel da Cachoeira** is located about 1,000 kilometers upstream from Manaus (about 2.5 hours by plane), in an area known as the High Negro River (Alto do Rio Negro). It sits near the Colombian border, which explains the presence of so many Brazilian troops. The area is home to about 10 percent of the Brazilian aboriginal population, some 30,000 indigenous

people and more than 35 different tribes. More than 80 percent of the population of the city of São Gabriel da Cachoeira is native or of native descent (including most of the armed forces in the area), and the city sits almost entirely on indigenous land, protected by Brazilian law. Some of these groups can be visited with the presence of guides (their handcrafts and customs are remarkable) and others are completely off-limits to visitors.

Besides the rich cultural landscape, the region is known for its dramatic topography. High above Rio Negro stands the Pico da Neblina, a great mountain peak inside the national park of the same name. Many have tried, but few make it to the top of the mountain to get a view of the entire region below. The hike takes several days to accomplish and you pass several native villages along the way. Most visitors prefer to stick to the river down below, where there are white-water rapids and sandy beaches in the dry season. Other natural attractions include the six lakes in the region—each one with a different water composition, giving it a unique color.

Much of the Pico da Neblina National Park lies outside of Brazil in Venezuela, where there are more indigenous tribes.

# Belém

Most people who come through Belém are looking to make their way up the Amazon River into the deep jungle. That's pretty much how it always has been for this city, which was built to guard one of the major arteries going into the Amazon region from the ocean. What you find in Belém is a unique mixture of cultures, economies, and topographies. It's not really part of the deep jungle due to its proximity to the ocean, yet it is surrounded by Amazonian flora and fauna. From Belém, you can visit sandy beaches (along with your choice of ocean or river water), jungle islands filled with tropical birds and other animals, native villages of artisans and fishermen, and rustic jungle ranches that offer rural adventures along with jungle excursions. In the city itself, you'll walk along the streets of Old Belém, lined with 17th-century colonial architecture. You'll also see buildings from the 18th, 19th, and 20th centuries in an eclectic mix of styles. Not to be missed is the great Ver-o-Peso public marketplace and the Estação das Docas, where you'll find the city's best restaurants and bars right on the old waterfront at the docks. Always present are the sights, sounds, and flavors of the aboriginal culture. Most remarkable are the native crafts and culinary delights. The presence of indigenous people and culture is strong, yet Belém also contains a strong Portuguese and Italian heritage. The mixture of cultures is present in the people and places of Belém, but especially in the legends, festivals, and folklore of the area.

## HISTORY

Like most of the major cities in the northern region of Brazil, Belém was chosen as a good location for a fort and in 1616 a wooden fort was built at the confluence of the Pará and Guamá Rivers to help protect the Portuguese colony from foreign invasions. Over the years, the city remained small and the fort was replaced by newer incarnations made of stone. The slow growth of exports from the jungle (cocoa, fruit, and nuts mostly) also brought some growth and architecture to Belém, which continued to serve as a way station for boats coming in and out of the Amazon. The semi-baroque architecture of the Italian Antônio Landi is a feature from this period. But it wasn't until the rubber boom in the late 1800s that the city began to explode. The influx of foreigners brought new urban works and architecture to the city, including paved streets (with stones from Portugal), electricity, telegraph with underwater cables, gas lamps to light the public thoroughfares, and the construction of several important buildings, including the Teatro da Paz and parts of the Mercado Ver-o-Peso complex. Workers came to Pará state from all over Brazil, but especially from the poor areas of the northeast, ranging from the states of Ceará to Southern Bahia. Many of these transplants did not acclimate well to the conditions they found here and remained poor in the jungle.

Along with Manaus and the rest of the region, Belém went into a period of decline after the rubber trade set sail for Asia, but Belém prospered in the mid-1900s with the discovery of metals and precious stones. *Garimpeiros* (miners of gold and jewels) came in from all over the country. Some got rich and many died trying. Today, the area is replete with metallurgical companies extracting bauxite and producing aluminum and other metals for export. In addition to tourism, beef and buffalo production, as well as harvesting the region's natural fruits and nuts, provide the general population with their livelihood. There is also a growing production of crops, including coffee and soy, being introduced into the region.

## SIGHTS IN OLD BELÉM

The historical center of Belém extends all along the waterfront from the docks on the bay side of the peninsula to the University of Pará on the Guamá River side—but the highest

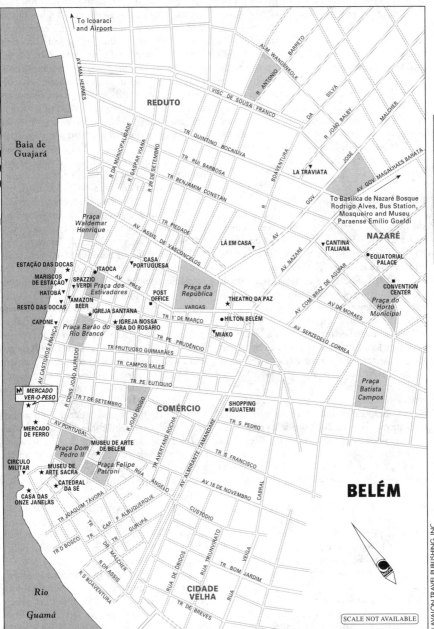

To Icoaraci
and Airport

AV MAL HERMES

Baia de
Guajará

REDUTO

R ANTONIO

AV M WANDENKOLK

BARRETO

DA                SILVA

VISC DE SOUSA FRANCO

R JOAO BALBY

MALCHER

TR QUINTINO BOCAIUVA

TR RUI BARBOSA

BOAVENTURA

JOSÉ

TR BENJAMIM CONSTAN

LA TRAVIATA

AV GOV MAGALHAES BARATA

R DA MUNICIPALIDADE

R GASPAR VIANA

AV 29 DE SETEMBRO

TR PIEDADE

GOV

To Basílica de Nazaré Bosque
Rodrigo Alves, Bus Station,
Mosqueiro and Museu
Paraense Emílio Goeldi

Praça
Waldemar
Henrique

AV ASSIS DE VASCONCELOS

AV

NAZARÉ

LÁ EM CASA

AV NAZARÉ

CANTINA
ITALIANA

EQUATORIAL
PALACE

CASA
PORTUGUESA

ESTAÇÃO DAS DOCAS
ITAOCA

MARISCOS
DE ESTAÇÃO
SPAZZIO
VERDI Praça dos
Estivadores

AV PRES

Praça da
República

AV COM BRAZ DE AGUIAR

CONVENTION
CENTER
Praça do
Horto
Municipal

HATOBÁ

AMAZON
BEER

POST
OFFICE

THEATRO DA PAZ

AV DE MORAES

RESTÓ DAS DOCAS

IGREJA SANTANA

VARGAS

TR 1' DE MARÇO

CAPONE

IGREJA NOSSA
SRA DO ROSÁRIO

HILTON BELÉM

AV CASTILHOS FRANÇA

Praça Barão do
Rio Branco

MIAKO

AV SERZEDELO CORREA

TR PE PRUDÊNCIO

TR FRUTUOSO GUIMARÃES

R CONS JOÃO ALFREDO

TR CAMPOS SALES

TR PE EUTIQUIO

Praça
Batista
Campos

MERCADO
VER-O-PESO

TR 7 DE SETEMBRO

R JOÃO DIOGO

COMÉRCIO

SHOPPING
IGUATEMI

AV PORTUGAL

TR S PEDRO

MERCADO
DE FERRO

TR AVERTANO ROCHA

MUSEU DE ARTE
DE BELÉM

TR S FRANCISCO

CIRCULO
MILITAR

Praça Dom
Pedro II

MUSEU DE
ARTE SACRA

RUA ANGELO

Praça Felipe
Patroni

AV ALMIRANTE TAMANDARE

AV 16 DE NOVEMBRO

CABRAL

BELÉM

CATEDRAL
DA SÉ

CASA DAS
ONZE JANELAS

TR JOAQUIM TAVORA

CUSTÓDIO

TR

CAP P ALBUQUERQUE

GURUPÁ

TR

DR MALCHER

R DH ASSIS

RUA DE ÓBIDOS

RUA TRIUNFIRATO

TR BOM JARDIM

VEIGA

TR D BOSCO

R S BOAVENTURA

Rio

Guamá

CIDADE
VELHA

RUA

TR DE BREVES

SCALE NOT AVAILABLE

© AVALON TRAVEL PUBLISHING, INC.

The Amazon

concentration of historical buildings is on the bay side. You can easily walk along the waterfront from the docks, through the Ver-o-Peso market, and over to Praça Frei Caetano Brandão, and you'll have seen a great many of the city's attractions. An easy stroll from the docks to the Praça da República gets you to the Theatro da Paz and some of the city's best hotels and restaurants. Farther into the city (away from the docks) is the Nazaré area, home to many mid-range hotels and restaurants, the Basilica de Nazaré, and the Emílio Goeldi Museum and Gardens. It's probably worth taking a taxi between the Nazaré neighborhood and Old Belém.

## Estação das Docas

During the rubber boom in the early 1900s, the docks in Belém were bustling with activity and commerce. But when American companies began to get their latex from Asian countries, the entire Amazon region fell into a state of disuse and disrepair. The docks in Belém were hardly required any longer, being used mostly by the tourist industry as a departure point for river excursions. Later, in 2000, inspired by the docks in Buenos Aires, Belém's Estação das Docas underwent a face-lift and the large warehouses and waterfront area became the city's hottest tourist and nightlife district. You'll find some of the city's best restaurants, bars, and shops here, as well as some interesting exhibitions of historical photos, arts, and crafts. There is also a theater and cinema. You can have breakfast here, with a variety of regional cakes and fruit juices. During the day, be sure to check out the various flavors of ice cream at one of the ice cream stands (*cupuaçú* and *acaí* are two fabulous flavors). In the afternoon, the docks provide an excellent view of the sunset over the Guarajá Bay and at night, there is always live music on the floating stage and plenty of activity in the bars and restaurants. If you are staying the night in Belém, you should probably take a taxi between the Estação and your hotel at night.

## Mercado Ver-o-Peso

The most striking and impressive structure in Old Belém is easily the Mercado Ver-o-Peso (open 9 A.M.–6 P.M. daily), sitting near the docks on the old waterfront. Originally created in 1688 by mandate of the Portuguese Crown, the Mercado was intended to help control the imports and exports of the city for purposes of collecting taxes. The name Ver-o-Peso comes from its original function of stopping ships along the Amazon River (generally on their way to or from Manaus) to *ver* (look) and *pesar* (weigh) their cargo. Currently used as the city's principal meat market, the original building was renovated in 1908 and given some contemporary touches, including its decorative staircase. An adjacent building, known as the **Mercado de Ferro,** or Iron Market, was constructed in 1901 from European materials. The Mercado and adjoining buildings are some of the oldest structures in the city and reveal the various stages of the city's history: colonial architecture in baroque style, neoclassic structures from the 19th century, and mixed nouveaux architecture from the early 20th century, remembrances of the *Ciclo de Borracha,* or rubber boom. A look at the outsides of these buildings is a lesson in the history of Belém and commerce in the Amazon region. At one end of the Mercado is the **Praça do Relógio** (Clock Square), with it's European timepiece and structure. Just outside the market along the waterfront are some great places to sit and relax with a cold drink and a snack.

Inside the Mercado structure is a mindboggling assortment of meat, fish, fruit, arts, crafts, herbs, and furnishings. Almost all of the merchandise in the Mercado is from the local area and often brought in from local aboriginal groups. Walking through the Ver-o-Peso provides an authentic view of the local culture. And you may find a cure for what ails you; one of the highlights of the Mercado is the assortment of alternative healers and herb vendors with their collections of leaves, twigs, bark, and seeds from all sorts of Amazonian plants—most containing medicinal qualities. If you're not quite ready to try the herbal concoctions, hike over to the fruit market, where you'll find an enormous variety of fruit from the Amazon region, including great quantities of *acaí* and *guaraná,* two of the most popular fruits in the region. Sampling the different flavors is one of the great pleasures of a trip to Belém, especially in the homemade ice creams made from these local fruits.

Note: The Ver-o-Peso market can be a moderately risky place to walk around. Pay careful attention to your belongings and don't bring anything that is not absolutely necessary. If you have a backpack, don't wear it on your back, but in front of you. Your wallet should be in a front pocket with your hand inside—or in a buttoned or zipped pocket. Even better, avoid using a wallet and just bring some cash and a copy of your passport for ID. Purses and cameras should be worn diagonally across your chest. Don't be fooled by misdirection schemes that take your attention away from your belongings, and don't walk into areas where you are the only person. If you wish, you can hire a guide to take you through the market and watch out for you along the way. You can find guides in the dock area. Look for those registered with EMBRATUR or the city agency of Belemtur. You can also just go directly to one of the Belemtur offices listed in the *Information and Services* section.

## Praça Batísta Campos

Not far from Old Belém in the neighborhood of Batísta Campos is the lovely Praça Batísta Campos, set into the landscape of the city during the rubber boom. The *praça* is actually a large park containing lakes, walking paths, bridges, and a small chunk of the Amazon forest. Some of the trees here are hundreds of years old.

## Praça Frei Caetano Brandão

Besides the Ver-o-Peso market, the most interesting architectural complex in the city is around the Praça Frei Caetano Brandão. On all sides and along the streets connecting to the *praça* are various colonial and neoclassic buildings from the city's glory days. Check out the Forte do Presépio, the Casa das Onze Janelas, and the homes along Ruas Padre Champagnat and Siqueira Mendes to see the highlights of the area.

## Theatro da Paz

At the end of the Rua da Paz in the Praça da República is the city's impressive Theatro da Paz (Rua da Paz, no number, Praça da República, tel. 91/3224-7355, 9:30–11 A.M. and 12:30–2:30 P.M. and 4–5 P.M. Mon.–Fri and 9 A.M.–noon on Sat.), a neoclassic structure inspired by opera houses in Italy (specifically the Teatro Scala in Milan). Built at the beginning of the rubber boom in 1878, the Theatro is still the city's principal stage for opera and classical music concerts, particularly during the summer months of July and August, when you'll find music competitions and festivals held there. Highlights inside the Theatro include the different colored woods used on the railings and furnishings, crystal mirrors, and the painted ceiling depicting Apollo in the Amazon. The Praça da República is a great place to have a picnic and stroll around to see the grounds. It's not a wild piece of the Amazon Jungle, but it does have a variety of Amazonian flora in its extensive garden areas.

# MUSEUMS AND CULTURAL CENTERS

## Casa das Onze Janelas

Originally used as the city hospital in the 1700s, the House of Eleven Windows (Praça Frei Caetano Brandão, tel. 91/3219-1105, 10 A.M.–6 P.M. Tues.–Fri. and 10 A.M.–8 P.M. weekends) is now a cultural center, producing art exhibits, theater performances, and cultural events throughout the year. Inside is a simple but terrific café where you can sit and look out over the Guajará Bay. It's located in the same *praça* as the Museu de Arte Sacra and the Catedral da Sé.

## Museu de Arte de Belém

If you walk down Rua Padre Champagnat from the historical complex at Praça Frei Caetano Brandão, you'll pass Praça Dom Pedro II, where the **Palácio Antônio Lemos** is located. Built in 1883 in a mixture of styles, the highlight inside is a grand marble staircase. Today, the palace is used as government offices, but the city shares the building with the Museu de Arte de Belém (Praça Dom Pedro II, tel. 91/3219-8217, 9 A.M.–5 P.M. Tues.–Fri. and 9 A.M.–1 P.M. weekends, R$1, free on Tues.). The museum has almost 1,000 pieces from the city's history, including paintings, sculptures, furnishings, pottery, and artifacts from the 17th–20th centuries. The museum also serves as a nucleus of preservation and restoration of the city's historical and cultural heritage.

## Museu de Arte Sacra

Sitting near the waterfront of Old Belém in the old Palácio Episcopal (1883) is the region's best collection of sacred art from the colonial period. The museum (Praça Frei Caetano Brandão, 10 A.M.–6 P.M. Tues.–Sat. and 10 A.M.–6 P.M. Sun., R$4 and free on Tues.) has more than 350 pieces on display, the majority being religious statuary from colonial churches of the 18th century. There are also documents, silver, and gold ornamentation, religious clothing, and furnishings. The architectural complex that comprises the museum is equally as impressive and includes the Santo Alexandre Church. There is also a coffee shop and souvenir shop inside.

# CHURCHES

## Basílica de Nazaré

Legend has it that in the mid-1700s a simple man from the region encountered a statue of Our Lady of Nazareth here, some five kilometers from shores of the Guajará Bay. Year after year, the statue would return to the same spot on the same day, so a simple mud chapel was erected to honor the miracle. Today, the site is where you'll see the Basílica de Nazaré (Praça Justo Chermont, 6:30–11:30 A.M. and 3–7 P.M. daily) and inside is the very statue, some 200 years old. Modeled after the great St. Paul's Cathedral in Rome, the Basílica de Nazaré is Belém's most important religious monument. It serves as the destination point of the great **Círio de Nazaré** procession that takes place in October, in honor of the great miracle of the

statue. The church was built in 1909 and contains stone mosaics along the walls, alabaster columns, a red-cedar ceiling, and bronze furnishings. The main altar is covered in marble. It's best to take a taxi out to the see it. From there, you can walk to the Emílio Goeldi Museum and Garden.

## Catedral da Sé

The Catedral da Sé (Praça Frei Caetano Brandão, 7 A.M.–noon and 2–7:30 P.M. Tues., Wed., and Fri. and 2–7:30 P.M. Mon., Thur., and Sat.) serves as the starting point of the great procession of Nazaré. It was built in 1748 by Antônio Landi, the Italian architect responsible for most of the city's colonial, baroque architecture. He gave this church a mixture of ornamental baroque and simple colonial touches. Perhaps most interesting from the outside (the facade is especially beautiful in the morning), the Catedral has some wonderful interior works in neoclassic style (added later), including paintings by Italian artist Domenico De Angelis and a great marble front altar. Other highlights include the pipe organ (eight meters tall) and a series of 18 copper candelabras. Sunday mass is 6–11 A.M. and 5–8:30 P.M.

## Igreja Nossa Sra. do Rosário

Like all Rosário churches in Brazil, the Igreja Nossa Sra. do Rosário (Rua Padre Prudêncio 339, tel. 91/3222-3482, 7 A.M.–noon and 5:30–8 P.M. daily) was built by the brotherhood of black slaves during the colonial period in the 1600s. The original chapel was reconstructed several times to reach its present form. Most of the Rosário churches across the country are small and modest on the inside. Here in Belém, you can see one of the richest and most elaborate of the bunch, with silver candle holders and rich sculpture and artwork throughout.

## Igreja Santana

One of Antônio Landi's most interesting (and most Italian) works, the Igreja Santana (Rua Padre Prudêncio 125, tel. 91/3222-6353, 8:30–11:30 A.M. and 3–5:30 P.M. Mon.–Fri.) was designed in the form of a cross, with high, vaulted

**The architecture of Antônio Landi is one of Belém's special features.**

ceilings, following Italian tradition. In the center of the cross is a grand cupola with stained-glass windows. The main altar is covered in carved marble. Parts of the present building were added in the 1800s, including the two front towers and most of the present facade.

# PARKS

## Bosque Rodrigues Alves

About 20 kilometers from the downtown area, the Rodrigues Alves Garden (Av. Almirante Barroso 2453, Macro neighborhood, 7:30 A.M.–5 P.M. Mon.–Sun.) is an oasis of green in the middle of the urban jungle. With 16 hectares of Amazonian flora and fauna (more than 2,500 species), the garden is a great place to get in touch with the jungle in a controlled environment. Inside are footpaths that lead past statuary and into the wooded areas, where you'll find huge and ancient trees (including Brazil nut and rubber trees), an artificial lake, and a small waterfall. There is also a cave, ruins of an old castle, and an orchid garden. Animal encounters include monkeys, sloths, and various types of tropical birds, but they also have

animal habitats and tanks in a kind of zoo, where you can see turtles, caimans, fish, and manatees. You can take a taxi there and back for about R$12 each way.

## Museu Paraense Emílio Goeldi

Known primarily as a museum, the Emílio Goeldi installation (Av. Magalhães Barata 376, São Brás neighborhood, tel. 91/3219-3369, 9–11:30 A.M. and 2–5 P.M. Tues.–Thur., 9–11:30 A.M. Fri., and 9 A.M.–5 P.M. weekends, R$1) is actually more of a botanical park and ecological research center. Recognized as the first research center for Amazonian studies, the park is dedicated to the study of all things Amazonian, including the flora, fauna, and native cultures. Inside is a botanical garden with more than 3,000 species of plants and trails to walk around and observe them. Animal habitats feature more than 600 animals, and fish tanks have various species from the local rivers. The museum exhibits a large collection of indigenous artifacts, including pottery and archeological finds, as much as 7,000 years old. There is also a botanical museum and geological museum. The park has 50,000 square

# STEP ASIDE, VIAGRA:
## APHRODISIACS OF THE AMAZON

Until Viagra hit the scene in recent years, most folks in the modern world dismissed aphrodisiacs as myth or fiction. At best, substances such as the legendary Spanish Fly, perhaps worked on animals, but could be dangerous for human use. But the FDA-approved Viagra has shown us that human sexuality, as complex as it may be, can indeed be stimulated, coaxed, and enhanced by chemical extracts.

The aboriginal people of the Brazilian Amazon have known this for centuries. They harvest leaves, tree bark, vines, and animal elements as part of their regular diet. Folks from this region will tell you straight out that these substances indeed work to stimulate desire and increase virility and sexual potency.

But categorizing the Amazon's aphrodisiacs and their effects is a challenge, since much remains unknown and untested concerning the many plants and foods of the region. Still, it's safe to point to two substances, *catuaba* and *marapuama,* as the legendary aphrodisiacs of the Amazon Jungle. Although the FDA steadfastly holds that all over-the-counter sexual stimulants are ineffective, throughout Brazil *catuaba* and *marapuama* are known to increase the libido and enhance eroticism in both men and women. Most reports on aphrodisiacs of the Amazon are non-scientific and none are sufficient to make any definite conclusions about their use. So if you decide to give any of these substances a try, you are advised to use caution and good judgment at all times.

Other extracts from the Amazon, such as *guaraná, unha de gato* (cat's claw), and *noz de cola* (cola nut), are considered general stimulants and can increase the intensity and duration of other sexual stimulants. Used alone, their stimulating qualities may or may not direct themselves to the libido. Finally, there are a few extracts that, although not mood altering or libido enhancing, assist in the flow of chemicals and blood to the genitalia. Some of these include pure cocoa powder and certain fish and spices.

### Catuaba

The most legendary of the Amazonian aphrodisiacs, *catuaba* comes from the bark of a tree that is indigenous to the Amazon Jungle. Used for centuries by the natives of the Amazon region as a sexual stimulant and general health tonic, *catuaba* has been tried and tested by thousands of non-Brazilians. Although single uses can result in powerful sexual impulses (especially when mixed with *guaraná* and other herbs), *catuaba* is not usually considered a one-time, mood-altering sexual stimulant. It is generally taken over several days or a week and may result in increased sexual appetite and/or erotic dreams. Besides these sex-specific qualities, *catuaba* is said to be a general health tonic that stimulates the immune system and increases stamina with antibacterial and anti-inflammatory qualities. Studies on *catuaba* are mostly linked to its stimulation of the immune system and not on its potential as a sexual stimulant. Scientists in Japan, for example, found that it may have some effectiveness in the "inhibition of HIV absorption to the cells" ("Effects of Catuaba extracts on microbial and HIV infection," Manabe H, Sakagami H, Ishizone H, Kusano H, Fujimaki M, Wada C, Komatsu N, Nakashima H, Murakami T, Yamamoto N, Horiuchi Itaro & Co., Ltd., Tokyo, Japan).

Combined with moderate amounts of alcohol, *catuaba* can be an effective sexual stimulant in single doses, but with somewhat limited and sporadic results. Nevertheless, *catuaba* bark, mixed with a mild apple wine, is available just about everywhere in Brazil and is a popular drink among young people. Most commonly, *catuaba* is mixed with other stimulants, including powdered *guaraná* and *unha de gato*. You can find *catuaba* in extract form, powdered (usually in capsules), and in dozens of mixtures sold as sexual stimulants.

### Marapuama

*Marapuama* has been used by the native people of the Amazon region for centuries. Usually mixed with *catuaba* and other herbs, *marapuama* comes from the leaves of a jungle plant. Although it does not produce erotic dreams like *catuaba*, *marapuama* is said to increase libido and sexual potency in men. It is often used as a food additive, since it is believed that its effects increase over extended use. You can find *marapuama* extract or even the dried leaves (which you can brew into a mild tea) in herb markets throughout the Amazon region.

### Guaraná

*Guaraná* fruit is used to produce one of the most popular soft drinks in Brazil. Like cola-based sodas, *guaraná* soda is loaded with natural stimulants, such as caffeine. The most potent way to take *guaraná* is in powdered form. The seeds, not the fruit, contain the most powerful concentration of elements and powdered, toasted *guaraná* seed is commonly used in foods and drinks throughout Brazil as a general stimulant. Together with *catuaba* or cocoa powder, *guaraná* can increase energy during sex and extend the effects of these other extracts. It's important to regulate the intake of pure *guaraná*, as it can be too powerful for effective use in aphrodisiacs. If too much is combined with cocoa powder, for example, it can produce overheating and excessive sweating. Besides chemical stimulation, *guaraná* also improves blood circulation.

### Unha de Gato

Although not an aphrodisiac in itself, *unha de gato* (oonya djee gah-too), or cat's claw, is used all over Brazil for circulation disorders (baldness, lethargy, skin problems, etc.) and as an anti-inflammatory for the prostate, ovaries, and genitals. Increased blood flow to these areas can also enhance sexual pleasure. The powder has been used to improve the overall functioning of the immune system and even as a food additive for weight-loss programs. *Unha de gato* is most commonly taken in powdered form in capsules, but the dried leaves can also be made into a tea.

### Cocoa

Pure cocoa powder is well-known as a sexual stimulant. It has been used in the Amazon region for centuries as a general health tonic and aphrodisiac. Originally, chocolate was not mixed with sugar, but eaten in its pure form in foods. The hot, bitter powder (what pure cocoa should taste like) improves circulation, stimulates the nervous system, and enhances the production of endorphins in the brain. Cocoa powder is best when mixed with other stimulants, such as cinnamon, clove, or peanuts. In the Amazon, cocoa is used in fish stews and other recipes to enhance potency in males and sexual desire in females.

### High-Potency Soup

Certain ingredients, when combined into soups and stews, are reputed as being aphrodisiacs. In the Amazon, the most well known of these recipes is piranha soup. The red piranha (and piranha in general) has long been considered a symbol of virility by the Tupi people and piranha soup, made with the jungle's herbs and spices, is said to have excellent effects on the libido. In other areas of Brazil, soup made with the bone marrow of a steer, called *mocotó,* is reputed as having similar qualities, and ranch hands in the Amazon and Pantanal regions make it a regular addition to their menu.

meters of space and is located only 15 minutes from Old Belém by car.

## MOSQUEIRO ISLAND

The Island of Mosqueiro was once a jungle beach haven for the many foreigners working the rubber trade in Belém in the early 20th century. When the sun got scorching hot in the winter months of June, July, and August, the many beaches bordering the island would fill up with British, American, and French workers. Today, the 18 different beaches around Mosqueiro are still a draw for locals and tourists alike. There are urbanized beaches with hotels and restaurants, and semi-deserted areas where you can get away from the crowds (except during the peak months of July and August, when locals swarm to the beaches from Belém to spend their holidays—you'd be well advised to avoid the island during this period).

The island is separated from the mainland by a narrow channel of water and sits facing the large Island of Marajó in the great body of semi-salty water known as the Marajó Bay. On the island is the city of Mosqueiro, where you can find hotels, restaurants, and tour guides to take you out on various excursions in the area. There is also a central market (Mercado Municipal) that has local arts and crafts, fruits, and snack stands.

### Mosqueiro Island Excursions

Excursions on the island include boat trips along the rivers and waterways around the island and trips to the smaller islands nearby. One of the most popular is the morning trip to Papagaios Island to see the flight of the parrots. This trip is detailed in the *Excursions and Activities* section.

A popular hike, known as the **Olhos da Agua Trail,** leaves from the docks at Mosqueiro by boat for about 40 minutes upstream. At that point, the hike begins—back in the direction of Mosqueiro—inside the Parque Ambiental de Mosqueiro. Along the way, you pass through a section of Amazon forest on a light trail that takes about two hours. You'll see some local

communities who live off the manioc and *açaí* harvest. The final stage of the journey is back onboard, flowing down a tributary into the Amazon River. You get a chance to stop for lunch on the bank of the river and even have a swim. The entire hike takes about eight hours to complete and you can get details in Mosqueiro at the tourist information stand (tel. 91/3771-3624) and in Belém at the Belemtur tourist office (tel. 91/3242-0900).

You can get to Mosqueiro by boat from Belém (25 nautical kilometers and about 30 minutes) or by bus from the Belém bus terminal (82 kilometers and about 1.5 hours). Buses also leave from Old Belém and you should check with a local tour agency or tourist information for details.

### Beaches

The most urbanized beaches on the island (and the most popular) are called **Murubira**, **Chapéu Virado**, and **Farol**. On these beaches, there are kiosks that sell food and drinks and provide beach chairs and umbrellas to get out of the sun for awhile. Lunch at one of these kiosks generally consists of *tacacá,* fried fish, or some kind of fish stew. Murubira is the main surfing and partying beach and in July it becomes a kind of Porto Seguro of the Amazon—with groups of young people doing group dances in the sand. Surfing is possible here because of an interesting fresh-water phenomenon involving high winds from the Marajó Island that create waves up to 4 meters tall when they finally reach Mosqueiro. It may be the only place in the world where you can see fresh water-waves of this magnitude. One of the more isolated beaches is Praia Baia do Sol, which has great swimming conditions.

## ILHA DE COTIJUBA

One of the most pleasant excursions from Belém is a trip to the Island of Cotijuba, just 35 minutes from Belém by boat. The principal activity on the island is sitting and sunning on the 20 kilometers of fresh-water beaches. Near the small village where the boat docks, the beaches are tourist oriented and offer beach bars and kiosks that serve lunch and snacks. Beaches with such services include Amor, Farol, Cravo, and Praia da Saudade. Farther out, the beaches get isolated and deserted. Worth visiting are Praia Vai Quem Quer, Sossego, and Flexeira. There is a local transit service that takes visitors to the various beaches, making it easy to find the one you prefer. You can hire a guide to take you on a jungle hike to the interior of the island, where you can see tropical birds and other animals and you can hike to the ruins of an old sugar plantation from the 18th century. You can get to Cotijuba Island from Belém via river transit, or from Mosqueiro or Icoaraci village (which you access from Belém).

## ALGODOAL

The Algodoal Island has some of the best beaches in the area but can be difficult to reach. The rough ocean tides make it impossible for ferryboats to make it to the island, so there are no cars and the island remains pristine and rustic. You should go by boat with a guide for an overnight trip, perhaps even taking the time to visit the beaches of Maracanã nearby. The most popular beach is **Praia da Princesa**, which has bars to serve guests and shady structures. You can get to this beach at low tide from the Village of Algodoal, or take a canoe. The beaches of Fortalezinha and Mococa require a hike through the forest to see and are semi-deserted and beautiful. You should only visit the island and its beaches with a guide. For a place to stay the night, try the **Chalés do Atlântico** (Vila do Algodoal, tel. 91/3226-9855, R$65). Peak season is in July.

## FESTIVALS AND EVENTS
### Festival do Cupuaçu
The sweet smell of the *cupuaçu* fruit has perfumed the homes on the Island of Mosqueiro for centuries. Just about every home on the island had a *cupuaçu* tree in the yard. Today, the island celebrates its love affair with the fruit by

way of a Cupuaçu Festival, generally held in March each year. Commonly used in juices, ice cream, and cakes, this delicious fruit can easily become a passion for those who taste it. *Cupuaçu* ice cream can be found all the way down to Southern Bahia, although the fruit is most commonly found in the Amazon region. If you don't happen to be in town for the festival, at least make a point to try some *cupuaçu* ice cream at the Estação das Docas in Belém.

### Procissão do Círio de Nazaré
Two hundred years ago, a simple *caboclo* (a person of indigenous and Portuguese descent) found a statue of Our Lady of Nazareth in the interior of Belém. As the legend goes, this statue would reappear on the same spot every year (from wherever it was being kept, one would imagine). That spot is now the site of the Basílica de Nazaré Church and the very statue resides inside all year long, except for a few days when it is used for the reenactment of the great miracle. The procession involves several phases. First, a great boat parade accompanies the image from Icoaraci to Belém, where it is then carried at night to the Catedral da Sé, along with many faithful followers carrying *círios* (huge candles). The night continues with fireworks and children dressed as angels running through the streets. The next morning, the image is carried over to its home in the Basílica five kilometers away, accompanied by more than one million followers, thus making it among the largest Catholic processions in the country. As the image moves down the street, it is protected by a rope, delineating a border that cannot be crossed by the masses. Touching or holding the rope along the trajectory has become a privileged position in the ritual and is believed to have curative powers. The Círio de Nazaré takes place on the second Sunday in October.

## SHOPPING

The enormous Ver-o-Peso market on the waterfront in Belém has items from the entire region for sale. This is, of course, the first place

*Marajoara* ceramics of the Amazon

to go for a shopping spree. On Sundays, there is an open-air market in the Praça da República, where you can find local crafts and souvenirs. There are also many food stands. If you want to get closer to the source of the region's ceramics, then you should pay a visit to the village of Icoaraci, out in the bay near the Island of Cotijuba. There, you'll find the actual potters who make the ceramic replicas of ancient indigenous artifacts. Originally, these artisans came from the Marajó Island and are therefore known as the *Marajoara* artisans. The **Cooperativa das Artesãos de Icoaraci** (Praça da Matriz) is the market where most of the artists in town display their wares, but you can also check out the **Feira do Paracuri** (Praça de São Sebastião). The prices are generally excellent. You can get there by boat in about 35 minutes from Belém and from there you can continue to Cotijuba or Mosqueiro if desired.

If you prefer the Tapajónica artisans, who are known for their decorative and sculpted pieces (rather than pottery), then you should visit Santarém, where you'll find most of the artisans of this style. These markets are usually running from 9 A.M.–5 P.M. daily during the peak season. Off-season hours are unpredictable.

## EXCURSIONS AND ACTIVITIES
### Jungle Trails
Belém and surrounding areas do not have the kind of tourist infrastructure that you find in Manaus. Hence, it's more difficult to find organized hikes into the jungle. There are trails and jungle experiences on the Island of Marajó, particularly those linked to one of the jungle lodges or *fazendas* on the island. There are also trails that enter the Parque Ambiental de Mosqueiro. The best trips are by boat and canoe.

### Papagaios Island: Flight of the Parrots
The best excursion is a trip to Papagaios Island. Generally, you leave very early in the morning (around 4 A.M.), so you can reach the small island in time to see the *papagaios* (parrots) wake up and fly out in a flurry of emerald feathers and a loud cacophony of songs. While out on

the islands, your guide will take you around to see other animals and bird species, although there are no facilities and the excursion generally returns to Mosqueiro before 8 A.M. Be sure to bring your camera or binoculars for this trip. You can get from Mosqueiro to the Islands of Cotijuba, Marajó, and Icoaraci. Check with tour guides in Belém or Mosqueiro.

## River Trips

The majority of river trips that leave Belém are going to some other destination to drop off passengers and goods. You can get to Manaus in about 98 hours, Santarém in about 55 hours, and just about any other destination along the river. The most economical way to go is via *embarcação* (a boat trip), which involves sleeping in a hammock onboard and is pretty much only for transportation between the two destinations. There are no special sightseeing excursions or comforts along the way, other than what you see from the boat. If you want to get to Santarém or Macapá, for example, and don't like the idea of flying, then an *embarcação* boat trip might be just the ticket. A couple of tips: Arrive early with your hammock to select a good location onboard for sleeping. Always keep your valuables with you, even in your hammock as you sleep. Bring plenty of snack foods and water. Although food is available onboard, you will want to have something else. Divide long trips into two or three stages. For example, go from Belém to Macapá, then from Macapá to Santerém, then from Santarém to Manaus. An *embarcação* from Belém to Manaus is jungle madness.

More elaborate and comfortable excursions are aboard floating hotels and include side trips and stops all along the way. Food, cool showers, and other services are also part of the package. There are long trips on floating hotels that go to Santarém, Parintins, and Manaus.

Boat excursions that stay around the Belém area include trips up the Guamá River. These trips generally pass some of the low-water, marshy areas to view the water plants and stop at one of the small islands in the river for a quick hike in the brush. They may include time for swimming in the river. These short Guamá excursions are only recommended if you are not heading out deeper into the jungle. After a few days in the jungle, these short river trips will seem like something designed for kids. Hence, if you want more of a jungle experience, and don't have time for a long trip to Santarém or Manaus, then you should head over to the Island of Marajó for some bird-watching, animal safaris, and piranha fishing.

Other boat trips from Belém go out to the islands of Cotijuba, Algodoal, and Mosqueiro—most of these are visited predominantly for their beaches and beach activities. There are also canoe trips you can take inside the Parque Ambiental de Mosqueiro that leave from the docks at Mosqueiro. Be sure to check for guides authorized by the city or with credentials from EMBRATUR. Finally, the Emílio Goeldi Museum has a jungle station about 15 hours from Breves (on the Island of Marajó) by boat. They have facilities for visitations, but you should check at the museum in Belém for details and to schedule a visit. Most of their facilities are for study and research purposes.

# ACCOMMODATIONS

If you want to get way out of town, try the **Pousada Trilha Dourada** (Ilha de Cotijuba, Praia Funda, tel. 91/3291-0025, R$45 s and R$65 d), which is considered a jungle lodge. It's located 45 minutes by boat from Belém, then another eight kilometers by land. It is very rustic with wooden cabanas and shared bath. They are near the beach and offer beach service as well as fishing and canoe excursions. They have a restaurant and bar. A good economical hotel is the **Manacá** (Tr. Quintino Bocaiuva 1645, Nazaré, tel. 91/3222-6227, R$65). They have 16 rooms with air, TV, and phone. Breakfast is not included.

Also pretty far out of town is **Parque dos Igarapés** (Augusto Montenegro, Km 7, tel. 91/3248-1718, fax 91/3248-7489, R$110), one of the most rustic and jungly of the hotels around Belém. They have 16,000 square meters of forested land on the edge of a river with a pool, restaurant, bar, and excursions. Their rooms are individual chalets with air, TV, and mini-bar. **Beira Rio** (Av. Bernardo Sayão 4804, Guamá, tel. 91/3249-7111, fax 91/3249-7808, R$135–185) along the Guamá River is slightly out of town, but features air, TV, and phone in the rooms, as well as a pool and a restaurant, which sits on an island in the middle of the Guamá River near the hotel. **Itaoca** (Av. Presidente Vargas 882, tel. 91/3241-3434, R$125–145) has 36 rooms with air, TV, and phone. They also have a restaurant and bar. **Equatorial Palace** (Av. Braz de Aguiar 612, Nazaré, tel. 91/3241-2000, www.equatorial-hotel.com.br, R$165–225) has 200 rooms with air and TV, and on the premises are a pool, restaurant, and bar. The **Ⓜ Hilton Belém** (Av. Presidente Vargas 882, Praça da República, tel. 91/3217-7000, www.hilton.com, R$365–425) has 350 rooms with air, TV, and phone; the facilities include a pool, restaurant, bar, sauna, and massage room. Breakfast is included.

## FOOD AND NIGHTLIFE
### Bars
Most of the bars in town are in the Estação das Docas area or along the Ver-o-Peso market. Try **Amazon Beer** (Blvd. Castilhos França, Estação das Docas, tel. 91/3212-5400, 5 P.M.–2 A.M. Mon.–Fri., 11–1 A.M. on weekends). There is also a place to drink a beer in the Casa das Onze Janelas with a view of the river. After the Estação das Docas in Belém, the next most active nightlife scene is in Mosqueiro along the urbanized beaches there.

### Casual Eats
**Ⓜ Spazzio Verdi** (Blvd. Castilhos França, Estação das Docas, tel. 91/3222-1166, 11:30 A.M.–midnight Tues.–Fri., 11:30–3 A.M. on weekends, R$20) is a self-service restaurant in the Docas area, with a good selection of items for a decent price. For an economical lunch plate, try **Bistrô da Rita** (Rua Ferreira Cantão 130, Centro, tel. 91/3230-0605, 11 A.M.–3:30 P.M. Mon.–Sat.). They have an executive plate for R$8 and other inexpensive meals off

the menu. Besides that, the best lunches in the area are on the beaches, where you can sample local recipes, such as *tucupi* and *tacacá,* or just have some grilled fish.

### Fish and Regional Favorites
**Mariscos de Estação** (Blvd. Castilhos França, Estação das Docas, Galpão 2, tel. 91/3242-7595, 10 A.M.–3 P.M. daily) is considered one of the city's best restaurants, serving fresh fish and duck for around R$50 per person. One of the local favorites is **Ⓜ Lá em Casa** (Av. Gov. José Malcher 247, Nazaré, tel. 91/3223-1212, lunch and dinner Mon.–Sat., lunch only on Sun.), which has a variety of local and international recipes. It will be about R$50 per person. They have a second location in the Estação das Docas. The **Círculo Militar** (Praça Frei Caetano Brandão, Old Belém, tel. 91/3223-4374, lunch and dinner daily) is a good bet for a reasonable price and if you're in the Icoaraci area, try **Na Telha** (Rua Siqueira Mendes 265, Icoaraci) for regional recipes at great prices. See the *Food* section of the *Know Brazil* chapter for details about these and other regional dishes.

### Italian
There are several Italian places in town, as Belém has had strong Italian connections since the 18th century. Try the **Cantina Italiana** (Tr. Benjamin Constant 1401, Nazaré, tel. 91/3225-2033, lunch and dinner daily, R$20) for an economical lunch or dinner. Also, **Capone** (Blvd. Castilhos França, Estação das Docas, tel. 91/3212-5566, lunch and dinner Tues.–Sun.) has good Italian concoctions. **La Traviata** (Av. Visconde de Souza Franco 1454, Nazaré, tel. 91/3241-3337, lunch and dinner Tues.–Sun.) is another excellent choice.

### Japanese
**Hatobá** (Blvd. Castilhos França, Estação das Docas, tel. 91/3212-3143, noon–midnight Mon.–Thurs., noon–3 A.M. Fri. and Sat.) has an authentic menu and is in the Docas area. You'll pay around R$35 per person there. Also, **Miako** (Tr. Primeiro de Março 766, Centro,

tel. 91/3242-4485, lunch and dinner Mon.–Sat., lunch only on Sun.) is a decent option for around the same price. Sushi made with fish from the local rivers is an interesting treat.

## Portuguese

The token Portuguese restaurant in town is **Casa Portuguesa** (Rua Sen. Manuel Barata 897, Centro, tel. 91/3242-4871, lunch and dinner Tues.–Sat., lunch only on Sun.), which offers river fish served up in Portuguese recipes for around R$35 per person.

## Other International

**Restô das Docas** (Blvd. Castilhos França, Estação das Docas, tel. 91/3212-3737, noon–midnight daily) has a varied menu with meat, fish, duck, and pasta for around R$25 per person.

# INFORMATION AND SERVICES

The two tourist information groups in Belém are Belemtur and Paratur, the city and state agencies, respectively. One or the other will have an office at main tourist centers around town. These include the main bus terminal in the São Brás neighborhood (tel. 91/3249-9190, 8 A.M.–7 P.M.), the airport (tel. 91/3210-6272, 8 A.M.–11 P.M.), the Ver-o-Peso market (tel. 91/3212-8484, 9 A.M.–5 P.M.), and Praça Waldemar Henrique on the other side of the Docas (tel. 91/3249-6250, 8 A.M.–5 P.M.).

The best place to find Internet connections and quiet phones is in the shopping malls around town. The closest is Shopping Iguatemi (Av. Almirante Tamandaré), just past the Praça da República. You can also find Banco do Brasil ATMs in the mall and in the Docas area. There is a branch office on Avenida Presidente Vargas, a couple of blocks from the docks. You can usually exchange money and traveler's checks at the tour agencies in town.

Most are located around the docks and on the inland streets parallel to the docks.

Belém is home to some foreign consulates. Following are some of them:
- France (Rua Presidente Pernambuco 269, tel. 91/3224-6818)
- Germany (Tr. Campos Sales 63, tel. 91/3222-5634)
- Japan (Av. Magalhães Barata 651, tel. 91/3249-3344)
- United Kingdom (Av. Governador José Malcher 815, tel. 91/3223-0990)
- United States (Tr. Padre Eutiquio 1309, tel. 91/3223-0613).

# GETTING THERE AND AROUND

Flights coming into Belém arrive at the International Airport of Belém (Av. Júlio César, Km 12, tel. 91/3210-6039). Local numbers for domestic flights include Penta (tel. 91/3210-6245), Surinam Airways (tel. 91/3210-6282), TAM (tel. 91/3212-2166), Transbrasil (tel. 91/3210-6390), Varig (tel. 91/3210-6262), and VASP (tel. 91/3257-0944). You can also check with agencies in town.

Most people do not arrive in Belém by bus, but there are some trips you can take that leave from the main bus terminal, such as the bus to Mosqueiro Island. The terminal is located in São Brás (tel. 91/3246-7442).

Boats going out of Belém generally leave from the Docas area. The most popular company for *embarcação* trips is Alves & Rodrigues (tel. 91/3225-1691), which services Santarém (60 hours with many stops) and Manaus (5 days). You can also look into Arapari (tel. 91/3212-4977), which services Ilha de Marajó (3 hours), and Enasa (tel. 91/3257-0299), which services Ilha de Marajó (3 hours) and Manaus (5 days). The Catamarã Atlântica (tel. 91/3225-0152) goes to Macapá (11 hours).

# Deeper into the Eastern Amazon

## ✦ ILHA DE MARAJÓ

During the rainy season, the entire east side of the Island of Marajó becomes a flooded marshland. Ironically, this is where most of the island's 250,000 inhabitants live. The rural and jungle lodges shut down during this season as it's difficult for tourists to get around. But in the dry season (June–January), the island is one of the Eastern Amazon's best destinations for jungle and rural adventures, with an emphasis on bird-watching, caiman focusing, canoe trips, and buffalo rides. The island is huge, about 50,000 square kilometers, and most of it is virgin jungle and wetlands. There is a cluster of towns along the eastern coast, across the bay from Belém. Boats coming from Belém generally dock at Salvaterra, where the island's best tourism facilities—and the best beaches—are located. Not far from Salvaterra are the towns of Soure (known for its ceramic artists and buffalo ranches, which are open for guest visits and overnight stays) and Cachoeira do Arari (known for its incredible waterways, lakes, and *caboclo* culture). Most visitors stick to these three centers, but if you're adventurous, you can take a boat trip out past Breves Straits on your way to Macapá. The trip from Belém to the Island of Marajó takes about three hours.

### Salvaterra

The main port of entry to the island and the largest center for tourism, Salvaterra is a favorite beach destination for residents of Belém. The most popular beach is called **Praia Grande,** and it has a number of kiosks and a semi-urbanized area. It also has fairly large waves that attract surfers from the city. You can walk from here to the lighthouse, which lets you see a more rustic area of the coastline. To find more secluded beaches, you can head to **Praia Joanes,** where you'll find a small village and the ruins of a Jesuit church along the beach. There are a couple of economical hotels in Salvaterra as well as the Pousada dos Guarás, one of the island's best accommodations.

### Soure

The road north from Salvaterra stops at the ferryboat into the small town of Soure. Anything beyond that point is difficult to access by land. The town is what has made the Island of Marajó famous for its buffalo, as the island's more significant farms are located in this region. In fact, here the buffalo outnumber the humans by more than two to one. No doubt, the macaws and caiman alligators also make humans a minority on the island. Buffalo meat is a common item on the menus in town and you can find leather goods at the leather-curing factory, the **Curtume Marajó** (Primeira Rua 450, Soure, no phone, 9 A.M.–5 P.M. daily). You'll find sandals, boots, hats, purses, and all kinds of personal items for pretty decent prices. You'll see buffalo all over town, pulling carts and carrying people from place to place. But if you want a closer look at a working buffalo ranch in the jungle, you can stay at the **Fazenda Bonjardim** (tel. 91/3242-1380, R$145), which provides a mixture of rural and jungle adventure. You can also spend a day at the **Fazenda Bom Jesus** (Quarta Rua, Km 8, tel. 91/3242-1380), a working buffalo farm about 10 kilometers from Soure. They specialize in day visits, where guests go on buffalo rides (getting on is the hardest part) and bird-watching excursions. A traditional island lunch is included for around R$20 per person for the day.

Besides buffalo, Soure is also famous for its rustic indigenous pottery in the Marajoára tradition. Here, you'll find some of the most recognized potters in the region, and you can pay a visit to their workshops. The most famous and respected of the island's potters is Carlos Amaral, whose works are found in museums around the world. To find his workshop, just ask around town. You might even get a ride there on a buffalo.

Finally, the coastline around Soure presents

The buffalo have the run of Marajó Island.

a few excellent beaches, most being quite secluded on weekdays but slightly more frequented on the weekends, when folks from Belém come to pay a visit to the island. Check out **Praia do Pesqueiro,** about 10 kilometers from Soure, with a few beach kiosks that serve seafood lunches. There are also some small sand dunes here, and during the week, it's fairly secluded. You can take a bus or taxi to get here. Also, there's **Praia do Araruna,** a more secluded beach that requires crossing a small waterway to reach. You can take a taxi most of the way there.

## Cachoeira do Arari

If you want to see the rare blue macaw, the enchanting blue egret, or the giant stork, then you should make your way down to Cachoeira do Arari, about 70 kilometers from Salvaterra. The area is full of waterways and lakes and is a haven for tropical birds. They are easy to spot around Lake Arari from a canoe or boat. Besides birdwatching, you can check out the caiman alligators at night, fish for piranha, and pay a visit to the **Marajó Museum** (Av. do Museu 1983, tel. 91/3758-1102, 8 A.M.–6 P.M. daily, R$2). The

museum has one of the best collections of original Marajoára pottery in the world, with pieces dating back more than 1,000 years. These are the pieces that present-day potters are trying to replicate all over the region.

You can get to Cachoeira do Arari from Salvaterra by boat (about five hours) or by car (about four hours along a difficult dirt road). You can also take a small plane and get there in 30 minutes. The best accommodations in the area are at the Fazenda Nossa Sra. do Carmo.

## Accommodations

The best hotel in town is the ▌ **Pousada dos Guarás** (Av. Beira Mar, Praia Grande in Salvaterra, tel. 91/3242-0904, www.pousadadosguaras.com.br, R$115). They have 50 rooms with air, TV, and phone. They offer beach service, pool, restaurant, and horseback excursions. They are located on Praia Grande and have an excellent restaurant that serves various buffalo-meat recipes. They also have multi-day packages that include all meals and excursions into the island. A more economical option is the **Pousada Ilha do Marajó** (Tr. 2 No. 10, Beira Rio in Soure, tel. 91/3241-3218, R$95).

They have a pool, restaurant, and 32 rooms with air and TV. Also, **Pousada Salvaterra** (PA-154 between 7th and 8th, tel. 91/3765-1390, www.engelhar.amazon.com.br, R$65) has eight rooms with air and TV.

## Jungle Ranches and Farms

The **M Fazenda Bonjardim** (Estrada para Cachoeira de Arari, tel. 91/3242-1380, fax 91/3212-3200, R$145–285) is a buffalo ranch and jungle lodge about 20 kilometers (30 minutes by boat) from Soure. They have five rooms with double beds and cool-water showers. They offer buffalo rides, farm activities, animal safaris by land and by boat (looking for blue macaws, monkeys, wolves, and other island species), nighttime caiman focusing (alligator searches), and piranha fishing excursions. Lunch and dinner on the farm often consist of barbecued buffalo meat. All meals are included.

**Fazenda Nossa Sra. do Carmo** (Estrada para Cachoeira de Arari, Beiradão, near Cachoeira do Arari, tel. 91/3241-2202, fax 91/3222-3575, R$150) is located on a small island. They have five chalets with ceiling fans and offer boat excursions, kayaking, and nature safaris.

## Information

You can find Banco do Brasil ATMs in Soure. You may be able to exchange money at one of the tour agencies in Salvaterra, but you're better off getting money in Belém before you come.

# MACAPÁ

A small city of about 300,000 inhabitants, Macapá has the distinction of being Brazil's second most northern capital city and what's more, it is right on the equator. Since it was built on the north bank of the Amazon River, it is effectively cut off from any road traffic from the country and thus remains relatively small and isolated. The only way to get to the city is by boat or plane. As a result, Macapá's economy is largely based on fishing and gathering of plants and fruits from the jungle. The

most significant monument in Macapá is the enormous fort, which was the impetus for the town's existence. On the outskirts of town are some interesting natural attractions, including two large waterfalls and the Pororoca phenomenon, which occurs at the mouth of the Amazon and Araguari Rivers.

## City Sights

If the Amazon River is like a snake winding its way through the jungle, then the **Fortaleza de São José do Macapá** (Av. Candido Mendes, tel. 96/3212-5118, 9 A.M.–6 P.M. Tues.–Sun., free) is one of the eyes on the snake's head. This huge fort was built in 1782 by the Portuguese (using African and indigenous slaves) to keep watch over the mouth of the Amazon River and thus control the extraction of goods from the jungle. At that time, the jungle was mostly producing spices, but the territory was heavily disputed between the Portuguese, the Dutch, and the British. Inside the fort are exhibition rooms, art galleries, and a restaurant. Visits are guided. Next to the fort is the **Casa do Artesão** (Av. Francisco Azarias Neto, tel. 96/3212-9156, 8 A.M.–6 P.M. Mon.–Sat. and 4–9 P.M. Sun., free), which is a collection of handcrafts from local aboriginal groups. The crafts use a combination of elements from the area, including latex from the rubber trees, feathers, and clay.

The **Parque Zoobotânico** (Rodovia Juscelino Kubitschek, Km 12, no phone, 8 A.M.–5 P.M. Tues.–Sun., R$3) has 440 hectares of forest where animals live in an open habitat. There are squirrel monkeys, sloths, and numerous bird species. There are also jaguars and other animals in controlled environments. **Marco Zero** (Rodovia Juscelino Kubitschek, Km 2) is a monument that marks the equatorial line running through the city.

## Distant Attractions

Most of the natural wonders that occur around Macapá are quite far from the city. Still, if you're spending a couple of days here before moving on up the Amazon or down to Belém, then it might be worth a trip out to the **Cachoeira do**

**Santo Antônio,** the largest and most spectacular in the region. To get there, you should hire a guide to take you the 200 kilometers outside of the city, then another hour by boat along the Jari River. When you arrive some 3.5 hours later, you'll see a spectacular waterfall that spans a wide area of the river and cascades about 40 meters. For information on guides and excursions, check with **Detur** (Rua da Independência 29, Centro, tel. 96/3212-5335).

## Accommodations

If you stay a night or two in Macapá, then look into the **M Hotel Macapá** (Av. Azanias Neto 17, Centro, tel. 96/3217-1350, R$145). They have rooms with air, TV, and phone and offer a restaurant, bar, pool, sauna and recreation area. Another option is **Hotel Milano** (Rua Raimundo Hozanan 23, Centro, tel. 96/3223-1522, R$125). Their rooms have air, TV, and phone.

## Food

For a decent dinner of regional fish and buffalo-meat dishes, try **M Chalé** (Av. Presidente Vargas 499, Centro, tel. 96/3222-1970, 11–1 A.M. Mon.–Sat., 11 A.M.–4 P.M. on Sun.). Also, **Bom Paladar** (Av. Presidente Vargas 456, Centro, tel. 96/3223-0555, 11–1 A.M. Mon.–Sat., 11 A.M.–4 P.M. on Sun.) has a mix of regional and international food.

# SANTARÉM

At the confluence of the Amazon and Tapajós Rivers is the city of Santarém, sitting about halfway between Belém and Manaus. Until recently, Santarém was a somewhat secluded jungle city, with an economy based primarily on wild harvesting and fishing. In the early 20th century, the city participated in the boom of the rubber trade and later participated in its bust. There were other economic activities in the area over the years, including some gold excavation, bauxite mining, and even an attempt by Henry Ford to create a huge rubber plantation nearby. The plantation was devastated by a disease that took out every tree. Recently revitalized by tourism, the city is home to some interesting sights and natural wonders that invite visitors to stop for a few days as they make their way between the two big cities.

The most popular attraction near Santarém is the beach area of Alter do Chão, which is located along the east bank of the Tapajós River. The river and lake in this area are especially beautiful with their turquoise-green water and sandy beaches. There are rustic kiosks and places to sit and rest between dips in the water. Hugging the east bank of the Tapajós River for a couple hundred kilometers south of Santarém is the Tapajós National Forest, a great place for jungle hikes and excursions. There are a couple of jungle lodges in the area to take you out.

In the Monte Alegre area, you'll find hot springs rich in sulfur and waterfalls; you can watch a flight of egrets in the evening. Most impressive are the 12,000-year-old paintings on stony cave walls high up in the hills.

## In Town

Two of the most interesting attractions in the city of Santarém are related to handcrafts. First is the **Centro Cultural João Fona** (Praça Br. de Santarém, tel. 93/3522-1383, 8 A.M.–5 P.M. Monday–Friday, free), where you'll see some of great examples of Tapajônica ceramic works, both reproductions by present-day potters and original pieces from excavations in the area. The museum buliding is a colonial structure from 1867 that served originally as the city hall and jail. The other artistic attraction is the studio of present-day craftswoman **Dica Frazão** (Rua Floriano Peixoto 281, Centro, tel. 93/3522-1026, 8 A.M.–noon and 2–6 P.M.). Now famous for her hand-made clothing, woven from plant fibers, leaves and feathers, Dica opens her studio (which she calls a museum) for visitation. Her creations have been word by world leaders and famous personalities. A final attraction that you can witness from town is the phenomenon known as the **Meeting of the Waters,** a slightly less dramatic version of the Meeting of the Waters in Manaus, where two different rivers join to form the Amazon River. Here, the Tapajós

River empties into the Amazon River and the two streams continue side-by-side without mixing for about six kilometers, the blue-green waters of the Tapajós contrasting with the brown water of the Amazon. You can see the Meeting on a short boat trip out onto the river, or watch it from the waterfront in Santarém.

## Alter do Chão

Lying about 35 kilometers to the south of Santarém along the bank of the blue Tapajós River are the sandy beaches of Alter do Chão. Home to some of the prettiest fresh-water beaches in the Amazon, Alter do Chão is a wide opening in the river that is surrounded by sandy beaches. One of the most popular is Ilha do Amor, which is a sand bar that jets out into the river. There are beach kiosks, restaurants, and relaxing places to sit and kick back. Other great beaches include Cururu, Jacaré, and Moça. Most of these are semi-deserted. Hikes from Alter do Chão include a 45-minute walk to Morro Alter do Chão, a local mountain peak, and a one-hour hike to Ponta do Cururu. You can get to Alter do Chão by boat (80 minutes from Santarém) or via bus that goes out Rua Everaldo Martins (50 minutes). Boat is the best way, as your guide can take you around to the various beaches in the area before stopping at your favorite.

Nearby is the **Centro de Preservação de Arte Indígena** (Rua D. Machado Costa 500, Vila Alter do Chão, Km 38, tel. 93/3527-1176, 9 A.M.–noon and 2–5 P.M. Tues.–Sun.). The center has an exhibit of more than 2,000 ceramic pieces from 72 different tribes of the Amazon and it represents the most impressive collection of native artifacts and pottery in Amazonas. There is also a souvenir shop where you can purchase reproductions and demonstrations of pottery-making techniques. If you see one museum of native ceramic works while you're in the Amazon, this should be the one.

## Ⓜ Monte Alegre

Down the Amazon River about six hours by boat is the city of Monte Alegre, sitting in the shadow of some tall, tropical mountains. Up in those looming mountains are some of the oldest cave paintings in the Americas, around 12,000 year old. Discovered by American archeologist Ana Roosevelt, the paintings provide some evidence that civilization in the Americas began in the Amazon region. A hike up to the cave paintings should be arranged in advance with the city of Monte Alegre and can be administered through Santarém Tour. A guide sponsored by the city of Monte Alegre is required. Besides the cave paintings, there are numerous waterfalls and beautiful vistas along the short but difficult hike up into the hills.

Another interesting excursion in the area is a trip out to the **Sulfur Springs Station** (Estância de Águas Sulfurosas), a structure from 1922 that was designed to capture the warm waters coming down from the Ererê Mountains. The 40°C waters are rich in sulfur and are excellent for certain health conditions or just relaxing and rejuvenating (a luxury of the rubber barons, no doubt). The station is about 15 kilometers from town along the PA-225 road.

After a day hiking and bathing in hot springs, there's nothing more enchanting than waiting for the return of the egrets to their evening perches around Monte Alegre. The spectacle takes place every day at sunset and you can catch it from a number of observation points in the city.

## Alenquer

Across the Amazon and upstream a piece (six hours by boat) is the town of Alenquer, home to some of the earliest Jesuit efforts to convert aboriginal groups to Catholicism. The area is also home to some dramatic scenery, including some impressive waterfalls. One of the finest is the **Cachoeira Açu das Pedras,** which requires a 30-minute hike and the crossing of a suspended bridge to reach. The water is clear and cold and you can go swimming. The trail starts about 30 minutes from Alenquer by car. A more extensive hike takes you to **Cachoeira Véu da Noiva** and requires a 3.5-hour hike going into the forest. At the end of the excursion is an immense canyon and a tall waterfall cascading down it. A multi-day hike into the canyon is an extreme sport, but possible with a guide and a few days of prior warning. The 10-kilometer trail starts about 100 kilometers from Alenquer along the PA-225 road. You can get to Alenquer by slow boat (six hours) or speedboat (two hours) from Santarém. Check with Santarém Tur for details before heading out to these locations.

## Excursions and Activities

You can take a canoe out to the *igarapés* (or still-water swampy areas near the banks of the river). One of the more interesting is the **Igarapé Açu,** which has all kinds of plants, including huge water lilies. At night, you can go out to the *igarapé* on a caiman focusing excursion, where you or your guide shines a light into the swamp to see the red, glowing eyes of the caiman looking back. Boats are available in the port of Santarém. Other favorite boat trips from the Santarém docks go out to the **Maicá Lake,** where you'll find all kinds of plant and animal species and out to **Furu do Jari** for piranha fishing. You can visit local villages around Santarém, such as the **Maguary Village,** where you'll see a small community of forest gatherers. Check with **Santarém Tur** (Av. Adriano Pimentel 44, Centro, tel. 93/3522-4847) for information about all of these excursions.

Longer hikes and deeper jungle excursions take place in Alenquer and Monte Alegre. You can hire guides in Santarém to take you out to these areas and along the different trails and waterways once you get there. You should plan in advance for most of these, since they sometimes require special guides or permissions. Boats going out to Alenquer and Monte Alegre can be hired from Antônio Rocha (tel. 93/3522-7947), Enasa (tel. 93/3522-1934), or Marques Pinto (tel. 93/3523-2828).

## Accommodations

A great place to stay while you're in the area is Alter do Chão. There are several hotels in the area, including some rustic jungle inns (not exactly jungle lodges, but close). You can try **Beloalter Hotel** (Rua Pedro Teixeira, Alter do Chão, tel. 93/3527-1247, www.beloalter.com.br, R$140–210), on the margins of Lago Verde. They have 20 rooms with air and TV, including a few in a very rustic style (wood and grass huts). They host excursions to remote beaches and into the jungle near the hotel and they have their own pool.

In Santarém, you can try **Amazon Park** (Av. Mendonça Furtado 4120, Liberdade, tel. 93/3523-2800, fax 93/3522-2631, R$165). They have 120 rooms with air, TV, and phone. They also have a pool, restaurant, and bar. The **Santarém Palace** (Av. Rui Barbosa 726, tel. 93/3523-2820, fax 93/3522-1779, R$75) has 44 rooms with air, TV, and phone. **Rio Dourado Hotel** (Rua Floriano Peixoto 799, tel. 93/3522-2174, R$65) has 20 rooms with air, TV, phone, and cold shower.

## Information and Services

Tourist information can be found at **Santarém Tur** (Av. Adriano Pimentel 44, Centro, tel. 93/3522-4847). There is also a tourist information center (Rua Floriano Peixoto 777, tel. 93/3523-2434). You can check with **Mãe Natureza Ecoturismo** (Praça Sete de Setembro 236, Alter do Chão, tel. 93/9651-5819) for excursions all around the area. Finally, you can check online with **Paratur** (www.paratur.pa.gov.br).

There is a Banco do Brasil in town, where you can get money.

From Santarém, you can travel 50 hours in either direction to either Belém or Manaus. Macapá is 40 hours downstream. Boats leave from the Arrimo Pier along Avenida Tapajós.

# The Pantanal

The Pantanal is quickly becoming the most popular area in Brazil for nature adventures outside the Amazon Jungle. In many ways, the Pantanal offers a more authentic wildlife experience than the Amazon, which is all too often touristy and commercial. In the Pantanal, tourism is not the main event, meaning the tourism industry has not run amok with the infrastructure, turning a natural environment into a hokey, staged animal show. Visits to the Pantanal are marked by authentic animal encounters, photographic safaris by day and night, observation of huge, colorful birds, and boat trips up the marshy wetlands filled with caiman alligators. Also memorable are the abundant lunches and dinners that provide a

taste of the regional foods, including succulent barbecued meats.

The lowlands known as the Pantanal comprise 140,000 square kilometers and are divided into various regions, called *pantanais,* which lie in the states of Mato Grosso and Mato Grosso do Sul, with some corners reaching into Bolivia and Paraguay. The water that fills the Pantanal—with its rich mixture of calcium and magnesium—comes cascading off the high mountains sparkling clear, but sadly undrinkable. The area is known to be the world's largest wetland and is home to an immense variety of wildlife, including at least 80 species of mammals, 650 species of birds, and 50 species of reptiles. Some of the most

# **M**ust-Sees

**Look for M to find the sights and activities you can't miss and M for the best dining and lodging.**

**M Rafting and Boat Safaris:** A boat journey up the rivers and waterways of the Pantanal is filled with animal encounters. Caiman alligators are probably the most plentiful species, but you'll also see exotic birds, capybaras, anteaters, monkeys, and numerous other species (page 506).

**M Snorkeling and Flotation:** One of the best ways to get face-to-face with the waters of Bonita is by putting on a mask and snorkel and floating effortlessly down a fresh-water corridor. For clarity of water and variety of fish, these river floatation adventures are difficult to beat (page 507).

**M Waterfalls and Swimming:** The rivers that flow down from the Bodoquena Mountains into the Pantanal are cool and clear and riddled with waterfalls and swimming holes. As you swing from a rope into one of these fresh pools, you may be overwhelmed with the desire to give out a Tarzan jungle call. That's perfectly natural (page 508).

**M Refúgio Ecológico Caiman:** The majority of the Pantanal species are represented on the vast lands of this preserve, and safaris will take you out to see the giant stork, pink flamingo, tiger heron, and numerous types of land animals. Their night safari reveals a whole different world of animals (page 512).

THE PANTANAL

*Refúgio Ecológico Caiman*
**M**

BOLIVIA

*Snorkeling and Flotation*
**M**

*Rafting and Boat Safaris*
**M**
Campo Grande

Bonito

*Waterfalls and Swimming*
**M**

PARAGUAY

Curitiba

ARGENTINA

Florianopolis

The Pantanal

© CHRISTOPHER VAN BUREN

a trip downstream

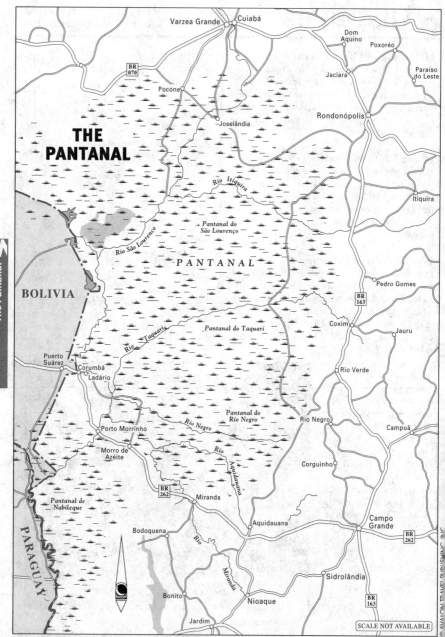

SCALE NOT AVAILABLE

celebrated of the Pantanal species are the jaguar, blue macaw, anteater, stork (the largest bird in the region), pink flamingo, snowy egret, red billed toucan, and the caiman (a crocodilian). You'll also find more than 1,000 different butterflies and countless fish species. The flora of the area is especially diverse, with a great many water plants, but also lowland chaparral, grasses, plains species, and dense forest.

There are two principal seasons in the Pantanal: the dry season and the wet season. The dry season, spanning June–September, is an excellent time for jeep safaris and bird-watching excursions, as many species are caring for their offspring during these months. This is generally the peak season in the Pantanal, since most people prefer to avoid the rain. It's easy to spot families of capybara and deer; and the ponds and marshlands are often filled with tiny caiman alligators. Egrets and storks protect their nests in the various trees of the area. The wet season, which spans October–March, is also a great time to visit. Waterways and lakes are brimming over, making boat safaris the favorite excursion of the season. The waterways, lakes, and marshlands themselves are interesting, with their many varieties of plants and different colors of water. Most of the area is swarming with caimans, the single most abundant species in the region, with numbers estimated at more than 30 million.

The second most abundant species in the Pantanal—more abundant than humans, which are third on the list—is the cow. Introduced into the region almost 200 years ago, cattle represent the area's most important resource, with an estimated 24 million head in Mato Grosso do Sul—5 million of which are in the Pantanal region. Interestingly, the impact of the cattle-farming industry is small on the delicate ecosystems in the Pantanal. About 98 percent of the Pantanal is privately owned and most of the owners are cattle ranchers. Thankfully, due to environmental protection laws, large ranches are required to preserve vast areas of wildlife. Many ranches have put up hotels or lodges in which you can stay and explore the wetlands via guided safaris in jeeps, in boats, on horseback, or on foot. The best safaris are at sunrise or after dark. Just about every nature lodge in the Pantanal, in addition to providing accommodations and adventures for tourists, is also a working cattle ranch. The fact that cattle production is more important and lucrative than tourism keeps the whole system from exploding out of control, as can be seen in the many beach towns of Brazil and in the Amazon to some extent. And you can even participate in a *boiadeira* (cattle drive) across the great fields of the Pantanal.

For most travelers, a highlight of their trip to the Pantanal is an adventure they had in the region around Bonito. Representing a kind of southern entrance to the Pantanal, Bonito is where many of the area's rivers begin, high up in mountains. The area is filled with freshwater rivers, natural springs, caves, waterfalls, and mountain peaks. Adventure travel is so abundant here that the area has turned into a huge adventure park where guides take groups out to see (and participate in) the many natural wonders of the area. You'll snorkel down clear, fresh-water streams, hike to tall waterfalls, swim in rivers and streams, rappel, scuba dive—the list goes on and on. As much as you'll be a mere observer in the Pantanal, you'll be an active participant in Bonito.

## PLANNING YOUR TIME

The experience of visiting Bonito is very different than staying in a nature lodge in the Pantanal. Most travelers like to spend some time in each destination. The best idea is to start in Bonito and finish in the Pantanal. The animal encounters and nature safaris of the Pantanal lodges will otherwise make Bonito somewhat anticlimactic. For some reason, it's more agreeable to get your adventure hikes and rappelling excursions out of the way before heading into the wetlands to observe the animals. You can do a good job of seeing Bonito in two days, but three is perfect. Plan another three days in the Pantanal.

Remember that the dry season is June–September, but the beginning of the dry season, and even the months leading up to it, are the best time to go. This time, from around mid-April through mid-August, is when the waters are beginning to recede back to the riverbeds and the great birds come down to feed on the fish that get caught in the small lakes and ponds that form. Bird-watching is at its best and there is still enough water to take the boat and canoe journeys up the smaller rivers. Note that July and August can get crowded and most hotels charge peak-season rates. That leaves May and June as the best months of all. Another idea is to catch the end of the dry season, when there are few crowds and rates are low in the hotels. The best months for this are September and October. Avoid Christmas, New Year's, and Carnaval (basically mid-December through mid-February) as these are peak months in the wet season and are crowded. Brazilians from São Paulo and Rio who detest Carnaval festivities often head out to the country to get away from it. The Pantanal is a preferred escape. Finally, avoid the school holiday break known as *Semana do Saco Cheio,* which occurs in the middle of October.

## HISTORY

This is Indian territory. At least as far back as 8,000 years ago. It was occupied by the Guaraní people mostly, but other tribes, such as the Paiaguá (now extinct) and Guató (found on one island in Matto Groso do Sul) also flourished here. It wasn't until 1524 that the Spanish from Paraguay sailed up the Paraguay River into the Pantanal territory, claiming it as their own. But with all the gold being discovered in Peru and other Spanish colonies, the swampy Pantanal was not very interesting at the time.

A little over 100 years later, the Portuguese immigrants of São Paulo, known as the *bandeirantes,* began scouring the country for gold and jewels with the support of the Portuguese Crown. They arrived in the Pantanal at the beginning of the 18th century and discovered gold in the area that is now the city of Cuiabá. To their dismay, the native tribes living in the region were not about to give up their lands without a fight and a series of bloody con-

### BRAZIL'S VALUABLE GREEN STEER

With all the colorful birds and exotic animals in the Pantanal, you might think that the green steer is a rare species of bovine, perhaps even greenish in color. In fact, the green in this steer's name refers to the natural and organic conditions with which it is raised and bred. In contrast to the increasing industrialization of cattle farming throughout Brazil, cattle ranchers in Minas Gerais and the Pantanal have recently jumped onto the "all natural" bandwagon. Not only does this cut costs of production, harking back to cheap, low-tech methods, but it also produces a higher-quality beef, which fetches a much higher price from today's demanding consumer.

Aside from being given all-natural feed, the green steer is also neglected hormones and other artificial additives. It is fed only at standard mealtimes (eliminating over-feeding, which is common in industrial cattle production), and green ranches even follow a code of environmental conduct. There are an estimated 300,000 head of green steer in the Triângulo Mineiro (the cattle ranching region in Minas Gerais) and each one will generate almost twice the income of normal beef, mostly from exportation to foreign markets.

flicts occurred between the indigenous people and the *bandeirantes.* The native inhabitants were eventually pushed deeper into the forest. Since they were theoretically occupying Spanish lands, the Brazilian settlers began erecting forts to protect their new lands and soon communities began to sprout up in the area. Cattle ranching and sugarcane plantations were the main economies until around 1864 when Paraguay decided that the territory belonged to them and entered into a conflict recognized as one of the bloodiest battles in Brazil's history, the Paraguay War. In the end, Brazil ended up with what is today known as the Southern Pantanal. To this day, the greater part of the Pantanal remains wild and untouched, although remarkably bereft of indigenous peoples.

# Campo Grande

Most travelers who come into Campo Grande are on their way out to Bonito or the Pantanal. Rightly so, since there's really nothing much in this spacious and uneventful city to deter one for very long. In terms of population, Campo Grande is a medium-sized city with 650,000 inhabitants. It's also a very large city geographically and has plenty of open spaces, parks, and wide streets. One of the highlights of the city are the great restaurants, featuring regional dishes of barbecued beef, *mocotó* (marrow soup), and game meats. Campo Grande is 700 meters above sea level in the Maracaju Mountains and has an average temperature of 22°C.

## SIGHTS

If you have some extra time, head over to the **Museu Dom Bosco** (Rua Br. do Rio Branco 1843, tel. 67/312-6491, 9 A.M.–5 P.M. Mon.–Fri., 10 A.M.–2 P.M. on Sat., R$3), also known as the Museu do Indio. It contains 5,000 indigenous artifacts, such as arrowheads, spears, bows, and cooking utensils. The headdresses and other clothing of the area's native peoples are most interesting of all. They also have about 1,500 of the region's animals stuffed and on display, with a focus on the birds and mammals. It's a bit dusty and you half expect them to get up and start singing and playing banjos, but it's a good way to get to know the various species of the region before you head out to the wilds to actually see them living and breathing. There are about 10,000 shells and sea fossils from all around the world, but the topper is the vast collection of butterflies (more than 8,000) and insects. You can walk around in about 20–40 minutes. It's only 15 minutes from the airport by taxi and makes a good time-killer if you're waiting for a plane or other connection.

The second most interesting sight in town is the **Memorial da Cultura Indígena** (Saida para Três Lagoas, tel. 67/341-6729, 8 A.M.–6 P.M. daily, R$3), where you'll find a replica of a Terena village made from bamboo and organic fibers. Inside are indigenous arts and crafts. One of the oldest buildings in the city is the **Morada dos Baís** (Av. Noroeste 5140, tel. 67/324-5830, 8 A.M.–7 P.M. Tues.–Sat. and 9 A.M.–noon Sun., free), a commercial building from 1918. It served as a boarding house until 1979 when it was converted into a cultural center. Today, it has art exhibitions, music productions, and is home to the Centro de Informações Turísticas e Culturais.

## RIO VERDE

If you find yourself in Campo Grande for awhile, you might consider a day trip out to Rio Verde, about 208 kilometers north of Campo Grande (3.5 hours by bus). It's a small town with only 20,000 inhabitants and the highlights are the great waterfalls and rivers that offer swimming, rafting, and various water sports. The great **Sete Quedas** is the most visited area. It has group of falls and pools that are perfect for swimming and relaxing. Rio Verde is also known for its industrial ceramic works.

## SHOPPING

You'll find a lot of indigenous arts and crafts at the **Centro do Artesão** (Av. Calógeras 2050, tel. 67/383-2633, 8 A.M.–6 P.M. Mon.–Fri. and 9 A.M.–3 P.M. on Sat.). There are many ceramic works, wood carvings, rugs, and fabrics, plus interesting foods and drinks from the native culture. The **Feira Indigena** (Praça Oshiro Takemori, 6:30 A.M.–8 P.M.), in front of the Mercado Municipal, is a market of indigenous works and products from the Terena tribe, who maintain connections with the merchants in the fair. If you need the refuge of an indoor shopping mall, head over to **Shopping Campo Grande** (Av. Afonso Pena 4909).

## ACCOMMODATIONS

If you get stuck a night in Campo Grande, you can stay at the classy **Bahamas Apart Hotel**

The Pantanal

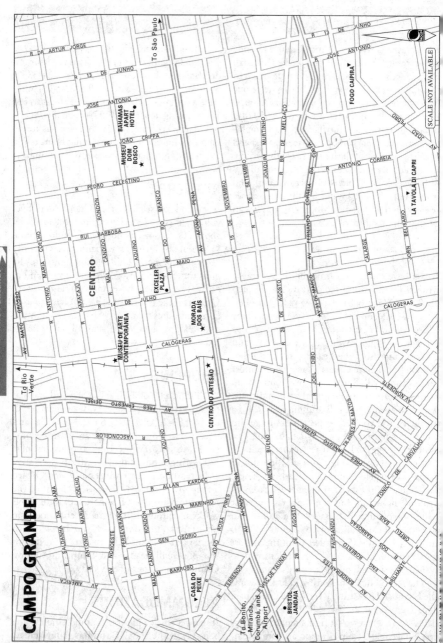

CAMPO GRANDE

(Rua José Antonino 1117, tel. 67/312-9393, www.bahamasaparthotel.com.br, R$255). They have professional facilities with a restaurant, bar, tobacco shop, pool, sauna, health club, and panoramic elevator. Rooms have air and cable TV. Also try the **N Bristol Jandaia** (Rua Barão do Rio Branco 1271, tel. 67/321-7000, www.jandaia.com.br, R$195). They offer a comfortable and modern facility at a decent price. It's not far from the airport.

You can also get set up at the **Exceler Plaza** (Av. Afonso Pena 444, tel. 67/312-2800, www.exceler.com.br, R$185). They have a pool, restaurant, and bar. Rooms have air, TV, and phone. Breakfast is included. An economical option that's close to the airport is the **Hotel Vale Verde** (Av. Afonso Pena 106, Centro, tel. 67/321-3355, www.hotelvaleverde.com.br, R$95). Rooms are simple but clean and they have air, TV, phone, and gas-heated showers. Services include a restaurant, bar, Internet, and 24-hour room service. Breakfast is included and they do not collect a service charge.

## FOOD

**La Tavola di Capri** (Rua Jornalista Belisário Lima 388, Vila Glória, tel. 67/724-2634, 6 P.M.–midnight, R$25) is one of the best Italian kitchens in town. For regional dishes, try the **Casa do Peixe** (Rua Dr. João Rosa Pires 1030, Amambai, tel. 67/782-7121, 6 P.M.–midnight daily, R$30) or **N Fogo Caipira** (Rua José Antônio Pereira 145, tel. 67/724-1641, 6 P.M.–11 P.M. Mon.–Sat., R$20), which specialize in barbecued meats. They both have a nice atmosphere and the prices are excellent.

## GETTING THERE AND AROUND

You'll probably hang around the **Airport Internacional de Campo Grande** (Av. Duque de Caxias, tel. 67/368-6000) until you catch your ground transportation into Bonito or the Pantanal. To hire an air taxi to one of the cities in the region, try **Amapil Taxi Aéreo** (Rua Belizário Lima 677, tel. 67/383-4382). The main **bus terminal** (Rua Joaquim Nabuco 200, tel. 67/383-1678) is where you can catch buses out to Bonito, Miranda, and Corumbá. When heading out to Corumbá, be sure to get a direct bus, as the economical buses stop many times and often in dangerous towns along the way. There have been reports of robberies on the buses at these stops.

If you want to rent a car and drive to Bonito and your other Pantanal destinations, you can try **Avis** (tel. 67/325-0072), **Localiza** (tel. 67/363-1401), or **Unidas** (tel. 67/363-2145). These are all represented at the airport.

## INFORMATION AND SERVICES

There is a good tourist information booth in the airport (tel. 67/363-3116) and another at the bus station. You'll also find tourist information at the Morada dos Baís (Av. Noroeste 5140, tel. 67/382-9244, 8 A.M.–6 P.M.). If you want to get in touch with the tourism department, see SEDEC (Rua Bahia 470, Jardim dos Estados, tel. 67/314-3580, www.pmcg.ms.gov.br).

There are international ATMs at the airport and you can change money with one of the tourism agencies in town.

# Bonito

Locals call this place The Kingdom of Clear Waters and for good reason. It is traversed by 10 rivers of amazingly transparent water, replete with natural pools, rapids, waterfalls, and spaces referred to as freshwater aquariums because of their clarity, stillness, and abundance of marine life. The rivers come down off the Bodoquena Mountains to feed the lower Pantanal. Here, in the highlands, the water is cool and crisp and very inviting. In fact, it's the rivers and waterfalls that are usually the first stop on visitors' lists. A trip out to the Estância Memosa would be an appropriate starting point. There, visitors enter the clear waters with masks and snorkels and swim around a fresh water aquarium to see dozens of species of fish. The excursion continues with a single-file float down a long water corridor to continue the underwater show. There are several such floatation excursions in the Bonito area.

At the Baía Bonita Park, you can dive into natural pools under great waterfall cascades and swim up under the waterfalls to explore the small caverns behind them. The park has a dozen of these cascades. On the Formoso River, you can take a mild white-water rafting trip that includes encounters with monkeys, caimans, parrots, and toucans along the banks of the river. You can hike to great waterfalls 120 meters tall and rappel down vertical caverns to greet the red macaws and other species that live there.

Among the highlights are the many great caves and caverns in the area, more than 70 of them, filled with stalactites and stalagmites formed by the water's rich calcium and magnesium deposits. Not to be missed is the Lago Azul, one of the world's largest underwater caverns. The lake at the bottom is perfectly still and an interesting refraction of light from the top of the cavern makes the water appear dark blue. In the Lagoa Misteriosa, no one has ever reached the bottom of the lake and divers have already exceeded 200 meters. For advanced thrill seekers, there's the Abismo Anhumas, a 72-meter rappel down to an underground lake, followed by a scuba dive in the lake.

Bonito is 260 kilometers from Campo Grande along the BR-060. The city itself is small, with only 20,000 inhabitants, but serves as one of the principal points of entry into the Pantanal. There are numerous hotels and inns at every budget level, plus restaurants and shops along the main road of town. Excursions around Bonito are all located on private properties that open their lands to guided visitations. Any trips out to these facilities require the presence of one of the local guides. The number and frequency of visitors is strictly controlled and only certified guides can bring groups into the sights.

## EXCURSIONS AND ADVENTURES

Bonito is all about the excursions you can take. Whether you're alone or in a group, you'll be going out to the rivers, caves, and waterfalls with a bunch of other people. That's how it works here; everything is done in controlled numbers to reduce the impact on the environment. Because of this, most visitors don't just show up in Bonito and head over to one of the tour offices to join a group. In Bonito, the best way to take in the sites and activities is to setup your trip ahead of time and contact tour guides in advance (see *Tour Agencies and Guides* in the *Information and Services* section for some options). Leaving things open-ended until you get there can work just fine at times, allowing you to pick and choose your excursions with some degree of freedom. Other times this technique may backfire. During peak season, most of the groups will be pre-established and you might have some trouble finding an opening. In the low season, you'll end up getting placed where there are openings in existing groups or where the numbers work out. So, whether you work with a tour agency in advance or leave things to chance at the last minute, you probably will not get to choose exactly which attractions you get to see. The truth is, it may be better that way, since guides can put together assortments of popular attractions, paying close attention to their proximity to each other and how they combine with one another. There are more than 35 different sights in the area and it can be difficult to choose the best ones and combine them for a day's activities. The information in this section will give you a good head start.

Note: Remember to wear tennis shoes or hiking shoes to any excursion and have a bathing suit and towel with you at all times. You never know when you'll be jumping into the water.

## Caves

Of the 78 caves that have been cataloged in the region, only four are open to the public. The image most commonly used in the Bonito travel guides is the dark blue water of the **Gruta do Lago Azul.** Sitting silently at the bottom of a large cavern is a lake of untold depth and incredible color. The water is thought to come from an underground river deep under the surface and the deep-blue color of the water is a result of refraction of the light entering the cave. This is an easy excursion that requires a mild hike down the cavern to the lake and back. It takes about 1.5 hours and costs R$30. Note that this excursion closes at 2 P.M. when the sun no longer illuminates the cave. There are no artificial lights inside. At the end of December and beginning of January, the sun is in a special position relative to the opening of the cavern and casts a beam of light down into the cave to the water. This is a very special time to see the Lago Azul.

## Radical Adventures

You can opt for some of the more radical adventures in the Bonito area, including scuba dives, beginner dives, rappelling, and heavy hikes up to mountain peaks. The **Cachoeiras do Aquidaban** is a difficult hike that takes you up to a series of beautiful waterfalls that include great pools for swimming. At the top is a waterfall with a 120-meter drop. You'll also get a panoramic view of the mountains around

Bonito with few people around to bother you. It takes the entire day and costs R$60 with lunch included. The hike out to **Boca da Onça** is similar. You hike out past numerous cascades and swimming holes to the 156-meter Boca da Onça falls and swim in the pools beneath it. If you're up for a dangle, you can then rappel beside 90 meters of canyon walls that are full of caves and caverns. At the bottom, there are pools of clear water for cooling off. It takes all day and costs R$210 with lunch included. A training session is required the previous day for all participants.

One of the most impressive sights in the region is the **Abismo Anhumas,** an underground cavern with a clear, blue lake at the bottom. You rappel down 72 meters into the cavern, passing stalactites along the way. At the bottom you can scuba dive in the silent, still lake. Scuba credentials and a day of training for the rappel are required for this one. For a true cave-diving experience, there's the **Gruta do Mimoso,** which has underwater galleries and a horizontal distance of 70 meters (vertical is around 18 meters). Cave-diving certification is required. R$100 with lunch. There are several other diving experiences, including the great **Buraco das Abelhas** (Bee Hole), where you can dive in underwater caves up to 50 meters deep, complete with fish and other cave species. This also requires cave-diver credentials. The **Lagoa Misteriosa** is a scuba experience into a lake whose depth has not been calculated. Divers have already gone more than 220 meters deep. The water is clear and relatively warm. You only need a normal diving credential for this. R$100 with all equipment included.

More in the area of scuba diving, you can take a beginner dive in either the Rio Formoso or the Rio Prata with a diving instructor and a few hours of instruction beforehand. The dive and all equipment and instruction costs R$140.

A unique adventure occurs at the **Buraco das Araras,** a huge vertical cavern 160 meters in diameter in which numerous bird species live, including the beautiful red macaw. You rappel down (optional) to get a closer look at the birds. A special area for descending has been designated. At the bottom, the lake is full

**BONITO AREA**

FAZENDA SAN FRANCISCO

REFUGIO ECOLÓGICO CAIMAN

Miranda

To Corumbá and Estrada Parque

FAZENDA BAIA GRANDE

Bodoquena

To Campo Grande

Boca da Onça

ENO BOKOTI

Cachoeiras Rio do Peixe

Rio Miranda

PARQUE DAS CACHOEIRAS

RAFTING AND BOAT SAFARIS

ESTÂNCIA MIMOSA

Rio Mimoso

Rio Formoso

Abismo Anhumas

HOTEL FAZENDA CACHOEIRA

Bonito

FAZENDA SEGREDO

PROJETO VIVO

Gruta do Lago Azul

BONITO AVENTURA

Rio Formosinho

Rio Sucuri

RIO SUCURI (FAZENDA SÃO GERALDO)

Rio Formoso

Rio da Prata

Rio Miranda

Rio da Prata

Guia Lopes

Lagoa Misteriosa

RECANTO ECOLÓGICO RIO DA PRATA

Buraco das Araras

Jardim

To São Paulo

FAZENDA JATOBÁ

SCALE NOT AVAILABLE

© AVALON TRAVEL PUBLISHING, INC

The Pantanal

of *jacarés sucuri* (yellow alligators). This adventure is near the town of Jardim.

See *Tour Agencies and Guides* in the *Information and Services* section for booking information for these activities.

## Rafting and Boat Safaris

The rafting safaris are some of the more mild excursions in the area in terms of physical demands placed on the participants. You ride in a large inflated raft down a river and past a series of small cascades (nothing close to white water but a thrill all the same). The main attraction is the nature safari you get along the borders of the river. You'll surely see monkeys, many kinds of birds, and caimans. A good trip is hosted by the **Fazenda Segredo** (10 km from Bonito, tel. 67/255-1872, www.pousadasegredo.com.br) and takes you down the Rio Formoso for about seven kilometers. Lunch is served at the *fazenda* afterward, and there are optional horseback excursions from there. Rafting and lunch are $50. The **Hotel Fazenda Cachoeira** (10 km from Bonito, www.hotelfazendacachoeira.com.br) also offers a trip down the Rio Formoso and a regional lunch afterward for R$50. Finally,  **Projecto Vivo** (32 km from Bonito, tel. 67/255-3803, www.projectovivo.com.br ) is a hotel-*fazenda* that has three rooms for guests, suspended trails, horseback excursions, and a boat trip down Rio Formoso. They allow day-use of their facilities for anyone to join. This package is R$50 with lunch. You can take your cameras on these trips as you won't get very wet, but keep it in a plastic bag all the same.

## Snorkeling and Flotation

If you've already been to the Parrachos in Natal or the great underwater pools in Porto de Galinhas on the north coast of Brazil, you might think that floating down a fresh-water river with a mask and snorkel could not possibly compare. You'll be surprised to discover that the flotation adventures in Bonito are some of the most compelling and exciting snorkeling excursions in the country. They generally begin with a short hike through the brush. You then enter a fresh-water pool, filled with an incredible variety of plants and fish, then float with the mild current along a river, viewing the fish swimming with you along the way. The water is amazingly clear (said to be some of the clearest in the world) and the wet suit helps keep you warm along the way. There are several flotation sites in the area and they all provide equipment and facilities for lunch and relaxation. One of the best is the **Reserva Ecológica Baía Bonita** (7 km from Bonito, tel. 67/255-1193, www.baiabonita.com.br), which has one of the most pristine aquariums in the area, with about 30 different types of fish. You begin in the aquarium, then commence floating downstream for about 1.5 kilometers. The water here is not as cold as other rivers and they have some excellent facilities, including a restaurant, outdoor showers, warm swimming pool, and relaxation cabana. The food is excellent and the suspended trail going out to the aquarium is an adventure in itself.

Another contender in the floatation game is

The Pantanal

rafting down Rio Mimoso

the **M Recanto Ecológico Rio da Prata** (54 km from Bonito, www.riodaprata.com.br). You begin with a light hike into the forest (40 minutes) where you can see monkeys and birds of the Pantanal. You come to a great natural pool of water, filled with fish and plant life and float down the current with your mask and snorkel, face down to watch the underwater world. The floatation lasts about an hour and 20 minutes. Afterward, there is lunch with regional cuisine and a relaxation area. They have an optional horseback excursion from there. The cost is R$90 with an additional R$15 for lunch. You can also check into the **M Rio Sucuri** (18 km from Bonito, tel. 67/255-1736, www.riosucuri.com.br), which is very much like the former site, with a floatation of about 1.5 kilometers in relatively cold but incredibly clear water. They have an abundant lunch with fish, chicken, and regional dishes. Optional horseback excursions or bike excursions are also available. It's R$100 including lunch and all equipment. **Bonito Aventura** (6 km from Bonito, tel. 67/382-2984, www.bonitoaventura.com.br) is the longest and deepest flotation, spanning 2.2 kilometers and up to five meters in depth at times. You pass through some mild cascades (an extra thrill) along the way. The adventure takes only three hours and there is no lunch included. The price is R$40. Finally, **Eno Bókoti** (32 km from Bonito, tel. 67/255-4023, www.enobokoti.com.br) is a full-day event, which includes a two-kilometer hike to a great waterfall and natural pool. There are also pools with swings and diving decks and you can take the optional flotation for 500 meters. Lunch is included for R$50, with an extra R$20 for the flotation.

## M Waterfalls and Swimming

There are some wonderful waterfall parks in the area where you can swim in the natural pools and sit under the cascades for a natural massage. Some of them are all-day experiences and others just take a few hours and can be combined with other excursions. The best one is the **M Estância Mimosa** (24 km from Bonito, www.estanciamimosa.com.br), which starts with a hike that follows the river past numerous waterfalls and pools to a few designated areas, where the pools are perfect for swimming. Some of the waterfalls have small caves behind them and there are cables and ropes for swinging into the water. The high-dive deck is a scream and you should swim up into the cave there to see a very special rock formation. Afterward, they offer an excellent regional lunch. There is an optional horseback excursion. It costs R$40 with an extra R$15 for lunch. The **Cachoeiras Rio do Peixe** (35 km from Bonito) involves a hike along the river until you arrive at the Rio do Peixe Waterfall, which is a large area with several cascades and great pools for swimming. Lunch is served back at the ranch. The excursion costs R$60 with lunch. A shorter version is available at the **Parque das Cachoeiras** (17 km from Bonito, www.parquedascachoeiras.com.br), which takes only three hours. You hike into the forest until you come to the waterfalls and pools, where you can swim and explore the natural cavern behind them. No lunch is offered and the cost is R$40.

## JARDIM

A smaller, more secluded version of Bonito, Jardim has many of the same kinds of excursions and nature adventures, with a specialty in adventure sports. The city is located in the southern rim of the Bodoquena Mountains near the Formoso, Peixe, Sucuri, and Prata Rivers. There are hotel-*fazendas* that provide the majority of excursions, which include rafting, river snorkeling, hiking, horseback riding, and rappelling. The Buraco das Araras is nearby and guides provide rappelling adventures down the hole to view the various species. It's close enough to Bonito that many of the surrounding attractions are just grouped together as part of the Bonito offerings. As in Bonito, all excursions in Jardim are hosted by private *fazendas* and require authorized guides.

one of the many waterfalls at the Estância Mimosa

## BODOQUENA

With a population of 9,000 inhabitants, Bodoquena is a small town that lies along the Bodoquena Mountain range, the principal range from which the rivers flow, feeding the Pantanal. You can get to Bodoquena from Bonito along a dirt road that takes a couple of hours to traverse, or you can drive in from Miranda along a nice, paved highway. The city is located inside the Bodoquena National Park and offers a pristine look at the mountains as they cascade down into the lower Pantanal area. The many rivers in the area are loaded with waterfalls and trails for snorkeling. There are numerous trails leading into caves and up to the mountain peaks, where you can rappel down, including a popular rappel of 90 meters at the Boca da Onça, which is one of the more distant attractions from Bonito. But Bodoquena has many of its own sights that are not listed among those in Bonito and you'll usually find them less crowded and equally as interesting. In addition, *pousadas* and hotel-*fazendas* in the area offer photographic bird-watching safaris, horseback excursions, and other adventures.

## ACCOMMODATIONS

A new hotel with an economical proposition is **Tapera Hotel** (Rod. Bonito Guia Lopes, Km 1, tel. 67/255-1700, www.taperahotel.com.br, taperahotel@vsp.com.br, R$90 s and R$120 d low season, R$120 and R$170 peak season), about one kilometer from the center of Bonito. They have a pool and restaurant and a large piece of property that is full of chickens and roosters (they can be noisy at night). They offer bicycles for their guests and their 46 rooms have air, TV, and phone. They do not offer transportation into the city, but the bikes help. They give excellent discounts for groups that stay in the same room. Their tour agency can help you plan your excursions.

One of the more reasonably-priced hotels in the area is the **Marruá** (Rua Joana Sorta 1173, Bonito, tel. 67/255-1040, www.marruahotel.com.br, marruahotel@bonitonline.com.br, R$124 standard, R$131 deluxe, and R$154 suite low season), which has basic facilities with no special charm, but they are clean and do the job for anyone not planning to spend much time at their hotel. They have a pool, gym, and restaurant where the breakfast (included) is served. Dinner is optional. They have about 55 rooms in a two-story complex and their low rates make them one of the most booked-up hotels in the area—particularly with Brazilians. Add about 60 percent to the price for peak season.

A great middle-level place to stay is the 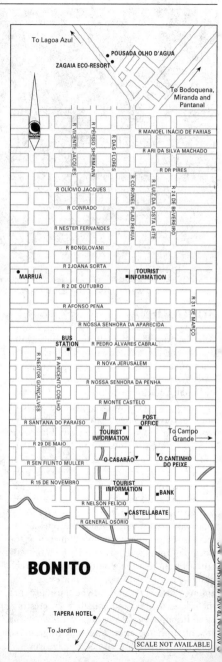 **Pousada Olho d'Água** (Caixa Postal 9, tel. 67/255-1430, www.pousadaolhodagua.com.br, bonito@pousadaolhodagua.com.br, R$145 s and R$230 d normal season), about three kilometers from the center of town. They have excellent grounds with individual chalets or apartment clusters. The 65 hectares of space provide a quiet and peaceful experience. They have a large pool, an inviting poolside patio area, and an excellent restaurant. The style is rustic, but comfortable and clean. Rooms have ceiling fans and hot-water showers.

The **Zagaia Eco-Resort** (Rodovia Três Morros, Km 3.5, tel. 67/255-1280, R$318, R$350, and R$390 s and R$414, R$455, and R$496 d) is probably the most elaborate setup in Bonito. As a resort-style hotel, they like to handle everything for you, from your flight into the area to excursions to all meals and leisure activities. There is no need to involve anyone else (although you're not required to use their services). Some people like that kind of total service and others prefer making some arrangements themselves. The grounds of the hotel are impressive. They have a cyber café, several pools, live music on weekends in their huge outdoor cabana area, a restaurant, beauty salon, bar, gym, sauna, tennis courts, massage rooms, and they are thinking of putting in a small golf course. Rooms come in standard, deluxe, and suite and they all have air and TV. Breakfast and dinner (three different buffets) are included.

## Fazendas and Rural Lodgings

If you want to combine your adventures in Bonito with the adventures of a working ranch, then you can stay at one of the hotel-*fazendas* in the area. Besides offering a more secluded locale, these places usually offer their own set of excursions, such as kayaking, horseback rides, swimming, fishing, and bird-watching safaris.

You'll be a bit farther out of town, so it's best if you have transportation of your own or have arranged transportation (along with the accommodations) through one of the tour agencies. Naturally, this will be easier to manage if you travel with a group.

In Bonito, there is the **Pousada Projecto Vivo** (Estrada para Ilha do Padre, Km 32, tel. 67/255-1500, www.projectovivo.com.br, R$179). They have three chalets that hold up to two people each, plus rafting on Rio Formoso and other attractions. They are located on the bank of Rio Formoso with beautiful surroundings. They are also open to the public for day-use with lunch services. In the Bodoquena area, you can stay at the Ⓜ **Fazenda do Betione** (Estrada para Três Irmãos, Km 70, tel. 67/687-1010, www.hotelbetione.com.br, R$195 low season and R$365 peak season). They have 16 rooms with air and they have a restaurant and bar. The grounds include a waterfall, swimming pool, and a working cattle ranch. They offer horseback excursions, biking excursions, and full use of the waterfall. In Jardim, to the south of Bonito, there's the **Fazenda Jatobá** (BR-267 para Porto Murtinho, Km 15, tel. 67/686-7026, fax 67/251-1713, R$85 low season and R$170 peak season), with eight rooms, a bar, restaurant, and horse ranch. They offer kayaking, swimming, horseback riding, and sportfishing, all in a rustic environment.

# FOOD

The interesting thing about food in Bonito and the Pantanal is that you're very likely to be eating either at your hotel or at one of the attractions. Lunch is almost never encountered outside of the attractions, since you don't really want to be wandering around town when you could be snorkeling down a river. Breakfast is almost always included with your hotel and most hotels also offer dinner—usually better than the restaurants in town. Nevertheless, if you find yourself seeking a restaurant in town for a dinner out, you can try **O Casarão** (Rua Cel Pilad Rebuá 1835, tel. 67/255-1970, 10:30 A.M.–3 P.M. and 6:30–11 P.M.

daily, closed during low season, R$25) for a variety of dishes, including regional foods. There's also **Castellabate** (Rua Cel Pilad Rebuá 2168, tel. 67/255-1713, 11 A.M.–2 P.M. and 6–11 P.M. daily, closed during low season, R$25), with regional food. You'll also find some cafés and bars along the main street of town, Rua Cel Pilad Rebuá. You can walk down this street to see the various shops and tour guide services. One of the most popular places in town is Ⓜ **O Cantinho do Peixe** (Rua 31 de Março 1918, tel. 67/255-3381, 11 A.M.–2 P.M. and 6–11 P.M. daily, closed during low season, R$25), which serves the local *urucum* fish in various ways. You can also get a piranha soup for starters.

# INFORMATION AND SERVICES

The Setuma tourist information office is at Rua Cel Pilad Rebuá 1780. You can get all the information you need from the tour guide offices in town. Useful websites include www.bonitoms.com.br and www.bonitonline.com.br.

## Tour Agencies and Guides

There are several tour groups in Campo Grande, Bonito, and the general Pantanal area that work with the various hotels, nature lodges, and guides to put together your trip. They sell pre-designed packages, but also just handle bookings and reception services at the airport in Campo Grande. They provide transportation to and from the sights and combine people into groups. Get in touch with a few of these in advance to see what types of packages they can put together for you. They will, of course, try to sell you on hotels and flights into town, which you can accept or not. These groups can also handle packages at the Pantanal nature lodges.

Try **Armadillo Ecoturismo** (Rua Rio Grande do Sul 1652, Campo Grande, tel. 67/325-1025, www.amadillotur.com.br), **Barauá Tour** (Rua Couto de Magalhães 98, Campo Grande, tel. 67/321-5406, www.baraua.com.br), and **Impacto Tour** (Rua Padre João Crippa 686, Campo Grande, tel. 67/325-1333, www.impactotour.com.br). Also **Aguas do Pantanal Tour**

(Av. Afonso Pena 367, Miranda, tel. 67/242-1242, www.aguasdopantanal.com.br) specializes in nature lodges in the Miranda area and receives guests in Campo Grande.

If you work with one of these agencies, they will handle all bookings with the local guides—the companies that are authorized to take groups into the attractions—and you will not have to shop for a guide at all. If you prefer to come to Bonito without a reception agency, then you should at least prearrange your adventures with one of the local guide services. This will ensure that you get scheduled for the adventures you want. Transportation to and from the sights will be up to you, but they may be able to help you with that, too. There are 35 authorized guide companies and they are all in the center of town. There is actually very little difference among them in terms of price, since the sights control their prices and give the same commissions to every agency. One of the best is **Ygarapé Tour** (Rua Cel. Pilad Rebuá 1853, Bonito, tel. 67/255-1733, www.ygarape.com.br). They can take you on hikes, floatations, and even work with scuba divers and the radical adventures. Another is **West Tour** (Rua Santana do Paraíso 808, Bonito, tel. 67/255-1443). You can also look into **Pitangua Tour** (Rua Cel de Rebuá 1701, Bonito, tel. 67/255-

1068, pitangua@bonitonline.com.br). Finally, there's **Naturatour** (Rua Cel Pilad Rebua 1830, Bonito, tel. 67/255-1544, www.naturatour.com.br).

## GETTING THERE AND AROUND

You can take a bus into Bonito from the Campo Grande *rodoviaria*. The Viação Cruzeiro do Sul line runs at 6 A.M., 11 A.M., and 3 P.M. Buses returning to Campo Grande run at 6 A.M., noon, and 4 P.M. By bus, the trip takes about five hours. There is also a bus between Bonito and Jardim on the same line that runs at 5 A.M., 11:50 A.M., 12:50 P.M., and 3:50 P.M.

Getting to and from the various attractions in Bonito is more tricky if you are not part of a tour group. First, you can enter open groups via the tour guide agencies in town. Just let them know that you are single and without transportation and would like to join a group if possible. In peak season, this might actually invoke laughter from the attendant, but in the off-season, it's very possible. If that fails, you can rent a car or take a taxi to your chosen attraction. The guides in Bonito should be able to check around for you and find an open spot or two in a van, including vans that leave from the various hotels in the area with closed groups.

# Miranda

For many visitors, the nature lodges around Miranda represent the best of the Southern Pantanal. This is where you can find nature safaris that bring you right up into the wetlands. You can count on seeing most of the great birds, reptiles, and mammals here, whether in the wet or dry season. The town itself is nothing to speak of, situated 194 kilometers from Campo Grande along the BR-262. It has 26,000 inhabitants and an average temperature of 35°C. When you drive into town, you'll see the main tourist stop, consisting of a restaurant, tourism agency, and souvenir shop (with some of the best souvenir items and prices in the area). Outside is a gas sta-

tion. Miranda sits in the middle of the Southern Pantanal, surrounded by numerous rivers and lakes, the very lifeblood of the wetlands. The area was originally inhabited by the Terena people and still has one of the largest indigenous populations in the region, which is visible in the cultural traditions, dances, arts, crafts, and foods.

## ◪ REFÚGIO ECOLÓGICO CAIMAN

Probably the most celebrated of the Pantanal nature lodges, the Refúgio Ecológico Caiman (tel. 65/242-1450, in São Paulo: tel. 11/3079-6622,

© CHRISTOPHER VAN BUREN

**an observation deck during the dry season**

www.caiman.com.br, caiman@caiman.com.br, around R$600 d) is a cross between a nature lodge, nature preserve/research center, and working cattle ranch. Actually, many of the lodges in the area have this same makeup, but Caiman offers the best in all three arenas.

As a place to stay, Caiman offers four separate lodges, each with cozy rooms and breakfast areas. The main lodge is located in the nucleus of the ranch, where the pool, barbecue area, restaurant, and bar are all located. In fact, the nucleus is almost a small village, since there are also separate houses occupied by the workers and executives of the ranch (some 300 people), an exhibit hall, and the main office of the Blue Macaw Project. The facilities here (11 rooms) are located in the main house and are extremely comfortable. Around the house are trees filled with blue macaws and toucans, which are some of the most up-close encounters you'll have here. There is a second lodge with six rooms located in the village area just a few hundred meters away on the bank of one of the area's small lakes. This is probably the coziest of the lodges and it's close to everything that's going on at the ranch. A satellite lodge, known as the Baiazinha has six rooms and is right up against a marshy lake riddled with caimans so close you could touch them. In the wet season, the lake comes right up to the edges of the lodge and guides will take you out on boat excursions from there. The pool at this lodge will satisfy that urge to jump in the water. The fourth lodge, called Corilheira, is built on stilts because during the wet season, it sits on top of the water. It has six rooms and an observation tower. Blue macaws sit in the trees that surround it and the waters are full of caimans—not for swimming!

As a nature preserve, Caiman is home to the Projeto Arara Azul (Blue Macaw Project), which is designed to study and assist the development of the endangered species. The Caiman land is one of the favorite breeding grounds of the colorful bird, with as much as 36 percent of the species' active nests. Besides the blue macaw, the majority of the Pantanal species are represented on the vast lands of the Caiman Ecological Preserve, and safaris will take you out to see the giant stork, pink flamingo, tiger heron, and numerous types of land animals. Their night safari reveals another world

## THE ENDANGERED HYACINTH MACAW

The rare and beautiful *arara azul*, or hyacinth macaw (scientific name: *Anodorhynchus hyacinthus*), is found in only three places in the world: the Island of Marajó in the Eastern Amazon, the Pantanal (including the parts in Bolivia and Colombia), and the mountains in-between, known as the Serras Gerais, south of the Amazon region. Aside from being the biggest bird of its kind (reaching up to four feet from its head to the tip of its tail feathers), its bright blue color and yellow facial markings make it one of the most beautiful and striking birds in the world. Like most of its kind, the hyacinth macaw is a social bird and often flies in small groups. Catching a dozen of these huge birds soaring together above the Pantanal wetlands is a rare and unforgettable pleasure. At times, a large group can be seen decorating the branches of a tree before taking flight again.

Like most parrots and macaws, the hyacinth macaw has a loud, screeching call and uses it quite frequently while flying. You can hear and see them quite easily around the Miranda area of the Southern Pantanal. They perch high up in the trees and stare watchfully at the tourists below.

The macaw's principal enemy is deforestation, since it makes its nest in only one or two species of tree and eats only a few types of fruit. Large-scale farming activities in the Pantanal, which are responsible for clearing the macaw's favorite trees, has placed the bird on the endangered species list. As luck would have it, the *manduvi* tree, one of the macaw's favorite nesting trees (it nests inside hollow cavities high up in the trunk) is perilous to cattle, which get sick from eating the leaves. Worse still, the hyacinth macaw has been prized by animal poachers, who sell live specimens to collectors for tens of thousands of dollars. More than 10,000 hyacinth macaws were illegally sold to foreign collectors in the 1980s, an astonishing number considering the total population of the species. Feathers and other parts of the bird are sold as souvenirs in tourist areas. Couples generally produce only one offspring every two years.

But thanks to the World Wildlife Foundation and the Hyacinth Macaw Project (www.projeto-araraazul.org.br), whereas once only a handful remained in the world, today there are around 3,000 hyacinth macaw's in Brazil. More than 30 percent of the nests appear in and around the protected Caiman Biological Reserve. To compensate for lack of *manduvi* trees, the project has experimented with artificial nests and many have been accepted by the birds. Through these efforts, the great hyacinth macaw is well on its way to recovery in Brazil.

of animals, including the elusive *onça pintada* jaguars, foxes, and wolves. Besides offering night and morning jeep safaris, they also organize walking safaris to see the many caimans on the ranch and horseback excursions.

Caiman is also a working ranch and you'll get the proof of that in the many excellent meals provided for the guests. Every Friday, a couple of steer are slaughtered for consumption by the employees and guests. Many of the fruits and vegetables used are also cultivated right on the ranch, which consists of 53 square kilometers of space, while the ecological preserve area is a mere 5 square kilometers. That's about how the division of land goes here in the Pantanal.

## FAZENDA SAN FRANCISCO

One of the most acclaimed lodges in the Southern Pantanal is the Fazenda San Francisco (Rua Calarge 349, Vila Glória, tel. 67/242-1088, tel. 67/325-6606, www.fazendasanfrancisco.tur.br, sanfco@zaz.com.br, R$65 s and R$135 d). They are located six kilometers off highway BR-262, on the way out to Corumbá. They offer photo safaris by boat and jeep, fishing excursions, night safaris, and horseback excursions. One of their special features is a suspended trail that leads into the brush and over rivers and waterways of the area. You are practically guaranteed to spot most of the region's mammals, birds, and reptiles here. Another feature is their Calana River boat ride, which takes you up to the São Domingas Lake, where you can fish for piranha. They operate a cattle ranch and rice farm on their extensive property and have great facilities and English-speaking guides. Their restaurant uses beef and elements from the farm in abundant feasts for its guests. All meals are included.

The *fazenda* is also home to several wildlife projects via the entity Sociedade de Defesa do Pantanal (SODEPAN), which supports projects like the Arara Azul Project, Animal Rehab Center, and Projeto Gadonça. The latter is aimed at studying the effects of the large cattle ranches on the jaguars of the region. The *fazendas* of the area are known to lose up to 300 cattle per year to the big cats. The ease by which the jaguars can capture these animals may be affecting their existence.

## FAZENDA BARRA MANSA

You have to take a small plane to get to Fazenda Barra Mansa (Rua Amazonas 947, Campo Grande, tel. 67/325-6807, bmansa@terra.com.br, R$250 s and R$480 d), but it's well worth the extra effort and expense. Here, you get a window into the heart of the Pantanal with very little civilization around. The facilities are rustic but nice and everything is included: meals, excursions, and accommodations. They have day and night safaris, fishing, caiman spotting, and horseback excursions. They use their own planes for taking guests to and from Campo Grande (for an extra fee). It's best and cheapest if you are in a group.

## FAZENDA BAÍA GRANDE

Sitting 18 kilometers from Miranda, the Fazenda Baía Grande (Estrada Miranda/Aldeia Lalima, Km 21.5, tel. 67/9984-6658, tel. 67/382-4223, R$150 s and R$300 d) is one of the more popular *fazendas* in the area. They offer all of the excursions you would expect, including nighttime caiman focusing, boat and horseback safaris, jeep safaris, and walk-ing safaris. They have comfortable facilities with access to the waterways. Rooms are rustic but comfortable.

## FAZENDA RIO NEGRO

The Fazenda Rio Negro (Rio Negro, tel. 67/326-8737, www.fazendarionegro.com.br, rionegro@conservation.org.br, R$285 s and R$550–$675 d) has excellent facilities and a superb location in the depths of the Pantanal wetlands. The *fazenda* has three principal buildings. The most inviting is the Casa Sede (Main House), which is used as the dining hall and bar. The country manor was built in 1920 and has great sitting areas and verandas for relaxing. There are also two suites and two standard rooms in the main house. The Guest House has five standard rooms with various arrangements of beds, from couples to groups of six. The Fisherman's House has four rooms for single guests. The *fazenda* is situated on the edge of a large lake in the Miranda area. They offer canoe excursions, boat safaris, jeep safaris, bird-watching treks, horseback safaris, and fishing excursions. The *fazenda* is home to the main office of the Centro de Pesquisa para Conservação (Conservation Research Center), which has numerous projects for studying and assisting the conservation of the Pananal flora and fauna.

You can get to the *fazenda* by a small plane that departs from Campo Grande and takes an hour to arrive. The *fazenda* offers this service for an extra fee. Land transportation is not provided, but the hotel will recommend services for guests. You can arrive by land only in the dry season.

## FAZENDA SANTA INESANTA INÊS

The Fazenda Santa Inês (Estrada Miranda/Aldeia Lalima, Km 21.5, tel. 67/9988-4082, tel. 67/362-9070, www.fazendasantaines.com.br, prata.msi@terra.com.br, R$150 s and R$300 d) is a working ranch with a focus on rural tourism. That means their excursions include

The Pantanal

## THE SOARING TUIUIU:
## SOUTH AMERICA'S LARGEST WINGSPAN

The *jaburu* stork, or *tuiuiu* (too-yoo-YOO) as it's known locally, is somewhat ungainly and awkward on the ground. It stands about four feet tall on one leg as it pokes its 16-inch, sharply pointed beak into the ponds and lakes of the Pantanal in search of mollusks, fish, frogs, and other amphibians. Sometimes it even snatches a baby alligator. If predators get too close (including humans on photo safaris), an entire group of these giant birds takes to the air in an instant. They circle around and land again not far away to continue their fishing activities. In the air, the *tuiuiu* (scientific name: *Jabiru mycteria*) is a high-flyer—graceful and elegant. With its eight-foot wingspan, it is among the largest birds of the western hemisphere and is found from Mexico to Argentina, east of the Andes.

The *tuiuiu* is mostly black and white: Its white body is offset by a black head and neck. Between these two colors is a strip of bright red at the base of its neck. Its red and black neck is not colored by feathers; rather, these are the colors of its naked skin, which stretches to accommodate the great quantities of small animals and fish that pass down its gullet. The *tuiuiu* lives in groups, but generally mates for life, creating 1–3 chicks each season from late July–September. It creates large nests out of interlaced sticks in the tops of tall trees and even goes back to the same nest each season to remodel and expand it.

It's easy to spot *tuiuius* in the Pantanal during their mating and incubation period, which corresponds to the region's dry season. Often, they stand up in their nests, keeping a lookout, or hang around in groups near small ponds and lakes. They are rather sensitive and don't let visitors get too close, so be sure to bring a good pair of binoculars to get an up-close look.

such things as horseback rides, cattle ranching, sportfishing, and hiking along the trails near the ranch. But they also work with a nearby nature preserve, called the Reserva das Figueiras. There, you can take canoe trips around the waterways to spot the many caimans and go on bird-watching excursions to snap pictures of the many species of the Miranda area. Plus, you can swim in fresh-water pools with all kinds of small fish (not caimans). The *fazenda* and preserve are located only 20 kilometers from Miranda and offer day use of their facilities, in case you're just passing through.

## POUSADA REFÚGIO DA ILHA

One of the more rustic facilities in the Southern Pantanal, the Pousada Refúgio da Ilha is located deep in the countryside on a small island in the middle of a river. Their rooms have air and ceiling fans. Excursions include snorkeling in the Solobra River (depending on clarity and conditions), nighttime caiman focusing, bird-watching, piranha fishing, and bike trails. They also have boat safaris, walking safaris, and horseback safaris. All meals and excursions are included. You can book this lodge through Pitanguá Tour (tel. 67/255-1068, R$240 s and R$320 d).

# Corumbá

Although on the western edge of Brazil, Corumbá is still in the middle of the Pantanal and is surrounded by some of the wildest and most beautiful country in the region. It sits on the bank of the Paraguay River and has an active harbor. Not far from Corumbá in the direction of Miranda you'll find the most popular nature lodges, where you can partake of great accommodations, regional food, and nature excursions into the Pantanal wetlands. A special feature of the Corumbá area is the sportfishing and the city attracts fishers from all over the world. The lakes and rivers in this part of the Pantanal are filled with large fish and most of the nature lodges and hotel-*fazendas* (working ranches) offer sportfishing among their excursions. Some of them have a catch-and-release philosophy and others provide the proper licenses for catching and eating. Besides the nature lodges, there are hotels situated on the banks of the Paraguay River near the city of Corumbá that offer a more fishing-oriented experience and floating hotels that offer full immersion into the sportfishing adventure.

Corumbá sits 413 kilometers from Campo Grande on the far west edge of Brazil, on the border of Bolivia. You can arrive by bus or plane from Campo Grande. The average temperature is 30°C and the city has 90,000 inhabitants.

## SIGHTS

The main attraction in Corumbá is **Forte Coimbra.** Built in 1775 to protect the city from the Spanish, the fort was involved in some important battles, including the great war with Paraguay. Its great white walls stand in contrast to the lush green forest that surrounds it. Situated way out in the Coimbra district, it's somewhat isolated from the city. The best way to see it is from the outside, passing by on a river excursion. **Forte Junqueira** (Rua Cáceres 425, access via the 17th batallion, 8 A.M.– 5 P.M. daily), is the city's other prominent fort. It was built in 1871 to fend off the Spanish

from Paraguay and offers a wonderful view of the river from its walls, which are five meters thick. There are many English cannons from the 19th century along the walls.

## ESTRADA PARQUE

The Estrada Parque is an area of the Pantanal just west of Corumbá that was opened up by a new road. Along this road, you'll find good hotels and restaurants, *fazendas,* and entrances to country lodges in the middle of the Pantanal. The road is mostly dirt and it can be tricky to get through in the wet season, but most of the lodges provide their own transportation, whether by boat or air. The idea behind the road was mostly to provide some tourist infrastructure for Brazilians driving through the Pantanal from Campo Grande to Corumbá. This is not something that I recommend for international tourists to attempt in a rental car.

## CITY ACCOMMODATIONS

One of the better hotels in town is the **Nacional Palace** (Rua América 936, tel. 65/231-6868, www.hnacional.com.br, R$80 s and R$100 d). It has 100 rooms with air, TV, and phone. Facilities include a pool and game room. On the bank of the river is the **Gold Fish Hotel** (Av. Rio Branco 2799, Saida para Ladário, Km 5, tel. 65/231-5106, www.candeias.com.br, R$79–145), set up specifically for fishing. They have a restaurant and fishing facilities on the lake and everybody in the hotel is awake at dawn. They also have a pool and are located near the city center. For economical accommodations, try the **Hostel Pantanal** (Av. Isaac Póvoas 655, Centro, tel. 65/624-8999, www.portaldopantanal.com.br, albergue@vsp.com.br, R$30 s and R$50 d). They have a 24-hour reception desk, lockers, TV room, Internet (extra fee), phones, community kitchen, and laundry facilities. They have group rooms and some private rooms for up to three people. They offer tour agency services and rides to and from the airport. Also, you can look into the **Santa Mônica Palace** (Rua Antônio Maria Coelho 345, tel. 65/231-3001, R$60 s and R$85 d).

# NATURE LODGES

## Fazenda Xaraés

The Fazenda Xaraés (Estrada Parque, Km 17, Abobral, Corumbá, tel. 67/232-4224, tel. 67/9906-9282, www.xaraes.com.br, R$225 pp) is a slightly less expensive version of a nature lodge, but every bit as interesting. They have a restaurant, bar, pool, tennis court, and landing strip for small planes that carry their guests back and forth from Campo Grande (check with them for group rates on these flights). They operate a working cattle ranch with 1,500 head of cattle. It was purchased by Portuguese investors in 2001 and remodeled to include better facilities for tourists. It has a capacity for 46 people, a restaurant, bar, barbecue area, game area, reading rooms, pool, sauna, and exercise equipment. Their apartments are close to the water and have air, phone, and veranda. They provide excursions like canoe trips, boat safaris, horseback safaris, jeep photo safaris, walking safaris, fishing, and nighttime caiman focusing—all with English-speaking guides. All meals are included.

They are 340 kilometers from Campo Grande and 130 from Carumbá, and they offer transportation from Campo Grande, Bonito, or Carumbá for an extra fee.

## Passo do Lontra Parque Hotel

One of the best-equipped nature lodges in the Southern Pantanal is the Passo do Lontra Parque Hotel (Estrada Parque, Km 8, tel. 67/231-6569, Campo Grande: tel. 67/356-4138, www.passodolontra.com.br, R$248 s and R$280 d). The hotel was built out of wood and brick and much of it is on stilts, above the Pantanal waters (in the wet season). They have suspended walkways and a fabulous restaurant that serves regional foods. Their rooms in the main lodge have air-conditioning and separate

chalets have living rooms, kitchens, and verandas. They offer boat and jeep safaris by day and night, sportfishing, river-boat excursions, and horseback safaris. Their guides can help with fishing safaris out onto the larger lakes. You can see many birds and caimans right from your porch. Choose between an individual chalet, regular suite, or an area for camping.

## Pousada Arara Azul

The Pousada Arara Azul (Estrada Parque, Km 135, tel. 67/9987-1530, pousadaarara-azul.com.br, R$190 s and R$320 d) has 25 rooms, a pool, TV room, game room, restaurant, and even meeting rooms. In the dry season, you can arrive by car, but the best way to get there yearround is by small plane. They have their own small landing strip, as well as a couple of lakes. They offer night and day safaris by truck, horseback safaris, photographic treks, and sportfishing. Rooms are simple and rustic, but comfortable. The area around the lodge is rife with plant and animal life and you are guaranteed to see caimans, storks, blue macaws, and many other species.

## Pousada Bela Vista

Located on a large open space, this working farm produces beef, lamb, and pork. It also has 13 chalets with air, ceiling fan, satellite TV, and phone. Despite apparently modern facilities, the Pousada Bela Vista ranch (Estrada Parque, Km 26, tel. 67/9987-3660, www.pousadabe-lavista.com, R$200 s and R$395 d) is very rustic. Nearby are waterways of the Pantanal, where you can see the giant otter, colored macaws, caimans, monkeys, and other animals. They offer safaris by horseback, kayak, and on foot, including night safaris by boat and jeep. They also offer a *chalana* (river-boat) excursion that includes sportfishing (catch-and-release style), onboard bar, and shower.

## Pousada Pantaneira Rio Vermelho

With only seven rooms and a capacity for 28 people, the Pousada Pantaneira Rio Vermelho (Rua Rui Barbosa 3538, Campo Grande, tel. 67/321-4737, www.pousadariovermelho.com.br, R$200 pp) is one of the smaller lodges in the area. Still, they offer a simple but comfortable environment, a private landing strip (which you'll need depending on the season), and plenty of boats for the wetland excursions. They also offer van pick-up service from Corumbá and Campo Grande (extra cost) and can arrange boat transportation during the wet season (extra cost). During the wet season, you have to take a boat or plane to get there. They are situated 250 kilometers east of Corumbá toward Miranda. Their excursions include caiman focusing, photo safaris, horseback safaris, and fishing. You'll also get to hang out with the cowboys on the ranch and watch them work. Rooms have air, ceiling fans, and private bath. All meals and excursions are included.

## FLOATING HOTELS

You can spend a few days on the *Millenium* (tel. 67/231-3372, tel. 67/231-3470, R$600 per person for a group of 16), a luxury floating hotel with great facilities, restaurant, and equipment for fishing. They go up and down the Paraguay River, stopping at different location for fishing, swimming, and other excursions. A similar boat is the *Sereia do Pantanal Barco Hotel* (tel. 67/287-2367, tel. 45/226-4769, a package of 6 days and 5 nights goes for around R$2,060 per person for 10 people and R$1,650 per person for 16 people), which has cabins with private bathrooms, air, and all equipment needed for fishing. They have a bar and kitchen onboard.

## FOOD

Fish recipes in the Corumbá area are often sweet and spicy at the same time. There are dishes served with coconut milk and palm oil, others with bananas, and some with sweet condensed milk. The best is *escabeche* sauce, which is made from tomato, green pepper, cilantro, and spices. Some fish come grated and served with cheese on top. The ℕ **Peixaria do Lulu**

(Rua Dom Aquino Correia 700, tel. 67/231-5081, lunch and dinner Mon.–Sat., lunch on Sun., R$20) offers all sorts of Pantanal fish, including the meaty *urucum* and the flavorful *pintado*. You can get a cup of piranha soup as an appetizer, which is considered an aphrodisiac. Also, try **Ceará** (Rua Albuquerque 516, tel. 67/231-1930, lunch and dinner Tues.–Sun., R$25) for regional dishes with a focus on fish. This place is actually located in a home, with tables and chairs spread around their patio and pool area. For meat, try **Restauante do Gaúcho** (Rua Frei Mariano 879, tel. 67/231-5220, 6–11 P.M. daily, R$25), which offers a *rodísio*-style barbecue with all the regional cuts.

## INFORMATION AND SERVICES

Tourist information is available at the airport, bus terminal, and the Porto Geral (the main port). You can also get in touch with **SEMATUR**, the government tourism office (tel. 65/231-6996, tel. 65/231-6899, 8:30 A.M.–noon and 3:30–6 P.M. Tues.–Fri. and 1–6 P.M. Mon.).

A couple of agents that handle reception services and bookings include **Corumbatur** (tel. 65/231-1532) and **La Barcatur** (tel. 65/231-3016).

## GETTING THERE AND AROUND

Flights come into Corumbá from Campo Grande and you can book flights at the Campo Grande airport. The main commercial carrier is TAM (tel. 65/231-7177, tel. 65/231-7299). There are other, small carriers that you can use as well. You should probably fly into Corumbá as there have been reports of assault on the roads between Miranda and Corumbá, specifically on the Estrada Parque road and especially with buses. If you stay at a hotel in the Estrada Parque area, make sure they provide you with *translado* transportation service between the Corumbá airport and their hotel.

# The Northern Pantanal

The Northern Pantanal is a bit less popular among travelers than the southern version, for several reasons. Primarily, the Northern Pantanal is farther away and more difficult to reach. Also, there are fewer tourist facilities in the area and the principal draw of the small towns that reach into the Pantanal (such as Poconé) is sportfishing. There are even sportfishing tournaments and festivals in the area. Visitors should be aware that the hotel-*fazendas* in this area is not nearly as well presented as those in the Southern Pantanal and facilities are often very rustic and uncomfortable. Most of them are more oriented to cattle ranching and fishing than to ecological or tourist activities. If you head to this area, stick with the recommendations in this book for the best hotel-*fazendas*.

The main point of entry into this region is via the city of Cuiabá, the capital of Mato Grosso. The city itself has very little to offer tourists, but from there you can make your way to one of the nature lodges or floating hotels in the area. Most of the Pantanal region is to the south of Cuiabá and accessible via the towns of Barão de Melgaço, Cáceres, and Poconé. Brazilians with off-road vehicles are known to make their way up to these cities from the south, following the Transpantaneira Highway. This highway is more than 150 kilometers long and has more than 100 wooden bridges that cross the various rivers and lakes of the region. Naturally, these bridges are high up off the ground to allow for the variation in water level between the wet and dry seasons. The trip up the highway is a fabulous ride and there are many hotel-*fazendas* along the way in which one can have lunch.

International tourists generally fly into Cuiabá or take a bus from Corumbá. To the north of Cuiabá is the extensive Guimarães National Park, filled with pristine forest, vast valleys, and rocky fissures. You can camp in the park or stay at one of the many *pousadas* there.

## POCONÉ

The road from Cuiabá to Poconé is 100 kilometers long and fully paved. Beyond the town of Poconé is the Northern Pantanal and its many rivers and lakes. A town of 30,000 inhabitants, Poconé is known mostly for its fishing excursions, but the residents there also make their living from cattle and mining activities. Poconé is at the northern tip of the Pantanal and the Transpantaneira Highway that cuts across the Nothern Pantanal from Poconé to Porto Jofre provides a radical 4-wheel-drive adventure through the wetlands, crossing over 100 wooden bridges (some in poor condition). There are also many waterways that run through the Northern Pantanal, including the Cuiabá River, which is a favorite for fishing excursions. You can find a few good nature lodges along the highway south of Poconé.

## SHOPPING

You can find indigenous arts and crafts in Cuiabá at the **Muxirum Cuiabano Bookstore** (Av. Presidente Getúlio Vargas 127, no phone, 10 A.M.–6 P.M. Mon.–Fri., 10 A.M.–2 P.M. on weekends) and at the **Mercado do Artesanato** (Rua Padro Celestino 300, tel. 65/623-1673, 8 A.M.–5 P.M. daily, closed for lunch). Perhaps the best place is the **Casa do Artesão** (Av. Calógeras 2050, tel. 65/383-2633, 8 A.M.–6 P.M. Mon.–Fri., 8 A.M.–noon on weekends), which gets its wares directly from the indigenous communities.

## ACCOMMODATIONS
### Cuiabá

The **Jaguar Palace Hotel** (Av. Getúlio Vargas 600, Cuiabá, tel. 65/642-4404, www.hoteljaguar.com.br, R$100) was built in the 1970s and looks like it. It's a bit old and worn, but the facilities are relatively modern and clean. It's one of the more economical hotels in town. A

Tamarin monkeys are also residents of the Pantanal.

newer option is the **Hotel Paiaguás** (Av. Historiador Rubens de Mendonca 1718, Cuiabá, tel. 65/642-9966, tel. 65/642-5353, www.hotelpaiaguas.com.br, R$185). They have a pool, sauna, restaurant, bar, and gym. The best hotel in town is the ⚑ **Eldorado Cuiabá** (Av. Isaac Póvoas 1000, tel. 65/624-4000, www.hoteiseldorado.com.br, R$145). They offer a pool, restaurant, and bar.

## Nature Lodges

When contacting a nature lodge in this region, you should ask about all extra costs involved in the package. Ask whether or not the excursions are included and if there are any costs for equipment or fuel involved in the excursions. Also, see if guides are included in the price and whether there are any extra costs for transportation to and from the hotel or excursions.

The **Hotel Fazenda Camalote** (Rodovia Transpantaneira, Km 73, tel. 65/682-4441, R$175 s and R$285 d) is a working ranch with 4,000 head of cattle. Their 10 rooms have air, ceiling fan, and private bathroom. It's situated on a lake that connects to the Cuiabá River and is far from everything and well into the Pantanal. The hotel offers fishing excursions and safaris via boat, horseback, jeep, and foot. English-speaking guides are available. Most of the Pantanal species are nearby, including capybaras, caiman alligators, monkeys, storks, and macaws. To get to the ranch, you travel from Cuiabá to Poconé, then take a boat for two hours down the Cuiabá River. You need to arrange this transportation with the hotel when you book.

The **Hotel Fazenda Santa Tereza** (Rodovia Transpantaneira, Km 67, tel. 65/971-9417, R$120 s and R$150 d) has decent facilities and offers a variety of excursions, including birdwatching and boat safaris. It's located about 1.5 hours south of Poconé along the Transpantaneira Highway. The ⚑ **Araras Lodge** (Rodovia Transpantaneira, Km 32, tel. 65/682-2800, www.araraslodge.com.br, araras@zaz.com.br, R$260 s and R$350 d) is fairly close to Poconé, only about 40 minutes down the highway. They offer 15 rustic-style rooms with air and ceiling fans. They also have a pool and restaurant. They have two suspended wooden trails that lead to a wooden observation tower for spying on the animals and offer boat, horseback, and walking safaris with English-speaking guides.

## GETTING THERE

Several domestic airlines travel into Cuiabá and Corumbá, from which you can access the Northern Pantanal. Check into Vasp (www.vasp.com.br), Varig (www.varig.com.br), TAM (www.tam.com.br), and Transbrasil (www.transbrasil.com.br). The best connections are from São Paulo.

## INFORMATION

Information and bookings are available from **Pantanal/Amazonas Turismo** (Avenida Dom Aquino, 101, Poconé, www.pantanal-pocone.net).

## CHAPADA DOS GUIMARÃES

Rising 70 meters above the plains that extend north from the Pantanal, the flat-top mountains of the Chapada dos Guimarães present a striking landscape. When you see the multi-layered, red rock cliffs of the Chapada, you can imagine the dinosaurs that roamed this great highland plateau in the Jurassic age. Waterfalls cascade down rocky formations and form cool swimming pools. There are more than 100 falls here, the tallest cascading 86 meters into a lush, forested area. The hills hold some 50 archeological sites with fossils and cave paintings, and most travelers hike past them on their way to the panoramic lookout points high in the cliffs. Highlights include the Aroe Jari Cavern with cave paintings on the walls and the Lagoa Azul, a clear-water lake cradled by the rocky surface of the Chapada. The area has many inns and restaurants to keep you comfortable between hikes and excursions.

The Guimarães National Park sits about 70 kilometers north of Cuiabá and there is a tourist information center in the small town of Chapada dos Guimarães (Praça Dom Wunibaldo 464, tel. 65/301-1393), about 30 kilometers from the entrance to the park. You should probably arrange a guided excursion up to the major sights on your first visit, as there is absolutely no assistance via signage or maps. There are guides available at the tourist information center. You can also check with **Eco Turismo Cultural Ltda** (Praça Dom Wunibaldo 464, Chapada dos Guimarães, tel. 65/301-1393, tel. 65/9952-1989).

Among the numerous waterfalls you can visit are the falls along the **Sete de Setembro River,** which goes way up into the depths of the canyon. A guide can take you out there in about 2.5 hours from the beginning of the park. Another highlight is the **Cidade de Pedra,** a canyon set into the *chapadas* and the site of several petroglyphs carved thousands of years ago into the stone walls of the canyon. Nearby is the **Casa de Pedra** cave and other interesting attractions. Be sure to bring a bathing suit, small towel, and biodegradable sunscreen and insect repellant (they ask you not to use chemical-based sunscreen if you are going to swim in the rivers and waterfalls). A good pair of hiking boots is a must and you might want binoculars as well.

You can stay overnight in or near the park at one of the *pousadas* in the area. Try the **M Solar do Inglês** (Rua Cipriano Curvo 142, tel. 65/301-1389, www.chapadadosguimaraes.com.br/solardoingles, R$175), which is a charming place with only seven rooms and excellent service. The owners speak English and they have a restaurant, bar, pool, and sauna. Cash only. You can also check into the **Villa Guimarães** (Village of Guimarães, no number, tel. 65/301-2970, www.chapadadosguimaraes.com.br/villaguimaraes, R$140), which is small and situated on a hill looking over the park. They have two pools as well as a sitting room and fireplace. The only *pousada* that is inside the park is the **Pousada do Parque** (Rodovia MT-251, Km 51, tel. 65/9971-6722, www.pousadadoparque.com.br, R$50–70). They have five rooms, a pool, and a fireplace.

To get to the Chapada dos Guimarães from Cuiabá, you can take the Viação Rubi or the Expresso Chapadense from around 5:45 A.M.–7:30 P.M. for R$7. The trip takes one hour.

# Curitiba and Paraná

People coming to Paraná almost always make a stopover in Curitiba. Most people are heading right out of town, but there are a few interesting sights in the city that could deter you for a day. The fact that you can see so many of Curitiba's attractions in such a short time via the city's organized bus tour is a big time-saver. Still, your next stop after arriving in Curitiba is where the excitement lies. For most travelers, that's the magnificent Foz de Iguaçu, the largest (not tallest) waterfall in the world. The falls occur in a couple of stages and come from two sides at the same time. The area is extensive and the rush of water a thrill beyond measure. You can see the falls from several observation decks or even come up close to the bottom of the falls on a boat from the Argentinean side. If money is no object, then take a short helicopter ride over the park, the only way to see the entire scene at once. However you decide to experience the falls, you will certainly not forget it. It's no wonder that the sights of Curitiba are somewhat lackluster after that. For sure, it's best to spend a day in Curitiba *before* you head out to Foz.

COURTESY OF CHRISTIAN KNEPPER/EMBRATUR

# Must-Sees

© CHRISTOPHER VAN BUREN

the Catedral Metropolitana at Praça Tiradentes in Curitiba

**M Praça Tiradentes and Curitiba's Historic Sector:** A central hub of traffic and activity in Curitiba, Praça Tiradentes is the starting point for the Linha Turismo city tour. It is flanked on one side by the Catedral Metropolitana, and on the other by the flower merchants of Curitiba (page 527).

**M Salto do Macuco Safari:** Although not the tallest falls in the world, **Foz de Iguaçu** is by far the most expansive, with dozens of roaring cascades crashing down from Brazil's wetlands into Argentina. The most popular way to see the falls from the Brazilian side is on this safari (page 538).

**M Paranaguá Bay Boat Excursions:** Take a boat to Ilha do Mel, Guaraqueçaba, or the Superagüi National Park. All of these require over-night stays, but the virgin forests and beaches are well worth the effort (page 545).

**M Superagüi National Park:** While you're on the coast of Paraná, take a day-trip out to this island village and hike over to the remote beaches across the island. You might catch a glimpse of the rare Black-Faced Tamarin monkey or see thousands of parrots flying across the islands in the late afternoon (page 547).

**M Salto Morato Nature Preserve:** One of the greenest pieces of planet Earth you'll ever see, the Salto Morato Nature Preserve is a protected wildlife area full of tropical flora and fauna and has a principal trail that leads to the Salto Morato Waterfall. At a height of 130 meters, the waterfall and surrounding pools make up one of the most beautiful visions in the area (page 547).

**CURITIBA AND PARANÁ**

Campo Grande

São Paulo

PARAGUAY

Salto do Macuco Safari

Salto Morato Nature Preserve

Curitiba

Praça Tiradentes and Curitiba's Historic Sector

Superagüi National Park

Paranaguá Bay Boat Excursions

Florianópolis

ATLANTIC OCEAN

URUGUAY

Heading out of Curitiba toward the coast presents another spectacular scene via the Serra Verde Express train ride. The train crosses an incredible stretch of mountains and passes through tropical forests and high cliffs. The panoramic views from the train are exhilarating. If you head all the way to Paranaguá, you'll have a chance to plan excursions to Ilha do Mel and Guaraqueçaba. On Ilha do Mel, you can hike along the many beaches, stopping to swim or drink in the view. At night, the two villages on the island offer up a selection of bars and restaurants in a charming, island atmosphere. Back in Guaraqueçaba, you'll get the chance to hike through some of the most beautiful tropical forest in the south of Brazil in the Superagüi National Park and the Salto Morato Nature Preserve.

## PLANNING YOUR TIME

Most travelers who come to this part of Brazil are here to see the great Foz de Iguaçu at the Argentinean border. This magnificent waterfall is not only one of the highlights of Brazil's southern region, but of the entire southern hemisphere. For sure, any trip to this region should include a visit to one of the natural wonders of the world. But if you are spending the time to visit the south of Brazil, then a quick sweep of Paraná state is perfectly in order before heading south to Santa Catarina.

When you return to Curitiba from Foz de Iguaçu, spend a day touring the sights of the city on the Linha Turismo, a convenient bus system that takes tourists to every important point in the city. On your way out of the city, be sure to take the legendary train ride to the town of Morrtes or, better yet, all the way to Paranaguá, where you can catch a boat out to Ilha do Mel for a couple of days or up to the Guaraqueçaba National Park (a day at each is not a bad idea). The entire trip, including two days and two nights at Foz de Iguaçu, should take 5–7 days. If you have more time, you can check out the town of Lapa to the south or visit the Vila Velha State Park while you're in Curitiba. But the truth is, after the 5–7 days outlined above, most travelers head down to Joinville to begin their tour of the Santa Catarina coast. Still, the Vila Velha State Park and other minor attractions in Paraná are detailed in this chapter for those who might be on an extended stay in Curitiba and would like to see the finer points of the state.

# Curitiba

Curitiba is the gateway to the south of Brazil. Just about all major highways pass through here on their way down the continent—certainly all the highways from the São Paulo area, which covers the majority of people. But while stopping in Curitiba is somewhat unavoidable if you're traveling by land, most people do not consider the place a destination point in itself. Rather, this clean and well-planned city is just a stopover on a continuing journey to Foz de Iguaçu or the southern coast. But that doesn't mean that you can't pause here for a moment and check out a few things the city has to offer. You can see most of the important sights in a day using the Linha Turismo city tour. Highlights include the Brasil Telecom Tower, with its panoramic view of the city,

and the Unilivre structure in the middle of a beautiful wooded grove. If you spend a night here, you should really partake of a great meal at one of the many incredible restaurants in town—especially those in the Italian colony of Santa Felicidade. And don't hesitate to try the local wines, as some of them are surprisingly good. There are also some food and nightlife options in the Betel neighborhood that should make you feel very much at home.

Curitiba, while clean and full of attractions, is somehow difficult for travelers to grasp and get close to. People here are friendly and courteous, but not particularly outgoing or accessible, so visitors have to make their own inroads to the city and its subtle offerings. This is difficult to do in a 24- or 48-hour stopover. So, if

# CURITIBA

SCALE NOT AVAILABLE

ROXINHO

AV PRES AFFONSO CAMARGO

RUA UBALDINO DO AMARAL

RUA AMINTAS DE BARROS

RUA XV DE NOVEMBRO

RUA GENERAL CAMEIRO

AV 7 DE SETEMBRO

RUA DR FAIVRE

RUA R B CONSTANT

RUA NILO CAIRO

AV SILVA JARDIM

RUA MARIANO TORRES

GOLDEN STAR HOTEL ●

RUA COM MACEDO

RUA TIBAGI

TEATRO GUAIRA

RUA C LAUBINDO

Passeio Público

UNIVERSITY OF PARANÁ (UFPR)

POST OFFICE ■

Praça Santos Andrade

SHOPPING ITÁLIA

Praça Senador Correia

RUA JOÃO NEGRÃO

GUARAPUAVA

AV V DE

ILÉ DE FRANCE ■

MABU ROYAL & TRADE HOTEL ●

TR DE LAPA

SHOPPING MUELLER ■

RUA 19 de Dezembro

RUA PRES FARIA

INTERPALACE HOTEL ●

RUA BR DO RIO BARANCO

RUA JOSÉ LOUREIRO

RUA PEDRO IVO

RUA ANDRE DE BARROS

RUA LOURENÇO PINTO

SOLAR DO BARÃO

SHOPPING MOUNIF ▼

RUA RIACHUELO

CENTRO

AV MAL FLORIANO

MUSEU ALFREDO ANDERSON ★

MUSEU JOÃO TURIN ■

AV LUIS XAVIER

RUA MATEUS LEME

CATEDRAL METROPOLITANA ■

MUSEU PARANAENSE ■

Praça Carlos Gomes

Praça Garibaldi

SÃO Sergio VILARIGNO da Ordem CAFÉ

IGREJA DO ROSÁRIO ★

SAL GROSSO ▼

PRAÇA TIRADENTES

LINHA TURISMO TICKETS ●

RUA DO ROSÁRIO

AV DR MURICY

RUA DES WESTPHALEN

SÃO FRANCISCO

DURSKI

RUA 13 DE MAIO

Praça João Cândido

CURITIBA MEMORIAL ★

SCHWARZWALD BAR ▼

RUA DAS FLORES

Praça Zacarias

MUSEU DA ARTE CONTEMPORÂNEA ★

RUA DR PEDROSA

RUA KELLERS

RUINAS DE SÃO FRANCISCO ★

MUSEU DE ARTE DO PARANÁ ■

MUSEU ANDRADE MURICY ■

HISTORIC SECTOR

BOUBON HOTEL CURITIBA ●

R E PEREIRA

RUA DAS FLORES

Praça Rui Barbosa

BATEL

RUA SALDANHA MARINHO

AL CABRAL

RUA VOLUNTÁRIOS DA PÁTRIA

Praça General Osório

SEMPLICE RESTAURANTE ●

RESTAURANTE ALAMEDA GRILL ▼

R V DE NACAR

RUA 24 HORAS

RUA C EMILIANO PERNETA

To Bus Station

RUA VICENTE MACHADO

RUA C ARAÚJO

GRAND HOTEL RAYON ●

GREEN LIFE ▼

OMAR SHOPPING ■

you're not here on an extended stay, then don't expect to leave town with your most exciting vacation memories. For that, you should take the slow train out of town to the beach.

## RUA DAS FLORES (THE CALÇADÃO)

Many great cities have pedestrian marketplaces. Paris has its Champs Élysées, Buenos Aires has its Avenida Florida, and Curitiba has its Rua das Flores. Although it was modeled and named after its Argentinean cousin, it is referred to by most people from the area as the Calçadão (the big sidewalk). Officially, it starts where the traffic is no longer permitted to enter the street. This happens at the end of Rua XV de Novembro, one of the main avenues in town that cuts directly through the middle of the downtown area, passing numerous *praças* and important structures (Teatro Guaíra, Universidade do Paraná, and the public library) along the way. When you reach Rua das Flores, the atmosphere changes. The street is lined with those traditional Brazilian cobblestones (the ones that decorate the boardwalk in Copacabana in wavy patterns) and people hurry back and forth with their purchases. Rua das Flores is home to numerous coffee shops, restaurants (toward the far end mostly), stores, and business offices. At the far end, you reach the Praça Osório, which leads to the landmark Praça 24-Horas. A walk from the beginning of Avenida XV de Novembro all the way to the Praça 24-Horas will take about an hour, given a few short stops along the way.

## ⚄ PRAÇA TIRADENTES AND THE HISTORIC SECTOR

A central hub of traffic and activity in the city, Praça Tiradentes is the starting point for the Linha Turismo city tour (and where you can purchase tickets). It is flanked on one side by the Catedral Metropolitana, a neo-gothic church built in 1883 (worth a look inside), and on the other side by the flower merchants of Curitiba. Just past the flower merchants is the Museu Paranaense, which is an interesting, historical building with a moderately interesting museum inside.

downtown historic sector

the Catedral at Praça Tiradentes

If you walk past the Catedral along Rua Barão do Cerro Azul (it's nearly impossible to know which direction you're walking because none of the Curitiba city maps includes direction indicators), you'll come to the foot of the historic sector of town at the intersection with Rua São Francisco. Turn left up São Francisco to pass the **Largo do Ordem,** where much of the city's nightlife occurs and where the **Curitiba Memorial** is located. The highlight at the Memorial is the trippy, free-standing spiral staircase in the middle. You can climb to the top for a view. The Memorial occasionally presents cultural events, art exhibitions, and it houses documents from the city's history. Continue past the Largo do Ordem to reach **Praça Geribaldi,** where you'll find several historic buildings, including the **Igreja do Rosário.** At the far end of the *praça* are the **Ruinas de São Francisco** and beyond that, the **Museu de Arte do Paraná.**

## SANTA FELICIDADE

The residents of this neighborhood like to refer to it as an Italian *colony* inside Curitiba. It was only a few decades ago that immigrants and their families spoke only Italian when in the neighborhood. Born in the late 1800s with an influx of Italians from the northern regions of Italy, the neighborhood enjoyed a kind of isolation and the children here grew up thinking that they were Italians, not Brazilians. The name of the area is homage to the Brazilian Dona Felicidade, who donated a part of her lands here to the hard-working Italian immigrants. In the 1950s, the area began to receive attention for its culinary arts and the growth of the area has not stopped since. Today, the neighborhood (colony) has some of the city's best and biggest restaurants, wineries (with production right here in Santa Felicidade), and home furnishing stores. The residents work hard to maintain their Italian culture and heritage and it shows in the architecture and personality of the area. Santa Felicidade is a long way from the center of Curitiba, but you can hop aboard a group tour that provides transportation there and back again for dinner (check with your hotel). If you take the Linha Turismo bus tour, you can get off in Santa Felicidade to give it a closer look during the day—and maybe purchase some local wines at the **Vinhos Durigan** winery. Santa Felicidade is the location of several annual festivals, including the Festival of the Grape, which takes place in January.

## RUA 24 HORAS

One of the city's landmarks, the Rua 24 Horas is a collection of restaurants, bars, and shops that resembles a shopping mall more than a street. It is, indeed, open 24 hours a day, and is a good place for a late-night snack or, for you insomniacs, a walk around the large bookstore at any time of the night. There is almost always live music playing until the wee hours and food here is reasonable, if limited in variety.

Curitiba and Paraná

# LINHA TURISMO, THE BEST CITY TOUR IN BRAZIL

Perhaps it's all that German ancestry in Curitiba that has resulted in such a well-engineered city tour, but whatever the reason, there is little doubt that the Linha Turismo is the best public tour of any city in Brazil, bar none. The Linha Turismo consists of several comfortable buses that circle the city, 30 minutes apart, visiting 25 of the city's tourist attractions. You can start anywhere along the line, although the official starting point is at Praça Tiradentes downtown, where you purchase tickets. For R$15, you get a set of four vouchers that let you enter and exit the bus four times, choosing your favorite attractions for the day's tour. If you want to see more, just purchase more vouchers and go around again. The loop around the city and four extended stops (you stay off as long as you like and reenter any of the passing buses) will probably take the better part of a day. If you prefer, you can even split your four stops over several days. When you get onboard, you should receive a copy of the Linha Turismo guide, which lists all of the attractions in order and bus schedules. The guide is written in Portuguese, English, and Spanish. If only the rest of Brazil's tourist industry functioned so well.

## PRINCIPAL SIGHTS

Curitiba is so well organized that not only is every important sight in the city presented on the Linha Turismo city tour, but most of the minor ones are as well. In fact, there are probably more options on the city tour than would interest the average visitor, so here is a list of the best sights in town. This is not necessarily the order in which the sights appear on the city tour.

### Jardim Botânico

The favorite attraction of many visitors, the Jardim Botânico is a huge green area (about 250,000 square meters) that has a tennis court, cycling lane, and the garden structure itself, now the main image on the postcards of Curitiba. The greenhouse building was inspired by the 18th-century crystal palaces in London and inside is a collection of tropical flora (most of which can be found in nature excursions around the state parks of Paraná, but the building is the most important thing here). Outside are fountains and flower gardens and even a café where you can sit and await the next Linha Turismo bus, which runs from 9:36 A.M.–6:06 P.M.

### Brazil Telecom Tower

The tower of the Brazil Telecom company was made primarily as a communications structure. It supports numerous satellite dishes and communications antennas. But the company also made it into a panoramic viewpoint for anyone wanting to see the far reaches of the city of Curitiba. The observation deck is 109.5 meters high and provides a 360-degree view of the city. Check out the interesting map of Curitiba made out of stone floor tiles. The tower is the only attraction on the Linha Turismo that has an extra cost. A trip up to the observation deck

the Brazil Telecom Tower

the Jardim Botânico and grounds

is R$3 and you can stay as long as you like. The front desk is also one of the city's tourist information points. The Linha Turismo bus passes from 11:09 A.M.–7:39 P.M.

Note: To get the best pictures, hold your camera lens right up to the glass to avoid reflection and turn off the flash.

## Museu Oscar Niemeyer

Brazil's fascination with the works of Oscar Niemeyer is a real mystery. But if you're into 1960s-style modern architecture with excess use of concrete and a flair for calling attention to itself, then you might like the exhibition of Niemeyer's work at the museum bearing his name. The building itself was created by Niemeyer for an African government but ended up going back to the state of Paraná, which used it for years as government offices. It opened in 2002 as a museum, displaying the works of various artists from the area (many worth seeing) as well as from the architect himself. The main exhibition hall is in the big "eye" in the front of the complex. There is a bookstore, coffee shop, and restaurant.

## Opera de Arame

The shape and design of this opera house were modeled after the Paris Opera, but this structure is made entirely out of iron tubing, giving it a kind of see-through effect. It has three stories with the bottom being used frequently for art exhibitions. There are 1,800 seats in the main theater area and another 46 box seats. The ceiling is a wire mesh. The whole thing is quite interesting and it fits perfectly into its surroundings, with a small lake in front, fed by a natural waterfall. Although it appears so, the lake is not polluted. It is loaded with algae and is home to many freshwater turtles and fish.

Next to the Opera de Arame is an outdoor concert area, where international bands have appeared, such as David Bowie and the Rolling Stones. There is a nice coffee house at the entrance to the Opera if you want a quick refreshment.

The Opera presents classical music and theater productions from time to time. During the day, the Linha Turismo passes from 10:28 A.M.–6:58 P.M.

the Opera de Arame

## Rodoferroviária and Mercado Municipal

This modern train station is one of the country's finest, but you'll see it up close when you take the scenic train to Morretes or Paranaguá. What you might want to check out at this point is the Mercado Municipal, which is where many of the city's restaurants purchase their food supplies. You'll find all kinds of imported and locally made goods, from wines to cheeses to various cuts of beef. The Linha Turismo passes this point from 9:43 A.M.–6:13 P.M.

## Teatro Paiol

Most interesting from the outside, the theater was once the old gunpowder stock house. Now it holds a theater-in-the-round where performances are presented throughout the month. If you get the chance, try to see a music production here one night. The Linha Turismo passes it from 9:27 A.M.–5:57 P.M.

## Ukrainian Memorial

The Ukrainian Memorial is said to be a replica of St. Michael's Church in the Ukraine. It has a bronze dome on top and inside is a memorial to the Polish immigrants in Paraná. It stands on the edge of the Tingui Park. The Linha Turismo passes here from 10:42 A.M.–7:12 P.M.

## Unilivre

The structure of the Universidade Livre do Meio Ambiente (Unilivre) is worth a look or two. It was designed after the spiral shape of the city's namesake, the pinecone (*curitiba* means "many pine seeds" in the Tupi-Guarani language). The structure is made entirely of eucalyptus wood and has a spiral ramp leading to the top that passes a number of classrooms in which environmental issues are discussed. At the top is a wonderful view of the surrounding Zanielli woods and lake. The Linha Turismo bus passes from 10:15 A.M.–6:45 P.M.

## MUSEUMS

If you're into museums, there are a few to check out in the downtown area. Thankfully, most are huddled pretty close together in or near the historic sector. The exception is the **Museu da Arte Contemporânea** (Rua Desembargador

Curitiba and Paraná

**Teatro Paiol**

Westphalen 16, tel. 41/3323-5328, 10 A.M.–7 P.M. Tues.–Fri. and 10 A.M.–4 P.M. weekends, R$3), located on the other side of Rua das Flores. The museum presents contemporary paintings and sculpture with an emphasis on artists from Paraná. The **Museu Andrade Muricy** (Al. Dr. Muricy 915, tel. 41/3321-4744, 10 A.M.–8 P.M. Tues.–Sun., R$3) is a small but well-manicured space that has temporary exhibitions from around the world. It's worth a look inside as you walk from the **Museu de Arte do Paraná** (Rua Kellers 289, tel. 41/3304-3300, 10 A.M.–5 P.M. Mon.–Fri., 11 A.M.–3 P.M. on weekends, R$3), which has a variety of paintings and sculpture from the region, mostly contemporary. Within walking distance from the Largo da Ordem is the **Museu Alfredo Andersen** (Rua Mateus Leme 336, tel. 41/3222-8262, 9 A.M.–6 P.M. Mon.–Fri. and 10 A.M.–4 P.M. weekends, R$2), dedicated to the works of the Paranaense painter. Also, the **Museu João Turin** (Rua Mateus Leme 38, tel. 41/3223-1182, 9 A.M.–6 P.M. Mon.–Fri. and 10 A.M.–4 P.M. weekends, R$3) is nearby and is dedicated to the works of this Paranaense sculptor.

For information on current exhibits, try the website www.pr.gov.br, which has links to most all the museums in town. It's in Portuguese.

## PARKS

The three principal parks in Curitiba are connected to one another and form what Curitibanos claim to be the nation's longest park. The three parks are Parque Tanguá, Parque Tingui, and Parque Barigui (with those names, who could keep them separate anyway?). **Tanguá Park** is the most interesting, with a terrific scenic viewpoint that looks out over a waterfall, lake, and large area of tropical forestation. In the wall of a stone quarry, a 45-meter tunnel was built that leads you to another observation point. There are places to sit and lanchonetes from which to buy snacks and cold drinks. The **Barigui Park** is most popular on the weekends with Curitiba residents. Many people come to the park to jog, sit by the lake, or fly model airplanes. There is also an exhibition hall, food court, and library. The Linha Turismo stops at both of these parks on its route through the city.

**Tingui Park** is probably the least accessible of the bunch and has fewer facilities for visitors.

# ENTERTAINMENT AND NIGHTLIFE

## After Hours

There are two principal gentlemen's clubs in downtown Curitiba. One is called **Metrô** and the other is **Café Paris**. They are both around the Rua 24 Horas area. You will pay a cover charge and three times the normal price for drinks.

## Bars and Clubs

There are two centers of night activity in Curitiba and they are both somewhat mild. This is not exactly a party town. The first place to check out is the Largo da Ordem, which is in the historic sector of town. There, you'll find several bars with outdoor seating, including **Sal Grosso** (Largo da Ordem 69, tel. 41/3222-8286, 11–2 A.M. daily) and the ever-popular **Shwarzwald Bar** (Largo da Ordem 63, tel. 41/3223-2585, 11–2 A.M. daily) next door. Both are pretty cool inside and start around 11 P.M. Nearby—actually a taxi from the Largo would be a good idea—is the **John Bull Pub** (Av. Mateus Leme 2204, tel. 41/3353-1793, www.johnbullpub.com.br), which features live rock music from 8 P.M. until the last person leaves, Tuesday–Saturday. Right there more or less in the historical sector is the **Vilarigno Café** (Al. Augusto Stellfeld 264, tel. 41/3323-8543. 8 P.M. daily, shows start around 10 P.M.), which presents live music and dance all week long, specializing in *forró* dancing on Wednesday nights.

One of the coolest bars in town is located on the other end of town (at the beginning of Avenida XV de Novembro) and is called **Roxinho** (Rua Mal. Deodoro 1285, tel. 41/3264-9421, www.roxinho.com.br, 4 P.M.–2 A.M. Sun.–Fri., 11:30 A.M.–1 A.M. on Sat.). The atmosphere here is hip, urban, and slightly alternative. They have a good selection of drinks and draft beer.

In the Betel neighborhood, there are a few good bars that specialize in happy hour, although they are open all night long. Try **Bar Brasil** (Av. Bispo Dom José 2481, tel. 41/3019-5800, 6 P.M. Tues.–Sun.) and **Armazém São José** (Av. Bispo Dom José 2459). Also try **Freguesia** (Rua Vicente Machado 642). To have a beer inside the Brahma brewery, head to **Bar Brahma** (Av. Getúlio Vargas 234, Reboucas, tel. 41/3224-1628, 5 P.M. Mon.–Sat.). Now, to give equal time to the competition, try **Cervejaria Original Antartica** (Av. Vicente Machado 627, tel. 41/3013-5800, 6 P.M. Tues.–Fri. and Sun., 4 P.M. Sat.) for draft beer and live samba music.

## Sidewalk Cafés

At the end of Rua das Flores is a series of outdoor cafés that get pretty busy with activity around happy hour. They close down at around midnight. Keep walking down Rua das Flores to the Praça Osório and you'll pass a number of other coffee shops and pizza joints. A great place for happy-hour drinks or coffee is **Exprex Caffé** (Rua XV de Novembro 784 at the University of Paraná, tel. 41/3232-9578, 8 A.M.–8 P.M. Mon.–Fri., 10 A.M.–2 P.M. on weekends). They have a nice atmosphere and plenty of different wines, cocktails, and coffee drinks—not to mention a pretty crowd.

## Theater and Classical Music

There are numerous theaters in Curitiba and you can pick up monthly guides at the magazine stands all over town. You can also call the theaters directly. Here are some of the major ones: **Guaira** (tel. 41/304-7900), **Opera de Arame** (tel. 41/354-3266), and **Teatro Paiol** (tel. 41/331-3300).

# FESTIVALS AND EVENTS

The Italian colony of Santa Felicidade hosts a **Grape Festival** (tel. 41/372-1417, acisf@brturbo.com) around the end of January each year. The wines produced here are very interesting and worth checking out.

# SHOPPING

The only central area for local arts, crafts, and souvenirs is at Praça Garibaldi in the historical sector of town. There, you'll find a number of stores. Curitiba has a bunch of modern shopping centers, including **Shopping Itália** and **Omar Shopping,** which are at either end of the Rua XV de Novembro and Rua das Flores. One of the larger shopping centers is **Shopping Mueller** (Rua Mateus Leme). There are about a half-dozen others spread around town. That's pretty much it; you can save your money for ceramics and leather goods on the outskirts of town.

## ACCOMMODATIONS
### Under R$100

The **Curitiba Eco-Hostel** (Rua Luiz Tramontin 1693, Campo Comprido area, tel. 41/3029-1693, www.curitibaecohostel.com.br, R$25 pp) is a cool place way on the outskirts of town. As a result, they have a lot of space and good prices. They offer a TV room, laundry facilities, parking, public telephones, tourist information, and 24-hour reception. Services include group rooms and some private rooms with breakfast. Internet is available. Be sure to check their website for details on how to get there. The **Golden Star Hotel** (Rua Mariano Torres 135, Centro, tel. 41/362-1798, www.goldenstar.com.br, goldenstar@goldenstar.com.br, R$79 s and R$89 d) is located at the beginning of Avenida XV de Novembro near the Passeio Publico. They have an old building with small rooms, but the service is good and the rooms are clean. Try not to get one on the street side as these are noisy. They offer assistance with booking excursions and vans into Santa Felicidade for dinner (free). Breakfast is included and is moderately good. They also provide free Internet. Rooms have gas-heated water, air, and TV. Note: Do not confuse this hotel with the Hotel Golden, which is a noisy, fleabag hotel on Praça Tiradentes for R$22 per person.

### R$100–200

The winner of the "Biggest Rooms in Latin America" award goes to the **Inter-Palace Hotel** (Av. XV de Novembro 904, tel. 41/223-5282, www.interpalace.com.br, info@interpalace.com.br, R$125), near the Uni-

versity of Curitiba. The rooms are a bit old and funky with Brazilian-style showers, but if you want space to practice those Capoeira moves, this is your place. They have a cool lobby with a glass elevator and a restaurant area where they serve breakfast (included). The **M Grand Hotel Rayon** (Rua Visconde de Nácar 1424, tel. 41/3027-6006, R$145 s and R$165 d, R$192 s suite and R$217 d suite) is next door to Rua 24 Horas in a tall, modern building with a comfortable lobby, lobby bar, non-smoking floors, 24-hour room service, pool, sauna and gym. Business center and services also available. Rooms have queen-size beds, cable TV, air, phone, safe, and bathtubs. The **Mabu Royal & Trade Hotel** (Praça Santos Andrade 830, tel. 41/219-6000, www.hoteismabu.com.br, R$118 s, R$128 d, R$315 suite) is near the University of Curitiba. They have a modern setup with a luxurious feeling to things, including a piano bar, restaurant, pool, and gym. Rooms have air, TV, and all the modern conveniences. In-room Internet is R$35 for 24 hours of service. They are very event-oriented, but they won't complain if you request a room for just two. They charge 15-percent service tax.

### R$200–500

Located about as downtown as you get, near Praça Tiradentes is the **M Boubon Hotel Curitiba** (Rua Cândido Lopes 102, tel. 41/221-4600, burbon.curitiba@burbon.com.br, R$175 s and R$197 d weekdays, R$150 s and R$165 d weekends, up to R$260 s suite and R$520 d suite). They have 175 rooms in a modern building with a gym, sauna, pool, and Jacuzzi. Rooms have air, central heat, voice mail, in-room Internet connection, cable TV, and safe. Breakfast is included.

## FOOD

It's not easy to locate Curitiba's best restaurants, as they are spread all over town. There are some focal points, however, where you can find many good restaurants grouped together. For starters, try the Santa Felicidade area, the city's Italian colony. Also, the Betel neighborhood serves a more business-oriented clientele. In these two areas, you can walk around and choose a restaurant on the spot if desired. Downtown, the offerings are more scattered and you should head directly to your chosen restaurant by taxi. One thing is for sure, Curitiba is a place where you'll eat well at a good price.

## Barbecue

One of the most popular places in town for barbecued meat and chicken is ☒ **Madalosso** (Av. Manoel Ribas 5875, tel. 41/372-2121, 11:30 A.M.–3 P.M. and 7–11 P.M. daily) in Santa Felicidade. This place has become something of a tourist attraction in itself. They have two restaurants across the street from one another. The old, smaller restaurant serves barbecued beef cuts along with a variety of salads, pasta dishes, and a plate of chicken. They have a good wine list and you should really try a bottle of the Aurora Merlot (if you're into rich, woody, dry red wines). The all-you-can-eat barbecue is only R\$16 per person. Their newer establishment across the street is one of the country's largest restaurants with a capacity to seat 5,000 people (not all in one room). They serve barbecued chicken, along with pasta and other side dishes. This is also R\$16 per person. There are tour vans that will bring you to Santa Felicidade and back to your hotel for free. Call the restaurant for details or ask at your hotel.

Another excellent barbecue is the **Restaurante Alameda Grill** (Al. Cabral 69, downtown, tel. 41/222-1851, 11:30 A.M.–3 P.M. and 6–11 P.M. Mon.–Sat., 11:30 A.M.–4 P.M. on Sun.). Here you'll find grilled meats along with pasta dishes, fried fish, and other seafood plates, including seafood paella. R\$18 per person.

## Italian

The **Barolo Trattoria** (Av. Silva Jardim 2487, Betel, tel. 41/243-3430, noon–3 P.M. and 7:30–midnight Mon.–Sat., noon–4 P.M. on Sun., R\$30) serves traditional Italian food with a modern twist, such as ravioli in mustard sauce. Open late. In the Centro, you have **Caffe Milano Ristorante** (Alameda Dr. Carlos de Carvalho 1066, Batel, tel. 41/3224-8429,

11:30 A.M.–3 P.M. and 7 P.M.–1 A.M. Mon.–Sat., 11:30 A.M.–3 P.M. on Sun.) which serves fresh fish with an Italian accent. Try the salmon in orange sauce. Meals are R\$20 per person. For an abundant pasta meal, try ☒ **Restaurante Famiglia Fadanelli** (Av. Manoel Ribas 5667, Santa Felicidade, tel. 41/3372-1616, 7 P.M.–midnight Tues.–Fri., noon–3:30 P.M. on weekends). They specialize in lamb and fresh pasta dishes. It costs about R\$20 per person. A great place for pasta and risotto is the elegant and well-lit ☒ **Semplice Restaurante** (Rua Dr. Pedrosa 208, Centro, tel. 41/3026-6661, noon–2:30 P.M. and 7 P.M.–midnight Mon.–Sat.). It's one of the best places in the downtown area—for about R\$20 per person.

## Japanese

**Tatibana Japanese Cuisine** (Rua Pasteur 106, Betel, tel. 41/3016-8284, 11:30 A.M.–3 P.M. and 7 P.M.–midnight daily) has a sushi lunch buffet and dinner off the menu with all the usual cuts you expect at a sushi bar. Meals run about R\$30 per person.

## Quick and Casual

There are casual eateries along Rua das Flores, where you can get self-service lunches, sandwiches, and finger foods. The best fresh juices are blended up at **Jungle Juice** (Av. Vicente Machado 1965, Betel, tel. 41/3023-7060, 11 A.M.–10 P.M. daily). You can find baked potatoes, salads, sandwiches, and the difficult-to-find bagel at **The Sub's** (Av. Dr. Carlos de Carvalho 974, Betel, tel. 41/3023-2353, 11 A.M.–midnight Mon.–Sat., 5 P.M.–11 P.M. on Sun., about R\$10 per person).

## Vegetarian

You'll find a huge salad buffet along with hot veggie dishes every day for lunch at **Green Life** (Rua Carlos de Carvalho 271, tel. 41/223-8490, lunch only from 11 A.M.–3 P.M. daily, R\$12).

## Other International

For Swiss potato pancakes filled with a variety of ingredients, try **Beto Batata** (Rua Prof. Brandão 678, tel. 41/3019-6969, 6 P.M.–midnight

Mon.–Fri., noon–midnight on weekends) in the Alto da XV area at the beginning of Avenida XV de Novembro. The environment is fun and friendly, and food costs around R$20 per person. You can find authentic Ukrainian food at **Durski** (Rua Jaime Reis 254, tel. 41/255-7893, 11:30 A.M.–3 P.M. and 7 P.M.–midnight Mon.–Sat., 11:30 A.M.–6 P.M. on Sun.), in the São Francisco neighborhood. Their influences are Polish and Russian. A meal will cost around R$25 per person. Traditional French cuisine is available at **Ile de France** (Praça 19 de Dezembro 538, Centro, tel. 41/3324-6499, 11:30 A.M.–3 P.M. and 7 P.M.–midnight Mon.–Sat., 11:30 A.M.–4 P.M. on Sun.) for around R$50 per person.

## INFORMATION AND SERVICES

There are several tourist information offices in Curitiba; they are located at Rua 24 Horas (8 A.M.–midnight Mon.–Fri. and 8 A.M.–10 P.M. weekends), the train station (8 A.M.–6 P.M. Mon.–Fri. and 8 A.M.–2 P.M. weekends), the Brasil Telecom Tower (10 A.M.–7 P.M. Tues.–Sun.), and the Alfonso Pena International Airport (7 A.M.–11 P.M. daily). You can call for information at **Disque Turismo** (tel. 41/352-8000, 8 A.M.–midnight Mon.–Fri. and 8 A.M.–10 P.M. weekends). You can also just dial 1516 while you're in town.

You'll find 24-hour Internet connections at **Get On Land & Cyber** (Visc. De Nacar 1388, tel. 41/232-6626, 9 A.M.–6 P.M. Mon.–Sat., 1 P.M.–1 A.M. on Sun.) near Rua 24 Horas. There are others along Rua das Flores near the sidewalk cafés. A good website for information on Curitiba is www.viaje.curitiba.pr.gov.br.

You can get money at the international ATMs in the train station, the airport, and in the shopping malls. You can also try the Banco do Brasil on Rua das Flores to see if one of their machines has international systems. Otherwise, look for Banco 24 Horas.

## GETTING THERE

What most people are concerned with is not getting *to* Curitiba, but getting *from* it, either to Iguaçu Falls or the southern coastline. The best way to get to Iguaçu Falls is on a short, domestic flight. These flights leave from the Curitiba domestic airport, called **Bacacheri** (Rua Cicero Jaime Bley, tel. 41/256-1441) in the Colombo district to the northeast of the city. You can check on flights with Vasp (tel. 41/221-7432), TAM (tel. 41/219-1250), Varig/Rio Sul (tel. 41/21-5200), or Gol (tel. 41/381-1735).

The international airport is called **Afonso Pena** (tel. 41/381-1515, www.infraero.gov.br) and hosts both domestic and international flights. It's in the southeastern outskirts of the city in the area called São José dos Pinhais, an area becoming known for its wines.

You can also take the bus to Iguaçu. Buses leave from the *rodoviaria*/train station (Av. Presidente Afonso Camargo 330, tel. 41/320-3000). Buses to and from São Paulo leave on the Cometa line for R$40 standard and R$60 executive. The executive bus gives you access to the VIP lounge both in São Pualo and Curitiba. If you're heading directly to Florianópolis, take the Catarinense bus line. Also, the Penha line has an executive bus that goes directly to Joinville for R$30. It leaves at 5:15 P.M. and is probably worth every penny.

Driving to Iguaçu is a perfectly good option. The trip takes in the neighborhood of eight hours. Local rental agencies include **Hertz** (tel. 0800/701-7300), **Localiza** (tel. 0800/992-000), **Unidas** (tel. 0800/121-121), **Thrifty** (tel. 41/3016-0909 or tel. 41/381-1333 at the airport, reservas@thrifty.com.br), **American Car Rental** (tel. 41/242-9322), and **Rent-a-Car** (tel. 41/3024-2427, reserva@arentacar.com.br).

To leave town by scenic train heading to Morretes or Paranaguá, get in touch with **Serra Verde Express** at the *rodoviaria*/train station (tel. 41/323-4007, www.serraverde-express.com.br). Most of Brazil's scenic train rides are in the southern region, and this is one of the most spectacular, crossing mountain caverns, hugging steep cliffs, and passing through long tunnels along a strip of countryside that will keep you glued to the window. At the time of this writing, the second half of the route, from Morretes to Paranaguá, was closed for re-

## ALL ABOARD THE SERRA VERDE EXPRESS

An impressive demonstration of engineering know-how, the Serra Verde Express train line was built more than a century ago to link Curitiba to the coast at the town of Paranaguá. Along the way, the train stops in Morretes, a small town that retains its traditional architecture and regional culture. The first segment of the trip is the most impressive—from Curitiba to Morretes. Many tours consist of the train ride to Morretes for lunch and a tour of the town, ending in a train or van trip back to the city. The train moves ever so slowly across the many steep hillsides and tall bridges of the Serra do Mar mountain range. When you're not in awe of the actual trajectory of the track, you'll be picking up your jaw from the amazing scenic views (which are best from the left side of the train).

There are three types of tours on the Serra Verde Express for three classes of compartments. The Turístico class is the most basic, offering a normal car, a soda, and a snack. First-class gives you a special car with large windows and comfortable seats, an English-speaking guide, and free beverages. The Litorina trip is actually made in a special train car with its own engine, separate from the other train and leaving about an hour later. You get extra stops along the way, plus a guide, air-conditioning, and hosted bar service. The trains take about three hours to get to Morretes, with a three-hour stopover before returning. Plan on an all-day affair if you are doing the roundtrip. An alternative is to head all the way to Paranaguá on your way out of Curitiba. At the time of this writing, the Paranaguá section of the track was undergoing repairs and was unavailable.

pairs on the line. If this part of the journey is not open, you can take a bus from Morretes to Paranaguá or a van back to Curitiba.

## GETTING AROUND

Curitiba is known for its wonderful bus system and, moreover, its interesting bus tubes that keep people safe and warm while waiting for the bus in the winter. It's a very civilized place, Curitiba. You can catch buses to all the major points in town and on the outskirts by catching a bus at Praça Tiradentes or Praça Rui Barbosa. Within the downtown area, you can walk to most everything, but you'll want to catch a taxi if you're going from one corner to the opposite corner. As mentioned earlier, the best way to see the sights in Curitiba is via the Linha Turismo. You can get tickets for R$15 at Praça Tiradentes. There are free vans that take tourists from downtown to the Santa Felicidade neighborhood for dinner. Check with your hotel or any tourist office for details.

# Foz de Iguaçu

One of Brazil's most impressive natural wonders, Foz de Iguaçu brings more than half a million visitors from around the world every year. It's an incredible rush of adrenaline to get up close to the rushing water, getting completely soaked in the process. You can stand at the various viewing decks and stare at the cascades for hours and most visitors do just that. You can also opt for one of the boat excursions, the most popular being the Salto do Macuco Safari, which takes you up close to the Garganta do Diabo, the main section of the falls. Other boat excursions travel up and down the rivers of the area. At night, there are options in all three countries, including samba and tango music and dance. Besides the falls themselves, there are a few interesting side attractions, including the Parque das Aves, where you can observe various bird species (including toucans) up close, the city of Ciudade del Este in Paraguay, where you can purchase all sorts of goods at incredible prices, and a peaceful Buddhist temple perched on the hills.

You can visit the falls at any time of the year, but try to avoid the peak of the rainy season, which is September–November.

During the day, giant rainbows arc over the 275 cascades that make up the falls, many of them as tall as 80 meters. The majority of the cascades are situated on the Argentinean side of the water, which means that they are all facing Brazil, giving the Brazil side of the fence a visual advantage. In the depths of the great fissure is the largest of the falls, known as the Garganta do Diabo (Devil's Throat). In the wet season, the wall of water is continuous and the rush and force of the falls is enthralling, even from a distance. The Iguaçu River, which empties in the Garganta do Diabo, is around 2,700 meters wide at the falls and drops nearly 6,500 cubic meters of water down the chasm every second. At the visitor's center of the park, you can walk out along various viewing decks to see the falls, including some that get close to the Garganta do Diabo. The viewing decks cost R$10 and there are double-decker buses that leave every 10 minutes from the visitor's center to take you through the park to the various viewing stations.

## THE ARGENTINEAN SIDE

The main reason for viewing the falls from the Argentinean side is to get up close, right up to the falling cascades. The boats that leave from the city of Puerto Iguazú in Argentina get their passengers completely wet from the spray of the falling water. The city itself is located only 10 kilometers from the city of Foz de Iguaçu in Brazil and has about 30,000 inhabitants. There is tourist information, an international airport that operates 24 hours a day, and transportation to the Iguazú National Park, where most of the excursions take place. Excursions include boat trips along the Iguaçu River, hikes in the Iguazú National Park, and photographic safaris. There is a free boat trip to the San Martin Island. The hike up to the peak at San Martin is difficult and time consuming but ends in an incredible view of the area. The most impressive excursions are the boat trips that go right into the Garganta do Diabo.

There are also a few museums on the Argentinean side and some ruins from the Jesuit missions that were based there in the 16th century. If you go there, be sure to bring your passport and ID. Dollars and Brazilian *reals* are accepted currencies (along with the peso, of course).

## M SALTO DO MACUCO SAFARI

The most popular way to see the falls from the Brazilian side in on the Salto do Macuco Safari. The safari starts with a trip by jeep into the forest, where you'll see some of the flora and fauna of the area. English-

The boat safaris get you right up into the falls.

speaking guides provide an orientation. Next, you hike about 600 meters to the great Macuco Falls, a 20-meter cascade of the Iguaçu River. Hiking down to the riverbank, you then begin a boat excursion that takes you out to the base of the great falls in the direction of the Garganta, passing various cascades and rocky canyons along the way. Here, you are sure to get soaked, as the boats get quite close to the falls. The trip takes about 2 hours and groups leave every 15 minutes. In the winter, the safari operates from 8:30 A.M.–5:30 P.M. Tuesday–Sunday and 1–5:30 P.M. on Monday. In the summer, hours are 8 A.M.–6 P.M. Tuesday–Sunday and 1–6 P.M. on Monday. For more information, check out www.macucosafari.com.br.

## PONTE DA AMIZADE

Created in 1965, the Friendship Bridge was designed to open up commerce between Brazil and Paraguay. What it opened up was a huge market for counterfeit goods created in Paraguay and unloaded in the Brazilian market. More than a few Brazilians make their living heading over to the bridge to purchase these goods and bring them back to Brazil to sell in street markets. The city of Foz de Iguaçu also became a major exportation center for Brazilian goods heading over to Paraguay and eventually making their way into Argentina. Commerce between Brazil and Argentina has been spotted with tension and various impediments over the years and the trade route through Paraguay has not helped things. The bridge is also a favorite spot for foreigners living illegally in Brazil to exit the country without detection, thus making it possible to enter again with a new passport stamp.

If you head over to the Paraguay side across the bridge, you'll enter a chaotic world of commerce and confusion. Keep an eye on your valuables and be smart about where you go. As for the bridge itself, it's a wonderful construction, spanning some 553 meters across the Paraguay River at a height of 32 meters above the water. It makes for some great photographs.

Curitiba and Paraná

## PARQUE DAS AVES

If you want to see some wild, tropical birds like toucans and macaws, take an excursion in the Parque das Aves (Bird Park; Rodovia das Cataratas, Km 11, www.parquedasaves.com.br, tel. 45/3529-8282, 8:30 A.M.–5:30 P.M. daily) at the beginning of the Iguaçu National Park. There, you can hike around a paved trail that takes you past the birds and get some excellent photo opportunities with birds that are quite used to the presence of humans. The park has more than 180 species from all over the world, a butterfly habitat, and a reptile exhibit. There is also a snack stand and souvenir shop.

## ZOO

The Municipal Zoo (Rua Tarobá 875, city of Foz de Iguaçu, tel. 45/523-9136, 9 A.M.–5:30 P.M. Tues.–Sun.) was created out of a deforested area around Foz and is home to exotic birds, reptiles, and mammals—with almost 700 animals in various habitats spread across an area of 40 square kilometers. It's not like a trip out to the Amazon or Pantanal, but if you want to see some exotic species, it may be worth a visit.

## BUDDHIST TEMPLE

If you need to integrate all that adrenaline produced by seeing the falls, you can head up to the Buddhist Temple (Rua Aluísio Ferreira de Souza 99, Jardim Nova Califórnia, tel. 45/524-5566, www.budismo.com.br, 9 A.M.–5 P.M. Tues.–Sat. and 10 A.M.–3 P.M. Sun.) for a time of meditation and contemplation. The temple was built in the Chinese tradition and has a number of Chinese Buddha statues on the grounds, including a giant Buddha (about 7 meters tall) that faces outward, looking over the hills. There are also 112 statues in the courtyard, slightly larger than life-size, that present a happy welcome to guests. There are lookout points, including a platform that looks out on the Paraná River, the Friendship Bridge, and even a piece of the falls.

## ENTERTAINMENT AND NIGHTLIFE

There is plenty going on at night in Foz de Iguaçu and many of the hotels in the area produce music and dance shows for guests and the public in general. If you don't like the samba and *forró* of Brazil, you can head over to Argentina for some tango. Downtown Foz de Iguaçu has bars and restaurants that also have live music and plenty going on. Try **Capitão Bar** (Av. Jorge Schimmelpfeng 228). In Argentina, there's **La Baranca** (Puerto Iguazú, on the river). Everything starts around 8 P.M.

## EXCURSIONS

Besides the Salto do Macuco Safari mentioned earlier, there are a few other boat trips worth investigating. The Triplice Fronteira (Triple Frontier) excursion takes you under the Friendship Bridge along the Iguaçu and Paraná Rivers from Port Meira in Foz de Iguaçu. You also pass the Espaço das Américas at the intersection of the two rivers and the Three Frontiers monument that marks the point at which the three countries meet. Just head over to the docks at Porto Meira and ask about programming and cost. It should be around R$35 per person.

Another excursion heads over to Puerto Bertoni, a historical village from the 19th century. You begin at Porto Meira in Foz de Iguaçu and head down the Iguaçu River in a comfortable yacht, passing the Espaço das Américas at the intersection with the Paraná River. Heading down the Paraná River, you finally reach Puerto Bertoni, where you continue on foot for about 30 minutes to the old Bertoni house, which is full of botanical and academic artifacts and studies made by Bertoni himself.

More information about these excursions is available at www.macucosafari.com.br.

The most impressive view of the falls is from above, via one of the helicopter tours you can take from the visitor's center area

looking down the Devil's Throat

(Rodovia das Cataratas, Km 16.5, tel. 45/529-7474). In 10 minutes, you pass over the entire area and even get close to the falls themselves. You can also take a quick pass over the hydroelectric plant. The company charges in dollars and you'll pay R$60–250 per person, depending on the length of the trip.

## ACCOMMODATIONS

For economical lodgings, try the **Albergue Paudimar** (Av. das Cataratas, Km 10, Remanso Grande, tel. 45/529-6061, www.paudimar.com.br, R$20 pp group rooms and R$45 d private rooms). They have 22 group rooms with shared bathrooms and two private rooms. They offer bike rentals, pool, and bar. The  **Recanto Park Hotel** (Av. Costa e Silva 3500, tel. 45/522-3000, www.recantoparkhotel.com.br, R$125–165) is a mod-

ern, business-style hotel with great facilities, including a restaurant, bar, sauna, pool, and game courts. Their rooms are clean and have air, TV, and phone. Another mid-range option is the **Hotel Panorama** (Av. das Cataratas, Km 6, tel. 45/529-8200, www.hotelpanoramaresort.com.br, R$150). They have a huge structure with 150 rooms in the shape of a semi-circle, gym, tennis courts, restaurant, and pool. They also have a miniature golf course and a water park in their facilities. The rooms are nothing special. A slightly more elaborate setup is the **Hotel San Martin** (Rodovia das Cataratas, Km 17, tel. 45/529-8088, www.hotelsanmartin.com.br, R$245). They offer air, TV, phone, restaurant, bar, sauna, pool, and tennis courts. Some rooms have views of the river. They also have bikes available for guests.

The more elaborate hotels include **Tropical das Cataratas Eco Resort** (Parque Nacional do Iguaçu, tel. 45/521-7000, www.tropicalhotel.com.br, R$350–550), which is located inside the national park with views of the falls from many of their rooms. They offer air, cable TV, phone, pool, playground, tennis courts, restaurant, and Brazilian-style recreation facilities. Another resort-style facility is the **Mabu Thermas e Resort** (Rodovia das Cataratas, Km 3, tel. 45/521-2000, www.hoteismabu.com.br, R$565). They offer a full-service package with all meals included. Their facilities are modern and comfortable with pool, bar, hot tubs, playground, tennis courts, restaurant, and massage room. Their hot tubs are supplied by thermal springs on the property and are around 34°C.

## FOOD

Food is a bit of a problem in Foz de Iguaçu, since most of the restaurants near the viewing decks are expensive and limited. My suggestion is to head into the city early and pick up fixings for a picnic lunch that you can enjoy while looking out over the falls. If you can make it back into town at lunchtime, you can try **Ver o Verde** (Rua Almirante Barroso 1713, tel. 45/3574-5647, 11:30 A.M.–3 P.M. daily, R$10) for a great self-service buffet at an excellent price. For an afternoon coffee, head over to **Café Laurent** (Av. Jorge Schimmelpfeng 550, tel. 45/3574-6666, 2 P.M.–midnight Mon.–Sat., noon–midnight on Sun.), where you can get a variety of coffee drinks and sweets.

## INFORMATION AND SERVICES

The tourist information center is located at the visitor's center at the Iguaçu National Park. You'll find English-speaking guides there. You'll find international ATMs at the visitor's center and in town along Rua Jorge Schimmelpfeng. A good website (in Portuguese) for information is www.cataratasdoiguacu.com.br.

# Paranaguá

The most important town on the bay, Paranaguá should be prettier and more charming than it is. It has all the elements of a lovely historical town: old, colonial buildings; an active tourist port, an arts and crafts market, and plenty of tourists passing through. But somehow this little village doesn't quite rank up there with its contemporaries (Olinda, Ouro Preto, or even the nearby São Francisco do Sul). The only logical reason for this is the presence of its huge, industrial shipping port (Porto Dom Pedro II) which ends up polluting the waterways around the islands and fishing villages of the area. As a result, the only thing really worth doing in Paranaguá is planning and preparing your excursions to Ilha do Mel and Guaraqueçaba. That may include a reluctant stopover in Paranaguá.

But don't let the run-down conditions of Paranaguá deter you from making your way out to the choice parts of the Paranaguá Bay. As soon as you touch base on Ilha do Mel, Ilha Superagüi, or the town of Guaraqueçaba, you'll be transported into a new world of tropical beauty and magical flora and fauna.

## THE VILLAGE AND SIGHTS

The humble village of Paranaguá is actually loaded with 17th- and 18th-century architecture, some of it handsomely restored and some not. The largest complex of historical buildings is right on the waterfront in front of the various small piers. This is called the Rua da Praia but is officially Rua General Carneiro.

The highlights of this area are the **Mercado do Artesanato** and the **Mercado do Café** across the street. These are both 19th-century buildings in a mixture of art nouveau and neoclassic styles. The Art Market is a great place to walk around and shop for souvenirs. There is a café-bar on one side. The Coffee Market also has some handmade baskets and souvenirs, but is mostly a place to have an economical lunch or morning coffee. Another great building on the waterfront is the **Palácio Mathias Bohn,** which is currently the tourist information center. It makes a picturesque view of old, colonial Paranaguá from the water if you happen to be sailing past on a clear day. Also, check out the **Praça Newton D. de Souza,** which has some interesting bas-relief sculptures on the adjoining wall.

Some highlights off the waterfront include the **Igrejas de São Benedito** and **Rosário** (Rua Conselheiro Sinimbu) a few streets inland from the bus terminal. Rosário was constructed in 1575 and is open for visitation from 8 A.M.– 6 P.M. São Benedito was built in 1784 by the brotherhood of slaves and has some interesting artifacts inside. Not far from the Rosário Church is the Casa da Cultura Monsenhor Celso (Largo Monsenhor Celso 23), an 18th-century cluster of buildings that are interesting enough on the outside and sport art exhibitions on the inside. The **Praça dos Leões** (Rua Hugo Simas) is a group of 16th-century buildings in a small *praça* and a picturesque example of the colonial architecture of the region. If you arrived by train, you will have already seen the

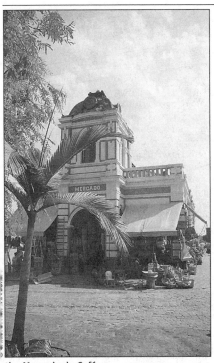

the Mercado do Café

old **Estação Ferroviaria.** If not, then head up to Avenida Arthur de Abreu to check it out. It was built in 1880 during the reign of Emperor Dom Pedro II.

## THE PARANAGUÁ BAY

### Antonina

When Bishop Francisco de São Jerônimo of Rio de Janeiro authorized the construction of a small chapel in honor of Nossa Sra. do Pilar in 1714, the small settlement of Antonina was born into a village. Originally known as Capela, it later became the town of Antonina when it began a robust shipping business, transporting coffee and grains out of the bay. It became a large shipping center but fell into disuse in the early 1900s and is now a small community once again. The town still has vestiges of the old, colonial buildings from the shipping era, including a historical sector in the middle of town. There are also several small colonial churches, several simple restaurants, and a few hotels and *pousadas*.

### Islands

The **Ilha dos Valadares** is closest to Paranaguá and was once owned by the Valadares

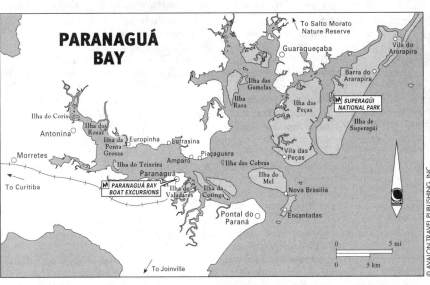

PARANAGUÁ BAY

To Salto Morato Nature Reserve

Guaraqueçaba

Vila do Ararapira

Barra do Ararapira

Ilha das Gamelas

Ilha do Coriscó

Ilha das Rosas

Ilha Rasa

Ilha das Peças

M **SUPERAGÜI NATIONAL PARK**

Antonina

Ilha da Ponta Grossa

Europinha

Eufrasina

Ilha de Superagüi

Morretes

Ilha do Teixeira

Amparo

Piaçaguera

Ilha das Cobras

To Curitiba

**PARANAGUÁ BAY BOAT EXCURSIONS**

Paranaguá

Ilha de Valadares

Ilha da Cotinga

Vila das Peças

Ilha do Mel

Nova Brasilia

Pontal do Paraná

Encantadas

To Joinville

0     5 mi
0     5 km

© AVALON TRAVEL PUBLISHING, INC.

# BRAZILIAN TOURISM AND THE SUPERLATIVE

Brazilians love to associate the words *best, first,* or *biggest* with tourist attractions and if a particular site merits a superlative in any way, you're likely to hear about it. But not all churches can be the first built in Brazil, so you'll also hear a host of second-tier claims, such as that a particular church is the first *Jesuit* church, or the first church in the Southern Region. When that doesn't apply, you might discover that you're looking at the first *church of Italian design* or of *non-Italian design* for that matter. Somehow a tour guide can muster up a bit more enthusiasm if he can show you the first non-baroque church in Caimu than just any old historical monument in town.

When an attraction can't be the first, it will often be the *longest, tallest, fattest,* or *most visited.* Albeit, it can be interesting to know that a certain monument is unique in some way and some of these particularities can be historically significant. "The San Francisco Convent is the only church in Pelourinho with a façade of sculpted stone..." Now that's an intriguing tidbit of information. It's not uncommon to hear that a monument is the second- or third-oldest, tallest, or largest and all of these little claims add color and character to the various city tours you'll be experiencing in Brazil. Rest assured, you aren't the first and you won't be the last to hear the wide variety of Brazilian superlatives.

family, who were heavily into the slave trade. Today, it's home to simple families that live mostly from fishing. On weekends, the island's beaches across from Paranaguá fill with locals. The **Ilha da Cotinga** has an interesting history. Its original occupants were the Carijós people, who live on the island to this day. Later, settlers from São Paulo built a small village on the island under the watchful eyes of the Carijós. There, you'll see the tiny Hermitage of Our Lady of Mercês, looking out over the bay. To get to the hermitage, you climb a stone stairway of 365 steps.

The most popular island in the Paranaguá Bay is **Ilha do Mel,** which is on the outermost edge of the bay and can be accessed from Paranaguá or Pontal do Sul. You may hear about the limiting of visitors on Ilha do Mel to only 5,000 per day. This is true, but it only affects people who are departing from Pontal do Sul. If you depart from Paranaguá, there are no restrictions. Actually, this is a sneaky way of limiting the number of low-income locals that visit the island, since almost no tourists (Brazilian or international) arrive on the island from the less expensive Pontal do Sul departures. This is because most tourists are coming from Curitiba.

Ilha das Peças and Ilha de Superagüi form the greater part of the Superagüi National Park. Officially, they belong to the municipality of

Guaraqueçaba and are thus detailed in that section, later in this chapter.

## Pontal do Paraná

This small municipality separated from Paranaguá in 1997. It is home to several beaches and the town of Pontal do Sul, where locals catch the boat over to Ilha do Mel. Because of its geographic position, most visitors do not enter Ilha do Mel through the Pontal, but go through Paranaguá. Still, if you are on your way down the coast after a visit to the island, you might consider crossing through Pontal do Paraná. There are numerous places to swim in the ocean, including the beaches of Praia de Leste and Shangri-La, where you can find waves suitable for surfing. The most popular beach on this part of the coast is the Balneario de Ipanema, which has plenty of restaurants and bars and an active nightlife.

## Porto Dom Pedro II

Considered one of the most important ports in Brazil, the industrial shipping activities of Porto Dom Pedro II specialize in moving grains around Brazil and internationally. The southern region of Brazil is a major producer of wheat, soy, and rice. You can take a short boat excursion out to the port and come up beside the big tankers docked at the port. Though it's a pretty interesting little journey for kids, it's not too special for adults.

## ENTERTAINMENT AND NIGHTLIFE

If you arrive late in the afternoon, you might find yourself stuck in Paranaguá for a night and you might as well make the best of it. There are bars with live music at both ends of the waterfront. One is called the **Ferradura** and the other is called **Praça Rosa Andrade.** These places stay open late and you can start at one of them and end up at the other (usually people migrate from the south end to the north end). They can get pretty crowded in the late evening and people have a tendency to drink a lot in this town (there's little else to do).

## PARANAGUÁ BAY BOAT EXCURSIONS

Visitors coming through Paranaguá are usually here to take one or more of the boat excursions around the bay. The principal excursions take you to Ilha do Mel, Guaraqueçaba, and the Superagüi National Park. All of these require overnight stays, which can be arranged by phone from Paranaguá. These are all detailed later in this chapter.

The official boat to **lha do Mel** leaves from the pier in front of the **Terminal de Embarque,** which is the ticket office and tourist information center. They are right on the waterfront in the most beautifully restored building facing the water. You can purchase tickets inside the terminal for R$21 round-trip (R$11 going to the island and R$10 returning). Boats leave from the pier directly in front of the terminal at 8:30 A.M., 9:30 A.M., 1 P.M., 3 P.M., and 4:30 P.M. Return trips leave the island at 8 A.M., 10 A.M., 1 P.M., 3 P.M., 4:30 P.M., and 5:30 P.M.

The Terminal de Embarque also has boats to **Guaraqueçaba** (from which you can see Salto do Morato and the Superagüi park), **Barra de Superagüi** (if you want to go directly to the park), and various islands and villages in the bay. Their trips to the Superagüi National Park are every bit are every bit as good as the ones leaving from Guaraqueçaba, so go ahead and plan your journeys from here. The tickets are R$21 round-trip. Boats leave at 8:30 A.M., 9:30 A.M., and 1 P.M. and return at 6 A.M., 1:30 P.M., and 3:30 P.M.

Excursions to Antonina and the inner reaches of the bay are not too interesting, as these areas are mostly industrial port towns (although Antonina has a small, historical section). Likewise, the short excursion for R$8 out to the Porto Dom Pedro II is pretty lame. Don't waste your time. There is an excursion that takes you out to the **Ilha da Cotinga** that is fairly interesting if you have a few hours to kill. Otherwise, the trip to Ilha do Mel passes along the inner perimeter of the island and gives you a pretty good view of the place from the water.

There are services besides the Terminal de Embarque that make all or most of these trips and they have different departure times. You can walk along the waterfront and ask at the various docks for details. Some possibilities include **Abaline** (tel. 41/455-2616), which has trips to Ilha do Mel at 9:30 A.M. daily and an extra trip at 1:30 P.M. on weekends. They also go out to Guaraqueçaba at 9:30 A.M. and 1:30 P.M. daily. You can also try **Sea Blue** (tel. 41/9978-3914) and **Mariner III** (tel. 41/422-6045) with trips every day from 10 A.M.–7 P.M.

Note: Private companies alter their schedules during low season if there are not enough passengers to warrant a trip.

## ACCOMMODATIONS

If you like to keep your schedule open-ended, you can probably just show up in town and start looking for a room. There's no need to reserve ahead of time in most cases, even during peak season. The **Hotel Continente** (Rua General Carneiro 300, tel. 41/423-3224, R$20 pp group room and R$45 private room) is the town's youth hostel and part of the HI chain. It's right on the waterfront and has plenty of rooms, mostly group but some individual with shared bathrooms. They have no air-conditioners, but rooms have fans. Rooms toward the front can be noisy, as they have a café/bar downstairs in front that stays open late. It's a decent place for meeting other international travelers. One of the nicer places in town (and that's relative) in terms of decent rooms with a decent atmosphere is the Ⓜ **Hotel Ponderosa** (Rua Presciliano Corrêa 68, tel. 41/423-2464, R$20 pp) a block off the water on the far end of town. They have a few rooms upstairs and most hold up to four people. Breakfast is included in their small but quaint breakfast nook. They are across the street from the Teatro da Ordem, in case you want to catch a play or something.

The town's top-end hotel is the **Dantas Executive Hotel** (Rua Visconde de Nacar 740, tel. 41/423-1555, dontashotel@dantashotel.com.br, R$85 s, R$105 d, and R$140 suite), located about three blocks inland from the far end of the village. They have a bunch of funky old rooms in an executive atmosphere and a restaurant where they serve breakfast (included) and lunch (not included but don't bother). Rooms have air, TV, and phone.

## FOOD

You'll find casual places for lunch and dinner all along the waterfront in the village. The kiosk bars at each end of the waterfront district serve a variety of fried foods and fish plates both for lunch and dinner. However, these places are best for drinking and not eating. There are casual eateries on the side of the fish market with economical lunch plates.

The best lunch or dinner buffet in town is at the **Restaurante Sun Shin** (Rua General Carneiro 394, tel. 41/3425-2329, 11 A.M.–3 P.M. and 7–11 P.M. daily), a Chinese restaurant with plenty of variety at a great price. The lunch buffet is only R$7 per person, all you can eat. They are also open for dinner until 11 P.M. If you ask, they can scrounge up some Chinese green tea from the back (it's not on the menu). The most elaborate buffet in town is at the Ⓜ **Danubio Azul Restaurante** (Rua XV de Novembro 95, tel. 41/3423-3255, 11:30 A.M.–4 P.M. and from 6 P.M.), which is on the far end of the waterfront in a white building that over-looks the ocean. They have a huge lunch and dinner buffet that includes several fish plates (including grilled salmon with capers and butter), pasta dishes, and salads. They also have some decent wines. It's R$22 per person for the buffet or about R$40 for two if you decide to order off the menu.

## INFORMATION AND SERVICES

There is a tourist information booth at the main bus terminal that can give you a basic orientation, maps, and brochures, but the best information center is on the waterfront at the Terminal de Embarque. There, you'll find a great wall map with diagrams of the available bay excursions, pamphlets, and all sorts of personal help. It's almost overkill for such a little village, but it's a nice change from the anemic information centers in Minas Gerais and the Nordeste. It serves as a reminder that you're in the south of Brazil, where the tourism industry actually invests in its infrastructure.

The Banco do Brasil (corner of Rua Mal. Alberto de Abreu and Rua Faria Sobrinho) has one ATM with the Plus and Cirrus systems. It's open until 10 P.M.

## GETTING THERE AND AROUND

When you arrive in Paranaguá, get off the bus and head to your right. You can walk right through the fish market, which is next to the bus terminal. You will pop out at the main *praça,* with the ocean and a small sandy beach on your right. The rest of the village is in front of you and on a few inland streets to the left. In about 15 minutes, you can walk to the far end of the village along the waterfront. If you want to leave your bags at the bus station while you walk around town, there is a *guarda volumes* (bag storage) desk that is open from 8 A.M.–6 P.M.

The train from Curitiba to Paranaguá was closed for maintenance during the writing of this book, but it could be open by the time you read this. (For details on this trip, see the sidebar *All Aboard the Serra Verde Express.*)

Buses from Curitiba to Paranaguá leave on the Graciosa line. There are 20 buses every day, 5:15 A.M.–11:15 P.M. The cost is R$15. If you took the train to Morretes, you can pick up a Graciosa bus from Morretes to Paranaguá.

If you're heading from Paranaguá down the coast to Joinville, be warned: Traffic along this coastal road can be heavy and the 2.5-hour trip can take as long as four hours. You might be happier returning to Curitiba and taking the direct bus along the main highways. Avoid the coastal route on weekend afternoons when everyone from Joinville is returning home from the northern beaches. During the week or weekends in the morning should be no problem. The trip includes a 15-minute ferryboat ride across the Cubatão River to Guaratuba. The Graciosa line goes there for R$13 and leaves at 7:40 A.M. and 3:45 P.M.

# Guaraqueçaba

One of the earliest settlements in the south of Brazil, Guaraqueçaba gets its name from the Tupi-Guarani word for a red-colored egret that flourished in the area. Here, you'll find a small town with a mixture of modern and colonial architecture. The town serves as a launching pad for many nearby forests and nature preserves, including the Reserva Natural Salto Morato, which is a pristine piece of tropical forest that has trails, campgrounds, and a visitor's center. From Guaraqueçaba, you can also catch a boat out to the Islands of Paças, Rasa, and Superagüi, the last being the principal location of the Superagüi National Park, which has a small, rustic village for those wanting to spend the night and explore the far reaches of the island. Although the town itself has hotels and restaurants, the attraction in this part of the region is in getting yourself far into the forests and natural parks. There are even some great hikes right from the edges of the town with incredible views of the waterways and marshlands from the hillsides.

## N SUPERAGÜI NATIONAL PARK

Made up of some 35,000 hectares of land and waterways, the Superagüi National Park is one of the most pristine areas in the south of Brazil. It consists primarily of the islands of Superagüi, Peças, Pinheiro, and Pinheirinho. The main area is the Superagüi Island and its principal port of entry is at Barra do Superagüi, a small village on the beach with a trail that leads into the island's topical beauty. Superagüi Island is not a natural island, but was cut-away from the mainland in the 1950s with the trenching of the waterways at the northern border between Paraná and São Paulo. This was done to improve shipping conditions in the area. From the village at Barra, you can hike about 1.5 hours to Deserta Beach through the thick tropical forest. Once there, you are free to continue along the beach for some 40 kilometers to the northern tip of the island, camping included, of course. One-day trips to Superagüi leave Guaraqueçaba daily and visit the Pinheiro Island along the way. The trip takes about an hour to arrive at Barra. Trips from Paranaguá generally include an overnight stay in one of the *pousadas* in Barra.

## N SALTO MORATO NATURE PRESERVE

One of the greenest pieces of planet Earth you'll ever see, the Salto Morato Nature Preserve (Salto Morato Foundation, tel. 41/482-1506, morato@founcacaoboticario.org.br) is a protected wildlife area with the capacity to receive visitors and campers (reservation required for camping). The area is full of tropical flora and fauna and has a principal trail that leads to the Salto Morato Waterfall. At a height of 130 meters, the falls and surrounding pools make up one of the most beautiful visions in the area. Along the way, you follow the stream with an opportunity to swim in some of the natural pools formed at a bend in the river. The hike takes only a couple of hours. You can also take a guided tour into a wet area of the park where the ecosystem is perfect for the proliferation of hundreds of tropical plants and animals. The tour takes about four hours to complete. If you don't arrive early enough to take both tours in one day, there are campgrounds where you can stay the night. The park has a reception area with souvenir shop, auditorium, research labs, snack shop, and picnic areas.

## MORRO DO QUITUMBÉ

Right outside the city of Guaraqueçaba is the Quitumbé Mountain, with an altitude of 80 meters. To hike up to the top, find the trail beside the Igreja do Nosso Senhor do Bom Jesus dos Perdões. There are signs along the trail, which is about one kilometer long. At the top is a fantastic view of the waterways and islands in the bay and the town below.

## ACCOMMODATIONS

The **Hotel Eduardo I** (Rua Paula Miranda 165, tel. 41/482-1225, hotelduardo@onda.com.br, R$45–65) is the main option in town. It's not fancy. You can also try the **Pousada da Yuassa** (Rua Inácio Barbosa Pinto 53, tel. 41/482-1291, R$25 pp).

## FOOD

Most likely, you'll be deep into a tropical forest or walking along a tropical beach at lunchtime, but if you're back in town for dinner, you can try **Restaurante Barbosa** (Rua Paula Miranda, tel. 41/3482-1248), which is open for dinner from 6:30 P.M. until the last client

leaves. Also on Rua Paula Miranda is the **Restaurante Guaricana**, (Rua Paula Miranda 35, tel. 41/3482-1235) which has the same hours. There are a couple more places on Rua Agricola Fonseca, including **Restaurante Marina da Diva** (Rua Agricola Fonseca 85, tel. 41/3482-1374, 11 A.M.–11 P.M. Tues.–Sat.) and **Restaurante Marina Guará** (Rua Agricola Fonseca 59, tel. 41/3482-1325, 8 P.M. until the last customer daily). Walk around town and check out these and other options to make your selection.

## INFORMATION AND SERVICES

You might be able to get some information at the IBAMA office (Rua Paula Miranda, tel. 41/3482-1262). Otherwise, try the tour agency **Cormorano Ecoturismo e Aventura** (Rua Luiz Ramos Figueira 145, tel. 41/3482-1546, www.cormorano.com.br). They can also set you up with boat trips and inland excursions. There are no banks here, so get your cash in Paranaguá before coming.

## GETTING THERE AND AROUND

You can get to Guaraqueçaba on a three-hour boat trip from Paranaguá. The trip makes a stop at the village on the Ilha das Peças. Once you're there, you can book passage to Superagüi, the Sebuí Preserve, or to some of the smaller islands in the area. You can also join a guided visit to Salto Morato Preserve, which gives you round-trip transportation. If you're heading back to Curitiba, the best way to return is via Paranaguá, where you can catch a bus to Curitiba. (You can go directly to Curitiba from Guaraqueçaba, but the road is long and full of potholes.)

# Ilha do Mel

The second most visited sight in Paraná, Ilha do Mel (the Island of Honey), is among the best spots on the southern coastline to find that cool, tropical beach atmosphere. The island has almost 28 square kilometers of space, most of it virgin forest. The inhabited part includes two charming villages with numerous *pousadas* and restaurants and 12 principal beaches, each with unique characteristics. You can hike to just about every corner of the island, most of it using well-defined trails that zig-zag through the hills and beaches. Visitors generally use the three main attractions on the island as destination points while walking along the trails. These include the lighthouse; the Fortaleza, in a more secluded part of the island; and the Enchanted Cave, accessible from the ocean or as a lookout point to the south. A short walk takes you up to the lighthouse with its panoramic view of the open ocean. From there, you can hike about three hours to the beach and village of Encantadas, passing many of the islands prettiest beaches and viewpoints along the way. Or you can walk in the other direction to see the old Fort of Nossa Senhora dos Prazeres.

There is a thin, sandy division between the two parts of the island. Just 25 year ago, this strip of sand was about 130 meters wide. Today, it's only about 30 meters wide and experts fear that it will soon be overcome by the ocean, creating two separate islands. In the meantime, you should not pass up the opportunity to walk along this sandy path out to the fort. At high tide, the ocean can completely cover this strip of sand, making it a terrific area for swimming and playing in the water, which is about one meter deep.

## NOVA BRASILIA AND THE LIGHTHOUSE

Most boats arriving on the island from Paranaguá drop off their passengers at the village of Nova Brasilia, situated to one side of the narrow strip of sand that connects the two principal parts of the island. Nova Brasilia is the island's main village and has the majority of *pousadas* and cafés. Nightlife on the island occurs principally in Nova Brasilia with some activities at Encantadas. Nova Brasilia actually extends to the other side of the island, along Praia das Conchas and Praia do Farol. If you arrive with luggage, you can have one of the baggage carriers put your bags in a wheelbarrow and haul them to you hotel with you running alongside. The cost for this is about R$20, depending on the number of bags and distance to your hotel. But it's best if you come to the island as light as possible, storing your larger bags, perhaps, in the bus terminal at Paranaguá.

You can walk around Nova Brasilia to choose your favorite *pousada* for the night. From there, you can hike to all of the island's attractions. Generally, you can find lodging without having to make reservations, but if you are visiting the island during the peak season (mid-December to mid-February) then it's best to get a confirmed room.

The hike up to the lighthouse, Farol das Conchas, is facilitated by a long staircase that brings you to the base. From there, you can see several beaches to the north and south, including the strip of sand that connects the two parts of the island.

## ENCANTADAS AND THE ENCHANTED CAVE

The Praia das Encantadas is the second most popular port on the island and many of the boats coming from the Pontal do Sul first stop and drop off passengers here. Along the hillside above the beach of Encantadas, there are a number of quaint *pousadas* from which to choose and they extend almost all the way over to the other side of the island at Praia das Encantadas de Fora, or Mar de Fora. From this point, you can access the entire southern part of the island, but it's not as convenient a position for exploring the island as is Nova Brasilia.

# ILHA DO MEL

POUSADA DOS PRAZERES

NOSSA SRA DOS PRAZERES FORT

Estação      Ecológica

I l h a      d o      M e l

PARQUE HOTEL
ILHA DO MEL

Praia
da Fortaleza

POUSADA
DONA CLARA

Praia    do    Limoeiro

FAROL DAS
CONCHAS

B a í a

Praia
do Farol

Praia das
Conchas

POUSADA PRAIA
DO FAROL

ENSEADA

Praia
de Fora

P a r a n a g u á

Nova Brazilia

CAIR
DO SOL

POUSADA
TREZE LUAS

Praia do Belo

Praia
Grande

Morro
do Meio

Praia do Miguel

POUSADA CORAÇÃO DA ILHA

Morro
Bento Alves

Morro
do Sabão

Prainha

Encantadas

Praia
Encantada
de Fora

POUSADA LUA CHEIA

A ILHA VERDE HOTEL

POUSADA PARADA
ALTERNATIVA

Enchanted Cave

SCALE NOT AVAILABLE

MOON

There is a decent nightlife in Encantadas for those staying in the area.

From the Encantadas Beach, you can walk over to the principal attraction of the area, the Enchanted Cave. The cave looks like something out of a Disney pirate movie and it carries with it a legend: Inside the cave were once a group of mermaids whose songs lured pirate ships toward the island where they would crash and sink. From above the cave, you can sit at a comfortable island bar with a terrific view to the south. You can also hire a boat to take you into the mouth of the cave from the Encantadas Beach.

## THE FORTRESS

The trail that leads to the fortress is a long one and it follows the extensive beach most of the way—unless, of course, the tide is high, in which case, you can use the inland trail to the fort. Either way, you will pass a few of the more out-of-the-way *pousadas* on the island. These are the best choice for anyone wanting to get away from the crowds and enjoy a little peace and quiet on a tropical island. The walk from Nova Brasilia to the fort takes about an hour or you can take a speedboat there in about 15 minutes. There is a small pier just after the fort where ships from the open ocean would dock in order to regenerate from long trips at sea. The view from the fort itself is stunning and on a clear day, you can see across to distant islands in the Paranaguá Bay. Inside the walls of the fort are plateaus holding rows of cannons, once used (literally once) to protect the bay.

## BEACHES AND TRAILS

Two very popular beaches for sunning and swimming are **Praia do Farol** and **Praia das Conchas** at Nova Brasilia. Nearby, you can find beach bars to keep you cool and refreshed. You can easily walk from the dock at Nova Brasilia to the lighthouse in about 20 minutes—passing these two beaches. On the other side of the lighthouse is **Praia de Fora,** where most of the island's surfing gets done. From Nova Brasilia to the fort takes about an hour each way and the path takes you all along the **Praia da Fortaleza,** about three kilometers long. It has medium waves and is one of the least-populated beaches on the island.

You can also hike from Nova Brasilia all the way to Encantadas in about 2.5 hours if you go directly there, but it's better to take your time and stop at some of the incredible beaches along the way. Before you go, be sure to find out about the tide, as you want to cross the island's beaches during low tide. If you leave from the lighthouse, you'll pass **Praia Grande,** one of the most popular beaches for surfing and sunning and about one kilometer long. Plus, there are small caves and tide pools around the outer edges. From Praia Grande, you can walk over Morro do Meio (Middle Mountain) to reach **Praia do Miguel,** one of the most pristine beaches on the island as it has no buildings whatever. Usually, this beach is semi-deserted, so you should pack your own water and snacks if you want to hang out here. It's one of the best locations for swimming on the island as the waves are calm and there are no crowds. After passing over and around the Morro de Sabão (Soap Hill), your next stop is **Praia de Fora,** also known as Mar de Fora and Encantada de Fora. From here, it's easy to get to the En-

chanted Cave via a trail that leads up the hill. Continue up and over, and you've reached your destination, **Praia das Encantadas,** the second most popular beach on the island for *pousadas,* bars, and village activities at night. A good way to take this trail is to go out in the morning low tide and back in the afternoon low tide. If you get stuck in Encantadas after high tide, then just charter a small boat back to Nova Brasilia. It takes only about 20 minutes.

Another popular trail on the island leads from Nova Brasilia to **Praia do Belo.** The trail is short and sweet (about 40 minutes) and leads through the island's vegetation, where you can see all types of tropical plants and small animals. The beach is a tiny, sandy inlet surrounded by rocks and tropical forest. It's a picture-perfect image of the island and worth every minute of the hike there.

## ACCOMMODATIONS

It's difficult to say whether you'd prefer staying in the village of Nova Brasilia/Farol or in Encantadas. They both offer a number of cozy *pousadas* and restaurants with activities going on at night. The Encantadas area is perhaps a bit more huddled together, with *pousadas* right next to one another and a nightlife that is perhaps more huddled together as well. In peak season, the Encantadas beach is said to be inappropriate for swimming due to run-off from the village into the ocean. That and the fact that it's not as centrally located for day hikes probably gives Nova Brasilia the edge. If you're interested in getting out and away from the crowd, then set yourself up in a *pousada* along the Praia da Fortaleza. You can check the website www.pousadasilhadomel.com.br for listings and photos of many of the *pousadas* on the island—although not all of them.

### Encantadas

If you land in Encantadas, you can easily walk around to most of the *pousadas* to check out their facilities before deciding. Some possibilities include **A Ilha Verde Hotel Pousada** (tel. 41/426-9036, www.ailhaverde.com.br, R$30 per person), **Pousada Coração da Ilha** (tel. 41/426-9043, www.pousadasilhadomel.com.br, R$20 per person), and **Pousada Lua Cheia** (tel. 41/426-9010, www.ilhadomelpousada-luacheia.com.br, ff.barros@uol.com.br, R$40 d). These are spread out in various corners of the Encantadas area. The **Pousada Parada Alternativa** (tel. 41/426-9035, www.paradaal-ternativa.com.br, reservas@paradaalternative .com.br, R$25 per person) is frequented by surfers and offers low-cost rooms.

Campgrounds near Encantadas include **Surf Camping Maninho** (tel. 41/426-9059, maninhosurfescola@ibest.com.br, R$10 per person) and **Tubarão** (tel. 41/426-9016, www .ilhadomelonline.com.br, R$10 per person).

### Nova Brasilia/Farol

Even if you visit on a busy summer weekend, you can probably find accommodations at the last minute without having to make reservations. The selection might be somewhat limited, however. On weekdays, you can walk around town and compare prices and facilities without a worry. You'll find that most *pousadas* in this area offer about the same types of facilities, which include a ceiling fan and breakfast. Some places to check out near the Farol include **Cair do Sol** (tel. 41/426-8016, pcairdosol@yahoo.com.br or pcairdosol@il hadomelpreserve.com.br, 75 s and R$125 d) and **Enseada** (tel. 41/426-8040, www.pousa-daenseada.com, pousadaenseada@uol.com.br, R$75 s and R$125 d). You can also take a look at **Pousada Praia do Farol** (tel. 41/426-8014, www.praiadofarol.com.br, R$70 s and R$110 d), which overlooks the Farol Beach, and **Pousadinha** (tel. 41/426-8026, www.pousadinha.com.br, R$35 s and R$50 d). A quaint little *pousada* in the area is **M Pousada Treze Luas** (tel. 41/426-8067, www.pousada-trezeluas.com, R$80 s and R$100 d).

### Near the Fort

The most distant and private *pousada* on the island is probably the **Pousada dos Prazeres** (4 km from Nova Brasilia, tel. 41/243-9649, www.pousadadosprazeres.com.br, R$35 s and

R$60 d) past the Fortaleza dos Prazeres. They have rooms in front with views of the ocean and beach service. They also have kayaks and boat service for guests. Just prior to the fort is the **Parque Hotel Ilha do Mel** (3.5 km from Nova Brasilia, tel. 41/426-8075, www.parquehotel-ilhadomel.com, R$50 s and R$90–R$135 d) which is a more elaborate setup with rooms facing the ocean and hotel facilities. The **Pousada Dona Clara** (Praia da Fortaleza, 3 km from the lighthouse, no number, tel. 41/426-8050, www.pousadadonaclara.com.br, R$40 s and R$90 d) is a charming place at a good price on the way to the fort.

Campgrounds near the fort include **Aloha** (Praia do Farol, tel. 41/426-8160, www .ilhadomelpreserve.com.br, aloha@ilhadomel-preserve.com, R$20 s and R$40 d) and **Recanto Verde** (tel. 41/426-8049, campingrecanto-verde@bol.com.br).

## FOOD AND NIGHTLIFE

In the Nova Brasilia/Farol area, there are several places to try. Starting with simple food, check out the **Lanchonete to Trapiche** (tel. 41/3426-8085, 10 A.M.–9 P.M. daily, around R$5 for snacks) at the lighthouse for simple snacks and beers. To make a picnic, you can purchase materials at the **Mercearia Cair do Sol** (tel. 41/3426-8016, 8 A.M.–9 P.M. daily). For pizza, check out the **Pizzaria e Bar Vila Farol.** The **Restaurante e Bar do David** is one of the best spots for afternoon and evening drinks and eats. Finally, the **Por do Sol Restaurant** (tel. 41/3426-8009, noon–4 P.M. and 8–11 P.M. daily, R$25) is a great place to eat and watch the sunset.

In Encantadas, the *pousadas* near the beach transform into bars and night spots. You can walk all along the beach and into the hills to choose your favorite location. Remember that away from the main villages, there is no light on the island, so a good flashlight is necessary. Check out the **Panificadora Encantadas** (tel. 41/3426-9089, 7 A.M.–11 P.M. daily) for simple baked goods and picnic items and the **Lanchonete Sonho de Verão** (tel. 41/3426-9044,

A.M.–11 P.M. daily) for snacks and finger foods. The **Restaurante Paraíso** (tel. 41/3426-0057, 9 A.M.–10 P.M. daily, R$25) in the hotel of the same name has lunch and dinner plates and the **Restaurante Ilha do Mel** (tel. 41/3426-0072, 9 A.M.–10 P.M. daily, R$25) is one of the nicer places in Encantadas.

## INFORMATION AND SERVICES

There is a tourist information booth in Nova Brasilia that's open 8 A.M.–7 P.M. and the *Jornal da Ilha do Mel* paper can tell you all about island happenings. There is an Internet café near the lighthouse heading toward Praia de Fora and some of the hotels have Internet access (a novelty on the island). There are no banks here, so be sure to get money before you embark in Paranaguá. There are small medical posts in Encantadas and Nova Brasilia

(open until 6 P.M.), but there is no pharmacy on the island, so be sure to pack anything you may need in that department. And don't forget the flashlight!

One of the official websites of Ilha do Mel is www.ilhadomelpreserve.com.br. Another is ilhadomelonline.com.br.

## GETTING THERE AND AROUND

Boats come to the island from Paranaguá and Pontal do Sul several times a day. See those sections for times and details. You can get off the island at just about any time between 8 A.M. and 7 P.M. (4:40 P.M. if you're heading to Paranaguá). The island's tourism authority has prohibited any type of motorized vehicle on the island. That includes cars, motorcycles, and off-road vehicles of any kind. You'll also have to leave your helicopter back on the mainland.

# Santa Catarina

Most travelers visiting the south of Brazil find Santa Catarina the most interesting of the southern states. The area from Joinville to capital city Florianópolis is one of the country's most diverse regions, both geographically—the emerald waters of the coastline make a striking contrast to the inland mountain towns—and culturally.

The area around Joinville is mostly rural, with many small farms and the relaxed atmosphere of the countryside. The hillsides here are covered in banana trees, the area's main agricultural product. The early settlers of the Joinville area were Portuguese from the archipelago of Azores and you'll hear a lot about the area's Azorian roots—particularly in the old, coastal towns, which are among the earliest colonial towns in the country.

Inland, in the mountainous areas, the main influence is German, from the relatively recent immigration in the first half of the 20th century. You'll see German culture in the architecture, food, and crafts. The small rural villages along the Caminho dos Principes (Road of the Princes) mix German culture and tropical landscapes. In the communities of Brusque and Pomerode, you'll often hear German spoken in the streets. Another highlight here are the mountains of Corupá loaded with rivers and waterfalls, which makes for some of the best hiking and camping in the region.

# **M**ust-Sees

Look for **M** to find the sights and activities you can't miss and **M** for the best dining and lodging.

**M São Francisco do Sul:** You can almost still hear the drunken laughter of the sailors who came to port here echoing from the 18th-century buildings that make up the old historical waterfront. Most interesting is the old shipping warehouse that today houses the Museu Nacional do Mar (page 562).

**M Parque Unipraias:** Just riding the gondola from Camboriú Beach to Laranjeiras is worth the price of admission. But you also get to stop at the nature park on the way, which has several spectacular view platforms and two great ropes courses for anyone wanting a little extra adventure. Praia Laranjeiras on the far end is a sea of colored umbrellas with blue-green water and plenty of bars facing the ocean (page 574).

**M Porto Belo:** Whether you have your scuba card or just want to go snorkeling in clear, shal-

Praia Laranjeiras is a sea of umbrellas.

© CHRISTOPHER VAN BUREN

low waters, there is something under the water for you here. Off the tip of Porto Belo Island are several underwater trails that you can follow with a mask and snorkel, viewing the abundant variety of marine life (page 580).

**M Florianópolis's Old City Center:** A loop around the historical center in Florianópolis makes an excellent half-day walking tour. Start at the Mercado Público, then stroll over to Praça XV de Novembro (page 586).

**M Praia Mole:** You won't find a more beautiful crowd of people than at Praia Mole. They'll be surfing, getting some sun, and modeling their latest swimwear for the onlookers (page 591).

**M Lagoinha do Leste:** The trail that leads up and over the mountains, then down into Lagoinha, has some spectacular views along the way. It's a challenging hike, so when you arrive, you'll be ready for a dip in the fresh-water lake or one of the small streams that feeds into it (page 592).

**M Solidão:** As its name implies (*solidão* meaning solitude or loneliness) this is a place that receives relatively few visitors. It requires a short hike down steep paths to arrive there, but the reward is well worth the trouble (page 592).

São Paulo

Curitiba

São Francisco do Sul

Porto Belo
Parque Unipraias
Solidão

Florianópolis
Praia Mole

Florianópolis's
Old City Center
Lagoinha
do Leste

**SANTA CATARINA**

ATLANTIC OCEAN

URUGUAY

Santa Catarina

As you work your way down the BR-101 highway, you can stop at the many vacation spots favored by South American tourists. Along the coast, the climate is quite different, especially as you enter the tourist beach of Balneario Camboriú, known as the Copacabana of the South. The similarity to Copacabana in Rio is made complete with a Cristo monument and a spectacular gondola ride to the peak of a coastal mountain. The beaches are crowded and the nightlife is high-volume. If you prefer a more quiet and quaint beach, you can set yourself up in Porto Belo. For many travelers, a visit to this part of the country is based on one primary goal: to dive in the emerald waters of the National Marine Preserve off the coast of Bombinhas. This is one of the few official marine preserves in the country, and one of Brazil's great diving locations.

Further south, Ilha de Santa Catarina is like a small country. It's big and diverse, each of the many smaller territories, towns, and neighborhoods within it offering its own unique personality. In addition to Florianópolis, the island offers 100 beaches (from urbanized to completely virgin), several lakes, and a variety of ecosystems. There are national parks, trails, major highways, and small villages. (It's worth noting that the entire island of Santa Catarina is often referred to simply as "Florianópolis" to avoid confusion with the larger state of Santa Catarina.)

## PLANNING YOUR TIME

If you want to see everything between Joinville and Florianópolis, you'll be zig-zagging your way between the coast and inland mountains. That's perfectly OK with most travelers, since the inland attractions are just as important as the coastal ones. Nowhere is this more true than up near Joinville itself—with Corupá's mountains and waterfalls to one side and the historical island of São Francisco do Sul on the other. Joinville itself, holds little interest for most people. So, when you get into town, head straight to the mountains of Corupá and spend your time trekking up the lush waterways. Plan two or three days there, depending on how much hiking you want to do. A single day (or even a half-day) on the island of São Francisco do Sul is enough time to see the village and Ocean Museum. Although Prainha Beach is quite pleasant, most travelers prefer the beaches to the south over those on the São Francisco do Sul.

The main highway from Joinville to Florianópolis heads straight down the coast, passing every significant beach along the way. The key intersection point is the coastal city of Itajaí, where you can head inland to the cities of Blumenau and Brusque. From Blumenau, you can head north a short way to visit Pomerode. If you don't have time to explore all of these, then head straight to Pomerode for a strong shot of old German culture.

There is a bus line that goes from Itajaí to Porto Belo, stopping at all the beaches in-between. The route takes about 1.5 hours and buses leave every 30 minutes until 1 A.M. Tripping up and down on this route is a great way to see this part of the coastline. After coming in from Pomerode, you can decide which beaches you like the best and return there to spend more time.

If you rent a car to make the trip from Joinville to Florianópolis, you'll find it smooth and effortless, with the exception of Balneario Camboriú, which can get quite congested in the summer. You should take this into consideration when making reservations there. Still, most travelers prefer to rent a car in Joinville and then again in Florianópolis and take buses between the two cities.

When you reach the island of Santa Catarina, you'll be confronted with the same dilemma as most visitors: How do I choose the best spot from so many possibilities? The island is so big and diverse that it's difficult to know where you're going to want to spend your time. It's possible to see most of the island's key locations in about 7–10 days but, frankly, not everything is going to appeal to everyone. The island is so diverse that most everybody needs to eliminate a few spots in order to keep it manageable; you don't want to waste your time on places that are not *sua praia* (your beach), as they say in Brazil.

So here's how to not waste your time in Florianópolis: Eliminate the northern half of the island (except for the village of Santo Antônio de Lisboa) and focus on downtown, the east coast, and the south. You will definitely enjoy the less crowded conditions of the southern beaches, including the enchanting island of Campeche. Plus, the south part of the island is where all the hiking and beautiful views can be found. If you like the idea of people-watching from a relaxing spot at a beach bar. . . well, the east coast has plenty of that at Praias Joaquina and Mole. And you won't want for a more beautiful crowd. The best nightlife is either downtown or at Lagoa da Conceição.

Where you stay and how you get around on Ilha de Santa Catarina depend largely on how much time and money you have. If you have five days and R$1,500, then spend a couple days downtown, where you can explore both downtown and the east coast. Take taxis back and forth to the east coast and Lagoa do Conceição. Next, move your base to Armação or Pântano do Sul for the rest of the time. From there, you can see the southern part of the island at a leisurely pace. If you like, you can rent a car to make it easier to get between these beaches.

If you're on a budget, then I suggest you get yourself installed in a reasonable hotel downtown or at Barra da Lagoa (the most economical) and take day trips from there (it's easier to take day trips from downtown). You can also camp out at Lagoinha do Leste, where you may decide to spend the rest of your time.

# Joinville

Visitors coming into Santa Catarina usually stop in Joinville for a look around before heading out to the beaches to the south. But Joinville has some interesting diversions that could keep one here for a few extra days. While most people are thinking about the coast, Joinville's most interesting attractions are in the opposite direction: in the mountainous areas inland toward Corupá. There, you can get a taste of how rural life must have been in old Germany (Germans who come into this area say that it reminds them of the rural countryside—that somehow got stuck in time—and that even the German spoken here is antique). This area is one of the largest suppliers of bananas in the country and you'll see endless banana plantations—one after the next—lining the hillsides in a very picturesque scene. There are trails that lead to incredible waterfalls that just invite you to dive in for a swim. You can also find some incredible adventure sports here, including rappelling and mountain climbing. Joinville is the largest city in Santa Catarina, with about 450,000 inhabitants, and is the first German-influenced city most people see when coming south from Curitiba. But as you get farther into the hillsides or visit some of the smaller cities to the south, you start to get some real German culture. Don't miss the opportunity to stop at an authentic bakery and try the strudels, macaroons, and other delights.

On the other side of Joinville is the coast and its main attraction, the historic village on the island of São Francisco do Sul. On the far side of the island are several interesting beaches, including Prainha with its crystal-clear waters and summer nights full of life both on the boardwalk and in the bars. Back in the city of Joinville itself, you'll find some decent beer gardens and interesting old hotels whose architecture speak of the German immigration to the area.

## TURISMO RURAL

The most interesting thing to do in Joinville is visit one or more of the rural areas that are set up to receive tourists. There are three of these areas and they are all west of the city in the inland hills and valleys. In these pockets

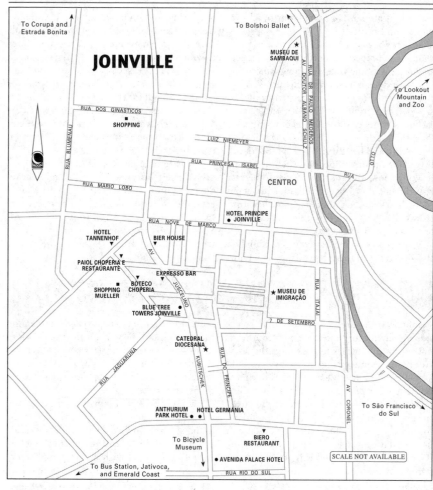

**JOINVILLE**

To Corupá and
Estrada Bonita

To Bolshoi Ballet

MUSEU DE
SAMBAQUI

To Lookout
Mountain
and Zoo

RUA DOS GINASTICOS

SHOPPING

RUA BLUMENAU

AV. DOUTOR ALBANO SCHULZ

AV. DR. PAULO MEDEROS

LUIZ NIEMEYER

RUA PRINCESA ISABEL

CENTRO

RUA OTTO

RUA MARIO LOBO

RUA NOVE DE MARCO

HOTEL PRINCIPE
JOINVILLE

HOTEL
TANNENHOF

BIER HOUSE

AV. JUSCELINO

PAIOL CHOPERIA E
RESTAURANTE

EXPRESSO BAR

SHOPPING
MUELLER

BOTECO
CHOPERIA

MUSEU DE
IMIGRAÇÃO

RUA ITAIAI

BLUE TREE
TOWERS JOINVILLE

7 DE SETEMBRO

RUA JAGUARUNA

CATEDRAL
DIOCESANA

RUA DO PRINCIPE

KUBITSCHEK

AV. CORONEL

To São Francisco
do Sul

ANTHURIUM
PARK HOTEL

HOTEL GERMANIA

To Bicycle
Museum

BIERO
RESTAURANT

AVENIDA PALACE HOTEL

To Bus Station, Jativoca,
and Emerald Coast

RUA RIO DO SUL

SCALE NOT AVAILABLE

of *turismo rural,* you'll see small farms, lakes, streams, and rural centers where you can stop at the local restaurants and visit the many shops. Besides the local arts and crafts, the highlights are the German bakeries and food confectioners. You'll find strudels, sweet jams and jellies, and some great restaurants that serve dishes like meat and potato stew, spiced sausages, and sweet-and-sour cabbage. There are three principal colonies: the Estrada Bonita to the north (the most popular), the Piraí area across from the main entrance to town

(the most extensive), and the Jativoca area to the south.

The best way to visit these areas is in a rental car as they are fairly distant and too large and spread out for visiting on foot once you get there (with the possible exception of the Estrada Bonita). They are easy to locate off the main BR-101 highway. Another way is to make a deal with a taxi to take you on a rural tour. You can usually get a brief city tour thrown in on your way out to the rural area—all for about R$80 (split as many ways as there are people in the taxi). An organized tour group will charge as much as R$150 per person, with no city tour included.

## LOOKOUT MOUNTAIN AND THE ZOO

On the east edge of the city is a small mountain called **Morro da Boa Vista** that is home to the Parque Zoobotanico, a vast area filled with waterways, lakes, and animal habitats. Some of the residents include various species of macaws, alligators, miniature monkeys, and other animals from around Brazil (most from the southern region and the Pantanal). Beyond the zoo at the end of a road that winds up to the top of the mountain is a lookout tower, offering a view of the Bay of Babitonga to the east. On a clear day, it's worth a trip up. The best way is by taxi or rental car, but you can walk all the way. It takes about an hour of uphill climbing.

## PRINCIPE BAY CRUISE

You'll hear a lot about the bay cruise on the *Principe de Joinville* mini–cruise ship. It takes you all around the bay with a stop for lunch on the Island of São Francisco do Sul. Sound interesting? Here's my take: Except for the stop in São Francisco do Sul, the cruise is mostly just a drive around the bay. You get to look at the islands from the deck of the boat. A better journey would be to catch a bus out to the island, where you can spend your time checking out the sights and, if you like, heading over to the beaches on the far side. There's a bay tour that departs from the São Francisco do Sul historical village and stops at one of the remote islands so you can have a swim. Spend the night on São Francisco do Sul if you like it there (bring a minimal overnight pack with you to the island), or head out later that afternoon or in the early evening. If you're on your way down the coast to Itajaí or Balneario Camboriú, be sure to leave from Joinville and not directly from São Francisco do Sul. You can leave your bags at

the Joinville *rodoviaria* while you're visiting the island.

## CITY SIGHTS

Joinville is not really a tourist city. There are only a few attractions and most of them will not wow you. There is a main avenue that cuts through the city, from one end to the other, passing most of the important areas along the way. This street changes names several times, but is mostly known as Avenida Juscelino Kubitschek. At the south end of this street near the train station is the **Bicycle Museum** (Rua Leite Ribeiro (old train station), tel. 47/4155-0372, 9 A.M.–noon and 2–6 P.M. Tues.–Fri., free), a small collection of antique bicycles and related items, including some from the 1800s. Coming north, you'll pass the **Catedral Diocesana** (Av. Juscelino Kubistcheck, tel. 47/433-3459, 9 A.M.–5 P.M. daily) on the right. This is a modern Catholic church with some mildly impressive stained glass around the perimeter. On the other side of the church is the historic district along **Rua do Principe,** which is now the main commercial district of the city. Nearby is the **Rua das Palmeiras** (Palm Tree Street, you can't miss it) with rows of tall imperial palms leading up to the **Museu de Imigração** (229 Rua Rio Branco, tel. 47/433-3736, 9 A.M.–5 P.M. Tues.–Fri. and 11 A.M.–5 P.M. weekends, R$2). The collection of documents and artifacts related to the history of immigration to the south of Brazil is housed in a beautiful 19th-century building that was once the royal family's summer house. Farther north and east on the way to the zoo is the **Museu de Sambaqui** (Rua Dona Francisca 600, tel. 47/433-0114, 9 A.M.–5 P.M. Tues.–Fri., 11 A.M.–5 P.M. on weekends, free) a collection of indigenous artifacts from archeological digs in the vicinity as well as information about the native cultures in Brazil.

## ENTERTAINMENT AND NIGHTLIFE

Joinville is not a huge nightlife center, but there are a few places to check out in the downtown

**Rua das Palmeiras**

area after dark. First, there's the **Expresso Bar** (Av. Juscelino Kubitschek 536, tel. 47/433-9451, 6 P.M. until 2 A.M. daily), which has several types of draft beer and plenty of whisky. It's popular among the locals. The food is mediocre. A more animated scene is at the **Paiol Choperia e Restaurante** (corner of Rua Pedro Lobo and Rua Visconde de Taunay, 8 P.M. until the last customer daily). They have live music nightly with plenty of folks sitting in a big indoor-outdoor space. Not far from this and located in front of Shopping Mueller is the **Boteco Choperia** (Rua Pedro Lobo 183, tel. 47/3026-7733, 6 P.M. until 2 A.M. Mon.–Sat.), which also has live music and lots of space, plus the food there is a bit better.

## SHOPPING

The main shopping center in town is **Shopping Mueller** (Rua Pedro Lobo, tel. 47/451-8154, 8 A.M.–6 P.M. Mon.–Fri., 8 A.M.–8 P.M. on week-

ends), which has just about everything you'd expect from a large mall, including a cinema, banks with international ATMs, restaurants, and plenty of stores. On a Sunday afternoon, it may be the best place in town (read: the only place in town) to get a meal. The best shopping is in the rural areas west of the city. You'll find some good prices on clothing around the bus station downtown (Rua Principe and Avenida XV de Novembro, not the *rodoviaria*, or main bus terminal). The square around the station and surrounding streets are full of clothing stores and *lanchonetes*.

## ACCOMMODATIONS
### Under R$100

The **Hotel Principe Joinville** (Rua Jerônimo Coelho 27, Centro, tel. 47/3028-4555, www.hprincipe.com.br, R$35 s and R$60 d), near the bus station downtown, is a small and somewhat aging hotel with simple and spacious rooms that have no special charm to them. However, the service is adequate and the rooms are clean, with air, TV, phone, and Brazilian-style showers. Breakfast is included. Another economical option is the **Avenida Palace Hotel** (Av. Getúlio Vargas 75, tel. 47/433-8070, R$28–47 s and R$50–72 d). They have three types of rooms: standard (fan, TV, phone), luxury (air, TV, phone), and executive (add remote control and mini-bar), all with Brazilian showers and any arrangement of beds you desire. Breakfast is included.

The best deal in town is the 🅼 **Hotel Germânia** (Rua Minístro Calógeras 612, tel. 47/433-9886, www.hotelgermania.com.br, germania@hotelgermania.com.br, R$76 s and R$96 d). They have a new building with modern facilities and super-clean, well-appointed rooms with wooden floors. Rooms also have king-size beds, cable TV, air, gas-heated showers, and phones. They speak English and other languages and have an excellent restaurant that is open to the public and serves meat, chicken, and fish for around R$25 per person. Breakfast is not included (available for R$8 extra).

Santa Catarina

## R$100–200

The most professional hotel in town is the **Blue Tree Towers Joinville** (Av. Juscelino Kubitschek 300, tel. 47/461-8001, reservas.joinville@bluetree.com.br, R$170 s, R$186 d, and R$230 suite), with executive-style rooms, a modern lobby, rooftop sauna and gym, and restaurant and bar with 24-hour room service. Rooms have air, cable TV, in-room Internet, 2-line phones, and comfortable beds with table space for working.

## R$200–500

Probably the most charming hotel in Joinville is the **M Anthurium Park Hotel** (Rua São José 226, tel. 47/433-6299, www.anthurium.com.br, reservas@anthurium.com.br, R$249 d). The building was once the Bishop Pio de Freitas Silveira's palace and you can even stay in the very room he used. The decoration is all from the 1800s and is quite elegant, while still being cozy and charming. They have a patio bar and outdoor garden, which is often used for weddings and events. Upstairs is a pool area with sauna. Rooms have gas-heated showers, air, TV, and phone.

## FOOD

There are plenty of coffee shops and bakeries for sweets along Rua do Principe, south of the Rua das Palmeiras. You can also find executive lunch plates in this area. The best lunch in town is at the **M Biero Restaurant** (Rua Minístro Calógeras 791, tel. 47/422-3016, open for lunch and dinner daily, music shows start around 9 P.M., call for show details or see www.biero.com.br)—turn left from Rua do Principe. They have a popular self-service buffet with tons of different dishes for around R$15 per person. Lunch only. Most of the bars listed in the *Entertainment and Nightlife* section are also full-scale restaurants.

Many of Joinville's best restaurants are inside the hotels. First, there's the restaurant at the top of the **Hotel Tannenhof** (Rua Visconde de Taunay 340, tel. 47/433-8011, lunch and dinner daily), which serves plenty of German dishes in a large buffet, plus you get a nice view of the city. Meals are around R$40 per person. For a relaxed, elegant atmosphere, try the restaurant in the **Hotel Germânia** (Rua Minístro Calógeras 612) for around R$25 per person. On the ground floor of the **Ibis Hotel** (Rua Nove de Março 806, tel. 47/489-9000, 24 hours) is a pizza and salad bar for around R$20 per person.

## INFORMATION AND SERVICES

There is a tourist information booth in the main bus terminal, but they tend to take very long lunch breaks, so get there in the morning or late afternoon. You can get maps and information at most hotels. There are Internet connections in Shopping Mueller and near the urban bus station on Rua Travessa Dr. Noberto Bachmann. There are international ATMs in Shopping Mueller; check on the bottom floor near the parking lot. Be advised that there are no banks in or around the main bus terminal. This is an unexplainable phenomenon that occurs at almost all of the bus terminals in the south of Brazil.

## GETTING THERE

The Penha and Graciosa lines comes into Joinville from Curitiba or Paranaguá. The Catarinense line comes in from Florianópolis and is generally very comfortable and well run. It continues all the way to Curitiba and you can catch it just about any time of the day or night for R$12.

To get to Saõ Francisco do Sul by bus, take the Verdes Mares line from the main *rodoviaria* at 8:50 A.M., 10:30 A.M., 3 P.M., 4 P.M., 5 P.M., and 7:20 P.M. Buses returning from the island leave throughout the day, 5:20 A.M.–6:45 P.M., with an extra Sunday bus at 8:30 P.M.

To get to Corupá, take the ViaSul/Canarinho bus, which leaves at 7:35 A.M., 9:50 A.M., 2 P.M., 3:30 P.M., and 6 P.M. It costs R$10. Buses return from Corupá at 7:30 A.M., 9:30 A.M., 12:30 P.M., 3:45 P.M., and 5 P.M.

Buses directly to Blumenau are on the Alto Viaçāo Catarinense line and leave 7 A.M.–midnight daily for R$18. To Itajaí, the same line leaves almost every hour of the day and night, 7 A.M.–1:10 A.M., for R$14.

## GETTING AROUND

You can walk to most bars and restaurants downtown. You might catch a bus or take a cab to the Bicycle Museum or the zoo, as these are fairly distant—although walking is possible. Catch buses at the downtown bus station at Rua XV de Novembro. If you want to save money on bus fare, buy your ticket at the booth and not on the bus. The discount is R$.60.

# Caminho dos Principes

## ◪ SÃO FRANCISCO DO SUL

This historical village contrasts sharply with the modern industrial port just a few kilometers to the north. The little pamphlets and maps you get to guide you around the island all talk about how São Francisco do Sul was discovered in 1504 by a Frenchman, one of the earliest dockings in the Americas, and was later populated (in 1658) by Manoel Lourenço de Andrade, who brought his family, his cattle, his mining tools, and his slaves to the island. What they don't mention is how, by the 1700s, this island village had become a wild port town stirred up by the many sailing ships that docked here to refuel and animated by the success of the shipping trade. This lasted into the late 1800s when Santa Catarina became one of the world's most productive whale-hunting regions, supplying the entire country and much of the world with whale oil and derivatives. You can still imagine the bawdy, bacchanalian atmosphere as you walk along the waterfront, looking up at the historical buildings that were once markets, supply houses, and, no doubt, houses of pleasure.

Today, the streets of the old historical center are rather quiet at night. They are mostly visited during the day by the tour groups that come to the island by boat. But the historical center still holds a kind of magic carried over from its heyday. In addition to the historic waterfront buildings, there are many colonial constructions just a block or two inland, including the lovely Nossa Sra. da Graça Church.

Besides the Centro Histórico, the island features a number of beaches, popular with the locals and residents from Joinville, mostly families and adolescents, who come for the weekend. The beaches vary from urbanized to semi-urbanized, but Prainha Beach is a little jewel in the rough, with clear water, mild waves, and pleasant bars and establishments lining the opposite side of the coastal road. If you are visiting the island for only one day, get here early enough to take the 10 A.M. bay tour, have lunch in the old town center, then head straight for Prainha for an afternoon on the beach and a drink at one of the beach bars.

### Centro Histórico

The highlight of the island is the old Centro Histórico and this is where most tours of the island begin and end. The **Waterfont Architectural Complex** is a long row of colonial buildings, many of them nicely restored, that represented the main part of town in the 1700s. These buildings line the street along the waterfront for about one kilometer. On one end (around the Praça da Bandeira) are some old family manors that are not open to the public (still in the family), but are probably most interesting from the outside anyway. There are some government buildings in this area (including the Secretary of Tourism office, which many maps show on the other end of the street). You'll also find some banks and a number of restaurants around here.

Walking to the other end, you'll pass numerous stores, coffee shops, and restaurants, including the **Mercado Municipal** building. Built in 1900, the Mercado served as the principal point of commerce on the island. Today, it houses local craft shops and simple *lanchonetes*. Continuing along, you'll pass a couple of hotels in converted colonial manors and the pier, where tour boats make trips out to the archipelago in the bay. Next to the pier is the Restaurante Por-

the waterfront at São Francisco do Sul

tela, right on the water (not recommended for dining due to the stench coming off the water in this area). Turn the corner at the end of the street and you enter the old shipping area, where you'll find the **Museu Nacional do Mar** (Rua Manoel Lourenço de Andrade 133, tel. 47/444-1868, 9 A.M.–6 P.M. Tues.–Fri., 11 A.M.–6 P.M. on weekends, closed Apr.–Nov.).

There are more historical buildings in the middle of town. The most prominent area is the **Praça Getúlio Vargas,** where you'll find the **Igreja Nossa Sra. da Graça.** The church was built in 1699 out of shells, whale oil, and sand. It was later renovated and a second tower added, along with the second-story windows. Inside are traditional sacred images and carvings, along with a pipe organ that was brought in from Rio de Janeiro in 1823. The *praça* beside the church is a main point for catching the circular buses that go all around the island. During Christmas season, the *praça* is dripping with lights and decorations.

Tip: If you're taking the bus to the island and heading straight to the Centro Histórico, then ask to get off at the *rodoviaria antiga,* the old bus station, which is just a stop along a

main street near the Centro. When you get off the bus, cross the street, walk to the left, and take the first street to the right into the Centro Histórico. You can purchase tickets for the bus back to Joinville at the *rodoviaria antiga* and catch the bus on the other side of the street.

## Museu Nacional do Mar

Touted as being the only museum of its kind in the Americas, the Museum of the Ocean is dedicated to the history and culture of boats and water travel. The museum is located in an old warehouse buildings from the town's shipping days, which no doubt served at one time as centers for processing and storing whale products. The museum is extensive and includes numerous exhibits, with different kinds of boats—both miniature and actual size—along with video and audio presentations. Some of the halls are made up to represent scenes from different types of fishing or boat-making activities, giving the museum a kind of amusement-park feel. It's definitely the only museum of its kind and it's a scream. At the end is a coffee shop with a cozy wooden loft, and at the entrance is a bar and outdoor seating area, where you can sit and

Santa Catarina

Prainha, the most charming beach on the island

watch the sunset or, in the other direction, the big industrial ships load and unload cargo. Entrance to the museum is only R$3.

## Beaches

There are beaches all around the island, including several small, sandy inlets on the far side of the industrial shipping port, but there are only a few beaches worth checking out for a possible swimming or sunbathing visit. Start with **Praia de Ubatuba,** which is on the edge of the Acarai River as it opens into the ocean. There is a mixture of salt and fresh water here and an interesting arrangement of sandbars and beaches. During the week, this is a cool area to go for a swim and walk along the sand. Unfortunately, this beach fills with masses of people from poor, local neighborhoods on sunny weekends and should be avoided. On the other side of the river mouth is **Praia da Enseada,** the most popular beach on the island and a destination point for families coming from Joinville. This urban beach has a bit of everything: hotels, shops, volleyball courts, a game kiosk (mostly chess), stands selling beer and coconut water, restaurants, beach bars, playgrounds, and

a narrow strip of sand for laying out in the sun. There is an arts and crafts area where you can find leather goods, jewelry, and other handmade items. There, you can also find henna artists. In the ocean are many boats (too many), but there is an area specifically designated for swimming. The water is calm and dark. At night, the beach is fairly active with adolescents.

**Prainha** is accessible by walking to the far end of Enseada and cutting through the village. You'll come out on the other side of the point at Prainha (on the point, there is a mountain with a scenic view at the top). Here, the water is clear and blue and great for swimming. The waves here are suitable for beginning surfers and you should be careful not to swim out too far, as the undertow can be strong. There are a couple of beach kiosks and surfboard rental booths on the sand and the boardwalk follows the beach's entire length of one kilometer, offering places to sit and watch the activities. Across the street are a few bars that serve all day long and into the evening, when activities light up for people of all ages. The best are **Bar do Banana** and **Ta Na Onda.** On busy summer weekends, both Prainha and Enseada overflow with youngsters

Santa Catarina

an island getaway near Saõ Francisco do Sul

from Joinville and the beach kiosks host music and dance festivals on the sand.

## Boat Tours

Tours leave from the pier on the old waterfront at around 10 A.M. but you should get there early just to be sure. There are more tours at noon, 3:30 P.M., and 5:30 P.M. The trip is two hours long, except for the noon trip, which is three hours to include lunch. The 5:30 P.M. trip affords a view of the sunset from the boat. You go past several islands in the bay, including a look at Ilha da Rita, which was a fuel stop for many ships in the bay, with its large coal deposit, deepwater perimeter, and proximity to the mainland. You will get a chance to swim at the beach of Ilha Grande and maybe see some dolphins going out from the bay to the open ocean for the evening. The tour is R$12 per person.

## Morro do Pão de Açúcar

The best view of the island and the surrounding ocean is from the top of Morro do Pão de Açúcar. You need to drive to the mountain and all the way up. From the top, you get a 360-degree panoramic view. If you are not traveling by car, then make a deal with a taxi driver for a trip there and back. From the Centro Histórico, it should cost around R$30.

## Accommodations

If you want to stay in the Centro Histórico (for quiet nights), then try the **Zibamba Hotel** (Rua Fernandes Dias 27, tel. 47/444-2020, zibamba@saofranciscodosul.com.br, R$90 s and R$130 d). It's located in a historical building and has a pool, restaurant, and cable TV. A more economical place in the center is the **Kontiki** (Rua Babitonga 211, tel. 47/444-2232, R$45 s and R$65 d), which is partially in a historical building and partially in a remodeled section. Avoid the economical **Hotel de Ilha** (Rua Marechal Deodoro 68) as the employees have attitude problems and can be quite rude.

On the beaches, try **Pousada Prainha** (Rua São Luís 41, Prainha, tel. 47/449-034, www.pousadaprainha.com.br, pousadaprainha@onda.com.br, R$40 s and R$55 d) on the far end of Prainha Beach. They have rooms with small kitchen facilities, ceiling fans, and minibars. It's popular with surfers. You can also try the  **Hotel Fragata** (Av. Atlântica 1738, tel. 47/449-1040, hotelfragata@ilhanet.com.br, R$80 s and R$100 d) on the far end of Enseada Beach. They have large, clean rooms and are quite comfortable for a beachfront hotel. Breakfast is included.

## Food

In the Centro Histórico, there are places to eat along the waterfront. For lunch, try **Conteiner Point** (Av. Atlântica, no phone, change hours above to 11–2 A.M.) at the south end. They have a great, all-you-can-eat lunch buffet for only R$7.50 per person. For dinner, try the **Restaurante Zinhabatista** (Rua Praça da Bandeira 58, tel. 47/444-3960, no phone, 11–2 A.M. daily) on the same end of town. They have seafood plates for around R$25 per person. There is a simple pizza restaurant in front of Zinhabatista and a good coffee shop, called **Café Show,** also in front.

## SCHROEDER

About half of the Shroeder municipality is located in the mountains. It's a very rural area, filled with small banana farms and residences. The town was first settled in the early 1900s by Germans of the Lutheran Evangelical denomination. Later, a host of Italian immigrants joined the party. The farmlands are generally situated at the foot of the mountains. Deeper and higher into the hills are beautiful rivers and waterfalls, with abundant flora and fauna of the region. A highlight is the **Vale do Rio Branco,** where the Bracinho River is born. Most of the area is an ecological preserve and you'll find places to practice all sort of nature activities, including rafting, canoeing, hiking, and rappelling. Look for the Arroio do Macaco, where you can hike up to several waterfalls, including the Macaco Waterfall, which is 40 meters high. The area has several trails and even campgrounds.

In the town of Schroeder, you'll find plenty of German culture and tradition, principally in the food and people. The streets of the city are clean and wide. There is an area on the bank of the Duas Mamas River called Prainha that has bars and restaurants with outdoor seating. In October, the city celebrates **Schroederfest** with German bands, parades, and outdoor events. It's a good time to visit the town.

## CORUPÁ

The 12,000 residents of Corupá are a quiet, reserved bunch, mostly of German descent. They go about their daily lives in this tiny rural village carrying on an intimate relationship with the banana. This region is responsible for most of the bananas grown in the country. As you wander around the village and up to the various mountains and waterfalls, you'll pass one banana farm after the next. Most farms are small and independent, but there are some large producers here, too. All told, the town is the largest producer of bananas in Brazil. In

one of the many banana plantations around Corupá

January, they have their **Festival of the Banana,** when you can find just about everything banana, from sweet and savory foods to crafts made from the peels.

But it's not really the banana that brings visitors to this region. Corupá is the portal to a world of water. The area is laced with rivers cascading down steep mountains, and is a sanctuary for anyone who loves waterfalls. Since this is a rural area, with homes and small farms, you won't have to do a lot of distant hiking into the mountains. Dirt roads lead past the farms and up into the hillsides. From these roads, short trails take you to the treasures within. Don't get the idea that this is an urbanized area. The town center is tiny and its paved roads do not extend very far. You can walk for hours without seeing much besides rolling hills carpeted with banana trees.

As you get out past the farms, you'll start climbing in altitude and getting close to the cascades. There is a waterfall park with designated trails that take you past 14 separate falls, many of which are open for swimming. There are campgrounds up in the mountains and a few hotels in town. Otherwise, you're pretty much on your own. This is one of the few areas in Brazil where you can enjoy the countryside without a guide and without worry. The best time to visit is March–May, just after the rainy season, or in September and October, just before the rainy season. In my opinion, this is the coup de grâce of the rural countryside west of Joinville and there's little reason to stop anywhere else.

## Sights

There are a few interesting sights right around the town of Corupá. First and foremost is the **Seminario Sagrado** (Rua Padre Gabriel Lux 900, tel. 47/375-1194, hours vary depending on the season and the weather. Call to confirm that they are open), a Catholic seminary built in 1929 that now contains a museum along with the main chapel and expansive grounds for walking and meditating. A taxi out to the Seminario is R$8. The **largest water lily in the world**—on record as reaching up to 2.5 meters in diameter and even bigger than those in the Amazon Jungle—is available for viewing between March and June at the charming home of Manfred Millnitz (Rua Francisco Antônio Piccione 540, tel. 47/375-2411, open Jun.–Sept., hours vary so call to confirm that they are open). The property also includes large gardens with paths for strolling and viewing the many rare tropical plants. There are places to sit and contemplate and a small souvenir shop. For a taste of the local fire water, head over to the **Alambique Linzmeyer** (Rua Roberto Serdel 2961, tel. 47/375-2214, no specific hours, call to let then know you're coming). There you can check out the small *cachaça* still and sample the goods. You should call ahead for all of these sights.

## Rural Walks

You don't want to miss the pleasant walks that you can take around the rural farmlands of Corupá by driving or taking taxis to all the major points outside of town. However, distances are rather challenging here, so you can't just set out walking from town without some kind of plan. Here are a couple of good ideas: Try a hike along the south road going out to the Seminario and then to the Alambique Linzmeyer. This is about nine kilometers there and back again and could take half a day. If you don't want to spend that much time, then have a taxi drop you off at the Praça da Figueira and from there you can walk back into town (about six kilometers on the south road). On your stroll back into town, you'll pass many of the town's sights along with some picturesque farmlands.

Another good walk is out to the Floricultura Chácara Bom Retiro to the north of town. It's only about five kilometers there and back. A hike out to the Cachoeira do Ano Bom up the Estrada Ano Bom takes you past many small farms before you get to the waterfall. It's about 11 kilometers there and back again. Again, an alternative is to take a taxi all the way to Cachoeira Braço Esquerdo and walk the eight kilometers back to town.

## Parque das Cachoeiras

The most popular excursion in the area is a trip to the Parque das Cachoeiras (Waterfall Park), about 20 kilometers from town up Rio Novo and into the Vale do Rio Novo (Rio Novo Valley). You can drive or take a taxi all the way to the base of the park, where you pay R$5 per person to go inside. At the base of the park are some stores and a simple restaurant (when open during the dry season). Two trails lead up the mountain past the waterfalls. One trail (three kilometers) passes the first 13 and the other (2.5 kilometers) passes the first and the last. Of the 14 waterfall stations that you can visit, a few are open for swimming (the first one at the bottom being one of the best). The hike is quite steep and you should bring good tennis shoes and light clothing and take your time. It takes about 1.5 hours to hike one of these trails. But since you'll want to make plenty of stops, you should plan on spending most of the day here. The last waterfall at the top is, as luck would have it, the most magnificent. Called *Salto Grande* (Big Drop), it's 125 meters tall. Its image is on most of the town's postcards and tourist materials.

If you do not have a car, then the best way to get to and from the park is by taxi. Going

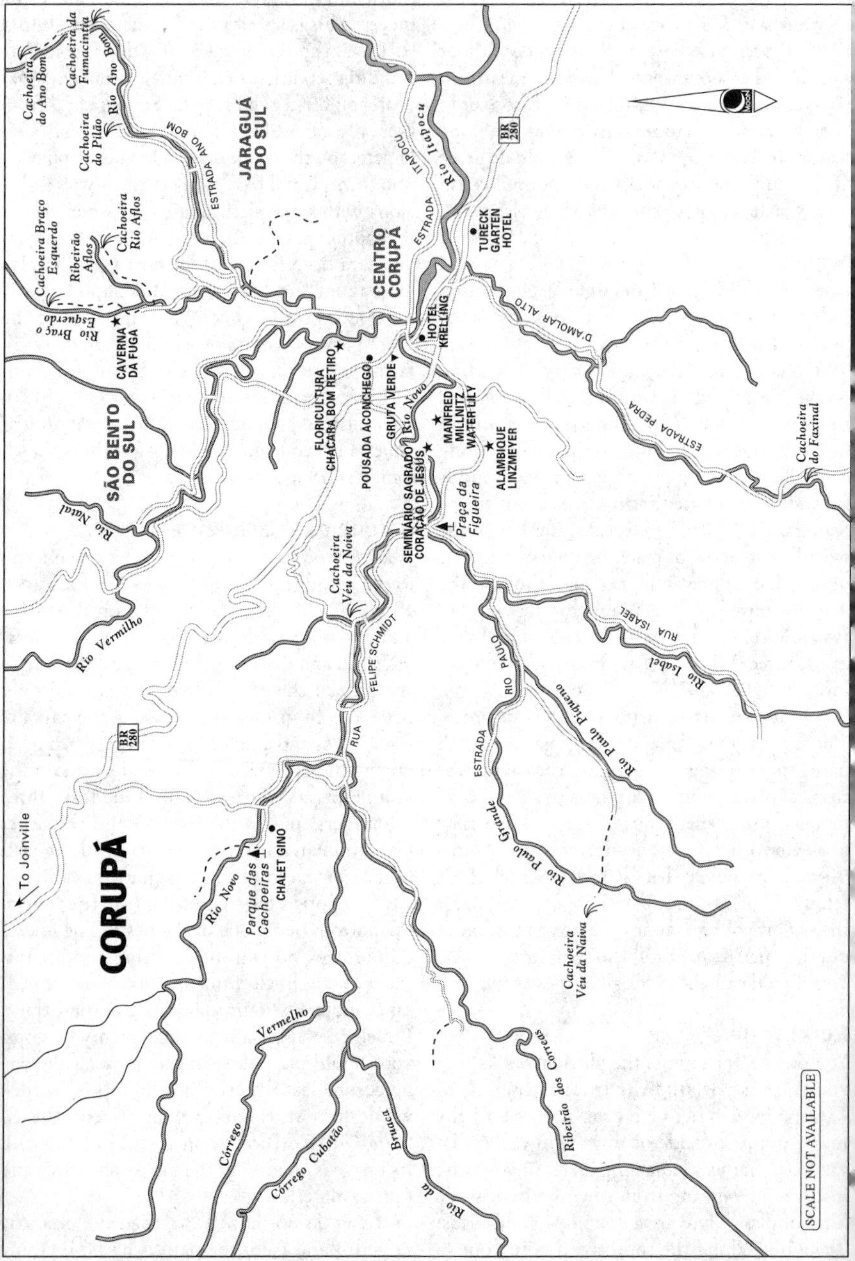

# CORUPÁ

To Joinville

**SÃO BENTO DO SUL**

**JARAGUÁ DO SUL**

**CENTRO CORUPÁ**

Cachoeira da Fumacinha
Cachoeira do Ano Bom
Cachoeira do Pilão
Rio Ano Bom
Cachoeira Braço Esquerdo
Cachoeira Rio Aflus
Ribeirão Aflus
Rio Braço Esquerdo
**CAVERNA DA FUGA**
ESTRADA ANO BOM

Rio Natal

Rio Vermilho

Rio Novo
Parque das Cachoeiras
**CHALET GINO**

Vermelho

Córrego

Córrego Cabatão

Rio da Bruaca

Ribeirão das Corredeiras

**FLORICULTURA CHÁCARA BOM RETIRO**
**POUSADA ACONCHEGO**
**GRUTA VERDE**
Rio Nova
**SEMINÁRIO SAGRADO CORAÇÃO DE JESUS**
Cachoeira Véu da Noiva
RUA FELIPE SCHMIDT

**HOTEL KRELLING**
**MANFRED MILLNITZ WATER LILY**
Praça da Figueira
**ALAMBIQUE LINZMEYER**

D'AMOLAR ALTO

ESTRADA ITAPOCU
Rio Itapocu

**TURECK GARTEN HOTEL**

BR 280

ESTRADA PEDRA
RUA ISABEL
Rio Isabel

Rio Paulo
ESTRADA
Rio Paulo Grande
Rio Paulo Pequeno
Cachoeira Véu da Noiva

Cachoeira do Faxinal

BR 280

out there and back will cost you around R$22. You can make a package deal with one of the taxi drivers for a round trip with an hour or two wait in-between for around R$40 for as many people as you can fit into the car. If you plan to stay longer, then make arrangements with the driver to pick you up at a specific time. Be sure to have him stop at the view point overlooking the Semenario on the way out.

## Ano Bom Waterfalls

The Estrada do Ano Bom on the east side of town, goes up to some great mountainous areas. To access the Estrada, you have to cross the train tracks on the south side of town and turn left when you reach the Estrada at the end. The paved road will end and you'll follow a dirt road the rest of the way. The best way to see these sights is to take a taxi most of the way and then hike. You can even walk back to town afterward if you're not too tired. Highlights include the **Cachoeira do Ano Bom** at the far end of the Rio Ano Bom (the highest point in the area), and the **Cachoeira do Pilão** along the same trajectory. An alterna-

tive path is up the Rio Braço Esquerdo (Left Arm River), which leads to the **Caverna da Fuga** (with a waterfall inside the cave—bring a flashlight), **Cachoeira Rio Aflos,** and the **Cachoeira Braço Esquerdo.** The latter is an entire area of small and large falls with facilities for rafting, camping, rappelling, climbing, and hiking.

## Accommodations

There is only one *pousada* in the town of Corupá and it has only three rooms. Called **Pousada Aconchego** (Av. Getúlio Vargas 586, tel. 47/375-1078, about R$50 per couple), it's in the home of Marialuise Stern, who rents her charming rooms. Call ahead for reservations. If you can't get into Marialuise's place, then you have a few other options. One is to stay at the funky, surreal fleabag **Hotel Krelling** (Rua Neiru Ramos, R$10), near the train tracks (bring your own toilet paper). The hotel and rooms look like something out of the film *Barton Fink,* but there are plenty of rooms and it's cheap, if a bit noisy from the trains. During the preparation of this book, the hotel was up

Small farms hug the hillsides in rural Corupá.

for sale, so it may not be there when you arrive. A second option is to stay outside of town at the **Tureck Garten Hotel** (Rodovia BR-280, tel. 47/375-1482, www.tureckgarten.com.br, hotel@tureckgarten.com.br, R$75), which is just off the highway coming into town. They have A-frame, chalet-style rooms with all the normal comforts of a hotel: pool, lake, restaurant, and clean rooms with wood floors, air, phones, and mini-bars.

There are two small chalets near the Waterfall Park called **Chalet Gino** (tel. 47/375-1428). These are great for couples or groups, especially if you arrive by car. Call Gino for prices, directions, and reservations.

Finally, you can camp at a number of different campgrounds in the area. There are two near the Waterfall Park. One is called **Recanto Dias** (tel. 47/375-2281, call on the weekend to make reservations) and another is called **Recanto das Cachoeiras** (tel. 47/375-2202), which has camping facilities and some private chalets.

Corupá is a paradise of waterfalls.

### Food
If you're in town for lunch, head over to **Gruta Verde** (Av. Getúlio Vargas 159, no phone) for a great lunch buffet for only R$7.50 per person. Although served from 11 A.M.–2 P.M., the food goes fast, so get there early. For snacks, head over to the bakery (across from the main *praça* where the bus stops, 6 A.M.–8 P.M. Mon.–Fri., 6 A.M.–2 P.M. on weekends). There, you can find great finger foods and even better German-style sweets, like banana and strawberry strudel, cakes, pies, and cookies. You'll also find banana chips and banana bread. The peanut macaroons are great for taking on hikes.

## Inland German Colonies

The mountain colonies that rest inland from the Emerald Coast in Santa Catarina are known for having the most German of the German communities in Brazil. But there are also many Italian, Polish, and Portuguese roots here, and the area is often called the European Valley. Three principal destinations await tourists, with Brusque and Pomerode being the most interesting. During the popular German festival of Octoberfest, these towns go into high gear with music, dance, and culinary wonders from northern Europe.

### BLUMENAU
Perhaps trying to compensate for the fact that it's not anywhere near as quaint as its neighbors Brusque and Pomerode, Blumenau puts on a heck of an **Octoberfest.** That's what brings most people to the city. That and the great prices on textiles (clothing, towels, bedding, etc.) that are manufactured here. Most likely, you're passing through town on your way to Pomerode, but if you have time to stick

around for awhile, there are a few attractions that might keep you interested.

## Rua XV de Novembro

The main part of town is around Rua XV de Novembro and this is where you'll find plenty of shops and restaurants. You'll also see some traditional architecture, such as the **Castelinho** (Rua XV de Novembro 1050) and the **Sociadade Dramático-Musical Carlos Gomes** (Rua XV de Novembro 1181). The latter is the location of many of the city's cultural presentations, including ballet and chamber music. It has a revolving stage and room for more than 1,100 people. While you're strolling along the street, check out the **Museu da Cerveja** (Rua XV de Novembro at Praça Hercílio Luz), which is inside the Continental Pub. Finally, you can take a look at the **Prefeitura Antiga** (Rua XV de Novembro 161), with its traditional German architecture. The building now serves as the city's tourist information center and cultural center. Inside, you'll find exhibitions from local artists and students.

## Vila Itoupava

One of the city's more interesting rural districts, Vila Itoupava is about 25 kilometers from the city and a world apart. Most of the 7,000 inhabitants speak German. There is a small village in which you can find typical baked goods and fruit preserves. The idea here is to stroll around the rural countryside and take in the unique culture and charming landscape.

## Parks

The largest designated park in the area, the **Spitzkopf Park** has more than 500 square kilometers of forest with rivers, waterfalls, and natural swimming holes. There are numerous trails in the area and you can hike up to the peak and look over the entire region. There are a few *pousadas* in the area if you decide that this is more to your liking than the downtown area. Only 15 kilometers from downtown, you can get here by bus or taxi. The **Parque das Nascentes** is located 23 kilometers from the city

and has numerous trails and roads to explore. There are several fresh-water springs and waterfalls here and you can find campgrounds and rooms for rent.

## Accommodations

If you decide to stay the night in Blumenau, check out the **Hotel Blumenhof** (Rua das Missões 103, Ponta Aguda, tel. 47/326-4868), which is a traditional German-style building with comfortable rooms and a good breakfast buffet (included). There's also the **Hotel Steinhausen Colonial** (Rua Buenos Aires 275, Ponta Aguda, tel. 47/322-5276, R$70 s, R$90 d), which is smaller and more quaint. For a modern hotel with comfortable rooms and good service, try the **Parthenon The Town House** (Rua Curt Hering 80, Centro, www.accorhotels.com, R$140 s, R$180 d).

# BRUSQUE

When you arrive in the center of Brusque, the first thing you'll probably notice is the northern European architecture. Rooftops are pointed to help keep the heavy snows from damaging the structures. One day, perhaps, it will snow here. Still, it's interesting to see the architecture in the middle of a tropical country. The best example is the **Mayor's Office** (Prefeitura Municipal), located in the Centro I area of town, along with most of the other sights. There, you'll also find great prices on textiles, including jeans, towels, and other articles that are made in the area. Highlights of the town also include the **zoo,** with its large archway entrance of German design. There, you'll find a huge park with animals from all over Brazil, including a small Pantanal area with lakes and animals from the Pantanal region. Inside the park, you can take a long chairlift up to one of the peaks while gasping at the incredible view from up there. For an underwater version, head to the **Brusquárium** at the other end of the chairlift, where you can look into 16 different aquariums. There is also an orchid garden inside the park.

Like most of the communities of this region, Brusque celebrates **Octoberfest** with a vengeance. Draft beer and traditional foods are the highlight, but there is plenty of German music and dance. A special feature of the Octoberfest in Brusque is the clothing fair, where the city's manufacturers, small and large, put their products up for sale at wholesale prices. The main event takes place in the Fenarreco Pavilion from morning to night.

If you arrive in the city and want to get right into sampling the beer, head over to the **Praça Barão de Schneeburg,** where you can sit and sip and watch the interesting characters of the town pass by.

## POMERODE

The most German of the towns in the European Valley, Pomerode is best known as the place where most people still speak German as their first language. Besides this, the town is famous for its **Festa Pomerana,** which takes place during the first half of January—a sort of preparation for Octoberfest. The festival is very authentic with children running around in knickers playing the accordion. There are children's parades, German square dancing, and traditional German games. Of course, this is all accompanied by traditional food and beer. For details, check out www.pomerode.com.br or www.pomerode.sc.gov.br/festapomerana.

If you want to do some shopping while you're in town, check out the **Centro de Artes e Artesanato** (Anexo ao Portal Turístico, no phones all of these are open from 10 A.M.–6 P.M Mon.–Fri., 10 A.M.–2 P.M. on weekends), where you'll find all kinds of crafts and souvenirs Also, there's the **Atelier Silvana Pujol** (Rua Testo Alto 1087), who will charm you with her painted eggs, and **Souvenir Ecke** (Rua XV de Novembro 821), with typical porcelain pieces and ceramics from the region.

You can stay at the **Hotel e Restaurante Bergblick** (Rua Georg Zeplin 120, tel. 47/387-0952, www.bergblick.com.br, R$85 s, R$155 d). They have five rooms, two master suites, and one large flat—all in German architecture with that special Germanic hospitality. You can also have a rural experience at the **Hotel Fazenda Mundo Antigo** (Rua Riberão Herdt 430, tel. 47/387-3143, www.mundoantigo.com.br), where you can partake of a working ranch. There is a restaurant that serves food from the farm.

# Balneario Camboriú

For travelers coming from Joinville, the first beach worth stopping to visit for a few days is Balneario Camboriú. Known as the Copacabana of the South, the situation here is very much like Copacabana in Rio. You have a long stretch of urban beach, full of sunbathers, volleyball players, cyclists, and joggers. There is a prominent boardwalk that follows the entire stretch of beach (about seven kilometers) and passes various kiosks that sell cold coconut water, beer, and snacks. Balneario Camboriú is a popular vacation spot for Argentineans and Paraguayans and the place can get very busy in the summer months. People can be seen drinking *chá matte* from their bowl-shaped hollow gourds—a tradition in the south of South America. The waves are calm, the water is warm, and the strip of sand is medium-wide. There are showers all along the beach and you can rent beach chairs and umbrellas if you find a spot at which you'd like to stay put for a while. Lined up along the coastal road are many tall buildings: a mixture of hotels, restaurants, and private condominiums. Like Copacabana in Rio, the street parallel to the coastal highway is full of shopping malls, boutique shops, restaurants, and all kinds of activity—even more so than the coastal road. Within 10 kilometers to the north and south of Camboriú Beach are various other beaches, each with a different personality.

Perhaps Balneario Camboriú does not have quite the grand scale that its Rio de Janeiro cousin has, and the city itself has none of the important historical monuments or internationally famous attractions. But what you won't find here in the south is the crime and pollution that sits like a dark cloud over Rio. Here, you can enjoy a night on the town without looking over your shoulder the entire time.

## THE BOARDWALK AND AVENIDA BRASIL

Two main roads pass through town, parallel to one another, and go the entire length of the beach. These are known as Avenida Atlantica and Avenida Brasil. If it weren't a total of 14 kilometers, it would be a great diversion to walk up one street and down the other. Alas, most travelers are not up for such a hike and end up catching the big red tractor bus (called the *bondindinho,* bown-djeen-DJEEN-yo) that makes the journey up one street and down the other 24 hours a day for only R$2.50. It's a great way to see everything in town and the best way to get to the far end of the beach, where several

things occur: During the day, you can catch a **boat excursion** on a schooner or pirate ship going out along the coastline to Praia Laranjeiras or ride the gondola into the **Parque Unipraias** and then over to Praia Laranjeiras. At night, the far end of town is where you'll find most of the bars and nightclubs that continue their festivities until sunrise.

There are several walkways, closed to traffic, that cross between Avenidas Atlântica and Brasil, forming pedestrian markets. These are great places for shopping and you can find things like restaurants, bars, Internet cafés, and money changers. One such street is **Avenida Central** (ask the *trocador,* or cashier, on the *bondindinho* to let you off there). About halfway along the boardwalk is the Praça Almirante Tamandaré, which is a central area with stands selling arts and crafts, outdoor stages, and plenty of activity during the day. Just inland from this *praça* on Avenida Brasil is the central part of town, where you'll find Atlântico Shopping, money changers, movie theaters, and lots of hotels.

**Balneario Camboriú from the Unipraias observation deck**

# ⓜ PARQUE UNIPRAIAS

The best way to get from Praia Camboriú to Praia Laranjeiras to the south is by taking the gondola up and over the hill that is the Parque Unipraias. But high-altitude transportation between the beaches is not the only reason for going. First, the gondola ride itself provides a spectacular view of the coast from an altitude of 240 meters. There are 47 gondolas that carry up to six people each (although most go out with just a few people in them, even in peak season). The mid-way point between the two beaches is the Estação Mata Atlântica (Atlantic Rainforest Station) and the main part of Unipraias Park. Here, you can exit the gondola and walk around the nature park to find the three scenic-view platforms. The views from here are at least as impressive as those from the gondolas. On the other side of the hill is what they call the Adventure Park, which offers two ropes courses built into the trees that take you through the forest. Each course has 12 activities and takes about 1.5 hours to complete. The courses cost an extra R$20 each. They are well built, secure, and the guides are excellent—a great value if you know ropes courses.

You can continue from the middle station to the third station, called Estação Laranjeiras, which brings you to the Laranjeiras Beach. The three stations are equipped with bathrooms, snack stands, and even art exhibitions. The first station at Camboriú Beach has a great outdoor seating area from which you can look out on the southern point of the beach.

Parque Unipraias gondolas operate 9 A.M.–8 P.M. and cost R$20 per person. Be sure to keep your ticket when you exit the Laranjeiras station, as this will be needed for your return trip. If you plan to partake of the course, then be sure to bring tennis shoes.

# PARQUE CYRO GEVAERD

There are two museums and a zoo at the Cyro Gevaerd Park. The **Museu Arqueológico** has various indigenous artifacts from the area and the **Museu do Artesanato Catarinense** is an exhibition of Azorian arts and crafts. The zoo has lots of tropical birds, some monkeys, and other mammals, as well as aquariums with fresh- and salt-water fish from the local waters. The grounds are extensive and lovely. You can catch a free shuttle out to the park or Avenida Brasil.

# CRISTO LUZ

To top off its similarity with Copacabana in Rio, Balneario Camboriú comes complete with a Cristo monument overlooking the ocean. This one is holding a light, which changes colors each night. During the day, you can visit the monument, which includes a restaurant with a panoramic view of the coast, a snack bar, shops, and areas to sit and look out over the city. You can catch a free ride to the Cristo monument along Avenida Atlantica.

# BEACHES TO THE NORTH

Beaches north of Camboriú include a few very small beaches on the north end of town and several others up the coast, 10–40 kilometers away. The small beaches on the north end of Camboriú are called **Canto** (a tiny, sandy area with small waves), **Buraco** (a nice beach with medium-sized waves and large hotel taking up most of it), and **Amores** (with strong waves for surfing and a popular area for sunbathing). Farther up the coast toward Itajaí is **Praia Brava**, a long stretch of sand that is semi-deserted and semi-isolated and has only a few beach bars spread out along the sand. There are dirt roads and few structures here, but this is an excellent beach for couples and anyone who wants to get away from the crowd. There are mild waves for surfing and the water is great for swimming (although not transparent). The best way to get to these northern beaches is by taxi.

## Itajaí

The next town to the north of Balneario Camboriú is Itajaí. The town is a kind of hub for buses coming in from Blumenau or heading down the coast to Porto Belo (the bus route is from Itajaí to Porto Belo and back, and buses make the trip every half hour). There are three principal parts to Itajaí: Navegantes, downtown, and the Cabeçudas beaches. The **Navegantes** area is accessed by taking a ferryboat across the Itajaí Açú River. It consists of a small urban area and an endless stretch of beach going up to the north. The beach here is not popular with tourists. If you go there to check it out, be sure to walk to the right when you get off the ferryboat.

The **downtown** area is where all the hotels are located. At the pier, where the cruise ships dock (Itajaí is a main stop for many cruises in the area), there is a small *praça* that hosts shows and activities during the summer months and a main commercial road heading into town, called Rua Hercílio Luz. Along this road is where all the nightlife in town takes place—especially at the Armazém Pub, which is near the *praça*. There are a couple of attractions in town, such as the **Igreja Matriz,** a huge structure that copies the neo-gothic style. It's best viewed from the outside, but there are some interesting stained-glass windows on the inside. The highlights are the carved wood doors and the life-sized statue of Moses. Another interesting building is across the street, called the **Barbosa Rodrigues** building. It contains the Museum of Itajaí and is best viewed from the outside.

The Itajaí bus terminal looks like it belongs in a city of two million inhabitants. It's quite impressive for such a little town. However, like so many of these bus terminals in the south of Brazil, there are no banks here, so your best bet is to come into town with cash. From the bus station, catch the yellow *Camboriú* bus for R$2 all the way to Balneario Camboriú or to the Matriz Church, where you can transfer to a bus going out to the Cabeçudas beach area, or just catch a cab for about R$10.

There are three beaches in the Cabeçudas area of Itajaí and the locals like to refer to them as the most charming beaches in Brazil. That's definitely an exaggeration, but the beaches do get extra points for being rather cute. The area around these beaches is full of upper-middle-class homes, so there are no monstrous buildings to break the skyline. **Praia Atalaia** is about 500 meters long and has a wide sandy area, perfect for volleyball and other beach sports. There are medium-sized waves here and some surfing goes on. The water is dark green and there is a bar on the far end. The next beach is **Praia do Papagaio,** one of the cutest beaches you'll ever see. It consists of a tiny sandy area surrounded by rocky hills on all sides. On one of the hills is a large stone formation that looks like a parrot's head. There is a grassy area above this beach that is great for picnics and you can go swimming here, as the waves are very mild. The final beach is **Cabeçudas,** a semi-urbanized stretch of sand with plenty of tourists mixed in with the locals. There is a boardwalk that extends along the entire one kilometer of beach and several kiosks to serve drinks and snacks. The sand is moderately crowded with folks getting sun and playing on the large rock formations in the water. There are a few beach bars on the other side of the coastal road, where there is plenty of shade under the trees.

From here, you can catch the bus back to the Matriz Church, where you can get to your next destination, or have one of the bars call you a taxi (there are no taxis waiting here) to take you straight to Balneario Camburiú (about R$20 to Atlantico Shopping).

## BEACHES TO THE SOUTH

The most interesting beach in the area is **Praia Laranjeiras,** and not just because you can get there from the Unipraias gondola. Laranjeiras is a small stretch of beach (less than one kilometer long) that is lined with bars and restaurants on a sort of extended deck that leans over the sand and surf. The music is constant, and the atmosphere is festive. You can sit on the deck area at one of the establishments or down on the sand, where the restaurants are only allowed to use the first meter or so—the rest of the sand is free space and you can rent a chair and umbrella and find a cozy little spot. Costumed vendors pass by with trinkets. When you're ready to cool off, you can swim out into the warm, blue-green water. On the far end

the rock formation at Praia do Papagaio

of the beach is a small pier where the pirate ships dock when coming in from Camboriú. There are small streets perpendicular to the beach that are lined with shops, making the whole scene a kind of quaint little village. On summer days, Laranjeiras is the most crowded beach in the area and you can hardly see the sand for all the colorful umbrellas.

Beaches south of Laranjeiras are much more private and the waves and tide along this part of the coast are somewhat rough. This especially goes for **Taquarinhas Beach,** just south of Laranjeiras, where swimming is not recommended. Still, sunbathing and sitting under an umbrella with a cool drink are perfectly acceptable. That's also true at **Praia Pinha,** as long as you're naked. Touted as Brazil's first nude beach, Pinha operates in an official way and guards keep couples and singles separate for good measure. It's probably one of the most populated nude beaches in the country, largely due to the many Argentineans that come here (Brazilians being somewhat conservative about public nudity that isn't part of a Carnaval parade).

The best way to get to these southern beaches is to walk or take a taxi from Laran-

jeiras Beach. It's about five kilometers from Laranjeiras to Pinha.

## ENTERTAINMENT AND NIGHTLIFE

There are activities going on all over town and all you have to do is ride the Bondindinho back and forth to make your selection. The most electric places are on the south side of town toward the Unipraias Park. One option in the area is **Mineirinho** (Av. Brasil at Rua 3300, no phone, 8 P.M. daily). The boardwalk stays pretty lively at night and Avenida Brasil is active until the wee hours.

## ACTIVITIES AND EXCURSIONS

There are boat excursions that head from the Camboriú River out along the beach and over to Laranjeiras. They cost R$10–15 per person. Some include a stop for swimming. Others offer activities on the boat itself. The appeal is mostly for kids and Brazilian and Argentinean families, since all the activities onboard take place in Portuguese and Spanish. A better idea is to take a short helicopter ride above the beaches or a fast banana-boat haul. All of this is available on the far end of the beach, toward Parque Unipraias. Boats line up along the river and the heliport is nearby as well. Also nearby is the Kiddie Car Park, where kids can go driving.

# ACCOMMODATIONS

There are hotels all over Balneario Camboriú. The largest cluster is near Atlantica Shopping where many restaurants and shops are also huddled. Naturally, the beachfront hotels are more expensive than those on Avenida Brasil or other inland roads. A good cluster of hotels is around the north end of the beach between the two avenues, and the cheapest hotels are out on the Avenida dos Estados on the north end of the beach. Here are some to get you started:

## Under R$100

The **Hotel Estrela do Mar** (Rua Antônio Bittencourt 417, tel. 47/367-3325, R$35 s and R$70 d peak season) is a very economical place with simple but clean rooms. It's located on the northern end of town a few blocks inland from the beach. Ask for discounts for low-season or extended stays.

## R$100–200

The **N Tropikalya Hotel** (Rua 401 15, tel. 47/367-2570, www.tropikalya.com.br, hoteis@tropikalya.com.br, R$40 s and R$70 d low season, R$80 s and R$120 d peak season) is a relatively modern place with a cozy feeling. It has 29 rooms, a restaurant, and parking. Rooms have air, TV, safe, and phone. A decent breakfast buffet is included. Next door is the best self-service lunch in town.

The other hotels in this group are all about the same and even appear in the same basic area of town. They are all in large, 30-year-old buildings and have no special charm to speak of. They offer pools, saunas, gyms, and restaurants inside. The rooms feature air, TV, mini-bar, safe, and phone. The service is all about the same and the prices are not much different either. **Hamburgo Palace Hotel** (Rua 1901, No. 333, tel.

47/367-1585, www.hamburgopalace.com.br, hotel@hamburgopalace.com.br, R$80 s and R$100 d peak season). They're about 15-percent less during low season. **Hotel Blumenau** (Rua 1001, No. 129, tel. 47/367-2100, www.hotelblumenau.com.br, R$100 s and R$130 d peak season). **HM Plaza Hotel** (Rua 1901, No. 291, tel. 47/367-3235, www.hoteishm.com.br, R$100 s and R$150 d peak season).

## Over R$200

Top-end hotels include the **N Hotel D'Sintra** (Av. Atlantica 1040, tel. 47/363-4080, R$350 d peak season), a beachfront hotel with a modern interior. Rooms have air, TV, phone, and safe, and some have an ocean view. The award for the "Most Charming Hotel in the Area" goes to the **N Pousada Felissimo** (Rua Alles Blau 201, tel. 47/360-6291, www.pousadafelissimo.com.br, info@pousadafelissimo.com.br, R$350–550 peak season), located on Praia Amores on the north end of town. They have a large, tropical garden area, pool, sauna, parking, and a gazebo bar with a cozy atmosphere at night. Rooms are super-clean and comfortable with king-size bed, air, phone, safe, CD player, and veranda.

# FOOD

The best self-service lunch in town is at the **N Restaurante Flamboyant** (Rua 401, tel. 47/366-7771), one block inland from Shopping Atlântico. They have an all-you-can-eat buffet with several types of meat, salads, and pasta dishes for only R$6 per person. They don't have a lot of space and they get crowded, so get there early. The **Oficina do Sabor** (Av. Brasil at Rua 3750, change address to Rua 3750, number 281 at Av. Brasil, tel. 47/361-8615, lunch and dinner daily, R$25) is a barbecue-style restaurant with all kinds of meat and chicken cooked over an open fire. For an Italian experience, try the **Villa Vecchia Trattoria** (Rua 511, No. 14, tel. 47/367-5645, 6 P.M.–midnight daily, R$35), next to Shopping Atlântico. They have fish and pasta dishes, including pasta with mussels, and all fresh ingredients. On the beachfront is

Ⓜ **Chaplin Bar e Restaurante** (Av. Atlântica 2220, tel. 47/367-0050, 6 P.M.–midnight daily, R$40), a great spot for hanging out, and they serve a variety of dishes.

## INFORMATION AND SERVICES

The information booth is on the road into town and if you're not driving into town, you'll miss it. You can try at the information office of the Parque Unipraias, which is located at the bottom of the Camboriú station (down the stairs to the parking lot, then outside to the offices in the back of the building on the side facing the river, not the ocean). They are not a tourist information office, but are there to assist large groups coming to the park. Just make like you're interested in returning with a group and they'll answer all your questions. There are Internet cafés all over town, especially around Shopping Atlântico. Some also have private phone booths for international calls (usually expensive). You can find money changers on Avenida Brasil near the shopping center. Try **Planet Cámbio** (Av. Brasil 601, no phone, 8 A.M.–6 P.M. daily). International ATMs can be found in the shopping center. Look for Banco do Brasil and Banco 24 Horas.

If you rented a car in Joinville to make the trip down the coast, then be sure to book a hotel that has parking facilities. The traffic in Balneario Camboriú can be treacherous in the summer.

## GETTING THERE AND AROUND

Buses coming from Joinville will stop first in Itajaí before heading to Balneario Camburiú. The main highway is BR-101. Getting between major beach towns along this part of the coast (Itajaí, Balneario Camburiú, Itapema, and Porto Belo) is easily accomplished by bus from about 7–1 A.M. for a cost of R$6–8. The bus passes each of the main bus terminals in Itajaí, Camboriú, and Itapema and makes a final stop in Porto Belo. Taxi rides between these towns will average about R$30 each.

# The Emerald Coast

The ocean along this part of the southern coast is so green that the area came to be known as the Emerald Coast. There's a 10-kilometer stretch going south from the center of Itapema that starts out urbanized and ends up semi-secluded. Farther down are the small beaches of Porto Belo with a highlight being the small, sandy inlets on the Island of Porto Belo. Finally, on the Bombinhas Peninsula are numerous beaches, mostly urbanized and popular on weekends with the locals. Off the coast of Bombinhas is the famous Arvoredo Marine Preserve, which is a sanctuary for marine life and an excellent place for snorkeling and scuba diving, with visibility of up to 25 meters.

The first thing to resolve is in which of these areas you want to make your home base. My advice: Stay in Porto Belo if you like quaint accommodations and don't plan on staying out late. Also stay there if you plan to visit the marine preserve most of the time. Stay in Itapema if you want nightlife and urbanized beaches with plenty of restaurants and bars and activity on the beach.

If you have a car, you can move among these three areas with ease. If you are taking the bus, remember that they run every 30 minutes until about 1 A.M. and less than once an hour on Sundays.

## ITAPEMA

Many travelers who visit this region prefer Itapema Beach over Balneario Camboriú, finding it to be smaller, less urbanized, and more accessible. It has only one main avenue and no crowded boardwalk and it doesn't have that feeling of being crammed with vacationers. The buildings here are smaller than those in Camboriú and the whole place has a more casual, alternative feel to it. There's even a small amusement park on one end, with a Ferris wheel and rides for kids.

## Itapema Beaches

Itapema is divided into two parts: Praia Central and Meia Praia. **Praia Central** is near the downtown area and the main bus terminal but is, ironically, the less active of the two sides, especially at night. There are plenty of hotels and *pousadas* here, many with ocean views. The waves are calm and the water is great for swimming. On the left side of the beach is an area called **Canto** that has almost no waves and is great for playing in the water. There are plenty of beach bars and restaurants on the coastal road to serve you here.

The more active part of Itapema is **Meia Praia,** where the bus leaves the highway and takes smaller roads the rest of the way. The beach here is long and medium-wide and there are only a few kiosks spread out along its five kilometers. That's because there is no coastal road for more than half of this beach. There are medium-sized waves and some surfing takes place here. All the activity at Meia Praia, including the nightlife, takes place on Avenida Nereu Ramos, which parallels the beach. There, you'll find hotels, bars, restaurants, and shops. At night, folks walk up and down, searching for the right restaurant or looking into the shops. On the south end of Meia Praia, you'll find the beaches of **Perequé** and **Costão das Vieiras** (or simply Vieiras). These are more secluded areas, frequented mostly by surfers. They are considered to be the most beautiful of the Itapema beaches. There are a few restaurants and bars here (it's not totally secluded).

The distance from one end of Itapema to the other (Canto to Vieiras) is about 12 kilometers on the beach, perhaps a bit too far to walk. Even walking from one end of the Meia Praia area to the other is quite a hike. You can catch a bus along Avenida Nereu Ramos to go from one end to the other. Be sure to let the driver know that you're only going a short distance *até*

*o final da praia* (to the end of the beach), so you don't get charged for a longer ride.

## Accommodations

Itapema is a decent place to set yourself up for exploring the beaches here and farther south. The hotels in this area are generally small two- or three-story buildings with no special charm to them, but most have decent facilities and service at a good price. (The more charming *pousadas* are in the Porto Belo area.) Check out the **Recanto do Guarapuvu** (Estrada Geral Sertão do Trombudo 4000, tel. 47/9977-5904) and the **Hotel Pousada Sete Mares** (Rua 109, No. 777, Centro, tel. 47/368-2247, www.7mares.com.br, R$90 s, R$180 d). This one is on the hill to the north of Canto Beach. Also in the Centro area is **Recanto Natural** (Rua 141, tel. 47/368-2466, Centro, recantonatural@terra.com.br). If you want to be closer to the Meia Praia area, try **Pousada da Aroeira** (Rua 260, Meia Praia, tel. 47/368-4784, www.pousadaaroeira.com.br, R$110 s or d).

## Food and Nightlife

There are excellent barbecue buffets at Meia Praia. Try **O Costelaça do Tonho** (Av. Nereu Ramos at Rua 284, tel. 47/368-7699, 6 P.M.–midnight daily) for a *rodísio*-style barbecue (all-you-can-eat, served at the table) for only about R$15 per person. There are great coffee shops and casual eateries all along the Avenida Nereu Ramos and in the Praia Central area. For pizza, try **Mi Casa** (Rua 234, No. 222, tel. 47/268-0808, 6 P.M.–midnight daily, R$25 for two) in Meia Praia, or the pizza and pasta *rodísio* at **Alberto's** (Av. Nereu Ramos 3910, tel. 47/368-4407, 6 P.M.–midnight daily, R$20). In the Praia Central area, the **Costão Restaurante** (Rua 109, tel. 47/368-3199, 6 P.M.–midnight daily, R$25) is good for seafood, specializing in mussels and oysters from the area.

## Information

There is tourist information at the *rodoviaria* in Itapema, but there are no banks there (as usual). You can find banks along Rua Nereu

Ramos. Note that there are no international banks in Porto Belo or Bombinhas, so this is the last money stop along this part of the coast. The official city website is itapema.sc.gov.br.

# ⓜ PORTO BELO

The town of Porto Belo was once just a small fishing village, with most of its inhabitants descendants of the Portuguese from the Azores Islands who came here some 250 years ago. Today, the place still looks like a small fishing village, but you'll notice some modern touches that speak of the growth of tourism in the area—hotels, restaurants, and boat excursions mostly. The village here is the quaintest part of the Emerald Coast and the hotels and *pousadas* are equally charming for the most part. The best beach in the area is Praia da Enseada, an inlet on the southern end of the village where you'll find clear, greenish water that is perfect for swimming. Just follow Praia do Baixo out and to the right until you reach the end. Also, be sure to spend a day on the Island of Porto Belo while you're here.

## Ilha do Port Belo

The Island of Porto Belo is the principal attraction of the area. It has a small beach with large stones scattered along its length, forming numerous little areas for layout out and catching some sun. There's a footpath that weaves in and out of these little nooks and crannies and there are two beach bars for getting in out of the sun for a cold drink. A restaurant on the hillside almost gives you the sensation that you're in a tree house. Everything here is a bit more expensive than other locations on the Emerald Coast, but it's the price you pay for so much charm. The water here is clear and clean, and you can take a boat around to the tip of the island for some snorkeling. There are even underwater trails that you can follow as you float along and check out the fish. For an extra R$3, you can take a hike along the **Trilha Ecológica** and look at the prehistoric rock carvings.

The best way to get to the island is to catch one of the small boats leaving from Praia do Baixo (just walk along the beach and you'll see plenty of boats getting ready to make the trip). These small boats cost around R$5–8 each way. The island is less then one kilometer from shore and the water is very calm and peaceful there. There is a tourist information center on the island and a kiosk that provides information on the snorkeling excursions.

Since the sandy area is not extensive, the island can get very crowded on weekends in the summer. Weekdays are the best. The island's website is www.ilhadeportobelo.com.br.

## Other Excursions

The **Porto dos Piratas** (Av. Governador Celso Ramos 1446, tel. 47/369-4245) is a group that has two or three ships that they use to take groups out to the various points in the area. There are three excursions offered: small, medium, and large. The small excursion is the only one worth taking, as it serves as transportation to the Island of Porto Belo and also gives you a look at the **Caixa D'Áço harbor,** where you can swim in the cool water among the boats. The longer excursions are pretty tedious and the guides offer their contrived games and festive dances in only Spanish and Portuguese. Even then, it's mostly for kids and families. If you take the small Caixa D'Aço excursion, you can get off at the island and return on a later trip. Be sure to ask them about return times so you don't end up paying for a small boat to bring you back.

You can rent bicycles for guided tours of the area. The scenic bike routes are quite lovely and you get a chance to go farther than you would on foot. Check with **Casa do Turista** (Av. Gov. Celso Ramos 2428, Porto Belo, tel. 47/369-5030).

## Music and Shows

**Café Pinhão** (Av. Colombo Machado Sales 1574, Perequê in Porto Belo tel. 47/369-8063, www.cafepinhao.com.br) is a large outdoor theater that presents shows just about every weekend in the summer. They have some occasional big names playing and the entire area

The Porto dos Piratas ship leaves from Porto Belo.

in and around the theater fills with crowds and becomes a big party scene. There is a pizza joint just outside and a couple of bars. On concert nights, you'll also find drink stations lined up along the street outside. The theater is less than one kilometer before the village of Porto Belo, across from the Pousada das Vieiras.

## Accommodations

The **Porto Belo Hostel** (Rua José Amancio 246, tel. 47/369-4483, www.portobelohostel.com, claudio@portobelohostel.com, R$25 pp), located in the village, offers group and individual rooms, open kitchen facilities, parking, and 24-hour reception. Breakfast is included. **Pousada Sonho Meu** (Rua São Luiz 500, tel. 47/369-4624, www.pousadasonhomeu.com, reservas@pousadasonhomeu.com, R$90 s and R$110 d) is a cozy place with chalets for 2–6 people, complete with hammock, veranda, TV, ceiling fan, and a view of the ocean from afar. The management is super-friendly and helpful. They have a really nice, alternative vibe.

It's on a side street before the village. Look for the sign. Near the beach in front of the village is the  **Pousada Baía do Porto** (Rua Manoel Felipe da Silva, tel. 47/369-4084, R$65 s without view and R$75 s with view, R$130 and R$150 d). They have a great location right on the beach with very cozy surroundings and an excellent restaurant. A charming breakfast is included.

## Information

If you're taking the bus into town, be sure to ask for the *Porto Belo vilarejo* if you want to get into the village or on the beach where you can take a boat out to the island. If you're staying at a *pousada* before the village, then you can ask to get off at *Porto Belo, antes do vilarejo*. There is a tourist information center on the main highway just before the *vilarejo* and another one at the entrance to the village. The official website of Porto Belo is www.portobelo.com.br. A lot of places here don't accept credit cards and you probably won't find an international ATM. The closest is back in Meia Praia in Itapema.

## BOMBINHAS AND ARVOREDO MARINE PRESERVE

Although the beaches of Bombinhas are extremely popular among local Brazilians, the main reason international travelers come to the area is to visit the Arvoredo Marine Preserve, recognized as the best location for diving in the south of Brazil. Here, you'll find water with a visibility of up to 25 meters and plenty of marine life around the three principal islands of the preserve. The diving schools in Bombinhas bring small groups out to the area for both scuba and snorkeling excursions (snorkeling is great near the islands). The trip takes an hour by boat and you get another hour or so of diving before heading back. Besides the marine preserve, there are plenty of good locations for snorkeling and diving right offshore in the Bombinhas area. Highlights include the rocks at the far end of Praia Bombinhas in an area called Praia da Conceição. You can swim from there to the edges of the Ilha do Macuco. You don't need a

**Bombinhas**

guide to snorkel around these beaches. To set up a trip to the preserve, check into the **Submarine** school (Rua Vereador Manuel José dos Santos, tel. 47/369-2223, www.submarinescuba.com.br, call to schedule a dive or appointment) or **Trek & Dive** (tel. 47/369-2137).

If you decide to spend the day on the beach, remember that Bombinhas Beach is the best and has the most facilities for tourists. It gets crowded on sunny weekends and during the peak season (mid-December through mid-February). There is nothing but private homes inland from the boardwalk areas. The best place to stay while you're in town is in the Porto Belo area.

For more information about Bombinhas and the Arvoredo Marine Preserve, check out www.bombinhas.sc.gov.br and www.guiabombinhas.com.br. Both are in Portuguese only.

## Florianópolis and Ilha de Santa Catarina

The Island of Santa Catarina contains within it many smaller territories, towns, and neighborhoods, each with a unique personality. It's an impressive mixture of elements in such a small place. There are four principal zones to the island. The first, **downtown Florianópolis,** on the west side, is the metropolitan center and is split into two parts, half on the island and half on the mainland—connected by a mere thread. It has some interesting historical buildings and a popular central market, where you can find products from all over the island.

The Beira Mar area is an upscale district with some of the city's finest restaurants and shopping centers. The **east coast** of the island includes the large Lake Conceição and has some of the most popular beaches for sun and fun in the sand. Around the lake is the island's most active nightspot, with restaurants and bars that stay open until the sun comes up. The beaches have fairly large waves and cool, clear water. On the **north side** are the urban beach towns, popular with Argentinean travelers. The beaches here have calm waters and plenty of places to

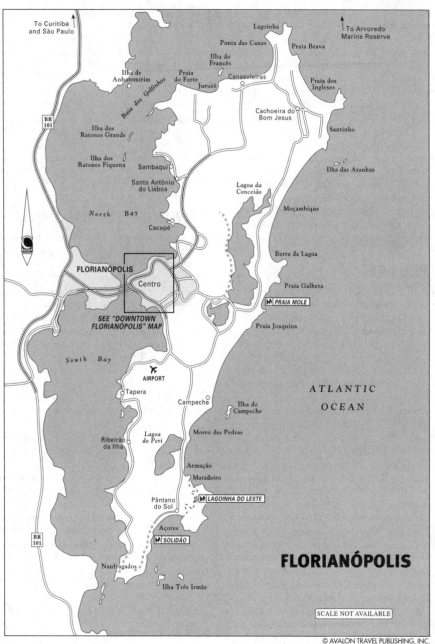

To Curitiba
and São Paulo

Lagoinha

To Arvoredo
Marine Reserve

Ponta das Canas

Praia Brava

Ilha do
Francês

Praia
do Forte

Canasvieiras

Jururê

Praia dos
Ingleses

Ilha de
Anhatomirim

Baía dos Golfinhos

BR
101

Cachoeira do
Bom Jesus

Santinho

Ilha dos
Ratones Grande

Ilha dos
Ratones Piquena

Sambaqui

Ilha das Aranhas

Santo Antônio
do Lisboa

Lagoa da
Conceião

Moçambique

North    Bay

Cacupé

Barra da Lagoa

Praia Galheta

FLORIANÓPOLIS

Centro

M PRAIA MOLE

SEE "DOWNTOWN
FLORIANÓPOLIS" MAP

Praia Joaquina

South   Bay

ATLANTIC

AIRPORT

OCEAN

Tapera

Campeche

Ilha do
Campeche

Morro das Pedras

Ribeirão
da Ilha

Lagoa
do Peri

Armação

Matadeiro

Pântano
do Sol

M LAGOINHA DO LESTE

Açores

M SOLIDÃO

BR
101

FLORIANÓPOLIS

Naufragados

Ilha Três Irmãs

SCALE NOT AVAILABLE

© AVALON TRAVEL PUBLISHING, INC.

sit with a cool drink and people-watch. The **south side** of the island is the most deserted, where you can find beaches with no urbanization whatever. The best trails are in this area, including a fabulous hike out to Prainha do Leste. There are some simple hotels in this region. From here, you can visit the island of Campeche, one of the highlights of any visit to Florianópolis.

The options here are endless: surfing, hiking, sunbathing (including a nude beach), kayaking, paragliding and hang gliding, and dining in some excellent restaurants. Speaking of food, the island is a major producer of seafood and shellfish and has a number of small offshore farms that produce mussels and oysters. Don't leave town without trying some of these locally-grown morsels. The best places are listed herein.

## HISTORY

It all started about 5,000 years ago with some indigenous tribes that were living on the islands in this region. They left their marks on many large stones and some of their bone tools have been found. They were probably the ancestors of the native tribes found in the area today, although their numbers have diminished significantly. Later, the islands in this area were populated by mandate of the Portuguese Crown. Groups of explorers from São Paulo were the first to settle here, but in the mid-1700s, the area attracted a different group, the islanders from the archipelago of Azores in Portugal. Groups of Azorians (Portuguese from the Azores Islands) settled along the coast of Santa Catarina, all the way down to Rio Grande do Sul. Much of the original colonization on the islands is Azorian in origin and you can still see their influences in the architecture, food, and fishing practices, not to mention the arts and crafts found in the area. At that time, the city of Florianópolis was known as the Village of Desterro and it was mostly a fishing village. Nobody would have guessed that it would be these fishing activities, specifically whaling, that would later bring a new vitality to the area.

Throughout the 19th century, the whaling business flourished in Santa Catarina and a number of structures were built to store and process the whale derivatives, principally the fat and oil. Such structures were known as *armações* and the quantity of whale fat that was processed and shipped to other parts of the country (and world) is staggering. In fact, it represented the near-extinction of most of the whales of the southern seas. It also represented the success of the Village of Desterro, and in 1823, it was renamed Florianópolis and became the capital of the state of Santa Catarina.

## DOWNTOWN FLORIANÓPOLIS

At one time, the people of Florianópolis had to get back and forth from the island using ferryboats and all kinds of floating devices. Then the Hercílio Luz bridge when up and put some 40,000 people out of work. Divided into two parts—one part on the mainland and the other on the island of Santa Catarina—the city of Florianópolis is one of the cleanest, most well-planned cities in Brazil. The capital of the state of Santa Catarina, Florianópolis is the second-largest city in the state, next to Joinville. The island of Santa Catarina is officially part of the city, equivalent to a county, and receives more visitors each summer (about 380,000) than its entire population (about 365,000). On the island, the city does not have a major-metropolitan feeling to it. Most of the major hotels are there, along with the historical part of town and a series of streets that are closed off to traffic, allowing people to do their shopping in a civilized manner. The *rodoviária* (main bus terminal) is on the island along with a modern municipal bus terminal for buses going all over the county. The city's international airport is also close to the downtown area on the island. During Carnaval, the island-half of the city is a major draw and is particularly popular with the gay community. Carnaval on the island is becoming known as the Gay Carnaval in Brazil.

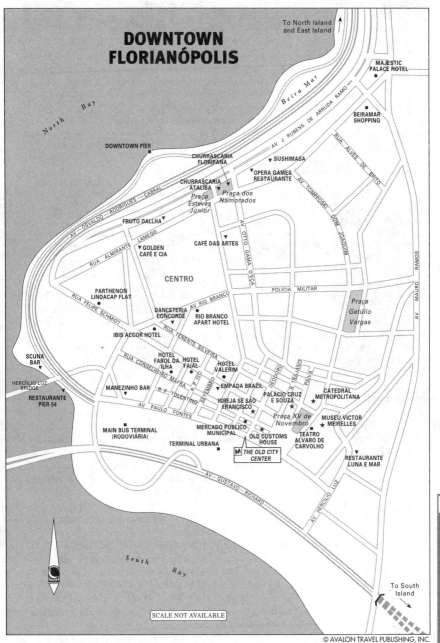

# DOWNTOWN FLORIANÓPOLIS

To North Island and East Island

North Bay

Beira Mar

MAJESTIC PALACE HOTEL

BEIRAMAR SHOPPING

AV J RUBENS DE ARRUDA RAMO

RUA ALVES DE BRITO

DOWNTOWN PIER

CHURRASCARIA FLORIPANA

SUSHIMASA

OPERA GAMES RESTAURANTE

AV TOMPOSKI DOM JOAQUIM

CHURRASCARIA ATALIBA

Praça Esteves Júnior

Praça dos Namorados

AV OSVALDO RODRIGUES CABRAL

FRUTO DALLHA

AV OTTO GAMA D'EÇA

LAMEGO

RUA ALMIRANTE

GOLDEN CAFÉ E CIA

CAFÉ DAS ARTES

CENTRO

POLICIA MILITAR

Praça Getúlio Vargas

PARTHENON LINDACAP FLAT

RUA FELIPE SCHMIDT

AV MAURO RAMOS

AV RIO BRANCO

DANCETERIA CONCORDE

RIO BRANCO APART HOTEL

RUA TENENTE SILVEIRA

IBIS ACCOR HOTEL

SCUNA BAR

HERCÍLIO LUZ BRIDGE

RUA CONSELHEIRO MAFRA

HOTEL FAROL DA ILHA

HOTEL FAIAL

HOTEL VALERIM

DEODORO

R TRAJANO

PAIVA

RESTAURANTE PÍER 54

MANEZINHO BAR

R F TOLENTINO

RE TENÓRIO

R PEDRO IVO

EMPADA BRAZIL

IGREJA SE SÃO FRANCISCO

PALÁCIO CRUZ E SOUZA

CATEDRAL METROPOLITANA

AV PAULO FONTES

Praça XV de Novembro

MUSEU VÍCTOR MEIRELLES

MAIN BUS TERMINAL (RODOVIÁRIA)

MERCADO PÚBLICO MUNICIPAL

OLD CUSTOMS HOUSE

TEATRO ÁLVARO DE CARVOLHO

TERMINAL URBANA

THE OLD CITY CENTER

RESTAURANTE LUNA E MAR

AV GUSTAVO RICHARD

AV HERCÍLIO LUZ

South Bay

MOON

To South Island

SCALE NOT AVAILABLE

© AVALON TRAVEL PUBLISHING, INC.

Santa Catarina

## THE STRONGHOLDS OF FLORIANÓPOLIS

Florianópolis was among the first locations along the southern coast of Brazil to be occupied by the Portuguese as part of their grand colony. The first settlers came from the more populated area of São Paulo, but soon Portugal sent a number of settlers from the Azores Islands to populate the south coast. To protect their interests, a series of forts were built along the northern end of the Island of Santa Catarina. Besides protecting the coast from foreign invasion, the forts served to patrol the bay for illegal contraband of goods from the colony. The three principal forts were Santa Cruz de Anhatomirim, Santo Antônio de Ratones, and São José da Ponta Grossa—all built in the last half of the 18th century. As the population and movement of goods grew, forts were constructed in the center of the island around the downtown area, including São Francisco Xavier, Sant'Ana, São Luis, and Nossa Sra da Conceição Forts.

In spite of all this protection and fortification, the Island of Santa Catarina fell into the hands of the Spanish when, in 1777, they sent over 100 ships to bombard the Portuguese stronghold. The Spanish controlled the island for only about a year before giving it back to the Portuguese in a treaty.

The most impressive and important of the forts is that of **Santa Cruz** on the Island of Anhatomirim. The architectural complex is from 1739 and includes several buildings that were used as the original government headquarters of the area. Having once served as a prison, the island has a fabulous view of the bay and, if you cross over to the fort at the right time of the day, you're likely to see dolphins coming in for the day or heading back to sea for the night. Other highlights include the Viveiro Beach, with its clear blue waters, aquariums with local marine species, and a souvenir shop. The **Santo Antônio de Ratones** fort includes hiking trails and an excellent view of the bay, while the **São José da Ponta Grossa** fort features local arts and crafts and some colonial buildings, including the humble Ponta Grossa Chapel. You can visit the forts by boat via **Scuna Sul** (tel. 48/225-1806, www.scunasul.com.br). English-speaking guides are available.

## The Old City Center

In the Praça da Alfândega and Rua Conselheiro Mafra (the first street in the downtown area across from the main bus terminal) is the **Old Customs House** (9 A.M.–6:30 P.M. Mon.–Fri. and 9 A.M.–noon on Sat.), which today houses a gallery of artists from Santa Catarina, arts and crafts stores, and a simple bar. It was built in 1876 to be the new customs house. Across the street is the **Mercado Publico Municipal** (9 A.M.–10 P.M. Mon.–Fri. and 9 A.M.–3 P.M. Sat.), built in 1898 as a new public marketplace (the old one was located in front of the Matriz church and was demolished in 1896). The Mercado has 140 stands, featuring bars, fish and meat markets, arts and crafts, herbs, clothing—you name it. The highlight is **Box 32,** a famous meeting place for locals and visitors and a great place to have a draft beer and oysters. Get

there just before happy hour, when the place fills up with activity. If you get into the habit of drinking *chá matte* while you're in the south of Brazil, you can find it in bulk in the Mercado. (Sadly, the Mercado burned almost to the ground in August 2005. The new, third version of the building should be up and running again by the end of 2006.)

At the end of Rua Conselheiro Mafra is the city's old town square, **Praça XV de Novembro.** It was here that the old village of Florianópolis began and many of the original buildings line the sides of the *praça*. Most are beautifully restored, along with the historical buildings in the pedestrian marketplace along **Rua Felipe Schmidt** and its many cross streets. In the middle of the *praça* is a large and majestic fig tree at well over 100 years old. Walking around the tree seven times is supposed to bring fortune in love and money. At the top of the *praça* is the striking facade of the **Catedral Metropolitana.** The church was built on top of an older church, which was built on top of another, older church . . . all originating from a chapel that was erected here in 1675 by a São Paulo *bandeirante.* Inside the church is an interesting, life-sized sculpture of the holy family fleeing to Egypt. There is also a pipe organ of German origin from 1924 and some stained-glass images. The facade of the church is most beautiful at night when it's lit from within. On the side of the *praça* stands the old **Palácio Cruz e Souza** (10 A.M.–6 P.M. Tues.–Fri. and 10 A.M.–4 P.M. weekends), built in 1770 as the governor's headquarters. It's a mixture of neoclassic and baroque architecture and today houses the Museu Historica de Santa Catarina, which presents a series of artifacts and documents from past governors who where headquartered here. Most impressive, for sure, is the building itself.

### The Bridge

Once bridging the two halves of the city of Florianópolis, the **Hercílio Luz Bridge** stands as one of the longest suspension bridges in the world, at 820 meters. Finished in 1926, the bridge was financed by U.S. banks and designed by American and Brazilian engineers. It was paid off in 1978 only four years before it was condemned and closed down. Today, it is mostly a visual element at the entrance to the city and for the various hotels and bars that have views of the bay.

### The Beira Mar

If you cut across town on Avenida Otto Gama D'eca, you'll end up at Avenida Beira Mar, looking out at the North Bay of Florianópolis. This is a kind of Gold Coast of the city and if you turn right and continue walking, you'll pass some of the city's best restaurants and waterfront hotels. There are a few bars here, where much of the downtown nightlife occurs. If you're walking past here during the day, be sure to stop at **Fruto da Ilha** for an all-natural juice and snack. At the far

end of town to the right is the **Beira Mar Shopping Center,** the city's best mall. On the left side of Avenida Beira Mar, you'll find a pier, where you can take boat excursions up the North Bay. Around the pier is a park and restaurant.

## NORTH ISLAND

Aside from the city of Florianópolis itself, the north side of the island is the most urbanized and developed part. Pretty much all the beaches here have small, urban centers where you can find hotels, restaurants, and shops along paved streets. Favored by Argentineans, the north side is often very crowded in the summer and offers a more active scene—both on the beach and at night in the bars. That's not to say that there aren't some small villages here, or even semi-deserted beaches. But these are not the norm. Even Lagoinha, the most distant beach on the northern tip of the island, is a sought-after destination for people staying in Jururé, Canasveiras, and Ingleses. The most secluded beach is on Ilha do Francês, off the coast of Canasveiras. Even if you don't want to visit the urban vacation beaches on the north end of the island, you might go up at least as far as Santo Antônio de Lisboa, where you can see a historical village and sample the local shellfish. It's a perfect place to watch the sunset with a great meal.

### Praia dos Canasveiras

Probably the oldest and most urbanized beach on the island, Canasveiras is a small beach town completely autonomous and independent of the rest of the island. There are banks, money exchange centers, car rental agencies, and a post office. This is a favorite location for visiting Argentineans and you'll hear mostly Spanish spoken in the streets. During the summer, it can get quite crowded here—especially on weekends. Within the town, you'll find restaurants, hotels, bars, Internet cafés, and lots of shops.

The bus going to Canasveiras takes about 45 minutes to arrive and stops a few kilometers

the pedestrian market on Rua Felipe Schmidt

from the town, so you need to catch another bus from the terminal into the main area. Catch the *Cachoeira* bus or any that go to the center of town. If you decide to walk, head out and to the right of the bus terminal. There are two principal streets here, in a T pattern, with most of the establishments along these roads. You'll find some great lunch buffet restaurants here with excellent prices, and be sure to stop at the **Capetaria Porto Seguro** for fresh juices. There are some arts and crafts stands on the left side of the T and you can walk for kilometers to the right side, eventually arriving at a second hub, where there are more shops and restaurants.

The beach here attracts families and a slightly older crowd (read: not a bunch of surfers). There is a long stretch of narrow beach with a few main bars along its length. Naturally, the point at the intersection of the T is the most crowded and has the largest bar and most people on the sand. You can rent umbrel-

las and beach chairs here. The farther you walk away from this, the less crowded the beach gets. The water is clear and greenish and has very mild waves, perfect for swimming or riding the banana boat. There are boat excursions that leave from Canasveiras out to **Ilha do Francês,** where you can find a small beach and some snorkeling and scuba diving spots. Boats also go out to Ilha dos Ratones Grandes, where you can see the **Forte de Santo Antônio.**

## Praia dos Ingleses

There are plenty of locals at Praia dos Ingleses and many of them are fishermen. In the winter months, the fishing activities here dominate, but in the summer, the beach at Ingleses is second in popularity to Canasveiras with Argentinean vacationers, and most of the establishments here have Spanish-speaking employees. The beach here is wider and longer than at Canasveiras (about five kilometers) and the water perhaps a little bluer. Mild waves attract beginning surfers, but this is not the preferred spot on the island for the sport. The town here is much less interesting than Canasveiras, although you'll find plenty of hotels and a few good locations for lunch and dinner. The small beach area on the far left side of Ingleses, called **Praia Tur,** is more interesting and has some bars and restaurants, as well as a small urban center. A few kilometers from the beach is a large area of sand dunes and you can take an excursion out to the dunes for a bit of sand skiing.

## Praia Jureré

Originally one of the north island's main fishing ports, Jururé is now home to the Santa Catarina Yacht Club and a huge planned community. The owners of these beach houses are mostly rich Argentineans and the establishments here are generally Spanish-speaking. You'll find bars and restaurants inside small shopping centers and plenty of beach access. The sand here is fine and the water calm, and the beach goes on for about three kilometers. This is a good place to find boat excursions out to the islands off the north coast.

## Praia Brava, Lagoinha, and Ponta das Canas

One of the hot spots on the island for surfing and beautiful people–watching, **Praia Brava** has tall waves and a nice selection of bars, beach kiosks, and hotels. In spite of its distant position on the northern tip of the island, Praia Brava is one of the islands more popular beaches. From here, you can easily get to **Ponta das Canas,** where the water is calm and clear, or up to **Lagoinha,** a small sandy beach about one kilometer long that is surrounded by hills. Here, the waves are calm and the water is warm. There are very few establishments to help you cool off on the beach, but you can walk over to Ponta das Canas for refreshments.

## Santinho

Favored by surfers, the waves here are considered to be the best on the northern part of the island. Hence, the beach is great for laying out and people-watching, but not as good for swimming. The sand here is wide, accommodating lots of people, and there are beach bars and restaurants to serve you.

## Santo Antônio de Lisboa

Visitors enter this small fishing village usually around lunch or dinnertime. That's because the place is known for its fine seafood, especially oysters and mussels, which are cultivated right here in farms offshore. The village also has the honor of being the oldest settlement on the island, where the original Azorian Portuguese came to settle. There is an old historical center where the Azorian architecture is intact and locals sell their traditional arts and crafts. The bus that goes up to Canasveiras makes a stop at the station here.

# EAST COAST

If you're young and single, then the east coast is probably where you want to be. Notwithstanding the cold water along the east coast, the beaches here are by far the most popular on the entire island—especially with surfers and anyone wanting to check out the latest in

bikini fashions (which are in abundance here). The Barra da Lagoa area is the island's best choice for economical lodging and a point of departure for many excursions—not to mention the access point to the Barra da Lagoa Beach, one of the longest and most interesting on the island. Not far away is the island's principal nightlife and gastronomic center, Lagoa da Conceição, which hugs the south end of the lake that bears the same name, the largest on the island. The lake offers some interesting options for water sports and there are some decent hotels in this area, too. The nights go on and on. Even if you're not young and single, you might want to check out some of the restaurants and bars in this area, as they are some of the best on the island.

## Lagoa da Conceição

The road going out to the lake from downtown Florianópolis passes though the eponymous town of Lagoa da Conceição, the main food and nightlife center of the island. It's also from this corner of the lake that you an access most of the water sports, including sailing, windsurfing, jet skiing, and kayaking, that take place in the warm water (an average of 26°C). You can also take boat trips from the docks at the town of Lagoa da Conceição. If you walk from the docks across the bridge that crosses the lake at a small bottleneck, you'll arrive at the main area for swimming and water sports. One of the most interesting activities is kayaking along Rio da Barra, which connects the lake and the ocean.

## Barra da Lagoa

One of the more economical areas on the island is the community of Barra da Lagoa, at the southern tip of Praia da Barra da Lagoa. The atmosphere here is perfect for backpackers and there are a few accommodations that specialize in serving this group, such as the **Backpackers Hostel,** a terrific place for communal lodgings. The village sits at the mouth of the Rio Barra, and you can find boating excursions out to the Island of Campeche right at the edge of the village. You can also rent boats and kayaks for going upriver to the lake. If you take the wooden suspension bridge that crosses the river from the tip of the village, you'll find some great *pousadas* and a trail that leads to a very quaint little beach, surrounded by rocks and vegetation, called **Prainha.** There's a bar on the hill above Prainha and it's a great place for contemplating the meaning of life (not just for backpackers). There are also trails that leave from the far side of the footbridge and go back toward the lake and down to Praia Galheta. There are also buses the go both north (to Ingleses) and south (to Mole and Joaquina).

On the village side of the river, you'll encounter the great **Barra da Lagoa Beach,** which goes on for about eight kilometers until Praia do Moçambique takes over and goes for another 14. The water here is clear and blue and the waves are on the small side. Some beginning surfers like it here, not only for the waves but for the atmosphere. The beach is excellent for swimming and the sand is white and powdery. There are some beach bars on the end near the village.

## Moçambique

If you like long walks along semi-deserted beaches with no homes, bars, or structures of any kind to remind you of civilization, then Praia Moçambique is your place. Here, the water is cold and the waves are rough, cutting down on the number of visitors that come here for the day. The 14 kilometers of soft sand are not easily accessible on foot from Barra da Lagoa, so you should get there by car via highway SC-406, then take the dirt road that branches off and parallels the beach.

## Praia Galheta

One of the few isolated and semi-deserted beaches on the northern half of the island, Galhetas is accessible only by way of a short trail that leads from either Praia Mole or Barra da Lagoa. The beach is completely fenced in by large hills that keep the place isolated, quiet, and semi-private. That's probably why many people strip down to their bare skin at this beach and have been doing so for more than 20 years. Nudity is not required here, but it's certainly welcomed (and officially permitted by city law). Nobody

Prainha at Barra da Lagoa—the cutest little beach on Ilha de Santa Catarina

will kick you off the beach if you're there with all your clothes on, so head on over to check it out. The beach itself is only about one kilometer long and has a wide swath of fine, white sand. The waves are decent here, and surfers come to practice their sport and check out the nude sunbathers (nude surfing has not caught on yet). There are no kiosks or beach bars, so if you come here, bring your own water and refreshments—or just hike back down to Praia Mole when you need to refuel.

## M Praia Mole

Getting its name from the *mole* (soft), pink sand that carpets the beach, Praia Mole is the most popular and fashionable beach on the island. Is it that surfers attract a young, beautiful crowd (a large number of surfing beaches in Brazil have turned into fashionable beaches for the upwardly mobile), or is it just a coincidence that Praia Mole is also one of the island's best surf spots? The waves here are long and tubular and the water is blue and sparkling, if somewhat cold. Although the conditions are not perfect for swimming, many folks venture a meter or so into the surf to cool off. A meter or so is all that's recommended here as the currents get rough farther out. There is no lack of refreshments, as there are numerous beach bars all along the interior of the beach, and many offer showers for washing off.

During peak summer months, this beach can get pretty crowded and traffic between Praia Mole and downtown can make the 20-minute trip last up to four hours!

## Praia Joaquina

Having been host to several surf competitions, Praia Joaquina boasts the best waves on the island. Not only do surfers flock to the place, though; visitors from all over the world come here to see and be seen. The beach here is wide and the sand is soft, but between the volleyball games, sunbathers, and beach kiosks, there's often very little room left for modeling your latest swimsuit. Still, Joaquina is probably the most agreeable beach on the island in terms of comfort for tourists. There are numerous restaurants and beach bars, outdoor showers, public bathrooms, and even lifeguards and police, should you need them. Although the ocean here is filled with surfers, there are calm areas where one can swim without any problem. The water is wonderfully clear. Shops and restaurants line the inside of the beach in case you decide to stay late and then head back over the hill to the downtown area.

## SOUTH ISLAND

For most, the south part of the island is the best. There, you'll find the most unspoiled, virgin beaches with semi-deserted conditions. What urban centers are there are small and still have the appearance of small fishing villages. In fact, many are only fishing villages and offer no accommodations whatever. Most of the accommodations here are in the Armação and Pântano do Sul areas. There are parks and trails throughout the south island, including a long trail that leads down to the tip of the island at Praia dos Naufragados. There are also many trails around the fresh-water lake, Lagoa do Peri. Although an active nightlife is not one of the main features of the south island, you will find plenty of late-night bars filled with tourists in Armação and Pântano do Sul, especially during the peak season.

## Armação

Perhaps the most charming village on the island, Armação is a small fishing village that fills with visitors during the peak months in the summer (and somewhat in the winter for whale-watching). You'll find some charming *pousadas* here and an ample selection of bars and restaurants. From Armação, you can catch a boat to the Island of Campeche. The beach here at Armação is not the best for swimming or sunbathing as the waves and currents are violent. Nearby is the small beach of Matadeiro, which is frequented by surfers and other visitors. Armação is an excellent place to stay if you want to spend most of your time exploring the trails and beaches on the southern tip of the island and on the Island of Campeche.

The word *armação* was given to the centers of the whaling business, where whale carcasses were processed and the fat and oils extracted and stored. The Island of Santa Catarina was one of the principal centers of whale products and the charming village of Armação was once a brutal force in the killing of these huge animals.

## Ⓜ Lagoinha do Leste

This is what you came to Florianópolis for. Lagoinha do Leste is probably the most beautiful area on the island. Besides having a small beach (about one kilometer long) with soft sand and blue ocean, it also boasts a fresh-water lake and plenty of small streams feeding into the ocean. The beach and lake are surrounded by the mountains of the Lagoinha do Leste Municipal Park, an area protected by the state and where it's forbidden to divide the land or create any structures. As such, the area is wild and natural and unspoiled by civilization. The park also has the effect of obstructing access to the beach and lake, keeping the number of visitors down. Since there are no constructions here, you will not find any kiosks or bars on the beach, so be sure to bring your own food and water and be prepared for a semi-difficult hike in order to arrive (be sure to use tennis shoes).

There are two trails leading to the beach—from Armação to the north and from Pântano do Sul to the south. The southern trail is the shortest and most popular. It takes about 1.5 hours and goes straight up the mountain. At the top, you can rest and take in the incredible view before making your descent into paradise. The trail from Armação passes through Praia Matadeiro and then into the forest. There are incredible views along this trail as it follows the coast. It takes about three hours to complete. Note: after heavy rains, the ground along these trails can be soft and dangerous and you should take care as you hike, especially when going downhill. These trails are characterized as semi-difficult.

You can camp out at Lagoinha do Leste around the lake area. There are signs indicating where you can pitch your tent. They ask you not to make a fire using the dry brush in the area but to bring your own materials. You can drink the water that comes in from the streams and small waterfalls.

## Pântano do Sul

An active fishing village, Pântano do Sul is where you'll find some of the best seafood on the island. Every day, the fishing boats come in with a fresh catch and the results are served up in the local restaurants. There are a number of Argentineans who have relocated here, looking for an easier lifestyle, and there are a few hotels in which visitors can stay. The beach here is about two kilometers long and has clear water and medium waves. It's a good place for swimming and there are lifeguards on duty. From here, you can access the enchanting Lagoinha do Leste or the semi-deserted beach of Solidão to the south.

## Ⓜ Solidão

As its name implies (*solidão* meaning solitude or loneliness) this is a place that receives relatively few visitors. Considered one of the prettiest beaches on the island, Solidão requires a short hike down steep paths to arrive there. But the reward is well worth the trouble as the water here is bright blue and beautiful. On the far end is a waterfall with a natural pool in which you can swim—opting for fresh water instead of salt water. All around you is the lush vegetation of the island. There is no civilization here, so bring all your own supplies. If you're up for a long hike, there's a trail that leads all the way from Solidão to Naufragados (The Shipwrecked) on the southern tip of the island. Naufragados is a lovely point, even more deserted than Solidão, and five times more difficult to access.

## Lagoa do Peri

The largest fresh-water lake on the island, Peri is a place for families to have a little fun. There is a large recreation area with barbecue pits, a bar, and a snack stand, and the lake is shallow, calm, and cool for swimming, perfect for kids who are just too small or too nervous to take advantage of the rough waves on the beaches. There is also a playground for little ones. What might attract travelers are the trails that lead from the lake into the mountains and past some small waterfalls. You can also visit an abandoned sugar mill.

## Ilha do Campeche

Any visit to the island of Santa Catarina should include a trip to the Island of Campeche. Known affectionately as Brazil's Easter Island, it is home to a number of mysterious petroglyphs—symbols and inscriptions carved into the stones around the island. The glyphs are said to be about 5,000 years old and are similar to those found on the main island and on the island of Porto Belo to the north. What befuddles most archeologists is the symbol known as the third eye, which is almost identical to prehistoric symbols found in Asia, Africa, and India. Also impressive is the inscription of the summer solstice, which was carved high upon a stone facade at exactly the location where rays of sunlight hit once a year on the longest day of the year.

The island is small, only about 1.5 kilometers long by 370 meters wide and its single beach, facing the island of Santa Catarina, is about 600 meters long. There, the water is blue and clear and you can wade far out into the shallow water. There are two simple beach bars on the island that serve cold drinks and lunch plates. Trails will lead you past the petroglyphs, and there are guides to keep the impact of the crowd to a minimum. While mass tourism is the greatest threat to the island, a secondary problem is the excessive population of raccoons, brought onto the island years ago by a hunting and fishing group—the same group that built the first houses on the island right on top of a native burial ground. They claim that the racoons were not brought to the island to be hunted, but now the group's raccoons have multiplied out of control and have practically exterminated many other species on the island, including snakes and birds. The same group is now responsible for the preservation of the island and the houses are used as headquarters for their efforts. Some of the workers have reported strange occurrences and noises in the middle of the night around the area of the houses.

In the winter months, the island sometimes receives visits by polar penguins and sea lions

and the large tail fins and shiny black skin of Australian whales is a common sight just offshore, as are dolphins in the channel between the two islands. At one time, the island was a processing station for the massive whale hunting that occurred in the south of Brazil, from the late 1700s to the late 1800s. The enormously successful whaling activities caused near-extinction in most of the whale species of the southern hemisphere. The tank that once held the whale fat is covered in sand near the beach. If you visit the island August–November, be sure to bring your binoculars because the whales are coming back.

To camp on the island, get in touch with the Associação Couto de Magalhães (tel. 48/224-8333).

### Ribeirão da Ilha

This small, historical village was once the only indigenous village on the island and later became the first village inhabited by Portuguese settlers in the 16th century. Later, a group of about 100 Portuguese from the Azores Islands settled in this village and it was this group that left the greatest mark here. The architecture and culture of the village retains its Azorian roots from the 1700s and represents the oldest village on the island. The principal activity here is fishing, but many of the residents present their arts and crafts for sale in the streets, not to mention their interesting recipes for sweets and other delights. From the village, you can walk down to the beaches, passing the various colorful homes and establishments, often with their inhabitants leaning out of the windows.

## SOUTH OF FLORIANÓPOLIS

### Garopaba

Despite the fact that the ocean around Garopaba is cold in some areas, the waves and beaches attract surfers from all over Brazil and South America. And where there are surfers, there are plenty of other young people hanging around. The most popular surfing beach is **Praia do Ferrugem,** which is not far from the town center. The beach gets crowded on summer days and even more so on summer nights. The nightlife here starts late and goes until sunrise. Other popular beaches are **Praia da Silveira** and **Praia de Garopaba.** The latter is in the town center and has calm waters and some boating activity. About 18 kilometers to the south (70 kilometers from Florianópolis) is the beautiful area of **Praia do Rosa,** where you'll find sand dunes, trails, waterfalls, and sandy beaches with little or no civilization on them. Just inland from the beach are two lakes.

May–November, this area is the breeding ground for hundreds of Australian whales (*eubalaena australis*), which can be seen from the coastline but even better via a boat excursion. The Garopaba region is one of the best places in the world for observing these creatures, which reach up to 18 meters in length and 60 tons. Today, the whales are increasing in numbers and are more easily spotted off the coast of Santa Catarina. Excursions leave from Garopaba.

About 35 kilometers inland from Garopaba is the **Serra do Tabuleiro Park,** where you'll find trails going into the lush tropical forest. A highlight is the Zanela Waterfall, where you might spot interesting bird species, including owls, toucans, and canaries. You can also take a dip in the waterfall to cool off. In this region, you can take horseback rides up the mountains and along sandy trails with incredible views of the beaches and sand dunes below.

You can find good restaurants with fresh fish and seafood in the town of Garopaba and Praia da Rosa (which is particularly famous for its shrimp). There are *pousadas* all over the area, the most economical are in Praia do Ferrugem. The most charming in the area is **M Pousada Quinta do Bucanero** (Estrada Geral do Rosa, tel. 48/355-6056, www.bucanero.com.br, R$255 with breakfast and dinner), which is far from the beach, across a small lake and up the side of a mountain. The view from the rooms is fantastic and they offer a boat ride across the lake for getting to the beach. They also have super-comfortable rooms with air, TV, and phone. Other features include a pool, bar, restaurant, and game room. No children allowed. Right on the beach is the **Fazenda Verde do Rosa** (Estrada Geral do Rosa, Km 5, tel. 48/355-6060, www.fazendaverde.com, R$335–385), with several different beachfront bars and restaurants. They offer surfing equipment, horseback rides, and other excursions for guests. Rooms are individual cabanas with fireplaces, phones, ceiling fans, and no TVs.

## Laguna

Laguna is one of the oldest cities in the south of Brazil and retains its historic architecture on the waterfront—giving the town a very charming profile. You can walk around the old waterfront or take a boat excursion along the coast. The beaches around Laguna are popular with surfers, especially **Prainha.** You can find *pousadas* in town and along Prainha Beach.

# ENTERTAINMENT AND NIGHTLIFE

## Sidewalk Cafés and Bars

It probably goes without saying that during the day, you'll be looking for lunch on one of the beaches. Most of the beaches on the island have snack stands, beach bars, or complete restaurants for sitting and enjoying a cold one while watching the waves. Naturally, the more urbanized the beach, the more you'll find in the area of cafés and bars. Some more urbanized spots are the beaches of Canasveiras, Santinho, Barra da Lagoa, Mole, and Joaquina.

## Lagoa do Conceição

When the beaches shut down for the evening, most people head out to the neighborhood of Lagoa da Conceição for drinks and happy hour activities. In fact, this area goes non-stop into the wee hours every night. If you take a bus to this area, you should walk out of the bus station to the right and straight ahead until you start seeing the restaurants and bars. The main street is Avenida das Rendeiras. You can't miss it. The best thing to do is walk around the area and look for a place you like. If you walk all the way to the end of Avenida das Rendeiras, you'll come to a park with an outdoor arts and crafts fair. There may be live music there, too.

Beyond this is the lake itself. On the edge of the lake are a few more places, including the late-night dance clubs in the area.

Some places to check out include **Suco da Saúde** (Av. das Rendeiras, Lagoa da Conceição) for great fruit juices, each mixture designed for a particular effect; **Café do Poeta** (R. Manoel Severino de Oliveira 620, Lagoa da Conceição, tel. 48/232-1730, 6 P.M. daily, R$ 20) for a great atmosphere and coffee drinks; **Confraria Chopp da Ilha** (Av. Afonso Delambert Filho 671, Lagoa da Conceição, 6 P.M. daily) for a good crowd and good beer.

The **Ⓝ Mandalla Restaurante e Bar** (Rodovia Admar Gonzaga 4700, tel. 48/234-8714, 6 P.M. daily.) is a perfect place to watch the sun go down and the lights around the lake light up. It has a perfect view of the lake from above and you can sit and enjoy a cold drink with the view. Access is by taxi or car.

There are some great places **downtown**— many of the favorites are in the Mercado Publico, starting with **Box 32** and **Zero Grao** across from it. Both places serve ice-cold beer and appetizers, and are open 10 A.M.–11 P.M. Mon.–Fri., and 10 A.M.–3 P.M. on Sat. **Café das Artes** (Rua Esteves Júnior 734, tel. 48/322-0609, 11:30 A.M.–11 P.M. Mon.–Fri., 4–11 P.M. on Sat. and Sun.) is located in an old Portuguese house and has a great atmosphere for drinks and appetizers. **Golden Café e Cia** (Rua Arno Hoeschel at Almirante Lamego, tel. 48/225-3400, 11:30 A.M.–3 P.M. daily) has German beer and plenty of space for people to hang out. The **Manezinho Bar** (Rua Henrique Valgas 296, tel. 48/222-1183, 8 P.M. daily) is located at the tip of downtown with a great view of the bridges and a great bar and outdoor patio. The **Scuna Bar** (Forte Santana 405, tel. 48/225-3138, 11 P.M. until sunrise Tues.–Sat.), under the Hercílio Luz bridge, has two bars, a dance floor, and a great view of the bridge and bay.

## Music and Dance

The **Danceteria Concorde** (Rua Rio Branco 729, downtown, tel. 48/222-1981, www.concordedanceteria.com.br) is a huge space for music and shows that opens for business on Saturday nights at midnight. **Mecenas** (Rua Lauro Linhares 770, Trindade neighborhood near downtown, tel. 48/334-2277, from 11 P.M. Thurs.–Sun.) is a dance club with three environments, DJs, and shows. There are other dance clubs in this neighborhood. In the Lagoa area, try **John Bull Pub** (Av. das Rendeiras 1047, Lagoa da Conceição) for late night music.

## Gay and Lesbian

It's said that Brazil is the third most popular vacation spot in South America among gay and lesbian travelers. Gay Pride parades and special festivals all over the country have brought in large crowds from the United States and Europe and represent one of the fastest growing segments of the tourism industry in Brazil. According to some authorities, almost 30 percent of visitors to São Paulo, Rio de Janeiro, and Florianópolis are from this market segment. In Florianópolis, one can find hotels that are not merely gay-friendly but predominantly gay, and guests are made to feel very much at home there. One hotel owner has even created a website to promote gay-friendly destinations in Brazil. You can find it at www.athosgls.com.br.

One of the fastest-growing gay-oriented festivals on the island is the Pop Gay competition that takes place during Carnaval. The competition judges beauty queens in various categories and attracted more than 15,000 participants in 2005, giving Florianópolis a newfound fame for hosting Brazil's gay Carnaval.

## Art

There's an art gallery beside the lake at Lagoa de Conceição called **Centro Cultural Bento Silverio** (Rua Henrique Vera 50, tel. 48/232-1514, 1–8 P.M. Mon.–Fri. and 2–5 P.M. weekends), which exhibits works from local artists. You'll also find exhibitions of local works in the main bus terminal on the second floor and in the Old Customs House in the downtown area.

## Festivals

The **Festa do Divino** occurs all over the island throughout May, June, and July. This is mostly a religious festival, but there are special events happening throughout these months. The big festivals in town are **Carnaval** and **New Year's Eve.** Both of these are centered in the downtown area but also spread throughout the island. During Carnaval, the old city center fills up with people and there is live music in Praça XV do Novembro. Naturally, the Lagoa de Conceição neighborhood is another hot spot. On New Year's eve, there are fireworks over the lake and along the Beira Mar area downtown.

## SPORTS AND RECREATION

### Excursions

A great boat trip is the one that goes from Praia do Forte out to the small Island of Anhatomirim, where the **Fortaleza de São José da Ponta Grossa** is located. You pass the Baia dos Golfinhos (Dolphin Bay), where you just might get a glimpse of some dolphins going out in the afternoon. You can also find excursions that give you a taste of the various beaches around the island, a sort of beach sampler. Another excursion takes you out to the waterfalls. A good source for these trips is **Turismo Vida Sol e Mar** (Rua Manoel Álvaro de Araújo 200, Praia do Centro, tel. 48/254-4199, www.praia-dorosa-brasil.com.br).

Boats to the **Island of Campeche** leave from Praia do Armação, Barra da Lagoa, and Pântano do Sul. From Armação, you pay about R$10 per person for the 20-minute trip on a small boat. From Barra da Lagoa, there are several agencies with larger boats that offer full-day excursions out to the island. They pass by the beaches of Mole and Joaquina along the way and stop for snorkeling near Campeche. They serve water and refreshments and charge around R$35 per person. Boats leave at 9 A.M. Try **Escuna Querubim** (tel. 48/232-3354) and **Lagomar** (tel. 48/232-7263), both in Barra da Lagoa near the footbridge.

### Trails and Hikes

Besides walking along the many beaches (some extensive, such as Moçambique and Joaquina), you can hike along well-marked trails located all around the island. One of the most rewarding is the hike from Matadeiro Beach to Lagoinha do Leste. This trail takes about three hours and passes some excellent lookout points before entering the forest. You break out at the lake and your reward is a fresh-water swim. The trail is considered advanced and has some very steep sections. The trail from Pântano do Sul to Lagoinha do Leste is just as difficult, but only takes 1.5 hours. This is the preferred method if your goal is to get to the lake. You can hike along the coast from Solidão Beach to Ponta do Pasto in about 2.5 hours. The trail is not difficult, but long. The hike to Naufragados starts at the end of the road going out to Caieira da Barra do Sul (actually, the road goes past Caieira). From there, you walk through the mountains and down to Naufragados. It takes about one hour. One of the longest trails on the island is the Costa da Lagoa trail, which passes along the inside of Lake Conceição and into the mountains. It takes more than four hours to complete, and along the way, you pass more than 30 mountain streams, walk on an antique cobblestone path, and pass abandoned mills. The final point is all the way up at Santinho Beach. Be sure to bring plenty of water for this one. The hike from Barra da Lagoa to Galhetas Beach is a favorite. You begin at the far side of the footbridge in Barra da Lagoa and turn right to follow the path. Along the way, you'll pass some petroglyphs. Your reward is a nude beach at the end. It takes about two hours. There are trails all over the Island of Campeche that pass the various petroglyphs on the island. A circle around the island takes as long as three hours to complete.

### Surfing and Water Sports

Surfing is probably the sport most practiced on the island, since a huge portion of the beaches on the ocean side have suitable conditions. Favorite beaches include Joaquina, Mole, Galheta (similar to Mole but smaller), Moçambique, Brava, Ingleses, and Matadeiro, the best being Joaquina and Matadeiro. You'll find surf shops all over the island, but mostly at Joaquina, Ingleses and in Barra da Lagoa. If you stay at the

Backpackers Sharehouse in Barra da Lagoa, you get free surfboards, fishing rods, boogie boards, and other fun stuff.

Water sports, such as windsurfing, kite surfing, canoeing, kayaking, and sailing, all take place along the bottom edge of the Lagoa da Conceição. An excellent kayak or canoe excursion is around the lake and out the Barra River to Barra da Lagoa village. A great source for lake adventures is **OpenWinds Action Sports** (Av. das Rendeiras 1672, tel. 48/232-5004, www.openwinds.com.br, the school is open from 2–5 P.M. during the week and 10 A.M.– 5 P.M. on weekends) in the Lagoa da Conceição area.

You can ski down large sand dunes in two principal areas of the island: in the area between Ingleses and Santinho (best access is from Santinho Beach) and in the area just south of Lake Conceição (best accessed from Joaquina). Sand boards are available at the location.

### Diving and Snorkeling

There are places to go diving and snorkeling all around Florianópolis. Snorkeling is best around the Islands of Campeche and Francês, but scuba diving is best in the National Marine Preserve off the northern coast. For that reason, most of the dive schools are located in Canasveiras. **Acquanauta** (Rua Antenor Borges 394, tel. 48/266-1137, www.acquanautafloripa.com.br) in Canasveiras offers a full scuba course, beginner dive, an equipment store, and excursions to special locations. You can also check with **Homem-Rã** (tel. 48/266-2096, www.homem-ra.com.br), meaning Frog Man, for similar services in Canasveiras. A more personal guide is **Karol Mayer** (karol@karolmayer.com), who takes groups of 4–8.

### Rappelling, Rock Climbing, and Rafting

Most of these radical rock-based sports take place in the Tabuleiro State Park, south of Florianópolis. Nevertheless, you can join excursions leaving from the island and heading out to the park for a day or two. Check with **Trekking Das Aguas** (Rodovia Princesa Leopol-

dina 68, Caldas da Imperatriz in Santo Amaro da Imperatriz, tel. 48/275-7279, www.trekkingdasaguas.com.br) or **Apuama Rafting** (Rua Dom Pedro II 7985, Poço Fundo in Santo Amaro da Imperatriz, tel. 48/245-1673, www.apuamarafting.com.br).

### Para-Sailing and Hang Gliding

There are excellent spots for para-sailing and hang gliding all over the island. The main points are around Lake Conceição and along the east coast. If you are not an experienced para-sailor, you can try a tandem ride with a licensed pilot. It's quite a trip. Try **Leandro** (tel. 48/9969-7034).

## ACCOMMODATIONS
### Downtown

Downtown hotels tend to be more professional and better equipped than those around the island. If you like the feeling of a business hotel or the comfort of a luxury hotel, then put yourself there. There are hotels with views of the bay so you don't forget that you're on an island. The least expensive hotels are along Rua Felipe Schmidt and the luxury hotels are near Shopping Beira Mar along the waterfront.

One of the best values in the downtown area is the **Hotel Valerim** (Rua Felipe Schmidt 705, tel. 48/2106-0200, www.hotelvalerim.com.br, R$67 s and R$89 d). It has freshly renovated rooms with modern interior, air, and TV. They have Brazilian-style showers. Breakfast is included. The **Hotel Farol da Ilha** (Rua Bento Gonçalves 163, tel. 48/225-3030, www.hotelfaroldailha.com.br, R$78 s and R$92 d) has decent rooms with air and cable TV. Breakfast is included. The **Ibis Accor Hotel** (Av. Rio Branco 37, tel. 48/216-0000, www.accorhotels.com, R$79) is a modern, business hotel in a great location at a good price. They have good facilities with no special frills. Breakfast is not included.

The **Hotel Faial** (Rua Felipe Schmidt 603, tel. 48/225-2766, www.hotelfaial.com.br, R$103 s and R$120 d) is one of the city's original business hotels. They offer excellent service (including English-speaking employees) and old but large rooms with air, TV, and gas-heated showers. There's a 20-percent service charge during peak season. Breakfast is included. They also have a terrific dinner buffet for R$16 per person. The **Parthenon Lindacap Flat** (Rua Felipe Schmidt 1102, tel. 48/225-4500, www.accorhotels.com, R$185) is a business-oriented hotel with good facilities and great service. They have a rooftop pool with a great view, sauna, gym, restaurant, bar, air, and cable TV.

The **Majestic Palace Hotel** (Av. Beira Mar 2746, tel. 48/231-8000, www.majesticpalace.com.br, R$200 s, R$240 d), across the street from Shopping Beira Mar has 261 rooms and one of the best locations in the downtown area, with an incredible view of the bay and the downtown area. They have been open since 2004 and offer comfortable beds, in-room Internet, 24-hour room service, pool, bar, and restaurant. Another option is the **Rio Branco Apart Hotel** (Av. Rio Branco 369, tel. 48/224-9388, www.riobrancoaparthotel.com.br, R$205–255), which is an executive-style hotel with excellent service and facilities. They have air, cable TV, pool, coffee shop, and restaurant.

## North Island

The hotels in Canasveiras and the north beaches are all about the same price and offer pretty much the same types of facilities. The only real difference is the condition of the buildings and decorations. You can try the **Ilhamar Canas Hotel** (Rua Vidal Ramos Neto 678, tel. 48/266-1648, www.ilhasol.cjb.net, R$165), which is moderately modern and clean. They have a pool and rooms with verandas, air, TV, and phone. They offer beach service. Breakfast is included. A slightly more modern version is the **Canasbeach Hotel** (Av. Madre Maria Villac 1150, tel. 48/266-1227, www.hotelcanasbeach.com.br, R$170). Another is the **Moçambique Praia Hotel** (Av. das Nações 375, tel. 48/266-1172, www.mocambique.com.br, R$140 s and R$155 d).

Note: Prices drop almost in half during low season for these hotels.

## East Coast

There are some great places to stay in the Barra da Lagoa area, including many super-economical hotels and several charming inns. If you want to be closer to the action, then try one of the hotels in Praia Mole or Joaquina and if you want to be right in the nightlife center, then stay in Lagoa do Conceição.

The best hotel for a communal experience is the **M Backpackers Sharehouse** (Barra da Lagoa, tel. 48/232-7606, thebackpackerssharehouse@hotmail.com, R$35 pp), across the bridge toward Prainha. They have only group rooms with breakfast included and a community TV room, barbecue area, and plenty of tourist information and help. They serve a decent dinner for R$8 per person and make a barbecue meal on Sundays for R$15 per person. Internet is available for R$4 per hour. The **Pousada Nunes** (Rua Servidão Manoel João Ferreira 47, tel. 48/232-7325, dilmonunes@yahoo.com.br, R$20 pp without breakfast) is a super value. They have basic rooms with shared bath, rooms with private bath, and *casas* with bath and small kitchen facility. It's not fancy but it books up in peak season. A more charming *pousada* in the Barra area is the **Villa del Este Pousada** (Beco dos Coroas 370, tel. 48/232-3253, www.villadeleste.com.br, R$230 s or d).

If you want to be close to the nightlife in Lagoa da Conceição, then try the **Cabanas Duna Sol** (Rua Vereador Osni Ortigo 2433, tel. 48/232-6666, www.dunasol.com.br, R$80). Also, the **Praia Mole Park Hotel** (Rodovia SC-406, No. 2001, tel. 48/232-5231, www.praiamole.com.br, R$120 s, R$144 d) has a view of the lake and is walking distance to Mole Beach. It's not fancy, but it's clean and well presented. Sitting on the lake with a great view is the **Pousada das Palmeiras** (Rua Laurindo J. da Silveira 2720, Canto da Lagoa. tel. 48/232-6267, www.pousadadaspalmeiras.com.br, R$185), with four separate cabanas offering space for up to four people each, air, and TV. Also on the lake is **Cabanas Duna'sol**

(Av. Vereador Osni Ortiga 2433, Lagoa da Conceição, tel. 48/232-6666, www.iaccess.com.br/dunasol, R$135), with individual chalets offering air, cable TV, and phones. They also have a pool, bar, and restaurant/kitchen.

The **Candice Apart Hotel** (Estrada Geral da Praia da Joaquina 1643, tel. 48/232-5700, www.candiceaparthotel.com.br, R$265–325) is right in front of the dunes at Praia Joaquina. They have a large, modern facility with specious rooms, great views, and a great breakfast buffet. They can help with excursions. Another option in the Joaquina area is **Cris Hotel** (Av. Praia da Joaquina 1, tel. 48/232-5101, R$205–225), with a view of the Joaquina Beach. They have air, TV, phones, and central heating.

### South Island

The south end of the island has some of the most charming hotels in the region. This is the perfect place for couples and anyone wanting a more relaxed and private experience.

**M Pousada Maré de Lua** (Av. Antônio Borges dos Santos 110, tel. 48/237-5068, www.maredelua.com.br, R$60 s, R$80 d) in the Armação area has simple rooms, suites, and a deluxe chalet, all in a very cozy setting only 100 meters from the sand. They have great views of the beach and Campeche Island.

**Pousada Vila Tamarindo** (Av. Campeche 1836, Campeche Beach, tel. 48/237-3464, www.tamarindo.com.br, R$80 s, R$100 d) has a series of different rooms, all well-appointed and clean with comfortable beds and verandas. They have basic rooms with ceiling fan and TV, larger suites with small kitchens, and luxury suites with private entrance, air, and ocean views. Also in Campeche is the **Hotel e Pousada Vila Tamarindo** (Av. Campeche 1836, tel. 48/237-3464, www.tamarindo.com.br, R$245), with ocean views, verandas with hammocks, pool, massage room, and extensive grounds. They help with excursions, including whale-watching and island trips and speak English, Spanish, and Italian.

### Camping

The island is full of campgrounds and many are frequented by the surfing community. Some are more rustic and cater to the true hiker/camper set. Here are a few to check into: **Camping Fortaleza da Barra** (Barra da Lagoa, tel. 48/232-4235, campingfortalezadabarra@yahoo.com.br, R$10 per person) rents tents and trailers and has small rooms for rent as well as the campgrounds. You can camp on **Ilha do Campeche**, but you have to work it out ahead of time with the authorities on the island. Call the Associação Couto de Magalhães (tel. 48/224-8333). One of the best camping areas is at **Lagoinha do Leste**, which is accessible by a trail. You'll need all your own gear as there is no infrastructure there.

## FOOD

There are so many restaurants and dining options on the island that one could write an entire guide to cover all the options. Naturally, the more urbanized areas have the most options; that means downtown, the Lagoa neighborhood, and the North Island. But there are some special spots for seafood that should not be missed. This section presents a few highlights in the culinary arts of Florianópolis.

### Quick and Casual

The best finger foods on the island are at **Fruto da Ilha** on Av. Beira Mar downtown. They have a variety of *pasteis* (meat pies). They also make terrific fresh juices and their prices are excellent. In Canasveiras, the **Capetaria** (10 A.M.–6 P.M. daily, R$3–8) is the place for fresh juices. You can't miss it on Avenida dos Nações, the main road in town. If you're looking for great coffee and snacks in the downtown area, try **Empada Brasil** (Rua Felipe Schmidt 413, tel. 48/224-3551, 9 A.M.–7:30 P.M. Mon.–Fri., 9 A.M.–4 P.M. on Sat., around R$5 for snacks), a small chain based in São Paulo that has some of the best *empadas* you'll every taste. What's an *empada*? Swing by and find out.

You'll find some large self-service buffets in the Canasveiras area. One example is the **Restaurante Candeias** (tel. 48/232-1286,

11 A.M.–11 P.M. daily ) on Av. dos Nações. You can get an all-you-can-eat lunch buffet with several varieties of fish and meat dishes, pasta, and salads for R$9 per person. Try the shellfish paella with mussels cultivated right on the island.

## Barbecues

The **Churrascaria Ataliba** (Av. Beira Mar 5050, tel. 48/333-0990, 11:30 A.M.–3 P.M. and 7 P.M.–midnight daily, R$30) has an all-you-can-eat barbecue with a buffet table of pasta dishes, salads, and desserts and so does the **Churrascaria Floripana** (Av. Beira Mar 1210, tel. 48/3052-4555, noon–3 P.M. and 7 P.M.–midnight Mon.–Sat., noon–4 P.M. on Sun., R$25) down the street. The latter is slightly more casual and less expensive.

In the Lagoa area, try **Olho de Boi Grill** (Est. Geral do Canto da Lagoa 2308, Rua Laurindo Januário da Silveira 2308, tel. 48/232-0197, 6P.M, until midnight daily, R$35) for a decent cut of meat.

## Fish and Seafood

**Sushimasa** (Av. Beira Mar, downtown, Travessa Harmonia 2, Centro, tel. 48/224-5124, 7 P.M.–midnight Mon.–Sat., R$30) is a great place for Japanese food in the downtown area. There are a number of Japanese restaurants in the Lagoa da Conceição neighborhood, including **Nigiri Sushi Bar** (Av. Afonso Delambert Neto 413, tel. 48/232-5761, 7 P.M.–midnight daily, R$50) and **Ichi-Ban** (Av. Rendeiras 200, tel. 48/232-0030, 6 P.M.–midnight Mon.–Fri., noon–midnight on weekends, R$35–55).

The **Restaurante Pier 54** (Forte Santana 405, tel. 48/225-3138, 6 P.M.–1 A.M. daily, R$25), under the Hercílio Luz Bridge, serves food from the island. That means they specialize in fish and seafood with an emphasis on mussels and oysters. They also boast a well-stocked wine cellar.

To really get a taste of the island's seafood marvels, head over to Pântano do Sul or Santo Antônio de Lisboa, where the fishing and shellfish harvesting activities are abundant.

## International

You'll find pizza and pasta at **Peperoni Restaurante e Pizzaria** (Rua Afonso Delambert Neto 688, tel. 48/232-0413, 7 P.M.–2 A.M. Mon.–Fri., noon–2 A.M. on weekends, R$20) in Lagoa da Conceição. Down the street is **Pizza na Pedra** (Rua Alfonso Delambert Neto 853), with a variety of wild pizza mixtures.

The **Opera Games Restaurante** (Av. Beira Mar 1280, tel. 48/225-1550, 6 P.M. until the last customer Mon.–Sat., R$30) is very well-known restaurant and piano bar in town. They have an elegant but casual atmosphere and an international menu. You can sit either in the piano bar room or the game room.

# INFORMATION AND SERVICES

There's a tourist information booth in the main bus terminal and in the airport. Internet is available all over the island, especially in the urbanized areas. You'll find plenty of options downtown and in the Lagoa neighborhood. International ATMs can be found in the main bus terminal, the airport, and the downtown area. You can also find them in the Lagoa neighborhood. Look for Banco do Brasil ATMs that have the Plus and Cirrus stickers on them or the Banco 24 Horas machines.

## Portuguese Classes

There's a group on the island that specializes in teaching Portuguese to gringos. If you're on the island for an extended stay, get in touch with **The Language Club** (Rua Afonso Delambert Neto 817, Lagoa da Conceição, tel. 48/232-1047, www.thelanguageclub.com.br). They even have weekly modules if that's all you have time for.

# GETTING THERE AND AROUND

If you're coming in from Itajaí or Balneario Camboriú by bus, you'll find buses leaving every hour, 6 A.M.–11 P.M. You can also come straight from Curitiba or Joinville on the Catarinense line. You'll arrive at the main bus terminal, which is on the island. Across from the bus terminal is the old downtown area, and next to the terminal, just a short walk down the street, is the **Terminal Urbana,** where you can find buses going to every location on the island. The buses are well-organized and on time. Just check out your destination on the directory outside to get the correct part of the terminal. Destination names are listed above the bus stop. If you need help, you can dial 1517 for the help line. If you plan to take the bus often, you can invest in a Tourist Ticket with values of R$10, R$20, and R$30 each. Look for a person in uniform at the terminal; they can sell you the ticket or direct you to someone who can.

If you decide to rent a car, you can call **Hertz** (tel. 48/224-9955) or **Dimas** (tel. 48/240-1111). If you need to call a taxi, try tel. 48/240-6951 or tel. 48/224-2777. The bus station phone number is tel. 48/224-2777 and the airport is tel. 48/331-4000.

# Know
# Brazil

## The Land

### GEOGRAPHY

Brazil is the fifth largest country in the world, both in terms of geography and population. Russia, Canada, China, and the United States are larger in terms of land, although Brazil is larger than the continental United States without Alaska. Brazil is the largest country in South America, comprising more than half of the continent and it shares borders with every South American country except Chile and Equador. Its total landmass is more than 8,500,000 square kilometers, with a diverse topography and numerous ecosystems. The majority of Brazil consists of lowland hills and coastal regions. There are some draught-ridden areas in the northeast and lowland plains in the interior states.

The highest peak in Brazil is the Pico de Neblina (Foggy Peak) in the northern region at the Venezuelan border, some 3,000 meters (9,800 feet) above sea level. These hills drop abruptly into the Amazon River Basin, which accounts for more than half of Brazil's territory and one third of Brazil's waterways. More than 200 tributaries feed into the Amazon River, helping to make it the world's largest river in terms of volume. Almost one fifth of the world's fresh water flows through the Amazon Basin. Covered in tropical jungle, the area also gets a huge amount of annual rainfall. In harsh contrast, the interior of the northeast region gets less than 50 centimeters of rain per year and is Brazil's driest and poorest area, plagued by drought and hunger.

Numerous mountain ranges follow a great portion of the coastline of Brazil. These ranges cut through most of the eastern states, such as the Serra do Cipó in Minas Gerais, and the Serra da Bocaina in Rio de Janeiro State. The highest of these ranges appear in the southern region, where the mountains drop abruptly before reaching the Atlantic. Once, the Atlantic Rainforest flourished in these mountains, but today, the lower foothills of these ranges are covered with vast plantations: sugar in the northeast, coffee in the southeast, and citrus, coffee, and bananas in the south. Brazil has almost 7,500 kilometers of coastline and much of it sits on a low shelf or plateau that overlooks the ocean, creating a natural division between the beaches and inland areas. Many coastal cities and towns are divided into high and low urban areas as a result. A great section of the northeast coastline is outlined by narrow reefs, comprised of mostly rock. The many coastal reefs, islands, and marshlands known as *manguezal* are home to a great many marine species, including several marine mammals. The reefs block much of the incoming surf and make the beaches calm and the water warm and shallow.

While the Amazon Basin is most famous for its massive waterways, the southern region also has a vast supply of fresh water, which comes down in a series of rivers from the Serra da Botoquena mountains and feeds the world's largest wetlands, the Brazilian Pantanal. In the wet season, the Paraguay River floods into the low marshlands of the Pantanal, creating huge lakes and waterways. When the waters recede in the dry season, the area becomes a rich hunting ground for diverse wildlife species. On the other side of these mountains, toward the state of Paraná, the waterways empty into the Paraná River, which eventually winds its way down to the great Foz de Iguaçu, the most expansive waterfall in the world.

If that's not enough water for one country, just imagine that a huge water table, often referred to as an underground lake, spans from lower Minas Gerais to Argentina under the states of São Paulo, Paraná, and Santa Catarina. The water table is known as the **Aquifero Guarani.**

### URBAN GEOGRAPHY

About 80 percent of Brazil's population are crammed together in the cities, a trend that began in the early 1900s with the industralizaion of farming and increasing wealth in the cities. In particular, the southeast cities of Rio de Janeiro, São Paulo, and Belo Horizonte, along with their outlying areas, comprise almost 40 percent of Brazil's population—with São Paulo in the lead at almost 20 million inhabitants. São Paulo is the third most populated city in the world. Rio de Janeiro is up there in the world's largest cities with a population of more than 10 million and is Brazil's second largest city. This out-of-control population shift to the southeast cities has created a host of problems, from lack of urban infrastructure to environmental issues to crime.

Belo Horizonte is Brazil's fourth largest city, with 3.2 million inhabitants. Salvador comes in third with almost 4 million inhabitants. A host of other cities come in at around the same count of between two and three million inhabitants, including Recife, Fortaleza, Manaus, and Porto Alegre. By far, most of Brazil's population is dotted along the coastline from Belém down to Porto Alegre. Brazil's five principal regions are divided into 26 states, which are further divided into municipalities.

## CLIMATE

Most of Brazil lies between the equator, which intersects Macapá at the mouth of the Amazon River, and the tropic of Capricorn, which intersects Ubatuba in the state of São Paulo. The rest is divided among a series of sub-tropical climates and one or two semi-arid areas. In general, Brazil is a very humid and wet country. A number of microclimates create variations in temperature and precipitation with the hottest and driest area being the northeast interior. The farther south you travel, the more dramatic the temperature varies, and some of the mountainous areas in the southern region see frost and even snowfall in the winter months.

The rainy season occurs during Brazil's summer months, with a variation of a few months between the northeast and the southeast regions (rains start in March in the northeast and in December in the southeast). The wettest regions are the Amazon Basin, which receives as much as 3,500 millimeters (138 inches) in some areas, and the southeast region around São Paulo and Rio de Janeiro. During the three months of wet season, rains bombard the stretch of mountains and valleys from Brasilia to Rio, including most of southern Minas Gerais and northern São Paulo. Floods are common in these areas and each year brings new disasters, with floods washing away poor neighborhoods built precariously on the hillsides along the outskirts of town. Some years, entire sections of São Paulo are filled with three or four meters of water rushing past with cars and lives in its currents. When it's not raining, the southeast region enjoys a warm, dry, and breezy climate, as do Salvador, Maceió, and Recife on the northeast coast. Natal and Fortaleza, because of their proximity to the equator, have little variation in temperature and are sunny and warm most of the year.

## ENVIRONMENTAL ISSUES

While the rest of the world looks on, Brazil continues to destroy and deplete the Amazon jungle at an astonishing rate of around 55 square kilometers per day. Much of this is a result of illegal logging activities by private landowners and local poachers, scrambling to satisfy the First World's hunger for timber. Although such activities are considered federal environmental crimes in Brazil, much of it goes on unchecked and unpunished. Corruption, greed, and feelings of entitlement among landowners account for much of the problem. But a large chunk of the blame can be placed on authorized mining and farming efforts. Huge tracks of the forest around Belém are being cleared for new crops and livestock. The main culprits are the cattle, which require not only space, but also plenty of soy protein for feed. The soy industry in Brazil has grown at an astounding rate and huge plantation are appearing in the southern states, Mato Grosso do Sul, upper Minas Gerais, and the Amazon region. In every case, there are environmental costs involved in this economic-growth industry. The debate continues as to whether some degree of environmental degradation is necessary to sustain economic growth. Looking to the United States and Europe as models, one would probably conclude that it is. In comparison to the wide-scale stripping of the old growth forests in the United States, Brazil is relatively tame in its use of natural resources for economic growth. In the Pantanal region, more than 40 million head of cattle live in relative harmony with the rest of the ecosystem.

Besides large-scale farming efforts, excessive fishing practices take their toll on indigenous species, such as the giant Pirarucu, the largest fresh-water fish in the world and a lucrative species for fishing communities throughout the Amazon. Some controls have been implemented in the central Amazon region, where the tourism industry helps keep watch on local fishermen in order to protect their valuable tourist attraction. Tourism, while it causes some damage, ends up helping to preserve the Amazon in some ways. It would be nice if tourist facilities were always created in good taste, but that's a matter of personal opinion.

Exotic species of birds and primates from these forests still carry high price tags on the black market, and attacks on key wildlife areas, such as the Amazon and Pantanal, are made by animal poachers.

While the deforestation of the Amazon continues to get the most attention among environmentalists, some of the greatest pollution problems are related to Brazil's metropolitan areas. Urban growth combined with a horrendous distribution of wealth creates huge poor areas on the outskirts of the cities (or in the case of Rio, right inside the city). These areas have practically no sewage treatment facilities, water treatment, or other urban infrastructure. Rivers and streams continue to serve as principal water sources and sewage systems for these populations. The rivers empty into the ocean and make most of the urban beaches unsafe for swimming. Sewage treatment is not ubiquitous in Brazil and many large coastal cities continue to dump untreated sewage into the oceans and rivers. In the case of Rio de Janeiro and São

the abundant underwater life in Brazil

Paulo, which do have sewage treatment facilities, the main problems are caused by heavy shipping activities and offshore oil drilling.

Thankfully, there are some bright spots in this tapestry. Brazil continues to be one of the world's most successful recycling nations, and government-sponsored protection activities are on the rise. Brazil is second in South America, behind Argentina, in its use of natural-gas vehicles, and cities like Salvador are slowly installing waste-treatment facilities to help keep the beaches clean. If tourists continue to spend money in Brazil to see the Amazon jungle, Pantanal, or whales swimming off the coast of Bahia and Santa Catarina, then local entities will scramble to help protect these resources rather than exploit them. Tourism is not a total solution and it adds some problems of its own, but the economic incentive it creates can be a start.

# History

## DISCOVERY AND CONQUEST

Not only were the Portuguese well positioned geographically to reach out across the great Atlantic, but they also possessed one of the greatest schools of marine navigation in Europe at the time, the Sagres school. Replete with naval maps and navigational devices, the school trained many of Europe's finest navigators in the 15th and 16th centuries.

The first half of the 16th century brought a series of discoveries along the eastern coast of South America, beginning with Vincent Pinzon of the Niña (one of Christopher Colombus's fleet) in April of 1500. Pinzon landed somewhere along the coast near present-day Fortaleza and although he recorded the discovery in Spanish navigational books, it was never revealed to the world. The territory he had discovered belonged to the Portuguese according to the Treaty of Tordesilhas (1494), which divided up the world among the southern European nations. It wasn't long, however, before Alvares Cabral discovered the same continent a bit farther south in what is currently Southern Bahia and claimed it for the Portuguese Crown. Later, Amerigo Vespucci sailed into the present-day Bay of All Saints and called it America. The name stuck.

These early opportunists found Brazil to be more difficult to tame than expected, what with all the indigenous people and dense forests. The only thing they managed to extract at first was the Pau Brasil tree for its hard wood and red dye—nothing near what was coming out of India at the time. The red dye made from the tree was as bright as the blaze of a fire and so it was named Brasil (blaze). In most cases, they were able to trade with the aboriginal groups for the right to remove the trees. Other products began to appear from the Amazon region, such as cocoa and spices, and the French and Dutch, not being parties to the Tordesilhas Treaty, began their own infiltration of the Brazilian coastline—principally to disrupt the plans of the Portuguese, but also in search of the Pau Brasil tree. They, too, did not get very far with the native people, but they were a thorn in the side of the Portuguese.

## THE SUGAR ERA

Everything changed with the discovery and cultivation of sugarcane, Brazil's most important cash crop to this day. The Portuguese invested in the colonization of this wild land and created 15 separate territories, which were given to 15 sea captains to govern and populate. They had varying degrees of success. João de Barros never set foot on his lands in the north and Francisco Pereira Coutinho shipwrecked off the coast of Salvador and was eaten by the Tupinambá people. In the second half of the 16th century, a different tactic was attempted and in 1549 Tomé de Souza was given governance of the entire colony. He set up his capital in Salvador da Bahia with about 1,000 workers, three key administrators, and a handful of prostitutes. He also counted on the help of the Jesuits to help dominate or convert the indigenous people, and little by little both the native inhabitants and their land came under the domination of the Portuguese. Indigenous people who did not convert to Christianity were enslaved and sent to work in the sugar trade. Where there were once as many as five million native individuals, today there are only around 70,000. Sugar grew from a small, boutique item into a huge export to Europe and turned key production areas (Salvador and Olinda mainly) into major trading centers with their own social and political structures. There emerged plantation owners, religious leaders, artists, architects, and governors from Portugal. For the most part, society was divided into two groups: the rich (plantation owners and governors) and the poor (slaves and poor European workers). Besides these two groups, there remained a great many indigenous people who were neither enslaved nor converted to Christianity by the Jesuits.

They regularly attacked the Portuguese settlers. The Jesuits were eventually expelled from the colony for their anti-slavery attitudes concerning the indigenous people.

## THE DUTCH INVASION

The French, Dutch, and English did not give up their attempts to snag a part of the new land for themselves and with the growing value of the sugar trade, the prospect became all the more attractive. They attacked regularly along the entire coastline of Brazil and played the native groups against the Portuguese settlers whenever they could. The Portuguese constructed numerous forts to protect themselves from both the European invasions and the indigenous attacks from within. But eventually, in 1630, the Dutch managed to dominate the coastline of Pernambuco and take over the city of Olinda, burning it to the ground. Soon, they conquered Salvador and the northern territories of Natal, Fortaleza, and São Luis. Their occupation of the colony lasted 24 years, destroyed Olinda's sugar production, and broke Portugal's monopoly of the sugar trade forever. When they were finally expelled by the Portuguese (assisted by native tribes), they removed numerous sugarcane seedlings on their way out.

## SLAVERY AND THE GOLD RUSH

When aboriginal slaves were not enough to maintain the growing sugar business, African slaves were brought into the colony by the tens of thousands. The Portuguese Crown divided the administration of the country into two parts: the sugar business and everything else. Those responsible for everything else were given permission to expand and explore the inner frontiers of the colony. It took almost 150 years, but the scouring of the colony paid off. During the 17th century, groups from the predominantly Jesuit town of São Paulo began to explore the area of Minas Gerais for gold and jewels. Carrying the banner of Portugal and other banners indicating their particular mission, these *bandeirantes* were usually accompanied by indigenous and black

## THE BRAZILIAN CIVIL WAR

Since the *bandeirantes* from São Paulo were the first to extract gold from Minas Gerais, they quickly became rather protective of their great backyard. Combine this with a racial tension between these *Paulistas* (who were Brazilians of mixed Portuguese and indigenous decent) and immigrant treasure-hunters. The result was a short but bloody civil war called the *Guerra das Emboabas.* The war began in Caeté, near Belo Horizonte, and was also fought on the hills of São João del Rei and Tiradentes, culminating with the burning of the Aldeia dos Paulistas near Ouro Preto, today known as the Morro da Queimada (Burned Hill). Not including the many separatist movements in the 1800s, the Guerra das Emboabas was the first of three rebellious uprisings in Brazil's colonial history. The second, the *Inconfidentes,* is described in a sidebar later in this chapter. The third was the successful independence of Brazil in 1822.

slaves. The many trips into the Minas Gerais area gave rise to small settlements used as bases for exploration. At long last, in 1698, a group of these *bandeirantes,* led by Antônio Dias, set out for the Pico do Itacolomi between Ouro Preto and Mariana where they had previously attempted to find gold. This time, one of their slaves discovered strange black stones along the banks of a small stream. The group sent a sample to Rio de Janeiro for analysis. When cut apart, it was discovered that the black stones were, in fact, pure gold that "shone like the sun."

By chance, they approached the peak from the Mariana side that day and so Mariana is credited as the first Minas town to have produced gold. Nevertheless, it was the area of Ouro Preto (then known only as the settlement of Antônio Dias) that was developed and grew to become the nucleus of the region's mining activities. Its fame soon attracted fortune hunters from Rio de Janeiro and even Portugal (often those escaping the Inquisition or other defectors). The area became wild and dangerous, with bandits and escaped slaves living in the hills and robbing caravans at night (some say it hasn't changed much). Many of the indigenous tribes in the region were still not yet "integrated" and offered other challenges for the gold hunter. Few of the early explorers were interested in anything but gold, so the agriculture of the area quickly became insufficient to feed the population. Supplies were shipped in from Rio at great expense and assaults on the roads were commonplace.

Naturally, the Portuguese Crown created a sort of infrastructure for taxing all this gold. First, anything found in the colony was to be taken to one of the official exchange houses, where it would be forged into bars and a fifth taken for the Crown. Important ports were set up in Rio de Janeiro and Paraty, where the gold was shipped out of the country. Quotas were put into place to set a minimum annual rate of production. If the quotas were not met, the Portuguese Crown would take the difference from the possessions of the population. All this wealth, taxation, and control evoked the rebellious instincts of the colonists and eventually gave rise to the Inconfidência Mineira, a liberation movement planned by a group of wealthy intellectuals for the independence of Brazil. They were captured and sent into exile in Africa. The supposed leader, known as Tiradentes, was hanged in Rio de Janeiro and his head was sent back to Ouro Preto for public display.

In the 70 years of the Brazilian *ciclo de ouro* gold rush, more gold was extracted from Brazil than during all preceding years combined and more than 10 times as much as was encountered in the California Gold Rush of 1849. The gold rush brought an increase in population and culture to the interior of Brazil (including an increase in Portuguese immigration) and moved the nucleus of power in Brazil from the northeast region to the southeast region, where it remains to this day.

## IMPERIAL BRAZIL AND INDEPENDENCE

While his crazy mother, Queen Maria Louca, was holding down the fort in Portugal, her son

Dom João VI and most of the court were spending a few years of exile in the colony, avoiding a potential confrontation with Napoleon. During their stay, their home base of Rio de Janeiro received a royal face-lift and became known as the Imperial City. Besides erecting numerous public and private buildings, parks, and monuments, Dom João also opened trade between Brazil and other allied nations (getting around Napoleon's sanctions on trade with England) and the colony turned into a kingdom within the Portuguese Empire. The result was a great economic and cultural boom for Brazil. Queen Maria died while Dom João was in Brazil (1818) and, now king of Portugal, Dom João VI returned to the homeland, leaving his son, Dom Pedro I, to govern the new kingdom/colony. When his father later demanded his return to Portugal and revoked all of Brazil's colonial rights, Dom Pedro I remained in Brazil and declared its independence from Portugal in 1822. He installed Brazil's first constitution. Only nine years later, he returned to Portugal, leaving his five-year-old son, Dom Pedro II, to rule the new kingdom. Dom Pedro I died three years later in Portugal in 1834.

Until Dom Pedro II was old enough to assume the throne in 1840, the country was divided among special interest groups and separatist movements. The country saw many regional battles, especially in the northeastern region. Even after assuming power, Dom Pedro II put down a number of separatist movements. He also entered into war with Paraguay, which ended in a massacre of the Paraguayans and destruction of their economy. During Dom Pedro II's reign, sugar and gold gave way to coffee as the main export and the area around São Paulo began to dominate economically.

## ABOLITION AND THE BRAZILIAN REPUBLIC

The sugar trade, continued mining activities throughout the country, and the new coffee trade all sustained themselves with slave labor. Slave traffickers from the north and northeast regions began to supply slaves to the southeast and central west states to work the new coffee boom, but with growing partisan movements in the government and rising support for the abolition of slavery, the transportation of slaves was forbidden. The modern coffee barons began to employ foreign immigrants in the fields. In the latter half of the 19th century, hundreds of thousands of Italian and Japanese immigrants were working in the coffee plantations and by 1888, slavery was abolished. In contrast to the bloody abolition movement in the United States just a few years earlier, abolition in Brazil took place over three phases and ended in parades and public celebrations. The next year, Dom Pedro I abdicated the throne to the new republic and its new constitution, which was inspired by those of Europe and the United States.

During the early days of the Brazilian Republic, most elections were fraudulent and the country was under the control of large farming interests. Brazil was essentially an oligarchy, dominated by the coffee barons of São Paulo and the cattle farmers of Minas Gerais, and the era was humorously known as the *Café com Leite* government. The capitalist tactics and manipulation of the government left many without land and gave rise to a number of *cangaça* or outlaw movements, not unlike the Jesse James gang in the United States. The most famous was the Lampião gang in Maceió in the state of Sergipe.

## THE VARGAS YEARS

The world economic crisis of 1929 weakened the Brazilian oligarchy and gave way for a military coup that placed Getúlio Vargas in power from 1934–1937. The period is known as the Vargas Constructional Government, a sort of fascist government focused on workers' rights. Vargas also led a new constitutional movement that implanted a minimum wage, vacation pay, and a number of workers' rights into the constitution. At the end of his term in 1937, Vargas, with the support of the military, took the presidency for another two terms in a military coup. His new program, called the New State, was marked by economic interventions in the

economy, giving special attention to the industrialization of agriculture and investments in metallurgy and petroleum—all three aimed directly at weakening the Café com Leite power structure. Trying to remain neutral during the initial years of WWII, Vargas knew he needed the financial support of the United States for his domestic plans to succeed, and finally sided with the Allies in 1942. In 1945, Vargas stepped down, but only six years later was re-elected (or elected for the first time, as some might say) and continued his policies with the creation of Petrobrás, Brazil's oil monopoly. Vargas shot himself after accusations of his involvement in the murder of an air force officer known to be his enemy, but many believe that the leftist opposition murdered him. His famous suicide note reads: "I exit life to enter into history."

## DICTATORSHIP IN 1964

Brazil's dictatorship came at the end of a utopian modernization period led by President Juscelino Kubitschek (J.K.) and his teams of cultural and urban reform artists. It was the golden era of samba and bossa nova, when Copacabana Beach was enjoying international fame and recognition. The presidency of J.K. was marked by many architectural and urban projects, many designed and implemented by his friends, architect Oscar Niemeyer and landscape designer Burle Marx. Kubitschek is most famous for his creation of the city and federal district of Brasília—not only a modern utopia and architectural showcase but, like the District of Columbia in the United States, a region that is constitutionally distinct and separate from the rest of the country. He claimed to have seen the plans for the city in a kind of vision. Brasília took the mantle of "Capital City" away from Rio de Janeiro and the presidency of J.K. caused an era of massive inflation. Following J.K., President Jânio Quadros took the helm for a short time. His resignation put leftist Vice President João Goulart into the presidency.

In addition to limiting freedom of the press, hunting down and torturing political enemies, and stacking political and executive power in

## HISTORY ACCORDING TO SAMBA

Samba music was originated in part to record and pass along the story of Brazil's colonization. Samba lyrics speak of the many stories associated with the European conquest. Here's a perfect example:

*O negro la na Africa era um rei* (The black man in Africa was a king)/
*Foi artesão e foi caçador* (He was an artist and a hunter)/*Guerreiro, feiticeiro camponês* (Warrior, mage and man of the wild)/*Exímio dançador* (An extraordinary dancer)/*Tinha sua propria lei e com a liberdade sim, pagou* (He had his own law and with his freedom, yes, he paid)/*O dono dos ouros, das pratas dos rios das matas* (To the lord of the gold and silver in the rivers and forests)/*O rei, senhor* (The King, his majesty)

*O dia chegou* (The day came)/*O branco invasor com armas na mão* (The white invader with guns in hand)/*Brutais e crueis, sangue pelo chão* (Brutal and cruel, blood staining the ground)/*Corrente nos pés em altas galés, lamentos de dor* (Chains on their feet in tall ships, wails of pain)/*Mas a escravidão surgiu* (But slavery prevailed)/*Zumbi que foi o rei libertador* (Zumbi was the liberator king)/*O tempo passou e a raça no Brasil* (Time passed and the Brazilian race)/*Tem uma nova cor* (Has a new color)

*João Nogueira and Paulo Cezar Pinheiros*
*"Rei Senhor, Rei Zumbi, Rei Nagô," 1985*

their favor, Brazil's various dictators and military leaders also led the country out of its financial morass and into a period of economic prosperity. That lasted until around 1970, when the ball dropped. Strikes, recession, and national debt were the themes for the next 15 years.

## BRAZIL'S DEMOCRACY SINCE 1985

In 1985 the people elected Tancredo Neves to the presidency, based on his campaign for elections without intermediate representatives. Although he came from the leftist dictatorship, his ideas were actually quite democratic. Unfortunately, he died of an unusual lung disease before taking office and his plans were not well carried out by his vice Josè Sarney. The economic crisis continued. Inflation in 1988 reached 100 percent and corruption and the national debt grew. What also grew was the democratization of the government and the end of the military and leftist control. This was evidenced by the impeachment of President Fernando Collor in 1992. During this time, the official currency in Brazil changed with the tide—passing through the *crusado, crusado novo, cruzeiro, cruzeiro real,* and finally stopping at the *real* in 1994.

## Government and Economy

# GOVERNMENT

Since its independence from Portugal in 1889, Brazil's constitution has changed six times, most recently in 1988. The country has passed through periods of monarchy, oligarchy, fascism, leftist dictatorship, and capitalist democracy. The recent back-to-back presidencies of Itamar Franco and Fernando Henrique Cardoso (both recognized economists), led the country through a series of capitalistic and democratic reforms, both politically and economically. In many ways, they put the country on a track of economic growth and stability after the disaster of the dictatorship era. But Brazil's unequal distribution of wealth (the third worst in the world) continues to damage progress and fuel popular leftist movements. Corruption in government and inflated salaries for politicians also causes discontent among the masses.

President Lula, from the leftist workers party (PT), has promised to increase the minimum wage, fight hunger, and control inflation, along with managing the national debt that increased under Franco and Cardoso. Ironically, Lula has amassed a personal fortune far greater than those of his predecessors Cardoso and Franco. It is yet to be seen whether his administration will be less corrupt than any of those before him.

Voting is mandatory in Brazil between the ages of 18 and 70 and voluntary between 16 and 18. Those who don't vote are fined and their federal privileges suspended (passports and work documents). With local and national elections occurring every two years, it seems like the country is constantly voting for something. The streets are frequently filled with annoying political campaigns and TV commercials run continually, giving equal time to each party.

The governmental structure is similar to that of the United States with a three-branch system (legislative, judicial, and executive). They have two houses of congress, which consist of *deputados* and *senadores,* elected representatives

of the 26 states. There are 14 political parties, including a communist party, a green party, and an assortment of liberal and conservative groups. About four of these parties are most commonly seen in government.

Brazil's armed forces are volunteer-based and considered some of the best opportunities in the country for the non-elite. In fact, most Brazilians can't get into the military schools because of their high standards. The military police are not part of the armed forces, but the federal police are considered a paramilitary group. Brazil spends about 2 percent of the GNP on its military.

# EDUCATION

Like military schools, federal universities are the best and most sought after by all classes in Brazil. Federal universities are free to those who get in. Basic public education starts at 6 or 7 years of age and continues for eleven years. Besides universities, Brazil has many public and private technical schools, which provide post high-school studies in specific areas, like computer science, chemistry, bookkeeping, and tourism. Technical schools also provide completion of the basic high school course, known as *segundo grão* or second-degree education. The literacy rate in Brazil is around 86 percent.

# ECONOMY

To foreign investors, Brazil remains a volatile economy and high-risk investment opportunity. Coming out of a series of currency changes and economic adjustments, Brazil has managed to keep its new *real* in a relatively stable position. Economic reforms under the presidency of Fernando Henrique Cardoso encouraged foreign investment and in 1998 the IMF joined with Brazil to create a US$45-billion nuclear power plant along the coast of Rio de Janeiro state near Angra dos Reis. The next year, the *real* was disconnected from the dollar and the economy experienced some mild growth along with the devaluation of the *real*. Ironically, the devaluation of the *real* causes a boost in exports, which translates to increased revenue. Therein lies the complexity of Brazil's economic situation: keeping internal economic growth, foreign debt, and international competitiveness in balance.

Brazil's most competitive industries include metallurgical interests (bauxite, gold, iron ore, and other metals), hydroelectric power, which it sells primarily to neighboring South American countries, and agricultural products (soy, beef, coffee, sugar, and other crops). Brazil's agribusinesses are gaining international acceptance with huge soy exports to Japan and beef to Europe. In addition, Brazil has more than 200 million orange trees and sells more than US$5-billion worth of orange juice each year. Brazil has a highly developed manufacturing sector, including automobiles and electro-domestic goods (blenders, refrigerators, etc.).

Brazil produces approximately 80 percent of what it consumes in terms of natural gas, petroleum, food products, and manufactured goods. Recent laws requiring all new cars sold in Brazil to run on alcohol will increase this self-sufficiency factor.

President Luis Ignácio Lula da Silva has promised to focus on keeping inflation under control, along with cutting government pension programs and reforming the tax system. In the first few months of his presidency, Lula disappointed many of his supporters with a number of tax increases. Since then, he has been working to expand Brazil's presence in foreign markets and has created trade agreements with many countries, including China and Western European nations. Brazil's inflation remains high at around 20 percent. As a result, interest rates also remain high. Despite the high cost of borrowing in Brazil, the country has a consistent rate of growth among small and medium-sized businesses.

# People and Culture

## DEMOGRAPHICS

Brazil's population is around 183 million and grows about 1.2 percent every year. There are slightly more women than men and the population is young, with an average age of 27. There are numerous distinct ethnic groups throughout the country including native indigenous groups, Italians, Germans, Japanese, Ukrainian, Swiss, Finnish, and Arabic. In keeping with the country's origins, there are also countless mixtures, beginning with the three principal groups: Portuguese, African, and indigenous. The mixture of Portuguese (technically considered to be white European) with African is called *mulato*, the mixture of Portuguese with indigenous is called *caboclo*, and the mixture of indigenous with African is called *cafuzo*. About half of the population has some mixture of these principal races. It's easy to recognize the basic distribution of races in main regions across the country. In the north you'll find more indigenous and *caboclo* people; the central west and southeast regions have large *mulato* populations; and the south region is predominantly white and unmixed foreign races (German, Japanese, Argentinean).

Racial tensions are not nearly as common in Brazil as are class tensions. The separation of castes has always been based more on economic status than on skin color, although people of African and indigenous descent tend to be poorer. The minimum wage in Brazil is R$300/month and that is what most manual laborers, domestic employees, and clerks earn. Workers with some technical training can earn up to R$1,000/month in the big cities, but usually earn around R$500/month. In contrast, a city council member in a city of around 100,000 inhabitants earns as much as R$6,000 per month.

# RELIGION

Brazil is 80 percent Catholic and remains a very traditional country both in public and family life. Traditional phrases fall off the tongues of all Brazilians in daily conversations, like *"se Deus quiser"* (God willing), *"graças a Deus"* (thank God), and *"vai com Deus"* (go with God). These phrases have become almost more Brazilian than Catholic. Attempts by Protestant evangelical movements to erode the Catholic stronghold have largely been unsuccessful. Recently, however, large evangelical movements are on the rise in poor areas throughout the country, gaining success by playing off the people's love of congregating in very large groups. Brazil also has a small Islamic population and an even smaller Jewish population. Buddhism, Hinduism, and various esoteric religions are all represented—especially in the modern centers of Brasilia, São Paulo, and Rio de Janeiro. Brazil is full of spiritual healers, UFO sightings, natural medicines, jungle cures, spiritualism, and channeling of energies and spirit guides. In Bahia, the Candomblé religion is prevalent, but not being evangelical in nature, it has not spread to many other parts of the country. Some might call soccer a religion in Brazil, but that's a matter of opinion.

# LANGUAGE

Brazil's official language is Portuguese, but Brazilian Portuguese contains thousands of words from Tupi-Guarani, the principal native language of the country. This is particularly common with names of animals, fruits, and places. Except for a few small, immigrant cultures, everyone in Brazil speaks Portuguese. There are, however, vast differences in pronunciation within Brazil's borders as well as regional slang and idiomatic expressions that can seem to foreigners like completely different languages. Today, there are also hundreds of English words sprinkled throughout the language and it's common to hear words like email, clean, freezer, diet (DAI-ech), high-tech, and know-how.

# MUSIC AND DANCE

One of Brazil's greatest national treasures is its musical heritage. The uniquely Brazilian forms of samba and bossa nova are recognized the world over. But Brazil has many musical traditions, including country, Afro-Brazilian, and pop. And there's nothing like a little Brazilian rap or hip-hop to start your day.

## Country Music

To some, the most genuinely Brazilian music is known as *chorinho.* Born in the Brazilian countryside, *chorinho* is based principally on the guitar and *cavaquinho* (mandolin) but often includes various small bamboo flutes and *pandeiros* (tambourines). It is characterized by an intricate and often high-velocity pickin' and strummin', not unlike the guitar and banjo playing of American bluegrass music. The most recognized piece of music in this genre is known as *Brasileirinho,* which would no doubt be recognized almost anywhere in the world. Carmen Miranda's musical accompaniment was basically *chorinho* music. There are usually no vocals involved in *chorinho,* but some of the slow serenades do include some heart-felt crooning.

*Chorinho,* which literally means whining music, is found primarily in the hillsides of the central west and southeast regions. It has a kind of folk character to it. From *chorinho* came Brazil's most popular and ubiquitous country music, known as *sertaneja.* Brazil's *sertaneja* music is reminiscent of other Latin American country music. It is dominated by male sopranos, singing sappy lyrics that are 90 percent likely to include the words *paixão* (passion), *coração* (heart), *solidão* (loneliness), and *traição* (ya done me wrong). It is associated with Brazil's cowboy culture, which is prevalent in the lower half of the country, but *sertaneja* can be heard everywhere in Brazil. The most traditional ranch hands in the Pantanal and Rio Grande do Sul prefer a guitar-based music, known as Moda de Viola (guitar-style music).

## Samba and Bossa Nova

The best place to hear samba music in Brazil is

n the samba capital of Rio de Janeiro. A mixture of African and Portuguese folk music, samba most likely grew up in the slave communities in the latter half of the 19th century, but did not emerge as a musical form until the early 1900s in its association with Carnaval and popular festivals. In addition to its music and dance forms, samba includes a kind of history-telling with a focus on colonial themes and, of course, Carnaval. In Brazil, any time you hear samba music, you'll probably see samba dancing. The sensual shuffle-step is especially designed for women, but includes some simple steps for men as well. Women commonly dance samba alone, as seen in the Carnaval parades. Men, however, always dance samba with a female partner.

The mellow, melodic bossa nova groove emerged in the 1950s and 1960s as a downtempo take on samba. It came specifically from the musical and rhythmic interpretations of João Gilberto, a poor and introverted guitar player from Bahia who made his way to Rio de Janeiro to try out his ideas. His association with songwriter Antônio Carlos Jobim and American jazz musician Stan Getz made a permanent mark in the history of music. Bossa nova is not commonly played in bars and establishments in Brazil these days, although you'll hear plenty of remakes of Jobim's compositions. Although Gilberto gained more international recognition, Tom Jobim has always been more popular inside Brazil. Astrud Gilberto, João Gilberto's first wife, while quite famous among American Bossa Nova fans, is practically unknown in Brazil.

## Popular Music

While the masses were dancing to samba, the upper crust was dancing to orchestral music, including the big band music of the United States. Brazil's orchestral music was extremely popular and influenced the next phase of popular music, called Musica Popular Brasileiro (MPB), which emerged in the 1960s and 1970s. Some of the more famous names in this genre include Caetano Veloso, Chico Boarque, and Rita Lee. MPB borrows its rhythms from samba, rock, and big band and so varies widely in its interpre-

tations. Some Brazilian compositions are famous the world over, such as *Aquarela do Brasil* (Ari Barroso) and *O Bêbado e a Equilibrista* (João Bosco). Both are sweet melodies that have become unofficial national anthems. On the hard end of MPB are Brazil's many rock groups. There are also funk, hip-hop, and techno music cultures in the larger cities.

## Dance Music

With the exception of samba, Brazil's most recognized dance music comes from Bahia and the northeast and incorporates the special Afro-Brazilian rhythms that originated there. Among the more popular styles are Axé, Afoxé, and Forró. Axé is most commonly heard during Carnaval and in the group dancing events throughout the northeast. People dance to Axé music individually in a kind of sexy, aerobic line dancing. The music is characterized by strong Afro-Brazilian beats and suggestive (often humorously vulgar) lyrics. Afoxé is a more traditional, folkloric music characterized by slow, almost hypnotic rhythms. It's commonly heard during Carnaval in Salvador as the marching beat for the parading groups. You can also hear it in the music of Gilberto Gil. Forró music originated in the 1940s when American soldiers were stationed in the northern states and got together with locals to throw large dance parties. The music was based on a traditional African dance music, known as Maxixe, but introduced new instruments like the guitar and accordion. Maxixe dancing was considered pornographic at the time and was prohibited from being practiced in public. The lighter Forró dance style is a cross between swing and lambada.

## ART, THEATER, AND CINEMA

Given the art world's myopic focus on European art, South America has never enjoyed the kind of recognition that it probably deserves. Travelers are often surprised at the variety and quality of Brazilian art and at how the Brazilian art scene has kept pace with the great European movements. Some artists worthy of note include **Guinard,** with his loose expressionistic style, reminiscent of Chegal and Kandensky, and **Di Cavalcanti,** with a powerful expressionism/cubism along the lines of Picasso's early figurative works. In a similar vein is the work of **Candido Portinari,** who moves from a kind of Diego Rivera mural style to the morbid German Expressionist style. There are many other famous names in Brazilian art, including Aldemir Martins (pop expressionism), Amilcar de Castro (abstract expressionism), and Burle Marx (cubism).

Many of Brazil's artists are from the interior state of Minas Gerais, where art has been part of the culture since the gold rush of the 18th century. A great many painters and sculptors came to Central Minas to help decorate the churches and religious structures being erected there. Among the most recognized include two artists from the Ouro Preto/Mariana region: the great sculptor Aleijadinho and the painter Atayde. Later, Guinard set up his home and studio in Ouro Preto and taught many of Brazil's most famous contemporary artists.

Brazil's contemporary art scene is quite varied, with artists working in all kinds of styles and media. Most cities have more than one cultural center to present exhibits by local and national artists. In some cities, a tour of contemporary art galleries makes a great excursion and provides an interesting look at the South American contemporary art scene.

The Brazilian film industry is finally beginning to enter the world with quality productions, as evidenced in the films *Central Station* and *Cidade de Deus,* nominated for an Academy Award (for best editing) in 2003. Brazilian films are almost always about Brazil, which could account for some of their limited acceptance internationally.

## SPORTS

Contrary to popular belief, Brazil does have sports other than soccer. It's just that soccer is one of Brazil's national passions and overshadows pretty much everything else. During the 2004 Olympic Games in Athens, Brazil watched in anticipation while their beloved gymnast Daiane do Santos did her floor routine and the men's volleyball team took the gold medal against Italy. It's safe to say that volleyball, including beach volleyball, is one of Brazil's most popular sports next to soccer. But Brazilians love any sport in which Brazil excels, so when tennis champion Gustavo "Guga" Querten went to Wembledon, Brazil was seriously into the sport. And Brazil has continued to produce top-notch Formula One racers since the 1960s, as evidenced by the presence of Rubens Barrichello on the Ferrari racing team.

# Food and Accommodations

## FOOD

Brazilian cuisine is as mixed and varied as are the Brazilian people. Also like the people, Brazilian food can be traced back to the mixture of three distinct groups. Native indigenous groups in Brazil were blessed with an abundant supply of fish, meat, wild fruits, and root vegetables. One of the staples among the native peoples was the manioc root, which they would pass over a sort of grate made of wood and sharp stones. The resulting mass was dried on leaves and used as a base for various dishes. They had

to cook it for hours before eating because the particular strain of manioc in the northern region is poisonous when eaten raw. Even after the poisons have been cooked out, the root can make your mouth numb if you eat enough of it. The cooked manioc flower turns into a paste that is then spiced with leaves or peppers. The dish, called *tucupi,* is common in the Amazon region where the aboriginal influences are still strong. Dry manioc flower became a staple in Brazilian cooking all over the country and is known as *farinha de manjioca.* Given a few basic spices, the course flower becomes the ubiquitous Brazilian ingredient called *farofa,* used as a breading on meats or thrown into a plate of beans or a bowl of soup.

Enter the Portuguese in 1504 and the indigenous ingredients begin to find their way into more elaborate recipes. The Portuguese were heavily into fishing and drying fish, but they also brought a taste for beef, chicken, and other cultivated animals. When they brought African slaves into the country, the cuisine changed again. The Africans brought with them new techniques and recipes using coconut, palm oil, hot peppers, and ochre. The mix of these three culinary influences—indigenous, Portuguese, and African—has made Brazilian food what it is today.

Traditionally, Brazilian kitchens use a wood-fired oven, called a *fogão de lenha.* On top of the oven, dishes were prepared in clay pots, which are still preferred to this day. In certain regions, such as in Minas Gerais, stone pots were also used. Because so many meals were prepared in pots, a lot of Brazilian dishes are saucy, soupy concoctions that cook for hours over a hot flame.

## Regional Foods

In the Amazon region, recipes resemble their indigenous origins. It's common to find *tucupi* spiced with different leaves and fruits, like the *jambu* fruit. This basic dish is combined with roasted duck in the popular Amazonian dish, known as *pato de tucupi.* Another dish from this region is *tacacá,* which is *tucupi* mixed with dried shrimp and hot pepper. Also common in the Amazon is the use of fish from the various rivers of the area, including dishes prepared with piranha and *tucunaré,* both used frequently in soups. The *tambaqui* fish is often grilled over an open fire. For desert, it's *tucupi* with honey.

Moving over to the northeast region, the dish found on every menu is *moqueca,* a rich fish or seafood stew made with palm oil and coconut milk. Other ingredients common to the northeast region include palm hearts, shrimp, and green kidney beans (chewy and pithy, but preferred by folks from the region). Of course, there is the manioc root, which is known in

the region as *macaxeira* (mah-kah-SHAY-rah). A common dish made with *macaxeira* and coconut is called *tapioca,* a kind of dry pancake stuffed with fish, meat, or cheese. There are also sweet *tapiocas* that are generally delicious. A wonderful dish in the northeast region is sautéed fish or lobster in *molho de camarão,* or shrimp sauce, and the presence of crab in the many mangroves of the region puts all kinds of crab dishes on the menu. In the meat department, it's always *carne de sol,* a leathery piece of sun-dried meat served in all kinds of ways, often with *macaxeira* and *mantega de garrafa* (liquid butter). For desert, it's sweets made with coconut, pineapple, and cashews. There is also an abundant use of bananas and mangos.

Bahian recipes are different than the rest of the northeast region due to the extensive African influences there. You find the famous *Acarajé,* a thick batter deep fried in palm oil and filled with shrimp and spices. The Portuguese had a preference for a strong white fish, called *bacalhau* (similar to codfish), which Bahians prepare in all sorts of ways.

The interior state of Minas Gerais is known all over Brazil for its country cooking, the area being loaded with cattle and small farms. In Minas, the tables are abundant with simple comfort foods: meats, chicken and pork sausages, corn meal, and plenty of greens. A typical dish is *frango com quiabo,* which is chicken simmered in ochre and mild spices, generally served over rice. Also, *mocotó* is a soup made of beef bone marrow and corn meal. *caldo de feijão* (bean soup) and *canja de galinha* (chicken soup) are staples in Minas. A sub-culture of the area is the Tropeiro culture, which is responsible for foods like *feijão tropeiro,* a dry mixture of beans, sausage, fried pork skin, and *farofa.*

In Rio and São Paulo, you find every type of food in the world with a special emphasis on Italian and Japanese. There are also many Arabic, French, and German immigrants that bring their country's recipes to the table.

Mato Grosso and the Pantanal area present some exotic meats, like alligator, deer, armadillo, and tapir. There are also turtle-egg omelets and roasted pigeons. A pungent fruit, known as *pequi* is used in soups and rice. The region is the original source of many of the country's food folklore, such as the idea that combining mango with milk will make you sick or that eating bananas at night can be deadly.

In the south of Brazil, the cooking goes cowboy, and barbecued meat is the main item on the menu. Barbecues are done Argentinean style with skewered meats leaning against an open fire on the ground. The *gaúchos,* or cowboys, from the region are very knowledgeable about the different cuts of meat and how to cook each one on the fire. For accompaniment, there's *pão de milho* (corn bread), black beans, and fried manioc root (like country fries). You almost never see a *gaúcho* without his *chimarrão,* matte herb drunk hot or cold from a hollow gourd. Sweets include rice pudding and fruit bars made from *goiaba* (guava), *pessego* (peach), and *batata doce* (sweet potato).

## The Elusive Brazilian Breakfast

Many foreigners, especially Americans, are baffled about breakfast in Brazil. It is a meal that is not traditionally eaten outside the home. For that reason, you won't find breakfast restaurants anywhere in the country (with a few exceptions specifically geared toward foreigners). A traditional breakfast inside the home often consists of fresh bread and butter with sliced *presunto* (ham), sweet bread or cake, and of course, coffee with loads of sugar. That's about it. Brazilians are well aware that Americans love their *big breakfast* as they humorously refer to it. It's customary for hotels to serve a more elaborate breakfast for their guests, consisting of various types of fresh bread, sweets, cakes, and juices. You'll always find sliced *presunto* and cheese. Many will also have some international items, like scrambled eggs, quiche, and cereals or granola with milk. An interesting creation that is very common throughout Brazil is a mixture of sliced hot dogs in a kind of light tomato sauce (do they think that's an American dish?). Some hotels put on a lavish buffet with a variety of these items as well as their regional dishes.

If you have to eat breakfast out, your best bet is to go straight to a *lanchonete* or *padaria* and order a *misto quente* (grilled ham and cheese), *pão com mantega quente* (hot bread with butter), or one of their pre-made finger foods, like *pão de queijo.*

## How Lunch Works

In the 1980s, a new craze hit Brazil that has turned into a national tradition: the self-service lunch buffet. Today, it's difficult to find a town or village that does not have some kind of self-service buffet, also called *comida a-quilo.* Interestingly, it's difficult to find self-service restaurants for dinner. The buffets work in various ways: Sometimes you pay one price and eat as much as you like (called *a vontade*) and other times, you pay one price for a single pass at the buffet and only one type of meat. Economical restaurants will offer a *prato feito* or ready-made plate that is generally about R$4 and is made for you by the staff. It's loaded with carbohydrates. An executive plate is an elaborate *prato feito.*

## Drinks

Brazil is by far the leading coffee producer on the planet. During the dictator years, most of Brazil's coffee production was motivated by quantity instead of quality and it's still difficult to find high-quality coffee outside of the big cities. But you can find great coffee in Brazil if you know where to look. Most of the best coffee is made for export, but some stays in Brazil. High-end shops in Rio and São Paulo carry the best beans. São Paulo state and Minas Gerais are the leading coffee-growing areas. Still, it's baffling how the world's leading producer of coffee can have so few coffee choices on a day-to-day basis, even in the better shops. Don't expect Starbucks here. Outside of Rio and São Paulo, don't even expect to find authentic mocha, latté, or cappuccino drinks.

Brazilians drink their coffee strong (usually run through the filter two or three times), sweet (often sugar or sweetener is already added for you), and in small doses. *Café com leite* is popular throughout the day and is usually about 70 percent milk. An alternative is *café*

the famous caipirinha

*pingado* (coffee with a drop of milk), which you can order *bem escuro* to make sure it's not all milk. Brazilians make fun of American coffee, which they say is 25 percent coffee and 75 percent hot water. Espresso, thankfully, is made the same way in Brazil as in Italy or the United States. If you don't want sugar in your coffee, get into the habit of asking first. The answer will be either *tem* or *tem não* (there is sugar, or there is not).

Tea is not as popular in Brazil as is coffee or soda, but you can find some popular tea blends in restaurants and cafés (and supermarkets for making in your hotel). Green tea can be difficult to find outside of São Paulo, where there is a large Asian population, but you can often find it in health-food stores or homeopathic pharmacies. Herbal teas are easy to find in markets and pharmacies and are frequently used as home remedies. Some of the most common are *carqueija* and *sete hervas*; both are excellent diuretics. *Chá matte* is like a black tea and *herva matte* is the green herb drink common in Argentina and southern Brazil.

Soda, known as *refrigerante* (heh-FREE-jeh-rahn-chee), includes Coke and Guaraná. The latter, having been repeatedly denied by the FDA for sale in the United States, is made from the *guaraná* fruit, which is high in caffeine. Powdered *guaraná* seeds can be used as a powerful stimulant. Another interesting soda is Matte-Couro, which tastes like cream soda. It's made with *erva matte* tea, an herb called *chapeu de couro* (literally, leather hat), and carbonated water.

Juices are a great bounty in Brazil and Brazilians love to put fruits and vegetables into blenders and spin up a concoction. Many juice stands offer fresh juices and some use frozen pulp. You can usually ask for your own mixture if you can remember all the vocabulary. Brazilians make juices with either milk or water and always add a lot of sugar, no matter how sweet the fruit is to begin with. Remember to ask for your juice *sem açúcar* if you don't want it super-sweet. (Note that *suco de maracujá,* or passion fruit juice, is barely drinkable without some sugar.) If you're worried about the water used in your juice, you can ask for *agua filtrada* or *agua mineral* in your juice.

Water is another of Brazil's greatest natural resources. In fact, scientists have recently found the world's largest underground water table in Brazil (under Brazil, actually), stretching from southern Minas Gerais all the way to Argentina. While most small streams and rivers in the metropolitan states of Rio, São Paulo, and Minas Gerais are polluted, clean water is not a problem to find, as witnessed by the variety of bottled waters across the country. Many small towns all over the country have their own mineral springs and wells and offer their inhabitants clean drinking water on tap. Still, it's always best to drink bottled water just to be sure. You'll find more on water under *Health and Safety* later in this chapter.

## Alcohol

*Cachaça* is to Brazil what sake is to Japan or wine is to France. Since Brazil's original cash crop was sugar, the hillsides all over the country were covered in sugarcane. Like moonshine stills in the backwoods of the United States, *cachaça* stills, or *alambiques,* could be found on just about every farm across the country. To this day, people from the *campo* (countryside) maintain *cachaça* stills to brew up a batch of the hot juice from the few sugarcane plants they keep on the farm. Some areas are famous for their *cachaça artesanal,* such as Bahia, Minas Gerais, and Goias. The area around Paraty in Rio de Janeiro is also famous for its small *cachaça* stills. Like the small wineries in France, the small *cachaça* makers in the backwoods of Brazil often produce the best product.

Like any other hard liquor, *cachaça* comes in various grades and qualities and there are many experts dedicated to the study of its production. Yellow *cachaça* is generally more flavorful and mellow and is considered a *cachaça* for sipping, while the white (actually clear) stuff is used for mixing and shooting. Some of the worst stuff is only slightly better than drinking the alcohol they put in cars and can do some damage to brain cells and stomach linings.

A drink favored by tourists, but also popular with Brazilians (although they don't like to admit it), is the caipirinha, made with crushed limes, sugar, and white *cachaça.* A version made with vodka is also popular, called a Caipivodka (or Caipiroska in Bahia). A delightful drink is a Caipifruita, which is made with tropical fruits; the best is with the sweet Brazilian pineapple.

Since the upper classes in Brazil are often preoccupied with being different from the masses, they have recently abandoned the consumption of *cachaça* and turned to whisky. Because mixed drinks are not common in Brazil, whisky is usually just drunk straight with ice. There are not many whiskies from which to choose, but a good bar will have two or three brands, including Jack Daniels and Jonny Walker.

All the above notwithstanding, there is little doubt that the national drink of Brazil these days is beer. In fact, the consumption of beer is right up there with soccer and Carnaval on the list of Brazil's favorite recreational activities and just about the entire country goes out on Friday and Saturday nights for a cold one. Ironically, there are only a handful of commercial beers and they all taste about the same to

foreigners: light and pale. Fortunately, there is a growing interest in microbreweries and it's possible to find excellent fresh beers in the larger cities. Likewise, it's easy to find imported beers in the cities.

Brazil's wine industry is getting better every year and some of the best wineries have even received international attention. Most of the wine is produced in the southern region, where the climate is best for grape growing. Over time, the region has been able to produce some excellent wines. Most of them are difficult to find outside of the south, but a well-stocked supermarket or wine specialty store (big city only) will have some. You should also be able to find some of the popular Chilean and Argentinean wines, although they are relatively expensive (about the same price you'd pay in the States). A decent Brazilian red wine is Miolo.

## ACCOMMODATIONS

Tourism in Brazil is a major industry and most hot spots have plenty of lodging for visitors, in all price and style categories. In many cases, you will be able to walk into a destination and shop for a room, even in peak season. However, because some spots get overbooked at this time, it is recommended that you make reservations in advance by phone or email if you are going to be traveling during peak months. You can usually call just a few days or a week ahead and book your room (Brazilians are notorious for making plans at the last minute). In the low season, you can make advanced reservations if you prefer not to hassle with shopping for a competitive price when you arrive. In some locations, walking from hotel to hotel is easy, and in other places hotels may be quite far apart. Walk-in travelers are often given a higher price than those making previous arrangements. The walk-in price is called the *preço do balcão* (counter or balcony price). This is the price listed behind the receptionist at the check-in counter. You should never pay this price, except when there are no other options available and the hotel is crowded. Simply state flat-out that you don't ever pay the counter price and want a discount. When making reservations by email or phone, you usually receive a discounted price. To be sure, always make it a practice to ask if you are receiving the balcony price or a discounted price (if they know that you are a foreigner, you might get the balcony price automatically). If you arrive at the desk and see that the balcony price is the same that you are paying, be sure to complain to the manager and ask for a discount before checking in. If your hotel does not list its prices, you can ask other guests what they are paying and tell the hotel to match it. If you've already paid, then ask for a discount on something else, like a free meal. Some hotels make it a point to not reveal their prices and try to avoid giving you a standard rate. These places are probably adjusting their prices depending on the nationality of the guest, the value of the dollar, and the time of year. It doesn't always mean that you're getting a bad price, but the policy leaves a bad taste. Personally, I avoid these places.

In some hotels, you are asked to pay a deposit to secure your room. If you are sure about the hotel, then go ahead and leave up to 50 percent. If you are asked to pay the entire price in advance, go to a different hotel. Only in the best hotels at the most popular locations during peak season (or festivals) will you encounter problems finding a room. When shopping for a room on the spot, you should pay attention to the neighborhood in which the hotel is located and the general condition of the building and interior. Most likely, if the building itself is not well kept, then the entire package will be substandard. In Brazil, you usually get what you pay for, and cheap hotels are probably going to have some kind of drawback, whether it be the location, the service, the condition of the rooms, or the type of facilities offered (for example, shared bathrooms). There are several types of accommodations in Brazil, but the lines between them are often very fuzzy. In general, you'll find the following:

## Motels

In Brazil, a motel is almost always a getaway for couples and rented by the hour. That doesn't mean they are all sleazy. On the contrary, there are both low-end and high-end motels and some are designed for middle-class, married couples. They offer all kinds of in-room facilities, including saunas, hot tubs, satellite TV, and CD players. They are usually very privacy-oriented and are designed to let guests enter and leave without being seen. The motel culture in Brazil comes from some very special conditions in the Brazilian domestic lifestyle. In particular, most people simply don't have any privacy at home. Even in middle and upper-class homes, families are crowded together and children live with their parents until they get married. Living alone is a very foreign concept to Brazilians. As a result, couples go to a motel for a few hours of privacy. Almost every reasonably-sized town in Brazil will have some motels lined up along the outskirts of town. For some strange reason, most motels are given American names, such as the Motel Las Vegas or Lone Star Motel.

## Hostels (Albergues)

Brazil is full of hostels and they vary widely in quality. Often, they are decent facilities that are located farther away from the main area. In some cases, they are right in the middle of the action, which may or may not be a good thing. Not all of the hostels in the Hostelling International chain are necessarily good and sometimes you can find a regular hotel or *pousada* around the corner for the same price with private facilities. The only way to really know for sure is to ask other travelers. You can start with the recommendations in this book. Hostels almost always have group facilities with shared bathrooms and one or two private rooms for couples. If the hostel is good, the private rooms will always be booked up, so you should reserve one in advance if that's what you want. You should ask if towels and *ropa de cama* (bedding) are included. There may also be an extra fee to store your bags, even if you're going to be checking in later that day. Most hostels have Internet, and you may want to ask whether or not it's free for guests. The best hostels are the ones that serve as central meeting places for travelers and offer group events, such as barbecues or excursions. There are particularly good hostels in Natal, Salvador, Olinda, Ouro Preto, Arraial d'Ajuda, São Paulo, and Florianópolis. All are listed in this book. The going rate for hostels is R$15–25 per person. Breakfast is usually included, but you should ask, just in case.

Note: If you end up sleeping in questionable conditions, you might want to invest in a bar of anti-bacterial, anti-parasitic soap. Look for the Foldan brand at any drug store.

## Budget Hotels

You can usually tell immediately if your budget hotel is going to result in a good experience; just look at the condition of the facilities, both inside and out. In most cases, these are old, dilapidated buildings, with uncomfortable beds, fuzzy TVs, small bathrooms, and Brazilian showers. The Brazilian shower is a most dumbfounding creation. It consists of an electric showerhead that heats the water as it passes through the head. There are exposed wires running along an aluminum pipe (sometimes PVC) and into the wall with 220 volts of electricity coursing through them. There you are, standing in a puddle of water with live wires dangling above your head. Since the device heats water on the fly, you never use up the hot water. However, the velocity of the water (i.e., the pressure) affects the temperature: The more water, the colder the shower. The more elaborate devices have several settings, including one for *inverno* that heats the water pretty well. Surprisingly, these devices are pretty safe and the worst that people ever experience is a mild shock. When shopping for budget hotels, always ask to take a look at the room and pay particular attention to the bed and bathroom. Budget hotels will cost anywhere from R$60 to R$120, depending on the popularity of your destination. They almost always include a simple breakfast.

## Mid-Range Hotels

Depending on the location, mid-range hotels can fall closer to the budget side or the high-end side of the fence. There are chains of mid-range hotels that offer streamlined, standardized rooms and service. These are usually excellent and economical, with gas-heated showers, clean rooms, and no breakfast

## BRAZIL'S MOST CHARMING INNS

Imagine finding a list of the most charming hotels in Brazil, each one located in an excellent tourist destination and offering the best conditions, most comfortable rooms, and most charming, rustic decoration of any hotel in its area. What's more, each inn is loaded with local arts and crafts and follows a code of environmental conduct. Sound like a hotel wish list you'd like to have? All you have to do is visit the **Roteiro de Charme** (Charm Circuit) website and check out the group's associate members. They are located at www.roteiros-decharme.com.br. Members of the Roteiro are generally among the most charming hotels in their respective areas and adhere to high standards of decoration, comfort, and service.

Besides being well designed and well run, inns in the Roteiro de Charme also follow a code of environmental conduct to help reduce their impact on the environment and support local environmental projects and activities. Their code of conduct includes the use of environmentally friendly products (and disuse of toxic or corrosive products), respect for local cultures and values, use of energy conserving products, and an active effort to recycle and use recycled products. This code of conduct is more than a piece of paper. The Roteiros de Charme organization signed a memorandum of cooperation with the United Nations Environmental Program (UNEP) to recognize and support each other's efforts. All member hotels in the Roteiro are contractually bound to follow the code. Many of the hotels in the Roteiro are listed in appropriate sections throughout this book.

included. They are almost always found in cities, as they are marketed to business travelers and not vacationers, so they may not be located close to the tourist activities. A good chain is the Ibis Accor (www.accorhotels.com). Other companies are beginning to copy the Ibis model and you'll find independent versions popping up all over Brazil.

Otherwise, mid-range hotels are generally clean and offer gas-heated showers, safe locations, and reasonably comfortable beds. They usually lack any sort of character or charm and sometimes appear to go out of their way to find tacky decorations for the rooms. Still, for the money, this can be an excellent category to seek out. Be sure to check if they have gas-heated or Brazilian showers. The price range is from R$100–200 and breakfast is always included (except as noted above).

## High-End Hotels

Perhaps the best category for cost-benefit is the high-end range, hotels that go for R$200–500. These offer semi-luxury experiences and will give you nothing to complain

about in most cases. Beds are comfortable, showers are gas-heated, and you get cable TV, phone, and often an in-room safe. Some are oriented to business travelers and provide desks, meeting tables, and in-room Internet connections. Hotels in this category usually put on an abundant spread for breakfast and almost always have a pool, gym, and sauna. With a few exceptions in the largest of cities, most high-end hotels are located in the best neighborhoods with views and easy access. Given the exchange rate, these hotels are an excellent value for anyone wanting a quality experience. Some of the high-end chains that you will encounter in Brazil are the Parthenon by Accor (www.accorhotels.com), the Atlantica Hotels (www.atlanticaho-tels.com.br), and the Meliá Hotels and Resorts (www.solmelia.com).

## Luxury Hotels

If you're interested in luxury accommodations and top-notch service, then look into the various luxury hotels located in cities and urban vacation spots all over the country. In most cases, you'll

one of the Roteiro de Charme inns in Porto de Galinhas

get a very comfortable room with gas-heated water, air-conditioning, good lighting, music, cable TV, telephone, and room safe. Facilities will almost always include a restaurant, bar, pool, and sauna. Some offer extensive facilities and border on full-scale resorts. You'll pay around R$500 for these rooms. Some groups that offer luxury accommodations in Brazil include the Blue Tree Hotels (www.bluetree.com.br), the Marriott (www.marriott.com), and Othon Palace Hotels (www.hoteisothon.com.br).

## Pousadas and Guest Houses

Most beaches and small towns that do not have high-rise buildings and high-end hotels, will offer a range of *pousadas,* bed-and-breakfast inns that usually offer more in the way of charm than their concrete cousins. *Pousadas* can range from extra rooms in somebody's home to four-star bed-and-breakfasts with award-winning restaurants. Prices also vary wildly, but on the whole, you get what you pay for. A *pousada* that costs R$45 double occupancy will probably be similar to a hostel, whereas a R$150 price tag is likely to get you a very charming place. One thing you can count on when you see the word *pousada* used is that it will not be in a multi-story building. The only way to know if a *pousada* is quaint and charming is to take a look around. The lobby will be your first clue. Many *pousadas* have rooms in separate chalets and these are usually the best. Places called guest houses are high-end *pousadas* where the owner lives in one of the rooms. They are often excellent places to stay.

# Sports and Recreation

## CAMPING

Camping out in Brazil is still an uncertain proposition on the whole. Before spending the night in a tent out in the open, you should be very sure about the safety of the campground or park in which you will be sleeping. Unfortunately, not all national parks are safe, so you cannot rely on that label to help. In general, you need to be more careful in the southeast and central west regions than anywhere else. Due to the large populations and huge poor areas, the parks and mountainous areas of these regions are often loaded with criminals waiting to assault anyone passing through. The national parks and campgrounds recommended in this book are safe. In addition, wherever you find closed conditions that require the presence of local guides, you can count on the area being patrolled and secure. Some examples include the Chapada Diamantina in Bahia and the Serra dos Orgãos in Rio State.

In addition, you can camp out on several beaches in Brazil, where the camping facilities are right on the beach. Some places include beaches around Paraty, Ilha Grande, and the south part of Florianópolis Island. You can also camp on the beach on the island of the Superagüi National Park in Paraná.

Unfortunately, Brazil has a long way to go to make conditions safe for people to camp out under the stars. Most foreigners prefer to stay in *pousadas* and create their adventures during the day.

## RADICAL SPORTS

The best way to participate in hang gliding, rappelling, mountain climbing, scuba diving, or other adventure sport is to set up your excursion in advance. If you are coming to Brazil specifically to participate in one of these endeavors, then try to arrange everything before you leave through one of the local agencies in the area that you will be visiting. There are phone numbers and websites listed throughout this book. If you prefer to plan your excursions after you arrive in Brazil, then try to plan at least three days in advance with local guides. Be sure to ask about equipment rental, transportation to and from the site, lodging, fees for guides, and if there are any other costs involved. Favorite places for jumping off cliffs with wings or parachutes include the Parque Florestal de Ibitipoca on the border between Minas Gerais and Rio de Janeiro state. For best results, check with guides in Rio for excursions. Also, the Chapada Diamantina in Bahia and the Parque Nacional da Serra do Cipó in Minas Gerais (check with Lirio at lirio.tour@bol.com.br) have rappelling and other sports. The Serra dos Orgãos National Park in Rio de Janeiro state has white-water rafting, climbing, and rappel. The beaches south of Rio de Janeiro have hang gliding and paragliding and you'll find kite surfing all over the coast.

## FISHING

Sportfishing is extremely popular in Brazil and you can find fishing excursions all over the coast and in the lakes and rivers inland. Ironically, the fresh-water fishing is more promoted as a tourist activity than ocean fishing and the Amazon and Pantanal regions have some of the most well-developed fishing programs in the country. For sportfishing, this is the best way to go, as tour agencies handle all required licenses and permissions. There is an endless supply of boats designed for multi-day excursions.

Brazil is one of the world's best locations for open-ocean fishing, especially during September–January, when the ocean currents bring warm waters to the coast of Brazil. One of the most sought-after places is along the cost of Espirito Santo state. Near the capital city of Victoria, you can find excursions that go out in search of the big game, including blue marlin and enormous white marlin. The Brazilian coastline is also frequented by tuna, swordfish, and barracuda.

Since most of the fishing off the coast of Brazil is either *artesanal* (subsistence fishing) or commercial, there are not as many programmed sportfishing adventures for tourists. However, the south of Brazil is known for its beach fishing adepts and numerous international competitions have been held on the beaches of Santa Catarina and Rio Grande do Sul.

For more information on fishing in Brazil, you can email the national sportfishing development group PNDPA at pndpa@embratur.gov.br. Some interesting information is also available at www.pescaventura.com.br.

## WHALE-WATCHING

From around July to November, the Antarctic region begins to freeze and thousands of whales make their way north to the warmer waters off the coast of Brazil. The migration also coincides with the gestation period of many species and their arrival is accompanied by the birth of new calves. Whales hang around during the entire season until their calves are strong enough to face the cold waters of the south. In the meantime, they dance and play near the surface of shallow waters, nurse their young, and mate again. Observing these activities is one of the most exciting excursions you can take during the winter months in Brazil. Boats get right up next to the whales and in some places, you can even see whales from the shore. Humpback whales are usually spotted along Brazil's northeastern coastline and the most popular place for whale-watching in this region is off the coast of Bahia. Centers for whale-watching excursions can be found in Praia do Forte, Itacaré, Arraial d'Ajuda, and the Abrolhos Islands/Caravelas.

In the waters of the southern region, the most common species is the Australian Whale, the huge, shiny black whale that weighs up to 40 tons. Once at the point of extinction, the *Baleia Franca,* as they are known in Brazil, now numbers in the thousands. Many of them come up to Brazil to give birth in the winter. The most active locations are along the southern coast from Florianópolis to the bottom of Brazil. Two particularly exciting locations are the Island of Campeche just off Florianópolis and along the coast near Praia do Rosa to the south of Florianópolis. In both of these locations, it's possible to see whales from the land, but excursions can take you out to meet them up close.

## SURFING

Not only is surfing one of the most popular sports in Brazil, but the surfer is given a kind of status among beach goers. More than a few of Brazil's most popular beach villages and vacation spots were first discovered by surfers between 1970 and 1990. It almost seems that wherever surfers congregate, others will eventually follow. It's difficult to point to just a few principal surf locations, when you have more than 7,000 kilometers of coastline to choose from. Every state and coastal region has its excellent surf spots. You even have the uncanny fresh-water surfing in the eastern Amazon region, where several rivers empty into the ocean (including the Amazon River) to create the river wave known as the Pororoca. There are also waves that reach up to four meters on the beaches near Belém, in the semi-salty Marajó Bay.

Other highlights include the village of Pipa to the south of Natal, and the beaches near Mangue Seco and Itacaré in Bahia. All of these locations have excellent surfing communities and condi-

tions. In the southeast region, some highlights include the beaches of Barra de Tijuca, south of Rio City. There are frequent competitions there and on the upper end of Ipanema Beach. Also, Trindade in Rio de Janeiro state has great waves at Praia Brava, and the beaches around Ubatuba are spectacular for waves and beautiful crowds of people. On the road from Rio to São Paulo, you should stop at Maresias, where many international competitions are held.

Heading to the southern states, you might stop at Prainha on the Island of São Francisco do Sul. The waves are about two meters and the water is clear and bright green. The best surfing conditions in the south are on the Island of Florianópolis, where you'll find about a dozen excellent beaches, including Praia Joaquina, where there have been a number of international competitions. Praia Mole and Praia Moçambique are two other highlights in Florianópolis. Most surfers stay in the Barra da Lagoa neighborhood, where there are many surf shops and excellent access to the rest of the island.

kite surfing

# SNORKELING AND SCUBA DIVING

Brazil's official tourism advocacy group, EMBRATUR (EMpresa BRAsileira, de TURismo), has recently declared scuba diving as one of nine principal tourism categories in Brazil. If nothing else, that means they recognize the value and importance of diving as an attraction in Brazil. With more than 7,000 kilometers of coastline, numerous islands, and an untold number of shipwrecks in local waters, Brazil is, indeed, one of the South America's best diving destinations. More and more areas of the Brazilian coastline are being turned into sanctuaries or aquatic parks, particularly for diving activities and preservation of marine life. There are official groups to protect the proliferation and habitats of sea turtles (TAMAR) and the *peixe boi* (sea cow, a salt-water cousin of the manatee). Numerous locations off Brazilian shores are favored by dolphins, and whales come to give birth to new calves in the warm Brazilian waters between June and October.

Just about every major diving spot in Brazil is home to a school with dive masters. It's easy to find equipment rentals, classes, and guides to take you out—from 4–70 meters down, day or night. A full scuba course with recognized certification takes 4–5 days and costs about R$600. This is a great way to spend a week on the coast of Brazil. A single beginner dive goes for about R$90 and many are performed in shallow ocean water.

The best months in which to visit Brazil for diving purposes are December–March, when the waters are clearest. Following are the best locations:

## The Northeast Coast

The most famous location for diving on the northeast coast (and perhaps in all of Brazil) is around the Island of Fernando de Noronha. Designated as a natural preserve, the island's waters are crystal clear, with visibility of up to 50 meters, and maintain an average temperature of 27°C. Fish range in size from small tropical species to dolphins, sharks, and even whales (diving is not permitted with whales and dolphins but they can be seen off the coast in great numbers). There are more than 250 species of fish and five different types of sharks in the area. It's also common to see huge sea turtles of up to 300 kilos. Favorite locations include the many natural underwater trails, or corridors, that are full of sponges, coral, lobster, tropical fish, and small sharks. There are dive schools on the island and back in the port of Natal.

On the coast around Natal is the largest area of underwater reefs in Brazil at the *Parrachos* of Maracajaú. There are also two accessible shipwrecks in the area. The water is super-clear and the bottom is a bed of white sand. Dive masters can be found in the Ponta Negra neighborhood of Natal.

Along the northern coast of Recife are a number of shipwrecks that are easily reached at about 30–40 meters. In fact, the Recife area is considered a ship cemetery due to the number of wrecks in the local waters. The area around the Island of Itamaraca has clear water with decent visibility and a variety of fish. In the south, there are the natural pools in the area of Porto de Galinhas, a haven for snorkeling but also excellent for less advanced scuba dives.

## The Coast of Bahia

In the south of Bahia, off the coast of Porto de Seguro is one of Brazil's marine parks, the Recife de Fora Marine Preserve. There is a great variety of crustaceans and reef species there. To the south is the unparalleled Archipelago de Abrolhos and the Abrolhos National Marine Park, about 70 kilometers from shore. Formed by an ancient volcano, the archipelago has shallow turquoise waters from as little as two meters deep (excellent for snorkeling as well as scuba diving). The area is considered to have one of the highest concentrations of fish on the planet and it's common to see manta rays and sea turtles. In the winter months, whales are commonly spotted splashing in these waters. There is even a shipwreck here of a 1939 Italian ship. Visibility in the summer months is as high as 30 meters. Boats generally leave from the town of Caravelas. Overnight trips are available with sleeping and dining arrangements on board. Dive masters can also be found in Porto Seguro and Arraial d'Ajuda.

The area of Itacaré and Barra Grande is becoming known as a scuba diving haven. Dolphins are often spotted offshore, along with whales in the winter. There are underwater pools all along the peninsula of Barra Grande. Dive masters are based in Itacaré.

## The Coast of Rio de Janeiro

The highlights in this area are the calm, clear waters of Ilha Grande and Angra dos Reis. On the Island of Ilha Grande, you'll find dive masters to take you all around the island, especially over to the far side, where there are a couple of shipwrecks. Around the islands in the Bay of Angra dos Reis, there are locations for divers of all levels, including snorkeling in the shallow waters around the Ilha de Paquetá. There, you find a variety of sea life, including octopus and manta rays. For more advanced divers, there are a number of shipwrecks in these waters and even an underwater cavern, some six meters below the surface. Other locations include the Ilha dos Meros and Laje Branca, both with clear water and depths of around 14–18 meters.

The Bay of Paraty is equally calm and clear and there are some favorite diving spots among the local dive masters—including around Ilha Comprida, Ilha dos Cocos, and Ilha dos Ratos. There are 65 islands in the Bay of Paraty and many have excellent conditions for diving with depths of up to 15 meters and visibility of around 8 meters. The waters are replete with starfish, sponges, and coral, along with many tropical fish. Several dive schools are based in Paraty. Other locations off the coast of Rio include the plant-filled waters around Arraial do Cabo and Cabo Frio, where the visibility is around 20 meters and you can dive to more than 80 different locations containing wreckage from ships. Seahorses, turtles, and colorful crustaceans are common here. Nearby are some interesting small islands around Buzios.

## The São Paulo Coast

One of the best locations for diving off the coast of São Paulo is off the coast of Ubatuba. With various islands spotting the bay, the options for diving are numerous. Favored locations include Ilha Anchieta, Ilha Vitória, Ilha das Palmas, and Ilha das Couves. Visibility in the area reaches 20 meters and the depths range from 5–25 meters.

Around the Island of Ilhabela is a marine sanctuary, where diving is actively encouraged. There is a great quantity of fish and lobster in this area and even a statue of Neptune six meters below the surface to honor the underwater world. There are several shipwrecks in these waters, including the Aymoré at a depth of only 12 meters. Others are resting peacefully in deeper waters.

## The Santa Catarina Coast

The Arvoredo Marine Preserve is the largest of Brazil's national marine parks and can be accessed from Bombinhas or Florianópolis. The visibility is the highlight here at around 30–40 meters. There are islands, sea mounts, and rock formations to explore with depths of 4–50 meters. You can also dive near the Island of Campeche off the coast of Florianópolis, where there are many sea turtles, sea lions, and even penguins in the winter months.

## The Pantanal

Divers interested in fresh-water dives should not miss the incredible opportunities in the Pantanal. There, the water is said to be some of the clearest in the world. You can dive in Rio Formoso and Rio Prata with numerous species of fish and water plants and take a dive down into the Lagoa Misteriosa, where the water is transparent and the bottom of the lake has not yet been calculated (more than 220 meters deep). The highlights are the cave-diving opportunities, including underwater caverns of 1,800 meters in length and 50 meters in depth.

# CARNAVAL

Most people think of either Rio de Janeiro or Salvador for Carnaval festivities. Indeed, these two cities host two of Brazil's most all-out, over-

# A COUNTRY OF MANY FESTIVALS

It seems like anywhere you go in Brazil, you'll find some kind of festival taking place. The number of local and regional festivals is almost endless. Many of these are Catholic in origin, but others celebrate local foods or special activities (dancing, fishing, sailing, etc.). There is almost always plenty of food, music, and dance involved. Here is a list of some of the country's principal festivals:

**January:** New Year's Eve in Copacabana, Ouro Preto, and Florianópolis; Festival de Cinema in Tiradentes.

**February:** Carnaval all over Brazil.

**March:** Semana Santa all over Brazil, but especially in Olinda, Ouro Preto, Congonhas, and S.J. del Rei.

**April:** Micarambe in Campina Grande.

**May:** Festival di Boteco in Belo Horizonte.

**June:** Festa Junina in Campina Grande and Caruaru; Fortal in Fortaleza; Ox Festival in Parintins.

**July:** Festival de Inverno in Minas Gerais and Campos de Jordão; Semana de Vela in Ilhabela; Dance Festival in Joinville; Festival de Cachaça in Belo Horizonte (at the Cerraria Souza Pinto, downtown); CarnaBelô in Belo Horizonte.

**August:** Cowboy Festival in São Paulo State (Barretos); Festival de Cinema in Gramado; Festival de Gastronomia in Tiradentes.

**September:** MaceióFest in Maceió.

**October:** Cirio de Nazaré in Belém; Octoberfest in Pomerode, Brusque, and Blumenau.

**December:** Christmas all over Brazil; Carnatal in Natal.

**Other Food Festivals:** Banana (Corumbá), Capuaçu (Mosqueiro Island in Belém), Ora Pro Nobis (Sabará), Potato (Ouro Branco), Jabuticaba (Sabará), Acai (Belém), Grape (Caxias); Wine Festival (Curitiba).

the-top Carnaval celebrations. But to complete the list, you'd have to add the Carnavals of Recife/Olinda and Florianópolis. By far the biggest production is given to the Carnaval in Rio de Janeiro, where the main event takes place in the Sambódromo, a special parade arena. This is the Carnaval that is televised all over the world (except perhaps in the United States, where nudity is not permitted on television). In Salvador, the festivities are divided into three main street parades and focus on drumming and music *blocos* that march down the streets in uniforms and costumes. These groups often march behind a *trio elétrico,* which is a large truck rigged with sound equipment and a stage. The main idea in Rio is to watch, whereas the main idea in Salvador is to walk with a group. The festivities in Recife/Olinda are some of the most traditional in the country, featuring elaborate costumes, folkloric music, and dancing. But don't get the idea that this is a small folk festival. The Recife Carnaval is probably larger than that in Salvador in terms of quantity of participants. More than one million people join the main parade at sunrise in the old city center. In Olinda, parades of huge papier-maché dolls hit the cobblestone streets, along with traditional costumes and dances in the *praças.* The Florianópolis Carnaval is probably the smallest of this group and occurs mostly in the old city center. It features *trio elétricos* with groups marching up and down the city streets, costumes, and a large participation by transvestites, who have helped it become Brazil's most gay Carnaval.

## Regional Events

Besides the big events, there are numerous regional Carnavals that take place in small cities and historical towns all over the country. A few worth noting include the very rowdy festival in Ouro Preto, which includes various small parades that roam the streets of the city, usually accompanied by drumming or marching bands. There are always live music shows in the main *praça* of town and floats with more festivities in the Barra neighborhood. Public drunkenness and noise is the main event here. A more mild and contained version of this is presented in

Diamantina, north of Belo Horizonte, where there are fewer college students than in Ouro Preto, and in the historical town of São Francisco do Sul off the coast of Paraná. These latter two festivals are mostly street festivals with plenty of eating, drinking, and dancing.

One of the most mobbed street scenes occurs in the town of Cabo Frio, where Carnaval is mostly celebrated by people from Minas Gerais. Hundreds of thousands of visitors swarm to the city in small groups to participate in the music and drinking that occur on the street in front of Praia do Forte. During the day, the beach itself is packed with people continuing the party out into the surf. A similar scene takes place on the beaches of Espirito Santo, principally Guarapari Beach.

## Off-Season Carnaval

Some of the best Carnaval festivals don't take place in February at the normal time. Instead, they are off-season events and usually go by special names. Two of the most popular of these occur in the cities of Natal and Fortaleza. The Fortaleza event, known as Fortal, occurs in June and consists of music, dancing, and general debauchery out in the street along the principal boardwalk at Meireles Beach. The Natal event is called CarNatal, and takes place around Christmas time. Festivities generally occur in the old city center, but also can be found all over town and along the south coast. In Belo Horizonte, you have CarnaBelô, which takes place in July along Rua Afonso Pena in the city center. It consists of various *blocos* marching down the streets of town with music and drumming. You can participate by joining a *bloco* (buying the uniform from one of the officials) or just watch. One of the largest and best-produced off-season Carnavals is the Ox Festival in Parintins, which takes place at the end of June. You can watch practice sessions beginning in April.

# Getting There

Even though Brazil has more than a dozen international airports, the majority of international flights come into three principal hubs: São Paulo, Rio de Janeiro, and Salvador. Some travelers coming from Europe fly directly into Fortaleza and Recife and, of course, travelers from other South American countries fly into all kinds of Brazilian airports and make connections throughout Brazil. Other international airports are located in Macapá, Manaus, Brasilia, Natal, Porto Alegre, and Belém. Brazil's own international airlines, Vasp and Varig, have flights into Paris, New York, and Miami, as well as most South American countries. Varig also services London. Brazil's discount airline, TAM, has flights into Miami and Paris. A good site for information on Brazilian airlines and airports is www.infraero.gov.br.

The airports in Rio, São Paulo, and Salvador are spacious and modern. They all have luggage carriers or carts, showers, and baggage storage areas. You can catch connecting flights to anywhere in the country from these airports or transfer to the interstate bus system. In São Paulo's Guarulhos airport, you can catch a taxi or bus to the local metro system, where you can enter the city or head to Congonhas airport for a domestic connection. The metro also stops at the Tietê bus station, where you can catch a bus to just about anywhere in Brazil. In Rio de Janeiro, there are courtesy buses that take passengers to the metro, but it's best to catch a taxi to your hotel or the bus station directly from the airport. In Salvador, you can take a bus or taxi from the airport into the city or to the bus terminal.

From North America, **United Airlines** (www.ual.com) has flights into São Paulo (Guarulhos) departing from Chicago, Los Angeles, New York, San Francisco, and Miami. They also have a flight out of Washington, D.C. From São Paulo, they continue to Brasilia, Florianópolis, Rio de Janeiro, Salvador, Manaus, Curitiba, and Porto Alegre. **American Airlines** (www.aa.com) flies direct to Brazil from Dallas and Miami. **Continental** (www.flycontinental.com) flies into Rio and São Paulo from Newark, New York, and Miami.

# Getting Around

Choosing a method of travel within Brazil will have a profound impact on the type of trip you have. You can either include interstate travel in your overall plan, or you can attempt to minimize its impact by using domestic flights. Brazil is a huge country, so if you plan to see a lot of it, you should consider using some domestic flights. Brazil has three major domestic airlines and a few discount lines. Domestic flights are available to and from just about any major city and are a very intelligent choice for long-distance interstate travel. No matter how comfortable the buses can be, a 30-hour trip up a windy highway with only short stops every few hours will put you to the test. All cities and towns have bus stations, called *rodoviarias,* for their interstate and local lines, and bus travel is relatively cheap and dependable. Within cities, you'll find municipal buses that vary widely depending on the city.

If you're determined to see the countryside, but don't like the idea of busing, then car rental may be an option. Comparatively speaking, car rental can be rather expensive in Brazil and is only recommended for local or regional travel. Plus, Brazil's decidedly corrupt and bureaucratic licensing mechanism for foreign drivers makes car rental a less attractive option. Those on extended trips might consider purchasing a simple vehicle to use through the duration of the trip and suffering through the licensing bureaucracy (see *Visas and Officialdom* later in this chapter for details). Driving from beach to beach up (or down) Brazil's coastline is a terrific way to vacation in Brazil.

## DOMESTIC FLIGHTS

Brazil's three largest interstate carriers are **Vasp** (tel. 11/258-0512, www.vasp.com.br), **Varig** (tel. 11/231-9381, www.varig.com.br), and **Tam** (tel. 11/0800-123100, www.tam.com.br). They all have hubs in Brazil's major cities. Vasp and Varig also have extensive international routs. Two smaller (and less expensive) interstate carriers include **Gol** (tel. 0300/789-2121, www.voegol.com.br) and **Fly** (tel. 11/256-9333), both of which have great deals on selected flights.

You can purchase tickets directly from any of these companies over the phone and pick up your tickets at the airport or at any local travel agency. You can also purchase tickets over the Internet, although a working knowledge of Portuguese might be required. The easiest way is to go through a local travel agency from the beginning. If you use an agency, you might want to call the airline first to get its direct prices for comparison. Agencies will vary on

# FLIGHTS AND TIMES BETWEEN KEY POINTS

Brasilia/Belo Horizonte: 740 km (1:10)
Curitiba/Florianópolis: 300 km (0:45)
Recife/Fortaleza: 800 km (1:20)

Rio/Brasilia: 1,150 km (1:35)
Rio/Belo Horizonte: 440 km (0:45)
Rio/Recife: 2350 km (2:45)
Rio/Salvador: 1,650 km (2:00)
Rio/São Paulo: 430 km (0:45)

São Paulo/Brasilia: 1,010 km (1:25)
São Paulo/Belo Horizonte: 590 km (1:10)

São Paulo/Campo Grande: 1,015 km (1:45)
São Paulo/Curitiba: 400 km (0:50)
São Paulo/Florianópolis: 700 km (1:10)
São Paulo/Manaus: 3,975 km (3:30)
São Paulo/Recife: 2,650 km (3:00)
São Paulo/Salvador: 1,960 km (2:20)

Manaus/Belém: 5,300 km (3:00)
Salvador/Fortaleza: 1,400 km (1:40)
Salvador/Recife: 840 km (1:15)
Salvador/Porto Seguro: 650 km (0:45)

the kinds of deals they access in their systems. It's always a good idea to ask if there are any discounts because in Brazil, if you don't ask for a discount they won't give you one. Most agencies will ask for cash or credit card payment in *reals* for domestic flights. International flights are usually priced in dollars, but can be paid in *reals* or dollars at the agency. As you might expect, if you want an exchangeable ticket, you will have to ask for that—and usually pay more. Most flights can be cancelled or changed with 24-hour notice, but be sure to ask when you purchase the tickets. No-shows usually result in loss of the ticket value.

Be sure to arrive a little early for your flight and ask for assistance at check-in. Otherwise, it's possible to mistake times, gates, or flight numbers and end up on a true adventure in some unknown city. Gate agents may not catch the mistake when taking your ticket. (In one of my first flying experiences in Brazil, I differed with a woman who claimed to have the same seat number as I had until I realized that I had boarded the wrong plane and sheepishly removed myself from the aircraft.)

## INTERSTATE BUSES

The interstate bus system is very well developed and you'll find that buses depart precisely on time. If you arrive one minute late for your departure, you will probably have missed your bus. Likewise, buses often arrive at their destinations ahead of schedule. This is not really a comment on the quality of Brazil's road system (on the contrary, you'll soon realize why there are so many tire repair stations, or *borracharias,* around the country); rather, it's a comment on how ubiquitous interstate buses have become and how well developed the whole busing system is. Everyone, from business execs to country folks take the bus. In most major cities, the bus station is a major hub of activity. There are dozens of bus companies with hundreds of lines to and from every city and small town. Interstate buses are generally clean and you will not be accompanied by chickens or goats . . . but a few screaming children or smelly people, per-

haps. That being said, some travelers like to carry anti-bacterial spray, to make their ride a bit more sanitary.

For trips of two hours or more, most companies have both common and executive lines—executive being more comfortable and sometimes including bottled water and coffee along the way. Executive buses may also have fewer stops. Most important, the profile of the executive passenger is a bit higher caliber. They are 25–45 percent more expensive than common buses. If it's important to you, then be sure to ask which type you're getting when you buy your ticket. Some time slots are executive slots, so asking for that time means getting an executive bus. The ticket agent may just assume you know that. Another thing to remember is that executive buses are usually air-conditioned and when Brazilians pay extra for something like air-conditioning, they want their bloody air-conditioning—even if they're freezing the entire trip. On long-distance executive trips, be sure to snag a blanket from your suitcase (which usually will go in the cargo hold) to keep with you in the cabin and don't hesitate to complain about the freezing compartment.

Except on major holidays or festivals, you can generally arrive at the bus station and catch the next available bus to your destination without any problem. If you are traveling on a holiday or to a major event or festival, you might pay attention to whether you actually have a seat or will be *de pê* (on foot) the entire trip. Another option is to get your ticket several hours in advance, which will usually assure your place. Most companies accept only cash for ticket purchases, but some of the larger companies accept credit cards in the major hubs. Inside the bus, be sure to keep your ticket stub, as it may be required for getting on and off the bus.

### Long Bus Trips

Bus trips of more than four hours will include a snack and smoke stop. Buses stop every three or four hours at designated snack stands, which are exactly the same across the entire country. But at 3 A.M. in the middle of nowhere, they make a welcome intermission. Most of these stops are pretty short—just enough time to hit the bathroom and grab a quick bite to eat. If you smoke, you'll have to hurry to get all three activities accomplished in one stop. If you do a lot of traveling by bus, you may find yourself evaluating the quality of each snack stand and even remembering the wonderful snack stop on that trip to Salvador or how that snack stand in João Monlevade had the best *pão de queijo*. Congratulations, you are now a formidable Brazil traveler.

Normally, you will not be able to access your luggage in the cargo hold, so be sure to take a daypack or handbag with you to your seat, loaded with your necessities for the trip. Items to consider keeping with you in the cabin include a light blanket or sheet, snacks, toothbrush, small neck pillow, CD player with headphones, and a hand towel for quick wash-ups along the way (bathrooms at the stops may not have paper towels). If you must access something in your luggage, a R$5 tip to the driver's assistant (or the driver if there is no assistant) will help get the cargo doors open in mid-trip. It's usually safe to leave your carry-on items on the bus when you exit for a snack stop. Bring your money with you and throw a blanket over anything that might tempt your neighbors. On arrival, it's a different story, so double- and triple-check for anything you might have left behind because odds are it will end up in someone else's bag before the last person has exited the bus.

## LOCAL BUSES

Municipal buses are plentiful throughout Brazil. So plentiful in the larger cities that it can be a daunting task to determine which bus to take and where to catch it. Generally, you can minimize errors by confirming your destination with the driver or *trocador* (money changer) before getting on. Fairs range from R$1.45 to R$3 in the cities and from R$.50 to R$1.50 in smaller towns. You don't have to have exact change. However, most of the cashiers will not accept a R$20 note and frown at a R$10 note.

When entering a municipal bus with a lot of packages or luggage, most Brazilians ask the driver (or offer some kind of signal) to open the side or rear doors so they can enter and set down their packages, thus avoiding the turnstile. The passenger then exits and reenters the bus with everyone else to pay his or her fair. Don't accept rides from people hawking trips outside *rodoviarias* (and sometimes inside) unless you're absolutely sure they are legitimate. Some are. But when there are established companies offering the same trip from within the *rodoviaria,* it's best to go for the sure thing, even if it means spending a bit more. Never give your luggage to "helpers" if their vehicles are not in sight, unless they are clearly *carregadores* (baggage carriers) sanctioned by the *rodoviaria*. Note that these baggage carriers get paid by the item, so they'll try to get you to put all your bags on the dolly. It's perfectly OK to carry some of your bags and let them carry the rest.

Note: Don't use CD players, computers, or cameras on municipal buses. It's alright to use them on interstate trips when you are outside city lines. Bring them with you, along with your money, passport, and wallet, when you leave the bus on food stops.

## TAXIS

Taxi drivers are famous the world over for their various scams and cons. Thankfully, Brazilian taxi drivers are not the worst you'll ever encounter. Most are capable of hiking up the fair or taking kickbacks from hotels or nightclubs, but they do not generally participate in outright criminal activities or robbery scams. Almost every taxi driver in the world will try to eek out a few more cents on the meter by driving as far as possible after you've reached your destination. And most will leave the meter running while helping get your bags out of the trunk. These petty games don't usually amount to much and you can just deduct them from any tip you intended to give. Some of the airports and bus terminals throughout Brazil sell pre-set taxi fairs at booths, thus standardizing prices and forcing drivers to collect the same fair for the same trip. If you find a driver that you like, get his phone number and call him for rides while you're in town. Otherwise, try to catch a taxi at a designated taxi line and always negotiate the fair before entering the taxi. At least get the driver to estimate the fair.

If you feel you're being ripped off by a taxi driver and feel you are in a safe place to complain (at the airport or bus terminal, for example), then ask the driver to call over a police officer to mediate, while you wait outside the taxi with your bags. Don't try this if you are not in a well-lit, public area as the driver could get angry that you've challenged his little scam.

## LOTAÇÃO

Many cities and towns will offer inexpensive and more frequent alternatives to the local buses. The service is called *lotação* and loosely refers to any private vehicle that carries groups of unrelated passengers. The most common vehicle is a white VW bus called a Kombi but you can find other types of vehicles, even taxis, that offer *lotação* services. Generally, the price is exactly the same as the bus, but the trip is faster and more frequent. The down side is that they pack as many people into these vans as possible and trips can be pretty uncomfortable. Still, in some areas *lotaçãos* are the best way to get around and they usually provide an entertaining and up-close view of the local people and lifestyle.

## DRIVING AND CAR RENTAL

It rarely makes sense to have a rental car in a big city. The cost of hiring drivers or taking taxis makes it easy to stay unencumbered by a car. Plus there's the hassle of parking and the risk of driving into a dangerous area. Likewise, it does not usually make sense to rent a car for long-distance travel between cities (the exceptions are noted below). The bus system is so complete and affordable that the hassle and expense of renting a vehicle is not justifiable. You're best off using rented vehicles only after you've arrived at your destination—to get out to the more distant sites, beaches, or villages. For example, you might fly

into Salvador, take a bus down to Porto Seguro, then rent a car from there to see the beaches and villages of the area.

The trip between São Paulo and Rio de Janeiro is a good one to make in a rented car and you might want a car if you're traveling in the south of Brazil, such as the trip from Joinville to Florianópolis, or all the way to Porto Alegre. A lot of Brazilians like to drive from Belo Horizonte to Salvador, stopping at the many sites in-between.

## BUYING A CAR OR MOTORCYCLE

It is possible to buy a car for an extended trip in Brazil, but the authorities do not make it easy. Paperwork is slow and cumbersome and you need to have it done by representatives, called *despachantes*, who may not always be reputable. Besides taking your documentation to the Department of Transportation (Detrans), they can also do a search for outstanding citations and IPVA (tax) payments. A good idea is to purchase a car through a dealership that has its own *despachante* who can handle your paperwork in-house.

Although natural gas is widely used in Brazil and a great option for economizing while reducing your impact on the environment, you're better off not purchasing a gas vehicle, due to the extra bureaucracy involved. An alternative is an alcohol-fueled car, which is cheaper and cleaner than gasoline and does not require any special paperwork. In Brazil, all new vehicles are required to accept alcohol, stimulating the Brazilian economy (sugar-cane alcohol is one of Brazil's biggest products) and reinforcing its self-sufficiency.

After buying a car, it may take a few days to get your paperwork in order, especially if your *despachante* does not know how to handle non-Brazilian documents. (I waited days because the Detrans clerk did not know where to enter a passport number into their computer system designed to hold the ten digits of a Brazilian ID card.) You'll need an address to enter into the system, as your permanent *recibo* (registration) and *registro* (pink slip) will be mailed to you.

You can probably use the *despachante*'s address if you trust him and drive with the temporary permit you will receive, which is good for only 30 days. As with a pink slip, you don't want to keep this document with the car. However, be sure to keep all your registration documents with you, as they will be checked frequently as you drive around the country.

If you purchase a car for an extended trip in Brazil, then you will undoubtedly be driving in all kinds of conditions and on all kinds of roads. Driving in Brazil is a challenging proposal. Brazilians could very well be the rudest and most dangerous drivers in the world. They do not respect right-of-way and can get dangerously angry if they feel you cut them off or otherwise interfered with their trajectory. I was once stopped and threatened in the middle of the highway by the driver of a car in front of me, who did not like how I merged onto the highway. In the cities, this is magnified by a great urban stress factor. On the interstate highways, it's amplified out of control by poor and over-crowded road conditions. Most interstate highways have only two lanes and passing is a high-risk venture that you have to take because the roads are full of slow-moving trucks and buses (although buses are often racing past you, pretending to be sports cars).

Other challenges include severe potholes and damaged roads that can snap your axle in a hurry. The roads around the big cities of Rio and São Paulo are generally good and the southern region of Brazil has very good conditions. The farther north and west you go, the worse the roads get. In rural areas, you have to be careful with animal crossings and weather conditions. Be especially careful in the fog and rain.

If you purchase a car that has any value, then you should get insurance for it. You can get this at Banco do Brasil and many of the other banks. I suggest, however, that you stick to a more humble vehicle, so that any fender benders are easily resolved (usually right on the spot with a cash payment) and outright theft will not be a major loss. There are lots of VW Beatles (called *fuscas*) and VW buses in Brazil that are cheap, easy to repair, and easy to sell when you leave.

Note: The best theft deterrent you can buy is a *corta circuita,* or *corta elétrica,* a system that cuts all electric power to the car until you push a hidden button.

## Civil Police

Unfortunately, the police that you will be dealing with in all traffic matters are the civil police, the most corrupt of Brazil's three police forces. It is not uncommon to be stopped at a border crossing and hassled about merchandise you have in your car. Generally, an item from your stock is what will get you through. Civil police also create frequent blitzes that require all cars on a given road to pass under their watchful eyes. They single out certain vehicles for document checking. If you have problems with your car, paperwork (including your driving permit), or merchandise inside the car, you will be cited or hassled. Most of the time, you will not have any problems, as civil police do not commonly pick on gringos but on low-income Brazilians. Civil police do not have any authority over your passport or visa issues. If you get into a minor accident, don't involve the police if you can avoid it. The best tactic is to work it out directly—perhaps even taking the car over to a shop for a quick estimate of damages. Get estimates without the other driver present if you can. It's very easy and tempting for the driver and shop owner to join forces against you.

Civil police may also be involved if you are caught breaking any Brazilian laws. If the infraction is minor, you are most likely going to encounter an elaborate ploy to get your money. Sometimes this will involve driving you to the nearest ATM where you can pull out money. In most cases, you can negotiate with them to get to a reasonable solution. If you feel they are going too far, then you can ask to call a lawyer, or *advogado.* If you are anywhere near a big city, you should have no problem finding a representative to help you.

## Driver's Licenses

If you plan to drive in Brazil, with your own car or a rental, then you should prepare some documentation ahead of time. You'll need a notarized copy of your driver's license (front and back) and copies of the Brazilian visa page and photo page of your passport. It may also help to get an International Drivers Permit, which is available from AAA or a number of online sources. If you plan to rent a car, take all of these documents to a local agency that has offices in Brazil (Hertz and Avis are common in Brazil) at least 30 days in advance. You will probably be required to pay a fee of around US$25–80. You may also be able to process your paperwork through your travel agent. Your Brazilian drivers permit is valid for one year if you will be driving only in small tourist areas, and you will probably not have any problem with just an International Drivers Permit and your valid license, even though these are not acceptable in Brazil officially.

## Visas and Officialdom

Brazil has a somewhat juvenile policy of exact reciprocity when it comes to foreign travelers from countries that restrict Brazilian travelers. This means that European travelers do not need visas to enter Brazil, whereas North American travelers do. This became almost comical when the United States began toughening security after 9/11, forcing travelers from many nations to pass through identification procedures upon entering the country. Brazil automatically forced the same rules upon American travelers until it was discovered that they didn't have the equipment to fingerprint and photograph so many people entering the country.

While in Brazil, try not to carry your passport around with you if you can help it. Leave it in your hotel room or in the hotel safe and carry a copy. You will need the original only when doing official business with the federal police, banks, or government agencies. If your passport is stolen, you should go immediately to the closest embassy office and go through the process of getting it replaced. You will receive an entrance receipt when you enter Brazil. It's usually a green and white paper stamped with your date of entry. It's important that you keep this and present it upon leaving the country.

The best place to get information about visas and other officialdom concerning Brazil is at the San Francisco Consulate General website: www.brazilsf.org. Information is in English and covers a wide range of topics, including a list of everything you need to bring and do before applying for your visa.

### TOURIST VISA

The tourist visa is the most common for travelers. It allows you to visit Brazil for three months with a three-month extension, for a total of 180 days out of every 365 days. That means that you have to stay out of Brazil for at least six months every year.

You must get the tourist visa at the Brazilian consulate nearest your home town and you will probably need to show your round-trip tickets and proof that you can support yourself on the trip (usually only required for stays of more than two weeks).

### Extensions

You must get your extension before the first 90 days of your stay are up. If you attempt to get it even one day late, they will not give it to you. If you are out of the country when this date passes, then you will likely not get back into the country again for another six months. Federal police are usually very strict about this. On the other hand, they will probably not ask you to leave the country if you stay past your limit. Brazil does not have a deportation policy and you are usually free to stick around and see if they catch you on the way out. If they do, you will be asked to pay R$8 for each day after your visa expired, whether 90 days or 180 days. You can get your three-month extension at the federal police station of most major cities. You will need your passport, ID, and the green entry receipt they gave you upon entering the country. There will be a small processing fee involved.

## Going to the Limit

Many visitors who wish to maximize their stay in Brazil get confused about the rules associated with their visa, especially if they are familiar with other South American countries where rules are different. A common mistake is the belief that exiting the country has an affect on the expiration of your 180 days. Another mistakes is the belief that the 180-day limit starts over again each calendar year. Neither of these ideas is true. Here's how it works: You have 180 days maximum stay (assuming you remember to get the extension before your first three months are up) out of every 365 days, starting from your first date of entry. That means that if you exit and reenter the country during this 180 days, it makes no difference to your required departure date. Your required departure date remains 180 days after the first date of entry that appears after any previous 180-day cycle. Once you complete a 180-day cycle and leave the country, your next entry begins the new cycle and nothing affects this. The new cycle cannot begin within 180 days of your last cycle. Federal police have been known to study passport stamps to calculate entry and exit dates and determine if visitors have gone over their maximum stay. This might be done when you apply for your three-month extension, when you leave the country, or when you attempt to reenter the country. It's also possible that upon leaving, the official will open your passport, stamp it, and ask you to move along. You never know.

What happens if you go over the limit? Usually, all that's required is payment of a small fine. They will often let you pay this when you reenter the next time. Fines are approximately R$8 per day with a ceiling of R$600. So, even if you stay three years past your exit date, your maximum fine is R$600.

## OTHER VISAS

There are several other common visas that can be obtained with connections in Brazil. Some of the most common are the student visa, teacher visa, journalist visa, artist visa, and re-

search visa. Except for the journalist visa, all of these require some type of sponsorship from Brazil. Students and teachers must get accepted by a school before applying for the visa. Artists will need a letter from a gallery or exhibition center. Journalists can get visas based on foreign sponsorship, such as a journalist from an American newspaper doing an assignment in Brazil. Just bring a letter from your publisher to the consulate for examination. Research projects usually need some connection to Brazilian institutions, as they want foreign research to occur in concert with Brazilian research. Most of these special visas are valid for two years, but can easily be renewed if the project or term of study is extended. You cannot work outside of the area for which your visa applies. Students, for example, are not allowed to work at all, while journalists can only work in journalism. Of course, this is seldom enforced.

If you are asked to work at a Brazilian company, then the company will likely get your paperwork in order for you to take to the consulate. If approved, your work visa will last for two or four years.

## Changing Visas

Brazil has a strict policy that all changes to visas must be done outside the country. If you change from a tourist to a journalist, for example, you'll have to leave the country and apply for the journalist visa on the outside. They ask that this is done at your home consulate, but you can actually change visas in any Brazilian consulate abroad. When switching visas, any dates and entry restrictions from your old visa will no longer apply. For example, if you switch to a journalist visa after spending the maximum 180 days on your tourist visa, you will still be able to reenter the country immediately under the new visa (assuming it's approved).

## CUSTOMS

You are allowed to bring up to US$500 worth of goods into Brazil without declaring anything at customs. You can also avoid the *bens a declarar* (goods to declare) line if you bring less than R$10,000 in cash and travelers checks. If you are bringing expensive equipment, such as cameras or computers, you should probably get a receipt from customs on your way into Brazil. If your equipment is brand-new or if you have more than one of something (two laptop computers, for example), they might charge you duty. Likewise, if they feel that your equipment is somehow not compatible with your purpose for visiting the country, they could require that you pay a deposit on the item, guaranteeing that you bring it out with you when you leave. You can attempt to argue your way out of this, but you will probably get nowhere. Remember, all of these items must have a value of more than US$500 to even worry about it. Most travelers play dumb and walk straight through customs, hoping no one will stop them and request registration of items. In many cases, you will not be stopped. Just in case, be prepared with receipts and any documents that support your activities. If you're a photographer, for example, bring your business cards and any other documents that help demonstrate that you are not going to sell your equipment.

## BRAZILIAN CONSULATES ABROAD

To apply for your visa or to get any other paperwork approved or questions answered, you should visit or write to your local Brazilian consulate. Check www.brazilsf.org for a list of offices throughout the United States or better yet, check the more friendly and informative Brazilian embassy in Great Britain (www.brazil.org.uk). The Brazilian embassy in the States is in Washington, D.C. (www.brazilemb.org). There are also offices in Boston (www.consulatebrazil.org), Chicago (www.brazilconsulatechicago.org), Houston (www.brazilhouston.org), Los Angeles

(www.brazil-consulate.org), Miami (www.brazilmiami.org), New York (www.brazilny.org), and San Francisco (www.brazilsf.org). For a list of offices in other countries, see www.mre.gov.br/ingles/endereco.

## FOREIGN CONSULATES AND EMBASSIES IN BRAZIL

In most cases, foreign embassies are located in Brasilia and consular offices appear in large cities, with Consular General offices in Salvador, São Paulo, and Rio de Janeiro. Other cities that have foreign consulates include Salvador, Belém, Recife, Manaus, Fortaleza, Curitiba, and Porto Alegre. Consular offices are listed in appropriate chapters throughout this book, under the *Information and Services* headings. The American embassy in Brazil can be accessed online at www.embaixada-americana.org.br.

## FEDERAL POLICE

The only police in Brazil that have authority over passport matters are the federal police. They are the most sophisticated of the three Brazilian forces and are usually quite educated. They also make a decent amount of money, so corruption among their ranks is not common. In fact, the federal police are usually very strict and follow the law to the letter. You should never attempt to bribe a federal police officer and anyone who tells you that they can is probably lying. It's very unlikely that you'll be able to buy your way around any of the rules associated with passports and visas. Federal police have the authority to deport you, especially if your papers are not in order and you are offensive in some way. This is extremely rare and most officers will simply tell you if you are over your limit and suggest that you do something about it (like leave). If they ask you to pay a fine, simply request to pay the fine when you exit the country.

# Conduct and Customs

## ENCOUNTERS

Brazil is a very informal country, even in the upper crust of society. You won't always get the polite *bom dia, boa tarde,* or *boa noite* when you pass people on the street, but if you offer it, they will always reply in kind. Most receptionists and servers will refer to you as *o senhor* or *a senhora* according to the formal custom. This is often done in the third person: "Can I do anything else for *o senhor.*" It's not important that you do the same, and the common *você* (you) is perfectly acceptable in every situation. In Rio de Janeiro and the southern states, it's common to hear the informal *tu,* but it's used almost as a replacement for *você* and is not considered informal or rude. Brazilians don't use *Dom* any more for men, ever since the country became a republic, but *Dona* is commonly used for women who have some position of authority. Young women in authority don't usually like it.

Brazilians use a couple of gestures that take foreigners by surprise. One is the attention-getting sound *pssssssiu,* which is often used in restaurants to call the waiter or waitress. It may also be used on the street to get your attention, usually so the person can beg from you or sell you something. You should probably get into the habit of ignoring this sound when you hear it. There is almost never anything worthwhile on the other end. The other mildly offensive gesture is the shaking of the first finger to mean *no.* You'll see this, sometimes accompanied by a *tisk tisk* sound, throughout Brazil. Most Americans remember this as a kind of ominous warning from our elders. In Brazil it simply means no.

## TIPPING

Most decent restaurants automatically charge a 10 percent service fee and tipping is not required or expected. Restaurants that do not charge this fee will usually let you know on the bill with the words *não cobramos 10 percent.* This is an indication that a tip would be welcome. Informal restaurants, self-service buffets, and *lanchonetes* usually don't charge a service fee and you are not expected to offer a tip. If you're in doubt, feel free to ask your server if there is a 10 percent fee included already: *"Já tem dez porcento na conta?"* They will be pleased that you asked. Any tip that you give in addition to the 10 percent or in a restaurant that does not charge 10 percent will be considered extremely gracious, even if it's just R$1. Your hotel probably also charges a 10 percent service fee, so you are not required to tip baggage handlers. But since most of the waiters and hotel staff will never see the 10 percent automatic charge, you might consider giving an extra few *reals* to your server if you think he or she is doing a good job. You should never leave tips on the table. Instead, hand them directly to the server.

## BARGAINING

Brazilians don't usually bargain with a lot of back and forth negotiation. In most cases, bargaining consists of the buyer asking for a discount on the price. This is true in public markets, hotels, boutique shops, and small stores. Give a reason why you're asking for the discount. Almost any reason is worth trying and better than no reason at all. The best is when you are paying in cash. You'd be surprised how many Brazilians pay on terms, even for the smallest items, so most small stores and merchants give cash discounts without a second thought. Even large chains have cash prices, so never hesitate to ask. If you don't ask, they will not give it to you. You can even ask if there is a cash discount in chain stores and shopping malls, but never in restaurants. Asking for a discount is not exactly bargaining in Brazil and there is little back and forth after they give you a lower price. If you don't like their discount, then tell them it's still too expensive and walk away. In most cases, they will not come down any farther. It would be considered rude to try to bargain lower than the discounted price unless you have an additional reason to give them (buying quantity for example but then only after you received the cash discount on a single item). You can also try stating what your limit is and see if they accept it: *meu limite é vinte reais* (my limit is 20 Reals). State this not as a final offer, but as a reason why you are not going to buy the item. Some places where bargaining is more acceptable include public markets (not all of them) and when dealing with individuals or street vendors. When making a private deal with an individual, the game is very much afoot.

## ON THE STREET

On the streets, it's common for working-class men to howl or whistle at women. In most cases, this is harmless and is only meant as a compliment. Brazilian men are generally very aggressive with women and are not shy about communicating their attraction. Despite the many prominent women in Brazilian society and the country's many technological advances, Brazil is still a very traditional country with plenty of machismo intact. Of course, this is more common the farther you get from the cities. Tips and advice for women traveling alone in Brazil appear later in this chapter.

One of the first things that foreigners notice in Brazil is how Brazilians litter. Even in middle-class areas, adults and children alike will peel the wrapper off some item or other and toss it right on the street without giving it a thought. People will almost always throw litter out of bus and car windows, even when there are trash receptacles in view. It comes as

a shock to many visitors. It's probably a carry-over from the master/servant mentality that prevailed in the country for three centuries. Anyone who cleans up is a servant and anyone who is cleaned up after is a master. The attitude that somebody else will clean it up is a kind of demonstration of your social caste and not considered irresponsible.

Brazilians can be both the nicest and the rudest people you'll ever meet and nowhere is the latter more noticeable than in public lines. It almost seems like a matter of personal pride for Brazilians to weasel their way in front of others or outright ignore lines. The *fila única* (single line) concept has not taken hold, even in the more European southern states. Another annoying aspect of public behavior is how Brazilians will not move out of the way to let others pass by. If they are in front of you, it's their right to stop where they want, when they want, and anyone behind them has to deal with their own problems. On buses, people will not make an effort to let you through and if you step aside to open a space for someone to pass, it's likely that they will stay right there in the space you temporarily opened up, making you stand in even more cramped conditions. Young people do not get up to let older people sit down.

A final word about public behavior in Brazil: noise. It's very difficult to get a moment of silence in Brazil. People are either shouting at each other, honking, or blasting music every waking hour and into the middle of the night. Even small towns out in the middle of nowhere can be unbearably noisy. As with the litter problem, there's very little you can do about this as a tourist. The best thing to do is head out to a secluded beach where all you hear is the sound of the ocean and the birds.

# Tips for Travelers

## WORKING IN BRAZIL

It's very easy to find jobs teaching English in Brazil. There are English schools all over the country, from small independents to national chains. You are most likely to find work at the independents if you don't have a work visa, as most of them will not ask for your paperwork. The large schools have more restrictions, but if you plan to teach in Brazil for a while, you can discuss opportunities with these schools ahead of time. The major chains are Fisk (www.fisk.com.br), CCAA (www.ccaa.com.br), and Number One (www.numberone.com.br). You can also check with some of the international organizations that help place teachers abroad, such as TEFL (www.tefl.com).

Opening a business in Brazil is fairly easy and many foreigners try their hand in tourism, clothing manufacturing, and food service, among other things. Some foreigners have purchased farms to grow exotic crops for export. Naturally, to get into any export business, you should pre-establish your contacts abroad before starting up in Brazil. You will probably need a Brazilian CPF card, which is a taxation ID. Without it, you cannot open a bank account or register a business officially in Brazil. Many foreigners report that this is extremely difficult to get, although there is no law that prohibits foreigners from having one. You just need to find an attorney or accountant who can set it up for you. If your business employs at least four Brazilians and you have a Brazilian partner, then it can become the basis for permanent residency in the country.

## ENVIRONMENTALIST ACTIVITIES

Anyone wishing to work in environmental activities in Brazil should contact Brazilian entities directly or go through a local organization that has ties to Brazil. Very few environmental organizations work independently in Brazil and access into the deep Amazon regions and other federally controlled areas is restricted. Although many large plantations and *fazendas* (working ranches) in the Amazon and Pantanal areas are privately owned, any official environmental activities performed by these groups are sanctioned by the government and therefore closely guarded and carefully administered.

The government's environmental agency is called the **Instituto Brasileiro do Meio Ambiente** (IBAMA; www.ibama.gov.br) and is responsible for administration of most of the government's environmental activities, including international studies inside Brazil. They have numerous projects, divided into a few principal sections. Some interesting divisions include RAN (management of reptiles and amphibians), CMA (management of marine mammals), CPB (protection of Brazilian primates), and CECAV (protection and research into caves and caverns). Each of these divisions has a host of projects and studies.

The government group responsible for the care and protection of indigenous groups is called **Fundação Nacional Assisténcia Indígena** (FUNAI; www.funai.gov.br). You can contact them for information on indigenous studies and internships.

Besides FUNAI and the IBAMA divisions, a number of non-governmental organizations (NGOs) in Brazil offer excellent opportunities for involvement. Some worth noting include the **Hyacinth Macaw Project** (www.projetoararaazul.org.br), which is dedicated to the study and protection of this endangered bird, the largest of its type (of the *psitacidae* family, which includes parrots, macaws, parakeets, etc.). This beautiful bird makes its home in only two places in the world: the Pantanal and Marajó Island in the eastern Amazon region. The project is supported by the WWF (World Wildlife Foundation) and various Brazilian organizations.

**Projeto TAMAR** (www.tamar.com.br) is dedicated to the protection and care of Brazil's sea turtles. Of the seven known species of sea turtle in the world, five make their home along the Brazilian coastline. TAMAR has been hugely successful in repopulating the species and involving local communities in their protection rather than in their use for food. For information on internships, go to their website and choose the Participe do Tamar—Estágios option. Their openings are usually reserved for students and graduates of related studies (oceanography, marine biology, etc.). They use interns for cultural education programs and for the care and protection of nests and nesting areas. You can enroll for an internship for 1–6 months.

**Projeto Peixe Boi** (www.projetopeixe-boi .com.br) works on the protection of the *trichechus manatus,* a salt-water manatee that frequents Brazil's coastal regions, particularly the northeast. They have programs for rehabilitating orphaned cubs and maintaining habitats for the replenishment of the species. Their main facility is in the Recife region, on the Island of Itamaraca.

**Conservation International do Brasil** (www .conservation.com.br) has a number of projects in which they watch and protect the environment. Their focus is on wildlife areas.

## WOMEN TRAVELING ALONE

Brazil's special combination of problems and cultural characteristics makes it a fairly dangerous place for women to travel alone. Robbery and assault are risks that apply to all travelers in Brazil, but a woman alone (or even two or three traveling together) will be considered easy targets and may actually attract problems. One piece of advice for women who do visit Brazil alone or with one other woman is to never actually be alone. Try to always have other travelers with you and never, ever go out on excursions with a male guide by yourself. This goes for hikes inside national parks as well as boat trips up the Amazon River or even a city tour. When going on hikes or walks on the beach, it's best to take someone with you. Traveling in a group is always safer than traveling alone or with one other person.

Besides robbery, there exists the possibility of personal injury or assault. If you are not able to travel in a group, you should be careful to use guides registered with EMBRATUR. You can check their registration number with the EMBRATUR office in Brasilia or online at www.embratur.gov.br. Guides registered with city or municipal agencies are also trustworthy. If you are on the beach, be sure that you stay in public areas and don't walk too far from the crowd. In the countryside, be sure to bring someone with you at all times. You should not trust anyone who you cannot easily track down through an agency or place of business. This especially applies to guides. At night, be careful when you walk anywhere that is not crowded. This includes major avenues in big cities, as well as main streets and *praças* in small towns. If you're out very late at night, be sure to have someone walk you to the taxi line, or have the establishment call a taxi to the door. Keep the phone number of any taxi driver that you've used before and trust and call the same driver every time.

Remember that you are most vulnerable when you have your backpack or bags with you. Anyone with a backpack walking in a touristy area is already a target and one or two women alone would be considered a great opportunity for assault. Also, be extra alert when you are walking around town and don't venture down deserted streets or into dubious territory alone. This is true for anyone, but especially for women.

As mentioned earlier, Brazilian men use somewhat aggressive dating tactics and can be very persistent—almost impossible to offend. Trying to pick up a woman, even failing, is an honorable vocation for Brazilian men. Even when done politely, a pick-up line or gesture (called a *cantada*) can seem aggressive to foreigners. In most cases, you can just ignore these come-ons or treat them with indifference. If someone is following you or hanging around you, you might have to ask them to leave you alone: *"Me deixa, por favor."* If you need to repeat it with a stronger energy, you can tell them to take off: *"Vai embora!"* If someone has weasled himself into a relationship with you in some way, you can tell him that you prefer to be alone: *"Prefiro ficar sem companhia agora, ta bom?"* If anyone touches you, immediately tell them to take their hand off: *"Tira mão!"* Don't hesitate to tell this to anyone who might be in your group; most Brazilian men will take it in stride.

Even with all these precautions, it's possible to be robbed during the day in the middle of a crowd. If this happens to you, the best tactic is to release your bag and let them run away with it. Brazilian hoodlums usually rob in groups, so it's probably not a good idea to use whistles, mace, or other modern self-defense tools.

## GAY AND LESBIAN TRAVELERS

Brazil is quickly becoming one of the world's favorite gay and lesbian travel destinations. In some areas, such as Salvador, Rio, São Paulo, and Florianópolis, the GLS market accounts for as much as 30 percent of tourism. These areas are known for their special events, including the Gay Pride parade in São Paulo and Pop Gay Carnaval in Florianópolis. Many cities have gay neighborhoods where the population can relax and be at home in public and there are numerous nightlife options in Rio and São Paulo.

When traveling outside of the cities, it's a good idea to exercise some caution. Brazil is a country full of contradictions and regional cultures and the countryside is not going to be very gay-friendly in most cases. In some places, where the macho, cowboy culture prevails, it can even be dangerous. A resource for gay and lesbian travel in Brazil is www.athosgls.com.br. The page is run and updated regularly by Samra Mougrabi and includes information on hotels and destinations for gay travelers. Other informative sites include **Now Voyager** (www.now-voyager.com), a gay-owned and operated travel agency in San Francisco, California and the **Álibi** agency (www.alibi.com.br), which is a Brazil-based agency that offers various packages for its clients.

## STUDENTS

Brazil has a great many Portuguese language, cultural studies, and environmental studies programs in which you can participate. Many of the language programs are offered by private schools, so you should carefully research each one before applying. Pay attention to where you will be based and how much immersion the program offers. Programs that include some kind of community or environmental project often get you more involved in the culture and language. Decide if you want to be based in an urban area or in a more remote setting. A good place to begin your research is at the **International Study and Education Service** (www.istudy.com). They have a list of universities in Brazil and their exchange programs, including language studies. Another great site is www.studyabroad.com, which has lists of international-study programs from private and academic organizations. You can go directly to their Brazil page at www.brazil.studyabroad.com.

A couple of specific programs worth mentioning include **International Cultural Exchange** (www.iceprograms.com), which has a number of programs in Brazil, including language and general studies. Also, **World Learning** (www.sit.edu) has a study-abroad program in Brazil that is based on Latin American issues, such as poverty, gender studies, human rights, and public health. Their program is based in Fortaleza and Salvador. Their Brazil information is at www.sit.edu/studyabroad/latinamerica/brazilcul.html. **CIEE** (www.ciee.org) has all sorts of Latin American study programs. In Brazil, they focus on cultural and language studies and are based in São Paulo and Salvador.

## TRAVELERS WITH DISABILITIES

Brazil has a long way to go before its cities and rural areas are accessible to all citizens. Mass urbanization over the last fifty years has caused enormous stresses on urban infrastructure and on the population in general. Streets are crowded, dirty, and unsafe. Little attention is paid to the pedestrian thoroughfare, so conditions continue to get worse as cities grow. Architectural design is only just beginning to include a vision for accessibility and only in the most modern areas of the country, such as São Paulo and Rio de Janeiro. Rio, in fact, has been implementing an urban revitalization program since 1994 that includes accessibility for physically impaired, pregnant, and elderly citizens. Many of the major tourist attractions, including Pão de Açúcar and the Cristo Redentor monument have wheelchair access and facilities for the visually impaired. Two good sites for information on accessible travel abroad are www.disabilityworld.org and www.access-able.com.

## TRAVELERS WITH CHILDREN

Brazil might not seem like a very kid-friendly place to travel, with all the adult-oriented festivals and beach activities designed for couples and singles, but nothing could be farther from the truth. Traveling with kids in Brazil can be a great experience and an excellent way to cross over cultural boundaries and make connections with Brazilian families. Brazilians love kids and travelers with kids are often given special treatment and attention. Brazilians often interact with kids and it's common to see people patting kids on the head as they pass by, something that might take some getting used to by foreign kids (and their parents).

Involve your kids early in the preparations and research for the trip and let them know what they are likely to encounter. This should be repeated during the trip for each destination. Encourage kids to make a journal (if they're old enough) or start some kind of collection along the journey, such as postcards or interesting objects. Also, be prepared with plenty of books and other activities for the long bus and plane trips. Experienced parents know that it's not always the principal attraction that catches their kids' imaginations, but often the relatively mundane situations. An extra degree of patience and flexibility will be essential throughout the trip. Kids require plenty of rest stops, snack breaks, and naps back at the hotel.

Speaking of snacks, you will find every-thing that kids like throughout Brazil, including candy, chips, and soda. Most products will be easily recognized, but trying out some of the local items could be a hoot for some kids. Since Brazil is one of the leading sugar-producing countries in the world, you might find it difficult to avoid sweets, if that's your goal. Most restaurants welcome kids with open arms and many come equipped with playgrounds where kids congregate while their parents enjoy their meal. Almost every town will have such restaurants and you should ask at your hotel for recommendations. Food in general will not be difficult for most kids; hamburgers, hot dogs, pizza, and other kid-friendly foods are extremely common. You can find deli items in most *padarias* (bakeries) if you want to make a lunch.

When planning your trip, take into consideration the interest level your children will have for a destination. Most kids will be more interested in nature than in historical monuments, for example, although long hikes without frequent rewards along the way will probably not go over well. Some beach areas are more adult-oriented than others are, so a glance at the appropriate sections in this book will help you choose the best destinations and prepare for them. Some good locations to start looking at include Porto de Galinhas, Maceió, Southern Bahia, Rio de Janeiro, Foz de Iguaçu, and the Pantanal. The Paraná coast is also excellent and the beaches along the Emerald Coast in the Santa Catarina have tons of activities for kids. The Amazon region is generally considered too hot and demanding for young kids and the Pantanal makes a much better encounter with nature. Plus, the adventures in Bonito near the southern Pantanal will probably be a huge hit.

You should have no trouble finding hotels with playgrounds and facilities for kids and many cities have special kids' parks and attractions that are not always mentioned in this book. You will almost always receive a discount for kids at attractions and for transportation. Many hotels have a special rate for children and in many cases kids under 12 are free.

# TRAVELERS WITH DIETARY CONCERNS

Healthy eating is on the rise in Brazil, but it still has a long way to go before anyone with serious restrictions is well accommodated. To many Brazilians, a vegetarian is someone who does not eat red meat. They may give you chicken or pork in compensation. In the cattle country of Minas Gerais, Mato Grosso, and Rio Grande do Sul, it may be extremely difficult to find meat-free menu selections. Your best bet is going to self-service buffets and focusing on the vegetable dishes. There will always be plenty of options. Many self-service buffets operate only for lunch, but if you ask around, you can usually find options for dinner. Of course, there will be more options in the cities than in the countryside.

Diabetics will find artificial sweeteners almost everywhere in the country. They are so commonly used that many cafés and restaurants automatically provide both sugar and sweetener. When ordering coffee, however, you should ask if it already has sugar before ordering: *"Já tem açúcar?"* Also remember that most places will add sugar to fruit juices, including orange juice. Be sure to order it *sem açúcar*.

# BUSINESS TRAVELERS

Before making a reservation, check that your hotel offers in-room, plug-and-play Internet service and ask if there is an extra fee for it. Most of the hotels in the Parthenon chain (www.accorhotels.com) offer this service for free. Hotel listings in this book include information about in-room Internet services whenever possible. Most business travelers find it worthwhile to hire a taxi on a daily basis. In big cities, like São Paulo, you can have a taxi for the entire day for around R$200. In smaller cities, you should be able to negotiate an even better rate.

If you are traveling with a laptop computer, never use it on a municipal bus, on the beach, or in parks or public spaces. You can use your laptop on commercial buses, but be sure to bring it with you when you leave for food stops. Avoid using laptops in cafés and bars, unless you are sure that it is safe (such as the bar inside your hotel or an Internet café). When traveling, keep your laptop stored in your normal luggage or backpack. Do not use a special case that advertises that you have a computer. The same is true for cameras. (See *Communications and Media* later in this chapter for more information on business travel in Brazil.)

# Health and Safety

## EATING AND DRINKING

Eating out in Brazil is usually a pleasant and safe experience, as much in the cities as in the small towns. In the cities, standards of cleanliness are generally higher as the culture in general is a bit more elevated. You'll find sophisticated restaurants and simple diners, all with excellent quality and standards. In small towns, especially in rural and farming areas, you're likely to get ingredients from the local farms—fresh chickens, eggs, produce, and fruits. In some places, avocados, mangos, and other fruits are so common that you can pick them from trees in public spaces. In most cases, you'll find the quality excellent.

The only caution that is worth noting involves the fast food *lanchonetes* and sidewalk food vendors. Although Brazil has cleanliness laws for food-service operators, many places—especially those in rural areas or on the outskirts of town—go unchecked. Small *lanchonetes* can vary widely in quality and cleanliness. You should be careful when eating at one of these places. Be sure to give the place a visual inspection when you enter. Check to see that the oil in the deep fryer is clean and that the display cases are kept in good condition and are not full of flies. Take a look at the employees to see if they are in uniform and if the cooks have masks and plastic gloves. Generally, the places with higher turn-over rates

**Know Brazil**

## ADVICE FROM AN AMERICAN ON A DIET

While in Brazil, I didn't find too much trouble sticking to my medical diet. In the bigger cities, the supermarkets have tons of fresh fruits and vegetables. I also found the villages to have plenty for sustenance in their small, neighborhood produce markets. If at all possible, do not pass up the opportunity to try Brazil's native fruits. I found *Caju* to be my favorite delight. I never knew that cashews came from the tops of this odd-tasting fruit, which I had never seen before.

When in restaurants, I found the Brazilian people to be characteristically hospitable and accommodating. Since I have a complicated diet, I found it quite useful to have an interpreter with me at all times. I recommend this if your diet is of critical importance and you do not know the language. In my situation, I need to have food with absolutely no flavorings, spices, garnishes, etc., and found the term *ao natural* helped greatly in conveying this!

The only big challenge I had was when I was on the road. Riding the buses is the most common system for getting around the country and you can be on one for several hours at a time. Please keep in mind that the stations have very limited food and drink selections and the stops the driver makes along the way are at small places with even more limits on varieties of food available. Do plan well ahead and bring plenty of things you know you can eat, such as nuts, easy-to-consume fruits, bread and cracker items, as well as bottled drinks. If you have any motion-sickness or stomach problems, you may want to be careful of consuming any or too much acid-containing items such as orange juice. Sometimes the roads taken are quite winding and can throw passengers back and forth.

If you are able, do make an effort to try some of the different types of mangos—many of which you can find only in Brazil. Here's a trick to eating this fruit (which is high in Vitamin C) neatly: Hold the fruit so that the stem is on top and the fruit is perpendicular to the surface below. Notice there are fuller sides on the fruit while looking at it head-on. Try to predict where the seed is and with a large sharp knife, cut vertically down those fuller sides. You will have two round-shaped pieces. With the skin side down, carefully (so that you do not cut through the skin, just the fruit inside) score the mango in a checkerboard pattern, crosshatching one way and then the other. Now, grab the skin and flip it inside out, exposing the cubes of pure delight. Now slide a fork under the chunks to separate them from the skin. Putting these into a bag or container makes them a convenient snack while traveling as opposed to the other popular way to eat them, which is skinning them and hacking away at it with your teeth!

*(Contributed by India Bonham, a freelance writer who recently returned from her first trip to Brazil.)*

(i.e., more popular places) will have fresher food and better conditions. In many *botecos* (diner/bars) and *lanchonetes,* food sits around for a long time on the counters and you should feel free to ask how long it's been there. If in doubt, pass it up for something you can be sure was cooked on the spot. When ordering juices, ask if they are using fresh fruit and take a look at the fruit as it's being used. As long as they wash it off, you're in pretty good shape. As this book was being written, 19 people vacationing in the south of Brazil (mostly Brazilians) got sick from contaminated *caldo de cana* (pure sugarcane juice) sold by a single street vendor who did not clean the stalks of sugarcane before extracting the juice. A rare and potentially deadly insect that is usually only encountered in the fields was crushed with the canes.

You do not have to be overly preoccupied with the purity of water in Brazil since most cities have water-treatment facilities and some small towns even have clean, potable water from local springs. Since you can never be 100 percent sure, just make it a rule to buy mineral water. There are numerous brands throughout the country and they are trustworthy. Tap water is called *agua da torneira* and Brazilians usually don't drink it without first running it through a dubious clay filter that probably only strains out dirt and particles. Most ice and juices are made with this water, which they call *agua filtrada*. Rarely are there problems involved with using this water, but if you prefer, you can ask any establishment to use *agua mineral* to make your juice. More elaborate carbon filtering systems are gradually becoming common in the cities and in some restaurants. You won't often get ice in your drink, since it's customary to serve drinks ice cold and Brazilians don't want ice taking up space in the glass. It's perfectly OK to ask at a hotel or restaurant if their ice is made with filtered or mineral water.

## VACCINATIONS

You will be required to get a yellow fever vaccination if you have visited (within 90 days) or will visit Angola, Benin, Bolivia, Burkina Faso, Cameroon, Colombia, Democratic Republic of Congo, Ecuador, French Guiana, Gabon, Gambia, Ghana, Guinea, Liberia, Nigeria, Peru, Sierra Leone, Sudan, or Venezuela before entering Brazil. If this does not apply to you, but you plan to enter the Amazon region, you should get this vaccination at least ten days before entering the Amazon. The vaccination is cheaper in Brazil than in the United States, but not all travelers can wait the ten days before going into the jungle. If you do want to get shots in Brazil, ask at any pharmacy for information on where you can get vaccinations locally.

## SUN AND SKIN

The sun in Brazil is fierce and you should remember to use sunscreen at all times. Apply a new coat every few hours or if you go into the water or sweat a lot. Be especially careful when you are snorkeling to protect your back, which will be out of the water and in the sun most of the time. Coconut water provides excellent temporary relief for sunburn, but if you have a

bad burn, you should seek medical attention. Any pharmacy should be able to help you. Almost all towns have at least one 24-hour pharmacy. Ask at your hotel for assistance.

## DEHYDRATION AND HEAT EXHAUSTION

Dehydration can occur if you've been sweating profusely and not drinking enough liquids. It is exacerbated by consumption of alcohol, which makes it a relatively common ailment among travelers in Brazil. You will not always feel thirsty when you are dehydrated. In fact, the unquenchable thirst symptom sometimes comes when you are already in danger of dehydration sickness. The sickness consists of violent temperature changes (chills and fever), diarrhea, dizziness, nausea, vomiting, and blackouts. The best way to avoid dehydration is to drink plenty of coconut water, which you'll find all over the Brazilian coastline. Interestingly, coconut water has the same composition as blood plasma. You can also create a saline solution using a liter of water, a teaspoon of sugar, and a couple pinches of salt. This solution will hydrate you faster than plain water. You can also find Gatorade in Brazil, which is rich in electrolytes and excellent for rehydration.

Heat exhaustion is usually accompanied by dehydration and the symptoms are similar. In addition to those mentioned above, you might experience paleness of skin, headache, and accelerated heart rate. The first order of business is to find or create some shade. Place some cold, wet towels on your head and neck, then drink plenty of coconut water as explained previously. Rest and even take a nap if you feel tired. People are prone to heat exhaustion if they are overweight, sensitive to heat, or if they've been drinking alcohol and over-extending themselves physically.

## MALARIA AND DENGUE

Malaria has never been as big an issue in the Brazilian Amazon as it is in other Latin American countries. That's because the principal tourist destination in the Amazon Jungle, Manaus, is located in a relatively mosquito-free zone. The water of the Rio Negro, where Manaus is located, is too acidic for mosquitoes and the region is mercifully free of the pests. As a result, malaria is not epidemic in this region. There are some minor risks in the eastern Amazon region, Minas Gerais, and some of the central west states, but most travelers do not go to the extent of taking malaria pills when they visit these areas, since the side effects can be rather unpleasant. Mosquitoes can also be the cause of the disease known as dengue, which has flu-like symptoms, along with achy joints and spiked fevers. Dengue is usually not fatal, but it should not go untreated. If you experience these symptoms, head to a medical post in Brazil and ask to be checked for dengue. Doctors in Brazil are very familiar with the symptoms and treatment of the illness and you should not hesitate to consult a doctor if you feel sick during your visit.

The best protection for these mosquito-based illnesses is to avoid getting bitten. You can decrease your exposure by wearing long pants and using repellent on your skin and clothing. You can use the natural repellants, such as citronella and eucalyptus oil, and they usually work pretty well. Still, bring a chemical repellant along as a backup. If your hotel room has air-conditioning, keep it on while you sleep and mosquitoes will disappear. Ceiling fans can be effective if they are strong enough and if the direction of the air is coming down toward the bed. Many switches allow you to change the direction of the fan and it does make a difference.

Spray mosquito netting and clothing with a permethrin-based spray. Mosquitoes have an uncanny way of biting through clothing and netting (if you are leaning against it) and they will find small openings in your mosquito netting. If you can, tuck the netting under the mattress on all sides to keep mosquitoes out. You can also try turning on a light in an adjacent room, which may attract many of the mosquitoes away from you. Smokers will find that their cigarette smoke repels mosquitoes, but they will likely return when the smoke clears. You can find incense sticks that act as repellants, both with their smoke and natural properties. They can help when used in concert with other precautions. Citronella candles, which are popular in Brazil, don't seem to work all that well.

## SEXUALLY TRANSMITTED DISEASES

There are a number of factors that make Brazil a high-risk area for sexually transmitted diseases, including HIV/AIDS, and sexual tourism is one of them. Sexual tourism is prevalent wherever international tourism and poverty are thrown together. In Brazil, there are significant epicenters where risk is especially high. Some areas include the northeast states, Rio de Janeiro, and Teófilo Otoni in Minas Gerais (frequented by international gem dealers). United Nations AIDS research claims that as much as 42 percent of all sex workers in Brazil are infected with HIV. This is among the highest-risk categories in the nation.

Almost 50 percent of the Brazil's population is under the age of 30 and Brazilian studies show that most infections occur in people between the ages of 20 and 35. The spread of AIDS among women and heterosexuals is on the rise although these remain among the lower-risk groups. Brazil's international drug trafficking and high rate of injected drug use add to the risk factors but also tend to concentrate AIDS in a smaller percentage of the population.

When all is said and done, Brazil accounts for more than half of all AIDS cases in Latin America and an estimated 600,000 Brazilians are said to be living with HIV/AIDS. Overall, Brazil appears to be making some headway in the control of new AIDS cases, as the rate of increase has been slowing over the past few years. This is probably due to an increase in public awareness and education about the use of condoms. For more detailed information, see the UNAIDS reports on Brazil at www.unaids.org.

## MEDICAL CARE IN BRAZIL

Brazil has an excellent health-care system and highly trained doctors can be found in every major city and many towns and villages. You can get excellent advice on medicines and cures for basic conditions at just about any drugstore. Drugstore technicians are often trained to administer shots and other medical procedures. Practically every small town in the nation has at least one medical treatment center, called a *posto medico,* and larger towns will have several, along with hospitals and medical centers. You can usually get medical care for free at a *posto medico,* if you don't mind waiting in line. If you have a serious medical problem, you should head to the nearest large city, where you can get the best medical attention and modern equipment and facilities.

Besides an overall competence in medical workers, Brazil is also known for its excellent quality and low-cost drugs. Many foreigners fill up their prescriptions in Brazil where the medicines are cheap and effective. Brazil is a leading producer of AIDS medications, which are available much cheaper than in other countries.

Finally, Brazil's dentists are considered to be some of the best in the Americas and dental care in Brazil is a fraction of the cost of that in the United States or Canada. Many Americans are shocked at how much money they could save on elaborate dental work by coming to Brazil. The difference can more than pay for the trip. Brazilian cosmetic surgery is already a hot item on the international market because of its incredible cost effectiveness. Hair transplants, implant surgery, and scar treatment are all popular procedures.

## ILLEGAL DRUGS

A small amount of marijuana (known as *erva* or herb) is probably not going to result in a prison sentence for a gringo in Brazil. But it will almost certainly result in loss of a lot of money. If you are caught with marijuana, you will probably be put through an exhausting game of "scare the gringo" before being taken down to the ATM where you can pull out all your cash. If they don't think you've paid enough, you might be taken to your hotel, so you can hand over your camera or other valuables. The general rule is as follows: If you do it, don't carry it. Cocaine is also common in Brazil and much more dangerous to deal with. A gringo caught with cocaine will probably be dealt with harshly and bribes may not be possible. You should avoid it at all costs. Newer drugs, such as ecstasy, are not common in Brazil outside of certain circles in major cities. The safety of taking any of these drugs is very uncertain.

## CRIME

The biggest enemy of Brazil's tourism industry is Brazil's crime. Every big city has its criminal element and dangerous zones and tourist attractions are often targeted by opportunists and hoodlums. By far the greatest number of offenses occurs in the southwest region in and around the three big cities: São Paulo, Rio de Janeiro, and Belo Horizonte. To complete the list of Brazil's top-five worst cities for crime, add Vitória (also in the southwest) and Recife. Not surprisingly, these cities are also the most active centers of drug trafficking and money laundering. Rio de Janeiro is practically out of control and wars between the police and traffickers often move out into the regular neighborhoods. Gangs commonly send out notices that businesses in a certain area should close down on a certain day as a demonstration of their control of the city. Businesses that do not comply are generally robbed and the owners harassed or killed. There have been large sweeps on the beaches of Rio de Janeiro, where hundreds of thieves from the *favelas* (squatter settlements) will swoop down on the beach, robbing everyone in sight. *Favelas* are known to be loaded with communications equipment, arms, and even anti-aircraft missiles. Despite their poor-looking conditions, the *favelas* in Rio de Janeiro are loaded with cash from drugs and Carnaval.

But what affects tourists more often are the petty crimes and robberies that occur every day in the streets. You should be cautious and alert at all times, but especially when you are in-transit with your bags. When taking a taxi, put your valuables in the trunk along with your passport and credit cards. Keep a bit of cash on you to pay the taxi and any other incidentals. Thieves are known to stake out hotels and bus stations waiting for foreigners to enter cabs with their luggage. They then call to motorcycle ambushes on the street, who ride up beside the cab pointing pistols at both the driver and passenger. If this happens to you, you should pull out the cash in your pocket and hand it over to the thief. Hopefully, you prepared yourself by keeping all your important bags in the trunk.

The same precautions apply to walking around town. Keep your valuable items in the hotel and walk around with only a bit of cash and a copy of your passport. Don't keep a lot of cash on you, ever. If you must travel with cash, it's best to break it up and store it in various places. Keep a small amount in your pocket or wallet and the rest should be hidden. Remember that most thieves know about money belts and halters. The best place to hide cash is said to be in your underwear, as thieves are not fond of fondling.

You can carry a day pack with you to hold your camera, but wear it in front of you on crowded streets or in markets. If you can, put your cash in a buttoned or zippered pocket and if you have plenty of cash on you, again, break it up into various pockets. Keep credit cards separate from your cash, preferably in a hidden money belt. In most cases, a thief will accept the money you pull out of your pocket and leave. The unnerving event will usually be over quickly and without too much loss. Never look directly at a thief in these situations. Cautious travelers will open a special bank account with a debit card attached and transfer small amounts

of money into this account throughout their trip. This creates a barrier to your larger savings or checking account in the unlikely event of kidnapping, extortion by the police, or other credit-card-related crimes.

Of course, you should never walk around wearing valuable jewelry, including earrings. They can be pulled off quickly and painfully. I've personally seen it happen many times on crowded city streets. When walking on crowded streets, be aware if anyone in front of you appears to be deliberately slowing you down or creating a jam, as there could be someone behind you ready to snatch your money. This is also true when getting on buses. Any confusion in the line in front of you should trigger you to grab your bags or put your hands in your pockets (if there's money in them). You should make a point of walking on the outside of the sidewalk (near the street) and not on the inside where you can be trapped against the wall.

Sophisticated scams aimed at gringos are not as common in Brazil as in other countries. The truth is, Brazilian thieves simply approach their targets with some kind of weapon and demand money. Nobody on the street will help. The exception to this applies principally to single men, who can become targets for more elaborate setups by women in bars and clubs. Never accept a drink from anyone you don't personally know when in a dance club atmosphere. It's liable to be drugged. And never leave your drink unattended. The *boa noite Cinderella* drug is quite common in touristy night spots. In such spots, you can assume that any woman who approaches you is after your money in one way or another. You can let your guard down as you become more comfortable with the situation.

# Information and Services

## MONEY

The best way to access your money while in Brazil is via the extensive network of ATMs. You can pull out your cash and usually get the best exchange rate on the spot. Most banks charge an extra fee for the international transaction, but it's usually only a couple dollars and worth the convenience and safety of using your ATM card. Pull out R$300 or R$500 at a time and put your ATM card away in your hotel safe until you need it again. You should look for Banco do Brasil and Banco 24 Horas ATMs, as they are most likely to have international systems, such as Plus and Cirrus. In most cases, machines that access international systems have the Plus and Cirrus stickers on the front of the machine. Usually only one or two machines in a Banco do Brasil branch will be equipped, so look at every machine to make sure. In large cities, you might also be able to find Citibank and HSBC branches with international machines. Most airports and some bus terminals have international ATMs on the premises.

Keep in mind that Brazil's ATMs are not open 24 hours. They open at 6 A.M. and shut down at 10 P.M. in most cases. You might find exceptions open 24 hours in airports, bus terminals, and major nightlife centers, but this is not something you should count on.

Besides your ATM card, you might want to bring a credit card or two. The best ones to use are Visa and MasterCard, but some places accept American Express and Diner's Club. You can use credit cards in most hotels and restaurants across the country. Many travelers like to open a temporary account with a debit card attached and keep their credit cards only for emergencies. If you bring more than one credit card, consider keeping them all in separate locations in case one gets lost or stolen. Don't bother with traveler's checks unless you want a few for backup purposes. They are difficult and costly to exchange. You can try Banco do Brasil first, but remote branches might not exchange them for you.

### Changing Money

There is no reason to bring foreign currency with you, but you should keep some of your own currency tucked away in your bag for your return trip home. There are money exchange centers in large cities and tourist towns, but it's better to use the ATM system and not carry all that cash around with you. Dollars, euros, and Argentinean pesos are easy to exchange at *cambio* offices, which always appear in tourist centers. You should never use money changers who are on the streets or in bus stations or airports. If you exchange a large amount, then Banco do Brasil is probably the best deal. They charge a hefty transaction fee, but their rates are the best. *Cambio* offices often charge no transaction fees but offer worse exchange rates. They are usually better for exchanging smaller amounts. The Amazon region near Manaus is the only place in Brazil where dollars and euros can be used to pay for things, although I once paid a taxi driver in dollars after I was pickpocketed in Copacabana and had no more Brazilian currency back at the hotel. It was late at night and naturally, I paid a premium for the transaction.

### Brazilian Money

Before 1994, Brazil used a number of different currencies, including the *cruzeiro, cruzado,* and *cruzado novo.* Inflation was off the charts in those days. Then, in 1994, the government created a single standard currency known as the *real.* Ironically named, the new currency was set artificially at one-to-one with the dollar and was even more valuable than the dollar for a short time. Later, the *real* dropped into a sort of equilibrium with the dollar and has been floating at around R$2.60–3 to the dollar for several years. *Reals* come in denominations of 1, 2, 5, 10, 20, 50, and 100 and each one has a unique color. Coins come in the same denominations as American coins: 1, 5, 10, 25, 50, and R$1.

You will find it difficult to change R$100 notes in many places (only large establishments accept them without complaining) and even R$50 notes will produce complaints in many shops and restaurants. You will probably have to wait while someone runs down the street to get change. In some cases, you might actually be turned away due to lack of change. You will even get asked for smaller bills at busy restaurants and establishments where you know for sure they are making decent money. In fact, most establishments remove excess money from their cash registers every couple of hours and don't always have change on hand. This practice serves to limit their losses in case of robbery. The bottom line is that you should try to get denominations of R$20 or smaller whenever possible, although you should be careful about walking around with money bulging out of your pockets. It's a bit of a catch-22.

## Banks and Money Wires

Every Banco do Brasil office is also a Western Union office, so you can receive or send money wires just about anywhere in Brazil. The sending party is required to specify the city in which you will be picking up the wire. In most cases, you just need to show up at a Banco do Brasil office in the specified city, give them the transaction code, and show them your passport. You will receive papers to sign and be asked to stand in the normal teller line to receive your cash. One note of caution: Be sure that the person who sent the money specifies your name exactly as it appears on your passport or you might run into problems picking up your wire in Brazil. Be sure to begin this process in the morning when the bank opens, because it can take hours to complete in some cases. The number of Brazilians who live overseas and send money wires to their families in Brazil is staggering. Billions of dollars enter Brazil via bank wires every year. You are likely to encounter a long line of Brazilians in front of you. Banks usually open at 10 A.M. and close at 4 P.M. but in some places they close earlier.

## COMMUNICATIONS AND MEDIA

### Phone Calls

Brazil's telecommunications system has changed dramatically since 2000 and is gradually becoming a first-rate service. Unfortunately, the cost of phone calls, both international and domestic, is still extremely high. Public phones work on prepaid phone cards, called *cartão telefone*, which you can purchase at drug stores and magazine stands. Lift the headset, insert the card, and hope that the machine recognizes it. The value of the card in units will appear on the phone's LCD screen. Cards come in 40 and 60 units. A 60-unit card is good for about 5–10 minutes of international calls, depending on the country, and costs around R$7. Note that not every public phone will call internationally. Different cities have different phone companies and some of the larger cities have several that offer public phone service. Phones from one company will allow international calls while those from another will not.

To call domestically, you need to know if you are calling outside of the local zone. If you are inside the local zone (calls within the same city, for instance), then you can just dial the seven- or eight-digit number and you'll be connected. If you are calling outside the local zone, then you need a long-distance service number (21, 31, 41, and 23 are the most common) and the area code, or DDD, of the party you are calling. This always has two digits. In front of these four numbers, you begin by dialing zero. The complete formula is *0 + long distance provider + area code + number.* For example, if you are calling from Rio de Janeiro to São Paulo, you would dial 021-11-2222-3344. What often makes this confusing is that some establishments, unable to let go of the old system, list their phone number with a zero in front of the area code. In fact, the zero goes in front of the long distance provider code and not the area code.

To call internationally, the formula is *00 + long distance provider + country code + number with local area code.* Calling the United States would look like 0021-1-415-555-1234. When

# BRAZIL'S TELEPHONE CODES

**B**razil's phone systems have been undergoing a lot of changes in recent years. One of the ramifications is that most of the country is being updated to have 8-digit phone numbers. This started around 2000 and is still in process, although most of the country has converted already. There are still some 7-digit numbers in São Paulo and the Southern Region, so if you have trouble with a 7-digit number at any time in Brazil, try it again by adding a 3 to the beginning, making it 8 digits. For example, the number tel. 71/251-4455 would become tel. 71/3251-4455.

**Know Brazil**

## Area Codes
Belém 79
Belo Horizonte 31
Boa Vista 95
Brasilia 61
Campo Grande 67
Cuiabá 65
Curitiba 41
Florianópolis 48
Fortaleza 85
João Pessoa 83
Macapá 96
Maceió 82
Manaus 92
Natal 84
Porto Alegre 51
Recife 81
Rio de Janeiro 21
Salvador 71
São Paulo 11

## Emergency Codes
Ambulance 192
Emergency 199
Federal Highway Police 191
Federal Police 194
Fire Department 193
IBAMA 152
Police 190
PROCON (consumer activist group) 151

## Country Codes
Argentina 54
Australia 61
Austria 43
Belgium 32
Brazil 55
Canada 1
Chile 56
China 86
Colombia 57
England 44
France 33
Germany 49
Ireland 44
Israel 972
Italy 39
Japan 81
Mexico 52
Netherlands 31
New Zealand 64
Peru 51
Portugal 351
Scotland 44
South Africa 27
Spain 34
Switzerland 41
United States 1
Venezuela 58

you use up the value on your card, you have a few seconds to insert a new card before the call is terminated.

You can use your international phone cards while in Brazil. Just dial the access number first to get an international connection. The major companies and their access numbers are AT&T (0800-890-0288), MCI (0800-890-0012), and Sprint (0800-890-8000). Unfortunately, most public phones in Brazil are on the noisiest streets and *praças,* and finding a quiet phone can be a real challenge. Your best bet is going to an indoor shopping mall. Some tourist towns have private phone booths with metered phones that you can use. These services, called *posto telefonico,* will offer different rates for different countries, so be sure to ask and compare. They are usually more expensive than using a public phone, but you get the benefit of a private and comfortable phone booth and you can sometimes pay with a credit card. Most hotels charge a service fee for using their phones and it can be abusive. Since this is not always the case, it's a good practice to ask when you make your reservations. The service fee is called a *taxa* (TAH-shah) *de serviço.*

## Cell Phones

Calling to a cell phone from a landline is very expensive in Brazil and many private phones are completely blocked from calling cell phones. It's cheaper to call from another cell phone. Even so, you may be aghast at the cost of a minute on a cell phone in Brazil. Depending on the package you purchase, calls are R$.65–1.90 per minute. The aforementioned calling procedure works equally from cell phones as from landlines. You can rent cell phones during your stay in Brazil and it's an excellent way of keeping in touch with your group. Rental services are listed in the *São Paulo* chapter.

Your own cell phone will work in Brazil if it is compatible with the CDMA, TDMA, or GSM 1800 standard and your service provider has a contract with one of the Brazilian cellular services, such as TIM, Claro, Telemig, or Oi. Roaming for Brazil is not automatic. Before bringing your cell phone, check with your phone company for roaming availability in Brazil. Vivo the largest cell phone company uses the same system as most American companies (CDMA). Claro, another cellular company, use two systems, one compatible with the U.S. (TDMA) and the other compatible with Europe (GSM) and a third company, TIM, is only GSM, like Europe. Your phone may not connect automatically to the local network, so you may have to connect manually when you arrive in Brazil. If you are not satisfied with the results of your connection, you may be able to switch to one of the other providers in Brazil. They might be listed in your phone's setup options under the above names or with numerical network codes. People calling you from your home country dial normally and they will be connected to you through the Brazilian network.

## Internet Connections

The best way to communicate while traveling is via email and you will have no trouble finding Internet cafés and LAN Houses throughout the country, even in small towns and on back roads. Multi-player, online games are extremely popular with young Brazilians and almost every town in the country has a LAN House full of screaming kids competing in online tournaments. You can use these locations for regular Internet connections, but they are usually set up for games, meaning that they are loud, dark, and the computers are usually bereft of accessories. High-speed connections are practically ubiquitous in Brazil, although services vary widely. Most LAN Houses use DSL lines, which can be fast or slow depending on the LAN setup. Some places have high-speed cable connections or even satellite. You'll find a lot of satellite connections in the Amazon region, allowing you to get online with a super-fast connection. These services, however, are generally quite expensive (I've seen prices as high as R$1 per minute). In many LAN Houses, you can make international phone calls using the net, so ask around.

## The Postal System

Brazil's postal system is generally very reliable

# BUSINESS TRAVEL TIPS

São Paulo and major Brazilian cities are not the jungle. Wireless technologies, wideband or wi-fi Internet access, cyber cafés, and LAN houses are all available and easily found. If you arrive in São Paulo, for example, the Guarulhos International Airport offers the Interconmax store (www.intercomox.com.br). There, you'll find more than Internet access; you can also get accessories and order map software for your palm or ipaq. Some other websites for maps include www.apontador.com.br and www.maplink.com.br.

Did you forget your notebook LAN connector, power supply, or palm pencil? Order it at the Guarulhos airport. Some other locations in São Paulo include the electronic and computer parts street fair on Rua Santa Efigênia downtown, Promocenter (Rua Augusta at Rua Luis Coelho, Jardins), and Casa do Notebook (Av. Faria Lima, www.casadonotebook.com.br).

Want to connect to the cellular networks here in Brazil? The providers include TIM (GSM), Vivo (CDMA), Claro (TDMA and GSM), and Nextel (trunking). Check with your local company for roaming availability before coming. You're likely to have a connection to one or more of these. Regarding hotel Internet and wi-fi availability, most chain hotels have both and some offer it for free. If it's important, check this before you make reservations.

For network connections, you'll find a list of LAN houses and wi-fi–equipped locations at www.link.estado.com.br or try the Link supplement of the *O Estado de São Paulo* newspaper Monday edition. Some free, dial-up access providers include www.ig.com.br, www.itelifonica.com.br, www.click21.com.br, and www.brfree.com.br.

Voltage in Brazil is normally 110v. AC 60hz, but you'll also find plenty of locations with 220v., especially in the northeast region. In most large cities, you'll find flat pin connectors (like those found in the United States) but you can also use round connectors like those used in Europe. Brazilian plugs generally accept both, but in some older places, only the round connectors work. Buy your converters here in Brazil. They are cheap and will work better than those little kits you get at travel shops.

*(Compiled by Marcelo Thalenberg, author of* Managing Your Business with Outlook For Dummies.*)*

and there are offices everywhere in Brazil. Sending mail within the country is usually fast and reasonably priced. A standard postcard costs about R$.55 within the country and arrives within a few days. An envelope costs around R$.75. Sending the same postcard to the United States will cost R$2.70 and the envelope around R$3.10. They take 7–14 days to arrive.

Sending and receiving packages is another matter altogether and can get pretty expensive, depending on the weight of the package and type of service you use. You can choose from economy service, which takes up to 30 days to arrive; registered mail, which takes around 15 days; and SedEx, which usually arrives within a week. Naturally, you'll pay quite a bit more for the faster services. A small package sent out of the country can cost R$25–65. You have to fill out paperwork declaring the value of everything in the box, which is more for the customs office abroad than for Brazil. However, there are some restrictions on what you can send out of the country and some shipments might get held up at the Brazilian customs office on the way out. This is especially true for works of art. If you buy a piece of sculpture or a painting, you should probably bring it back with you rather than mail it. To send art out of the country, you must get a clearance from the Instituto de Patrimónia Histórica e Artística Nacional (IPHAN). This requires you to pick up special forms at a local IPHAN office, fill them out, and return them with photos of the works you are sending. About one week later, you'll receive clearance forms to send with the art, which you should attach to the package

Know Brazil

or give to the shipping service you are using. Without these clearance forms, your package is almost certain to be returned. If you buy a piece of art from a gallery and have it shipped, the gallery will have to go through these same procedures, so don't expect your package to arrive quickly.

Postal employees are strict about boxes being clean and advertising-free, so make sure you wrap any packages with brown paper before taking them to the post office. They are also strict about your putting a return address on the package. The best idea is to use your hotel's address and make sure you leave instructions with the hotel, in case it is returned. If you are not confident in your hotel, then ask the post office to use their own address, explaining that you are a temporary visitor with no local address. Do not use a return address that is not within the zone of the post office, as returned mail gets sent to the post office from which it came. This is determined from the postal stamp and not from your return address. The local post office then sends the returned package to the return address on the box. If the return address is not in their area, they will send the package to storage, from whence it shall never return. If the return address is the post office itself, then they will keep it for up to 90 days on site.

Sending packages from Brazil can be slow and expensive, but the service is reliable and trustworthy. However, if you prefer, you can find Federal Express, DHL, and UPS in most large cities. In most cases, these services will pick up and deliver from your hotel or place of residence.

Receiving packages in Brazil is a mixed bag. In most cases, your package will be delayed in Brazilian customs. It's common to receive packages 2–3 months after they are delivered. If your package is determined to have saleable merchandise in it, you will be charged duty, which is sometimes based on the value that the sender placed on the international shipping forms and sometimes based on their own determination. I was once sent a CD-ROM with only computer data on it, but the customs office determined that I should pay R$8 duty, which is the fee for music CDs. I have also received large boxes full of products from the United States and paid no duty whatever. If you want your packages to arrive quickly, then have the sender use Federal Express or UPS International.

## MAPS AND TOURIST INFORMATION

### Maps

The most detailed road maps of Brazil are in the *Guia Quatro Rodas Brasil* guidebook (www.guia4rodas.abril.com.br/loja). The company that publishes this guide also has smaller, individual guides for different regions, cities, and states. These guides are designed to help people who are driving around Brazil, so their maps are especially well done and detailed. Besides the complete guides, which are all in Portuguese, they also publish maps separately. You can find their products at most bookstores and even many magazine stands, but you will probably get an incomplete selection. To see their complete catalog, purchase from their website. You can place an international online order for their products before your trip if you want to study the maps before leaving. You can also check at www.apontador.com.br and www.maplink.com.br. These sites also have maps and location software for Palm and Pocket PCs. If you fly into the São Paulo Guarulhos airport, you can find map software at the Intercomax store (www.intercomax.com.br).

Most cities in Brazil have their own maps and they are usually available at tourist information offices and bookstores. Free tourist maps are also generally available at hotels and tourist information centers.

### Tourist Information

Each city or tourist area will have its own tourist information entities and some areas have two. Sometimes they are connected to the city or state government and sometimes they are private. However, the official tourism entities will at least be sanctioned by the city or state government. All tourist information offices listed throughout this book are official entities.

They usually have *tur* at the end of their names, as in RioTur, BeloTur, and ManausTur. Many of these have websites and many are listed in the *Information and Services* sections throughout this book. Most of these agencies are also sanctioned by EMBRATUR, the country's national tourism advocacy and regulatory group. Any agency, tour guide, tourism office, or other entity that bears the EMBRATUR logo has theoretically been checked out and approved. You can get in touch with EMBRATUR if you want to check up on any group. Their website is www.embratur.gov.br.

In addition, you can get in touch with the Convention and Visitors Bureaus in many cities for more information. Most of these bureaus will be happy to send you information on their city and its convention capabilities. They can also refer you to other sources of information. Most of the CVBs have English-speaking staff. You can get a list of Brazil's CVBs at www.fb-cevb.com.br.

## PHOTOGRAPHY

### Film and Processing

Film-processing labs are abundant in Brazil and you should never have a problem finding one. Most offer one-hour processing for print films. The quality of these labs varies widely. The best print film is also the cheapest, called Kodak Pro Image. It comes in 100 and 200 speed. Fuji makes a comparable film for the same price. You'll pay about R$8 for a roll of 36.

Slide and black-and-white films are difficult to find and even more difficult (and expensive) to get developed in Brazil. If you use these films, you should probably bring your own and don't develop the film until you get home. There are some professional labs in São Paulo and Rio de Janeiro, but they are expensive and slow compared to pro labs in the States.

### Digital Services

Many film-processing labs in Brazil offer a range of digital services. Large cities have numerous digital labs available. They are usually easiest to find in shopping malls, and one of the largest and best-equipped chains is the Fuji processing labs. Services include downloading and storage of images from memory cards onto various types of media, digitization from negatives and prints, and printing of digital images. If you bring a digital camera, be sure to have several high-capacity cards with you, especially if you are gong to be trekking through remote areas. Also make sure you bring any card adapters or special cables required by your camera.

Some labs can digitize your film at the time it is being chemically processed and this is usually the cheapest way to go. While on extended trips around Brazil, I always use this service and ask for no paper prints so I don't have to carry the heavy paper around with me. I get a CD with all my photos (several rolls on one CD) and pay around R$12–15 per roll for both developing and digitizing. You may not find these services in small towns, but most large cities offer it. Digitizing prints after the film has been developed is much more expensive at around R$1 per photo.

You'll find repair services, equipment, and accessories in just about every large city in Brazil. The best place for equipment and service, however, is São Paulo, where the prices are most competitive, variety is greater, and service is more professional. Many repair shops around the country just send your camera to São Paulo anyway. Prices are about 30 percent higher than those in the United States. You can find camera batteries all over Brazil. One more thing: Don't use a professional carrying bag for your equipment as it will call attention to the fact that you have expensive equipment with you. Instead, arrange space in a daypack or shoulder bag and you can protect the equipment with soft rags.

### Snapping Photos

Brazilians take serious offense at anyone snapping their picture without permission, even in crowded public spaces. You should be careful about doing so. The best way to get pictures of crowds and street scenes is with a telephoto lens. However, carrying around a heavy lens may detract from the enjoyment of your trip. In tourist locations, you should always ask before photographing the locals. They will usually hit you up for a couple *reals*. If you take more than one photo, feel free to negotiate a package deal. Street vendors will usually let you take their picture if you buy something from them, but you should ask before paying for the item or they'll probably hit you up for another couple *reals*. Be careful taking pictures on a crowded beach. Automatic-focus cameras come in handy so you can snap quickly and get away. Otherwise, if you appear like a professional photographer, with plenty of equipment, who is setting up a shot with a tripod and team of assistants, you will probably not be assaulted by your subjects. Somehow a professional photographer who is just doing his job is more accepted than some foreigner with a nice camera popping off shots on the beach. You can usually take pictures at will during festivals, but you'll probably need a flash and a bodyguard. Don't assume that you can photograph Capoeira demonstrations just because they are on the street. It's best if you ask one of the participants first.

A telephoto lens is absolutely necessary for animal shots in the Amazon or Pantanal. You will also need a great deal of patience and a delicate step. Often, the best way to get a shot is to stay in one place and wait for the animals to come to you. However, the photographic safaris in these regions will usually pass through fairly quickly. If you're serious about getting animal shots, you should hire a guide to take you on a private photo excursion. For architectural shots, you may want to have a translator with you since the best shots are usually captured from neighboring buildings. You may need a native speaker to explain why you want to go into the building.

## WEIGHTS, MEASURES, TIMES

Brazil uses the metric system for everything and you'll find a metric conversion chart at the back of this book. They also use the 24-hour clock and you'll encounter this every time you look at a bus or plane schedule. There are four time zones in Brazil, but most of the country is united in the same zone, which they call Brasilia Time (GMT -3). Much of the year, this is one hour ahead of New York, but while the United States is on Daylight Savings Time, Brazil is also changing their clock. . . in the opposite direction. This puts the country three hours ahead of New York in December and only one hour ahead in July. To make matters more confusing, there are a couple of months when the United States has changed the clocks but Brazil has not and the difference is two hours.

The Amazon region all the way to Santarém in Pará is one hour behind Brasilia time and this extends down to Mato Grosso and Mato Grosso do Sul. The state of Acre on the western tip of Brazil is two hours behind Brasilia time. The Island of Fernando de Noronha is one hour ahead of Brasilia time.

# Portuguese Phrase Book

## PRONUNCIATION

Most foreigners who have had some exposure to Spanish are left completely dumfounded when they hear Portuguese. Although based on the Spanish language and structurally very similar, the differences in pronunciation are vast. In addition, Portuguese has far more accents and contractions than Spanish has. Interestingly, most Brazilians can understand Spanish fairly well, but Spanish-speaking people require some retraining of the ear to understand Portuguese. Moreover, Portuguese has many pronunciation rules and subtle differences in vowel sounds. A common joke among Brazilians is how foreigners pronounce *pão* (bread) exactly like *pau* (stick and slang for penis). The former is completely nasal and the latter is not. The difference between *vó* (grandma) and *vô* (grandpa) is extremely subtle. The former is slightly more open sounding like the 'ah' in "fall." Finally, don't pronounce the m at the ends of words like *tem* (is there, are there) and *sim* (yes).

Common mistakes made by Spanish speakers: The word *não* has a distinct nasal quality and is not "no," as in English or Spanish. Likewise, *eu* (I) is not pronounced like the Spanish *yo* but more like 'ehoo.' Words that are similar to Spanish words often require new pronunciations, like *simpatica,* which uses the 'chi' sound in place of 'ti,' and some require re-learning, such as *porto* instead of *puerto* and *uma* instead of *una*. It can also be difficult to remember that in Portuguese, the letter r is often pronounced like an h. Brazilian Portuguese never ends words in the Spanish *cion* but uses *ão* at the end, like a cat's "meow." There are a few excellent books designed to teach Portuguese to Spanish speakers.

## Vowels

**a**—like the 'ah' in "hah": *casa* (CAH-sah), *garota* (gah-RO-tah).

**e**—pronounced like 'eh' as in "fell": *sede* (sehdj), *prego* (PREH-go). When e is fol-lowed by an m or n, the sound becomes more nasal (see m and n below). At the end of a word, e is pronounced like 'ee,' as in "speed": *ele* (EH-lee), *pente* (PAYN-chee).

**i**—pronouned 'ee,' as in "speed": *polícia* (po-LEE-cee-ah).

**o**—like the 'o' in "home": *sofre* (SO-free), *esposa* (ehs-PO-zah). At the end of a word, it sounds more like the 'oo' in "boot": *caminho* (kah-MEEN-yoo), *minuto* (mee-NOO-too).

**u**—like the 'oo' in "moon": *muito* (moo-EEN-too).

## Consonants

**c and ç**—pronounced like 'k' when followed by a, o, u, or any consonant: *caboclo* (kah-BO-klo). When followed by i or e, the c becomes an 's,' as in "see": *reciclar* (reh-see-KLAGH), *alface* (al-FAH-see). The ç is al-ways pronounced like an 's': *poço* (PO-so).

**d**—in most cases, it's pronounced like 'd' in "dome": *delícia* (deh-LEE-see-ah). When followed by an i, it's pronounced like the 'j' in "jeep" which we'll indicate with 'dj': *divulgar* (DJEE-vool-gagh). At the end of a word followed by an e, it takes on the same jeep sound: *parede* (pah-DEH-djee), *de nada* (djee NAH-dah).

**em, en**—pronounced as you would expect, except at the end of a word, when they be-come a nasal-sounding 'aing': *Belém* (beh-LAING), *trem* (traing).

**im, in**—similar to the above, but with an 'eeng' sound: *mim* (meeng), *cupim* (coo-PEENG).

**h**—usually combined with l and n to make a 'y' sound, as in *linha* (LEEN-yah) or *filho* (FEEL-yo). In its rare appearance without l or n, it is generally silent, as in *hotel* (O-tel) or *Bahia* (bah-EE-ah).

**r**—pronounced like 'h' as in "hope" when it appears at the beginning of a word: *rapido* (HA-pee-doo), *rato* (HAH-too). In the mid-dle of a word, r is pronounced like a very quick and light 'd' in English, as in the word "ready": *garota* (gah-DO-tah). When at the end of a word, r is pronounced with a throaty sound (a glottal slide), which we'll indicate as a 'gh' sound, although it's much more scratchy in your throat: *fedor* (feh-DOGH), *melhor* (mel-YOGH), *vir* (veegh). In some parts of São Paulo, you'll hear r pronounced like the American 'r' in "fort."

**rr**—pronounced like the 'h' in "hope": *forró* (fo-HO), *barra* (BAH-hah). In the south of Brazil and in the countryside, you'll hear rr pronounced like the Spanish rolled 'r'.

**s**—is a bit of a trouble-maker. In general, it's pronounced like an s when at the beginning or end of a word: *solteiro* (sol-TAY-roo), *dedos* (DEH-doos). When in the middle of a word, it's usually pronounced like a z: *casa* (KAH-zah). However, after following en or er, it becomes an s again, except with the prefix "trans": *transatlântico* (tranz-aht-LAHN-chee-ko).

**t**—similar to d, it's normally pronounced like the 't' in "temple": *até* (ah-TAY). When followed by an i, it's pronounced like the 'ch' in "cheese": *tive* (CHEE-vee). At the end of a word, followed by an e, it's pronounced like the same cheese sound: *leite* (LAY-chee).

**x**—is either an s sound or a 'sh,' depending on where it appears. When following an e, it's usually pronounced like an s: *ex-marido* (EHS mah-DEE-doo), *extrato* (EHS-trah-too). In most other cases, it's a 'sh': *caixa* (KAI-shah).

## Accents

Portuguese has three principal accents and they are all used to alter vowel sounds. The **til** is the most common and it changes word stress where stress would otherwise be on a wrong syllable. In other words, it forces stress on the vowel over which it appears, such as *cafuné* (kah-foo-NEH). The **agudo** accent appears with a and o and forces a nasal sound, as in the common ending *ção*, which is pronounced like the 'saoo' in "sound" but even more nasal. This accent can also be used with the letter o, and is commonly used to turn words that end in *ção* into plurals. The plural of *nação* (nation) becomes *nações* (nas-OYZ), where the *ões* gets a nasal

treatment as if you pinched your nose while saying it. The **chapéu** (little hat) accent makes vowels more open and 'ahh'-sounding. The ô becomes almost an 'ahh' sound as in the word "fauna." *Antônio* is pronounced an-TAH-nee-oo. The ê becomes an 'eh' sound, as in "ethnic." *você* is pronounced vo-SEH and not vo-SAY.

## USAGE

### Diminutive

Brazilians win first place in the use of the diminutive in everyday language. It's common to hear all kinds of *inhos* and *zinhos* attached to the ends of words, like *trenzinho* (little train) and *irmãozinho* (little brother). If you order a *cafezinho* at a lunch stand, you'll probably get less than half a cup. Brazilians even stack the diminutives on top of each other for more emphasis. *Pequeno* is small, *pequenino* is smaller and *pequenininho* is almost too small to imagine. Diminutive can also be used figuratively to lessen the effect of something, such as a *minutinho*, which is probably the same amount of time as a minute, but it feels shorter. If *rapidinho* is any faster than *rapido,* it's merely psychological. Of course, this gives way to using the diminutive for no real alteration of the original word whatever, but merely to communicate affection or dearness. One man might have a *namorada* while another has a *namoradinha.* Neither has any bearing on the size of the girlfriend. Children have their *amiguinhos,* which are no smaller than regular *amigos.*

In colloquial usage, you can never be totally sure if the diminutive is sincere or ironic. Someone might refer to his *casinha* (little house) and *filinho* (little son), but when you arrive, you're surprised to see a mansion and a seven-foot-tall basketball player. Finally, there are some cases where the diminutive version of a word creates a completely different word. A *camisa* is a shirt, whereas a *camisinha* is a condom. *Cebola* is an onion, but *cebolinha* is green onion.

### Questions

Questions are formed mostly by voice inflection, since the sentence structure for a question is the ame as for a statement. The phrase *você tem medo* (you are afraid) becomes a question simply by raising the tone at the end of the sentence. Many questions, however, are stated in the negative (aren't you afraid?) and in many cases, an extra *não* is placed at the end of the sentence for good measure: *Você não tem medo não?*

## Commands

Brazilians form requests and commands in a much more blunt way than in English. They do not prep requests with "could you. . ." or "when you have a minute. . ." and doing so could even be misinterpreted. The most common way to ask for something is in a command: *"Me da um suco, por favor"* (Give me a juice please). This is not considered rude as long as the *por favor* is used. An alternative version is, *"Quero uma cerveja, por favor"* (I want a beer please). You'll also hear a lot of . . . *para mim* (. . . for me) in Brazil, such as, *"Faz um suco para mim, por favor"* (Make me a juice please). Brazilians who have traveled to England or the United States often have stories about how they got a dirty look from the clerk when they "asked" for something in a store in the typical Brazilian manner.

## ADDRESSING PEOPLE

I—*eu*
you—*você*
he/him—*ele*
she/her—*ela*
we/us—*nós*
we/us (the group)—*a gente*
you (plural)—*vocês*
they/them—*eles* (m)/*elas* (f)
Mr.—*senhor* or *seu* (casual)
Mrs./Madam—*senhora* or *dona*
young man—*moço*
young woman—*moça*
guy (generic)—*rapaz* or *cara*
boy/girl—*garoto/garota*
child—*criança*
baby—*neném*
brother/sister—*irmão/irmã*
father/mother—*pai/mãe*
wife—*esposa*

husband—*marido*
son/daughter—*filho/filha*
grandmother—*avó*
grandfather—*avô*
friend—*amigo*
acquaintance—*conhecido*
colleague—*colega* (m or f)
boyfriend/girlfriend—*namorado/namorada*
generic third party—*fulano* (m)/*fulana* (f)

Note: *Dona* is used as a title for women while *a senhora* is used when addressing women. For men, it's *senhor* or *seu* for titles and *o senhor* for addressing.

## MEETING PEOPLE

hello—*olá*
hey—*oi*
good morning—*bom dia*
good afternoon—*boa tarde*
good evening—*boa noite*
How's it going?—*Como vai?*
How are you? (formal)—*Como você está?*
very well—*estou bem*
so-so—*mais ou menos*
And you?—*E você?*
excuse me (sorry)—*me desculpa*
excuse me (getting attention or moving through a crows)—*com licença*
Nice to meet you.—*Um prazer.*
What's your name?—*Como você se chama? / Qual é o seu nome?*
My name is. . .—*Meu nome é. . .*
Do you speak English?—*Você fala inglês?*
thank you—*obrigado* (m)/*obrigada* (f)
Would you be so kind. . .—*Por gentileza. . .*
You're welcome.—*De nada.*
She's very nice.—*Ela é muita simpática.*
I like her.—*Gostei dela.*
What?—*O quê?*
I don't know.—*Não sei*
I mean. . .—*Quero dizer. . .*
I don't understand.—*Não entendi*
Please speak slowly.—*Fala devagar, por favor.*
Can you repeat that?—*Fala de novo?*
What happened?—*O que foi?*
just a minute—*só um minuto*

Wait a minute.—*Espera aí.*
How do you say. . .—*Como se fala. . .*
That's right/that's it.—*Isto mesmo.*
Let's go.—*Vamos.*
I have to go.—*Tenho que ir.*
goodbye—*tchau*
See you later.—*Até mais tarde.*
See you soon.—*Até breve, até logo.*
Let's meet. . . tomorrow morning, at my hotel.—*Vamos encontrar. . . amanhã de manhã, em meu hotel.*
I'll call you tomorrow.—*Eu te ligo amanhã.*
I'll see you tomorrow.—*Eu te vejo amanhã.*
I'll come back tomorrow.—*Eu volto amanhã.*

Note: Brazilians use the past tense for compliments and criticism given in the present moment. For example, they say, *"Gostei do seu cabelo"* (I liked your hair), instead of, *"Gosto do seu cabelo"* (I like your hair). This applies to in-the-moment comments and not direct questions: *"Você gosta do meu cabelo?"* (Do you like my hair?), *"Sim, eu gosto"* (Yes, I like it), although many people will ask this question in the past tense.

## ACCOMMODATIONS

Do you have a room for tonight?—*Tem quarto para hoje?*
just one night—*uma noite só*
Can I see it?—*Eu posso ver?*
Is breakfast included?—*O café está incluido?*
single room, bed—*quarto de solteiro, cama de solteiro*
double room, bed—*quarto de casal, cama de casal*
two single beds—*duas camas de solteiro*
I need another blanket, towel, pillow.—*Vou precisar de mais um cobertor, uma toalha, um travesseiro.*
Is that the counter price?—*Este é o preço de balcão?*
Can you give me a discount?—*Pode me dar um desconto? Não tem desconto?*
Do you have a cash discount?—*Tem desconto a vista?*
Can you wake me up at 9 A.M. tomorrow?—*Acorde-me as nove da manhã?*

What time is check out?—*A que horas é o check out?*
Can I check out a little late?—*Posso fazer check out um pouco mais tarde?*
I'm paying in cash/by credit card.—*Vou pagar com dinheiro/com cartão.*
There's a problem with the bathroom.—*Tem problema no banheiro.*
When does the sauna close?—*A que horas fecha a sauna?*
I'd like to change rooms.—*Quero mudar de quarto.*
Are there special towels for the pool—*Tem toalha de piscina?*
What is this charge for?—*O que é este valor?*
Can you make a reservation for me at this hotel?—*Pode me ajudar com uma reserva neste hotel?*

## RESTAURANTS

Are you hungry—*Está com fome?*
thirsty—*sede*
I'm hungry.—*Estou com fome.*
Let's go eat.—*Vamos comer.*
What do you want to eat?—*Onde você quer comer?*
I don't eat meat.—*Não como carne.*
I'm a vegetarian.—*Sou vegetariano.*
Do you have a menu?—*Tem cardápio?*
Do you have a prepared plate?—*Tem algum prato feito?*
Do you have any specials?—*Tem alguma promoção?*
How does it work here?—*Como funciona aqui?*
Is it all-you-can-eat?—*Come a vontade?*
Do you have any fresh juices?—*Tem suco natural?*
I just want a light snack.—*Só quero lanchar.*
nothing fancy—*nada formal*
mineral water—*agua mineral*
plain—*sem gás*
carbonated—*com gás*
I'd like a plate of french fries.—*Me da uma porção de fritas, por favor.*
Does this serve two people?—*É para duas pessoas?*

Can you make a single portion?—*Pode fazer meia porção?*

I'm full.—*Estou satisfeito.*

I ate a lot.—*Comi muito.*

one more beer please—*mais uma cerveja, por favor*

Do you have wine?—*Tem vinho?*

dry—*seco*

sweet—*suave*

red—*tinto*

white—*branco*

Do you have tea?—*Tem chá?*

I'd like coffee.—*Queria um café.*

black—*puro*

with a little milk—*pingado, com pouco leite*

with milk—*com leite*

that's fine/like that—*assim está bom*

Can you make a real cappuccino?—*Pode fazer um cappuccino verdadeiro?*

Can you bring me silverware please?—*Pode trazer talheres, por favor?*

bill please—*a conta, por favor*

Is the tip included?—*Já tem taxa de serviço na conta?*

Let's go somewhere else for coffee.—*Vamos num outro lugar para café.*

dessert—*sobremesa*

drinks—*bebidas*

It was delicious.—*Foi delicioso.*

Compliments to the chef.—*Parabéns ao chefe.*

Note: Brazilians rarely answer questions with yes or no. Instead, they repeat the verb in the first person. For example, if someone asks, *"Você quer comer?"* (Would you like to eat?), you answer, *"Quero"* (I would like).

## TRANSPORTATION AND DIRECTIONS

Where is the. . . (permanent object or building)?—*Onde é. . . ?*

Where is. . . (temporary object)?—*Onde está. . . ?*

How do I get to. . . the park, the church, downtown?—*Como eu posso achar. . . o parque, a igreja, o centro?*

How do I get from downtown to Copacabana?—*Como eu chego em Copacabana do centro?*

Can you help me?—*Pode me ajudar?*

Can you call me a taxi please—*Pode chamar um taxi para mim, favor?*

Where can I find a taxi?—*Onde ficam os taxis?*

Is it far?—*Está longe?*

Is this the bus to. . . ?—*Este é o onibus para. . . ?*

Are you the taxi driver?—*Você é o taxista?*

Is this taxi free?—*Está livre, o taxi?*

How much is it to downtown?—*Quanto que é até o centro?*

Can you give me an idea?—*Pode me dar uma ideia?*

to the bus station please—*até a rodoviaria, por favor*

You can take this bag?—*Pode levar esta mala?*

I'll take this bag.—*Vou levar esta mala.*

Where is the exit/entrance?—*Onde está a saida/entrada?*

It's close to. . . —*Está perto de. . .*

Do you go past Barra, the lighthouse, downtown?—*Você passa na Barra, no farol, no centro?*

You can stop here.—*Pode parar aqui.*

next right, left—*a próxima direita, esquerda*

Turn here.—*Vire aqui.*

at the corner—*na esquina*

straight ahead—*direto*

Can you slow down please?—*Pode andar mais devagar, por favor?*

where are we going?—*Onde vamos?*

Where are you taking me?—*Para onde você está me levando?*

Can you pick me up here at 10 P.M.?—*Pode me buscar aqui as vinte duas horas?*

there (over there)—*lá*

there (where you are)—*aí*

there (right over there)—*ali*

## MONEY AND SHOPPING

How much is it?—*Quanto que é?*

cash price—*preço a vista*

What if I buy three?—*E se eu comprar três?*

Do you take credit cards?—*Aceita cartão de credito?*

Can you change this bill?—*Pode trocar esta nota?*

It's too expensive.—*É um pouco caro.*
It's way too expensive.—*É caro demais.*
I'll take it.—*Vou levar.*
It's for my husband.—*É para meu marido.*
Can you put it in a box?—*Pode colocar numa caixa?*
Can you deliver this to my hotel?—*Pode entregar em meu hotel?*
Can you send this out of the country?—*Pode enviar pelo exterior?*
I'd like to pick it up later.—*Gostaria de buscar mais tarde.*

## COMMUNICATIONS

phone call—*ligação, chamada*
international phone call—*ligação internacional*
I want to call. . .—*Quero ligar para. . .*
collect call—*a cobrar*
phone card—*cartão telefonico*
dial—*discar*
I'd like to speak with. . .—*Queria falar com. . .*
I'd like to mail these letters.—*Queria enviar estas cartas.*
What are the options?—*Quais são as opcões?*
What's the most economical?—*Qual é mais econômico?*
What's the fastest?—*Qual é mais rápido?*
postal insurance—*seguro*
Can I use your tape?—*Posso usar seu durex?*
return address—*remitente*
addressee (person receiving)—*destinatário*
Do you have a high-speed connection?—*Tem conexão de alta velocidade?*
It's very slow.—*Está muito lento.*
I need to use my own disk/CD.—*Preciso usar meu proprio disco.*
I have finished.—*Já terminei.*
private phone booth—*cabine*
quiet public phone—*telefone publico num lugar quieto*

## HEALTH AND EMERGENCIES

Help!—*Socorro!*
Help me please.—*Me ajuda, por favor.*
I was mugged/robbed.—*Fui assaltado/roubado.*

I feel sick.—*Estou passando mal.*
Call a doctor.—*Chama um médico.*
Take me to the hospital.—*Me leva ao hospital.*
Is there a drugstore nearby?—*Tem drogaria por perto?*
I have a headache.—*Tenho dor de cabeça.*
a stomach ache—*dor no estomago*
acid indigestion—*azía*
a cold—*gripe*
an allergy—*alergia*
nausea—*náusea*
toothache—*dor nos dentes*
a fever—*febre*
sunburn—*queimada de sol*
cramps (women)—*colica*
diarrhea—*diarréia*
constipation—*prisão de ventre*
I sprained my ankle.—*Torci minha canela.*
I feel dizzy.—*Estou tonto.*
I need to lie down.—*Preciso deitar.*
I need aspirin.—*Preciso aspirina.*
ointment—*crème, pomada*
sanitary napkins—*absorventes*
tampons—*O.B.*
toothbrush—*escova de dentes*
antacid—*sal de fruta*
anti-bacterial soap—*sabonete anti-bactericida*
condom—*preservativo*

## NUMBERS

zero—*zero*
one—*um/uma*
two—*dois/duas*
three—*três*
four—*quatro*
five—*cinco*
six—*seis*
seven—*sete*
eight—*oito*
nine—*nove*
10—*dez*
11—*onze*
12—*doze*
13—*treze*
14—*quatorze*
15—*quinze*
16—*dezesseis*

M

17—*dezessete*
18—*dezoito*
19—*dezenove*
20—*vinte*
21—*vinte e um*
30—*trinta*
40—*quarenta*
50—*cinquenta*
60—*sessenta*
70—*setenta*
80—*oitenta*
90—*noventa*
100—*cem*
500—*quinhientos*
600—*seis centos*
1,000—*mil*
10,000—*dez mil*
100,000—*cem mil*
100,000,000—*milhão*
one half—*metade*
in the middle—*no meio*
average—*a media*
one third—*um terco*
one fourth—*um quarto*
one fifth—*um quinto*
first—*primeiro/primeira*
second—*segundo/segunda*
third—*terceiro/terceira*
fourth—*quarta*
fifth—*quinta*
sixth—*sexta*
seventh—*setima*
eighth—*oitava*
ninth—*nono*
tenth—*decimo*
eleventh—*decimo primeiro*
twentieth—*vigesimo*
twenty first—*vigesimo primeiro*
even—*par*
odd—*impar*
every other one—*um sim, um não*
every two days—*de dois em dois dias*

## DAYS AND MONTHS

Monday—*segunda-feira*
Tuesday—*terça-feira*
Wednesday—*quarta-feira*

Thursday—*quinta-feira*
Friday—*sexta-feira*
Saturday—*sabado*
Sunday—*domingo*
today—*hoje*
yesterday—*ontem*
tomorrow—*amanhã*
this Friday—*sexta-feira que vem*
next Friday—*sexta-feira proxima*
next week—*semana proxima*
January—*janeiro*
February—*fevereiro*
March—*março*
April—*abril*
May—*maio*
June—*junho*
July—*julho*
August—*agosto*
September—*setembro*
October—*outubro*
November—*novembro*
December—*dezembro*

## TIME

What time is it?—*São quantas horas? Tem horas?*
It's 9 o'clock.—*São nove horas.*
at 9 o'clock in the morning—*as nove horas da manhã*
It's 1 in the afternoon.—*É uma hora da tarde.*
tomorrow morning—*amanhã de manhã, amanhã cedo*
3:30—*três e meia*
3:15—*três e quinze*
3:45—*três e quarena e cinco, quinze para as quatro*
Do you mean 2 o'clock or in two hours?—*Quer dizer as duas horas ou em duas horas?*
once—*uma vez*
at one time—*de uma vez*
every thirty minutes—*de trinta em trinta minutos*
every two hours—*de duas em duas horas*

## VERBS AND BASIC GRAMMAR

Like Spanish, Portuguese is a very verb-driven language. Most of the fundamental grammar is about conjugating verbs in different ways for different tenses and pronouns. In Portuguese, there are three types of verbs: those that end with ar, er, ir. They are conjugated like this:

to speak—*falar*
I speak—*falo*
you, he, she, it speaks—*fala*
we speak—*falamos*
they speak—*falam*

to sell—*vender*
I sell—*vendo*
you, he, she, it sells—*vende*
we sell—*vendemos*
they sell—*vendem*

to sleep—*dormir*
I sleep—*durmo*
you, he, she, it sleeps—*dorme*
we sleep—*dormimos*
they sleep—*dormem*

Pretty easy, right? Especially if you know Spanish. Here are some more regular verbs that you should find useful:

to ask—*perguntar*
to collect, charge—*cobrar*
to come, draw near—*chegar*
to cook—*cozinhar*
to delay, take a while—*demorar*
to eat—*comer*
to fall—*cair*
to feel—*sentir*
to find—*achar*
to finish—*terminar*
to give—*dar*
to have dinner—*jantar*
to have lunch—*almoçar*
to intend—*pretender*
to leave (exit)—*sair*
to leave (something)—*deixar*
to lie down—*deitar*
to like—*gostar*
to look—*olhar*
to look for—*procurar*
to need/to want—*precisar*

to pay—*pagar*
to pick up—*pegar*
to place, put—*colocar*
to play—*brincar*
to play (instrument)—*tocar*
to play (sports)—*jogar*
to promise—*prometer*
to remain, stay, stay with—*ficar*
to scare—*assustar*
to send, deliver—*enviar*
to swim—*nadar*
to tell (story)—*contar*
to think—*pensar*
to try—*tentar*
to wake up—*acordar*
to walk—*andar*

Unfortunately, some of the most useful and important verbs are irregular and you have to learn them separately. Here are some important irregular verbs and the specific conjugations that are irregular:

to be (temporary)—*estar*
I am—*estou*
you are, he, she, it is—*está*
we are—*estamos*
they are—*estão*

to be (permanent)—*ser*
I am—*sou*
you are, he, she, it is—*é*
we are—*somos*
they are—*são*

to see—*ver*
I see—*vejo*

to come, arrive—*vir*
I come—*venho*
you come, he, she, it comes—*vem*
they come—*vêem*

to want—*querer*
you, he, she, it wants—*quer*

to bring—*trazer*
I bring—*trago*

you, he, she, it brings—*traz*

to be able—*poder*
, can—*posso*

to have—*ter*
I have—*tenho*
you, he, she, it has—*tem*

to lose—*perder*
I lose—*perco*

to listen/to hear—*ouvir*
I hear—*ouço*

to obtain/to manage—*consiguir*
you, he, she, it manages—*consegue*

Note: Like Spanish, Portuguese has two forms of the verb to be. Use *estar* for temporary conditions and states of being: *"Estou bem"* (I am well), *"ele está em Paraty"* (He is in Paraty). Use *ser* for permanent conditions or locations: *"O museu é grande"* (The museum is big), *"Eu sou da Inglaterra"* (I am from England).

In addition to its normal meaning, the verb *ficar* is used in many different expressions, like *"Fico com fome"* (I get hungry), *"Fica quieto"* (Be quiet), *"Fica bem em você"* (Looks good on you), and *"Minha casa fica longe"* (My house is far).

The verb *ter* is used for "there is/are" and to ask "is/are there" questions: *"Tem cobras lá?"* (Are there snakes there?). It can also be used for "do you have" questions: *"Tem café?"* (Do you have coffee?).

# Glossary

**aldeia**—a rustic, aboriginal village

**a quilo**—by the kilogram, a self-service restaurant that charges by weight

**arara**—Macaw or parrot

**armação**—a station or building where whales were processed during the whaling era

**arraial**—settlement

**a vontade**—at will, used to mean "as you wish" or "make yourself at home"

**baía**—bay

**baixa**—below, under, underneath

**bandeirante**—literally, a flag bearer; this name is given to the Brazilians from the São Paulo area who first explored and populated the interior of the colony.

**banho**—bath or swimming hole

**barqueiro**—boat keeper, captain of a small boat

**barraca**—tent, stand, small makeshift house, beach kiosk or bar

**beco**—alley or small street

**bloco**—parade group

**boiada**—cattle, group of cows

**boiadeiro**—ranch hand, cowboy

**boite**—nightclub, dance club, strip club

**bosque**—wooded area, grove

**boteco**—small bar, greasy spoon, diner, dive bar

**cachoeira**—waterfall

**cachorro**—dog

**calçadão**—boardwalk, pedestrian walkway

**camarão**—shrimp

**caminho**—way or street, road

**caranguejo**—crab

**casa**—house

**casarão**—big house, main house, manor, old house

**chopp**—draft beer

**cia**—abbreviation of *compania,* company

**cidade**—city

**comida**—food

**coroa**—crown, small island of sand

**dentro, de dentro**—inside, on the inside, inner

**embarcação**—journey, trip, economic transportation

**enseada**—inlet, beach

**estância**—station, old mill house, factory

**falésias**—cliffs, faults

**farol**—lighthouse

**favela**—shantytown settlement on city outskirts, especially of Rio de Janeiro

**fazenda**—farm, plantation, ranch, country house

**feira**—fair, outdoor market, farmers market, marketplace

**fora, de fora**—outside, on the outside, outer

**foz**—mouth of a river

**galinha**—chicken

**gruta**—cave

**guaraná**—a carbonated soft drink made from the Guarana fruit and high in caffeine

**guerra**—war

**igreja**—church

**ilha**—island

**jangada**—small boat, rowboat, flat-bottom boat

**jardim**—garden

**ladeira**—hillside

**lagoa**—lake

**lagosta**—lobster

**lanchonete**—lunch stand, fast-food stand, diner

**largo**—space, area between buildings, small square

**lua**—moon

**leste, do leste**—east, eastern

**litoral**—coastline

**mangue**—marsh area on the banks of rivers, usually near coastal areas where the water is semi-salty

**maré**—tide

**morro**—mount, small mountain, hill

**norte**—north

**orla**—coastal margin, beach, waterfront

**palácio**—palace

**parque**—park

**parrachos**—underwater reefs and pools formed by rock formations and reefs, usually with a sandy ocean floor. These are preferred areas for snorkeling and diving activities.

**pão**—bread (pronounced with a nasal sound)

**passarela**—walkway, footpath, overpass

**pau**—stick (pronounced "pow")

**peixe**—fish

**piscina**—pool

**ponta**—tip or point

**ponto**—point, meaning place or locale

**porção**—appetizer, portion

**porto**—port

**pousada**—inn, small hotel, bed-and-breakfast

**praça**—square, city square, plaza

**praia**—beach

**queda**—fall, drop, cascade

**recife**—barrier reef

**republica**—fraternity, republic

**revellon**—New Years Eve

**rodísio**—rotating or alternating, a type of restaurant where different types of food are brought to your table throughout the meal

**rodoviaria**—central bus station, main bus terminal

**salgado**—finger food, snack, salty food item, salty, torturous (slang)

**seco**—dry

**suco**—juice

**sul**—south

**trevo**—roadside stop, turnout

**viagem**—voyage, trip

**vilarejo**—village

# Internet Resources

## TRAVEL INFORMATION AND GUIDES

### The Brazilian Consulate in San Francisco
### www.brazilsf.org

This is an excellent compilation on Brazil, with great sections on visas and officialdom. You'll also find a list of consulates in the United States as well as links to related sites.

### The Brazilian Embassy in London
### www.brazil.org.uk

One of the best general resources for information about Brazil, links, and advice on getting your visa and other documentation in order. They also have some basic tourist information on Brazil's main tourist attractions.

## Brazil for You
## www.brazil4you.com

Brazil4you.com is a fairly complete guide to Brazil destinations and tourism in general. You'll find basic background information on principal destinations as well as lists of hotels. This is a good place to augment your existing information.

## BrazilMax
## www.brazilmax.com

This site is owned and operated by Bill Hinchberger, an American journalist living and working out of São Paulo. Bill keeps his site pretty well updated and full of interesting articles.

## Brazil Tourism
## www.braziltourism.org

This organization has a great site with lots of information on Brazil, destinations, and activities like fishing, golf, surfing, diving, etc. It's worth a look to augment any information you already have.

## Brazzil Magazine
## www.brazzil.com

You'll find some great articles and informative stories about Brazil from an informed gringo's perspective at this site. Numerous stories and back issues are also available. This is a more honest source of information than the standard media's take on Brazil.

## South American Explorers
## www.saexplorers.org

This site includes background information, travel tips, and resources for travelers heading to South America with an emphasis on Spanish-speaking nations, but their Brazil section is growing. It's worth a look.

# DESTINATIONS

## Amazonas by Viverde
## www.amazonastravel.com.br

Run by a travel agency, this site has lots of great information on culture, hotels, floating hotels, excursions, and destinations within the central Amazon region. You may decide to book through this company or just access the site for reference. All information is available in English, Spanish, and Portuguese.

## Bahia.com.br
## www.bahia.com.br

One of the most complete sites about Bahia, this website has information in English and covers everything in the region, with plenty of information on Salvador, the Discovery Coast, and Chapada Diamantina. Basic information covers attractions, hotels, restaurants, and events.

## Foz do Iguaçu
## www.fozdoiguacu.pr.gov.br/turismo

This site has an excellent collection of facts and photos about Foz do Iguaçu, with some pages in English and German.

## Ipanema.com
## www.ipanema.com.br

Written totally in English, this site is packed with information about Rio de Janeiro. It's a bit difficult to navigate, but you'll find all kinds of interesting resources as you click around. You'll find lots of picture tours, virtual tours, and advice on getting around the city.

## Maraú
## www.barragrande.net

This excellent site has information in Portuguese, English, and French and covers a wide range of topics about the Maraú Peninsula, south of Salvador.

## Pantanal Regional Park
## www.parqueregionaldopantanal.org.br

You'll find a lot of background information about the Pantanal region at this site, including details about the various sections of the Pantanal, flora, fauna, history, and culture. There's plenty of information in English.

### Radio Bahia Online
**www.bahia-online.net**

An American runs this Internet radio site, which streams music from Bahia. He has also put together some interesting information about Salvador, including a great background on Carnaval and information on flights.

### RioTur
**www.rio.rj.gov.br**

The city government put together this impressive site in both English and Portuguese. They compiled information on just about everything you might need before and during your visit to Rio de Janeiro. The lists of hotels and restaurants are exhaustive and a bit difficult to use for choosing the best options. Still, the site will give you lots of information on attractions, events, and Carnaval.

### Santa Catarina
**www.sc.gov.br**

Created by the state government, this site has plenty of general information on Santa Catarina to whet your appetite for a visit. There are plenty of pages in English.

## SCUBA DIVING

### Abrolhos
**www.abrolhos.com.br**

This is the best site on the Abrolhos Islands, with information on diving, places to stay, and links to other national parks in Brazil. They have some information in English.

## NATURE AND ECOLOGY

### Amazon Watch
**www.amazonwatch.com**

Not specifically focused on Brazil, the Amazon Watch organization keeps an eye on the entire Amazon and reports newsworthy events regularly. Their focus is on exposing environmental hazards and risks.

### GORP
**www.gorp.com**

Hikers and trail blazers should take a look at this site for information on great hiking adventures in Brazil. Click on the locations tab to find a world map. You'll arrive at small articles about various adventures throughout Brazil.

### IBAMA
**www.ibama.gov.br**

This site is in Portuguese, but it contains complete details about all of Brazil's official environmental projects. The home page has an animated list of each one of their main groups, where you can get more detailed information.

### Planeta
**www.planeta.com**

This online journal provides information and links about ecotourism, local resources, and global environmental and tourism conferences. They have a great links page for Brazil.

# Index

# Acknowledgments

My wife, Edna, helped me all throughout this project, with travel arrangements, research, phone calls, fact checking, hotel evaluations, and all kinds of other assistance in the field. She also gave a final proof to the manuscript to correct problems with accents and the Portuguese in general. Above and beyond all that, she gave me constant moral and personal support throughout the entire project. The tipmeister, Marcelo Thalenberg, provided all kinds of tips and connections, especially related to São Paulo, but also throughout Brazil. Mike Richey, American abroad, provided refuge, as well as phone and Internet access, during Brazil's Spring Break, when all the hotels on the coast were booked solid.

I had lots of help in the Southwest Region. Natalia Arbex from the São Paulo CVB got me in touch with all kinds of important people, including Bia Morano, formerly with EMBRATUR, who helped with some special travel arrangements, and Rosa and Andreia from Anhembi who gave Edna and me a terrific orientation to São Paulo. Maira Taques from Accor Hotels helped set us up in São Paulo, where they have some of the best hotels in the city. Virginia Gaia from Atlantic Hotels and Milai Muniz from nh Hotels also treated us extremely well. We got excellent private tours from the Sala São Paulo, the Theatro Municipal, the Mercado Municipal, the Catedral da Sé, and the Pinacoteca Museum.

Ricardo Merzvinskas from EasyGoing Travel gave me some ideas for the São Paulo Coast chapter and an orienatation to the area in general. Gabriel from Vila Bebek Hotel in Camburi gave us an orientation and materials for the São Sebastião area, plus an excellent stay at his charming hotel. Rosilene and the staff at SETUR (Secretary of Tourism) in Minas Gerais provided all sort of research materials and maps and Carlos Felípe and Rosangela de Albuquerque at the Belo Horizonte CVB gave me an expert orientation to everything Minas has to offer. Vitório from the Hotel Solar do Rosário in Ouro Preto and Carlos from Pouso de Bartolomeu in Tiradentes provided wonderful accommodations and access to their cities.

In the Northeast, we stayed a week or so in the home of Arlete and Ico Moraes while exploring Natal and Fortaleza. Hopefully, we convinced them to visit Pipa by now. Henrique at the incredible Toca da Coruja Pousada in Pipa connected us with the Roteiro do Charme and gave us a great couple of days in town. His is one of my favorite places to stay on the Brazilian coast. Kiki Zonari from the Pousada Tabapitanga gave us a great background and tour of Porto de Galinhas. In Maceió, Nilo from the Pousada do Toque presented us to São Miguel dos Milagres and included us in his family, as he does with all his guests and Edival from the Brisamar Hotel in Barra de São Miguel took great care of us and even drove us to a hilltop overlooking the ocean, so I could get the best photos of the area.

We were especially blessed in Morro de São Paulo, where Luciano from the Pousada Praia do Encanto set us up in his beautiful island retreat, connected us with the locals, and provided me with plenty of research materials, not to mention some of his special home-brewed cachaça, some of the best in the region. Also, Laura and João Carlos at the Pousada Via Brasil treated us like old friends and helped with all kinds of small details. In Salvador, Janet from the Pousada Encanto da Itapoan gave us a complete orientation to the northern beaches and a great stay at her charming pousada. She also reviewed the Salvador chapter for me and provided a few important facts.

Making our way down the coast, we were lucky to land at the Ilha Verde Pousada in Itacaré, where Nicole and Christof gave us an orientation to the area, along with great hospitality and wonderful energy. In Porto Seguro, we stayed a couple of nights at the Vela Branca

Resort, which was quiet and peaceful and offered an incredible breakfast. Thanks to Evandro for that. In Arraial d'Ajuda, we stayed at the Pousada Pitinga, the best place in town, where we took the most incredible midnight swim under the full moon. Beth and Luiz Ricardo got us all set up there. Vera and Peter at the Pousada Agua Marinha showed us the north end of town and made us feel like part of their family during our stay there. Finally, Luila at the Pousada Estrela d'Agua in Trancoso gave us a complete orientation to the village and its many offerings and put us up for a couple of nights in great comfort and style.

At Avalon Travel Publishing, Chris Jones ran the project with great competence and equanimity, while Kevin Anglin handled the making of maps from my mock-ups and Amber Pirker put the photos into place. Rebecca Browning put the entire thing into motion with her confidence in me as the author. Maria Moreira (my mother-in-law in Brazil) provided many wonderful lunches and a warm nucleus during the heavy months of writing in João Monlevade. In many ways, my greatest debt is to my mother, Dona, and sister, Barbara, for coming to my rescue and reminding me what it is to have a family.

# U.S.~Metric Conversion

| | | |
|---:|:---:|:---|
| 1 inch | = | 2.54 centimeters (cm) |
| 1 foot | = | .304 meters (m) |
| 1 yard | = | 0.914 meters |
| 1 mile | = | 1.6093 kilometers (km) |
| 1 km | = | .6214 miles |
| 1 fathom | = | 1.8288 m |
| 1 chain | = | 20.1168 m |
| 1 furlong | = | 201.168 m |
| 1 acre | = | .4047 hectares |
| 1 sq km | = | 100 hectares |
| 1 sq mile | = | 2.59 square km |
| 1 ounce | = | 28.35 grams |
| 1 pound | = | .4536 kilograms |
| 1 short ton | = | .90718 metric ton |
| 1 short ton | = | 2000 pounds |
| 1 long ton | = | 1.016 metric tons |
| 1 long ton | = | 2240 pounds |
| 1 metric ton | = | 1000 kilograms |
| 1 quart | = | .94635 liters |
| 1 US gallon | = | 3.7854 liters |
| 1 Imperial gallon | = | 4.5459 liters |
| 1 nautical mile | = | 1.852 km |

To compute Celsius temperatures, subtract 32 from Fahrenheit and divide by 1.8. To go the other way, multiply Celsius by 1.8 and add 32.

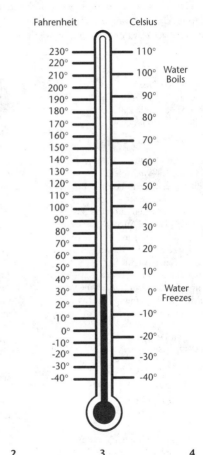

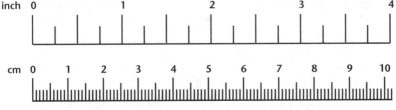

# Keeping Current

Although we strive to produce the most up-to-date guidebook humanly possible, change is unavoidable. Between the time this book goes to print and the moment you read it, a handful of the businesses noted in these pages will undoubtedly change prices, move, or even close their doors forever. Other worthy attractions will open for the first time. If you have a favorite gem you'd like to see included in the next edition, or see anything that needs updating, clarification, or correction, please drop us a line. Send your comments via email to atpfeedback@avalonpub.com, or use the address below.

*Moon Handbooks Brazil*
Avalon Travel Publishing
1400 65th Street, Suite 250
Emeryville, CA 94608, USA
www.moon.com

Avalon Travel Publishing
An Imprint of Avalon Publishing
Group, Inc.

AVALON
publishing group incorporated

Editors: Christopher Jones, Kathryn Ettinger
Series Manager: Kevin McLain
Acquisitions Manager: Rebecca K. Browning
Copy Editor: Kim Marks
Graphics and Production Coordinators:
 Amber Pirker, Gerilyn Attebery, Elizabeth Jang
Cover Designer: Kari Gim
Interior Designer: Amber Pirker
Map Editor: Kevin Anglin
Cartographers: Suzanne Service, Kat Kalamaras,
 Kat Smith, Kansai Uchida, Christine Markiewicz
Proofreaders: Sabrina Young, Pearl Wu
Indexer: Rachel Kuhn

ISBN-10: 1-56691-896-0
ISBN-13: 978-1-56691-896-1
ISSN: 1555-9742

Printing History
1st Edition—January 2006
5 4 3 2 1

Text © 2006 by Christopher Van Buren.
Maps © 2006 by Avalon Travel Publishing, Inc.
All rights reserved.

Some photos and illustrations are used by permission and are the property of the original copyright owners.

Front cover photo: © Stefan Hess/Tyba/Brazil-Photos.com

Printed in the USA by Malloy